The Rocky Mountains

written and researched by

Alf Alderson, Christian Williams and Cameron Wilson

www.roughguides.com

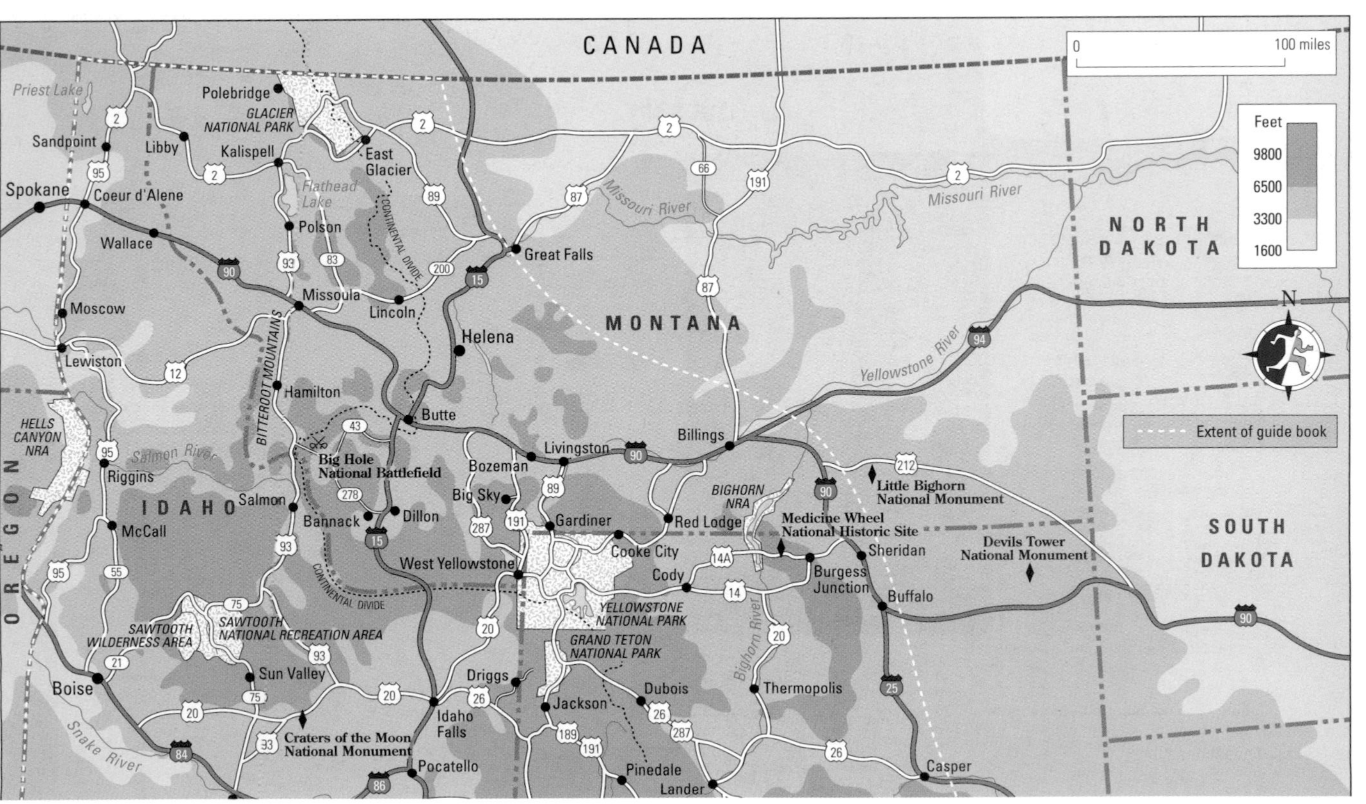
CANADA
0
100 miles
Feet
9800
6500
3300
1600
NORTH DAKOTA
SOUTH DAKOTA
MONTANA
IDAHO
OREGON
N
Extent of guide book
Priest Lake
Polebridge
GLACIER NATIONAL PARK
Sandpoint
Libby
Kalispell
East Glacier
Spokane
Coeur d'Alene
Flathead Lake
Polson
Wallace
CONTINENTAL DIVIDE
Great Falls
Missouri River
Missoula
Lincoln
Moscow
BITTERROOT MOUNTAINS
Helena
Lewiston
Hamilton
Yellowstone River
Butte
HELLS CANYON NRA
Salmon River
Big Hole National Battlefield
Bozeman
Livingston
Billings
Riggins
Big Sky
BIGHORN NRA
Little Bighorn National Monument
Salmon
Bannack
Dillon
Gardiner
Red Lodge
Medicine Wheel National Historic Site
McCall
Cooke City
Sheridan
Devils Tower National Monument
West Yellowstone
Cody
Burgess Junction
Buffalo
YELLOWSTONE NATIONAL PARK
SAWTOOTH WILDERNESS AREA
SAWTOOTH NATIONAL RECREATION AREA
GRAND TETON NATIONAL PARK
Bighorn River
Sun Valley
Driggs
Boise
Dubois
Thermopolis
Jackson
Idaho Falls
Craters of the Moon National Monument
Snake River
Pocatello
Pinedale
Lander
Casper

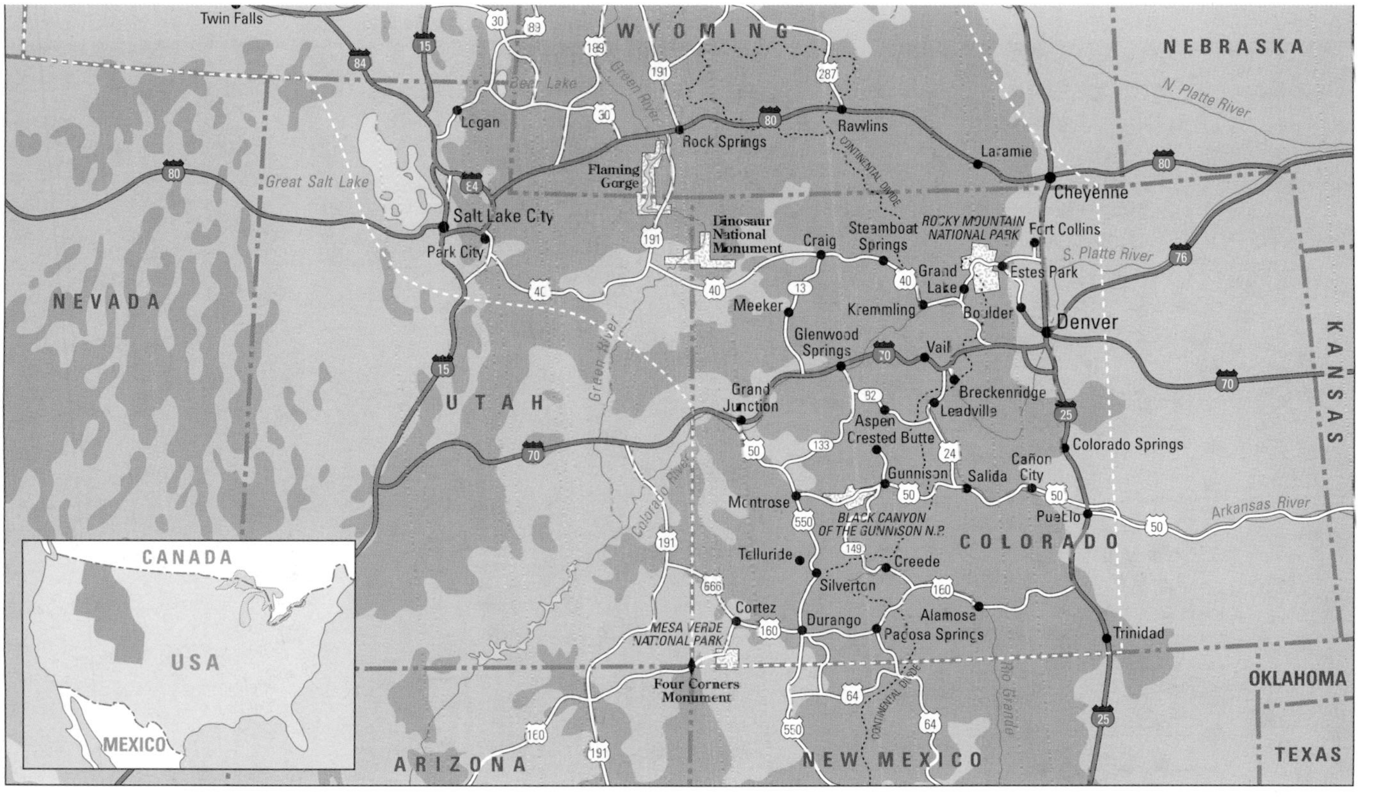
NEBRASKA
KANSAS
OKLAHOMA
TEXAS
WYOMING
NEVADA
UTAH
COLORADO
ARIZONA
NEW MEXICO
Twin Falls
Logan
Salt Lake City
Park City
Rock Springs
Flaming Gorge
Rawlins
Laramie
Cheyenne
Fort Collins
Estes Park
Denver
Boulder
Dinosaur National Monument
ROCKY MOUNTAIN NATIONAL PARK
Craig
Steamboat Springs
Grand Lake
Meeker
Kremmling
Glenwood Springs
Vail
Breckenridge
Leadville
Grand Junction
Aspen
Crested Butte
Colorado Springs
Gunnison
Salida
Cañon City
Montrose
Pueblo
BLACK CANYON OF THE GUNNISON N.P.
Telluride
Creede
Silverton
Alamosa
Cortez
Durango
Pagosa Springs
Trinidad
MESA VERDE NATIONAL PARK
Four Corners Monument
Great Salt Lake
Bear Lake
Green River
N. Platte River
S. Platte River
Arkansas River
Colorado River
Rio Grande
CONTINENTAL DIVIDE
CANADA
USA
MEXICO

Glacier National Park

Introduction to the Rocky Mountains

Forming the backbone of the American West, the Rocky Mountains own the most spectacular mountain landscapes in the so-called lower 48. They assert themselves most strongly in Colorado, Wyoming, Montana, Idaho and the northern chunk of Utah, areas filled with breathtaking alpine forest, dramatic mountain passes, thrilling wildlife, some charming urban centers and enough one-horse towns to make those looking to get away from it all long for some company. It may not be the final frontier, like Alaska, but if you're looking to head to the great outdoors, and still have civilization right on the doorstep, you can't do much better.

Unlike many of the world's classic mountain ranges, such as the Alps and the Himalayas, which are characterized by steep peaks and spires shooting from valley floors towards the sky, the Rockies are bulky and broad-shouldered, building steadily from the high-altitude basins and grassy plains east and west of the Continental Divide to the highest reaches of around 14,000 feet. But the scenery is nevertheless striking, particularly on the mountainsides – cloaked in forests of aspen, pine, spruce and fir, and capped by wildflower-flecked alpine tundra.

Much of this is best played out in the series of national parks running from north to south: Glacier, Yellowstone, Grand Teton, Rocky Mountain,

Sunrise over Yellowstone Lake

and Mesa Verde. You could spend entire vacations hiking round their boundaries and exploring the geological – and in the case of Mesa Verde, the archeological – wonders within. Even then, of course, you'd be missing out on huge swathes of untrammeled wilderness – trail-laced Idaho, the most rugged Rocky Mountain state, doesn't even have a national park. Certainly most who come to the region do so for outdoor activities. Warm, dry summers open up thousands of miles of spectacular, lonely trails, offering perfect conditions for hiking and mountain biking. Spring run-offs keep the myriad rivers and lakes busy with fly-fishermen and whitewater rafters, while climbers, campers and other assorted adventurers all get their day in the sun as well. And in winter, huge piles of powdery snow are dumped onto some of the most incredible ski terrain on the planet – with no shortage of world-class resorts from which to take advantage of it.

Beyond the obvious appeal of the outdoors is the somewhat intangible, but undeniable, Wild West feel that permeates much of the range. The endearingly gritty, old mining towns hearken back to the era when the Rockies were home to resilient nomadic Indians, hardy mountain men, grizzled miners and maverick outlaws like Butch Cassidy and the Sundance Kid. And the thinly spread population, especially in Wyoming, the least populous US state, coupled with plenty of ranchland and wildlife to roam around it – everything from grizzly bears, wolves and mountain lions, herds of bison and bighorn sheep, to elk, moose, mule deer and pronghorn antelope – ensure that the cowboy way still prevails.

Where to go

Physically, the Rocky Mountains emerge far north of the US-Canada border, rumbling and rolling their way south through Montana, Idaho, Wyoming, Utah and Colorado, before petering out amid the deserts of New Mexico, almost 1500 miles away.

To explore even relatively small portions of this vast region, you'll need to have a car. In some instances, driving yourself is indeed the only feasible option and one that not only offers one of the Rockies' real delights – coaxing a car along the tight switchback roads that wind over precipitous mountain passes – but also allows for the flexibility to pause and take in the landscape, or better still strike out on a remote trail on foot or by mountain bike.

Beyond the obvious appeal of the outdoors is the somewhat intangible, but undeniable, Wild West feel that permeates much of the range

As the only major metropolis in the Rockies, friendly and sophisticated **Denver** is its most obvious gateway but is often overlooked as a destination in its own right. And while it's not the cultural powerhouse of many of the US's coastal cities, it, and the nearby liberal college town of **Boulder**, offer an ideal balance of outdoors pursuits and urban frivolity in

Southern Colorado's Sangre de Cristo mountains

Rocky Mountain High

High altitude comes with the territory when you're in the Rockies. Even in the region's major metropolis, the "mile high" city of Denver, its effects are felt – as evidenced by the greater number of home runs that whistle through the thin air of Coors Field. Still, it's not until you head higher up into the mountains, past the 10,000 feet mark – and note that Colorado alone has fifty peaks over 14,000 feet, let alone 10,000 – that you'll really notice the scarcity of oxygen in the air. At its worst, this deprivation can lead to altitude sickness (see box on p.20), but if you're relatively fit and let your system adjust by taking it easy the first few days, only progressively picking up the pace, you should be fine.

themselves. Additionally, both are within easy striking distance of the grand **Rocky Mountain National Park**.

To tackle the Colorado heartland by road, you could strike out on a clockwise loop from Denver, heading south to the strongly Hispanic San Luis Valley, location of the remarkable **Sand Dunes National Monument**. West from here are the San Juan Mountains, where the quest for gold and silver gave rise to scores of Victorian mining camps – some of which are now quaint bases for exploring vast networks of trails and backroads. The energetic college town of **Durango** is the main center in the San Juans and also the best jumping-off point for **Mesa Verde National Park**, created to protect the intriguing ruins of the once great Ancestral Puebloan civilization. North from Durango, the precipitous and winding San Juan Skyway takes in small mountain gems like **Silverton** and **Ouray** and leads to the trendy ski-town of **Telluride**. To complete the loop from here, follow the Gunnison and the Arkansas river valleys; pause to gaze into the depths of the **Black Canyon of the Gunnison**, or make time to hike, bike or ski around **Crested Butte**.

Colorado's most visited towns are strung along the state's main east–west interstate highway, I-70. Here you'll find the clutch of incredible ski areas for which Colorado is famous: glitzy **Vail** and **Aspen**, egalitarian **Winter Park**, and the resorts of Summit County which include

Breckenridge and **Copper Mountain**. A detour north along I-40 brings you to **Steamboat Springs** – widely acknowledged as one of the country's best all-round wintersports destinations.

Northwest of Colorado, the Rockies emerge briefly in Northern Utah, where the 2002 Winter Olympics have boosted the profile of the ski resorts of **Park City** and the Wasatch Canyons. In **Salt Lake City** itself, the Mormon Church's world headquarters still dominate the city skyline, even as the church's influence on cultural and political life in Utah continues its slow decline. Salt Lake City makes a useful access point for getting into the mountains too; it's a six-hour drive from downtown via I-15 and I-89 to the breathtaking scenery of Wyoming's twin jewels, **Yellowstone National Park** and the impossibly picturesque vistas of **Teton National Park**. Due south of these is the prime tourist town of **Jackson**, a top winter playground with three world-class skiing and boarding resorts nearby.

In central Wyoming highlights include the stunning Wind River

Mining times

While go-it-alone fur-trappers were the first whites to begin fruitful exploration of the Rockies, the first major wave of permanent settlers came only after major gold strikes in the 1850s. Upon arriving, settlers quickly carved up the land, chiseling into hillsides and leaving the landscaped pockmarked with tailings and old mine workings. The legacy adds an atmospheric twist to the

present-day scenery of the region, and some old mines are still open for tours, but the real contribution of mining to visitors today is the way its infrastructure has opened up the mountains. The network of old railroads, dirt roads and pack trails provide unusual platforms to view the surroundings wilds by less conventional means – including steam trains, four-wheel drive vehicles and mountain bikes. In addition, the century-old, ramshackle mining boom-towns continue to nurture the frontier feel of Rocky Mountains, though the bars and brothels of old have been renovated to house a mix of boutiques, galleries, outfitters and restaurants. The most authentically preserved mining towns in the region are dotted about both southern Colorado (see p.101) and Montana's Gold Country (see p.489).

Mountain Range – which offers peerless backcountry hiking, climbing and angling – and the friendly town of **Lander**. The spa town of **Thermopolis** can be easily added to a Wyoming driving itinerary, and it provides some real surprises in the form of the world's largest mineral hot springs and some extraordinary dinosaur fossil finds. In the far north of the state, Buffalo Bill is seemingly immortalized in every brick and beam of the town of **Cody**, while the sparser southern portion of the state is home to **Cheyenne** and **Laramie**, both best seen during the summer rodeo and festival season when their unique cowboy-cultures shine brightest.

To the north of Wyoming, Montana has imposing mountains, rivers that offer some of the best fly-fishing in the US and some very big bears –

Close encounters

Of all the safety measures discussed among hikers, the ones that provoke the most macabre ponderings and snippets of gallows humor are those related to bear encounters. Is ringing a bear-bell really akin to ringing a dinner-bell? Can I keep my lip-balm inside the tent, or do I need to hang that from a tree a hundred yards upwind too? For answers to these queries and more, turn to p.550. But, before heading out in a full suit of armor or, even worse, canceling an overnight hike, keep in mind that during the last twenty years in Yellowstone National Park, there have been about twenty-five known injuries to humans by bears, or one recorded attack for every 2.2 million visitors. Play by the rules, and your trip should work out as smoothly as planned.

scenic **Glacier National Park** has the largest concentration of grizzlies in the country. The park is also home to the Going-to-the-Sun Road, a can't-miss drive past roaring waterfalls, brooding glaciers and craggy mountains. Though not as well known for its urban centers, both the lively university town of **Missoula** and sophisticated **Bozeman**, just an hour's drive from Yellowstone, make for pleasant extended stays year round. The state's evocative nickname finds itself attached to **Big Sky Resort**, which quietly goes about exploiting some of the best (and earliest) snow in the Rockies every year, while up-and-coming **Big Mountain** is handily situated by the town of **Whitefish**, where you'll find the liveliest apres-ski community in the state.

Of the five states covered in this guide, Idaho is perhaps the least well known. Though home to no national parks, the state proudly boasts the largest wilderness area in the lower 48 (the **Frank Church-River of No Return Wilderness**). Indeed, Idaho is the most rugged state in the Rockies, where wild country impinges upon you at almost every turn, from the black cinder landscape of **Craters of the Moon National Monument** in the south to the densely forested slopes of the **Selkirk Mountains** in the north. In between, though, are a handful of surprisingly sophisticated towns and cities like friendly **Boise** and the glitzy ski town of **Sun Valley** making the case that not all comforts are lost.

Skiing and snowboarding

For a fair share of visitors and locals alike, winter is the star season on the Rocky Mountain calendar. On average, there's enough decent snow on the ground by mid-December to warrant a jaunt out to the slopes, but those with only one opportunity for a trip should play it safe and wait for January or, even better, February and March, when the powder days begin seriously piling up. Keep in mind also that in most years the riding season runs well into April, and you'll certainly long remember that first day's spring skiing in the Rockies, spent barreling downhill wearing little more than a t-shirt, sunglasses and an idiot grin. Regardless of when you go, be sure to try to hit more than just one resort. The high density of ski hills throughout the region mean the resorts are often virtually lined up side-by-side, giving enthusiasts the opportunity to experience both different terrain and overall atmosphere effortlessly. See p.53 for more on the skiing and boarding scene.

When to go

The overriding assumption made by many people is that visiting the Rockies requires a hard-and-fast choice between a **summer** hiking vacation or a **winter** ski-trip. There is some basic sense to this seasonal dichotomy, and certainly the three months of summer (June–Aug) and of winter (Dec–Feb) do draw the bulk of visitors who come to explore the mountains. But crowds at the marquee national parks like Yellowstone, Glacier and Rocky Mountain thin out nicely in the **fall**, which is also the time that many animals become more active as daytime temperatures begin to drop. And while **spring** is rather unglamorously known as the "mud season," it can still deliver fine ski conditions to go with warm mountain sunshine. At lower elevations, the spring run-off is manna from heaven for whitewater enthusiasts, with rivers at their highest and fastest providing plenty of high-energy rafting and kayaking excursions. In broad terms, those wanting to hike and climb in comfortable, non-hazardous conditions will want to avoid any place still snowbound; this varies according to altitude and local climate, but the majority of mountain trails below 10,000 feet are usually passable between mid-May and late September.

Average Temperatures and rainfall

	Jan	Feb	Mar	Apr	May	June	July	Aug	Sept	Oct	Nov	Dec
Boise												
(Max °F)	36	46	51	61	71	82	90	87	78	66	47	36
(Min °F)	21	26	31	38	44	50	57	56	47	39	32	21
(inches)	1.4	1.1	1.3	1.2	1.2	0.8	0.5	0.4	0.9	0.8	1.5	1.5
Cheyenne												
(Max °F)	37	41	44	54	64	75	82	79	70	59	44	38
(Min °F)	15	19	22	31	38	47	54	52	43	33	24	17
(inches)	0.4	0.4	0.9	1.3	2.3	2.1	2.2	1.7	1.3	0.8	0.5	0.5
Denver												
(Max °F)	42	46	52	60	71	80	88	84	76	65	52	42
(Min °F)	15	20	25	34	44	51	58	56	47	35	25	16
(inches)	0.5	0.7	1.2	1.6	2.4	1.9	1.9	1.5	1.1	1	0.8	0.6
Jackson												
(Max °F)	23	30	37	47	59	70	80	76	66	54	36	25
(Min °F)	-1	3	10	20	30	35	41	38	31	22	13	1
(inches)	2.5	2	1.7	1.4	1.9	1.9	1.3	1.3	1.4	1.2	2.2	2.4
Missoula												
(Max °F)	31	37	47	57	66	73	83	83	71	57	42	30
(Min °F)	15	22	25	31	35	45	52	50	39	31	25	15
(inches)	1.3	0.8	1.1	1.1	1.8	1.9	1.1	1.2	1.1	0.8	0.8	1.2
Salt Lake City												
(Max °F)	37	42	52	60	71	81	90	88	80	66	49	38
(Min °F)	17	23	27	37	45	55	62	61	50	39	29	19
(inches)	1	1.1	1.9	2.1	1.8	0.9	0.8	0.9	1.4	1.4	1.4	1.4
Vail												
(Max °F)	28	31	37	43	54	66	74	72	64	55	38	31
(Min °F)	0	1	7	17	25	32	38	37	30	22	11	1
(inches)	0.9	1	1.1	1.2	1.3	1.2	1.7	1.8	1.3	0.8	0.7	1
West Glacier												
(Max °F)	28	36	41	54	65	72	80	79	67	54	38	29
(Min °F)	13	17	23	29	35	44	48	47	38	34	24	18
(inches)	3.3	2.3	1.8	1.8	2.6	3.1	1.9	1.8	2	2	3.1	3.3
West Yellowstone												
(Max °F)	23	31	37	45	58	67	77	76	64	52	35	23
(Min °F)	0	3	10	19	28	36	41	38	31	22	11	1
(inches)	2.1	1.5	1.8	1.4	2	2.5	1.7	1.7	1.9	1.3	2.2	2.1

36 things not to miss

It's not possible to see everything that the Rocky Mountains have to offer in one trip – and we don't suggest you try. What follows is a selective taste of the region's highlights: famous national parks, breath-taking natural wonders, unforgettable outdoor activities and stirring events. They're arranged in five color-coded categories, which you can browse through to find the very best things to see and experience. All entries have a page reference to take you straight into the guide, where you can find out more.

01 Grand Teton National Park Page 436 • Home to the most photogenic mountain range in North America.

02 Devil's Causeway hiking trail Page 305 • Narrowing to four feet wide as it drops away 1500 feet on either side, this trail in northern Colorado's Flat Tops Wilderness is not for the faint-hearted.

03 Denver Pow-Wow Page 82 • Held in early March, this pow-wow is one of the country's largest annual gatherings of Native Americans and features the Grand Entry, a massive dance complete with 1000 participants.

04 Riding Lone Mountain Page 471 • The hair-raising black- and double black diamond-only runs from the exposed summit at Big Sky Resort in southern Montana should satisfy even the most hard-core riders.

05 Mesa Verde National Park Page 161 • The country's only national park exclusively devoted to archeological remains, Mesa Verde is laced with scores of cliff dwellings, a particular highlight being the stunning Cliff Palace, once home to some 250 Ancestral Puebloans.

06 Driving the Going-to-the-Sun Road Page 547 • Cross the Continental Divide and snake past stupendous ice-carved mountain peaks on Glacier National Park's scenic throughway.

07 Skiing Steamboat Page 302 • Shadows and Closet are the resort's classic aspen tree-runs, where you'll find stashes of Steamboat's famous "champagne powder."

08 Silverton Page 167 • Located along the dramatic San Juan Skyway, Silverton is the final stop on the Durango & Silverton Narrow Gauge Railroad and one of the most atmospheric Victorian mining towns in Colorado.

09 Million Dollar Cowboy Bar Page 452 • One of Jackson's many aprés-ski spots; straddle a bar-side saddle for a quintessential, if hokey, saloon experience.

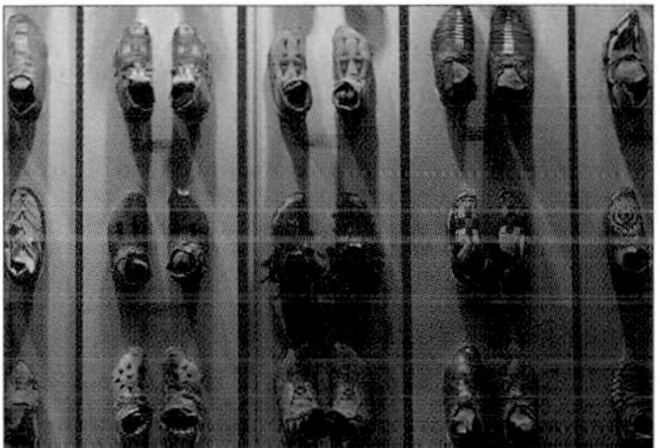

10 Buffalo Bill Historical Center Page 383 • An extraordinary museum loaded with mint examples of Western Americana, from Native crafts to famous Western painters and, of course, artifacts from the life and times of Buffalo Bill.

11 Frontier Days Page 357 • Cheyenne's premier annual event features the country's most prestigious outdoor rodeo — known locally as "the Daddy of 'em all."

12 Great Sand Dunes National Monument Page 137 • Tucked up against the contrasting Sangre de Cristo mountains, these fifty-square-miles of constantly shifting sand rising up to 700 feet make up the tallest sand dunes in the country.

13 Cirque of the Towers Page 396 & 405 • For hikers and climbers alike, this cluster of glaciated peaks is the jewel in the crown of the mighty Wind River mountains.

15 Bishop's Castle Page 130 • A tribute to eccentricity in southern Colorado's Wet Mountains, this is one man's wild and rather rickety creation, built entirely from hand-hauled stones.

14 Skiing Vail Page 229 • Exceptional snowfalls – the annual average hovers around 350 inches – and the largest ski area in the region virtually guarantees a fantastic day on the slopes.

16 Rocky Mountain National Park Page 275 • The best hiking in Colorado along with the chance to spot bighorn sheep in their natural habitat.

17 Mountain biking in Sun Valley Page 598 • The lift-accessed trails at Sun Valley offer top notch excitement in summer as well as during the snowy months.

18 Leadville Page 232 • Come as close as you can to experiencing Colorado during its mining days in this ramshackle, unpretentious old mining town.

19 Artist Point Page 423 • Arrive early in the day to beat the crowds and get the best light conditions for this dramatic viewpoint, Yellowstone National Park's quintessential photo opportunity.

20 Galena Summit Page 610 • This high mountain pass gives fine views over the fantastically serrated ridges and peaks of the Sawtooth National Recreation Area's mountains; in winter, the local cross-country skiing is unsurpassed.

21 Museum of the Rockies Page 465 • Bozeman's top attraction – a perfect rainy day hideaway – holds a fine collection of items pertaining to Montana's history from geological times to the present.

22 Montana's ghost towns Page 489 • Get an atmospheric insight into the mining boom-times of the late 1800s by visiting one of several atmospheric ghost towns in and around Montana's Gold Country region.

23 Old Faithful Page 420 • Though dozens of geysers are dotted about Yellowstone National Park, Old Faithful – as the name implies – is the most dependable, erupting some twenty times a day.

24 Devils Tower Page 376 • Though not part of the Rockies per se, a day-trip out to hike around this sacred national monument in Wyoming's northeast corner is well worth the effort.

25 Backcountry boarding and skiing Page 55 • Though not without its dangers, heading out into the backcountry in search of virgin snow via helicopter, snowcat or on foot is a must for experienced big mountain riders.

26 Raspberries Page 348 • Enjoy one of the world's finest raspberry shakes by the shores of turquoise Bear Lake.

27 Fly-fishing in Southern Montana Page 460 • The land that inspired *A River Runs Through It* unsurprisingly is home to some of the finest-fly fishing in the US.

28 **Hiking in the Maroon Belles** Page 246 • Fifteen miles from Aspen's leafy pedestrian core stand these towering purple-grey peaks, two of the most attractive "fourteeners" in the state.

29 The Mountain Man Rendezvous Page 402 • The legend of the mountain man lives on in the Green River country around Pinedale, Wyoming.

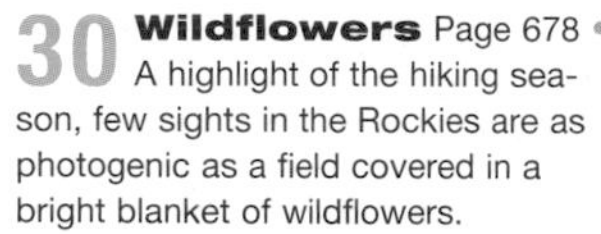

30 Wildflowers Page 678 • A highlight of the hiking season, few sights in the Rockies are as photogenic as a field covered in a bright blanket of wildflowers.

31 Brown Palace Hotel Page 76 • A perfect foil to the Rockies' rugged mountain-scapes, Denver's landmark hotel – a plush Italian Renaissance-style edifice opened in 1892 – is home to a breathtaking eight-story atrium lobby.

32 Temple Square Page 322 • The heart of Salt Lake City, this square is the cradle of Mormon culture, home to both the towering Temple and renowned Mormon Tabernacle.

33 McCall Winter Festival Page 620 • The little resort town on the south shores of the Payette Lake comes alive during Idaho's biggest winter festival, featuring ice-sculptures, sled-dog races and fireworks.

34 Boise Page 567 • Fly-fish in the leafy downtown greenbelt and then head out for an authentic Basque meal in Idaho's friendly state capital.

35 Park City Page 335 • By day, ski the broad, fast groomed runs at Deer Valley Resort; by night sample the myriad restaurants of Main Street, at their busiest during the Sundance Film Festival.

36 Whitewater rafting Page 56 • Scores of churning rivers throughout the region provide ample adventure for everyone from first-timers to hardcore daredevils.

contents

Using the Rough Guide

We've tried to make this Rough Guide a good read and easy to use. The book is divided into five main sections, and you should be able to find whatever you want in one of them.

color section

The front color section offers a quick tour of the Rocky Mountains. The **introduction** aims to give you a feel for the place, with suggestions on where to go. We also tell you what the weather is like and include interesting boxes on the region. Next, our authors round up their favorite aspects of the Rockies in the **things not to miss** section – whether it's an amazing sight, a superb festival, or a great place for outdoor activities. Right after this comes the Rough Guide's full **contents** list.

basics

The Basics section covers all the **pre-departure** practicalities to help you plan your trip. This is where you'll find out which airlines serve the Rockies, what to do about money and insurance, public transport, car rental, food, and accommodation, along with how to best explore the outdoors. In short, Basics contains just about every piece of **general practical information** you might need.

guide

This is the heart of the Rough Guide, divided into user-friendly chapters, each of which covers a specific state or region. Every chapter starts with a list of **highlights** and an **introduction** that helps you to decide where to go, depending on your time and budget. Likewise, introductions to the various towns and smaller regions within each chapter should help you plan your itinerary. We start most town accounts with information on arrival and accommodation, followed by a tour of the sights, and finally reviews of places to eat and drink, and details of nightlife. Longer accounts also have a directory of practical listings. Each chapter concludes with **public transport** details for that region.

contexts

Read Contexts to get a deeper understanding of how the **Rocky Mountains** tick. We've included a brief history and a look at the region's **landscape** and **wildlife**, along with a detailed further reading section that reviews dozens of **books** relating to the area.

index + small print

Apart from a **full index**, which includes maps as well as places, this section covers publishing information, credits and acknowledgments, and also has our contact details in case you want to send in updates and corrections to the book – or suggestions as to how we might improve it.

chapter map of **The Rocky Mountains**

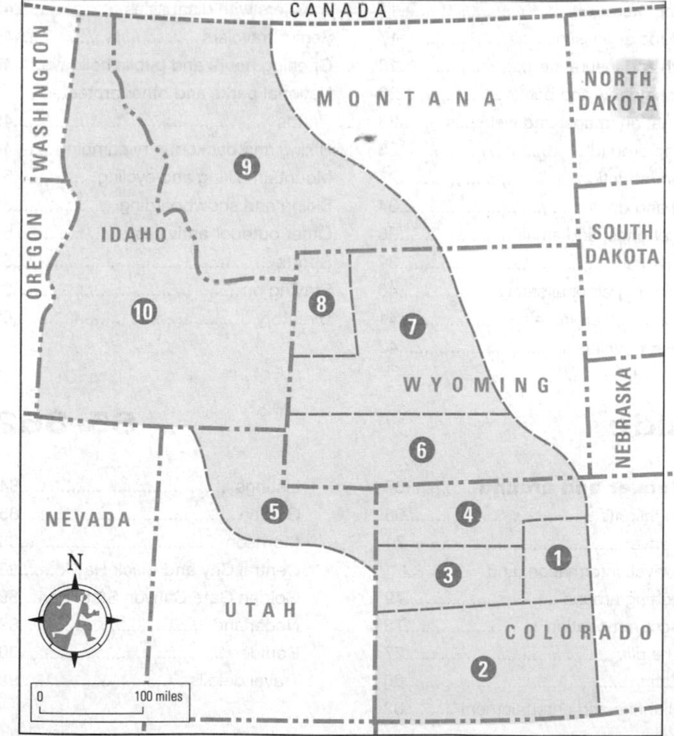

contents

color section i–xxiv

basics 9–64

guide 65–662

contexts 663–684

index and small print 685–695

map symbols

maps are listed in the full index using colored text

International boundary
State boundary
Chapter division boundary
Continental divide
Interstate
US Highway
Highway
Other roads
Pedestrianised street
One-way street
Path
Railway
River
Point of interest
Mountain peak
Mountain pass
Waterfall
Spring
Campground
Chalet
Customs

Accommodation
Restaurant
Ruins
Castle
Museum
Ski area
Golf course
Airport
Bus stop
Parking
Hospital/medical center
Tourist information
Post office
Building
Cathedral
Stadium
Cemetery
Park
Forest
Indian reservation
Beach

basics

basics

Getting there

The Rockies were all but inaccessible to travelers right up until 1869, when the two halves of the country's first transcontinental railway finally met in northern Utah. A great deal has changed since, and there are now convenient air links to a number of centers throughout the region. The main hubs for reaching the Rocky Mountains by air are Denver, Colorado and Salt Lake City, Utah – both of which are serviced by a number of international and domestic airlines. If your objective is the northern reaches of the Rockies, such as Glacier National Park in Montana, you might consider flying in to Spokane, Washington or Missoula, Montana – both of which have regular connections to Denver and Salt Lake City. Seeing as the purpose of most people's trip to the mountains is to see out-of-the-way places, it also makes perfect sense to arrive in the Rockies by car.

If flying, remember that airfares depend on the **season**. In the Rockies, there are two high seasons – summer and the snowy winter months – with cheaper flights available in the spring and fall. Note also that flying on weekends is typically more expensive; price ranges quoted below assume midweek travel. You can often cut costs by going through a **specialist flight agent** – either a consolidator, who buys up blocks of tickets from the airlines and sells them at a discount, or a **discount agent**, who in addition to dealing with discounted flights may offer special student and youth fares and a range of other travel-related services such as car rentals, tours and the like. Some agents specialize in **charter flights**, which may be cheaper than anything available on a scheduled flight, but again departure dates are fixed and withdrawal penalties are high. For some of the more popular destinations, you may even find it cheaper to pick up a bargain **package deal** from one of the tour operators listed below and then find your own accommodation when you get there. A further possibility is to see if you can arrange a **courier flight**, although you'll need a flexible schedule, and preferably be travelling alone with very little luggage. In return for shepherding a parcel through customs, you can expect to get a deeply discounted ticket. You'll probably also be restricted in the duration of your stay.

Booking flights online

Many airlines and discount travel websites offer you the opportunity to book your tickets online, cutting out the costs of agents and middlemen. Good deals can often be found through discount or auction sites, as well as through the airlines' own websites.

Online booking agents and general travel sites

Ⓦ **www.cheapflights.com** Flight deals, travel agents, plus links to other travel sites. UK only.
Ⓦ **www.cheaptickets.com** Discount flight specialists.
Ⓦ **www.etn.nl/discount.htm** A hub of consolidator and discount agent Web links, maintained by the nonprofit European Travel Network.
Ⓦ **www.expedia.com** Discount airfares, all-airline search engine and daily deals.
Ⓦ **www.flyaow.com** Online air travel info and reservations site.
Ⓦ **www.gaytravel.com** Gay online travel agent, concentrating mostly on accommodation.
Ⓦ **www.hotwire.com** Bookings from the US only. Last-minute savings of up to forty percent on regular published fares. Travellers must be at least 18 and there are no refunds, transfers or changes allowed. Log-in required.
Ⓦ **www.lastminute.com** Offers good last-minute holiday package and flight-only deals. UK only.
Ⓦ **www.priceline.com** Name-your-own-price website that has deals at around forty percent off standard fares. You cannot specify flight times (although you do specify dates) and the tickets are nonrefundable, nontransferable and nonchangeable.
Ⓦ **www.princeton.edu/Main/air800.html** Has an extensive list of airline toll-free numbers and websites.

ⓦ **www.smilinjack.com/airlines.htm** Lists an up-to-date compilation of airline website addresses.
ⓦ **www.travelocity.com** Destination guides, cheap web fares and best deals for car hire and accommodation. Provides access to the travel agent system SABRE, the most comprehensive central reservations system in the US.
ⓦ **www.travelshop.com.au** Australian website offering discounted flights, packages, insurance, online bookings.
ⓦ **http://travel.yahoo.com** Incorporates a lot of Rough Guide material in its coverage of destination countries and cities across the world, with information about places to eat, sleep, and etc.

Getting there from North America

Getting to the main cities in the Rockies from anywhere else in **North America** is rarely a problem. Flying is the quickest but most expensive way to get there, and most major airlines operate daily scheduled flights to Denver and Salt Lake City from across the country. The least expensive method is traveling by bus, though the great distances and frequent stops make for slow going. Trains are not much of an option due to the sparse rail network through the region. Seeing as you'll need a car to get around much of the region, the most effective option is driving yourself.

By air

Denver (DIA) and to a lesser extent Salt Lake City (SLC) are the main **air** hubs into the Rocky Mountains. Both have excellent links to the rest of the USA and Canada, and from each there are daily flights to most major towns and cities in the region.

Barring a fare war, round-trip prices to both Denver and Salt Lake City start at around $250 from New York, $225 and $150 respectively from Los Angeles, and around CAN$400 from Vancouver and Toronto. What makes more difference than your choice of carrier are the conditions governing the ticket – whether it's fully refundable, the time and day and most importantly the **time of year** you travel. Least expensive of all is a non-summer-season midweek flight, booked and paid for at least three weeks in advance. Also keep in mind that one-way tickets are sometimes more expensive than round-trip tickets. While it's good to call the airlines directly to get a sense of their official fares, it's also worth checking with a reputable **travel agent** to find out about any **special deals** or student/youth fares that may be available.

Travelers intending to fly from **Canada** are likely to find that fares are somewhat higher than they are for flights wholly within the US. You may well find that it's worth the effort to get to a US city first, and fly on to the Rockies from there.

Onward flights within the Rockies from Denver and Salt Lake City can be surprisingly expensive, to the point where it's worth considering car rental instead. Examples of round-trip fares from Denver include Boise ($350), Missoula ($280), and Cheyenne ($250), and from Salt Lake City the same destinations are respectively $85 (a good deal with Delta), $230, and $390.

Airlines

Air Canada ⓣ1-888/247-2262, ⓦwww.aircanada.ca.
America West Airlines ⓣ1-800/235-9292, ⓦwww.americawest.com.
American Airlines ⓣ1-800/433-7300, ⓦwww.aa.com.
American Trans Air ⓣ1-800/435-9282, ⓦwww.ata.com.
Continental Airlines domestic ⓣ1-800/523-3273, ⓦwww.continental.com.
Delta Air Lines domestic ⓣ1-800/221-1212, ⓦwww.delta.com.
Frontier Airlines ⓣ1-800/432-1359, ⓦwww.flyfrontier.com.
JetBlue ⓣ1-800/538-2583, ⓦwww.jetblue.com.
Northwest/KLM Airlines domestic ⓣ1-800/225-2525, ⓦwww.nwa.com.
Reno Air ⓣ1-800/433-7300, ⓦwww.aa.com. Part of American Airlines.
Southwest Airlines ⓣ1-800/435-9792, ⓦwww.southwest.com.
TWA domestic ⓣ1-800/221-2000, ⓦwww.twa.com.
United Airlines domestic ⓣ1-800/241-6522, ⓦwww.ual.com.
US Airways domestic ⓣ1-800/428-4322, ⓦwww.usairways.com.

By train

Anyone who has ever traveled through the Alps by rail knows that, in theory, the Rockies would be a perfect destination for **train travel**. Unfortunately there are very few rail services in the area, and those that do exist tend to be quite expensive.

The most northerly **Amtrak** route, the Empire Builder, heads east from Seattle, calling in at Sandpoint in Idaho and at Libby, Whitefish, West Glacier, Essex, East Glacier Park, and Browning in Montana before dropping down onto the plains and on to Minneapolis and Chicago. The California Zephyr, which runs from Chicago to San Francisco (53 hours), calls in at Denver, Fraser-Winter Park, Glenwood Springs, and Grand Junction in Colorado as well as Salt Lake City in Utah. In southern Colorado, the Southwest Chief from Los Angeles cuts through the towns of Trinidad, La Junta, and Lamar before heading on to Kansas City and Chicago.

Before being swayed by the romance of rail travel, bear in mind that Amtrak **fares** are often more expensive than flying, though off-peak discounts and special deals can make the train an economical choice. One-way cross-country fares are around $285, though if you're traveling round-trip you can take advantage of **Explore America** fares, which are zone-based and allow three stopovers – within 45 days – in between your origin and eventual return. Travel within the West (from Denver to the Pacific) costs $229 between September and May or $259 from June to August; within the West and Midwest (west of Chicago) costs $299/359; and for the entire USA the cost is $359/419. While Amtrak's basic fares are decent value, if you want to travel in a bit more comfort the cost rises quickly. **Sleeping compartments**, which include meals, small toilets and showers, start at around $150 per night for one or two people.

For all information on **Amtrak fares and schedules**, and to make reservations, use the toll-free number ⓣ1-800/USA-RAIL or website (ⓦwww.amtrak.com). Do not call individual stations.

By bus

Bus travel is the most tedious and time-consuming way to get to the Rockies, and, for all the discomfort, it won't really save you much money. **Greyhound** (ⓣ1-800/231-2222, ⓦwww.greyhound.com), the sole long-distance operator, has an extensive network of destinations throughout the area. A one-way ticket from New York to Denver costs $109 ($184 round-trip), with cheaper deals if you buy in advance.

The only reason to go Greyhound is if you're planning to visit a number of other places en route; Greyhound's **Ameripass** is good for unlimited travel within a certain time, and costs $199 for seven days, $299 for fifteen days and $399 for thirty days.

Smaller regional bus companies provide services between towns and cities within individual states and shuttle services to ski resorts – these are detailed in the relevant chapters.

By car

Driving your own car gives the greatest freedom and flexibility. If you don't have one, **renting a car** is the usual story of phoning your local branch of one of the majors (Avis, Budget, Hertz, Thrifty, etc – listed on p.27). Most have airport offices and addresses and phone numbers are comprehensively documented in the *Yellow Pages*.

Also worth considering are **fly-drive deals**, which give cut-rate (and sometimes free) car rental when buying an air ticket. They usually work out cheaper than renting on the spot and are especially good value if you intend to do a lot of driving.

One thing to bear in mind when driving in the Rockies is that conditions can often be extreme. Snow and subzero temperatures in winter, highs of over 100°F in summer, altitude and some pretty gnarly roads once you get off the beaten track mean you really need a reliable vehicle for major journeys, and in many cases a 4WD is preferable.

Package tours

Many operators run **all-inclusive packages** that combine plane tickets and hotel accommodation with (for example) skiing, sightseeing, wining and dining, or excursions to tourist sites. Even if the "package" aspect doesn't thrill you to pieces, these deals can still be more convenient and sometimes even work out to be more economical than arranging the same thing yourself, providing you don't mind losing a little flexibility. With such a vast range of packages available, it's impossible to give an overview – major travel agents will have brochures detailing what's available.

Tour operators

Abercrombie & Kent ⓣ630/954-2944 or 1-800/323-7308, ⓦwww.abercrombiekent.com. Easy adventure travel for the well-heeled in Colorado and Utah, but expect to pay up to $2000 for a week's rafting, biking, hiking, etc.

Adventure Center ⓣ510/654-1879 or 1-800/228-8747, ⓦwww.adventure-center.com. Guided hiking and "soft adventure" specialists, including an all-inclusive fifteen-day hiking tour starting in Yellowstone and heading south for more hikes in Colorado and Utah ($975).

AmeriCan Adventures/Roadrunner Worldwide Hosteling Treks ⓣ1-800/873-5872, ⓦwww.americanadventures.com. Van and small bus tours aimed at active hosteling types; a nineteen-day Western national park tour starts at around $1000.

Backroads ⓣ510/527-1555 or 1-800/462-2848, ⓦwww.backroads.com. Well run cycling, hiking, and multisport tours. A biking, hiking, and rafting tour from Telluride to Silverton in Colorado runs around $2000, including some very fine lodging choices.

Holidaze Ski Tours ⓣ1-800/526-2827, ⓦwww.holidaze.com. Rocky Mountain ski holidays.

International Gay & Lesbian Travel Association ⓣ1-800/448-8550, ⓦwww.iglta.org.

Mountain Travel-Sobek ⓣ1-888/687-6235, ⓦwww.mtsobek.com. A well-established US-based adventure travel company offering intricately planned activity holidays. A six-day rafting tour of the Middle Fork of the Salmon River, including day-hikes and very fine backcountry cookouts, costs $1700.

REI Adventures ⓣ1-800/622-2236, ⓦwww.rei.com. Climbing, cycling, hiking, cruising, paddling, and multisport tours. A week-long winter snowshoe/cross-country ski tour of Yellowstone and Grand Tetons national parks – including fine ranch accommodation – costs $1500.

Getting there from Britain and Ireland

Although you can fly to the US from many of Britain's regional airports, the only **non stop flight** into the Rockies leaves from London Gatwick and heads to Denver. The flight, a daily service with British Airways, takes around ten hours. **For one-stop flights** travelers can choose between either Continental, which also flies to Denver from Gatwick, but via Houston six times per week; or United Airlines who offer two daily flights to Denver from London Heathrow, one via Newark, the other via Chicago. Most other carriers flying from Britain to the US will also be able to put you on a connecting flight to Denver – or the other big regional hub, Salt Lake City. Typically you end up changing planes and waiting times between flights vary wildly. A basic round-trip economy-class ticket will cost around £500 in high season and about £100–200 less during other times.

The best choices for those who don't live around London are a bit different. The quickest services will involve taking a flight to the US from a regional airport like Manchester or Glasgow (both offered by Continental), then a connecting flight from a US airport. The cheapest services are, however, usually offered by European carriers, who will fly you to a hub like Paris, Amsterdam, or Frankfurt for a connecting flight to the US, then another on to Denver. These trips can become eighteen- to twenty-hour odysseys, but might be worth it if the fare is right.

Travel agents (see opposite) can offer cut-price seats on direct **charter flights**. These tend to be limited to the summer season, be restricted to so-called "holiday destinations," and have fixed departure and return dates. Brochures are available in most high street travel agents, or contact the specialists direct. **Packages** – fly-drive, flight/accommodation deals, and guided tours (or a combination of all three) – can also work out cheaper, and there are scores of tour operators willing to help book a trip (see opposite).

> One word of **warning**: it's not a good idea to buy a **one-way** ticket to the States. Not only are they rarely good value compared to a round-trip ticket, but US immigration officials usually take them as a sign that you aren't planning to go home, and may refuse your entry.

Airlines

Air France ⓣ0845/084 5111, Republic of Ireland ⓣ01/605 0383, ⓦwww.airfrance.co.uk.

British Airways ⓣ0845/773 3377, in Republic of Ireland ⓣ0141/222 2345, ⓦwww.britishairways. com.

Continental ⓣ0800/776464, Republic of Ireland ⓣ01/814 5311, ⓦwww.flycontinental.com. Six times per week to Denver via Houston.

Delta ⓣ0800/414767, Northern Ireland ⓣ028/9048 0526, Republic of Ireland

Ⓣ1800/414767, Ⓦwww.delta.com.
KLM Ⓣ0870/507 4074, Northern Ireland Ⓣ0990/074074, Republic of Ireland Ⓣ0345/445588, Ⓦwww.klmuk.com.
Lufthansa Ⓣ0845/773 7747, Republic of Ireland Ⓣ01/844 5544, Ⓦwww.lufthansa.com.
United Airlines Ⓣ0845/844 4777, Republic of Ireland Ⓣ1800/535300, Ⓦwww.ual.com.

Travel agents

Bridge the World Ⓣ020/7911 0900, Ⓦwww.bridgetheworld.com. Specializing in round-the-world tickets, with good deals aimed at the backpacker market.
Destination Group Ⓣ020/7400 7000, Ⓦwww.destination-group.com. Good discount airfares as well as inclusive packages.
Flightbookers Ⓣ020/7757 2444, Ⓦwww.ebookers.com. Low fares on an extensive selection of scheduled flights.
The London Flight Center Ⓣ020/7244 6411, Ⓦwww.topdecktravel.co.uk. Long-established agent dealing in discount flights.
North South Travel Ⓣ & Ⓕ 01245/608291, Ⓦwww.northsouthtravel.co.uk. Friendly, competitive travel agency, offering discounted fares – profits are used to support projects in the developing world, especially the promotion of sustainable tourism.
STA Travel Ⓣ0870/160 6070, Ⓦwww.statravel.co.uk. Worldwide specialists in low-cost flights and tours for students and under-26s, though other customers welcome.
Trailfinders, Ⓣ020/7937 5400; Ⓦwww.trailfinders.com. One of the best-informed and most efficient agents for independent travelers; produce a very useful quarterly magazine worth scrutinizing for round-the-world routes. Branches nationwide.
usit CAMPUS Ⓣ0870/240 1010, Ⓦwww.usitcampus.co.uk. Student/youth travel specialists, offering discount flights throughout North America.

Tour operators

Airtours Ⓣ0870/241 2567, Ⓦwww.airtours.co.uk. Large tour company offering good-value ski packages to Colorado and Utah's larger resorts.
American Adventures Ⓣ01892/512700, Ⓦwww.americanadventures.com. Organize small-group tours, like the thirteen-day Western Adventure, which includes lots of activities, though the more expensive like whitewater rafting are extra, for £600.
American Holidays Belfast Ⓣ028/9023 8762, Dublin Ⓣ01/679 8800 or 679 6611. Specialists in travel to USA.
Explore Worldwide Ⓣ01252/760000, Ⓦwww.explore.co.uk. An upscale operator whose two-week tours include visits to several national parks and activities like hiking, canoeing, and whitewater rafting for around £1200.

Flights from Ireland

There are no direct flights to the Rocky Mountains from Ireland, so you're best bet is either to take Aer Lingus to New York and get a connecting flight there, or fly to London for one of the services from there. The **cheapest flights** from Ireland – if you're under 26 or a student – are available from usit. Student-only return fares to Denver range from €800 to €570. Ordinary Apex fares are only marginally higher.

Travel agents in Ireland

CIE Tours International Dublin Ⓣ01/703 1888, Ⓦwww.cietours.ie. General flight and tour agent.
Joe Walsh Tours Dublin Ⓣ01/872 2555 or 676 3053, Cork Ⓣ021/277950, Ⓦwww.joewalshtours.ie. General budget fares agent.
Liffey Travel Dublin Ⓣ01/878 8322 or 878 8063. Package tour specialists.
McCarthy's Travel Cork Ⓣ021/270127, Ⓦwww.mccarthystravel.ie. General flight agent.
Trailfinders Dublin Ⓣ01/677 7888, Ⓦwww.trailfinders.com. One of the best-informed and most efficient agents for independent travelers.
usit NOW Belfast Ⓣ028/9032 7111, Dublin Ⓣ01/602 1777 or 677 8117, Cork Ⓣ021/270900, Derry Ⓣ028/7137 1888, Ⓦwww.usitnow.ie. Student and youth specialists for flights and trains.

Getting there from Australia and NZ

There are no direct flights from **Australia** and **New Zealand** to Denver or Salt Lake City. Whether you go via the Pacific or the more roundabout route through Asia, you'll have to touch down on the US West Coast – in Los Angeles or San Francisco – before going on to the Rockies. Via the Pacific most flights are nonstop, with traveling time between Auckland/Sydney and the US West Coast twelve to fourteen hours; some flights allow for stopovers in Honolulu or one of a number of the South Pacific Islands. If you go via Asia, you'll usually have to spend a night, or the best part of a day, in the airline's home city.

Airfares vary throughout the year, with seasonal differences generally working out around A/NZ$200–300. For most airlines, **low season** is from mid-January to the end of February and October to the end of November. **High season** runs mid-May to the end of August and December to mid-January and **shoulder seasons** cover the rest of the year. Seat availability on most international flights out of Australia and New Zealand is limited, so it's best to book several weeks ahead.

Traveling from Australia's east-coast cities, **fares** to Denver and Salt Lake City cost much the same, while from Perth they may be A$300–400 more. There are daily flights from Sydney to Denver and Salt Lake City via Los Angeles or San Francisco on United and Qantas/American from A$1900 (low season). Via Asia, the best deal is often on JAL (A$1800–2100), which includes a night's stopover in Tokyo in the fare. If you don't want to spend the night, Cathay Pacific and Singapore Airlines can get you there, via a transfer in the home cities of Hong Kong and Singapore, for A$2000–2200.

From **New Zealand**, most flights are out of **Auckland** (add NZ$200–250 for Christchurch and Wellington departures), with the best deals on Air New Zealand (either nonstop or via Honolulu, Fiji, or Tonga) and Qantas (direct or via Sydney) to Los Angeles, where you would link with American for the onward flight to Denver or Salt Lake (NZ$2200–2600). United Airlines have regular deals on fares all the way to Denver or Salt Lake that may undercut their competition. Via Asia, Singapore Airlines has convenient connecting services to LA and San Francisco from NZ$2300, while the best value for money (NZ$1950–2350) is on JAL via Tokyo.

If you intend to take in the Rockies as part of a world trip, a round-the-world (**RTW**) ticket offers the greatest flexibility. Many international airlines are now aligned with one of two globe-spanning networks: the "Star Alliance," which links Air New Zealand, United, Lufthansa, Thai, SAS, Varig, and Air Canada; and "One World," which combines routes run by American, British Airways, Canadian Airlines, Cathay Pacific, LAN Chile, and Qantas. Both offer RTW deals with three stopovers in each continental sector you visit, with the option of adding additional sectors relatively cheaply. Fares depend on the number of sectors required, but start at around A$2300/NZ$2700 (low season) for a US–Europe–Asia and home itinerary.

Airlines

Air New Zealand New Zealand 09/357 3000, ⓦwww.airnz.co.nz.
American Airlines Australia ⓣ1300/650 747, New Zealand ⓣ09/309 0735 or 0800/887 997, ⓦwww.aa.com.
Cathay Pacific Australia ⓣ13 1747 or 02/9931 5500, New Zealand ⓣ09/379 0861, ⓦwww.cathaypacific.com.
JAL Australia ⓣ02/9272 1111, New Zealand ⓣ09/379 3202.
Qantas Australia ⓣ13 1313, New Zealand ⓣ09/357 8900 or 0800/808 767, ⓦwww.qantas.com.au.
Singapore Airlines Australia ⓣ13 1011 or 02/9350 0262, New Zealand ⓣ09/303 2129 or 0800/808 909, ⓦwww.singaporeair.com.
United Airlines Australia ⓣ13 1777, New Zealand ⓣ09/379 3800, ⓦwww.ual.com.

Travel agents

Anywhere Travel Australia ⓣ02/9663 0411 or 018 401 014, ⓔanywhere@ozemail.com.au.
Budget Travel New Zealand ⓣ09/366 0061 or ⓣ0800/808 040.
Destinations Unlimited New Zealand ⓣ09/373 4033.
Flight Centre Australia ⓣ13 1600 for nearest branch, New Zealand ⓣ09/358 4310, ⓦwww.flightcentre.com.au.
Northern Gateway Australia ⓣ08/8941 1394, ⓔoztravel@norgate.com.au.
STA Travel Australia ⓣ13 1776 for nearest branch, New Zealand ⓣ09/309 0458 or 366 6673, ⓦwww.statravel.com.au.
Student Uni Travel Australia ⓣ02/9232 8444, ⓔAustralia@backpackers.net.
Thomas Cook Australia ⓣ13 1771 or ⓣ1800/801 002, New Zealand ⓣ09/379 3920, ⓦwww.thomascook.com.au.
Trailfinders Australia ⓣ02/9247 7666.
usit BEYOND New Zealand ⓣ09/379 4224 or 0800/788 336, ⓦwww.usitbeyond.co.nz

Specialist agents

Adventure World Australia ⓣ1300/363 055, New Zealand ⓣ09/524 5118, ⓦwww.adventureworld.com.au. Agent for a number of adventure travel companies that offer group trips in the Rockies, including Trek America (Yellowstone and such for

18–38s; ⓦwww.trekamerica.com) and Explore Worldwide (hiking trips in the Rockies, tailored to a slightly older market; ⓦwww.exploreworldwide.com).

Canada and America Travel Specialists Australia ⓣ02/9922 4600, ⓦwww.canam.com.au. Wholesaler of Greyhound Ameripasses plus flights and accommodation in North America.

Silke's Travel Australia ⓣ1800/807 860, or 02/9380 5835, ⓦwww.silkes.com.au. Gay and lesbian specialist travel agent.

The Ski and Snowboard Travel Company Australia ⓣ02/9955 5201 or 1800/251 934, ⓦwww.skiandsnowboard.com.au. Customized skiing holidays in Colorado, Wyoming, and Utah.

Snow Bookings Only Australia ⓣ03/9809 2699 or ⓣ1800/623 266, ⓦwww.snowbookingsonly.com.au. Skiing in the USA.

Sydney International Travel Centre ⓣ02/9299 8000, ⓦwww.sydneytravel.com.au. US flights, accommodation, city stays, and car rental.

Red tape and visas

Under the Visa Waiver Scheme, citizens of Andorra, Argentina, Australia, Austria, Belgium, Brunei, Denmark, Finland, France, Germany, Iceland, Ireland, Italy, Japan, Liechtenstein, Luxembourg, Monaco, Netherlands, New Zealand, Norway, San Marino, Spain, Sweden, Switzerland, and the United Kingdom visiting the United States for a period of less than ninety days only need a passport and a visa waiver form. The latter will be provided either by your travel agent or by the airline during check-in or on the plane, and must be presented to immigration on arrival. Prospective visitors from other parts of the world not mentioned above must have a valid passport and a nonimmigrant visitor's visa. To obtain a visa, fill in the application form available at most travel agents and send it with a full passport to your nearest US Embassy or Consulate. Visas are not issued to convicted criminals. You'll need to give precise dates of your trip and declare that you're not intending to live or work in the US (if you are intending to do either of these things, see "Staying on", p.6).

Immigration controls

During the flight, you'll be handed an **immigration form** (and a customs declaration; see overleaf), which must be given up at immigration control once you land. The form requires details of where you are staying on your first night (if you don't know, write "touring") and the date you intend to **leave** the US. You probably won't be asked unless you look disreputable in the eyes of the official on duty, but you should be able to prove that you have enough money to support yourself while in the US – $300–400 a week is usually considered sufficient – as anyone revealing the slightest intention of working while in the country is likely to be refused admission.

US Embassies and Consulates

Australia Moonah Place, Canberra ⓣ02/6214 5600, ⓦwww.usis-australia.gov.

Denmark Dag Hammerskjölds Allé 24, 2100 Copenhagen ⓣ35 55 31 44, ⓦwww.usembassy.dk.

Ireland 42 Elgin St, Ballsbridge, Dublin ⓣ01/688 8777.

Netherlands Lange Voorhout 102, 2514 EJ, The Hague ⓣ70/310 9209, ⓦwww.usemb.nl.

New Zealand 29 Fitzherbert Terrace, Thorndon, Wellington ⓣ644/472 2068.

Norway Drammensveien 18, Oslo ⓣ22 44 85 50.

Spain Serrano 75, 28006 Madrid ⓣ915 872 200, ⓦwww.embusa.es

Sweden Dag Hammarskjölds Väg 31, SE-11589 Stockholm ⓣ08/783 5300, ⓦwww.usis.usemb.se.

UK 24 Grosvenor Square, London W1A 1AE ⓣ020/7499 7010, ⓦwww.usembassy.org.uk; 3 Regent Terrace, Edinburgh EH7 5BW ⓣ0131/556 8315; Queens House, 14 Queen St, Belfast BT1 6EQ (ⓣ028/9032 8239).

Customs

Customs officers will relieve you of your customs declaration and ask if you have any fresh foods. You'll also be asked if you've visited a farm in the last month: if you have, you may well have your shoes taken away for inspection. The **duty-free allowance** if you're over 17 is 200 cigarettes or 50 cigars (*not* Cuban), a liter of spirits (if you're over 21), and $100 worth of gifts, which can include an additional 100 cigars. As well as foods and anything agricultural, it's prohibited to carry into the country any articles from North Korea, Iran, Iraq, Libya, Sudan, or Cuba, obscene publications, drug paraphernalia, lottery tickets, chocolate liqueurs. Anyone caught carrying drugs into the country will not only face prosecution, but be entered in the records as an undesirable and probably denied entry for all time. If you take prescription medicines, it's a good idea to carry a letter from a doctor explaining the exact nature of the pills you are carrying.

Extensions and leaving

The date stamped on your passport is the latest you're legally allowed to stay. Leaving a few days later may not matter, especially if you're heading home, but more than a week or so can result in a protracted, rather unpleasant interrogation from officials, which may cause you to miss your flight and be denied entry to the US in the future. Your American hosts and/or employers could also face legal proceedings.

To get an **extension** before your time is up, apply at the nearest **US Immigration and Naturalization Service** (INS) office; the address will be under the Federal Government Offices listings at the front of the phone book. They will automatically assume that you're working illegally and it's up to you to convince them otherwise. Do this by providing evidence of ample finances, and, if you can, bring along an upstanding American citizen to vouch for you. You'll also have to explain why you didn't plan for the extra time initially.

Health and insurance

Though the worst that befalls most travelers through the Rockies is a sunburn or common cold, you will still want the security of health insurance. Even though EU healthcare privileges apply throughout the Rockies, residents of the United Kingdom would do well to take out an insurance policy before travelling to cover against theft, loss, and illness or injury. Before paying for a new policy, however, it's worth checking whether you are already covered: some all-risks home insurance policies may cover your possessions when overseas, and many private medical schemes include cover when abroad. In Canada, provincial health plans usually provide partial cover for medical mishaps in the US, while holders of official student/teacher/youth cards in Canada and the US are entitled to meagre accident coverage and hospital inpatient benefits. Students will often find that their student health coverage extends during the vacations and for one term beyond the date of last enrollment.

After exhausting the possibilities above, you might want to contact a specialist travel insurance company, or consider the travel insurance deal we offer (see box, opposite). A typical travel insurance policy usually provides cover for the loss of baggage, tickets, and – up to a certain limit – cash or checks, as well as cancellation or curtailment of your

Rough Guide travel insurance

Rough Guides offers its own travel insurance, customized for our readers by a leading UK broker and backed by a Lloyds underwriter. It's available for anyone, of any nationality, traveling anywhere in the world.

There are two main Rough Guide insurance plans: **Essential**, for basic, no-frills cover; and **Premier** – with more generous and extensive benefits. Alternatively, you can take out annual multitrip insurance, which covers you for any number of trips throughout the year (with a maximum of sixty days for any one trip). Unlike many policies, the Rough Guides schemes are calculated by the day, so if you're travelling for 27 days rather than a month, that's all you pay for. If you intend to be away for the whole year, the **Adventurer** policy will cover you for 365 days. Each plan can be supplemented with a "Hazardous Activities Premium" if you plan to indulge in sports considered dangerous, such as skiing, scuba-diving or trekking. Rough Guides also does good deals for older travelers, and will insure you up to any age, at prices comparable to SAGA's.

For a policy quote, call the Rough Guide Insurance Line on US freefone ⓣ1-866/220-5588; UK freefone ⓣ0800/015 0906, or, if you're calling from elsewhere ⓣ+44 1243/621046. Alternatively, get an online quote at ⓦwww.roughguides.com/insurance.

journey. Most of them exclude so-called **high-risk activities** unless an extra premium is paid: in the Rockies, this can mean off-piste skiing and snowboarding, rock climbing, hiking, downhill mountain biking, white-water rafting, and snowmobiling, though probably not kayaking or jeep safaris. Many policies can be chopped and changed to exclude coverage you don't need – for example, sickness and accident benefits can often be excluded or included at will. If you do take medical coverage, ascertain whether benefits will be paid as treatment proceeds or only after return home, and whether there is a 24-hour medical emergency number.

When securing **baggage cover**, make sure that the per-article limit – typically around $500 – will cover your most valuable possession. If you need to make a claim, you should keep receipts for medicines and medical treatment, and in the event you have anything stolen, you must obtain an official report from the police containing a reference number.

Health

If you have a serious **accident** while in the Rockies, emergency services will generally get to you quickly (depending on how remote the location) and charge you later. For emergencies or ambulance, dial ⓣ911, the nationwide emergency number (or whatever variant may be on the information plate of the pay phone).

Should you need to see a doctor, lists can be found in the *Yellow Pages* under "Clinics" or "Physicians and Surgeons." The basic consultation fee is $50–100, payable in advance. Medications aren't cheap either – keep all your receipts for later claims on your insurance policy.

Foreign visitors should bear in mind that many pills available over the counter at home require a **prescription** in the US – most codeine-based painkillers, for example – and that local brand names can be confusing; ask for advice at the **pharmacy** in any **drugstore**.

Health issues specific to the Rockies include **altitude sickness** (see box, overleaf), **dehydration/heat stroke** in summer, and **hypothermia** in winter, both of which are easily avoided by drinking plenty of fluids and by wearing a layered system of clothing in the case of the latter.

Encounters with "dangerous" animals are rare and not too difficult to avoid. Although **bears** (see box p.550) get the bulk of the publicity, more people are killed by moose and snakes each year in the US, and all of these are invariably acting in self defense. In all cases, by using common sense, making the animal aware of your presence and avoiding a surprise encounter, you should easily survive your encounter with the wild.

Water quality is excellent throughout the Rockies and it's quite safe to drink from

Altitude sickness

At higher elevations, you should be aware of the possibility of **altitude sickness**, especially if you've traveled high up straight from sea level. The symptoms, including lightheadedness, weakness, headaches, nausea and breathlessness, are brought on by the body having problems trying to process less oxygen at higher altitude. Although there isn't actually less oxygen in the atmosphere, the barometric pressure is lower so you absorb less oxygen from the air.

At the kind of heights attained in the Rockies, altitude sickness is unlikely to bring on serious problems such as pulmonary odema (water on the brain), but if you start to feel any of the above symptoms you should descend as quickly as possible to a considerably lower level, take plenty of fluids (not alcohol), eat well and rest. The problem should sort itself out within 24 hours. If you're at a ski resort, head for the ski patrol or local clinic, who should be able to help you with a small dose of supplemental oxygen.

The problem can be exacerbated by pushing it too hard on your first day in the mountains, and by fatigue, poor nutrition and hangovers.

taps. However, while mountain streams may look clean and inviting, water should be chemically treated, boiled, or filtered before you drink it to avoid the risk of *giardia* contamination.

Another small nuisance are **ticks**, which can pass on Colorado Tick Fever and Rocky Mountain Spotted Fever. Both have similar symptoms – headaches and muscle aches, nausea, vomiting, skin rash, and abdominal pain. Ticks are most likely to attach themselves to bare legs or feet when walking through brush, forest or grassland. If you find a tick burrowing into you skin, grab it by the head with a pair of tweezers and gently pull it out. If any of the above symptoms occur within two weeks, contact a doctor.

It's also worth carrying insect repellent for **mosquitoes**, which can get amazingly annoying in the woods in summer.

Costs, money, and banks

To help with planning your vacation in the Rockies, this book contains detailed price information for accommodation and eating as well as a range of activities. Unless otherwise stated, the hotel price codes (explained on p.30) are for the cheapest double room during peak travel times; note however, that the price codes do not include local hotel taxes, which usually range from five to ten percent, but can soar as high as twenty percent. Meal prices listed include food only and not drinks or tip. For museums and similar attractions, the prices we quote are generally for adults; you can assume that children get in half-price. Naturally, costs will increase slightly overall during the life of this edition, but the relative comparisons should remain valid.

Costs

Accommodation is likely to be your biggest single expense. Few hotel or motel rooms in the Rockies cost under $35; it's more usual to pay between $40 and $80 for anything halfway decent in a city or town, while rates in ski resorts can go much higher. Although some of the larger towns and some resorts have hostels offering dorm beds – usually around $15 – they are by no means everywhere, besides which they save little money for two or more people traveling together. Camping, of course, is cheap, ranging from free to about $20 a night per site.

As for **food**, $15 a day is enough for an adequate life-support diet; on a daily total of around $30 you can dine pretty well. Beyond this, everything hinges on how much sightseeing, drinking and socializing you do. Much of any of these, and you're likely to go through upwards of $50 a day.

The rates for **traveling around**, especially on buses, may look inexpensive on paper, but the distances involved mean that costs soon mount up. For a group of two or more, **renting a car** is a very good investment, not least because it enables you to camp or stay in the ubiquitous budget motels along the interstate highways.

Remember that a **sales tax** is added to virtually everything you buy in stores except for groceries. In Colorado the sales tax varies from three to four percent; in Wyoming it's four percent; Idaho five percent; Utah six percent. Montana currently has no state sales tax.

Cash and travelers' checks

Most people on vacation simply draw **cash** as needed from automatic teller machines (**ATMs**), since most banks' cards are linked to one of the major international networks like Plus or Cirrus – if in doubt about your own card's usefulness overseas, check with your bank before you leave.

ATMs are pretty easy to find, even in far-flung corners of the Rockies. In addition to banks, many supermarkets and convenience stores have outlets where you can withdraw cash for a small transaction fee (usually around $1–2).

Major banks in larger cities like Denver and Salt Lake will **change foreign travelers' checks** and **currency**, but it's highly unlikely you'll be able to exchange your British Pounds or Australian Dollars in a small mountain town. In any case it's far better to take only **US dollars checks** with you, as these can be used as cash in many stores. The most recognized kind are American Express and Thomas Cook, available from their various agencies or from banks in your home country (the usual fee for travelers' check sales is one or two percent). It pays to get a selection of denominations, from $20 to $100. Make sure to keep the purchase agreement and a record of check serial numbers safe and separate from the checks themselves. See p.41 for what to do if your checks are lost or stolen.

Credit and debit cards

Credit cards are a very handy backup source of funds, and can be used either in ATMs or over the counter. MasterCard, Visa and American Express are accepted just about everywhere, but other cards may not be recognized in the US. Remember that all cash advances are treated as loans, with interest accruing daily from the date of withdrawal; there may be a transaction fee on

Money: a note for foreign travelers

Regular upheaval in the world money markets causes the relative value of the US dollar against other currencies to vary considerably. Generally speaking, one Canadian dollar is worth between 75¢ and 85¢; one Australian dollar is worth between 50¢ and 60¢; and one New Zealand dollar is worth between 40¢ and 50¢. Over the last five years, the dollar/sterling rate has remained remarkably stable at between $1.55 and $1.65 to the pound.

US currency comes in bills of $1, $5, $10, $20, $50, and $100, plus various larger (and rarer) denominations. It's a good idea to check each bill carefully, as all are the same size and color. The dollar is made up of 100 cents, with coins of 1 cent (known as a penny, and regarded as worthless), 5 cents (a nickel), 10 cents (a dime), and 25 cents (a quarter). Quarters are very useful for buses, vending machines, parking meters, and telephones, so always carry plenty. Coin collectors might want to look out for the new "state" quarter designs currently being introduced, and also the golden "Sacagawea" dollar coin – named after the Shoshone woman who assisted Lewis and Clark on their expedition through the Rockies – issued in 2000. Very occasionally you might come across JFK half-dollars (50¢), Susan B. Anthony dollar coins, or a two-dollar bill.

Visa Travel Money (ⓦ www.visa.com)

This is a disposable debit card prepaid with dedicated travel funds which you can access from over 660,000 Visa ATMs in 120 countries with a PIN that you select yourself. When your funds are depleted, you simply throw the card away. Since you can buy up to nine cards to access the same funds – useful for couples/families traveling together – it's recommended that you buy at least one extra as a backup in case your first is lost or stolen. For 24-hour customer assistance within the US, dial ⓣ800/847-2399. In the UK, many Thomas Cook outlets sell the card.

top of this. However, you may be able to make withdrawals from ATMs using your debit card, which is not liable to interest payments, and the flat transaction fee is usually quite small ($1–2). Make sure you have a personal identification number (PIN) that's designed to work overseas.

Wiring money

Having money **wired** from home using one of the companies listed below is never convenient or cheap, and should be considered a last resort. It's also possible to have money wired directly from a bank in your home country to a bank in the US, although this is somewhat less reliable because it involves two separate institutions. If you go this route, your home bank will need the address of the branch bank where you want to pick up the money and the address and telex number of that bank's state head office, which will act as the clearing house; money wired this way normally takes two working days to arrive, and costs around £25/$40 per transaction.

Money-wiring companies

In North America

American Express Moneygram ⓣ1-800/926-9400, ⓦwww.moneygram.com.
Thomas Cook ⓣ1-800/287-7362, ⓦwww.us.thomascook.com.
Western Union ⓣ1-800/325-6000, ⓦwww.westernunion.com.

In Australia

American Express Moneygram ⓣ1300/139 060, ⓦwww.moneygram.com.
Western Union ⓣ1800/649 565, ⓦwww.westernunion.com.

In New Zealand

American Express Moneygram ⓣ09/379 8243 or 0800/262 263, ⓦwww.moneygram.com.
Western Union ⓣ09/270 0050, ⓦwww.westernunion.com.

In the UK and Ireland

Moneygram ⓣ0800/018 0104, ⓦwww.moneygram.com.
Thomas Cook ⓣ01733/318922, Belfast ⓣ028/9055 0030, Dublin ⓣ01/677 1721.
Western Union Money Transfer ⓣ0800/833833, ⓦwww.westernunion.com.

Youth and student discounts

Various official and quasi-official **youth/student ID cards** are available to full-time students and under-26s, but they bring few benefits to foreign visitors to the US. Full-time students are eligible for the International Student ID Card (ISIC), which may entitle the bearer to special air, rail and bus fares and discount entry to some attractions. For Americans there's also a health benefit, providing up to $3000 in emergency medical coverage and $100 a day for sixty days in the hospital, plus a 24-hour hotline to call in the event of a medical, legal, or financial emergency. The card costs $22 for Americans; Can$16 for Canadians; A$16.50 for Australians; NZ$21 for New Zealanders; and £6 in the UK.

The **International Youth Travel Card**, which costs US$22/£7, is for under-26s and carries the same benefits. Teachers qualify for the **International Teacher Card**, offering similar discounts and costing US$22, Can$16, £5, A$16.50, and NZ$21. All these cards are available in the US from Council Travel, STA, Travel CUTS, and, in Canada, Hostelling International (see p.32 for addresses); in Australia and New Zealand from STA or Campus Travel; and in the UK from usit CAMPUS and STA.

Information, maps, and websites

Advance information on any of the states in the Rocky Mountains can be obtained from the various statewide organizations listed below. Once you've arrived, you'll find most towns in the region have visitor centers of some description – often the chamber of commerce – as well as a United States Forest Service (USFS) office nearby: all are listed in the *Guide*. These will give out detailed information on the local area and can often help with finding accommodation. Free newspapers in most areas carry news of events and entertainment.

State tourist agencies

Colorado Colorado Travel and Tourism Authority, 1672 Pennsylvania St, Denver, CO 80203 ⓣ303/832-6171 or 1-800/265-6723, ⓦwww.colorado.com.
Idaho Idaho Recreation and Tourism, PO Box 83720, Boise, ID 83720, ⓦwww.visitid.org.
Montana Travel Montana, 1424 9th Ave, PO Box 200533, Helena, MT 59620 ⓣ406/444-2654 or 1-800/047-4868, ⓦwww.visitmt.com.
Utah The Utah Travel Council, Council Hall/Capitol Hill, Salt Lake City, UT 84114 ⓣ801/538-1900 or 1-800/200-1160, ⓦwww.utah.com.
Wyoming Wyoming Tourist Board, College Drive, Cheyenne, WY 82002 ⓣ307/777-7777 or 1-800/225-5996, ⓦwww.wyomingtourism.org.

Most of the tourist offices mentioned can supply you with good **maps**, either free or for a small charge, and, supplemented with our own, these should be enough for general sightseeing and touring. Rand McNally (ⓦwww.randmcnallystore.com) produces decent low-cost state maps and its *Road Atlas* covering the whole country plus Mexico and Canada, is a worthwhile investment if you're traveling further afield. For driving or cycling through rural areas, the *Atlas & Gazetteer* published for each state by DeLorme ($16.95 each; ⓦwww.delorme.com) are invaluable companions, with detailed city plans, marked campsites and reams of national park and forest information. The American Automobile Association (ⓣ1-800/222-4357, ⓦwww.aaa.com) has offices in most large cities and provides excellent free maps and travel assistance to its members, and to British members of the AA and RAC.

For detailed **hiking maps**, ranger stations in parks and wilderness areas all sell good-quality local maps for $1–3, and camping stores generally have a good selection too. Most bookstores will have a range of local trail guides, the best of which we've listed in Contexts, p.679.

Map and travel book outlets

USA and Canada

Adventurous Traveler Bookstore PO Box 64769, Burlington, VT 05406 ⓣ1-800/282-3963, ⓦwww.AdventurousTraveler.com.
Book Passage 51 Tamal Vista Blvd, Corte Madera, CA 94925 ⓣ415/927-0960, ⓦwww.bookpassage.com.
Complete Traveller 199 Madison Ave, New York, NY 10016 ⓣ212/685-9007.
Distant Lands 56 S Raymond St, Pasadena, CA 91105 ⓣ1-800/310-3220, ⓦwww.distantlands.com.
Elliot Bay Book Company 101 S Main St, Seattle, WA 98104 ⓣ206/624-6600 or 1-800/962-5311, ⓦwww.elliotbaybook.com.
Forsyth Travel Library 226 Westchester Ave, White Plains, NY 10604 ⓣ1-800/367-7984, ⓦwww.forsyth.com.
Globe Corner Bookstore 28 Church St, Cambridge, MA 02138 ⓣ1-800/358-6013, ⓦwww.globecorner.com.
GORP Adventure Library online only ⓣ1-800/754-8229, ⓦwww.gorp.com.
Map Link Inc. 30 S La Patera Lane, Unit 5, Santa Barbara, CA 93117 ⓣ805/692-6777, ⓦwww.maplink.com.
Phileas Fogg's Travel Center #87 Stanford Shopping Center, Palo Alto, CA 94304 ⓣ1-800/533-3644, ⓦwww.foggs.com.
Rand McNally 444 N Michigan Ave, Chicago, IL 60611 ⓣ312/321-1751, ⓦwww.randmcnally.com;

150 E 52nd St, New York, NY 10022 ⓣ212/758-7488; 595 Market St, San Francisco, CA 94105 ⓣ415/777-3131; around thirty stores across the US – call ⓣ1-800/333-0136 ext 2111 or check the website for the nearest store.

Travel Books & Language Center 4437 Wisconsin Ave, Washington, DC 20016 ⓣ1-800/220-2665, ⓦwww.bookweb.org/bookstore/travelbks.

The Travel Bug Bookstore 2667 W Broadway, Vancouver, BC V6K 2G2 ⓣ604/737-1122, ⓦwww.swifty.com/tbug.

World of Maps 1235 Wellington St, Ottawa, ON K1Y 3A3 ⓣ613/724-6776, ⓦwww.worldofmaps.com.

UK and Ireland

Blackwell's Map and Travel Shop 53 Broad St, Oxford OX1 3BQ ⓣ01865/792792, ⓦwww.bookshop.blackwell.co.uk.

Easons Bookshop 40 O'Connell St, Dublin 1 ⓣ01/873 3811, ⓦwww.eason.ie.

Heffers Map and Travel 20 Trinity St, Cambridge CB2 1TJ ⓣ01223/568568, ⓦwww.heffers.co.uk.

Hodges Figgis Bookshop 56–58 Dawson St, Dublin 2 ⓣ01/677 4754, ⓦwww.hodgesfiggis.com.

James Thin Melven's Bookshop 29 Union St, Inverness IV1 1QA ⓣ01463/233500, ⓦwww.jthin.co.uk.

John Smith and Sons 26 Colquhoun Ave, Glasgow G52 4PJ ⓣ0141/552 3377, ⓦwww.johnsmith.co.uk.

The Map Shop 30a Belvoir St, Leicester LE1 6QH ⓣ0116/247 1400.

National Map Center 22–24 Caxton St, SW1H 0QU ⓣ020/7222 2466, ⓦwww.mapsnmc.co.uk.

Newcastle Map Center 55 Grey St, Newcastle upon Tyne NE1 6EF ⓣ0191/261 5622, ⓦwww.traveller.ltd.uk.

Ordnance Survey of Northern Ireland Colby House, Stranmillis Ct, Belfast BT9 5BJ ⓣ028/9066 1244, ⓦwww.osni.gov.uk.

Ordnance Survey Service Phoenix Park, Dublin 8 ⓣ01/820 6100, ⓦwww.irlgov.ie/osi/.

Stanfords 12–14 Long Acre, London WC2E 9LP ⓣ020/7836 1321, ⓦwww.stanfords.co.uk; maps by mail or phone order are available on this number and via ⓔsales@stanfords.co.uk. Other branches within British Airways offices at 156 Regent St, London W1R 5TA ⓣ020/7434 4744, and 29 Corn St, Bristol BS1 1HT ⓣ0117/929 9966.

The Travel Bookshop 13–15 Blenheim Crescent, London W11 2EE ⓣ020/7229 5260, ⓦwww.thetravelbookshop.co.uk.

Australia and New Zealand

The Map Shop 6 Peel St, Adelaide ⓣ08/8231 2033, ⓦwww.mapshop.net.au.

Mapland 372 Little Bourke St, Melbourne ⓣ03/9670 4383, ⓦwww.mapland.com.au.

Mapworld 173 Gloucester St, Christchurch ⓣ03/374 5399, ⓕ03/374 5633, ⓦwww.mapworld.co.nz.

Perth Map Center 1/884 Hay St, Perth ⓣ08/9322 5733, ⓦwww.perthmap.com.au.

Specialty Maps 46 Albert St, Auckland ⓣ09/307 2217, ⓦwww.ubd-online.co.nz/maps.

Useful Rocky Mountain websites

Travel

Rough Guides ⓦwww.roughguides.com Post any of your pre-trip questions – or post-trip suggestions – in Travel Talk, our online forum for travelers.

Daily newspapers

For information on both local and national news, weather updates, sports scores and entertainment happenings, check out the following sites:

The Denver Post ⓦwww.denverpost.com

High Country News ⓦwww.hcn.org

The Rocky Mountain News ⓦwww.rockymountainnews.com

Outdoor pursuits

Backpacker Magazine ⓦwww.backpacker.com Online site of magazine focusing on hiking and backpacking – includes good Rocky Mountain state overviews along with a wide array of detailed trail listings. Also a good place to look before purchasing new gear.

Dirt World ⓦwww.dirtworld.com Site dedicated to mountain biking; has a good section devoted to trails in the various Rocky Mountain states.

Great Outdoor Recreation Pages ⓦwww.gorp.com A top online resource for all outdoor activities and related topics. Especially good on hiking, climbing, biking, and kayaking information. Highly recommended.

SkiMaps ⓦwww.skimaps.com The latest snowfall reports, plus the snow-base depth and trail maps for all the major skiing and snowboarding resorts in the Rockies.

Native culture

Pow Wows ⓦwww.powwows.com Thorough listings of upcoming Native American powwows, as well as explanations on the various outfits worn and dances performed.

Getting around

Having your own transport is definitely the preferred option for getting around the Rockies, and is absolutely essential if your trip is focused on national parks and other backcountry destinations. Amtrak can get you to Denver and Salt Lake City, and also travels across northern Montana and northern Idaho, as well as portions of central and southern Colorado; Greyhound and associated bus lines do get to many towns throughout the Rockies, but their coverage is nothing like comprehensive. Although distances can be great, driving through the Rockies is such a fantastically scenic experience that long hours behind the wheel won't seem much of a bother at all.

By bus

If you're traveling on your own, and making frequent stops, **buses** are a pretty cheap way to get around. The main long-distance service is **Greyhound** (ⓣ1-800/229-9424, ⓦwww.greyhound.com), which links all major cities and many smaller towns, and also networks with other bus lines such as Powder River Coach USA to provide the broadest possible service. Timetables for the entire network appear on the Greyhound website.

In many parts of the Rockies, buses are scarce or nonexistent; some private shuttle services pick up the slack, but there are many places you simply can't reach without a car. Greyhound buses are slightly less uncomfortable than you might expect, and it's feasible to save on a night's accommodation by traveling overnight and sleeping on the bus – though you may not feel up to much the next day.

It used to be that any sizeable community would have a Greyhound station; in many places, a gas station now doubles as the bus stop and ticket office. Reservations on the toll-free number are not essential but recommended – if a bus is full you may be forced to wait until the next one, sometimes overnight or longer.

Bus passes

Foreign visitors and US and Canadian nationals can all buy a **Greyhound Ameripass**, offering unlimited travel within a set time limit: most travel agents can oblige or you can order online at ⓦwww.greyhound.com. A seven-day pass costs $199; ten days is $249, fifteen days $299 and thirty days $399 (passes for 45 days and sixty days also available). All kids under twelve go half-price, and there are discounts for US students and seniors.

By train

The **Amtrak rail service** (ⓣ1-800/USA-RAIL, ⓦwww.amtrak.com) is generally very good, with reliable trains that are clean and well staffed. Unfortunately, coverage of the Rockies region is quite limited, and in any case there are few stations that give immediate access to the mountain towns and national parks that are probably your intended destinations. The three Amtrak services of potential use in the Rockies are the Empire Builder, the California Zephyr and the Southwest Chief. The Empire Builder goes from Chicago across the vast North Dakota plains and into northern Montana (including Glacier National Park) and northern Idaho, before heading on to Seattle or Portland. The California Zephyr leaves Chicago for Kansas City and then goes to Denver and Salt Lake City and on to the southern California coast. The Southwest Chief from Los Angeles cuts through the towns of Trinidad, La Junta, and Lamar in Colorado before heading on to Kansas City and Chicago.

Train passes

An **Amtrak Rail Pass** may be worth considering if you're engaged in broader travels within the US. Outside the peak travel season in particular, a rail pass may represent good value if you have a few long-distance hauls to do in a few days – and is a far more pleasant experience than travelling by bus.

Amtrak Rail Passes are available to anyone except residents of the US and Canada; they're valid for either fifteen or thirty days and include unlimited stops. A fifteen-day pass costs $325 during the peak travel season, which is June to early September ($200 the rest of the year); the thirty-day pass costs $405/270. For further details, check the website ⓦwww.amtrak.com. If a US citizen, the best deals going are **Explore America** passes; see p.13 for details.

Agents for Amtrak rail passes

UK and Ireland

usit CAMPUS ⓣ0870/240 1010, ⓦwww.usitcampus.co.uk. See p.15 for further contacts.

Australia and New Zealand

Rail Plus, Australia ⓣ1300/555 003 or 03/9642 8644, ⓔinfo@railplus.com.au; New Zealand ⓣ09/303 2484.

By car

Driving is by far the best way to get around the Rockies. Many smaller towns, national and state parks, and ski areas are only served by infrequent public transportation or private shuttle buses – if at all. What's more, if you are planning on doing a fair amount of camping, renting a car can save you money by allowing access to less expensive, out-of-the-way campgrounds.

Gas will cost anywhere between $1.10 and $1.90 a gallon (3.8 liters). Driving conditions in the Rockies are excellent in summer, with the major distractions for drivers being attention-grabbing mountain scenery and unwary wildlife wandering onto the roads. During winter, however, driving can be difficult indeed, particularly at high elevations where snow and ice accumulate on roads.

Car rental

Drivers wishing to **rent** cars are supposed to have held a license for at least one year (though this is rarely checked); those under

Winter driving

If you're unaccustomed to driving in icy conditions, it's best to be very conservative and to avoid driving during snowstorms if possible. Basic **equipment** for winter driving in the mountains includes snow-tires and/or chains, an ice-scraper for clearing your windshield and a shovel for clearing away built-up snow. It also pays to have warm clothes, blankets and extra food and water in case you do get stuck.

If your car has **snow tires** (you should definitely double-check this when booking a rental car for a winter trip into the mountains) you'll be in good shape for general highway and town driving in winter. Major roads are regularly cleared throughout the winter, as are town and city streets, though you should not rely on smaller county roads and such being cleared every day. At times you may see road signs indicating that drivers are required to carry **chains** in a certain area. If in doubt about the conditions on a certain route, check with a tourist office, USFS office or at a gas station.

Even with the best of precautions, you may find yourself on a stretch of road covered in an unbroken sheet of **ice**. Even snow tires won't help you much, and if you have no alternative but to keep driving, you'll need to be very careful indeed. The reaction to skidding on ice depends on whether your car is equipped with anti-lock brakes (ABS). If it is not, firmly pump the brakes until the car is back under control. If equipped with ABS brakes, your car should automatically pump the brakes after pressing down the pedal, keeping the wheels from locking up.

25 pay a higher insurance premium. A credit card is essential, as rental companies (listed below) will rarely accept a cash deposit.

You may prefer to rent a **4WD** vehicle, but this will be at least $10 per day more expensive than a regular sedan. All the major towns, national parks and so forth are accessible in a regular car, so a 4WD is probably only necessary if you're planning to drive lots of backcountry roads – although they are a good choice for winter driving too. Not also that **ski/bike racks** can often be requested as well.

It's often worth booking in advance via the internet to get a good deal on rentals of a week or more. Otherwise you can phone the major firms' toll-free numbers and ask for their best rate – most will try to beat the offers of their competitors, so it's worth haggling. Be sure too to have written confirmation of your booking to present when collecting your vehicle.

One oddity about the rate for car rental is that **cheaper deals** are almost always done by the week; for example, a car rented at $45 per day can often be had for $200 a week. Rental companies' strict adherence to weekly discounted rates can lead to the bizarre situation where it's cheaper to rent a car for fourteen days than for twelve.

Important details to check are whether the rate includes free unlimited mileage, and what the insurance cost will be. When looking at some of the cheaper rental firms, keep in mind that there's a big difference in the quality of cars from company to company; industry leaders like Hertz and Avis tend to have newer, lower-mileage cars, often with air-conditioning and decent stereo systems – no small consideration on a long drive through the mountains. Virtually all US rental cars have automatic transmissions.

When you rent a car, read the small print carefully for details on the **Collision Damage Waiver (CDW)** – sometimes called a Liability Damage Waiver (LDW) or a Physical Damage Waiver (PDW) – a form of insurance that usually isn't included in the rental charge but is well worth considering. Americans may already be covered by their own vehicle insurance (check before you leave home) but foreign visitors should definitely consider taking this option. It specifically covers the car that you are driving, as you are in any case insured for damage to other vehicles. At $10–14 a day, it does add considerably to the daily rental fee, but without it you're liable for every scratch to the car – even those that aren't your fault. Some credit card companies offer automatic CDW coverage to anyone using their card; again, check before leaving home.

You should also check your **third-party liability**. The standard policy often only covers you for the first $15,000 of the third party's claim against you, a paltry sum in litigation-conscious America. Companies strongly advise taking out third-party insurance, which costs a further $10–12 a day but indemnifies the driver for up to $2,000,000.

If you **break down** in a rented car, you can normally call an emergency assistance number, printed on your rental contract. If you're not carrying your own, you might consider renting a **mobile telephone** from the car rental agency (or from outlets at major airports) – you often only have to pay a nominal amount until you actually use it. Having a phone can be reassuring at least, and a potential lifesaver should something go terribly wrong.

Car rental agencies

Alamo ⓣ1-800/522-9696, ⓦwww.alamo.com.
Avis ⓣ1-800/331-1084, ⓦwww.avis.com.
Budget ⓣ1-800/527-0700, ⓦwww.budgetrentacar.com.
Dollar ⓣ1-800/800-6000, ⓦwww.dollar.com.
Enterprise ⓣ1-800/325-8007, ⓦwww.enterprise.com.
Hertz ⓣ1-800/654-3001, ⓦwww.hertz.com.
National ⓣ1-800/227-7368, ⓦwww.nationalcar.com.
Thrifty ⓣ1-800/367-2277, ⓦwww.thrifty.com.

Motoring organizations

In North America

American Automobile Association (AAA) ⓣ1-800/222-4357, ⓦwww.aaa.com. Each state has its own club – check the phone book for local address and phone number.
Canadian Automobile Association (CAA) ⓣ613/247-0117, ⓦwww.caa.com. Each region has its own club – check the phone book for local address and phone number.

In the UK and Ireland

AA ⓣ0800/444500, ⓦwww.theaa.co.uk.

AA Travel Dublin ☎01/617 9988, ⓦwww.aaireland.ie.
RAC ☎0800/550055, ⓦwww.rac.co.uk.

In Australia and New Zealand

Australian Automobile Association ☎02/6247 7311.
New Zealand Automobile Association ☎09/377 4660.

Renting an RV

Besides cars, Recreational Vehicles or **RVs** (camper vans) can be rented for around $500 a week, although outlets are surprisingly rare, as people tend to own their RVs. The Recreational Vehicle Rental Association, 3930 University Drive, Fairfax, VA 22030 (☎703/591-7130 or 1-800/336-0355, ⓦwww.rvra.org), publishes a directory of rental firms in the US and Canada ($10, $15 outside North America). Some of the larger companies offering RV rentals are Cruise America (☎1-800/327-7799, ⓦwww.cruiseamerica.com) and Moturis (☎1-877/668-8747, ⓦwww.moturis.com).

On top of the rental fees, take into account the cost of gas (some RVs do twelve miles to the gallon or less) and any drop-off charges, in case you plan to do a one-way trip across the country. Also, it is rarely legal simply to pull up in an RV and spend the night at the roadside – you are expected to stay in designated parks that cost $20–30 per night.

Roads

You will encounter several types of roads in the Rockies. The best for covering long distances are the wide, straight and fast interstate highways (eg I-80), usually six-lane motorways. Driving on these roads is easier than it first appears, but you need to adapt to the American habit of changing lanes: US drivers do this frequently, and overtake on both sides. Big overhead signs warn you if the road is about to split towards two different destinations (this happens quite often), or if an exit's coming up. Sometimes a lane *must* exit, so it's possible to wind up leaving the interstate unintentionally – no great calamity as it's easy enough to get back on again.

A grade down are the state highways and the US highways, which may be two or four lanes wide. Some major roads in cities are technically state highways but are better known by their local name. In the Rockies, you'll also come across much smaller County Roads; their number is preceded by a letter denoting their county. In cities and large towns, streets are arranged on an easy-to-manage grid system and are labeled at each junction.

Foreign drivers

UK, Canadian, Australian, and New Zealand citizens can all drive in the US on a regular driving license; International Driving Permits are not required. If in any doubt about your driving status in the US, check with your local motoring organization (see overleaf). Remember too that it's safer not to set off on a long drive immediately following an international flight.

Some foreign travelers have problems at first adjusting to **driving on the right**. In terms of technical skills, it's actually pretty easy to make the switch; a more common problem is that people simply forget and set out one morning on the left – you might try taping a reminder note to your steering wheel.

Rules of the road

Although the law says that drivers must keep up with the flow of traffic, which is often hurtling along at 75mph, the maximum **speed limit** on the interstates varies between 65 and 75mph, with lower sign-posted limits – usually 35–45mph – in built-up areas, and 20mph near schools when children are present. If the **police** flag you down, don't get out of the car, and don't reach into the glove compartment until you're given the OK to do so; simply sit still with your hands on the wheel, be polite and don't attempt to make jokes.

Apart from the obvious fact that Americans drive on the right, various rules may be unfamiliar to **foreign drivers**. US law requires that any alcohol be carried unopened in the trunk of the car; it's illegal to make a U-turn on an interstate or anywhere where a single unbroken line runs along the middle of the road; to park on a highway; and for front-seat passengers to ride without fastened seatbelts. At junctions, you can turn right on a red light if there is no traffic approaching from the left; and some junctions are **four-way stops**: a crossroads where all traffic must stop before proceeding in order of arrival.

It can't be stressed too strongly that **Driving Under the Influence** (DUI) is a very serious offence. If a police officer smells alcohol on your breath, he/she is entitled to administer a breath, saliva, or urine test. If you fail, they'll lock you up with other inebriates in the "drunk tank" of the nearest jail until you sober up. Your case will later be heard by a judge, who can fine you several hundred dollars or in extreme (or repeat) cases, imprison you for thirty days.

The usual advice given to **hitchhikers** is that they should use their common sense; in fact, common sense should tell anyone that hitchhiking in the US is a **bad idea**. It is, however, still practiced between the various mountain towns. Women should never, ever, hitch alone.

Cycling

In general, **cycling** is a cheap and healthy method of getting around, although it's important to choose your routes carefully to ensure you don't take on an entirely unrealistic trip through extreme mountainous terrain.

Bikes can be **rented** for around $25 a day, and $90–100 a week from most bike stores (we've listed rental options where applicable throughout the *Guide*). During the summer months, you'll encounter few problems besides sunburn; cycling about in the Rockies during winter is impractical and would be highly unpleasant.

For **long-distance cycling**, you'll need maps, spare tires, tools, panniers, a helmet (not a legal necessity in every state, but essential equipment nonetheless), and a good quality multispeed bike. Don't immediately splurge on a mountain bike, unless you are planning a lot of off-road use – good road conditions and trail restrictions in national parks make a touring bike an equally good or better choice. The most pleasant routes are along quieter roads; cycling on interstate highways is illegal (and very dangerous).

Accommodation

Accommodation standards in the Rockies – as in the rest of the US – are high, and costs inevitably form a significant proportion of the expenses for any trip to the state. It is possible to haggle, however, especially in the chain motels, and if you're on your own costs can be pared down by sleeping in dormitory-style hostels, where a bed will cost $12–20. Unfortunately, these are few and far between in the Rockies. However, groups of two or more will find it only a little more expensive to stay in the far more plentiful motels and hotels, where basic rooms away from the major cities typically cost around $40–50 per night. Some hotels will set up a third single bed for around $5 to $10 on top of the regular price, reducing costs for three people sharing. By contrast, the lone traveler will have a hard time of it: "singles" are usually double rooms at an only slightly reduced rate. Prices quoted by hotels and motels are almost always for the actual room rather than for each person using it.

Motels are plentiful on the main approach roads to cities, around mountain resorts and by the main road junctions in some country areas. High-rise **hotels** are common in the larger cities and also around some of the region's largest resorts. In major cities, **campgrounds** tend to be on the outskirts, if they exist at all. Outside of cities, however, they're just about everywhere.

Wherever you stay, you'll be expected to

Accommodation price codes

Throughout this book, **accommodation** has been price-coded according to the cost of the least expensive **double room** throughout most of the year; we have given individual prices for **hostels** and whole apartments. Expect prices in most places to jump into the next highest category on Friday and Saturday nights. However, with the exception of the budget interstate motels, there's rarely such a thing as a set rate for a room. A basic motel in a mountain resort may double its prices according to the season, while a big-city hotel which charges $200 per room during the week will often slash its tariff at the weekend when all the business types have gone home. Particularly in scenic areas, prices might leap into the next higher category at weekends. Watch out also for local events, which can raise rates far above normal.

Fees quoted for state and federally-run campgrounds include taxes; price codes for hotels, motels, and B&Bs do not and state lodging taxes vary. In Colorado, the average tax is two percent, though in Denver it's twelve percent. Utah has a baseline tax of six percent, but can vary from town to town (see p.315 for more.) In Montana tax is four percent, up to eight percent in Wyoming, and Idaho rates range from six to nine percent.

❶ up to $30	❹ $60–80	❼ $130–180
❷ $30–45	❺ $80–100	❽ $180–240
❸ $45–60	❻ $100–130	❾ $240+

pay in advance, at least for the first night and perhaps for further nights too, particularly if it's high season and the hotel's expecting to be busy. Payment can be in cash or in dollar travelers' checks, though it's more common to give your credit card number and sign for everything when you leave. **Reservations** are only held until 5pm or 6pm unless you've told them you'll be arriving late. Most of the larger chains have an advance booking form in their brochures and will make reservations at another of their premises for you.

Since cheap accommodation in the cities, mountain resorts, and close to the major national parks is snapped up fast, **book ahead** whenever possible.

Hotels and motels

While **hotels** and **motels** essentially offer the same things – double rooms with bathroom, TV and phone – motels tend to be slightly cheaper and are often located beside the main highways away from city centers, easily accessible to drivers. The budget ones are pretty basic affairs, but in general there's a uniform standard of comfort everywhere and you don't get a much better deal by paying, say, $50 instead of $35. Over $50, the room and its fittings get bigger and more luxurious, and there may be a swimming pool which guests can use for free. Paying over $100 brings you into the realms of the en-suite hot tub.

A growing number of hotels are providing a **complimentary breakfast**. Sometimes this will be no more than a cup of coffee and a roll, but increasingly it is a sit-down affair likely to comprise fruit, cereals, muffins, and toast. In the pricier places, you may also be offered made-to-order omelettes.

In some places you'll be able to find cheap one-off hotels and motels simply by keeping your eyes open – they're usually advertised by enormous roadside signs. Alternatively, there are a number of budget-priced **chains**, such as *Econolodge*, *Days Inn* and *Motel 6*, whose rooms cost $30–45. Mid-priced options include *Best Western*, *Howard Johnson*, *Travelodge* and *Ramada* – though if you can afford to pay this much ($50–100) there's normally somewhere nicer to stay. When it's worth blowing a hunk of cash on somewhere really atmospheric we've said as much in the guide. Bear in mind the most upscale establishments have all manner of services which may appear to be free but for which you'll be expected to **tip** in a style commensurate with the hotel's status – ie big. For more on tipping see p.63.

Also note that distances between towns in the Rockies can be substantial, and there may be no accommodation in between –

while this isn't exactly life threatening it can mean driving for several hours without finding the kind of lodgings you're looking for.

Discount options

During **off-peak periods**, many motels and hotels struggle to fill their rooms and it's worth **haggling** to get a few dollars off the asking price. Staying in the same place for more than one night will bring further reductions. Motels in particular also offer small but worthwhile discounts for seniors and members of various organizations, particularly the American Automobile Association (AAA). Additionally, pick up the many **discount coupons** which fill tourist information offices. Read the small print, though: what appears to be an amazingly cheap room rate sometimes turns out to be a per-person charge for two people sharing, and limited to midweek.

For the benefit of overseas travelers, many of the higher-rung hotel chains offer prepaid **discount vouchers**, which in theory save you money if you're prepared to pay in advance. To take advantage of such schemes, British travelers must purchase the vouchers in the UK, at a usual cost of £30–60 per night for a minimum of two people sharing. However, it's hard to think of a good reason to buy them; you may save a nominal amount on the fixed rates, but better-value accommodation is not exactly difficult to find in the US, and you may well regret the inflexibility imposed upon your travels. Most UK travel agents will have details of the various voucher schemes.

Bed and breakfasts

B&Bs in the Rockies are typically a luxury – the bed-and-breakfast inns, as they're usually known, are often small, restored Victorian buildings filled with antiques and/or local folk art. Even the larger establishments tend to have no more than ten rooms, often without TV and phone but with plentiful flowers, stuffed cushions and a homey atmosphere; others may just be a couple of furnished rooms in someone's home, or an entire apartment where you won't even see your host. Victorian and Romantic are dominant themes; while selecting the best in that vein, we've also gone out of our way to seek out those that don't conform.

While always including a huge and wholesome breakfast (five courses is not unheard of), prices vary greatly: anything from $70 to $250 depending on location and season. Most fall between $85 and $125 per night for a double, a little more for a whole apartment. Bear in mind, too, that they are frequently booked well in advance, and even if they're not full, the cheaper rooms, which determine our price code, may be already taken.

Useful **websites** covering B&Bs in the Rockies include the B&B Channel (ⓦwww.bbchannel.com), Inn Site (ⓦwww.innsite.com) and ⓦwww.bedandbreakfastsinns.org.

Dude ranches

The Rockies are dotted with **dude ranches**, where you can experience everything from the full-on cowboy lifestyle of rising at dawn, mucking out the stables and tending to the cattle to a luxury lifestyle involving horseback riding, fly fishing, hiking, etc that just happens to be centered on a ranch.

Prices vary enormously depending on the level of luxury you require – cheaper options in basic, rustic cabins with no-frills communal meals start at around $100 per day, while ranches providing more opulent accommodation and gourmet meals will set you back considerably more.

A good dude ranch will provide you with the nearest you're likely to get to cowboy-style living short of signing on for a job. For more details contact the Dude Ranchers' Association, PO Box F-471, Laporte, CO 80535 (ⓣ970/223-8440, ⓦwww.duderanch.org).

YMCA/YWCAs and hostels

At an average of around $15 per night per person, **hostels** are clearly the cheapest accommodation option in the Rockies other than camping. That said there are only a handful of them throughout the region, with Colorado home to the widest selection.

There are three main kinds of hostel-type accommodation in the US. The first are **YMCA/YWCA** hostels (known as "Ys"; ⓣ1-800/872-9622, ⓦwww.ymca.com) offering accommodation for both sexes or, in a few cases, women-only accommodation. Though sporadically located throughout much of the region, the vast majority of Ys in the Rockies are basically low-budget health clubs that do not offer accommodation. Those that do, though, typically offer dorm rooms from around $12 and single and double rooms for upwards of $60 and facilities often include a gymnasium, a swimming pool, and an inexpensive cafeteria.

The second and most prevalent type of hostel in the Rockies are the **HI-AYH** hostels (the prefix is usually shortened to HI in listings) located in major cities and popular mountain resort areas. Most urban hostels have 24-hour access, while rural ones may have a curfew and limited daytime hours. HI also operates a couple of small "home hostels"; though similar to other hostels you need to reserve in advance or there may be no one there to receive you. Rates at HI hostels range from $12 to $18 for HI members; nonmembers generally pay an additional $3 per night.

Particularly if you're traveling in high season, it's advisable to **book ahead**. Within North America you can call toll-free at ⓣ1-800/909-4776, followed by a two-digit code for the required hostel, which is published in the *Hostelling International Guide to North America* and is listed on the HI **website** (ⓦwww.hiayh.com). For a small fee you can also reserve on ⓣ202/783-6161, and when booking from outside North America you can use the IBN booking service. Some HI hostels will allow you to use a **sleeping bag**, though officially they should (and many do) insist on a **sheet sleeping bag**, which can usually be rented at the hostel. The maximum stay at each hostel is technically three days, though this is again a rule that is often ignored if there's space. Few hostels provide meals, but most have **cooking** facilities. Alcohol, smoking, and, of course, drugs are banned.

The final type of hostels in the Rockies are **independent** hostels, usually a little less expensive than their HI counterparts, and with fewer rules. The quality, though, is not as consistent; some can be quite poor, while others, which we've included in this book, are absolutely wonderful. In popular areas they compete fiercely for your business with airport and train station pick-ups, free breakfasts and free bike hire. There is often no curfew and, at some, a party atmosphere is encouraged at barbecues and keg parties. Their independent status may be due to a failure to come up to the HI's (fairly rigid) criteria, but often it's simply because the owners prefer not to be tied down by HI regulations. Many have now loosely affiliated themselves under an assortment of bodies, mostly designed to encourage you to move on to a sister hostel.

All the information in this book was accurate at the time of going to press; however, hostels are often shoestring organizations, prone to changing address or closing down altogether. Similarly, new ones appear each year; check the noticeboards of other hostels for news.

Youth hostel information

Hostelling International Guide to North America, the HI guide to hostels in the USA and Canada, is available free of charge to any overnight guest at an HI-AYH hostel or direct for $3 from the HI National Office in Washington DC. For overseas hostelers, the two-volume *Hostelling International Guide* provides a full list of hostels and is available from your local association headquarters as well.

To make hostel reservations from outside the US using the IBN system, call your nearest credit card Booking Center:

Australia ⓣ02/9261 1111
Canada ⓣ1-800/663 5777
England ⓣ01629/581418
New Zealand ⓣ03/379 9970
Northern Ireland ⓣ028/3231 5435
Republic of Ireland ⓣ01/830 4555
Scotland ⓣ054/155 3255

You can also book online at ⓦwww.hostelbooking.com.

USA

Hostelling International-American Youth Hostels (HI-AYH) 733 15th St NW, Suite 840, PO Box 37613, Washington, DC 20005 (ⓣ202/783-6161, ⓦwww.hiayh.org). Annual membership for adults (18–55) is $25, for seniors (55 or over) is $15, and for under-18s is free. Lifetime memberships are $250.

Canada

Hostelling International/Canadian Hostelling Association Room 400, 205 Catherine St, Ottawa, ON K2P 1C3 (ⓣ1-800/663-5777 or 613/237-7884, ⓦwww.hostellingintl.ca). Rather than sell the traditional one- or two-year memberships, the association now sells one Individual Adult membership. The length of the term depends on when the membership is sold, but a member can receive up to 28 months of membership for just $35. Membership is free for under-18s and you can become a lifetime member for $175.

England and Wales

Youth Hostel Association (YHA), Trevelyan House, 8 St Stephen's Hill, St Albans, Herts AL1 2DY (☎0870/870 8808, ⓦwww.yha.org.uk and ⓦwww.iyhf.org, ⓔcustomerservices@yha.org.uk). Annual membership £12.50, for under-18s £6.25.

Scotland

Scottish Youth Hostel Association 7 Glebe Crescent, Stirling FK8 2JA (☎0870/155 3255, ⓦwww.syha.org.uk). Annual membership £6, for under-18s £2.50.

Ireland

An Óige 61 Mountjoy St, Dublin 7 (☎01/830 4555, ⓦwww.irelandyha.org). Adult (and single parent) membership €15; family (2 parents and children under 16) €30; under-18s €8.
Hostelling International Northern Ireland 22–32 Donegall Rd, Belfast BT12 5JN (☎028/9032 4733, ⓦwww.hini.org.uk). Adult membership £10; under-18s £6; family £20.

Australia

Australia Youth Hostels Association 422 Kent St, Sydney (☎02/9261 1111, ⓦwww.yha.com.au). Adult membership rate A$49 for the first twelve months and then A$32 each year after.

New Zealand

New Zealand Youth Hostels Association 173 Gloucester St, Christchurch (☎03/379 9970, ⓦwww.yha.co.nz). Adult membership NZ$40 for one year, NZ$60 for two and NZ$80 for three.

Camping

Rocky Mountain **campgrounds** range from the primitive (a flat piece of ground that may or may not have a water tap) to those that are more like open-air hotels, with markets, restaurants, washing facilities, game rooms, and so on. When camping in national and state parks, as well as national forests, you can typically expect a large site designed to accommodate up to two vehicles, six people and all the paraphernalia that Americans like to take with them. There'll be a picnic table and fire pit on the site, with a short walk to an outhouse and a drinking water tap.

Naturally enough, **prices** vary accordingly, ranging from nothing for the most basic plots, up to $20 a night for something comparatively luxurious. There are plenty of campgrounds, but often plenty of people intending to use them as well: take care over plotting your route if you're intending to camp in the big national parks, or anywhere at all during national holidays or the summer, when many grounds will be either full or very crowded. Vacancies often exist in the grounds outside the parks – where the facilities are usually marginally better – and by contrast, some of the more basic campgrounds in isolated areas will often be empty whatever time of year you're there. Payment method for the latter is often a simple box in which you slide money in the slot provided.

Look out too for **hiker/biker** or **walk-in** campgrounds, which, at $3 per person per night, are much cheaper than most sites but only available if you are traveling under your own steam.

Much of the Rocky Mountain region is in the public domain, and, if you're backpacking, you can **backcountry camp** pretty much anywhere you want in the gaping wilderness areas and national forests. However, in the more heavily hiked areas (we've indicated the relevant areas in the text), you must first get a **wilderness permit** (almost always free), and usually a free **campfire permit** (even if you are using a cooking stove). Campfire permits are available from park rangers' offices and once obtained are usually valid for a year. You should also take the proper precautions: carry sufficient food and drink to cover emergencies, inform the park ranger of your travel plans, and watch out for bears and rattlesnakes, as well as the effect *your* presence can have on *their* environment; see "Backcountry camping" on p.50 for more information.

You can camp in some but not all **state parks**, and fees and facilities vary between parks. Expect to pay on average $1–4 per vehicle entry, and around $12 per night for camping. Annual passes allowing unlimited access to all state parks are available for around $30.

Campground reservations

Campgrounds in popular national parks, state parks and national forests soon fill up in summer, especially during the July and August school vacation, so it pays to **reserve** as far in advance as you can. Phone and website reservations can often be made several months in advance, but must be lodged a minimum of two days before you plan to arrive. When making reservations, be sure to have dates, locations, number of people, a mailing address, and alternative sites picked out. Reservations can be made on the following numbers and websites:

Kampgrounds of America (KOA), PO Box 30558, Billings, MT 59114 (Ⓣ406/248-7444, Ⓦwww.koa.com). Oversees a multitude of family-style campgrounds throughout the Rockies, most of them with a wide range of facilities, and usually located close to urban and/or city areas.

National Forests: contact the National Recreation Reservation Service Ⓣ1-877/444-6777, ⓌReserveUSA.com.

National Parks: Ⓣ1-800/365-2267, Ⓦreservations.nps.gov.

State Parks: call Destinet Ⓣ916/638-5883 or 1-800/444-7275, Ⓦwww.reserveamerica.com/usa/ca. Also see below for individual state contacts.

State park contacts

Colorado State Parks 1313 Sherman St, Room 618, Denver, CO 80203 (Ⓣ303/866-3437, Ⓦwww.parks.state.co.us).

Idaho Dept of Parks and Recreation PO Box 83720, Boise, ID 83720-0065 (Ⓣ208/334-4199, Ⓦwww.idoc.state.id.us/irti/).

Montana Fish Wildlife & Parks 1420 E 6th Ave, Helena, MT 59620 (Ⓣ406/444-2535, Ⓦwww.fwp.state.mt.us).

Utah State Parks 1594 W, North Temple, PO Box 146001, Salt Lake City, UT 84114 (Ⓣ801/322-3770, Ⓦwww.parks.state.ut.us).

Wyoming Division of State Parks and Historic Sites 2301 Central Avenue, Cheyenne, WY 82002 (Ⓣ307/777-6323, Ⓦwww.wyo-park.com).

Food and drink

Outside the major towns and tourist centers, old-fashioned American food dominates restaurants throughout the Rockies region. Particularly in the cattle ranching regions, red meats are almost synonymous with the term food. Preparation techniques are also of the pre-health conscious era, with frying the main discipline in greasy spoon diners and truck stops – chicken-fried steak, a hunk of steak breaded and fried, is the cornerstone of many menus. Thankfully, ethnic foods have helped expand the range of choices, and you'll find pockets of good Mexican food throughout the region, and some respectable Asian food as well. In college towns, the health-conscious vibe of the regions comes through strongest and you'll have a wide range of decent veggie places to choose from. The last decade has also seen an increase of restaurants at the gourmet end of the scale, many of which successfully blend local ingredients like beef, trout, lamb, buffalo, or elk with international cooking styles.

Breakfast

For the price (on average $4–7), breakfast is the best-value and most filling meal of the day. Go to a **diner**, **café**, or **coffee shop**, all of which serve breakfast until at least 11am, with some diners serving them all day. There are often special deals at earlier times too, say 6–8am, when the price may be even lower.

The breakfasts themselves are pretty much what you'd find all over the country. Various egg and omelette combos with ham or bacon, pancakes, French toast, and waffles appear on nearly every menu. Wherever you eat, a dollar or so will entitle you to wash the meal down with as much coffee or tea as you can stomach.

Lunch and snacks

Most restaurants that open for lunch will serve a range of smaller meals that include sandwiches, burger, salads, and even pizza by the slice. Many Mexican restaurants are good options for cheap quick lunches, and are represented in the chain market by the likes of *Taco Bell*, which sell swift tacos and burritos for around $1, and more upmarket chains like *Chipotle*. And of course the **burger chains** are as ubiquitous here as anywhere in the US: *Wendy's*, *Burger King* and *McDonald's* are the familiar names.

Dining out

In spite of the presence of fashionable regional and ethnic cuisines, **traditional American cooking** – burgers, steaks, fries, salads, and baked potatoes – is found all over the Rocky Mountains. Cheapest of the food chains is the regionwide *Denny's*, although you'll rarely need to spend more than $10 for a solid blowout anywhere. Vegetarians will usually find something on the menu – the best standby in many traditional burger and steak joints being the humble baked potato.

Some upscale restaurants flout a new line in "Rocky Mountain Cuisine," with an emphasis on dishing up local produce, and if it is native to the region then all the better: hence the interest in serving salmon, trout, elk, venison, and buffalo (bison). One unique, eye-catching item on many menus are **Rocky Mountain Oysters**, which you may or may not want to try once you find out that the bull providing the food was castrated rather than killed.

Although technically ethnic, **Mexican** food is so common that it often seems like (and, historically, often is) an indigenous cuisine, especially in southern Colorado. What's more, day or night, it's the cheapest type of food to eat: even a full dinner with a few drinks will rarely be over $12 anywhere except the most upmarket establishments. In the main, Mexican food here is different from what you'll find in Mexico, making more use of fresh vegetables and fruit, but the essentials are the same: lots of rice and pinto beans, often served refried (ie boiled, mashed and fried), with variations on the versatile **tortilla**. You can eat a tortilla as an accompaniment to your main dish; wrapped around the food and eaten by hand (a burrito); filled and folded (a taco); rolled, filled, and baked (an enchilada); or fried flat and topped with a stack of food (a tostada). One of the few options for vegetarians in this meat-oriented cuisine is the chile relleno, a green pepper stuffed with cheese, dipped in egg batter and fried. Veggie burritos, filled with beans, rice, lettuce, avocado, cheese, and sour cream are another prevalent option for those averse to meat.

Other ethnic cuisines are common too. **Chinese** food is everywhere, and often good value at lunchtime. **Japanese** is more expensive and fashionable. **Italian** food is very popular, but can be expensive once you leave the simple pizzas and pastas to explore more specialist Italian regional cooking. **French** food, too, is available, though always pricey, and the cuisine of social climbers and power-lunchers, rarely found outside expensive resorts and the larger cities. **Thai**, **Korean**, **Vietnamese**, and **Indonesian** food is similarly city-based, though usually cheaper; **Indian** restaurants, on the other hand, are thin on the ground just about everywhere and often very expensive.

Tipping

Foreign visitors should note to top up the bill in restaurants by 15–20 percent; a little less perhaps at the bar.

Drinking

Even though the goldrush is now long gone, the Rocky Mountain towns still hold a strong contingent of old-fashioned, get-drunk **bars** that are fun to spend an evening in even if you don't plan to get legless. Many of the longer-standing and remoter bars in particular are still filled with trophy heads and jukeboxes playing nothing but Country – likely venues for some of the most evocatively Western experiences. Additionally the wave of **brewpubs** that has swept the US over the last couple of decades is nowhere better represented than in the Rockies. Nearly every sizeable town has one, and though occasionally hit and miss, you're always guaranteed at least an original pint.

Regulations governing the purchase and consumption of alcohol are similar in all the Rocky Mountain states (except Utah; see p.317). You need to be 21, and could well be asked for ID even if you look much older. **Licensing laws** and **drinking hours** are among the most liberal in the country (though laws on drinking and driving are not; see p.29), and alcohol can be bought and drunk any time between 10am (in some states and counties as early as 6am) up until 2am (except in Idaho, where it's 1am in some counties), seven days a week (except in Colorado, where liquor stores aren't permitted to sell alcohol on a Sun). As well as bars and clubs, restaurants are nearly always fully licensed too.

American **beers** fall into two diametrically opposite categories: wonderful and tasteless. The latter includes light, fizzy brands such as Budweiser, Coors, Miller and Michelob. The alternative is a fabulous range of **"microbrewed" beers**, the product of a wave of backyard and in-house operations that has now matured to the point that many operations pump out over 150,000 barrels a year and are classed as "regional breweries." Head for one of the brewpubs and you'll find handcrafted beers such as crisp pilsners, wheat beers and stouts on tap, at prices only marginally above those of the national brews. Along the same lines, a wide range of bottled microbrews are available throughout the Rockies.

Alternatively, do what many locals do and stick to **imported** beers, especially the Mexican brands Bohemia, Corona, Dos Equis, and Tecate. Expect to fork out $3 for a glass of draft beer, about the same for a bottle of imported beer. Taste aside, imported beers gain advocates for their comparative alcoholic strength.

Don't forget that in all but the most pretentious bars, several people can save money by buying a half-gallon **"pitcher"** of beer for $6–8. If bar prices are a problem, you can stock up with **six-packs** from a supermarket ($3–7 for domestic, $5–9 for imported and microbrews).

Cocktails are extremely popular, especially during **happy hours** (usually any time between 5pm and 7pm) when drinks are often half-price and there may be a free or very cheap buffet thrown in as well.

Mail, phones, and email

Visitors from overseas tend to be impressed by the speed and efficiency of communication in the US. In some small towns you may have to hunt around to find the nearest public phone, but even national park visitor centers almost always have them, so in general, keeping in touch is easy. Every town in the Rockies has a post office, or at least a postal depot operating from out of the general store. Even the internet reached the mountains some years ago, and is readily accessible in all but the smallest towns – though it's still mercifully hard to find a public computer terminal in a national park.

Mail

Post offices are usually open Monday to Friday from about 9am until 5pm (though some open earlier), and in some cases on Saturday from 9am to noon or later; there are blue **mail boxes** on street corners in cities and the larger towns. **Ordinary mail** within the US costs 34¢ for letters weighing up to an ounce; addresses must include the **zip code** (postal code), and a return address should be written in the upper left corner of the envelope. **Air mail** from the western US to Europe generally takes about a week. Aerograms and international postcards cost 70¢, letters weighing up to one ounce (a couple of sheets) cost 80¢.

Letters can be sent c/o **General Delivery** (what's known elsewhere as **poste restante**) to the one relevant post office in each city, but must include the zip code and will only be held for thirty days before being returned to sender – so make sure there's a return address on the envelope. If you're receiving mail at someone else's address, it should include "c/o" and the regular occupant's name, or it is likely to be returned. To send a package out of the country, you'll need a green **customs declaration form**, available from the post office.

Telephones

Public telephones can be found everywhere – on street corners, in train and bus stations, hotels, bars, and restaurants. They take 5¢, 10¢, and 25¢ coins. The cost of a **local call** from a public phone is usually 35¢; when necessary, a voice comes on the line telling you to pay more.

Pricier are long-distance calls, for which you'll need plenty of change. Long-distance calls are much less expensive if made between 6pm and 8am – the cheapest rates are after 11pm and at weekends – and calls from private phones are always much cheaper than those from public phones. Detailed rates are listed at the front of the telephone directory (the *White Pages*, a copious source of information on many matters).

There are very few **area codes** in use among the Rocky Mountain states; Montana (☎406), Wyoming (☎307), and Idaho (☎208) each have just one code, while Colorado (☎303, ☎970 and ☎719) has three and Utah (☎801 and ☎435) two. It is always necessary to include the area code when dialing beyond the local area, even though you may be in the same area code. For example, although ☎307 is the code for all of Wyoming, a call from Cheyenne to Jackson is a long-distance call, and so the prefix ☎1-307 must be dialled first and long-distance charges will apply.

Making telephone calls from **hotel rooms** is always more expensive than from a pay phone; however, some hotels offer free local calls from rooms – ask when you check in.

Many government agencies, car rental firms, hotels and so on have **toll-free numbers**, which always have the prefix ☎1-800, ☎1-888 or ☎1-877. Within the US, you can dial any number starting with those digits free of charge, though some numbers are only available if you're calling from outside that local call area: it isn't apparent from the number until you try. Numbers with the prefix ☎1-900 are pay-per-call lines, generally quite expensive and almost always involving either sports, psychics, or phone sex.

Useful numbers

Emergencies ☎911; ask for the appropriate emergency service: fire, police, or ambulance
Directory information ☎411
Directory inquiries for toll-free numbers ☎1-800/555-1212
Long-distance directory information ☎1- (Area Code)/555-1212

Phoning home

International calls can be dialed direct from private or (more expensively) public phones. You can get assistance from the **international operator** (☎00), who may also interrupt every three minutes, asking for more money, if you're on a public phone. An operator can also put through a collect (reverse charges) call for you. The **lowest rates** for international calls to Europe operate between 6pm and 7am, when a direct-dialed three-minute call will cost roughly $5.

In **Britain**, it's possible to obtain a free **BT Chargecard** (☎0800/345144), with which all calls from overseas can be charged to your domestic account. To use these cards in the US, or to make a **collect call** using a

BT operator, contact the carrier: AT&T ☎1-800/445-5667; MCI ☎1-800/444-2162; or Sprint ☎1-800/800-0008. To avoid the international operator fee, BT credit card calls can be made directly using an automated system: AT&T ☎1-800/445-5688; MCI ☎1-800/854-4826; or Sprint ☎1-800/825-4904.

To call **Australia and New Zealand** from overseas, telephone charge cards such as Telstra Telecard or Optus Calling Card in Australia, and Telecom NZ's Calling Card can be used to make calls abroad, which are charged back to a domestic account or credit card. Apply to Telstra (☎1800/038 000), Optus (☎1300/300 937), or Telecom NZ (☎04/801 9000).

The alternative to the various phone charge cards is to buy a **prepaid calling card**, available in increments of $5, $10 and $20, from a grocery store or gas station. These are reasonably good value and can be used from both private and public phones.

International dialling codes

For calls TO the US, dial your own country's international access code, then +1+ area code.

For calls FROM the US, the codes are as follows:

Australia: 011+ 61+ area code
New Zealand: 011+ 64+ area code
UK and Northern Ireland: 011+ 44 + area code
Republic of Ireland: 011+353+ area code

Mobile phones

If you want to use your **mobile phone** abroad, you'll need to check with your service provider whether this is possible, what it will cost and how the call charges will work. Unless you have a tri-band phone, it is unlikely that a mobile bought for use outside the US will work inside the States. They tend to be very expensive to own in the US, too, as users are billed for both incoming and outgoing calls. Calling a US mobile, however, costs no more than making a call to a landline in that area code.

Email

One of the best ways to keep in touch while travelling is to sign up for a free internet email address that can be accessed from anywhere, for example Yahoo Mail or Hotmail – accessible through Ⓦwww.yahoo.com and Ⓦwww.hotmail.com. Once you've set up an account, you can use these sites to pick up and send mail from any internet café, or hotel with internet access.

Cyber-cafés are found in most towns of any size, though many travelers resort to the **free internet access** provided by public libraries. Generally you just drop in, or otherwise phone and reserve a half-hour slot. A third alternative is to find a commercial photocopying and printing shop, such as Kinko's, whose stores are scattered throughout the Rockies region (open 24hrs; 20¢ per minute for use of a computer).

The media

Newspapers

The *Rocky Mountain News* and the *Denver Post*, who collaborate on weekend editions, compete as the most influential **newspapers** in the region. Both are parochial affairs, slim on news, not to mention quality journalism for events outside the region. Nearly every community has at least a few **free newspapers**, found in street distribution bins, cafés and bars, or just lying around in piles. It's a good idea to pick up a full assortment: some simply cover local goings-on, others provide specialist coverage of interests ranging from long-distance cycling to getting ahead in business – and the classified and personal ads can provide hours of entertainment. Many of them are also excellent sources for bar, restaurant, and nightlife information; the most useful titles are mentioned throughout the guide. A prime example of a fine local newspaper is **Denver's** free weekly *Westword*, with considered and witty features along with an indispensable guide to what's going on. In **Wyoming**, the only newspaper of any note is the *Casper Star-Tribune*, which does a good job of state coverage. In **Montana** several papers have statewide coverage, the right-wing *Billings Gazette* offering some decent national coverage, while the rather introverted, but mercifully progressive *Missoulian* has the best state news coverage. The nondescript, Boise-based *Idaho Statesman* is the main daily in **Idaho**.

TV

TV in the Rockies is pretty much the standard network barrage of sitcoms, newscasts and talk shows. **PBS**, the national public television station, broadcasts a steady stream of interesting documentaries, informative (if slightly dry) news programs, and educational children's television. Many motel and hotel rooms in the region are hooked up to **cable**. The number of channels available to guests varies from place to place, but fifty is common and eighty isn't unheard of. Most cable stations are no better than the major networks (ABC, CBS, NBC, and FOX), though some of the more specialized channels are consistently interesting.

Radio

Like with TV, the majority of **radio** stations stick to a bland commercial format. Except for news and chat, stations on the **AM** band are best avoided in favor of **FM**, in particular the nationally funded public (NPR) and college stations, typically found between 88 and 92 FM. These provide diverse and listenable programming, and they're also good sources for information on local nightlife.

Crime and personal safety

Crime in the Rockies is remarkably low-key – residents of smaller towns boast of being able to leave their doors open day and night, although in larger cities the doors are most likely double locked and the usual precautions are advisable. Wherever you are in the region, by simply being careful, planning ahead, and taking care of your possessions, you should have few real problems.

In recent years right-wing **white supremacist and militia** groups have given northern Montana and Idaho an undeserved notoriety, but it's highly unlikely you'll meet any of these people while you're traveling. Of more concern for most visitors is backcountry safety, especially bears (see p.550), and to a lesser extent rattlesnakes (see p.259), mountain lions (see p.286), and altitude sickness (see p.20). Again, by using common sense, encounters with any of these can be avoided.

Mugging and theft

The biggest problem for most travelers is the threat of **mugging**. It's impossible to give hard and fast rules about what to do if confronted by a mugger. Whether to run, scream, or fight depends on the situation – but most locals would just hand over their money.

Of course, the best thing is to avoid being mugged, and a few obvious basic rules are worth remembering: don't flash money around; don't peer at your map (or this book) at every street corner, thereby announcing that you're a lost stranger; even if you're terrified or drunk (or both), try not to appear so; avoid dark streets, especially ones you can't see the end of; and in the early hours, stick to the roadside edge of the pavement so it's easier to run into the road to attract attention. If you have to ask for directions, choose your target carefully. Another idea is to carry a wad of cash, perhaps $50 or so, separate from the bulk of your holdings so that if you do get confronted you can hand over something of value without it costing you everything.

If the worst happens and your assailant is toting a gun or (more likely) a knife, try to stay calm: remember that he (for this is generally a male pursuit) is probably scared too. Keep still, don't make any sudden movements – and hand over your money. When he's gone, you should, despite your shock, try to find a phone and **dial ☎911**, or head to the nearest police station. Here, report the theft and get a reference number on the

Losing your passport

For a foreign visitor, few disasters create a bigger headache than losing your passport. If the worst happens, the closest British consulates are in San Francisco (☎415/981-3030) and Chicago (☎312/346-1810) and they will issue emergency passports, provided you have sufficient ID. Call and give an address where they can mail you an application form. When you return the filled-out application, you'll need to include a notarized (i.e. specially stamped at any major bank) photocopy of any ID you might still have plus a $38 reissuing fee. The resulting emergency passport is only a one-way travel document, good for return home. In non-emergency situations, the only way to get a new passport is through the British Embassy in Washington, DC (☎202/588-7800). The passport issuing process normally takes two weeks, but can take as long as six weeks. If you're in a real hurry, let them know and they will usually be as accommodating as possible. Australian citizens should contact the Australian Embassy, 1601 Massachusetts Ave, Washington, DC 20036 (☎202/797-3000).

Stolen travelers' checks and credit cards

Lost or stolen **travelers' checks** are a common problem. As long as you keep a record of the numbers of your travelers' checks separately from the actual checks, you should have little trouble getting new ones reissued. First, ring the issuing company using one of the toll-free numbers listed below. They'll ask you for the check numbers, the place you bought them, when and how you lost them and whether it's been reported to the police. All being well, you should get the missing checks reissued within a couple of days – and perhaps an emergency advance to tide you over.

American Express (TCs) ⓣ1-800/221-7282; (credit cards) ⓣ1-800/528-4800
Citicorp ⓣ1-800/645-6556
Diners Club ⓣ1-800/234-6377
MasterCard ⓣ1-800/307-7309
Thomas Cook ⓣ1-800/223-7373
Visa ⓣ1-800/227-6811

report to claim insurance and travelers' check refunds. If you're in a big city, ring the local Travelers Aid (their numbers are listed in the phone book) for sympathy and practical advice. For specific advice for women in case of mugging or attack, see overleaf.

Another potential source of trouble is having your **hotel room** or **car burglarized**. Always store valuables in the hotel safe when you go out; when inside, keep your door locked and don't open it to anyone you don't trust. If they claim to be hotel staff and you don't believe them, call reception to check. If you must keep valuable equipment in your car, keep it out of sight and locked away in the trunk if at all possible. If toting a bike or ski equipment along, do not leave it unattended for even short period of time. And in the evenings, bring all your gear into wherever you are staying – both for peace of mind and also to not give burglars any specific targets.

Gay and lesbian travelers

In contrast to the gay scene on either US coast, the mountains are at best underdeveloped, at worst hostile to same sex liaisons. Particularly in rural areas, gay couples may well attract unwanted attention and will find it in their interest to postpone displays of affection. Almost the entire Rocky Mountain gay scene, such as it is, is based in relatively cosmopolitan Denver and Boulder, though Aspen, too, has a small scene and is the preferred mountain destination for many gays. Leading gay publications in Colorado include the biweekly *Out Front* and the monthly *Quest*. Outside Colorado, the gay scene is limited to small social groups, usually based in college towns. The best contact for information on gay issues is the Gay, Lesbian & Bisexual Community Services Center of Colorado, 1245 E Colfax Ave, Suite 125, PO Box 18E, Denver, CO 80218-0140 (ⓣ303/831-6268). Montana has two branches of the national gay and lesbian organization PRIDE that can also help with information; PO Box 755, Helena, MT 59674 (ⓣ406/442-9322 or 1-800/610-9322) and PO Box 7380, Bozeman, MT 59771 (ⓣ406/388-1481).

US Gay and lesbian resources

National **publications** to look out for, most of which are available from any good bookstore, include the range of guides produced by The Damron Company (ⓣ415/255-0404 or 1-800/462-6654, ⓦwww.damron.com).

These include the *Address Book* ($15.95), a pocket-sized yearbook full of listings of hotels, bars, clubs, and resources for gay men; and the *Women's Traveler*, which provides similar listings for lesbians ($12.95). *The Advocate* ($3.95; ⓦwww.advocate.com) is a bimonthly national gay news magazine, with features, general info, and classified ads (not to be confused with *Advocate Men*, which is a soft-porn magazine). The nation's most widely circulated gay and lesbian publication, *Out* ($4.95), is more progressive. *Instinct* (ⓦwww.instinctmag.com) and *Genre* (ⓦwww.genremag.com) are two more popular (if somewhat fluffy) nationals for gay men. For women, *Curve* (ⓦwww.curve.com) is the leader, with *Girlfriends* (ⓦwww.gfriends.com) running not far behind. Another useful lesbian publication is *Gaia's Guide* (132 W 24th St, New York, NY 10014; $6.95), a yearly international directory with a lot of US information.

Women travelers

Practically speaking, though a woman traveling alone is certainly not the attention-grabbing spectacle in the Rockies that she might be elsewhere in the world, the odds that you'll come across some sort of harassment are pretty high. In most cases, it won't be any more serious than the odd offensive comment. Still, rape statistics in the US are high, and it goes without saying that women should never hitch alone – this is widely interpreted as an invitation for trouble, and there's no shortage of weirdoes to give it. If you can, avoid traveling at night by public transportation – deserted bus stations, while not necessarily threatening, will do little to make you feel secure, and where possible you should team up with another woman. On Greyhound buses, follow the example of other lone women and sit as near to the front – and the driver – as possible.

Small towns in rural areas are not blessed with the same liberal attitudes toward lone women travelers that you'll find in the cities. If you have a **car**, be careful whom you pick up: just because you're in the driver's seat doesn't mean you're safe. If you have a **vehicle breakdown** in a country area, walk to the nearest house or town for help; don't wait by the vehicle in the middle of nowhere hoping for somebody to stop – they will, but it may not be the kind of help you're looking for. Should disaster strike, all major towns have some kind of rape counseling service available; if not, the local police station will make adequate arrangements for you to get help, counseling, and, if necessary, get you home.

The **National Organization for Women** (ⓦwww.now.org) is a women's issues group whose lobbying has done much to affect positive legislation. NOW branches, listed in local phone directories and on their website, can provide referrals for specific concerns, such as rape crisis centers and counseling services, feminist bookstores and lesbian bars. Specific **women's contacts** are listed where applicable in the city sections of the guide.

Travelers with disabilities

Travelers with mobility problems or other physical disabilities are likely to find the Rockies – as with the US in general – to be much more in tune with their needs than anywhere else in the world. All public buildings must be wheelchair-accessible and have suitable toilets; most city street corners have dropped curbs; subways have elevators, and most city buses are able to kneel to make access easier and are built with space and handgrips for wheelchair users. Most hotels, restaurants and theaters (certainly any built in the last ten years or so) have excellent wheelchair access.

Contacts and resources

US and Canada

Access-Able Ⓦwww.access-able.com. Online resource for travelers with disabilities.

Directions Unlimited 123 Green Lane, Bedford Hills, NY 10507 ⓣ914/241-1700 or 1-800/533-5343. Tour operator specializing in custom tours for people with disabilities.

Mobility International USA 451 Broadway, Eugene, OR 97401 Voice and TDD ⓣ541/343-1284, Ⓦwww.miusa.org. Information and referral services, access guides, tours, and exchange programs. Annual membership $35 (includes quarterly newsletter).

Society for the Advancement of Travelers with Handicaps (SATH) 347 5th Ave, New York, NY 10016 ⓣ212/447-7284, Ⓦwww.sath.org. Non-profit educational organization that has actively represented travelers with disabilities since 1976.

Travel Information Service ⓣ215/456-9600. Telephone-only information and referral service.

Twin Peaks Press PO Box 129, Vancouver, WA 98661 ⓣ360/694-2462 or 1-800/637-2256, Ⓦwww.twinpeak.virtualave.net. Publisher of the *Directory of Travel Agencies for the Disabled* ($19.95), listing more than 370 agencies worldwide; *Travel for the Disabled* ($19.95); the *Directory of Accessible Van Rentals* ($12.95) and *Wheelchair Vagabond* ($19.95), loaded with personal tips.

Wheels Up! ⓣ1-888/389-4335, Ⓦwww.wheelsup.com. Provides discounted airfare, tour and cruise prices for disabled travelers, also publishes a free monthly newsletter and has a comprehensive website.

UK and Ireland

Ⓦwww.everybody.co.uk Provides information on accommodation suitable for disabled travelers throughout the UK, including Northern Ireland.

Disability Action Group 2 Annadale Ave, Belfast BT7 3JH ⓣ028/9049 1011. Provides information about access for disabled travelers abroad.

Holiday Care 2nd floor, Imperial Building, Victoria Rd, Horley, Surrey RH6 7PZ ⓣ01293/774535, Minicom ⓣ01293/776943, Ⓦwww.holidaycare.org.uk. Provides free lists of accessible accommodation abroad – European, American, and long-haul destinations – plus a list of accessible attractions in the UK. Information on financial help for holidays available.

Irish Wheelchair Association Blackheath Drive, Clontarf, Dublin 3 ⓣ01/833 8241, Ⓕ833 3873, Ⓔiwa@iol.ie. Useful information provided about traveling abroad with a wheelchair.

Tripscope Alexandra House, Albany Rd, Brentford, Middlesex TW8 0NE ⓣ08457/585641, Ⓦwww.justmobility.co.uk/tripscope. This registered charity provides a national telephone information service offering free advice on UK and international transport for those with a mobility problem.

Australia and New Zealand

ACROD (Australian Council for Rehabilitation of the Disabled) PO Box 60, Curtin, ACT 2605 ⓣ02/6282 4333; 24 Cabarita Rd, Cabarita, NSW 2137 ⓣ02/9743 2699. Provides lists of travel agencies and tour operators for people with disabilities.

Disabled Persons Assembly 4/173–175 Victoria St, Wellington, New Zealand ⓣ04/801 9100. Resource centre with lists of travel agencies and tour operators for people with disabilities.

Getting there and around

Most **airlines**, transatlantic and within the US, do whatever they can to ease your journey, and will usually let attendants of people with serious disabilities accompany them at no extra charge. The Air Carriers Access Act of 1986 obliged all domestic air carriers to make the majority of their services accessible to travelers with disabilities.

Almost every **Amtrak train** includes one or more coaches with accommodation for disabled passengers. Guide dogs travel free, and Amtrak will provide wheelchair assistance at its train stations, adapted seating on board and a fifteen percent discount on the regular fare, all provided 24-hours' notice is given. Passengers with hearing impairment can get information on ⓣ1-800/523-6590.

Traveling by **Greyhound** and **Amtrak Thruway** buses, however, is not to be recommended. Buses are not equipped with lifts for wheelchairs, though staff will assist with boarding (intercity carriers are required by law to do this), and the "Helping Hand" scheme offers two-for-the-price-of-one tickets to passengers unable to travel alone (carry a doctor's certificate). For assistance on Greyhound, call ⓣ1-800/752-4841 at least 48 hours before you intend to travel.

The major **car rental** firms can, given sufficient notice, provide vehicles with hand controls (though these are usually only available on the more expensive models, and you'll need to reserve well in advance). The American Automobile Association (see p.27) produces the *Handicapped Driver's Mobility Guide* for drivers with disabilities.

Outdoor activities

Citizens or permanent residents of the US who have been "medically determined to be blind or permanently disabled" can obtain the **Golden Access Passport**, a free lifetime entrance pass to those federally operated parks, monuments, historic sites, recreation areas and wildlife refuges that charge entrance fees. The pass must be picked up in person, from the areas described, and it also provides a fifty percent discount on fees charged for camping, boat launching and parking, and the like. The **Golden Bear Pass** (free to the disabled) offers similar concessions to state-run parks, beaches and historic sites.

The biggest effort to offer the disabled the same opportunities as the fully abled has been made by the **National Sports Center for the Disabled** (ⓣ970/726-1540, ⓦwww.nscd.org), based in Winter Park, Colorado. This accomplished center is best known for its program of instruction for disabled skiers, which has taught more than 45,000 students with either mental or physical disabilities. The resort has also created a program of summertime activities that include rafting, horseback riding, hand crank and tandem biking, rock climbing and sailing. Other organizations providing support for skiers at various resorts include the **Breckenridge Outdoor Education Center** (ⓣ970/455-6422), which offers assisted skiing for those with mental and physical disabilities along with adaptive equipment. The BOEC program also serves Arapahoe Basin, Copper Mountain, and Keystone. Based at Snowmass, the **Challenge Aspen/B.O.L.D.** (Blind Outdoor Leisure Development; ⓣ970/925-0578) offers its programs at all four mountains. Challenge Aspen caters to all disabilities; B.O.L.D. to visually impaired participants. The **Vail/Beaver Creek Resort Disabled Skiers Program**, ⓣ970/479-4445, offers a similar program.

Senior travelers

For many senior citizens, retirement brings the opportunity to explore the world in a style and at a pace that is the envy of younger travelers. As well as the obvious advantages of being free to travel for longer periods during the quieter, more congenial, and less expensive seasons, anyone over the age of 62 can enjoy the tremendous variety of discounts available. Both Amtrak and Greyhound, for example, and many US airlines, offer (smallish) percentage reductions on fares to older passengers.

Any US citizen or permanent resident aged 62 or over is entitled to free admission for life to all national parks, monuments, and historic sites using a **Golden Age Passport**, for which a once-only $10 fee is charged; it can be issued at any such site. This free entry also applies to any accompanying car passengers in their car or, for those hiking or cycling, the passport-holder's immediate family. It also gives a fifty percent reduction on fees for camping, parking, and boat launching.

The annual **Golden Bear Pass** ($5 to those 62 and over) offers a fifty percent discount on admission to state-run parks, beaches, and historic sites, subject to a means test. There is also a Senior Citizen Discount (based on proof of age only) giving $1 off parking and $2 off family camping, except where the fee is less than $3.

But before heading out to the Rockies its worth doing your homework on health matters first. The high-altitude of the region in general and the mountain passes specifically can aggravate certain conditions: those with heart problems should tread carefully over around 10,000ft – getting advice from a physician before your trip is best if you are in doubt. Respiratory conditions can also be aggravated – those with emphysema should avoid high altitudes completely – and again it's worth checking with your doctor before you go. Bear in mind that many spots in the Rockies are far from healthcare facilities or hospitals.

Contacts for senior travelers

American Association of Retired Persons 601 E St NW, Washington, DC 20049 ⓣ1-800/424-3410, membership hotline ⓣ202/434-2277 or 1-800/515-2299, ⓦwww.aarp.org. Can provide discounts on accommodation and vehicle rental. Membership open to US and Canadian residents aged 50 or over for an annual fee of $10 or $27 for three years. Canadian residents only have the annual option.

Elderhostel 75 Federal St, Boston, MA 02110 ⓣ1-877/426-8056, ⓦwww.elderhostel.com. Runs an extensive worldwide network of educational and activity programs, cruises, and homestays for people over 60 (companions may be younger). Programs generally last a week or more and costs are in line with those of commercial tours. In the Rockies, Elderhostel courses are available at a number of locations, including Boulder, Larmie, Boise, and Bozemon.

Saga Holidays 222 Berkeley St, Boston, MA 02116 ⓣ1-877/265-6862, ⓦwww.sagaholidays.com. Specializes in worldwide group travel for seniors. Saga's Road Scholar coach tours and their Smithsonian Odyssey Tours have a more educational slant.

Vantage Travel ⓣ1-800/322-6677, ⓦwww.vantagetravel.com. Specializes in worldwide group travel for seniors.

Opening hours and public holidays

Shops and services are generally open Monday to Saturday 8am/9am–5pm/6pm. Many stores are also open on Sundays, and larger towns and cities will invariably have 24-hour supermarkets and drugstores.

Post offices are usually open 8.30am–5.30pm Mon–Fri, with those in larger towns and cities open on Saturday mornings too.

Public holidays

The biggest and most all-American of the **national festivals and holidays** is Independence Day on the Fourth of July, when the entire country grinds to a standstill as people get drunk, salute the flag, and take part in firework displays, marches, and more, all in commemoration of the signing of the Declaration of Independence in 1776. Halloween (October 31) lacks any such patriotic overtones, and is not a public holiday despite being one of the most popular yearly flings. Traditionally, kids run around the streets banging on doors demanding "trick or treat," and are given pieces of candy. More sedate is Thanksgiving Day, on the last Thursday in November. The third big event of the year is essentially a domestic affair, when relatives return to the familial nest to stuff themselves with roast turkey, and (supposedly) fondly recall the first harvest of the Pilgrims in Massachusetts – though in fact Thanksgiving was already a national holiday before anyone thought to make that connection.

January 1 **New Year's Day**
January 15 **Martin Luther King Jr's Birthday**
Third Monday in February **Presidents' Day**
Varies (Usually Early April) **Easter Monday**
Last Monday in May **Memorial Day**
July 4 **Independence Day**
First Monday in September **Labor Day**
Second Monday in October **Columbus Day**
November 11 **Veterans' Day**
Last Thursday in November **Thanksgiving Day**
December 25 **Christmas Day**

On the national public holidays listed above, banks and offices are liable to be closed all day, and shops may reduce their hours. The traditional summer season for tourism runs from Memorial Day to Labor Day, though obviously the ski resorts and other cold-weather destinations have their peak season through the winter.

National parks and other protected lands

The various protected backcountry areas that you'll encounter in the Rockies fall into a number of potentially confusing categories, and include several different types of federally administered lands as well as state parks. The three main federal bodies entrusted with overseeing public lands and their use are the National Parks Service (NPS), the Department of Agriculture (USDA), which manages the national forests via its US Forest Service (USFS), and the Bureau of Land Management (BLM).

National parks and national monuments

National parks are large, federally controlled and preserved areas of great natural beauty, and most comprise several different features or ecosystems. These are rightly considered to be the country's flagship public lands, showcasing the most spectacular scenery, flora, and fauna in the US. **Entry fees** range from $10–20; if you have plans for repeat visits within a year or you have a few parks on your itinerary, pick up an **annual national parks pass** ($50). The pass is good for entry to all national parks within the US, for the pass-holder, spouse, and children, and can be purchased at any national park entrance station, or in advance by phone (within the US ⓣ888/467-2757), the internet (ⓦwww.nationalparks.org) or post (National Parks Pass, 27540 Avenue Mentry, Valencia, CA 91355; add $3.95 for postage). For an additional $15, you can upgrade your pass with a **Golden Eagle Hologram** – this adds free entry to all national forest areas that charge an entry fee as well as BLM sites.

National Parks contacts

For all national parks information, check the NPS website (ⓦwww.nps.gov). Contact phone numbers for the individual Rocky Mountains national parks are as follows:
Colorado Black Canyon of the Gunnison National Park ⓣ970/641-2337; Mesa Verde National Park ⓣ970/529-4465; Rocky Mountain National Park ⓣ970/586-1206.
Montana Glacier National Park ⓣ406/888-7800.
Wyoming Grand Teton National Park ⓣ307/739-3300; Yellowstone National Park ⓣ307/344-7381.

Fittingly, Yellowstone was designated as the **world's first national park** in 1872; this extraordinary geothermal wonderland was set aside by the US Congress "as a public park or pleasuring ground for the benefit and enjoyment of the people." The urge to protect unique public lands gathered further momentum into the early twentieth century, as the importance of a number of Native American sites was being recognized. Most of these were solitary structures or archeological sites rather than large ecosystems, and so the term **national monument** began to be applied. Some, such as Devil's Tower in Wyoming, retain the title, while the archeological preserve of Mesa Verde in Colorado, originally a national monument, has since been expanded into a national park.

National parks are otherwise distinguished from other federal public lands by the high level of public services they provide. Roads and trails are well marked and maintained, and even restrooms are provided at strategic points throughout each park. Typically a national park will also have one or more visitor centers, staffed by rangers on hand to ensure the safety, comfort and education of visitors, while enforcing the rules that protect the park's environment. Among the services typically provided at visitor centers are ranger-led nature walks, education programs, video presentations, and even group instruction on anything from wildlife photography to fly-fishing. Visitor centers also distribute a range of maps and information brochures (many of them free) and may offer a selection of books, maps, and photos for sale.

National forests, Bureau of Land Management (BLM) and wilderness areas

Large swaths of the Rockies are designated **national forests**, which differ from national parks in that they enjoy less protection; more roads run through them, and limited commercial activities including logging and mining may be pursued, subject to government approval. In some cases, ski resorts are permitted to operate on land leased from the United States Forest Service (USFS). National forests are managed to be as multipurpose as possible, allowing for the pursuit of a wide array of interests in an attractive environment. However, these areas tend to be categorized to some extent, with mountain biking only allowed on certain trails, snowmobiles restricted to particular areas, and so forth. You can camp at developed USFS campgrounds in the national forests ($5–15), or often camp for free, where permitted, in the backcountry.

USFS contacts

For all information on USFS areas and campgrounds, check the website ⓦwww.fs.fed.us. The central toll-free number for information and campsite reservations is ⓣ1-800/280-2267.

The **Bureau of Land Management** (BLM) administers some 264 million acres of public land, much of it in the western US. There are fewer restrictions than for national forests, with most areas open for unrestricted hiking, biking, and camping. For information on each state's BLM sites, check the website ⓦwww.blm.gov.

National forests, national parks, and land under BLM care can all contain **wilderness areas**, where the aim is to preserve the land in its most natural state. In practice this means commercial activities, motorized vehicles and bicycles are prohibited, as are firearms and pets. Dispersed camping in wilderness areas is allowed, but permits for this are usually required (free–$5). A number of wilderness areas that offer particularly fine opportunities for hiking and climbing and so forth are detailed throughout the guide.

State parks

As the name suggests, **state parks** are administered by the individual states, and tend to be fairly small areas focused on specific features such as lakes and dams used for recreation, or sites of geological or historical importance. **Daily usage fees** for these range from $3–5; it's worth noting that the usage fee is typically in addition to any overnight fee for camping in a state park.

State park contacts

For all information on individual state parks, check the website ⓦwww.stateparks.org. Contact phone numbers of the central administration offices for each state are as follows:

Colorado ⓣ303/866-3437
Idaho ⓣ208/334-4199
Montana ⓣ406/444-2950
Utah ⓣ801/538-7220
Wyoming ⓣ307/777-6323

Hiking and backcountry camping

Even in the planning stage of a trip to the Rockies, you're very likely thinking about hikes on high mountain trails, taking in the peerless beauty of the region first-hand. Between the national parks, national forests, and wilderness areas, there are enough superb hiking opportunities to keep you busy for decades.

It's worth keeping in mind that the well-known national parks such as Yellowstone are not automatically the best places in which to do your hiking. Certainly if solitude is an important goal, you may be better off heading for a less-visited wilderness area or national forest – several of which offer superb hiking without the strains of overcrowding. An excellent example of this is Wyoming's stunning Wind River region; overshadowed by two famous national parks nearby (Yellowstone and Grand Teton), the Wind River area is nevertheless widely considered to be the state's best for backcountry hiking. It may be, however, that the facilities, such as visitor centers, well-marked and maintained trails, and ranger-led activities available at established parks and recreation areas suit you best.

Details of specific hiking destinations, including local conditions and descriptions of some of the best trails, are included in individual accounts throughout the guide. If you're planning extensive exploration of one or two areas, you might consider investing in one of the comprehensive hik-

Hiking highlights

Colorado Rocky Mountain National Park: forested trails, plenty of wildlife and seemingly endless stretches of wild alpine tundra; The Sawatch Mountains around Leadville: a morning is all that's needed to hike up Colorado's highest mountain, Mt Elbert; Colorado National Monument: the huge rock arches of Rattlesnake Canyon are tailor made to be explored on foot.

Idaho Sawtooth National Recreation Area: easily accessible trails beneath some of the most rugged peaks in the Rockies; Frank Church-River of No Return Wilderness: 2600 miles of trails through impeccable, wildlife-rich backcountry waiting to be explored.

Montana Glacier National Park: spectacular mountain peaks and glaciers in the heart of grizzly and black bear country; Bob Marshall Wilderness: some of the best backcountry hiking in the Lower 48.

Utah Logan Canyon: family-friendly hikes to alpine lakes, past explosions of wildflowers in spring and summer; Big Cottonwood Canyon: access to lots of mostly moderate hikes, and within easy range of downtown Salt Lake City.

Wyoming Grand Teton National Park: peerless scenery bounded by lakes and the majestic Teton peaks; Wind River Mountains: Wyoming's best-kept secret offers great trails for extended backcountry trips and hundreds of stunning alpine lakes.

ing guides reviewed in Contexts at the back of this book.

Equipment

It's worth investing some thought and financial resources to ensure that you have the basic **hiking equipment**, and that it's comfortable. First and foremost in order of importance are sturdy **hiking boots**. The main considerations when purchasing them are whether to get heavy-duty ones or something lightweight, and whether they need to be waterproof or just water-resistant. If you don't plan on spending days on end scrambling about in the backcountry, it may be best to go for a fairly light, flexible boot. There are several varieties of boots available that mimic the comfort and flexibility of a running shoe, but also have grip and support appropriate for light to moderate hiking. If you're heading on a longer expedition and plan on carrying a heavy pack, you will certainly need a high-cut waterproof boot with a good quality sole. In either case, it's well worth being choosy and trying plenty of different styles before making a decision; indeed, you should only purchase boots from a reputable store with a knowledgeable staff that will run a series of tests to make sure the boot is right for you. Most importantly, you need to break in your boots by walking about in them for a few weeks before beginning your trip.

On most day-hikes, it's fine to wear T-shirt and shorts, although you should always have a **waterproof jacket** and a **fleece top** on hand in case the weather turns nasty, and a **hat** with a wide brim to protect your face and the back of your neck from the sun. You will be most comfortable in a shirt made from polypropylene or similar synthetic, as these don't absorb water and stay dry even as you sweat. Many hiking enthusiasts go as far as insisting that **"cotton'll kill ya"**; certainly damp cotton clothing will quickly chill you to the bone in a cold breeze at high altitude. For the same reasons, avoid cotton **socks** and splurge on a couple pairs of wool or synthetic wool-like socks instead.

Just what constitutes essential hiking gear is entirely dependent upon the duration and difficulty of the hike you're undertaking; for example, there's little need to carry tons of emergency supplies when you're doing an up-and-back three-hour walk on a marked trail in Rocky Mountain National Park. However, you should always carry at least a basic trail map, and if you're delving into backcountry areas, a compass and (waterproof) detailed topographic map become standard equipment. The most important general items to carry on any hike are plenty of water (you'll easily get through three liters a day in the mountains), sunscreen, energy snacks like chocolate bars and such, and some warm and waterproof gear. Use the

Hiking gear

For an overnight hiking trip, you'll need at least the "Essential" items listed below; you may want to pack a few from the "Additional" selection too.

Essential
waterproof tent
sleeping bag
boots
wool socks
long underwear
fleece
waterproof gear
first aid kit
stove and fuel
pots, pans, and utensils
food (including emergency supply)
sturdy water bottle
matches
thirty feet of nylon cord
pocket knife
flashlight, lantern, or candles
sunscreen

Additional
sleeping pad
bear spray
water purifier
hat and gloves
toilet paper
bug spray
binoculars
camera
tarp/ground cover
journal
entertainment; books, playing cards, etc.

checklist above to review your own requirements for both day-hikes and overnight backcountry trips.

Safety

Safety issues in regard to hiking in the Rockies have much to do with **altitude**; dehydration occurs quickly in the thin, dry air of the mountains, and altitude sickness is an ever-present danger (see box on p.20 for more information). **Mountain weather** is notoriously unpredictable, and snowstorms can appear at any time of the year. When hiking above the treeline you'll be completely exposed to the sun – in which case a lightweight long-sleeve shirt is a very good idea, in addition to a hat. If **lightning** is a potential threat, you should head back down below the treeline; if you're stuck in the open, crouch between a couple of boulders, or hunker down on top of a small one, preferably on some insulating material such as a foam sleeping mat.

The most common problems come down to errors of judgment rather than natural disasters. Most can be averted simply by making sensible decisions based on your level of backcountry experience. There are lots of fantastic hiking opportunities available in well-traveled areas with clearly marked trails, so you're better off sticking to these if your backcountry experience is limited. Remember too that a detailed topographic map and compass are only helpful if you know how to use them.

Hiking alone is not recommended, and you should ideally let someone know what your plans are and when you expect to return. Heed the advice of rangers, and use any self-registration system, such as logsheets at trailheads, wherever you're expected to do so.

Encounters with large animals such as elk, bison, moose, bears, and mountain lions simply demand awareness and respect (for details on encounters with bears, see p.550; for mountain lions, see p.286). You're far more likely to be bothered by such things as ticks and mosquitoes.

Backcountry camping

The Rocky Mountain region is the US's preeminent **backcountry camping** location. Nearly every national park and forest, wilderness and recreation area allows for it at minimal or no cost – though a permit is often required. While the idea of heading off into the hills with your tent may sound appealing, remember that there are certain responsibilities you take on when you do so. The reason that so many cliched backcountry camping mantras – "good camp sites are found, not made" and "leave only footprints behind" are two most often heard – exist is that the advice they give continues to be ignored. Few things are as disheartening as spending a full day labouring under a heavy pack only to find that your backcountry site resembles the local landfill.

Before leaving, be sure to let someone – preferably a ranger – know where you're heading for and when you intend to return. Also check with the local ranger office for detailed maps and regulations on local camping grounds, and for weather forecasts and any potential hazards along the way, such as local wildlife, avalanche areas or rivers that may need to be forded.

When camping rough, always **pack out what you pack in** (or more if you come across some other inconsiderate soul's litter), and avoid the old advice to burn rubbish; wildfires have been started in this way. Regarding fires, always check before departing to see if fires are permitted in the first place; if they are, only use deadwood and fallen wood. Where there are no toilets, **bury human waste** at least four inches into the ground and a hundred feet from the nearest water supply and camp. A growing problem is giardia, a water-borne protozoan causing an intestinal disease, symptoms of which are chronic diarrhea, abdominal cramps, fatigue, and loss of weight, that requires treatment. To avoid catching it, **never drink** directly from rivers and streams, no matter how clear and inviting they may look (you never know what unspeakable acts people – or animals – further upstream have performed in them). Before you drink **water** that isn't from taps, it should be boiled for at least five minutes, or cleansed with an iodine-based purifier or a giardia-rated filter, available from camping and sports shops.

Finally, don't use **soaps or detergents** (even special ecological or biodegradable soaps) anywhere near lakes and streams; folk using water purifiers or filters downstream won't thank you at all. Instead carry water at least a hundred feet (preferably two hundred) from the water's edge before washing.

Mountain biking and cycling

Though all wilderness areas and national park trails are out of bounds to mountain bikes, fat tires are welcome on almost all national forest and BLM trails. These include thousands of miles of single track and many more miles of old logging and mining roads. Whether you are a skilled mountain biker after technical challenges or a more leisurely cyclist looking to explore the countryside on traffic-free trails, it's hard to think of a place better suited to exploration by bicycle. The mountainous topography and high altitude of course means that it pays to be fit, particularly if you have a longer multiday tour in mind. For those looking for more thrills with less climbing, many resorts open their ski-lifts to bikes in the summer.

The Great Divide Trail

King of all the off-road trails in the region is the **Great Divide Trail**, which runs from Canada to Mexico, through Montana, Wyoming, Colorado, and New Mexico. The 2465-mile route was dreamt up and managed by the Adventure Cycling Association, PO Box 8308-GP, Missoula, M 59807 (☎406/721-1776 or 1-800/755-2453) who can provide trail maps, information, and run tours.

Almost every good-sized mountain town in the Rockies will have a bike shop offering **rentals** to visitors. The quality of the bikes is reliably good – almost all have good front suspension and if you want to hire a full suspension rig, it's usually not too hard to find one. Prices hover around $25 per day for front-suspension, $40 for a full suspension. Bike shops are usually happy to change pedals for those who wish to use their own clip-in system with a rental bike – the best option to creating a comfortable bike without bringing your own. But many serious bikers will want to bring their own rides; check out your **airline's policy** on bike handling *before* booking. Generally you will be charged around $70 to carry your bike on a domestic flight, while those flying in from abroad will be allowed to bring their bike in free – in lieu of one of the two pieces of luggage allowed. Also check to so if your carrier requires bikes to be boxed – at the very least you will probably be asked to remove pedals, deflate tires and turn handlebars.

Local bike shops are the best source of advice and **information** about nearby trails. Another good resource, particularly if you will be exploring one state for a while, are the topographic atlases produced by DeLorme published on a state-by-state basis and sold at many gas stations.

Over the last decade, several areas have emerged as popular **mountain biking hubs** (see below). Wherever you bike the accepted **trail etiquette** is that bikers yield to hikers and horseback riders and if encountering another cyclist, the biker descending should give way to the biker climbing. **Helmets** are not required by law in any of the Rocky Mountain states, but clearly make good sense, particularly when riding off-road.

Biking highlights

Colorado

The ultimate adventure in the state is the Colorado Trail (see p.87) which crosses Colorado from Durango to Denver – a journey just short of 500 miles – and is open to bikes along its entire length. Crested Butte is one of the birthplaces of mountain biking, with several world-class trails to choose from (see box on p.187). The best ski resorts to hit up for lift-serviced trails are Winter Park, Keystone, Vail and Breckenridge. Winter Park in particular has a huge network, while all the trails in Keystone are fairly hard – a couple of sections are the most technical lift-serviced sections in the state – while at Vail you can ride the remnants of past years' World Cup cross-country and downhill courses.

Idaho

The entire Sawtooth NRA area has worthwhile trails, one of the finest (with plenty of steep singe track downhill action) being the Fisher Creek-Williams Creek Trail (see p.662). The Route of the Hiawatha Trail (see box on p.660) is the most popular trail for touring cyclists and follows a converted railway line over several high trestles and through the memorable Taft Tunnel.

Montana

Cyclists visiting the state often choose to ride the 52 mile Going-to-the-Sun Highway through Glacier National Park. Though scenically stunning, the experience is rather marred by traffic, so choosing a more remote road in the area is recommended. For lift-serviced downhill biking, both Big Sky and Big Mountain serve up a wide array of routes.

Wyoming

Medicine Bow National Forest, two miles south of Arlington, is particularly popular, with trails including the incredible Rock Creek Trail along a granite ledge high above forests of lodgepole pines, spruces, and aspens. Grand Teton National Park is not as dangerous as Yellowstone National Park (where drivers pull over erratically and constantly).The main roads here provide decent room for bikers and the views are unforgettable.

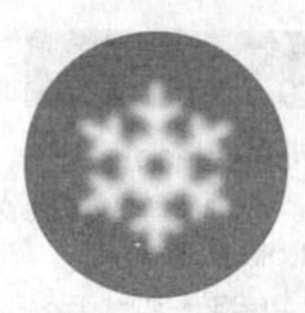

Skiing and snowboarding

To many, the Rocky Mountains are synonymous with winter sports and with around sixty ski areas in the region, it's easy to see why. Alongside the big name resorts like Aspen, Vail, Breckenridge, Telluride, Jackson Hole, Big Sky and Sun Valley that draw all the crowds, the Rockies have dozens of smaller, less-glitzy and cheaper ski areas – all with their own personality and some dramatic ski terrain of their own. Even more so than the terrain – rugged ridges, steep drops, dense glades and lonely bowls – the quality and amount of local snowfalls, dubbed "champagne powder," keep people coming back for more. Those used to icy slopes elsewhere will be surprised by how forgiving the snow is and are sure to be blown away after experiencing a legendary powder day – skiing or riding in light, thigh- or waist-deep snow.

Though exact **season** dates vary, depending on the location of a resort within the mountain range, typically resorts run their lifts from late-November to mid-April. Taken as a whole, the choice of ski resorts in the Rocky Mountain region is intimidatingly large. If you're traveling in from well outside the region, the most tempting option is clearly to go for one of the larger resorts. If your time is limited to a week or two, you'll probably also want to spend the minimum amount of time in transit. Many skiers fall into these groups, which is why around a fifth of all U.S. skier days occur in Colorado. But the other Rocky Mountain states have their own significant, world-class ski hills and are generally a good deal less crowded. Utah is particularly popular, despite its watered-down après-ski scene, with its resorts extraordinarily convenient from Salt Lake City, as shown during the recent Salt Lake City Olympics. If **après-ski** is important to you, then you should definitely head to Colorado, where ski towns party much harder than further north – the best rule of thumb being that the older the associated town the better the nightlife. So former mining towns like Aspen, Breckenridge, Telluride, and Crested Butte are good bets for raucous partying and leagues ahead of newer rivals – particularly the all-inclusive resorts which largely attract families.

Costs

Those familiar with Europe's more palatable lift-ticket prices, or used to skiing lesser resorts on the US eastern seaboard, might be a little shocked by the **cost of skiing** in the Rockies. The most expensive place to ski is consistently Aspen, where tickets are hovering around the $70 mark for a one-day adult day-ticket. Thankfully, the typical price of a ticket at a larger resort is around the $50 per day – still rather costly, though – with kids skiing at around half-price. There are of course ways you can save money on tickets. Strategies include scanning the websites of resorts for ticket offers or once there checking adverts in local newspapers and supermarkets for deals designed to attract locals. The purchase of multiday tickets will also cut the cost of a day's skiing as will visiting later in the season – often killer deals are offered in April when the snows are still good but many have lost interest in skiing. Early and late in the season you can also often pick up a couple of nights lodging and skiing for around $200 per person at major resorts like Winter Park and even Aspen. Check websites at the last minute for details. Other ways to cut costs include packing a lunch to avoid pricey slope-side options and commuting in from cheaper accommodation outside the resort area – which is likely however to mean a super-early start in the morning and put you far out of reach of any après-ski action.

In contrast to the price of lift tickets, **equipment rental** is much better value and there is keen competition around resorts. Packages for basic skis, poles and boots start at around $15 per day, though if you are more advanced you'd do well to spend a little more on equipment or even try out a

Skiing and snowboarding highlights

Colorado The most popular place to ski in Colorado is Summit County, where Breckenridge, Keystone, Copper Mountain, and Arapaho Basin are all within close proximity. Within a short drive of Summit County are several other major ski areas, including the varied and challenging Winter Park, the idyllic backcountry paradise of Berthoud Pass and the massive slopes of Vail. The other major resorts in Colorado are harder to get to and include the four ski areas at Aspen, the state's après-ski capital; laid-back Steamboat Springs in northern Colorado; and the enjoyable Crested Butte and Telluride in southern Colorado – each large enough to warrant their own airports.

Idaho Best known for the Sun Valley Resort, loaded with steep mogul runs and fine, long, intermediate level cruising opportunities. Other top resorts include Schweitzer Mountain Resort near Sandpoint and Silver Mountain Resort near Kellogg.

Montana Big Sky, half-hour drive north of Yellowstone National Park, has the biggest vertical drop of any resort in the US (over 4000ft), and is known for its good mix of intermediate-level terrain as well as a clutch of scary expert trails. Big Mountain, near Whitefish, is another large and very worthwhile resort, known for varied skiing and great glade skiing in between snow-covered trees – so-called snow ghosts. The ski area of Red Lodge Mountain is beside a happening party town and close to an outstanding network of cross-country trails.

Utah Nearly all of the state's major resorts are clustered within an hour's drive of Salt Lake City, and huge quantities of light, legendary snow fall consistently. Alta (for skiers only) and Snowbird, both in Little Cottonwood Canyon a half-hour from Salt Lake City, are renowned for their laid-back nature and incredible terrain. In nearby Big Cottonwood Canyon are Brighton and Solitude, while the state's other most famous resorts – Park City, Deer Valley, and the Canyons – are lined up in a row a few miles to the east.

Wyoming Judged by many to be the best in the country, the ski scene here is dominated by the world-class monster of Jackson Hole Mountain Resort – a challenge for even the most extreme of skiers. Not far away are a couple of other good resorts: Snow King Resort in Jackson and Grand Targhee Resort in Alta, reachable via Idaho only.

demo package of the latest gear – usually around $35 per day. Rates for renting a board and boots start at around $25. If you need rental gear and plan on taking lessons, it's well worth waiting until you get to the mountain since most resorts offer rental gear, a lesson and lift-ticket packages at a fraction of the cost of the sum of their parts.

Ski and snowboard events

Being blessed with so many fine venues for skiing and snowboarding, the Rockies see their fair share of international **skiing and snowboarding competitions**. At least a couple of official World Cup events are held each year at North American resorts; favored Rockies venues in recent years include Aspen, Vail, Breckenridge, and Park City. The resorts around Park City will presumably be firmly in the reckoning for major competitions in coming seasons, following its turn as host of the **2002 Winter Olympics**.

As spectator events go, **downhill skiing** and boarding are somewhat less than ideal, since all you can realistically do is stand beside the course and watch a competitor come hurtling downwhill before disappearing below you. There's plenty of whooping and hollering from the crowd as each competitor flies past, so it's more about the communal experience than actually seeing a lot of skiing or boarding. Much better from a spectator's standpoint are more static events such as aerial **freestyle** and **half-pipe competitions**. Because all the competitors perform in a small area – either a jump-plus-landing-zone, or in a half-pipe which is usually less than 100 yards long – spectators can watch an entire competition from one position. These events are also served up with plenty of hype – loud music and usually an MC calling each jump or run.

A full season's schedule of skiing events, including World Cup races, is available online at ⓦwww.irisco.net/ski; for snowboarding check ⓦwww.expn.go.com.

Cross-country and backcountry skiing

The opportunities for **cross-country (Nordic) skiing** in the Rocky Mountains are vast, with thousands of miles of trails in national forests and national parks being joined by scores of cross-country ski areas with groomed terrain. These cross-country areas are commonly run alongside downhill-skiing facilities and support the activity with lessons, rentals and a couple of warming cabins. But despite the attractions of a well-managed and supported network, it's often also worth exploring beyond the environs of busy ski resorts, to accessible locations with more scenic splendor – particularly national park areas like Rocky Mountain National Park or Mesa Verde National Park in Colorado and Yellowstone National Park in Wyoming. Recently there has also been a surge in interest in **hut-to-hut skiing**, exploring a network of trails, between backcountry cabins, furnished with enough comforts for a pleasant overnight stay and designed to be a stopping stone on a multiday skiing trip. The popularity of the sport means that reservations for huts such as those in the 10th Mountain Division hut system (see p.237) must be made at least a month in advance.

Backcountry skiing takes Nordic skiing one stage further, the adoption of telemark skiing equipment allowing skiers to both travel cross-country and drop down steep slopes along the way. A difficult skill, telemarking is best learnt in the confines of a resort before it becomes a skill you'd want to depend on in the wilderness. Exploring the backcountry is also understandably popular with snowboarders and downhill skiers. However, making your own way into the backcountry carries with it some grave dangers, particularly from human-triggered avalanches. Steep, treeless slopes always pose a serious risk. Under no circumstances should you head into the backcountry without prior instruction, and in most cases a snow shovel and receiver should be taken along as well. The Rockies are known for **fickle weather**; what starts out as a bright day can turn nasty within minutes; wear sunglasses or goggles and sunscreen and drink plenty of water to guard against sunburn, windburn, and altitude sickness. Those confident of their abilities and backcountry expertise will find conditions to be optimum later on in the season when your skills are at their sharpest and snows have firmed up a little, making them easier to walk on as well as diminishing avalanche dangers.

A much tamer and less spectacular way to enjoy the backcountry is strapped to a pair of **snowshoes**. Thanks to today's high-tech models, gone are days when walking on these cumbersome items required much skill and practice. Now it's easy and worthwhile to hire a pair from a local ski shop and strike out, exploring empty local forest trails.

Other outdoor activities

Though hiking, biking, skiing, and snowboarding have the highest profile in the Rockies, several other outdoor pursuits are followed just as religiously by locals and visitors alike.

Climbing and mountaineering

With an abundance of peaks in the 12,000–14,000ft range, plus hundreds of precipitous walls of granite, limestone, and ice and clusters of huge boulders, the Rocky Mountains serve up abundant **climbing** and **mountaineering** opportunities. Whether your own preference is for summiting a mighty peak, employing technical equipment and skills to scale a granite wall or a sheer sheet of ice, or undertaking some unfettered free-climbing or bouldering, you'll find plenty of routes to choose from all across the Rockies.

In the US, the system used to classify the levels of technical difficulty in mountaineering is the **Yosemite Decimal System**; climbs that require technical expertise and equipment will come under the system's category 5, which breaks down further into classifications from 5.2 to 5.14. An approximate comparison with the UIAA system would be: 5.2-5.9 equals I-VI; 5.10-5.14 equals VI+-X.

Top climbing spots

Colorado **Ouray:** home of the Quray Ice Park, one of the top ice-climbing destinations in the US; Rocky Mountain National Park, where the prime target of summiteers is Long's Peak.

Idaho **Sawtooth National Recreation Area:** year-round climbing with a real alpine feel and few other climbers to share it with; City of Rocks, east of Pocatello: amazing granite pinnacles thrusting out of the desert provide a test for all abilities; Chimney Rock near Priest Lake: the Panhandle's top vertical challenge.

Montana **Hyalite Canyon:** some of the best ice-climbing in the Rockies, within easy reach of Bozeman.

Wyoming **Grand Teton National Park:** for technical and non-technical climbs in the stunning Teton Range; Cirque of the Towers, in the Wind River Mountains: a popular hike to cluster of 12,000ft-plus peaks in a superb setting; Vedauwoo Recreation Area, east of Laramie: offers several freestanding granite formations with challenges to suit every proficiency level.

Whitewater rafting, kayaking, and canoeing

You'd be hard pressed to find many other regions in the world with as many **whitewater rafting** opportunities as the Rockies. There are several fast moving rivers throughout the region (see opposite) fit for everyone from first timers to experienced pros. If the former, you'll be in need of a river guide; contacts for the best are listed throughout the guide.

The whitewater **season** runs from late April through to September, though the early part of this season is for hardened paddlers as the waters tend to be very fast and very cold. The months of May and June typically see rivers at their highest as a result of spring runoff, making for a faster ride and bigger rapids. Though the water flow decreases in the second half of the season, trips can be just as enjoyable as the warmer waters make for more pleasant swimming and splashing about.

The most popular method of floating down is on a **raft**, followed by **kayaks** and **canoes**. Regardless of the craft, just getting out onto the water is a thrill, and one that allows you to take in a great deal of natural beauty, spy on wildlife and often cast a line or two.

Rafting

A major reason behind the popularity of **rafting** is that anyone, including those who have never floated a river before, can participate. It's not unusual for even novice rafters, after a short riverside safety course, to bash through Class III or even occasionally Class IV rapids (see box, opposite, for breakdown of classifications) in the hands of a good river guide.

The majority of rafters book their trip through a **commercial outfitter**, who will take care of any necessary **permits** and supply

River classifications

Class I Very Easy. Small regular waves and riffles. Few or no obstructions and little maneuvering is required.

Class II Easy. Waves up to three feet. Wide, clear channels that are obvious without scouting. Low ledges and small rock gardens. Some maneuvering required.

Class III Medium. Rapids with numerous high irregular waves capable of swamping an open canoe. Strong eddies. Narrow passages that often require complex maneuvering. May require scouting from shore.

Class IV Difficult. Long, difficult rapids with irregular waves, dangerous rocks, boiling eddies, and constricted passages that require precise maneuvering. Scouting from shore is necessary and conditions make rescue difficult. Generally not possible for open canoes.

Class V Very difficult. Long, violent rapids with wild turbulence and highly congested routes that must be scouted from shore. Rescue conditions are difficult and there is significant hazard to life in the event of a mishap.

Class VI Limit of navigation and a definite hazard to life.

the necessary **safety gear** (life jackets, helmets, and, in cold water conditions, wet suits). Costs for commercial trips vary from $50 for a half-day to around $1500 for a week-long journey, including transport to and from put-in and take-out points and all meals while on the river. It's highly advisable to use a well-established company as their guides will know the river well and are trained in first aid skills in the rare event they may be required.

Various types of craft are used for rafting. **Paddle rafts** are up to 14ft long, hold six to eight paddlers and a guide, and are a heap of fun in rapids. One or two-person inflatable kayaks, known as "**rubber duckies**" may also be available for more adventurous paddlers who want to take on the rapids alone. **Oar rafts** are up to 22ft long, controlled and paddled with a rear oar and used to transport camping gear and equipment downriver, and are often manned only by a guide and partner. Some companies also use traditional wooden or steel-hulled **dories** that are also controlled by paddles, but are less mobile than modern rafts. Occasionally, motorized **jet boats** are used as well.

Top rivers

While the Rockies region contains scores of rivers to raft down, details of which are given in individual regional accounts throughout the guide, here are some of the standouts:

Colorado Cache la Poudre River: a designated "wild and scenic river" with Class III–V rapids; The Arkansas River: the busiest stretch of whitewater in the States, thanks to long runs of continuous Class III water as well as the unremitting "Numbers section" or the chunky waves at the base of the Royal Gorge, both Class IV–V.

Idaho The Middle Fork of the Salmon, flowing through the heart of the Frank Church-River of No Return Wilderness Area; a real backcountry experience with exciting Class III–IV rapids.

Montana Alberton Gorge on the Clark Fork River – a thrilling, rapid-rich experience within easy reach of Missoula; Gallatin River near Big Sky: highlights of the III–IV rapids include the heart-pounding "Mad Mile."

Wyoming Snake River from Jackson Hole: Class III–IV rapids, plus the state's most scenic float trips, right past the majestic Teton Range.

Kayaking

Many of the rivers used by rafters are also popular with **kayakers**, although on all but the gentlest of rivers kayaking requires a certain amount of experience and the ability to roll the craft. Since kayakers are more likely to ride the river independently, a good knowledge of the river and/or the ability to read river maps are vital. If you're in any doubt about your ability, go for a rafting trip instead.

Canoeing

Canoeing is a relaxing way to discover calmer waterways and lakes, and most major lakes in the Rockies will have outfitters who can rent canoes by the hour, half-day or longer. This quiet and traditional Native American method of water transport allows you to get close to waterfowl, pull up and enjoy picnics on secluded lakeside or riverside beaches, or just get in a nice, low-key workout.

Fishing and hunting

The Rocky Mountains are a natural draw for **hunters** and **anglers**, with some of the finest stocks of fish and game in the Lower 48. It's impossible to list the best fishing rivers in the Rockies simply because there are so many, but details are given in individual regional accounts throughout the guide. Suffice to say there are enough "Blue Ribbon" or "Gold Medal" rivers throughout the region to make such terms nearly meaningless. In many places it's possible to fly-fish virtually from the roadside or even within some city centers, and if you're looking for solitude the lakes and rivers of the backcountry will provide infinite variety. Good access sites are often signposted, but don't necessarily assume you can fish anywhere you choose – some rivers run through private land and permission must be given by the landowner before you cast a line. It's often best to stop in to discuss spots and possible guided tours with a local outfitter; again, these are listed throughout the guide.

The main fishing **season** is June to October, although it's quite possible to fish year-round in many areas; ice fishing is a popular lake option in winter. License fees for each state are listed below.

Hunters will find a huge variety of **game**, from waterfowl and game birds to big game such as elk, bear, and moose. The main season is from late September to early December, when deer and elk are the big draw, especially on BLM and national forest land. License fees and seasons vary enormously – for instance a nonresident elk-hunting license in Colorado runs $250, while the same in Idaho costs $340. In any case, contact the relevant wildlife management department (see below) for full details of the animal you're interested in tracking down. Note that hunting and fishing licenses are nearly always also available from ranger stations, sporting goods stores, and local outfitters.

A note for **hikers**; if you're in the backcountry in the main hunting season ensure you make yourself very visible – some greenhorn hunters can get jumpy and may mistake you for their prey if it's not entirely obvious that you're a human and not an elk.

State Hunting and Fishing Licenses and Fees

Note that all fees are for nonresidents.

Colorado Colorado Division of Wildlife, 6060 Broadway, Denver, CO 80216 (T 303/297-1192, W www.dnr.state.co.us/wildlife/). A seasonal fishing license costs $20, a one-day license $5, five days $18. The fishing season is year-round with certain exceptions on some waters.

Idaho Idaho Dept of Fish and Game, 600 S Walnut St, Boise, ID 83707-0025 (T 1-800/635-7820, W www.state.id.us/fishgame). A seasonal fishing license costs $75, $10 for one day, $4 for additional consecutive days, and a three-day salmon/steelhead license costs $31. Lakes and reservoirs are open year-round, but there are seasonal restrictions on rivers and streams.

Montana Montana Fish, Wildlife and Parks, PO Box 200701, Helena, MT 59620-0701 (T 406/444-4720, W www.fwp.state.mt.us/). A seasonal fishing license costs $45, a two-day license is $10, but you must have a conservation license ($5, valid for life) to obtain these. Most lakes and reservoirs are open year-round, but there are seasonal restrictions on rivers and streams.

Utah Utah Division of Wildlife Resources, PO Box 146301, Salt Lake City, UT 84114-6301 (T 801/538-4700, W www.wildlife.utah.gov). A seasonal fishing license costs $46 per year, a one-day license $8, a seven-day license $21. Most lakes and reservoirs are open year-round, but there are seasonal restrictions on some rivers and streams.

Wyoming Wyoming Game & Fish Dept, 5400 Bishop Blvd, Cheyenne, WY 82006-0001 (T 307/777-4600, W www.gf.state.wy.us/). A seasonal fishing license costs $65 per year, a one-day license $6. Most lakes and reservoirs are open year-round, but there are seasonal restrictions on rivers and streams.

Golf, horseback riding, and other miscellaneous pursuits

The pursuit with the longest pedigree in the region is, of course, **horseback riding**. Though some stables will hire horses to experienced riders, more common is a guided trail ride for anything between an hour (costing around $15) to multiday overnight forays of up to $150 per day. Such guided backcountry trips usually require a party of at least two. For a full immersion into Western life, you might like to spend time at a dude ranch; see p.31.

Golf has also taken off as a popular summertime pursuit. The region has always had its share of good smaller 9- or 18-hole public courses, but these have been joined by more expensive world-championship standard courses run by resorts as a summer alternative to skiing. At the height of summer tee times at these courses are booked up to a couple of weeks in advance. A goodregionwide publication is *The Guide to Golf in the Rockies* by Breckenridge Publishing Company, which includes full course descriptions, fees, and contact information.

Of all the high-end sports offered in the mountains, the most thrilling, memorable, and expensive is **hot-air ballooning**. Short half-hour flights are the cheapest way to go and will cost around $100. Most companies, though, aim for a more leisurely experience, with at least an hour of air-time. Flights are offered by companies based in many Colorado towns including Boulder, Steamboat Springs, Vail, Aspen, and Colorado Springs. You can also get airborne in Jackson, Wyoming and near Glacier National Park and Whitefish in Montana. The greatest annual hot-air balloon spectacle is held in a July Rally in Riverton, Wyoming and in Rock Springs Wyoming around the same time. In Colorado both Grand Junction and Crested Butte have hot-air balloon festivals.

An alternative to soaring high above the mountains is to explore deep within them, and **caving** attracts a small and dedicated number of fans to the area. The largest concentration of limestone bedrock, creating caverns perfect for exploration by experienced cavers, in the region is in Wyoming and a key publication for spelunkers is *Caves of Wyoming* by Hill, Sutherland, and Tierney (University of Wyoming). In Montana, one of the few options is Azure Cave in the Little Rocky Mountains between Zortman and Landusky. Those that want to see a cave in the presence of a guide should head to the Cave of the Winds near Manitou Springs, Colorado; the Glenwood Fairy Caverns in Colorado; or the Lewis and Clark Caverns State Park, near Bozeman in Montana.

Sports

The Rocky Mountain states have just a few teams at the top professional level in baseball, basketball, and football; naturally these are based in the large population centers of Denver and Salt Lake City. A number of college towns throughout the Rockies do, however, boast collegiate equivalents in basketball and football. College football is the fiercest of the school-based sports, and the chance to see rival schools in particular going head-to-head is not to be missed. During summer, the quintessential spectator event in the Rockies is the rodeo – a unique celebration of cowboy culture.

Football

Football in America attracts some of the most wild and devoted fans of any sport, perhaps because there are relatively few games played – only sixteen in a season, which lasts throughout the fall and culminates in the **Super Bowl** at the end of January. With many quick skirmishes and military-like movements up and down the field, it's ideal for television, and nowhere is this more apparent than during the **televised games** which are a feature of many bars on Monday nights – though most games are played on Sundays.

The only NFL team residing in the Rockies are the **Denver Broncos**, who enjoy enormous support with home games typically sold out for the entire season in advance. Happily, watching a **college game** is an equally fun – and far less expensive (tickets $15–60) – alternative. If you think you've seen a sporting crowd get emotionally involved, check out a game between traditional rivals such as Colorado State (Fort Collins) and the University of Colorado

(Boulder). Games are typically played on Saturday, and feature cheerleaders, marching bands and lots of rowdy student fans.

Teams

Professional teams

Denver Broncos ⓣ720/258-3333, ⓦwww.denverbroncos.com. The team's long-time home field, Mile High Stadium, was torn down at the end of the 1999–2000 season, and its replacement subject to furious debate over its proposed corporate name. In the end, the compromise "Invesco Field at Mile High" was arrived at, in time for the 2001–2002 NFL season. **Tickets** cost $30–90.

Collegiate teams

Air Force Falcon Stadium, Colorado Springs, CO ⓣ719/472-1895 or 1-800/666-8723.
Boise State Bronco Stadium, Boise, ID ⓣ208/426-4737.
Brigham Young University LaVell Edwards Stadium, Salt Lake City, UT ⓣ801/378-BYU1 or 1-800/322-BYU1.
Colorado State Hughes Stadium, Fort Collins, CO ⓣ970/491-RAMS or 1-800/491-RAMS.
Montana State Bobcat Stadium, Bozeman, MO ⓣ406/994-2287.
University of Colorado Folsom Field, Boulder, CO ⓣ303/830-8497.
University of Montana Washington-Grizzly Stadium, Missoula, MO ⓣ406/243-4051 or 1-888/666-8262.
University of Wyoming War Memorial Stadium, Laramie, WY ⓣ307/766-4850 or 1-800/922-9461.

Baseball

Baseball, much like cricket in its relaxed, summertime pace and seemingly Byzantine rules, is often called "America's pastime." Games are played – 162 each season – all over the US almost every day from April to early October, with the playoffs and the World Series (a best-of-seven playoff), lasting through the end of October.

If you're not familiar with the game, the subtleties involved in playing will more than likely escape you, at least until you've watched several games and asked a lot of questions. Still, anyone can have a grand day out sitting in the sun in the bleachers, a beer and a hotdog in hand, joining in a chorus of "Take me out to the ballgame." This is without doubt a true American cultural experience.

The **Colorado Rockies** are the sole major league team in the Rocky Mountain region, and the state-of-the-art Coors Field, their home turf in Denver, has proven to be one of the most popular ballparks in the country since the Rockies moved there from the (former) Mile High Stadium in 1995.

Teams and tickets

Colorado Rockies Coors Field, Denver, CO ⓣ1-800/388-ROCK, ⓦhttp://rockies.mlb.com. **Tickets** for games cost $5–75 per seat, and are generally available on the day of the game.

Basketball

Basketball is one of the few professional sports that is also actually played by many ordinary Americans – hardly surprising since all you need is a ball and a hoop. The professional game is governed by the **National Basketball Association** (NBA), which oversees a season running from November until the playoffs in May. Games last for an exhausting 48 minutes of playing time, though with stoppages and commercial breaks games typically take around two hours to complete. **Tickets** to NBA games cost $20–80.

The two Rockies-based NBA teams are Salt Lake City's **Utah Jazz** and the **Denver Nuggets**. The Jazz are still one of the league's highest profile teams, and have consistently figured in the playoffs over the last decade, while the more middle of the road Nuggets seem unlikely to make any immediate impact on the league.

The **Women's National Basketball Association** (WNBA) was launched amidst a media blitz in late 1996, and its credibility and profile has risen steadily since. The WNBA season takes place in the summer; **Utah Starzz** are stablemates to the Utah Jazz, and are also based at Salt Lake City's Delta Center. **Tickets** to WNBA games, more reasonable than their NBA counterparts, cost $10–60.

Teams

NBA

Denver Nuggets Pepsi Center, Denver, CO ⓣ303/405-1212, ⓦwww.nba.com/nuggets.

Utah Jazz Delta Center, Salt Lake City, UT ⓣ801/325-SEAT, ⓦwww.nba.com/jazz.

WNBA

Utah Starzz Delta Center, Salt Lake City, UT ⓣ801/325-SEAT, ⓦwww.wnba.com/starzz.

Ice hockey

Understandably in a region known for winter sports, **ice hockey** enjoys considerable popularity in the Rocky Mountain states. The only NHL team in the Rockies, though, is the Denver-based **Colorado Avalanche**, winners of the **Stanley Cup** in 1996 and 2001. As the "Avs" are one of the league's most dominant teams, it's usually difficult to get tickets to see them play. The NHL seson runs between October and June.

Teams and tickets

Colorado Avalanche Pepsi Center, Denver, CO ⓣ303/830-8497. Tickets cost $20–175.

Rodeo

Bad-tempered bulls and bucking broncos ridden by lean, laconic, tobacco-spitting types clad in tight blue Wrangler jeans and plaid shirts. If this is your idea of the key ingredients of a **rodeo**, then you've got it absolutely right. This, happily, is one sporting spectacle that has changed very little over the years, and it remains a true cultural bastion in the Rocky Mountains.

The main events are the spectacular **bull-riding** and **bronc-riding** competitions. Each ride is scored according to how hard the animal bucks and how well the cowboy rides – while keeping one hand swinging free in the air at all times. A minimum eight seconds is the time required to earn a score. **Calf-roping** is another crowd favorite, for its combining of daring, skill, and speed. A cowboy pursues the calf on horseback, hurls a lasso around its neck, dismounts at a full run then tackles the animal to the ground before trussing three of its legs together, thus rendering it immobile. Sounds like an afternoon's work, but in fact under ten seconds is considered a good effort. Cowgirls often feature in the **barrel-riding**, which demands great riding skills as competitors turn tight figure-eights around barrels at a full gallop. Among other events are races and such for kids, the grand tradition of the rodeo being that everyone can be involved. **Details** of specific rodeos are included in the individual city and town accounts throughout this guide.

Staying on

Besides students, anyone planning an extended legal stay in the United States should apply for a special working visa at any American Embassy *before* setting off. Different types of visas are issued, depending on your skills and length of stay, but unless you've got relatives (parents or children over 21) or a prospective employer to sponsor you, your chances are slim at best.

Illegal work is not as easy to find as it used to be, now that the government has introduced fines as high as $10,000 for companies caught employing anyone without a **social security number** (which effectively proves you're part of the legal workforce). Even in the traditionally more casual establishments, like restaurants and bars, things have really tightened up, and if you do find work it's likely to be of the less-visible, poorly paid kind – dishwasher rather than waiter. Making up a social security number, or borrowing one from somebody else, is of course completely illegal, as are **marriages of convenience**; usually inconvenient for all concerned and with a lower success rate than is claimed.

Those with the necessary work visa, or social security number will however, find no problem in finding casual, seasonal work in all the main ski areas – as long as you apply early. Ski resorts and nearby businesses will start to hire from early November, those looking for summer staff will usually have all vacancies filled from early June. Most of the work available is doing menial work in shops, hotels, or restaurants, although if you have special skills relevant to the service industry or a sport you might find a position in your field. In the hunt for work, heading towards the larger resort towns makes the most sense in winter (Breckenridge or Aspen in Colorado; Jackson Hole in Wyoming; Big Sky in Montana; Sun Valley in Idaho), while in summer a good place to look are the gateway towns to national parks (especially Estes Park in Colorado; West Yellowstone or Whitefish in Montana). Don't expect to make much more than the minimum wage ($5.15) doing casual work – but at least you'll get a free ski pass, or at least one for next to nothing.

Foreign students have a slightly better chance of a prolonged stay in the Rockies, especially those who can arrange a "year abroad" through their university at home – most universities have semester abroad programs to different countries. Otherwise you can apply directly to a university; if they admit you (and you can afford the painfully expensive fees charged to overseas students) it can be a great way to get to know the country, and maybe even learn something useful. The US grants more or less unlimited visas to those enrolled in full-time further education. Another possibility for students is to get onto an **Exchange Visitor Program**, for which participants are given a J-1 visa that entitles them to accept paid summer employment and apply for a social security number. However, most of these visas are issued for jobs in American **summer camps**, which aren't everybody's idea of a good time; they fly you over, and after a couple of months' work you end up with around $500 and a month to six weeks to blow it in.

For young women (in most cases) working as an **au pair** is a viable option (see below). For other work opportunities check with contacts below or pick up a copy of the useful *International Jobs: Where They Are, How to Get Them* published by HarperCollins.

Study and work programs

From the UK and Ireland

BUNAC (British Universities' North America Club) 16 Bowling Green Lane, London EC1R 0QH ⓣ020/7251 3472, ⓦwww.bunac.org. Organizes working holidays in the US for students, typically at summer camps or training placements with companies.

Camp America/Au Pair in America 37 Queen's Gate, London SW7 5HR (camps ⓣ020/7581 7373, ⓦwww.campamerica.co.uk; au pairs ⓣ020/7581 7311, ⓦwww.aupairamerica.co.uk). The Camp America scheme is similar to that of Camp Counselors USA (see below). The Au Pair scheme is open to both men and women aged 18–26, though women are mostly preferred. There is a placement fee of £40, a £67 contribution towards insurance and a good-faith deposit of £268; the combined amount includes the interviewing and selection process, visa (covering you for thirteen months, twelve months working plus optional one month travel at the end) and flight to the US. On-the-job payment while in the US is about US$150 per week; on completion of the twelve months you get your good-faith deposit back in American dollars (about US$400), which you can then use to fund further US travels.

Camp Counselors USA Green Dragon House, 64–70 High St, Croydon CR0 9XN ⓣ020/8688 9051, ⓦwww.campcounselors.com. Volunteer summer work (nine weeks from anytime in June) for over-18s; you need to have experience with children (except for support staff, who must be full-time students) and be a specialist in an area like arts and crafts, drama, or sport. A charge of £215 covers a return flight to New York (and ten weeks to travel at the end of the camp program), visa, insurance and travel to the camp. Food and board is provided and some pocket money.

Council Exchange 52 Poland St, London W1F 7AB ⓣ020/7478 2000. International study and work programs for students and recent graduates in North America and Central America, Europe, Asia, Pacific (including Australia), China and Japan; notably recruits for the JET program (Japan Exchange and Teaching) and Internship USA.

Work Experience USA Green Dragon House, 64–70 High St, Croydon CR0 9XN ⓣ020/8688 9051, ⓦwww.campcounselors.com. For full-time students only, a chance to live and work in a regular job in the USA. £695 covers flights, insurance, guaranteed job offer, orientation, and help with tax forms and other paperwork. Minimum ten weeks, maximum four months, plus one month's travel. They also offer a scheme as above but you find your own job in the USA for £595.

From Australia and New Zealand

Australians Studying Abroad 1/970 High St, Armadale, Melbourne ⓣ1800/645 755 or 03/9509 1955, ⓦwww.asatravinfo.com.au. Study tours focusing on art and culture.
Council on International Educational Exchange Level 8, University Centre, 210 Clarence St, Sydney ⓣ02/9373 2730, ⓦwww.councilexchanges.org.au. International student exchange programs to USA.

Directory

Addresses Generally speaking, roads in built-up areas are laid out to a grid system, creating "blocks" of buildings: addresses of buildings refer to the block, which will be numbered in sequence from a central point, usually downtown; for example, 620 S Cedar will be six blocks south of downtown. In small towns, and parts of larger cities, "streets" and "avenues" often run north–south and east–west respectively; streets are usually named (sometimes alphabetically), avenues generally numbered.

Cigarettes and smoking Smoking is a much-frowned-upon activity in the US, and especially so in Utah where smoking is banned in all indoor public places with the exception of bars. In fact, it's really only in a few old-style cowboy saloons that you're likely to come across many smokers at all. Cigarettes are sold in virtually any food shop, drugstore or bar, and also from vending machines.

Departure tax All airport, customs and security taxes are included in the price of your ticket.

Electricity 110V AC. Most plugs are two-pronged and rather insubstantial. Some travel plug adapters don't fit American sockets. British-made equipment won't work unless it has a voltage switching provision.

Floors In the US, what would be the ground floor in Britain is the first floor, the first floor the second floor and so on.

ID It's a good idea to have at least one piece of photo ID with you at all times – ideally either a passport or driving license.

Measurements and sizes Measurements are in inches, feet, yards, and miles; weight in ounces, pounds, and tons. American pints and gallons are about four-fifths of Imperial ones. Clothing sizes are always two figures less what they would be in Britain – a British women's size 12 is a US size 10 – while British shoe sizes are half a size below American ones for women, and one size below for men.

Time The majority of the Rocky Mountain region is on Mountain Time, which is two hours behind the US east coast and seven hours behind Greenwich Mean Time (GMT). Roughly the northern half of Idaho, though, is actually on Pacific Time, an hour behind Mountain Time.

Tipping You really shouldn't leave a bar or restaurant without leaving a tip of at least fifteen percent and about the same should be added to taxi fares. A hotel porter should get roughly $1 for each bag carried to your room. When paying by credit card you're expected to add the tip to the total bill before filling in the amount and signing.

Videos The standard format used for video cassettes in the US is different from that used in Britain and Australasia, though some modern VCRs will play both formats. You cannot buy videos in the US compatible with a video camera bought in Britain.

guide

guide

Denver and around

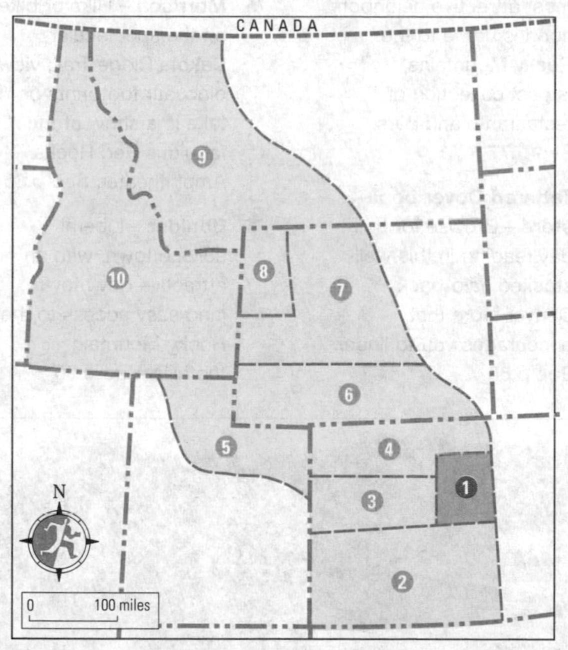

CHAPTER 1 Highlights

* **Brown Palace Hotel** – Denver's landmark hotel; a triangular Italian Renaissance-style structure with an eight-story atrium lobby. See p.76
* **LoDo** – Centered around Larimer Square, Denver's most attractive neighborhood is home to the Rocky Mountains' largest collection of restaurants and bars. See p.77
* **Tattered Cover bookstore** – Browse for holiday reading in this well-stocked, laid-back Denver store that encourages you to linger. See p.80
* **Denver Pow-Wow** – One of the country's largest annual gatherings of Native Americans, featuring the Grand Entry, complete with 1000 dancers. See p.82
* **Morrison** – Hike or bike on the spectacular Dakota Ridge Trail, view dinosaur footprints or take in a show at the fabulous Red Rocks Amphitheater. See p.86
* **Boulder** – Liberal college town, with an attractive downtown and easy access to the Rocky Mountain foothills. See p.90

1

Denver and Around

A good six hundred miles from another city of even vaguely similar size, **Denver** and its surrounding area is unique in the Rockies for its great mix of urban diversions and outdoor adventure. Flanked by the impressive mountain peaks of the Front Range – the foothills of the Rocky Mountain range that rise from the plains along a north–south axis – the Denver area has always been closely connected with serving the needs of the mountain towns; first acting as a string of supply centers when ores were the main source of wealth, and now providing the gateway for vacationers heading to the mountains. Indirectly, the nearby mountains even contributed to current high-tech industry growth, giving the area a reputation for easy access to numerous mountain pursuits, and attracting college graduates wanting to escape the prices and congestion of eastern and western seaboards. The pool of intelligent labor here consequently attracted numerous high-tech corporations also keen to benefit from the low rents. In the 1990s up to two thousand people per week migrated into the Denver area, doubling its population to well over two million. And while the inevitable congestion, soaring real estate prices and suburban sprawl that have followed cause native Denverites to grumble, most consider it a reasonable price for the transformation of a flagging cowtown and declining oil-center to a high-tech boom-town.

Encouraged by consistently good weather – more sunshine, in fact, than either San Diego or Miami – Denver bustles with life all year round, as does its northern neighbor, the progressive college town of **Boulder**. Most precipitation lands on the Rockies themselves and snow, when it settles in the Front Range, never stays for more than a couple of days). But beyond their leafy pedestrian malls, neither town has an abundance of attractions to explore, though the citizens of the towns have proudly sponsored the purchase that has created large public parks in the foothills of the Front Range. Tourism in the

Accommodation price codes

All accommodation prices in this book have been coded using the symbols below. For **hotels**, **motels**, and **B&Bs**, rates are given for the least expensive double room in each establishment during peak season; variations are indicated where appropriate, including winter rates for all ski resorts. For **hostels**, we've given a specific price per bed; for **camping**, the overnight cost per site is given. For a full explanation see p.30 in Basics.

❶ up to $30	❹ $60–80	❼ $130–180
❷ $30–45	❺ $80–100	❽ $180–240
❸ $45–60	❻ $100–130	❾ over $240

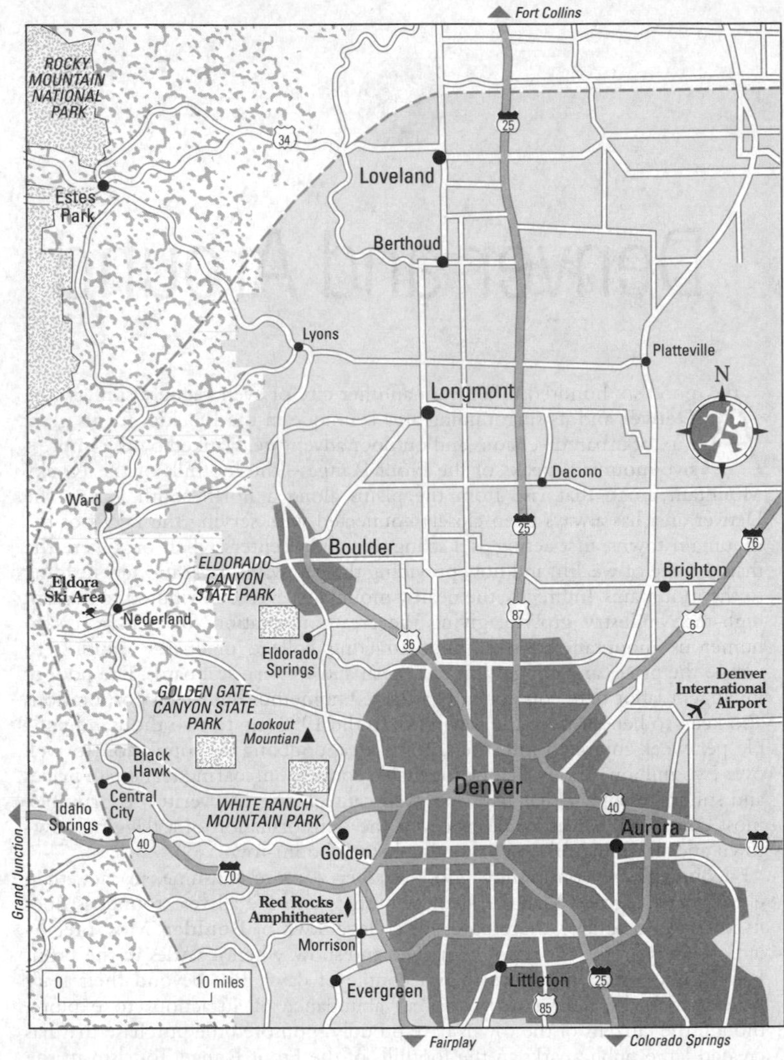

area is based more around these parks and along the I-70 highway corridor to the stunning landscapes and greater outdoor recreation opportunities of the rest of the Rocky Mountains. Located at the base of this highway as it enters the mountains, the sleepy brewery town of **Golden** is well-placed for these outdoor adventures and close to the start of the stunning **Peak-to-Peak** highway. A great way to travel to Rocky Mountain National Park (see p.275), the Peak-to-Peak cuts its way through alpine scenery and small mining towns like the rather crassly made-over, casino hot spots of **Black Hawk** and **Central City**, or laid-back, rustic **Nederland**.

Denver

Its skyscrapers marking the final transition between the Great Plains and the American West, **DENVER** stands at the threshold of the Rocky Mountains. Despite being known as the "Mile High City," it is itself uniformly flat, perched on the last few acres of Colorado's arid eastern plains. The grand peaks of the Rockies, though, are clearly visible, rising roughly fifteen miles west of downtown, though urban sprawl spreads out far in all directions, even lining the base of the Front Range's foothills.

Mineral wealth has always been at the heart of the city's prosperity, with all the fluctuations of fortune that this entails. Its original foundation in 1858 was pure chance; this was the first spot where small quantities of **gold** were discovered in Colorado. There was no significant river, let alone a road, but prospectors came streaming in, indifferent to any prior claims on the land – least of all those of the **Arapaho**, who had supposedly been guaranteed ownership of the area by the Fort Laramie Treaty of 1851. Various local communities had their own names for the settlement, but, with the judicious distribution of whiskey, one faction persuaded the rest to agree to "Denver" in 1859. Their hope was to ingratiate themselves with territorial governor **James Denver**, who, humorously, had already resigned.

With actually very little gold in Denver itself, the infant town swarmed only briefly with disgruntled fortune-seekers, who soon decamped after receiving news of a massive gold strike at Central City. Despite this, and the various fires and floods that all but destroyed the city in the 1860s, Denver cagily survived as a supply town, prospering further with the discovery of silver in the mountains. All sorts of shady characters made this their home, including the entrepreneurial Jefferson "Soapy" Smith, who acquired his nickname here by selling bars of soap at extortionate prices under the pretence that some contained $100 bills.

Once strengthened in its role as supply center for the mountains and market for the prairies, Denver outflanked Central City and Golden to become the **state capital** in the 1860s. When the first railroads bypassed Denver in the late 1860s – the death knell for so many other communities – the citizens banded together and built their own connecting spur. This in turn drew ranchers, who used the rail lines to get their product off to market. By the 1880s, **cattle** became as, if not more, important than mining, and within fifty years gigantic stockyards dominated much of the landscape.

In the first half of the twentieth-century Denver consolidated its reputation as a quintessential cow-town, replete with the pool halls, saloons and flophouses that Jack Kerouac so enthusiastically wrote about in *On the Road*. The city polished itself up somewhat over the next few decades largely thanks to the attentions of the oil and gas industry, whose drilling operations in the region were profitable until the mid-1980s oil recession. Nonetheless, the citizens of Denver continued to strive to improve their city, electing the charismatic Federico Peña as mayor in 1983. He in turn embarked on an adventurous program of investment in the city – persuading citizens to pay more taxes and developing some extravagant infrastructure, including the foundation for the $5 billion, ultramodern Denver International Airport. But it wasn't until the city's 1990s high-tech boom that money became available to really modernize its downtown. Now rejuvenated, Denver's main pedestrian mall bustles with the city's huge, young graduate population. Downtown building work also produced a superb and atmospheric ballpark for the major-league

Colorado Rockies to play their baseball, and with two 1990s Superbowl victories under the belts of the fanatically supported Denver Broncos football team, the city has begun the new millennium burgeoning and optimistic.

Arrival, information, and getting around

The colossal, high-tech **Denver International Airport** (ⓣ303/342-2000 or 1-800/247-2336, ⓦwww.flydenver.com) lies on the plains 24 miles northeast of downtown, its dramatic tented roof of Teflon-coated fiberglass fashioned into peaks resembling the nearby mountains. Shuttle trains connect its three vast concourses with the main terminal and the baggage-claim areas, sensibly located alongside the numerous transport options heading downtown.

The cheapest way into the city is on one of Skyride's **buses**, which run to both downtown's Market Street Station (55min; $6/$10 round-trip) and over to Boulder (75min; $8/$13 round-trip). Both services run daily from 7am–11pm and depart from just outside exit 506 at the eastern end of the Central Concourse and from exit 511 at its western end. Slightly more expensive are the **shuttle-buses** heading to a number of locations downtown (45min); two of the best are Super Shuttle (ⓣ303/370-1300 or 1-800/258-3826) and Denver Airport Shuttle (ⓣ303/342-5454 or 1-800/525-3177). These run around $15 per person, though the price can double for door-to-door services, becoming similar to **taxi** charges ($40).

All the major **car rental** companies (see p.27) are located within the terminals near baggage claim, but it's worth noting that it can be considerably cheaper to pick a car up once in town. Some less expensive local firms that don't have spots in the terminal will pick you up if you phone ahead. The airport's only road connects with C470, which heads south to the I-70, the main interstate that runs past downtown before continuing west into the mountains. When heading downtown, stick to I-70 until it intersects with the I-25 and take the latter south into the city. There's plenty of paid **parking** downtown (typically around $12 a day) in both open lots and parking garages.

Amtrak (ⓣ303/825-2583 or 1-800/872-7245) **trains** arrive at the grand nineteenth-century **Union Station** at 1701 Wynkoop St (ⓣ303/534-2812), within easy walking distance of downtown Denver. Amtrak's famous California Zephyr travels a scenic route across the Continental Divide and through Glenwood Canyon linking Denver to Salt Lake City and, eventually, Oakland, California. In the winter months, the Ski Train (ⓣ303/296-4754, ⓦwww.ski-train.com) to Winter Park also departs from here, leaving at 7.15am and returning at 6.15pm (2hr each way; $40).

The **Denver Bus Terminal** (ⓣ303/293-6555 or 1-800/231-2222), from where Greyhound buses operate, is every bit as close to the action, at 1055 19th St (at Arapaho). A twice-daily service to Wyoming and Montana, operated by the Powder River Coach company (ⓣ1-800/442-3682), also leaves from here.

Colorado Shuttles

Numerous direct bus services run from Denver airport to many of Colorado's most popular resorts, making it unnecessary to rent a car if you plan on being based in only one place. For services to Aspen, see p.239; Boulder p.91; Colorado Springs p.107; Estes Park (for Rocky Mountain National Park) p.268; Steamboat Springs p.298; Summit County p.212; Vail p.227; and Winter Park p.207. Note that these should be booked as far in advance as possible, and many of the shuttle companies have desks in the airport itself near baggage claim.

City transport

Negotiating downtown Denver **on foot** is pretty straightforward, though the free **buses** (daily 6am–lam) that run for a mile up and down the pedestrian 16th Street Mall at the heart of the city's grid-like street pattern are hard to pass up. RTD, Denver's excellent public transportation network (ⓣ303/229-6000, ⓦwww.rtd-denver.com), also runs the regular bus service ($1.25 during rush hour; 75¢ at other times); frequent services to the various sports arenas and airport leave from the underground **Market Street Station** at Market and 16th. The city's well-developed bus network is supplemented by a light railway running from Littleton in the southwest, across the 16th Street Mall and up to Five Points in the northeast (same local fares as buses). From mid-May to September, you can also buy a day-pass for the Cultural Connection Trolley (every 30min; 9.30am–10pm; $3), which links Denver's main points of interest; passes can be purchased on the trolleys. The **green route** links downtown with the City Park area and the **red route** loops around downtown and runs to Cherry Creek Mall, via the Capitol Hill area. All RTD services are designed to carry bikes (free) and accommodate wheelchair users.

For a **walking tour** of the Denver's downtown, pick up a self-guided booklet from the visitor center (see below) or join one of their free two-hour-long walking tours that leave from the clock tower on 16th Street and Arapahoe on Tuesdays, Thursdays, and Saturdays at 10.30am (ⓣ303/571-9456).

Information

Denver's main **visitor center** is conveniently located in the Tabor Center, directly off pedestrian-only 16th Street at 1668 Larimer St (Mon–Sat 8am–5pm, Sun 10am–2pm; ⓣ303/892-1112 or 1-800/233-6837, ⓦwww.denver.org). Besides running an accommodation reservation service, the center offers some useful magazine-style visitor guides as well as *The Mile High Trail*, good for a self-guided walking tour of Denver's historic downtown. There's also an **information booth** near the airport's baggage-claim area (same hours, though printed information is always available).

Accommodation

Denver has a good selection of downtown **accommodation**, ranging from simple hostels and motels to homey B&Bs and grand historic hotels. The Denver visitor center (see above) can help with reservations. Some cheaper options, particularly **motels** and **hostels**, cluster around the somewhat seedy but relatively safe Colfax Avenue, within walking distance of downtown. More motels, mostly franchise operations, have located further out on Colfax and alongside many of Denver's major cross-town highways, and northeast of the city, around the defunct Stapleton airport – with many of these offering free shuttles to the airport and downtown. Highway 6, the most direct route from downtown to the mountains, has also attracted a few motels. If you're desperate to **camp**, the drab *Camping Denver North*, I-70 exit 229 (ⓣ303/452-4120 or 1-800/851-6521; $16), is the most central option – but you'd do better heading twenty miles out of town to Boulder, Golden, or further into the mountains.

Hostels

Denver International Youth Hostel 630 E 16th Ave (office hours daily 8–10am & 6–9pm) ⓣ303/832-9996, ⓦwww.youthhostels.com/denver. Located in a not-entirely safe area four blocks from the capitol, this is the city's cheapest option. You certainly get what you pay for as the $9 dorm beds are cramped, grotty, and worn out. No curfew.

Hostel of the Rocky Mountains 1530 Downing St ⓣ303/861-7777, ⓔhostel-denver@sni.net. Institutional and unfriendly hostel a fifteen-minute walk east from the State Capitol down seedy E Colfax, with the usual array of dorm accommoda-

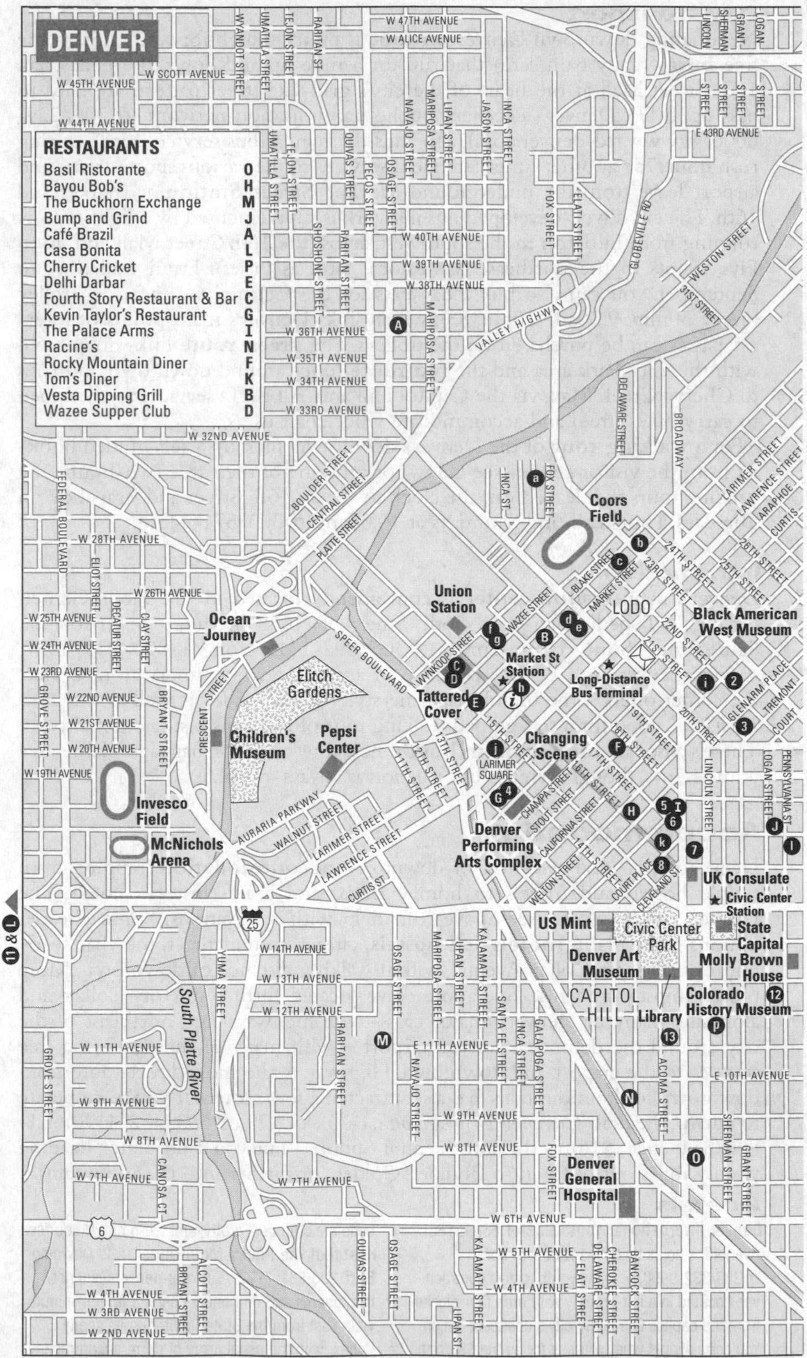
DENVER
RESTAURANTS
Basil Ristorante O
Bayou Bob's H
The Buckhorn Exchange M
Bump and Grind J
Café Brazil A
Casa Bonita L
Cherry Cricket P
Delhi Darbar E
Fourth Story Restaurant & Bar C
Kevin Taylor's Restaurant G
The Palace Arms I
Racine's N
Rocky Mountain Diner F
Tom's Diner K
Vesta Dipping Grill B
Wazee Supper Club D
Coors Field
Union Station
Ocean Journey
LODO
Black American West Museum
Market St Station
Long-Distance Bus Terminal
Elitch Gardens
Tattered Cover
Children's Museum
Pepsi Center
Changing Scene
Larimer Square
Invesco Field
McNichols Arena
Denver Performing Arts Complex
UK Consulate
Civic Center Station
US Mint
Civic Center Park
State Capital
Denver Art Museum
Molly Brown House
Capitol Hill
Library
Colorado History Museum
Denver General Hospital
South Platte River
Speer Boulevard
Valley Highway
Auraria Parkway
Federal Boulevard
Broadway
W 47th Avenue
W Alice Avenue
W Scott Avenue
W 45th Avenue
W 44th Avenue
E 43rd Avenue
W 40th Avenue
W 39th Avenue
W 38th Avenue
W 36th Avenue
W 35th Avenue
W 34th Avenue
W 33rd Avenue
W 32nd Avenue
W 28th Avenue
W 26th Avenue
W 25th Avenue
W 24th Avenue
W 23rd Avenue
W 22nd Avenue
W 21st Avenue
W 20th Avenue
W 19th Avenue
W 14th Avenue
W 13th Avenue
W 12th Avenue
W 11th Avenue
E 11th Avenue
E 10th Avenue
W 9th Avenue
W 8th Avenue
W 7th Avenue
W 6th Avenue
W 5th Avenue
W 4th Avenue
W 3rd Avenue
W 2nd Avenue
11 & 12
25
6

ACCOMMODATION
Adam's Mark 8
Broadway Plaza Motel 13
Brown Palace 6
Capitol Hill Mansion 12
Comfort Inn Downtown 5
Denver International Youth Hostel 9
Four Points Hotel 14
Hampton Inn DIA 1
Hostel of the Rocky Mountains 10
Hotel Teatro 4
Melbourne Hostel 2
Queen Anne Inn 3
Ramada Inn Downtown 11
YMCA 7
BARS AND CLUBS
Bluebird m
Breckenridge Brewery c
Brendan's h
Charlie's o
The Church p
Comedy Works j
Cruise Room Bar g
Duffy's Shamrock k
El Chapultepec e
The Grand l
Herman's Hideaway q
Mercury Cafe i
Ogden n
Polly Esthers b
The Soiled Dove d
Tracks a
Wynkoop Brewing Co f
Denver Coliseum
Denver Zoo
Denver Museum of Nature & Science
Botanical Gardens
University Hospital
1 & Denver International Airport
Cherry Creek Mall
P
N
0 500 yards
E COLFAX AVENUE
PARK AVENUE
COLORADO BOULEVARD
BRIGHTON BOULEVARD

tion ($12) as well as a few pleasant doubles ($40 with shared bathrooms; three-night maximum stay) in neighboring buildings. No curfew.
Melbourne Hostel 607 22nd St ⓣ303/292-6386, ⓦwww.denverhostel.com. Located in a stylish but run-down former hotel, this hostel is an easy – if not all that safe – walk northeast of downtown. Beds in clean dorms (sleeping up to six) cost $15, with a three-night maximum stay in summer, when reservations are advised. Many of the rooms are private ($30), some with their own bathroom. There's no curfew and free email.
YMCA 25E 16th Ave ⓣ303/861-8300. Clean, secure and comfortable, with plain private rooms ($46 for an en-suite room) in a prime downtown location. Staying entitles free use of the excellent fitness center, which includes an indoor pool, running tracks, exercise equipment, and handball and racquetball courts. Weekly rates available and reservations advised.

Hotels, motels, and B&Bs

Adam's Mark Hotel 1550 Court Place ⓣ303/893-3333, ⓦwww.adamsmark.com. A giant, 1200-room luxury hotel adjacent to the 16th Street Mall. Excellent facilities include in-room dataports, a fitness center, steam room, outdoor heated pool, and a sundeck. ❶
Broadway Plaza Motel 111 Broadway ⓣ303/893-0303. Within walking distance of downtown, this plain but friendly motel has large and clean rooms (with phones and cable TV), free parking and reasonable daily and weekly rates. ❹
Brown Palace Hotel 321 17th St ⓣ303/297-3111 or 1-800/321-2599, ⓦwww.brownpalace.com. Beautifully maintained downtown landmark that's been in continuous operation since 1892. The Italian Renaissance structure has elegant dining rooms and public area based around a sunlit, eight-story atrium lobby with tiers of iron railings. It's worth popping in even if not staying to marvel at the craftsmanship and to relax in the comfortable leather armchairs strewn about. Weekend nights have cheapest rates ❽
Capitol Hill Mansion 1207 Pennsylvania St ⓣ303/839-5221, ⓦwww.capitolhillmansion.com. A luxurious B&B housed in a turreted Victorian sandstone mansion built shortly before the 1890s silver crash. Located on a leafy street near the State Capitol, each of the eight antique-furnished rooms are delightful; several include large whirlpool tubs. ❻
Comfort Inn Downtown 401 17th St ⓣ303/296-0400 or 1-800/221-2222. A central location, along with a skywalk connecting it to the *Brown Palace Hotel*'s elegant restaurants and lounges, make this arguably the best downtown bargain. Continental breakfast served daily. ❺
Four Points Hotel Denver Cherry Creek 600 S Colorado Blvd ⓣ303/757-3341 or 1-800/325-3535. Inexpensive Sheraton hotel located five miles out of the city center. Amenities include a heated outdoor pool, restaurant and lounge, and the Cherry Creek Mall (see p.80) is within walking distance. A courtesy shuttle is offered to several downtown locations. ❹
Hampton Inn DIA 6290 Tower Rd ⓣ303/371-0200 or 1-800/426-7866, ⓦwww.hamptoninn-suites.com. One of several functional hotels a short ride from the Denver International Airport, and fine for a one-night stay; shuttle is free, as are the cereal, pastries, and terrible coffee that make up the continental breakfast. ❺
Hotel Teatro 1100 14th St ⓣ303/228-1100, ⓦwww.wyndham.com. Housed in the renovated 1911 Tramway Tower, this sophisticated downtown business hotel is stylishly themed around the theatre, with photos and props from theater performances scattered between chic Art Deco furnishings. In-room facilities include dataports, faxes, copiers, and scanners. There's also a small fitness center. ❼
Motel 6 12020 E 39th Ave and Peoria St ⓣ303/371-1980. Located off of I-70's exit 281, this plain and cheap motel is well outside of the downtown core, but a free shuttle service is on offer. A second branch of the *Motel 6*'s spartan chain (ⓣ303/232-4924) is located west of downtown and alongside Hwy 6 – the most direct route from downtown to the mountains. ❸
Queen Anne Inn 2147 Tremont Place ⓣ303/296-6666 or 1-800/432-4667, ⓦwww.queenannebnb.com. Central and hospitable nineteenth-century B&B overlooking a small park and pretty back garden (where breakfast can be eaten). A few of the fourteen individually decorated rooms contain extravagant murals, while others are themed after a particular artist (Calder, Remington, Rockwell). The "Rooftop Room" has the most decadent feature – an outdoor hot tub overlooking Denver's skyline. ❺
Ramada Inn Downtown 1150 E Colfax Ave ⓣ303/831-7700. Good-value, straightforward motel on Denver's seedy E Colfax. The location is handy for both downtown and City Park, and facilities include a heated outdoor pool and hot tub. ❹
Sheraton Four Points Inn 3535 Quebec St ⓣ303/333-7711. Standard chain hotel off I-70 and convenient for Denver International Airport (shuttle costs $8). Facilities include an indoor swimming pool, hot tub, and exercise area that opens onto a courtyard with gazebo and picnic tables. ❺

The City

Though a hectic spate of high-rise construction in the early 1980s means that **downtown Denver** is barely recognizable as the Gold Rush town of the 1860s, it's still easy – on a map at least – to pick out its oldest section. It's the area which, in a city that stretches out for miles in a regimental grid, stands at a sharp angle to the rest. Cutting diagonally through downtown's tightly packed streets is **16th Street**, where much of Denver's day-to-day activity is centred. Except for its free buses, it's a pedestrian zone and a fine place to wander, window shop, and stop to eat when hunger strikes. Since the mall is given over largely to eating and shopping, you'll need to head west to the refurbished warehouses of **LoDo** or southeast to the **capital district** to see anything of note.

LoDo

At downtown Denver's western end, in between Wynkoop, Larimer, 14th, and 20th, lies the revitalized district of lower downtown, colloquially known as **LoDo**. In the late-1980s, this area was made up mostly of slums and abandoned brick warehouses, which artists had begun using as studios and galleries. This gentrification spread rapidly during the early 1990s, and today it's a high-rent district populated with speciality shops, restaurants, bars, and only the occasional gallery.

It was in LoDo's **Larimer Square**, off of Market Street between 14th and 15th, that William Larimer built Denver's original log cabin, with doors made out of coffin lids. Many of the buildings in this area were the first in Denver to be built with bricks, and also the first to be restored, some years later, to their late-Victorian appearance with plenty of colorful awnings and hanging flower baskets. Today the square provides a lively focus for shops, bars, and restaurants in LoDo. An **information booth** in Larimer Square can provide a walking-tour pamphlet that gives more detailed information on the history of Denver's oldest streets.

On opposite side of LoDo to the northwest is the lovely **Coors Field**, 2001 Blake St, home to Denver's Major League baseball team the **Colorado Rockies** (season: April to early Oct; ⓣ303/292-0200 or 1-800/388-7625, ⓦwww.coloradorockies.com). You can take ninety-minute **tours** of Coors field that head to the press boxes, clubhouses, and dugouts (April–Oct Mon–Sat 10am–3pm; Nov–March Mon–Sat 11am–2pm; $5; ⓣ303/762-5437).

The Capitol area

For a quick appreciation of Denver's geographical position, head for the opposite end of downtown to the **State Capitol** at Broadway and East Colfax Avenue (Mon–Fri daily 9.30am–2.30pm). The thirteenth step on the way up to its entrance is exactly one mile above sea level; turn back and look west, and you get a commanding view – zealously protected by building regulations – of the Rockies swelling on the horizon. The Capitol is a rather predictable copy of the one in Washington DC, but with the novelty that almost all of the building's materials are indigenous to the state – including the pretty red onyx, of which the world's entire supply is located in Colorado. The free tours are pleasantly informal, and include a climb up into the dome for an even better view.

Right in front of the State Capitol is **Civic Center Park**, home to two of Denver's finest museums. The most interesting features of the **Colorado History Museum**, one block southwest of the Capitol at 1300 Broadway (Mon–Sat 10am–4.30pm, Sun noon–4.30pm; $4.50; ⓦwww.coloradohistory.org), are found in its lower galleries. Several intricate dioramas, made under the auspices of the WPA in the 1930s, show historical scenes of Colorado in fascinating detail, starting with the Anasazi of Mesa Verde, and following up with trappers meeting with Indians at a "fair in the wilderness" in the early 1800s. An exhaustive archive of photographs of the early West showcases the work of W.H. Jackson, and there's also a model of Denver in 1860, before it was leveled by fires and floods a few years later.

The glass-tile covered **Denver Art Museum**, one block west at 100 W 14th Ave (Tues–Sat 10am–5pm, Wed 10am–9pm, Sun noon–5pm; $4.50; Ⓦ www.denverartmuseum.org), has a solid collection of paintings from around the world, but is most noteworthy for its superb examples of Native American art and crafts. Items in the massive collection, which includes pieces from over a hundred different tribes, include marvelous beadwork by Plains tribes and some finely detailed Navajo weavings. The pre-Columbian Central American art – particularly the extraordinary Olmec miniatures – is also spectacular. The museum runs free **tours** daily at 1.30pm and also at 11am on Saturdays.

Also near to the State Capitol, a short walk west along Colfax Avenue at no. 320, is the **US Mint** (Mon–Fri 8am–3pm; free; Ⓦ www.usmint.gov), where free tours reveal millions of fresh coins gushing from presses in a flurry of flashing metal. Avaricious fantasies are checked, though, once you notice the machine-gun turrets on the exterior, mounted here in the depth of the Depression.

On the opposite side of the State Capitol, two blocks southeast, is the **Molly Brown House**, 1340 Pennsylvania Ave (June–Aug Mon–Sat 10am–3.30pm, Sun noon–3.30pm; Sept–May same schedule, closed Mon; $6; Ⓦ www.molly-brown.org). The "unsinkable" Molly Brown was famous for surviving the sinking of the *Titanic* (she'd already lived through a typhoon in the Pacific) and raising money for poor immigrant survivors and their families. A poor Irish girl who went West to marry a millionaire, she ended up mixing with high society in Denver, becoming a suffragette and eventually running for the US Senate in 1914. Sadly, the house tours concentrate more on what the Browns owned and what the preservationists have managed to authenticate than on illuminating her extraordinary life.

City Park and around

A couple miles northeast of downtown stands **City Park**, an enormous grassy area crossed by paths and dotted with trees and including a golf course. The top attraction is the **Denver Museum of Nature and Science**, 2001 Colorado Blvd (daily: 9am–5pm; museum and planetarium $6, IMAX cinema $6, all three $9; Ⓣ 303/322-7009 or 1-800/925-2250, Ⓦ www.dmns.org). Highlights include the "Prehistoric Journey" exhibit, showcasing wonderful dinosaur displays alongside a working fossils lab, and scores of wildlife scenes featuring animals from as far as Australia and Africa. There's also the obligatory IMAX theater, as well as a good deal of anthropological material on Native Americans, which, though fascinating, does seem rather out of place. City Park is also home to the large, popular **Denver Zoo** (daily: April–Sept 9am–6pm; Oct–March 10am–5pm; $8; Ⓦ www.denverzoo.org), whose four-thousand inmates include a couple of huge lowland gorillas in a large thickly wooded sanctuary. Six blocks south of the zoo, adjacent to Cheeseman Park, the tranquil **Denver Botanic Gardens**, 1005 York St (daily: 9am–5pm; $3; Ⓦ www.botanicgardens.org), contain an excellent array of beautifully displayed gardens, including a rock alpine garden featuring local mountain flora.

Northwest of City Park is Denver's most prominent black neighborhood, the old Five Points district, originally created to house black railroad workers in the 1870s. Here, the **Black American West Museum**, 3091 California St (May–Sept Mon–Fri 10am–5pm, Sat & Sun noon–5pm; Oct–April Wed–Fri

△ Denver's State Capitol, open since 1886

10am–2pm, Sat & Sun noon–5pm; $6; Ⓦwww.coax.net/people/lwf/bawmus.htm), is dedicated to telling the story of black pioneers and outlaws in the Old West, including the myth-debunking fact that one-third of all cowboys are thought to have been black, many of them slaves freed after the Civil War.

The Platte River area

Beside the Platte River on the west side of town are a number of Denver's larger attractions, connected to each other via the **Platte River Trolley** (mid-May to Sept daily 11am–4pm; Oct to mid-May Sat & Sun same times; $2). The most high profile is a slick new aquarium, the **Ocean Journey**, 700 Water St (May–Sept Mon–Fri 9am–6.30pm, Sat & Sun 9am–8pm; Oct–April daily 10am–6pm; $15, kids $7, parking $5; Ⓦwww.oceanjourney.org), dedicated to the ecosystems of the Colorado and Indonesian Kanpur rivers. A number of plants, mammals, and birds lend authenticity at the headwater end of the visitor trail through the aquarium, which eventually leads to tunnel sections where fish and other sea-creatures completely surround the visitor.

South along the Platte River is the **Children's Museum of Denver**, 2121 Children's Museum Drive (May–Sept daily 10am–5pm; Oct–April Tues–Sun noon–5pm; $5; Ⓦwww.cmdenver.com), relying on interactive playscapes to get kids to learn. The outdoor challenge center, where kids (and adults) can learn to skate, snowboard and ski year-round is the museum's most popular feature (two hours instruction costs around $10). Kids will also love the nearby **Elitch Gardens** theme park, 2000 Elitch Circle (June–Sept daily 10am–10pm; Oct–May irregular hours; $33; Ⓣ303/595-4386, Ⓦwww.sixflags.com/elitchgardens), for its white-knuckle rides – including the *Mind Eraser*, which catapults you at 60mph through terrifying corkscrew loops – and **water park**.

For something quieter, the glitzy **Cherry Creek Mall**, a few miles southeast of downtown, is second only to the 16th Street Mall as Denver's most popular shopping center. Opposite its main entrance is one of the best bookstores in the US, the **Tattered Cover Bookstore** at 2955 E 1st Ave (Ⓣ303/322-7727), which spreads over four extremely well-stocked floors.

Eating

Though Western-themed steak and barbecue places abound, many of Denver's **restaurants** have begun to embrace a more refined "Rocky Mountain cuisine," emphasizing game and other local products like trout and lamb. Additionally, southwestern-style food options are plenty, and there's also a cosmopolitan selection of international restaurants to choose from. Of the several distinct restaurant districts, LoDo and in particular Larimer Square is the most easily accessible on foot. Several of the city's brewpubs also serve good-quality meals; see "Nightlife and Entertainment" p.82. For further dining information, check the reliable reviews in the **free weekly** *Westword*, available from bars, restaurants, and sidewalk dispensers.

Basil Ristorante 846 Broadway Ⓣ303/832-8009. Great homemade Italian food, including hand-rolled ravioli and fresh pastas, as well as baked breads and desserts. A build-your-own approach to entrees (around $8) allows lots of combos on pastas, sauces, meats, and vegetables. The house speciality is its own style of panini: bread dough wrapped around vegetables and cheeses and topped with marinara sauce. Open for dinner only.

Bayou Bob's 1635 Glenarm Place Ⓣ303/573-6828. Authentic and good-value Louisiana-style Cajun lunches and dinners keep this inexpensive no-frills bistro busy. Choose from options like jambalaya, red beans and rice, a po'boy sandwich, shrimp gumbo, or fried catfish. Closed Sunday lunch.

The Buckhorn Exchange 1000 Osage St Ⓣ303/534-9505. Opened in 1893, the oldest restaurant in town was started by a keen hunter who coated the walls with over five hundred stuffed trophies. Nowadays, the natural history museum-like dining areas set the tone for the meaty menu, featuring various game dishes, steak, and novelty items like rattlesnake and alligator tail. Dinner entrees are expensive ($20 and up), but lunches more reasonable at about half-price. There's live folk and cowboy music in the saloon upstairs Thursday through Saturday nights. Closed for lunch on Saturday and Sunday. Reservations are recommended.

Bump and Grind 439 E 17th Ave ⓣ303/861-4841. Cheap café/bistro just outside downtown that's the flamboyant hub for the local gay social scene – particularly during Sunday brunch when the wait-staff is almost exclusively transvestite. The food is excellent, creative and inexpensive; the eggs-Benedict on sourdough bread costs $6.

Café Brazil 3611 Navajo St ⓣ303/480-1877. Unassuming, tiny, and cheerful Brazilian restaurant serving excellent food at moderate prices. Particularly good are national dishes like the *feijoada completa*; a black-bean stew full of sausages and accompanied by fried plantains. Open for dinner only and closed Sunday and Monday. Moderately priced – two courses cost under $20.

Casa Bonita 6715 W Colfax Ave ⓣ303/232-5115. A short drive out on Colfax, this absolutely wild Mexican restaurant seats 1200 diners and features staged gunfights, cliff dives and "abandoned mines" you can explore. The only weak link is the food itself, but it's a lot of fun (especially for kids) and far from expensive.

Cherry Cricket 2641 E 2nd Ave ⓣ303/322-7666. Excellent burgers and Mexican food served up in a generally dingy sports-bar ambience make this a great place (near Cherry Creek Mall) to nurse a hangover – or even work on getting one (120 different beers on offer) while watching televised sports. Open 11am–2am.

Delhi Darbar 1514 Blake St ⓣ303/595-0680. Relaxed haunt with decent North Indian food, including a number of unusual tandoori dishes like quail, shrimp or lamb sausage. The $6 lunch buffet is an inexpensive way to sample the food, but otherwise it's on the expensive side with a two-course dinner running around $25.

Fourth Story Restaurant & Bar 2955 E 1st Ave ⓣ303/322-1824. Gracing the top floor of the Tattered Cover Bookstore (see opposite), this relaxed restaurant has a wonderful front lounge with overstuffed couches and chairs, and a stylish restaurant serving snacks and meals (lunch and dinner) from a frequently changing creative American menu. The wine list is superb. A very popular place to hang out, especially during the Sunday brunch when there's live music.

Kevin Taylor's Restaurant *Hotel Theatro*, 1106 14th St ⓣ303/820-2600. This formal restaurant serves up imaginative and eclectic contemporary dinners – including seared New York State foie gras, Maine lobster ravioli with asparagus and sweetcorn, and roasted rack of Colorado lamb – charging around $25 for two courses. *Jou Jou's*, the cheaper, more casual bistro next door, has the same management and is also open for breakfast, lunch, and dinner. Both also serve relatively good-value pre-theater set meals.

The Palace Arms *Brown Palace Hotel*, 321 17th St ⓣ303/297-3111. This small and classy restaurant tucked in the *Brown Palace Hotel* (see p.76) is the ultimate splurge in town. The menu features mostly seasonal game specialties like pheasant, buffalo, and venison, all which run over $30. The interior is decorated using antiques from the Napoleonic period – including a pair of Napoleon's dueling pistols.

Racine's 850 Bannock St ⓣ303/595-0418. Just south of downtown, this large, laid-back place is a Denver institution. Housed in a former auto showroom, the inexpensive restaurant serves excellent egg-based breakfasts (try the superb Florentine Benedict) and a range of great classic salads, imaginative pastas, and reliably good sandwiches along with some Mexican entrees later in the day. The in-house bakery provides superb desserts including juicy carrot cake and some excellent brownies.

Rocky Mountain Diner 800 18th St ⓣ303/293-8383. Diner with big booths and a Western theme serving up standard fare like good Yankee pot roast and mash potatoes, along with more creative dishes like roast-duck enchiladas. Breakfast or lunch costs around $7, dinners about $13 for two courses.

Tom's Diner 601 E Colfax Ave (and Pearl). Wonderfully gritty and authentic 24-hour diner, providing cheap deals on big portions of stock diner food at the seedy end of town.

Vesta Dipping Grill,1822 Blake St ⓣ303/296-1970. Attractive restaurant in a renovated LoDo warehouse serving tasty food in unusual combinations; its menu, rather pretentiously, is based around the "art" of dipping, but it actually works. You can personalize each entree – including a range of kebab-style meat or veggies – in a spectrum of flavors (Mediterranean, Asian, Mexican…); try the tuna roll in a wasabi cream sauce to start. Two courses will set you back around $20,and there's live jazz on Thursdays.

Wazee Supper Club 1600 15th St ⓣ303/623-9518. Well-established LoDo dining room, serving good cheap burgers, deli sandwiches, and superb pizzas, plus a full range of beers, in a retro, Art Deco atmosphere. One of few places open really late (1.30am most nights).

Denver's continued Western traditions

High-tech boom or not, Denver is still a cradle of Western US culture, as evidenced by two of its larger festivals. In mid-January, the **National Western Stock Show and Rodeo** takes over the Denver Coliseum, 4600 Humboldt St (Brighton Blvd exit off I-70; ⓣ303/297-1166, ⓦwww.nationalwestern.com). Having taken place annually for almost a century, this stock show is one of the most significant in the Rocky Mountain region. However, it's the large-purse rodeo, one of the US's largest, that attracts most of the 600,000 people here over the festival's sixteen days. Other attractions include live Country music, line-dancing and Native American food and crafts. Admission runs about $10 to get into the show and around the same again for rodeo tickets.

Also at the Denver Coliseum is the **Denver March Pow-Wow** (ⓣ303/934-8045), a three-day event in early March that's attended by around 100,000 spectators and focused around the swirling and rhythmic dancing of Native Americans in sensational traditional costumes. The highlight of this powwow, one of the country's largest annual gatherings of Native American peoples, is the Grand Entry, a massive dance with up to a thousand participants. Native American oral traditions are also kept alive by storytelling events, as are traditional arts and crafts through workshops and sales. The entry fee is $6.

Nightlife and entertainment

Though business still booms for Denver's numerous downtown brewpubs, an onslaught of sports bars in the LoDo district, particularly near Coors field, have mostly taken over as the city's liveliest nightlife area. Still, if sports bars don't appeal, there are plenty of other more stylish or relaxing places to drink here as well. Most places close around 1am, except Saturdays when many have extensions until 2am.

Though you'll find some **live music** downtown, much of Denver's live music scene is outside downtown. Denver's best-known larger concert venue is the remarkable **Red Rocks Amphitheater** near Golden (see p.871). But the larger capacities of **Fiddler's Green**, 6350 Greenwood Plaza Blvd, and the **McNichols Arena**, near Mile High Stadium (event information for both venues ⓣ303/640-7330), mean they tend to attract the bookings of the big acts. For news of musical happenings of all sizes, consult Wednesday's free *Westword*, the free monthly *Freestyle*, or the "Weekend" section of the *Denver Post*.

High-culture can most easily be found in the modern **Denver Performing Arts Complex** (the "PLEX") on 14th and Curtis (ⓣ303/893-4100 or 1-800/641-1222, ⓦwww.denvercenter.org), home to the Denver Center Theater Company, Colorado Symphony Orchestra, Opera Colorado, and the Colorado Ballet. Facilities include the **Symphony Hall** (in the round, giving it superb acoustics), as well as eight individual **theaters**. Cheaper and often more experimental performances take place in the **Changing Scene**, 1527 Champa (Thurs–Sun; ⓣ303/893-5775), a theater which does world premieres exclusively; tickets are normally around $10.

In the hunt for **tickets**, both Ticketmaster (ⓣ303/830-8497) and Ticketman (ⓣ303/430-1111) can usually help. You can try the Ticket Bus, parked on 16th Street and Curtis, in person (daily:10am–6pm), where you'll often find last-minute deals on shows that have yet to sell out.

Bars and clubs

Breckenridge Brewery 2220 Blake St ⓣ303/297-3644. Atmospheric brewpub opposite Coors Field where you can watch the beers being brewed while snacking on pub grub like burgers and chicken sandwiches and various salads, and soups.
The Church 1160 Lincoln ⓣ303/832-3528. A dance club located inside a gutted cathedral, this significant downtown nightlife landmark combines a wine bar, sushi bar, and three invariably busy dance floors get down to mostly garage, hard-house, and techno. $5–15 cover.
Comedy Works 1226 15th St ⓣ303/595-3637. Right off Larimer Square, Denver's major comedy venue is the most likely place to find visiting big-name stand-up acts. Two-drink minimum and closed Mondays.
Cruise Room Bar 1600 17th St ⓣ303/628-5400. Inside the *Oxford Hotel*, this bar a worth a stop for the atmosphere – it's a replica of the Art Deco bar on the *Queen Mary* ocean liner – and its mean martinis.
Duffy's Shamrock 1635 Court Place. Friendly local downtown bar that also serves food, including good Southern-fried chicken. Open from 7am until 1.30am daily.
Mercury Cafe 2199 California St ⓣ303/294-9281. When there's not jazz on here, there's swing dancing, poetry readings, or some other form of entertainment. The club is combined with a good-value restaurant, serving lots of healthy choices, many vegetarian.
Polly Esthers 2301 Blake St ⓣ303/382-1976. Massive and consistently popular club with seventies and eighties hits playing on two floors. Cover $5–10.
The Soiled Dove 1949 Market St ⓣ303/299-0100. Massively popular bar with an often rowdy rooftop overlooking Market St. There's an eclectic variety of live music almost every night; from local to national names and from jazz to rock.
Stampede Steak House and Dance Emporium 2430 S Havanna St and Park Rd ⓣ303/337-6909. The massive antique saloon bar is the centerpiece of this Country and Western pick-up joint. Located in suburban Aurora, it's only worth the drive if you're in a boot-scooting frame of mind.
Wynkoop Brewing Co 1634 18th St ⓣ303/297-2700. The state's first brewpub serves up good home-brewed beers and great bar food opposite Union Station. There's an elegant pool hall upstairs, and live entertainment Thurs–Sat. Brewery tours, with free samples, are given on Saturdays (1–5pm).

Live music venues

Bluebird 3317 E Colfax ⓣ303/333-7749. Art Deco 1914 former film theater that now hosts a good range of local microbrews and a variety of live bands.
Brendan's 1624 Market St ⓣ303/595-0609. Small basement pub in the LoDo with regular live blues; big-name acts pop by a few times a month and cover is rarely more than $10.
El Chapultepec 20th and Market St ⓣ303/295-9126. Tiny, very popular LoDo jazz venue that's been hosting acts for more than fifty years. Local bands play nightly, and bigger names occasionally stop by.
Grizzly Rose 5450 N Valley Hwy ⓣ303/295-1330. Celebrated Country and Western venue a ten-minute drive north of downtown on I-25 (exit 215). The huge venue has bands every night, attracts famous names regularly, and has been named the Country's Best Country Music Club by the Country Music Association several years running. Cover $5–10.
Herman's Hideaway 1578 S Broadway

Gay nightlife

Providing without doubt the most vibrant **gay and lesbian scene** in the Rockies, Denver has around thirty bars serving the local community, several of which are in the 16th Avenue area, southeast of downtown. Weekend nights buzz at the upscale piano bar *The Grand,* 538 E 17th Ave and Pearl (ⓣ303/839-5390), which puts on live music and cabaret and attracts a mix of gays and lesbians. Another popular choice is *Tracks*, 2975 Fox St between 20th and Chestnut Street (ⓣ303/292-6600), where DJs spin to a packed dance floor. The gay scene is fused with traditional Denver culture at the Country and Western music bar *Charlie's*, 900 E Colfax Ave and Emerson (ⓣ303/839-8890), whose popular restaurant serves lunch and dinner. The local gay newspapers with listings are *Out Front* and *H Ink*; for listings on the web, check ⓦwww.outindenver.com and ⓦwww.denvergay.com.

☎303/777-5840. Located just south of I-25, *Herman's* is one of Denver's best rock clubs, with live music from Wed–Sat. Cover $5.

Ogden 935 E Colfax ☎303/830-2525. Small gritty joint featuring dense crowds and mostly local rock bands.

Listings

Banks There are numerous ATMs and banks with full exchange facilities downtown. For travelers checks, Thomas Cook is at 1625 Broadway (☎303/571-0808) and American Express at 555 S 17th St (☎303/298-7100).

Consulates A British consulate is located in the World Trade Center Tower at 1675 Broadway (☎303/592-5200, Ⓦwww.britainusa.com); the Australian consulate is at 50 S Steele (☎303/321-2234).

Cycling The Colorado State Division of Parks and Recreation, 1313 Sherman St #618 (☎303/866-3437), has information and maps on the 400 miles of cycle paths in the Denver area. The Platte River Greenway is one of the most picturesque, while the Cherry Creek bike path, connecting the mall, downtown, and several attractions west of downtown, one of the most convenient. Blazing Saddles, 1426 Market St (☎303/534-5255), rents out bikes from $20 per day. Two Wheel Tours (☎303/798-4601) runs day-trips in Denver and the Front Range from around $70/day with bikes and food included.

Emergency ☎911

Golf An information line (☎303/964-2563) has details of numerous courses in the Denver area. The public City Park course, E 25th Ave and York St, is the most central ($19 for 18 holes; ☎303/295-4420). One of the most beautiful however is the Arrowhead Golf Club near the red-rock Roxborough State Park 45-minutes drive southwest of Denver at 10850 W Sundown Trail (☎303/973-9614).

Internet There are plenty of free public internet terminals spread over the seven floors of the impressive central Denver Public Library, 10 W 14th Ave (☎303/640-6200).

Laundry In the northeast, try the *Melbourne Hostel* ; Cycles Laundry, 320 Broadway, is your best southeast-side option.

Medical Walgreen's, 2000 E Colfax Ave (☎303/331-0917) operates a 24hr pharmacy. To locate medical help, try the local dental (☎1-800/428-8773) or medical (☎303/425-2929) referral services. The University Hospital is at 4200 E 9th Ave and Colorado Ave (☎303/399-1211); Denver General Hospital at 6th Ave and Bannock St (☎303/436-6000).

Post office The main downtown branch is at 951 20th St (Mon–Fri 8am–5pm; zip code 80201).

Spectator sports The fanatically supported and consistently sold-out **Denver Broncos** (season: Sept–Dec; ☎303/433-7466, Ⓦwww.denverbroncos.com) football team play their home games in Invesco Field (1900 Eliot St, I 25 exit 210B), to which you're unlikely to find tickets for much under $70. Also not far from downtown is the Pepsi Center, 1000 Chopper, nicknamed "The Can," where the NHL **Colorado Avalanche**, the 2001 Stanley Cup winners (season: Oct–April; ☎303/405-1100) play their ice hockey. For transport to downtown sports events contact the public transportation company RTD (☎303/299-6000, Ⓦwww.rtd-denver.com) who organize shuttles to games, using a park-and-ride system, from numerous locations throughout the Denver Metro area.

Sporting goods Major local sports retailer Gart Bros has a branch within walking distance of downtown at 1000 Broadway (☎303/861-1122). In a huge former railway building, the outdoor goods giant REI, 1416 Platte St (☎303/756-3100), is also a short walk away from downtown.

Taxis Yellow Cab (☎303/777-7777); Metro Taxi (☎303/333-3333); and the cheapest company in town, Zone Cab (☎303/444-8888).

Tours: GrayLine (☎303/289-2841 or 1-800/348-6877, Ⓦwww.coloradograyline.com) operates bus tours of Rocky Mountain National Park and the surrounding area (May 15–Oct 15). Best Mountain Tours (☎303/750-5200, Ⓦwww.bestmountaintours.com) do similar tours, together with day-trips to the Pikes Peak area and other nearby Front Range attractions. Tours cost around $65/person.

Vehicle rental The RV specialist Cruise America is at 8950 N Federal Blvd (☎1-800/327-7799). Moturis, 5300 Colorado Blvd, Suite 2 (☎303/295-6837 or 1-888/295-6837, Ⓦwww.moturis.com) rents out motorcycles, including Harley Davidsons, and motorhomes of various sizes too.

Golden

Wedged between the mountains and Denver's suburbs, the sleepy town of **GOLDEN** is more interesting for its location near several superb mountain parks (see box overleaf) and the Buffalo Bill Memorial Museum, than for its small-town charms. First a mining camp that dwindled in the absence of much ore, the town only rose to fame briefly as the seat of legislative assemblies in the mid-1860s. Since then Golden's notoriety has come as the site of the **Coors Brewery**, the world's largest single brewery (daily 10am–4pm; free; ⓣ303/277-2337). Located three blocks east of Washington Avenue, Golden's main thoroughfare, the brewery serves up one-and a-half-hour-long tours full of corporate self-promotion. The tour ends in a tasting session of their numerous products (including the light beer for which the company's most famous). The town's other big employer, the Colorado School of Mines, runs a small **geology museum** at 16th Street, and Maple (Mon–Sat 9am–4pm, Sun 1–4pm, though hours may vary; free; ⓣ303/273-3823). There's a diverting selection of pre-electricity mining lamps here, as well as a good selection of rock and ores, but sadly no free beer is handed out upon completion of a tour. Another small-scale attraction is the **Golden Pioneer Museum**, 923 10th St (Mon–Sat 10am–4.30pm; free; ⓣ303/278-7151, ⓦwww.henge.com/~goldenpm), which has a mostly predictable array of pioneer artifacts, though there's an unusual picture manufactured entirely from the hair of one family.

Buffalo Bill museum

High above town on Lookout Mountain, **Buffalo Bill's Memorial Museum** (May–Oct daily 9am–5pm; Nov–April Tues–Sun 9am–4pm; $3) is the final resting place of William Cody, famed frontiersman, buffalo-hunter, army scout and showman, who died in Denver in 1915 (see p.384). At the time of his death there was some debate if this was his site of choice, and some citizens of Cody, the city he founded in Wyoming, still claim he's buried in the wrong place. In the years following his death the threat of disinterment was such that the National Guard was brought in to watch over the gravesite – with the aid of a tank. Occasionally billed as the "Graceland of the Rockies," the museum itself does a thorough job of outlining Buffalo Bill's past, a man who first did almost every quintessential Wild West job, then went on to create and fortify many of its myths in his travelling circus. Some of the more gruesome, yet intriguing elements on display include a pistol whose handle has been fashioned from human bone, and an account of Bill scalping a Native American – a group he mostly got on with and also integrated in his world-traveling circus show. The restaurant next door (in the former museum building) serves buffalo burgers and other snacks.

Practicalities

Buses from downtown Denver (at least hourly; leaving from 15th St and California) stop beside Golden's central **chamber of commerce**, 10th Street and Washington Street (Mon–Fri 8.30am–5pm, Sat & Sun 10am–4pm; ⓣ303/279-3113 or 1-800/590-3113, ⓦwww.goldenchamber.org).

For a small town, Golden has a large number of **accommodation** possibilities. The cheapest option is the *Clear Creek RV Park* (ⓣ303/278-1437), a few blocks west of downtown on 10th Street. It has a pool, hot tub, and $17 sites, set up mostly for RVs. The modest *Golden Motel* (ⓣ303/279-5581; ③), south of downtown on 24th and Ford Street, offers basic units, some with kitchenettes. Friendlier and more central is the *Williamsburg Inn*, 1407 Washington

Denver's mountain parks

One perk of living in Denver and part of the reason so many flock to live here is the easy access to the countryside, made possible by the presence of a large amount of public land in the Rocky Mountain foothills beside the city. Though if you have more time you're better off heading deeper into Colorado's mountains, for a couple of hours of hiking, biking, or snowshoeing these mountain parks are hard to beat – particularly since many offer stupendous views out over the plains.

One good park that's rarely busy, but is within easy striking distance of Denver only a couple of miles outside Golden, is **White Ranch**. The secluded nature of the hiking trails here make it easy to forget how close you are to a city, until, at regular intervals trees thin to offer stunning views over the plains. To get to White Ranch follow Hwy-93 north from Golden, then onto 56th Street for half a mile, the main trailhead parking lot is near the junction with Pine Ridge Road. A second trailhead is an extra ten minutes of driving along 56th Street and Golden Gate Canyon Road, and has the advantage of cutting out a large climb up into the park. Leaflet dispensers are on hand at both trailheads to provide maps to the park. The density of the trail network makes it easy to find a route length to suit most hikers – while only skilled mountain bikers will enjoy the steep, rough terrain here.

Several public bodies have over the last hundred years acquired land in the parks and now administer them for conservation and public recreation. Organizations administrating open space in the foothills include Denver Parks and Recreation Department (ⓣ303/964-2462, ⓦwww.denvergov.org) and **Jefferson County Open Space** (ⓣ303/271-5925, ⓦwww.co.jefferson.co.us). The cumbersome websites of both these government departments have good information about their public lands. More user friendly, though, is the chamber of commerce in Golden (see overleaf), which keeps a good stock of leaflets on the local public lands.

St (ⓣ303/279-7673; ❹). Breakfasts are included in room rates here, as at *The Dove Inn B&B,* 711 14th St (ⓣ303/278-2209 or 1-888/278-2209, ⓦwww.doveinn.com; ❹), a former 1860s pioneer home that makes for another pleasant central lodging option. The modern *Golden Hotel,* 11th Street and Washington (ⓣ303/279-0100 or 1-800/233-7214, ⓦwww.golden-hotel.com; ❺), includes amenities like an exercise room, hot tub, and pool, along with an airy Western-decorated lobby and rooms.

Simple, cheap, and filling is the order of the day in most of Golden's downtown **restaurants**. *Kenrow's,* 718 12th St, has a good buffet breakfast for $3, with burgers and sandwich lunches and prime-rib dinners starting at around $6; it's also one of Golden's most popular bars, with pool tables and live music most weekends. If you're looking for a bit of a splurge Golden-style, head to the *Mesa Bar & Grill,* 1310 Washington Ave (ⓣ303/271-0110) in the *Table Mountain Inn*, which serves mostly American specialties – prime rib of buffalo, grilled salmon – spiced and prepared in a southwestern style.

Morrison and around

There's not much to **Morrison**, thirty miles south of Denver, besides its close vicinity to both the world-famous Red Rock Amphitheater and impressive Dakota Ridge. If you've got kids in tow, you may want to stop by **Tiny Town**, 6249 S Turkey Creek Rd (May-Sept daily 10am–5pm; Oct Sat & Sun 10am–5pm; $3; ⓣ303/697-6829), where there's a hundred or so engaging miniature buildings on display. And if you're feeling peckish, a visit to the *Morrison Inn*, 301 Bear Creek Ave, for good Mexican food and great margari-

The Colorado Trail

Judged to be the state's ultimate long-distance backpacking trail, the Colorado Trail runs for 470 miles from Denver to Durango (see p.155). The route is not an easy one, following the continental divide for much of the way and visiting eight mountain ranges, seven national forests, six wilderness areas and five river systems as it passes through wonderful craggy mountain scenery on its way southwest. This classic mountain adventure takes at least a month to complete on foot. For books, maps, advice, and information on volunteer opportunities along the trail, contact the Colorado Trail Foundation (Ⓣ303/384-3729, Ⓦwww.coloradotrail.org).

The Denver end of the trail begins southwest of town from the dirt road along the steep-sided Waterton Canyon – five miles south of Littleton along Wadsworth Boulevard and CO-121 – that's also home to a group of easily-spotted bighorn sheep.

tas is in order. Otherwise, head to the impressive **Dakota ridge** – part of a fourteen-mile-long ridge known as "the hogback." A varied four- to five-hour hiking trip (beginning at a parking lot just south of the I-70) over the rocky ridge takes in panoramic views of Denver, before looping around (and crossing a main road) onto the **Red Rocks trail**. It then returns to the parking lot via numerous contorted, red-sandstone rocks. Skilled mountain bikers can do this trail, one of the most challenging in the area, in around two hours. It's worth making a couple of worthwhile side-trips along the route as well: a part of Dakota Ridge known as **Dinosaur Ridge** is noted for its fossilized dinosaur footprints, dotted alongside Hwy-26 that crosses the ridge. The world's first large dinosaur discovery (a Stegosaurus) occurred here in 1877, quickly setting off "the dinosaur gold rush" in which numerous scientists converged, excavating over seventy species. A tiny **visitors' center** (daily: 9am–4pm; Ⓣ303/697-3466, Ⓦwww.dinoridge.org) beside the road on the eastern side of the ridge has more information on discoveries. The Dakota Ridge trail drops down onto the western side of the ridge before crossing a road to link up to the Red Rocks trail. A spur off this trail runs to the remarkable **Red Rocks Amphitheater** (Ⓣ303/694-1234, Ⓦwww.red-rocks.com), though if you are driving it's best to pull into its main entrance just west of Morrison. The 9000-seater amphitheater has been the venue for thousands of rock and classical concerts, though none more famous than U2's *Under a Blood Red Sky*. Squeezed between two 400ft red-sandstone rocks that glow under the late evening sun, the setting is a beautiful one, with commanding views over Denver, and it's open free of charge during the day.

The Peak-to-Peak Highway

The scenic **PEAK-TO-PEAK HIGHWAY** begins in Idaho Springs and runs seventy-odd miles north through the casino towns of **Central City** and **Black Hawk**, then past **Golden Gate Canyon State Park** and **Nederland** (around one-third of the way north) to Estes Park and the adjacent Rocky Mountain National Park (see p.265–286). Views on much of the route are splendid, with the high peaks of the Continental Divide to the west and thousands of square miles of plains to the east. Though a popular drive on summer weekends, traffic is rarely busy enough to be a problem except around Central City and Black Hawk, when the addition of casino traffic can slow things down.

Central City and Black Hawk

Once crumbling Victorian mining towns, **Central City** and the adjoining smaller town of **Black Hawk** each spent the last decade transforming themselves into shiny, pseudo-Victorian casino centers. With little else to drive the economy, it's easy to understand why the local electorate, with the proviso that casinos had to be located in historic buildings, turned to legalized gambling. Still, though an economic success, it's hard to cheer the fact that the once potent atmosphere of these fabled mining towns has been forever lost to the clatter of slot machines.

Central City originally began as an amalgamation of mining camps along steep-sided Gregory Gulch. Soon dubbed "the richest square mile on earth" it grew quickly, partly thanks to publicity of *New York Tribune* writer Horace Greely. Having been shown a "salted" mine here – one into which local miners had shot gold dust – Greely returned back east to write the famous lines, "Go West young man and grow with the country." By the time of the Civil War, the city had grown to 15,000 strong, making it the largest settlement in the territory. It was by all accounts a rough place; city records from 1861 list 217 fist fights, 97 gunfights, 11 Bowie knife fights and one dog fight (though amazingly no one was killed until 1896). Even Kerouac's writings in the 1950s found Central City to be a wild outpost. Today the last vestige of this is found on the third Saturday in June, **Madame Lou Bunch Day**, named after the last (officially) operating madam in town, when locals dress up as Victorian prostitutes and patrons. The highlight is the Brass Bed Race, complete with its occupant posing as a "sporting house girl."

Central City had a softer side too, its **Central City Opera House** (Ⓣ303/292-6700 or 1-800/851-8175, Ⓦwww.centralcityopera.org) in the center of town showing off a cosmopolitan air. The opera season here runs mid-July to mid-August and includes both classical and modern pieces. The nearby **Teller House**, 120 Eureka St (10am–4pm; $3; Ⓣ303/582-3200), is a former hotel in which Horace Tabor kept a large suite for his mistress "Baby Doe" (see Leadville p.232). It's now curiously famous for a face painted on the bar-room floor – a confusing tale best explained by the helpful staff. A good impression of what the frontier town must have been like in the mining days can be gained at both the **Gilpin County Historical Museum**, 228 E High St (May–Sept daily 11am–4pm; $3; Ⓣ303/582-5283), and the **Thomas House**, 120 Eureka St (May–Sept Fri–Mon 11am–4pm; tours on the hour; $3). The latter, a Greek Revival residence built in 1894, was boarded up in 1917 and reopened years later to give a time-capsule-like look at domestic life in the early 1900s.

Practicalities

Information can be found at **Gillian County Chamber of Commerce** 141 Nevada St (Ⓣ303/582-5251 or 1-800/542-2999). Most of the **accommodation** options in both towns are in the larger casinos. In Central City, *Harvey's Wagon Wheel Hotel and Casino,* 321 Gregory St (Ⓣ303/582-0800 or 1-800/924-6646; ⑤), has basic modern rooms, some with good views over town, and free breakfasts. In Black Hawk, the massive *Isle of Capri Casino*, 401 Main St (Ⓣ1-800/743-4753, Ⓦwww.isleofcapricasino.com; ⑥) is a resort aspiring to Las Vegas proportions, featuring restaurants as well as (predictably cheesy) live music and a cabaret on site. More homey options include the *Shamrock Inn,* 351 Gregory St (Ⓣ303/582-5513; ③), which has four small and plain rooms, and the more upmarket *High Street Inn B&B,* 215 W High St (Ⓣ303/582-

0622; ❺), located in a beautiful Victorian building. Two miles above Central City past its old cemeteries is the *USFS Columbine Campground* (late-May to mid-Oct; ☎303/567-2901), which accommodates both RVs and tents ($9). Thanks to casino deals like prime rib and fries for $3, there are few other **places to eat** in town. One longstanding local institution, the *Black Forest Inn,* 260 Gregory St (☎303/279-3333), serves up German-style wild game and schnitzel entrees from around $9.

Golden Gate Canyon State Park

While traveling the Peak-to-Peak highway, it's well worth stopping off to appreciate the landscape from the other side of the car windshield. One excellent place to do this is **Golden Gate Canyon State Park** ($4/vehicle; ☎303/582-3707, Ⓦwww.coloradoparks.org) where 35 miles of trails cross through aspen forests and lush meadows, and give fantastic views over the Indian Peaks Wilderness and the Continental Divide.

The park is eleven miles from Black Hawk along Hwy-119 and Golden Gate Canyon Road and only thirty miles from downtown Denver. This makes the park a popular day-trip for Denverites, who come here to escape the summer heat of the plains and hike, bike or fish. While in the winter the park is popular for cross-country skiing, snowshoeing, ice-fishing, skating, and sledding.

For an overview and good introduction to the park, head to the visitors' center (daily: 9am–5pm; ☎303/582-3707), at the park's eastern fringe. The center also dispenses free permits for backcountry sites and the use of several Appalachian-style backcountry shelters in the park. Several serviced campgrounds ($5–12; reservations ☎303/470-1444 or 1-800/678-2267) are also available in the park, including the massive *Reverend's Ridge Campground* or the much more pleasant *Aspen Meadow* ground with its 35 tent sites.

Nederland

Affectionately known as Ned, the mountain backwater **NEDERLAND** is a laid-back old mining center that's become a hippie favorite. Sprawling across an entire valley floor eighteen miles north of Central City and seventeen miles east of Boulder, it sits in an attractive location at the head of a reservoir, surrounded by the **Roosevelt National Forest** and backdropped by the snow-capped peaks of the **Indian Peaks Wilderness Area**. Most activity in town centers around a shopping mall and a short street of old clapboard houses nearby, where in the evenings the wooden bar-room floors vibrate with the bluegrass and acoustic acts of the town's surprisingly vibrant music scene. But it's the town's mountain and forest setting along the Peak-to-Peak Highway that generally attracts visitors to hike and bike in the warmer months. Two miles beyond the Eldora (see below) turnoff is a relatively small wooded recreation area, **West Magnolia**, where there's a dense network of trails including some good single-track mountain biking.

The big draw in winter is the **Eldora Ski area** (mid-Nov to mid-April; snow reports ☎303/440-8700, lodging ☎1-800/444-0447, Ⓦwww.eldora.com), just four miles south of town. While not exactly one of Colorado's flagship resorts, the relatively cheap lift tickets ($40/day) and convenient location keeps the healthy mix of snow-riders who attend happy. Rated twenty percent beginner, fifty percent intermediate and thirty percent expert, the slopes feature some solid glade runs as well as a steep half-pipe much-loved by Boulder's student boarders. Its 45 miles of cross-country tracks make it a good venue for Nordic skiing too.

Practicalities

Bus "N" from Boulder (six/day; $2) stops in front of the **visitor information** cabin (unreliable opening hours; ⓣ303/258-3936 or 1-800/221-0044) and continues, in winter, to the Eldora ski area. Visitor information is just beside the town's roundabout and adjacent to a small area of old wooden buildings, containing shops and a couple of bars. The *Best Western Lodge*, 55 Lakeview Drive (ⓣ303/258-9463 or 1-800/279-9463; ④), provides fine modern rooms in the center of town, and the outdoor hot tub and the lodge's reasonable Eldora ski packages make it particularly enticing in the winter. Further down along the main road (Hwy-119), opposite the shopping mall, is the small *Nederland Hostel* (ⓣ303/258-7788) which has dorm beds ($12) and some newly refurbished private rooms ($30). About four miles east out of town in the village of Eldora is the cozy, antique-furnished *Goldminer Hotel*, 601 Klondike Ave (ⓣ303/444-4705 or 1-800/422-4629, ⓦwww.goldminerhotel.com; ⑥), where both hiking and cross-country skiing trails begin from just outside the back door. To **camp**, try the *USFS Kelly-Dahl Campground,* three miles east along CO-119, which has pretty lakeside sites ($9) with excellent views and a number of trailheads nearby.

Nederland has quite a few places to **eat**. In the old railway carriages in the center of town, *Cools Beans Espresso* is a popular morning hangout, serving excellent espressos, vast slabs of cardamom cake and thick chocolate brownies. Opposite, *Once Again Books and Café* (ⓣ303/258-3695) can provide a number of snacks along with an internet service and a fine collection of used books. Up in the historic district, the popular *Neapolitan's*, 1 W 1st St, bakes massive pizzas, served alongside vast portions of good pasta ($6) in a candlelit, cabin-style restaurant. Across the road, the all-wood *Pioneer Inn* is open all day and late into the night, serving breakfasts, burgers, and Mexican dishes like green chili burritos ($7). The bar here is busy with locals all day and really gets going with live music on Fridays. The most upmarket eating choice is the *Black Forest Restaurant*, just above the shopping mall; it has the same owners, style and menu as the longtime favorite in Central City (see overleaf).

Boulder

BOULDER, just under thirty miles northwest of Denver on US-36, is one of the country's liveliest college towns, filled with a youthful population that divides its time between phenomenally healthy daytime activities and almost equally unhealthy evening ones. Founded in 1858 by a prospecting party who erroneously felt that the nearby **Flatiron Mountains** – enormous sandstone monoliths that lean against the first swell of the Rockies – "looked right for gold," Boulder bloomed with the addition of a railroad and university in the 1870s, and hasn't stopped growing since. Thanks largely to the presence of the **University of Colorado-Boulder** and its 26,000 students, the small town has fostered an offbeat, liberal vibe, making it one of the West's major centers for alternative medicine and spirituality. Additionally, Boulder's mountainous location – ideal for cycling, hiking, and climbing – has attracted scores of outdoor enthusiasts, who continue to flock here despite closely guarded city restrictions on growth. Consequently, overcrowding is a major topic of concern, mirroring an Arapahoe **curse** placed on the town when the natives were forced into the mountains. According to the hex, all those setting eyes on the area would be unable to leave, thereby overpopulating and ultimately destroying it.

Arrival and getting around

The main point of entry and departure for local and long-distance **buses** is the Transit Center, 14th and Walnut (☎303/442-1044). Regular services to Denver ($3) and the Denver International Airport ($8) depart from here as well. To get around locally, HOP shuttle buses (every 15min Mon–Sat 7am–7pm, until 10pm Thurs-Sun during university terms; 75¢), links downtown, the university, the trendy student district known as "The Hill," and the major shopping center Crossroads Mall. The SKIP (Mon–Fri 5.30am–midnight; Sun 7.30am–10.30pm; 75¢) is another useful service, running back and forth along most of Broadway; it picks up every ten minutes during weekdays, every thirty minutes after 7pm and on weekends. For a **taxi**, try either Boulder Yellow Cab (☎303/777-7777) or Metro Taxi (☎303/333-3333).

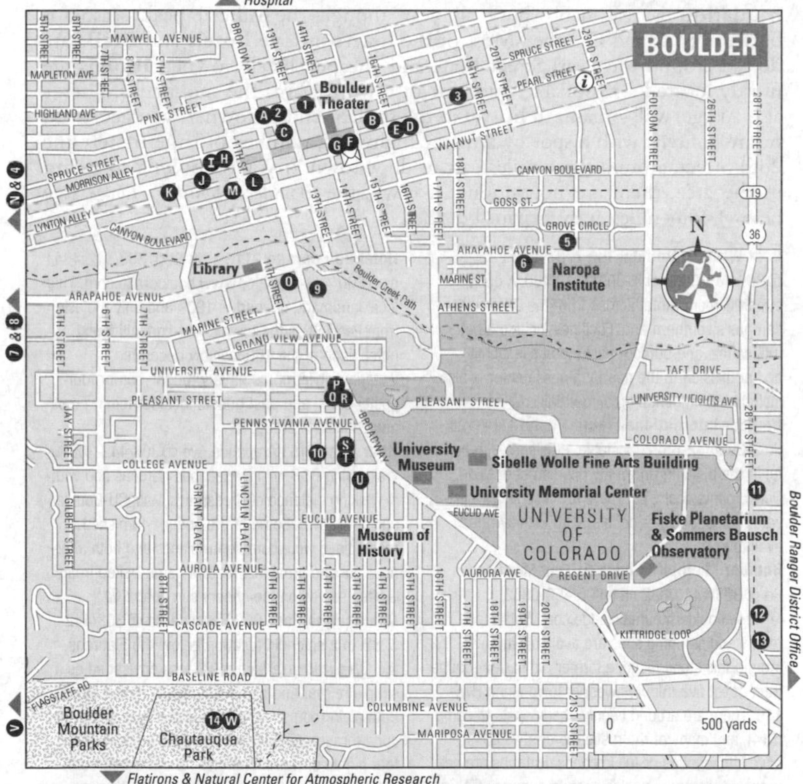

ACCOMMODATION

- Best Western Boulder Inn 13
- Boulder International Youth Hostel 10
- Boulder Mountain Lodge 4
- Boulder Victoria Historic B&B 1
- Hotel Boulderado 2
- Briar Rose 5
- Chautauqua Park 14
- Econo Lodge 6
- Foot of the Mountain Motel 7
- Holiday Inn 12
- Lazy L Motel 11
- Pearl Street Inn 3
- Silver Saddle Motel 8
- University Inn 9

RESTAURANTS

- Alfalfa O
- bd's Mongolian Barbecue E
- Chautauqua Dining Hall W
- Dot's Diner P
- Flagstaff House V
- Illegal Pete's U
- Little Russian Café F
- Moshi Moshi Bowl D
- Mountain Sun Pub & Brewery B
- Pasta Jay's I
- Red Lion Inn N
- Redfish New Orleans Brewhouse C
- Rhumba K
- Rocky Mountain Joe's Café G

BARS & CLUBS

- Catacombs A
- The Foundry L
- Fox Theater S
- K's China Q
- La Iguana R
- 'round Midnight H
- Tulagi T
- The Walrus M
- West End Tavern J

Information

The hospitable, low-key **visitor center** is at 2440 Pearl St (Mon–Fri 9am–5pm; ⓣ303/442-2911 or 1-800/444-0447, ⓦwww.visitor.boulder.net). For information on public land around Boulder, contact the City of Boulder Open Space & Mountain Parks Department (ⓣ303-441-3440), who manage large chunks of land in the neighboring foothills. The **USFS Boulder Ranger District Office**, 2995 Baseline Rd (ⓣ303/444-6600, ⓦwww.fs.fed.us/ r2/arnf/), provides information and camping permits for the Roosevelt National Forests and the adjacent Indian Peaks Wilderness near Nederland (see p.89).

Accommodation

Due in large part to the university's busy schedule of events, Boulder **accommodation** is reasonably busy all year, though the official peak season is between May and October. Most of the town's upscale **hotels** and **B&Bs** are dotted around the Pearl Street Mall, and cheaper, locally owned **motels** are mostly located a reasonable walk out of town towards the mountains. There's also a large, well-organized **hostel** in the student end of town. If you get stuck, or are content with a spot by a major highway, a number of large motels line 28th Street, around three miles east of downtown. If you're looking to **camp** in the area, there are no options in town; the *Boulder Mountain Lodge* (see below), four miles away, is your best bet.

Best Western Boulder Inn 770 28th St ⓣ303/449-3800 or 1-800/233-8469. A plain, hundred-room motel across from the CU-Boulder campus's southern end. Facilities include a hot tub, sauna, and outdoor pool (open seasonally), and admission to the nearby fitness center is also included. Continental breakfast daily. ❺

Boulder International Youth Hostel 1107 12th St ⓣ303/442-0522. Sociable, efficiently-run hostel in the bustling university hill district of town. Dorm rooms cost $15. There are also several private rooms ($40 per double) with weekly rates available.

Boulder Mountain Lodge 91 Four Mile Canyon Rd ⓣ303/444-0882 or 1-800/458-0882, ⓦwww.bouldermountainlodge.com. Both motel rooms and camping sites are available in and around this stone lodge, a former old narrow-gauge train depot five minutes west of town along Hwy-119. There are around twenty shady spots to camp ($14), and many of the rustic motel-style units have kitchenettes or full kitchens. Hot tubs are next to the creek, and a pool is open in summer. ❹

Boulder Victoria Historic B&B 1305 Pine St ⓣ303/938-1300, ⓦwww.bouldervictoria.com. Small, high-class Victorian inn a block from the Pearl Street Mall with elegant antique-furnished rooms, with brass beds, down comforters, and dried-flower decorations. Afternoon tea and port wine served in the evening. Breakfast includes great homemade fruit breads and muffins. ❼

Hotel Boulderado 2115 13th St ⓣ303/442-4344 or 1-800/433-4344, ⓦwww.boulderado.com. This local landmark, opened in 1909 and only a block from Pearl St, is the town's first and still finest hotel. Each of the 160 lavishly decorated, Victorian-style rooms have wrought-iron or four-poster beds, and past guests include Robert Frost and Louis Armstrong. ❼

Briar Rose 2151 Arapahoe Ave ⓣ303/442-3007. Welcoming B&B with landscaped gardens and within walking distance of Crossroads Mall, CU-Boulder and downtown. Some of the antique-furnished rooms have woodburning fireplaces and both afternoon tea and breakfast feature home-baked treats – often served on the cheery sun porch. ❼

Chautauqua Park 900 Baseline Rd ⓣ303/442-3282. In a splendid location below the Flatirons, the *Chautauqua* (see p.94) was envisaged as a simple retreat and has successfully remained so. Both plain rooms and cottages are available from June through August, but can only be booked for four nights or more. The one- to three-bedroom cottages have full kitchens, but no telephones, air-conditioning, or TVs. They do, though, have one of the most beautiful locations in town and are often booked up six months in advance. ❷

Econo Lodge 2020 Arapahoe Ave ⓣ303/449-7550 or 1-800/449-7550. Tidy motel within walking distance of downtown and the university. Rooms have cable TV and the motel also offers an indoor pool, hot tub, and sauna. A coffee and doughnut breakfast is included in rates. Refrigerators and microwaves available in some units. ④

Foot of the Mountain Motel 200 Arapahoe Ave ⓣ303/442-5688. Clean and friendly log-cabin-style motel, nine blocks from downtown beside Boulder Creek at the foot of Flagstaff mountain. All rooms have refrigerators and cable TV. ④

Holiday Inn 800 28th St ⓣ303/443-3322 or 1-800/HOLIDAY. Well-maintained motel with 165 large, clean rooms. The on-site "Holidome" includes a large indoor pool, hot tub, sauna and exercise room. Like all the other hotels along this part of 28th St, it's also very close to the university. ⑥

Lazy L Motel 1000 28th St ⓣ303/442-7525. No-nonsense inexpensive motel on the 28th St strip. Units come with kitchenettes and there's a pool. ④

Pearl Street Inn 1820 Pearl St ⓣ303/444-5584 or 1-888/810-1302, ⓦwww.pearlstreet.com. Elegant bed and breakfast with antique-furnished rooms overlooking a quiet central courtyard three blocks east of the Pearl Street Mall. Thanks to a high fence around its pretty gardens, the B&B maintains a secluded feel. Afternoon refreshments are also included. ⑥

Silver Saddle Motel 90 Arapahoe Ave ⓣ303/442-8022 or 1-800/525-9509, ⓦwww.silversaddlemotel.com. Large motel on the edge of town, around twenty-minutes' walk from the center along the Boulder Creek path. All units have fridges and microwaves. ④

University Inn 1632 Broadway ⓣ303/442-3830 or 1-800/258-7917, ⓦwww.u-inn.com. The most central motel in town is nothing fancy, though rooms have cable TV and there's free coffee and doughnuts for breakfast. There's also a tiny pool (alongside the busy Broadway Ave) and laundry facilities available. ⑤

The Town

It's the town's students, hippies, and New Age residents who have made Boulder offbeat and a popular tourist destination. In fact, there are few attractions in the renovated Victorian **downtown** area and mostly visitors just browse up and down its pedestrian mall. To the south, the lively **University** district also has only a couple of modest museums, though again just wandering around is pleasant enough. Pretty soon you'll probably find yourself heading out of town, along with the locals, to the town's real gems; the easily accessible **mountain parks** just west of town that have become an adventure playground for hikers, bikers, and climbers.

Downtown Boulder

Downtown centers on the leafy pedestrian mall of **Pearl Street**, lined with all sorts of lively cafés, galleries, and stores that can easily take a few hours to explore. The most notable sight around here is the redbrick **Hotel Boulderado**, just north of the mall at 2115 13th St. It's hard to believe that only a few decades ago this magnificently restored structure, built in 1909 and complete with a cherry cantilevered staircase and an Italian stained-glass ceiling, was on the verge of total decay. Like the rest of downtown, the hotel was hit hard by the decline that hit the area as businesses moved into the suburbs. In the 1960s snowstorm the glass ceiling crashed in; cooks hung bait to deter rats; and vagrants slept in its empty rooms. From May through September, informative **tours** of the hotel, along with the rest of town, are given by Boulder Historic Tours ($4; ⓣ303/444-5192).

A few blocks south, on the opposite side of the Pearl Street Mall, runs the **Boulder Creek Path**, cutting through downtown between Canyon Boulevard and Arapahoe Avenue. The nine-mile-long path follows the creek through a canyon and out to the eastern plains, making for a great jog, skate, or bike ride. On hot summer afternoons, walking west from downtown, then **floating** back down the creek on inflated truck inner-tubes is hard to beat. The tubes are on sale at local gas stations (more cheaply outside downtown).

The University district

Boulder owes much of its identity to the **University of Colorado** (☎303/492-1411). Its pleasant landscaped redbrick-and-tile **campus** bustles with life during term-time, as does the adjacent shopping district known as "The Hill." In the 1960s, the campus environs were seen as a regional counterculture stronghold, attracting hippies and generally propagating dissent, earning the town the "People's Republic of Boulder" tag that's since stuck. Though the town of Boulder still has a very enlightened liberal attitude, today this stems much less from the activities of CU students – many of whom are far more likely to engage in the almost annual frat-house riots than experiment with politics.

Campus tours (daily: 9.30am & 1.30pm; ☎303/492-6301) and maps are available at the **Memorial Center**, Broadway and Euclid, though meandering through the leafy campus alone is easy enough. Of the several museums here, the **CU Art Gallery** in the Sibell-Wolle Fine Arts Building has the most impressive collection (Mon–Fri 10am–5pm, Sat noon–4pm; free); around five thousand wide-ranging works by the likes of Rembrandt, Hogarth, Picasso, and others. The **University Museum**, 15th and Broadway (Mon–Fri 9am–5pm, Sat 9am–4pm, Sun 10am–4pm; free), is worth a peek for its collection of dinosaur skeletons.

Not associated with the University of Colorado, but just southwest of campus on University Hill is the **Boulder Museum of History**, 1206 Euclid Ave (Tues–Fri 10am–4pm, Sat & Sun noon–4pm; $2). Built in 1899 as a summer home by a New York merchant, the building is known as much for its impressive nine-foot-tall Tiffany stained-glass window as for its assortment of memorabilia on Boulder County's history. The ragtag collection downstairs relates mainly to mining, ranching, and everyday life in Boulder, while the second floor holds a sizeable costume gallery.

Likewise unaffiliated but nearby is the Buddhist-inspired **Naropa Institute**, on the north edge of the university campus at 2130 Arapahoe Ave (☎303/444-0202). This unconventional liberal arts college blends Eastern intuition with Western logic, including writing courses at the Allen Ginsberg founded Jack Kerouac School of Disembodied Poetics. The institute is also the venue for various performances and workshops throughout the year, and visitors are welcome to look around at any time, or join a tour (Mon–Fri 2pm).

Boulder Mountain Parks and around

On the southwest fringe of town, the landmark Flatirons are the centerpiece of the Boulder Mountain Parks. This network of rocky peaks and valleys is laced with some 8000 acres of trails and copious amounts of rough **climbing** taking in Bear Peak, Green Mountain, Flagstaff Mountain, and Mount Sanitas. The Flatirons themselves are part of a string of formations along Front Range that include the Garden of the Gods (see p.111) in Colorado Springs and Red Rocks (see p.87) near Denver. All are former oceanic sediments tilted in the fold-and-thrust construction of the mountain range over the last 65 million years. Hugely popular with climbers, the Flatirons offer superb no-bolt sport **climbing**; the first and second flatirons are frequently free-climbed, but the third (counted north to south) definitely warrants ropes.

Almost at the foot of the Flatirons lies the **Boulder Chautauqua**, 900 Baseline Rd (☎303/440-3776, ⓦwww.chautauqua.com). This community of wooden cabins and houses was first opened as a retreat for Texans in 1898, as part of a movement that built around 400 retreats around the US to foster adult education and cultural entertainment. Centered around the grand **Chautauqua Auditorium** and **Dining Hall** (see p.97), the grounds also provide the venue for summer cultural and educational events like the **Colorado Music Festival** (ⓣ303/449-1397, ⓦwww.coloradomusicfest.com), a well-regarded classical music event beginning mid-June.

On the Chautauqua's western edge, the **Ranger Cottage** (Mon–Fri 8.30am–5pm, irregular weekend hours; ⓣ303/441-3408 ⓦwww.ci.boulder.co.uk/openspace/index.htm), run by Boulder Mountain Parks, is staffed by rangers who happily dispense information on local hiking. The *Boulder Mountain Parks Trail Map* ($5) is sold here and provides information on the 100 miles of hiking trails throughout the Boulder area. Of the trails that begin beside the Ranger Cottage, one of the best is the **McClintock Trail**, an easy and mostly shady hike that follows the contours of the mountain below the **Flatirons**. The trail climbs gently for two miles beyond the Ranger Cottage and joins the **Mesa Trail** which heads south to Eldorado Canyon (see below) a further five miles away. But only a mile past the intersection of the two trails is the **Natural Center for Atmospheric Research** (Mon–Fri 8am–5pm; Sat & Sun 9am–3pm; ⓣ303/497-1000, ⓦwww.ncar.ucar.edu) a facility that researches and monitors climate, and a three-hour round-hike from the Ranger Cottage. While free tours of the center are given daily at noon, self-guided ones can be taken at any time. Unfortunately, the exhibits on climate change and weather research are disappointing, as is the uneventful sight of some of the world's beefiest computers performing billions of calculations per second.

Striking out in the opposite direction as the McClintock Trail, Baseline Road passes the Chautauqua complex to ascend **Flagstaff Mountain**, also part of Boulder Mountain Park. Local cyclists like to climb this road, and the hike or drive up are also obvious excursions for views over the plains and further into the Rockies. Hiking routes here avoid the steep road for the most part and take considerably longer than the drive up, so it's generally better to drive to one of the trailhead parking lots ($5/day-use fee) alongside the road to get access to scenic hikes away from the road. **Mountain bikers** should follow Flagstaff Road further, part of the way back down the west side of the mountain, to the **Walker Ranch loop** a wooded and mostly straightforward eight-mile single- and double-track loop (popularly done counterclockwise) that takes around two hours to bike. The forest trail here feels wild, and there's a relatively good chance of spotting mountain lions or black bears. The loop twice crosses a sizeable creek, with good **fly-fishing** holes.

Eldorado Canyon State Park

Though there's no shortage of great rock in the Boulder Mountain Parks, expert climbers in the area often head out to the sheer cliffs of **Eldorado Canyon State Park** (open Aug–Jan, otherwise closed to protect raptor nesting sites $2/person or $4/vehicle; ⓣ303/494-3943), eight miles southwest of Boulder along CO-93 to CO-170. With vertical cliffs up to 850ft high, the park is known as one of the country's premier sites for difficult (class 5.6 to 5.9) **climbing**. Perhaps the park's climbers are inspired by Ivy Baldwin, an eccentric daredevil who tightrope-walked across a 500ft cable spanning the Bastille, a rock tower on the south side of the canyon, and the Wind Tower to the north, 89 times between 1906 and 1926. If you're not into daredeviling, there's also good rainbow trout **fishing** in the canyon's creek and **hot springs** to soak in at Eldorado Springs, a small resort just east of the state park (June–Aug 10am–6pm; $5; ⓣ303/499-1316).

Boulder's outdoor activities and outfitters

With a population that seems almost universally keen on outdoor recreation, there's no shortage of places to get sports equipment and advice about where to go. For **hikers** and **climbers**, the obvious destinations largely boil down to Boulder Mountain Park and Eldorado Canyon State Park (see overleaf). For further suggestions around town and further west in the Indian Peaks Wilderness, head to Mountain Sports, 821 Pearl St (Ⓣ303/443-6700), or go south out of town to the well-stocked climbing, hiking, and Nordic ski specialist, Neptune Mountaineering, 633 S Broadway (Ⓣ303/499-8866) in the Table Mesa shopping center. The seminal work on climbing in the area – Richard Rossiter's *Boulder Climbs South* (Chokestone Press) – is available in the store's excellent book department. Also of interest to climbers might be a local climbing school, the Boulder Rock School (Ⓣ303/447-2804 or 1-800/836-4008, Ⓦwww.boulderrock.com), with courses for climbers of all skill levels and ages.

Seeing as **mountain bikers** are banned from the trails in Boulder Mountain Park and there's very little for them in the Eldorado State Park, heading west out of town into the mountains is the best option. Besides the popular Walker Ranch loop (see overleaf), another great ride can be had along the rugged four-wheel-drive **Switzerland Trail**. An excellent 30-mile day-trip starting from either Nederland (see p.89) or Boulder, the relatively flat route leads through little-visited forests on mostly four-wheel-drive tracks. To end in Boulder, take the bus to Nederland (6 daily; $2; bikes ride free) from where you cycle south down the Peak-to-Peak highway for eight miles to the turn-off at CR-120 (not signposted). The CR-120 leads to a number of different trails, including the Switzerland Trail (also not signposted) alongside the peaceful Fourmile Canyon, all culminating at the conical Sugarloaf Mountain. The Sugarloaf Road begins here, heading downhill back to Boulder. Just two miles from the main road (CO-119) you pass the **Betasso Reserve** where there's an excellent two-mile single-track loop (clockwise) with great views down into Boulder. From here into Boulder you only need to spend a couple of (largely downhill) miles on the road before you can link up with the western end of the Boulder Creek path leading downtown. For further riding suggestions, refer to the extremely useful *Boulder County Mountain Bike Map* ($9). It's available from all Boulder bike shops, including Full Cycle, 1211 13th St (Ⓣ303/440-7771), who rent out mountain bikes on University Hill; front suspension models cost $25/day. Similar rental prices are found downtown at University Bicycles, Pearl and 9th Street (Ⓣ303/444-4196).

Local **kayakers** head to Boulder Creek, but for longer trips ask at the Paddle Shop, 1727 15th St (Ⓣ303/786-8799) or at the Boulder Outdoor Center, 2510 47th St (Ⓣ303/444-8420), which can both offer kayak instruction, raft trips, and rentals. For advice on local **fishing** visit the Front Range Anglers, 629-B S Broadway (Ⓣ303/494-1375) or, on University Hill, Kinsley Outfitters, 1155 13th St (Ⓣ303/442-6204 or 1-800/442-7420).

For **ski and snowboard** rentals contact Doc's Sports, 633 S Broadway (Ⓣ303/499-0963), who also do overnight repairs; or Boulder Ski Deals, 2404 Pearl St (Ⓣ303/938-8799), where cut-price lift tickets for some resorts can often be had.

Eating

From hippie-styled vegetarian cafés to all-American burger bars and elegant dining options, **restaurants** in Boulder are surprisingly diverse. Most can be found either downtown around **Pearl Street** or in the **University Hill** area.

Alfalfa 1651 Broadway. Huge wholefood supermarket with deli, serving pizza slices ($3) and grilled chicken, a huge salad bar and juice bar. A great place to stock up for a picnic.

bd's Mongolian Barbecue 1600 Pearl St. As with other Mongolian bbq spots, customers do most of the work here. Food is a buffet DIY style; pile your plate high with meat, veggies, oils, and seasoning, then have it fried on a massive hotplate. Healthy but not too cheap.

Chautauqua Dining Hall 900 Baseline Rd ☎303/440-3776. Thoughtfully prepared selections are served on the lovely patio overlooking the park, or in a large dining hall with a slightly institutional feel. Try the berry waffles for breakfast ($8); a selection of salads, the grilled vegetable and goats' cheese sandwich, or the grilled salmon melt for lunch ($10); and grilled lamb or Rocky Mountain trout for dinner ($20). Good fruit pies make the perfect dessert.

Dot's Diner 2716 N 28th St and 1333 Broadway. Reliable, busy local diner with all the usual inexpensive favorites for breakfast or lunch, including some of the best buttermilk biscuits in town, along with good huevos rancheros. In two locations, one near the town's motel row, the other just below the University Hill district.

Flagstaff House 1138 Flagstaff Rd ☎303/442-4640. A good upmarket choice – it's the only restaurant the Emperor and Empress of Japan deigned to dine in on their 1994 visit to the States – with superb views from its 1000ft-high vantage-point above town. Good local game dishes are sprinkled among the more than thirty gourmet entrees on offer; two courses run to about $40. Jacket and tie required.

Illegal Pete's 1320 College. Bustling takeaway or eat-in Mexican food restaurant. Large portions of low-priced food are served into the small hours of the night. Try the huge and excellent potato burrito ($5).

Little Russian Café 1430 Pearl St ☎303/449-7696. Lots of filling Eastern European specialties, including good borscht and goulash (around $12 for two courses), and dozens of flavored vodkas. There's live music and often dancing on weekends.

Moshi Moshi Bowl 1628 Pearl St ☎720/565-9787. Cavernous and stylish Japanese fast-food joint a short walk east of Pearl Street Mall. Perfect for a quick bowl of noodles or a fix of inexpensive sushi.

Mountain Sun Pub and Brewery 1535 Pearl St ☎303/546-0886. Bright, ethnic-style décor, hippie ambience, and a laid-back crowd make this popular microbrewery feel very Boulder. The huge beer selection – seven beers are made on the premises – accompanies inexpensive sandwiches, burgers, burritos, and fish and chips. Weekend nights often see live bluegrass. Open for both lunch and dinner.

Pasta Jay's 1001 Pearl St. A warm, exposed-brick trattoria with bright red-check tablecloths and large, fresh portions of pasta. Try the excellent gnocchi or tortellini ($7) with any of their tasty homemade sauces. Open for lunch and dinner.

Red Lion Inn Boulder Canyon Drive, 2.5 miles west of town on the road to Nederland (☎303/442-9368). Rustic restaurant that has served Central European and wild game dishes, like wild boar, for as long as anyone can remember. Though now fairly mainstream American, the menu still contains Austro-German influences like red cabbage and spaetzle noodles. Cheap early dinner deals are available before 6pm – after that expect to pay around $15 for a dish.

Redfish New Orleans Brewhouse 2027 13th St. Trendy exposed-brick restaurant featuring excellent but pricey helpings of Cajun food. The menu changes frequently, but appetizers usually include seafood gumbo, crawfish Caesar, and fresh oysters. Entrees are also mostly based around fresh seafood, though there are some good steaks here too. Six home-brewed beers are on offer and the wine list is extensive.

Rhumba 950 Pearl St. Slightly pretentious, but nonetheless popular bar and restaurant serving great rum cocktails (happy hour 4–6pm) and zingy Caribbean cuisine: snapper roasted in banana leaves, conch chowder, catfish egg-rolls, and jerk chicken. Open daily for lunch (except Mon) and dinner.

Rocky Mountain Joe's Café 1410 Pearl St. Open daily until 2pm and decorated with local historic photos, Joe's serves numerous breakfast options and wholesome quiches, soups, and sandwiches for lunch. The excellent fresh muffins and tasty banana bread are both worth stopping in for.

Nightlife and entertainment

For a town of only 100,000 people, Boulder more than does itself justice once night rolls on thanks largely to the gregarious CU crowd. Not only do they keep the few small bars on University Hill lively, they also spill downtown onto **Pearl Street** where the combination of revelers and evening buskers often keep it as busy on summer nights as it is during the day. And while the bulk of the local nightlife (including the brewhouses listed above) is dotted around the pedestrian mall, the live music scene is centered up on the Hill. The **Fox Theater**, 1135 13th St (☎303/447-9848), a converted movie theater, and the longstanding **Tulagi**, 1129 13th (☎303/442-1369), both pull in local and decently well-known national bands. While dance and theater performances are put on by the University in various campus halls, the major venue in town is the **Boulder Theater** (ⓣ303/786-7030), where the **Boulder Philharmonic** (ⓣ303/449-1343, ⓦwww.boulderphil.com) often plays on Fridays and Saturdays. Up-to-date listings can be found in the "Friday" magazine in the *Daily Camera*, available from newsagents, and the free *Boulder Planet* and *Boulder Weekly* papers found in cafés and numerous downtown dispensers. A note to **smokers**: Californian-style restrictions on smoking in public buildings are enforced throughout Boulder, so to take a drag you'll have to head out onto the street or into a sealed room within a bar.

Catacombs *Hotel Boulderado*, 2115 13th St. Atmospheric vaults beneath the oldest hotel in town that draw a mixed crowd – not just students – to its almost nightly live blues, jazz, and acoustic music.
The Foundry 1109 Walnut St ⓣ303/447-1803. The bulk of the club's huge area is devoted to a dozen or so full-size pool tables. The small bar beside offers numerous draft beers and hums on weekend nights when jazz and blues plays alongside the tiny dance floor.
K's China 1325 Broadway ⓣ303/413-0000. Budget Chinese restaurant, whose role as late-opening (until 2am), crowded, and boisterous rooftop bar – from where there are superb views of downtown Boulder and the Flatirons – has long overshadowed its importance as an eatery.
La Iguana 1301 Broadway ⓣ303/938-8888. Gregarious large outdoor bar, often with cheap deals on Mexican beers, at the northern end of the Hill district.
'round Midnight 1005 Pearl St ⓣ303/442-2176. The packed weekend dance floor is your best bet for getting your groove on downtown. On weekend nights the dance floor vibrates to mainly hip-hop. A $3 cover is charged.
The Walrus 1911 11th St. Good atmosphere in a consistently bustling bar, with pool tables, a jukebox, plenty of neon, and shells from free peanuts scattered throughout by self-consciously grungy college crowd that heads here to party.
West End Tavern 926 Pearl St ⓣ303/444-3535. Great venue for live jazz and comedy, with local microbrews and spectacular Flatiron views from the roof terrace.

Listings

Banks ATMs located all along the Hill and Pearl St. The Norwest Bank, just beyond the pedestrian mall on 1242 Pearl St (ⓣ303/442-0351), offers most other banking services.
Books Boulder Bookstore, 1107 Pearl St (ⓣ303/447-2074 or 1-800/244-4651), is the best all-round bookstore in town. There are also several special-interest bookshops along Pearl St.
Car rental Alamo ⓣ1-800/327-9633; Avis ⓣ303/499-1136; Dollar ⓣ1-800/800-4000; Price King ⓣ303/545-6600.
Emergency Call ⓣ911. Otherwise, call the Boulder police on ⓣ303/441-4444.
Golf The Par 70 Flatiron course, 5706 Arapahoe (ⓣ303/442-7801) costs $27 for eighteen holes and is one of five local courses.
Internet The public library, 1000 Canyon Drive (ⓣ303/441-3111), has numerous free public terminals.
Laundry Dozy Duds, 1150 University Ave (7am–11.30pm), is one of a number of places around the University Hill area.
Medical King Soopers, 1650 30th St (ⓣ303/444-0164) is a supermarket with a 24hr pharmacy. Boulder Community Hospital, 1100 Balsam Ave (ⓣ303/440-2273), is off N Broadway.
Post office The main post office is at 1905 15th St.

Travel details

Flights

(all services United Airlines unless otherwise stated)
Denver to: Alamosa CO (3 daily; 1hr); Aspen (14 daily; 45 min); Boise ID (7 daily; 1hr 55min); Cheyenne WY (6 daily; 40min); Cody WY (6 daily; 1hr 50min); Colorado Springs (17 daily; 40min); Cortez CO (4 daily; 1hr 20min); Durango (11 daily; 1hr 20min); Eagle (Vail) (5 daily; 45min); Grand Junction (12 daily; 1hr 10min); Gunnison (8 daily; 1hr); Hayden (Steamboat) (12 daily; 50min); Jackson Hole WY (4 daily; 1hr 55min); Laramie WY (4 daily; 50min); Pueblo (4 daily; 40min); Salt Lake City UT (16 daily; 1hr 20min; Delta, Frontier and United); Telluride (5 daily; 1hr 10min).

Trains

(all services are Amtrak):
Denver to: Glenwood Springs (1 daily 6hr 27min); Granby(1 daily 3hr 10min); Grand Junction (1 daily 8hr 35min); Salt Lake City(1 daily; 25hr 50min); Winter Park (1daily; 2hr 40min).

Buses

(all buses are Greyhound unless otherwise stated)
Denver to: Alamosa (1daily; 5hr 50min; TNM&O); Boulder (24 daily; 50 min; RTD); Cheyenne WY (3 daily; 3hr 20min); Cody WY (1daily; 12hr 10min); Colorado Springs (11 daily; 1hr 40min; TNM&O and Greyhound); Craig (2 daily; 5hr 40min); Durango (1 daily; 11hr 50min); Fort Collins (3 daily direct; 1hr 15min); Glenwood Springs (4 daily; 3hr 45min); Granby (2 daily; 2hr); Grand Junction (4 daily; 5hr 50min; TNM&O and Greyhound); Gunnison (1 daily; 7hr 30min); Hot Sulphur Springs (2 daily; 2hr 35min), Kremmling (2 daily; 3hr); Hot Sulphur Springs (2 daily; 2hr 40min); Montrose (2 daily; 9hr 50min); Ouray (1daily; 8hr 30min); Pueblo (11 daily; 2hr 40; TNM&O and Greyhound); Salida (1 daily; 5hr 45min); Salt Lake City (5 daily; 12hr 30min); Silverton (1 daily 9hr 40min); Steamboat Springs (4 daily; 4hr 30min); Trinidad (2 daily; 4hr 30min; TNM&O); Vail (4 daily; 2hr 10min).

Southern Colorado

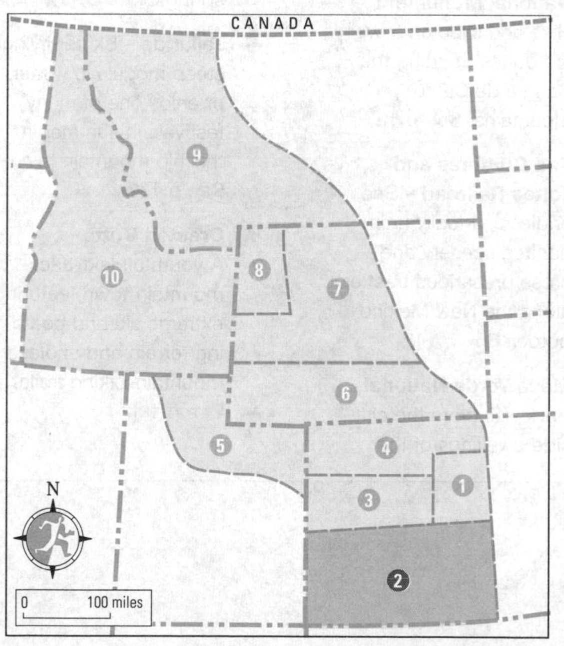

CHAPTER 2

Highlights

* **Bishop's Castle** – Forty miles west of Pueblo stands this bizarre spectacle, built by one man entirely from hand-hauled stones. See p.130

* **Great Sand Dunes National Monument** – Hike and slide on towering dunes abutting the Sangre de Cristo Mountains. See p.137

* **The Cumbres and Toltec Railroad** – See endless, virtually uninhabited scenery and cross precarious trestles along the New Mexico border. See p.142

* **Mesa Verde National Park** – Explore the cliff-side dwellings of the Ancestral Puebloans, the first major civilization in the region. See p.161

* **Orvis Hot Springs** – Bathe naked under the starry sky in the shadow of the mountains at this small, friendly hot springs. See p.172

* **Telluride** – Ski terrifyingly steep moguls in winter, or enjoy one of many festivals in summer in this hip mountain town. See p.173

* **Crested Butte** – A youthful, laid-back mountain town featuring extreme ski and boarding terrain and endless mountain-biking trails. See p.184

Southern Colorado

Though lacking the high-profile ski resorts for which Colorado is best known, some of the state's most stunning, peaceful alpine landscapes, richest historical heritage and best outdoor adventure venues are in **SOUTHERN COLORADO**. This is due in large part to the impressive mountain ranges here which make much of the region relatively inaccessible; the only interstate skirts the very eastern edge, making the most distant, southwest corner of the region a ten-hour drive from Denver.

At one time, the mountains here were home to large settlements of ancient Ancestral Puebloan civilization, mostly concentrated along what is now the southern border with New Mexico. The next major wave of settlers came from the south as well, when the land south of the Arkansas River fell into Mexican hands, leaving vestiges of Hispanic culture not only in the present-day names of the region's towns and mountains, but also in its architecture and food. Once in Anglo-American hands in the mid-nineteenth century, the region underwent its most dramatic changes, as hillsides were ripped open in search of precious ores and tourism, then the fashionable pursuit of the wealthy, prompted the emergence of spa towns. Eventually boom turned to bust in the mining towns, and now most towns in the region rely most heavily on tourism for their major industry. The old Victorian properties, formerly the bars, brothels, gambling dens, and hardware stores of the mining era, have been renovated to host art galleries, outdoor shops, and bakeries – serving not only the needs of the visitor, but also the teleworkers and young bohemians that have been attracted into the area to pursue outdoor sports.

With the exception of the touristy **Pikes Peak** region, it's mostly this lure of the outdoors that brings visitors here as well – camping, hiking, biking, fishing, rafting, and in winter skiing and snowboarding at excellent, lesser-known resorts. The road south of the Pikes Peak region heads into sparsely populated **South**

Accommodation price codes

All accommodation prices in this book have been coded using the symbols below. For **hotels**, **motels**, and **B&Bs**, rates are given for the least expensive double room in each establishment during peak season; variations are indicated where appropriate, including winter rates for all ski resorts. For **hostels**, we've given a specific price per bed; for **camping**, the overnight cost per site is given. For a full explanation see p.30 in Basics.

① up to $30	④ $60–80	⑦ $130–180
② $30–45	⑤ $80–100	⑧ $180–240
③ $45–60	⑥ $100–130	⑨ over $240

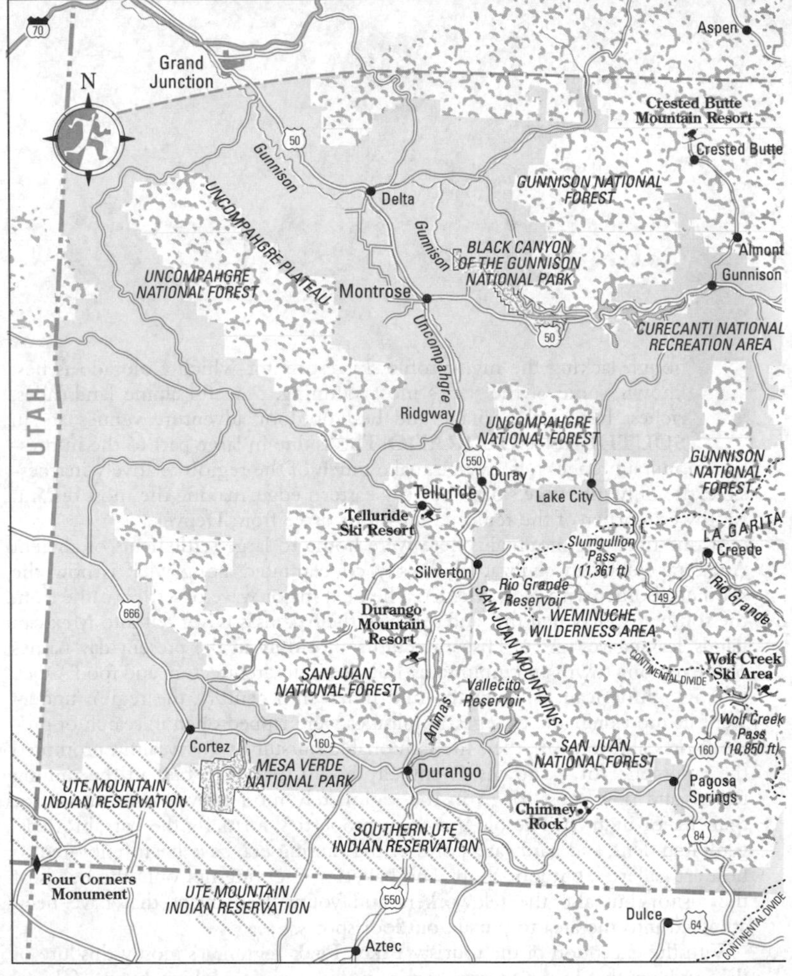

Central Colorado, where the Hispanic influence is marked both in the sleepy towns along the Southern Front Range and in the vast alpine **San Luis Valley**. At the center of the region are the barely penetrable Sangre de Cristo mountains, up beside which lays the **Sand Dunes National Monument**. Most visitors only stop here briefly before heading further west to where the **San Juan Mountains** begin their rise, starting off as almost rolling hills in the east and becoming savage jagged peaks further west along the Continental Divide. Most of the towns in these parts were former Victorian mining camps, whose ramshackle buildings are slowly being renovated to house galleries and outdoor sports shops. Heading still further west, the character of these mountains changes again, forming rolling hills and shrub-covered mesas of the Four Corners

Region, more part of the Southwest than the Rocky Mountains proper. It's in these foothills that the Ancestral Puebloans chose to build their incredible towns, most famously the cliff-dwellings of **Mesa Verde National Park**. A similar dry, dusty landscape lies on the northwest side of the San Juan Range – a surprise after the nearby maze of spectacular ridges and thickly forested peaks. But as you move east through this no man's land between the well-defined mountain ranges to the south and busy central Colorado to the north, the landscape surrounding the fertile **Gunnison** and **Arkansas** river valleys begins to get greener. And with some of the region's largest highways through them, both form a sort of regional crossroads – though in themselves they're marvellous destinations with world-class rafting, mountain biking, hiking, and fishing opportunities.

The Pikes Peak Region

Slightly more than an hour south of Denver on I-25, the crowded and touristy **PIKES PEAK REGION** is Colorado's most popular summer-time destination. Once the goal of gold prospectors heading west with "Pikes Peak or bust" daubed on their wagons, the area now attracts six million annual visitors to sample an array of rather naff delights. Despite these commercial attractions, the region is saved by the presence of the Rocky Mountain foothills, an unheralded and worthwhile destination for hikers and bikers.

Far and away the largest city in the region – and almost synonymous with it – is busy, but mostly bland **Colorado Springs**. Directly alongside it to the west, the small town of **Manitou Springs** rests at the foot of **Pikes Peak** – known around these parts as "America's Mountain." The area is undoubtedly Colorado's capital of cheesy attractions, keeping it jammed with road-tripping families throughout the summer. The surrounding countryside, thankfully, provides an easy escape, and although there's a railway and road up the side of Pikes Peak, it is still both a terrific sight and vantage point. Also in the vicinity is the diverting **Florissant National Monument** – a geological freeze-frame of huge petrified sequoia stumps – and the old gold-rush town of **Cripple Creek**, now a casino center. A short drive south, the striking **Royal Gorge** – a deep canyon through which the foaming Arkansas is pressed – is located beside sleepy **Cañon City**.

Colorado Springs

Seventy miles south of Denver on I-25, where the plains meet the foothills of the magnificent Pikes Peak, is uninspiring **COLORADO SPRINGS**, Colorado's second-largest city. The city was developed in the 1870s as a vacation spot by railroad tycoon William Jackson Palmer, who wished to entice his fiancée here from New York. He built the city several miles east of the raucous Old Colorado City, banning the sale of alcohol and hoping to make it "the most attractive in the west for homes – a place for schools, colleges, literature, science, first-class newspapers, and everything the above implies." But essentially, Palmer saw the town grow to rival other spa towns such as Saratoga Springs, attracting numerous tuberculosis sufferers seeking mountain air and the spring water nearby. The start of the twentieth century was a crucial time in the history of the developing town. The town's fortunes were tied in with those of miners in booming Cripple Creek (see p.120), many of whom built grand mansions around the base of Cheyenne Mountain on the southwest side of town. The massive, Italian-Renaissance style *Broadmoor Hotel*, completed in 1918, was built here by mining mogul Spencer Penrose, also drawn to the notion of developing a spa town. But as most of the mines in Cripple Creek were played out by the 1920s, the town had to look elsewhere for wealth. Building on the town's spa-town image, investment was directed at tourism, and developments included the building of the Pikes Peak Highway. Less predictable was the town's appeal to the military, attracted into the area in increasing numbers from the 1940s on with the building of the United States Air Force Academy and the North American Air Defense Command Headquarters

(NORAD). The town has grown dramatically with this influx and now around a third of the town's population are directly involved with the military, which has helped the town develop into the state's bastion of conservatism.

But in Palmer's former spa town, tourism is still going strong. In the last few decades, Colorado Springs has enthusiastically marketed a number of tawdry tourist traps outside town and around its made-over historic suburb of **Old Colorado City**.

Arrival, information, and getting around

There are a number of inexpensive **flights** from Denver's DIA to Colorado Springs' airport (ⓣ719/550-1900 or 1-800/462-6774, ⓦwww.flycos.com). Alternatively you can book the Colorado Springs Shuttle (ⓣ719/578-5232) or the Super Shuttle (ⓣ303/370-1300 or 1-800/525-3826). Both run services to downtown Colorado Springs from DIA ($27) or the local airport ($13), from where Ride Finders Transportation Center (ⓣ719/385-7433) provides a much cheaper bus service downtown. Otherwise taxis cost around $20. The downtown **bus terminal**, where the Greyhound and TNM&O (ⓣ719/635-1505) buses stop, is at 120 S Weber St. The bus station is also the hub for local public transportation run by Colorado Springs Transit (ⓣ719/475-9733). Bus #1 is a useful service for visitors, with frequent departures to Manitou Springs and the Garden of the Gods (until 6.15pm; $1).

Colorado Springs' **visitor center**, 104 Cascade St (daily: June–Sept 8.30am–5pm; Oct–May 10am–4pm; ⓣ719/635-7506 or 1-800/368-4748, ⓦwww.coloradosprings-travel.com), produces a useful *Official Visitors Guide* and an up to date events guide. These can also be picked up at the visitor information booth at the airport near baggage carousel #2. The Pike National Forest Ranger Service, 601 S Weber St (Mon–Fri 8.30am–4pm; ⓣ719/636-1602), can provide information about the nearby national forest areas, including Pikes Peak. For **guided local tours** contact Pikes Peak Tours (ⓣ719/633-1181 or 1-800/345-8197), who do a good range of trips, as well as organizing trips rafting on the Arkansas.

Accommodation

Apart from the slew of chain lodging off I-25 at the north end of town, most of the town's **accommodation** is concentrated either downtown or around Old Colorado City four miles west on Colorado Avenue heading towards Manitou Springs. A large number of posh B&Bs have also set up shop in both areas, but most exclusive of all is the famous *Broadmoor* resort, outside most people's budgets. In all cases rooms in Colorado Springs regularly get scarce in the summer months. **Camping** options are pretty limited in the immediate environs, although a handful of busy commercial campgrounds, like the *Garden of the Gods Campground*, line Colorado Avenue to the west of town. The nearest USFS camping options are near Rampart Reservoir (see p.113) or along the Gold Camp Road (see p.112).

Central Colorado Springs

The Antlers 4 S Cascade Ave ⓣ719/473-5600 or 1-800/444-2326, ⓦwww.adamsmark.com. Classy modern high-rise on the site of the historic hotel built by the town's founding father William Jackson Palmer. A plush marble lobby sets the establishment's tone, and both the spacious rooms and the well-equipped fitness center on the building's west side have superb views of Pikes Peak. ❼

Hearthstone Inn 506 N Cascade Ave ⓣ719/473-4413 or 1-800/521-1885, ⓦwww.hearthstoneinn.com. Fine B&B in downtown Colorado Springs. Antique-furnished rooms are spread across two properties – one a former sanatorium. Fantastic hearty breakfasts served daily. ❺

Holden House B&B 1102 W Pikes Peak Ave

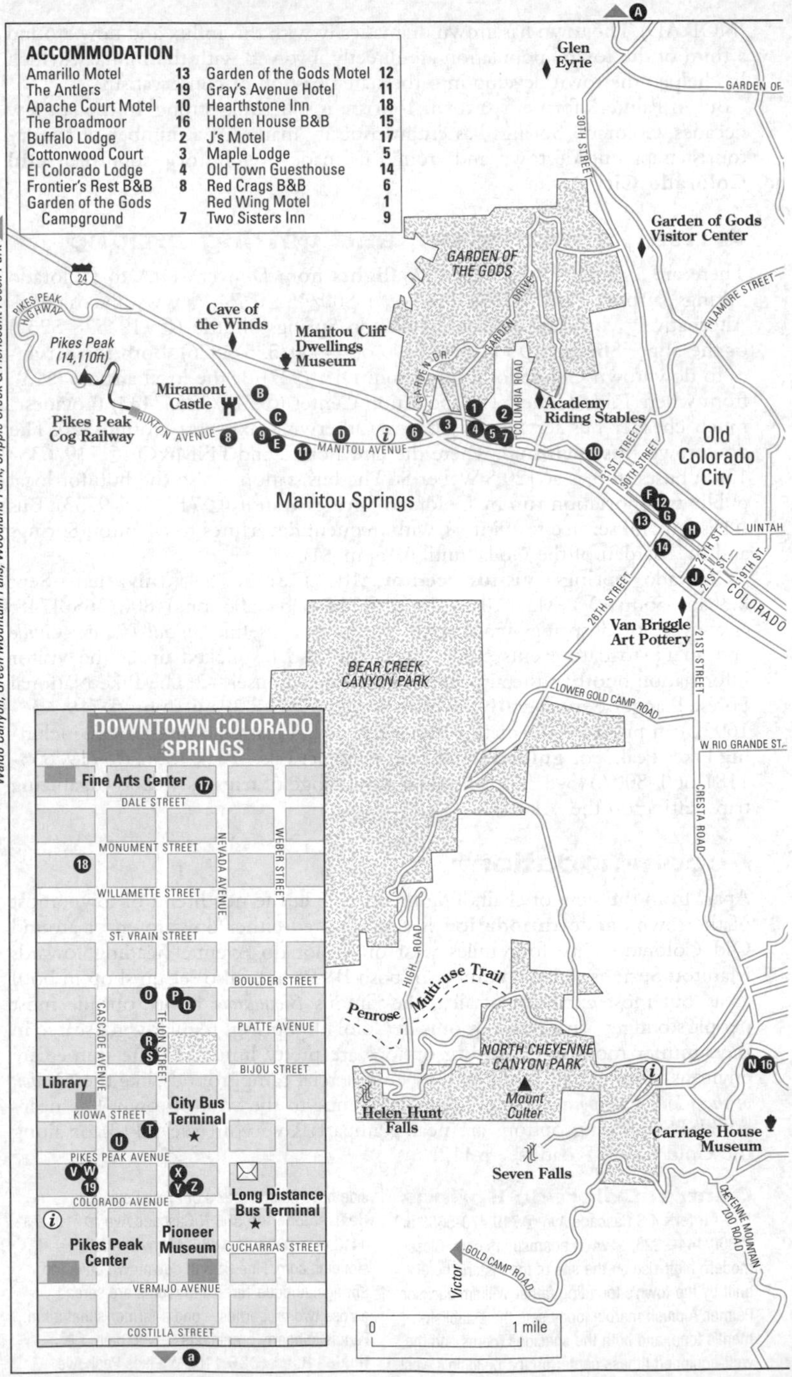

ACCOMMODATION

Amarillo Motel	13	Garden of the Gods Motel	12
The Antlers	19	Gray's Avenue Hotel	11
Apache Court Motel	10	Hearthstone Inn	18
The Broadmoor	16	Holden House B&B	15
Buffalo Lodge	2	J's Motel	17
Cottonwood Court	3	Maple Lodge	5
El Colorado Lodge	4	Old Town Guesthouse	14
Frontier's Rest B&B	8	Red Crags B&B	6
Garden of the Gods		Red Wing Motel	1
Campground	7	Two Sisters Inn	9

Waldo Canyon, Green Mountain Falls, Woodland Park, Cripple Creek & Florissant Fossil Park

Glen Eyrie
Garden of Gods Visitor Center
GARDEN OF THE GODS
Cave of the Winds
Manitou Cliff Dwellings Museum
Pikes Peak (14,110ft)
Miramont Castle
Pikes Peak Cog Railway
Academy Riding Stables
Old Colorado City
Manitou Springs
Van Briggle Art Pottery
BEAR CREEK CANYON PARK
NORTH CHEYENNE CANYON PARK
Penrose Multi-use Trail
Helen Hunt Falls
Mount Culter
Seven Falls
Carriage House Museum
Victor
PIKES PEAK HIGHWAY
RUXTON AVENUE
MANITOU AVENUE
GARDEN DR
GARDEN DRIVE
COLUMBIA ROAD
30TH STREET
31ST STREET
GARDEN OF
FILAMORE STREET
UINTAH
24TH ST
21ST ST
19TH ST
COLORADO
26TH STREET
21ST STREET
LOWER GOLD CAMP ROAD
W RIO GRANDE ST
CRESTA ROAD
HIGH ROAD
GOLD CAMP ROAD
CHEYENNE MOUNTAIN ZOO ROAD
0 1 mile

DOWNTOWN COLORADO SPRINGS

Fine Arts Center
DALE STREET
MONUMENT STREET
WILLAMETTE STREET
ST. VRAIN STREET
BOULDER STREET
PLATTE AVENUE
BIJOU STREET
KIOWA STREET
PIKES PEAK AVENUE
COLORADO AVENUE
CUCHARRAS STREET
VERMIJO AVENUE
COSTILLA STREET
NEVADA AVENUE
WEBER STREET
CASCADE AVENUE
TEJON STREET
Library
City Bus Terminal
Long Distance Bus Terminal
Pioneer Museum
Pikes Peak Center

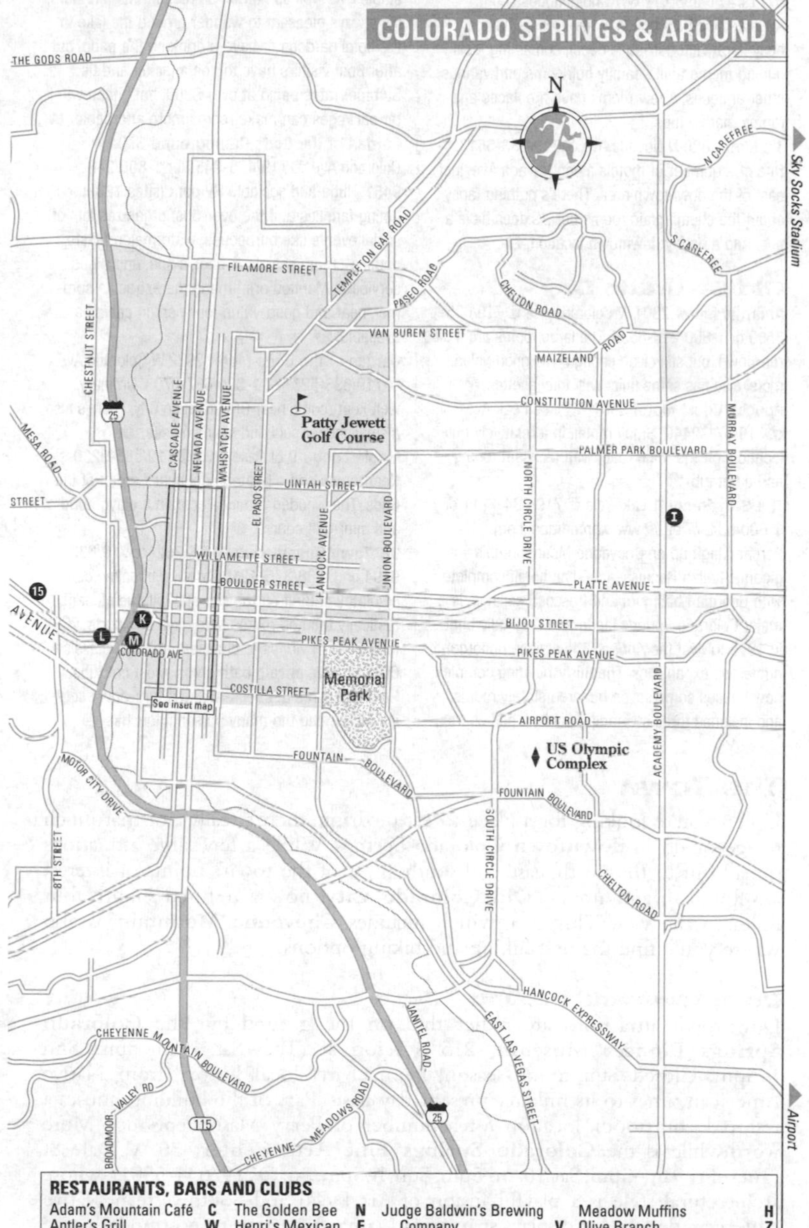

RESTAURANTS, BARS AND CLUBS

Adam's Mountain Café	C	The Golden Bee	N	Judge Baldwin's Brewing Company	V	Meadow Muffins	H
Antler's Grill	W	Henri's Mexican	F	La Baguette	J	Olive Branch	Z
Briarhurst Manor	D	Hide and Seek	L	La Crêperie Restaurant	S	The Phantom Canyon Brewing Co	U
Dutch kitchen	B	HW Brigges Pizza	P	Laffs Comedy Corner	I	Poor Richard's Feed & Read	O
El Tesoro	K	Ichiban	Q	Luigis	a	The Ritz Grill	X
Flying W Chuckwagon	A	Jack Quinn	Y	Manitou Bakery & Café	E	Rum Bay	T
Gertrude's	G	Jose Muldoon's	R				
Giuseppe's Depot	M						

ⓣ719/471-3980, ⓦwww.holdenhouse.com. Another nice B&B option, where rooms have a busy floral Victorian-style décor, containing local mining memorabilia, family heirlooms and various other antiques. A few rooms have fireplaces and roomy marble tubs. 6

J's Motel 820 N Nevada Ave ⓣ719/633-5513. One of a number of motels along Nevada Ave, just east of the downtown area. There's nothing fancy about the cheap, plain rooms but *J's* does have a pool and a handy downtown location. 3

Old Colorado City

Amarillo Motel 2801 W Colorado Ave ⓣ719/635-8539 or 1-800/216-8539. The large rooms are a bit run-down, but still clean enough. The good-value motel also has some units with kitchenettes. 2

Apache Court Motel 3401 W Pikes Peak Ave ⓣ719/471-9440. Small motel, in a relatively quiet location, off the main road, with pleasant rooms and a hot tub. 3

The Broadmoor 1 Lake Ave ⓣ719/634-7711 or 1-800/634-7711, ⓦwww.broadmoor.com. Perched high up on Cheyenne Mountain, this gigantic Italian Renaissance-style hotel, complete with Georgian ballroom and frescoed ceilings, is a major Colorado Springs landmark. Originally built in 1918 to rival the *Antlers*, it has since undergone numerous expansions. The thirty-building complex now houses some seven hundred stately rooms, and includes three swimming pools, a golf course, stables, as well as numerous restaurants and bars. It's always pleasant to wander around the lake in the hotel gardens or have a drink on the patio, but after 6pm visitors have to don a jacket and tie. Summer rates begin at over $300, but cheap winter packages can make rooms more affordable. 9

Garden of the Gods Campground 3704 W Colorado Ave ⓣ719/475-9450 or 1-800/248-9451. Huge and sociable RV park (sites $23) targeting families and the over-50s; organizes lots of social events like barbecues, watermelon feasts, and ice-cream socials. A pool, a spa, and a bus service to Manitou are among the extras. In summer, neat and good-value four-person cabins are available. 2

Garden of the Gods Motel 2922 W Colorado Ave ⓣ719/636-5271 or 1-800/637-0703. Ordinary, well-kept rooms near Old Colorado City. There's also a small indoor pool and sauna on site. 4

Maple Lodge 9 El Paso Blvd ⓣ719/685-9230. Neat rooms and a heated pool near Garden of the Gods. The wooded grounds contain a playground and mini-golf course. 3

Old Town Guesthouse 115 S 26th ⓣ719/632-9194 or 1-888/375-4210, ⓦwww.bbonline.com/co/oldtown. Built on the site of a jail, the elegant, rustically themed rooms here have dataports, VCRs (hundreds of videos to choose from), and classical CDs. All have private bathrooms, most hot tubs. Hors d'oeuvres at check-in and a turn-down service are among the many personal touches. 5

The Town

Unless you're looking for a place to eat or drink, there's really not that much to see or do in **downtown** Colorado Springs. While a few large attractions spread out to the north, east, and south, most of the town's points of interest are found in and around **Old Colorado City**, now a restored suburb four miles to the west. This area, which includes **Cheyenne Mountain**, is also where you'll find the best hiking and biking options.

Downtown and around

Downtown attractions are rather thin on the ground but the **Colorado Springs Pioneer Museum,** 215 S Tejon St (Tues–Sat 10am–5pm, Sun 1–5pm; Closed Sun in off-season; free), charts local history from Native American times to its military present-day basis. Part of the building houses a restored courtroom, location for a number of Perry Mason episodes. More worthwhile is the **Colorado Springs Fine Arts Center**, 30 W Dale St (Tues–Fri 9am–5pm; Sat 10am–5pm; Sun 1–5pm; $6; ⓣ719/634-5581), whose architectural style is a playful fusion of Art Deco and Southwestern Native American design. Art displays span from Native American to postmodern, and some of the more famous pieces include works by Georgia O'Keeffe, Peter Hurd, and Edward Hopper.

A short bus ride (#1; every 30min; $1) east from downtown is the **United States Olympic training center**, 1 Olympic Plaza, Boulder Street and Union

Boulevard (June–Sept Mon–Sat 9am–5pm, Sun 10am–5pm; free; Ⓦwww.usoc.org). Located on a former airforce base, a huge number of athletes, among them swimmers, wrestlers, and cyclists, train here. Free guided **tours** of the training complex – mostly gyms, courts, and pools – leave every half-hour, after an introductory movie that will make you proud to be an American. It's best to arrive early, when you are more likely to see athletes at work, rather than tour around an empty and consequently uninspiring training facility

North of downtown

Surprisingly, the most popular man-made attraction in Colorado is the **United States Air Force Academy**, located fifteen miles north of town on I-25 (daily 9am–5pm; free; Ⓦwww.usafa.af.mil), where beyond observing cadets in formation there's precious little to see. Most entertaining is the **noon formation** (12.30pm), where over four thousand cadets assemble and march to lunch, and observing practice take-offs from the Thunderbird Airmanship Overlook.

Near the Academy's north entrance, the low-key **Western Museum of Mining and Industry**, 125 Gleneagle Drive (June–Sept Mon–Sat 9am–4pm, Sun noon–4pm; $6; Ⓦwww.wmmi.org), displays a vast amount of mining equipment from the Cripple Creek area, including working steam-powered engines and a sluice box where you can pan for gold. More of Western culture is explored south (I-25 exit 147) at the **Pro Rodeo Hall of Fame**, 101 Pro Rodeo Drive (daily 9am–5pm; $6; Ⓣ719/528-4764, Ⓦwww.prorodeo.com). Videos and displays here explain the sport's various disciplines and how it developed out of the needs of early ranch work. The Pikes Peak or Bust Rodeo, held at Penrose Stadium, 1045 W Rio Grande Ave (Ⓣ719/635-3547), in early August, is a major stop on the professional rodeo circuit.

South of downtown

South of town just off CO-115 on the way to Cañon City, located in a nuke-proof set of tunnels on giant shock-absorbers deep within Cheyenne Mountain, is the **North American Air Defense Command Headquarters (NORAD)**, which is and will hopefully remain a chilling souvenir of the Cold War. Nine miles further south is the **May Natural History Museum of the Tropics**, 710 Rock Creek Canyon Rd (May–Sept 8am–8pm; $4.50). The turnoff is marked by a giant beetle, and inside you'll find a massive and quite engaging collection of insects – the lifetime work of one John May. Rather incongruously, the site also contains the **Museum of Space Exploration**, located in a musty trailer full of clippings about the US space program and an assemblage of junk that has the feel of yard-sale pickings.

Old Colorado City and around

Due west of downtown Colorado Springs is **Old Colorado City**. Like many frontier towns, Old Colorado City was a rough place, harboring gambling, drinking and prostitution; by all accounts serving the hypocritical needs of the Victorian gentry of Colorado Springs as much as servicing the desires of miners. Ironically once spurned (at least officially) by decent society, today the core of the old town is now a chic neighborhood. Wooden storefronts and redbrick buildings have been restored to a gussied-up version of their former selves, but now harboring boutiques, restaurants, and bars.

The most rewarding sight hereabouts is the incredible **Garden of the Gods** (daily 5am–11pm; free), on the northern side of Old Colorado City along 30th Street. Made from former dunes and sea beds, this gnarled and warped red-sandstone park was lifted up at the same time as the nearby mountains (around

65 million years ago), but has since been eroded into finely balanced overhangs, jagged pinnacles, and massive pedestals. The **visitor center**, at the park's eastern border (daily: summer 8am–9pm; winter 9am–6pm; Ⓦwww.gardenofgods.com), has details of hiking and mountain-biking trails. Skip the movie ($2) and instead relax with a drink from the center's snack bar, which has great views over the park.

Further north on 30th Street, around two miles north of Colorado City, **Glen Eyrie** (tours at 1pm, sometimes more; $5; Ⓣ719/594-2289), is the former mansion of the Colorado Springs' founder William Jackson Palmer. The 67-room, Tudor-style castle reveals his affection for European finery, including roof tiles off an old English church and a fireplace hand-carved by Benedictine monks in the Middle Ages. Today the mansion is in the hands of a ministry, The Navigators, who allow the public to drive through the grounds and arrange regular tours.

Cheyenne Mountain and around

South of Old Colorado City and southwest of downtown Colorado Springs is Cheyenne Mountain. Its large, gently sloping base holds the grand *Broadmoor Hotel* (see p.110) and leafy suburban districts, close to the superb North Cheyenne Canyon Mountain Park. Several small attractions have clustered around the *Broadmoor Hotel*, including the **Carriage House Museum** (Mon–Sat 10am–noon & 1–5pm; free), opposite the hotel's main building on Lake Circle. The museum houses over thirty vehicles from the collection of Spencer Penrose, also the main force behind the building of the Pikes Peak Highway. About a mile south of the *Broadmoor*, the **Cheyenne Mountain Zoo** (June–Aug 9am–4pm; Sept–May 9am–5pm; $8.50; Ⓦwww.cmzoo.org) provides a mountain setting for around five hundred animals.

Further west on Cheyenne Mountain is **Seven Falls** (mid-May to Aug 8am–11pm; Sept to mid-May 9am–4pm; $7; Ⓣ719/632-0741), an attraction focusing on a nearly 200-foot-long waterfall cascading down the steep-sided South Cheyenne Canyon. Without a doubt a spectacular spot, particularly during the spring snowmelt, it's unfortunate that the adulteration of the waterfall by additional piped-in music, colored lights, elevators, and Native-American dances only lessens their natural beauty.

The falls are better kept at a distance and viewed from **North Cheyenne Canyon Park** (daily: June–Sept 5am–11pm; Oct–May 5am–9pm; free), just north of Seven Falls. The park is based around a steep-sided and densely vegetated canyon, entered into beside the park's information center (daily 9am–5pm; Ⓣ719/578-6146), who organize free events like children's wildlife programs and introductory climbing sessions and provides a free map of canyon hikes. From here, the road climbs up the canyon, past trailheads for the Mount Culter Trail and, as it rises to a switchback the beginning of the hike to Helen Hunt Falls (see box, opposite). Beyond the trailhead the road climbs up to a large dusty parking lot and junction of three dirt roads. From here, two are open to motor vehicles – **High Drive** and the **Lower Gold Camp Road** – and both are scenic drives leading to the western edge of Colorado Springs, passing **Bear Creek Regional Park** – where two miles of easy nature trails have been set out – en route. The third dirt road, the **Gold Camp Road**, follows the course of an old railroad track to Victor, a 36-mile tour that takes two-and-a-half hours to navigate (road conditions Ⓣ719/385-5940). The start of the trail is closed off to motor vehicles, but you can join it part way along from the **Old Cripple Creek Stagecoach Road**. Though not signposted, the start of this route to Cripple Creek is found fairly easily by taking the Old

Stagecoach Road, the continuation of Cheyenne Mountain Boulevard, from Penrose Boulevard, about a mile south of the *Broadmoor Hotel*. The craggy, mountain scenery in the shadow of Pikes Peak along this route was felt by Theodore Roosevelt to "bankrupt the English language." The road passes a couple of Forest Service **campgrounds** as well.

Outdoor activities and outfitters around Colorado Springs

Though few come to the area specifically for outdoor recreation, the **hiking** and **biking** trails laced through the mountain parks and national forest lands around Colorado Springs are well worth hitting up. Some of the most spectacular and convenient are in **North Cheyenne Canyon Park** (see opposite). One of the easiest hikes here is the satisfying 3.5 mile round-trip **Mount Culter Trail**, which climbs 500ft with views of the distant Seven Falls. Further up the valley, another small information booth sits at the base of the trail to **Helen Hunt Falls**. From the road it's a five-mile round-trip to the scenic mountain waterfall, plunging into the narrow North Cheyenne canyon. In addition to these short and popular trails, there are also several good longer ones, including the excellent single-track **Mt Buckhorn Trail**, a two-hour ride or a good four-hour hike through woodland with views over Colorado Springs. The trail begins from the Upper Gold Camp Road as the unmarked Buckhorn Cutoff (just before crossing North Cheyenne Creek), which zigzags its way up to the top of Mt Buckhorn for good views over Cheyenne Canyon. From here it's a sandy single-track descent to **Captain Jack's** – a parking lot on the High Drive road. By crossing High Drive you can get onto the **Penrose Multi-use** which heads north then east before descending down a (sometimes slippery) luge-like single-track to the Lower Gold Camp Road, which you can climb back to the start.

Another great trail for both hikers and bikers, with great views of Pikes Peak, is a seven-mile loop that takes in the lush **Waldo Canyon**. Beginning from an easily missed parking lot ten miles northwest of Colorado Springs along Hwy-24, the popular trail takes around three hours to hike and about two hours to mountain-bike – though the steep, loose nature of some of the single-track demands some skill and experience. The loop starts steeply, soon working its way clear of the highway and up into beautiful wooded terrain, with some of the area's best views of Pikes Peak and Cheyenne Mountain. The trail begins to descend, then heads to an intersection where mountain bikers usually turn left to complete a clockwise loop, returning back to this point.

Woodland Park, eighteen miles northwest of Colorado Springs along Hwy-24, is a gateway to recreational opportunities in the Pike National Forest. In particular, the **Rampart Reservoir** is a good spot to explore as it offers some excellent hiking, mountain biking and fishing (rainbow trout) along with great views of Pikes Peak. To get to Rampart Reservoir from Woodland Park, take the turnoff at the southern end of town, beside the *McDonald's* and Team Telecycle bike shop (ⓣ719/687-6165; front suspension mountain bikes from $25/day) onto Baldwin Street. This soon becomes Rampart Range Road, with Rampart Reservoir signposted four miles further on. The **Rainbow Gulch** trailhead is three miles beyond this sign, and the path here follows alongside a crystal stream leading to the shores of the placid reservoir, which is encircled by twelve miles of undulating single track. This makes for a superb three-hour mountain bike ride (five-hour hike) with no real climbing, but enough challenging sections to keep experts awake.

Colorado Spring's best outfitters include Mountain Chalet, on 226 N Tejon St (ⓣ719/633-0732), and Blick's Sporting Goods, 119 N Tejon St (ⓣ719/636-3348), which contains the Pikes Peak Angler, good for advice on local fishing and gear. For **bike rentals** try Bicycle Village, 5660 N Academy Blvd (ⓣ719/265-9346, ⓦwww.bicyclevillage.com), who rent out front-suspension mountain bikes for $25/day.

Eating and drinking

Though there's a cosmopolitan range to choose from, Colorado Springs has a fairly small number of **restaurants**. Most are downtown, though a few worthwhile options operate out of Old Colorado City. The city's downtown **bars** and **brewpubs** are often good sources for cheap, filling, quality food. If nothing catches your eye, nearby Manitou Springs extends the local dining opportunities (see p.116).

Downtown Colorado Springs

Antler's Grill *Antler's Hotel*, 4 S Cascade Ave. The excellent-value breakfast buffet ($11) and Sunday brunch offer up plenty of choices, and the dark-wood restaurant opens for upscale dinners too, serving Rocky Mountain favorites like elk, buffalo, and trout. On Fridays, wild game is offered at half-price.

El Tesoro 10 N Sierra Madre St. The former brothel now doubles as an art gallery and restaurant serving excellent northern Mexican and New Mexican food; the menu features creative departures like mango quesadillas or spinach and mushroom burritos sautéed in white wine ($12). Killer margaritas too. Closed Sun.

Giuseppe's Depot 10 S Sierra Madre St. Views over the railroad yards can make for interesting scenery while eating great pizzas, subs ($6), steaks ($15), seafood, or the superb lasagna.

HW Brigges Pizza 333 N Tejon ⓣ719/471-9984. Student-friendly sports bar serving good-value slabs of pie. Various sports paraphernalia dangle throughout the cavernous restaurant, which turns into a bustling bar later on. Wednesday night is an affordable all-you-can-eat pizza night.

Ichiban Japanese Cuisine 333 N Tejon. Decent-value, carefully prepared sushi for lunch and dinner in a spacious redbrick restaurant. Prices are cut by thirty percent from 5–8pm.

Jose Muldoon's 222 Tejon St. The combination of a bar and a restaurant here makes *Muldoon's* a reliable choice for ordering a margarita to wash down Mexican food (entrees around $8) on an outdoor patio. The restaurant holds the record for world's largest margarita (4756.5 gallons); more notable perhaps is the fact that the huge vat was emptied inside four days. Open for lunch and dinner.

Judge Baldwin's Brewing Company *Antler's Hotel*, 4 S Cascade Ave. The first brewpub in town serves up a good range of beers and serves excellent inexpensive bar food; burgers, quesadillas, soups, and salads (all around $6). Open for lunch and dinner.

La Crêperie Restaurant 204 N Tejon Ave ⓣ719/632-0984. Stylish and small, this popular restaurant serves up a variety of delicious savory crepes ($9) and other French fare; filet mignon and veal cutlets ($20) also make an appearance on the slightly pretentious sounding menu. Unsurprisingly, sweet crepes ($3) are available for dessert.

Luigis 947 S Tejon. A longstanding family-run institution located nine blocks south of downtown. The superb homemade Italian food makes it a deservedly popular local stop-off; pastas ($9) are offered in a wide range of sauces.

Olive Branch 23 S Tejon. Best known for its huge breakfast menu, featuring numerous types of omelettes ($5). The good vegetarian food served for lunch and dinner features a large selection of salads.

The Phantom Canyon Brewing Co 2 E Pikes Peak Ave. A great place for microbrews, authentic pub food and even some refined seafood options. Lunch entrees are around $7, dinners $11. Popular evening haunt too, with a number of pool tables.

Poor Richard's Feed and Read 824 1/2 N Tejon St. Popular with the college crowd for healthy vegetarian fare and a full range of sandwiches ($6) and pizzas eaten among numerous piles of books. Open until 10pm.

Old Colorado City

Flying W Chuckwagon Supper 3300 Chuckwagon Rd, north past Garden of the Gods (mid-May to Sept daily 7.15pm; Oct to mid-May Fri & Sat 5pm & 8pm; $15–19; ⓣ719/598-4000, ⓦwww.flyingw.com. A fun and vast outdoor picnic with accompanying wrangler and Western music show. Baked beans, beef, and fresh biscuits are doled out to up to 1400 guests seated at long picnic tables. Arrive early (from 4.30pm) to view the reconstructed Old West town – including a jail, smithy, and various knickknack shops.

Gertrude's 2625 W Colorado. Upscale restaurant that takes pride in its eclectic menu, including plenty of vegetarian options amongst the fresh baked goods, salads, soups, pasta, and grilled meats on offer. Open for breakfast, lunch and dinner. Closed Monday evening.

Henri's Mexican 2427 W Colorado Ave ⓣ719/634-9031. Family-owned favorite that pulls in the crowds for home-style cooking like stuffed sopaipillas and shrimp chiles rellenos ($9). Both their mole sauce and potent margaritas are superb. Live music on Fridays and Saturdays.

La Baguette 2417 W Colorado. Breakfast here kicks off at 7am and includes fantastic blueberry croissants. Lunches consist of great simple fare like salads, pasta, soups, and, as the name implies, great bread.

Nightlife and entertainment

Weekend nights downtown are best spent bar- and club-hopping along Tejon Street. The most popular venue for more sedate events is the sleek **Pikes Peak Center**, 190 S Cascade Ave (☎719/520-7469), which hosts regular symphonies, as well as touring theater and dance performances in the summer. For detailed entertainment listings, check out Friday's "Scene" in the *Gazette Telegraph*, or the free weekly events guide *Go!*, available in stands all over town.

The Golden Bee International Center, *Broadmoor Hotel*. This "authentic" British pub was shipped in pieces and rebuilt here and now serves supposed English favorites like kidney pies along with yards of ale while a ragtime piano player encourages a party atmosphere.

Hide and Seek 512 W Colorado ☎719/634-9303. A massive gay bar, complete with Country, sports and dancing-themed areas, that's been open since the 1970s. There's also an onsite restaurant.

Jack Quinn 21 S Tejon. Cheerful and popular downtown Irish pub with local bands on weekend nights.

Laffs Comedy Corner 1305 N Academy Blvd ☎719/591-0707. Stand-up comedy club east of downtown; mostly local hopefuls but occasionally a nationally-known act stops by.

Meadow Muffins 2432 W Colorado Ave ☎719/633-0583. This boisterous and friendly Old Colorado City bar is one of area's best, festooned with trinkets and local memorabilia. There are quite a few pool tables and weekend nights (no cover) see live music, late opening (until 2am) and a heaving dance floor. If the munchies strike, try the quirky Jiffy burger – topped with peanut butter and bacon.

The Ritz Grill 15 S Tejon. By day an Art Deco-style grill serving American favorites, by night a packed bar attracting a mix of age groups, with live pop music on weekends.

Rum Bay 20 N Tejon. A vague Caribbean theme is played out throughout this large downtown bar and club, where the youngish crowd seems most intent on drinking and shaking on the tiny dance floor. Small cover charge.

Listings

Car rental Most of the major names in car rental can be found in town or at the airport. Enterprise, 803 W Colorado Ave (☎719/636-3900), will pick-up and deliver their cars; Budget, 303 W Bijou St (☎719/574-7400 or 1-800/831-2847), are conveniently located beside I-25 near downtown. A local company with low rates is Xpress Rent-a-Car, 2021 E Platte Ave (☎719/634-1914 or 1-800/634-1914, Ⓦwww.bnm.com/xpress).

Golf The municipal and reasonably central Patty Jewett, 900 E Española St (☎719/578-6825) has 27 holes. A more interesting course, with elevation changes, numerous bunkers, trees, creeks, and lakes, is the eighteen-hole Pine Creek, 9850 Divot Trail (☎719/594-9999).

Horseback riding Academy Riding Stables, 4 El Paso Blvd (☎719/633-5667 or 1-800/700-0410, Ⓦwww.arsriding.com), organize one- to two-hour jaunts to the Garden of the Gods ($20).

Internet The downtown Penrose Public Library, corner of Kiowa and Cascade, has free access.

Laundry King's Cleaners, 1536 S Nevada St, is just south of downtown.

Medical Walgreen's operates a 24hr pharmacy at 2727 Palmer Park (☎719/473-9090). Local referral services exist for both dentists (☎719/598-5161) and doctors (☎719/444-2273). May Hospital, 1400 E Boulder St (☎719/475-5000), is east of downtown.

Police ☎719/635-6611; call ☎911 for emergencies.

Post office The main post office is at 201 E Pikes Peak Ave (zip 80903).

Spectator sports Superb atmosphere, cheap tickets, and good seats make the minor league baseball team, the Sky Socks (April–Sept; from $4; ☎719/597-3000), well worth watching. They play in Sandcreek Community Park in the Stetson Hills; exit 146 off the I-25, six miles east on Austin Bluffs Parkway, right onto Barns Rd for two miles. The college football team, the Air Force Academy Falcons (☎719/472-1895 or 1-800/666-USAF), are very popular; games on Sat from Aug–Nov.

Taxis Yellow Cab (☎719/634-5000).

Manitou Springs and around

Despite being an incorporated city, the limits of **Manitou Springs** blend nearly seamlessly with Old Colorado City, making it feel like another historic suburb of Colorado Springs, ten miles to the east. Long before these towns existed, though, Native American tribes – Arapaho, Cheyenne, Kiowa, and particularly the Ute – considered the mineral springs here sacred, stopping off during annual migrations to buffalo hunting grounds. As early as the 1820s, whites began reporting on the water's health benefits, and within fifty years Colorado Springs founder William Jackson Palmer, along with Dr William Bell, an English physician convinced of the springs' miracle cures, had turned the once tranquil valley into a European-style spa town. Within a few years, bottled concoctions of the spring water, like the optimistically named Manitou Ginger Champagne, were being shipped across the country; as the spa's profile grew, notables like presidents Roosevelt and Ulysses S. Grant, P.T Barnum, and Thomas Edison all came for a dip. While few make the pilgrimage today solely to soak, Manitou continues to attract visitors with a motley assortment of attractions and its location near Pike Peak. The busy center has managed to retain some of its historical feel, but due to a preponderance of gift shops and tacky attractions, it ultimately comes across as a tourist trap.

Information and accommodation

The chamber of commerce (ⓣ719/685-5089 or 1-800/642-2567, ⓦwww.manitousprings.org), along with the Pikes Peak Country Attractions Association (ⓣ1-800/525-2250, ⓦwww.pikes-peak.com), provide a **visitor information center** on the eastern end of town at 354 Manitou Ave (daily 9am–5pm). For tours, a **town trolley** (hourly: May–Sept 9am–8pm), complete with historic commentary, runs up and down Manitou Avenue; tickets operate as day-passes allowing you to hop on an off the service.

Dozens of Ma-and-Pa **motels** line busy Manitou Avenue (called Colorado Ave further east) on its way into town from Old Colorado City. A few **bed and breakfasts** have also clustered around the side streets near the historic core, offering more luxurious rooms. To avoid the humdrum of town in favor of a peaceful mountain setting, consider heading west of Manitou Springs along Hwy-24, either six miles to the town of Green Mountain Falls, or fifteen miles to Woodland Park.

Manitou Springs

Buffalo Lodge 2 El Paso Blvd ⓣ719/634-2851 or 1-800/235-7416, ⓦwww.buffalolodge.com. The creekside location helps with the rustic charm of a number of different accommodation options that range from badly worn motel rooms to fancy renovated lodgings. Heated pool and hot tubs available and continental breakfast included. ④

Cottonwood Court 120 Manitou Ave ⓣ719/685-1312 or 1-888/227-8047, ⓦwww.cottonwood-court.com. Small and neat motel rooms, most of which are set back from the busy road. All units include microwave and fridge, cable TV, and phones. Rates also include use of the small swimming pool and a continental breakfast. ③

El Colorado Lodge 23 Manitou Ave ⓣ719/685-5485 or 1-800/782-2246. Economical southwestern-style cabins, many with fireplaces and beamed ceilings; most have kitchenettes and some sleep six. ③

Frontier's Rest Bed and Breakfast 341 Ruxton Ave ⓣ719/685-0588 or 1-800/455-0588, ⓦwww.colorado-springs-inn.com. Four tasteful, country-style rooms, including a particularly roomy suite with its own hot tub, in an 1890s residence with a pleasant porch. Close to downtown and a short walk from the Pikes Peak Railway and several hiking trails. Excellent breakfasts. ⑥

Gray's Avenue Hotel 711 Manitou Ave ⓣ719/685-1277 or 1-800/294-1277, ⓦwww.pikespeakmall.com/graysb&b. Bed and breakfast with large common rooms and a big front porch overlooking Manitou Ave. All rooms have private baths. The outside hot tub is open all year. ④

Red Crags B&B 302 El Paso Blvd ⓣ719/685-1920 or 1-800/721-2248, ⓦwww.redcrags.com. Beautifully located property, a mile east of downtown Manitou Springs, with views of Pikes Peak and the Garden of the Gods from its landscaped grounds, duck pond, and outdoor hot tub. Built by town founder Dr Bell sometime around 1880. ⑤

Red Wing Motel 56 El Paso Blvd ⓣ719/685-5655 or 1-800/RED-9547, ⓔredwingmotel@pikes-peak.com. Clean and simple rooms near the southern entrance of the Garden of the Gods – one of the quietest locations in town. Rooms include basic kitchens and the grounds include a small heated pool and a playground. ③

Two Sisters Inn 10 Otoe Place ⓣ719/685-9684 or 1-800/274-7466, ⓦwww.twosisinn.com. Originally a late-1800s boarding house for teachers, this inn retains a fine Victorian feel. Breakfast, eaten with silverware, is a decidedly gourmet affair. ⑤

Green Mountain Falls and Woodland Park

Campground at Woodland Park 1125 Bowman Ave, Woodland Park ⓣ719/687-7575 or 1-800/808-2267. Relatively small campground off Hwy-67 a couple of miles outside Woodland Park with both RV ($25, full hookup) and tent ($20) sites dotted among pine trees. There are also a few two-person cabins here ($35). Facilities include laundry, hot tub, swimming pool, and mini-golf.

Elwell's Cabins 2220 Lee Circle Drive, Woodland Park ⓣ719/687-9838. Five rustic log cabins, well spread-out and furnished with hand-hewn log furniture and antiques, sleep up to four. ③

Falls Motel Green Mountain Falls ⓣ719/684-9745. Small roadside motel where many rooms have kitchens and there's a communal hot tub; has an inviting shady picnic area beside a small lake. ③

The Lofthouse 222 E Henrietta, Woodland Park ⓣ719/687-9187. Clean comfortable motel on the hill above town; units have kitchenettes. ④

Sky Vue Motel Green Mountain Falls ⓣ719/684-2611. A slightly dated hotel with spacious units containing fridge and microwave along with clear mountain views. Good-value weekly rates ($150). ③

Woodland Inn B&B 159 Trull Rd, Woodland Park ⓣ719/687-8209 or 1-800/226-9565, ⓦwww.bbonline.com/co/woodland. A pleasant B&B located on twelve wooded acres that provide great Pikes Peak views; rooms are spacious and breakfast is served in a fireplace-warmed dining room. ③

The town and around

Sandwiched in a circular redbrick building in between trinket shops, the **Shoshone Spring** is the most obvious spring in the center of town, where you can step up and drink the water. For a greater variety of waters, head east along the main road to the small **Soda Springs Park**, where the Cheyenne, Soda, and Navajo springs can be sampled. Despite the decidedly "medicinal" taste of the waters, a walking tour around the rest of the springs is worth the effort and the chamber of commerce (see opposite) can provide a self-guided tour leaflet.

Besides the springs, the only real site in town is **Miramont Castle**, 9 Capital Hill Ave (June–Aug 10am–5pm; Sept–May 11am–4pm; $4; ⓣ719/685-1011). The extravagant former residence of a French priest, who came looking for a cure for his tuberculosis, is a medley of six architectural styles, with Swiss chalet, San Francisco Victorian, and medieval castle included in the mix. Most of the furnishings are period pieces and various rooms contain odd collections (like dolls) which help make a visit worthwhile.

The outlying attractions

Several **attractions** have accumulated around Manitou Springs, including entirely-missable ones like the improbably located North Pole and Santa's Workshop. Of them all, the most high profile is the **Cave of the Winds**, just north of town beside US-24 (daily: May–Sept 9am–8pm; Oct–April 10am–5pm; ⓣ719/685-5444, ⓦwww.caveofthewinds.com), a series of labyrinthine underground caverns that walks the fine line between dramatic natural beauty and crass tourist tat. The tacky, 45min **discovery tour** ($15) should be avoided in favor of the atmospheric **lantern tour** ($18), which takes you around pretty much the same route, but with only the guidance of hand-held light. Better still is the opportunity to do some more genuine speleology, crawling around the narrow, twisting caverns in old clothes on the **explorers trip** ($80). The huge limestone walls of the canyon below the caves are used for nightly **laser shows** (9pm; $7); predictably overhyped and cheesy – yet still impressive thanks to the beauty of the natural backdrop.

A short way further east along US-24, the **Manitou Cliff Dwellings Museum** (June–Aug 9am–8pm; Sept–May 9am–5pm; $7; ⓣ719/685-5242, ⓦwww.cliffdwellingsmuseum.com) centers around a number of cliff dwellings hauled here in the early 1920s from Montezuma, around 300 miles southwest. Similar to those used by the Ancestral Puebloans around Mesa Verde (see p.161), the structures, allegedly under threat of souvenir hunters, were moved here in a painstaking process, whereby each stone was carefully marked by its position prior to disassembly, then repositioned exactly to replicate the 600-year-old originals. Sadly, no reference is made to this background in the museum itself. In fact, there's very little illuminating information in the museum at all, though the much larger **gift shop** nearby has plenty to say (and sell). In front of the dwellings, a rather fuzzy cultural link is made with regular frantic dances by plains Indians; a European cultural equivalent might be Scottish country dancing displays outside a medieval French chateaux.

Eating and drinking

Gathered around Manitou's historic area are a surprising number of good **restaurants**, serving up a wide range of food. The **bar** scene, however, is tiny and rarely exciting.

Adam's Mountain Café 110 Cañon Ave ⓣ719/685-1430. A grandma's-parlor-style café serving mainly Southwestern nouvelle cuisine. Breakfasts include egg burritos as well as excellent muffins and juices. The lunch menu features mainly sandwiches and pasta ($6–10), the dinner menu catering to a wider range of tastes, including Thai-style vegetables and a few good pasta dishes. Dinner entrees run around $10. Closed Sun & Mon evenings.

Briarhurst Manor 404 Manitou Ave ⓣ719/685-1864. Former house of the town's founder, Dr William Bell, now a decidedly high-end and romantic place to eat. Summer evenings see string quartets play on the patio. The fine gourmet food uses mostly organic ingredients and also features local produce like Colorado lamb, or Rocky Mountain trout. The Wednesday night buffet is good value ($18). Open Monday to Saturday; smart-casual dress required.

Dutch kitchen 1035 Manitou Ave. Small family-owned restaurant that makes a good lunch stop for its popular range of sandwiches and splendid fruit pies.

Manitou Bakery & Café 729 Manitou Ave. Bohemian bakery that makes for a good place to start the day with slabs of French toast ($6) or numerous baked goods. Good for sandwiches at lunch, too.

The Pantry Green Mountain Falls. Classic American cuisine dished out in a peaceful setting beside the village's small lake; has a superb reputation in Manitou Springs for filling home-cooked meals. Open for breakfast, lunch, and dinner.

Pikes Peak

Though there are thirty taller mountains in Colorado, **Pikes Peak**, just west of Colorado Springs, is the state's most famous. For years the symbolic gateway to Colorado's goldfields, today it's better known as the summit that inspired Katherine Lee Bates to write a poem entitled "America the Beautiful" – set to music, it quickly became the United State's unofficial second anthem. The 14,110ft peak is named for Zebulon Pike, who crossed its path during an expedition in 1806. After failing an attempt to climb it, he wrote that "no human being could have ascended to its summit." Fourteen years later, Dr Edwin James bagged the peak, and by the end of the century trails had been built to carry rich tourists like Ms Bates to the top. Zebulon, though, must have really rolled in his grave when in 1929, Texan Bill Williams took twenty days and 170 changes of trousers to scale the mountain, while pushing a peanut with his nose. Nowadays, around a quarter of a million people head up each summer via a curvy road, long hike, or quaint railway. Whichever route you choose, set off early, since afternoons tend to be cloudier and often frequented by thunderstorms.

Ascending by car or bike

The most obvious way up is the **Pikes Peak Highway** (May–Sept 7am–7pm; Oct–April 9am–3pm; $10 per person or $35 per car; Ⓣ719/385-7325 or 1-800/318-9505, Ⓦwww.pikespeakcolorado.com), which begins near the town of Cascade, three miles west of Manitou Springs. Though only nineteen miles long (twelve of which are unpaved), the twisting and turning 1916 toll-road takes around two hours to drive. Drivers in the **Pikes Peak Auto Hill Climb** (Ⓦwww.ppihc.com), an annual Fourth of July race held since the 1920s, do it in much less time – the record run took just over ten minutes. Naturally there are superb views from many places, although the peak, dominated by a big parking lot, is a bit of a disappointment. Staying at the *Black Bear Inn*, 5250 Pikes Peak Hwy (Ⓣ719/684-1051 or 1-877/732-5232, Ⓦwww.blackbearinnpikespeak.com; ⑤), partway along the road to the peak, allows plenty of time to enjoy views. Rooms have private baths and there are a few cabins here too. The road can also be used by **cyclists**, and companies like Challenge Unlimited, 204 S 24th St (Ⓣ719/633-6399 or 1-800/798-5954, Ⓦwww.bikithikit.com), rent bikes and have shuttles to the top, allowing you to freewheel back down – tours start at $26.

Ascending by rail

The **Pikes Peak Cog Railway** (mid-May to Nov; $22, reservations advised; Ⓣ719/685-5401, Ⓦwww.cograilway.com) was the first mechanical form of transport to ascend the peak, built by mattress magnate Zalmon G. Simmons after he found his mule ride up overly jarring. Opened in 1891, the red carriages of the thrilling railway grind their way up an average of 847ft per mile on a ninety-minute journey to the summit; from 11,500ft onwards they cross a barren expanse of tundra, scarred by giant scree flows. From the bleak and windswept top, it's possible to see Denver seventy miles north, and the endless prairie to the east, while to the west mile upon mile of giant snowcapped peaks rise into the distance. The train leaves from 515 Ruxton Ave in Manitou Springs; round-trips take 3 hours 15 minutes, including a 40-minute stop on the chilly summit.

Ascending by foot

Though there are trails up from elsewhere (including near Cripple Creek), the **Barr Trail** is the most popular route up Pikes Peak. The thirteen-mile path begins near the Cog Railway terminus, and the steepest part of the entire trail comes first, leveling out as it ascends to the *Barr Camp Cabins* (reservations ⓣ719/630-3934), seven miles from the trailhead and a mile-and-a-half below the treeline. Beyond here, the alpine tundra takes over, harboring numerous delicate plants, flowers, and bighorn sheep. As the air gets thinner the last few miles of switchbacks make the rocky slopes a hard climb. Average hikers manage the trail in twelve hours: eight hours up and four hours down.

Florissant National Monument

Protecting part of a massive expanse covered by volcanic ash 35 million years ago, **Florissant National Monument** (daily: June–Aug 8am–7pm; Sept–May 8am–4pm; $2; ⓦwww.nps.gov/flfo) is an arid mountain valley littered with fossil-filled rocks and petrified trees. Thirty miles west of Colorado Springs on US-24, the lightly wooded monument contains one of the most perfect records of Eocene natural history found anywhere; an era when Colorado was lush with palm trees, redwoods, and willows and thousands of species of insects thrived around the long-gone Lake Florissant. First discovered by settlers unearthing the skeleton of a mastodon, the area soon became a huge fossil quarry for both scientists and souvenir hunters. And although ninety percent of the unearthed fossils here have been carted away, none of the huge petrified sequoias – despite numerous attempts – could be budged. Various short trails lead between them, such as the shade-free **Petrified Forest Loop**, along which free hour-long tours regularly go. The half-mile **Walk Through Time Loop**, behind the visitors' center, is also a worthwhile walk – mostly to see the unusual sight of conifers growing from petrified stumps. Another ten miles of hiking trails lead around the area's rolling hills and have become particularly popular with cross-country skiers and snowshoers in winter.

The whole area is still incredibly rich with fossils and it is not hard to find them around the monument. These of course must be left behind, but back on the road to **Florissant** the **Florissant Fossil Quarry**, near the minor road's junction with Hwy-24 (10am–4pm; $7.50), allows you to souvenir-hunt through rocks in an even richer fossil bed. At the main crossroads of the tiny Florissant, the rustic *Fossil Inn* (7am–8pm) offers a particularly good selection of American dinner entrees ($13).

Cripple Creek and Victor

Once the richest goldfield in the Rockies, **CRIPPLE CREEK** has produced twice as much gold as California's famed mother lode and more, in fact, than any other single geological deposit in the world. The much-chronicled gold camp, fifty miles from Colorado Springs via US-24, nestles in a grim volcanic bowl on the west flank of Pikes Peak. The gold rush here began in 1891, when cowhand Bob Womack, discovered gold on poor cattle-raising land. Though at first no one believed Crazy Bob's tale, he eventually sold his share for $500 (the El Paso mine ultimately proved to be worth around $5 million) and spent most of it on whiskey. Others were more fortunate and Winfield Scott Stratton became the most famous of Cripple Creek prospectors. Formerly a carpenter making hand-carved fireplaces, he took a second look at his claims after a few years of fruitless searching and a leave of absence (due to promises to his wife), finding a rich vein that would become the Independence Mine. He didn't work it for long and with the proceeds of the sale built a hospital and gave bicycles for the poor. He died a wealthy and much-loved philanthropist. By 1900, sixty thousand people lived in a town boasting eight newspapers, hundreds of saloons, splendid hotels, elegant homes, and even a stock exchange. In 1915 the price of gold plunged, and within five years most mines were played out. All but a handful of mines had shut by the 1960s, the economy becoming increasingly desperate. But since 1991, when gambling was legalized in Cripple Creek, the new gold mines in town are its **casinos**. Most of its Victorian buildings have been converted into these, a sprucing-up that has markedly changed their character. What these structures used to be like before gambling set in can be seen seven miles south of Cripple Creek at **Victor**, whose run-down state preserves a more acute sense of history.

Downtown Cripple Creek and around

The now casino-lined main street (**Bennett St**) of this 650-inhabitant-strong town still backs onto a forbidding rocky plateau, pockmarked by scars and mine dumps. It has always been the main business area in town and, at its eastern end, the **Cripple Creek District Museum** (daily late May to mid-Oct 10am–5pm, rest of year weekends only noon–4pm; $2.50) is the best place to gain an appreciation of the frontier town's raucous history. A model of local gold mines made with multiple sheets of glass with mine workings inked on gives an idea of the complexity and density of mining operations here. The museum is in the old railroad station, where, in the camp's heyday, a train passed through every six minutes. Some of these were ferrying workers out to various mines on a route that the **Narrow Gauge Railroad** (June to mid-Oct daily every 45min 10am–5pm; $8; ⓣ719/689-2640), boarded at the depot beside the museum, still trundles. It's a scenic four-mile tour past several abandoned mines, including the site of Bob Womack's original strike.

A block south of Bennett Street runs **Myers Street**, once one of the West's most notorious red-light districts. Its history remembered in fun tours of the **Old Homestead Museum**, no. 353 (daily 11am–5pm; $3; ⓣ719/689-3090), a former high-class brothel filled with many original furnishings. In the opposite direction, heading west from Bennett Street, is an unpaved road leading out of town to the small, conical Mount Pisgah, surrounded by **city cemeteries**. At the beginning of the nineteenth century the local murder rate averaged eight per month, making some headstones particularly interesting reading. One tombstone was simply inscribed "He called Bill Smith a liar"– but has since been stolen from the cemetery.

One of the last mines to close in the area was the **Mollie Kathleen Gold Mine** (May-Oct daily 9am–5pm; $11), one mile north on Hwy-67, which now gives tours led by ex-miners to gold veins a thousand feet underground. The informative tours take around forty minutes and include a free sample of gold ore. A few mines do still work the area, and although around $8 billion (at today's prices) has already been extracted, eighty percent of the area's ore is still thought to be underground; many speculate about a rich mother lode deep in Pikes Peak.

Victor

There are far fewer attractions in nearby **Victor**, where the streets are literally paved with gold – no one could be bothered with the low-grade ore at the time, so it was used for road surfacing – though the metaphor is rendered worthless by the scrappy town's collection of decaying buildings. But at least the formerly grand buildings have preserved a certain ramshackle authenticity that's been lost in Cripple Creek. One of the few well-preserved buildings is the stately **Imperial Hotel**. Just downhill of it is the modest **Lowell Thomas Museum** (June–Oct daily 9am–5pm; free), dedicated to a local boy turned journalist and adventurer. Among the commemorative articles, photos, and memorabilia, a few artifacts from Victor's past have crept into the collection too. But Victor's finest attraction is the **American Eagles Scenic Overlook**, a couple of miles east on a dirt road above town accessed from Diamond Avenue, the road running a block above the main street (Victor Ave). A handful of old mine buildings are open for exploration, with interpretive boards provided, but far more memorable are the stunning views west over surrounding valleys and several mountain ranges beyond.

Practicalities

Cripple Creek's **chamber of commerce**, located between the district museum and the scenic railway at 337 E Bennett St (Ⓣ719/689-2169 or 1-800/526-8777, Ⓦwww.cripple-creek.co.us), provides a self-guided auto-tour leaflet of the area. **Ghost Town Tours** (Ⓣ719/689-2466) offer excellent one and a half-hour walking tours (run depending on demand).

The grand 1896 *Imperial Hotel*, 123 N 3rd St (Ⓣ719/689-7777 or 1-800/235-2922; ④), is the last of Cripple Creek's gold rush **hotels**, and it shows in the numerous antique features, including claw-foot bathtubs and steam-heat radiators. Most patrons, though, seem more interested in the large onsite casino. Another hotel with casino, the *Double Eagle Hotel*, 442 E Bennet Ave (Ⓣ719/689-2646 or 1-800/711-7234; ⑤), is also very central. If you're looking for amenities like a pool and a hot tub, you'll have to head a short way out of town to the *Holiday Inn Express*, 601 Galena St (Ⓣ719/689-2600 or 1-800/445-3607; ⑤). Of the town's half-dozen bed and breakfasts, the most central is the *Cherub House*, 415 Main St (Ⓣ719/689-0526 or 1-800/679-7366; ④), which has rooms with either private or shared baths as well as a hot tub. *Cripple Creek Gold Campground* (Ⓣ719/689-2342), on 12654 CO-67 seven miles out of town on Hwy-67 to Divide, has pretty **campsites** for both RVs and tents (sites from $15); they also offer short horseback-riding trips in the local Pike National Forest.

The casinos along the main street provide the only **restaurants** in town, and often some cheap deals, including *Bronco Billy's* 49¢ breakfast (two eggs, bacon, hash browns, and toast); *The Palace Hotel's* full stack of pancakes for $1.99; The *Gold Rush Hotel and Casino's* $2.99 New York Strip Steak Special or the *Creeker Casino's* decent $10 Sunday buffet.

In **Victor**, the town's pride is the Victorian *Victor Hotel*, on 4th Street and Victor Avenue (Ⓣ719/689-3553 or 1-800/748-0870; ④), whose straightforward modern rooms are above a grand lobby, formerly used as a bank and now providing what little tourist **information** is needed. A few doors down, the *Two Mile Deli* is an inexpensive choice for cheap basic breakfasts and lunches. Opposite, *It's Someplace Else* not only has a classy collection of bras hanging above the bar but also serves up pizzas and Mexican food.

The Shelf Road

From Cripple Creek and Victor, three roads head south to Cañon City and the Arkansas River valley – around twenty miles away as the crow flies. The most interesting of these is the narrow, winding **Shelf Road**, a dirt road set in precipitous terrain, passing down Helena Canyon, home to bighorn sheep, and close to areas well-known for superb **rock-climbing** in the **Shelf Road Recreation Area**, eight miles out of Cripple Creek. In co-operation with the Bureau of Land Management (BLM) of Cañon city (see below), more than four hundred climbing routes have been established across a network of steep cliffs and walls that's so extensive that climbers are unlikely to ever feel crowded. Thoughtfully placed expansion bolts open up all manner of technical pitches, bulges, cracks, and slabs. The BLM have a couple of **campgrounds** available in the area, including the *Bank* campsite ($4) near Red Canyon, where most of the good climbing is. Generally flat and with only light traffic, the Shelf Road also makes for good, reasonably easy out-and-back **cycle** rides along washboard dirt roads.

Cañon City and the Royal Gorge

Approaching this sprawling mass of motels and prisons, its easy to see how **CAÑON CITY**, nearly fifty miles south of Colorado Springs, has largely been defined by its thirteen state penitentiaries. But it's the spectacular nearby **Royal Gorge**, to the west, from which the city gets its name, which attracts visitors. Most settle for views down into the gorge and the foaming Arkansas River at its base, where the adventurous are busy **whitewater rafting**.

The town's present-day form and economy dates back to its 1868 decision to be the site of the state penitentiary (in preference to hosting the State University, which consequently went to Boulder), shaping Cañon City as a stable, rather dull, administrative place. Since the 1930s, it has also developed as a tourist destination, thanks to the building of the Royal Gorge Bridge west of town. But since most of the visitors who head here are either on day-trips from Colorado Springs, or on their way to Arkansas rafting trips, the city's small core, a block north of the main drag, has retained its small-town feel – even though it's sprawled a good way east along Royal Gorge Boulevard (Hwy-50), a road lined with motels and chain restaurants.

Arrival, information and accommodation

Daily Greyhound/TNM&O **buses** running between Pueblo and Grand Junction stop at the Video House, 731 Main St (Ⓣ719/275-0163). For information, stop by the **chamber of commerce**, 403 Royal Gorge Blvd (Ⓣ719/275-2331); from June through August they also operate an info booth in the city park. For details on camping or hiking in the local national forests, check with the **USFS/BLM** office, 3170 E Main St (Mon–Fri 7.45am–4.30pm; Ⓣ719/269-8500) on the east side of town.

There's no shortage of **motels** in and around Cañon City and the Royal Gorge area. Rates can fall as much as half outside the peak season, so be sure to ask around. The majority of **camping** options are located near the Royal Gorge, though free dispersed camping is also possible in the Wet Mountains portion of the San Isabel National Forest, six miles south of town (along Oak Creek Grade Rd).

Hotels and motels

Best Western Royal Gorge 1925 Fremont Drive T719/275-3377. Reliable chain hotel, with a good range of amenities, including a pool, hot tub, playground, and laundry room. 5

Cactus Rose 44058 W Hwy-50 T719/269-7673. Friendly family-run motel near the Royal Gorge, recently renovated with all rooms receiving an Old West makeover. 4

Cañon Inn 3075 E Hwy-50 T719/275-8676 or 1-800/525-7727, Wwww.canoninn.com. A relatively high-end motel with 152 large rooms, all with cable TV. There are also several hot tubs and a heated outdoor pool. 6

Holiday Motel 1502 Main St T719/275-3317. Standard inexpensive motel accommodation on the main highway a couple of minutes drive from downtown. Units are worn, but clean and come with phones, cable TV, and a/c. 2

Parkview Motel 231 Royal Gorge Blvd T719/275-0624. Located across from the leafy Veterans Memorial Park, this is one of the best-value and most central motels in town. 2

St Cloud Hotel 631 Main St T719/276-2000 or 1-800/405-9666, Wwww.stcloudhotel.com. A Victorian four-story brick hotel with a good central location. Built in 1883, the *St Cloud* was actually moved from Silvercliffe, 51 miles away, once the silver mines there had been played out. Many of its antique-furnished rooms contain original fittings like clawfoot tubs. 6

Campgrounds

Buffalo Bill's Campground 30 County Road 3A T719/275-1900 or 1-800/787-0880, Wwww.coloradovacation.com/camp/buffalo. Located conveniently rather than picturesquely, this RV park is at the busy intersection of Hwy-50 and Royal Gorge Rd (tent sites from $18). Showers here cost nonguests $4.

Cañon City Campground between Hwy-50 and the Royal Gorge's northern tollgate. The isolated sites of the sprawling free campground are the best choice, but only if you're fine with the limited facilities (toilets, but no water).

The town and around

Though most visitors skip Cañon City and head directly west towards the Royal Gorge, there's a handful of attractions in the town's older core worth stopping off at. Of these, the unusual **Colorado Territorial Prison Museum**, 1st Street and Macon Avenue (May–Oct Mon–Fri 8.30am–6pm; Oct to April Fri & Sat 10am–5pm; $3.50), is the most compelling. It's located in the 1871 Colorado Territorial State Penitentiary, which makes up the bulk of Cañon City's west end of and still houses some seven hundred inmates. The hulking gas chambers – last used in 1967 – in the forecourt of the complex sets the tone for the museum, which details a rather gruesome 120-year history of incarceration. This jail was decommissioned in the 1970s when its conditions were deemed too "cruel and unusual" a punishment. Now its cells are used to display a variety of restraining mechanisms, as well as an antique electric chair – the last seat for more than one hundred people. There's also displays on some its more notorious inmates, including the locally infamous Alferd Packer, jailed for murder and cannibalizing (see p.151).

Much less depressing, but no less interesting is the **Dinosaur Depot**, 330 Royal Gorge Blvd (June–Aug daily 9am–5pm; Sept–May Tues–Sat 10am–4pm; $3; Wwww.dinosaurdepot.com), marked by the life-sized allosaurus in front of the old train station along Hwy-50. Exhibits here relate mainly to the work of local scientists attracted to the area due to the presence of the nearby bone-rich **Garden Park Fossil Area** five miles north of town along Field Avenue (the start of the Shelf Rd; see box, overleaf). In the Dinosaur Depot lab, workers painstakingly remove from the rock a stegosaurus skeleton (the only complete one in the world) that was found in the Garden Park. The Depot also organizes informative **tours** of Garden Park (Fri & Sun 10am; $5 includes museum entrance). If you're more interested in the area's more recent history, then the mixed bag of local treasures at the **Cañon City Municipal Museum**, 612 Royal Gorge Blvd (Tues–Sun 10am–4pm; closed Sun Sept–April; $1; T719/269-9018), is worth a quick look. These include Ute artifacts, fossils, guns, the mounted heads of the last of the area's wild buffaloes (shot by poachers in 1897), as well as a log cabin and stone settlers house from the 1880s.

The Royal Gorge

Part incredible geological feature, part tawdry tourist trap, the **Royal Gorge**, a remarkably narrow and steep-sided thousand-foot chasm eight miles from Cañon City, has become an awkward fusion of natural wonder and unbridled commercialism. But the tacky roadside trade – like the mildly diverting Bucksin Joe Frontier Town and Railway, often used as a movie set for Westerns – en route to the Royal Gorge is easily forgotten once you peer into its vertigo-inducing depths. The Royal Gorge is linked to Hwy-50 around six miles west of Cañon City by a loop of road that passes the north entrance, to cross the Royal Gorge Bridge and rejoin Hwy-50. You can visit the gorge from either end, paying at a tollbooth at either side of the bridge. However, if you're not interested in paying to see the gorge you should come in from the northern entrance (the one nearest Cañon City) and drive to the **free viewing point** just before the tollbooth.

Since its construction – specifically to attract tourists – in 1929, the most popular way of viewing the gorge is from the **Royal Gorge Bridge** (daily until dusk; $15; ⓣ719/275-7507 or 1-888/333-5597, ⓦwww.royalgorgebridge.com), allegedly the world's highest suspension bridge. You can drive over the gently swaying bridge (no RVs, buses, or trailers) or just walk on it – the better way to appreciate the dizzying views of the gorge's solid rock walls and the foaming white waters of the Arkansas far below. Entrance to the bridge also allows you to descend to the base of the canyon on the world's steepest incline railway or use an aerial tramway for yet another view of the gorge.

Another way to experience the Royal Gorge is to take the **Royal Gorge Route Train** (daily: mid-May to mid-Oct 9am, noon & 3pm; mid-Oct to mid-May noon; $27, reservations recommended; ⓣ303/569-2403 or 1-888/RAILS4U, ⓦwww.royalgorgeroute.com) from Cañon City. Departing from 401 Water St, the 24-mile round-trip takes around two hours, and runs along a precarious ledge at the base of the narrowest and most rugged portion of the gorge.

The most expensive, but most exciting and memorable way to see the gorge is from an inflatable **raft** on the foaming Arkansas at its base. The run through the canyon includes difficult Class V rapids and is particularly challenging when the river is at full flow in late May and early June – though trips are run through here until late August. For further information on rafting the Arkansas see p.195.

Finally, if you are heading in the direction of Cañon City from the Royal Gorge and have a head for mountain driving you should definitely investigate **Skyline Drive**, a giddying roller-coaster road along the spine of a ridge. Built by convicts to provide a thrill for tourists, the one-way highway begins about a mile west of town, climbs up onto the narrow ridge and follows its undulating course – with incredible views in all directions – before plunging into the western end of town. In total it's a ten-minute detour from Hwy-50.

Eating and drinking

The town center contains several cheap Mexican **restaurants** as well as a couple of classier joints and a couple of friendly neighborhood bars. For the usual array of fast-food joints, head east along Hwy-50.

Merlino's Belvedere 1330 Elm Ave ☎719/275-5558. This moderately expensive restaurant is one of the city's main fine-dining establishments. Italian favorites, as well as salmon, shrimp, and prime rib, are complemented by over-indulgent desserts.

My Brother's Place 625 Main ☎719/275-9954. Smoky local hangout serving mostly domestic beers to pool players.

Old Mission Deli 1905 Fremont. Good range of cheap (entrees $5–7) Mexican food: burritos, chimichangas, chorizo, and superb homemade green chilerellenos.

Ortega's 2301 E Main St ☎719/275-9437. Reliable choice among the many budget Southwestern-style restaurants in town. The standard Mexican choices are on offer, including great chile rellenos, as well as some Italian and American dishes. Open for breakfast, lunch, and dinner.

The Owl Cigar Store 626 Main St. Bought with money won playing poker, this Cañon City institution is the place to go for vinyl booths, old-school jukebox, and inexpensive traditional American diner food like burgers and thick malts. A local watering hole for over a hundred years, its walls are lined with all sorts of artifacts – hunting trophies, photographs, license plates – and there's also a few pool tables.

Wild Sage Café & Bakery 325 Main St. Good bakery in the center of town that's open for breakfast and lunch; an espresso bar sets up patrons will all manner of frothy drinks. Closed Sun.

South central Colorado

Part plains and part mountains, most visitors don't really know what to make of **SOUTH CENTRAL COLORADO** and so leave it well alone. But it's the contrast between the sharp, jagged profile of the **Sangre de Cristos** at the center of the region and the flatlands on either side, along with a deep-rooted Hispanic culture, that gives the area its character – akin more to the Southwest than Colorado's mountain towns.

For the initial part of its settlement until the end of the Mexican–American War in 1859, when south central Colorado was finally ceded to the US, most of this area was in Spanish hands, with traders busy on the Santa Fe trail and ranchers pioneering the **San Luis Valley**.

In contrast to the rest of the mountains of the Front Range that rise dramatically from the plains beside Colorado Springs, Denver, and Boulder, the **Southern Front Range**, south of the Arkansas River, sees a much more gradual transition; wide-open sagebrush plains around dull, post-industrial **Pueblo**, the region's largest town, becoming the rolling **Wet Mountains** to the west. Further west, the virtually impassable granite Sangre de Cristo Mountains run as an unbroken chain for 75 miles, joining the Arkansas Headwaters in the north to the **Spanish Peaks** in the south – a small and pretty range of mountains that has begun to foster small artist communities, whose main life-line is the run-down and uneventful **Trinidad**, near the New Mexican border.

To the west of the Sangre de Cristos, sandwiched between them and the San Juans, is the San Luis Valley. The vast, pancake-flat area feels more like a giant hunk of plains that have been dropped into the mountains, though the ring of frequently snow-covered mountains on either side attest to its valley status. Again, few visitors venture into this area, although the **Great Sand Dunes National Monument**, is definitely worth a visit.

The Southern Front range

South of the Arkansas River, the **SOUTHERN FRONT RANGE** and its green valleys back away from its main artery, I-25, where the landscape is predominantly rolling sagebrush plains. From gritty **Pueblo**, the interstate runs south through sparsely inhabited areas past the road junction town of **Walsenburg** up to uneventful **Trinidad**, close to the New Mexican border. As these towns are devoid of Colorado's more typical alpine splendor, there's not much here to keep visitors. Indeed, even the local populace is leaving, making these the few towns in the state that are actually shrinking. Only the tiny communities of the **Wet Mountains**, west of Pueblo, and the small **Spanish Peaks** region, west of Trinidad, are growing, mainly thanks to artists taking advantage of the low rents and inspiring landscape.

Pueblo

Starting as a trading post and goldmining supply center, **PUEBLO** quickly grew into Colorado's second-largest city after it was chosen by the Colorado Fuel and Iron Company to be the site of a huge steel mill in the 1870s. For more than one hundred years, coal transported up from Trinidad (see p.133) helped keep the mill's smokestack's fuming, but by the 1980s the mill had all but shut down, leaving an unappealing townscape and an economic void. Still shrinking, Pueblo is now the state's third-largest city, and if there's any cause for optimism it's in the fact that Pueblo has bounced back from being down and out before. During the Christmas celebrations of 1854, the fledgling community decided to invite local Ute into town to celebrate; the natives quickly butchered all but a handful of the drunken revelers. And in 1921, the Arkansas River overflowed, submerging and destroying most of downtown, claiming scores of lives. Given the range of much more enticing opportunities elsewhere in the region, few visitors make it to Pueblo, except during the late-August State Fair, when beds in town are hard to come by.

Arrival, information, and accommodation

Buses from both Denver and Grand Junction arrive at the Greyhound and TNM&O bus depot on 703 US-50 W (Ⓣ719/544-6295), near I-25 (exit 101). Opposite, on Elizabeth Street and US-50, is an **information center** (daily: Jun–Sept 8am–6pm; Oct–May 8am–4pm Ⓣ719/543-1742), from where a shuttle to Cripple Creek departs six times per day ($15, though you get $7 worth of gambling chips on arrival; Ⓣ719/545-8687). Another visitor center is in the Pueblo **chamber of commerce** at 302 N Santa Fe Ave (Mon–Fri 8am–5pm; Ⓣ719/542-1704 or 1-800/233-3446), the city's principal downtown street. Downtown, there's a **post office** at 1005 W 6th St.

A large number of **hotels** and **motels** have settled a couple of miles north of the city center, around I-25's exit 101. There's little accommodation downtown, and little available anywhere during State Fair in late August. One of the cheapest and most basic deals near the interstate is the *Al-Re-Ho Motel*, 2424 N Freeway (Ⓣ719/542-5135; ❶). The nearby *Days Inn*, 4201 N Elizabeth St (Ⓣ719/543-8031; ❹), with its Southwestern-style rooms and pool is quite a bit smarter. Downtown, the *Travelers Motel*, 1012 N Santa Fe Ave (Ⓣ719/543-5451; ❷), is a dreary though cheap and central option. The odd-one out in the town's bland lodging selection is the lovely and laid-back *Abriendo Inn*, 300 W

△ The Cumbres and Toltec Scenic Railroad

Abriendo Ave (Ⓣ719/544-2703, Ⓦwww.bedandbreakfastinns.org/abriendo; ❺). Its reputation as one of the finest B&Bs in the state is well earned; the house features plenty of stained glass and antique furniture, and some rooms – all of which are en suite – have four-poster beds and hot tubs.

The town

Without a doubt the city's premier event is the roughly two-week-long **Colorado State Fair**, which takes place in large purpose-built grounds found by taking I-25 exit 97A, heading one block north to Northern Avenue, which you follow west two miles before going north on Prairie Street ($5; Ⓣ719/830-8497 or 1-800/444-3247, Ⓦwww.coloradosfair.com). Starting in late August, Colorado's biggest fair combines an important rodeo with lots of live music; from big band to Country to rock. If the fair's not on, you can always visit the nearby, **El Pueblo Museum**, 324 west 1st St (Mon–Sat 10am–4.30pm, Sun noon–3pm; $2.50), which re-creates the adobe 1842 Fort Pueblo trading post, one of the town's first buildings.

At other times, Pueblo's premier attraction is the **Rosemount**, 419 W 14th St (June–Sept Mon–Sat 10am–2pm; Sun 2–3.30pm; Oct–May Tues–Sat 1–3pm, Sun 2–3pm, closed Jan; $6; Ⓦwww.rosemount.org), an opulent 37-room Victorian mansion that contrasts with much of the rest of the rather run-down downtown area. Built in 1893 for local banker John Thatcher, the antique-furnished home includes original Tiffany chandeliers and an elaborate thirteen-foot-tall stained-glass window dedicated to two of Thatcher's children who died young. An Egyptian mummy and a number of other strange souvenirs are also on show.

On the western side of downtown, by the Arkansas River, is the **Union Avenue Historic District**, where the refurbishment of numerous old railway and warehouse buildings has seen several restaurants and boutiques move in.

Eating, drinking, and nightlife

Near the strip of hotels and motels out by the interstate, *Don's Café*, on Elizabeth Street just south of CO-50 (Ⓣ719/543-5814), is a cheap blue-collar diner serving good meals throughout the day. Downtown, *Rita's*, 302 N Grand Ave Ⓣ719/542-4820 (off 3rd St, two blocks west of Santa Fe Ave), serves a good range of Mexican food, including enormous combination platters for only $5. A more upmarket option downtown is *Rendezvous*, 218 W 2nd St, which offers a pretty eclectic menu – Mexican to Continental – including good-value lunches from $6; Fridays feature live jazz. For a more jumping atmosphere and regular live music head to the *Irish Brewpub and Grill*, 108 W 3rd St (Ⓣ719/542-9974), which also serves good bar food, including unusual offerings like buffalo burgers and alligator sausages. The most reliable nightclub in town is *Peppers Pueblo Hot Spot*, 4109 Club Manor Drive (just west of the I-25 and Hwy-50 intersection; Ⓣ719/542-8629), where occasional live bands are augmented by a steady diet of sixties, seventies and eighties pop along with the occasional techno night.

The Wet Mountains

South from Pueblo, I-25 zips through 48 miles of dry, uneventful desert landscape to Walsenburg. But a worthwhile detour – the odd **Bishop's Castle** – lies in the craggy Wet Mountains, 25 miles west of Pueblo on Hwy-96. Further west, separating the eastern and western halves of the San Isabel National Forest, is the Wet Mountain Valley, a 35-mile-wide belt of rolling hills that make for ideal ranching country. At the valley's center, the small communities of **Westcliffe** and **Silvercliff** are bordered to the west by the virtually impassable Sangre de Cristo Range, home to numerous trails and climbing routes.

Bishop's Castle

Touted as the world's largest one-man construction project, **Bishop's Castle** (always open; by donation; ⓣ719/485-3040, ⓦwww.bishopcastle.org), 34 miles west of Pueblo on Hwy-78, is a tribute to determination and eccentricity. The massive pseudo-medieval castle, a ramshackle affair rising up as high as 160 feet, is the work of Jim Bishop, a former Pueblo steelworker who's been building it stone-by-stone for over thirty years. Over one thousand tons of hand-gathered local rocks have gone into the structure, which contains an entertaining mix of dungeon-like rooms, stained-glass windows, flimsy iron spiral staircases, and numerous stone turrets, spires, and flying buttresses – enter at your own risk. Bishop's still potting away on his surreal masterpiece, and you'll probably spot him working on something or another if you visit. Interestingly, he had no intention of building the castle when he first bought this land – he was only building a small stone cottage, but in response to frequent comments by visitors that it looked like a castle, he decided to go ahead and make it one. Since then, the structure has hosted over seventy weddings and gets more visitors than anything else in the Wet Mountains – all while remaining free, dedicated to the "hardworking poor people of the world."

Westcliffe and Silver Cliff

Twenty-nine miles west of Bishop's Castle, off the junction of Hwys 69 and 96, the small ranching towns of **WESTCLIFFE** and **SILVER CLIFF** enjoyed their heydays a century ago. The fomer began as the local railroad terminus for the line from Cañon City, and the latter, smaller and virtually attached to Westcliffe's eastern fringes, was for a brief spell Colorado's third-largest after silver had been found in 1877. Both proceeded to near ghost town status, though in recent years, Westcliffe has become a bit of a base for exploring the outdoors and its Main Street is now filled with realtor's offices, Western art galleries and twee emporiums selling Old West gifts and ice cream. Not all of the town's agricultural basis has been forgotten, though, as proven by the **Westcliffe Stampede**, a rodeo, held in late June. This is overshadowed, though, by the far bigger **Jazz in the Sangres** festival (ⓣ719/783-3785), held on the second weekend of August.

Other than wander around gift shops, there's not really much to do in Westcliffe or Silver Cliff other than stock up before heading into the mountains. A small **museum**, 713 Main St (Memorial Day–Labor Day Thurs–Sun 1–4pm; free), charts their history via a predictable but diverting collection of relics and old photos housed in a nineteenth-century former fire station. The only other real local attraction is **Mission Wolf** (9am–sunset; free; ⓣ719/746-2919), a sanctuary for former pet wolves in Blue Spring, 41 miles from Westcliffe along Hwy-69 (for 27 miles) and Gardner Road. Around fifty wolves and wolf-dog hybrids are looked after here in environments that try to simulate their natural habitat.

Outdoor recreation around Westcliffe

Westcliffe, on the doorstep of the Sangre de Cristo, is well-placed to give access to a range of generally underused outdoor recreation possibilities. Since most of the Sangre de Cristo mountains, which include 35 peaks over 13,500ft, are hard climbs – the majority requiring some climbing equipment and expertise – most of the hiking in the area centers either around the easy **Rainbow Trail** or trails up to mountain passes from where there are good views up and down the imposing jagged range. Originally built for forest firefighters, the Rainbow Trail follows the contours of the base of the range. Mountain bikers can also use this trail, since it's outside the Wilderness Area that covers much of the Sangre de Cristo range.

A good place to access the Rainbow Trail is from the *USFS Alvarado Campground* – see practicalities below. Here you can also pick up a trail to Venable Lakes, a six-mile return hike to a pair of pretty alpine lakes above the timberline (favorites with anglers for good-sized brook trout). Before heading out, check in with the USDA Forest Service, 5 Hermit Lane (ⓣ719/783-2481), or the Sangre de Cristo Fly Shop, 104 Main St (ⓣ719/783-2313), who sell Michael O'Hanlons' *The Colorado Sangre De Cristo – Complete Trail Guide* (Hungry Gulch Press; $13), the definitive guide to trails in the Sangre de Cristos range. If you're interested in exploring the Wet Mountains, then pick up a copy of Nadia N. Brelje's *Southern Front Range Trail Guide* (self-published; $15), which reviews trails within a 50-mile radius of Pueblo – and is sold at Bishop's Castle.

Practicalities

Westcliffe's **information center** (Mon–Sat 10am 4pm, Sun noon–4pm; ⓣ719/783-9163, ⓦwww.custercountyco.com), is on the junction of Main Street and the northward bound Hwy-69. The **USDA Forest Service**, in Silver Cliff on 5 Hermit Lane (ⓣ719/783-2481), has details on the surrounding San Isabel National Forest.

Of the decent range of **accommodation**, the cheapest option is the *Antler Motel*, 102 S Main (ⓣ719/783-2426; ❷), a bit scrappy but still clean. A better option, a mile south along Hwy-69, is the *Westcliffe Inn* (ⓣ719/783-9275; ❸), where facilities include a hot tub and most rooms have great mountain views. At the more luxurious end of the scale, the central *Main St Bed and Breakfast*, no. 501 (ⓣ719/783-4000 or 1-877/783-4006, ⓦwww.mainstreetbnb.com; ❺), offers antique-furnished rooms (with private bath) in a renovated Victorian home. In Silver Cliff, *Yoder's High Country Inn*, 700 Ohio St (ⓣ719/783-2656; ❸), is a clean, family-run motel whose rates include a continental breakfast. Campers should head to the San Isabel National Forest to the west. The USFS office (see above) can supply details of all the **campgrounds**, but one that's particularly conveniently located by trailheads is the *USFS Alvarado Campground* (mid-May to mid-Sept; $9), which has thirty RV sites and seventeen tent sites. To find it, head south from Westcliffe on Hwy-69 for three miles, then right on CO-302 for seven more.

There's a more limited range of **places to eat**. For breakfast and lunch, try *Karen's Gourmet Coffee*, 104 Main St (daily 7.30am–2pm), a small restaurant with a fine range of food – omelettes for breakfast and more adventurous daily specials like chicken quesadillas and buffalo burgers with blue cheese ($6.25). Further east along Main Street at no. 212, *Shining Mountains* is a lunch-only restaurant with decent Mexican dishes, along with wraps, burgers, and sandwiches served out on its adobe patio. For dinner, Silver Cliff is the best option, with *Yoders*, 700 Ohio St (closed Sun and Wed afternoon), serving dishes like grilled ham steak ($6) and Polish sausage, and the vegetarian friendly *Pizza Madness*, 715 Main St, where there's a big outside patio.

The Spanish Peaks

Unlike most of the rest of the Rockies, the twin **Spanish Peaks** (12,683ft and 13,626ft) are the result of volcanic activity rather than folding and faulting. As a result, they have a more conical shape than mountains in neighboring ranges, and are nearly symmetrical. Like much of the rest of the Southern Front range, the trails that crisscross the mountains here are relatively undiscovered, meaning there's plenty of good peaceful hiking, biking, and riding to be had here.

The northern gateway to the Spanish Peaks is the junction town of **Walsenberg**. From here the most usual route south to Trinidad heads south 37 miles on the I-25. An alternative route is the scenic **Highway of Legends** (largely Hwy-12). This takes twice as long to drive, but is much more attractive, as it cuts through the southern portion of the San Isabel National Forest traveling past the **Great Dikes**, a series of impressive volcanic rock formations.

Walsenberg and La Veta

The northern gateway to the Spanish Peaks, nondescript **Walsenberg** has little going for it besides its location at the convergence of major roads linking the Front Range with Colorado's southwest. Unless you need to stop at the **Huerfano County Chamber of Commerce**, 400 Main St (☎719/738-1065), which is the best source of information for the region, there's really little reason to linger.

Around sixteen miles southwest of Walsenberg on Hwy-160 is neat little **LA VETA**, kept lively by an enthusiastic artist community. Huddled around a short main street, everything in town, including its handful of accommodation options and restaurants, are within easy walking distance, making it a handy stopover. The town is also a good place to check out local art, on display at The Gallery, on W Ryus Avenue, at the center of town, or as a hub for exploration of the surrounding area. A useful outfitter is Wahatoya Base Camp, 22 Main St (☎719/742-5578), who run outdoor classes and trips – from courses in local botany and bird-watching to mountain-biking trips – and also provides outdoor gear sales and rental.

The main sight in town is the **Fort Francisco Museum** (May–Sept Wed–Sat 10am–4pm, Sun 1–4pm; $2) on Main Street in the center of town, which was built in 1862 to protect settlers from Comanche attacks. A number of its buildings now serve as an open-air museum. The local history covered includes material on the Ludlow Massacre (see p.134) and the carved and painted *santos* of the Penitente brotherhood – an important force in the church both locally and in the San Luis Valley.

The Fort Francisco Museum can also provide **visitor information**, although a better source for those wanting to explore nearby is the **San Isabel National Forest Ranger Station**, 103 E Field St (☎719/742-3681). If staying on, campsites ($15) are available from *The Rustic Shack*, 404 S Oak St (☎719/742-6221 or 1-877/460-6221; ❸), which also runs good-value cabins. The *La Veta Inn* (☎719/742-3700; ❹) on Main Street and Ryus Avenue at the center of town, is the town's only hotel; rooms in the Victorian hotel have their own bath. *Hunter House Bed and Breakfast*, 115 W Grand Ave (☎719/742-5577; ❹), offers rooms with shared bath in a small home. The *Mainstreet Diner* at the south end of Main Street has cheap and filling breakfasts. For a selection of baked goods, try the *Ryus Avenue Bakery*, 129 W Ryus Ave, where sandwiches and light lunches are also served (until 1.30pm). The *La Veta Inn* (see above) is a good choice for a standard range of American dishes, while the nearby *Covered Wagon Steakhouse,* 205 S Main St, serves more basic bar food, as well as steaks.

Along the Highway of Legends

The first opportunity to view some of the **Great Dikes**, a landform scattered throughout the Spanish Peaks area, comes a short way south of La Veta along the Highway of Legends. These narrow rock walls, up to 100 feet high and several miles long, were formed by molten lava being forced into volcanic cracks, cooling there as hard rock. **Cuchara**, eleven miles on, is a pleasant little place, best visited during the winter to take advantage of the **Cuchara Mountain Ski Resort** two miles west of town (mid-Dec to early April 9am–4pm; $30; ⓣ719/742-3163 or 1-888/282-4272, ⓦwww.cuchara.com). The resort's vertical drop is 1542ft; its terrain divides as forty percent beginner; forty percent intermediate and twenty percent advanced, of which only a tiny part is expert terrain. Despite attempting to market themselves as a year-round destination, both the town and the resort – which allows mountain biking in summer – are pretty dead outside the winter season. Cuchara Valley Sports Guides (ⓣ719/742-5544) can help with finding warm-weather activities, including four-wheel-drive tours, bike rental, and fly-fishing trips.

Though you leave the national forest a short way beyond Cuchara Pass, Hwy-12 continues to wind its way through rolling green hills and passes several smaller communities with low-key recreation facilities. These include **Monument Lake Park** ($2), 36 miles west of Trinidad, a small park around a lake popular for trout fishing, horseback riding, hiking, and some mountain biking. There are several USFS campgrounds here as well as the municipally-owned *Mountain Lake Resort* (ⓣ719/868-2226 or 1-800/845-8006; ④; closed in winter), which provides Southwestern-style rooms and cabins along with campsites ($10) with RV hookups.

Only eight miles from Trinidad on Hwy-12, the **Cokedale National Historic District**, preserves a former coke-producing town that once worked to feed Pueblo's steel mills. Now it's a ghost town, complete with numerous abandoned homes, huge ovens and giant black slag-heaps. Leaflets at the parking lot provide more information about the site; one of few places locally where workers paid a fair rent for homes and were not forced to shop at factory-owned stores – unlike workers at the Colorado Fuel & Iron Company (see box overleaf). A good way to link a visit to Cokedale with a hike is to follow a five-mile hiking trail up here from **Trinidad Reservoir and State Park** (ⓣ719/846-6951 or 1-800/678-2267; ⓦwww.coloradoparks.org/trinidad) on the edge of Trinidad. Highway-12 also passes by this park, which is popular locally for watersports and fishing. You can camp at *Carpois Ridge Campground* (tents $9, RVs $12; ⓣ303/470-1144 or 1-800/678-2267) west of the dam.

Trinidad

Once a bustling railhead for freighting local coal, **TRINIDAD**'s formerly grand brick-paved streets are now lined with boarded-up businesses. The cityscape is overshadowed by the interstate flyover and, strangely enough, the town's industry seems to center around sex-change operations, with over 3500 having been performed here to date.

Originally a major stop along the Santa Fe Trail, Trinidad has always contained a mix of US and Mexican cultures, perhaps best displayed at the excellent **Trinidad History Museum**, 300 E Main St (May–Sept Mon–Sat 10am–4pm; $5), comprising several buildings. One houses the **Santa Fe Trail Museum**, while the other two properties tell the intriguing tales of two of the town's leading families, one Hispanic, the other Anglo-American, in more prosperous

Ludlow Massacre Monument

Ten miles north of town (one mile west of I-25 exit 27) a monument commemorates the 1914 **Ludlow Massacre**, a tragic episode in American labor history. Having called a strike to gain more humane working conditions and union recognition, miners and their families were evicted from the (overpriced) Colorado Fuel & Iron Company housing and forced to live in a huge tented city. After frictions and clashes between the mine guards and miners (mostly poor Italian, Irish, and Greek immigrants) the National Guard was called in. They sided with the mine owners and, as tension escalated, the National Guard torched the 1200-strong tent-city, in which several asphyxiated women and children were later found. Mine leaders mysteriously died in captivity, but National Guard leaders, though deemed responsible for the murders, were never punished. Sadly too, the miners returned to work, despite no concessions having been granted. Eventually, Federal legislation would take into account their demands – but too late for most of those involved to benefit.

times. The relatively plain adobe Baca House was the former home of a rancher, shipping magnate, and politician; while the opulent Bloom House was the Victorian mansion of a ranching and banking family. Much of the impetus to preserve these residences came from Arthur Ray Mitchell, a local artist famous for illustrating pulp-fiction Westerns. His work is commemorated in the **A.R. Mitchell Memorial Museum of Western Art**, 150 E Main St (April–Sept Mon–Sat 10am–4pm; free; ⓣ719/846-4224), where an insightful collection of photos charting local life from the 1870s onwards can also be seen.

Practicalities

Greyhound (ⓣ1-800/231-2222) and TNM&O **buses** (ⓣ719/543-2775) stop at JR's Travel Shoppe, 639 W Main St. The daily Amtrak services between Chicago and Los Angeles stop at the depot alongside Purgatoire river on Commercial Street. Information is available at the **Colorado Welcome Center & Trinidad Chamber of Commerce**, 309 Nevada Ave (ⓣ719/846-9285, ⓦwww.trinidadco.com), beside the elevated I-25 (exit 15). The **Trinidad Trolley** (May–Sept 10am–5pm; free) starts its tour of the main shops and attractions from here.

One of the cheapest **accommodation** options in the area is the *Budget Host Derrick Motel*, south of town (I-25 exit 11) at 1031 Santa Fe Drive (ⓣ719/846-3307; ❸). Located beside a landmark derrick, the motel has pretty mountain views as well as tent and RV sites ($15). Two B&Bs provide more personal, historic lodging: the *Inn on the Santa Fe Trail,* W Main and Animas (ⓣ719/846-4636; ❹), is in a late nineteenth-century residence where all rooms have private baths; the *Stone Mansion Bed and Breakfast,* 212 E 2nd St (ⓣ719/845-1625 or 1-877/264-4279; ❹), has smart, spacious bedrooms with private bathrooms and gourmet breakfasts. There are quite a number of good cheap **restaurants** in Trinidad. A good place for breakfast is the *Main St Bakery*, 121 Main St, where fresh pastries and pancakes are served along with simple lunches and dinners (Thurs–Sat nights). Further along Main Street, the *El Paso Café*, no. 1101, has some of the best Mexican food in town. At the west end of town (I-25 exit 14A), *Monte Leone's Deli/Nana and Nono's Pasta House*, 415 University St, is a cheerful cheap restaurant serving up excellent Mexican and Italian food side-by-side. There's also a deli here, good for stocking up on picnic items.

The San Luis Valley

The largest alpine valley in the world, the uniformly flat **SAN LUIS VALLEY** contrasts dramatically with the rest of the Colorado Rockies. Flanked by the impressively jagged and often snowcapped Sangre de Cristo range to the east and the bulky San Juans to the west, the semi-arid grass and sagebrush plain is dotted with isolated farms and the occasional small town. Both the valley's geography and culture make it more reminiscent of New Mexico's southwestern charms than Colorado's wealthy mountain resorts, and though you're likely to be just passing through, the valley's secluded backcountry, Hispanic culture and cheap accommodation make it worth a look.

When Europeans first arrived, the valley was home to the Ute, who had taken full advantage of the valley's plentiful bison herds. They zealously protected this area, thwarting settlement attempts until the 1850s when Mexican colonists from nearby Taos (New Mexico) successfully established the town of **San Luis**. The US took possession of the area at the end of the Mexican–American War in 1859, but even today Spanish is still the first language of over half the valley's population.

On the valley's eastern side, the spectacular **Great Sand Dunes National Monument**, nestling beside the magnificent peaks of the **Sangre de Cristo Mountains**, definitely warrants a detour. There's not much in **Alamosa**, the geographical and social center of the valley, though the nearby wetland bird sanctuaries are a favorite nesting ground for bald eagles and both sandhill and whooping cranes. To the southwest, along the New Mexico border, the antique **Cumbres and Toltec Railroad** passes through almost pristine land at the southern end of the Rio Grande National Forest. Both here and north around **Monte Vista** and **Del Norte** on to the headwaters of the Rio Grande, large trout populations attract fishermen in the summer. Also on the valley's western side, tiny **La Garita** is best known for its superb rock climbing and good hiking. Here and elsewhere in the **Rio Grande National Forest** that all but encircles the valley, the numerous backcountry trails are used more by bighorn sheep than people.

The southeastern valley

Travelling in from the east, wide Hwy-160 sweeps from Walsenberg (see p.132), past the Spanish Peaks and over the wooded La Veta Pass into the San Luis Valley. The first settlement you come to here is a tiny town named after the adobe buildings of **Fort Garland** (April–Oct daily 9am–5pm; Nov–March Thurs–Mon 8am–4pm; $3; ⓣ719/379-3512), beside the road to San Luis. Built in 1858, the fort was used mainly to flex military muscle and police the new US territory (see box, overleaf). Now a museum, the most interesting building here – decked out simply with period furnishings – is a reconstruction of the residence of Kit Carson, the west's most notorious Indian fighter. Carson came here in 1866, his final posting before death, and was able to use his close friendship with the Ute chief Ouray to help secure a relative peace in the region. Another notable exhibit sheds light on little-recognized black army regiments from this time, dubbed "buffalo soldiers" by local Indian enemies in recognition of their considerable bravery and fighting skill.

A few miles beyond the town of Fort Garland is the dull litte farming town of **Blanca**, the closest stop on Greyhound and TNM&O bus lines to the Great Sand Dunes National Monument. You can camp in town where shaded sites at the *Mt Blanca RV Park* go for $12 or stay just three miles southeast of Blanca,

The Bloody Espinozas

For the 25 years that Fort Garland served as a military fort, almost its entire time was spent policing southwestern Colorado. The most high-profile case to have attracted the fort's attention involved two Hispanic brothers, known locally as "**The bloody Espinozas**," who in response to a vision of the Virgin Mary decided it was God's desire that all Anglos be driven from the region. The two bandits headed north from the San Luis Valley, ambushing and murdering travelers on roads near Buena Vista apparently at random. When local soldiers were sent to catch them, they did little but return with the corpses of dead men the Espinozas had ambushed, though they did give chase to an innocent man for fifteen miles (terrified, he ran in his bare feet!), until they realized their error. On suspicion that a local rancher was harboring the brothers, a local posse hastily headed over and extracted a young man, who protesting his innocence (rightfully) was duly lynched. The comedy of errors eventually ended after local soldiers caught up with the Espinozas and killed one in a shootout. The other escaped to furtively live with an uncle in the Sangre de Cristo – until the Fort Garland military scout Tom Tobin was dispatched to capture the remaining brother and uncle – which he did, returning to Fort Garland with a sack, which when emptied out at his commanders feet produced two bloody, severed Espinoza heads.

down a dirt road (signposted "airport"), in pleasant rooms at the *Mt Blanca Game Bird and Trout B&B* (ⓣ719/379-3825 or 1-800/686-4024, ⓦwww.mtblanca.com; ❺). Several stocked lakes and the option of clay and upland bird shooting here should appeal particularly to fishermen and hunters.

San Luis

The tourist trail in the San Luis Valley usually continues west from Fort Garland and Blanca to the Great Sand Dunes National Monument, meaning that **San Luis**, sixteen miles south of Fort Garland on Hwy-159, is rarely visited. But if you're destination is the Toltec Railroad, this way is slightly more direct and in any case it's worth dropping into the small town if you are interested in sampling some authentic Colorado-style Hispanic culture – and the associated good food.

San Luis was founded in 1851, making it the earliest major white settlement in Colorado. The **San Luis Museum**, 402 Church Place (May–Sept daily 8am–4.30pm; Oct–April Mon–Fri 8am–4.30pm, Sat & Sun 10am–3pm; $2), does a good job of introducing the history of the valley and includes an impressively detailed and brightly colored collection of small religious woodcarvings known as *santos*. Also inside is a recently reconstructed Penitente chapel of the type that formerly served the local lay brotherhood, once an important part of the local Catholic church, and whose practices included self-flagellation. The church still has strong local ties; in 1995 Pope John Paul II visited the **stations of the cross** shrine above town. Beginning near the junction of CO-159 and CO-142, a short trail leads up to an impressive, onion-domed church, past fourteen life-sized statues by local sculptor Humberto Maestas, depicting the crucifixion of Christ. The view from the top of the mesa is an inspiring one; indeed, the crimson sunsets viewable from here are said to have given the Sangre de Cristo – "Blood of Christ" – Mountains their name.

The plush new *San Luis Inn Motel*, 138 Main St (ⓣ719/672-3399 or 1-877/672-3331; ❸) offers a good standard of motel **accommodation** and has an indoor hot tub. More authentic Southwestern accommodation can be found in *El Convento B&B,* a former convent at 512 Church Place (Ⓣ719/672-4223; ④). Rooms contain handcrafted furniture and fireplaces. A little gallery shares the same building and is a good place to view and buy contemporary San Luis Valley **crafts**, particularly pictorial quilting. The excellent *Emma's Hacienda,* 355 Main St, is a long-running family **restaurant** serving superb Southwestern fare, including delicious red and green enchiladas ($7).

The Great Sand Dunes National Monument

Fifty square miles of shifting sand, the **Great Sand Dunes National Monument** are located in a surprising and picturesque location forty miles north of Fort Garland, huddled against the contrasting Sangre de Cristo mountains. Over millions of years, fine glacial sands from the San Juan mountains have been blown east and deposited at the base of the Sangre de Cristos. Looking for a way through the mountains, the prevailing southwest winds have been channelled towards the lower part of the range – near the Music, Medano and Mosca passes – where they've buffeted against the mountains, dropping their load at their base and forming the dunes.

Though the tallest sand dunes in the country (some rising to around 700ft), their beige color makes it hard to gauge the scale. One reason why they can grow so high is the relative stability afforded by their unusually high moisture content. Although footprints and other surface marks are quickly blown away, the dampness of the sand only a foot below the surface means that the general shapes remain unchanged for centuries. The dunes also harbor a number of small creatures, including two species of beetle, the giant sand-treader camel cricket, and the small kangaroo rat – whose water-efficient kidneys eliminate its need to drink. Most visitors go little further than the "beach" beside Medano creek, but the climb up the dunes themselves, though incredibly tiring, is not to be missed – especially for the fun **slide down** on dune boards (available for rent) or torn pieces of cardboard. A walk along the sandy trails, squeezed between the Dunes and the mountains, and a night spent out at one of the underused backcountry **campsites** is also worthwhile. But for the best views of the whole monument, head south to **Zapata Falls**.

Exploring the monument

At the monument entrance (daily: May–Sept 8am–6pm; Oct–April 8.30am–4.30pm; $4 per vehicle; Ⓣ719/378-2312; Ⓦwww.nps.gov/grsa), you'll receive a useful **map**; three miles on, the **visitors' center** can inform you about organized nature walks and various events put on at the *Pinyon Flats* campground. Downhill behind the visitors' center is the **Mosca picnic area** – the main gateway to exploring the monument and conveniently located near some of its largest dunes. You can walk to these via the southern flank of the dunes, from where you can choose any line of ascent up – though first, depending on the season, you may need to ford **Medano Creek**.

Park Safety

Some careful preparation is advised for the harsh dune environment. Temperatures up to 140°F have been recorded in summer, though summer nights can get cold – and winters even see snow. The glare from the bright sands makes sunscreen and sunglasses vital. Long sleeves and long pants also help against the huge numbers of mosquitoes around the creek in summer. To avoid the worst of these conditions and the afternoon winds, it's wise to explore early in the day.

Along the eastern boundary of the monument, outside the actual body of dunes, trails head north towards **Mosca Pass**. The shortest is the **Montville nature trail**, east of the visitors' center, that runs half a mile beside Mosca Creek providing fine views of the dunes along the way. The **Mosca Pass trail** to the east of the visitors' center betters these views, higher up along this former toll road once used by trappers and prospectors travelling across the mountains into the valley. The trail climbs through a range of vegetation on a seven-mile round-trip to the top of pass: pinyon-juniper forest, aspen groves, and spruce-fir forest lead eventually on to lush meadows in the Sangre de Cristo Mountains.

Further north the single road that passes through the park terminates at the *Pinyon Flats Campground*. Just before this, a turnoff onto a four-wheel-drive track known as the **Medano Pass primitive road** leads up to an eponymous pass east through the Sangre de Cristo Mountains. You can drive this road for two miles in an ordinary car, but beyond the **Point Of No Return** parking lot you'll need a four-wheel-drive vehicle or mountain bike, both of which will need to run on low tire pressure for the numerous sandy sections (free air hoses for reinflating are available at the *Pinyon Flats Campground*). The Medano Pass road heads north alongside Medano Creek, then turns east into the mountains to the pass eleven miles away. After around two and a half miles you will pass ghost trees – ponderosa pines killed by encroaching sands at Castle Creek. About a mile and a half further, the pines have been peeled by Utes, who used their barks for food and medicine.

The trailhead for the **Little Medano Pass Trail** is also at the Point Of No Return. This sandy trail roughly parallels the primitive road, rising and dipping through thorny shrubs, cacti, and wild grasses. Eventually, 5.5 miles further on, beyond the primitive *Little Medano Campground*, it becomes the **Sand Creek Trail**. It's a further six miles to the *Sand Creek Campground*, the most distant part of the accessible dunescape. Deer, elk, black bears, and mountain lions are regularly spotted from this remote trail, and the primitive *Cold Creek Campground*, a mile from the end, is a particularly beautiful spot, sandwiched between the dunes and a rugged valley in the Sangre de Cristos.

Practicalities

The most unforgettable way to stay here – and one that will leave sand in your gear for weeks – is to pitch on the dune mass itself. Virtually no one bothers to because of the slog up the dunes, but if you're up for it the visitor's center has the necessary and free **backcountry permits**. A backcountry permit is also needed to use the seven lightly used primitive backcountry sites ($10) in the park. Convenience dictates that most campers stay at the large *Pinyon Flats Campground* ($10), the only site in the park accessible by car and usually crowded with RVs. It is run on a first-come, first-served basis, and is often full in July and August.

The *Great Sand Dunes Oasis Store* (Ⓣ719/378-2222) just before the monument entrance offers showers, laundry, and arid tent sites ($10) as well as a small number of basic cabins (❸). They also conduct two-hour-long **four-wheel-drive tours** (June–Aug daily 10am & 2pm; May Sept & Oct daily 11am; $14) along part of the Medano Pass road. Behind the store, the *Great Sand Dunes Lodge* (Ⓣ719/378-2900, Ⓦwww.gsdlodge.com; ❺) has a restaurant, indoor pool, and pleasant rooms with dune views.

Zapata Falls

Some of the best views over the Sand Dunes are had from outside the park's boundaries, around six miles south of the park along CO-150 at **Zapata Falls**.

A gravel road, beside a roadside signpost, climbs four miles to the picnic and parking area and trailhead, from where there are excellent views of the dunes, their smooth curves elegantly contrasting with the ridge of jagged peaks behind. The falls are only a half-mile round trip from here, though the final sections along the rocky slippery riverbank and stepping-stones leading to the vigorous torrent are a bit tricky. Below the parking area several interconnecting trails make for pleasant hiking with occasional grand views of the San Luis Valley and Sangre de Cristo mountains. The trails also provide some relatively flat, mellow single-track mountain biking.

The Northeastern valley

Heading **northeast** from the Sand Dunes, the valley's long, straight, and flat roads cross little more than ranchland. It feels like driving Colorado's eastern plains and there's really very little here to stop for save a couple of eccentric attractions and a large collection of spiritual centers in tiny Crestone.

As out of place in the valley as the dunes themselves, the **San Luis Valley Alligator Farm** (daily: May–Sept 7am–7pm; Oct–April 10am–3pm; $5; Ⓦwww.gatorfarm.com), on Hwy-17, nineteen miles east of the sand dunes, originally began as a fish farm. The introduction of alligators only came about as an ingenious way of processing waste. The creatures are mostly intriguing as they seem so out of place – both the fish and reptiles survive the valley winters thanks to hot springs at the farm. The location of the **UFO Watchtower** (May–Sept 11am–10pm; free; Ⓣ719/580-7901, Ⓦwww.ufowatchtower.com), nine miles north of the alligator farm, is best explained by the owners, who built it on a whim in response to the many alleged sightings that have taken place in the valley. They can also offer ten campsites ($10) and a gift shop for alien souvenirs.

Crestone and around

A turnoff at the hamlet of Moffet, another ten miles along Hwy-17, leads thirteen miles to the spiritual village of **Crestone**. Formerly a tiny, ex-mining community, much of Crestone has been subdivided, with lots donated to various faiths by a rancher with a vision of international spiritual harmony in 1978. In its New Age form Crestone now attracts thousands of people from around the world to its various spiritual festivals, and a small community of artists and writers have also settled here.

The village itself is no more than a collection of houses around a general store, and most of the spiritual lots are a little further out of the center – and for the most part tucked away and largely obscured by woodlands. But if you hunt around, you'll find Buddhist (containing one of the largest *stupas* in the western hemisphere), Carmelite, and Zen centers, together with an Ashram and a few environmental projects.

A rudimentary **information board** on the county road that leads to the town can help with orientation and gives an idea of courses available at the various centers. If you are more interested in hiking here, it's best to stop by the Rio Grande National Forest headquarters (Ⓣ719/852-5941), near Monte Vista (p.142), first. One trip worth asking about is the **South Crestone Creek Trail**, which climbs up to South Crestone Lake on a ten-mile round-trip into bighorn sheep country. More trails leave from out of the *North Crestone Creek Campground* ($8) reached on the Alder Terrace road out of town. On the same road, the *Alder Terrace Inn* (Ⓣ719/265-4975; ③) has rooms with kitchens and a laundry in the same building. The modern *Rainbow B&B* (Ⓣ719/265-4110 or

1-800/530-1992; ❷) provides rooms with shared bath south of town – right at intersection to information board, then south around 1.5 miles.

Back on the main north–south road, CO-17, Salida (p.188) is 39 miles north of Moffat and there's really very little en route save the **Mineral Hot Springs Spa** (Thurs–Tues 10am–10pm; $10; ⓣ719/256-4328), a mile south of the junction with CO-285 (32 miles south of Salida). It's an elegant place to soak, offering a number of different massage styles as well.

Alamosa and around

As the one-time northern terminus of the Denver and Rio Grande railway, many of the utilitarian buildings in **Alamosa** were virtually thrown up overnight, having been brought in as portable buildings on flatbed rail cars. Despite the decline of the railroad industry, the town has remained an important trading and supply center and nucleus for the whole San Luis Valley. There's no denying it's a functional town, but its low rents have attracted a fair number of artists and craftsmen, and the small Adams State College is also a lively influence. For visitors, the town is usually just a stop off on the way across the San Luis Valley or down to the Cumbres and Toltec Railroad that starts from Antonito, south on the New Mexico border.

Arrival, information and accommodation

The TNM&O bus line serves Alamosa on their Denver to Albuquerque route; the stop is outside SLV Van lines, 8480 Stockton St (ⓣ719/589-4948), on the west side of town. Alamosa's **visitors' center** (ⓣ719/589-3681 or 1-800/258-7597, ⓦwww.alamosa.org) is beside Cole Park and the Rio Grande, and is the best source of information for the entire San Luis Valley. Alamosa Sporting Goods, 1114 Main St (ⓣ719/589-3006), can advise on hunting and fishing regulations for national forest areas fringing the valley.

The Alamosa KOA Juniper Lane, north of US-160 ⓣ719/589-9757. A KOA located three miles east of town; tent sites go for $16, fully hooked-up RV plots for $21.

Alamosa Lamplighter Motel 425 Main St ⓣ719/589-6636 or 1-800/359-2138. Two large locally-owned good-value motels under the same management at the center of town, separated by a few blocks. Rooms are nondescript standard motel fare, but guests at either have use of an indoor swimming pool, a sauna, and a hot tub. There are laundry facilities and some rooms come with kitchenettes. ❹

Best Western Alamosa Inn 1919 Main St ⓣ719/589-2567 or 1-800/528-1234, ⓦwww.bestwestern.com/alamosainn. Large, recently refurbished rooms. Facilities include hot tub, sauna, indoor pool, and a restaurant. ❺

Cottonwood Inn 123 San Juan Ave ⓣ719/589-3882 or 1-800/955-2623, ⓦwww.cottonwood-inn.com. A number of antique-furnished rooms with clawfoot tubs in a leafy Victorian neighborhood. The inn, also a gallery showcasing local art, offers packages that include the Cumbres and Toltec train, tours of local hot springs, horseback riding, and golf. ❹

Sky-Vue Motel 250 Broadway ⓣ719/589-4945 or 1-800/805-9164. Basic adobe-styled motel with simple rooms, some with kitchenettes. Often the cheapest deal in town. ❷

The town and around

Much of Alamosa centers around the main road, CO-160 (Main St), which crosses the Rio Grande on its way through town. For a brief (30min) tour, start just east of the river, on the opposite bank to the shady cottonwoods of **Cole Park**, following the riverside trail north. Less than a mile along you pass the public **Cattails Golf Course** (ⓣ719/589-9515), where golfers take advantage of the valley's average of 350 days of sun. Cross back over the river at State Avenue, taking it as far as 3rd Street, which heads back to Cole Park, to the visitor information center and the **San Luis Valley History Center** (June–Sept

10am–4pm; ☎719/587-0667). This houses a small, but reasonably diverting, collection of old local photographs and artifacts charting the valley's multicultural history.

If you're in town in the spring or fall (March–May/Sept–Nov), head three miles east out of town on Rt-160 to the **Alamosa National Wildlife Refuge**, 9383 El Rancho Lane (refuge: daily sunrise–sunset; office: Mon–Fri 7.30am–4pm; ☎719/589-4021). The massive wetland area around a meandering stretch of the Rio Grande is popular with migrating and nesting waterfowl. Around 20,000 sandhill and whooping cranes (an endangered species with 8ft wingspan) stop here along their migratory routes, and bald eagles nest here too in the spring.

Eating and drinking

Bauer's Campus Pancake House 435 Poncha Ave ☎719/589-4202. Good place to start the day with a large cinnamon roll. The place caters mainly to a student crowd – probably why breakfast is served until closing at 2pm. Closed Tuesdays.

El Charro Café 421 6th St ☎719/589-2262. Basic ambience and what's locally considered staple fare: entrees like the huge and excellent guacamole tostada ($5). The unlicensed café is two blocks south of the visitors' center and closed Mondays.

Mrs Rivera's 1019 6th St ☎719/589-0277. Locally considered one of the best, *Mrs Rivera's* does great chile rellenos ($6). There are also good margaritas in the restaurant's cheery Mexican atmosphere. A block south of Main St; open for lunch and dinner.

St Ives Pub and Eatery 719 Main St ☎719/589-0711. On top of the selection of microbrewed beers, cheap bar food like New York deli sandwiches, salads, and hamburgers are served. Open until midnight but closed Sundays.

True Grits Steakhouse 100 Santa Fe Ave ☎719/589-9954. Noisy basic steakhouse combined with a shrine to John Wayne. Reasonably priced steak lunches ($7) and dinners come in massive oversized portions. Located a couple of blocks east of the Rio Grande.

South to Antonito and the Cumbres and Toltec railroad

The road south is a dusty affair, as is the town of Antonito, the terminus of the Cumbres and Toltec railroad, 28 miles south of Alamosa. On the way, though, there are a few diversions worth a look. Nine miles west of uneventful La Jara, in tiny Capulin, is **Eppie Archuleta's Studio** (☎719/274-5019). Five generations of Archuletas (including Eppie's mother, aged over one hundred) weave here using traditional looms. Some of Eppie's weaving has been displayed as regional folk art in Washington DC's Smithsonian and though the studio's not really run as a tourist attraction, those passing by are welcome to stop in, and some pieces are on sale. Back on the main highway, three miles south of La Jara is the USFS Conejos Peak Ranger District Office (☎719/274-8971), a good place to pick up information on the fishing and hiking possibilities to the west. A couple of miles further on is the turnoff for the almost entirely Mormon town of **Manassa**. Here in the log cabin birthplace of the Manassa Mauler is the **Jack Dempsey Museum**, 401 Main St (May–Sept Mon–Sat 9am–5pm). The museum uses clippings and artifacts to celebrate the life of the heavyweight boxing great who went on to win the world title in 1919 after years of prize-fighting in mining camp saloons like those in Cripple Creek.

Unappealing and run-down, **Antonito** is only notable as a terminus of the **Cumbres and Toltec Scenic Railroad** (see box, overleaf), though there's good backcountry fishing and hiking west along the Conejos River Valley. TNM&O buses between Denver and Albuquerque stop at the Texaco store in town once a day, and Twin Hearts Express (☎505/751-1201) run a **shuttle** service from the *Holiday Inn*, 333 Santa Fe Ave, in Alamosa, to the railroad. Round-trips cost $20. Opposite the railroad depot, the **visitors' center** (☎719/376-2049 or 1-

The Cumbres and Toltec Scenic Railroad

The **Cumbres and Toltec Scenic Railroad** (ⓣ719/376-5483 or 1-888/286-2737, ⓦwww.cumbrestoltec.com) was originally conceived as a link for a grand railroad to El Paso and Mexico City before it became part of a narrow-gauge railroad serving mining camps by connecting with Farmington, Durango, and Silverton. Clearly a must for railroad buffs, the 64-mile run in open cars is an atmospheric tour through pine and aspen groves cut along the mountainous border between Colorado and New Mexico, the line running as far as **Chama** (New Mexico). On its unhurried, meandering route, the steam trains ascend the spectacular **Cumbres Pass** and run on high wooden trestles above deep pristine gorges like the one at **Toltec**. In early trials, one trestle above Cascade Creek was the site of a derailment – the last for over a century up to the present.

Since both trains depart daily (May–Oct) from Antonito and Chama, the two trains meet during a stop for lunch at mountain ghost town **Osier**. By riding one or both trains and using company buses, four different round-trips are possible. From Antonito: to Osier (departs 10am, returns 4.45pm; $38); to Cumbres, returning by bus (departs 10am, returns 4pm; $58); to Chama, returning by bus (departs 10am, returns 6pm; $58); to Chama by bus, return by train (departs 9.15am returns 4.45pm; $58). A similar array of options is also possible from Chama and in all cases under-11s pay half-price. Whichever trip you make, take plenty of clothing, since the mountain passes and open cars can get cold.

800/835/1098) can provide information and directions to **Tres Piedras,** a location for good **rock climbing** around thirty miles south, in New Mexico.

Some of the most pleasant **accommodation** is west of town along the Conejos River, where numerous campsites and cabins are located. However, most of these are closed between October and May, when the cheap and basic *Park Motel* (ⓣ719/376-5582 or 1-888/892-5701; ❷) and the slightly plusher *Narrow Gauge Railroad Inn* (ⓣ719/376-5441 or 1-800/323-9469; ❸) in Antonito itself may be the best options. The *Dutch Mill Café* can provide standard diner fare and good Mexican dishes. Heading west five miles on CO-17 (in the direction of Chama), *Cottonwood Meadows* (ⓣ719/376-5660; ❸) is well set up for **fishing,** not only renting comfortable two-person cabins, but also running an equipment and tack shop.

The Western Valley

Heading northwest along the Rio Grande, through a rich agricultural area that has **Monte Vista** at its heart, the mountains get closer and good **hiking** and **biking** opportunities abound. This is also the start of great trout **fishing** in the headwaters of the Rio Grande located upstream of **Del Norte**, a former supply center and now a gateway to the superb **climbing** further north at **La Garita**.

Monte Vista

Pretty much the only reason you'll want to pop into the nondescript farming town of **Monte Vista**, seventeen miles west of Alamosa on Hwy-160, is to stop by a couple of **informational offices** that are useful for planning time in the mountains. Material on hunting or viewing wildlife can be had at the Colorado Division of Wildlife office, 722 S CO-1, south of Hwy-160 (Mon–Fri 8am–5pm; ⓣ719/852-4783), while west out of town the Rio Grande National Forest Headquarters, 1803 W US-160 (8am–4.30pm; ⓣ719/852-5941) has information and maps on the national forest on both sides of the valley. If looking for a **place to stay**, the most novel option is the 1950s style *Movie Manor Motel,* two miles west of town (2830 W Rt 160; ⓣ719/852-5921 or 1-800/771-9468; ⓦwww.coloradovacation/motel/movie.com; ⑤). The otherwise bland motel units here all look out onto the big screen of the next door *Star Drive-In Movie Theatre*, and soundtracks for the films – screened April to September – are piped into each room.

Mountain bikers and **hikers** visiting Monte Vista, should head for the fifteen-mile loop on single-track trails through dense stands of aspen around **Cat Creek**, thirteen miles south of Monte Vista (CO-15, right onto Forest Road 250 for seven miles and follow signs for Deer Creek on Forest Road 271). The trailhead begins at a sign for the Cat Creek Horse Trail. The first leg climbs the rutted four-wheel-drive Deer Creek Trail (Forest Road 271); turn onto the single-track climb up Forest Road 703, for the final ascent across to the fantastic views of the San Luis Valley from Blowout Pass Overlook; then descending alongside Cat Creek (Forest Road 704) on single-track. The trail takes around two hours to bike and around five to hike, though longer after rainstorms, when it quickly gets muddy. Kristi Mountain Sports, Villa Mall, Alamosa (ⓣ719/589-9759), rents out front-suspension mountain bikes for $15/day.

La Garita

La Garita, twenty miles north of Monte Vista off US-285, has earned a superb reputation in the world of rock-climbing. In nearby **Penitente Canyon**, four hundred (mostly bolted) climbs on both gigantic boulders and sheer walls span the full range of skill levels. Before heading to the canyon, a former nineteenth century chapel, built by an offshoot of the Penitente lay brotherhood (see San Luis p.136), might be of interest. It now houses the **San Juan Art Center**, a co-operative venture displaying and selling Hispanic folk art (May–Sept, Mon–Fri, 10am–5pm; Sat 1–5pm).

To find the canyon, go one mile west from the La Garita store (which has information on the backcountry camping at free local BLM **campgrounds**), veer left after the pavement ends, then turn right off the main road which heads south – taking the middle of three roads. Looking like a huge bullet-hole in the volcanic dyke, **La Ventana**, a vast natural arch, has commanding views over the San Luis Valley. It's eight miles further south of Penitente Canyon (three miles on 38A; three miles on 32A; right at the second fork once inside the national forest, then two miles to parking area) and is a short but steep scramble up from the dirt road. Around 100 **bighorn sheep** live here, so have your camera ready.

Del Norte

A supply center for the Rio Grande headwater area, **Del Norte**, fourteen miles west of Monte Vista, can also supply information on local hiking and climbing, as well as gear at Casa de Madera, 680 Grande Ave (ⓣ719/657-2336). Check with Del Norte Ranger District Office, 13308 W Hwy 160 (ⓣ719/657-3321), for the special catch and tackle restrictions applying to the local, so-called Gold Medal fishing areas. **Rio Grande County Museum**, 580 Oak St (Mon–Fri 11am–4pm; $1), explores the multicultural history of the Rio Grande headwaters area with some ancient petroglyphs among its general information on rock-art sites. Relics relating to the exploration of the area by mountain men are also displayed here – particularly from the failed expedition in quest of a winter-time route over the Continental Divide, in which a third of the 33-man expedition died. A couple of **motels** at the eastern end of US-160 into town have straightforward rooms: *The El Rancho,* 1160 Grande Ave (☎719/657-3332; ❷); and the slightly smarter *Del Norte Motel and Café,* 1050 Grande Ave (☎719/657-3581 or 1-800/372-2332; ❸), where breakfast and lunch is also served. *Stone Quarry Pizza*, 580 Grande Ave (☎719/657-9115), has a good salad bar and of course pizzas, served inside or on an outdoor patio; the *La Fuente Supper Club*, 540 Grande Ave (☎719/657-3492), does steaks, seafood and good traditional Mexican fare at low prices.

San Juan Mountains

The **SAN JUAN MOUNTAINS**, which form the Continental Divide in Colorado's southwest corner, are the largest, wildest, and least populated range in the state. For backcountry explorers, it's the state's premier playground, a jumbled mass of often inaccessible deep-green forest slopes and jagged peaks. While all other ranges in the state are relatively narrow and consequently less remote, in the San Juans you really can get away from it all. But even less-adventurous travelers sticking to the area's main routes can easily appreciate the scenery in what's been dubbed the "Alps of America" via scenic roads, a steam train, four-wheel-drive vehicles, mountain bikes, or by foot.

The range's **eastern** side rises gently from the San Juan Valley and is home to the dynamic little towns of **Creede** and **Lake City**. Heading west leads to the Continental Divide, where the **Wolf Creek** ski area auspiciously sits receiving Colorado's highest average snowfall, and over to the modest town of Pagosa Springs, little more than a pit stop (albeit with a nice hot soak) for travelers on the way to laid-back **Durango**. A base for healthy young bohemians enjoying some of the state's best year-round outdoor recreation, Durango is also the gateway to the arid Southwest Four Corners region: where the borders of Colorado, New Mexico, Arizona, and Utah meet. The highly organized Ancestral Puebloans (formerly known as the Anasazi – a term now considered offensive by modern Puebloans as it means "Ancient Enemy" in Navajo) populated cliffside pueblo towns, leaving the extraordinary remains in the region. The most spectacular include the ceremonial structures at **Chimney Rock** near Pagosa Springs and cliff dwellings – clinging precariously like eagle's nests in the high rocky alcoves of the red-rock canyon walls – at both **Mesa Verde**

Accommodation price codes

All accommodation prices in this book have been coded using the symbols below. For **hotels**, **motels**, and **B&Bs**, rates are given for the least expensive double room in each establishment during peak season; variations are indicated where appropriate, including winter rates for all ski resorts. For **hostels**, we've given a specific price per bed; for **camping**, the overnight cost per site is given. For a full explanation see p.30 in Basics.

❶ up to $30	❹ $60-80	❼ $130–180
❷ $30–45	❺ $80-100	❽ $180–240
❸ $45–60	❻ $100–130	❾ over $240

National Park and the more remote **Ute Mountain Tribal Park**. Durango is also an access point to the spectacular mountain region bisected by the **San Juan Skyway** to the north. The highway darts through a series of stunning high mountain passes before looping its way through a trio of great stopovers; the atmospheric mining town of **Silverton**, the touristy Victorian resort town of **Ouray** and the spectacular ski-town of **Telluride**.

The Eastern Mountains

In contrast to the western side of the San Juan range where Durango and Telluride typically throb with visitors, the **eastern side** of the range is a remote backwater. Small **South Fork** is really only notable as it's the eastern gateway to the San Juan Mountains. From here, Hwy-149 cuts north to **Creede**, **Lake City**, and eventually the Gunnison region (see p.177), while Hwy-160 heads east to Durango via **Pagosa Springs**. Besides perhaps using the town as a lodging alternative when skiing at **Wolf Creek**, you'll most likely speed right through, though "Biggin," a 24-foot-tall wooden lumberjack at the main highway junction, might catch your eye.

Creede

Sheer, gaping canyon walls form the picturesque backdrop of the quirky, slightly ramshackle town of **CREEDE**. Some twenty miles north of South Fork on Hwy-149, this one-time mining boomtown is the seat for the surrounding Mineral County, 95 percent of which is national forest. Not surprisingly then, the opportunities for outdoor recreation here are seemingly boundless. Creede also makes a good base from which to explore the area's mining history along a maze of four-wheel-drive roads extending in all directions. One such road also heads to the most remarkable landscape in the area, the **Wheeler Geologic Area**, a geological oddity that's well worth the difficult trek.

The town was named after Nicolas Creede who, poking around in the ground during a lunch stop above Wagon Wheel Gap in 1889, uncovered ore and is said to have exclaimed "Holy Moses, I've struck it rich!" He had, finding the richest silver lode in Colorado, and the Holy Moses Mine began a rush that quickly created a town of around 10,000 citizens, half miners and half colorful hangers-on. Indeed, the local newspaper at the time claimed that "some of her citizens would take a prize at a hog show," though legendary characters like "Calamity Jane" Canary, "Poker Annie" Tubbs, and Denver's infamous conman Jefferson Randolph "Soapy" Smith (see p.71) were probably too busy pulling off scams to take much offense.

Information and accommodation

For information, head to the small but obvious **visitor center** cabin on Main Street (June–Sept Mon–Sat 8am–5pm; Oct–May Mon–Fri 9am–5pm; Ⓣ719/658-2374 or 1-800/327-2102, Ⓦwww.creede.com), which has a good map outlining a walking tour of the tiny downtown. Before embarking on any outdoor exploration, call in at the **USFS Divide District Ranger Station**, 3rd Street and Creede Avenue (May–Nov 8am–4.30pm; Ⓣ719/658-2556), loaded with information on both the Forest Service lands surrounding town and also the nearby Weminuche Wilderness Area (see p.169).

There are virtually limitless opportunities for dispersed **camping** around Creede, since it is entirely surrounded by national forest land. In addition,

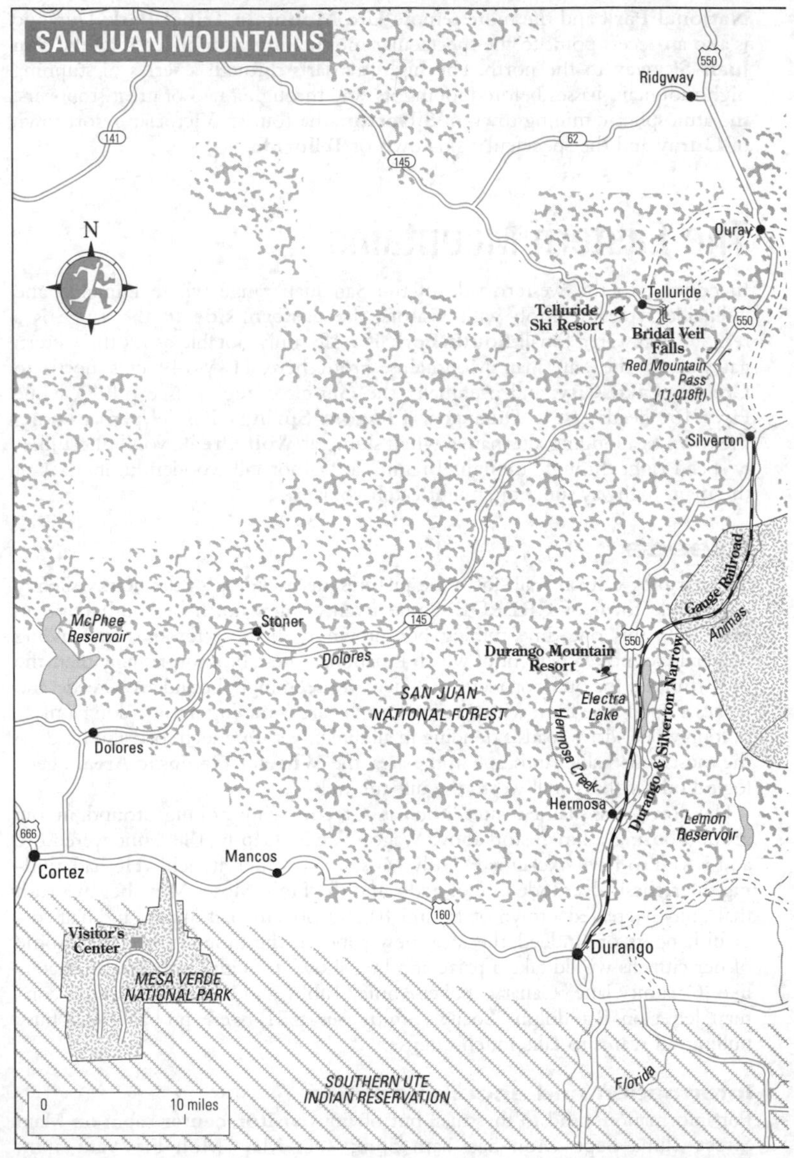

campers will find about a dozen USFS **campgrounds** within twenty miles of town. The most convenient (and most popular, so make reservations) are the *Marshall Park Campground*, seven miles southwest of Creede on Hwy-149, and the *Rio Grande Campground* another seven miles along the same road ($10; ⓣ1-800/280-2267). Creede's Victorian main street contains several **B&Bs** and a **hotel**. The cheapest central option is the *Snowshoe Lodge* (ⓣ719/658-0212; ③)

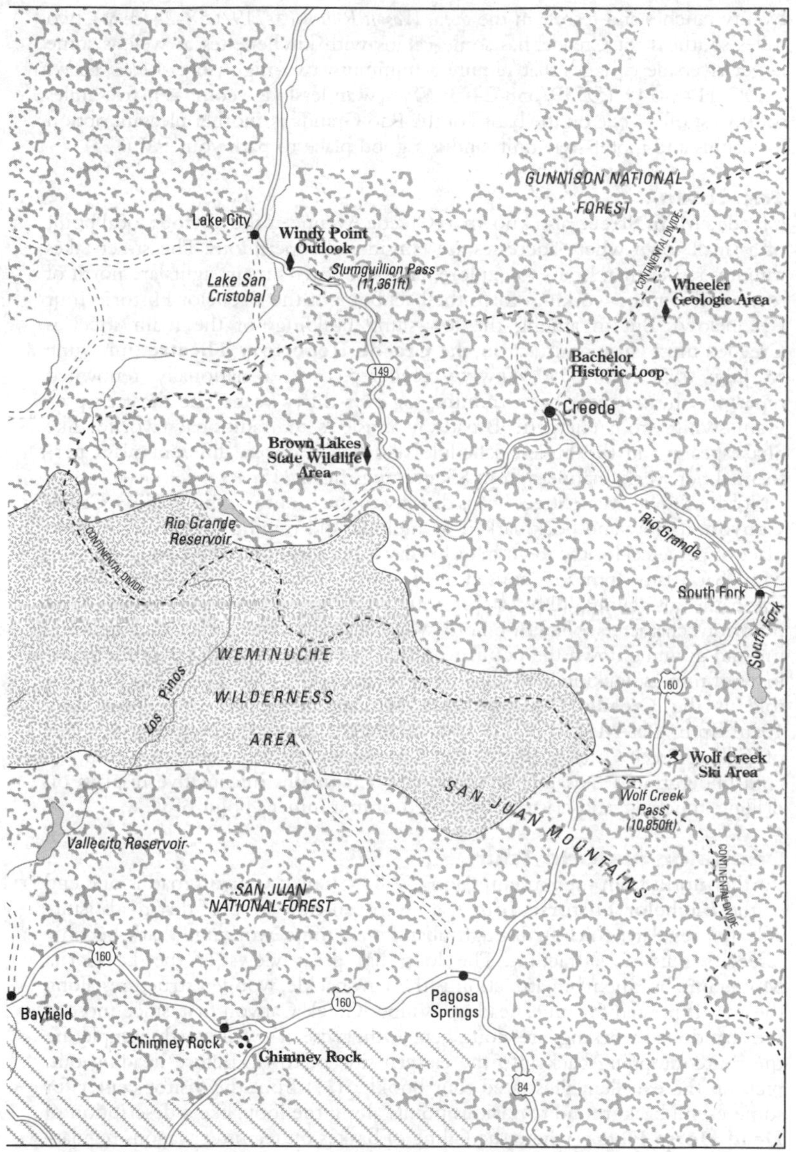

whose clean motel rooms are on the southeast edge of town. Not much more expensive is the classy *Creede Hotel B&B* (☎719/658-2608; Ⓦwww.creedehotel.com; ❹; May–Oct), in the heart of town beside the repertory theatre where rates include a good breakfast. Slightly further down the road is *The Old Firehouse No. 1 B&B*, Main Street (☎719/658-0212; ❺; May–Oct), with a pleasant communal sitting room decorated with old firefighting memorabilia. Of the twenty ranches and resorts in the area, *Wason Ranch* (☎719/658-2413; ❸), two miles southeast of Creede, has some cabins with kitchenettes as well as some larger riverside cottages that require a minimum two-night stay. *Antlers Lodge*, 26222 Hwy-149 (☎719/658-2423; Ⓦwww.antlerslodge.com; ❺), five miles southwest of Creede on the banks of the Rio Grande is another pleasant option for cabins and motel-style units and is a good place to park your RV ($23).

The town

Creede's **Main Street**, also known as Creede Avenue, is the obvious focal point of a small town where addresses are considered superfluous. The street takes minutes rather than hours to explore, since the town's main sights are north of town where mine workings form the backbone of the Bachelor Historic Tour (see below). But in among the low-slung buildings of the main street is Creede's most curious attraction, the **Creede Repertory Theatre** (mid-June to July; ☎719/658-2540, Ⓦwww.creederep.com), a nationally renowned repertory theatre that's been running for over thirty years. The theatre's program swings from energetic Broadway musicals to traditional favorites like Shakespeare, and the busiest schedule sees half a dozen different plays performed per week; matinees from $5, evenings from $15.

North of town, Main Street heads directly to the mouth of the **Willow Creek Canyon**, narrow and pockmarked by multiple old mining operations. A good place to get a feel for the town in its heyday is the **Creede Museum** (June–Aug Mon–Sat 10am–4pm; $1), housed in the town's former railroad depot behind city park. Entertaining displays concentrate on biographies of the town's more notorious characters – like Bob Ford, who became a town pariah after ambushing and gunning down the popular outlaw Jesse James – rather than the trainloads of miners flocking here during the town's boom days. The miners' story is told at the **Creede Underground Mining Museum** (June–Sept daily 10am–4pm; Oct–May Mon–Fri 10am–3pm; $5), north of town near the start of Willow Creek Canyon. Blasted and dug specifically as a mining museum, the cold underground museum, a constant 51°F, contains informative displays on drilling, mucking, and blasting, explained from a miner's point of view.

Bachelor Historic Tour

Further north from the museum along Willow Creek Canyon road is one end of the **Bachelor Historic Tour** – a seventeen-mile loop of dirt roads (suitable for regular vehicles) through abandoned mine workings that's become Creede's must-do attraction. The loop has great views of the La Garita Mountains, but the main attraction is the ramshackle, wooden structures along the way. If pressed for time, head up Willow Creek Canyon first, since most of the abandoned workings are along here. Otherwise, it's well worth completing the route, dropping back into the eastern side of town. Before heading out, pick up the excellent illustrated tour booklet ($1) from the visitor center for some useful background to various points along the loop, like a description of **Dead Horse Flats** – where the failing of brakes on teamster wagons regularly sent animals to their death. It also has information about **Bachelor City**, whose 1200 bachelors made the place rough even by Creede standards – strange to imagine, when all that's left now is just a meadow with some scattered rocks and a downed cabin.

Wheeler Geologic Area

The result of repeated volcanic ash flows that hardened to be carved by wind and rain into a small 60-acre town of spiny spires and dank caverns, the

Wheeler Geologic Area is quite the surprise in an area dominated by hanging valleys and smooth high-alpine meadows. Framed by evergreen forests, its dramatic, contorted landscape of spires and molten mounds began life around 40 million years ago, with violent eruptions of lava from volcanoes melting together to form a rise 4000 feet thick and over 9000 square miles wide. A million years later another major eruption caused accumulations of ash up to 3000 feet deep. Volcanic debris – dust and pebbles – settled into layers on the ground called tuff. Occasional rock fragments (brecca) – sometimes two or three feet in diameter – were also thrown out to nestle in the tuff beds. Under its own weight, the tuff hardened into rock and these brecca lodged in the rock strata were subsequently less susceptible to erosion than the surrounding tuff. Consequently small areas of tuff, protected by pieces of brecca above, survived the wind and water erosion that cleared other material, leaving spindly minarets precariously topped by brecca. Water running from these towers helped not only deepen the gaps between them, but also carved tiny erosion gullies in the form of twisted wrinkles into the rock below.

Whichever means you choose, the route to the monument is not an easy one. You can hike, cycle or four-wheel drive to it, but as hikers have a separate, more direct path, it's around a five-hour round-trip regardless of how you travel. The road, when open (usually late May to Oct), is around fifteen miles long, making for a thirty-mile round trip, hikers need to cover only half that distance to get to the monument along the hiking trail. The road and hiking trail begin beside one another, eighteen miles south of Creede – take Hwy-149 eleven miles in the direction of South Fork, then follow Pool Table Road (Forest Road 600) seven miles east.

Outdoor activities

Though most drive the Bachelor Historic Tour, it also makes a good three-hour loop on a **mountain bike**; generally done clockwise to get most of the climbing out of the way in the first four miles. The loop begins near the cemetery, marked by a small sign on off Hwy-149 on the town's southern perimeter. Mountain bikes ($18 per day) can be **rented** from San Juan Sports (Ⓣ719/658-2359 or 1-888/658-0851), a block west of Main Street. They also rent out backpacking and mountaineering gear, making it a good first stop for any **hikers** as well. One of the area's prettiest hikes is up to the high alpine meadow of Phoenix Park, past waterfalls and beaver ponds along the way; the trailhead is at the top of East Willow Canyon, the next valley east of the Bachelor Historic Tour, by the defunct King Solomon Mill.

The Creede area is also well-known for excellent **fishing** as the waters of the Rio Grande start their 1900-mile journey to the Gulf of Mexico. The river snakes past town two miles to the south, but some of the best places to fish are several miles further south on Hwy-149 around USFS *Marshall Park* and *Rio Grande* campgrounds (see p.146). Another popular fishing spot is the Brown Lakes State Wildlife Area, 25 miles west of Creede along Hwy-149, where large browns and native cutthroat are the main attraction. If you're in the area, it's also worth pausing to see **North Clear Creek Falls**, a little further west along Hwy-149 than the Brown Lakes turnoff and just half-a-mile from the highway. The impressive falls plunge into a deep gorge here and can be viewed from an outlook from the gorge's edge. Creede Guide & Outfitters (Ⓣ719/658-2482) on Creede Avenue has a good stock of fishing supplies, sells licenses, and runs lessons and trips, including wade trips from $50 and float trips from $80.

Eating and drinking

Considering the size of Creede, the selection of **places to eat** isn't too bad. A good place to start the day with a healthy breakfast or a pastry is *Journeys* (Ⓣ719/658-2290) on the west side of Main Street, which also does good natural-food lunches. Just southeast of the center the *Bears' Den* (Ⓣ719/658-2423) on 7th Street and La Garita Avenue is the town's main diner, patronized by plenty of locals thanks to its good-value home-cooked omelettes, burgers, and steaks for breakfast, lunch, and dinner. The *Bears' Den* bar is also a lively place at night, as is the *Tommy Knocker Tavern* (Ⓣ719/658-0138), just east of Main Street at the center of town, a small popular bar serving Mexican food with regular live music. The pick for fine dining in town is the *Creede Hotel Dining Room*, Main Street (May–Sept; Ⓣ719/658-2608), a popular pre-theatre venue, when reservations are advised. Lunches here include the usual burgers and sandwiches for $6–10; while the homemade entrees (from $13) served for dinner include tamari-honey chicken, prime rib, and baked salmon.

Lake City

Located fifty miles from both Creede to the southeast and Gunnison to the north, **LAKE CITY** is one of the remotest towns in the Colorado Rockies. Lake San Cristobal, Colorado's second largest, is only a short way west of town, hemmed in by the huge Slumgullion earthslide (see below). Unlike most mining camps, Lake City was never a particularly rowdy place, attracting mostly optimistic pioneers who built a small town full of Greek and Gothic Revival architecture. After the gold rush, the town's population, which peaked at around 5000, steadily dwindled, and by the 1960s it was virtually abandoned. But in the last decade, it has started to burgeon again, curiously largely with Texans looking for summer homes. It's easy to see why they're attracted, as the peaceful town is a great launch pad from which to explore a network of four-wheel-drive tracks and there's also easy access to the **Big Blue** and **Powderhorn Wilderness** areas, both offering secluded backpacking and superb fishing.

A short line of proud Neoclassical buildings have survived intact to form the town's historic core along **Silver Street**. A few of the buildings here now house craftsy shops and some restaurants, but the main point of interest is the **Hindsdale County Museum** ($2), at the southern end of the street, at the junction with 2nd Street. Some exhibits here chart the town's history, but the lion's share of the museum is devoted to the macabre exploits of Alferd Packer (see box opposite).

The most stunning approach into town is from the south over Slumgullion Pass. Just north of the pass is the **Windy Point** outlook, where great views of both Mount Uncompahgre in the distance and the nearby **Slumgullion Slide** are had. The mudslide itself came in two distinct thrusts, the first eight hundred years ago when a huge amount of mud slid five miles down to block the valley, damming the Lake Fork of the Gunnison River and forming Lake San Cristobal. The second, slower and still persisting slide began around 350 years ago. It's easy to pick out the active portions as they're barren of trees.

Outdoor activities

Many visitors to Lake City are here to go off-road exploring with four-wheel-drive jeeps, typically heading along the **Alpine Loop Backcountry Byway**, 65 miles of mostly rough four-wheel-drive road that passes old ghost towns and mining centers to link Lake City with both Ouray and Silverton. There are a number of places hiring four-wheel-drives, including the *Gingerbed & Breakfast* (see overleaf) who do rentals from around $80 per day.

Hikers will find good trails leading through mixed forest and small alpine meadows to beautiful mountain lakes in virtually any direction. One particularly good trip is the approximately fifteen-mile loop to Thompson, Larson, and Crystal Lakes, beginning from the trailhead near the cemetery at the north of town. Despite a couple of steep sections, the trail is generally easy and makes an ideal overnight trip, leaving time for some fishing. Of the many longer and more ambitious hiking options within striking distance of town, the most obvious places to head to are the **Big Blue Wilderness**, which includes the 14,000ft-plus Uncompahgre, Wetterhorne, and Handies peaks, to the east of town, and the **Powderhorn Wilderness** to the west. Obviously the altitude makes any of the fourteeners harder to bag, but ascending **Handies Peak** is relatively straightforward and the views no less glorious than elsewhere. The trail begins around twenty miles southwest of Lake City off CR-34 – a minor road beyond Lake San Cristobal, heading up the north side of Grizzly Gulch. From the top of the peak you can continue on down to Sloan Lake to make a loop with CR-34 and avoid retracing your steps. This loop is a full day's work at around ten miles long.

Both wilderness areas are also premium elk habitat and popular for their good trout **fishing**. The fishing in Henson Creek, just east of town is also good for a short trip, but if you're planning to fish in the area for a while be sure to pick up the guide to local fishing spots ($1) produced by the chamber of commerce. Cannibal Outdoors, 355 S Gunnison Ave (Ⓣ970/944-2559, Ⓦwww

Colorado's Cannibal

South of Lake City on Hwy-149 near its junction with CO-30, sits a memorial to five prospectors butchered by the locally infamous **Alferd Packer**. Packer was originally hired as a guide to lead the prospectors from Montrose to the Breckenridge Gold Strike in February 1874. Against the advice of local Indians, including chief Ouray, who feared the winter weather would spell disaster for the party, they set off, leaving town with only seven days' worth of provisions. Nothing was seen of the party until April, when relatively healthy Packer turned up alone in Lake City, claiming to have endured near-starvation when his companions left him behind due to an injury. But Packer had little interest in food, being more interested in stiff drinks for which he paid with money from several wallets. Suspicions were naturally aroused and Packer soon changed his story, claiming his companions had developed frostbite and asked him to go ahead without them, taking their personal possessions as some kind of precautionary measure. Nobody believed this story either, and upon further questioning Packer eventually broke down and admitted tearfully that his companions had died one by one, and yes, the remaining survivors had used the bodies when legitimate food supplies ran low. Asked to lead a search party to the remains of the others, he lost his memory on several attempts and the bodies were not found. Packer was jailed anyway in Saguache, in the northern San Luis Valley, from where he escaped before he could be tried. As spring melted the snows around Lake City, local Ute found strips of human flesh, and in June, a *Harper's Weekly* artist stumbled on the skeletons – one had been shot in the back and the others had their skulls crushed. Ranching under an assumed name in Wyoming, Packer was recaptured nearly a decade later in 1883 and was convicted of murdering and cannibalizing his companions. The conviction was overturned on a technicality; three years later he was retried, convicted, and received a forty-year sentence, during which time he became a vegetarian. He was eventually released on health grounds and died in 1907 – he now lies in Littleton cemetery, on the southwestern edge of Denver.

.cannibaloutdoors.com), can answer fishing questions as well as set you up with gear. For **bike rentals**, contact San Juan Mountain Bikes (ⓣ970/944-2274) at the north end of town, who hire out front-suspension bikes for $25 per day.

Practicalities

Conveniently, the local chamber of commerce is combined with the USFS and BLM to provide a very useful **visitor center** at Gunnison Avenue and 8th Street on the north side of town (ⓣ970/944-2527 or 1-800/569-1874, ⓦwww.lakecity.net). For its size, Lake City has a surprisingly good range of **accommodation** options. These include two downtown **campgrounds**; the *Lake City Campground* (ⓣ970/944-2668) on Bluff Street, where facilities include a laundry and public showers (tents $12, RVs $16); and the *Henson Creek RV Park* at Henson Creek Bridge (ⓣ970/944-2394) which has similar facilities, but a slightly prettier location beside a creek ($17). The town's stock of standard motels include the *Matterhorn Lodge* (ⓣ970/944-2210 or 1-800/779-8028; ❸; May–Oct), a block from the center on the west side of town on Bluff Street. In addition, several local ranches in the area have set themselves up as rustic resorts, including the exclusive *Crystal Lodge*, Rt 149 S (ⓣ970-944-2201; ❻), tucked away in the forest near Lake San Cristobal with several lodging options ranging from simple rooms to luxury cabins. The resort has a gourmet restaurant, a hot tub, and several hiking trails – as well as splendid views of Crystal Peak. *Gingerbed & Breakfast B&B* (ⓣ970/944-2888 or 1-800/421-5509; ❺), in a Victorian home just outside the center of Lake City, offers private baths, hot tub, and cable TV.

Lake City has a fair number of **restaurants**, many catering to expensive, gourmet tastes. The *Lake City Bakery*, 922 Hwy-149 (ⓣ970/944-2613) at the north end of town near the Lake City Market, is a good place to start the day with a varied collection of fresh-baked goods. Later on, the *Blue Iguana*, 808 N Gunnison Ave (ⓣ970/944-1618), is a simple cantina that's a good choice for Mexican food; most of the filling combination plates run around $7. In the heart of old downtown, *Mammy's Kitchen & Whiskey Bar*, 304 Silver St (ⓣ970/944-4142), is a perennial favorite for both its restaurant and bar. The mains, including steaks, trout, and roasted duck, are all served with fresh bread and soup. Entrees are $10–15 and the bar stays open until 2am.

Wolf Creek Ski Area

Perched on the Continental Divide between South Fork and Pagosa Springs, the **Wolf Creek Ski Area** (ⓣ970/264-2268 or 1-800/754-9653, ⓦwww.wolfcreekski.com) gets more snow than any other resort in Colorado – around 450 inches per year – and some of the earliest, with the season starting in early November. It's particularly popular with those searching for steep glades and chutes. The relatively small ski area covers 1600 acres and is served by a mere six lifts that carry skiers and boarders up almost 1500 feet to superb views from an elevation of nearly 12,000ft. The ski area has a choice of fifty trails; the terrain divides up as twenty percent beginner, fifty percent intermediate, and thirty percent advanced. Though evenly split, it's the advanced runs that have made this a local favorite. Extreme skiers and boarders particularly enjoy the Knife Ridge area, a breathtakingly exposed ridge, from where you can often launch yourself into chest-deep clouds of fluffy snow through glades, chutes, and in bowls. Strong intermediate skiers can try the milder, but equally impressive Water Fall area, and even beginners will find good runs here. The resort infrastructure at the base of the lifts is minimal, although rentals are available. The relatively inexpensive tickets (adult day-pass is $42) and reliably minimal lift lines make Wolf Creek a consistently popular ski area.

Pagosa Springs

Swooping down from the densely wooded Wolf Creek Pass, Hwy-160 arrives in the rolling landscape of the San Juan River Valley, at the center of which nestles the modest town of **Pagosa Springs**. The town owes its location here beside the San Juan River, to the presence of one of North America's major geothermal springs and has sprawled out along the main highway to capitalize on its attractiveness to visitors. The hot springs themselves have long been held sacred among Native Americans; a no man's land where weapons of feuding tribes, including Ute, Navajo, and Apache, would be laid down and healing mud packs applied. Nearby archeological evidence – a spear point and the foundations of a shelter – also suggest human use of the springs as long as 9000 years ago, making it highly likely that the Ancestral Puebloan people living in nearby **Chimney Rock** also came here. As white settlers moved here in the 1880s, the springs became the focus of attempts at creating a spa town, but the remote location west of Wolf Creek Pass stymied all attempts of creating a large, Manitou Springs-like resort. That's not to say that wallowing in the pools isn't popular – in winter, they're an après ski favorite, while in summer they're the perfect cap to a day spent hiking, biking, or fishing.

Information and accommodation

At the center of town and beside its only stop-light is the **chamber of commerce** (Ⓣ970/264-2360 or 1-800/252-2204, Ⓦwww.pagosa-springs.com), which publishes the annual *Pagosa Country* magazine – a compendium of local attractions and activities. For more detailed information on national forest campsites contact the **USFS Pagosa Ranger Station** (Ⓣ970/264-2268), corner of 2nd and Pagosa streets.

There's a good selection and quantity of **accommodation** both downtown and more-isolated options an easy drive from town. Rates tend to drop in the winter and the **Pagosa Central Reservations** (Ⓣ970/731-2215 or 1-800/945-0182, Ⓦwww.pagosaaccommodations.com) is open year-round. The eight USFS **campgrounds** in the Pagosa Springs area should keep campers happy – two of the larger, pleasant options are the nonreservable *Wolf Creek* and *West Fork* campgrounds, thirteen miles northeast of town along Hwy-160 and Forest Road 684, where sites cost $8.

Echo Manor Inn 3366 Rt 84 Ⓣ970/264-5646, Ⓦwww.echomanorinn.com. Eccentric-looking lodge where the previous owners, inspired by a visit to Disneyland, added towers and gables. The present owners have run with the notion, filling the house with an eclectic array of antiques and collectables. Many of the rooms have great mountain views. Use of a hot tub and a shuttle service to both airport and ski area is included. ❻

Pagosa Lodge 3505 W Hwy-160 Ⓣ970/731-4141 or 1-800/523-7704. Huge resort hotel with around a hundred rooms and extensive leisure facilities – including golf course, tennis courts, and a swimming pool – gathered around a lake, three miles west of town on Hwy-160. ❻

Sky View Motel 1300 Hwy-160 W Ⓣ970/264-5803 or 1-888/633-7047. Small wood-clad motel units on the western edge of town that are not only usually the cheapest local option but are also regularly offered as part of winter ski packages. RV hookups ($18) are also available. ❸

Spa Motel 317 Hot Springs Blvd Ⓣ970/264-5910 or 1-800/832-5523. Tidy, simple motel rooms in the center of town that come with use of a couple of on-site geothermally heated pools – rather dowdy compared to those at the *Spring Inn*. ❹

The Spring Inn Ⓣ970/264-4168 or 1-800/225-0934. Standard motel that happens to own the best hot springs facility in town. Rates for the average rooms are a bit steep, though they include off-hours use of the hot springs. In winter, they offer good packages that include Wolf Creek lift tickets. ❺

Downtown Pagosa

The town's obvious attractions are the steaming **hot springs** at its center. The prettiest collection of pools are at the *Spring Inn* ($10; see overleaf for details) set in a landscaped area on the banks of the San Juan River. The interconnected pools are a variety of temperatures, the hottest being the painful 112°F Lobster Pot. Modest competition exists over the road at The Spa at Pagosa Springs (Sun–Thurs 8am–9pm, Fri & Sat 8am–10pm; $7.50), whose far less attractive mineral baths include an outdoor hot tub and swimming pool and an indoor steam room.

Downtown Pagosa Springs is quickly explored, but for an appreciation of the town's history, it's worth heading to the **San Juan Historical Society Pioneer Museum**, 1st and Pagosa streets (June–Aug Mon–Fri 9am–5pm; $2). Most of the museum's highlights are from the late 1800s, including early domestic items like a horsehide coat along with a fully equipped blacksmith's shop. Those interested in popular Western art should head two miles west of town along Hwy-160 to the **Fred Harman Art Museum** (Mon–Fri 10.30am–5pm; $2; Ⓦwww.harmanartmuseum.com), devoted to the cartoonist's work, the most famous of which was his "Red Ryder" cowboy comic strip, estimated to have had around 45 million readers in the 1950s.

Outdoor activities

If you've stopped in Pagosa Springs to stretch your legs, it's worth exploring the town's centrally located web of hiking and biking trails around **Reservoir Hill**. One trailhead to the area is located a couple of hundred yards southeast of *The Spring Inn*; turn east down San Juan Street, then south after a block to the parking area and trailhead. A variety of options for hikes and bike rides on the hill's woodland single-track are detailed here on a signpost, along with estimated times. There are of course plenty of **longer hiking trips**, including a good five-mile round-trip hike starting from the West Fork trailhead found fourteen miles northeast of Pagosa Springs via Hwy-160 and CO-648. The trail to the unmarked **Rainbow Hot Springs** follows the course of the river up the valley, past a couple of free primitive campsites en route.

As always in the San Juans you don't have to look far to find good **mountain biking** routes as well. The best advice is doled out at Juan's Mountain Sports, 155 Hot Springs Blvd (Ⓣ970/264-4730, Ⓦwww.juansmountainsports.com), who rent mountain bikes for $25 per day. If you are looking for places to **fish**, there are reliable spots in the San Juan River to the north, in the Piedra River about twenty miles west, and at Echo lake (five miles south of town along US-84). For guided fishing trips in local waters contact Colorado Fishing Adventures (Ⓣ970/731-4141).

Eating

The selection of **restaurants** in downtown Pagosa Springs is minimal, while the larger selection alongside Hwy-160 west of town is generally unexciting. Perhaps the best downtown option, open for both lunch and dinner, is the *Elkhorn Café* at 438 Pagosa St (Ⓣ970/264-2146), which serves inexpensive (entrees from $5) American standards like meatloaf and pot roast as well as a nice line in fiery Mexican fare. On the eastern edge of town, the *Branding Iron Bar-B-Q*, 4101 Hwy-160 (Ⓣ970/264-4268), doles out grilled meat, potatoes, and corn ($8 mains) in a ranch-style setting. Not much further along is *Ole Miners*, 3825 Hwy-160 (Ⓣ970/264-5981), where rusty mining artifacts hang on the walls and the food is a classier assortment of mostly seafood, including king crab legs, flounder, and shrimp; entrees start from around $12.

Chimney Rock

Named for the twin rock spires overlooking a collection of mesa-top ruins, **Chimney Rock** (mid-May to mid-Sept daily 9am–4.30pm; $5; ⓣ970/264-2268), seventeen miles west of Pagosa Springs via Hwy-151 and Hwy-160, is the most spectacularly situated Ancestral Puebloan ruin in Southern Colorado. Although only partially excavated, archeologists surmise the site was occupied by around 2000 natives between 925–1125, making this the most distant colony of the huge Ancestral Puebloan settlement at Chaco Canyon in New Mexico, ninety miles away.

The ruins can only be visited on guided tours (daily: 9.30am, 10.30am, 1pm and 2pm) that lead past a number of restored ruins. The tours are rather uninformative, as answers to the key questions about why it was built remain unknown. Most striking on the site is the positioning of several huge *kivas* – circular, stone-lined ceremonial pits or buildings – with the spires of the Chimney Rock, which is thought to be related to astrological events. This would clearly suggest that the entire settlement had ceremonial significance, borne out by its inconvenient location 1000ft above the nearest water source. There's also evidence that this outpost served as a logging center – perhaps offering an explanation for the rapid demise of the settlement with the disappearance of all the area's useful timber.

Durango

DURANGO, named after Durango, Mexico, is the largest town in southwestern Colorado and the best hub for exploring the Four-Corners region. Founded in 1880 as a refining town and rail junction for Silverton, 45 miles north, steam trains continue to run along the spectacular old mining route through the Animas Valley, though nowadays tourists, not sacks of gold, are the money-making cargo. Before the sightseers came, though, the town slid into a post-boom poverty that was only really broken in the 1950s with the arrival of **Fort Lewis College** and by a growth in tourism to nearby Mesa Verde National Park soon after. The town continues to bustle with students and tourists, but it has also taken advantage of the computer technology boom, and hosts a large influx of long-distance computerized teleworkers. Combine them with outdoors enthusiasts, who come to ride and hike the area's superb trails, and during the day at least, the place has an unexpectedly youthful, energetic buzz. In the evening, it seems everyone's a bit too wiped-out to do very much.

Arrival, information, and tours

Greyhound (TMN&O) **buses** between Denver and Albuquerque call in at the main station, 275 E 8th Ave (ⓣ970/259-2755). From here services also head along a route to Grand Junction via Ouray and Montrose. **La Plata County Airport**, eighteen miles east of Durango, is served by frequent shuttle buses provided by Durango Transportation (ⓣ970/259-4818); seats should be booked at least two hours in advance.

Durango's **visitor center** (summer Mon–Fri 8am–7pm, Sat 10am–6pm, Sun 11am–5pm; rest of year Mon–Fri 8am–6pm, Sat 8am–5pm, Sun 10am–4pm; ⓣ970/247-0312 or 1-800/525-8855, ⓦwww.durango.com) is beside the Animas River in a park west of town. The best source of information about activities on public lands, however, is the **San Juan and Rio Grande**

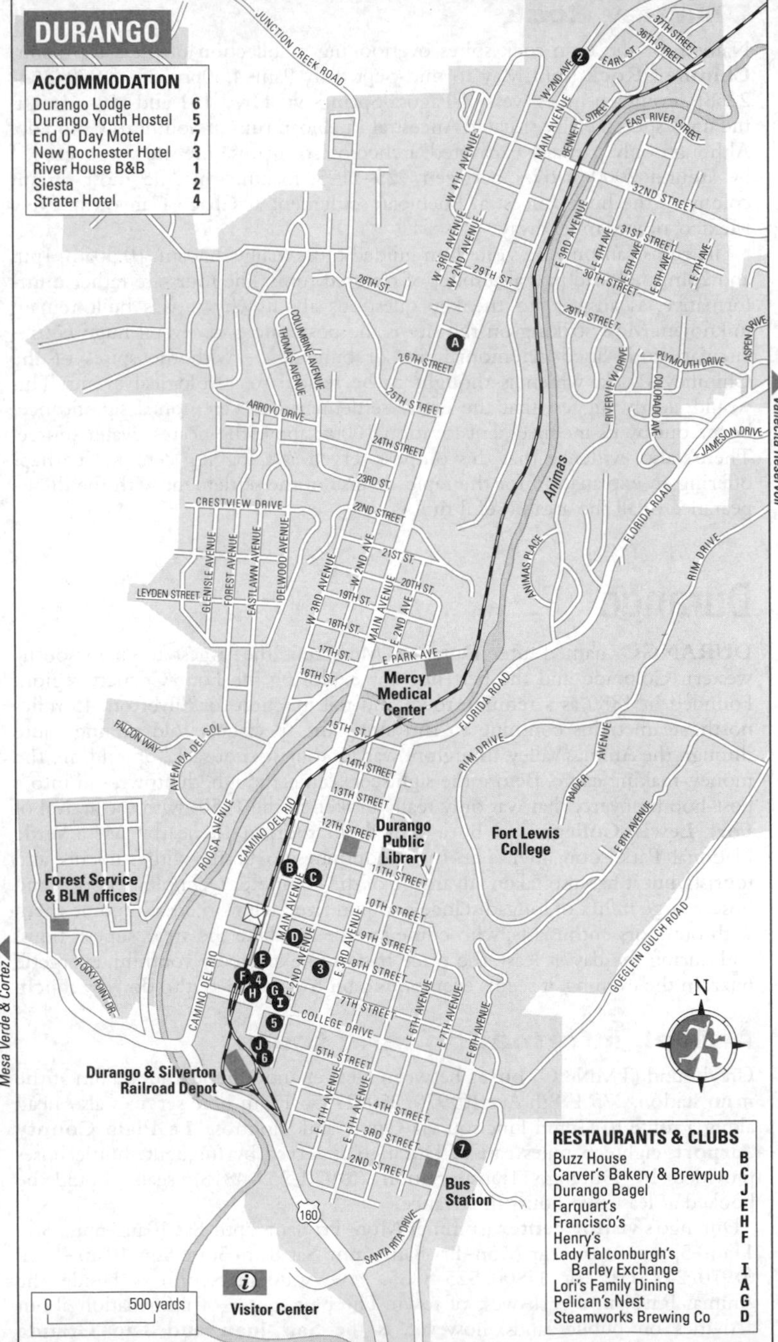
DURANGO
ACCOMMODATION
Durango Lodge 6
Durango Youth Hostel 5
End O' Day Motel 7
New Rochester Hotel 3
River House B&B 1
Siesta 2
Strater Hotel 4
RESTAURANTS & CLUBS
Buzz House B
Carver's Bakery & Brewpub C
Durango Bagel J
Farquart's E
Francisco's H
Henry's F
Lady Falconburgh's Barley Exchange I
Lori's Family Dining A
Pelican's Nest G
Steamworks Brewing Co D
Colorado Trail & Junction Creek Campground
Trimble Hot Springs, 1, Durango Mountain Resort & Silverton
Vallecita Reservoir
Mesa Verde & Cortez
Airport & Pagosa Springs
Mercy Medical Center
Durango Public Library
Fort Lewis College
Forest Service & BLM offices
Durango & Silverton Railroad Depot
Bus Station
Visitor Center
Animas
0
500 yards
N

National Forest and BLM office at 710 Camino Del Rio 301 (Mon–Fri 8am–4.30pm; ⓣ970/247-4874), west of town off the road to Cortez.

Since many visitors are in town on their way to Mesa Verde National Park, it's worth noting that a couple of companies organize **daily tours** of the park from Durango. These include Mesa Verde Tours (ⓣ970/247-4161 or 1-800/626-2066) and Durango Transportation (ⓣ970/259-4818), and costs hover around $60 per person.

Accommodation

Only a handful of **accommodation** options are concentrated in Durango's downtown area, including pricey hotels and a grotty hostel. The bulk of the town's beds are in the motels north of town along Main Avenue. Few are within walking distance of downtown, though an inexpensive and frequent trolley service (see overleaf) does the forty-block run up and down the Main Avenue. Summer is peak season in Durango, and for help in finding a vacancy, contact Durango Central Reservations (ⓣ970/247-8900 or 1-800/979-9742).

The nearest USFS **campground** to town is *Junction Creek*, five miles north of town on Junction Creek Road ($12; April to mid-Nov), which has 34 sites suitable for both tents and RVs. In addition, several USFS campgrounds can be found around the Vallecito Reservoir, twenty miles northeast of town. A good commercial campsite is *Hermosa Meadows* (ⓣ970/247-3055 or 1-800/748-2853), with showers, laundry, and shaded tent sites ($15) beside the Animas River eight miles north of town

Country View Lodge, 28295 Hwy-160 E ⓣ970/247-5701. Large well-maintained hostel with friendly owners, beside Hwy-160 six miles east of Durango. On offer are dorm beds ($13); basic private rooms ($30); and camping ($10) in the grassy area behind the hostel: a sociable area sheltered from traffic and beside a mountain stream. Facilities include a large kitchen, lounge, and laundry.

Durango Lodge 150 5th St ⓣ970/247-0955. One of the most central motels – hence the slightly higher rates – close to the railroad depot with unremarkable rooms, a pool, and hot tub. ❺

Durango Youth Hostel 543 E 2nd Ave ⓣ970/247-9905. Shabby but sociable downtown hostel lacking any real facilities (except a cramped kitchen) offering dorm beds ($13) and a basic private room for $30.

End O' Day Motel 350 E 8th Ave ⓣ970/247-1722. Small and comfortable motel at the southern edge of town is one of the cheapest deals in town and only a ten-minute walk from downtown. ❸

New Rochester Hotel 721 E 2nd Ave ⓣ970/385-1920 or 1-800/664-1920, ⓦwww.rochesterhotel.com. This very central hotel has swung between having some of the town's grandest lodgings in the 1890s to being its cheapest flophouse. But renovated in the 1990s, it's now a luxurious, period-furnished B&B decorated with cowboy movie memorabilia. Gourmet breakfasts included as is use of a hot tub. ❼

River House B&B 495 Animas View Drive ⓣ970/247-4775. Beautifully located beside railroad tracks (used solely by the Durango steam train) and the Animas River north of town. Great gourmet breakfasts are served in the sunny atrium, guest facilities include sauna and exercise room. ❻

Siesta 3475 Main Ave ⓣ970/247-0741. One of Durango's cheapest motels is way out on its northern fringes. Facilities are minimal, though all rooms have phones and TV, some kitchenettes. ❸

Strater Hotel 699 Main Ave ⓣ970/247-4431 or 1-800/247-4431, ⓦwww.strater.com. Antique-furnished rooms embody the frontier elegance of this longstanding Durango hotel. At one time the fourth floor housed a brothel. Later Western writer Louis L'Amour kept a suite where he wrote several novels based in the area. Rates include a great buffet breakfast heaped with fresh fruit, muffins, pasties, pancakes, waffle, eggs, and meats. ❻

Downtown Durango

The north–south **Main Avenue** is unsurprisingly the hub of Durango's urban action. Though some forty blocks long, traversing its length is the Main Avenue Trolley (every 30min, daily: 6.45am–6.15pm; 50¢). Its northern end is a charmless strip of motels and fast-food joints, but in the Victorian center, things become much more attractive. Here, the street is lined with restaurants, souvenir shops, Southwestern art galleries and sporting goods stores – almost all housed in century-old Victorian redbrick buildings. At Main Street's southern end stands the squat depot of the **Durango & Silverton Narrow Gauge Railroad**, the town's main tourist attraction. The train runs up to four round-trips daily between May and October, from a depot at 479 Main Ave (all leave in the early morning; $55 round-trip; ⓣ970/247-2733 or 1-888/TRAIN-07, ⓦwww.durangotrain.com). Using the same route once used to transport ore from mining districts to the north of town, the steam train shoots out dark plumes of smoke as it chugs through glorious mountain scenery, passing through forests and glades before hugging precarious ledges and crossing exposed trestles high above the roaring Dolores River. The round-trip takes around seven hours, including a lunchtime stopover in Silverton. Shorter excursions, running to Cascade Canyon and covering the most scenic areas of the route, run between late November and early May (daily 10am; $42). For all trips, try and reserve tickets at least three weeks in advance; if not possible, it's always worth checking early on the day to pick up a cancellation.

Outdoor activities

Lying beside the Animas River, Durango is at the transition of the landscape from lush-wooded steep mountains and rolling meadows to a land of wide slumbering rivers and slickrock deserts. Opportunities for **outdoor activities** are in as great abundance as scenic variety and various pursuits draw visitors in about equal measure; rafting, biking, hiking, fishing, and in winter the terrific Durango Mountain resort. Whatever your poison during the day, a good place to soothe aches afterwards is at **Trimble Hot Springs** (daily 9am–10pm; $8; ⓣ970/884-2473, ⓦwww.trimblehotsprings.com) six miles north of Durango. Here since 1883, the rebuilt resort has a large swimming pool along with smaller, hotter soaking pools.

Rafting

Whitewater rafting on the Animas River is second only to the Narrow Gauge Railroad as the local must-do activity – and some trips even include a ride on the steam train as well. Several companies offer rafting trips in Durango, most of which are easily found in small wooden booths scattered along the downtown portion of Main Avenue. The most popular trips sold here are the fairly tame family-friendly trips on the **Lower Animas**; Class II and III waters south of town. Half-day trips run around $38; full-days on the water $65. But the real gem for those with the courage, money, and time are the rafting trips further upstream. Dropping steeper and faster than almost any other river in the state, the 28 miles of the **Upper Animas River** south of Silverton provides an excellent venue for one- or two-day whitewater raft and kayak trips; continuous Class III water with several Class IV and V sections. Trips include maneuvering around giant boulders scattered throughout No Name rapids, camping at Needleton and a take-out at Rockwood – below which the canyon narrows too much to make it runnable. From here many companies

Biking in Durango

Since hosting the inaugural mountain-bike world championships in 1990, Durango has become a world-class center for off-road biking. Such is the town's relationship with the sport that numerous stars have either chosen to live or retire here, and it again hosted a round of the Mountain Bike World Cup in 2001. Durango's also famous as the venue for one of the largest bike races in the US – the Memorial Day **Iron Horse Bicycle Classic** – an event in which up to 2000 riders race the narrow-gauge railway train 47 miles to Silverton. The event began in 1972 as a friendly wager between two brothers and has since mushroomed into a major three-day carnival, including several other bicycle races and events. For rentals, equipment, and advice contact Mountain Bike Specialists, 949 Main Ave (ⓣ970/247-4066), or Southwest Adventures, 780 Main Ave (ⓣ970/259-0370), who'll both rent out front-suspension machines from $25 per day. You can also get bike rentals up at Durango Mountain Resort, where several ability-graded trails have been laid out. Classic local trails include:

Telegraph hill There's no set route around this network of single-track on the eastern side of town, but it's challenging and fun enough to have been incorporated into the 2001 World Cup cross-country course. Head up Horse Gulch road (the eastern end of 3rd St) and explore; don't miss riding down the rocky technical Raider Ridge (on northwest side of Horse Gulch road) with its stunning views over Durango.

Haflin Creek Trail Highly challenging 22-mile loop northeast of town. Experienced riders take around five hours to grind up the long, well-graded climb and the steep, at times death-defying, descent into Haflin Canyon.

Hermosa Creek trail Wonderful, largely downhill, 21-mile trail northwest of town. The generally smooth single-track trail cuts through thick, pristine forests and is best done by setting up a shuttle to Durango Mountain Resort (contact Southwest Adventures). Done one-way the ride takes around five hours.

arrange for rafters to load gear onto the narrow-gauge railroad to cover the last thirty miles to Durango by steam, a memorable itinerary that runs around $200 per day per person. Reputable companies offering a full range of local trips include; Mountain Waters Rafting (ⓣ970/259-4191 or 1-800/748-2507, ⓦwww.durangorafting.com), at the corner of College Drive and Main Avenue; or Mild to Wild Rafting (ⓣ970/247-4789 or 1-800/567-6745, ⓦwww.mild2wildrafting.com) on Camino Del Rio and 11th Street. Several stretches of the Animas are also popular among kayakers, and in late June kayakers from all over the US descend on Durango for the **Animas River Days** – a national-level whitewater competition.

Hiking and fishing

Though Durango hasn't built up the kind of cult status amongst **hikers** as it has amongst mountain bikers, the town still has plenty of fine hiking options. Many of the favorite trails of bikers (see box above) are also great options for bikers; the ultimate challenge is the almost 500-mile **Colorado Trail** (see p.87) to Denver that starts seven miles northwest of town near the *Junction Creek* campground. For a short, good hike near town try the five-mile round-trip hike on the **Animas Trail Mountain**, with good views of the Animas Valley and river and is a likely place to spot elk and deer. The trail starts on the northern fringes of Durango – take 32nd Street west, then W 4th Avenue north to the end of the road.

For river fishing in the Durango area, the obvious place to head is the **Animas River**, around town – particularly the stretch between Lighter Creek

Durango Mountain Resort

Durango Mountain Resort (☎970/247-9000 or 1-800/525-0892, Ⓦwww.ski-purg.com), formerly known as Purgatory, 25 miles north of Durango along Hwy-550, is a good mid-sized resort. The total ski area, 1200 acres, is served by eleven lifts that create a 2029ft vertical drop; terrain is divided as 23 percent beginner, 51 percent intermediate, and 26 percent advanced. Adult day-passes cost $43; though if you're an absolute beginner a Columbine lift ticket ($17) makes learning the basics much cheaper. The resort is known to get good powder days regularly, although the annual snowfall is only a modest 260 inches. Though the temptation for experts is to head to the far reaches of the resort straight away, a good place to find untracked powder are black-diamond runs above the base area: Styx and Lower Hades particularly.

Though primarily a day-use area, there is a fair bit of accommodation around the resort; the best point of contact for deals and the full selection of local accommodation is Durango Central Reservations (☎1-800/962-4077). An additional five miles north of the Mountain Resort the **Durango Resort Ski Touring Center** (☎970/245-9000) offers rentals, ski lessons, and ten miles of groomed trails. Backcountry Nordic skiers should try to investigate options around Haviland Lake and Molas pass.

and the Purple Cliffs below town. A quieter place to look for trout in numerous small streams is along the **Hermosa Creek Drainage area**, west of and accessed from Durango Mountain Resort. For lake fishing and hooking trout, kokanee salon, northern pike, or walleye, **Vallecito Reservoir**, 25 miles northeast of Durango, has become a popular place – with five marinas renting out fishing boats – though with 22 miles of accessible shoreline it's hardly ever crowded. For fishing, licenses, and classes call in at Durango Fly Goods, 139 E 5th St (☎970/385-4081). For guided trips contact Flyfishing Durango (☎970/382-0478).

Eating and drinking

The c.1900 redbrick buildings along Main Avenue house a plethora of **restaurants**; some with their sights set on affluent train passengers, others aimed at young bikers. Northwest of downtown is where you'll find the familiar fast-food spots and local diners.

For a university town, the **nightlife** scene is surprisingly quiet, though dependably sociable venues include *Lady Falconburgh's*, *Steamworks*, *Carvers,* and *Farquart's* (see below), the latter two of which have live music at weekends. For a mellower night, head to the *Pelican's Nest*, 656 Main Ave, where there's live jazz nightly, or look into seeing one of the melodramas regularly performed at the *Strater Hotel* (June–Sept; from $15).

Buzz House 1019 Main Ave. Popular coffeehouse with lots of healthy veggie snacks, smoothies, and a large array of coffee drinks. Open for breakfast and lunch only.

Carver's Bakery & Brewpub 1022 Main Ave ☎970/259-2545. Bakery by morning, brewpub by night, *Carver's* opens at 6.30am for big breakfasts that include excellent granola pancakes. The lunch and dinner menu features tasty, inexpensive Southwestern options like beef or chicken fajitas along with Western dishes like bison, best accompanied by one of four varieties of home-brewed beer.

Durango Bagel 106 E 5th ☎970/385-7927. No-frills café near the train depot, offering a huge variety of bagels for breakfast and lunch.

Farquart's 725 Main St ☎970/247-5440. Serves what just may be Durango's best pizza, a well-balanced wholewheat crust creation that can be matched with a huge range of toppings. The linguini and meatballs in marinara sauce is another a strong choice, as are the Mexican entrees on offer from around $8. The loud and smoky bar, typically full of students, has a good range of imported and domestic suds.

Francisco's Restaurante y Cantina 619 Main Ave ☎970/247-4098. The large Santa Fe-style dining room is a popular choice for the best, moderately priced Mexican food in town. Usual Mexican favorites are offered along with more adventurous choices like Enchiladas Durango ($8.50): beef wrapped in blue corn tortillas smothered in a zesty green chili.

Henry's *Strater Hotel* (see p.157) ☎970/247-4431. Ornately decorated with red leather booths and Tiffany lamps, *Henry's* is a Durango institution. The moderately pricey menu is based around good American and classy Italian fare. Entrees vary dramatically in cost from $9 to $22; but include veal occo bucco, deep lasagnas, and the longstanding house favorite the pepper steak Herbert in chutney and cognac. The salad bar is outstanding and varied.

Lady Falconburgh's Barley Exchange Century Mall, 640 Main Ave ☎970/382-9664. Popular basement pub in the heart of downtown serving fried snacks and some larger burger and salad-type meals as well. The big draw isn't the food, though, but the extensive beer menu, featuring well over a hundred varieties in bottle and on tap.

Lori's Family Dining 2653 Main Ave ☎970/247-1224. Popular diner on motel row, serving filling breakfasts from around $5, as well as lunch and dinners that include a good salad bar.

Steamworks Brewing Co 801 E 2nd Ave ☎970/259-9200. Vast brewpub with good food like oven-fired pizzas, best eaten on the sunny outdoor patio. The good selection of beers is best tried by ordering a sampler – half a dozen small glasses for $10.

Listings

Internet Durango Public Library, 1188 E 2nd Ave.

Laundry North Main Coin Laundry, 2980 N Main Ave (☎970/247-9915).

Medical Mercy Medical Center, 375 E Park Ave (☎970/247-4311).

Police Durango Police Dept, 990 E 2nd Ave (☎970/247-3232).

Post Office The main post office is at 222 W 8th (☎970/247-3434).

Mesa Verde National Park

In the southwest corner of Colorado, the mountains quickly flatten out towards the Four Corners Region and **MESA VERDE NATIONAL PARK**, 37 miles west of Durango along Hwy-160, the only national park in the US exclusively devoted to archeological remains. Between the time of Christ and 1300 AD, Ancestral Puebloan civilization expanded to cover much of the area known as the Four Corners. Settlements here appear to have been the northern outpost of a civilization that dominated the southwest for centuries and evolved into the modern-day Pueblo Indians. The earliest dwellings were simple pits, but before vanishing the Ancestral Puebloan people had developed the architectural sophistication needed to build the extraordinary complexes high on the plateaus of Mesa Verde and, more famously, castle-like stone pueblos carved into cliffside niches. It's an astonishing place, so far off the beaten track that its extensive ruins were not fully explored until 1888 – hard to imagine given the well-preserved nature of the archeological sites, as well as the huge numbers visiting them today.

Though the area was named in the seventeenth century, the ruins in Mesa Verde weren't noted for another two hundred years. Though photographer William Henry Jackson recorded some lesser sites in 1874, the outside world only really took note of the place after a snowstorm in 1888 when local rancher Richard Wetherill stumbled upon the Cliff Palace. Along with a few others, the Wetherill's soon spawned an industry out of finding and selling Ancestral Puebloan artifacts. One particularly good customer was the Swedish Count Gustaf Nordenskjöld, who shipped caseloads of ancient pottery to Europe in the 1890s and gave the National Museum of Finland the world's finest collection of Mesa Verde artifacts. These activities prompted the Antiquities Act of

A History of Mesa Verde

Although archeological finds in the Montezuma Valley around nearby Cortez (see p.165) date back as far as 5500 BC, the **Ancestral Puebloans** who made **Mesa Verde** their home between 500 and 1300 AD appeared to be the area's first residents. Their earliest homes here were pit-houses dug into cave floors, and it's known that they were skilled potters who led a stable agricultural life. Around 1100 AD, they moved out of the pit-houses to intricate walled villages on the mesa tops, where an extensive system of irrigation ditches and reservoirs was also created. At this time, it's thought that the Mesa Verde population reached its peak of around 2500, meaning it was still only the eighth or ninth largest surface Pueblo community in the Montezuma Valley.

Around a century later, the Mesa Verdeans moved again, this time constructing the spectacular multistory cliff-dwellings for which the park is most famous. Surprisingly, archeologists regard these as an indication that the culture was now in decline, noting that the rather haphazard structures are far less sophisticated than the mesatop pueblos. The cliff-side dwellings, in practice, must have also been less ideal, dangerous for both the elderly and for children, who must have been continuously supervised to avoid fatal falls. Moreover, though each complex was near the seep or spring that had originally created the alcove, many will have run dry, making fetching water a constant chore.

Given their shortcomings, it's not known for sure why the cliff dwellings were built in the first place. While reasonable to suggest that it was for defensive reasons, there's also no evidence that the Mesa Verdeans were ever attacked. Still, the idea that this was a peaceful group was recently dashed after archeological finds suggested cannibalistic tendencies, and it's thought that the other Pueblo communities in the Montezuma Valley were hostile to those living here. Some also argue that the move occurred to open up more space on the mesa tops for agricultural purposes as arable land was at such a premium. The biggest mystery of all, though, is why the cliff dwellings were abandoned after only a century. It may have been a long drought, though that can't explain the exceptional quantity of artifacts – including jewelry, weapons and kitchen utensils – left behind. On the other hand, there's no evidence of a catastrophic or violent end to the civilization either. Whatever happened, evidence suggests that the inhabitants of Mesa Verde headed south to join similar people where Arizona and New Mexico are today, establishing pueblos where their descendants, the modern Pueblo Indians, still live.

1906, which prohibited dealing in archeological treasures, and the creation of Mesa Verde National Park in the same year.

Mesa Verde's "green table," a plateau densely wooded with juniper and piñon, overlooks distant mountains and arid plains and is cut at its southern edge by sheer canyons dividing the land into narrow fingers. Given these natural barriers there are few hiking opportunities in the park and it's really only the ruins that make it a worthwhile stop-off. Since the ruins are easily accessible, the park can get crowded in summer, making the best months to visit May, September and October – when the summer heat also begins to ease off. Since it's blanketed in snow in winter, only the park's main museum and the Spruce Tree House ruin are open year-round and hiking trails attract snowshoers and cross-country skiers.

Arrival, information, and tours

The access road to Mesa Verde climbs south from Hwy-160 a little more than a half-hour drive west of Durango. Once past the **entrance station** ($10 per vehicle), the road climbs and twists through a barren, burnt-out 23,607-acre area, the result of the virulent Bircher Fire in July 2000 – which was larger than the combined size of all other forest fires the park has seen since records began. Mercifully the areas around the ruins were spared, and by the time you reach the **Far View visitor center** (late April to late Oct daily 8am–5pm; ⓣ970/529-4461, ⓦwww.visitmesaverde.com), fifteen miles from the entrance, the landscape is back to its green self. Exhibits inside the center cover Navajo, Hopi and Pueblo crafts and jewelry. Immediately beyond here, the road forks south to the Chapin Mesa area and west to the Wetherill Mesa.

There are free overlooks at most of the ruins, but to tour any of the three major attractions you must buy **tickets** ($1.75) at the visitor center. On Chapin Mesa, Cliff Palace is usually open between 9am and 5pm daily from late April until early November, and Balcony House for the same hours between late April and mid-October; at busy times, you can't tour both on the same day. Tours of Long House over on Wetherill Mesa run between late May and early September and operate 9am–4pm daily.

Several commercial operators run **tours** of the park if you don't want to go it alone. Most leave from Durango (see p.157 for details), though at the park there's the option of joining a bus tour ($16 half-day, $21 full day) from the *Far View Motor Lodge* and *Morefield Campground*; contact either establishment for details (see "Practicalities," overleaf). **Horseback rides** through the park's hilly piñon and juniper forest are offered by Mesa Verde Riding Stable, 27758 Rt 145 (ⓣ970/562-3808), who also hire out horses to experienced riders who wish to strike out alone.

Chapin Mesa

A couple of miles from the visitor center on the road to Chapin Mesa stands **Far View**, a mesatop pueblo abandoned early in the thirteenth century. It's one of the structures that predates the cliff-dwellings. Nearby is the artificial **Mummy Lake**. Like so many other objects in the park, opinion on its origins is divided – thought for a long time to have been a reservoir, some now believe that this vast depression, capable of holding half a million gallons, might have been an open-air plaza. Four miles onwards is the **Chapin Mesa Archeological Museum** (daily: summer 8am–6.30pm; rest of year 8am–5pm), which holds the park's best displays on the Ancestral Puebloans and also sells tour tickets after the visitor center closes in late fall. A couple of fairly dull two- to three-mile-long nature trails start here, but far more rewarding is the short, steep hike down to **Spruce Tree House** – the only ruin open in winter. It's a neat little village of three-story structures snugly molded into the recesses of a rocky alcove and fronted by open plazas. One *kiva* has been reroofed to give visitors a feel for the structure in its original state.

Beyond the museum, two one-way, six-mile loops known as the **Ruins Road** (April to early Nov daily 8am–dusk) split off to the park's major sites. The **western** loop, the one to skip if pressed on time, first stops at the **Square Tower House**, where an easy stroll leads to views of an eighty-room alcove complex based around the four-story, 26-feet-wide Square Tower, the tallest tower in the park. Further along the road is **Sun Point Overlook**, a great viewpoint to appreciate the clustering of twelve distinct cliff dwellings at the other side of Spruce Canyon, including the Cliff Palace, which gives a good appreciation of just how crowded the canyon was in its heyday. In contrast to the cliff sites, the mesatop **Sun Temple**, next up on the loop, was built to premeditated plans, and though never finished, it may have been intended to be a major ceremonial center. However, little of its shape and function can be appreciated by walking around its walls, making the exploration of the ruin unrewarding.

Cliff Palace

The star of the **eastern loop** of Ruins Road is **Cliff Palace**, the largest standing Ancestral Puebloan cliff dwelling in existence. The incredible location, tucked a hundred feet below an overhanging ledge of pale rock, is made more so when you realize the two hundred plus rooms here once housed a community of around 250 people. Though you can get a great view from the promontory below the parking lot, entering the ruin on a tour is the way to go. Especially on quieter days, walking through empty plazas and past mysterious *kivas* provides a haunting evocation of a lost and little-known world. Fading murals are still be discerned inside some of the structures and a metal stairway leaving the site through a narrow crevice climbs past the original toe- and footholds of the Ancestral Puebloans.

Balcony House

Beyond here, the loop briefly passes into small portion of Ute Mountain Tribal Park (see opposite) before arriving back into the park around **Balcony House**, one of the few Mesa Verde complexes clearly geared towards defense. Access to the network of rooms here is very difficult, and it's not visible from above. Hourly guided tours involve scrambling up three hair-raising ladders and crawling through a narrow tunnel, teetering all the while above a steep drop into Soda Canyon. Park authorities present it as more "fun" than the other ruins, but unless you share the fearless Ancestral Puebloan attitude to heights, you might prefer to give it a miss.

Wetherill Mesa

Beside a ranger station and snack kiosk at the end of the twisting, twelve-mile drive from the visitor center to **Wetherill Mesa** (late May to early Sept daily 8am–4.30pm; excluding large vehicles like RVs) is the terminus of a free **miniature train**, which loops around the tip of the mesa. Time spent waiting for the next train can be occupied by walking down to investigate the **Step House**, where there's a restored pit-house dated to 626 as well as a single alcove pueblo from 1226.

The train stops at various trailheads for hikers wishing to explore minor early mesatop sites and alcove overlooks, but its principal destination is the **Long House**, the park's second-largest ruin set in a large cave. Hour-long tours descend around sixty steps to reach a central plaza, before scrambling around the 150 rooms and 21 *kivas*. These ruins, though more ramshackle than those at Chapin Mesa, are considered some of the most authentic in the park, since they have been simply stabilized rather than subject to the extensive rebuilding programs at the other main sites early in the twentieth century.

Park practicalities

As most of the park is inaccessible in winter, services such as gas, food, and lodging only operate between late April and mid-October. While most visitors **stay** in nearby towns, there is the *Far View Motor Lodge*, in the park itself near the visitor center (Ⓣ970/529-4421 or 1-800/449-2288; ⑤; late April to early Oct). The rooms are rather basic (no phones or TV), though the views from its mesatop location are fantastic. You can **camp** at the pleasant and large *Morefield*

Campground (ⓣ970/529-4421; $10 per site; late April to mid-Oct), four miles up from the entrance and thus a long way from the ruins. **Food** available year-round at *Spruce Tree Terrace* restaurant near the Chapin Mesa museum and also one of the facilities available in season at the *Far View*, across from the visitor center – which has a gas station.

Cortez and the Ute Mountain Tribal Park

CORTEZ, strung out along one long curve of Hwy-160, is roughly 25 miles north from the Four Corners Monument marking the meeting place of Colorado, New Mexico, Arizona and Utah. Nothing in town commands much attention, though the giant Sleeping Ute Mountain to the southwest, visible from all over, makes a dramatic backdrop, looking uncannily like a warrior god asleep with his arms folded across his chest. Around town, though, the scrubby mesas and canyonlands of the Montezuma Valley offer an amazing array of remote archeological sites, including the spectacular **Ute Mountain Tribal Park**.

In addition, the magnificent collection of Ancestral Puebloan artifacts at the **Anasazi Heritage Center** north of Cortez is well worthwhile visiting. If you want a chance to find some new artifacts, the **Crow Canyon Archeological Center**, five miles northwest of Cortez on Hwy-666 at 23390 CO-K (June to mid-Sept Tues–Thurs 9am; mid-Sept to mid-Oct Tues & Thurs 9am; ⓣ970/565-8975 or 1-800/422-8975), organizes digs at a variety of Ancestral Puebloan sites in the valley. You can join a dig for anything from a day or longer from around $40.

Ute Mountain Tribal Park and the Anasazi Heritage Center

Abutting Mesa Verde National Park, the **Ute Mountain Indian Reservation** was one of several reservations created when the Victorian-era silver mining boom pushed the native peoples westward. One part of this reservation, the out of the way **Ute Mountain Tribal Park**, contains a collection of Ancestral Puebloan cliff dwellings that are just as enthralling as Mesa Verde's but far less visited. This is probably because the only way to visit them is by joining a Ute-led tour, arranged at the tribe's **visitor center** (ⓣ970/565-9653 or 1-800/847-5485, ⓦwww.utemountainute.com), housed in a former gas station at the intersection of Hwy-160 and Hwy-666. The tour schedule varies according to demand, and although you can theoretically join a tour by turning up at 8am, it's much safer to arrange in advance. Both full- (8.30am–4pm; $30) and half-day (8.30am–noon; $17) tours are offered; the latter covers not only the petroglyphs and a potsherd-scattered mounds concealing surface-level pueblos at the base of the cliffs, but also follows a remote dirt road to several cliff dwellings built at the same time as those at Mesa Verde. These include the eighty-room **Lion House** and the precarious **Eagle's Nest Cliff** perched in a cavernous natural alcove. It also involves a fair bit of walking and climbing – pack plenty of water – and five tall ladders, though only a couple will bother vertigo sufferers. While the tours require you to bring your own (sturdy) vehicle to access the sites, an extra $5 allows up to a dozen visitors to ride in the guide's van, allowing you to both preserve your vehicle and receive a much more detailed commentary on the park.

Six miles north of Cortez, the **Anasazi Heritage Center** (daily 9am–4pm; $3; ⓣ970/882-4811, ⓦwww.co.blm.gov/ahc/hmepge.htm) is housed in a couple of twelfth-century pueblos. The collection here, which comes mostly from excavations from an area now drowned by the nearby McPhee Dam, includes sandals, blankets, and embroidery, a reconstructed pit-house helping to give a sense of what life was like. The well-equipped museum also has some hands-on displays – one of which keep kids busy grinding corn. Near the center is the **Escalante Ruin**, which dates from around 900–1300 AD and was named for the eighteenth-century Spanish friar who noted the traces of prehistoric Indians in a 1776 expedition to the area.

Practicalities

Cortez's **visitor center**, 928 E Main St (daily 8am–6pm; ⓣ970/565-4048 or 1-800/253-1616), is on the edge of the city park and, as a Colorado Welcome Center, has information on the entire state. **Accommodation** in town centers on a clutch of very similar motels on the main strip, including the clean and basic *Aneth Lodge*, 645 E Main St (ⓣ970/565-3453 or 1-877/263-8454; ❸). Fine B&B accommodation is offered at *Kelly's Place* (ⓣ970/565-3125 or 1-800/745-4885; ❹), ten miles west of town at 14663 CO-G, where there are eight en-suite rooms. The best range of local **camping** possibilities are on the banks of the McPhee Reservoir around ten miles north of town on Hwy-145.

Far and away the best place to **eat** in Cortez is the *Dry Dock Restaurant*, 200 W Main St (ⓣ970/564-9404), which dishes up great seafood in a pleasant garden setting. A cheaper alternative is the old-time Western diner *Homesteaders*, 45 E Main St (closed Sun in winter), where there's a decent selection of barbecued meals and Mexican fry-ups – most entrees around $8. *Francisca's*, 125 E Main St (ⓣ970/565-4093), is the best place in town for authentic Mexican food, and is often packed.

San Juan Skyway

North of Durango, a number of old Victorian mining towns tucked deep into isolated valleys of the San Juan Mountains are connected by the **San Juan Skyway** (Hwy-550), easily one of Colorado's finest drives passing some of the most rugged and scenic country in the state. The first stretch north up the Animas River Valley begins tamely, but things heat up as the road climbs over Molass Pass – which due to its height and remoteness is said to have the purest air in the US – and into the quaint, slightly ramshackle town of **Silverton**. From here, the road is known as the **Million Dollar Highway** as it twists and turns its way to **Ouray**, passing abandoned mine workings and rusting machinery along the way. Though this portion of the highway cost a fortune to build – over $1000 dollars a foot at the time – it owes its name to the gold in the ore-bearing gravel used in its construction. Marketers long ago decided that the landscape around Ouray justifies the tag little Switzerland, and they're not too far wrong – the valleys in this part of the range are narrow, the peaks high and craggy. So inaccessible is this part of the range that although the year-round resort town **Telluride** is only around ten miles away as the crow flies, the wall of gunmetal-gray peaks in between forces the road to curve and twist for fifty between the two towns. That said, those with courage can nudge a **four-wheel-drive** vehicle to Telluride a more direct way on one of the most spectacular off-road routes in an area renowned for its network of tough backroads. Though these routes are also open to **cyclists** and **horseback riders**, the best ways to explore this area is on foot. **Hikers** are spoilt for choice in the region, which is on the doorstep of the **Weminuche Wilderness** (see box on p.169) and filled with challenging peaks, narrow gorges, forests, and bleak, imposing stretches of high alpine tundra.

Silverton

Journey's end for the narrow-gauge railroad from Durango (see p.158), **SILVERTON** is one of Colorado's most atmospheric mountain towns, with wide, dirt-paved streets leading off towards the hills on either side of its one main road. The town boomed after the railroad came in 1882, and thanks to the sheer quantity of ore around Silverton – a name said to come from a miner's comment that "there's no gold here, but silver by the ton" – the town fared better than most after the 1893 Silver Crash. Zinc and copper mining continued until a little more than a decade ago, and while the population has dropped since then, those that remain have so far resisted suggestions that its future lies in gambling to draw in the tourists. They are, however, extremely reliant on the seasonal tourist train; so while the false-fronted stores along "Notorious Blair Street" remind of the days when **Wyatt Earp** dealt cards in the Arlington saloon, the town is defined by the restaurants and gift shops that fill up between 11am and 2pm when tourists are deposited in town. From November to March the town goes into hibernation, with few visitors and the bulk of businesses closing for the season – although the creation of a new ski area nearby may breathe life into the town's winter economy.

Arrival, information, and accommodation

TMN&O buses between Durango and Grand Junction, pull into Silverton and stop in front of the *Lunch Box Café*, 1124 Green St. The town's helpful **visitors' center** (daily: 9am–5pm; ⓣ970/387-5654 or 1-800/752-4494. ⓦwww.silverton.org) is at the southern edge of town at the junction of Greene Street and US-550. Although tourism makes Silverton tick, it's pretty quiet here in the evenings as most visitors are on day-trips with the train. In winter, it's positively dead at most times. There are several USFS **campgrounds** in the area, the most convenient being the free riverside *South Mineral*, around five miles west on Hwy-550 and Forest Road 585.

Grand Imperial Hotel 1219 Greene St ⓣ970/387-5527 or 1-800/341-3340. In the center of town, this grand 1882 hotel has forty creaky, antique-furnished rooms, each with private bath, cable TV, and views down the main street or over the mountains. Rates drop by half between November and April. ❺

Silverton Hostel 1025 Blair St ⓣ970/387-0015. Friendly, but thin-walled hostel run by a potter, with studio on premises. Options include $13 dorm beds or budget double rooms ($32–42). Check-in between 8–10am and 4–10pm. Also offers showers for $3.50.

Teller House Hotel 1250 Greene St ⓣ970/387-5423 or 1-800/342-4338. Former miners' boarding house now provides Victorian-style guestrooms in a central location, some with private baths. Non smoking. ❹

Triangle Motel 848 Greene St ⓣ970/387-5780. Functional and unappealing, but well-run motel at the south end of town. There are some good-value two-room suites, and rooms have queen beds and cable TV. ❸

Wyman Hotel and Inn 1371 Greene St ⓣ970/387-5372 or 1-800/609-7845, ⓦwww.thewyman.com. One of Silverton's finest establishments features comfortable and elegant antique-furnished rooms and common areas. Amenities include gourmet breakfasts, a selection of six hundred videos and whirlpool tubs in some rooms. Nonsmoking. ❻

The town and around

Luckily for those arriving by train and departing a couple of hours later, a wander around **downtown Silverton**, between colorful false-fronted buildings, is not a time-consuming affair. The bulk of the town's business are spread down Greene Street, the Main drag a block west of Blair Street where the steam train arrives. Around the rudimentary train depot particularly are a cluster of cheerfully cheesy souvenir shops, but at least their presence is not too crass to destroy the Victorian appeal of the town. First stop should be the **San Juan County Museum**, 1559 Greene St (June–Aug daily 9am–5pm; Sept to mid-Oct daily 10am–3pm; $3). Housed in the former county jail, the most captivating exhibits relate to anecdotes told about the building's role in preserving law and order in the mining camp. For a better impression of a miner's daily toil, head to the **One Hundred Mine** (daily: May–Sept 10am–4pm; $13; Ⓣ970/387-5444 or 1-800/872-3009, Ⓦwww.minetour.com), three miles northeast of town on Hwy-110 E. Mine tours head a third of a mile into Galena Mountain, where old mining tools aren't just exhibited but operated as well. Tours begin with a three-minute underground train ride to a large cavern, where there are noisy air-powered stoppers and a mucker scooping rock into a cart.

Further down the road is the partially restored and extraordinarily beautifully located ghost town of **Animas Forks**. Although a sign along the way states that two-wheel-drive vehicles should go no further, it's easy in dry conditions to coax a regular car all the way. Located by the headwaters of the Animas River, all that's left of this once 500-strong town are a few ruined private homes and old mine buildings; all neatly evoking the struggle of life here. To travel on the rough dirt roads that lead to Ouray and Lake City from Animas Forks, four-wheel-drive vehicles are a must (see below).

Outdoor activities

Silverton is also well-placed to take advantage of some of the wildest areas in the San Juans. Three national forests are around town: the Uncompahgre National Forest in the north; the Rio Grande National Forest in the east; and the San Juan National Forest in the south and west. The area also has lots of BLM-managed lands, but, more significantly, is close to the **Weminuche Wilderness** (see box opposite).

The local visitor center is a good source of local hiking information since they've prepared a number of free trail leaflets. This includes a description of the **Molas Pass Trail**, a pretty six miles out-and-back trail which begins at Molas Lake beside Hwy-550, dropping a steep thousand feet to the Animas river and offering a hard return climb.

Four-wheel driving is almost as popular here as it is in nearby Ouray (see box p.172), good, rough, dirt roads spread out in almost every direction: east to Creede and Lake City; west to Telluride. If you're over 25 and have proof of insurance, you can rent a jeep in town from the *Triangle Motel* (see overleaf) for $120 per day. Otherwise, take a tour with San Juan Backcountry, 1121 Greene St (Ⓣ970/387-5565 or 1-800/494-8687, Ⓦwww.silverton.org/sanjuanbackcountry), who charge $35 per person for two-hour tours. Four-wheeling combined with backcountry camping is also offered for $150 per person, per night.

The big winter news here is the rugged **Silverton Mountain** (Ⓣ970/387-5706, Ⓦwww.silvertonmountain.com; $25), which opened in time for the 2001/2002 season. An experts-only facility with only one chairlift, it's probably the only mountain in the Lower 48 that can guarantee first tracks and idyl-

Weminuche Wilderness

Weminuche Wilderness, named after a group of Utes, is crossed by the Continental Divide and is the largest roadless area in Colorado, making it one of the best places to head for genuinely remote **backcountry hiking** experiences. Lower portions of the area are open from late June, but you need to wait until late July for snow to clear at higher altitudes. One of the best times to hike is in late summer and early fall (Aug and Sept), when the virulent mosquitoes, busiest during the snowmelt, are less of a problem and parts of the forest erupt into fall colors. Before heading off into the wilderness, you'd be well advised to discuss your route and preparations with the forest service in Durango first. The most popular long-distance trail through the wilderness is the **Chicago Basin** route to Creede, 75 miles away – a trip which necessitates taking the steam train to the trailhead and usually takes backpackers around a week. Otherwise **Silverton** is the most convenient access point, the Weminuche Wilderness beginning around six miles southeast of town. To access it cross the bridge over the Animas River to follow trails alongside Kendall Mountain and up Deer Park Creek. In Silverton, Outdoor World, 1234 Greene St (☎970/387-5628), is on hand to discuss hikes in the wilderness, as well as supply any equipment you might need. The best access points to the Wilderness near **Durango** are from trailheads around Vallecito Reservoir (see p.160).

lic backcountry conditions. Note you'll need an avalanche receiver, shovel, and backcountry experience – there's a short test – before being allowed up. The other skiing opportunities in town remain much flatter, with many good backcountry **cross-county skiing** possibilities (hire equipment available at the *French Bakery*; see below). The town also maintains a free **ice rink**, with skate hire available at the public library.

Eating and drinking

The selection of places **to eat** in Silverton varies markedly depending on what time of day – and year – you turn up. Summer lunchtimes see the largest selection as many places shutter up when the train leaves town and close completely in winter. **Nightlife** is limited basically to occasional live music in *Handlebars*, drinking and shooting pool at the spit-and-sawdust *Miners Tavern*, 1069 Greene St, and a mixed bag of theater performances at **Miners Union Theater**, 1069 Greene St (July–Sept; ☎970/387-5337).

The French Bakery 1250 Greene St ☎970/387-5976. Part of the *Teller House Hotel*, this bakery also serves good omelettes, sandwiches, and soups through to full meals. Its location near the train depot means it's generally packed at lunch. Closed Nov–Feb.

Grand Imperial Hotel 1219 Greene St ☎970/387-5527. Well-known as having the best buffet breakfast; only $6.95 and with many cooked options. Served from 7am and available to non-guests. You can also pick up decent burgers and sandwiches here later in the day; full meals – including pepper stuffed chipotle steaks ($17) in the evening.

Handlebars 117 13th St ☎970/387-5395. Atmospheric restaurant and saloon covered in hundreds of antiques and curios ranging from old wooden skis to musty mooseheads. The menu ranges from regular bar grub to more lavish dinner entrees, including breaded and fried Rocky Mountain oysters from $8. Closed Nov–Feb.

Pickle Barrel 1304 Greene St ☎970/387-5713. Located in an all-wood, former general store, the *Pickle Barrel* serves good sandwiches for lunch and more substantial entrees like steak and trout for dinner.

Romero's 1151 Greene St ☎970/387-0123. An enjoyable Mexican cantina, with tasty, authentic food and fantastic salsa. Prices start from around $8 for entrees.

Rocky Mountain Funnel Cakes & Café, 1249 Greene St ☎970/387-5450. Jolly little café with low prices offers the best possible introduction to funnel cakes (big puffy pancakes); an exhaustive array of options range from simple icing sugar to a full Mexican version with beans and guacamole.

Ouray

From Silverton, the Million Dollar Highway (Hwy-550) climbs a series of switchbacks past ruins of mines and mills, cresting the aptly named Red Mountain Pass (11,018ft) – where the bare rock beneath the snow really is red – before twisting down into **OURAY**, 23 miles to the north. Beautifully situated in a natural amphitheater-like box canyon 5000ft below surrounding peaks, Ouray began life in the early 1880s as a booming silver town, but was saved after the silver-market crash by the discovery of gold in 1896, allowing the Ouray economy to hum on along.

Unlike its closest neighbors, Ouray has not developed tourism based on either skiing or a railroad. Instead it's concentrated, since Victorian times, on promoting its hot springs, nowadays along with a furious promotion of **four-wheel driving** on the numerous local rough mountain tracks. Ouray also seems to take its self-proclaimed status as the Switzerland of America rather seriously, constructing a huge **ice-climbing** wall in a narrow gorge near town every winter.

Arrival, information, and accommodation

Daily TNM&O buses (Montrose station: ⓣ970/249-6873) between Durango and Montrose stop in Ouray. Note that since there's no established stop in town it's critical to find a place where the bus can pull over if hailed. The **visitor center** (daily 8am–6pm; closed Mon & Tues in winter; ⓣ970/325-4746 or 1-800/228-1876, ⓦwww.ouraycolorado.com) is beside the hot springs on the north side of town and publishes the useful *Ouray County Vacation Guide* that includes a four-wheel-drive map of routes in the area. For detailed information on the local national forests, contact the **Public Lands Office**, 2505 S Townsend (ⓣ970/249-3711) in Montrose (see p.182).

From the campgrounds and motels on the outskirts of town to pricey B&Bs downtown, there are quite a few places to bed down in Ouray. Those places staying open in the winter usually offer not only a substantial discount, but can usually also provide half-price lift tickets at Telluride. Of the nearby **campgrounds**, the *Amphitheater Campground* (ⓣ970/249-3711 or 1-800/280-2267), around a mile from its signpost on Hwy-550 at the southern end of town, is one of the most picturesque, perched an almost vertical 700ft above Ouray and offering thirty primitive sites ($14). In town, you can pitch a tent at *4J+1+1*, 709 Oak St (mid-May to mid-Oct; ⓣ970/325-4418), for $16.

Box Canyon Lodge 45 3rd Ave ⓣ970/325-4981 or 1-800/327-5080, ⓦwww.boxcanyonouray.com. Mid-range motel in an Alpine-style timber building below Box Canyon Falls Park, where you can bathe in cask-like hot tubs. ❸

Manor B&B 317 2nd St ⓣ970/325-4981 or 1-800/628-6946, ⓦwww.ouraymanor.com. Renovated three-story Victorian home, built in 1890, where each room is decorated with an Old West theme – most with private baths and mountain views. There's a hot tub in the gardens and a full breakfast is served daily. ❻

Ouray Hotel 303 6th Ave ⓣ970/325-0500 or 1-800/216-8779. Grand, central Victorian property with straightforward, comfortable hotel rooms (with private baths); ranging from dark economy rooms to roomy suites. Open May–October. ❸

Ouray Victorian Inn 1-800/864-8729, ⓦwww.ouraylodging.com. Quality motel rooms that are the lodging of choice for winter ice-climbers – for whom rates are slashed by half (and a free breakfast included) by the friendly manager (who lives to ice-climb). ❻

Riverside Inn & Cabins 1805 N Main St ⓣ970/325-4061 or 1-800/432-4170, ⓦwww.ourayriversideinn.com. Large modern property on the northern edge of town, near the Ouray Hot Springs, has a wide variety of accommodations from great-value rustic cabins to pricey roomy suites. ❸

St Elmo Hotel 426 Main St ⓣ970/325-4951, ⓦwww.stelmohotel.com. Luxurious B&B located on the main drag and home to its own venerable, high-class restaurant. Inside, it's a harmonious combination of polished wood and brass, period furnishings, and stained glass, and all rooms are finely decorated and en suite. Outdoor hot tub as well. ❻

Wiesbaden Hot Springs and Lodgings ⓣ970/325-4347, ⓦwww.wiesbadenhotsprings.com. Small spa hotel with its own private hot springs-fed outdoor pool, a hot tub, and some dingy, atmospheric, underground vapor caves. The elegant rooms come in a variety of shapes and sizes; some are suites and some have kitchens. ❻

Downtown and around

As with many former mining towns dotting the San Juans, Ouray's small downtown area is lined with grand Victorian structures, built with the spoils of silver and gold mining – an industry detailed in a local museum **Ouray County Historical Society Museum**, 20 6th Ave (May–Oct Mon–Sat 10am–4pm; Nov–April Mon–Fri 1–4pm; $3; ⓣ970/324-4576). A better choice, though, are the hourly mine tours of the **Bachelor-Syracuse Mine**, 1222 CO-14 (late May to mid-Sept daily 9am–6pm; $12; ⓣ970/325-4500). The tours head 3350ft into a cold hill from which gold, silver, lead, zinc, and copper were once extracted.

What helps set Ouray apart from the other mining towns, though, are its famed **hot springs**. There are several options in the area, the largest of which is **Ouray Hot Springs** (daily: June–Aug 10am–10pm; Sept–May noon–9pm; $7; ⓣ970/325-4638), beside the Uncompahgre River at the north end of town. The complex contains a large swimming pool and smaller soaking pool, but has a rather institutional feel. Much more intimate and unique are the facilities offered by the **Wiesbaden Vapor Cave**, 625 5th St (daily 8am–9.45pm; $10; ⓣ970/325-4347), on the east side of town. Run by a hotel (see above), nonguests can pay for use of the vapor cave (a steam room in a roughly hewn underground cave) and pool, as well for a massage or mud wraps. Another slightly unconventional soaking option is available at the Orvis Hot Springs near Ridgeway (see overleaf).

Outdoor activities

Traditionally the town's major outdoor attraction has been **Box Canyon Falls Park** (daily 8am–dusk; $2), a mile south of town. As in Victorian times, visitors come to walk up a 500ft trail, partly along a swaying wooden parapet, that leads into a dark and narrow box canyon. At the far end, falls thunder 300ft through a tiny cleft in the mountain, and a clamber up rocks to the lip of the canyon allows visitors to stand high above them on a vulnerable-looking steel suspension footbridge. With the creation of the **Ouray Ice Park** (ⓦwww.ourayicepark.com; free) in 1995, winters in the canyon also court vertigo. The attraction began with an eccentric idea to set sprinklers on the edges of a narrow crevasse in the canyon, spraying water down the walls – creating sheets of ice a hundred feet tall and half a mile long in the process. Ice-climbers now swarm here to strike their way up the walls, particularly during the **Ouray Ice Festival** held here the third weekend in January.

With so many trails and mining roads in the area, mountain bikers and hikers are obviously well-served. For a mellow ride exploring the Uncompahgre River Valley, head ten miles to Ridgeway along CO-17. Largely devoid of traffic, this road parallels Hwy-550 along an old Rio Grande Southern Railroad bed and is so flat that it makes absorbing the surrounding scenery positively relaxing. If you like to expend even less energy, the San Juan Mountain Outfitters, 2882 CO-23 (ⓣ970/626-5659), run a variety of half- to multiday **horseback-riding** trips. For **rental equipment**, Ouray Mountain Sports, 722 Main St (ⓣ970/325-4284), is the place to go. In winter they hire out cross-country skis and ice-climbing gear, and in summer they switch over to mountain bikes.

Four-wheeling

More than anywhere else in the San Juans, the Ouray area is known for its plethora of great **jeeping** roads running along steep cliffsides and through old mining camps. One of the easier popular local drives is to **Yankee Boy Basin**. The route starts at Camp Bird Road south of Ouray and heads alongside Canyon Creek to Camp Bird Mine, then eastward through flowering meadows. A number of other popular jeep roads head over passes to Telluride. More experienced drivers will enjoy the harder but very scenic **Imogene Pass** to Telluride via the abandoned Tomboy Mine and the remains of a guard station used during some of Telluride's labor-management conflicts. But it's the heart-stopping **Black Bear Pass** that's the most famous local drive. Not only does it include the insanely steep, uneven "staircase" section, it also drops into Telluride on far and away the most memorable route; suddenly the town appears cradled in the bowl of surrounding mountains far below. Colorado West Tours, 701 Main St (Ⓣ970/325-4014 or 1-800/648-JEEP, Ⓦwww.coloradowest-tours.com), is one of a number of operators in Ouray that runs four-wheel-drive tours (May–Oct); prices begin at $45 for a half-day tour. They also rent to those with their own vehicle insurance ($120 per day; $25 per hour). You'll find similar rates at the *Riverside Inn* (see p.170), who have a fleet of modern jeeps and are one of the few places in town to welcome those who don't have their own insurance.

Eating and drinking

Bon Ton 426 Main St Ⓣ970/325-4951. Accomplished Northern Italian food served up in the *St Elmo Hotel*'s atmospheric redbrick basement. At $7, the great Sunday brunch is an unmissable deal; otherwise it's an expensive choice.

Buen Tiempo, 515 Main St Ⓣ970/325-4544. Good range of Southwestern and Mexican food – spinach enchiladas and chile-rubbed prime rib – and a dozen margaritas, served in a lively restaurant where dexterous bartenders have stuck hundreds of dollar bills on the high ceiling.

The Cottage Shoppe 400 Main St. Heavenly homemade ice creams and frozen yogurts; and a few good focaccias ($6) for light lunches.

Grounds Keeper Coffee House and Eatery 524 Main St Ⓣ970/325-0550. Central café serving espresso drinks and healthy light lunches that includes a fine veggie lasagna.

Ouray Brewing Co 522 Main St Ⓣ970/325-4265. The town's nonsmoking brewpub is a popular choice for an evening drink.

Piñon 737 Main St Ⓣ970/325-4334. Modern café serving some great healthy food like a veggie burrito, stuffed with beans, zucchini, carrots, and more.

Pricco's 736 Main St Ⓣ970/325-4040. Long standing local favorite with a menu that features steaks, salads, hoagies, and spicy Santa Fe-style chicken, along with some veggie options too. Moderate.

Ridgeway

Though only ten miles north of the craggy alpine scenery of Ouray, the red rocks and sparse sagebrush around **RIDGEWAY** seems a world apart. The broad ranching valley in which the town sits is almost universally flat, and while the area has attracted the rich – Ralph Lauren has a ranch nearby – it's really best used as a cheap jumping-off point to both Telluride and Ouray. Visitors staying here in winter qualify for half-price lift passes at Telluride, forty miles away, and have the added bonus of being able to soak slope-weary bones a the town's only attraction of note, the slightly nonconformist **Orvis Hot Springs** ($12; Ⓣ970/626-5324). Located a couple of miles south of town on Hwy-550, this pretty collection of pools, sauna, and private indoor hot tubs is among the best hot-springs facilities in the state thanks to the fantastic views of surrounding mountains and the night sky. The atmosphere is generally chilled-out, although its clothing optional rule may not be to everyone's taste.

In summer, **campers** can stay at the nearby, lakeside **Ridgway State Park** ($4 day-use fee; campsites $12–16), a popular place for trout fishing. There's a dependable *Super 8 Motel* (☎970/626-5444 or 1-800/368-5444; ④) with pool and hot tub in town, but a good year-round hotel option in town is the *Chipeta Sun Lodge* (☎970/626-3737 or 1-800/633-5868, Ⓦwww.chipeta.com; ⑥), an adobe-style building with good views and rustic, Southwestern-style rooms. Big creative breakfasts are served and a solarium and the hot tub, inside the third-floor's turret, are an added bonus. One of the small number of places to **eat** in town is the *True Grit Café*, 123 N Lena (☎970/626-5739), where burgers and sandwiches are served amidst stacks of John Wayne memorabilia – his movie *True Grit* was filmed around these parts back in the late 1960s.

Telluride

Lying at the flat base of vast steep-sided mountains, **TELLURIDE**, is located in one of the most picturesque valleys in the Rockies. Beginning as a mining village, settlement began to take off here from 1875, even though Ute ownership of surrounding lowlands forced prospectors over high mountain-passes. In the 1880s, Telluride was briefly home to the young Butch Cassidy, who robbed his first bank here in 1889, but the town didn't really develop until the following year when the Grand Southern Railroad pulled into town. It quickly grew to over 5000, but was still considered so far off the beaten track that the train's conductors traditionally yelled "to-hell-you-ride" on arrival into town. By 1930, though, all the mines had closed and the town's population was down to 512. The town seemed destined for oblivion until 1968, when a Californian investor starting developing the surrounding slopes and the town's reputation as a great ski area was launched – albeit only for the committed, since it remained hard to get to. The building of a local airport changed all that and these days Telluride rivals Aspen as the prime winter destination for the stars – and one that has become too expensive for many locals to continue to live in. Like Aspen, Telluride has also launched a supremely successful program of summer-season festivals that, together with the array of good hiking and biking trails, has turned the town into a strong year-round destination. Thankfully, the town remains a laid-back place and both the town's Victorian core and overall offbeat but cool vibe have been preserved, making it a worthy trip winter or summer.

Arrival and information

The **Telluride Airport**, five miles east of town, handles a large amount of traffic with daily services to Denver and frequent flights to Phoenix, Chicago, Houston, and Newark. **Skip's Taxi and Shuttle Service** (☎970/728-6000) meet flights from the airport for the short ride into town.

The **visitor center**, 666 W Colorado Ave (daily: summer 9am–7pm; winter 9am–5pm; ☎970/728-3041 or 1-800/525-3455, Ⓦwww.telluridemm.com), is beside the highway into town. **Free buses** from here run on a loop along Pacific and Colorado avenues, though it's hardly slower to walk into town. Either way it's generally best to leave your car here, as spaces in the center are hard to come by and everything is within walking distance anyway.

Accommodation

Finding somewhere to stay in Telluride year-round is nearly always a struggle, particularly if you're not after the condo accommodation that the town has

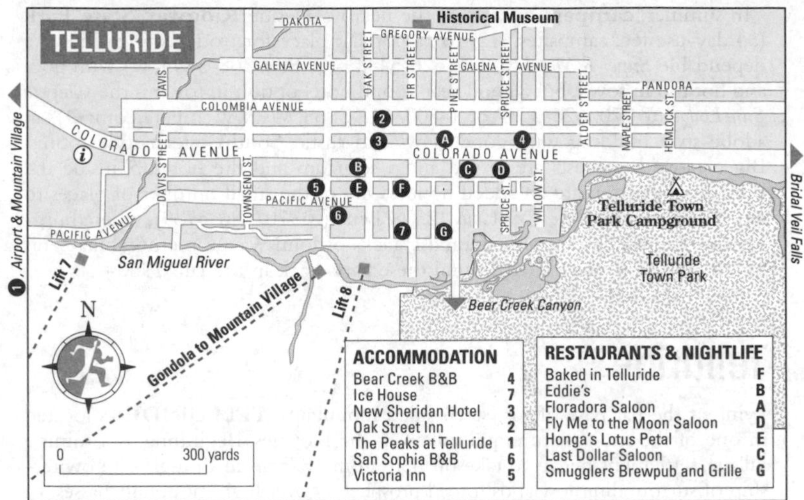

eagerly bred over the last decade or so. The best bet is to book as far ahead as possible. The visitor center-run **Telluride Central Reservations** (☎970/728-4431 or 1-800/525 3455) can help secure a bed in advance, though their prices are a little above walk-in rates. If looking for **condo accommodation** – the best deal if in a group – try contacting Telluride Resort Accommodations (☎970/728-6621 or 1-800/538-7754); a two-bedroom, four-person condo works out around $170 and up a night during the ski season. The only way to really cut costs is to **camp**: *Telluride Town Park Campground* (☎970/728-9645; mid-May to Oct;) has forty sites near the center of town ($15) that have access to showers, swimming, and tennis facilities. The nearest **USFS campgrounds**, fifteen miles away on Hwy-145, are the primitive *Sunshine* ($10) and the *Matterhorn* ($16), which includes showers and hookups.

Bear Creek Bed & Breakfast 221 E Colorado Ave ☎970/728-6282 or 1-800/338-7064, ⓦwww.bearcreektelluride.com. Good, central B&B offering a variety of rooms, all en suite and with access to a rooftop hot tub. ❺

Ice House 310 S Fir St ☎970/728-6300 or 1-800/544-3436. Average hotel rooms located in a fusion of Scandinavian and Southwest decor a little over a block from the lifts. Continental breakfast included. Facilities include hot tub and steam room. ❺

New Sheridan Hotel 231 W Colorado Ave ☎970/728-4351 or 1-800/200-1891. This 1895 hotel filled with period decor offers some of the cheapest rooms in town in both winter and summer (when rates drop by half). Only some of the rooms have private bath, but guests have use of a hot tub and exercise room. ❺

Oak Street Inn 134 N Oak St ☎970/728-3383. An AYH youth hostel with private rooms, a sauna, and a sociable TV lounge. ❹

The Peaks at Telluride 136 Country Club Drive ☎970/729-6800 or 1-800/789-2220. Large resort and spa development on the Telluride Mountain side of town. Ski in and ski out in winter, play golf just beside it in summer, and avail yourself to over fifty different spa treatments year-round. The excellent sports include an extensive fitness center with pools and hot tubs, tennis courts, racquetball, and even a climbing wall. ❽

San Sophia B&B 330 W Pacific St ☎970/728-3001 or 1-800/537-4781. Stylish, upscale B&B whose enthusiastic owners serve both fantastic breakfasts and great après-ski snacks. Each room is wonderfully decorated and the hot tub out back makes for a perfect end to the day. ❽

Victoria Inn 401 W Pacific Ave ☎970/728-6601 or 1-800/611-9893. Clean motel-standard doubles and a sauna. ❻

Downtown and the Mountain Village

Thankfully, despite the influx of the chic, Telluride has not lost all of its old-time character: the wide main street, a National Historic District has low-slung buildings on either side, and is still surrounded by gingerbread Victorian homes. For a detailed tour of the historic center of Telluride, largely scattered along W Colorado Avenue, the town's main street, it's worth following the **walking tour** printed in *Telluride* magazine, available from the town's visitor center. However, this guide is no real substitute for joining the **guided walking tours** run by Historic Tours of Telluride (June–Sept daily 10am; $10; ⓣ970/728-6639), beginning from Elk's Park, which also includes a look at some of the less obvious historic landmarks. The **San Miguel County Historical Museum**, 317 N First St ($3; ⓣ970/728-3344), is the town's modest local museum which recalls days when the town had 26 saloons and twelve brothels, and miners sledded down from mines on their shovels in winter.

The bulk of the ski-related developments at **Telluride Mountain Village** are hidden on the other side of a 2000ft-high mountain ridge. Mountain Village and Telluride proper are connected to one another by a gondola (May to mid-October & mid-Nov to March; free) which heads up one side of the ridge, then down the other – the two are three miles away by road. Though many ski runs descend into Telluride itself, the Mountain Village is really the heart of the ski area; a collection of million-dollar homes, all-inclusive resorts and condos and with its own golf course.

Winter activities

With most of Telluride's awesome black-mogul fields looming over town, it's easy to see where the most brutal downhill action takes place, but hidden behind this foreboding face, surrounding Telluride Mountain Village is the true center of winter sports activities in the valley. **Cross-country** skiers visiting town are also well served both around town and in the mountain village by the twenty miles of free tracks maintained by the **Telluride Nordic Center** (ⓣ970/728-7260), who also offer affordable rentals. More adventurous Nordic skiers should try to use some of the cabins operated by the **San Juan Hut System** (ⓣ970/728-6935, ⓦwww.telluridegateway.com/sjhuts), which are about six miles apart and linked by easy cross-country ski trails suitable even for beginners.

Telluride Ski Area

With an awesome vertical drop of 3552ft and terrain that begins to rival the Alps for scenic beauty, the **Telluride Ski Area** (ⓣ1-800/525-3455, ⓦwww.telski.com), is one of the most exciting and dramatic places to ski in Colorado. As with most other resorts in the state, Telluride gets plenty of light, dry powder – the season usually running from late November to early April – which covers all its varied slopes, from the incredibly demanding double black diamonds with massive bumps on the town side of the mountain, to the mixture of mellower terrain on the resort side.

The ski area's eighty-plus runs break down as 21 percent beginner; 47 percent intermediate; and 32 percent advanced and expert – all served by twelve lifts and the gondola. Though slightly tamed over the last few years to make more terrain available to intermediate riders, it remains one of Colorado's toughest mountains. Expert-only runs like the incredibly steep Plunge and Spiral Staircase, both dotted with massive moguls, will give even the most advanced a run for their money, and the recently expanded Prospect Bowl area has glade and bowl challenges for all upper levels. See Forever, at nearly three miles long, is a top intermediate run with panoramic views stretching into Utah. Telluride is also a world-class freestyle snowboarding destination, as evidenced by the huge Surge Air Garden **terrain park**, host to several championship competitions.

As a one-day **lift ticket** is a steep $65 it's worth investigating what deals are available through Telluride Central Reservations (see p.174), who can often offer heavily reduced rates in conjunction with accommodation. You can also claim a fifty-percent discount on lift passes by staying in neighboring towns such as Ridgway or Ouray. As you'd expect, a number of businesses in both the town and the resort side of the mountain offer equipment **rental**, including Paragon Sports, 213 W Colorado Ave (Ⓣ970/728-4525).

Summer activities

By June much of the snow on the surrounding mountains has melted, leaving behind flower-covered slopes, high alpine ridges and trails that draw outdoor enthusiasts of all stripes. Some of the finest hiking options are around the 10,500ft ridges in the ski area, accessed via the free gondola. One of the finest excursions away from the resort area is the three-mile round-trip hike to 365ft **Bridal Veil Falls** – the largest in Colorado. To reach the trailhead, follow Colorado Avenue west to where it ends at Pioneer Mill. Another good short hike is the 1000ft trek up **Bear Creek Canyon** to a multitiered waterfall; follow Pine Street south to the trailhead.

Mountain bikers can also use the gondola for free and there are a variety of trails leading back down either side of the mountain, including some challenging and rocky single track runs cutting through beautiful stands of aspens on the Mountain Village side. The ultimate local ride, though, is the 215-mile tour to Moab, Utah, that crosses over from alpine tundra into slickrock desert, using the **San Juan Hut System**. The shelters, a series of six hut groups evenly spaced along the route, are prestocked with more than enough food, covered (along with your lodging) by the $400 per person usage fee (Ⓣ970/728-6935, Ⓦwww.telluridegateway.com/sjhuts). For details on more routes in the area, pick up Dave Rich's local guide *Tellurides*, or stop by Telluride Sports, 150

Telluride summer festivals

Telluride stands apart from most ski-resorts in having an off-season program of worthwhile **festivals** that actually draw crowds from both near and far. Highlights include:

Bluegrass festival (Ⓣ970/449-6007 or 1-800/624-2422, Ⓦwww.bluegrass.com). A four-day festival in late June which attracts around 10,000 visitors for big-name acts. A four-day ticket to the festival costs around $170, with around another $50 charged for a spot to camp near town.

Jazz Celebration (Ⓣ970/728-7009, Ⓦwww.telluridejazz.com). Held since the 1970s in the first week of August, this jazz fest has included performances by Herbie Hancock and Etta James in the past.

Chamber Music Festival (Ⓣ1-800/525-3455, Ⓦwww.telluridemm.com). Another longstanding August festival begins with an outdoor sunset concert and ends in the elegant surroundings of the Victorian Sheridan Opera House.

Film Festival (Ⓣ603/643-1255, Ⓦwww.telluridefilmfestival.com). Held on the first weekend in September, past premieres at this 25-year-old film festival have included *The Crying Game* and *The Piano* and free films are screened in an outdoor theatre. Needless to say, tickets go fast.

W Colorado Ave (☎970/728-4477), where day-rentals run around $25 for a front-suspension bike.

The old mining roads around town are also popularly explored with **four-wheel-drive vehicles**, including the many high-pass routes over to Ouray; see box on p.172 for more details. To pick up a tour in town contact Telluride Outside (☎970/728-3895). Other possibilities include touring the area the old-fashioned way on **horseback**; Telluride Horseback, 9025 Rt 145 (☎970/728-9611), offer rides from $30 per hour.

Eating, drinking, and entertainment

Telluride's **dining** scene has taken its lead from its lodging options: it's often overpriced, though the standard of quality is high. Nightlife in town mostly revolves around boisterous bars lining Colorado Avenue, often with live music. If that doesn't appeal, there's also the option of seeing a play performed by the Telluride Repertory Company (☎970/728-6363) at the Sheridan Opera House. Special events are usually listed in the local *Daily Planet* newspaper.

Baked In Telluride 127 S Fir St ☎970/728-4705. One of the most affordable options in town where good muffins and pastries are served early on, while pizza slices and huge portions of the hearty specials are served throughout the day. The bar is also a lively evening hangout.

Eddie's 300 W Colorado Ave ☎970/728-5335. Sports bar serving good Italian food alongside home-brewed ales. For light feeds you can pick up pizza by the slice or a range of salads and sandwiches.

Floradora Saloon 103 W Colorado Ave ☎970/728-3888. Serving fine food in an Old West saloon atmosphere, this busy restaurant is named after two of the town's most popular Victorian call-girls. Food runs from teriyaki-glazed salmon and wild mushroom pasta to standard Mexican and burger favorites, and there's a fine salad bar as well. Closed October and November.

Fly Me to the Moon Saloon 132 E Colorado Ave ☎970/728-6666. Noisy and boisterous bar with nightly live bands during the ski and festival seasons: typically rock, reggae, and R&B.

Honga's Lotus Petal, 133 S Oak St ☎970/728-5234. Variety of good Asian dishes at unusually reasonable prices. The range of food represented here spans Japanese, Korean, Thai, and Indonesian to Chinese; entrees from around $12. Dinner only.

Last Dollar Saloon 100 E Colorado. Gritty, smoky and loud spit-and-sawdust place where locals hang out.

Smugglers Brewpub and Grille San Juan and Pine ☎970/728-0919. Lively evening hangout with a decent menu of bar food and some good local microbrews.

The Gunnison and Arkansas headwaters

Containing two of Colorado's most impressive rivers and flanked by some of the state's highest mountains, the **Gunnison and Arkansas headwaters** represent Colorado at its best: relatively uncrowded and unspoilt, with superb recreation possibilities at nearly every turn, both in the rivers and on the mountains.

The western gateways to the Gunnison region, **Montrose** and **Delta** are dull little crossroads towns but close to the magnificent **Black Canyon of the**

Gunnison National Park**. Further upstream the Gunnison River has been dammed, forming the vast **Blue Mesa Reservoir**, surrounded by the bleak lands of the **Curecanti Recreation Area** and close to the bland workaday town of **Gunnison** further east. Although there's some great fishing in the area, most pass quickly through Gunnison on to **Crested Butte**, a gorgeous nineteenth-century mining village turned laid-back ski resort that's almost as busy in summer for its hiking and biking routes.

East along the broad Gunnison River Valley the land rises to the 11,846ft Monarch Pass, site of the **Monarch Ski Area**, to drop into the **Arkansas River Valley**. Like the Gunnison River Valley, it's an empty, windswept, and for the most part sparsely-populated valley. But flanked between a magnificent line of soaring fourteeners of the **Collegiate Range** to the west and the montane Pikes Peak region to the east, the scenery is much more spectacular. The valley is also a point of convergence for several major highways. From the energetic town of **Salida** in the south highways head south to the San Luis Valley or east to Cañon City, while from the small whitewater rafting town of **Buena Vista** further north roads branch to Denver or to the band of development along the I-70 to the north.

Black Canyon of the Gunnison National Park and around

Splitting a mesatop above the Uncompahgre Valley, the Black Canyon of the Gunnison runs 53 miles from near Delta west towards Gunnison. The most spectacular portion, a fourteen-mile stretch of canyon, fifteen miles from Montrose along Hwy-50 and Hwy-347, became **The Black Canyon of the Gunnison National Park** (Ⓣ970/249-7036, Ⓦwww.nps.gov/blca/index.htm) in 1999. Here the canyon's dark-gray cliffs and jagged spires of Precambrian schist, gneiss, and quartz plunge 2689ft at the highest point to the foaming Gunnison River below. For those who've visited the Grand Canyon, a comparison is inevitable – and while the scale of the Black Canyon is not as impressive, its dimensions certainly are. In several places, the canyon is obviously far deeper than it is wide, and the relative closeness of the two rims makes the visit a more intimate experience.

Formed over two million years by the erosive powers of the mighty Gunnison, the deep gorge was considered a dangerous place by the Ute, whose legends declared you could not return alive from a visit into the canyon. In the 1850s, geologist Wallace R. Hansen challenged the legend and lived to map much of the canyon, writing that "No other canyon in North America combines the depth, narrowness, sheerness and somber countenance of the Black Canyon." Three years later, John W. Gunnison led a party to the canyon's upper reaches, though the trip was ultimately abandoned short of the gorge floor, leaving a first detailed exploration of its floor to Ferdinand V. Hayden (veteran explorer of Yellowstone) in 1874. But it was not until 1901 that the first recorded trip along its whole length took place when the Denver and Rio Grande railroad sent an exploratory party out to check the feasibility of laying a railroad along its base. The party navigated as much of the river as it could on air mattresses, swimming and scrambling where they had to, and eventually covered the 33-mile stretch in nine days. This exploration led to a six-mile diversion tunnel of water for the farms of the nearby plateau, but the railroad was never extended from nearby Cimmaron into the actual Black Canyon itself.

△ Laid-back Telluride, home to Butch Cassidy's first bank robbery in 1889

Exploring the park

Most people explore the park along the **south rim**, hopping between hikes of varying lengths – from a few yards to over a mile in length – that lead to impressive canyon viewpoints. It's easy to get a **backcountry permit** to enter the canyon (from the visitors' center on the south rim or the ranger station on the north rim), but it's such an arduous and dangerous undertaking that few people take up the opportunity.

Just beyond the **south rim** park entrance ($7 per vehicle; includes detailed map), the East Portal Road heads east to the *East Portal Campground* ($9) in the Curecanti National Recreation Area (see below), while the South Rim Road passes the *South Rim Campground* (102 sites; $9) and heads on to the **visitors' center** (May–Oct daily 8am–6pm; ⓣ970/249-1915) on the canyon rim. The center is a good starting point for the southern rim's only longer hike – the **Rim Rock Trail** – that heads along the canyon rim, before looping around along the Uplands trail which connects the Oak Flat Trail and heading back to the visitors' center in a two-hour loop. From the visitors' center it's another five miles west to **High Point** – the western terminus of the road that joins a series of overlooks and nature trails beside the precipitous canyon walls. From High Point a trail heads another three-quarters of a mile further west to **Warner Point**, a good vantage point to admire both the northern rim and a portion of the southern rim. The patient wildlife spotter may also see golden eagles, red-tailed hawks, and turkey vultures negotiating the canyon's air-currents below.

The more remote **north rim** (closed in winter) road is reached by a long, unpaved road from the little town of Crawford (near Delta, see p.182) along Hwy-92. While there are a couple of long, secluded hikes here, the views are not nearly as rewarding as those elsewhere and only the headiest climbers should think about heading this way.

Curecanti National Recreation Area

Abutting the eastern boundary of the Black Canyon of the Gunnison, the **Curecanti National Recreation Area** offers a range of recreation opportunities around three reservoirs created by dams across the Gunnison River. The recreation area spans from the **Morrow Point Reservoir** which snakes along the upper part of the Gunnison River Gorge, to the west, while to the east sprawls the **Blue Mesa Reservoir**, the largest body of water in Colorado.

Rafting through the Black Canyon

Rafting or **kayaking** through the Black Canyon of the Gunnison is a severely hard undertaking and one fraught with portages around unrunnable rapids and through large stands of poison ivy on slippery rocks. Needless to say, few bother. But just west of the national park lies the **Gunnison Gorge wilderness area**, surrounding the western extension of the Black Canyon, where the river squeezes itself between sheer black-granite cliffs. Most of this stretch is accessible only by raft, and although the rafting itself is generally straightforward (few rapids above Class III), the impressive scenery, the remoteness of the location and the excellent trout fishing make the trip – which generally requires an overnight camping stop – well worthwhile. One of the few commercial outfits that have a license to run this river is the experienced Wilderness Aware Rafting (ⓣ719/395-2112 or 1-800/462-7238, ⓦwww.inaraft.com) in Buena Vista (see p.192), who offer both overnight rafting and fishing trips in the gorge from around $350.

Bleak and windy, most of the land around the reservoirs isn't particularly attractive, though there is great float-fishing for rainbow, mackinaw, brook, and brown trout along with kokanee salmon. Boating and water-skiing also draw people in, as do cross-country skiing, snowmobiling, and ice-fishing in winter.

Two visitors' centers beside Hwy-50 serve the recreation area: the **Cimarron Visitors Center** (daily 8am–4.30pm) is near the Morrow Point Reservoir; the **Elk Creek Visitors Center** (daily 8am–4.30pm; ⓣ970/641-2337) is six miles west of the junction with Hwy-149 to Lake City. **Boat rentals** are available from marinas near each of the visitor centers, though the park service also runs guided boat cruises with good views of the upper canyon; these depart from the Morrow Point Reservoir daily (ⓣ970/641-0402; reservations required).

One of the few local features that the creation of the reservoirs haven't changed is the Curecanti Needle – a 700ft-high granite spire – that give the park its name. This can be seen up close by hiking down the parched and rugged **Curecanti Creek trail** (four miles round trip; 2–3hr), which begins at Pioneer Point Overlook off Hwy-92, six miles from the junction with Hwy-50. By contrast, **Neversink trail** (1.5 miles), off Hwy-50 five miles west of Gunnison, is far more verdant, running by the Gunnison River and perfect for bird-watching, including great blue herons.

The recreation area includes eight **campgrounds** with over 300 sites costing around $9 per night. Many are overrun with RVs and are fairly soulless, though the *East Portal Campground* near the Black Canyon National Park has some stunning views from the nearby rim.

South of the Black Canyon: Montrose

A hub for ranchers and hunters, parched and sprawling **MONTROSE** is the largest settlement between Grand Junction and Durango, on the stark and arid western slope of the Colorado Rockies. Besides using the town as a stopover en route to the Black Canyon, the only other reason for stopping here is to visit the **Ute Indian Museum**, 17253 Chipeta Drive (daily: mid-May to Sept 9am–6pm; Oct to mid-May 10am–5pm; $3). This small museum sits on land once farmed by the last great Ute chief, **Ouray** (1833–80), who's best known for negotiating a fragile peace with the Federal government in 1873. As part of the peace, he helped negotiate Ute withdrawal from eastern Colorado into the San Juan Mountains, though after his death this agreement was broken pushing the Ute west into semi-arid areas around Montrose and into present-day Utah, in return for a tokenistic payment of $25,000 dollars per year when mineral deposits were found in the mountains. The small museum does a good job describing Ute culture, thought to have had the longest continuous history among all the various tribes who at one time inhabited Colorado. Top exhibits include presentations on the bear dance and a display of the ceremonial garb worn by Ouray during treaty negotiations in Washington DC. The most interesting exhibits of the **Montrose County Historical Museum** on W Main Street (Memorial Day–Sept Mon–Sat 9am–5pm; $2; ⓣ970/249-2085) also relate to the Ute presence in the area with a great collection of arrowheads and some superb historical photos, including snaps of Ouray and his wife Chipeta.

Practicalities

TNM&O **buses** from Grand Junction, Durango, and Pueblo stop at the bus depot at 132 N 1st St. There's also a small **airport** (ⓣ970/249-8455), which sees the most use in winter when poor weather shuts Telluride's (see p.173) airport down. Shuttles to Telluride are run by Telluride Transit (ⓣ970/249-6993; $30 per person). Local information is doled out at the **Montrose Visitor Information Center**, 1519 E Main (Mon–Fri 9am–5pm; ⓣ970/249-5000 or 1-800/923-5515), though the **Montrose Public Lands Office**, 2505 S Townsend Ave (ⓣ970/240-5300), is a better choice if looking for outdoor information. The bulk of Montrose's **motels** line Hwy-50 (also Main St) on the eastern side of town, including the *Black Canyon Motel*, 1605 E Main St (ⓣ970/249-3495 or 1-800/453-4911; ❸), a standard, modest motel, and the slightly more luxurious *Best Western Red Arrow Inn*, 1702 E Main St (ⓣ970/249-9641 or 1-800/468-9323; ❹). **Campers** intent on staying near town should head east to the *Hangin' Tree RV Park*, 17250 Hwy-50 (ⓣ970/249-9966), where there are laundry facilities and full hookups.

All the usual chain **restaurants** are found on the highways out of Montrose, though pickings in town itself are slim. The *Daily Bread*, 1st Street and Cascade Street, is a good early morning stop-off, while decent Mexican and Southwestern-style food can be had at the *Whole Enchilada*, 44 S Grand St (ⓣ970/249-1881), where most entrees cost around $10.

North of the Black Canyon: Delta

Strung along Hwy-50, **DELTA** bills itself as a "City of Murals" after the vast gaudy paintings on several downtown stores. Located thirty miles south of Grand Junction (see p.255), Delta offers a handy place to stop for supplies before heading out to the Black Canyon. Other than traveling down to Montrose to reach the main park entrance, it's also possible to take the slower but hugely scenic Hwy-92 to the park's northern rim and the Curecanti Recreation Area. Even if you don't intend to visit the park itself, there are several good places along the road to stop and peer into the canyon. As seen at the Ute Indian Museum in Montrose (see overleaf), this region still contains some of the last vestiges of contemporary Ute culture in the state, best seen at the annual **Pow-wow Festival** (ⓣ1-800/874-1741, ⓦwww.counciltreepow-wow.org) held on the fourth weekend in September. But the main museum in Delta is a living-history museum, with costumed custodians who cheerfully perform displays of early pioneering activities at **Fort Uncompahgre** ($3.50; ⓣ970/874-8349), a reconstructed 1852 French fur-trading fort, in the Riverside Confluence Park, just north of Delta. The town's **visitor center**, 3rd Street and Main Street (Mon–Fri 9am–5pm; ⓣ970/874-8616), can supply more information on the powwow.

Gunnison

The workaday ranching/farming town of **GUNNISON** passes by in a blur, notable mainly as the turnoff point for Hwy–135 that leads 25 miles north to Crested Butte. Scratch the surface, though, and you'll find that this town does a good job of tapping into the **Gunnison National Forest** to the north, making for a good stopover for hikers, bikers, and especially anglers. Gunnison can also be used as a cheap base for activities around Crested Butte – though you'll only make worthwhile savings during the ski season.

For a quick appreciation of Gunnison's history, visit the **Gunnison County Pioneer and Historical Society Museum**, 110 S Adams (June–Sept Mon–Sat 9am–5pm; $4), on the eastern side of town. The most memorable item in the museum's collection is a restored narrow-gauge steam train from the Denver and Rio Grande Western Railroad.

Far more exciting are the numerous fishing areas around Gunnison. Just west of town, the **Gunnison River**, as it runs to the Blue Mesa Reservoir (see p.180), is a particularly productive stretch of water. East of Gunnison, the **Taylor River**, one of the main tributaries of the Gunnison, is also highly regarded for its excellent trout fishing. The Taylor River runs to Gunnison from the quiet **Taylor Park Reservoir**, thirty miles away – an idyllic spot for float-fishing, while above the reservoir's extent, the **Roaring Judy State Wildlife Area** is a favorite for committed fly-fishing enthusiasts. Fishing **outfitters** in the Gunnison area include Gene Taylor's Sporting Goods, 201 W Tomichi (☎970/641-1845); the Three Rivers Resort and Outfitting (☎970/641-1302), eleven miles north along Hwy-135 to Crested Butte; and the Taylor Park Boat House (☎970/641-2900) beside the Taylor Park Reservoir, who also rent out boats.

Hikers and bikers will want to head southwest of town to the **Hartman Rocks**, several piles of red-granite landforms surrounded by sage, pine, and juniper clinging to the sandy soil. The area provides an interconnected network of trails pleasantly unlike the wooded trails in the rest of the region, and conveniently the most interesting ones are within a mile of the parking lot. Here, the bulk of the igneous ring dykes – where lava-injected magma has cooled and hardened below the earth's surface before being heaved up above it in a series of uplifts – are located. The rocks are reached by traveling along Hwy-50 west for one-and-a-half miles before turning south on CO-38 (Gold Basin Rd) for four miles.

Practicalities

Gunnison is served by TNM&O **buses** from Pueblo and Montrose, which pull in at **Gunnison County Airport** (☎970/641-2304). The airport is at its busiest during the ski season, when Alpine Express (☎970/641-5074 or 1-800/822-4844) offers a shuttle service to Crested Butte for $40. For town **information**, contact the chamber of commerce, 500 E Tomichi (☎970/641-1501 or 1-800/323-2453); for details of opportunities on forest lands contact the Gunnison National Forest, Taylor and Cebolla Ranger Districts, 216 N Colorado (Mon–Fri 7.30am–4pm; ☎970/641-0471).

The strip of standard **motels** along Hwy-50 (Tomichi Ave) through town includes the basic *ABC Motel*, 212 E Tomichi Ave (☎970/641-2400 or 1-800/341-8000; ❸), and the slightly plusher *Hylander Inn*, 412 W Tomichi Ave (☎970/641-1061; ❹). The *Mary Lawrence Inn*, 601 N Taylor St (☎970/641-3343; ❻), is a small and comfortable B&B on one of the town's leafy side-streets. There are over thirty USFS **campgrounds** within an hour's drive of town, and the forest service office in town can provide a full list. If closed, head in the direction of the Taylor Park Reservoir, where campgrounds are dotted along the road.

When it comes to **eating out**, the *Sidewalk Café*, 113 W Tomichi Ave (☎970/641-4130), is good for cheap breakfasts, and the similarly inexpensive *Sundae Shoppe Restaurant* (☎970/641-5051) takes care of dinner, with offerings of chicken-fried steak and chimichangas followed by wonderful dessert sundaes. The ranch-style *Cattlemen Inn*, 301 W Tomichi (☎970/641-1061), is the town's answer to fine dining with an assortment of steaks, chicken, and seafood entrees starting at around $10. Of the handful of **bars**, *The Trough*, 37550 W Hwy-50 (☎970/641-3724), is the best bet with comedy shows on Thursdays and live bands on Friday and Saturday nights.

Crested Butte

The beautiful Victorian mining village of **CRESTED BUTTE** began as a thriving gold camp in the early 1880s, but became far more important for the rich seams of coal discovered here a few years later. While coal deposits began to run out in the late 1950s, the town was saved by the development of 11,875ft Mount Crested Butte into a world-class ski resort a few years later. Now a mountain-bikers' paradise as well, this picturesque former mining town can justifiably claim to be the best year-round resort in Colorado. Unlike other resort towns that have given in to commercialization, downtown Crested Butte is resplendent with gaily painted clapboard homes and local businesses, and zoning laws ensure that condos and chalets are confined to the resort area, **Mount Crested Butte**, tucked behind the foothills three miles up the road. The peaceful, nature-first vibe that permeates the town is threatened though by a possible mining resurgence: Mt Emmons – the 12,392ft mountain that watches over town – is home to the world's largest molybdenum deposit, whose estimated value lies at around $7 billion. For twenty years locals have fought a plucky battle against a large mining conglomerate, but still the threat of mining operations moving back into the area remains.

Arrival and information

Crested Butte is not an easy place to get to, especially in winter and spring when roads are often cut off by heavy snow. Most skiers fly in: ten **flights** per day from Denver, and at least one per week from Atlanta, Dallas, and Houston, touch down at Gunnison Airport, under thirty miles away (see ovrleaf). Once in Crested Butte there's no need for a car as **buses** ply the three-mile route between the town and resort every fifteen minutes. The **visitor center** is at Elk Avenue and 6th Street (daily 9am–5pm; ⓣ970/349-6438 or 1-800/545-4505, ⓦwww.visitcrestedbutte.com) and produces a good weekly events guide for the area. The closest ranger office is the one in Gunnison.

Accommodation

The big **accommodation** choice in Crested Butte lies between staying up at the ski area or downtown; you're likely to flit between the two areas every day, so it's only worth staying at the mostly more expensive mountainside lodgings if you're obsessed with getting first tracks. In either case, be sure to reserve a room as far in advance as possible during winter. From June to September, there are plenty of camping opportunities in the surrounding national forest, including the primitive *USFS Lake Irwin Campground* (ⓣ1-800/280-2267; $14) ten miles west of Crested Butte on CO-Road 2 and Forest Road 826.

Claim Jumper B&B 704 Whiterock Ave ⓣ970/349-6471. Six variously themed rooms amid a jumble of Americana and other assorted odds and ends makes this historic log home one of the most enjoyable B&Bs in Colorado. Big breakfasts, a hot tub, sauna, and friendly owners help keep things happy. ❺

Crested Butte International Hostel 615 Teocalli Ave ⓣ970/349-0588. Large, friendly, ultraplush hostel (swipe-card access to rooms), where dorm beds cost $17 in summer, and $24 – assuming you manage to get one – in winter. A large public laundry is on site as well.

Crested Butte Lodge Crested Butte Mountain Resort ⓣ970/349-4660 or 1-800/544-8448. Built in the 1960s, this is the oldest and most characterful place to stay in the resort, with its own indoor pool and spa. ❺

Crested Butte Marriott 500 Gothic Rd ⓣ970/349-4000. The most exclusive hotel in town is right beside the chairlifts at Mount Crested Butte. All rooms are outfitted luxuriously, including whirlpool baths; communal facilities include indoor and outdoor hot tubs, a pool, sauna, and gym. ❽

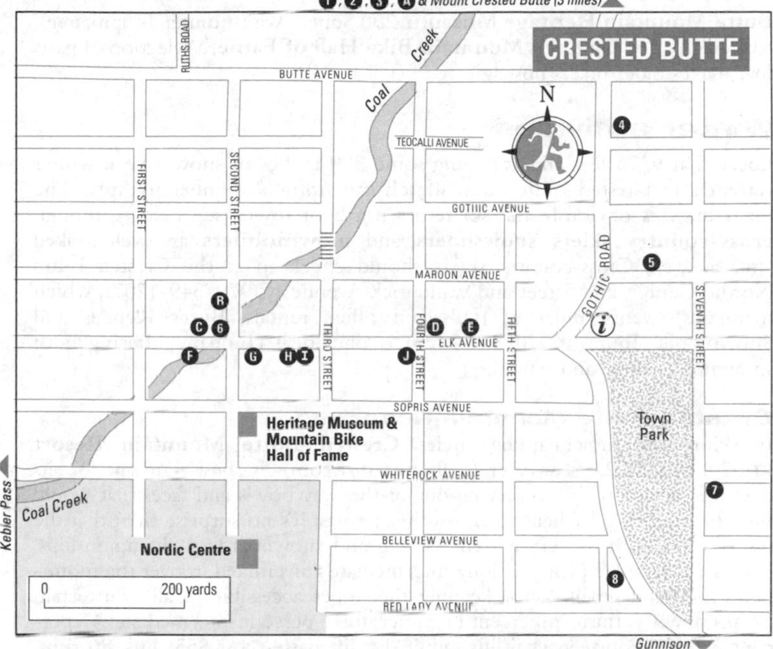

ACCOMMODATION			
Claim Jumper B&B	7	Cristiana Guesthause	5
Crested Butte International Hostel	4	Forest Queen Hotel & Restaurant	6
Crested Butte Lodge	1	Manor Lodge	3
Crested Butte Marriott	2	Old Town Inn	8

RESTAURANTS & BARS			
Bacchanale	G	Kong's Asian Cuisine	E
Bakery Cafe	D	Powerhouse	F
Donita's Cantina	J	Soupçon	B
Idle Spur Brewpub	I	The Rafters	A
Kochevar's Bar	C	Wooden Nickel	H

Cristiana Guesthause 621 Maroon Ave ☎970/349-5329 or 1-800/824-7988. European ski-lodge-style B&B in the center of Crested Butte. All rooms are en suite, and a hearty continental breakfast is served daily. Sauna, outdoor hot tub, and fabulous mountain views round out the package. 5

Forest Queen Hotel & Restaurant 129 Elk Ave ☎970/349-5336 or 1-800/937-1788. Built in 1881, the "Queen" has seven clean and basic hotel rooms. Located in the center of Crested Butte. 4

Manor Lodge 650 Gothic Rd ☎970/349-5365. Small, no-frills motel rooms – usually the cheapest deal in town outside the hostel – near the ski lifts in Crested Butte Mountain Resort and with access to a sauna and hot tub. 4

Old Town Inn Hwy-35 and Belleview Ave ☎970/349-6184. Standard motel rooms beside the main highway at the southern edge of town. 5

Downtown Crested Butte

Pretty as it is, it doesn't take long to take in Crested Butte's tiny **downtown**. Colorfully painted and lined by the original and eye-catching work of two local artists, who've used chrome bumpers to make a series of striking and unusual sculptures, the six short blocks of **Elk Avenue**, the town's main drag, is lined with a pleasing array of cafés, Wild West saloons, and outdoor outfitters. Keep an eye out downtown for some of the two-story buildings with doors on the second floor, there to allow easy access during deep winter snowdrifts: one is in the alley behind Company Store at Elk Avenue and 3rd Street. To get a quick introduction to the town's history, head over to the **Crested**

Butte Mountain Heritage Museum, 200 Sopris Ave (summer 1–6pm; free), particularly popular for its **Mountain Bike Hall of Fame**; a selection of parts that makes older bikers nostalgic.

Winter activities

Located at 9375 feet and averaging some 300 inches of snow a year, winter activities in Crested Butte often stretch out from November to April. The main draw is obviously the ski resort north of town (see below), though **cross-country skiers**, **snowshoers**, and **snowmobilers** are well looked after as well. Cross-country skiers should check in at the Crested Butte Nordic Center, 2nd Street and Whiterock Avenue (ⓣ970/349-1707), which maintains twenty miles of trails and offers rentals. Burt's Rentals and Snowmobile Tours (ⓣ970/349-7423) is one local company offering both snowmobile tours and rentals.

Crested Butte Mountain Resort

In skiing and snowboarding circles, **Crested Butte Mountain Resort** (ⓣ970/349-2222, ⓦwww.crestedbutteresort.com) is best known for its extreme terrain, with lifts serving out-of-the-way bowls and faces that would only be accessible by helicopter at other resorts. It's no surprise then that the resort hosts both the US extreme skiing and snowboarding championships. That said, there are plenty of long intermediate runs mixed in over the mountain's thousand skiable acres, keeping the slopes accessible to all (the terrain breaks down as thirteen percent beginner; forty percent intermediate; 47 percent expert). Fourteen chairlifts (adult day-lift passes cost $55) link 86 runs, which are usually uncrowded thanks to the resort's isolated location. Paradise Bikes and Skis (see box, opposite), and Gene Taylor's Sporting Goods, 19 Emmons Loop at the base of the lifts (ⓣ970/349-5386), are two good places to **rent** gear.

Summer activities

Once the snow melts and the summer season begins, the Nordic ski trails that dot the valley emerge as scenic **hiking** and **mountain bike** routes, crisscrossing through the valley's wildflower-covered meadows. This assortment of blossoms – including purple and white columbine, orange scarlet gilia, yellow mule's ear sunflowers, blue lupine, pink wild rose, and violet flax – are celebrated during July's **Wildflower Festival** (ⓣ970/349-2571), when a program of photography, painting, and herbal medicine workshops are offered. While mountain biking is the big story around these parts, hikers are also spoilt for choice; with many of the best areas used by both (see box opposite). To wander around the area's best-preserved ghost town, head eight miles north of Crested Butte, passing through the Mountain Resort to **Gothic**. The visitor center (see p.184) or the adjacent Alpineer outdoor store have plenty more advice on nearby trails.

The best **kayaking**, **rafting**, and **fishing** in the area is found south near Gunnison; see p.182. The local CB Rafting and Adventures, 309 Gothic Rd (ⓣ970/349-7423), run rafting tours, as well as horseback, mountain bike, and even dog-sledding adventures.

Biking in the Butte

In summer, **mountain bikers** all but outnumber cars around the town, especially during July's **Fat Tire Week**, a festival that according to local legend evolved from a race over the rocky 21-mile **Pearl Pass** to Aspen on newspaper bicycles in the 1970s. Though claims that Crested Butte is the birthplace of mountain biking are disputed by Californians from Marin, no one argues that this is premier mountain-bike country. While the visitors' information can help out with a basic map for the main trails, it's usually best to get a route map and information from a local **bikeshop** before heading out. The Alpineer, 419 6th St (ⓣ970/349-5210, ⓦwww.alpineer.com), is a good source of info and equipment as is Paradise Bikes and Skis, 224 Elk Ave (ⓣ970/349-6324) at the base of the lifts in the mountain resort – where a good network of trails (lift-serviced; $15) has been built. Both rent front-suspension bikes for around $30 per day. No mountain-bike holiday in the area is complete, though, without tackling these three classic trails:

Trail 401 Without doubt one of the most incredible rides in Colorado. Starts as a seven-mile grind north from Gothic to Schofield Pass on FS-317. From the pass, it's single-track all the way back; starting with a short sharp section of climbing to fantastic views over surrounding peaks before leading into some of the best smooth and fast single-track possible. The trail swings down countless hairpins as it follows the side of the East River Valley back to Gothic. The best part is above the intersection with the dirt road to Schofield pass, though if you've still got the energy it's better to continue on Trail 401 back to the start than retrace your bike tracks along the road. The loop is around fifteen miles long and typically takes 3–4 hours.

Dyke Trail The beautiful single-track trail through stands of aspen heading south-west from Lake Irwin is part of a four-teen-mile loop that uses the Kebler Pass Road, a former railroad bed, to link the two ends of the trail. Expect to spend around three hours riding the loop, which starts from Lake Irwin, twelve miles west of Crested Butte along Kebler Pass Road.

Deadman's Gulch Trail A superb longer loop that encompasses a great variety of trails and terrain including some long climbs and fast descents and a series of famed rolling switchbacks to finish off with. Typically this twenty-mile ride takes around five hours. To reach it, head seven miles south of Crested Butte on Hwy-135 then a further seven miles along the unsurfaced Cement Creek Road (CO-740).

Eating and drinking

Crested Butte lays claim to a surprising number of gourmet **restaurants**, happily charging much less than their equivalents in the more glitzy resorts. Good, inexpensive food is also easy to find; even around the ski lifts, a filling lunch can be had for $5. The early après-ski center is *Rafters,* right by the lifts. But by early evening most visitors have found their way to downtown to rowdy local bars like *Kochevar's*. In the summer, there's virtually nothing going on up at the ski area.

Bacchanale 208 Elk Ave ⓣ970/349-5257. Intimate restaurant with a varied Northern Italian menu including good veal and cannelloni along with a range of specialty desserts. Open for dinner only; entrees start at around $10.

Bakery Cafe 3rd St and Elk Ave ⓣ970/349-7280. Best breakfast in town – oven-fresh muffins, breads and pastries, plus wide selection of coffees and juices and cooked breakfasts.

Donita's Cantina 330 Elk Ave ⓣ970/349-6674. Excellent Mexican restaurant famed for its tasty homemade salsa. The large, inexpensive portions of chile rellenos, fajitas, or the more unusual spinach enchilada are all well worth trying. Lots of veggie options.

Idle Spur Brewpub 226 Elk Ave ⓣ970/349-5026. Definitive Colorado microbrewery; a rowdy cavernous hall with rough-hewn beams, a roaring fire in winter and the usual hearty American bar food: burgers, salads, and pastas. On Thursday, Friday, and Saturday nights, there's live music in back room.

Kochevar's Bar 127 Elk Ave ⓣ970/349-6745. Sociable neighborhood bar, with the feel of an Old West saloon; pool tables, foosball, free popcorn, and regular live bands keep things buzzing loudly and happily.

Kong's Asian Cuisine 425 Elk Ave ⓣ970/349-2758. Despite its unlikely location in the heart of the Rockies, *Kong's* serves up good inexpensive, MSG-free, Far Eastern food, from Cantonese to Thai dishes.

Powerhouse 130 Elk Ave ⓣ970/349-5494. The Mexican food is comparable to the cheaper *Donita's Cantina*, though the setting here – a fondly-restored 1880s generating station with a huge wooden bar and 65 varieties of Tequila on offer – gives the *Powerhouse* a slight edge.

The Rafters Crested Butte Mountain Resort ⓣ970/349-2298. Big bar at the base of the lifts with a big deck that packs out during happy hour 3–6pm when a wheel's spun on the half-hour to determine drinks specials. Many make the most of the reasonable bar food (burgers, chili, salads, and sandwiches) and stay for the live bands that follow.

Soupçon 127 Elk Ave ⓣ970/349-5448. Housed in a rustic log cabin, this restaurant is home to gourmet French cuisine. The menu changes daily but often includes escargot, shrimp, oysters, lamb, and homemade soups. The wine list is extensive and entrees start at around $20.

Wooden Nickel 222 Elk Ave ⓣ970/349-6350. The oldest bar and restaurant in town is unsurprisingly cluttered with antiques and curios. Only open for dinner, the menu includes filling favorites that range from potato skins to steak or lobster. After dinner, it becomes a busy drinking hole until final call around 1.45am.

Salida

Driving through **SALIDA** on Hwy-50 (Rainbow Blvd), you'd be forgiven for thinking that the town is little more than an unappealing strip of chain eateries and budget motels. The interstate, though, passes to the south of Salida's Victorian downtown area by a good twelve blocks. This old district of redbrick buildings huddled alongside the Arkansas River is one of the state's most historically significant clusters of buildings, home to a laid-back collection of small local shops, quaint B&Bs and modest restaurants.

Despite its ready accessibility from both Denver and Colorado Springs, Salida is often overlooked as a tourist destination, most visitors just passing the old railroad town en-route to whitewater **kayaking**, **rafting**, and **fishing** trips on the Arkansas River in summer (particularly mid-May to late June) and **skiing** at the Monarch Ski Area. But recently the town has started to lose its undiscovered status, and has come into its own as a base for the superb **mountain biking** and **hiking** on its doorstep. And while it has yet to go a long way to embrace visitors in the way many of Colorado's other mountain towns like Durango or Breckenridge have, the town's laid-back, modest redbrick downtown is a good base to return to after a day in the mountains.

Information and accommodation

The main source for local visitor **information** is the so-called Heart of the Rockies Chamber of Commerce, 406 W US-50 (June–Sept daily 9am–5pm; Oct–May Mon–Fri 9am–5pm; ⓣ719/539-2068, ⓦwww.nowthisiscolorado.com). It's worth popping in to pick up the free *Chaffe County Guide*, loaded with details for both Salida and Buena Vista, and for the free guide to local mountain biking if you intend to ride locally. A few hundred yards further east, the **Salida USFS Ranger Station**, 325 W Rainbow Blvd (Mon–Fri 8am–4.30pm; ⓣ719/539-3591) is the best source of information on local hiking trails and camping in the area. The information offices of the **Arkansas Headwaters Recreation Area**, 307 W Sackett St (Mon–Fri 9am–5pm, Sat & Sun 9am–4pm;

☎719/539-7289), can provide information on recreation and camping opportunities throughout the Headwater Area encompassing the area surrounding the Arkansas between Buena Vista and Cañon City.

There's a good stock of **accommodation** in and around Salida, including numerous motels lining Hwy-50 on the town's southern side and an impressive array of B&B's downtown. Generally rates in both will be a little higher in summer than in winter. **Campers** have several choices locally, including a free public-land campground three miles south of town along Hwy-50 beside the Arkansas River and the *4 Seasons RV Park* (☎719/539-3084 or 1-888/444-3626) has full hookups ($20) and grassy sites ($15). The Forest Service and Arkansas Headwaters offices in town (see opposite) can help with many others. Finally, more accommodation is available year-round beside the Monarch Ski Resort to the west (see p.191).

Gazebo Country Inn 507 E 3rd St ☎719/539-7806 or 1-800/565-7806, ⓦwww.gazebocountryinn.com. Once the home of a prominent early twentieth-century merchant, this two-story B&B now offers pleasant, florally-decorated guest rooms that look out onto even more flowers in the garden, white picket fences and the surrounding mountains. There's a hot tub out back and all rooms are en-suite. 5

Mountain Motel 1425 E Rainbow Blvd ☎719/539-4420. This attractive motel featuring wood-clad cabin-style rooms with kitchens is one of Salida's best values. 3

Piñon & Sage B&B 803 F St ☎719/539-3227 or 1-800/840-3156, ⓦwww.pinonandsage.com. Southwest-style rooms (some with private bath) in an airy restored Victorian residence a five-minute walk from downtown. The friendly owners serve superb breakfasts and give excellent advice about all sorts of local activities. The large outside patio is a great place to hang out and there's a relaxing outdoor hot tub too. 4

River Run Inn 8495 CO-160 ☎719/539-3818 or 1-800/385-6925, ⓦwww.riverruninn.com. In a picturesque location beside the Arkansas River (good mountain views and trout fishing) northwest of Salida, this inn, built in 1882, provides both B&B and hostel accommodation in what was once the county poor farm. Today, you have to pay rather than work for your board and lodging; $27 for a dorm room, or choose from a room with or without private bath. ⑤

Super 8 Motel 525 W Rainbow Blvd ☎719/539-6689 or 1-800/800-8000. Reliable chain motel located opposite the hot springs pool (see below), but with its own hot tub and pool as well. Rates include a continental breakfast. ④

Woodland Motel 903 W 1st St ☎719/539-4980 or 1-800/488-0456. Small motel seven blocks northwest of downtown featuring good-value, spotless rooms – some with kitchens, some with mountain views, and all with access to a hot tub. ③

Outdoor activities

If you're interested in hiking one of the local "fourteeners," try the strenuous ascent of **Mount Shavano** (14,229ft), a four-mile hike from a trailhead fifteen miles west of Salida (take Hwy-50, to CO-250 then take CO-252 to its end). Salida is also close to a couple of major long-distance hiking trails, portions of which can make for good day-trips from town. The five-hundred-mile **Colorado Trail**, which runs between Denver and Durango, travels over the Monarch pass a half-hour drive west. The hundred-mile **Rainbow Trail** begins around twenty miles southwest of town, south of Marshall Pass, and runs east – passing within about four miles of Salida – before following a route along the eastern side of the Sangre de Cristo mountains.

A favorite with those worn out by a day spent outdoors is the **Salida Hot Springs Pool**, 410 W Rainbow Blvd (June–Aug daily 1–9pm; Sept–May Tues–Thurs 4–9pm, Fri–Sun 1–9pm; $6; ☎719/539-6738). Heated water is piped in from five miles away to a large municipal pool and half a dozen hot tubs. The main pool is also used for kayak instruction, call for details.

Biking

The classic **mountain-biking** trail in the area – and perhaps one of the classics in Colorado – is the **Monarch Crest Trail** that begins from the Monarch Ski Area 34 miles from Salida and runs along the Continental Divide for around 25 miles. For a large part, the route follows the Colorado Trail and runs past a string of thirteen-thousand-foot peaks, supplying absolutely incredible views in all directions. Though the most satisfying variant of the trail is suitable only for experienced bikers, the route can easily be cut short by those running out of energy. The trail is generally rideable from around mid-June to September and best attempted early in the day – since thunderstorms often make the exposed Continental Divide a bit dicey later on in the afternoon. If you want to **shuttle** up and avoid the road section of the route up to Monarch Pass from Poncha Springs, contact High Country Shuttle (☎719/539-6089 or 1-800/871-5145, Ⓦwww.monarchcrest.com; $16). If renting, stop by Absolute Bikes, 300 W Sackett St (☎719/539-9295 or 1-888/539-9295, Ⓦwww.absolutebikes.com) downtown beside the river, where an impressive collection of vintage mountain bikes are also on display.

Rafting

Though sandwiched between two challenging and exciting stretches of the Arkansas, the stretch of river around Salida itself is rather quiet, best for those in search of more sedate, though still scenic, float trips. The only real noise made on the river occurs during downtown's boisterous **FIBArk** (First in Boating on the Arkansas) festival, held for five days around the third weekend in June. The festival features concerts and various rafting and kayaking events, including the popular Hooligan Race where crafts are awarded for originality as much as speed, encouraging participants to enter vessels like Viking longboats, beer-keg rafts, and brass beds. Throughout the summer, Canyon Marine, 129 W Rainbow

Monarch Ski and Snowboard Area

Though not one of Colorado's most famous resorts, the small, 670-acre **Monarch Ski and Snowboard Area** (Nov to mid-April; ⓣ719/539-373 or 1-800/996-7669, ⓦwww.skimonarch.com) still has a well-deserved reputation for excellent downhill skiing for all ability levels. Located on the Continental Divide, the terrain breaks down as 21 percent beginner, 37 percent intermediate and 42 percent advanced. There's 1171ft of vertical drop, and only five lifts. Its reliable abundant snow cover (around 300 inches each year; for conditions call ⓣ719/228-7943), the lack of crowds – particularly midweek – and its relatively inexpensive lift tickets ($36) have attracted a small but deeply committed group of followers. **Rentals** are available slopeside, but to save time and cash you can get your gear in Salida the night before from the Mt Shavano Ski and Snowboard Shop, 16101 W Hwy-50 (ⓣ719/539-3420 or 1-800/678-0341). Monarch has also become famous for its excellent **snowcat-serviced skiing**, which adds nine hundred acres of backcountry terrain packed with deep, untracked powder suitable for well-heeled, hardcore enthusiasts. A group of twelve skiers can rent a snowcat for $1800 a day for an expensive but unforgettable experience.

The nearest resort **accommodation** is the *Monarch Mountain Lodge* (ⓣ719/539-2581 or 1-800/332-3668, ⓦwww.monarchmountainlodge.com; ❻), a hotel three miles from the lifts where rooms have kitchens and access to a pool, hot tub, sauna, and tennis as well as racquetball courts. Adjacent to the hotel are the *Ski Town Condominiums* (ⓣ719/539-7935 or 1-800/539-7380; ❺), which sleep four and include a kitchen.

Blvd (Hwy-50; ⓣ719/539-7476 or 1-800/643-0707, ⓦwww.canyonmarine.com), runs relaxed **guided float trips** around Salida from around $35. They also offer wilder, more expensive rides on the roaring portions of the Arkansas north around Buena Vista (see overleaf) or east through the Royal Gorge (see p.125).

Eating and drinking

Cornucopia Bakery & Café 168 F St. Popular breakfast and lunch spot overlooking Salida's shady riverside park. On offer is a range of soups and salads for around $7, hot or cold sandwiches and some good baked goods, particularly the scones. Opens at 6.30am.

1st Street Café 137 E 1st St ⓣ719/539-4759. Friendly, laid-back haunt with a good range of cooked breakfasts, and a predictable (though still good) range of American favorites – burgers, sandwiches, and salads – as well as a decent selection of Mexican food. Moderate prices.

Il Vicino Wood Oven Pizza and Brewery 136 E 2nd ⓣ719/539-5219. Hip brewpub with great pizzas and pastas for around $7. Great place to quaff a couple of the exceptional ales too – but only until 11.30pm.

Laughing Ladies Café 128 W 1st St ⓣ719/539-3546. A good range of imaginative food is served in this trendy, art-lined redbrick restaurant. Lunches include tasty sandwiches – a good crispy snapper option – and salads, most under $6. Dinner entrees run twice that price and include thick steaks with butter garlic sauce, goats-cheese enchiladas and honey-grilled pork chops. Microbrew beers are also available. Closed Tues & Wed.

Victoria Hotel and Tavern 143 N F St ⓣ719/539-4819. Spit and sawdust place, with beers served in the can, is the most popular downtonwn nightspot and packs out at weekends, when there's often live music.

Windmill Restaurant 720 E Rainbow Blvd. On the main highway, the inexpensive menu here includes fajitas, taco salads, steak, and seafood. The food is good and filling, and there's a wonderful and extensive collection of old advertising memorabilia strewn about.

Listings

Banks Pueblo Bank & Trust has an ATM on 200 F St.

Golf Salida Golf Club (ⓣ719/539-1060) runs a pretty nine-hole course near downtown with inexpensive green fees ($15)

Laundry There's a self-service laundromat at 14th and E St (6am–10pm)

Medical Center The Heart of the Rockies Regional Medical Center, 448 E 1st St (ⓣ719/539-6661) provides 24-hour emergency care.

Post Office The most central is at 310 D St.

Showers Salida Hot Springs Pool, 410 W Rainbow Blvd (ⓣ719/539-6738) charges $2 for a shower and opens for showers at 9am.

Buena Vista

Buena Vista, a small ragtag town 26 miles north of Salida, has amazing views indeed. The **Collegiate Peaks**, a cluster of towering 14,000ft mountains, loom to the west, and the town sits alongside the foaming Arkansas River, arguably America's busiest stretch of whitewater. The river is the town's lifeblood, and all the action in town centers around the **Buena Vista River Park**, where rafters and kayakers put in and fishermen cast into the Arkansas. Besides the river, the town has no sights to speak of, though a few nearby **hot springs** resorts (see below) attract folks tired out and sore after a day spent out on the river or on local trails.

Arrival, information and accommodation

Though not serviced by public transport, Buena Vista is an easy 115-mile drive east from Denver on Hwy-285. This highway arrives on the southern edge of town, but a couple of minutes north along Hwy-24 soon brings you to the downtown area. Housed in a small chapel in a park beside busy Hwy-24 as it cuts through town is the friendly **visitor center** (daily: 9am–4pm; ⓣ719/539-2068, ⓦwww.nowthisiscolorado.com). If you're looking for in-depth info on the Arkansas Headwaters Recreation Area, you'll need to head to their office in Salida (see p.188). If you need to clean up and dry off after a day on the water, there's a **laundry** at 10 Linderman Ave (7am–10pm), and 24hr coin-operated **showers** near Buena Vista River Park.

In the summer (particularly weekends), **accommodation** in Buena Vista fills up fast with rafters looking for somewhere close by. Outside the rafting season, things quiet down and prices generally drop by at least a third, making this an affordable though slightly inconvenient base for skiing in Vail or Monarch. If **camping**, the surrounding national forest land harbors plenty of sites. These include some convenient options due west of town along CO-306 (W Main St), like the *Cottonwood Lake* campground ($12; first-come, first-served). There's a further cluster of options south of town near the *Mount Princeton Hot Springs Resort* (see below), including three small USFS campgrounds near Chalk Creek: *Mt Princeton*, *Chalk Creek*, and *Cascade* (mid-May to mid-Sept; ⓣ1-800/280-2267; all $12). All take both tents and RVs, but should be booked in advance as they fill fast.

Cottonwood Hot Springs Inn 18999 CO-306 ⓣ719/395-6434. This hot-springs resort, five miles west of Buena Vista on CO-306, offers a buffet of lodging options that include cabins, motel rooms, dorm beds (some in tepees), and a couple of unattractive tent sites. Though lodging seems a little overpriced at first – for a slightly shabby beatnik place – free entry to the laid-back hot spring pools by the creek make the deals pretty reasonable. ❹

Mount Princeton Hot Springs Resort 15870 CO-162, Nathrop ⓣ719/395-2447 or 1-888/395-7799, ⓔmtphs@chaffe.net. A modern lodge with spacious rooms thirteen miles from Buena Vista

Rafting the Arkansas

Replete with chunky waves and hungry holes, the varied array of wild rapids on the Arkansas attract whitewater kayakers and rafters in the thousands. Thankfully the season is a long one – ranging from late May to late September – meaning the river only gets congested on summer weekends. The favorite stretches of river are between Buena Vista and Cañon City, with the most exciting sections at either end of the stretch. The **Royal Gorge** section of the river has far and away it's most spectacular scenery, but before you get to the thrilling Class IV and V sections at the bottom of this huge canyon there's a long stretch of Class III waters to negotiate. For a more sustained Class IV whitewater experience, you're better off doing the **Numbers**, a quick succession of Class IV and V rapids that at high water leave little room for error. Those who don't find this thrilling enough should try the daring run down **Pine Creek**, where hard Class V rapids put off the majority of commercial operators.

If you want to run the Royal Gorge section near Cañon City (see p.123), top operators include Echo Canyon River Expeditions, 45000 Hwy-50 W (Ⓣ1-800/748-2953, Ⓦwww.echocanyonrafting.com) in Cañon City, or Arkansas River Tours (Ⓣ1-800/824-3795, Ⓦwww.arkansasrivertours.com) in Cotopaxi near the start of the section. Two experienced operators offering raft trips in the Buena Vista area are Four Corners Rafting (Ⓣ719/395-4137 or 1-800/332-7238, Ⓦwww.fourcornersrafting.com), based in Nathrop to the south, and Wilderness Aware Rafting (Ⓣ719/395-2112 or 1-800/462-7238; Ⓦwww.inaraft.com), located at the southern end of Buena Vista on Hwy-285. With all of the above, expect to pay around $70–90 for a full days' rafting including a picnic lunch.

Next to rafting, **kayaking** is the most popular way to navigate local rivers. The skills needed to tackle the most interesting parts of the Arkansas river can be learnt at The Rocky Mountain Outdoor Center, 10281 Hwy-50 (Ⓣ719/942-3214 or 1-800/255-5784, Ⓦwww.rmoc.com), in Howard between Salida and Cañon City.

(eight miles south on Hwy-285 to Nathrop, then five miles west along CO 162). It's the latest, and most modest, of a string of hotels that has inhabited this site since the 1920s, taking advantage of the hot springs here. ❻

Silver Wheel Motel 520 S US-24 Ⓣ719/395-2955. Basic and clean motel rooms, the cost of which are slashed by around half in winter. ❸

Trout City Inn Near junction of Hwy-24 and Hwy-285 Ⓣ719/395-8433. Unusual B&B with four guestrooms in a couple of old narrow-gauge railroad cars eight miles east of Buena Vista on the 9346ft Trout Pass. Each carriage is decorated with elegant Victoriana, to provide for a surreal and memorable stay. ❻

Vista Court Cabins 1004 W Main St Ⓣ719/395-6557. Cheerful, good-value cabins a short way west of downtown. Some even less expensive lodge rooms are also available, with substantial winter discounts offered on both. ❹

Vista Inn 733 N US-24 Ⓣ719/395-8009 or 1-800/809-3495, Ⓦwww.vtinent.com/vistainn. Large, new motel with comfortable and well-equipped rooms – with fridges and microwaves – and three outdoor hot tubs with views of the mountains that put the Vista into the *Vista Inn*. The B&B deal includes an extensive continental breakfast. ❺

Fly-fishing

Though most people's attention is focused on the whitewater of the Arkansas, the river and many of its tributaries are also world-class places to go **fly-fishing** – particularly for brown trout, although rainbow, cutthroat, and brook are also abundant in many tributary streams. In spring and fall, anglers can expect to catch brown and rainbow averaging around a foot. Cottonwood Lake, ten miles west of Buena Vista on Hwy-306 (starts as Main St), is particularly legendary for big rainbow trout. Note that many good stretches of the Arkansas are private property, so take careful advice where to fish from local outfitters like Hi-Rocky Fishing Tackle, 111 Cottonwood (Ⓣ719/539-2144), or Ark Anglers, 545 N

Hwy-24 (Ⓣ719/539-4223, Ⓦwww.arkanglers.com), who also run a variety of fishing trips; half-day float trips for $145.

Hiking and biking

The obvious target for serious hikers visiting Buena Vista are the **Collegiate Peaks**, Colorado's greatest concentration of 14,000-foot peaks just west of Buena Vista. These comprise Mount Oxford (14,153ft), Mount Harvard (14,420ft), Mount Columbia (14,075ft), Mount Yale (14,196ft), and Mount Princeton (14,197ft), named for the Ivy League schools whose mountaineering teams were the first to summit the peaks in the early twentieth century. A long and challenging ascent requiring no special equipment here is the 8.5-mile trail to the summit of **Mount Harvard**. The upper portion follows the Colorado Trail and is best begun from the Collegiate Peaks Wilderness Area just west of town (along CO-306). You can also strike out on an easy eight-mile out-and-back hike to **Kroenke Lake** from here. Another good short hike in the Collegiate peaks, with a hundred-year-old prospectors cabin as its terminus, begins from the Denny Creek Trailhead, two miles west of Buena Vista (along CO-306). The trail climbs four miles to Brown's Pass on the Continental Divide then descends half-a-mile to Brown's Cabin.

Further west towards the barren Independence Pass on a road leading to the Taylor Park Reservoir and eventually Gunnison is a trail to **Ptarmigan Lake** – actually a couple of lakes nestling among damp meadows just above the timberline and surrounded by bleak high-alpine scenery. The rocky trail also makes a good out-and-back ride for experienced mountain bikers, taking around two hours from the trailhead beside CO-306, about ten miles west of Buena Vista.

Before heading out, drop in at the visitor center (see p.192) for the free guide to ten of the area's most popular hikes. And, if in need of **equipment** or **rentals**, stop at The Trailhead, 707 Hwy-24 N (Ⓣ719/395-8001), where mountain bikes go for $25 per day or $85 per week.

Eating and drinking

Antero Grill Hwy-285 sixteen miles south of Buena Vista Ⓣ719/530-0301. Expensive restaurant serving "Modern American cowboy cuisine," basically ranch favorites fused with gourmet ingredients that makes for the finest dining for miles around. Appetizers include rock shrimp quesadillas while entrees like braised rabbit or vegetable torte with beef tenderloin tips and roasted sweetcorn mashed potatoes are sure to fill you up. Great dry-aged steaks are also available. The cowboy decor here includes a predictable but atmospheric collection of paintings and lassos.

Blue Parrot 304 E Main St. Friendly bar that's a good place to unwind after a day on the river.

Casa Del Sol 303 Rt24. Superb, moderately priced Mexican restaurant serving not just the usual Tex Mex-style food, but also a range of dishes from different parts of Mexico – from seafood quesadillas to *pollo en mole*.

Coyote Cantina W Hwy-285. Good filling inexpensive Mexican food in a busy bar on Hwy-285 to Denver.

Evergreen Café 418 N Hwy-24 Ⓣ719/395-8984. A good stop for its extensive breakfast menu (opens 6.30am) and simple burger or sandwich lunches.

Shanghai Chinese Restaurant 527 W Lake St Ⓣ719/395-4950. Cheap and unexciting Chinese food at bargain prices.

Travel details

Buses

(all buses are Greyhound unless otherwise stated)

Colorado Springs to: Cheyenne WY (6 daily; 6hr 30min); Denver (11 daily; 1hr 40min; TNM&O); Pueblo (11 daily; 1hr; TNM&O); Trinidad (2 daily; 2hr 50min; TNM&O); Vail (4 daily; 4hr 55min).

Denver from: Alamosa (1 daily; 5hr 50min; TNM&O); Montrose (2 daily; 9hr 50min); Ouray (1 daily; 8hr 30min); Pueblo (11 daily; 2hr 40min; TNM&O); Pueblo (9 daily; 2hr 50min); Salida (1 daily; 5hr 45min); Silverton (1 daily, 9hr 40min); Trinidad (2 daily; 4hr 30min; TNM&O).

Durango to: Grand Junction (2 daily; 5hr; TNM&O); Montrose (2 daily; 4hr 20min; TNM&O); Salt Lake City (1 daily, 12hr; TNM&O); Silverton (1 daily; 2hr; TNM&O).

Grand Junction from: Cañon City (1 daily; 6hr; TNM&O); Gunnison (1 daily; 2hr 45min; TNM&O); Montrose (2 daily; 1hr 30min; TNM&O); Pueblo (1 daily; 6hr 45min; TNM&O); Salida (1 daily; 4hr 45min; TNM&O); Silverton (1 daily; 3hr; TNM&O).

Flights

Denver from: Alamosa (3 daily; 1hr); Aspen (14 daily; 45min); Colorado Springs (17 daily; 40min); Cortez (4 daily; 1hr 20min); Durango (11 daily; 1hr 20min); Eagle (Vail) (5 daily; 45min); Gunnison (8 daily; 1hr); Pueblo (4 daily; 40min); Telluride (5 daily; 1hr 10min).

3

Central Colorado

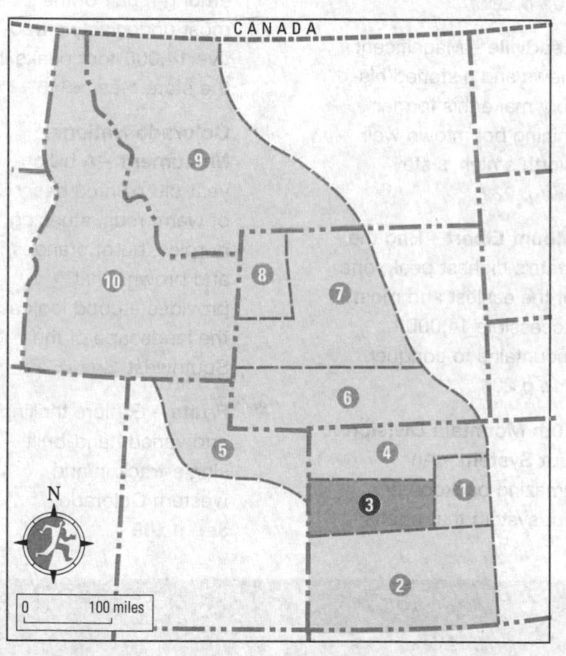

CHAPTER 3 **Highlights**

* **Breckenridge** – Jib the rails and ride off huge jumps in one of the finest snowboard parks in the country. See p.218

* **Vail** – Lose yourself in endless back-bowls of great skiing and riding. See p.229

* **Leadville** – Magnificent views and a storied history make this former mining boomtown well worth a night's stay. See p.232

* **Mount Elbert** – Bag the state's highest peak, one of the easiest and most accessible 14,000ft mountains to conquer. See p.236

* **10th Mountain Division Hut System** – An amazing backcountry hut system that opens up hundreds of miles of cross-country skiing and mountain biking. See p.237

* **Maroon Belles** – A popular spot near Aspen, so head out early for some relatively secluded hiking among a pair of the most undeniably attractive 14,000-foot peaks in the state. See p.246

* **Colorado National Monument** – A billion-year-old painted desert of warm reds, stunning purples, burnt oranges, and browns that provides a good look at the landscape of the Southwest. See p.258

* **Fruita** – Explore thrilling and varied hand-built single-track in arid western Colorado. See p.259

Central Colorado

Colorado's image and unrivalled reputation as a formidable winter resort destination derive from the cluster of incredible ski areas not much more than a snowball's throw from one another at the heart of **CENTRAL COLORADO**. As throughout the Rocky Mountains, the original impetus to turf out the native Ute Indians came from the underground wealth here. The mining boom ended abruptly with the 1893 silver crash – but not before the major towns were decorated with grand Victorian mansions and opera houses. The economy then limped along until its focus began to switch from the rich seams of precious ore buried deep within the mountainsides to the precious winter snows above them. Initially, the area served as a training ground for the ski-based troops of the **10th Mountain Division**, who honed their winter skills here prior to heading off to fight in World War II. But the mountain division's influence on the area would be much more far-reaching, and although veterans didn't invent the idea of creating downhill resorts in Colorado, indirectly they went a long way to creating the industry. Of course, the reliable continental weather patterns that drop most of the wet snow on the Californian sierras, blessing the Rockies with dry, fluffy "champagne powder," played a major role as well.

While the region's reputation for winter sports largely speaks for itself, almost all the ski resorts are now also devoting huge amounts of energy to promoting themselves as summer destinations, when the region is not only much less crowded, but also much more economical to visit. While some of this is undoubtedly forced marketing, the region as a whole – containing seemingly boundless alpine tundra, thick dark forests, and immense peaks, which give way to gorgeous forested mesatops and dusty semi-arid areas on the Utah border – is certainly a legitimate haven for excellent hiking and biking, fishing, and kayaking.

Accommodation price codes

All accommodation prices in this book have been coded using the symbols below. For **hotels, motels**, and **B&Bs**, rates are given for the least expensive double room in each establishment during peak season; variations are indicated where appropriate, including winter rates for all ski resorts. For **hostels**, we've given a specific price per bed; for **camping**, the overnight cost per site is given. For a full explanation see p.30 in Basics.

❶ up to $30	❹ $60–80	❼ $130–180
❷ $30–45	❺ $80–100	❽ $180–240
❸ $45–60	❻ $100–130	❾ over $240

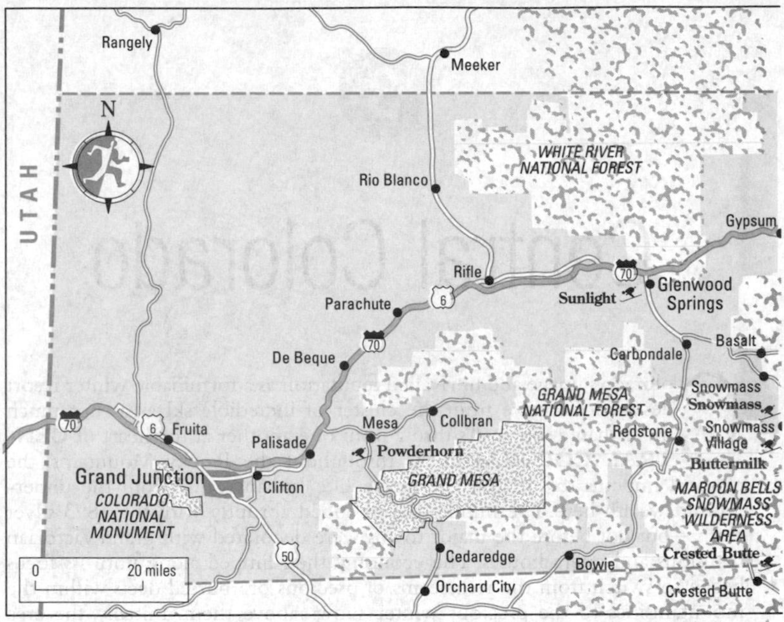

Colorado's major interstate, I-70, heads due west from Denver to Utah, irrespective of the tricky mountain terrain that's forced the construction of hugely expensive tunnels and multilevel roadways along the way. While these allow the I-70 to plough west relatively unhampered, the Continental Divide still marks an important regional divide. The communities and resorts to the east, which include the affordable ski resort of **Winter Park**, are much more modest and less commercial than those west of the Continental Divide in **Summit County**, home to a thick cluster of ski areas around **Lake Dillon** and **Breckenridge**. From Summit County, the I-70 climbs up over Vail Pass to drop down and skirt the northern portions of the huge **Sawatch and Elk Mountains**, which harbor the famous Rocky Mountain ski resorts of **Vail** and **Aspen**, along with the evocative mining town of **Leadville** and the enjoyable modest spa town of **Glenwood Springs** on the eastern and western fringes respectively. Continuing west out of the mountains towards the Utah border, the landscape rollercoasts through a patchwork of granite peaks, raging rivers and red-sandstone canyons, winding up as the semi-arid environments that surround **Grand Junction** and the memorable **Colorado National Monument**.

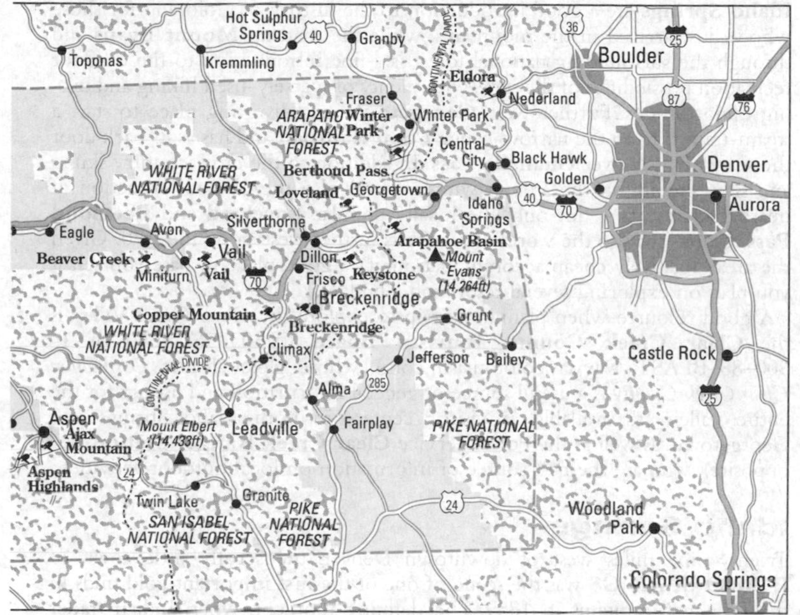

The Clear Creek Valley and around

On Denver's doorstep and just east of the Continental Divide, the **Clear Creek Valley** is much less glitzy and commercial than the areas immediately west of the watershed. The valley includes the modest historic community of **Idaho Springs**, gateway to the majestic **Mount Evans**, and the well-preserved, Victorian **Georgetown** further west, terminus for the magnificent Georgetown Loop Railroad. In winter the valley also boasts downhill skiing at **Loveland** and **Berthoud Pass**, a couple of low-key but enjoyable ski resorts. Just north of the valley the road drops down beyond Berthoud Pass into the understated, yet world-class ski resort of **Winter Park**, owned and run by the city of Denver and every bit as good a summer destination for hikers and mountain bikers.

Clear Creek Valley

The **Clear Creek Valley**, which runs fifty miles west from Denver's fringes to the Loveland Pass, sees far more through-traffic than visitors. But in fact there's plenty to detain the inquisitive along here. The **historic mining sites** around

Idaho Springs are a good introduction to the history of Colorado for those who've just arrived in the mountains, while the road up **Mount Evans** and through the surrounding national forest is a fine introduction to the outdoor recreation possibilities of the state, with plenty of sparsely-used hiking and biking opportunities. Further west, **Georgetown** is a diverting place to start a steam-train ride on the narrow-gauge **Loop Railroad** and has as its back door the scenic byway over **Guanella Pass**. In addition to the cross-country skiing and snowshoeing in the area in winter, there's also the obvious attraction of nearby ski resorts – not only the locally popular **Loveland** and **Berthoud Pass** resorts, but also the world-class resorts further west along the I-70. Given the area's relatively cheap accommodation, it's a good place to base yourself if you plan on exploring several resorts on a budget.

A good resource when planning a trip to explore the Clear Creek Valley is the **Clear Creek County Tourism Board** (ⓣ303/567-4660 or 1-800–88–BLAST, ⓦwww.colotourism.com), whose glossy leaflet *Destination Clear Creek County* is a useful source of general information and listings for the entire valley. It's available at visitor centers in both Idaho Springs and Georgetown, as well as the Forest Service **Clear Creek Ranger Station** (see opposite), who are the best source of information on local outdoor activities.

Idaho Springs

Twenty-nine miles west of downtown Denver, the scruffy little town of **IDAHO SPRINGS** was the scene of one of the first important gold finds in the Rocky Mountains in 1859. The defining moment, when Indian trader George Jackson dug his knife into frozen ground and came out with gold, is now marked by a monument a quarter-mile up Hwy-103. Within a week of his chance find Jackson had pulled out $2000-worth, which sparked the gold rush that founded the settlement. It was silver, however, that became Idaho Spring's really lucrative ore, with the town growing to be a hub for a silver district that included Black Hawk and Central City. Once the town's mining days were over, the enterprising Jackson took advantage of the town's natural hot mineral springs and invested some of his earnings in creating the Radium Hot Springs Resort, which still exists as the *Indian Springs Resort* (see opposite). Today, the town attracts a smattering of visitors, either resting on their way into the mountains, pausing to explore the town's mining history or halting en route on a drive up **Mount Evans**.

The Town

While the handful of nineteenth-century buildings downtown along Miner Street reflect the town's Victorian pedigree, the real clue to Idaho Spring's **mining past** come from the floes of yellow tailings spilling from holes dotting the mountainsides along the I-70 corridor. A good introduction to this history can be had on a driving tour along the evocatively named **Oh My God Road** to Central City (see p.88). This narrow, potholed road northwest of Idaho Springs is easily driven in a regular two-wheel-drive car and well worth it to see hillsides pockmarked by hundreds of holes and tailings that suggest how busy this area once was. Back in town, you can get a closer glimpse into the town's mining past at the commercialized **Argo Gold Mill Museum**, 2317 Riverside Drive (May–Oct daily 9am–6pm; $9; ⓦwww.historicargotours.com), the biggest structure on the north side of the valley. Alongside the obligatory gold panning and staged shootouts, visitors get to see the furnaces where ore was turned into gold ingots, and the high-security vaults in which they were stored. More enjoyable is the **Phoenix Mine** (daily 10am–6pm; $9; Ⓦwww.phoenixmine.com), located a mile west of exit 239 along Frontage Road (which runs parallel to I-70) to Trail Creek Road. Mining still takes place here, but is now secondary to entertaining tours given by ex-miners, in which visitors head down 600ft to view a three-foot-long vein of gold ore, wield nineteenth-century excavating tools and try their luck at panning for gold.

To get up-to-date on your mining history you should visit the **Edgar Experimental Mine**, 365 8th Ave (mid-June to Aug Tues–Sat 9.30am & 1pm), an old 1870s mine, now furnished with the latest mining techniques and technology and used to tutor students at Golden's School of Mining. For yet another perspective on mining in the area visit the modest **Underhill Museum**, 1416 Miner St (Ⓣ303/567-4709), which at one time was an assay office and now houses information on the process of analyzing ore, together with some reconstructed living accommodations from the era – an aspect of a miner's life on which light is rarely shed.

Idaho Springs' natural **hot mineral springs** can be sampled at the *Indian Springs Resort*, 302 Soda Creek Rd (daily: 7.30am–10.30pm; Ⓣ303/567-2191. Facilities include a covered mineral water swimming pool ($10), geothermal caves ($14), private baths (reservations required; $14 per hr), and the unusual Club Mud ($8), a gooey mud pool allowing for total immersion. There are discounts for combining activities, and facilities are free to those staying at the resort.

Mount Evans

Together with Pikes Peak (see p.119), **Mount Evans** (14,264ft) is Colorado's easiest 14,000ft peak to bag, since there's a narrow road (typically open June–Aug; $6 per vehicle) almost all the way to the summit from Idaho Springs fourteen miles away. As the dominant peak in the Rocky Mountain skyline when viewed from Denver, Mount Evans is also an exceptional local vantage point and with few other fourteeners in this part of the range, clear days promise views one hundred miles in all directions. The easy quarter-mile hike from the parking lot to the summit is only an introduction to what the mountain has to offer. Protected by a wilderness area, it is crisscrossed by more than a hundred miles of hiking trails, which pass through ancient stands of bristlecone pine forests, yielding great views and sheltering ample wildlife – including yellow-bellied marmots, bighorn sheep, pikas, and mountain goats. The best point of contact for information on recreation opportunities here is the **Clear Creek Ranger Station** (daily 8am–5pm; Ⓣ303/567-2901) at the base of the road up Mount Evans, on the western side of Idaho Springs (I-70 exit 240). **Echo Lake**, on the route up, contains not only a picnic area but also the reservable *USFS Echo Lake Campground* (sites $10; Ⓣ1-800/280-2267) and a little restaurant at *Echo Lake Lodge* (Ⓣ303/567-2138).

St Mary's Glacier

One of the few glaciers in Colorado, **St Mary's Glacier**, is used by both backcountry skiers and snowboarders year-round – though it's mostly a playground for the latter group, often found near the steeper bottom portion launching off jumps. To get there, leave I-70 at exit 238 two miles west of Idaho Springs and then head twelve miles on Fall River Road to the old ghost town of **Alice**, today nothing more than an old schoolhouse and a couple of log cabins. From here it's a half-mile walk to St Mary's Lake above the eponymous glacier.

Practicalities

For information and an introduction to the area head to the **visitors center** at the west end of Colorado Boulevard (ⓣ303/567-4382 or 1-800/685-7785, ⓦwww.idahospringschamber.com). A small onsite heritage museum, half-devoted to the local Argo water treatment works, has some old mining relics on display.

As you enter Idaho Springs from the east, half a dozen **motels** line Colorado Boulevard. These include the basic *Idaho Springs Motel* at no. 2631 (ⓣ303/567-2242; ❷), where some rooms have kitchenettes, and the more cheerful *H&H Motor Lodge* at no. 2445 (ⓣ303/567-2838 or 1-800/445-2893; ❸), where in addition to kitchenettes there's access to a hot tub and sauna. The obvious place to stay in town, however, is the *Indian Springs Resort*, 302 Soda Creek Rd (spa facilities: 7.30am–10.30pm; ⓣ303/567-2191, ⓦwww.indianspringsresort.com; ❸), which has a range of options from unexciting motel rooms to more comfortable quarters. Sites at the resort's **campground** cost $18. More secluded USFS campsites can be found at Mount Evans (see overleaf) and to the north in the Arapahoe National Forest; contact the Clear Creek Ranger Station for further information.

Though you won't find gourmet dining in Idaho Springs, the town does have a good selection of friendly **restaurants** serving big, inexpensive portions of American favorites. A good place to start the day is *Mainstreet, A Restaurant*, 1518 Miner St, a homey place serving good full breakfasts and sandwich or burger lunches. Another local favorite is *Beau Jo's Colorado Style Pizza*, 1517 Miner St (ⓣ303/567-4376), which has a huge range of imaginative toppings and a plentiful salad bar. In the evenings try the *Buffalo Bar and Restaurant*, 1617 Miner St (ⓣ303/567-2729), where buffalo meat is served up alongside pizza, salads, and soups in a dining room packed with old mining and pioneering artifacts.

Georgetown

Nestling deep in the head of a valley beside a lake and surrounded by 12,000ft mountains, **GEORGETOWN**, 45 miles from Denver, has a marvelous setting – but for the I-70 running so close past the town. But to drop off the highway here is to step back several decades, since the sleepy town, thanks to the hard work of its volunteer fire brigade which spared it a major fire, is one of the best-preserved Victorian mining towns in Colorado. Georgetown made its fortunes in both gold and silver, and until the strikes at Leadville in 1878 was the major silver town in the territory. But even after Leadville's boom took off, mining continued in the Georgetown area, leading to the construction of an ambitious narrow-gauge railroad, the **Georgetown Loop Railroad**, for which the town is today most famous.

The town

The grandeur of the town's mining days lives on in many of its elegant buildings, and at weekends the local historic society leads ninety-minute **tours** of the downtown area (10.30am & 1.30pm; $5), leaving from the community center at 613 6th St. The tours include an informed look at two of the town's most outstanding buildings, the Gothic revival **Hamil House**, 305 Argentine St (daily: June–Sept 10am–5pm; Oct–May noon–4pm; $5), once considered one of the most elegant Victorian homes in the Rockies, with a luxuriously furnished, polished hardwood interior containing some odd touches such as camel-hair wallpaper, and the **Hotel de Paris**, 409 6th St (daily: June–Sept 10am–5pm; Oct–May noon–4pm; $4), a far more eccentric operation run by

French aristocrat Louis Du Puy. By all accounts a headstrong, maverick character, Du Puy was known as a dedicated misogynist who refused to pay taxes and regularly turfed guests off the premises if he took a dislike to them during their stay.

Georgetown is however best known as the starting point of the **Georgetown Loop Railroad**, 1106 Rose St (May to early Oct daily 10am–3.20pm; $14; ⓣ303/569-2403 or 1-800/691-4386, ⓦwww.gtownloop.com). On the line, 1920s steam trains run a six-mile round-trip to Silver Plume, on a route which loops in big arcs – added to enable the engines to overcome the six-percent climb – and includes a trip across a precarious trestle above Clear Creek. A much-vaunted engineering marvel at its completion in 1884, the railroad was disbanded and finally sold for scrap in 1939, before being revived and entirely rebuilt by enthusiasts in 1984. Along the route to Silver Plume (where you can also pick up the train from 9.20am to 4pm), the train stops at the Lebanon Mine ($5), a former mine now offering tours 600ft down into the cold, damp mine. If you stop at the mine you can catch the next train, which will make a round trip of around two and a half hours; skip the mine and the return rail journey takes around an hour.

Practicalities

Georgetown runs a **visitor information** service on 6th Street (ⓣ303/569-2888 or 1-800/472-8230, ⓦwww.georgetowncolorado.com) during the summer months. There's not much in the way of **accommodation** in town, although the *Georgetown Motor Inn*, 1100 Rose St (ⓣ303/569-3201; ❸), can provide standard, clean motel rooms with access to a hot tub. More upscale lodging options are available in the tiny town of **EMPIRE** five miles east; here the *Peck House*, 83 Sunny Ave (ⓣ303/569-9870; ❹), is the oldest B&B in Colorado, with the cheapest rooms sharing bathrooms; the *Empire House Bed and Breakfast*, 268 E Park Ave (ⓣ303/569-2557, ⓦwww.empirehousebb.com; ❺), is another good B&B in town.

For **food**, head to the *Happy Cooker*, 412 6th St (ⓣ303/569-3166), which does superb home-cooked meals, though service is on the slow side. Great breakfasts include filling egg dishes and fluffy waffles, and later in the day soups, served with thick slabs of homemade bread. There's also quiche, creative salads, or chunky sandwiches, with great pies for dessert. A decent place to grab a burger or other bar basics like prime rib is the *Red Ram*, 606 6th St (ⓣ303/569-2300), a neighborhood pub serving lunch and dinner.

Loveland and Berthoud Pass ski areas

The two closest places to ski near Denver are **Loveland** and **Berthoud Pass** along the I-70 corridor, both good, unpretentious, no-nonsense ski areas blessed with some extreme terrain, relatively low prices, and – thanks to their location on major passes – fine snow. The skiers here are almost all day-trippers from Denver, an easy hour's drive away. In consequence neither ski area has developed more than a basic base area, and though you won't go hungry or want for rental equipment here, there's **no resort lodging**.

Loveland Ski Area

The **LOVELAND SKI AREA** (ⓣ303/571-5580 or 1-800/736-3754, ⓦwww.skiloveland.com) lies 71 miles from Denver along the I-70, beside the Eisenhower Tunnel – which separates Clear Creek Valley from Summit County. The resort divides into a gentle beginners' mountain, Loveland Valley, and the original mountain, Loveland Basin; the two are connected by a free shuttle and a horizontal chairlift. Most of the skiing in the resort is on broad bowls and open snowfields, and much is above treeline, which allows panoramic views of the surrounding mountains but often causes the runs to be windy. The ski area's 65 **trails** cover 1265 **skiable acres** (designated 25 percent beginner, 48 percent intermediate and 27 percent advanced and expert), but experienced skiiers who don't mind hiking a bit will find some great extreme out-of-bounds skiing on the craggy peaks when blizzard and avalanche threats are low. Skiing actually began on nearby Loveland Pass in the 1930s as an adventurous backcountry pursuit; skiers were driven to the top of Loveland Pass via Hwy-6 and skied back down, a practice that many backcountry experts still continue. The resort receives almost 400 inches of **annual snowfall**, which combines with the resort's **altitude** – the base is at 10,600 feet – to produce a **long season**, typically running from mid-October to late May. Adult one-day **lift tickets** cost $39.

Berthoud Pass Ski Area

BERTHOUD PASS SKI AREA (☎970/726-0287 or 1-800/SKI-BERT, Ⓦwww.berthoudpass.com), Colorado's oldest resort, is highly acclaimed by expert level skiers and snowboarders in search of lift-served powder, extreme skiing, and exciting off-piste action. The ski area straddles Berthoud Pass – which separates the Clear Creek Valley from Winter Park – with spectacular views of surrounding mountains and skiing on both the north and south sides of the pass. Key to the resort's enthusiastic reception amongst the winter-sports community is its **elevation** – the base area is at 11,340ft – which means that snow stays soft hours, sometimes days, longer than elsewhere. Despite the presence of gentler slopes beneath the two lifts, the real reason many come here is to head into off-piste-style conditions on the **65 runs** that radiate over 1000 acres of terrain (twenty percent beginner, thirty percent intermediate and fifty percent expert). Almost uniquely among Colorado resorts, most skiers and snowboarders spend more time on buses than on lifts. All the best runs leave the immediate resort area to descend both the north and south slopes of the pass through glades and long narrow runs to the two stops served by shuttle buses on either side of the pass. It's the most convenient backcountry-style skiing experience that most advance skiers will ever enjoy – but, like proper backcountry skiing, it's not without its dangers. Ominously on the resort's opening day in 1937, two skiers died in an avalanche. Today **avalanche safety courses** and **powder-skiing clinics** are available from $60 per person per half-day. Thankfully ticket prices are more in line with the minimal resort infrastructure than the quality of the skiing, with **day-passes** costing around $37; discounts are available according to how many of the expected 500 annual inches of fresh snow have landed in the past few days.

Winter Park

The former railroad center of **WINTER PARK**, 67 miles northwest of Denver, is little more than a sprawling agglomeration of condominiums, outfitters, and shopping malls, there to service the eponymous **ski resort** two miles to the south. Five miles north of Winter Park, life in workaday **FRASER** revolves around workers for the ski industry. In the absence of any attractions in either town, visitors to the valley generally get straight down to business – skiing in winter and hiking and biking in summer.

Arrival, orientation, and information

Year-round service to Winter Park is provided by **Greyhound**, by **Amtrak** on the California Zephyr to Fraser, and by Home James **shuttles** from Denver International Airport (Ⓣ303/726-5060 or 1-800/451-4844; $34). The **Winter Park Ski Train** (reservations required Ⓣ303/296-4754, Ⓦwww.skitrain.com; $45; 2hr) operates round trips from Denver every Saturday and Sunday during ski season, leaving at 7.15am and starting back at 4.25pm, and on Saturdays only between mid-June and mid–August.

It's easy to **orientate** yourself in Winter Park and Fraser, since virtually everything – lodging, dining, and shopping – is situated along Hwy-40 and is visible from the road. The swank new **visitor center** (daily 8am–5pm; Ⓣ970/726-4118 or 1-800/903-7275, Ⓦwww.winterpark-info.com), at the junction of Hwy-40 and Vasquez Road, in Winter Park is no exception, and can provide a very helpful service to all visiting the area – including useful free summer trail maps. An additional useful resource for visitors in the area is the county website Ⓦwww.grand-county.com, which also covers the Grand Lake and Granby area (see pp.271 and 294).

An excellent network of **free shuttle buses** renders cars unnecessary in town, connecting Winter Park and nearby Fraser every ten to fifteen minutes in winter, hourly in summer. Free buses also take passengers from restaurants and bars to the doorstep of their accommodation on Friday and Saturday nights until 2am.

Accommodation

Winter Park offers the best choice of accommodation among Colorado resorts, ranging from condos on the mountainside to B&Bs and motels in town. **Winter Park Central Reservations** (Ⓣ970/726-5587 or 1 800/453-2525, Ⓦwww.skiwinterpark.com) can arrange lodging in more than fifty condominiums, motels, hotels, lodges, inns, and B&Bs (❹ and up), and also offer flexible packages including activities like biking, golfing, and, of course, skiing. Another useful contact if you are looking for a condo in the area is **Winter Park Adventures** (Ⓣ970/726-5701 or 1-800/525-2466, Ⓦwww.winterparkadventures.com), who can organize units from $60 per night as long as you stay a minimum of two nights.

In summer there are almost limitless opportunities for backcountry **camping** in the surrounding national forest – a popular place to head is along Moffat Road in the direction of Rollins Pass (see p.210). The USFS also runs several campgrounds in the area, including the *Idlewild Campground* ($9) south of Winter Park Resort along Hwy-40.

Beaver Village Lodge 79303 Hwy-40, Winter Park Ⓣ970/726-5741 or 1-800/666-0281, Ⓦwww.beavervillage.com. Very economical downtown lodge, with extensive facilities including a hot tub, pool, laundry room, and ski shop. ❸

Engelmann Pines 1053 Cranmer Ave, Winter Park Ⓣ970/726-4632 or 1-800/992-9512. Friendly B&B three miles outside Winter Park, furnished with European heirloom furniture. Facilities include a guests' kitchen and living room. All bathrooms have hot tubs. Open May–October. ❹

Gasthaus Eichler 78786 Hwy-40, Winter Park Ⓣ970/726-5133 or 1-800/543-3899. German alpine chalet-style house with fifteen stylishly-plain but comfortable hotel rooms with down comforters and whirlpool baths. The room rate (halved late April to Nov) includes a delicious breakfast and gourmet dinner as well as a shuttle to the ski area. ❼

Iron Horse Resort 257 Winter Park Drive, Winter Park Ⓣ970/726-8851 or 1-800/621-8190, Ⓦwww.ironhorse-resort.com. Prestigious condo-hotel property at the center of the ski area with cheerful Southwestern-style accommodation which ranges from studios to two- and three-bath premium suites with full kitchens and sundecks. Facilities include a heated outdoor pool, four hot tubs, an exercise room, a lounge, and free shuttles. 7

Olympia Motor Lodge 78572 Hwy-40, Winter Park ⓣ970/726-8843 or 1-800/548-1992. This standard, though comfortable downtown motel has rooms with queen beds, some with kitchenettes. 4

Snow Mountain Ranch 1344 CO-53, 7 miles north of Fraser along Hwy-40 and CO-53 ⓣ970/726-4628, ⓦwww.ymcarockies.org. Lodges and cabins run by the YMCA that draw almost 50,000 visitors a year, many attracted by the good group rates. Facilities include free ski shuttles, a large indoor pool, whirlpool, indoor roller rink, volleyball and basketball courts, gym, restaurant, a Nordic center, and a ski rental shop. 4

Viking Lodge Copper Creek Square, Winter Park ⓣ970/726 8885 or 1-800/421-4013, ⓦwww.skiwp.com. Clean and well-maintained downtown motel, usually the cheapest deal in town. Coffee and a continental breakfast are included, and facilities include a game room, whirlpool, and sauna. 3

Vintage Hotel 100 Winter Park Drive, Winter Park ⓣ970/726-8801 or 1-800/472-7017, ⓦwww.vintagehotel.com. Condo-hotel just feet from the ski area where accommodations range from small hotel rooms with kitchenettes to three-bedroom condos with full kitchens. Facilities include a game room, a lounge, hot tubs, a sauna, and a courtesy shuttle to town. 5

The Winter Park Mountain Lodge 81699 Hwy-40, Winter Park ⓣ970/726-4211 or 1-800/726-3340, ⓦwww.winterparkhotel.com. Modern chain hotel with indoor pool, hot tubs, a sauna, and laundry facilities. 5

Winter activities

The majority of winter visitors come to Winter Park to ski (see below), but there are a variety of other activities on offer. You can **snowmobile** the Continental Divide on a one-hour tour with Trailblazers in Fraser (ⓣ970/726-8452; $35), or around a 25-mile course with Mountain Madness (ⓣ970/726-4529; $35 per hour), just north of town. For more traditional **sleigh rides**, contact Jim's Sleigh Rides (ⓣ970/726-0944), who tow up to twenty guests per sleigh ($18 per person) along the Fraser River, with a stop in the woods for a snack. Other popular evening activities are the **Tubing Hill** at Fraser (Mon–Fri 4–10pm, Sat & Sun 10am–10pm; $10; ⓣ970/726-5954), half a mile behind the Safeway store, where you get towed to the top of an icy run to slide down on an oversized truck inner-tube. Alternatively, you can ice-skate at the outdoor **Fraser Ice Rink**, 601 Zerex Ave (ⓣ970/726-8882), where bonfires are lit at night.

Winter Park Resort

WINTER PARK RESORT (ⓣ970/726-5514 or 1-800/729-5832, snow conditions ⓣ303/572-SNOW, ⓦwww.skiwinterpark.com), the oldest continuously operating resort in the country, first opened its lifts in 1944 as a municipal facility – a winter park for Denverites. Its success lies in it being modest and good value (particularly for season pass-holders – an adult **day-ticket** costs $55) and of course in it having regular installments of good snow – an average of 370 inches per year. The resort's **121 trails** spread over its 2581-acre terrain are clearly skewed towards better skiers (designated nine percent beginner, 21 percent intermediate, and seventy percent advanced and expert), but beginners will be pleased to find the almost self-enclosed 200-acre Discovery Park.

Winter Park Resort divides into four interconnected ski areas: the core base area and three distinct peaks. The most renowned of these peaks is the rugged **Mary Jane** mountain, whose steep, long runs – up to 4.5 miles long – are sprinkled with narrow, bumpy ridges harboring some of the best mogul runs in Colorado. The fluffy snows of the high-alpine **Parsenn Bowl**, which at 12,060ft acts as a magnet for deep powder, also has its fans for its above-timberline vistas and fantastic secluded glades. The third major peak, the uncrowded **Vasquez Ridge**, is gateway to the backcountry idyll **Vasquez Cirque**, whose undeveloped, ungroomed off-piste challenges include cornices and rock outcrops. Winter Park also has three good, imaginatively designed **terrain parks** – features of which are incorporated into the **Spring Slash** course, when on the last day of skiing in Winter Park, skiers don shorts and bathing suits and follow a bizarre course down the mountain to plunge into a sixty-foot pond of ice water at its base.

Cross-country skiers consider the 150-odd miles of cross-country trails in the area, which include plenty of good backcountry options, one of the best networks in the state. Down the valley from the downhill area is the great cross-country center of **Devil's Thumb Ranch**, 3530 CO-83, Tabernash (ⓣ970/726-8231 or 1-800/933-4339), where nearly eighty miles of groomed trails fan out into the forest from a central meadow. To get there, drive west from Winter Park to the town of Fraser and turn right onto CO-83. Tickets are $12 for adults, and lessons and equipment rental are also available.

Winter Park is also known for its **National Sports Center for the Disabled**, the largest and most successful of its kind, which provides low-cost lessons and special adaptive equipment for 2500 people a year, and trains serious competitors for its Disabled Ski Team.

There's no shortage of places to **rent** ski and snowboard gear in Winter Park. Basic ski rental packages cost around $20 per day, a little more for some top-notch demo gear. Ski Depot Sports (ⓣ970/726-8055 or 1-800/525-6484) are a popular choice, with four locations around town and in the resort itself, and one of the best selections of demo gear locally. Power Play Sports, 535 Zerex, Fraser (ⓣ970/726-5359), is a good local snowboard specialist.

Summer activities

Winter Park has worked hard to attract **mountain bikers**, and cycling is now the main summertime activity in the valley. The resort has built some 45 miles of terrific trails – arguably the best collection of trails run by any Colorado ski resort – which can be accessed via the Zephyr Express chairlift; tickets (adult day-pass $21) can be purchased as a package with a mountain bike (front-suspension bike $49). The real gem in the valley, however, is the 600 miles of marked, mapped, and maintained trails throughout the Winter Park and Fraser Valley. These trails include the five-mile, paved **Fraser River Trail** between the two towns, which is an easy ride, good for families and in-line skaters too. More adventurous riders should definitely try the delightful, rolling, single-track of the **Tipperary Creek Trail**, west of Fraser. For the best views, the **Moffat Road** (see box, overleaf) makes a good cycle ride – on easy terrain, with the knowledge that however far you manage to go, it's all downhill back into town. A free trail map is available at the many local bike stores or from the visitor center. **Bike rentals** are available from Winter Park Sports Shop, in Winter Park at 78336 Hwy-40 (ⓣ970/726-5554 or 1-800/222-7547, ⓦwww.winterparkbike.com), which has a good selection and knowledgeable staff, or Winter Park Rental and Repair Shop, at the base of the mountain (ⓣ970/726-5514 ext 1809). Rental rates at both are competitive, at around $20 per day for a front-suspension bike.

The bowl of mountains surrounding the Winter Park and Fraser Valley is also a tempting prospect for those looking for multiday **hiking** trips, particularly along the Continental Divide trail which loops around the southern and eastern sides of the valley. The visitor information center can provide free **trail maps**, while a good place for information and gear is Flanagan's Ski Rental and Black Dog Mountaineering, 78902 Hwy-40, Winter Park (ⓣ970/726-

The Moffat Road

For an appreciation of Winter Park's setting and history, take a twelve-mile drive east to the Rollins Pass via the rough and rutted **Moffat Road** (also known as the Corona Pass Rd), generally passable with regular two-wheel-drive vehicles from June until early November. The railroad once came this way – when the route was the valley's lifeline and the main reason for its existence as a timber camp for Denver – before the construction of the Moffat Tunnel below made this section of line superfluous. The views over Indian Peaks Wilderness to the north are astonishing, and from the summit of the pass four-wheel-drive vehicles can head further east to Rollinsville and the Peak-to-Peak highway (see p.87). For detailed information about remaining railroad sections and a history of the road's construction, pick up *The Moffat Road* leaflet ($1) from the visitor center in Winter Park.

4412), which has a good stock of camping equipment, tents, sleeping bags, and backpacks.

Other popular summertime activities include the super-fun, mile-and-a-half-long alpine slide ($6), a climbing wall and a maze at the Winter Park Resort. Also in the valley is the **Pole Creek Golf Course** (☎970/726-8847 or 1-800/511-5076), eleven miles northwest of Fraser on Hwy-40 in the town of Tabernash, one of the best in Colorado.

Eating and drinking

Winter Park may lack the selection of **restaurants** that the Summit County resorts or Vail offer, but the range still isn't half bad except in Fraser, where options are much more limited.

Arpeggios 78785 Hwy-40, Winter Park ☎970/726-5402. Wonderfully authentic, but pricey Northern Italian fare downtown. The excellent Chicken Fantasia comes with a creamy sauce, nuts and grapes tossed in with pasta. Reservations recommended.

Carlos and Maria's Copper Creek Square, Winter Park ☎970/726-9674. Reliably good, inexpensive Mexican restaurant with low-cost margaritas during the daily happy hour from 3.30 to 6pm.

Carvers Behind Copper Creek Square, Winter Park ☎970/726-8202. Large variety of reasonably priced big breakfasts and some good sandwiches for lunch. Its bakery is a good place to stock up on picnic items.

Crooked Creek Saloon & Eatery 401 Zerex Ave, Fraser ☎970/726-5727. Occasionally wild dining and nightlife venue, serving Mexican and American food and plenty of beer. Regular live music.

Deno's 78911 Hwy-40, Winter Park, ☎970/726-5332. Sports bar serving unexpectedly good food – including pasta ($10), steaks, and spicy Cajun seafood – plus a hundred or so varieties of beer.

Fontenot's Cajun Cafe Park Plaza, Hwy-40, Winter Park ☎970/726-4021. Downtown local favorite with fresh fish, pasta dishes, crawfish, and gumbo on the menu.

Gasthaus Eichler 78786 Hwy-40, Winter Park ☎970/726-5133. Austrian and German specialties (around $20) like schnitzel, *sauerbraten*, or bratwurst with sauerkraut are served with a gourmet twist in this quaint upscale alpine ski lodge downtown. Reservations recommended.

The Last Waltz Restaurant 78336 Hwy-40, Winter Park ☎970/726-4877. This place opens at 7am to serve satisfying egg-combination breakfasts (the eggs Benedict is great). The lunchtime and dinner menus are more varied, but always include good Mexican food and some superb home-baked desserts.

Lodge at Sunspot Winter Park Resort ☎970/726-5514 ext 1727. Head to the top of Winter Park Resort where views over the Continental Divide make for a memorable four-course dinner that will set you back at least $40 per person – gourmet offerings include fresh trout, local lamb, and various wild game options. Reservations advised. Open Thurs, Fri & Sat nights.

The Shed 78672 Hwy-40, Winter Park ☎970/726-9912. Decent, filling Southwestern-Mexican fare is served up at this popular joint, but it's better known as a margarita-drinking and pool-

playing hangout, with a well-priced happy hour.
The Slope Winter Park Resort, just north of the base of the lifts ☎970/726-5727. Nightlife kicks off here at the base of the ski lifts before progressing downtown. Regular live music.

Summit County

Appropriately named, the spectacularly mountainous **Summit County** just east of the Continental Divide, and around an hour and a half's drive from Denver, harbors the greatest concentration of ski resorts in the Rocky Mountains. Many of the purpose-built ski resorts, old mining towns, snow-covered peaks, alpine meadows, and crystal lakes that make up Summit County lie clustered around the large **Lake Dillon** reservoir. Adjacent towns bustle as rather dreary service towns offering plentiful ski accommodation and including a couple of pleasant, but unexciting resort towns. By far the liveliest of Summit County's towns is the charismatic Victorian mining town of **Breckenridge** south of here.

Four major **ski areas** – Arapahoe Basin, Keystone, Breckenridge and Copper Mountain – are within a half-hour drive of each other. A fifth gigantic ski area, Vail (see p.226), is hardly much further, just over the Vail Pass. Tickets at all the Summit County resorts, except Copper Mountain, are interchangeable (Vail can be included on multiday passes), allowing skiers and snowboarders to visit several resorts on one lift ticket. Moving between ski areas is further encouraged by the efficient, free Summit County shuttle bus service, making a car unnecessary.

Although winter is still the busiest time in Summit County, **summer activities** are becoming increasingly important to the area's economy. Several of the resorts, but especially Keystone and Breckenridge, have gone out of their way to create and promote summertime pursuits, in particular by building scenic hiking trails and challenging, lift-serviced mountain-bike runs. Golf is also becoming a major industry, with the swanky Keystone Ranch Golf Club – which now occupies the meadow where the Ute pitched their tepees during the summer hunting season – a particularly popular place for a round.

For advance **information** on the area visit Summit County's website Ⓦwww.summitnet.com, which has information on accommodation, restaurants, activities, and events in both the Lake Dillon communities and Breckenridge.

Around Lake Dillon

Sprawled out beside the I-70 on the shore of the large, earth-dammed Lake Dillon reservoir are several communities based largely on serving the nearby ski resorts. Of these communities **Frisco**, on the lake's southwestern side, is the oldest and, stretching sedately along a quiet valley, the most attractive too, appealing to those looking for a less hectic pace; as the center of the county's free transit system, it's also the handiest base in the area. On the northern side of the lake lie **Silverthorne** and **Dillon**, straddling the west and east side of the I-70 respectively. Both are dreary, though the former contains dozens of cut-price factory outlet stores and the latter some fairly inexpensive condo accommodation. A short drive east of Dillon, and on the way to **Arapahoe Basin** is the slick, but unexciting resort village of **Keystone** around the base of the eponymous ski area. Another superb modern, self-contained major ski resort, **Copper Mountain**, is only six miles southwest of Frisco. In addition to the good downhill skiing, the area around Lake Dillon is also known for its Nordic ski opportunities, with several ski centers and a well-organized, extensive network of trails used as cycle paths in the summer. As one of the largest bodies of water in Colorado, Lake Dillon itself also invites sailors and anglers.

Arrival, information, and getting around

By car, Summit County is about two hours from Denver. **Greyhound buses** heading west from Denver ($11 one-way) and east from Grand Junction stop in Frisco at the transit center (see below). There are also **shuttles** from Denver International Airport. Resort Express serves Dillon, Frisco, Silverthorne, Keystone, and Copper Mountain (Ⓣ970/468-7600 or 1-800/334-7433, Ⓦwww.resort-express.com; $45), while Supershuttle (Ⓣ1-800/258-3826) and Colorado Mountain Express (Ⓣ1-800/222-2112) run a more expensive door-to-door service to your hotel.

The main **visitor center** (daily 9am–5pm; Ⓣ970/668-2051 or 1-800/424-1554, Ⓦwww.townoffrisco.com) stands by the lake at the end of Frisco's Main Street. An excellent **free public transportation** system, the Summit Stage (Ⓣ970/453-1339), operates from its hub, the **transit center** in Frisco behind the Safeway supermarket near the I-70. From here frequent shuttle buses run throughout the Lake Dillon area and Breckenridge, with less-frequent buses heading to Copper Mountain (half-hourly) and Vail. Shuttles have facilities for carrying several bikes, allowing cyclists using the local cycle paths to skip sections or ride one-way along routes.

Accommodation

Lodgings in Summit County cover all budgets, with prices often almost halving in summer. The centralized booking system for hotels, B&Bs, and condominium complexes in Frisco, Silverthorne, and Dillon is **Summit County Central Reservations**, 330 Fiedler Ave (Ⓣ970/468-6222 or 1-800/365-6365), who offer rates as low as $50 in the summer, and can also organize car rentals and airport transfers along with discounted lift tickets during the ski season. For resort accommodation in the **condo units** strewn around the base of the ski mountains contact **Keystone Resort** (Ⓣ970/496-4500 or 1-877/753-9786); guests have access to swimming pools, saunas, and hot tubs and receive a "mountain passport" for various indoor and outdoor activities in both summer and winter: including guided snowshoeing, cross-country skiing, yoga, and tennis clinics. The accommodation is first class, but so too are the prices, with virtually nothing costing under $100 a night.

Similarly all the accommodation at **Copper Mountain** is in pricey condos or hotel rooms, though all have free access to the top-notch Copper Mountain Racquet & Athletic Club; in winter you're unlikely to find a room for under $120 per night. The best bet is to call Copper Mountain Resort (Ⓣ970/968-2882 or 1-800/458-8386).

In summer, there's also the option of **camping** in Summit County. A number of large USFS campgrounds are well-placed on the shores of Lake Dillon and cost around $10. These include *Heaton Bay*, on Dam Road a mile east of Frisco's N Summit Boulevard on Hwy-9, and *Pine Cove* and the *Prospector*, further along the south shore of the lake.

Frisco

Best Western Lake Dillon Lodge 1202 N Summit Blvd ⓣ970/668-5094 or 1-800/727-0607. Dependable motel with large rooms – some with lake views – an indoor pool, hot tub, and ski shop. Family rooms with three double beds also available. Under-18s stay free. ❺

Frisco Lodge 321 Main St ⓣ970/668-0195. Simple, motel-style accommodation in an old railroad inn – usually the cheapest deal in town. Units have kitchenettes and access to a hot tub. ❹

Galena Street Mountain Inn 106 Galena St ⓣ970/668-3224 or 1-800/248-9138. Modern B&B near the bike path and a local shuttle bus stop, a half-block back from Main St. Amenities include a sundeck, living and dining room, hot tub, and sauna. ❺

Sky-Vue Motel 305 2nd Ave ⓣ970/668-3311. Quiet and inexpensive motel two blocks from Main St. Some rooms have kitchenette units and there's an indoor pool and hot tub. ❹

Snowshoe Motel 521 Main St ⓣ970/668-3444. Centrally located budget choice with no-frills rooms, though some have kitchenettes. ❹

Twilight Inn 300 Main St ⓣ970/668-5009. B&B with a variety of rooms, including some Victorian-style antique-furnished quarters and some rooms that share bathrooms. Amenities include hot tub and laundry facilities. ❺

Woods Inn 205 S 2nd St ⓣ970/668-3389 or 1-800/668-4448. Inexpensive B&B in a pine-log building originally built below Lake Dillon. The cozy communal area has a fireplace and there's a hot tub available. ❹

Silverthorne

Alpen Hütte Lodge 471 Rainbow Drive ⓣ970/468-6336. Clean hostel bunkrooms in comfortable environs. Rooms are closed for cleaning daily from 9.30am to 3.30pm, the office from noon to 3.30pm and there's a midnight curfew. Dorm rooms cost $25 in winter, $18 in summer. Private, motel-style rooms are also available. ❹

Wildernest Condominiums 204 Wildernest Rd ⓣ970/468-7851 or 1-800/554-2212. Massive 200-unit development beside the interstate exit. Lodging options range from modest studios to grander multibedroom apartments. The complex's clubhouse includes a pool, hot tub, and sauna, and there are free shuttle services to nearby ski areas and towns. ❺

Dillon

Best Western Ptarmigan Lodge 652 Lake Dillon Drive ⓣ970/468-2341. The only hotel near Dillon's marina and its lakefront public areas has fairly plain rooms, all with balconies and some with kitchenettes and fireplaces. Included in the price is use of the hot tub and sauna and a continental breakfast. At the height of ski season, a five-night minimum stay is usually required. ❺

Super 8 Motel 808 Little Beaver Trail ⓣ970/468-8888 or 1-800/843-1991. Reliable, mid-priced motel, with free continental breakfast. ❺

Keystone

Paradox Lodge 5040 Montezuma Rd, Keystone ⓣ970/468-9445. Pretty self-contained cabins sleeping up to five, plus four guestrooms available in a tranquil spot, at the head of the Peru Gulch Trail six miles east of Keystone, surrounded by Arapaho National Forest land. A generous continental breakfast is included, as is use of a living room, sundeck, and fire-heated hot tub. ❼

Copper Mountain

Club Med 50 Beeler Pl, Copper Mountain ⓣ970/968-2161 or 1-800/CLUB-MED. Self contained resort offering **all-inclusive packages**; including meals, lift passes, instruction, and an evening entertainment program; for around $1500 per adult for one week. Open mid-November to early May. ❽

Winter activities

Far and away the most popular winter activity in the Lake Dillon area is either downhill skiing and snowboarding at the three local ski-areas – **Keystone**, **Arapahoe Basin**, and **Copper Mountain** – or cross-country skiing. But other winter activities are also available locally, including both **snowmobiling** and **dog-sledding**; Good Times, 6061 Tiger Rd (ⓣ970/453-7604 or 1-

800/477-0144; ⓦ www.snowmobilecolorado.com), offer tours of both, including a half-day snowmobile tour following a route that climbs up 1500ft past abandoned mines and cabins to the Continental Divide ($70). Snowmobile rental is also available for those who want to strike out alone, exploring the company's own trail system. Another company offering both snowmobile and dog-sled tours is Tiger Run, 15945 Hwy-9 (ⓣ 970/453-2231 or 1-800/318-1386, ⓦ www.tigerruntours.com), who take guests up to an old mining town. Evenings, horse-drawn **sleigh rides** are offered to Soda Creek Homestead (ⓣ 970/468-2316 or 1-800/222-0188; $51), one of the original ranches in the tree-covered valley. Following the trip, guests tour several of the old outbuildings, before being served dinner. A similar package towed by **mules**, the area's traditional working animals, is offered by Below Zero Dinner Sleigh Rides, Frisco Nordic Center, one mile south of Frisco on Hwy-9 (Mon–Sat; $45; ⓣ 970/453-1520 or 1-800/571-MULE).

Additionally Keystone Resort offers the opportunity to go **snow-tubing** ($10) or **ice skating** (late Nov to early March daily 10am–10pm; from $8) – the latter on a large five-acre former beaver pond – now the largest maintained outdoor ice-skating rink in North America; skate rental costs $6, and hockey sticks are also available.

Keystone Ski Area

Owned and operated as part of a resort, the **Keystone Ski Area** (ⓣ 970/496-2316 or 1-877/625-1556, snow conditions ⓣ 970/494-4111, ⓦ www.keystoneresort.com) extends beyond a pleasantly bland alpine-style base village to cover 1755 acres and encompasses a little of everything from easy beginner runs to powder stashes in back-bowls. As the first major resort along the I-70 corridor from Denver, Keystone tends to get crowded on weekends and holidays, when the resort's superb range of beginner and intermediate terrain pulls many families here. There's an excellent **Children's Center**, with extensive child-care facilities and lesson programs, as well as Gold Rush Alley, a kids-only terrain garden with a mining theme. Despite its popularity, even in busy times the resort's relatively small but challenging expert area, **The Outback**, which includes a number of great glade and mogul runs along with two treeless back-bowls, never really gets crowded. In addition to its good range of runs (**92 trails** on terrain that divides as 13 percent beginner, 36 percent intermediate, and 51 percent advanced), Keystone is best-known for its notable snowmaking capability, which usually allows it to open earlier than its neighbors (the **season** typically running mid-Oct to late April), and for having a large **night-ski** operation, with seventeen runs illuminated until 8pm. Adult all-day **lift tickets** cost around $59 – and are also valid in Arapahoe and Breckenridge.

Arapahoe Basin Ski Area

Arapahoe Basin Ski Area (ⓣ 970/486-0718 or 1-888/ARA-PAHO, snow conditions ⓣ 970/468-4111, ⓦ www.arapahoebasin.com), tucked just west of the Continental Divide, ninety miles west of Denver, has cult status as a no-nonsense ski area – the drug of choice for scruffy young hard-core skiers and riders who revel in its raw, taxing terrain and the fact that the small number of lifts (only five) and spartan amenities largely keep the crowds away. Thanks to its mighty **elevation** (the base is at 10,800ft) and decent **snowfall** (around 360 inches annually) the **season** here at "A-Basin" spans from mid-November until at least June, when mild temperatures encourage the donning of bikinis or Hawaiian shirts. As the highest resort in the country, A-Basin offers great above-treeline bowl skiing across a relatively tiny 490-acre **ski area**, of which ninety percent is rated intermediate and expert, making it a poor training ground for novices. Absolute beginners will, however, enjoy being able to use one lift and one run for only $5 per day. But the more skilled will have a great time here on the insane double black diamond mogul runs, particularly those around the Palavincini lift. **Lift tickets** cost around $40 for an all-day adult ticket; $59 for those also good at both Keystone and Breckenridge. A frequent bus service to Keystone, a fifteen-minute ride away, means that it's perfectly viable to include a couple of runs here in a day of skiing at Keystone.

Copper Mountain Ski Resort

Constructed as a self-contained resort village in the early 1970s, **Copper Mountain Ski Resort** (ⓣ970/968-2882 or 1-800/458-8386, snow conditions ⓣ970/968-2100 or 1-800/789-7609, ⓦwww.ski-copper.com), on the western edge of Summit County beside I-70, is an unpretentious resort with skiing on a par with Vail, but without its neighbor's fame or glitz. And while Copper Mountain is only half the size of Vail – though at more than 2400 acres it's still the biggest **ski area** in Summit County – it has roughly as many separate **runs**, 166 in total. With more than two-thirds of its terrain rated intermediate or advanced (the exact breakdown is 23 percent beginner, 36 percent intermediate, 41 percent advanced), the resort is an enticing place for experienced skiers, though there are plenty of good areas for beginners too. In fact a key part of the resort's success is the way in which the terrain divides so readily between harder and easier skiing areas, keeping beginners, intermediates and experts out of each other's way. Steeper pitches are to the east, gentle slopes such as those in the beginner-friendly Union Creek area are to the west, while behind the mogul runs on the front slopes of the resort stretch out steep, lonely back bowls – the Copper, Union, and Spaulding Bowls. A one-day adult **lift ticket** costs around $55, though budget deals are often available via King Soopers grocery stores in Denver and Boulder.

Cross-country skiing

Cross-country skiing is incredibly popular in the Lake Dillon area thanks to an excellent network of trails along the area's bikepaths, some great backcountry opportunities, and extensive facilities. Of these, the largest and most significant is the **Frisco Nordic Center**, one mile south of Frisco on Hwy-9 (winter daily 9am–4pm; $10; ⓣ970/668-0866). Designed by Olympic silver-medallist Bill Koch, the center offers 23 miles of groomed trails, many of which overlook Lake Dillon. Free afternoon lessons for beginners are available, as well as more advanced lessons and rentals and use of cabin for breaks. The center shares an interchangeable trail pass with the Breckenridge Nordic Center (see p.222). To explore more ungroomed terrain, head to the **Keystone Cross-Country Center**, two miles east of Keystone on Montezuma Road (ⓣ970/496-4386). The center has just a dozen miles of groomed trails in the Snake River Valley, but an extensive 32 miles of backcountry trails in the Arapaho National Forest. Again, it offers rentals and lessons as well as tours – including one under the full moon. The **Copper Mountain resort** also includes a cross-country center near the Union Creek base area (ⓣ970/968-2318 ext 6342), from where eighteen miles of machine-set tracks and skating lanes wind on enjoyable undulating terrain through the rolling wooded valleys of Arapaho National Forest. You can book rentals, lessons, and overnight hut trips through the center.

Summer activities

Though excursions to the factory outlet stores at Silverthorne seem to be the most popular activity in the summer, there are plenty of opportunities for more energetic outdoor pursuits in the Lake Dillon area. The **Adventure Center** at Keystone Resort (Ⓣ970/668-0866 or 1-800/545-4FUN) offers a range of activities including horseback riding, rafting, fly-fishing, and hikes with llamas, as well as a good range of children's programs. The resort also runs the swank **Keystone Ranch Golf Course** three miles to the south (Ⓣ970/496-4250 or 1-800/451-5930), though it's often hard to get tee-time here. An alternative is the less-expensive Eagles Nest Golf Club (Ⓣ970/468-0681) in Silverthorne.

For those wanting to leave the well-developed Lake Dillon area well behind, there are great **hiking** opportunities at the **Ptarmigan Peaks Wilderness** and **Eagles Nest Wilderness** either side of Silverthorne. Get hold of the free *Summer Trailhead Guide*, available from the Frisco visitor center.

Sailing and fishing

Too cold for swimming, Lake Dillon is popular with sailboats, kayaks, and fishing boats, though inexperienced sailors should beware of unpredictable late-afternoon heavy winds, channeled from the bowl of surrounding mountains. Between May and October various craft are available for rent from **Dillon Marina** (Ⓣ970/468-5100, Ⓦwww.dillonmarina.com) and Osprey Adventures (Ⓣ970/668-5573 or 1-888/780-4970) at **Frisco Bay Marina**, who rent paddle boats ($12 per hr); motorboats ($75 for 2hr); canoes ($25 for 2hr); kayaks ($15 for 2hr); and sailboats ($60 for 2hr). Lake **anglers** will find good spots to fish along the lakeshore south of Frisco, while for fly-fishermen the 34 miles of the Blue River between Dillon Dam and the Colorado River is the main local fishing artery. Columbine Outfitters (Ⓣ970/262-0966) offer guided trips, a half-day trip for two people costing around $140.

Mountain biking

Both **road cyclists** and **mountain bikers** will be delighted by what they find in the Lake Dillon area, even before they swing a leg over their bike, thanks to the excellent, comprehensive and free *Summit County Bike Trail Guide* available from the Frisco visitor center that gives a thorough rundown of road and mountain bike possibilities in the county, with route maps and trail descriptions.

Frisco is at the heart of a superb 100-mile network of bike trails that include spurs to Breckenridge (10 miles), Dillon (5 miles), Keystone (12 miles), Copper (8 miles), and Vail (19 miles). **Keystone** is the best base for mountain-bike trips. The resort provides a (sadly overpriced) **gondola** service up the mountain (June–Sept; daily 9.30am–3.30pm; day-pass $25), from where there's a maze of entertaining riding – from plenty of beginner-level snaking single-track, to loose gnarly drops on technical runs like Wild Thing. Even if you are not planning to use the lift or even ride the resort's trails, it's worth picking up the free local trail map from the gondola ticket offices. This covers trails well beyond the confines of the resort – which can be accessed either via the gondola or a grind up the face of the mountain. Technically adept riders should try one of the trails heading east to the tiny community of Montezuma, while all riders should at some point try the portion of the **Colorado Trail**, just southwest of the resort. This almost entirely smooth single-track trail passes through pristine stands of pine and aspen before dropping down via a series of kamikaze switchbacks to Hwy-9 at the *Tiger Run RV Resort* six miles south of Frisco. You can also do this ride as a 25-mile (approximately 3hr) loop from the *RV Resort* (free

Lake Dillon area outfitters

Antlers Ski and Sport Shop 900 Summit Blvd, Frisco ⓣ970/668-3152. Ski and bike rentals and a good selection of camping and fishing supplies.

Christy Sports Ski 849 N Summit Blvd, Frisco; 817 Hwy-6, Dillon ⓣ970/468-2329; Copper Mountain ⓣ970/968-6250. The area's biggest, though not necessarily cheapest source of rentals – but convenient since you can pick up, drop off or swap your equipment at any one of the other thirty outlets in all the major Central Colorado resorts.

Mountain Sports 167B Merilay Way, Silverthorne ⓣ970/262-2836. Rents and sells skis, snowboards and snow shoes in the winter, in-line skates, hiking boots, sleeping bags and camping gear in the summer.

Mountain View Sports Hwy-6 Mountain View Plaza, Keystone ⓣ970/468-0396. Located beside Keystone's ski slopes; skis, snowboards and snowshoes, bikes and in-line skates rental.

Recycle Ski and Sport 842 Summit Blvd, Frisco ⓣ970/668-5150. Huge second-hand sporting goods retailer with tons of used ski and snowboard equipment in winter, bikes and camping gear in summer.

Wildernest Sports 171 Blue River Pkwy, Silverthorne ⓣ970/468-8519. Rents out bikes and skis and has a good range of hiking gear, maps and guide books.

parking lot beside Hwy-9), heading along Tiger Run Road and Middle Fork Road (FS-6) to a point nine miles from Hwy-9 where you double back onto the Colorado Trail, following this well-marked trail fifteen miles back to the start.

Local **bike rental** costs around $30 for front suspension, $55 for full suspension; see the box, above, for details of rental outfits.

Eating, drinking, and nightlife

The Lake Dillon area hasn't developed a reputation for fine dining, though two notable exceptions are the *Alpenglow Stube* restaurant at Keystone Resort (see overleaf) and the $70-per-head **dinner cruises** arranged by Dillon Marina (ⓣ970/468-5100; May–Oct). Frisco also has its moments, and good burgers or burritos are never too far away.

Frisco

Barkley's 620 Main St ⓦwww.barkleys.com. Mexican food and an extensive selection of margaritas at Frisco's only late-night venue, complete with live music and billiards.

Blue Spruce Inn 120 W Main St ⓣ970/668-5900. Frisco's best upscale restaurant is a worthy splurge, though you pay at least $15 for its tasty veal, beef, and seafood entrees.

Butterhorn Bakery 408 W Main St ⓣ970/668-3997. Good local bakery for breads, bagels, and cakes. Well-known for its huge breakfast burrito ($6) and smoked salmon omelette ($7), and at lunch a good range of sandwiches and burgers are served for around $7. Closed Tues.

El Rio Cantina & Grill 450 Main St ⓣ970/668-5043. Healthy inexpensive wholefood Mexican dishes and excellent margaritas.

Moose Jaw 208 Main St ⓣ970/668-3931. Dark wooden bar serving mediocre burgers and a dreary selection of beers until 2am – but a popular local hangout nevertheless.

Pika Bagel Bakery & Cafe 401 Main St ⓣ970/668-0902. Friendly outlet for a fruit smoothie and a bagel.

Uptown Bistro 304 Main St ⓣ970/668-4728. Elegant, upscale restaurant with seafood and Asian specialties including house-cured marinated salmon and Indonesian noodle salad. Entrees cost around $20.

Silverthorne

Matteo's 122 W 10th St ⓣ970/262-6508. Super happy-hour deals; serves salads, pasta, and pizza by the slice.

Old Dillon Inn 321 Blue River Parkway

☎970/468-2791. Impressive nineteenth-century bar that gets packed with skiers for the inexpensive Mexican food and margaritas and the energetic Country and Western music.

Dillon

Arapahoe Café and Pub 626 Lake Dillon Drive ☎970/468-0873. Good generous and healthy breakfasts and a range of entrees like trout, roast duck, and veggie pasta for lunch – most around the $6 mark. Also open for dinner, though only serving lighter meals.

Dillon Dam Brewery 100 Little Dam Rd ☎970/262-7777. Good microbrew ales and inexpensive quality bar food – salads, burgers, and pasta – with entrees from around $8.

Keystone

Alpenglow Stube Keystone Resort ☎970/496-4386. The best dining experience in Summit County – take the free gondola ride to the top of 11,444ft North Peak and feast on New American cuisine with a Bavarian edge in beautiful surroundings. At $70 for a six-course meal, it doesn't come cheap though. Smart dress required (denim banned). The restaurant closes during the spring and fall shoulder seasons, when the gondola doesn't operate. Reservations advised.

Snake River Saloon 23074 Hwy-6 ☎970/468-2788, ⓦwww.snakeriversaloon.com. A full menu of bar food, steaks and prime rib is served in this locally popular bar that's one of the best venues for live rock in the area.

Copper Mountain

O'Shea's base of American Eagle lift ☎970/968-2318 ext 6504. Inexpensive selection of bar food including nachos, burritos, and hamburgers.

Pesce's Fresco Mountain Village ☎970/968-2318 ext. 6505. Moderately expensive changing menu with soups, salads, and pastas for lunch and full meals later on.

Breckenridge

One of the most well-rounded ski-towns in Colorado, **Breckenridge** couples a well-developed resort and its huge varied ski area with a pleasant Victorian mining town that knows how to party at night, and all at prices that are less shocking than at Vail or Aspen. Breckenridge was established in 1859, the year gold was discovered. The ebb and flow of various local gold-mining booms and busts over the years left behind many dilapidated ghost towns in the area, but the one settlement to survive was Breckenridge, thanks partly to its role in silver as well as gold mining – the former said to be sparked-off by a barber's comment about the presence of silver dust in a customers hair. Today, the brightly-painted gingerbread Victorian houses, shops, and cafés that line the main street as you roll into town are the twee core of a huge skiing operation – one of the busiest in Colorado – which has seen the limits of the town continually expand over the last decade. Summer is also a busy time, when bikes are rolled out onto local paths and trails and golfers take advantage of good-value packages in ski lodges.

South of Breckenridge along Hwy-9 over the 11,541ft Hoosier Pass lie the straggly minor communities of **Alma** and **Fairplay**, which sit on the huge flat expanse of the South Park Basin.

Arrival, information, and getting around

From Denver International Airport, Resort Express serves Breckenridge (☎970/468-7600 or 1-800/334-7433, ⓦwww.resort-express.com; $40), while Supershuttle (☎1-800/258-3826) runs a more expensive door-to-door service to your hotel. Either way the journey takes around two and a half hours.

The **Welcome Center** is on the north side of town at 309 N Main (daily: 9am–5pm; ☎970/453-6018, ⓦwww.gobreck.com), and there's another helpful visitor information center in the center of town at 137 S Main St (daily: 9am–5pm; ☎970/453-5579). Both dispense the useful free *Breckenridge*

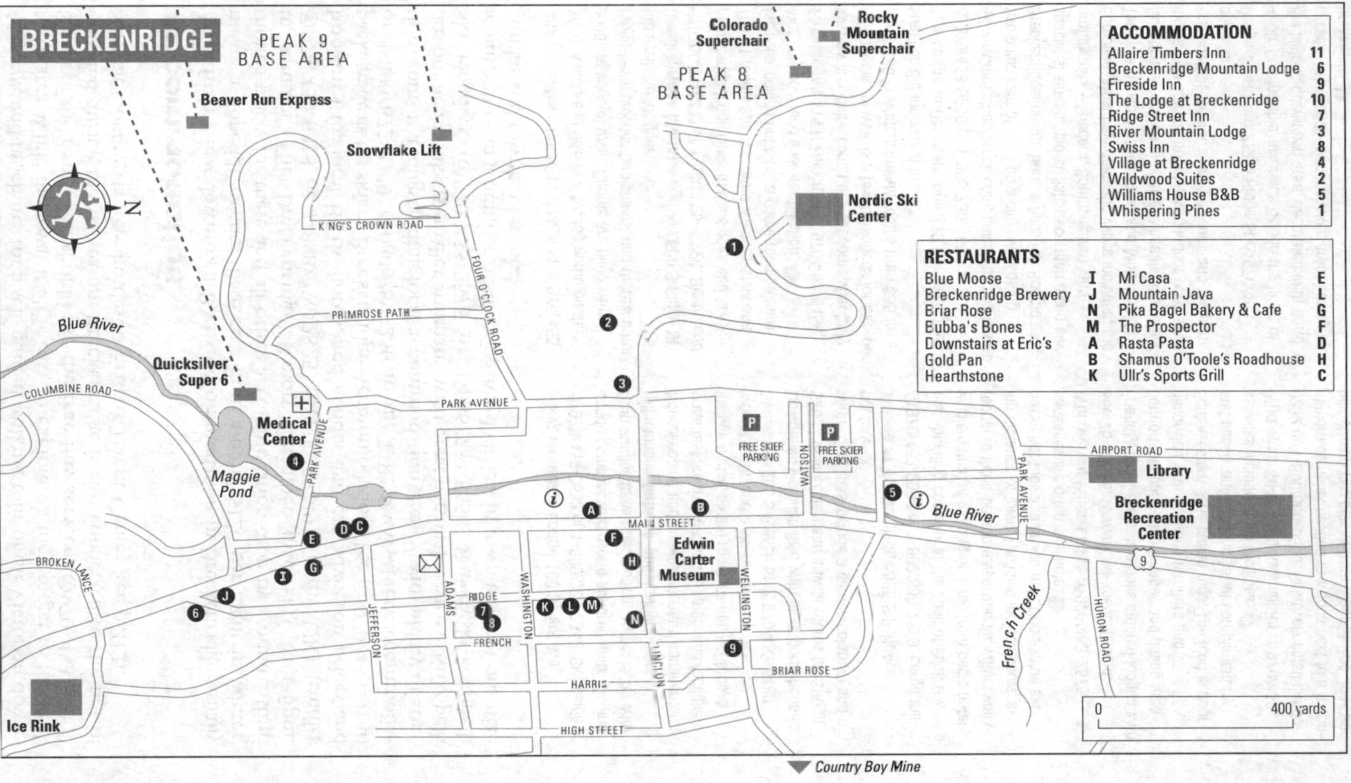
BRECKENRIDGE
PEAK 9 BASE AREA
Beaver Run Express
Snowflake Lift
PEAK 8 BASE AREA
Colorado Superchair
Rocky Mountain Superchair
Nordic Ski Center
N
KING'S CROWN ROAD
FOUR O'CLOCK ROAD
PRIMROSE PATH
Blue River
Quicksilver Super 6
COLUMBINE ROAD
Medical Center
Maggie Pond
PARK AVENUE
MAIN STREET
RIDGE
FRENCH
ADAMS
WASHINGTON
JEFFERSON
HARRIS
HIGH STREET
LINCOLN
WELLINGTON
BRIAR ROSE
WATSON
FREE SKIER PARKING
Edwin Carter Museum
AIRPORT ROAD
Library
Breckenridge Recreation Center
HURON ROAD
French Creek
BROKEN LANCE
Ice Rink
10, 11 & Fairplay
Country Boy Mine
Golf course & Frisco
0
400 yards
ACCOMMODATION
Allaire Timbers Inn 11
Breckenridge Mountain Lodge 6
Fireside Inn 9
The Lodge at Breckenridge 10
Ridge Street Inn 7
River Mountain Lodge 3
Swiss Inn 8
Village at Breckenridge 4
Wildwood Suites 2
Williams House B&B 5
Whispering Pines 1
RESTAURANTS
Blue Moose I
Breckenridge Brewery J
Briar Rose N
Bubba's Bones M
Downstairs at Eric's A
Gold Pan B
Hearthstone K
Mi Casa E
Mountain Java L
Pika Bagel Bakery & Cafe G
The Prospector F
Rasta Pasta D
Shamus O'Toole's Roadhouse H
Ullr's Sports Grill C

Magazine and brochures for a self-guided walking tour of the Victorian downtown area. While the town itself is easy to explore on foot, to get to the Peak 8 area of the resort, you should use the **free bus service** (Ⓣ970/453-5000), operated during the ski season. Breckenridge is also connected to the rest of Summit County via free shuttles to Frisco's Transit Center (see p.212).

Accommodation

Aside from a few downtown B&Bs, accommodation in Breckenridge usually means a slopeside condo; these cost from around $120 per night in winter, though prices for these and all other accommodation drop by around a third in summer. The Breckenridge Resort Chamber (Mon–Fri 8am–5pm; Ⓣ970/453-6018 or 1-888/796-2825, Ⓣ0800/897491 in the UK) handles **bookings** for local B&Bs, hotels, and condos and can advise on prices and package deals for skiers. Breckenridge Accommodations Inc (Ⓣ970/453-9140 or 1-800/872-8779, Ⓣ0800/899236 in the UK, Ⓦwww.breckaccommodations.com) is a longstanding local accommodation agency with plenty of condos on their books. A smaller company with great personal service is Kokopelli Ski Holidays. (Ⓣ970/453-2575 or 1-866/754-5656, Ⓦwww.ski-kokopelli.com), who run a number of luxury catered chalets in town and can organize condos and townhouses too.

Allaire Timbers Inn 9511 S Main St Ⓣ970/453-7530. A high-end B&B in a big log home on the southern edge of town. Rooms are filled with rough-hewn wooden furnishings, and there's a hot tub available for guests. ❼

Breckenridge Mountain Lodge 600 S Ridge St Ⓣ970/453-2333 or 1-800/525- 2224. Rustic and picturesque lodge close to the slopes and town. The 71 rooms are decorated Western-style and facilities include hot tubs, a game room, a summer-only pool, and a ski-rental shop. ❺

Fireside Inn 114 N French St Ⓣ970/453-6456, Ⓦwww.firesideinn.com. Cozy but somewhat tatty B&B rooms, as well as a few bunk beds for $25 per night ($30 in winter), private rooms from $55 in summer. Big indoor hot tub. ❻

The Lodge at Breckenridge 112 Overlook Drive Ⓣ970/453-9200 or 1-800/736-1607, Ⓦwww.thelodgeatbreck.com. Luxurious spa resort two miles east of town on a cliff overlooking Breckenridge, beside Boreas Pass Rd. Rooms are spacious, simple, and stylish, decorated along several themes – Western, Southwestern, and European. Most have fantastic views including the Ten-mile Range, Hoosier Pass, and Mount Baldy. Guests have access to a superb health club offering various spa treatments, with indoor pool, several hot tubs, sauna, a weight room, and racquetball courts. ❼

Ridge Street Inn 212 N Ridge St Ⓣ970/453-4680. Comfortable, luxurious B&B in the heart of the historic downtown area, decorated with floral excess. The friendly owner makes great hearty breakfasts. ❻

River Mountain Lodge 100 S Park Ave Ⓣ970/453-0533 or 1-800/325-2342. Slopeside condo complex with over a hundred units ranging from studios to two-bedroom apartments, all with full kitchens, terraces, and washer/dryers. Housekeeping and a complimentary continental breakfast are included in the rates, and facilities include a pool, steam room, sauna, hot tubs, a weight room, and a ski-rental shop. ❺

Swiss Inn 205 S French St Ⓣ970/453-6489. Downtown Victorian B&B with eight dorm beds for $28 ($38 in winter) and private rooms for $90 in winter. Facilities include a garden solarium and a hot tub. ❺

Village at Breckenridge 535 S Park Ave Ⓣ970/453-2000 or 1-800/800-7829. Large thirteen-building complex at the base of Peak 9 with a whole gamut of lodging options, from basic hotel rooms to three-bedroom apartments, within walking distance of town. Facilities include pools, a dozen hot tubs and an ice rink. Good-value ski packages are often available. ❼

Whispering Pines Lodge Ⓣ970/453-2575 or 1-866/754-5656, Ⓦwww.ski-kokopelli.com. Friendly, small-scale, luxurious catered lodges with comfortable open-plan lounges and dining area decorated with Colorado furniture and Southwestern-style Indian rugs. The food is gourmet quality and the long list of complimentary services include email facilities. ❽

Wildwood Suites 120 Sawmill Rd Ⓣ970/453-0232 or 1-800/866-0300. Relatively small condominium complex nestled in woods next to a mountain stream two blocks from Main St. The one- and two-bedroom condos are in a ski-in location and have access to large outdoor hot tubs, a sauna, a massage service, and a ski-rental shop. Continental breakfast included. ⑤

Williams House Bed & Breakfast 303 N Main St ⓣ970/453-2975. Elegant nineteenth-century home with period furniture and antiques and an outdoor hot tub. ⑥

The town and around

Set at the base of a glorious bowl of mountains, Breckenridge's snug Victorian downtown spreads over a compact twelve square blocks. The old multicolored gingerbread buildings along Main Street, the core of town, have been well preserved and are now taken over by restaurants and gift shops – which pull in large numbers, particularly in the summer. The town's local history museum, the **Edwin Carter Museum**, on the corner of Wellington and Ridge streets (Mon–Fri 1.30–3pm; $3), is good for its insight into the local characters that shaped the town's beginnings. But the bulk of the exhibits are given over to Edwin Carter, a naturalist from New York, who in the late nineteenth century built a phenomenal local collection of flora and fauna, while campaigning for the protection of the local environment as it was progressively attacked by open-cast mining methods. To complete the picture of what the early days of Breckenridge were like, head two miles northeast of town to the **Country Boy Mine**, 542 French Gulch Rd (phone for hours; $10; ⓣ970/453-4405), where the mine tours include drilling and dynamite demonstrations.

Winter activities

For those skiing or riding on the mountain slopes around town and those who've just finished a day there, there are plenty of other good winter diversions in the area, from ice-skating, through snowmobiling and dog-sledding to evening sleigh rides.

The best place to go ice-skating in Breckenridge is at the **Breckenridge Ice Rink**, 0189 Boreas Pass Rd (daily 10am–10pm; $4; ⓣ970/547-9974), a new, covered outdoor rink at the south end of town. Skate rental costs $3 for ice skates and $5 for in-line skates. For a cozier experience you can also skate at **Maggie Pond** at 535 S Park Ave, a small pond in the Village at Breckenridge (daily 10am–10pm; $6; ⓣ970/453-2000); at the base of Peak 9, where admission includes an hour of skate rental.

Dinner sleigh rides, incorporating a stop for gourmet food at an out-of-the-way cabin, have become a popular splurge in recent years; these are offered by Eagles Nest Equestrian Center (ⓣ970/468-0677) and Nordic Sleigh Rides (ⓣ970/453-2005), and generally cost around $55, although cheaper non-dinner rides are also available ($30).

Breckenridge Ski Area

Breckenridge Ski Area (ⓣ970/453-5000 or 1-800/221-1091, snow conditions ⓣ970/453-6118, ⓦwww.breckenridge.com) spans four peaks and offers ideal terrain for its one million annual skiers, with 139 **trails** over 2043 skiable acres (designated 20 percent beginner, 31 percent intermediate, and 49 percent advanced and expert) and a **season** that lasts from early November to late April. Note, however, that the resort is one of the most crowded in Colorado, since it is not only a popular destination for Denverites, but also the most convenient central Colorado resort for those living in Colorado Springs. If possible, it's best to restrict visits to weekdays.

The resort has two main centers; around **Peak 9**, accessed by the consistently overcrowded Quicksilver lift from the town's southern edge and from **Peak**

8, the original mountain, a free shuttle bus ride from town. The bulk of both peaks 8 and 9 consists of a good mix of intermediate and beginner runs with the odd harder one thrown in. The large and highly-respected six-acre **Freeway terrain park** with its plentiful and well-designed rails, jumps, and a half-pipe, is on Peak 8. The main expert areas – almost exclusively so – are at peaks 7 and 10. **Peak 7**, on the northern side of Peak 8, is a bleak, treeless series of ungroomed back bowls, that's generally the best hangout on powder days, particularly for its awesome Imperial Bowl which requires a half-hour hike in. **Peak 10**, to the south of Peak 9, has some great mogul runs, along with some of the best steep, powdery glade runs on the mountain in The Burn.

An adult **day-pass**, also valid for Keystone and Arapahoe, costs $59; a three-day lift ticket, also good for a day at Vail or Beaver Creek, is around $150. Skiers driving in to the resort have a choice of expensive pay parking near the base of peaks 8 and 9, or leaving their car in one of the town's free public lots alongside Hwy-9 on the north side of town and taking a free shuttle to the slopes. For **disabled skiers**, adaptive skiing with special seats and equipment is offered by the Breckenridge Outdoor Education Center (ⓣ970/453-6422).

There are plenty of outfitters in Breckenridge, though comparatively few at the actual base of the lifts. **Rental rates** start at around $15 per day for basic ski gear, doubling for top-notch demo gear. Among those offering rentals are Lone Star Sports, corner Four O' Clock Road and Park Avenue (ⓣ970/453-2003), a longstanding local ski store, specializing in personalized fitting services, custom ski tuning, and overnight repair services. Carvers Ski and Snowboard Shop, 203 N Main St (ⓣ970/453-0132, ⓦwww.carverskishop.com), usually has some of the best rental rates in town.

Cross-country

Breckenridge is also well-equipped for cross-country skiers. The largest network of groomed trails in the area is maintained by **Breckenridge Nordic Center**, 1200 Ski Hill Rd (ⓣ970/453-6855), which grooms around sixteen miles of trails in the valleys below peaks 7 and 8. A trail pass is $10 and is interchangeable with that of the Frisco Nordic Center (see p.215). To get further away from the resort scene, try the ten miles of groomed cross-country trails maintained by **Whateley Ranch**, off Hwy-9 north of Breckenridge (ⓣ970/453-2600). The Breckenridge area also has some good **backcountry** Nordic skiing opportunities, particularly south of town near the **Hoosier Pass**, where snow conditions are usually excellent. Several trails from the top of the pass are a good place to start on explorative forays. There are more cross-country skiing opportunities south of Breckenridge at Fairplay (see p.224), and to the west at Copper Mountain (see p.215).

Summer activities

Though winter is still by far the busiest time in Breckenridge, the town is fast becoming a popular destination in summer too, with visitors taking advantage of the cheaper accommodation and plentiful opportunities to hike, bike, fish, and play golf. A popular local **hike** for those looking for some serious exercise is the ascent of Bald Mountain (13,684ft) southeast of Breckenridge, a three- to four-hour round trip from a trailhead off Boreas Pass Road. Another good choice is the Gold Hill Trail south of Breckenridge, which leads hikers up to the crest of the Tenmile Range overlooking a tundra of craggy bald peaks and graceful valleys. The visitor information center can provide printed hiking guides for many routes in the Arapaho National Forest.

The center also supplies the excellent free *Summit County Mountain Bike Guide*, an invaluable resource for **cyclists** exploring the area. Racer's Edge at 114 N Main St in Breckenridge (ⓣ970/453-0995), and Carvers on the same street at no. 203 (ⓣ970/453-0132, ⓦwww.carverskishop.com), both rent good front-suspension bikes for around $30 per day. As at Keystone, Breckenridge Resort runs chairlift rides to the top of the mountains (adult day-pass $18), which, as well as offering stunning views, provide access to great hiking and mountain-biking trails – though expert mountain bikers will find the more exciting terrain at Keystone. Breckenridge Resort also offers **toboggan rides** down the dry SuperSlide (summer daily 9am–5pm; $8), minigolf ($6), and a giant maze ($5).

If you'd like to explore the surrounding mountain range on **horseback** rather than on foot, Breckenridge Stables (ⓣ970/453-4438) offer two-hour trail rides from $32. The Blue River runs through Breckenridge and is a favorite **fly-fishing** spot; Mountain Anglers, 31 S Main St (ⓣ970/453-4665), can provide the requisite licenses and equipment and also organize guided fishing trips. Once voted by *Golf Digest* the top public course in Colorado, **Breckenridge Golf Club** on Tiger Run Road (ⓣ970/453-9104) has green fees of around $70.

Eating

There's a good variety of places to **eat** in Breckenridge and though few are particularly cheap, prices here have a fair way to go before they begin to reach those at Vail or Aspen. Most of the town's nightlife venues offer decent bar food, so check these listings too.

Blue Moose 540 S Main St ⓣ970/453-4859. Inventive international menu, with lots of vegetarian dishes for well under $10. Open for breakfast, when good inexpensive wheat pancakes are on offer, and for lunch, when sandwiches, soups, and salads take over.

Briar Rose 109 E Lincoln St ⓣ970/453-9948. Upscale restaurant in a modern building made atmospheric by addition of old relics – in particular a wonderfully atmospheric Victorian-era saloon bar. The speciality is wild game like elk and venison though there's a dependable range of posh steak and seafood dishes on the menu too.

Bubba's Bones 110 S Ridge St ⓣ970/547-9942. Authentic Southern-style barbecue – hickory-smoked and with a range of homemade sauces – at reasonable prices; entrees cost around $10.

Hearthstone 130 S Ridge St ⓣ970/453-1148. Fine upmarket dining choice in a restored Victorian building. Serving so-called "Rocky Mountain cuisine," the menu includes rack of elk, trout, wild mushrooms, and some delicious slow-roasted prime rib.

Mi Casa 600 S Park Ave ⓣ970/453-2071. The best Mexican food in Summit County, including fine chili rellenos. Most entrees, like the tangy fajitas, are below $10 and the daily happy hour (3–6pm) is also good value. Open for lunch and dinner.

Mountain Java 118 S Ridge St ⓣ970/453-1874. Cozy, book-lined coffeehouse serving healthy lunches, low-fat muffins and gourmet breads along with steaming espresso drinks.

Pika Bagel Bakery & Cafe 500 S Main St ⓣ970/453-6246. Cheerful place to pick up a New York-style bagel sandwich and a fruit smoothie.

The Prospector 130 S Main St ⓣ970/453-6858. Tasty traditional home-cooked breakfasts (including a spicy and excellent huevos rancheros) and lunches that involve traditional American favorites like roasts or meatloaf. Prices are among the lowest in town.

Rasta Pasta 411 S Main St ⓣ970/453-7467. Large helpings of relatively cheap pasta with a Caribbean twist, set against a reggae music soundtrack.

Nightlife

Breckenridge offers the best choice of nightlife in Summit County and has several late-night music venues. Local papers such as the *Summit County Journal* and

Ullr Fest

Horned helmets are de rigeur at the **Ullr Fest** (pronounced "oo-ler"), a Breckenridge festival in honor of the Norse god of snow. Usually beginning in the third week in January, festivities generally kick off on a Monday with the annual International Snow Sculpture Championships and events in the Ullympics, such as Broom Ball and volleyball with snowshoes, and run into the weekend when there's a parade and fireworks. There are a variety of different events and activities daily, including freestyle ski competitions in ski ballet, mogul skiing, and aerial jumping, plus concerts and the opportunity for kids to go ice skating with cartoon characters.

the *Summit Daily News* are a good source of information about what's going on. The **Backstage Theater** by Maggie Pond in the Village at Breckenridge (July–Sept; ☎970/453-0199) put on nightly performances in summer.

Breckenridge Brewery & Pub 600 S Main St ☎970/453-1550. This huge brewpub was one of the first in Colorado and is now a landmark at the southern edge of town. The Avalanche Ale is a superb amber ale and the pub-brewed root beer is also worth a try. The pub's also a dependable option for good bar food – burgers, sandwiches, and salads – from around $7.

Downstairs at Eric's 111 S Main St ☎970/453-1401. Lively basement sports bar, with a good range of microbrews – 120 beers on offer – and a massive menu of filling bar food for the outdoorsy types that gather here.

Gold Pan 103 N Main St ☎970/453-8499. The only place you could get a drink in Colorado during Prohibition, nowadays the *Gold Pan* is a lively saloon and pool hall. There's a daily happy hour from 4 to 7pm, and they serve burritos, pizzas, and soup.

Shamus O'Toole's Roadhouse 115 S Ridge St ☎970/453-2004. Dingy-looking bar attracting a motley crew of bikers, bohemians, and boozers. Rowdy, fun, and with a generous happy hour.

Ullr's Sports Grill 401 S Main St ☎970/453-6060. Small, neighborhood-style sports bar in the center of town with regular promotions and cheap drinks on Tuesdays.

South of Breckenridge: Alma and Fairplay

Ten miles south of Breckenridge lies **Hoosier Pass** (11,541ft), surrounded by terrific high-alpine scenery. The views are particularly spectacular on the southern side, as Hwy-9 swoops down from the Continental Divide into the **South Park Basin**, a windswept basin of flat ranchlands, passing through the tiny no-nonsense community of **Alma**, surrounded by wonderful old mine workings and pristine high-alpine landscapes. To best explore the area, turn off Hwy-9 along CO-8, which starts beside the Alma Fire House. The well-graded dirt road heads west for around six miles before coming to a fork in the road. From here the trails become much rougher, though they're still suitable for two-wheel-drive vehicles. One trail heads north to **Windy Ridge**, a stunningly bleak glacial bowl where you can explore several marked trails. The other trail heads northeast to the **Bristlecone Pine Scenic Area**, one of several alpine areas in Colorado where stunted, slow-growing trees have contorted themselves into wild, twisted shapes over thousands of years in front of stark surrounding treeless ridges. The oldest of the specimens are thought to be among the oldest living organisms on earth, approximately 5000 years old – twice the age of California's giant redwoods. Alma is also the trailhead (marked on highway just south of town) for one of Colorado's most fabled four-wheel-drive routes, over the **Mosquito Pass Road** to Leadville (see p.232) 21 miles away. The first seven miles are fine for regular cars, but the pass soon turns steep and rocky requiring a four-by-four vehicle.

Further south along Hwy-9 is **Fairplay**, where you'll find the refreshingly uncommercialized **South Park City Museum** (mid-May to mid-Oct daily

△ Aspen grove

9am–5pm; $5; ☎719/836-2387), a collection of 35 old buildings moved from abandoned mining towns to form an open-air museum. All the buildings – which include a bank, stagecoach station, general store, and a small onsite brewery – are well preserved or restored, and the 50,000 period artifacts within them give one of the best glimpses into life as it must have been during Colorado's early mining days.

The Sawatch and Elk Mountains

The **Sawatch** and **Elk Mountains** contain Colorado's most famed ski resort towns: **Vail** and **Aspen**, both of which offer undeniably fantastic skiing. They are, unfortunately, also cursed by high prices and glitzy pretentiousness that make the other local towns, including the splendid old mining town of **Leadville** and the modest, rather functional **Glenwood Springs**, seem like a breath of fresh air. But love them or hate them, you have to admit that both Vail and especially Aspen lie in a beautiful part of the country and one which teems with high, picturesque mountains harboring some of the finest outdoor recreation opportunities in the state. So even if the monetary excesses of the major resorts aren't to your taste or in your budget, it's worth taking the time to explore the area and particularly in summer it's easy to be part of the action without blowing all your money.

Vail and around

Compared to most other Colorado ski towns, **VAIL**, 120 miles west of Denver on I-70, is a new creation. Only a handful of farmers lived here before the resort was opened in 1952. Built as a relatively unimaginative collection of Tyrolean-style chalets and concrete-block condominiums, at least the town is a compact and pedestrian-friendly place, albeit pockmarked by pricey fashion boutiques and high-priced, often painfully pretentious, restaurants. Vail Resorts who operate the ski area at Vail also own its exclusive sidekick, **Beaver Creek**, eleven miles farther west on I-70. This gated resort, full of Alpine-castle-style resort hotels, is even more exclusive than Vail, but both skiers and snowboarders visiting the area will enjoy the fact that tickets between the two are interchangeable, creating a formidable winter sport offer. Between the two large resorts lie a couple of modest little towns: Miniturn, a small railroad town next to the Eagle river, is dotted with galleries and antique stores and Avon is a nondescript sprawling service town. Neither are of too much consequence to visitors, though you might find them useful as a source of less-expensive accommodation or food.

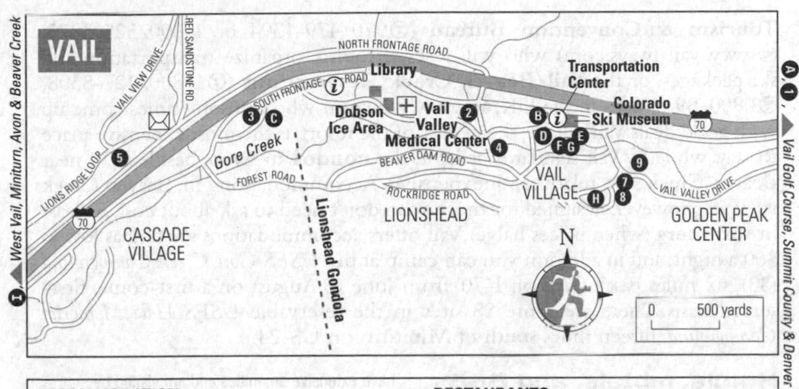

ACCOMMODATION				RESTAURANTS			
Best Western Vailglo Lodge	3	Roost Lodge	5	Blu's	F	Pazzo's	D
Chateau Vail-Holiday Inn	2	Simba Run	1	Covered Bridge Coffee	E	Seasons at the Green	A
Christiania Lodge	8	Sonnenalp Resort	4	DJ's Classic Diner	C	Sweet Basil	G
Manor Vail Lodge	6	Tivoli Lodge	7	Hubcap Brewery	B	Vendetta's	H
				Jackalope	I		

Arrival, information, and getting around

From Denver International Airport, several companies offer **shuttles** to Vail and Beaver Creek, including Supershuttle (☎1-800/258-3826) and Colorado Mountain Express (☎1-800/222-2112); expect to pay around $60 one-way for the three-hour trip. Less convenient, but far cheaper is the **Greyhound bus**, which stops at the Vail Transportation Center, 31 S Frontage Rd, on its way back and forth between Denver and Grand Junction. **Eagle County Airport** lies just 35 miles west from the resort. Vail Valley Transportation (☎970/476-8008 or 1-800/882-8872) offers shuttles from the airport to Vail for $32.

Vail has two main **visitor centers**, one at the Transportation Center (see above; ☎970/479-1394) and a Lionshead office (☎970/479-1385) beside the parking garage. An additional visitor service, the **Vail Valley Hotline** (☎970/476-8696) provides up-to-date prerecorded information on road conditions and current local events. For information on local national forest lands, contact the **White River National Forest Holy Cross Ranger Station** (☎970/827-5715), near the I-70 junction with US-24 to Miniturn.

Vail spreads for eight miles along the narrow valley floor, with successive nuclei from east to west at Vail Village, Lionshead, Cascade Village, and West Vail. The entire complex is pedestrianized with no charge for the central parking lots in summer – in winter only those on the very edge of Vail remain free – and is served by free shuttle buses to the lifts. **Vail Buses** (☎970/328-8143) also run free shuttles year-round between different areas of town; schedules are printed in the *Vail Valley* magazine. Public buses also run to **Beaver Creek** and **Avon** ($3), in winter, on the half-hour 6am–2am. Vail Resorts Express (☎970/469-8245) runs a shuttle service to **Summit County** resorts.

Accommodation

In winter finding an affordable **place to stay** can be a problem as the valley's filled with grand lodges and luxury hotels: because the town is new, friendly little B&Bs are all but absent. Your best bet is to contact the **Vail Valley**

Tourism & Convention Bureau (Ⓣ970/479-1394 or 1-800/525-3875, Ⓦwww.vailalways.com) who will reserve rooms, organize transportation and ski packages, or the **Vail/Beaver Creek Reservations** (Ⓣ1-800/427-8308, Ⓣ0800/891772 from the UK; Ⓦwww.vail.com) who can sometimes come up with good deals. Vail Village, the center of the resort, is the most expensive place to stay, while by Vail standards at least, the **condos** in Avon, beside I-70 near Beaver Creek, are relatively inexpensive. Accommodations in Beaver Creek itself are, however, designed for those who don't need to ask about cost. At least in **summers** (when prices halve), Vail offers accommodations starting as low as $60 a night, and in addition you can camp at the *USFS Gore Creek Campground* ($8), six miles east of Vail on I-70, from June to August on a first-come, first-served basis. There are more $8 sites in the reservable *USFS Hale Memorial Campground*, fifteen miles south of Miniturn on US-24.

Hotels, motels, and B&Bs

Best Western Vailglo Lodge 701 W Lionshead Circle, Vail Ⓣ970/476-5506 or 1-800/528-1234. Pleasant chain lodgings a handy two-minute walk from the Lionshead gondola. Rates include a continental breakfast and access to the pool, sauna, and guest laundry. 6

Chateau Vail-Holiday Inn 13 Vail Rd, Vail Ⓣ970/476-5631 or 1-800/451-9840. Central upscale chain motel, with functional rooms, an outdoor pool and hot tub and its own bar. 6

Christiania Lodge 356 E Hanson Ranch Rd, Vail Ⓣ970/476-5641. Bavarian-style suites, rooms and condos in central Vail, within walking distance of the lifts. Rates include a complimentary breakfast, outdoor pool, and sauna. 7

Comfort Inn 161 W Beaver Creek Blvd, Avon Ⓣ970/949-5511 or 1-800/423-4374. Economical chain hotel, though the nearest restaurants are a drive away. There's a pool and continental breakfast is included. 6

Eagle River Inn 145 N Main St, Miniturn Ⓣ970/827-5761 or 1-800/344-1750. B&B decked out in tasteful Santa Fe-style in the small town of Miniturn, seven miles south of Vail on US-24. 7

Hyatt Regency Beaver Creek 136 Thomas Pl, Beaver Creek Ⓣ970/949-1234 or 1-800/233-1234. The hub of Beaver Creek village has almost three hundred spacious and luxuriously furnished rooms. Amenities include fitness center with classes, full-service spa, pool, hot tubs, restaurants, a concierge, and ski and parking valets. 8

Miniturn Inn 442 Main St, Miniturn Ⓣ970/827-9647. Friendly B&B where rooms have been decorated along local themes – including angling and Nordic skiing. Some rooms have their own fireplace and hot tub and there's a sauna. 6

The Pines Lodge 141 Scott Hill Rd, Beaver Creek Ⓣ970/845-7900 or 1-800/859-8242. Opulently decorated lodge close to Chair 12 – which provides a cross-resort ride to the base area. Rooms have extensive amenities and are visited by housekeepers three times a day. Included are a full breakfast, après-ski snacks and afternoon tea as well as ski waxing and valet, laundry service and use of an outdoor pool, whirlpool, saunas, fitness equipment, and a library. 8

Roost Lodge 1783 N Frontage Rd, Vail Ⓣ970/476-5451 or 1-800/873-3065. Generally Vail's cheapest lodging option, this A-frame lodge offers motel-standard rooms on the north side of the interstate in West Vail. Rates are inclusive of a continental breakfast and a free hourly shuttle to town and ski areas. Facilities include an outdoor pool and hot tub. 6

Sonnenalp Resort 20 Vail Rd, Vail Ⓣ970/476-5656 or 1-800/654-8312, Ⓦwww.sonnenalp.com. Terrific resort bang in the center of Vail's pedestrian area. Accommodations are split between three equally delightful, but distinct buildings: the Bavaria Haus, the Austria Haus, and the Swiss Chalet, decorated in the corresponding styles. The hotel offers a splendid fitness facility with pools and hot tubs, and rates include the superb breakfasts. The best deals are packages that can include the likes of skiing, golf, and spa treatments from $150 per person per day. But during the winter peak season you won't get a room here for under $450 per night. 9

Tivoli Lodge 386 Hanson Ranch Rd, Vail Ⓣ970/476-5615 or 1-800/451-4756. One of Vail's more inexpensive options in a handy location, midway between Vail Village and Golden Peak. Room rates include a continental breakfast and use of an outdoor pool, whirlpool, and sauna. 6

Condos

Christie Lodge 47 E Beaver Creek Blvd, Avon Ⓣ970/949-7700 or 1-800/551-4326. Dreary looking condo with small basic suites, but with kitchenettes and fireplaces at prices that are cheap by Vail standards. Handy for skiing Beaver Creek, use of a pool, hot tubs, sauna, athletic club, and laundry are included. ⑤

Manor Vail Lodge 595 E Vail Valley Drive, Vail ⓣ970/476-5651 or 1-800/950-VAIL. Revamped 1960s condo complex at the base of Golden Peak. All units have kitchens, fireplaces, and balconies or patios and access to an outdoor pool, hot tub, and sauna. ⑦

Simba Run 1100 Fall Line Drive, Vail ⓣ970/476-0344 or 1-800/321-1489. Less-expensive condo complex in West Vail. All the spacious units are privately owned and so vary in decor. A private shuttle runs into town during the winter. The complex is served by a large indoor pool, an exercise room, a hot tub, and a steam room. ⑥

Vail

According to *SKI* magazine, **Vail** (ⓣ970/476-5601 or 1-800/525-2257, snow report ⓣ970/476-4888, ⓦwww.vail.com) is the top ski destination in the US – but not for its aesthetic beauty. What lures the ultra-rich (more conspicuous here than in Aspen) between mid-November to late April is the exceptional quality and quantity of snow (annually 346 inches), the sheer variety of terrain, and the huge number of lifts that serve the ski area – at 5289 acres the largest in the US.

Vail's real forte is its bowl skiing and boarding. The ski-area extends from one vast treeless bowl to another, providing an experience unlike that anywhere else in Colorado. Each of Vail's seven, largely ungroomed, back bowls has its own distinct personality – and certainly different parts are better at different parts of the day. On powder days, snowboarders, in particular, will enjoy being able to carve fat turns, swinging across the sprawling bowls – before heading to the long half-pipe on Golden Peak or Lionshead. But with 87 percent of these back-bowls classified as expert terrain (though large areas are suitable for confident intermediates), the most exciting parts of the resort are rather wasted on the beginner. As a whole the resort's terrain breaks down as 18 percent beginner, 29 percent intermediate, and 53 percent advanced. As with all else in Vail, skiing here is an expensive affair (**lift tickets** costing around $65 a day), as is eating at lifttop restaurants. *Camp 21* at the top of Chair 14 is the only budget choice for food and even has some self-service microwaves to use if you're brown-bagging it. Among the many **outfitters** in Vail are Vail Sports, who have six branches around town including one at, 227 Wall St (ⓣ970/479-0600), near the Vail Village ticket window. If you feel you have exhausted the vast possibilities of Vail's terrain, consider hiring a snowcat to more pristine, **backcountry skiing**. Nova Guides 82 E Beaver Creek Blvd, Avon (ⓣ970/949-4232) shuttle skiers and boarders into the backcountry in the White River National Forest around Vail. Half a day costs around $60.

The Colorado Ski Museum

For a look at the development of skiing in Colorado investigate the excellent **Colorado Ski Museum and Hall of Fame**, 231 S Frontage Rd (Tues–Sun 10am–5pm; free; ⓣ970/476-1876). Exhibits, videos, and wonderful old photos chart the evolution of the sport here – from Finnish-style snow-glide-shoes used as early transportation, to today's high-tech recreational skiing and snowboarding. The museum also has early gear from 10th Mountain Division, the famed mountain regiment (see p.237), some of whose veterans have been included in the Hall of Fame for their role in developing the local ski industry.

Beaver Creek

Newer and snootier than Vail, **Beaver Creek** (☎970/949-5750 or 1-800/622-3131, snow reports: ☎970/476-4888, Ⓦwww.beavercreek.com) was developed by Vail Associates in 1980, when a successful lettuce-growing valley was transformed into a gated resort of luxury lodges and condos, connected by outdoor escalators. Like Vail, Beaver Creek is blessed with good snow, with around 330 inches falling annually. But while Vail's bleak back-bowls are missing from the terrain here, Beaver Creek has a fine array of glades and 146 mostly narrow runs spread across the mountain. The 1625-acre terrain – divided up as 34 percent beginner, 39 percent intermediate, and 27 percent advanced – is spread across the mountain in a rather odd way, with the large beginner area being near the top while some of the steepest expert runs descend into the base area. This makes Bachelor Gulch, to the south of the mountain a better beginner area. Intermediate level skiers will enjoy village hopping on groomed intermediate runs that link sections of the mountain together, while experts will be at home on the challenging World Cup terrain of the acclaimed Birds of Prey race course area. Whatever the level of your skiing, Beaver Creek's **ski school** is considered as good as any in the US. Tickets to ski Beaver Creek are interchangeable with those for Vail ($65). Those not staying at the resort are best off parking near Avon and taking a free shuttle up to the slopes.

Other winter activities

Vail and Beaver Creek operate three cross-country ski centers, the largest of which is the **Beaver Creek Cross Country Ski Center** (☎970/845-5313), which maintains fifteen miles of trails at both the bottom and top of the Strawberry Park lift. In Vail, the golf course clubhouse becomes the **Vail Nordic Center**, 1778 Sunburst Drive (☎970/476-8366 or 1-800/525-2257) in winter, grooming its grounds for ten miles of track skiing and skating. Also in Vail is the **Golden Peak Cross Country Ski Touring Center** (☎970/845-5313), which has the best backcountry access to Vail Mountain and the White River National Forest. On Thursdays an all-day nature tour from here includes a gourmet lunch and costs around $70.

Opportunities to do other winter activities are well developed at Vail, which has its own mountaintop activity center, **Adventure Ridge** (winter only; 9am–10pm; ☎970/476-9090) at the top the Lionshead Gondola. Facilities here range from an outdoor **skating rink** ($4) and a **tubing hill** ($12 an hour) to the chance to speed down a 3000ft **bobsleigh** run at $15 a time.

To explore the area by **snowmobile**, contact Nova Guides 82 E Beaver Creek Blvd, Avon (☎970/949-4232), who will pick you up from your hotel to take one of a number of their tours – from an hour ($50) to the day-long Top of the Rockies tour ($150) that climbs to 13,000ft. If you'd rather be pulled by a dozen dogs try Wolf Canyon Mushers (☎970/328-6930), who charge around $125 a person for a half-day tour through forests.

Summer activities

As the regular host of the Mountain Bike World Cup, Vail is well placed to offer visitors lots of quality **mountain biking** trails. The most obvious place to head is to the 100 miles of trails in the ski area, serviced by two of its lifts (mid-June to Aug daily 10am–4.30pm; $16) and marked on free maps available from the lift ticket offices. While the hairiest parts of the World Cup downhill courses have either been tamed down or removed, riders of all abilities will find plenty of good riding on the hill. The cross-country course is at the base of the hill and can comfortably be ridden without using a lift. Best of the local stores offering rentals (front-suspension for $30 per day) is Vail Bicycle Services, 450 E Lionshead Circle (℡970/476-1233). Local **road bikers** like to head on the Canyon Trail cycle-path over Vail pass, an eight-mile climb on the way to Frisco another 11 miles from the top of the pass.

It's possible to **hike** around Vail's ski area but the bald runs and ski-infrastructure spoil the outdoor experience. Better to head to Beaver Creek, where it's easier to leave the resort trappings behind. A good six-mile round-trip heads out-and-back to Beaver Lake, taking around three or four hours. There are many more hiking trails outside the ski areas and a particularly convenient network from Vail is the North Trail system; a twelve-mile multiple-use trail network on the valley's north side. One easily accessible trailhead to this network lies beside a parking lot off Red Sandstone Road on the edge of town. The difficult Notch Mountain Trail, which climbs just short of 3000 feet in under five miles, also begins in Vail and heads to the Mount of the Holy Cross, a peak made famous in the black-and-white photos of one William Henry Jackson. The local visitors' center in Vail can help out with details of these and other local hikes, as can the Vail Nature Center, 841 Vail Valley Drive (℡970/479-2291). The best source of information for longer trips, however, is the USFS Ranger office near Miniturn (see p.227).

If you're in the Vail valley in May, consider donning a wetsuit to go **white-water rafting** in the Eagle river, running the fun Class IV Dowd Chutes before moving on to more sedate Class II and III water further down. Trips usually run for half a day and cost around $65. After May local waters are a little too low for good rafting, but are still ideal for learning how to **kayak**; Alpine Kayak & Canoe, 40690 US-6 in Avon (℡970/949-3350), offers a two-day beginner course costing $135, including all rental gear. One adventurous local company that runs river-trips throughout the summer are Lakota River Guides (℡970/476-RAFT or 1-800/274-0636, Ⓦwww.lakotariver.com), who also do several extreme trips that few other commercial companies offer. This includes the local Gore Canyon in August and September, generally considered one of the ultimate commercially raftable challenges in state. Tours begin with a 500ft rappel, before crossing the river on a harness system to get to the put-in. The river itself is full of Class V rapids that require a pretty gung-ho attitude.

Golfing holidays are a big summer money-maker for Vail, and golfers have a selection of nine courses in the valley, ranging from the pricey Beaver Creek Resort Golf Club (℡970/949-7123) to the fun and more affordable Eagle-Vail Golf Course (℡970/949-5267), the public course between Vail and Avon.

Eating

Eating out in Vail is expensive, and in Beaver Creek – where reservations are required at most restaurants – even more so. But at least the food is generally of a very high standard. It's also worth heading out to Miniturn to dine at places frequented by the local workforce, where there's some good inexpensive Mexican food to be had.

Beano's Cabin *Beaver Creek Resort* ℡970/949-9090. It's unlikely lettuce farmer Frank Bienkowski ever expected his secluded cabin to become the poshest place to dine in the valley. In winter diners are towed here by snowcat-drawn sleigh to a six-course gourmet meal ($85), in summer on horseback or by horse-drawn wagon, for the one-hour trip. The food is superb and there are plenty of entrees to choose from. Open mid-Dec to Sept.

Blu's 193 E Gore Creek Drive, Vail ℡970/476-

3113. Relaxed restaurant with some of Vail's most modest prices; serves American breakfasts, soups, salads, pizzas for lunches and dinners (entrees from around $10), and great desserts.

Chili Willy's 101 Main St, Miniturn ☎970/827-5887. Casual, inexpensive place in Miniturn is a good place to dig into great Tex-Mex – particularly the fajitas – and knock back a couple of margaritas.

Covered Bridge Coffee ☎970/479-2883. Good place to start the day with a coffee, pastries, bagels, and to nip into for a lunchtime deli sandwich.

DJ's Classic Diner 616 W Lionshead Circle, Vail ☎970/476-2336. A breath of fresh air in the otherwise fairly stuffy dining scene comes in the form of this fairly priced 24hr diner (during ski season, shorter hours outside). Pick up all the usual American favorites, omelettes or burritos, or enjoy the Vail touch – dessert crepes and a wine list.

Hubcap Brewery Vail Village ☎970/476-5757. Bustling brewpub, with some good ales and a dependable menu of inexpensive bar food based largely around steaks and burgers.

Jackalope West Vail Mall ☎970/476-4314. Lively saloon and pool hall serving affordable basic food, even breakfasts, including a large, satisfying huevos rancheros for $7.

Pazzo's Willow Bridge Rd ☎970/476-9026. Pizza by the slice and good hearty portions of lasagna ($10) make *Pazzo's* a ski-bum favorite.

Seasons at the Green Restaurant Vail Golf Course, 1778 Vail Valley Drive ☎970/476-8057. The gourmet food at one of Vail's top restaurants is only half of the attraction – the horse-drawn sleighs to and from the restaurant, around Vail Golf Course, make up the other half. The experience costs around $55 and reservations are required.

Sweet Basil 193 E Gore Creek Drive ☎970/476-0125. Snug expensive bistro overlooking Gore Creek and serving imaginative dishes – like the apple and jicama salad or the portobello mushroom and goat's cheese tarts – as well as having a good line in seafood pasta. Entrees start around $20.

Turntable Restaurant 160 Main St, Miniturn ☎970/827-4164. One of several inexpensive options in Miniturn, the *Turntable* is decorated with railroad memorabilia and serves cheap, filling breakfasts, burgers, tacos, and burritos (from $5). Open 5.30am–10.30pm.

Vendetta's 291 Bridge St, Vail ☎970/476-5070. Elegant restaurant with views of Vail Mountain (you can dine outside on a deck in summer) serving fine Italian lunch specials and pasta dinners; entrees start from $15.

Nightlife

Nightlife in Vail revolves around Bridge Street in Vail Village. Most people tour between the bars and discos, most of which regularly host live music; the local *Vail Daily* is good for listings. The checklist of places to see and be seen includes *The Club* (☎970/479-0556), a basement bar with loud rock; the *Hong Kong Café*, 227 Wall St (☎970/476-1818), a small venue where crowds spill outside and loud music rules upstairs at *Vendetta's* (the ski patrol hang-out); and *Nick's* (☎970/476-5011), below *Russell's Restaurant*, which plays reasonable dance music. The *Hubcap Brewery* (see above) is another dependably busy option, with regular live music. For those wishing to hear piano or blues, head to the laid-back *Club Chelsea* (☎970/476-5600) which tends to attract a much older crowd.

In July and August, free Tuesday night concerts are held at 6.30pm at the Gerald Ford Amphitheater, 530 S Frontage Rd (☎970/476-2918). The music varies drastically between the likes of jazz, soul, and rock. Classical performances, part of the Colorado Music Festival (☎970/827-5700) can be heard on weekends during the same months.

Leadville and around

Sitting at an elevation of over ten thousand feet, the wonderfully atmospheric old mining town of **LEADVILLE** has magnificent views across the base of the wide, flat Arkansas Valley to broad-shouldered, ice-laden mountains. Approaching the town, located 38 miles south of Vail on US-24, your

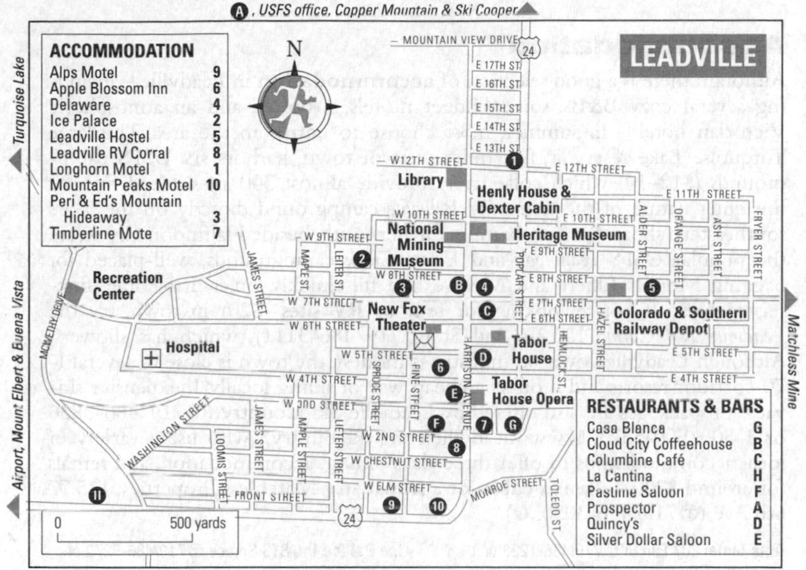

first impression is likely to be of giant slag heaps and disused mining sheds. Don't let this put you off: Leadville is rich in character and romance, abounding with tales of gunfights, miners dying of exposure, and graveyards being excavated to get at seams.

The town boomed in the 1880s due to the area's phenomenally high concentrations of precious ores; not only gold and silver, but also molybdenum, manganese, and zinc. It was then the largest smelting center in the country, boasting around 15,000 residents served by four churches, 120 saloons and 188 gambling houses. Over the last century the town has shrunk to an eighth of its former size, and while most of its former businesses have disappeared, a large network of old mining trails around town remain. This network offers splendid opportunities for mountain biking and, in winter, exploration on cross-country skis or snowmobiles. These trails are the setting for Leadville's outrageously hard endurance bike and foot races – both a hundred miles long – held in late August. Leadville is also best placed for ascents of Colorado's two tallest peaks: **mounts Elbert** (14,433ft) and **Massive** (14,421ft), which are both relatively easy to bag, and so are busy with hikers throughout the summer.

Arrival and information

Leadville is not served by any form of public transportation, so the best option for those without a car is Dee Hive Tours & Transportation (Ⓣ719/486-2339), who charge $65 for their **shuttle service** to Denver – but stipulate a four-person minimum. Leadville's helpful **visitor center**, 809 Harrison Ave (June–Sept daily 10am–5pm; Ⓣ719/486-3900 or 1-800/939-3901, Ⓦwww.leadvilleusa.com), is at the north end of downtown. For detailed information on the local national forest areas contact the USFS Leadville Ranger Station, 2015 Poplar St (Ⓣ790/486-0749), on the northern edge of town.

Accommodation

Although there is a good selection of **accommodation** in Leadville – including several cozy B&Bs, some budget motels, a hostel, and an atmospheric Victorian hotel – in summer, most choose to **camp** in the area. The large Turquoise Lake reservoir, five miles west of town, harbors six USFS campgrounds ($12–14) which collectively provide almost 300 sites. Head first for the quiet nature of the tent-only *Bellevue* campground directly on the lake's southeastern shore. Around six miles further south, beside Halfmoon Creek, are the popular USFS *Halfmoon* and *Elbert Creek* campgrounds, well-placed for bagging Mounts Elbert and Massive and fill quickly on a first-come, first-served basis. If you're looking for tent or RV sites ($20) in town, try the *Leadville RV Corral*, 135 W 2nd St (ⓣ719/486-3111), which has showers. Although Leadville's own ski industry is modest, the town is close to several I-70 corridor resorts and it offers a cheap way of skiing locally. Inexpensive ski-vacation packages are also offered by Leadville Ski Country (ⓣ719/486-3836 or 1-800/500-5323, ⓦwww.leadville.com/skicountry), who use a variety of local accommodations to offer three-days' skiing, accommodation, and rentals for around $200. To rent a **cabin** or a **house**, try Matchless Properties, 115 W 6th Ave (ⓣ719/486-3030; ❻).

Alps Motel 207 Elm St ⓣ719/486-1223 or 1-800/818-2577. Great-value, clean motel on the southern edge of town. Some units have fridges and microwaves; all have phones and cable TV. ❸

Apple Blossom Inn 120 W 4th St ⓣ719/486-2141 or 1-800/982-9279, ⓦwww.colorado-bnb.com/abi. Centrally located and stylish B&B in wonderful old Victorian property – most rooms are regal affairs, paneled in dark wood, some with stained glass. Top floor apartment sleeps up to nine but is good value even for four. The breakfasts are first rate, as are the afternoon brownies. The hot tub is in a peaceful spot in the back garden. ❺

Delaware Hotel 700 Harrison Ave ⓣ719/486-1418 or 1-800/748-2004, ⓦwww.delawarehotel.com. Grand old Victorian-era hotel in the center of town, that in the 1880s provided lodgings for the likes of Doc Holliday and Billy the Kid. Despite extensive restoration, the period look has been maintained with floral carpeting and polished oak, brass beds, and lace curtains. The good-value room-rates include a simple cooked breakfast. Ski packages are offered in the winter. Hot tub available. ❹

Grand West Village Resort 99 Grand West Rd ⓣ719/486-0702 or 1-800/691-3999, ⓦwww.grandwest.com. Modest condo complex between Leadville and Ski Cooper, in a forest overlooking the Arkansas River Valley, and handy for outdoor activities. Units have gas fireplaces, TVs with VCRs, jetted tubs, and shared laundry facilities. ❻

Ice Palace Inn 813 Spruce ⓣ719/486-8272 or 1-800/754-2840, ⓦwww.icepalaceinn.com. B&B located on Capitol Hill a few short blocks west of town where the town's Ice Palace once stood and built from lumber retrieved from it. Rooms are richly decorated with lots of old curios – friendly hosts can offer good advice on local hikes and cook gourmet breakfasts. Hot tub. ❺

Leadville Hostel 500 E 7th St ⓣ719/486-9334, ⓦwww.leadvillehostel.com. Friendly hostel, where dorm beds run $15–20 depending on season. Facilities include a large kitchen, games room, laundry, and internet. The accommodating owner will also arrange shuttles to trailheads. ❷

Longhorn Motel 1515 Poplar St ⓣ719/486-3155. Budget motel close to town. With small refrigerators, phones, and cable TV. Good-value weekly rates. ❷

Mountain Peaks Motel 1 Harrison Ave ⓣ719/486-3178 or 1-888/215-7040. Clean, comfortable motel just north of downtown. Some units have kitchenettes. ❷

Peri & Ed's Mountain Hideaway 201 W 8th St ⓣ719/486-8272, ⓦwww.mountainhideaway.com. Creaky old house close to the center of town, with friendly landlady (providing hearty breakfasts) and good communal guest facilities: kitchen, lounge, games-room, and a scenic outdoor hot tub. ❸

Timberline Motel 216 Harrison Ave ⓣ719/486-1876. Slightly institutional-feeling, clean and economical downtown motel with cable TV and phones as well as communal hot tub. ❸

The Town

The best place to start an exploration of the town and its surroundings is at the town's **visitor center** (see p.233). The center is not only replete with activity-specific recreation maps, but also screens (on demand) a short film on the town's local history, a simple affair but featuring evocative oral histories. You can also pick up the magazine-format *Leadville Walking Tour* here, which gives you the salient details for most of the older buildings along the town's main street.

In the light of the insight the film offers, visiting Leadville's rambling **National Mining Hall of Fame and Museum**, 120 W 9th St (summer daily 9am–5pm; rest of year Mon–Fri 10am–2pm; $3.50), is a patchy experience. It's best to skip the museum's mining industry propaganda films (global warming isn't all bad and landscapes can look better after mining) in favor of the lurid globs of precious minerals, reconstructed mine-passages and atmospheric old photos of weatherbeaten prospectors. The museum's hall of fame is dedicated to mining's kingpins – mostly graying white gentlemen – and also of little interest.

For a more illuminating romp through the town's grim early history, head for the **Heritage Museum**, further down the road at 102 E 9th St (mid-May to Nov daily 10am–6pm; $2.50). Glass cases hold snippets on local fraternal organizations, quack doctors, music-hall stars and the like, while a host of smoky photographs portray the lawless boomtown that in two years grew from a mining camp of 200 people into Colorado's second-largest city. Some old gear of the 10th Mountain Division (see p.237) is on display as well. The museum also has a large foam reconstruction of Leadville's **Ice Palace**, which had been a fanciful attempt by the town to pull in visitors and create jobs. The ice structure – which featured ice walls eight-feet thick and fifty feet high surrounding a ballroom, skating rink, restaurant, and even a peep show – took three months to build, went ten times over budget and despite attracting gawkers in the thousands, was a struggle to maintain. Eventually all investors pulled out, leaving it to melt.

Horace Tabor and Baby Doe

Of all Leadville's extraordinary tales, the story of **Horace Tabor** is perhaps the most compelling – a classic account of rags-to-riches and back again. Having given up on his own luck to find gold in Colorado, Tabor became a storekeeper in Leadville, supplying goods to prospectors in exchange for a share in potential profits. He hit lucky when two prospectors developed a silver mine that produced $20 million inside a year. Tabor collected a one-third share and left his wife to marry local blue-eyed waitress "Baby Doe" McCourt in *the* wedding of 1883 in Washington DC, which was attended by President Chester Arthur. For a long time Tabor lived a lifestyle that involved trading mines by day and sleeping in silk nightshirts with diamond buttons by night. But by the time of his death in 1899, he was financially ruined thanks to both investment errors and the 1893 silver crash. On his death, **Baby Doe** returned to Leadville to his only remaining mine, hoping for a turn of fortune in the industry, only to become a recluse during her 36 years of residence in the mine's simple cabin, before finally dying there, emaciated and frostbitten. The wooden outhouses of the **Matchless Mine** still stand, two miles out on 7th Street, and in the crude wooden shack in which she died, guides recount the story of Baby Doe's bizarre life in full, fascinating detail (daily 9am–4.15pm; $3).

Also worth a look are two of the town's earliest remaining houses, **Healy House** and **Dexter Cabin** (June–Aug 10am–4.30pm; $3.50), up behind the Heritage Museum. The former is a grandiose Greek-revival clapboard house, the latter a modest rough-hewn cabin mostly used as a gambling den. While you can poke around the Dexter Cabin on your own, you'll be given a tour of the Healy House which was, for a time, a boarding house, and has now been furnished to represent that purpose and era. One exhibit in the house is a sheet signed by local bigwigs, and subsequently embroidered to represent a kind of Victorian *Who's Who* for the town – amongst the names is the mark of the now legendary Horace Tabor (see box, overleaf).

Also downtown, don't miss the **Tabor Opera House**, 308 Harrison Ave (June–Oct Sun–Fri 9am–5.30pm; $4), where you're free to wander onto the stage and around the eerie, dusty old dressing rooms while recorded oral histories tell tales of the grand old theater's golden days. They give no details, sadly, of the time in 1882 when Oscar Wilde, garbed in black-velvet knee britches and diamonds, addressed a host of dozing miners on the "Practical Application of the Aesthetic Theory to Exterior and Interior House Decoration with Observations on Dress and Personal Ornament." For a closer look into the Tabor story, visit the **Tabor House**, ($2), 116 E 5th St. It's now been reconstructed to look as at did in 1877 when Horace resided here with his first wife, Augusta.

Outdoor activities

The obvious attractions for fit **hikers** are the ascents of **Mount Massive** and **Mount Elbert**, most popularly started from the Colorado Trail trailheads beside Halfmoon Creek around seven miles southwest of town. Both are strenuous hikes, although the trail up each is relatively straightforward, with no real scrambling or full-body climbing involved. The average time for the return trip to the top of either peak from Halfmoon Creek is around six hours – and, due to frequent afternoon lightning storms, it's worth planning to have the hike completed around midday. A good level hike, ideal for acclimatization, goes around the northern and eastern perimeters of **Turquoise Lake**. From around the lake there are great views over the water of the Mount Massive Wilderness, with the eponymous mountain at its center.

Mountain bikers also use the lakeside trail, the most technically challenging riding in the area. If combined with a road climb northeast from the lake, this can be made into a good twenty-mile loop descending on a fast dirt road beside the St Kevin Gulch after reaching fine views over town. A section of this route is used for the **Leadville 100**, the town's August hundred-mile mountain-bike race. Another high-energy route, detailed in a free guide from the visitors' center, is the **Mineral Belt Tour** – which guides you around an excellent twelve-and-a-half-mile loop, half of which is through the old Leadville mining district, while the other half snakes through aspen groves, conifer forests, and wildflower meadows. Bill's Sport Shop, 225 Harrison Ave (☎719/486-0739), **rents** out basic rigid mountain bikes for $25 per day.

In **winter** there's no end of excellent **cross-country ski** opportunities in the area, from quick jaunts on the groomed Mineral Belt Tour (see above) to the huge sprawling network of backcountry trails connecting the 10th Mountain Division Hut System (see box, opposite). The most popular areas to ski are however north of town off US-24 before it crests the Continental Divide to drop into Miniturn. Here the **Tennessee Pass Trail System**, around thirteen miles from Leadville, offers a network of ski trails tailored to the needs of novice to intermediate skiers. There are further cross-country skiing opportunities on more regularly groomed trails from the local ski resort **Ski Cooper** (Ⓣ719/486-3684, Ⓦwww.skicooper.com), which lies just eight miles north of Leadville along US-24. Of course, more people come to the small down-to-earth resort to downhill ski or snowboard – attracted by the unpretentious atmosphere, uncrowded slopes, and inexpensive tickets. It's one of Colorado's smaller ski areas with only four lifts and 26 runs, spread over 365 acres (thirty percent beginner, forty percent intermediate, thirty percent

10th Mountain Division and its Hut System

Set up during World War II, the **10th Mountain Division** was envisioned as an elite corps of crack troops for missions against the Nazis in the snow-covered regions of mountainous Europe. America's only winter warfare unit, the Mountain Divison not only made several indispensable contributions to the war, but later, as veterans returned, became a major force in the development of skiing as a major recreation pursuit.

The 14,000 mountain troops were originally stationed at Camp Hale (dubbed Camp Hell) near Vail, which became the hub for exercises in which soldiers would strike out into the backcountry with ninety pounds of gear in their rucksacks, skiing on seven-and-a-half-foot-long hickory boards at altitudes of over 13,000 feet. Conditions were extraordinarily tough although great pains were taken to make life easier. The first snowmobiles, motorized toboggans, and snowcats were all developed as a result of these endeavours. The Division's most significant entry into the history books came on the night of Februrary 18, 1945 near Florence, Italy. Having climbed the 2000ft escarpment of Riva Ridge in the dark, the division ambushed the German forces in foggy conditions, taking first the ridge, and on the next day Mount Belvedere. Both actions were later hailed as turning points in the war. During the fighting 992 10th Mountain men were killed (more than 4000 wounded); a memorial to the dead stands at the summit of Tennesse Pass, on the Continental Divide south of Camp Hale.

On their return, many 10th Division soldiers seemed naturally attracted to stay near snow and on skis: over 2000 became ski instructors, and it is claimed that 62 present-day American ski resorts were either founded or originally run by veterans. In Colorado, these included the development of both Aspen and Vail.

The development of the **10th Mountain Division Hut System**, 1280 Ute Ave, Aspen (Ⓣ970/925-5775, Ⓦwww.huts.org), was also the brainchild of a former 10th Division soldier. The system enables access to hundreds of miles of scenic backcountry mountain trails that sprawl over 34 square miles of national forest between Leadville, Aspen, and Vail. Well-marked and well-used trails connect the seventeen huts and a maze of side routes enable the creation of any number of different multiday routes to ski, hike, or bike. While these routes are suitable for less-experienced skiers, skiing hut-to-hut requires a high level of fitness and winter wilderness skills; flawless map, route-finding, and compass skills are essential.

Each of the huts is furnished with basic necessities like wood, a stove, electric lights, and cookware; mattresses up the comfort level of the sleeping quarters. Most sleep around sixteen people. Two of the nicest huts are the Shrine Mountain Inn and the Fowler/Hilliard huts. To reserve a place in a hut (between $22 and $35 per person per night) call 10th Mountain Division Hut System, who can also reserve places for the even more remote Alfred A. Braun Hut System, which encompasses six huts between Aspen and Crested Butte. Reservations should be made well in advance for winter and are taken from June 1st for the following season. Paragon Guides (Ⓣ970/926-5299, Ⓦwww.paragonguides.com) run fully supported three- to six-day mountain biking or Nordic skiing trips between the huts.

advanced and expert). But there's a good variety of terrain, from gladed tree skiing and challenging moguls to groomed open slopes. And for those with the skill and the cash there's the opportunity for some adventurous snowcat-accessible skiing on Chicago Ridge where 1800 acres of untracked powder by the Continental Divide beckon – at $200 per day. Otherwise a day of skiing at the resort costs $29.

Eating and drinking

Leadville has a gratifying choice of inexpensive places to **eat** and **drink**. The southern end of town has long been a Hispanic stronghold and still provides a number of good Mexican food cantinas. Nightlife is concentrated at the weekends and focuses on simple pleasures: pool and heavy drinking.

Casa Blanca 188 E 2nd St ⓣ719/486-9969. Great margaritas and decent Southwestern renditions of Mexican favorites.

Cloud City Coffee House and Deli 711 Harrison Ave ⓣ719/486-1317. Relaxed café where bagels, buns, and good espressos are served in a grand old hotel lobby. Opens at 7am.

Columbine Café 612 Harrison Ave ⓣ719/486-3599. Inexpensive and imaginative fresh food including Creole dishes and lots of vegetarian options, served in simple diner surroundings. Opens early (5.30am weekdays, 7am weekends) to deliver hearty breakfasts; stays open for lunch too.

La Cantina one mile south on US-24 ⓣ719/486 9021. Spartan restaurant where great inexpensive Mexican and Southwestern food is served to diners in worn booths; good homemade tamales or tortillas smothered in a spicy green chili sauce and served with a great homemade fresh salsa.

Pastime Saloon 120 W 2nd St ⓣ719/486-9986. The bar of choice for many locals, it has a great mountain view from its patio and delicious wings and burgers.

Prospector Restaurant 2798 Hwy-9 ⓣ719/486-3955. Upscale joint three miles north of town serving homemade soups, aged steaks, and Cajun food. Leadville's best smarter choice.

Quincy's 416 Harrison Ave ⓣ719/486-9765. Friendly pub with reasonable steaks, filet mignon for only $6, prime rib at $8 and has a good line in cocktails.

Silver Dollar Saloon 315 Harrison Ave ⓣ719/486-9914. Old wood paneled gin-joint, patronized by Oscar Wilde after his performance at the Opera House, is today a welcoming place, thick with Irish memorabilia.

Aspen

Coffee-table magazines might have you believe that a tollgate outside **ASPEN** only admits film stars and the super-rich. This elite ski resort, two hundred miles west of Denver via Leadville, is indeed home to the likes of Cher, Jack Nicholson, and Goldie Hawn, but in summer it can be an affordable, and very appealing place for anyone to come – unless you're on an absolute shoestring budget. Visiting in winter requires more cash, though you can save money by staying in the Glenwood Springs (see p.249) area and commuting in – as much of the local workforce does.

From inauspicious beginnings in 1879, this pristine mountain-locked town developed slowly, thanks to its remote location, to become one of the world's top silver producers. By the time the silver market crashed fourteen years later, it had acquired tasteful residential palaces, grand hotels, and an opera house. Miners were quick to leave and within a year of the crash only a quarter of the populace remained. In the 1930s, with the population slumped below seven hundred, it was ironically enough the anti-poverty WPA program that gave the community the cash to build its first crude ski lift. Entrepreneurs seized the opportunity presented by the varied terrain and plentiful snow, and the first chairlift was dedicated on Aspen Mountain (now known as **Ajax**) in 1947.

Skiing has since spread to three more mountains – **Aspen Highlands**, **Snowmass**, and **Buttermilk Mountain**, and the social jet set arrived in force during the 1960s. Development is a burning political issue, but the last decade has seen yet more Scandinavian-style lodges, condo blocks, and giant houses (the average price of a home exceeds two million dollars) built. And while many Colorado mountain towns have looked on Aspen as a blueprint for the development of their own economies, many of their local residents fear becoming "another Aspen" and finding themselves priced out of town by second-homers.

Arrival, information, and getting around

In winter, Independence Pass on Hwy-82, which provides the quickest access to Aspen, is closed, and the detour through Glenwood Springs adds an extra seventy miles to the trip from Denver. Many instead choose to fly into **Sardy Field**, the small airport four miles north of town on Hwy-82; if you fly into Denver, connecting flights bought in advance only cost another $60 or so. Or you can take a shuttle (make sure to book in advance) from Denver International Airport; shuttle companies include Supershuttle (ⓣ1-800/258-3826) and Colorado Mountain Express (ⓣ1-800/222-2112). Another option is to fly into Eagle County Airport near Vail, an eighty-minute drive away. Several **car rental** agencies have counters at Aspen's airport, including Avis (ⓣ970/925-2355 or 1-800/331-1212) and Thrifty (ⓣ970/920-2305 or 1-800/367-2277).

Once in Aspen, the Roaring Fork Transit Agency (ⓣ970/925-8484) runs free shuttle **buses** between the four ski mountains and also serve the airport and outlying areas. Conveniently, the winter bus service to the resort area of Snowmass, twelve miles northwest of Aspen, continues to operate until 2.30am ($2). Aspen's bus terminal is the Rubey Park Transit Center in the center of town on Durant Avenue. A **taxi service** is provided by High Mountain Taxi (ⓣ970/925-8294).

The town's best source of visitor information is the **visitor center** at 425 Rio Grande Place (Mon–Fri 9am–5pm; ⓣ970/925-9000 or 1-800/262-7736), next to a multistory parking lot that's the best place to leave your car while you explore town. The free *Aspen Daily News* ("If you don't want it printed, don't let it happen") is an excellent source of local gossip, news, and food and drink offers. Another helpful source of information when planning your trip is the huge Aspen-Snowmass website (ⓦwww.aspenonline.com). For information on local forests and the three wilderness areas around Aspen – the Hunter Fryingpan, Maroon Bells, and Collegiate Peaks – contact the **White River National Forest's Aspen Ranger Station**, 806 W Hallam St (Mon–Fri 8am–4.30pm; ⓣ970/925-3445).

Accommodation

The basic choice of **accommodation** is either a hotel, B&B, or condo in Aspen itself, or a slopeside lodge or condo over in Snowmass. Snowmass tends to be a shade cheaper, though in summer it's dead and in winter you're likely to spend a good deal of your time on shuttles heading to the bulk of the area's restaurants and nightlife in Aspen. Both **Aspen Central Reservations**, 425 Rio Grande Place (ⓣ970/925-9000, 925-4444 or 1-800/262-7736; ⓦwww.aspen4u.com) and **Snowmass Central Reservations**, 38 Village Square, Snowmass (ⓣ970/923-2000 or 1-800/598-2005) run superb services. Other useful contacts for winter accommodation are the Aspen Skiing

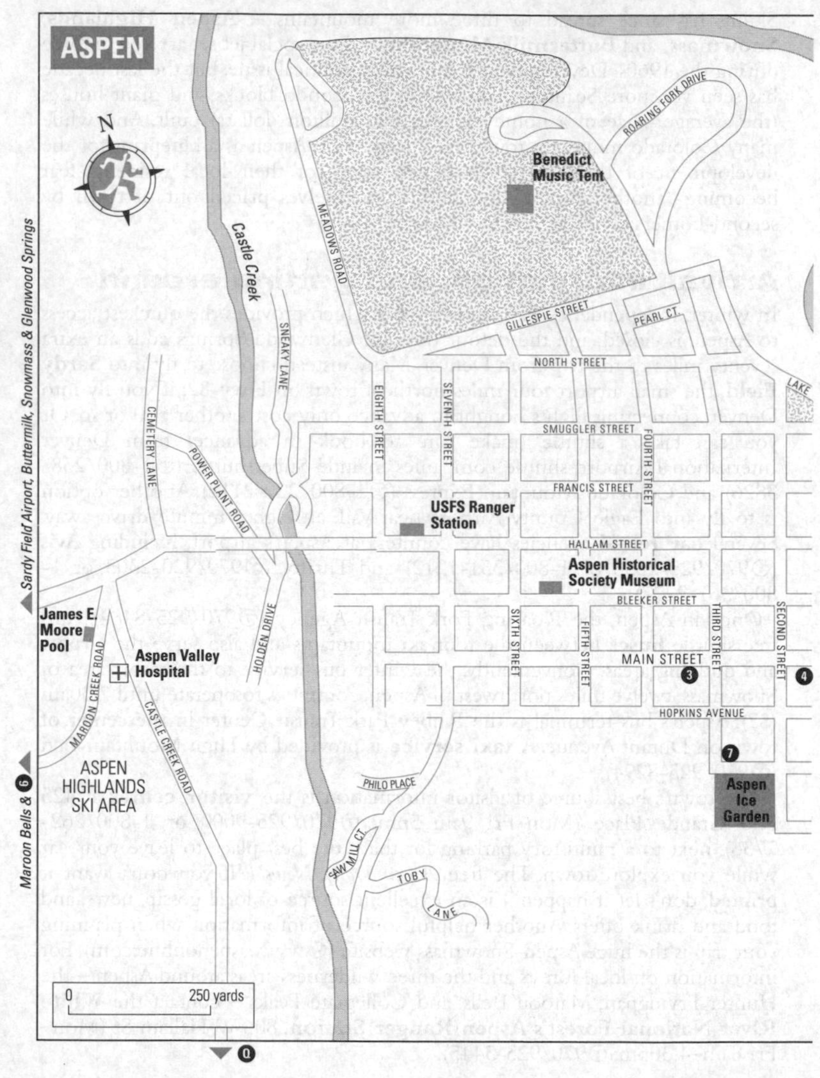

Company (☎970/925-1220 or 1-800/525-6200), who organize condo bookings, and Affordable Aspen (☎970/527-6451 or 1-800/243-9466), an agency devoted to finding cheap lodgings – though these are often reserved up to a year in advance. Prices in the entire area as much as halve during the **summer**, when **camping** is also a good cheap option; There are nine USFS campgrounds around Aspen, of which only a handful of sites are reservable (☎877/444-6777). Several campgrounds are on Maroon Creek Road south of Aspen, and some smaller options out toward Independence Pass, including the serene *Lincoln Gulch Campground*. Free dispersed camping is offered along Lincoln Creek, eleven miles southeast of Aspen.

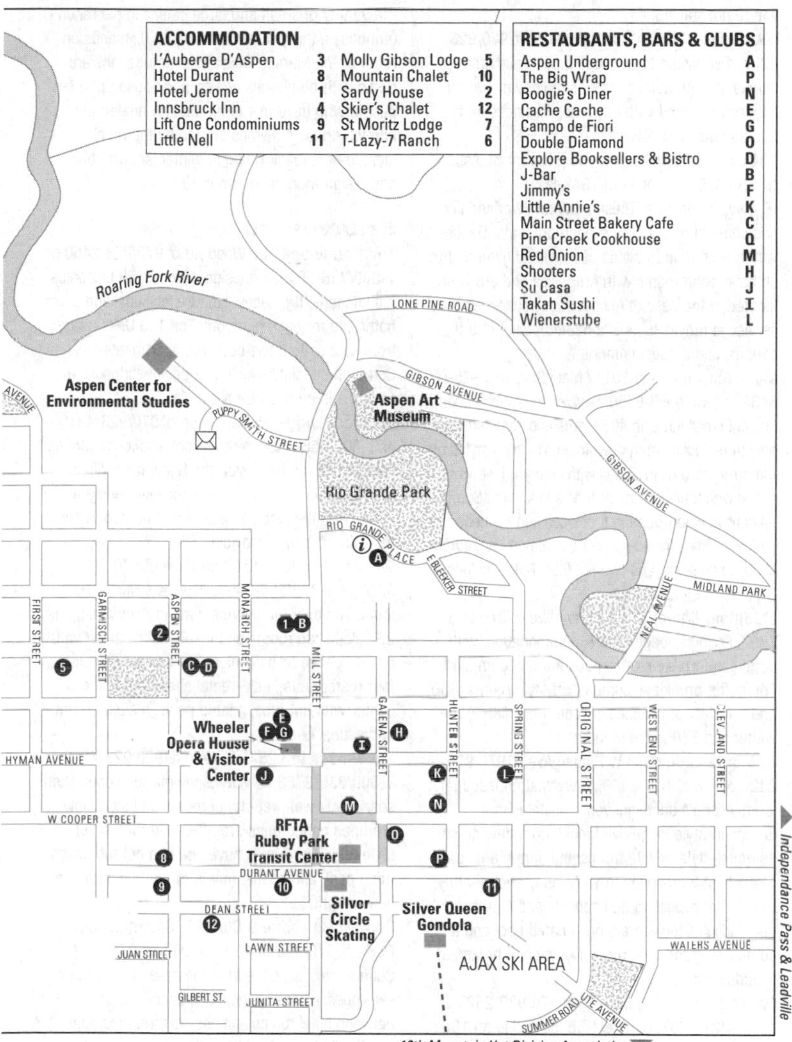

Aspen

Hotel Durant 122 E Durant St ⓣ970/925-8500, ⓦwww.preferredlodging.com. Comfortable and friendly small hotel a couple of blocks from the town center that's one of Aspen's cheapest deals; includes hot tub, use of a pleasant little communal lounge area, and a continental breakfast. 7

Innsbruck Inn 233 W Main St ⓣ970/925-2980, ⓦwww.preferredlodging.com. Austrian-style lodge with hand-carved beams and bright basic rooms, a few blocks from downtown; with a continental breakfast, and in winter aprés-ski snacks. 8

Hotel Jerome 330 E Main St ⓣ970/920-1000 or 1-800/331-7213, ⓦwww.hoteljerome.com. Stately downtown landmark built at the height of the 1880s silver boom by the then Macy's president Jerome B. Wheeler. Each of the spacious rooms features period wallpaper, antique brass and cast-iron beds, along with a gamut of modern amenities. The central lobby elegantly combines Victorian splendor and Rocky Mountain chic and, along with the hotel's bar, the *J-Bar*, is worth a look even if you're not staying. ⑨

L'Auberge D'Aspen 435 W Main St ⓣ970/925-8297, ⓦwww.preferredlodging.co. Idyllic little cabins, in a great location close to downtown and superbly outfitted with kitchens, fireplaces, hot tub, stereos, and VCRs. ⑦

Lift One Condominiums 131 E Durant St, Aspen ⓣ970/925-1670 or 1-800/543-8001, ⓦwww.liftone.com. These moderately priced condos come in one- to three-bedroom units. Decor varies according to tastes of individual owners, but all have living rooms with fireplaces and are well located at the base of Ajax. A daily housekeeping service is provided, as is a heated pool, hot tub, saunas, and a guest laundry. ⑧

Molly Gibson Lodge 101 W Main St ⓣ970/925-3434 or 1-800/356-6559, ⓦwww.mollygibson.com. Elegant small inn with fifty rooms and some suites only three blocks from downtown. The nine styles of room run from plain rooms with courtyard views to suites with four-person hot tubs and lounge. Some units have wood-burning fireplaces and kitchens. Lodge facilities include a courtesy airport van, après-ski bar, two pools, and two hot tubs. Rates include a continental breakfast. ⑦

Mountain Chalet 333 E Durant Ave ⓣ970/925-7797. Friendly, lodge-type accommodation, with large comfortable rooms, pool, hot tub, gym, and fine buffet breakfast, some dorm-style rooms ($30) and a variety of qualities of room from $80 in the winter and $40 in the summer. ⑤

St Moritz Lodge 334 W Hyman Ave ⓣ970/925-3220 or 1-800/817-2069, ⓦwww.stmoritzlodge.com. Aspen's unofficial youth hostel is in a European-style lodge five blocks from downtown. Its motel-style private rooms and dorms are some of the best bargains in town (weekly and monthly rentals are available) and consequently hard to get. Facilities include a small heated pool and a comfortable common room. Continental breakfast included. ⑥

Sardy House 128 E Main St ⓣ970/920-2525 or 1-800/321-3457. Genteel B&B located in an 1892 Victorian home. Decor is Laura Ashley-style and all rooms are opulently furnished, largely with antiques. Guestrooms have their own hot tubs, and there's a sauna and swimming pool. ⑧

Skier's Chalet 233 Gilbert St ⓣ970/920-2037 or 1-800/262-7736. Dated chalet accommodation retaining much of the 1950s and 1960s, when the complex was built. But it's close to the skiing action and draws in a younger, fun-loving crowd, who don't care about the basic rooms and limited facilities; though there is a pool. ⑥

T-Lazy-7 Ranch 3129 Maroon Creek Rd ⓣ970/925-4614, ⓦwww.tlazy7.com. Western-style decor in one of its most appropriate locations – a variety of small and large cabins in old ranch outhouses, three miles from Aspen Highlands en route to the Maroon Bells. Accommodations are rustic with no phones or TVs, and house up to ten people who have use of an outdoor heated pool and whirlpool. Activities offered by the ranch include horseback riding in winter, snowmobile and sleigh tours in summer. ⑤

Snowmass

The Crestwood 400 Wood Rd ⓣ970/923-2450 or 1-800/356-5949. Slopeside condos with balconies, full kitchens, fireplaces, laundry facilities, and a bathroom for each bedroom. The 120 Units range from studios to three-bedroom apartments. Communal facilities include a pool, whirlpools, a sauna, and an exercise room. ⑤

Pokolodi Lodge 25 Daly Lane ⓣ970/923-4310 or 1-800/666-4556, ⓦwww.pokolodi.com. Modest motel-style rooms beside the Snowmass Village Mall; also offer snug quarters for four people to share. Facilities include a pool and hot tub. A courtesy airport bus is provided. ⑤

Silvertree Hotel 100 Elbert Lane ⓣ970/923-3520 or 1-800/525-9402, ⓦwww.silvertreehotel.com. The only full-service hotel in Snowmass has 262 slopeside rooms and luxury suites, most with private patios or balconies. The complex includes four restaurants, a ski-rental shop and a fitness center with hot tubs, heated pools, a steam room, and sauna. ⑦

Snowmass Inn 25 Daly Lane ⓣ970/923-4202 or 1-800/635-3758, ⓦwww.snowmassinn.com. Both sparklingly well-kept hotel rooms and incredibly cramped condo units are offered in this chalet-style building. Guests have use of a hot tub, swimming pool, and sauna. In winter the minimum stay is five nights. ⑤

Snowmass Lodge & Club 239 Snowmass Club Circle ⓣ970/923-5600 or 1-800/525-0710. Country-club-style resort at the base of Snowmass' ski slopes, whose accommodations are split between hotel rooms and one- to three-bedroom condos. A slopeside ski concierge and a courtesy shuttle to Aspen are available; facilities include a splendid fitness center – with hot tubs, steam rooms, indoor tennis, squash and racquetball courts, and ski rentals. The minimum stay is usually two nights. Good-value golf and ski packages are sometimes offered. ⑥

Wildwood Lodge 40 Elbert Lane ⓣ970/923-3520 or 1-800/525-9402, ⓦwww.wildwood-lodge.com. The smaller, plainer brother of the *Silvertree Hotel* shares many of its facilities – including the health club – but is more economically priced. Breakfast is included in room rates. ⑥

The town and around

There's not all that much to do in Aspen itself. Strolling around the town's leafy pedestrianized streets or browsing in the chichi stores and galleries is a pleasant way to spend a couple of hours. Beyond that, you may want to call in at the **Aspen Historical Society Museum**, 620 W Bleeker St (daily 9am–5pm; $3), located in the former home of Jerome Wheeler. Generally considered the town's founding father, Wheeler's up-and-down fortunes closely mirrored that of Leadville's Harry Tabor (see box p.235). The society offers tours of the house and hour-long walking tours of Aspen in the summer ($10).

Before Wheeler went bankrupt, he built its two most magnificent Victorian buildings. At the center of town, beside the pedestrian mall, the **Wheeler Opera House**, 320 E Hyman Ave (daily 9am–5pm; $2; Ⓦwww.wheeleroperahouse.com), attracted the nation's top performers in its heyday and is still in use for various arts performances. Two blocks to the north the **Hotel Jerome** (see p.241) is an equally famous landmark. Step inside to marvel at the lobby's distinctive Rocky Mountain chic in its Victorian decor and then take a look at the photos beside the adjacent *J-Bar* which show it before its 1985 restoration.

Just north of downtown on the northern side of the Roaring Fork River, is the **Aspen Art Museum**, 590 N Mill St (Tues–Sat 10am–6pm, Sun noon–6pm; $3 (free Sat); Ⓣ970/925-8050). In the absence of a permanent collection this can be a bit of a hit-and-miss affair, though usually its visiting exhibitions are dependably good. Still, the many commercial galleries sprinkled about town often have bigger names on display – a testament to the bank accounts of local citizenry. Another more spectacular cultural installation in town is the **Benedict Music Tent**, an impressive permanent structure on the northwest edge of town – it reputedly cost $11 million to build – and the main venue for the summertime Aspen Music Festival (see box p.247).

A good aperitif for more adventurous sorties into the wilds is a visit to the **Aspen Center for Environmental Studies**, 100 S Puppy Smith St (Dec–April Mon–Fri 9am–5pm; May–Nov Mon–Sat 9am–5pm; $2 donation; Ⓣ970/925-5756). The Center is beside the small Hallam Lake Wildlife Sanctuary – a first-rate reserve to watch wildfowl – and summer and winter offer a wide range of guided hikes or snowshoe tours (bring your own snowshoes) led by naturalists. One tour offered by the center in summer is the free hour-long tour (Mon, Wed & Fri 10am) of **Ashcroft** (mid-June to Aug; $3; Ⓣ970/925-3721), eleven miles west up Castle Creek Road. Once the largest town in the area with a population of over 2500, its mines attracted investment from Horace Tabor who stood the town drinks when Baby Doe came to visit. Today only nine buildings remain and it's hard to imagine two bustling main streets that housed three hotels and a newspaper office, but an information booth at the site manned by the Aspen Historical Society and various placards help paint a picture of what it was once like.

Skiing, snowboarding, and other winter activities

Aspen's resorts – **Ajax**, **Aspen Highlands**, **Buttermilk**, and **Snowmass** – are four excellent but distinctively different mountains. Conveniently, all are run by the Aspen Ski Co (Ⓣ970/925-1220 or 1-800/525-6200, Ⓣ1-888/277-3676 for conditions, Ⓦwww.aspensnowmass.com) and connected by free shuttles (8am–4.45pm; every 15min). Daily **adult lift tickets**, good for all four mountains, cost $65 (the most expensive in Colorado, though you can save by buying in advance). The rental of skis, boots, and poles usually costs from around $18 a day and can be conveniently rented via the Aspen Ski Co's own slopeside stores. Independent shops in town include Aspen Sports, with four locations including 408 E Cooper Ave (Ⓣ970/925-6332), which stocks a good range of both skiing and snowboarding gear.

Ajax

Overlooking Aspen itself, the mogul-packed monster of **Ajax** is for experienced skiers only; its 75 trails break down as 35 percent intermediate, 65 percent advanced and expert. A small ski area of only 673 acres, Ajax (summit elevation 11,212ft) consists of three ridges (Ruthie's, Bell, and Gentleman's) between which trails and glades zip down gullies. First thing in the morning, consider taking lift 1A in preference to lining up with the crowds at the Silver Queen gondola. If you're in search of deep powder, Bear Paw Glade and Silver Queen, both in the Ruthie's Ridge part of the mountain are usually among the best places to find it. Later in the day, the best skiing and snow are near the summit, though it's wise to ski all the way down the mountain to make use of the speedy Silver Queen gondola to the summit, rather than get caught in slower moving lift lines further up.

Aspen Highlands

With a ridgetop setting on Lodge Peak, **Aspen Highlands** (top elevation 11,675ft) offers splendid scenery as a backdrop for some of Colorado's best adventure skiing and riding. Known primarily for its expert terrain (although the 714 acres of terrain divide up as 20 percent beginner, 33 percent intermediate, and 47 percent advanced), Aspen Highlands is the least crowded of the four resorts and most enjoyable for those who enjoy moguls or are looking for a backcountry-like experience in gladed terrain or in the bleak, double-black diamond Highland Bowl. Good expert-level powder stashes can be found around Steeplechase, and the adjacent gladed Temerity. The resort also has a couple of distinct beginner and intermediate areas at its center. Intermediates looking for good powder are likely to find it early in the day on the Upper Robinsons – usually one of the last runs on the mountain to see much traffic. Snowboarders looking for good cruising runs should stick to blue runs; one superb top-to-bottom tour cobbles together Broadway and Hayden Meadows with Prospector Gulch before hooking onto Jerome via Golden Barrel. Aspen Highlands has also become well known for its **Freestyle Fridays**, when local talent get to show off their aerial trickery in front of hordes of onlookers.

Buttermilk Mountain

Buttermilk Mountain is the most novice-friendly of the Aspen resorts. Originally developed as an easy alternative to Aspen Mountain, Buttermilk is one of the nation's finest teaching and learning mountains. One particularly nice feature for novices is that they can explore the highest points on the mountain as well as parts further down. Still, there are some harder runs in the small 420-acre resort, and the area divides up as 35 percent beginner, 39 percent intermediate, and 26 percent advanced. The longest advanced run is Tiehack, which often retains lots of great powder after a storm. Since the boom in snowboarding, the wide-open, blissfully uncrowded cruising runs of this ski area have attracted riders in droves. Buttermilk's excellent ski school offers a three-day guaranteed "Learn to Snowboard" program. And a superb snowboard park is located at the base of Main Buttermilk – the center of Buttermilks' annual **Aspen Boardfest**, held in December, during which skiers are banned from the mountain.

Skate, sleighs, and sledges

If you've still got energy after the slopes have closed – or are just looking for a relaxing day off – **ice skating, sleigh** and **sledge rides** are popular in Aspen. The prettiest spot to skate in town is at Silver Circle Skating, 433 E Durant Ave (Ⓣ970/544-0303; $6.50), while the Aspen Ice Garden, 233 W Hyman Ave (Ⓣ970/920-5141; $4) is a larger year-round indoor rink. Call ahead for opening times as they tend to vary. Dog-sled rides are offered by Krabloonik, 4250 Divide Rd, Snowmass (Ⓣ970/923-4342 or 923-3953). Half a day costs around $200. To be pulled up the Maroon Creek Valley by horses or take part in a snowmobile tour, contact *T-Lazy-7 Ranch*, 3129 Maroon Creek Rd (Ⓣ970/925-4614), which rents out snowmobiles for $170 per day. Both Krabloonik and the *T-Lazy-7 Ranch* also organize evening sled or sleigh trips to gourmet restaurants.

Snowmass

The wide-open runs of **Snowmass** offer an incredible venue for intermediate skiers, though there are also pockets of testing runs in the resort. Far and away the biggest Aspen resort, Snowmass spreads over a series of four distinct ridges, linked by a multitude of intermediate runs. The 2585-acre terrain divides as 7 percent beginner, 55 percent intermediate, and 38 percent advanced. Consequently, beginners will find very little here, while those looking for expert runs will spend all their time in two excellent, relatively small areas of glades and chutes of the Hanging Valley, and bowl skiing in the cirque. Of the other areas, Elk Camp is best known for enjoyable above-treeline cruising runs. The next best intermediate ski area is Big Burn. There's good bowl riding around the cirque, while freestylers will enjoy the varied terrain park Trenchtown – despite its rather forced-hip feel with piped music and a chill-out yurt – and the world's longest snowboard half-pipe on Assay Hill.

Cross-country skiing

Aspen's "Fifth Mountain" is easily its best value, since the fifty miles of **cross-country** ski trails groomed by the Aspen/Snowmass Nordic Council (Ⓦwww.aspennordic.com) is one of the most extensive free cross-country trail networks in the US. The network can be accessed from both the Aspen Cross-Country Center, 308 S Mill St (Ⓣ970/925-2849 or 925-2145), or the Snowmass Club Cross-Country Center, 239 Snowmass Club Circle (Ⓣ970/923-3148). Both centers are on golf courses offering easy novice-level skiing and offer rental equipment and lessons. Should you tire of these trails you can also explore the 22 miles of beautifully-groomed trails maintained by Ashcroft Ski Touring Unlimited (Ⓣ970/925-1971; $12), centered on the old ghost town of Ashcroft eleven miles west up Castle Creek Road. Those in search of **backcountry adventure** on Nordic skis should contact the 10th Mountain Division Hut System office in town (see box on p.237). Ute Mountaineers, 308 S Mill St (Ⓣ970/925-2849), is a fantastic source of local equipment for cross-country skiers and has **snowshoe** rentals as well.

Summer activities

Though far more summer visitors go to Aspen for its festivals and boutique shopping, the town's mountain setting also makes it a good hub for hikers and mountain bikers who want to explore trails in the spectacular Sawatch and Elk Ranges. To this end, the free *Ute Scout Hiking and Biking Guide*, available free from the visitor center, is an excellent resource. One of the best short local

hikes is the Ute Trail, which begins from the southeastern corner of town along Ute Avenue. This trail zigzags steeply upwards to quickly give you great views over town. The Ute Trail is done by most as an hour-long out-and-back trail, though the trail goes further to hook up to the network serviced by the nearby **Silver Queen Gondola**, 601 Dean St (daily 10am–4pm; $18 day-pass, $32 week-pass; ⓣ970/925-1220), which climbs to the summit of Aspen Mountain. You can join one of the free guided nature walks provided (set off on the hour from 11am to 3pm). Another good longer local hike, which leads to natural hot springs on Conundrum Creek, starts from a trailhead five miles south of Aspen on the road to Ashcroft (see p.243). The easy creek-side trail leads south down a narrow valley for nine miles to two pools perfect for soaking. Camping is allowed at designated backcountry sites, making the out-and-back hike a good overnight adventure.

Despite plenty of other good options in the area, the most alluring are in the glacial landscape around the twin purple-gray peaks of the soaring **Maroon Bells**, gathered around above the dark-blue Maroon Lake fifteen miles to the southwest. The Bells are reached via the eleven-mile-long Maroon Creek Road, closed between 8.30am and 5pm to all except overnight campers with permits, disabled travelers, bikers, and in-line skaters, and RFTA buses, which leave from the Rubey Park transit center (every 30min 9am–4.30pm; $5 round-trip, or $19 combination ticket with a ride on the Silver Queen Gondola – see above). From the end of the road, visitors are funelled down a single trail to Maroon Lake. From here, it's best to head on a rough track up to Crater Lake – an out-and-back trail (four miles out-and-back) that takes a couple of hours and gives you some of best possible views of the Bells. Beautiful as the Maroon Bells are, the surrounding Wilderness area is somewhat overused. Those looking for a more pristine, secluded experience should visit the **Hunter-Fryingpan Wilderness**, which spreads to the east of Aspen. Details on hiking are available from the ranger station (see p.239).

Even more so than hiking, **cycling** seems to be the main summer pursuit, with the **Rio Grande Trail** the most convenient and popular ride. The trail cuts through town on its easy, but busy, four-mile length beside the Rio Grande along an old railroad grade. For more challenging riding, head up **Smuggler Mountain**. Going right to the top on the well-graded track is quite a slog, with more than 2500ft of climbing, so most cyclists go only as far as the lookout – about a quarter of the way up – for the fine views over Aspen and the Roaring Fork Valley. Continuing upwards leads to a fork in the path; the left trail heads down to a section of fun single-track which winds down to Hunter Creek and then back to the northern side of town. The Hub, 315 E Hyman Ave (ⓣ970/925-7970), has a wide choice of rental bikes, while Timberline, 516 E Durant St (ⓣ970/925-3586 or 1-800/842-2453), has some of the cheapest mountain-bike rentals, and organizes tours.

The Roaring Fork River, surging out of the Sawatch range, is excellent for **kayaking** and **rafting** during a short season that's typically over by July. In addition, sections of Class V water can be dangerous and every summer sees a few fatalities. Blazing Paddles, 407 E Hyman Ave (ⓣ970/925-5651; $50 for a half-day float trip) is a good guide choice. In addition to adrenalin activities, the Roaring Fork and its tributaries offer splendid **fly-fishing**, although many coming to the area to fish head straight to **Basalt**, eighteen miles northwest of Aspen. Here a long stretch of clear public water surrounded by reddish bluffs, forests, and mountains is, thanks to regular insect hatches, the idyllic location of one of Colorado's premier fly-fishing venues. For fishing gear and information on local access, check in with the Aspen Outfitting Company, 315 E Dean Ave

Aspen's summer festivals

Ever since 1949, when the Chicago industrialist Walter Paepcke celebrated the 200th birthday of German writer Goethe by bringing together a mix of musicians, philosophers and scientists to celebrate here, summer festivals have been an important part of life in Aspen. The flagship event is the nine-week-long **Aspen Music Festival** (☎970/925-9042), between late June and late August, when orchestras and operas feature well-known international performers, as well as promising students who come to learn from musical masters. Shows are more or less nightly. The main venues are the Wheeler Opera House, the Harris Concert Hall, at the north end of 4th Street, and Benedict Music Tent. And while concerts are the cornerstone of the event, it's well worth attending a workshop or rehearsal as well. Also in the summer are the **Theatre in the Park** (☎970/925-9313), a two-month series of contemporary plays, and the five-day **Aspen Filmfest** (☎970/925-9313). Another of Aspen's major festivals is the six-week-long **DanceAspen Festival**, which starts in late June and usually contains reliably good contemporary shows; ticket prices start at $14. During the summer a free daily guide to what's on is available from Aspen's visitor centers and tickets to all events can be purchased at the **Wheeler Opera House** (☎970/920-5570, ⓦwww.wheeleroperahouse.com) whose program of concerts, plays and dance performances runs year-round.

(☎970/925-3406), or Aspen Sports, 303 E Durant St (☎970/925-6332).

Given the wealth in the area, both **hot-air ballooning** and **golf** have become popular sports – though many visitors are likely to be put off by the expense of either. For $200 the Aspen Unicorn Balloon Company of Colorado, 300B Aspen Airport Business Center (☎970/925-5752 or 1-800/468-2478), offers a three-hour flight concluding with a champagne toast. Visiting golfers are likely to enjoy the long flights of balls at altitude here. The Aspen Golf Course (☎970/925-2145) is a relatively inexpensive eighteen-hole public course just outside town with green fees from around $60.

Eating

Many of Aspen's classy **cafés** and **restaurants** charge over $25 for a main course, but good budget places exist and competition is keen. Note that most of the bars serve good, reasonably priced food as well (see "Nightlife", overleaf).

Aspen Underground 455 Rio Grande Place ☎970/925-6050. Budget-priced Mexican food is available for lunch in this basic restaurant beside the library and municipal parking facility. Avoid the gourmet wraps in favor of traditional items: burritos, soft tacos, quesadillas.

The Big Wrap 520 E Durant Ave ☎970/544-1700. Small café with inventive wraps ($7), summing up various cusines; from the American mashed potatoes with grilled steak and roasted veggies to the Mexican fajita burritos. Good line in healthy smoothies too ($4).

Boogie's Diner 534 E Cooper Ave ☎970/925-6610. Worth stepping into for the 1950s diner-style experience alone, the restaurant is lined with vinyl and chrome and serves terrific meatloaf and mashed potatoes ($8.50) and killer shakes ($5), along with a few tofu-rich veggie options.

Cache Cache 205 S Mill St ☎970/925-3835. Elegant restaurant decorated in pastel hues serving items like rostisserie chicken with kalamata olives and capers, an outstanding *osso buco*, and a duck salad with candied walnuts ($12). The lively bar serves up smaller, cheaper helpings of excellent food as well.

Campo de Fiori 205 S Mill St ☎970/920-7717. Cramped and noisy bistro with great Italian foods – particularly good selection of antipasta and unusual pastas, like the *malfatti* dumplings – complementing the wide range of fine Italian wines. Moderate to expensive.

Explore Booksellers and Bistro 221 E Main St ☎970/925-5336. Great bookstore with high quality creative vegetarian food, good espresso and pastries, and a shady roof terrace. Open 10am–10pm.

Il Poggio 73 Elbert Lane, Snowmass ☎970/923-4292. Lively, moderately expensive Italian joint is the pick of the bunch in the unexciting Snowmass dining scene: good pasta and pizza and decent fresh antipasta.

Little Annie's 517 E Hyman Ave ☎970/925-1098. Lively, popular, and unpretentious saloon-style restaurant decorated in huge quantities of international golfing memorabilia. Hard to beat for good ol' down-home cookery: potato pancakes, hearty stews and excellent burgers for lunch; huge trout, barbecued chicken, beef, or rib for dinner – platters for around $15.

Main Street Bakery Cafe 201 E Main St ☎970/925-6446. Casual café busy in the mornings when serving massive, fresh fruit-packed breakfasts – and you can pick up good baked goods here too.

Pine Creek Cookhouse 11399 Castle Creek Rd, Ashcroft ☎970/925-1044. Ski in or ride a horse-drawn sleigh 1.5 miles from the ghost town of Ashcroft to a gourmet lunch or dinner. Dinner entrees include Rocky Mountain trout, Cornish game hen, quail, and lamb. Dinner prices vary with the menu but cost around $60, including the sleigh ride. The price is lower for skiers.

Su Casa 315 E Hyman ☎970/920-1488. Splendid authentic Mexican food – with a number of excellent *carnitas* (fried pork) dishes, but also a big range of good veggie options like the spinach and mushroom enchiladas. Good margaritas served in an enjoyable courtyard. Moderately expensive.

Takah Sushi 420 E Hyman Ave ☎970/925-8588. Phenomenally good sushi and pan-Asian cuisine, in a buzzing, cheerful atmosphere. Highly recommended yet quite expensive, sushi running around $5 a piece.

Wienerstube 633 E Hyman Ave ☎970/925-3357. The best breakfast in Aspen: eggs Benedict, Austrian sausage, and Viennese pastries among other things. Also does decent renditions of Austrian cuisine; wienerschnitzel ($17), sauerbraten ($17).

Wildcat Café Snowmass ☎970/923-5990. No-frills eating option in Snowmass. From breakfast to dinner all options are inexpensive and reliably satisfying enough to make locals regulars.

Nightlife

Going out in Aspen, the capital of **après-ski**, is fun year round and need not be expensive. The scene is dynamic and bars frequently change hands, but those listed below are largely dependable favorites. Note that nightlife, which in Aspen generally means serious drinking, is not just restricted to bars – many restaurants also have bar areas that stay open just as long. In summer, several top-notch festivals (see box, overleaf) add a bit of verve to the otherwise laid-back scene.

Double Diamond 450 S Galena St ☎970/920-6905. Aspen's top live-music venue. Usually free before 10pm and the drink prices are reasonable.

J-Bar *Hotel Jerome* ☎970/920-1000. The grand bar in the historic *Hotel Jerome* is a good place to soak in the hotel's atmosphere and rub elbows with well-heeled hotel guests.

Jimmy's 205 S Mill St ☎970/925-6020. Reliably buzzing bar with a sociable deck and a superb selection of tequilas. There's also a restaurant that serves top steaks and traditional American comfort food like meatloaf and pork chops.

Red Onion Cooper St Mall ☎970/925-9043. Aspen's oldest bar is a popular après-ski spot; generally raucous and with a lethal line in jello shots. In summer it's also fairly busy with street-side tables in the Mall allowing for entertaining people-watching. Also serves big portions of standard American pub fare (good burgers) and some Mexican food.

Gay Aspen

Though Colorado has traditionally been one of the least **gay-friendly** states – for a long time boycotted by the gay community for its discriminatory laws – Aspen is, outside Denver, the state's exception. Not only does it have some of the oldest anti-discrimination laws in US but it has developed a small gay scene. Still, the town has no real gay hangouts or bars – except during Gay Ski Week in late January when it seems hard to find a straight bar. For local information contact the Aspen Gay and Lesbian Community Information Hotline ☎970/925-9249.

Shooters 220 S Galena St ☎970/925-4567. Swinging Country and Western bar which also holds a popular Tuesday night non-Country disco.

Woody Creek Tavern Upper Never Rd, Woody Creek ☎970/923-4585. Unpretentious local bar, where ranch hands and rock stars shoot pool, guzzle fresh lime-juice margaritas and eat good Tex-Mex. The bar is in tiny Woody Creek – seven miles north of Aspen along Hwy-82, right on River Rd, and then first left.

Listings

Laundry Sunshine Laundry, 465 Puppy Smith St (☎970/925-5378).

Medical Aspen Valley Hospital, 401 Castle Creek Rd (☎970/925-1120).

Post Office 235 Puppy Smith St; 1106 Kearns Rd, Snowmass.

Showers and swimming James E Moore Pool, 895 Maroon Creek Rd (Mon–Fri 8am–7.30pm, Sat & Sun 10am–6pm; ☎970/920-5145).

Glenwood Springs

Bustling, touristy **GLENWOOD SPRINGS** sits at the end of impressive Glenwood Canyon, within easy striking distance of Aspen (forty miles southeast) and Vail (sixty miles east). The **hot springs** for which the town were named were long used by the Utes as a place of relaxation, later attracting miners before becoming the target for unscrupulous speculators who broke treaties and established resort facilities in the 1880s. For some time, Glenwood Springs was every bit as chic as Vail or Aspen are today. Today, though, the town has largely become a service center for nearby resorts, beset by faceless malls, motels, and fast food outlets along I-70 and Hwy-6 south out of town. The downtown area is still an attractive place, but there's really not much to explore besides the hot springs, which are particularly welcome after a day of skiing at the modest nearby **Sunlight Mountain Resort**. In summer, the best local activities include biking along the base of **Glenwood Canyon** just east of town and exploring the spectacular landscape along the **Crystal River Valley** to the south.

Arrival, information, and getting around

Amtrak **trains** – with daily services from Denver – pull in at the depot on 413 7th St, downtown by the Colorado River. Greyhound **buses**, arriving three times a day from both Denver and Grand Junction, pull in at the *Ramada Inn*, 124 W 6th St. Shuttle services from Denver International Airport include Aspen Limo (☎970/925-1234 or 1-800/222-2112), who charge $60 one-way; they also run shuttles from Aspen's airport for $20. If commuting to the slopes in Aspen, RFTA buses run daily trips (6am–10pm; 1 hr; $6; ☎970/925-8484), leaving from W Glenwood Mall (see below). If you intend to do the trip several times buy a $10 punch ticket, which effectively makes rides half-price.

The **visitor center**, 1102 Grand Ave (open 24 hours, staffed Mon–Fri 8.30am–5pm, Sat & Sun 9am–3pm; ☎970/945-6589) stocks the useful *Glenwood Springs Official Guide*, and the **USFS White River National Forest Office** is at 900 Grand Ave (☎970/945-2521). Getting around town is easy enough as Glenwood Trolley buses (50¢) run every half-hour between W Glenwood Mall at the west end of town and Roaring Forks Marketplace at its southern end.

Accommodation

Accommodation tends to fill up quickly, so reservations in summer are recommended, especially if you're hoping to stay downtown. In winter, lodging in town is one of Colorado's best deals, with rates often dropping by half. If you're

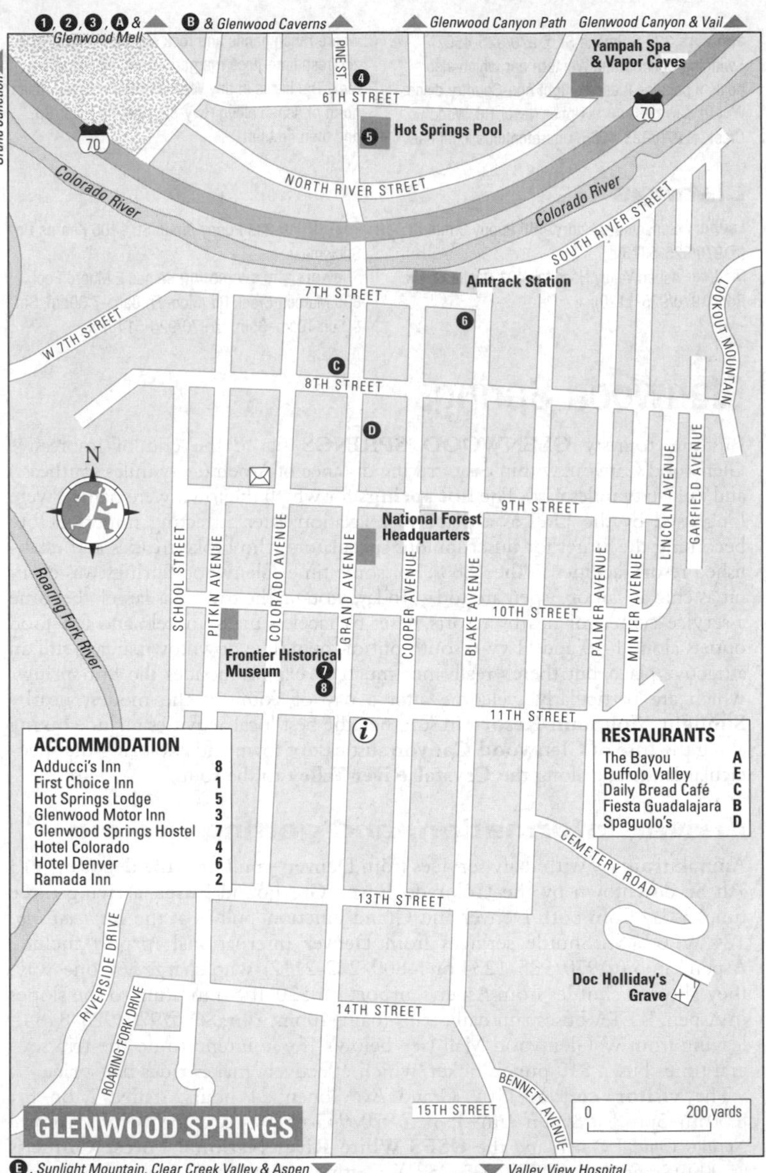

skiing Sunlight, you can get an even better deal with one of their sleep, ski, and soak packages which include lodging, lift tickets, and passes to hot springs from around $60 per night (call the resort for details of participating accommodations). **Campers** will find plenty of sites in nearby White River National Forest, including in the Crystal River Valley near Marble (see p.253), though the only sites close to town are at the *Hideout Campground and Cabins* (see opposite).

Adducci's Inn 1023 Grand Ave ☎970/945-9341. Extremely good-value lodgings in an old Victorian house; rooms share a bath and a large full-breakfast is included. ❷

Brettelberg Condominiums 11101 CO-117, ☎970/945-7421 or 1-800/634-0481. Fairly basic old condo lodge, with great slopeside location. On offer are functional studio and one-bedroom units (sleeping up to six) with full kitchens, VCRs, and fireplaces. Facilities include an outdoor hot tub. The nearby base lodge can provide meals in the winter, but in the summer the nearest food's in town. ❸

Hotel Colorado 526 Pine St ☎970/945-6511 or 1-800/544-3998. Modeled after a stately Italian townhouse, this striking sandstone is a town landmark. Located near the hot springs, parts of the antique-furnished hotel are a little worn but charming nonetheless; facilities include a basement health club and a hot tub. ❻

Hotel Denver 402 7th St ☎970/945-6565 or 1-800/826-8820. Plush Art Deco-style turn-of-the twentieth century hotel, remodeled in the 1990s to be the most luxurious place in town. Close to the hot springs, extras include extensive fitness facilities, fresh cookies at check in, and a hot muffin delivered with the morning paper. ❺

First Choice Inn of Glenwood Springs 51359 6th St ☎970/945-8551 or 1-800/332-2233. Great-value standard motel at the west end of town, with a guest laundry, striking view of the red mountain faces to the south and a free, good breakfast. ❸

Glenwood Motor Inn 141 W 6th St, ☎970/945-5438 or 1-800/543-5906. This motel, just a few blocks from the hot springs, is the best deal downtown. Some rooms have refrigerators and microwaves. Facilities include a hot tub and a sauna. ❸

Glenwood Springs Hostel 1021 Grand Ave ☎970/945-8545 or 1-800/9-HOSTEL. Enthusiastically run hippie hostel with a spacious dorm (beds $12–14) and cheap private rooms ($26) with shared bath, plus kitchen facilities and a giant record collection. Can also arrange tours and whitewater trips. Office closed 10am–4pm.

Hideout Campground & Cabins 1293 CO-117, ☎970/945-5621 or 1-800/987-0779. Huddled in the woods off the road to Sunlight Mountain, the *Hideout* has a number of modern cabins ranging from studios to three-bedroom units (sleeping up to twelve). Some have fireplaces; all have access to the guest laundry. There's also space for both tents ($18) and RVs ($19). ❸

Hot Springs Lodge 415 E 6th St ☎970/945-6571 or 1-800/537-SWIM. Adjacent to the hot springs, where soaking is both convenient and discounted. The 107 rooms are fairly standard motel rooms, decorated in a Southwestern style with either a patio or balcony. Facilities include guest laundry, outdoor hot tub, and a shuttle to the train station. ❹

Inn at Raspberry Ridge 5580 CO-3, Marble ☎970/963-3035. Small home with a handful of twee country-style rooms and good breakfasts in the exceedingly peaceful little village of Marble, around 45 miles south of Glenwood Springs (see p.253). ❺

Ramada Inn of Glenwood Springs 124 W 6th St ☎970/945-2500, 1-800/332-1472 or 1 800/228-2828. The largest chain hotel in town, two blocks from the hot springs, is reasonably priced. Facilities include a fitness center and pool. ❸

The Redstone Inn Redstone ☎970/963-2526. Elegant B&B in an out-of-place, yet still magnificent Tudor-era building in the village of Redstone (see p.253), thirty miles south of Glenwood. Facilities include a health spa with pool, a hot tub and tennis courts adjacent to a creek. The restaurant serves swanky meals, including a popular Sunday brunch. ❻

Sunlight Mountain Inn 10252 CO-117 ☎970/945-5225 or 1-800/733-4757. B&B in a traditional-style ski lodge near the base of Sunlight's slopes. Simple rooms are rustically outfitted with pine-board walls, and the onsite restaurant serves great full breakfasts included in the rates. ❻

The town

Of the few historic sights in Glenwood Springs, the most celebrated is the grave of **Dr John R "Doc" Holliday**, who lies buried on a bluff overlooking the town in the picturesque **Linwood Cemetery**. Holliday, a dentist better known as a gambler and gunslinger, came to the springs for a cure to his chronic tuberculosis but died months later in November 1887, aged 35. In the paupers' section lies the grave of Harvey Logan, alias bank robber Kid Curry, a member of Butch Cassidy's notorious Hole-in-the-Wall gang (see p.310). A good place to brush up on local outlaw history is the **Frontier Historical Museum**, 1001 Colorado Ave (daily: June–Aug 11am–4pm; rest of year 1–4pm; $3), which also focuses on the indigenous Ute as well as the area's pioneering history. Displays inside include pioneer-era clothing, a bed used by Horace Tabor and his mistress Baby Doe (see p.255) and some illuminating old maps and photos of town.

Heading north from downtown and crossing the Eagle River, the town's main attraction, **Glenwood Hot Springs Pool**, 410 N River St (daily: summer 7.30am–10pm; rest of year 9am–10pm; $8; ⓣ970/945-6571), is announced by its sulfurous smell. Billed as the "world's largest outdoor mineral hot springs pool," the complex has a rather institutional feel, though the large square pools are made more interesting by the presence of a water slide and special seats into which water is jetted. Next door, you can destress in the natural subterranean steam baths of the **Yampah Spa Vapor Caves**, 709 E 6th St (daily 9am–9pm; $9), where cool marble benches are set deep in a series of hot, humid ancient caves. Massages ($30) and other treatments are offered here as well.

Also on the north side of town are the **Glenwood Fairy Caves**, 508 Pine St (June–Nov; daily, call for tour times; ⓣ970/945-4228), an old Victorian-era attraction that's recently reopened. The caverns extend for two miles, with some chambers reaching a height of fifty feet. There are two sightseeing options here; the regular two-hour Family Tour ($10) that includes views over Glenwood Canyon from an overlook high above; and the more adventurous four-hour dimly lit Wild Tour ($40; no kids). The caves are connected to town by shuttles leaving from outside the *Hotel Colorado* – call for times.

Outdoor activities

During the snowy months, the family-oriented **Sunlight Mountain Resort** (ⓣ970/945-7491 or 1-800/445-7931, ⓦwww.sunlightmtn.com), ten miles south of Glenwood Springs via Hwy-82 and CO-117, offers some of the least-expensive skiing in the region (**lift tickets** $28). It's also a forgiving place to learn the sport before heading to Aspen. The resort divides into about sixty trails covering 460 acres stretching up to 2010ft above the simple base area; terrain breaks down as 20 percent beginner, 55 percent intermediate, 25 percent advanced. Beginners will find ideal practice areas around the Enchanted Forest. From the top of the 10,000ft **Compass Mountain**, more difficult runs, including some mogul fields and Sunlight Extreme, which has one of the steepest sections in any US resort, branch off. There's also a decent snowboard park east of the base lodge. For **cross-country** enthusiasts, the resort also grooms twenty miles of unusually wide tracks, the venue for the annual 10km Coal Dust Classic, one of the state's oldest amateur cross-country races. Shuttle buses from Glenwood Springs (ⓣ970/945-7491; $1) run from West Glenwood Mall.

In summer, consider heading up the twenty-mile-long cycling trail along the narrow **Glenwood Canyon**, east of town and sandwiched between precipitous 2000ft-high walls. Long impassible, today you'll share the canyon with both the railroad and the four-lane I-70 highway. Thankfully the latter has been largely shielded from the cycle path through a combination of tunnels and stilts. The path starts from the east end of 6th Street in town and along it are several trailheads for hikes into narrow canyons, of which the 1.2-mile uphill hike to **Hanging Lake**, where waterfalls feed an idyllic deep-blue lake, is the most popular. The trailhead for this hike is ten miles from Glenwood Springs along the cycle path. **Bike rental** at Canyon Bikes, 319 6th St (ⓣ970 945-8904) in the *Hotel Colorado*, will provide a shuttle service so you can follow the path downhill east-to-west back to Glenwood Springs for an additional $10.

Crystal River Valley

Relatively few visitors head out to the out-of-the-way **Crystal River Valley**, but along it are a couple of interesting low-key and unusual mining towns. The larger settlement is **Redstone**, a former coal town largely built by a philanthropist owner, including the lavish, Tudor-style *Redstone Inn* (see p.251), originally built to house workers. But the real reason to head up the Crystal River Valley is to explore the area around **Marble**, famous for quarrying the eponymous material. The town began as a hub for the nearby Yule Marble Quarry, it's population at one point exceeding 1500 and linked to the outside world by a train service. Today, you'll need your own vehicle to get here and visit the ruined old marble mill and the scatter of houses that still makes up the town. From beside the old mill, a road climbs up four miles beside Yule Creek to the huge 10,000-square-foot old quarry area, from where the rock for the Tomb of the Unknown Soldier and the Lincoln Memorial in Washington DC came; marble continues to be quarried here.

The other road out of Marble continues east of town, past the small Beaver Lake before becoming rough enough to warrant a four-wheel-drive vehicle for the journey to the hamlet of Crystal. The track can be the first section of a superb twelve-mile **mountain-bike loop** (3–4hr) with great views of the Elk Range. The secluded route begins on CO-314 and follows the idyllic Crystal River closely to the hamlet of **Crystal City** at the center of a large aspen grove. Just before arriving is the much photographed Sheep Mountain Mill, a restored 1882 vintage powerhouse precariously perched on a rocky outcrop. From Crystal City, take the left turn onto the Lead King Basin road (CO-315), from where the uphill route begins in earnest and views over the Maroon Bells and Snowmass Wilderness Area open up. The climb is a steady one and only gets worse once you cross a bridge over a creek, though at least the thousands of pretty wildflowers here in July and August offer an excellent distraction, as do the captivatingly gigantic mountains that surround the route. Having ground up numerous switchbacks the trail begins to level until you come to a number of trails – follow the lowest for the fast roller coaster-style ride back into Marble. Other than a couple of nearby campgrounds there are few places to stay in Marble, and there are no restaurants – the town is served only by a small general store.

Eating and drinking

Despite a good range of inexpensive **dining** options, Glenwood Springs is rarely an exciting place for a night out – though there are a couple of modest neighborhood bars along Grand Avenue. In summer, you can catch free Wednesday night (6.30pm) jazz concerts in the Two Rivers Park.

The Bayou 52103 Hwy-6 ⓣ970/945-1047. Though the menu's claim that the moderately priced food here is "so good you'll slap yo' mama" is slightly overblown, the spicy Cajun dishes – including a fine gumbo and blackened chicken – are worth the short drive out. Summer weekends see live music on the patio.

Buffalo Valley Restaurant 3637 Hwy-82 ⓣ970/945-5297. Locally popular saloon-like joint a mile and a half south of downtown, with good moderately expensive Western fare like buffalo steaks and barbecue chicken. Also has a large dance floor with live music, often Country, on weekends.

Daily Bread Cafe and Bakery 729 Grand Ave ⓣ970/945-6253. Popular downtown spot for breakfast, dishing out delicious and fresh baked goods and egg dishes. Lunches are equally worthwhile here, with a good range of chunky sandwiches, soups, and massive salads.

Devereux Room *Hotel Colorado* ⓣ970/945-6511. Though rather formal, lunch mains – burgers, soups, and salads – can be had for around $7. Prices more than double for dinner, when various Southwestern influenced gourmet dishes are rolled out.

Fiesta Guadalajara 503 Pine St ⓣ970/947-1670. Decent family-run Mexican place near the hot springs. Huge variety of filling options including more than two dozen combination plates, all priced around $9.

Glenwood Canyon Brewpub *Hotel Denver*, 402 7th St ⓣ970/945-1276. Small friendly brewpub with pool tables and a number of good local hand-crafted microbrews, including a good pale ale named Vapor Cave.

Rosi's 141 W 6th ⓣ970/928-9186. Diner-type restaurant in the *Glenwood Motor Inn*; best for a cheap cooked breakfast.

Spagnolo's 812 Grand Ave ⓣ970/945-8440. Affordable bistro with large helpings of standard Italian food; the thin-crust pizzas are excellent.

Grand Junction and around

Along the last fifty-mile stretch of I-70 that heads west into **Grand Junction**, you can trace Colorado's transition from fertile valleys to full-blown desert. To the north, the town is flanked by the Little Bookcliffs, a row of mesaside cliffs to the northwest, to the south the towering soft red-rock canyons and cliffs of the **Colorado National Monument**. The monument is separated from town by the wide, lazy Colorado River, which looks a little out of place, until a glance back east reveals a skyline dominated by the huge, verdant tabletop mountain of **Grand Mesa**, one of the mountainous areas at its source.

Grand Mesa

Sprawling over fifty square miles and soaring up to 10,000ft, the thickly forested **Grand Mesa** is the world's largest flat-topped mountain, known for excellent **fishing** in a multitude of stocked lakes and a huge network of **hiking** trails. In winter, these trails are turned over to **Nordic skiers** and **snowshoers**, when there's also the option of downhill skiing at **Powderhorn** resort.

The road up onto Grand Mesa, Hwy-65, begins from the I-70 twenty miles east of Grand Junction. Around tweny miles from the interstate, in the mesa's foothills, is **Powderhorn Resort** (ⓣ970/268-5700 or 1-800/241-6997, ⓦwww.powderhorn.com) a small (only 500 acres), but inexpensive ($35) ski resort. Although the terrain breaks down as twenty percent beginner, fifty percent intermediate and thirty percent advanced, those seeking black runs will find the half-dozen trails on offer pretty limiting. The best reason for expert skiers to come here is on powder days, and with 250 inches of snow per year, the resort sees its share between December and March.

From Powderhorn, the twisting Hwy-65 heads south up to the plateau left here by a period of 600 million years of erosion working on soft rock that surrounded this huge tongue of lava. With over three hundred lakes and reservoirs surrounded by pine and aspen groves, the landscape is remarkably idyllic and tranquil thanks to the absence of any real development. One of the best car impressions of the area can be had by following **Lands End Road**, a well-graded eleven-mile dirt track that heads east from Hwy-65 (starting around thirty miles south of I-70). The road leads to a stunning panorama: lakes, plains, sand hills, and smaller mesas separate thick forest on the left from desert on the right, with the snowcrested San Juan peaks far off in the background. But as usual, the best way to really see the landscape is to **hike**. The best trail, with startling ridge views, is the ten-mile-long **Crag Crest Trail**, best started from an eastern trailhead beside FS-121 (east off Hwy-65). This end offers some of the most spectacular panoramas, so even if you don't intend to walk the whole leg, it's worth heading along here for a couple of hours on an out-and-back hike.

Practicalities

The helpful **visitors center** near Cobbet Lake junction of FS-121 and Hwy-65 on the southern side of the Mesa can suggest good places to mountain bike and where to head out on cross-country skis or snowshoes in winter. The **Grand Junction Ranger District Office** (Ⓣ970/242-8211) can also help with advance planning and can supply details on their dozen pretty USFS **campgrounds** (reservations Ⓣ1-800/280-CAMP; $6-10; late-May–September). Of these, several dot the east side near Alexander Lake, as does a basic café and the *Alexander Lake Lodge* (Ⓣ970/856-6240; ⑤), which offers motel-style rooms and cabins. At the bottom of the Mesa, five miles north of **Cedaredge**, the hospitable *Llama's B&B* on Hwy-65 (Ⓣ970/856-6836; ④) has fantastic breakfasts served on a sundeck, along with the chance to meet resident llamas. In Cedaredge, the *Log Cabin B&B* (Ⓣ970/856-7585, Ⓦwww.logcabinbedandbreakfast.com; ⑤) is in an 1891 log cabin, surrounded by two forested acres. Rooms are decorated with antique tools and cowboy artifacts.

Grand Junction

Given its parochial nature, it's hard to believe that **GRAND JUNCTION** is the largest city between Denver, 246 miles east on I-70, and Salt Lake City 287 miles west. One of many towns that sprang to life with the arrival of the railroads in the 1880s, it now makes its living primarily through the oil and gas industries and as the center of a buoyant local farming industry, centered on the orchards and vineyards around **Palisade**. Not surprisingly, dusty, sprawling and generally unattractive Grand Junction is often neglected as a destination, even though its immediate environs abound with outdoor opportunities. Particularly splendid is the network of hiking and biking trails, many cutting through rugged and spectacular desert country. Especially enticing for **hikers** is the remarkable scenery of the **Colorado National Monument**, while **mountain bikers**, should relish the prospect of smooth, rolling single-track trails around **Fruita**. Both activities are possible year-round, and are in fact generally more pleasant in the winter months.

Arrival, information, and accommodation

Amtrak's daily California Zephyr stops at 2nd Street and Pitkin Avenue, while Greyhound **buses** pull in at 230 S 5th St. The helpful **visitor center**, 740 Horizon Drive (daily 8.30am–5pm; Ⓣ970/244-1480 or 1-800/962-2547), is beside I-70 three miles from downtown. Additionally, the town runs an info booth in the Amtrak station. Conveniently, the local **USFS** office is located by the visitor center at 2777 Crossroad Blvd (Mon–Fri 8am–5pm; Ⓣ970/242-8211).

An absolute glut of chain **motels** line I-70 three miles north of town, but if you want to actually see anything of the downtown area, you're better off staying in one of the budget motels there. There's a large amount of good **camping** spots in the national forest around the town; contact the USFS office for details.

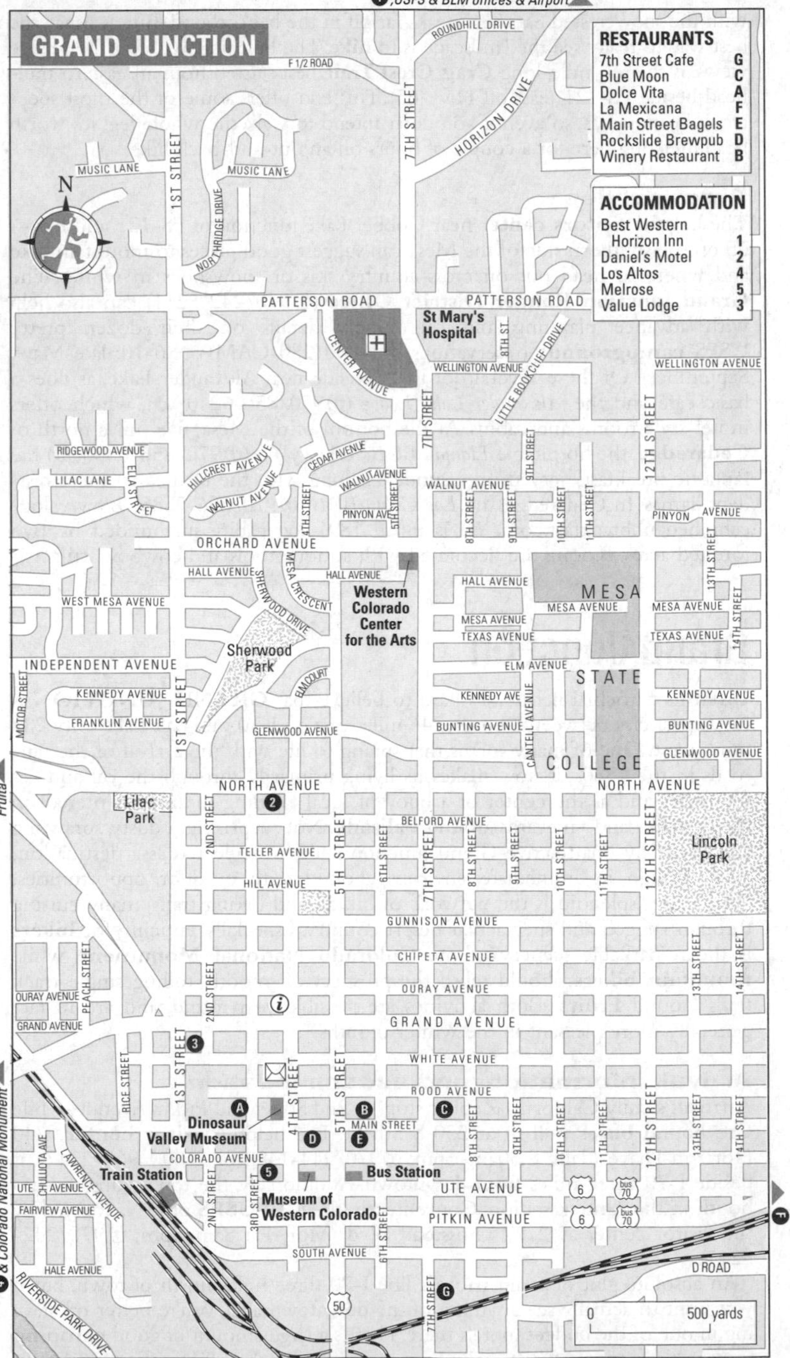
GRAND JUNCTION
1 USFS & BLM offices & Airport
RESTAURANTS
7th Street Cafe G
Blue Moon C
Dolce Vita A
La Mexicana F
Main Street Bagels E
Rockslide Brewpub D
Winery Restaurant B
ACCOMMODATION
Best Western Horizon Inn 1
Daniel's Motel 2
Los Altos 4
Melrose 5
Value Lodge 3
ROUNDHILL DRIVE
F 1/2 ROAD
7TH STREET
HORIZON DRIVE
MUSIC LANE
1ST STREET
NORTHRIDGE DRIVE
N
PATTERSON ROAD
St Mary's Hospital
CENTER AVENUE
8TH ST
LITTLE BOOKCLIFF DRIVE
WELLINGTON AVENUE
RIDGEWOOD AVENUE
ELLA STREET
LILAC LANE
HILLCREST AVENUE
CEDAR AVENUE
WALNUT AVENUE
PINYON AVENUE
ORCHARD AVENUE
HALL AVENUE
MESA CRESCENT
SHERWOOD DRIVE
Western Colorado Center for the Arts
WEST MESA AVENUE
MESA AVENUE
TEXAS AVENUE
MESA STATE COLLEGE
Sherwood Park
INDEPENDENT AVENUE
ELM AVENUE
ELM COURT
KENNEDY AVENUE
FRANKLIN AVENUE
MOTOR STREET
GLENWOOD AVENUE
BUNTING AVENUE
CANTELL AVENUE
NORTH AVENUE
Fruita
Lilac Park
BELFORD AVENUE
TELLER AVENUE
HILL AVENUE
Lincoln Park
GUNNISON AVENUE
CHIPETA AVENUE
OURAY AVENUE
PEACH STREET
GRAND AVENUE
WHITE AVENUE
RICE STREET
ROOD AVENUE
Dinosaur Valley Museum
MAIN STREET
COLORADO AVENUE
Train Station
Bus Station
UTE AVENUE
CHULUOTA AVE
LAWRENCE AVENUE
FAIRVIEW AVENUE
Museum of Western Colorado
PITKIN AVENUE
SOUTH AVENUE
HALE AVENUE
D ROAD
RIVERSIDE PARK DRIVE
4 & Colorado National Monument
2ND STREET
3RD STREET
4TH STREET
5TH STREET
6TH STREET
9TH STREET
10TH STREET
11TH STREET
12TH STREET
13TH STREET
14TH STREET
6
bus 70
50
0 500 yards
Delta

Best Western Horizon Inn 754 Horizon Drive ⓣ970/245-1410. Reliable, good-value chain hotel with amenities that include a pool, spa, and free continental breakfast. ❸
Daniel's Motel 333 North Ave ⓣ970/243-1084. Basic clean motel rooms; the rates are hard to beat and the location convenient to downtown. ❷
H-Motel 333 Hwys 6 & 50, Fruita ⓣ970/858-7198. Fruita's only lodging option; a cheap, but clean, motel with cable TV and phones. ❷
Los Altos 375 Hill View Drive ⓣ970/256-0964 or 1-888/774-0982. Friendly B&B, located in a picturesque location southwest of town at the foot of the Colorado National Monument. Communal areas on the third floor make the most of views and there's a large outdoor deck too. Breakfast includes tasty home-baked goods. ❻
Hotel Melrose 337 Colorado Ave ⓣ970/242-9636 or 1-800/430-4555. Sociable downtown hostel in a Victorian-era hotel that's still furnished with antiques. Both private rooms ($30; some with private bath) and dorm beds ($12) are on offer, and facilities include a kitchen, lounge, and outdoor bbq area.
Value Lodge 104 White Ave ⓣ970/242-0651. Another affordable motel close to downtown, with cable TV, phones, and swimming pool. ❷

The town and around

After driving through the unsightly sprawl of light industry and commercial forecourts that make up Grand Junction's outskirts, the leafy **downtown** core comes as a pleasant surprise. Here, Main Street is lined with an affable mix of c.1900 buildings and a number of creative bronze busts and other sculptures. Though the Dinosaur National Monument (see p.311) is ninety miles north on Hwy-139, Grand Junction is in many ways a better place to get an impression of these prehistoric reptiles as it's home to both the Devil's Canyon Science and Learning Center (see below) and the extensive and enjoyable **Dinosaur Valley Museum**, 362 Main St (summer daily 9am–5pm; rest of year Tues–Sat 10am–4.30pm; $4.50). The museum's collection includes reconstructed reptiles, replica eggs, and casts of footprints and giant bones excavated locally – all helping to create a vivid picture of these beasts.

Two blocks south along the main drag stands the **Museum of Western Colorado**, 248 S 4th St (Tues–Sat 10am–4pm; $2), a small but diverting museum that does a good job of summing up the history of western Colorado with artifacts including well-preserved Ute baskets, bows, and arrows. The **Western Colorado Center for the Arts**, 1803 N 7th St (Tues–Sat 9am–4pm; $2; ⓣ970/243-7337), is also a good place to get a handle on the area; it displays a permanent collection of impressive Navajo rugs and is also home to rotating collections of other Native American and contemporary Western art.

If you have kids in tow, you should also make time for the diverting **Devil's Canyon Science and Learning Center**, in nearby Fruita at 550 Jurassic Court (daily 9am–5pm; $5.50). The interactive displays here include an earthquake simulator, mock dinosaur quarry, and some amazingly lifelike robotic dinosaur simulations.

For a more adult attraction, you can tour **wineries** around the small, sprawling and rather nondescript town of **Palisade**, twelve miles west of Grand Junction and the epicenter of Colorado's little-known, but underrated wine industry. The town appears to be particularly well placed for fruit cultivation – not only do many of the succulent Colorado peaches hail from Palisade, but the hot days here allow grapes to build up sugar while cool nights are said to add a distinctive crispness to local wines. Though the area's wine-growing tradition spans over a hundred years, the ripping out of vines during Prohibition largely put the industry into hibernation, until the last couple of decades when interest has resurfaced. Around half a dozen vineyards include relaxed places to enjoy the wines, including Plum Creek Cellars, 3708 G Rd (daily 10am–5pm; ⓣ970/464-7586), who've been producing wine since 1984; and the Carlson Vineyards, 462 35 Rd (daily 11am–6pm; ⓣ970/464-5554), who like to give their wines jolly names like the Tyrannosaurus Red or the Prairie Dog Blush.

Harvest time, in mid-September, is a particularly good time to visit Palisade, since it's the scheduled time for the **Colorado Mountain Winefest**, where the areas wineries club together to provide live music and appetizers free of charge (Ⓣ1-800/704-3667, Ⓦwww.coloradowine.com).

Colorado National Monument and Rattlesnake Canyon

Millions of years of wind and water erosion have gouged out the brightly colored rock spires, domes, arches, pedestals, and balanced rocks of the **Colorado National Monument**, on cliff-edges overlooking the valley four miles southwest of Grand Junction. This billion-year-old painted desert of warm reds, stunning purples, burnt oranges, and browns is also home to a high arid vegetation of piñon pine, yucca, sagebrush, and Utah juniper.

The Monument has two entrances ($5) at either end of the single 23-mile **Rim Rock Drive** that passes through it; one at its southern close to Grand Junction, the other at Fruita. Along with your park pass, you'll receive a leaflet on the monument, a map, and the main points of interest along the way. Even just driving the length of the twisting and curving road is a spectacular experience, and though too busy to enjoy on a **bike** during weekends, during the week it makes for an invigorating ride. Bikes are banned on all park trails, though, so to explore beyond the road you'll have to strike out on foot. One of the best short hikes is the one-hour **John Otto's Trail**, which affords close-up views of several monoliths. Longer trails get right down to the canyon floor: the six-mile **Monument Canyon Trail** weaves through a series of scenic spots. All trails are depicted on the leaflet you receive on entering, but for more detailed information call in at the **visitors' center** at the north (Fruita) end of the monument (May–Sept 8am–7pm, rest of year 9am–5pm; Ⓣ970/858-3617, Ⓦwww.nps.gov/colm). The monument's only campground, the basic *Saddlehorn Campground* ($10), is near the visitors' center; campers looking for solitude should take advantage of the fact that you're allowed to pitch a tent anywhere more than a quarter of a mile off the road for free. Out of Fruita, Rimrock Adventures (Ⓣ970/858-9555) offer **horseback-riding** trips around the monument and also arrange rafting trips in the area.

Though outside the monument itself, **Rattlesnake Canyon**, which contains some huge spectacular hundred-foot-wide natural rock arches, is most easily reached from the southern end of Rim Rock Drive. Amid bizarrely eroded Entrada sandstone canyons, the hardy can strike out, hiking or biking (or even four-wheeling if you have a vehicle with plenty of clearance), to the twelve natural rock arches. The largest, Rainbow bridge, spans around one hundred feet and is particularly photogenic late or early in the day when its shadows lengthen. To get there you need to follow the **Black Ridge Access Road**, which starts eleven miles from the northern (Fruita) entrance to the monument and is signposted at the Glade Park Store. It's a thirteen-mile drive to the trailhead and high clearance 4WD vehicles are required for the last mile and a half; do not attempt this drive in wet conditions as the road gets very slippery and dangerous. From the end of the road, a trail drops down through one arch on the start of a two-mile loop that visits all the main arches in the group. En route, watch your step – the canyon was named Rattlesnake Canyon for a reason (see box, opposite), though you're highly unlikely to have a problem. The canyon, once a national monument itself, is now managed by BLM, who have an office in Grand Junction at 2815 H Rd (daily Mon–Fri 7.30am–4.30pm; Ⓣ970/244-3000).

Rattlesnakes

Of all the snakes in the Rockies, the only poisonous one you are likely to meet is the **rattlesnake**. You might not be able to tell a rattler from any other kind of snake; in fact many rattlers don't rattle at all. If in doubt, assume it is one. When it's hot, snakes lurk in shaded areas under bushes, around wood debris, old mining shafts, and piles of rocks. When it's cooler, they sun themselves out in the open, but they won't be expecting you and if disturbed will attack. A bite is initially like a sharp pin-prick, but within hours the pain becomes severe, usually accompanied by swelling and acute nausea. Forget any misconceptions you may harbor about sucking the poison out; it doesn't work and even tends to hasten the spread of venom. Since venom travels mainly through the lymph system just under the skin, the best way of inhibiting the diffusion is to wrap the whole limb firmly, but not in a tourniquet, then contact a ranger or doctor as soon as possible. Do all you can to keep calm – a slower pulse rate limits the spread of the venom. Keep in mind that even if a snake does bite you, about fifty percent of the time it's a dry – or non-venomous – strike. Snakes don't want to waste their venom on something too large to eat. However, it's a wise precaution to carry a snake-bite kit, available for a couple of dollars from most sports and camping stores.

Outdoor activities

Though the Colorado National Monument is the obvious draw in the area, there are many more worthwhile trails around Grand Junction. The rippled, purple-gray **Bookcliffs**, paralleling the town on the north side, whose subtle changes of color throughout the day are a delight, are a good venue for **hiking**. The area is managed by the BLM as a reserve to protect wild horses, but is open to use by hikers, horseback riders, mountain bikers, and campers. The cliffs themselves also attract rock climbers. In Grand Junction, Summit Canyon Mountaineering, 549 Main St (Ⓣ970/243-2847), can supply you with relevant information and gear.

Lauded by the mountain-biking press as the next Moab (Utah), Fruita, thirteen miles northwest of Grand Junction, is an off-road paradise. Indeed, Fruita is connected to the mythical Moab by the 128-mile-long **Kokopelli Trail**, a stupendous off-road adventure. Obviously, most riders in the area concentrate on riding shorter loops. These include the smooth, rolling single-track at the base of the Fruita end of the Bookcliffs north of town, or the more rugged trails that roller coaster south of town, overlooking the broad Colorado River and the parched landscapes in neighboring Utah. For more information, head to Over the Edge Sports, 202 E Aspen Ave (Ⓣ970/858-7220), a block east of the roundabout at the center of Fruita. Their knowledge of current local conditions is indispensable, and a map of local trails can be picked up for $1; front-suspension bikes are rented for $28 per day. You can also rent bikes and pick up route details at several shops in Grand Junction, including Bicycle Outfitters, 248 Ute Ave (Ⓣ970/245-2699).

Eating and drinking

Blue Moon Bar & Grill 120 N 7th St Ⓣ970/242-5406. Busy bar, with a decent range of bar food, sandwiches – including a tasty kalamari steak sandwich in pita bread ($6) – and salads ($6) for lunch; steaks and pizza in the evening. There's often live music here at weekends.

Dolce Vita 336 Main St Ⓣ970/242-8482. Good Northern Italian food with unusual dishes like polenta with wine-marinated portobello mushrooms or an angel-hair pasta tossed with chicken, capers, and artichoke hearts. Moderately expensive.

La Mexicana 1310 Ute Ⓣ970/245-2737. A very lively Mexican place, particularly at weekends when there's folk dancing. The food is as authentic as the atmosphere, and prices reasonable. Closed Sunday and Monday.

Main Street Bagels 559 Main St ⑦970/241-2740. Huge variety of bagels for breakfast or lunch; take out or eat in the large, laid-back dining area.

Rockslide Brew Pub 401 Main ⑦970/245-2111. Serves up a good variety of beers, but is most popular for its huge portions; both the burgers ($7) and cobb salad ($8) are recommended.

The Rose 2993 North Ave (⑦970/245-0606). Cornerstone of the local Country and Western scene. There's live music here almost nightly, making it a reliably busy bar.

7th Street Café 832 S 7th St ⑦970/242-7225. A retro, 1950s diner with the standard array of good-value meals; from meatloaf to burritos.

The Winery 642 Main St ⑦970/242-4100. A fairly expensive but stylish restaurant – exposed brick, stained glass, dark wooden beams – serving reliable steak, prime rib, and shrimp dishes to be accompanied by a comprehensive array of local wines.

Travel details

Trains

(all services Amtrak)

Grand Junction to: Denver (1 daily; 8hr 35min); Glenwood Springs (1 daily; 1hr 55min); Salt Lake City (1 daily; 17hr 15min).

Buses

(all buses are Greyhound unless otherwise stated)

Denver from: Frisco (4 daily; 1hr 45min); Glenwood Springs (4 daily; 3hr 45min); Grand Junction (4 daily; 5hr 50min; TNM&O and Greyhound); Vail (4 daily; 2hr 10min).

Grand Junction to: Cañon City (1 daily; 6hr; TNM&O); Denver (4 daily; 5hr 50min; TNM&O and Greyhound); Durango (2 daily; 5hr; TNM&O); Gunnison (1 daily; 2hr 45min; TNM&O); Montrose (2 daily; 1hr 30min; TNM&O); Pueblo (1 daily; 6hr 45min; TNM&O); Salida (1 daily; 4hr 45min; TNM&O); Salt Lake City (1 daily; 6hr 50min; TNM&O); Silverton (1 daily; 3hr; TNM&O).

Flights

Aspen to: Denver (14 daily; 45min);

Eagle (Vail) to: Denver (5 daily; 45min);

Grand Junction to: Denver (12 daily; 1hr 10min); Salt Lake City (7 daily; 1hr 20min).

Northern Colorado

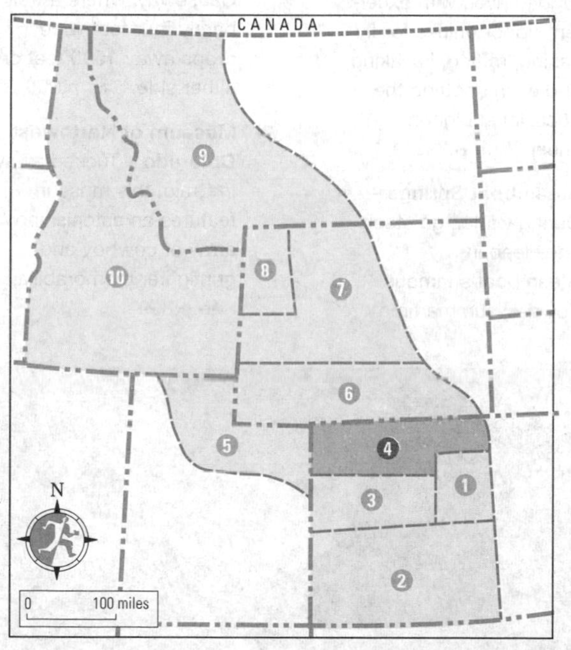

CHAPTER 4 Highlights

* **Rocky Mountain National Park** – The state's best hiking, plus the chance to view moose, elk, deer, and even black bear. See p.275

* **Cache la Poudre** – A rugged river, with excellent opportunities for fly-fishing, rafting, kayaking, and even spotting the occasional bighorn sheep. See p.292

* **Steamboat Springs** – During winter, go steep-and-deep in Steamboat's famous powder; summertime brings endless sunshine to go with rafting, mountain biking and even hot-air ballooning. See p.296

* **The Flat Tops Wilderness** – Real get-away-from-it-all hiking; a highlight is the Devil's Causeway, where a trail barely four feet wide drops away 1500 feet on either side. See p.305

* **Museum of Northwest Colorado** – Tucked away in Craig, this museum features an astonishing array of cowboy and gunfighter memorabilia. See p.309

Northern Colorado

Barely a century ago, outlaws like Butch Cassidy and the Sundance Kid found it easy to evade capture in picturesque **NORTHERN COLORADO** simply because the region was so sparsely populated. Today, much remains the same, though this scarcity of people now favors not outlaws but those who fancy secluded trails, wildlife spotting, and high-altitude rivers and lakes where peace and quiet are teamed with beautiful mountain terrain. There's a subtle shift in mood once you branch north from I-40, and the cowboy towns hereabouts show little sign of the self-conscious Old West makeover that is so prevalent in central and southern Colorado. It's not all abandoned mining towns and ghosts of cowboys past though, as shown by northern Colorado's two high-profile destinations – **Rocky Mountain National Park** and **Steamboat Springs** – that give the region plenty to boast about besides cultural and geographic separation from the "busier" parts of the state.

The area's main artery is the stretch of I-40 between **Granby** and **Craig**, taking in the tiny highway town of **Kremmling** – a favorite of hunters and fisherfolk – and the mineral spa resort of **Hot Sulphur Springs** on the way to Steamboat Springs, one of Colorado's most appealing ski destinations. Leaving Granby, I-34 raises the scenery stakes still further as it travels northeast via **Grand Lake** through majestic Rocky Mountain National Park, and on to the heavily touristed gateway town of **Estes Park**. The nearest thing to a city in Colorado's northern reaches, **Fort Collins** is a pleasant university town less than fifty miles from the park's eastern edge, and with even handier access to the excellent fishing and rafting of the **Cache la Poudre River**. The dry and dusty northwestern corner of the state is still revealing an exceptional collection of fossilized dinosaur bits in an area designated as **Dinosaur National Monument**. Meanwhile, the **Flat Tops Wilderness**, flanked on the west and

Accommodation price codes

All accommodation prices in this book have been coded using the symbols below. For **hotels**, **motels**, and **B&Bs**, rates are given for the least expensive double room in each establishment during peak season; variations are indicated where appropriate, including winter rates for all ski resorts. For **hostels**, we've given a specific price per bed; for **camping**, the overnight cost per site is given. For a full explanation see p.30 in Basics.

❶ up to $30	❹ $60–80	❼ $130–180
❷ $30–45	❺ $80–100	❽ $180–240
❸ $45–60	❻ $100–130	❾ over $240

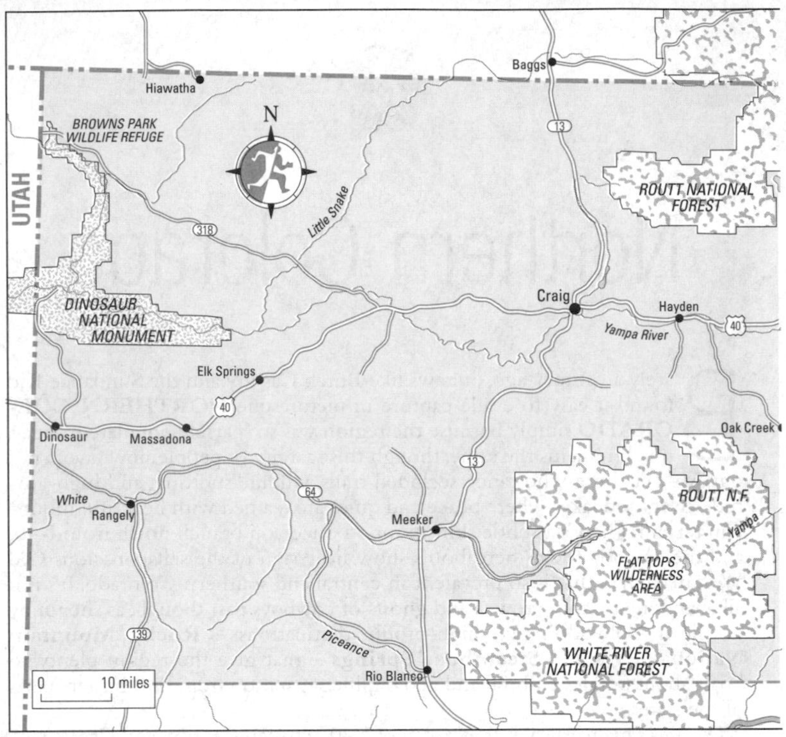

east respectively by the towns of **Meeker** and **Yampa**, is a backcountry gem that gets less attention than it deserves.

As far as the region's **history** goes, the colonization by white people of the northern reaches of Colorado is a familiar story, with greedy prospectors unable or unwilling to continue the positive relationships that had been established between nomadic fur-trappers – the so-called "mountain men" – and the native Ute people. The US government, meanwhile, was also doing its best to alienate the indigenous inhabitants of the region; between 1860 and 1873, it enacted and then broke four separate treaties with the Utes. The government finally enforced a "relocation program," which essentially saw the Utes herded out of Colorado en masse and onto reservations in Utah.

The possibility of finding gold may have been initially responsible for drawing folk on horseback and in wagon-trains into the remoter reaches of Colorado, but coal and beef cattle would become, by the turn of the twentieth century, the staple livelihoods of those who remained. Union Pacific Railroad railheads in southern Wyoming provided essential, if not entirely convenient, access to markets out east, and once the Denver & Rio Grande Railroad had snaked its way to Steamboat Springs, the connection with the rest of the country was complete.

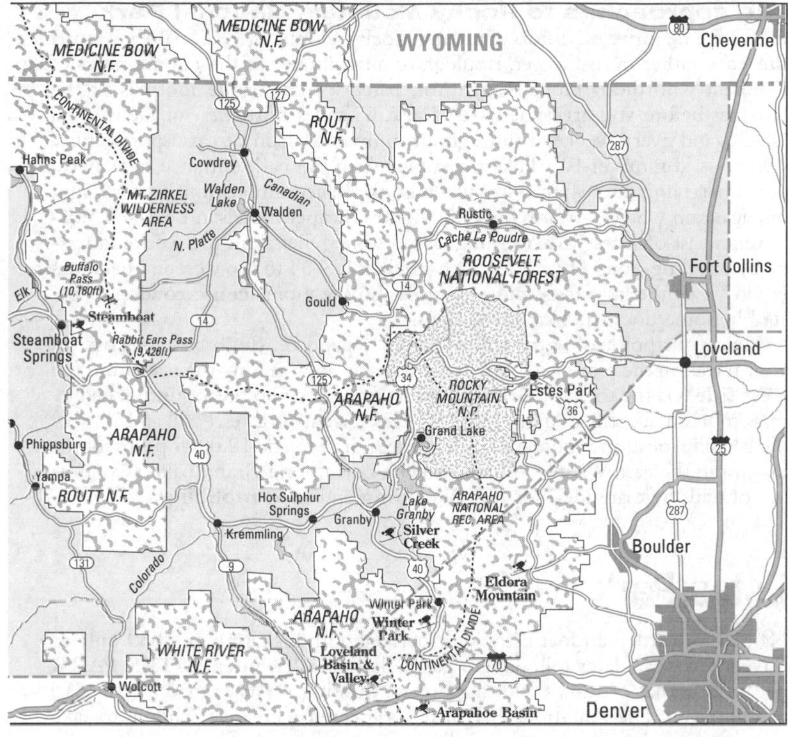

Rocky Mountain National Park and around

Any foray into northern Colorado should include a visit to **Rocky Mountain National Park**, which offers arguably the best hiking in the state along with excellent wildlife-viewing opportunities. The main question when heading to the park is whether to camp within its boundaries or to establish more civilized digs in a nearby town and visit the park from there. Fortunately, the choices for the latter option are quite clear-cut, with three obvious bases – **Grand Lake**, **Estes Park**, and **Fort Collins** – that each have their own merits. An hour's drive from the park's eastern entrance, Fort Collins does not qualify strictly as a gateway town, but it does make an excellent alternative to the hurly-burly of summer tourism in the towns nearer the park. Grand Lake, which straddles the park's western boundary, has unbeatable "doorstep" access to several trailheads, while larger Estes Park on the eastern border offers a greater range of accommodation choices, shopping, fast food, and amusements for kids.

The approaches to Rocky Mountain National Park

By far the majority of visitors approach Rocky Mountain National Park **from the east**, either from Denver, Boulder, or any number of the communities of Colorado's northern Front Range. You barely penetrate the foothills of the Rockies before you arrive at **Estes Park**, 65 miles northwest of Denver via US-36, and every weekend throughout summer a chain of cars, sports utility vehicles and monster RVs links the capital with the park entrance here. Most people arriving after 4pm without prebooked accommodation head straight out again on US-34, towards the only slightly cheaper motels in Loveland, thirty miles east of Estes Park. You might find some relief from the weekend traffic by traveling along Hwy-72, which parallels US-34 to the west and becomes Hwy-7 over the last fifteen miles – this is also the more **scenic road**, punctuated by some dramatic rock formations.

While your point of entry will probably depend on the broader picture of your travels in the region, it's worth considering approaching the park from the **west side**, via the town of **Grand Lake**. Although by no means untouched by mass tourism, it's still a far cry from the tacky scene at Estes Park, and it's scenic lakeside location is bordered by a number of dramatic 12,000ft peaks looming just to the east. **Winter** visitors will fare best around Grand Lake, as a number of trails here are ideal for **Nordic skiing** and **snowmobiling**.

Estes Park

Named for cattleman Joel Estes, who arrived with his family in 1859 only to leave a few years later following a particularly harsh winter, **ESTES PARK** became, by that century's end, the private hunting preserve of the Irish Earl of Dunraven. The ambitious Earl had engineered a creative scheme to take possession of virtually the entire valley: at a time when land ownership in the valley was restricted to 160 acres per person, Dunraven "sponsored" land purchases by various drifters and layabouts – and even some occupants of the local cemetery – and then transferred ownership of every parcel to himself. It's not clear how Dunraven's mini-empire unravelled, but in 1903 a far more progressive influence arrived in the person of **Freelan O. Stanley**, inventor of the "Stanley Steamer," a steam-powered automobile. Stanley came in search of relief from his respiratory ailments and ended up erecting the stunning *Stanley Hotel* in 1909 (see "Accommodation", p.269); the town soon began to take on the more democratic function it still serves, of providing visitors to Rocky Mountain National Park with food and lodging. Unfortunately, as the park's **main gateway**, Estes Park now has a wide array of tacky tourist shops, mini-golf and amusement arcades, along with all the traffic nightmares expected in a town whose population fluctuates seasonally between four thousand and 35,000, with up to three million people passing through annually.

The cheery news is that the problem is a bit less dramatic outside the peak holiday period (June–Aug), and the scenery around Estes Park is undeniably beautiful, the green foothills of the Rockies dotted with photogenic rock formations. By mid-fall, most tourists have gone, many businesses are closing down for the winter, and herds of elk arrive in numbers, often setting up camp right in the middle of town.

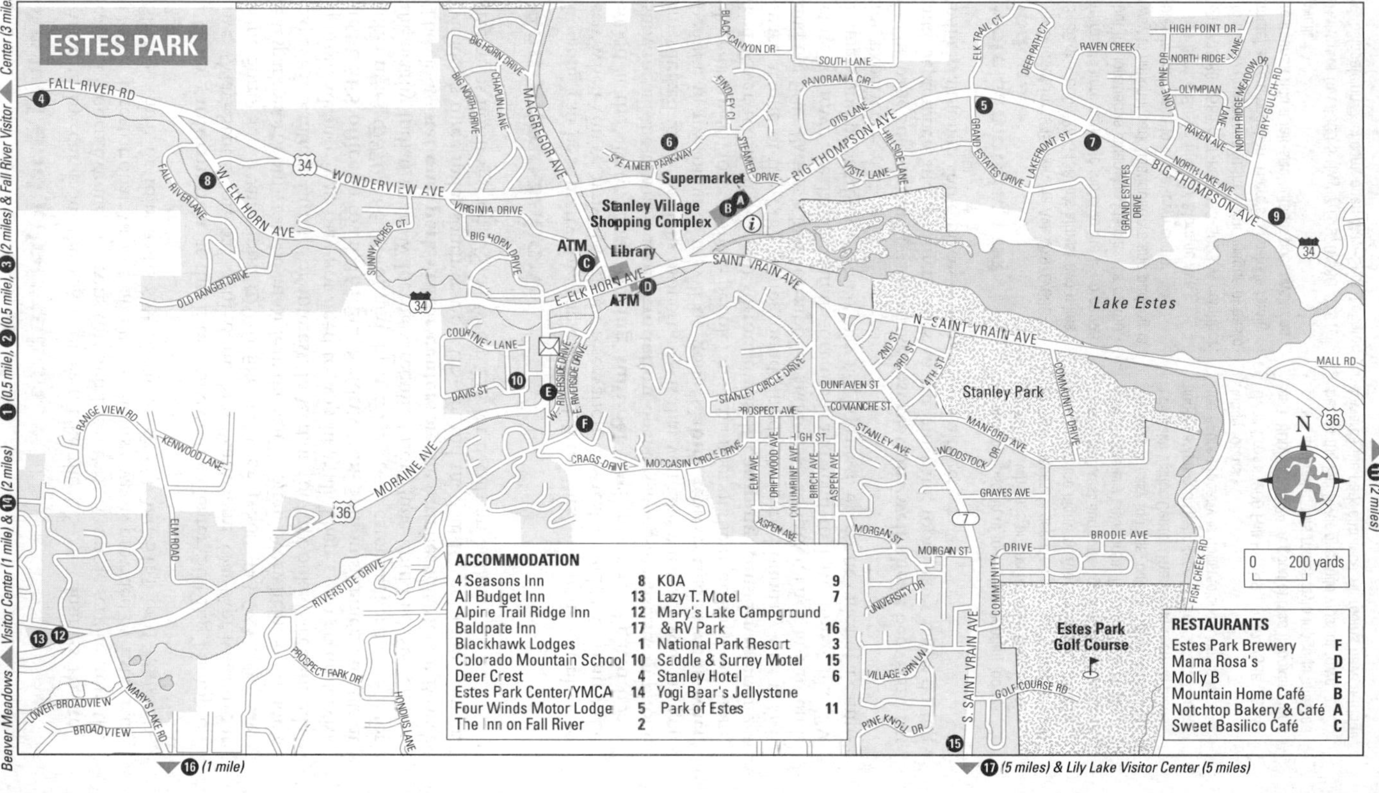
ESTES PARK
Beaver Meadows Visitor Center (1 mile) & 14 (2 miles)
1 (0.5 mile), 2 (0.5 mile), 3 (2 miles) & Fall River Visitor Center (3 miles)
16 (1 mile)
17 (5 miles) & Lily Lake Visitor Center (5 miles)
11 (2 miles)
ACCOMMODATION
4 Seasons Inn 8
All Budget Inn 13
Alpine Trail Ridge Inn 12
Baldpate Inn 17
Blackhawk Lodges 1
Colorado Mountain School 10
Deer Crest 4
Estes Park Center/YMCA 14
Four Winds Motor Lodge 5
The Inn on Fall River 2
KOA 9
Lazy T. Motel 7
Mary's Lake Campground & RV Park 16
National Park Resort 3
Saddle & Surrey Motel 15
Stanley Hotel 6
Yogi Bear's Jellystone Park of Estes 11
RESTAURANTS
Estes Park Brewery F
Mama Rosa's D
Molly B E
Mountain Home Café B
Notchtop Bakery & Café A
Sweet Basilico Café C
0 200 yards
N
Lake Estes
Stanley Park
Estes Park Golf Course
Supermarket
Stanley Village Shopping Complex
Library
ATM
FALL RIVER RD
W. ELK HORN AVE
E. ELK HORN AVE
WONDERVIEW AVE
MACGREGOR AVE
BIG THOMPSON AVE
SAINT VRAIN AVE
N. SAINT VRAIN AVE
S. SAINT VRAIN AVE
MORAINE AVE
RIVERSIDE DRIVE
W. RIVERSIDE DRIVE
E. RIVERSIDE DRIVE
COMMUNITY DRIVE
FISH CREEK RD
GOLF COURSE RD
MALL RD
DRY GULCH RD
STEAMER PARKWAY
STEAMER DRIVE

Arrival and information

Arriving **by car** from the south or east, take the US-34 "Business Route," called Elkhorn Avenue as it runs through Estes Park. A shuttle service from the Denver International Airport, about two hours away, is provided by Estes Park Shuttle (three or four daily, $39 one-way; ⓣ970/586-5151 or 1-800/950-3274).

Getting **information** at the Estes Park Visitor Center, 500 Big Thompson Ave (May–Sept Mon–Sat 8am–8pm, Sun 9am–5pm; Oct–April Mon–Sat 8am–5pm, Sun 10am–4pm; ⓣ970/586-4431 or 1-800/443-7837, ⓦwww.estesparkresort.com), can be an ordeal; the staff is often overwhelmed, so don't expect too much warmth or interest. Indeed, if you've booked accommodations in advance, you may not need to stop in at all. There's also an undervisited **USFS office** in town, 161 2nd St (daily 9am–5pm in summer, variable at other times; ⓣ970/586-3440), and the staff here issue camping permits ($5) for the nearby Indian Peaks Wilderness, required from June until mid-September. The closest **national park visitor centers** are the park headquarters at Beaver Meadows three miles southwest on US-36, and the Fall River Visitor Center, five miles northwest on US-34 (see p.278 for details on both).

Accommodation

Lodging can be a pretty sore topic around Estes Park, and finding a place to stay when you've arrived without reservations is a real scramble. Certainly the mood at the visitor center **during summer** – when a huge, lighted board showing all the town's **accommodation** operates alongside a series of phone lines linked to the various properties – is that you take whatever you can get, because in five minutes it will be gone. **Cabins** represent good value when shared between four or more people, and a number of them are lined out along Fall River Road in peaceful surroundings. If **camping**, consider reserving a space at one of the NPS campgrounds inside the park boundary (see p.278) and use Estes Park as a base for supplies and to take a shower. The campgrounds close to town are largely family-oriented, and tend to have things like TV lounges and pool tables – which may not equate to everyone's idea of a camping experience.

The basic rule of thumb is to make **reservations well ahead** between May and September, and at other times to bargain hard; room rates halve during winter, although some places will be closed altogether.

Hotels, motels, and lodges

All Budget Inn 945 Moraine Ave ⓣ970/586-3485 or 1-800/628-3438. It's almost two miles from this unremarkable motel to the town center, but the location is otherwise ideal as it's on the way to national park headquarters and parking is a breeze compared to in the town center. ❹

Alpine Trail Ridge Inn 927 Moraine Ave ⓣ970/586-4585 or 1-800/233-5023. A neighbor to the *All Budget* and in the same league of basic motel accommodation. There's a no-frills family restaurant and a fair-size outdoor pool onsite as well. ❹

Baldpate Inn 4900 S Hwy-7 ⓣ970/586-6151, ⓔbaldpateinn@aol.com; open May–Sept. Located seven miles south of town, this wooden lodge-style B&B, which is on the National Register of Historic Places, is secreted away in a wooded spot away from the highway. Attractions here include bird-filled forest surroundings and proximity to trails in the Lily Lake area. The turnoff from the highway is easy to miss, but it's right beside the Lily Lake Visitor Center. The dining room is pleasingly casual and rustic (see "Eating", p.270), and the entire property is nonsmoking. Cabins ❼, lodge rooms ❺

Deer Crest 1200 Fall River Rd ⓣ970/586-2324 or 1-800/331-2324. A good choice if looking for peace and quiet, this motel-style lodge is situated beside the Fall River one mile west of town towards the park entrance. All rooms have a fridge and microwave, and there's also a pool and hot tub. No smoking and no children under 12. ⑥

Estes Park Center/YMCA 2515 Tunnel Rd Ⓣ970/586-3341. Primarily a group-oriented, activities-based center, with a range of fairly spartan four- to ten-person cabins and four- to six-person lodge rooms on an 860-acre property. Really only a good option for families keen on organized outings such as horseback riding. Cabins $70–240, lodge rooms ④

4 Seasons Inn 1130 W Elkhorn Ave Ⓣ970/586-5693 or 1-800/779-4616. Cozy and quiet are the watchwords at this motel lodge, where kids and pets and all other things noisy are verboten. All rooms have a queen bed, fridge, coffee-maker, and microwave, plus private bath. ⑥

Four Winds Motor Lodge 1120 Big Thompson Ave Ⓣ970/586-3313 or 1-800/527-7509. These motel rooms are set back far enough from the road to enjoy a quiet night, and they have coffee-makers and small fridges too. Facilities include a large outdoor heated pool, indoor sauna and hot tub and you can picnic or barbecue on the lawn out front. ④

Lazy T Motel 1340 Big Thompson Ave Ⓣ970/586-4376 or 1-800/530-8822. A basic motel with garish pink and green exterior, but the rooms are clean, there's a small outdoor pool, and it's among the least expensive options in town. ③

Saddle & Surrey Motel 1341 S St Vrain Ave Ⓣ970/586-3326 or 1-800/204-6226. At a mile south along Hwy-7 it's still pretty close to town, and the owners are friendly and cheerful. There's an outdoor pool and hot tub, and some rooms have kitchenettes. ④

Stanley Hotel 333 Wonderview Ave Ⓣ970/586-3371 or 1-800/976-1377. Built in 1909, complete with a fantastic mountainside location, this is the town's architectural showpiece and prestige lodging property. The building has further claim to fame for having inspired former hotel guest and author Stephen King to invent his creepy, rambling hotel creation in *The Shining*; the management has turned this to advantage by hosting an annual "The Shining" Halloween Ball. ⑦

Cabins

Blackhawk Lodges 1750 Fall River Rd Ⓣ970/586-6100, Ⓦwww.estesparkresort.com/blackhawk. Ten cabins in a quiet spot by the river, each with a fireplace, full-equipped kitchen, and TV; the largest of them can accommodate six people comfortably. There's a riverside hot tub and trout fishing onsite. Summer ⑥–⑦; winter rates also available.

The Inn on Fall River 1600 Fall River Rd Ⓣ970/586-4118 or 1-800/255-4118, Ⓦwww.innonfallriver.com. These two-bedroom riverside cabins are ideal for families, and have their own kitchen, fireplace, and patio or balcony. Motel-style rooms also available (⑤). Cabins ⑦. Open year-round.

National Park Resort 3501 Fall River Rd Ⓣ970/586-4563. Located close to the Fall River park entrance, the resort offers a variety of motel rooms, and simple cabins that can accommodate up to six people. The cabins have fully-equipped kitchens, bathrooms, and TV, and most have fireplaces and riverside decks. Some also have small outdoor hot tubs. Cabins (⑥) open year-round, motel rooms (④) open May–Sept. Shaded tent sites are also available for $25 for two people.

Hostel and camping

Colorado Mountain School 351 Moraine Ave Ⓣ970/586-5758, Ⓕ586-5798, Ⓦwww.cmschool.com. The closest thing to a hostel in town, but there is no communal kitchen or living area, bathroom facilities are minimal and the building is sorely in need of overall maintenance. On weekends, all the beds may be booked for groups on climbing courses – which is the actual purpose of the place (see p.284). Dorm beds $20, includes towel and soap.

KOA 2051 Big Thompson Ave Ⓣ970/586-2888 or 1-800/KOA-1887; May to mid-Oct. Along with the usual shared shower and laundry facilities there's a TV lounge and small grocery store. Tent sites $22, camper cabins with bunk beds $45.

Mary's Lake Campground & RV Park 2120 Mary's Lake Rd Ⓣ970/586-4411 or 1-800/445-6279; May to mid-Sept. Although primarily an RV park, there are some shaded tent sites too, and the location – beside the lake for which the campground is named – is a good one. There's a small heated pool plus a game room complete with pool table. Tent sites $21, sites with full hookup $26.

Yogi Bear's Jellystone Park of Estes 5495 I-36 Ⓣ970/586-4230 or 1-800/722-2928; open May–Sept. Among the family-fun attractions here are a large heated pool, basketball court, game room, TV lounge, and wagon rides for kids. As well as tent and RV sites there are three camper cabins ($40–50) and five fully-equipped cabins with kitchen and bathroom that can sleep up to eight people ($100–260). Tent sites $21. RV $26.

The town

No one comes to Estes Park to visit Estes Park; there are no quaint frontier-era buildings, no Western-style boardwalks, and really no reason to be here other than the proximity to the national park. A stroll along central Elkhorn Avenue does reveal a fair degree of commercial enthusiasm, but it's mostly of the tacky souvenir-store variety. An unavoidable landmark is the **aerial tramway**, which has little to recommend it unless you don't plan to go any further for a view of the mountains; it takes you to the top of Prospect Mountain from 420 E Riverside Drive (June–Aug daily 9am–dusk; $10).

While there's nothing much about the history of Estes Park itself that bears exploring, you can get to grips with some of Rocky Mountain National Park's history at **Enos Mills' Cabin**, c.1885, eight miles south of town along Hwy-7 (summer Tues–Sat 11am–5pm; winter Sat & Sun 11am–5pm; free). Here the work of naturalist Enos Mills, the man who pushed for Congress to create the national park, is preserved in the form of books of his writings as well as some interesting news clippings and letters. There is also a small display of Mills' photos taken at various locations in the park between 1900 and 1922 – the year he died.

Outdoor activities

While you'll probably use up your energy hiking in the national park, there are a few other diversions to consider, such as spending a day cycling about town or along trails around Glen Haven, seven miles northeast of Estes Park (no off-road cycling is permitted inside the national park). For advice on area rides and for **bike rental**, try Estes Park Mountain Shop, 358 Elkhorn Ave (Ⓣ970/586-6548 or 1-800/504-6642), or Colorado Bicycle, 184 Elkhorn Ave (Ⓣ970/586-4241); both rent mountain bikes from $22 per day. The USFS office (see p.268) has some basic free maps of forest trails too.

National Park Village Stables (Ⓣ970/586-5269) and Sombrero Ranch (Ⓣ970/586-4577, Ⓦwww.sombrero.com) both offer gentle nose-to-tail **horserides** into the national park, from 1hr to overnight pack trips. The best whitewater **rafting** is well north of town in the Cache la Poudre Canyon (see p.292); both Rapid Transit (Ⓣ970/586-2303 or 1-800/367-8523) and Estes Park Mountain Shop (Ⓣ970/586-6548 or 1-800/504-6642) run half-day trips from here for around $45, including transportation.

Eating and drinking

Considering the high concentration of tourists, Estes Park is a bit lacking in really notable **places to eat**. Being largely a domain for climbers, hikers, and families on vacation, you'll be stretched to find any really lively **nightspots** – food and sleep are generally more pressing subjects than carousing after a day or two out in the mountains.

Baldpate Inn 4900 S Highway 7, seven miles south of town Ⓣ970/586-6151. A standout for its location and setting, the *Baldpate Inn* has no menu, just an $11 all-you-can-eat soup-and-salad bar, a must visit for its hearty soups, fresh-baked gourmet breads, and a good range of salads, with cheese and crackers to finish. Dinner only; reservations are essential and they stop serving at 8pm.

Estes Park Brewery 470 E Riverside. If you're just after a pizza to go with a beer and perhaps a game of pool, then this should suffice. As it's basically just a pub, and not quite in the town center, there are usually fewer "vacationers" and more hikers and climbers.

Mama Rosa's 338 Elkhorn Ave Ⓣ970/586-3330. The Italian standards – lasagne, veal, and pizzas – on offer are decent if unspectacular; prices are moderate and it's very central, with outdoor seating in a small plaza. Open daily for lunch and dinner.

Molly B 200 Moraine Ave ☎970/586-2766. This restaurant is a real stalwart, with a surprising variety of dishes and prices – some cooked breakfast combo's go for diner prices. At lunch there are sandwiches, salads, seafood quesadillas and vegetarian lasagna, while the moderately priced dinner menu stretches to trout, salmon, steaks, and even a vegetarian Indian stir-fry. Daily: May–Oct 6.30am–9pm; Nov–April for breakfast and lunch only.
Mountain Home Cafe upper Stanley Village. A good spot to fill up early in the day, with big breakfast combo's at $4–5, plus huge burgers at lunchtime; veggie choices include mushroom or garden burgers. Daily 7am–2.30pm.
Notchtop Bakery & Cafe upper Stanley Village ☎970/586-0272. The name doesn't quite do justice to a mix of food that stretches from fresh baked goods, omelettes, and pancakes for breakfast to pasta, seafood, and stir-fry specials for dinner, followed by a late-night menu of soups, desserts, speciality coffees and microbrews. There's even occasional live entertainment, and the place is completely smoke-free; it's worth calling ahead in the evening. Daily 7am–10pm (until 11pm Fri–Sat).
Sweet Basilico Cafe 401 E Elkhorn Ave ☎970/586-3899. Popular and inexpensive place for pizzas ($10), pasta dishes, and Italian specialities based on chicken or veal ($8–11); the $5 focaccia with your choice of toppings includes soup or salad. Daily 11am–9 or 10pm; closed Wed in winter.

Listings

Banks First National Bank has ATMs at 334 E Elkhorn Ave (center of town) and right behind the town park at cnr MacGregor Ave and Park Lane; Key Bank ATM is in upper Stanley Village.
Internet access Public Library, cnr Elkhorn and MacGregor avenues (Mon–Thurs 9am–9pm, Fri–Sat 9am–5pm, Sun 1–5pm; ☎970/586-8116; free access, but phone ahead during summer to reserve a terminal); The Peace Pilgrims Shop, upstairs at 165 Virginia Drive (summer daily 10am–9pm, winter hours vary; ☎970/586-9301; $12 per hour).
Laundry Dad's Maytag Laundry, upper Stanley Village (daily 7am–9.30pm; ☎970/586-2025); public showers $3.
Medical Center Estes Park Medical Center, 555 Prospect Ave (☎970/586-2317), has 24hr emergency care; normal consultation hours are Mon–Fri 8am–5pm & Sat 8am–noon.
Pharmacy inside Safeway, upper Stanley Village (Mon–Fri 9am–9pm, Sat 9am–6pm, Sun 10am–4pm).
Police 170 MacGregor Ave (☎970/586-4000; emergencies ☎911).
Post office 215 W Riverside Drive (Mon–Fri 9am–5pm, Sat 10am–2.30pm).
Supermarket The Safeway in upper Stanley Village is open 24hr.
Tours and transport Emerald Taxi ☎970/586-1991 offers a 4hr guided tour of the national park from $25 per person, and shuttle service to/from Denver (4–6 times daily) for $30 one-way; Estes Park Shuttle & Mountain Tours ☎970/586 5151 runs similar trips at slightly higher rates.

Grand Lake

Following its days in the late 1800s as a tiny, lakeside supply stop for prospectors who were heading into the neighboring mountains, **GRAND LAKE** was always going to eventually attract a fair number of summer vacation "cabin-dwellers." The lake itself is the largest natural body of water in Colorado, and back in 1901 that was reason enough to inaugurate the Grand Lake yacht club, which remains a prominent fixture today. Even so, the town miraculously remained something of an unheralded hideaway for much of the twentieth century. For better or worse, a Denver travel writer in the early 1980s trumpeted Grand Lake as Colorado's last "Shangri-la," and people have since arrived in numbers – a trend that cannot now be reversed.

The town's winter **population** of around four hundred nudges close to five thousand over summer, and the presence of two mini-golf courses and a ten-pin bowling center further confirms, at least for some, the direction in which the town is headed. Others would say that to really appreciate Grand Lake, you only have to spend a day in Estes Park. In any case, the town's **lakeside setting**

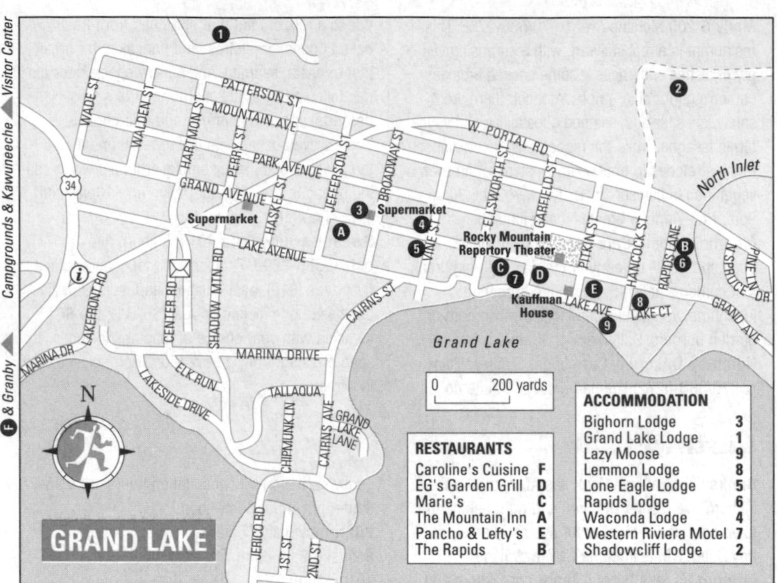

is superb, and the cluster of peaks that looms over the town to the east confirms that – bumper-to-bumper summer weekends notwithstanding – Grand Lake makes an excellent base for exploring Rocky Mountain National Park.

Arrival and information

It's a gentle uphill run once you leave I-40 at Granby and turn north onto I-34 to cover the fourteen-mile stretch up to Grand Lake. The tourist **information** office (Mon–Sat 9am–5pm, Sun 10am–4pm, winter hours variable; ⓣ970/627-3402, ⓦwww.grandlakechamber.com) is a tiny hut perched just off US-34 at the entrance to town. It's easy to drive past it as you turn off the highway, and it doesn't offer much useful information anyway – the only town map available is very poor, and information on Rocky Mountain National Park is dispensed at the Kawuneeche Visitor Center (see p.278) up the road. Downtown Grand Lake is the four blocks of Grand Avenue between Vine and Hancock streets lined with an Old West-style boardwalk. Almost everything is within reasonable walking distance except for *Grand Lake Lodge*, while *Shadowcliff Lodge* is several-minutes' walk up a very steep hill.

Accommodation

With trailheads leading directly from Grand Lake into Rocky Mountain National Park, you can have the convenience of decent **accommodation** coupled with immediate access to a pristine mountain environment. You won't be able to drive much of a bargain at any of the **motels** or **lodges** between May and September, and between June and August some may insist on at least three-nights' stay. **Cabins** are a great option for groups of four or more, but should be booked at least three months ahead. **Reservations** are essential during peak season, ideally several weeks in advance; some places close for the winter, but although things are slower then, they're certainly not quieter, thanks to enthusiastic snowmobilers.

Excellent **hostel** accommodation is available at *Shadowcliff Lodge*, and both private and public **campgrounds** are scattered about the town's outskirts.

Motels and cabins

Bighorn Lodge 613 Grand Ave ⓣ970/627-8101 or 1-800/341-8000. Conveniently central motel with clean rooms. Open year-round; minimum stay may be required during peak times and on weekends. ⑤

Grand Lake Lodge 15500 US-34, via a signposted turnoff half a mile north of town ⓣ970/627-3967, ⓕ627-9495; open June to mid-Sept. The lodge itself is a National Historic Landmark, but accommodations are in the rustic cabins clustered around it – and these are often booked up a year in advance. Facilities include a restaurant and bar with unparalleled views and occasional live music, plus there's an outdoor pool and hot tub; the larger cabins have kitchens, and are good value for 4–8 people. No TVs, no telephones, and no smoking. Four-person cabins from $145 per night. Minimum length of stay is usually 2–3 nights. ⑤

Lazy Moose 1005 Lake Ave ⓣ970/627-1881, ⓕ627-1877, ⓦwww.lazymoose.com. Choose between a one-bedroom lakeside cabin with fully-equipped kitchen ($110) and a simpler studio-style cabin with queen-size bed and small bathroom. Open year-round, with some good winter deals; rates usually slightly lower for three nights or more. ④

Lemmon Lodge beside the Grand Lake Yacht Club summer ⓣ970/627-3314, winter 725-3511; open mid-May to Sept. Twenty cabins with wildly varying rates commensurate with facilities, although all have own kitchen and bathroom but no TV or telephone. Location is superb, quiet, and shady beside the lakeshore. The most basic four-person cabin is $100 per night. ⑤

Lone Eagle Lodge 712 Grand Ave ⓣ970/627-3310 or 1-800/282-3311. Basic motel rooms, friendly proprietors and a Grand Ave address make this a good choice in the middle range. ⑤

Rapids Lodge 209 Rapids Lane ⓣ970/627-3707, ⓦwww.rapidslodge.com. The original log-pine lodge is almost a century old, and there are now cabins and several condominiums at this low-key riverside location too, as well as Grand Lake's finest restaurant. Rates on cabins and condos – some of which have kitchens and fireplaces – vary according to size and facilities. All rates are slightly lower for stays of two nights or more. Riverview condo (⑦); two-bedroom condo for 4–6 people (⑦); basic lodge room or cabin for two (⑤).

Waconda Motel 725 Grand Ave ⓣ970/627-8312, ⓔwaconda@rkymtnhi.com. A central location and comfortable rooms make this motel a popular choice, and it's breakfast menu is one of Grand Lake's more favourable. ④

Western Riviera Motel 419 Garfield St ⓣ970/627-3580, ⓕ627-3320. This motel is a good first choice for its lakeside location, simple but comfortable rooms and outdoor hot tub. ⑤

Hostel and camping

Elk Creek Campground a half-mile north of town and just west of US-34 ⓣ970/627-8502 or 1-800/355-2733, ⓔelkcreek@rkymtnhi.com; open May–Oct. Tent sites for $18, sites with full hookup $23, and bare-bones "camper cabins" for $40. There's nothing terribly attractive about the site but the bathroom facilities are well-maintained and there's a small shop for necessities.

Green Ridge Campground three miles south of Grand Lake ⓣ970/887-0056 or 1-877/444-6777. A USFS campground just below the Shadow Mountain Reservoir. Amenities include bathrooms (but no showers) and the sixty sites go for $12 a night.

Shadowcliff Lodge perched on the hillside just above West Portal Rd ⓣ970/627-9220; open late May to Sept. This gorgeous, rambling, log-built lodge offers some of the finest budget accommodation anywhere in the state. Dorm beds are six to a room, and there are clean, comfortable motel rooms with great views; big, hummingbird-visited terraces, and a serene chapel open to all. Other facilities include a small guest kitchen and a communal living area with a library and open fireplace. There are also three cabins which sleep 6–8 people ($70–80 per night), but these are generally booked a year in advance. *Shadowcliff Lodge* is a nonprofit church-affiliated enterprise, and most guests cheerfully help out with a small chore during their stay. Dorms $10 ($12 for nonmembers); doubles ②.

Stillwater Campground five miles south of Grand Lake ⓣ970/887-0056 or 1-877/444-6777. On the western shore of Lake Granby, this large USFS campground (130 sites) includes restrooms and showers for $16 a night.

Winding River Resort a mile-and-a-half north along I-34; the turnoff is signposted opposite the Kawuneeche Visitor Center ⓣ970/627-3215, ⓕ627-5003; open year-round. Tent sites for $18 and shaded cabins which can accommodate 2–6 people ($80–90). The main attraction here is proximity to the park, although it's also a pleasantly wooded spot.

The town

It doesn't take long to stroll the four boardwalk-lined blocks which mark the center of Grand Lake village, but people nevertheless manage to amuse themselves by poking about in tourist knickknack stores, watching the yachts out on the lake or just wandering up and down the boardwalk. **Grand Lake Chocolates**, 918 Grand Ave (daily noon–10pm), is hard to ignore, for its handmade chocolates and enormous ice-cream cones in a multitude of flavours. Apart from the "family entertainments" of two mini-golf courses and a ten-pin bowling center, there's not much by way of diversions – but then a little mooching about is just the thing after a days' hiking in the national park.

The town's small **museum** is the 1892 log-built **Kauffman House**, at 407 Pitkin St (summer daily 1–5pm; free); one of Grand Lake's original hotels, it now houses a fairly unremarkable assortment of period furniture and other bits-and-pieces.

Outdoor activities

Seeing as **mountain bikes** are not allowed off-road inside the national park, most people head for the trails in the Arapaho National Forest just west of town. A handy biking trail map, produced by the Grand Lake Metro Recreation District (Ⓣ970/627-8328), can often be nabbed at Rocky Mountain Sports, 830 Grand Ave (Ⓣ970/627-8124), which also rents mountain bikes for $16 per half-day ($22 per day). More trails can be explored with Sombrero Ranch (Ⓣ970/627-3514), who offers sedate **horserides** along trails in the national park, from one hour ($30) to a half-day ($50); longer backcountry excursions can also be arranged. If looking to get out onto the lake, Boaters Choice, 1246 Lake Ave (Ⓣ970/627-9273), has a range of pontoon **boats**, **canoes**, skiffs, and motorboats for hire at various hourly and daily rates; Rocky Mountain Sports (see above) rents **sea kayaks** ($25 half-day, $35 full day).

Despite the recent national park ban on **snowmobiling** (see box on p.285), this is still a popular area base from which to rev about in the neighboring national forest. On the Trail, at *Winding River Resort* (Ⓣ970/627-2429), and Lone Eagle, 720 Grand Ave (Ⓣ970/627-3310), have snowmobiles for $80–100 per half-day.

Eating, drinking, and nightlife

There are a number of highly satisfying **places to eat** in Grand Lake, from cheap diners to elegant restaurants with ambitious menus and prices; don't miss breakfast at the *Grand Lake Lodge* (see opposite). The town has two mid-size **supermarkets**, both with slightly higher than average prices (see "Listings" opposite). The **pubs** in Grand Lake are your basic barstools-and-sawdust affairs, and while they're fine for a beer, you're not likely to get a decent meal at any of them. For an occasional live rock or country band, you could look in at the *Lariat Saloon* (1121 Grand Ave) or the *Stagecoach Inn* (920 Grand Ave), which are almost opposite one another in the town center. For a change of pace, check out what's playing at the highly regarded **Rocky Mountain Repertory Theater** (Ⓣ970/627-3421; June–Sept; tickets $15), which is also bang in the middle of town. A tiny box office on the boardwalk sells tickets for the current show; there are usually four different productions each season, mostly musicals, satire, and pantomime.

Restaurants

Caroline's Cuisine 9921 US-34 ☎970/627-9404. Although the local word is that *Caroline's* has slipped just a notch in recent times, the menu is still quite a read and might just be worth the five-mile drive to peruse. Frogs legs, escargot, port-glazed venison, and linguini rock shrimp are usually featured (entrees $14–26). Open for dinner daily, lunch Wed–Sun; closed Mon in winter.

EG's Garden Grill 1000 Grand Ave ☎970/627-8404. Good quality food served up in a cozy, colorful dining room – the menu ranges from burgers to grilled wild boar sausages, New York steak and seafood specials like marlin and grilled salmon. You can sit indoors or in the beer garden, where happy hour runs Mon–Sat 5–7pm. Moderate prices; open daily for lunch and dinner.

Grand Lake Lodge 15500 US-34 ☎970/627-3185; open June to mid-Sept. Even if you're not staying here, a meal at the lodge should be a priority for the outstanding view over Grand Lake. Dinner entrees such as tortilla-dusted rack of lamb, elk, and other fresh game or seafood don't come especially cheap (entrees $15–25), but the all-you-can-eat breakfast buffet, which includes the lodge's famous Belgian waffles, is an exceptional value at $7. Reservations are advised, and essential for the champagne brunch on Sunday (9.30am–1.30pm). Breakfast Mon–Sat 7.30–10am, lunch Mon–Sat 11.30am–2.30pm, dinner nightly from 5.30pm.

Marie's 928 Grand Ave ☎970/627-9475. The old style stools and countertop go nicely with the predictable diner menu and prices. The simple breakfasts are probably the best value; a stack of pancakes plus coffee will get your day started for around $4. Closed Mon and Tues, and evening hours can be a bit unreliable; dinner reservations required for six or more people.

The Mountain Inn 612 Grand Ave ☎970/627-3385. This popular, inexpensive, and rustic restaurant serves up very good steaks ($12–17) and burgers ($7–9) but not too much else; great for carnivores but nothing doing if you have vegetarian leanings. Daily for dinner.

Pancho & Lefty's 1120 Grand Ave ☎970/627-8773. This bustling Mexican bar-restaurant is popular for its inexpensive Mexican standards (entrees $8–12), and the big, sunny deck overlooking the lake. Open daily for lunch and dinner, reservations for dinner advised during summer.

The Rapids Restaurant 209 Rapids Lane ☎970/627-3707. The busy but picturesque Tonahutu River runs right past the huge windows of this quiet, elegant dining room, which is the prime spot for a truly fine meal in Grand Lake. For a Northern Italian-influenced meal of linguini with prawns, chili oil, lime, and herbs, followed by sauteed rainbow trout or veal marsala, dessert, and wine, you can expect to spend $50 per person. Daily for dinner, reservations advised.

Waconda Motel 725 Grand Ave ☎970/627-8312. The small motel dining room primarily serves guests each morning, but all are welcome and the excellent, moderately priced breakfasts are highly recommended. Breakfast daily.

Listings

Banks The only 24hr ATM is located at West Star Bank on Pitkin St; the ATM inside Lone Eagle Gas Station is accessible 8am–7pm.

Internet access Juniper Library, on the east side of the town park (Mon & Wed noon–6pm, Thurs, Fri & Sat 10am–3pm, closed Tues & Sun; $4 per 30min).

Post office 520 Center Drive, fifteen-minutes' walk west of the town center (Mon–Fri 8.30am–5pm).

Supermarket Circle D Foods, at the corner of Broadway and Grand Ave (daily 9am–7pm); Mountain Food Market is at the west end of town on Grand Ave (Mon–Sat 9am–7pm, Sun 9am–5pm).

Taxi Mountain Goat Tours (☎970/627-1226 or 1-888/950-1226) runs charter tours of the national park and also does shuttle runs to the Bear Lake parking lot for hikers who have left their cars at the trailhead.

Rocky Mountain National Park

Based on its name alone, one might easily imagine that a visit to **ROCKY MOUNTAIN NATIONAL PARK** is essential in order to appreciate the full splendor of the Rockies. In fact, the park, totalling 415 square miles, takes up a relatively minuscule section of the range. A tenth of the size of Yellowstone, it attracts almost as many visitors – around three-and-a-half million per year –

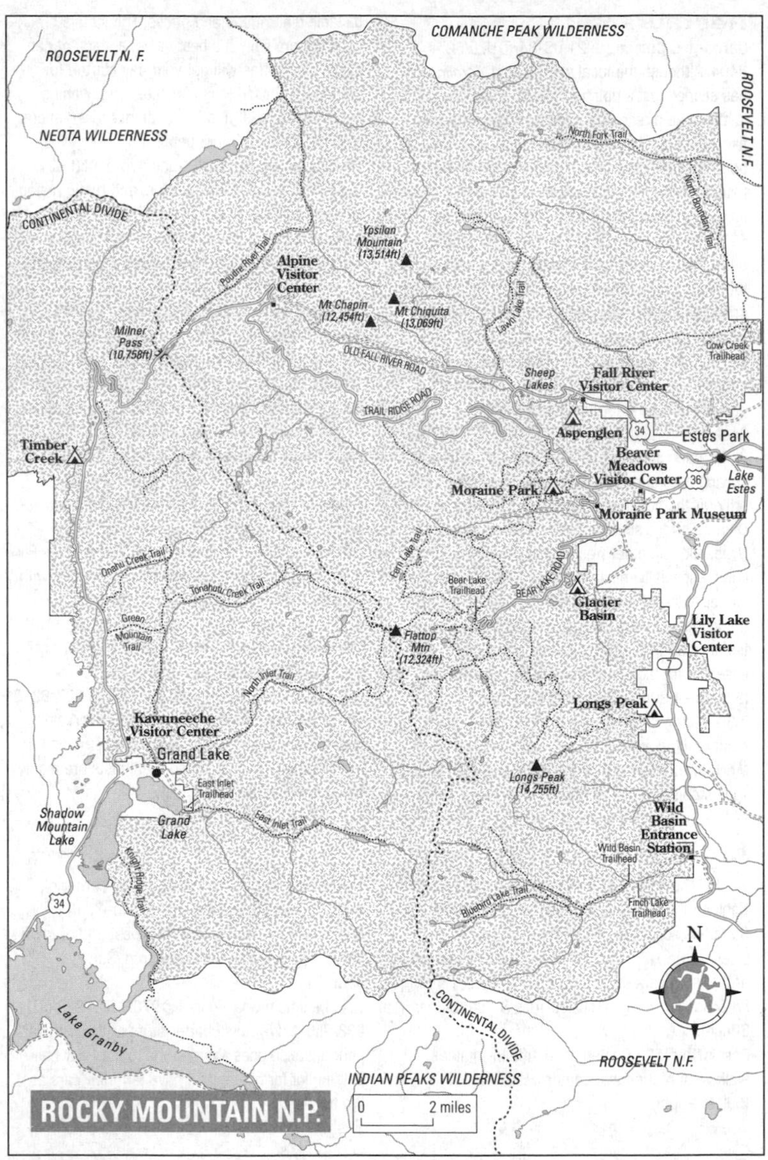

and with the bulk of those coming in high summer, its lone arterial highway, **Trail Ridge Road**, can get incredibly congested. However, it is undeniably beautiful, straddling the Continental Divide at elevations in excess of ten thousand feet, while an even fairer measure of what to expect is the number of **summits over 12,000ft** – there are 76 of them. A full third of the park is above treeline, and large areas of snow never melt; the name of the **Never Summer Mountains** speaks volumes about the long, empty expanses of **arc-**

tic-style tundra. Lower down are patches of lush greenery which support the park's grazing animals, and you never know when you may stumble upon a sheltered mountain meadow flecked with wildflowers.

Although there's never any shortage of people making a quick foray into the park from Denver or Boulder, it would be a mistake to attempt to see anything much on a **day-trip**, since you could only realistically manage to dip a few miles into the park's eastern fringes. About the furthest base that makes for a comfortable day-trip is Fort Collins; at 49 miles from the park's eastern entrance it's not a lot closer than Denver, but the drive is much easier. It's also worth noting that the west side of the park enjoys more **rainfall** – around twenty inches annually, compared with fifteen inches at Estes Park – so the forests and meadows here are notably green and lush. And while it's certainly possible to take in the alpine splendor of the park from your vehicle, you should ideally try to set aside three or four days to **hike** some trails, perhaps pitch a tent in the backcountry, and drive Trail Ridge Road at a leisurely pace.

Some history

For all its natural appeal, this is not an area that humans have ever made their permanent home. During the warmer summer months, though, the Ute people would come here to hunt, before being driven west of the Continental Divide by the Arapaho. The Colorado gold rush of the 1860s and 1870s saw some hardy prospectors gravitate towards the region, but by 1879 the land had yielded little by way of mineral wealth, and the miners' shanty towns crumbled almost as quickly as they had appeared.

The dedicating of these mountains as Rocky Mountain National Park was largely the work of one man, **Enos Mills**, a naturalist who wrote and lectured on the area for much of his life. Mills lobbied Congress to create the country's tenth national park, and his wish was granted on January 26, 1915. The original proposal was for it to be much bigger, extending from the Wyoming border south to Pikes Peak (see p.119), but the boundaries were drawn up as a compromise, following negotiations with Colorado's powerful logging and mining interests. There has been just one small land acquisition since – 465 acres on the eastern edge around Lily Lake, absorbed into the park in 1990.

But the real creative forces at work here were not bureaucrats or naturalists – rather, they were the mighty **glaciers**, huge beds of ice and rock which solidified and shifted under the power of their own accumulated mass, sliding and scouring their way through steep canyons, widening them as they went. Showing scant regard for seniority, the 10,000–15,000-year-old glaciers slid across rock that had risen from the earth millions of years earlier, carving out broad valleys between the peaks. When the last Ice Age ended and the glaciers receded, huge deposits of rock and debris called moraines were left behind, effectively damming parts of some valleys and creating lakes, some of which would in turn become meadows – delicate touches added to the massively sculpted mountain terrain.

Information, books, maps and accommodation

For a private vehicle, the park **entrance fee** is $15, valid for seven days; cyclists and motorcyclists pay $5. Keep your receipt to be able to leave and re-enter the park during that period. An annual pass costs $25. For general **information**, phone park headquarters (Ⓣ970/586-1206), or check the park's **website** (Ⓦwww.nps.gov/romo).

There are five **visitor centers** servicing the park (see below), each stocked with maps, brochures and books, exhibits, and interpretive displays. One curious feature about the park is that three of the five visitor centers – Kawuneeche, Lily Lake, and Fall River – are located outside the park, and a number of trailheads also begin beyond park boundaries. It is thus perfectly feasible to collect maps and information at a visitor center, and then do any number of hikes without ever going through an entrance station and paying for a park permit.

The two essential pieces of printed material you'll require are available **free** from any entrance station or vistor center: a park **map** and a copy of the quarterly *Rocky Mountain Park High Country Headlines*. The latter includes comprehensive **listings** of the excellent, free ranger-led activities such as guided walks and campfire talks that are well worth taking advantage of.

A number of detailed **topographic maps** are available at the visitor centers, including the waterproof 1:59,000 Trails Illustrated map ($9.95). However, between the free park map, the well-marked and maintained trails, and the various free handouts with trail and campsite descriptions, you could explore the park for weeks without needing to purchase any additional paperwork.

Visitor centers are also well stocked with **books**, covering every topic from hikes and climbs to geology and wildlife. The most **useful hiking guide** available is *Hiking Rocky Mountain National Park*, by Kent and Donna Dannen; this is a comprehensive, no-frills guide to trails inside the park as well as the Indian Peaks Wilderness just to the south. For a more offbeat read, try *Long's Peak Tales* by Glenn Randall, a series of tall-tales-and-true, including pioneering routes to the summit and several ill-fated climbing expeditions – some comic, some tragic – representing over one hundred years on Long's Peak.

Park Visitor Centers

Alpine Visitor Center halfway along Trail Ridge Rd at Fall River Pass (May–Aug 9am–5pm daily; Sept 10am–4pm daily; closed Oct–April). This marks the center of the park, and it's really the only requisite stop for any visitor who is happy enough to see the alpine tundra by car. The center has exhibits relating to the flora and fauna of the tundra and there are good positions for wildlife viewing a little further east along Trail Ridge Rd.

Beaver Meadows Visitor Center two miles west of Estes Park on US-36 (daily: June–Aug 8am–9pm; Sept–May 8am–5pm; ⓣ970/586-1206). This is the official park headquarters, and also the location of the main backcountry office. There are several wildlife exhibits and regular audiovisual presentations as well.

Fall River Visitor Center five miles west of Estes Park on US-34 (May–Sept daily 8am–8pm; winter hours variable). Opened in May 2000, this is the newest visitor center in the park. In the tacky tradition of Estes Park, the center's information desk and interpretive center are tiny in relation to the gift shop. The cafeteria here has a salad bar, burgers, cinnamon rolls, and clean restrooms.

Kawuneeche Visitor Center one mile north of Grand Lake on US-34 (daily: May–Sept 8am–6pm; Oct–April 8am–5pm; ⓣ970/627-3471). For people entering the park from the western side, this is the only visitor center and an essential port of call for maps, information, and backcountry camping permits. A large, three-dimensional map of the park highlights the major peaks, including Long's.

Lily Lake Visitor Center (daily May–Sept 9am–4.30pm; closed in winter). This small visitor center is far less busy than the rest, but you can collect a park map and other information, and it's a handy place to check conditions on nearby Long's Peak.

Camping in Rocky Mountain National Park

The only overnight facilities within park boundaries are provided at five NPS **campgrounds**. **Reservations** can be made up to five months ahead and a credit card is required for sites at *Moraine Park* and *Glacier Basin* (ⓣ301/722-1257 or 1-800/365-2267, ⓦwww.reservations.nps.gov). Both are located on the eastern side of the park and fill daily in summer. *Aspenglen*, *Timber Creek*, and *Long's Peak* campgrounds all operate on a first-come, first-served basis – try to claim a spot before noon. There's little to separate the campsites in terms of facilities or attractiveness, so your choice should be made according to which areas of the park you're planning to explore. The **maximum length of stay** is generally seven nights, except for *Long's Peak*, which has a three-night limit. All campgrounds have toilet **facilities**, water, and firewood, but no showers or electrical hookups. *Long's Peak* is the only campground without a public phone. Each campsite allows for one vehicle and one camping unit (tent, RV, or trailer). All sites are $16 per night (the rate drops to $10 for Oct–April for the three campgrounds that remain open, and at these drinking water is no longer available).

Aspenglen (elevation 8230ft), just inside the Fall River entrance on the eastern edge of the park. Open May–Sept, though exact dates vary according to the weather; 54 sites, no reservations.

Glacier Basin (elevation 8600ft), on the east side of the park, just off Bear Lake Rd. Open May–Sept, though it tends to open a week or so later than *Aspenglen* and close a week earlier. Handy to a number of gentle, scenic trails; 150 sites, reservations required.

Long's Peak (elevation 9400ft), beside the Long's Peak trailhead. Open year-round, but with running water only late May to mid-September, this campground primarily serves climbers intending to tackle the peak; 26 sites, tents only, no reservations.

Moraine Park (elevation 8150ft), just west of the Moraine Park Museum, off Bear Lake Rd. Open year-round (running water mid-May to late Sept), with access to several popular trails that lead up to the Continental Divide via a series of alpine lakes; 247 sites, reservations required between May and September.

Timber Creek (elevation 8900ft), the only serviced campground on the west side of the park, at the northern end of the Kawuneeche Valley. Open year-round (running water late May to mid-September), it's close to both the gentle and scenic Colorado River Trail and the more challenging Timber Lake Trail, in an area that offers a good chance for viewing moose; 100 sites, no reservations.

Backcountry camping

The alternative to staying at the established campgrounds is to camp in the **backcountry**. The advantages of this are numerous: you'll leave most of the day-hikers behind; your tent won't be hemmed in by RVs and trucks; you're far more likely to see wildlife behaving naturally (ie ignoring you); and the best way to experience the dizzying highs of the alpine tundra is to camp just below treeline, from where you can hike at leisure across terrain with the park's finest views and perhaps bag a 13,000-foot peak.

There are two main park offices which issue **backcountry permits**: the small building one hundred yards east of the Beaver Meadows Visitor Center (Ⓣ970/586-1242 for information as well as advance bookings of backcountry campsites), and inside the Kawuneeche Visitor Center. From mid-May until the end of September reservations are only accepted in person or by mail; write to receive a map of backcountry sites plus a request form (Rocky Mountain National Park, Estes Park, CO 80517). During summer only, backcountry permits are also available at the Long's Peak and Wild Basin ranger stations (daily 8am–4.30pm); a $15 administration **fee** is levied from May–Oct. The permit covers one person for up to seven days; however, a new one is required for each separate trip into the backcountry. Put simply, if you do a three-day hike and then drive to another trailhead to begin hiking a different route, you need a new permit. If you want to book a site in advance, it's worth phoning and asking about the more secluded or scenic sites; there are also a small number of group sites where an open fire is allowed, which adds greatly to the evening atmosphere.

The campsite at **Sprague Lake**, which is accessible by car, is specifically designed to accommodate **disabled visitors**, up to twelve people plus six wheelchairs at a time, for a maximum stay of three nights. The half-mile nature trail around the lake is level and wheelchair-accessible too. A backcountry permit is required, and reservations should be made through the backcountry office at park headquarters (see overleaf).

Exploring the park

The showpiece of Rocky Mountain National Park is **Trail Ridge Road**, which connects Estes Park and Grand Lake. This 45-mile stretch of I-34, the highest paved highway in the US, affords a succession of tremendous views, and there are several trailheads that start from parking lots along the way. There are **no gas stations** en route, and rangers advise that you should allow three to four hours' driving time. The road is normally open from Memorial Day to mid-October. As winter progresses and the snow falls, it is blocked progressively lower down, but you can always expect to get as far as **Many Peaks Curve** from the east or the **Colorado River Trailhead** from the west (snowfall is typically heaviest during March and April). The definite highlight is the stretch of road on both sides of the Alpine Visitor Center; here the peaks and alpine tundra literally take your breath away.

During summer, you can also drive along the unpaved **Old Fall River Road**; completed in 1920, this was the first road to be built in the park. Running one-way (east–west) through the bed of a valley carved by glaciers into a U-shape, it does not have open mountain vistas, but it is much quieter than the Trail Ridge, and offers a good chance of spotting **wildlife**. Although the drive is only nine miles, it's worth investing in the *Old Fall River Road* guide (available at visitor centers; $1), which leads you through its history, geography and geology, as well as the variations in landscape and wildlife habitat. The speed limit is 15mph, and there are several short trails along the way that lead off to waterfalls, streams, and lakes.

Just inside the park, near the Estes Park entrance, a spur road, open year-round, leads south to two small and pristine alpine lakes. On the way, the **Moraine Park Museum** (summer only daily 9am–5pm; free) has a well laid-out set of exhibits on the park's natural history. The broad, marshy meadow of Moraine Park is a rare example of development in reverse; there were three hotels, a post office, and a golf course here until the 1950s, when the National Parks Service removed the buildings and set about restoring the landscape to its original state.

Beyond here, to ease traffic, a free **shuttle bus** from the Glacier Basin parking area runs the last few miles up to **Bear Lake** (June–Aug daily 8.30am–5.30pm every 15–30min; Sept service is less frequent, check at the visitor centers for the day's schedule). The classic viewpoint here is probably the park's most photographed, the mountains framed to perfection beyond the cool, still waters. Also here is the Bear Lake trailhead, by far the park's busiest (see p.282).

Hiking

Recommending any one **hiking** trail above another is not necessary as there are literally dozens of superb hikes to choose from. Instead, think about what sort of experience you want to have – photographing a particular animal, fishing an alpine lake, hiking across the Continental Divide – and then plan around that with a ranger's help.

The best way to gain a sense of this extraordinary environment is to begin a hike at a relatively low elevation (around 8000ft), and head right up onto the **alpine tundra** (11,500ft). Along the way you take in the ponderosa pine,

Hiking hazards in Rocky Mountain National Park

There are a number of special safety considerations that apply to hiking in Rocky Mountain National Park that you may not have encountered elsewhere in the Rockies. The park's lowest elevations are around 8000ft, and some of the hiking and climbing routes top 13,000ft; by way of comparison, the highest point at most Colorado ski resorts is well below 11,000ft. The **potential dangers** are all related to altitude: **dehydration** and **altitude sickness** are not uncommon, while afternoon thunderstorms regularly produce **lightning strikes** on the exposed alpine tundra. Several lives are lost in the park every year, so a healthy measure of respect for this dramatic mountain environment is essential. Plan your hikes conservatively, keep an eye on the weather and heed the advice of rangers.

If you've recently arrived from somewhere near sea-level, let your system adjust to the altitude before you try hoofing it up a five-mile trail to 12,000ft. A perfect way to start is with a scenic trail that's not very steep; you get to enjoy the surroundings as you keep an eye out for wildlife – just drink plenty of water. With that under your belt, you may feel ready to hike up to the treeline at around 11,000ft. It's extremely unwise to be exposed above the trees when the lightning storms roll in, so start out early and plan to be heading down by early afternoon. The key to enjoying yourself while hiking is to stay properly hydrated and don't push too hard; plan on walking about two miles an hour, and drinking about five pints (three liters) of water a day. Note too that distances marked at trailheads are one-way; a four-mile hike is actually eight miles there and back. For general tips on hiking safety, see p.50 in Basics.

lodgepole pine and Douglas fir forests of the **montane** ecosystem (7000–9500ft), then feel the air start to cool and thin as you reach the stands of subalpine fir and Engelmann spruce in the **subalpine** strata (9500–11,000ft). Finally, you break out above the treeline onto the windswept tundra, where the sun is as strong as the air is bracing. From this vantage, it's easy to appreciate the sheer size of the mountains and the effect of glacial shifts upon their shape, and to reflect upon the stark changes in the environment, apparent as you pass through the three distinct ecosystems.

Around Grand Lake

Three popular trailheads that start from just outside the park in Grand Lake are the Tonahutu, North Inlet, and East Inlet trails. The **Tonahutu** and the **North Inlet** link into a moderate loop which takes you up onto the alpine tundra at just over 12,000ft; it takes every bit of two days to cover the complete circuit, but many people simply hike three or four miles along either forested trail, before retracing their steps. At almost four miles along the Tonahutu trail you reach Big Meadows, where elk and moose often graze in the early evening.

The **East Inlet** trail, a fourteen-mile round-trip, is also an excellent place to start, as it offers views of some spectacular peaks, meadows frequented by deer, elk, and moose, and several picturesque alpine lakes as you get into the upper reaches. The first couple of miles are a gentle climb, the stretch leading up to Lone Pine Lake gets progressively steeper, and you can carry on via three more lakes – although this requires a very early start or a night out in the backcountry.

A few miles north of the Kawuneeche Visitor Center are a couple more promising trailheads. The **Green Mountain** trail links up with Tonahutu near Big Meadows, and allows for a moderate 7.5-mile loop beginning at either the Green Mountain or **Onahu** trailhead. Having completed one of the easier day-hikes, **Timber Lake** makes a great warm-up for a more ambitious backcountry expedition; in the course of 4.9 miles you gain 2060ft in elevation – a strenuous hike to 11,000ft, with a pristine lake as your reward.

Most people planning to stay **overnight** in the backcountry have the high alpine reaches as their goal, and for many the icing on the cake is to cross the Continental Divide. The only trail which crosses the divide is the **Flattop Mountain** trail, which meets the North Inlet-Tonahutu loop at around 12,000ft in the shadow of Flattop Mountain (see below). It's worth noting that there is a somewhat disheartening series of switchbacks on the North Inlet trail, which is why most people covering this loop over two or three days elect to go up via Tonahutu and descend on the North Inlet.

Around Alpine Visitor Center

Perched high on the tundra at 11,796ft, the Alpine Visitor Center is usually jammed with people admiring the breathtaking mountain vistas; however, that's typically all they do as there are few hiking trails anywhere in this area because the flora is so fragile and lightning an ever-present danger. Nevertheless, the four-mile trail down to **Milner Pass** is a bracing way to take in this harsh but stunning environment. A more challenging option is to pick up the **Chapin Creek trail** from Old Fall River Road below the visitor center and climb to the top of **Mt Chapin** (12,454ft); from there you can walk down the adjoining saddle and up to the peak of **Mt Chiquita** (13,069ft), and continue on to **Mt Ypsilon** (13,514ft). It's a tough 3.5 miles (one-way) at this altitude, but it's also a unique opportunity to bag three peaks during a single hike. There is no actual trail beyond Mt Chapin, but you can see where you're headed and the park rangers don't mind a few people walking across the tundra, although they do ask you not to walk single-file so that the impact is spread a little. It's important to start early and watch the weather, as there's no cover if a lightning storm hits.

Around Bear Lake

The fact that there's a 250-space parking lot at the **Bear Lake** trailhead, plus more parking below near *Glacier Basin* campground and a bus which shuttles people in between, should provide some idea of just how heavily used this area is. The trails here are also maintained so that older or disabled visitors and young children can enjoy them. It's a very short hike both to the aptly named **Dream Lake** and the one-mile interpretive nature trail that circumnavigates **Nymph Lake**; this is also the closest point of access for hikers heading to the Flattop Mountain trail (see below). While the parking lots and trails can be hopelessly crowded, it's still easy enough to enjoy this area simply by visiting early or late in the day; try to arrive by 8am, or else wait until after 3pm – weather permitting.

If you have in mind to tackle the trail to **Flattop Mountain**, pack weather-proof gear and lots of water; what looks like a reasonably short hike on the park map is in fact 4.4 miles with an elevation gain of almost 3000ft. Allow about three hours to reach the base of the mountain, and if you intend spending some time on the tundra, don't begin hiking any later than 9am. Many people take this trail so that they can cross the Continental Divide, spend a night in the backcountry, and then hike right down to the park's western boundary. Very few have the stomach for the return trip, however, and having left a vehicle parked at the Bear Lake trailhead, find themselves hitchhiking down to Grand Lake in search of an (expensive) shuttle ride back to their car (see p.275).

Long's Peak

Officially the **highest point** in Rocky Mountain National Park, 14,255-foot **Long's Peak** gets all the attention it deserves from both hikers and climbers.

△ Bighorn sheep, the classic high-country dwellers

The nontechnical route to the summit is known as The Keyhole, and even this approach does not guarantee a successful assault. Note too that the Keyhole route does demand technical equipment and expertise when under winter conditions; snow may persist from mid-September until early or mid-July.

Some planning is required for this hike, which from the trailhead is about eight miles one-way with an elevation gain of 4855ft. To have a realistic chance of reaching the top ahead of the afternoon weather, most people start out well **before sunrise**, having camped at *Long's Peak* campground (see box on p.279) beside the trailhead. Another option is to camp at one of the backcountry sites closer to the peak; this alleviates some of the urgency of time, so you might even consider a sunrise stop at Chasm Lake, from where it's worth trying for a photo of **the Diamond**, the (diamond-shaped) east face of the mountain favoured by technical climbers. Even if you don't intend scaling the peak, the hike in to **Chasm Lake** is highly rewarding.

Climbing

There are some popular destinations nearby for **rock climbers** besides the high-profile Long's Peak, including **Lumpy Ridge**, two miles north of Estes Park via Devil's Gulch Road, which offers a good variety of mostly short climbs. Assaults on many of the alpine summits require a night spent camping close to the base or even on the rock-face itself; a special bivouac permit (free) is available to technical climbers for overnight stays in certain areas – contact the backcountry office at park headquarters for details (see p.278). The Colorado Mountain School, 351 Moraine Ave, Estes Park (ⓣ970/586-5758, ⓦwww.cmschool.com), is a good point of contact for climbing information and instructional courses, including a technical climb of Long's Peak. The school is currently the only company authorized to take people climbing in Rocky Mountain National Park; prices for its highly regarded climbing courses start at $175 for one day, and some courses include ice-climbing or even an overnight mountain bivouac. Estes Park Mountain Shop, 358 Elkhorn Ave (daily 8am–9pm; ⓣ970/586-6548 or 1-800/504-6642), has an indoor climbing gym right in town ($20 for a full day) and offers indoor and outdoor instruction.

Fishing

Many of the park's lakes and streams have been stocked with brown, brook, and rainbow trout, and some support small numbers of endangered native greenback cutthroat and Colorado River cutthroat trout. Seeing as **regulations** vary depending on the species and area – fishing is banned altogether in some waters – you'll need the park's *Fishing Information* leaflet to sort things out. A standard Colorado **state fishing license** is required – available at sporting goods stores in Grand Lake and Estes Park, but not sold within the park itself. Generally speaking, the lakes at higher altitudes support the fewest fish. The best stretch of river for **fly-fishing** is the North Fork of the Big Thompson, in the northeast corner of the park; this is accessed via a service road off Devils Gulch Road, which leads to the North Fork Trailhead. The seven miles between the trailhead and Lost Falls offer fine fishing, and there are a dozen scenic backcountry campsites over the three miles between Lost Falls and Lost Lake too.

Wildlife viewing

The mix of excitement and frustration borne by people hoping to **spot particular animals** stems, of course, from the fact that the park's animals are wild; they don't show up on demand, and the more intelligent and secretive of them

Winter in Rocky Mountain National Park

As in summer, a **winter experience** of Rocky Mountain National Park is a tale of two climate zones. The western side receives a great deal more snow than the east, so while cross-country ski enthusiasts and snowshoers are startling wildlife along trails from Grand Lake in January, hikers heading in from Estes Park and other eastern points may well find themselves on terrain that is virtually snow-free.

Some excellent and fairly moderate **Nordic skiing** can be had north of Grand Lake in the Kawuneeche Valley and along trails that lead into the Arapaho National Forest. Popular routes include the East Inlet trail into the national park from Grand Lake, and the Continental Divide trail which heads west into the Arapaho National Forest from *Winding River Resort* (see p.273). Among several recommended **winter hikes** on the east side of the Continental Divide are easy walks to Cub Lake (2.3 miles one-way; park at road closure on Moraine Park Rd and walk to Cub Lake trailhead) and The Pool (2.5 miles one-way; start from the Fern Lake trailhead, a half-mile beyond the Cub Lake trailhead). Hiking can be a labored and dangerous affair in deep snow, so it's important to check current conditions before setting off during winter.

Snowmobiling has been a highly controversial winter activity in the park for several years, with packs of snowmobilers making their presence felt on trails in and around Grand Lake. From the winter of 2000–2001, however, the machines were officially banned from the national park, although Grand Lake is likely to continue to attract snowmobilers to the national forest trails just outside park boundaries which are still open to them (see p.274).

make a point of avoiding **human contact** altogether. The largest of the animals you're most likely to encounter is the **elk** (also called *wapiti*, an appropriately descriptive Native American word meaning "white rump"). There may be as many as four thousand of them inside the park during summer, the larger bulls weighing up to nine hundred pounds and sporting huge antlers. The most dramatic time to observe the elk is during the **fall rut**, which generally begins in September and may go on into early November. The most extraordinary part of this display is an unearthly call by the bulls to a potential mate, called **bugling**; rather than the macho bellow one might expect, it's an ear-piercing squeal which lasts several seconds.

Although not originally native to the area, a few of a group of **moose** transplanted into the adjacent Arapaho National Forest in 1978 wandered across to the Kawuneeche Valley at the park's western edge, and soon established themselves in the marshy meadows alongside the Colorado River. There are now thought to be about thirty roaming the park, and they are still seen almost exclusively along the wetter western boundary in the **Kawuneeche Valley** – notably the half-mile north of Onahu Creek trailhead. Another member of the deer family, **mule deer**, are also quite common; look out for them along both the stretch of US-34 between the Fall River entrance station and Endovalley and along the Bear Lake Road.

The title of Rocky Mountain National Park mascot goes, of course, to the extraordinary **Rocky Mountain bighorn sheep**. Nearly eliminated from within the park's boundaries by the early twentieth century, a reintroduction and management program has since seen sheep numbers return to over one thousand animals. Rams put on an extraordinary display during the **rutting season**, roughly mid-November through December, when they square off and crack horns with a sickening impact. Bighorns are the archetypal high-country dwellers; look for them in the Horseshoe Park area, particularly around Sheep Lakes, or check with staff at Alpine Visitor Center for current viewing spots.

It is a source of some disappointment to many visitors that bears are very rarely seen, and indeed there are few of them residing in the park. The grizzly population was wiped out a century ago, and today around thirty or so **black bears** have scavenging rights pretty much to themselves. Though an opportunistic animal might forage in one of the campgrounds, contact with humans is otherwise minimal. For detailed advice on bear behavior and encounters, see p.550. The park's other major predator, also seldom seen, is the **mountain lion**. There are no reliable lion-watching spots, as these solitary animals keep to rugged and remote corners of the park. Note, however, that encounters with humans are not unheard of, and lone hikers in particular should be aware of their possible presence (see box, below).

Among the other interesting animals for which you need a fair bit of luck to see are the bobcat, badger, beaver, river otter, raccoon, muskrat, weasel, and pine marten. More common are the **pika**, a small but rotund rodent which announces its presence by squeaking loudly as it pops out from its rocky hideaway, and the **yellow-bellied marmot**, which closely resembles a groundhog. **Bird-watchers** will see plenty of hummingbirds, mallards, mountain bluebirds, and red-tailed hawks, among others, while less commonly seen are the golden eagle, peregrine falcon, blue grouse, and white-tailed ptarmigan. Bald eagles are known to pass through the area, although there are most likely no nesting sites within park boundaries.

Mountain lions

The **mountain lion** is the most secretive predator in the Rocky Mountains. Also referred to as a puma or cougar, this sleek, tawny-colored animal wears its Latin name best of all – *felis concolor*, the one-colored cat. Easily the largest of North America's cats, the male of the species may reach eight feet in length and weigh up to 180 pounds, while females can grow to seven feet and weigh up to 100 pounds; both male and female have a tawny-colored coat and black-tipped ears and tail.

Little is known about the mountain lion's status in the Rockies, or anywhere much else for that matter. Sightings have increased in recent years – notably here in Colorado, where the lion population is thought to be 1500–3000 – though that's not necessarily good news. While some suggest more sightings equals an expanding population, it's more likely that their habitat is shrinking, bringing them into closer proximity with humans. The mountain lion's range covers much of the western US, including the entire length of the Rockies; specific **habitat** tends to be dictated by the presence of deer, their favorite prey.

There have been occasional attacks by mountain lions on humans, although known fatalities number less than ten over the past century. These cats prefer remote, rugged country where human contact is rare; however, **encounters with humans** do occur, and it's as well to be aware of their possible presence, especially when hiking, jogging, or biking alone. Mountain lions silently stalk their prey or lie in ambush, and are more likely to take an interest in pets and small children than in full-grown adults. If you do come across a lion, do not approach it, but move slowly away while facing the animal and staying fully upright; running or cowering may trigger its instinct to attack. If a lion appears to be a genuine threat, appear as formidable as possible by opening your jacket and raising your arms while talking loudly but firmly. In the event of an actual attack, throw stones and sticks or arm yourself with a tree-branch – lions have been driven away by prey that fights back.

Fort Collins

With a rising population of almost 120,000, **FORT COLLINS** straddles the fine line between big town and small city. In its first incarnation as an 1862 military post, it was humble Camp Collins, established to protect traders traveling through the region. When the camp was washed out in a flood in 1864, the new settlement was given grown-up status as a fort. Today, Fort Collins is largely known as the home of **Colorado State University**, somewhat secondary in status to Boulder's Colorado University. You may even hear the town referred to as "Boulder, without the hippies" – although this description probably causes some dismay among the hippies who do amble about the streets of Fort Collins. In any event, it is the town's proximity to Rocky Mountain National Park – fifty miles, and just under an hour's drive from the park's eastern entrance – and neighboring **Cache la Poudre Canyon**, together with the energy which accompanies any college population, that have combined to put Fort Collins near the very top of the list of ideal "lifestyle" cities in the US.

Arrival, information, and getting around

Driving in to Fort Collins from just about any direction can be a little dispiriting. There's not much mountain romance about the bland stretch of I-25 which runs from Denver via Fort Collins and on to Laramie, Wyoming, while much of I-287 – the road between Loveland and Fort Collins – is lined with car dealers and a succession of depressing shopping malls and fast-food outlets. Things brighten considerably, however, as soon as you reach the CSU neighbourhood around College Avenue and Laurel Street, and historic Old Town just a few blocks further north. The **bus terminal** for Greyhound and Powder River buses is at the junction of Riverside Avenue and East Mulberry (office open daily 7.30am–12.30pm & 2.30–6.30pm; ⓣ970/221-1327).

The town's **tourist office** is actually a storefront for Colorado State Tourism, with the Fort Collins Chamber of Commerce also headquartered there. It's in an isolated spot four miles east of town at 3545 Prospect Rd (ⓣ970/491-3388 or 1-800/274-3678, ⓦwww.ftcollins.com), near I-25 exit 268. There is also a **USFS office** at 1311 S College Ave (Mon–Fri 8am–4.30pm; ⓣ970/498-2770), which offers useful information on recreation in the nearby Cache la Poudre Canyon (see p.292).

The **local bus** network, Transfort (ⓣ970/221-6620), operates fifteen routes throughout Fort Collins; pick up a schedule including color-coded route maps from a visitor center or on board a bus. The single fare is $1 and transfers are free.

Accommodation

Accommodation in Fort Collins is most booked during summer, when some national park visitors use it as their base. It's otherwise hard to predict when the town will be busiest, since a college event or football game can be enough to stretch lodging resources on any weekend. Most of the more desirable places to stay are clustered around the university, while the town center, several blocks to the north of the campus, is inexplicably short on accommodation of any kind. There's no hostel in Fort Collins, but the cheapest hotel in town – the *Mountain Empire Hotel* – is also the most central (see below). If you've arrived by car and don't have a reservation, you may well find yourself resorting to one of the standard chain **motels** strung along E Mulberry (Hwy-14).

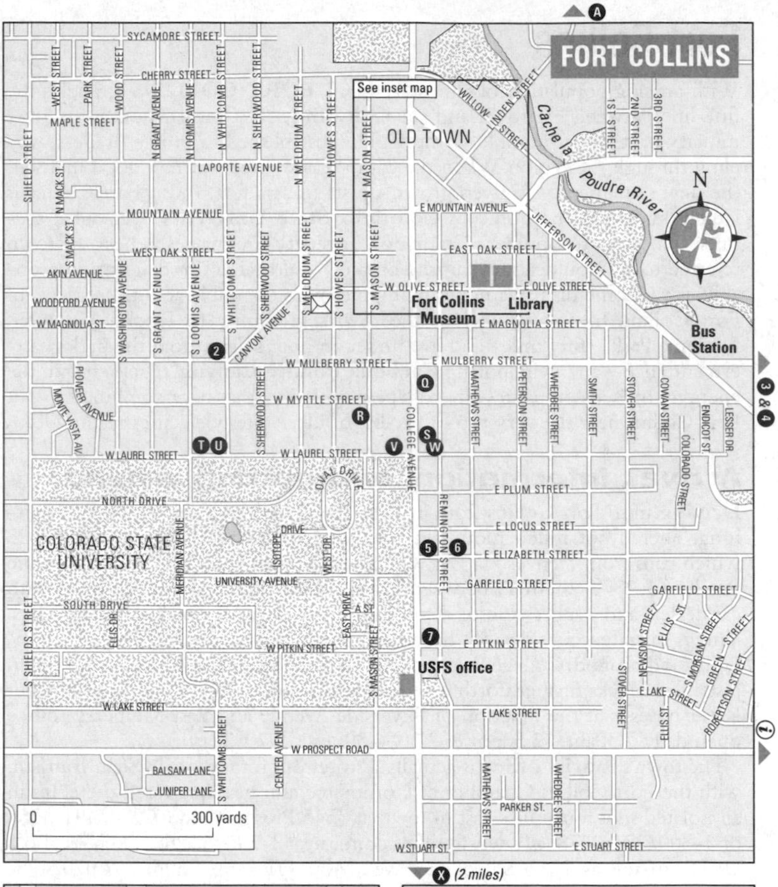

FORT COLLINS

A
See inset map
OLD TOWN
SYCAMORE STREET
CHERRY STREET
MAPLE STREET
LAPORTE AVENUE
MOUNTAIN AVENUE
WEST OAK STREET
AKIN AVENUE
WOODFORD AVENUE
W MAGNOLIA ST
W MULBERRY STREET
W MYRTLE STREET
W LAUREL STREET
NORTH DRIVE
COLORADO STATE UNIVERSITY
UNIVERSITY AVENUE
SOUTH DRIVE
W PITKIN STREET
W LAKE STREET
W PROSPECT ROAD
BALSAM LANE
JUNIPER LANE
W STUART ST.
WEST STREET
PARK STREET
WOOD STREET
N GRANT AVENUE
N LOOMIS AVENUE
N WHITCOMB STREET
N SHERWOOD STREET
N MELDRUM STREET
N HOWES STREET
N MASON STREET
SHIELD STREET
N MACK ST.
S MACK ST.
S WASHINGTON AVENUE
S GRANT AVENUE
S LOOMIS AVENUE
S WHITCOMB STREET
S SHERWOOD STREET
S MELDRUM STREET
S HOWES STREET
S MASON STREET
CANYON AVENUE
PIONEER AVENUE
MONTE VISTA AV.
SHERWOOD STREET
OVAL DRIVE
DRIVE
ISOTOPE
WEST DR.
MERIDIAN AVENUE
ELLIS DR.
EAST DRIVE
A ST.
S SHIELDS STREET
S WHITCOMB STREET
CENTER AVENUE
COLLEGE AVENUE
E MOUNTAIN AVENUE
EAST OAK STREET
W OLIVE STREET
E OLIVE STREET
Fort Collins Museum
Library
E MAGNOLIA STREET
E MULBERRY STREET
E PLUM STREET
E LOCUS STREET
E ELIZABETH STREET
GARFIELD STREET
E PITKIN STREET
USFS office
E LAKE STREET
E LAKE STREET
PARKER ST.
E STUART STREET
WILLOW STREET
LINDEN STREET
JEFFERSON STREET
Cache la Poudre River
N
1ST STREET
2ND STREET
3RD STREET
Bus Station
MATHEWS STREET
PETERSON STREET
WHEDBEE STREET
SMITH STREET
STOVER STREET
COWAN STREET
ENDICOT ST.
LESSER DR.
COLORADO STREET
REMINGTON STREET
NEWSOM STREET
ELLIS ST.
S MORGAN STREET
GREEN STREET
ROBERTSON STREET
STOVER STREET
ELLIS ST.
3 & 4
0 300 yards
X (2 miles)

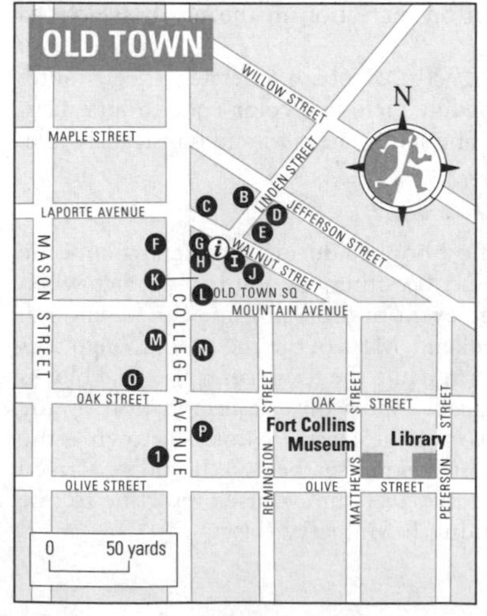

ACCOMMODATION

Best Western Kiva Inn	3
Best Western University Inn	5
Elizabeth Street Guest House	6
Helmshire Inn	7
Mountain Empire Hotel	1
Mulberry Inn	4
Sheldon House	2

RESTAURANTS, BARS AND CLUBS

Aggie Theatre	P	Pickle Barrel	V
Avogadro's Number	R	Silver Grill Cafe	C
Big City Burrito	Q	Starlight	F
Cafe Bluebird	T	Starry Night	N
Coopersmith's	J	Suite 152	K
Cozzola's Pizzas	B	Surfside	G
Deja Vu Coffee House	S	Taj Mahal	O
Elliot's Martini Bar	D	Thai Pepper	W
Linden's	E	Vault	H
Lucky Joe's	L	Woody's	U
The Matrixx	A	Young's Cafe	X
Nico's Catacombs	M	Zydeco's	I

Best Western Kiva Inn 1638 E Mulberry ⓣ970/484-2444 or 1-888/299-5482, ⓕ970/221-0967. The newest of the chain properties east of town, with scrupulously clean rooms and impressive facilities which include a pool, sauna, and hot tub; a decent continental breakfast is included in the rate. ❻

Best Western University Inn 914 S College Ave ⓣ970/484-1984 or 1-800/528-1234, ⓕ970/484-1987. This no-frills motel, handily positioned right across from the CSU campus, is ageing fairly gracefully. Facilities include an outdoor pool and hot tub, and a basic continental breakfast is included. ❹

Elizabeth Street Guest House 202 E Elizabeth St ⓣ970/493-2337, ⓕ493-6662. Although located right on a street corner, this B&B, built in 1905, is in a peaceful spot and set on perfectly trimmed, leafy grounds; there are four comfortable rooms with homey touches – only two have private bath. ❹

Helmshire Inn 1204 S College Ave ⓣ970/493-4683, ⓕ495-0794. Any of the *Helmshire Inn*'s 24 large, comfortably furnished rooms are a good choice for the price; all have fridges and microwave ovens and are smoke-free. The place feels more like a large B&B than a small hotel, and it's located right across from CSU. ❹

Mountain Empire Hotel 259 S College Ave ⓣ970/482-5536. With little accommodation of any description in downtown Fort Collins, the *Mountain Empire* stands alone for its location and value. Though the building itself is somewhat gone-to-seed and its elevator is old and cranky, the management is helpful, the rooms are clean and nonsmoking, and there are good-value singles on offer. Ask to see a couple of rooms, as furnishings in some are newer than in others. ❷

Mulberry Inn 4333 E Mulberry ⓣ970/493-9000 or 1-800/234-5548, ⓕ970/224-9636, ⓔmulberry@verinet.com; $65. As long as you have a car you probably won't mind being four miles from downtown at this comfortable mid-range motor lodge. Space is not at a premium out here, so the rooms are huge and there's no shortage of parking either. There's no free breakfast, although you do get packaged muffins and terrible coffee in the lobby until about 10am. ❹

Sheldon House 616 W Mulberry St ⓣ970/221-1917, ⓕ495-6954, ⓔblackerbyj@aol.com. A centrally located B&B with friendly, helpful owners; breakfasts are deliciously creative, served in a light and airy dining room. Three double rooms, and one cheaper single. ❻

The town

The most popular daytime activity in Fort Collins is perambulating about **Old Town**, a small but proudly maintained precinct of buildings that date from around 1860 to 1900. Prominent among the smartly renovated buildings in and around the Old Town Square are several restaurants and pubs – ideal for an outdoor lunch – while in the block or two north and west of the square there's an array of used clothing spots, friendly bookstores, and various antique dealers. You can take a more studied interest in this part of town with the help of a free brochure, available at visitor centers, which sets out a Fort Collins **Historic Walking Tour**.

An equally fine and leisurely summer option is to sit in the square and listen to a free concert while sampling a microbrew. Fort Collins is a noted locale for beer production; its **breweries** are big business, and no less than six currently offer **free tours**, with requisite samples at the end. The most generic of the bunch is undoubtedly Anheuser-Busch (2351 Busch Drive, just north of I-25 exit 271; ⓣ970/490-4691), brewers of Budweiser, where the real attraction is the chance to see the famous **Budweiser Clydesdale horses** (tours available June–Aug daily 9.30am–5pm; Sept daily 10am–4pm; Oct–May Thurs–Mon 10am–4pm; phone to check that the horses are not away on tour). Coopersmith's, 5 Old Town Square (tours Sat 1–4pm; ⓣ970/493-0483), Linden's Brewing Company at 212 Linden St (call to schedule a tour; ⓣ970/482-9291), and New Belgium Brewing Company at 500 Linden St (self-guided tours Mon–Sat 10am–5pm; guided tours Mon–Fri at 2pm & Sat hourly 11am–4pm; ⓣ970/221-0524) are the three closest to, or within, Old Town. Brewery enthusiasts may wish to obtain a complete list of tours from visitor information. The annual **Colorado Brewers' Festival**, held in late

June, provides further grist (or yeast) for connoisseurs of the amber liquid in the form of tastings and beer-themed celebrations.

For a non beer-related cultural experience, the **Fort Collins Museum**, 200 Matthews St (Tues–Sat 10am–5pm, Sun noon–5pm; free, donations accepted), has a collection of artifacts depicting the town's professional and civic life, much of it from the early twentieth century. Among the more evocative items are a physician's kit from 1925 and an old telephone switchboard, still in pretty good condition; a room devoted to revolving photographic exhibitions takes up a third of the museum's space.

There's not much happening on the **university campus**. During the fall months, though, it's well worth getting out to see Colorado State's football team (the Rams) play a game at the campus's Hughes Stadium (Ⓣ970/491-RAMS, Ⓦwww.csurams.com). They've built quite a fanatical following in recent seasons on the back of several courageous wins, including a couple over their historically superior rivals over in Boulder.

If looking to get into the great **outdoors**, your best bet is the Cache la Poudre Canyon, which begins just ten miles north of town (see p.292).

Eating, drinking, and nightlife

You won't be in town very long before someone informs you that, per capita, per square mile, and pound-for-pound, Fort Collins has more **restaurants** than any place else in Colorado. From top-notch affordable student places to a surprising range of ethnic restaurants, you can eat well regardless of your budget. Fort Collins is further blessed with two very good **ice-creameries**: *Kilwin's*, which also has homemade chocolates and fudge (114 S College Ave; Mon–Thurs 10am–9pm, Fri–Sat 10am–10pm, Sun noon–6pm), and the slightly cheaper *Walrus Ice Cream* (125 Mountain Ave; daily 11am–10 or 11pm).

Naturally enough, you'll find plenty of musical happenings, although when school is out there's very little going on. For places to get down, you don't need to go much beyond Old Town Square, as this is where the **DJs and dancefloors** are. For full **listings** of happenings, including live bands, dance events and happy hours, pick up a copy of the monthly *Scene Magazine* (free) from a streetstand or coffeeshop. During summer, check the schedule of shows coming up at the **Mishawaka Amphitheater**, which is 25 miles west of town in the Cache la Poudre Canyon; big-name artists and a fine outdoors setting make for some inspiring concert events.

Restaurants

Avogadro's Number 605 S Mason St Ⓣ970/493-5555. A college favorite for burgers, microbrews, hanging out, and sometimes even dancing. On any night of the week you could encounter anything from a bluegrass band to a poetry reading. Open daily, closing time varies.

Big City Burrito 510 S College Ave. Does a great job serving students with gigantic custom-made burritos ($4–6); you get to choose the type of tortilla wrap, from spinach to jalapeno, as well as from a variety of meats, salsas, salads, and three types of beans. Mon–Sat 10am–10pm, Sun 11am–10pm.

Cafe Bluebird 524 W Laurel St. A bit more expensive for breakfast than the *Silver Grill*, but its campus-side location ensures that prices don't get out of hand. Plenty of vegetarian items, plus homemade breads and soups and tasty breakfast dishes, including an excellent eggs Benedict. Mon–Fri 6.30am–2pm, Sat–Sun 7am–2pm.

Cozzola's Pizzas 241 Linden St Ⓣ970/482-3557. Conveniently central, and folk allegedly drive from Laramie in Wyoming to quell their pizza craving here. A monster sixteen-inch pie goes for $13–16. Open for lunch and dinner Tues–Sat, dinner only Sun, closed Mon.

Deja Vu Coffee House 646-and-a-half S College Ave. This is the university neighborhood's coffee place; there are light lunches and soups available, but most people just sit in for a chat over coffee with a muffin or piece of carrot cake. Mon–Sat 6.30am–10pm, Sun 8am–3pm.

Nico's Catacombs 115 S College Ave ☎970/484-6029. The surest way to divest yourself of student dining company is to settle in at *Nico's* for an evening of Continental cuisine and ambience. The filet mignon gets doused in a rich, boozey sauce, but then so does just about everything else, while the extensive wine list will provide you with further reason to indulge. Entrees $25–35. Mon–Sat; dinner only.

Pickle Barrel 122 W Laurel St. A prime college hangout, because the sandwiches are big and very good and the microbrews flow freely. Open daily; closes early Sun.

Silver Grill Cafe 218 Walnut St. This bright and cheerful diner-grill is quite literally where Fort Collins goes for breakfast – enormous cinnamon rolls ($1.95) are what they're famous for, and you need to get in early if you want one topped with pecans. The lunch menu is popular as well, featuring a good range of inexpensive grills, sandwiches, and salads. Mon–Sat 6am–2pm, Sun 7am–2pm.

Starry Night Coffee Company 112 S College Ave. Downtown coffee place with low-key, casual interior. There are usually some fairly exotic pies to go with the range of coffees, along with light meals such as a veggie pita pocket, soups, and focaccia. Daily 7am–10pm.

Taj Mahal 148 W Oak ☎970/493-1105. Dependable and central Indian restaurant, with plenty of vegetarian items on the menu, including a fine tandoori eggplant. The $6.95 lunch buffet makes for an inexpensive all-you-can-eat range of textures and flavors; entrees $11–15. Mon–Sat for lunch and dinner; lunch buffet 11am–2.30pm.

Thai Pepper 109 E Laurel St ☎970/221-3260. Range of fresh and delicious Thai standards including yellow, green, and red curries with your choice of meat and vegetables, and a delicious Pad Thai. Entrees $6–8; Mon–Sat for lunch and dinner, closes at 9pm.

Woody's 510 W Laurel St. Basically a beer and pizza joint, staffed and largely patronized by college kids, but the Monday dinner special is the best deal in town – $4.99 for all the (surprisingly good) wood-fired pizza, soup, and salad you can eat. The system for determining what pizza combinations are dished up is impressively fair and democratic too: if you yell "chicken-pineapple-mushroom-and-barbecue-sauce" loud enough, then that's what they'll make. Daily 11am–2am.

Young's Cafe 3307 S College Ave #114 ☎970/223-8000. An award-winning Vietnamese restaurant well worth the five-minute drive from downtown – it's tucked into a mall, so look for the *Red Lobster* sign on your right as you drive south. Bird's Nest Chicken and Vietnamese-style Duck are among the specialities, and everything is excellent, fresh, and well-presented. Entrees around $12. Sun–Thurs 11am–9.30pm, Fri–Sat 11am–10pm.

Bars, clubs, and live music

Aggie Theatre 204 S College Ave ☎970/407-1322. Having undergone numerous makeovers, the *Aggie*'s most recent effort to please some of the people all of the time has resulted in the installing of several pool tables and a "foosball lounge." It otherwise remains the town's largest live-music venue and hosts the bigger touring acts that come by – the place is usually given over to bands Thurs–Sat, although special events such as the Hip-Hop Holocaust and female mud-wrestling contribute to a varied calendar.

Coopersmith's Pub & Brewing 5 Old Town Square. The biggest of the brewpubs in the square, this is also the most popular among them for outdoor dining; there are usually some steak and seafood specials to go along with the standard list of burgers, sandwiches, appetizers, and Mexican items. Daily from 11am.

Elliot's Martini Bar 234 Linden St. This stylish, low-lit bar makes a nice change from the beery places nearby. Their speciality is, of course, martini's – lots of different kinds – along with other exotic cocktails and cigars, and the interior represents a fair stab at Art Deco too. Mon–Sat evenings until late.

Linden's Brewing Company 214 Linden St ☎970/482-9291. A high-ceilinged brewpub which is worth checking before most of the rest for its consistent roll-call of live bands; does some decent food too, as well as a renowned spicy Bloody Mary. Open daily from 11am, closing time and cover charge varies.

Lucky Joe's Sidewalk Saloon 25 Old Town Square ☎970/493-2213. The crowd here is pretty mixed, though at times thick with tourists. There are big-screen TVs for sporting events, a good range of microbrews, there's hardly ever a cover charge and the music is nonthreatening – mostly solo singer-guitarists. Open daily from 11am.

The Matrixx 450 Linden Center Drive ☎970/407-0738. Decked out in stark techno-moderne, supposedly in keeping with the movie *The Matrix*, this is the most genuinely dance-oriented club in town, where DJs spin a fair mix of techno, new R&B, and occasionally New Metal. Mon–Sat 10pm until late.

Starlight 167 N College Ave ☎970/484-4974. This is currently the down-and-dirty home of mostly college bands, which means the mood is very "rock" and the quality variable. Check the posters out front before you commit; cover charge and closing time varies.

Suite 152 Old Town Square ⓣ970/224-0888. Upstairs is a bar-restaurant, downstairs is a cavern with a DJ and dance floor. The music or fashion theme could be anything, although one night per week is "college night" (cheap booze), while another is set aside for under-21s (no booze) – usually Wednesday or Sunday.

Surfside 150 N College Ave. This dimly lit bar rarely has live music, but it's popular with students for its solid bar menu of appetizers, salads and burgers as well as the inevitable microbrews.

Vault 146 N College Ave ⓣ970/484-0995. One of the more appealing buildings among the music venues, this historic former bank occasionally hosts smaller bands and duos, but seems to be metamorphosing into a mellow lunch-and-supper club, judging by the increased number of solo acts and the improved menu. Mon–Fri 11.30am–2am, Sat 6pm–2am.

Zydeco's 11 Old Town Square ⓣ970/224-4100. Rounding off the clutch of bars in the square with a pub menu, small dance floor, occasional DJs, and various themed happy hours. Daily from noon.

Listings

Airport shuttle Airport Express ⓣ970/482-0505 runs a dozen services daily between Fort Collins and Denver International Airport; $17 one-way, trip takes almost 2hr, departing Fort Collins from *Holiday Inn University Park* (425 W Prospect Rd) and *Courtyard Marriott* (1200 Oakridge Drive); pick-up elsewhere in Fort Collins is $4–7 extra. Shamrock Airport Shuttle ⓣ970/686-9999 departs from the *Hampton Inn* (1620 Oakridge Drive), will also pick up elsewhere, and is slightly cheaper.

Banks Two downtown ATM locations are Key Bank at 300 Oak St, and Home State Bank, cnr Matthews and Mountain streets.

Bike and skate rental Lee's Cyclery, 202 W Laurel St (Mon–Fri 9am–7pm, Sat 9am–6pm, Sun 11am–5pm; ⓣ970/482-6006) rents mountain bikes from $25 per day and $30 for 24hr; The Wright Life, 200 Linden St (Mon–Wed & Sat 9.30am–7pm, Thurs–Fri 9.30am–9pm, Sun 10am–5pm; ⓣ970/484-6932) rents in-line skates; $7 for 4hr, $15 for 24hr.

Bookshop Old Corner Bookshop, 216 Linden St (Mon–Sat 10am–6pm, Sun noon–4pm), buys, sells, and trades a range of used books.

Car rental Advantage ⓣ970/224-2211; Avis ⓣ970/229-9115; Budget ⓣ970/407-1770; Dollar ⓣ970/203-1809; Enterprise ⓣ970/224-2592; Midtown ⓣ970/484-7443; Price King ⓣ970/490-1512.

Hospital Poudre Valley Hospital, 1024 S Lemay Ave ⓣ970/495-7000, has 24hr emergency care.

Internet access Fort Collins Public Library, 201 Peterson St (Mon–Thurs 9.30am–9pm, Fri 10am–6pm, Sat 10am–5pm, Sun 1–5pm; ⓣ970/221-6687; free); Kinko's Copies, 130 W Olive St (open 24hr; $12 per hour).

Laundry American Coin Laundry, 415 S Mason St (daily 7am–11pm).

Police 15 Old Town Square (Mon–Fri 9am–5pm; ⓣ970/419-3375); for emergencies dial ⓣ911.

Post office cnr W Olive and Howes streets (Mon–Fri 7.30am–5pm, Sat 10am–2pm).

Sporting and outdoors equipment EMS, 101 E Foothills Parkway, just off College Ave about three miles south of downtown (Mon–Sat 9am–9.30pm, Sun 11am–6pm); Gart Sports, cnr College Ave & Mulberry St (Mon–Sat 9am–9pm, Sun 10am–7pm); REI, 4025 S College Ave (Mon–Sat 9am–9pm, Sun 10am–5pm).

Supermarket Safeway, cnr College Ave and Mulberry St (daily 5am–midnight; pharmacy hours Mon–Fri 9am–9pm, Sat 9am–6pm, Sun 10am–2pm).

Taxi Shamrock Taxi ⓣ970/686-5555.

Cache la Poudre Canyon

Those frivolous French fur-trappers of the 1800s get the credit for so many imaginative names on Rocky Mountains maps that they deserve special mention for an uncharacteristic show of pragmatism when it came to naming this picturesque canyon. The story goes that a group of trappers were caught in a fierce snowstorm in the winter of 1836, and, desperate to lighten the loads they were carrying, decided to bury some barrels of gunpowder along the riverbank with the plan to return for them the following spring.

Today, the powder stashes have been recovered but the canyon road (Hwy-14) is well worth driving as a scenic route, with – at the very least – a stop for a picnic lunch coupled with the chance to view some bighorn sheep. The river itself is officially classified a "**National Wild and Scenic River**," which means the flow of water is uninterrupted by dams and other impediments and the banks have been left in their natural state, and offers superb opportunities for fly-fishing, whitewater rafting, and kayaking. The section which runs from the junction of Hwy-14 and I-287 just outside Fort Collins to the tiny village of Gould 66 miles further west contains the best scenery, fishing, and rafting possibilities. A **bighorn sheep viewing station**, little more than a raised platform beside the road, is 41 miles west of the highway junction.

Outdoor activities

A useful brochure entitled *Cache la Poudre – a Wild and Scenic River* is available at the USFS office in Fort Collins, and it provides a concise overview of camp sites, trailheads, and points of interest, and details the **fishing** regulations that vary over different stretches of the river. Around the town of **Rustic**, anglers go after wild trout under tightly regulated conditions; other sections of the river are regularly stocked with hatchery-raised rainbow and brown trout. Rocky Mountain Adventures, in Fort Collins (Ⓣ970/493-4005 or 1-800/858-6808), runs guided fly-fishing (half-day $80) and fishing float-trips (full day $130) on the Cache la Poudre.

The absence of dams along the Cache la Poudre accounts for much of its appeal for **rafting and kayaking**; the flow of water is uncontrolled however, so conditions are not easy to predict. June is the most reliable month for running the river, but suitable conditions for rafting may persist from mid-May until early August. Rafting companies based in or near Fort Collins including Rocky Mountain Adventures (see above), A Wanderlust Adventure (Ⓣ970/484-1219), and A-1 Wildwater, Inc. (Ⓣ970/224-3379 or 1-800/369-4165), all of whom run regular half-day ($55-60) and day-trips ($75-80) through Class III and Class IV rapids; extremely demanding Class V trips are available too, subject to private arrangement.

Trailheads that lead off into the Comanche Peak Wilderness south of the Highway and the Rawah Wilderness to the north are marked on the canyon brochure too. The USFS Arrowhead Lodge outpost just east of Rustic at 34484 Poudre Canyon Rd (summer only Thurs–Sun 9am–5pm) has information on area hikes as well.

Staying in Cache la Poudre Canyon

There are eleven riverside USFS **campgrounds** dotted alongside Hwy-14, all of which have pit toilets but no showers or drinking water. From east to west, the following campgrounds appear before you reach the tiny hamlet of Rustic: *Ansel Watrous* (22 sites; $10), *Stove Prairie* (12 sites; $12), *Narrows* (12 sites; $8), *Dutch Gorge Flats* (25 sites; $12), *Mountain Park* (55 sites; $13), *Kelly Flats* (38 sites; $10), *Big Bend* (9 sites; $10); beyond Rustic are *Sleeping Elephant* (19 sites; $10), *Big South* (4 sites; $8), *Aspen Glen* (8 sites; $9), and *Chambers Lake* (45 sites; $13). Contact the USFS office in Fort Collins for more information (see p.287). In Rustic itself, you can rent attractive, fully-equipped **cabins** for a minimum two-night stay at *Bighorn Cabins*, 31635 Poudre Canyon Rd (Ⓣ970/881-2142; ❹). The nearby *Glen Echo Resort*, 31503 Poudre Canyon Rd (Ⓣ970/881-2208 or 1-800/348-2208), has modern cabins with private bathrooms (❹) and rustic cabins with shared facilities (❸) as well as a small grocery store and restaurant.

Northern mountains

There's no place in the NORTHERN MOUNTAINS that tops the splendor of Rocky Mountain National Park, though that doesn't mean venturing in and around the various small towns and national forests that make up this part of the state isn't rewarding. The scenic drive west from Grand Lake along I-34 and then I-40 towards the northern mountains takes in Granby – Amtrak's last port-of-call in northern Colorado – and the tiny spa resort town of Hot Sulphur Springs before heading on to Kremmling, one of Colorado's most popular hunting and fishing bases. A few miles further west the aptly-named Flat Tops hove into view, their dramatic table-top peaks and plateaus a home to pristine wilderness hiking; the tiny town of Meeker serves as a handy western gateway. As the highway spikes northward, towns are fewer and further between, and inside each pub hunting and ranching may be the dominant topics of conversation. But just when you think that the towns and the hills can only get smaller, Steamboat Springs, a ski resort which more than stacks up to the likes of Vail and Aspen, appears. It's a fine old cowboy town that has grown up just enough to become one of North America's premier winter-sports destinations. Further west is the cheerful ranching community of Craig, while out on the Utah border the parched landscape reveals some of the earth's prehistoric secrets at Dinosaur National Monument.

Granby

Sitting high, dry, and windy at the junction of I-40 and I-34, the town of **GRANBY** is notable only because it has the most northerly **Amtrak** station in Colorado. It may also come in handy as a last-ditch choice for accommodation and services within reach of Rocky Mountain National Park – fourteen miles north – though Grand Lake (see p.271) makes a much finer base. During winter, Granby motels also take some of the spillover of weekend ski crowds heading to Winter Park (see p.206).

The **USFS office**, 62429 I-40 at the east end of town (May–Sept Mon–Sat 8am–4.30pm; ⓣ970/887-3331), has information and backcountry camping permits ($5) for the Indian Peaks Wilderness area just to the north (see box below). If you need **to stay**, there are several inexpensive **motels** here, the tidiest of which are the *Blue Spruce* (ⓣ970/887-3300; ❹) and *Littletree Inn* (ⓣ970/887-2551; ❸). For a bite to eat, check the family-friendly menu at

Indian Peaks Wilderness

Appearing on maps almost as an adjunct to Rocky Mountain National Park, the **Indian Peaks Wilderness**, encompassing nearly 75,000 acres of mountainous terrain below the park's southern edge, hosts thousands of hikers and climbers every year. The attraction is a fine collection of 13,000-foot-plus tundra-covered peaks, and a network of trails and backcountry campsites allowing access to them. Camping permits are required from June until September 15 ($5), and these, along with trail maps and information on hiking conditions, are available at the USFS office in Granby (see above); permits are also sold from Ace Hardware in Nederland (see p.89). *Colorado's Indian Peaks – Classic Hikes and Climbs*, by Gerry Roach (Fulcram publishing; 1998), is the comprehensive guide to this wilderness area.

Windy Gap Wildlife Viewing Area

Two miles west of Granby on I-40 is the **Windy Gap Wildlife Viewing Area**, by a small dam that is home to a variety of animals and waterbirds. A series of interpretive signs helps in identifying the various species of raptors, shorebirds, and waterfowl that inhabit the area, and there are coin-operated binoculars to assist you; a wheelchair-accessible trail runs along the north side of the dam. With a little luck and a sharp eye, you might see otters or even beaver ducking amongst the flotsam and jetsam near the banks, and white-tailed deer are known to come down for a drink in the early evening too.

Remington's, just off the highway on N 4th Street, or *Mad Munchies* across the road, where you can get good sandwiches and subs made to order.

Hot Sulphur Springs

Perched on I-40 between Granby and Kremmling and with a population of just 480, **HOT SULPHUR SPRINGS** exudes an altogether more genteel air than its neighbors. The eponymous town springs – allegedly loaded with such health-giving goodies as sodium, chloride, magnesium, potassium, calcium, and fluoride – are now enclosed in a peaceful spa resort, which, together with a decent town museum, comprise fair reasons for a day-visit or even an overnight stay.

The **Grand County Museum**, 110 Byers Ave (daily June–Aug 10am–5pm, rest of year variable hours; ⓣ970/725-3939; $4), features a meticulous collection of buildings salvaged from elsewhere in the region. The main building is a 1924 schoolhouse that now contains Native American artifacts, clothing and firearms from pioneering times, and an exhibit on the emergence of winter sports in Colorado.

The riverside **Hot Sulphur Springs Resort and Spa**, 5617 CO-20 (ⓣ970/725-3306, ⓦwww.hotsulphursprings.com; ❺), has twenty pools and private baths, offers body wraps and massage, and makes no apologies for its policy of "No smoking, drugs, alcohol, or pets!" Accommodation is in bright motel-style rooms, none of which has a TV; **day-use** of the spa facilities is also available (daily 8am-10pm; $14, towel rental $1). Other places to **stay** include the *Canyon Motel*, 221 Byers Ave (ⓣ970/725-3395; ❷), and the *Ute Trail Motel*, 120 E I-40 (ⓣ970/725-0123 or 1-800/506-0099; ❸). The *County Seat Grill*, 517 Byers Ave, is about the only place of note to **eat** – the menu runs to steaks, burgers, and decent pizzas.

Kremmling

The tiny town of **KREMMLING**, at the junction of I-40 and Hwy 9, is best known for it's **excellent fishing**; the Blue River, Colorado River, Muddy Creek, Williams Fork River, Williams Fork Reservoir, and Green Mountain Reservoir all are nearby. If you're not prepared to just wade in and take your chances with rod-and-reel, you can have a blue-ribbon fishing experience with Elktrout (ⓣ970/724-3343; $375 per day for two people), plying their private trout waters on the Colorado and Blue rivers with a guide. If you'd rather get on the Colorado River than in it, the highly regarded Mad Adventures **rafting** company, at the east end of town (ⓣ1-800/451-4844), has half-day ($36) and full-day ($55) Class II trips on the Colorado River. In autumn, Kremmling switches gear slightly, hosting a steady flow of **hunters** heading into the bountiful Arapaho and White River national forests south of town, in search of a trophy elk, moose, and even black bear.

The Kremmling tourist **information** office (Mon–Fri 9am–5pm, Sat 10am–5pm, Sun 9am–noon; ⓣ970/724-3472), a tiny log cabin in the "town square," can help with fishing and hunting advice. For fishing licenses and equipment, stop by the Fishin' Hole at 310 Park Ave, right on I-40 (Mon–Sat 8am–7pm, Sun 8am–5pm). The most venerable **place to stay** is undoubtedly the *Eastin Hotel*, 105 2nd St (ⓣ970/724-3261 or 1-800/546-0815, ⓦwww.hoteleastin.com; ❸), a 1906 boarding house that has operated as a hotel since 1913. If looking **to eat**, *Big Shooter Coffee*, 204 Park Ave (Mon– Fri 6.30am–6pm, Sat–Sun 7am–5pm), is an amiable coffehouse serving up fresh muffins, cinnamon rolls, and ice cream, while the *Quarter Circle Saloon* is the *de rigueur* saloon-restaurant, with burgers, steaks, and Mexican dishes from 11am until 10pm.

Beyond Kremling, I-40 winds its way north to Steamboat, crossing back and forth over the Continental Divide at four separate points within four miles. This stretch of highway, which culminates at the 9426ft crest of **Rabbit Ears Pass**, demands a fair degree of driver vigilance during winter, as well as appropriate tires or chains.

Steamboat Springs and around

The frequently stolen highway sign at the southeastern edge of **STEAMBOAT SPRINGS** simply reads "Welcome to Ski-Town USA." As a piece of self-aggrandizement it would perhaps be better suited to one of Colorado's snootier ski resorts, but Steamboat actually earned the title for producing, at last count, more **winter Olympians** than any other ski area in the country – 43 of them.

The indigenous Ute people were the first to make use of the **mineral sulphur springs** in this part of the Yampa Valley at least eight hundred years ago, and groups of them would stay by the Yampa River for much of the summer. The "Steamboat" tag came much later courtesy of French trappers, whose imaginations ran away with them over the chugging sound made by one particular spring – which remains the official "Steamboat Spring" today. As **miners** in search of silver and copper arrived in increasing numbers throughout the late 1800s, a town site grew and the name stuck.

By 1900, the small-time gold prospectors had given up and given way to "proper" mining companies – which extracted huge deposits of **coal** from the low-lying hills to the south – and **beef cattle** ranches. Both industries pushed for the Denver & Rio Grande **railroad** to extend its line north into Steamboat; its arrival in 1908 spelt boom times for them, and by 1913 more cattle were being transported from Steamboat than from any other single point in the US. The town remained largely a ranchers' domain until the next cultural shift occurred – the opening of the first ski-lifts on nearby **Mount Werner** in 1964.

Steamboat's appeal as a winter-sports destination lies equally in the consistent dumps of light dry snow and the fact that the town still feels as much a home for its residents as it does a playground for its visitors. This lack of pretension may be only slightly apparent in the stylized cowboy-pioneer architecture of the buildings downtown, but events like a summer rodeo series, and the winter "Cowboy Downhill" – in which cowboys race on skis down the mountain before saddling a horse on which to cross the finish line – leave little doubt as to the town's historical and cultural allegiance. And if the locals feel at all hurt that movie stars take up residence in Aspen rather than here, they do a good job of concealing their disappointment.

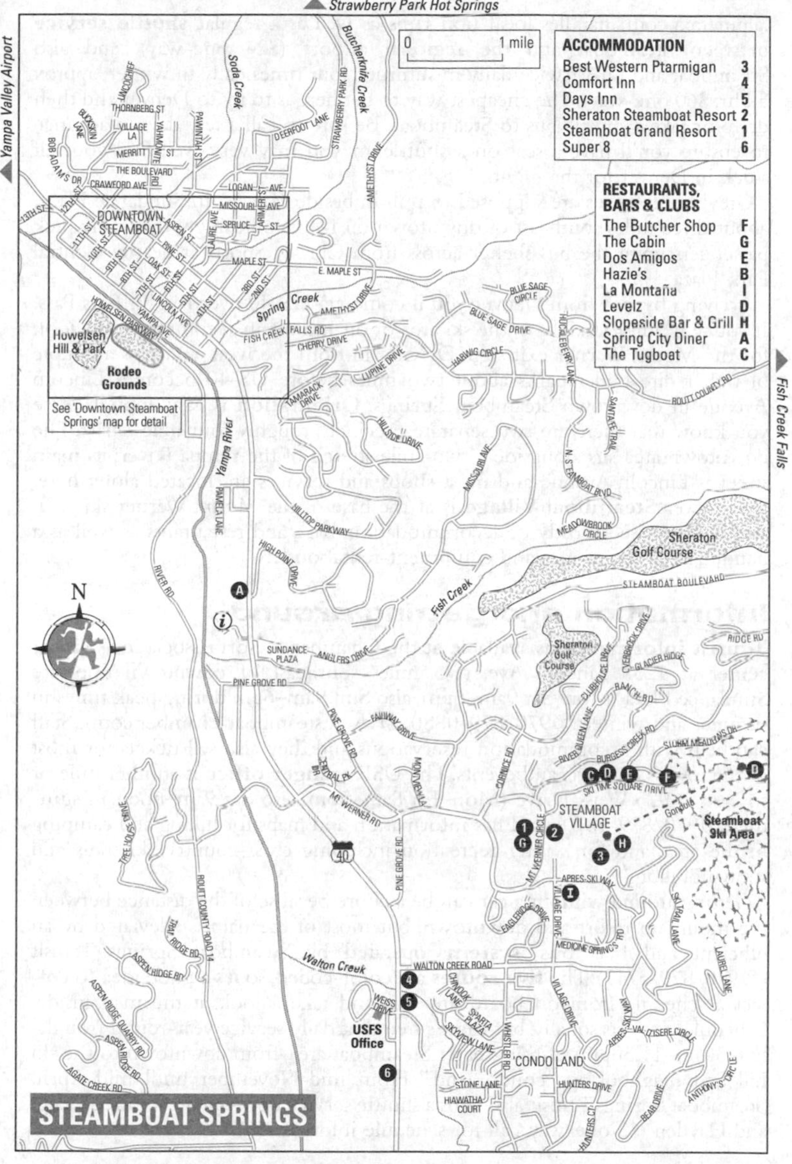

Arrival and orientation

Yampa Valley Regional Airport (Ⓣ970/276-3669) is 22 miles from Steamboat, and during the ski season is serviced by regular **flights** from Denver, Chicago, Houston, Cleveland, Minneapolis, and New York (Newark); at other times of the year there is just one United Express flight daily from Denver. Alpine Taxi (Ⓣ970/879-8294 or 1-800/343-7433, Ⓦwww

.alpinetaxi.com) handles local **taxi** runs as well as a regular **shuttle service** between Steamboat and the regional airport ($24 one-way), and also Steamboat and DIA (twice daily in summer, four times daily in winter; approx 3.5hr; $60 one-way). The cheapest way to get here is to fly to Denver and then drive or take a shuttle bus to Steamboat. Be sure to call a few days in advance to ensure you'll have a seat on a shuttle, or you may very well find yourself stuck in Denver for the night.

Greyhound **buses** are supposed to pull in beside *Wendy's* in Sundance Plaza, about three miles southeast of downtown on I-40; confusingly, they only pick passengers up at the bus shelter across from Christy Sports at nearby Central Park Plaza.

Arriving **by car** from Denver you'll come via US-40 over Rabbit Ears Pass. If you're heading straight to the ski area or on-mountain accommodation, look for the Mount Werner exit sign. Driving in from the west, you pass a couple of rather dire trailer parks about two miles before US-40 becomes Lincoln Avenue in downtown Steamboat Springs. **Orientation** is easy enough once you know that there are two separate precincts, roughly four miles apart. The downtown area sits alongside a two-mile stretch of the Yampa River; its main street is Lincoln Avenue and most shops and services are located along here. The newer **Steamboat Village** is at the base of the Mount Werner ski area, and is comprised mostly of accommodation, bars, and restaurants as well as a handful of ski boutiques and equipment-rental outlets.

Information and getting around

Tourist information is available at the Chamber Resort Association's visitor center at 1255 Lincoln Ave, two miles southeast of downtown opposite Sundance Plaza (Mon–Sat 9am–6pm, also Sun 9am–6pm during peak times in summer and winter; Ⓣ970/879-0880, Ⓦwww.steamboat-chamber.com). Staff can help with accommodation reservations and they also sell tickets for most of the town's concerts and events. The USFS **ranger office** is another mile or so east, at 925 Weiss Drive (Mon–Fri 8am–5pm, also Sat 9am–noon in summer; Ⓣ970/879-1870), and has information and maps for hiking and camping in the area, and for winter recreation including cross-country ski trails and snowmobiling.

Getting around without a car can be a chore because of the distance between the mountain resort and downtown, but most of the pain is alleviated by an efficient and free **bus system**, operated by Steamboat Springs Transit (Ⓣ970/879-3717). The **five routes** are color-coded, so it's a good idea to collect a schedule from on board any bus and take a look at the map inside. Schedules vary seasonally, but there's frequent daily service year-round (roughly 6.30am–11.30pm) of the greater Steamboat area, from downtown to the ski hill and neighboring "condo land." From mid-November until mid-April, Steamboat Springs Transit also runs a shuttle service between Steamboat, Craig, and Hayden ($3 one-way, call for schedule information).

Accommodation

Steamboat's **accommodation** offerings include five-star resort hotels, mid-range chain properties, some basic motor lodges and a little traditional B&B hospitality for good measure. Prices are highest during winter, and you'll need to reserve well in advance during the peak ski season. On summer weekends, many of the cheaper places are taken over completely by large groups attending various events, so don't count on just showing up and finding a room even then. Best value are the motor lodges downtown on Lincoln Avenue, as Steamboat has no hostel accommodation. Steamboat Central Reservations (ⓣ970/879-4074 or 1-800/922-2722) can supply information on ski packages and all accommodation, including condo rental – well worth considering for a stay of a week or more.

There is one **campground** in Steamboat and three state park campgrounds within thirty miles of town; the latter incur a day-use charge of $4 per day in addition to a camping fee. At a pinch, the *Dry Lake Campground* (eight sites; $10) is the closest USFS campground, six miles from Steamboat, but it has no drinking water; drive northeast on CO-36, then east on CO-38.

Hotels and motels

Alpiner Lodge 424 Lincoln Ave ⓣ970/879-1430. This motor lodge boasts nothing fancier than a central, downtown location. Rooms are clean, and not bad value even in ski season, when you can probably negotiate a rate if you book and pay for several days well in advance. Summer ④, winter ⑤

Best Western Ptarmigan Inn 2304 Apres Ski Way ⓣ970/879-1730 or 1-800/538-7519, ⓦwww.steamboat-lodging.com. This is where you'll find the cheapest hotel rooms on the mountain – although juxtaposed with the *Sheraton* and *Steamboat Grand*, that's not really saying much. Ski-in, ski-out from this property, whose rooms have tiny bathrooms but a few handy extras like a bar-fridge, coffee-maker, and even internet access in some. Summer ⑥, winter ⑦

Hotel Bristol 917 Lincoln Ave ⓣ970/879-3083 or 1-800/851-0872, ⓦwww.steamboathotelbristol.com. The rooms are tiny, but this is as central as you could be in downtown Steamboat. The place feels agreeably relaxed and homey, and a decent free breakfast – which is a step up from your basic hotel continental – is a nice bonus; weekend rates are thirty percent higher year-round. Summer ④, winter ⑥

Days Inn at the junction of Walton Creek Rd and I-40 ⓣ970/971-1219. This standard chain motel has bright rooms and a communal hot tub, and although it's somewhat isolated between town and the mountain, it's pretty close to the ski resort. And if this one is full there's a *Comfort Inn* and *Super 8 Motel* nearby. ⑤

Harbor Hotel 703 Lincoln Ave ⓣ970/879-1522 or 1-800/543-8888, ⓕ 879-1737. The interior is comfortably old-fashioned, and while the carpet and furnishings in some of the rooms is a bit worn, it still feels homey rather than dowdy. Facilities include two indoor hot tubs and a sauna, and the location is as central as you can get, and great value for the price. Condo units with kitchens and family rooms are also available. Summer ⑤, winter ⑥

Nite's Rest Motel 601 Lincoln Ave ⓣ970/879-1212 or 1-800/828-1780, ⓦwww.nitesrest.com. Although it doesn't look too promising from the outside, the *Nite's Rest* has clean, basic rooms to go with its central location. Summer ④, winter ⑥

Nordic Lodge Motel 1036 Lincoln Ave ⓣ970/879-0531 or 1-800/364-0331. This is your basic 1960s motor lodge, but the simple rooms are fastidiously clean, and there's an outdoor pool and hot tub. Best of the rooms are those with their own fridge and microwave, a real bonus for skiers. Summer ③, winter ④, all rates $10–20 higher on weekends.

Rabbit Ears Motel 201 Lincoln Ave ⓣ970/879-1150 or 1-800/828-7702, ⓕ970/870-0483, ⓦwww.rabbitearsmotel.com. The motel's large pair of pink, neon rabbit's ears marks the eastern edge of downtown Steamboat. It's a friendly, comfortable place to stay, with useful features in rooms which include microwave, coffee-maker, and fridge, and the rates include a simple continental breakfast. There are 65 rooms of varying sizes, and some can accommodate four people – ideal for a cozy ski vacation. Summer ④, winter ⑥

Sheraton Steamboat Resort 2200 Village Inn Court ⓣ970/879-2220 or 1-800/848-8877, ⓕ879-7686, ⓦwww.steamboat-sheraton.com. Quite a venerable fixture by the ski lifts these days, but this is still top-drawer (and top-price) slopeside resort living, with restaurants, bars, three rooftop hot tubs, a fitness room, and private golf course. There are standard rooms, two-bedroom condos and some brand new four-bedroom suites. The hotel normally closes for six weeks twice each year (mid-April to May & mid-Oct to Nov). Summer ⑦, winter ⑧

Steamboat Bed and Breakfast 422 Pine St ⓣ970/879-5724, ⓕ870-8787, ⓦwww.steamboatb-b.com. Situated two blocks behind Lincoln Ave, this bright and airy seven-room B&B enjoys a quiet but very central location. The interior feels like a very well-kept home, the managers are cheerful, and breakfast is a chatty affair. Rates are often negotiable for stays of three or more nights; advance bookings for winter are essential. Summer ⑥, winter ⑦

Steamboat Grand Resort Hotel 2300 Mt Werner Circle ⓣ970/871-5500 or 1-877/269-2628, ⓕ970/871-5051, ⓦwww.steamboatgrand.com. The latest addition to on-mountain accommodation, the upmarket *Steamboat Grand* has rooms that range from a standard king-bed studio to a five-bedroom penthouse. There are amenities to match, including restaurants, bars, a full fitness center, outdoor pools and hot tubs, sauna and steam room; *The Cabin* restaurant is one of Steamboat's most elegant fine-dining choices too (see p.306). Summer ❼, winter ❽

Western Lodge 1122 Lincoln Ave ⓣ970/879-1050. This motor lodge is looking a bit tired and its bleak carpark would not look out of place in front of a supermarket, but most rooms have been renovated fairly recently and the larger ones have two queen beds and a fridge and microwave to boot. Summer ❹, winter ❺

Campgrounds

The following all have toilets, drinking water, and garbage collection, but showers only where indicated.

KOA two miles west of downtown on I-40 ⓣ970/879-0273. This well-appointed campground has summer-only shaded tent sites on their own little island in the Yampa River, and a handful of no-frills cabins which are available year-round. The laundry and shower block is immaculate, and there is even a communal outdoor hot tub. Tent sites $20, cabins $40.

Pearl Lake State Park twenty-six miles north via CO-129 ⓣ970/879-3922. 38 sites; electrical hookups $14, tent sites $10. There are also a couple of very comfortable six-person yurts (a circular canvas tent-like hut) available for rent at Pearl Lake; each has one double futon and four single bunk beds, power, light, and screened windows. $40 for two, plus $5 per additional person.

Stagecoach State Park seventeen miles south via state Hwy 131, then CO-14 ⓣ970/736-2436. Good fishing in Stagecoach Reservoir and Morrison Creek is a plus; showers available. 100 sites; $9.

Steamboat Lake State Park twenty-seven miles north via CO-129 ⓣ970/879-3922. The camper services building at Dutch Hill Marina has laundry and shower facilities. Fishing (rainbow and cutthroat trout), swimming, and boat hire available, and there's a brand new visitor center too (Sun–Thurs 8am–7pm, Fri–Sat 8am–10pm). 198 sites; sites with electrical hookups $14, tent sites $10.

Downtown Steamboat

The ten blocks of Lincoln Avenue that comprise downtown Steamboat is where you'll find most of the town's restaurants and bars, as well as clothing and outdoor-wear shops. As Steamboat's "old town," it's pleasantly redolent of a **ranching history**, with a touch of the Old West in the storefronts, not to mention an impressive rodeo arena just across the river (see box p.302). Of course, between the ski resort and the summer recreation opportunities, you may not be spending much time hanging about Lincoln Avenue. But there's no doubting that one of the real niceties of visiting a ski town with a one-hundred-year history – Steamboat's official centenary was in 2000 – is that it's not just a bunch of hotels thrown up in front of a ski lift.

Really the only two things you might consider doing in downtown are a (smelly) **walking tour** of the various sulphur springs, and a visit to the **museum** (see opposite). To examine the springs, you need nothing besides your two legs and the visitor center's free hot springs walking-tour map. You can otherwise indulge yourself a little at the **Steamboat Springs Health and Recreation Center**, 135 Lincoln Ave (6.30am–10pm; $5, $10 including gym), which offers hot mineral pools, an outdoor lap-pool and waterslide, as well as workout facilities. Better still are the secluded 105°F **Strawberry Park Hot Springs** (10am–6pm $5; 6pm–midnight $10), six miles north of town, and only accessible by 4WD once winter sets in. Here you can slip – naked, if you prefer – into a hot pool in a forest setting; the effect is probably best at night when it's snowing, making this one of Steamboat's true aprés-ski traditions.

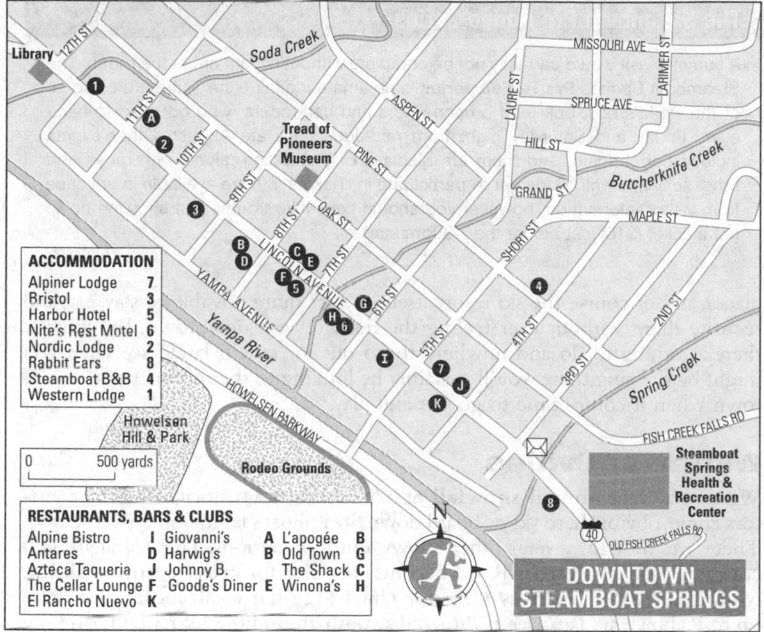

Tread of Pioneers Museum

With a collection of exhibits representing the past century of life in northwest Colorado, Steamboat's **Tread of Pioneers Museum**, 800 Oak St (summer daily 11am–5pm, winter Tues–Sat 11am–5pm; $5), is most worthy of attention for its **ski exhibit**. The display pays homage to an impressively large group of local stars of skiing and snowboarding, as well as Steamboat's father-figure of skiing, Norwegian Carl Howelsen (see p.303), and it's fun to see for yourself the evolution of skis, boots, and poles. Some of the old metal ski-boots would not look out of place in a film of a lunar landing, while most of the ancient wooden poles prove not all designs have changed so greatly.

A small firearms collection and the display of Ute artifacts upstairs are all staples of these sorts of museums, while two more distinctive items are a lovely square parlor-style grand piano, c.1868, which you can actually play, and an extraordinary piece of 1939 film footage of the spectacular fire which destroyed Steamboat's *Cabin Hotel*, killing two people. Built in 1909, the *Cabin* was the hub of social activity in Steamboat; watching the place burn from the perspective of the photographer – who presumably had just climbed out a window to safety – is quite an eerie experience.

Steamboat Village and around

Of the six-mile sprawl that Steamboat has become, the two sections besides downtown in which you may find yourself are **Steamboat Village**, the development on and immediately around the Mount Werner ski area, and the aptly nicknamed "**condo land**," a mini district of homes and condo buildings on the south side of Walton Creek Road. There's plenty to do around Steamboat Village, which has its own clutch of bars, restaurants, equipment- and bike-hire

The Steamboat Pro Rodeo Series

A summer visit would certainly not be complete without a night out at the rodeo. The Steamboat Springs **Pro Rodeo series** is no amateur affair either – it features some of the world's best bull- and bronco-riders and calf-ropers, who go head-to-head every Friday and Saturday night from mid-June until late August. Other events include barrel-riding, and there are displays of trick-riding, along with races and other activities which kids get to participate in. Tickets ($9) are available in advance from visitor information; however you should have little trouble just showing up to get a ticket ($10) just before the 7.30pm start.

places, and of course the ski resort itself, and it's quite possible to stay, eat, and recreate there without ever feeling the need to visit downtown. By contrast there's nothing to do and nowhere to go out in "condo land," so while you might be sleeping there, you'll certainly be looking to the mountain or downtown when it comes time to go out and play.

Winter activities

With an average **annual snowfall** of 320 inches, the majority of winter visitors come, obviously, to ski or board down Steamboat's large slopes (see below). There are, though, several other snowy outdoor options. The *Sheraton*'s golf course just off Mt Werner Road becomes the base for **cross-country skiing** (Ⓣ970/879-8180; trail pass $12, gear rental $11), but locals mostly just drive up to Rabbit Ears Pass (see p.296) and swoosh around the USFS trails on long skis (or gallop about on **snowshoes**). The USFS office (see p.298) has an excellent cross-country skiing map and directory covering this area. There are designated **snowmobile** trails north of town in the neighborhoods of Hahn's Peak and Buffalo Pass, and on the north side of I-40 on Rabbit Ears Pass. Again, the USFS office is the place for more information. If looking for backcountry adventure, check in with Steamboat Powder Cats (Ⓣ970/871-4260, Ⓦwww.powdercats.com), which takes groups of advanced skiers and boarders **cat-skiing** in the Buffalo Pass area.

Steamboat Resort

Famous for its prodigious falls of light dry snow – "champagne powder" as it's called hereabouts – **Steamboat Resort** (Ⓣ970/879-6111 or 1-800/299-5017, Ⓦwww.steamboat.com) boasts the second-highest lift-served mountain in Colorado, and is generally considered one of the country's best all-round winter-sports venues. Besides offering great conditions for skiers and boarders of all abilities, Steamboat has in recent years become something of a haven for telemark enthusiasts, with locals increasingly embracing the technical demands of the deep knee-bend turn.

The summit of Mount Werner is the resort's **highest point** at 10,568ft, allowing for a very tidy **vertical drop** of 3668ft. The **skiable area** of 2939 acres is crossed with 142 **trails**, rated 13 percent novice, 56 percent intermediate and 31 percent expert. The highly efficient lift system comprises seventeen **chairlifts**, along with the eight-seater Silver Bullet **gondola**. **Lift tickets** are $59 per day, and there are the usual multiday passes; all in all, however, Steamboat is a hard place in which to find a cheap way to ski.

A great deal of the downhill action is centered around the **Sunshine lift** at the southern end of the resort. All of the intermediate runs out here are wide, fast, and bathed in Colorado sunshine, the black runs like **Rolex** and **Two**

Outfitters and equipment rental

Steamboat is a popular launch point for horsepacking, hunting, and fishing expeditions that require gear and local knowledge, and there are several **outfitters and ranches** in the area that fit the bill. Trips are generally tailored to meet the requirements of each party so prices are negotiable, but a **guided trip** including horses, equipment and meals is likely to run $120–200 per day, with **hunting** trips much more. Del's Triangle Ranch, roughly twenty miles north of Steamboat near the town of Clark (☎970/879-3495, ⓦwww.steamboathorses.com), offers two-hour horseback rides right up to five-day hunting camps in the Mt Zirkel Wilderness; *High Meadows Ranch*, 24 miles south (☎970/736-8416 or 1-800/457-4453, ⓦwww.hmranch.com), has self-contained log chalets with kitchen, bathroom, and woodstove, and offers a similar range of horseback trips.

During **winter** you can still safely access remote backcountry areas, thanks to Rocky Mountain Ventures (☎970/870-8440), which offers **snowshoeing and cross-country skiing** day-trips to Rabbit Ears Pass, and also **ice-climbing** instruction (call for information and prices). Mountain Recreation Company (☎970/871-1495, ⓦwww.mountainrec.com) runs guided trips for skiers and snowshoers in the Hahn's Peak area, 25 miles north of Steamboat.

If you simply want to **rent** ski and snowboard equipment, try Christy Sports, Central Park Plaza (☎970/879-1250), or Clock Tower Square, by the gondola (☎970/879-9011). You can get rental gear for cross-country touring or snowshoeing at Straightline, 8th Street and Lincoln Avenue (☎970/879-7568). The retailers, as well as most others, have brochures at the visitor center that give a **discount of twenty percent** on regular rental prices.

O'Clock are bumpy without being life-threatening, and all roads lead back towards the amenities and restaurants at Thunderhead Lodge. On a powder day, head straight for the **Priest Creek liftline** and the adjacent tree runs, **Shadows** and **Closet**, where the snow really piles up for skiers and boarders with steely nerves and sturdy helmets. Thus far, Steamboat Resort does not have any big backcountry bowls, although there will likely be some expansion along those lines soon. Three small **terrain parks** and a **half-pipe**, meanwhile, keep those looking for big air happy.

Howelsen Hill

Carl Howelsen arrived from Norway in 1913 and introduced ski-jumping to the ranching folk of Steamboat, who inexplicably elected not to run him out of town, and instead enrolled their kids in ski-jumping lessons. **Howelsen Hill** (☎970/879-8499), located directly opposite downtown Steamboat on the other side of the Yampa River, is officially the oldest continuously operating ski area in Colorado, and Howelsen himself – the "Flying Norseman" – is rightly revered as the state's father of skiing. Steamboat's Winter Sports Club, formed by Howelsen in 1915, was the first official ski club west of the Mississippi. Today, the five jumping ramps at Howelsen Hill is where the US Ski Jumping Team trains; there are also seventy acres of skiable terrain serviced by two surface tows and one chairlift. Snowboarders can make use of a small terrain park and half-pipe, and the hill is lit for **night skiing** (4–9pm). **Lift tickets** cost $11.

The **Howlesen Ice Arena**, 234 Howelsen Parkway (☎970/879-0341; $4.75, skate rental $2.75), beside the rodeo grounds is Steamboat's only public ice-skating rink, although public skating hours are limited to a couple of sessions daily, so you should phone ahead.

Summer activities

Contrary to popular belief, Steamboaters don't hibernate during the snow-free months; whether hiking in the **Flat Tops**, biking around **Rabbit Ears Pass**, or just fishing or floating the **Yampa River**, locals manage to wring just as much from summer as they do from the winter. The Steamboat "Outdoor Activity Map," free from the visitor center, has some useful tips on spots for hiking, fishing, biking, and kayaking in the area.

Fishing and rafting

Fly-fishing for brown and rainbow trout in the Yampa is popular almost year-round, and Bucking Rainbow Outfitters, upstairs at 402 Lincoln Ave (☎970/879-8747 or 1-888/810-8747), has fishing gear to buy or rent, licenses and guided trips on their private waters. Another leisurely river activity is **tubing** – cruising the rapids on an old tyre inner-tube; Buggywhip's (☎970/879-8033 or 1-800/759-0343) rents tubes for $10. On any summer's day you'll also see people in kayaks and rafts, although the Yampa is by no means the most challenging white-water **rafting** experience to be had. Buggywhip's and Bucking Rainbow both offer a range of summer rafting opportunities on the Yampa or Colorado rivers (both Class II), Elk or Eagle rivers (both Class III), and Cross Mountain Canyon (July–Aug only; Class IV). Trips start at $43 for the Yampa, $59 for a half-day on the Colorado, and $115 for the hair-raising Cross Mountain expedition. For **kayak** rental and instruction, contact Mountain Sports Kayak School (☎970/879-8794); a basic class in learning to roll and recover a kayak costs $25 for an hour, while a half-day's river instruction runs about $100.

Biking

A well-maintained **bike** path runs the length of downtown Steamboat, much of it alongside the river. The most popular mountain-bike trails within easy reach of Steamboat are those on Mount Werner itself, and you can ride up from the gondola base – but only if you've got thighs and buns of steel. Plan B – riding the Silver Bullet **gondola** with your bike – will get you straight onto a network of winding trails before you barrel back down the hill (weekends only early June and late Sept, and daily late June to early Sept; $23).

A great out-of-town option is to ride out to the **Mad Creek** trailhead, six miles north along CO-129, from where you have a fairly technical climb on a rocky trail alongside the western edge of the Mt Zirkel Wilderness. The backcountry trails and service roads around **Rabbit Ears Pass** are great for biking too, but you'll have to rack the bikes and drive to the pass, since riding up there along I-40 is both exhausting and dangerous. Steamboat Trading Company, 1850 Ski Time Square Drive (☎970/879-0083), and Ski Haus, at I-40 and Pine Grove Road (☎970/879-0385), **rent bikes** for $20–30 per day. If you have some ambitious biking in mind, it's a good idea to stop in at the USFS office (see p.298) to collect some trail maps and fine-tune your plans.

Hiking

Of the **hiking** opportunities near town, **Fish Creek Falls** is the most popular trail and definitely worth doing. The trailhead is four miles up Fish Creek Falls Road from behind the post office; the parking area ($3) is just below a wheelchair-accessible quarter-mile trail. A second trail from here switchbacks across Fish Creek for three strenuous miles to the falls themselves – where your reward is in the form of several pools ideal for a fresh mountain dip – and

Hiking the Flat Tops

The 235,000 acres of the **Flat Tops** comprise the second-largest wilderness area in Colorado, their distinctive tabletop headlands dominated by the broad grasslands of the White River Plateau. Even from a distance, this chunky, squared-off mountain range looks like an upturned box, punctuated by a handful of daunting 13,000–14,000-foot peaks. The fact that the area is home to the largest **elk herd** in Colorado has hunters dewy with anticipation each September, but otherwise the animals are left alone and the Flat Tops retain an air of remoteness beloved of hiking enthusiasts.

Although billed as a Colorado Scenic Byway, unsealed CO-8, which makes its winding way across the Flat Tops, is not really worth driving just for driving's sake; it does, however, provide access to many of the 39 trailheads that lead in to the heart of these mountains. The towns of **Yampa** and **Mecker** mark the east and west gateways respectively, and each has a USFS office which supplies free detailed **trail maps** that include informative narratives of many hikes along with the hard facts on distance, elevation, and level of difficulty. There are no "must-do" hikes in an area whose selling point is the chance to experience a little lonesomeness, but the destination which you're likely to hear plenty about is the **Devil's Causeway**. This is a section of the plateau divide which separates the Bear River and Williams Fork drainages; a steep, three-mile hike takes you to a point at 11,800ft where the plateau narrows to a heart-thumping four feet wide, with a sheer drop of fifteen hundred feet into the valley on either side. The trail that leads to the causeway begins beside Stillwater Reservoir, about fifteen miles from Yampa along Forest Road 900 (take Forest Road 7 west from Yampa for six miles and then drive a further nine miles on Forest Road 900). This same trailhead also allows access to trails to **Trappers Lake**, a popular fishing and recreation spot (five miles one-way; also accessible by car via Trappers Lake Rd) and **Flat Top Mountain**, which commands a panoramic view of up to one hundred miles from its elevation of 12,354ft (four miles one-way). There are also a number of trails which provide access to secluded streams and lakes which support populations of various types of trout; best of these are the Marvine and East Marvine trails, located 35 miles east of Meeker via the scenic byway.

To collect information and maps in Yampa, visit the USFS office at 300 Roselawn Ave (Mon–Sat 8am–5.30pm; ☎970/638-4516); for details on access to the Flat Tops from the town of Meeker, see p.309. Thirteen USFS campgrounds ($11–13) are scattered throughout the Flat Tops too; most are open from mid-May until mid-November, although the area is crawling with hunters from late September so few hikers are inclined to stay out overnight during the fall. Check with a USFS office for a map of campgrounds and for information on amenities and current conditions.

another two miles on to Long Lake. More secluded hiking is to be had in the **Mt Zirkel Wilderness** (trail map available complete with backcountry campsites available from the USFS office), north of town, although the whole area has been littered with downed timber, following a huge storm and "blowdown" that occurred in October of 1997. The very best hiking in the area, though, is in the nearby Flat Tops (see box above).

Eating, drinking, and nightlife

While Steamboat stands pretty tall alongside the other big Colorado resorts when it comes to **eating**, it doesn't have a really notable **nightlife** scene. This is due to the fact that the slopeside hotels, bars, and restaurants are a fifteen-minute drive from those in downtown; in short, this isn't a place where you can visit every club on a single night on foot. Steamboat is also something of a family vacation destination, and thus not quite among the most swinging spots in the Rockies.

Steamboat's **restaurants** include a broad range of cuisines and menu prices, with plenty of cowboy staples like steaks and Mexican food, but also fine French and Italian places and a couple of excellent traditional diners too. The lion's share are downtown, though satisfying meals are still easy to come by if staying near the slopes.

The free local daily rag, *Steamboat Today*, is available from newsstands all over town and is an excellent source of information on visiting bands, nightclub happenings, and dining specials.

Restaurants

Alpine Bistro 521 Lincoln Ave ⓣ970/879-7757. The menu here leans towards western Europe, with schnitzel and cheese fondue ($18), alongside a chocolate fondue dessert ($8 per person). The food is uniformly good and prices moderate – given there's an award-winning chef presiding over the pots and pans – but the tables are rather crammed together and the ambience doesn't amount to much. Summer lunch and dinner daily, winter dinner only.

Antares 57-and-a-third 8th St ⓣ970/879-9939. Well in the running for the title of Best in Town, *Antares* has a warm and opulent bistro feel that would not be out of place in midtown Manhattan; there's even a bar where you can schmooze and watch the bartender polish whiskey tumblers while you wait for a table. Promising something called "New World Cuisine," the menu has things like honey sriracha shrimp ($17), tournedos of beef "LeBrun" ($26) and sesame-crusted ahi tuna salad ($16). Two huge bonuses are a carefully stocked wine-cellar and some fabulously indulgent desserts – go for a chocolate cappuccino mousse torte or a Meyer's Rum creme brulee ($6). Daily 6pm until late.

Antler's Cafe 40 Moffat Ave, Yampa ⓣ970/638-4555. It's worth the forty-minute drive to take in the funky Western ambience and friendly vibe at this historic pub-restaurant. Fragrant sausages of venison and such feature along with hearty soups, grilled fish and steaks (entrees $14–23). There's even live music occasionally outside on summer weekends. Dinner daily, also brunch on Sundays only; reservations advised.

Azteca Taqueria 402 Lincoln Ave ⓣ970/870-9980. For great, inexpensive Mexican food on the go, you can't do better than this. With just a couple of tables inside and three more out front on a sunny deck, locals cheerfully line up at the counter to order burritos, enchiladas, or daily specials like the $6 pork green chili. The enormous $5 breakfast burrito will easily set you up for a day's hiking or skiing. Daily 9am–8pm.

The Butcher Shop Ski Time Square Drive ⓣ970/879-2484. Family owned since 1971 and with a genuinely rustic Western atmosphere, this carnivores' delight would probably be better known were it not tucked away from the rest of the on-mountain action. Entrees, including prime cut of beef, rack of lamb or sauteed elk loin, are priced between $18–30 and are each served up with fresh bread, baked potato, and all the salad you can eat (salad bar on its own is $11). Daily 5.30–10pm.

The Cabin inside *Steamboat Grand Resort* at 2300 Mt Werner Circle ⓣ970/871-5500. Simple elegance defines the interior of this new hotel restaurant. The former personal chef to John Denver oversees proceedings, and has created a menu which tackles the Rocky Mountains theme – lots of beef and lamb – with considerable panache. The rack of lamb or filet mignon are both excellent choices ($28–35), but there are seafood options such as sea bass and salmon as well, and the chilled king prawns come with a spicy cocktail sauce that's at least two parts vodka. Daily for dinner; expensive.

Dos Amigos 1910 Mt Werner Rd ⓣ970/879-4270. Another Mexican restaurant which pulls a good aprés-ski crowd every afternoon. Standard dishes like enchiladas and fajitas are $10–13, a New York strip $15 (dinner only). Aprés-ski munchies include free chips and salsa and half-price appetizers 4.30–6pm, and if there's nowhere special you have to be for a while, try a "Chick-arita," a sort of rocket-fuel margarita created by a former barman ("Chick"), which tastes really pleasant – just before it lands on you like a ton of bricks. Daily: summer from 3.30pm, winter from 2.30pm, until late.

Giovanni's 127 11th St ⓣ970/879-4141. Best of the more expensive Italian restaurants in town, with an extensive wine list, excellent fresh pasta entrees ($13–18) and plenty of seafood dishes ($18–28) with a Southern Italian bent. Daily for dinner.

Harwig's 911 Lincoln Ave ⓣ970/879-1919. Serviced by the same kitchen as *L'apogée* (see below), *Harwig's* is a sort of diet version, with more casual ambience where people nibble samplers of pâté and cheese or stuffed mushrooms ($6–8) at the bar over a glass of red. Among some light and appealing dishes are the warm duck salad, Tuscan fish chowder, and an excellent Thai green chicken curry. Entrees $13–22. Daily 5pm–midnight/1am.

Hazie's at the top of the gondola on Mount Werner ⓣ970/879-6111. While there's undoubtedly a certain kind of romance to dining here on a winter's night with a view of the Yampa Valley, the must-do at *Hazie's* is the summer-only Sunday all-you-can-eat brunch. It's a phenomenal spread that includes hot breakfast favorites, all manner of pastries and desserts, fresh prawns, smoked salmon, and sea bass. The price includes the gondola ride up, and on a sunny Sunday you could virtually make a full day of it, walking (slowly) back down the mountain after eating. Keep an eye open too when you're skiing, for occasional two-for-one lunchtime entrees; another great value is the soup-of-the-day plus a basket of fresh bread for $6. Sunday brunch is 10am–1.30pm (mid-June until Labor Day; $20), dinner in summer Fri–Sat only, winter Tues–Sat, reservations essential.

Johnny B. Goode's Diner 738 Lincoln Ave. Pretty solid all round for a standard American breakfast, lunch or dinner; best value are the daily specials like a burger, fries, and a shake for $6 – which you'll see advertised on a sandwich board out front. Daily 7am–10pm.

La Montaña 2500 Village Drive ⓣ970/879-5800. A big hit with moneyed visitors, the chef at *La Montaña* is undoubtedly a very good exponent of Southwestern and Mexican cuisine, but locals will tell you that the prices are a bit much for what is pretty straightforward fare (entrees $16–28). Dinner only, 5–10pm; closed Mon or Tues (except winter).

L'apogée 911 Lincoln Ave ⓣ970/879-1919. Steamboat's upscale French entry, complete with low lighting, attentive staff, and silly prices; a meal takes 2–3hr to get through, so it's for a special occasion only. Escargot, oysters, foie gras or an exotic charcuterie selection are first up, followed by entrees such as scallopini of milk-fed veal flamed with cognac and cream. Entrees $24–40. Daily for dinner only.

Old Town Pub & Restaurant 600 Lincoln Ave ⓣ970/879-2101. The fine pub menu here features great steaks, fish, and pastas, though prices are into the $16–24 range. There are some cheaper pub standards like sandwiches, and the place is agreeably bustling most nights. During Tuesday's "burger night," a large burger with fries can be had for just $4. Daily for lunch and dinner.

The Shack 740 Lincoln Ave. This is the prime breakfast haunt in downtown for eggs or some pecan or blueberry pancakes. It can be a real ordeal getting a seat in the morning, especially on weekends. Lunches include a range of burgers and sandwiches, among them a good rib-eye teriyaki steak sandwich for $11. Daily 7am–2.30pm.

Spring City Diner on I-40 about two miles east of downtown (opposite the Dinosaur gas station). Address-less and isolated between town and the mountain, this diner is mainly visited by locals, who enthuse about the fresh home-cooking and great value. Big combination grills and omelettes ($5–8) are the go for breakfast, while lunch and dinner entrees include burgers, steaks, and pastas; try a grilled chicken salad ($7) for lunch, and herb-crusted salmon ($14) for dinner. Daily 7am–10pm.

Winona's 617 Lincoln Ave ⓣ970/879-2483. It's worth reserving a table here for the excellent breakfasts – variations of "eggs Benny," pancakes, waffles, and muffins. Otherwise you can grab something fresh on the run from the in-house bakery – the $2 cinnamon rolls are top-notch. Open daily for breakfast and lunch.

Bars and nightclubs

The Cellar Lounge 703 Lincoln Ave ⓣ970/871-8917. A good bet for live rock and bands, and it's also where Steamboat's young and grungey crowd tends to congregate. There's a small dance floor, chunky lounge chairs, and a separate tiny smokers bar out the back (the main bar is non smoking after 9pm). Cover charge $2–10, although entry is often free before 9 or 10pm.

El Rancho Nuevo 421 Lincoln Ave ⓣ970/879-0658. The *El Rancho*'s lounge bar has evolved in recent years into one of the regular aprés-ski haunts for Steamboat natives. Happy hour (summer 5–7pm, winter 4–6pm) features margaritas for $2.50, $1.50 microbrews (pints) and free chips and salsa; the entertainment runs to two pool tables and a couple of televisions. Daily 4pm until late.

Levelz Ski Time Square Drive ⓣ970/870-9090. A welcome new addition, this club takes up three "levels" across from the gondola and its winter roster includes bands and DJs most nights, with less-frequent live acts during the summer; you have a choice of activities too, as one floor is basically just a bar plus pool tables. Cover charge ranges from $5–20. Daily until late.

Slopeside Bar & Grill Ski Time Square. Another of Steamboat's quasi-eateries, *Slopeside* has a family-friendly menu of wood-fired pizzas ($8–11), pastas, burgers, and ribs, and its daily happy hour is one of the best in town; $6 for any of the excellent wood-fired pizzas on the menu, and $2 for your pick of any microbrew by the pint (10pm–midnight peak season, 7 or 8–11pm rest of year). Daily 11am–midnight.

The Tugboat Grill and Pub 1860 Mt Werner Rd ⓣ970/879-7070. The pub food here is not at all bad, with soups and nachos to steak dinners on the menu, but it's really a drinking, dancing, and hollering kind of place – at least when it's busy in winter. Being right on the mountain, the *Tugboat* tends to get the well-heeled crowd that's staying nearest the slopes, so it can get overrun with smoochy vacation couples. The band line-up is fairly reliable, lots of funky R&B, blues-rock, and reggae; there's usually a cover charge for the bands ($5–12), although you're likely to get in free before 9pm on any night.

Listings

Banks Community First Bank, 555 Lincoln Ave (Mon–Thurs 9am–5pm, Fri 9am–6pm) and Wells Fargo, cnr Lincoln Ave and 3rd St (Mon–Thurs 9am–5pm, Fri 9am–5.30pm) both have currency exchange and 24hr ATMs.

Car rental Avis ⓣ970/879-3785, Checkpoint ⓣ970/879-1996, and Economy ⓣ970/879-1179 have branches in Steamboat; Avis ⓣ970/879-276-4377 and Hertz ⓣ970/879-276-3304 have rental desks at the regional airport in Hayden, 22 miles west of town.

Internet access Bud Werner Memorial Library, 1289 Lincoln Ave (Mon–Thurs 9am–8pm, Fri 9am–6pm, Sat 9am–5pm, Sun noon–5pm; ⓣ970/879-0240; free).

Laundry Spring Creek Laundromat is downtown at 235 Lincoln Ave (daily 9am–9pm; ⓣ970/879-5587); Cheryl's Laundromat, 1815 Central Park Plaza (daily 24hr; ⓣ970/879-0440).

Medical center Yampa Valley Medical Center, 1024 Central Park Drive ⓣ970/879-1322, ⓦwww.steamboathealthcare.org, has a full range of medical services, specialist consultants and 24hr emrgency care.

Pharmacy Lyon's Corner Drug, 840 Lincoln Ave (Mon–Fri 8.30am–9pm, Sat 9am–9pm, Sun 10am–6pm; ⓣ970/879-1114).

Police 840 Yampa St ⓣ970/879-1144; emergencies ⓣ911.

Post Office 200 Lincoln Ave (Mon–Fri 8.30am–5pm, Sat 9am–noon).

Supermarket City Market, Central Park Plaza (daily 6am–11pm; pharmacy hours Mon–Fri 8.30am–8pm, Sat 8.30am–6pm, Sun 10am–4pm). Safeway, Sundance Plaza (daily 6am–midnight).

Taxi Alpine Taxi ⓣ970/879-8294 or 1-800/343-7433.

The northwest corner

Most visitors to the Rockies who find themselves driving through **Colorado's northwest corner** will be heading to or from the mountains of northern Utah (see Chapter 5). There's little by way of diversions along the ninety-mile stretch of I-40 that runs from **Craig** to the Utah border, although a small detour north takes you into **Dinosaur National Monument**. The tiny town of **Meeker**, sitting midway between the parallel arteries of I-40 and I-70, is the place to access the **Flat Tops Wilderness** from the western edge; it's busy only in the fall, when thousands of hunters arrive to go after trophy elk, deer, and even mountain lion.

Craig and around

Driving the forty miles along Hwy-40 west from Steamboat to the gritty coal town of **CRAIG**, the Rocky Mountains begin to recede and you find yourself entering an entirely different landscape of small mountain ranges and rocky desert basins. Most of the outsiders coming here are hunters and, unusually for Colorado, Craig's economic base – as supplier of electricity to three states – is firmly industrial. The list of local attractions is a short one, though the **Museum of Northwest Colorado** (see opposite) is worthwhile, as is a short, enjoyable hike along the **Sandstone Trail**. To reach the latter, a good vantage point from which to spot local elk as well as investigate a number of Native

American petroglyphs, head to the western end of Alta Vista Drive (follow 9th St to Alta Vista Drive). If you've come to **hunt** and **fish**, drop in at Craig Sports, 124 W Victory Way (☎970/824-4044), for licenses and supplies.

West of Craig is a desolate arid stretch of shale badlands that sees only a smattering of visitors drawn through the area on their way to the Dinosaur National Monument (see box p.311). It's in this remote region that various outlaws would traditionally hide out, most famously at what is now the **Browns Park Wildlife Refuge** (daily 7.30am–dusk; ☎970/365-3613), ninety miles west via Hwy-40 and Rt-318. Once the notorious hideout of Butch Cassidy and the Sundance Kid (see box, overleaf), today it's a pristine spot to watch elk and pronghorn antelope. Note that the route to the refuge is unclear in places so it's best to call in advance for accurate directions.

The Museum of Northwest Colorado

Tucked away at 590 Yampa Ave is the excellent **Museum of Northwest Colorado** (Mon–Sat 8.30am–5pm; free). Along with some quirky oddities such as a record-weight mountain lion, stuffed and displayed together with the photo taken at the scene of its demise, the museum is home to a world-renowned collection of **cowboy and gunfighter memorabilia**, assembled over a lifetime by Bill Mackin. Among a host of highlights are a c.1900 saddle that was custom-made for Buffalo Bill Cody, and an ivory-handled "Peacemaker," allegedly used in an 1890s double killing in Wyoming. This is as good a collection of antique guns, saddles, spurs, and cowboy gear as you're likely to find, and worth the forty-mile drive west of Steamboat, ideally on some damp or chilly afternoon.

Practicalities

Greyhound-Trailways **buses** pull into town at 470 Russell (☎970/824-5161), and **information** is available at the chamber of commerce on 360 E Victory Way (☎970/824-5689). Good budget accommodation is to be had at the basic *Craig Motel*, 894 Yampa Ave (☎970/824-4491; ❷), usually the cheapest place in town though all rooms have phones and cable TV. For a little more money, you get a lot more facilities at the *Holiday Inn*, 300 Hwy-13 (☎970/824-4000; ❹), a notch above most motels in town and has a good little fitness facility which includes an indoor pool, a hot tub, and an exercise room. Craig has an impressive quantity of mediocre fast-food joints and family **restaurants**, the best of which is the casual *Golden Cavvy Restaurant and Lounge*, 538 Yampa Ave (☎970/824-6038), serving a selection of soups, salads, sandwiches, steaks, and plenty of deep-fried goodies. If you like Mexican, you're better off heading to the modest *Plaza Restaurant*, 994 Yampa Ave (☎970/824-7345), for some excellent burritos.

Meeker

South of Craig, Hwy-13 heads fifty miles south before arriving at the proud and quiet community of **MEEKER**, a favorite destination for hunters who book up all the accommodation throughout the fall **hunting season** and gateway to the lightly visited **White River National Forest**. Sadly, the town gets its name for the Meeker Massacre that occurred here in 1879 and which saw Indian agent Nathan C. Meeker and ten other government employees fall foul of a Ute war party. By all accounts, Meeker seemed to have done his best to provoke the Ute. He not only tried forcing the nomadic nation to become sedentary farmers, but also insisted on ploughing up some of their premier pastures. The final straw came with Meeker's building of an irrigation ditch across

Butch Cassidy and the Sundance Kid

Without doubt the two most engaging characters to roam the Rocky Mountains of northern Colorado and southern Wyoming, **Butch Cassidy** and the **Sundance Kid** remain legends not only of the Old West but of a romantic outlaw existence in which breaking the law became an expression of personal freedom. Thanks in large part to being mythologized in the classic 1969 Hollywood film *Butch Cassidy and the Sundance Kid* (which starred Paul Newman and Robert Redford), these two former thieves and cattle rustlers continue to cast a long shadow across the Rockies.

Butch Cassidy was born **George LeRoy Parker** in the Mormon town of Beaver, Utah, on April 6, 1866. Taught the fine art of cattle rustling by local ranch-hand Mike Cassidy, George borrowed his mentor's last name, then picked up the handle "Butch" while working as a butcher in Rock Springs, Wyoming. He pulled his first bank job in Telluride, Colorado in 1889, and soon found himself in the company of a like-minded group of villains known collectively as the **Wild Bunch**. Among their number was one **Harry Longabaugh** – the Sundance Kid – who picked up his nickname following a jail stint in Sundance, Wyoming. The Wild Bunch were eclectic in their criminal pursuits, and the gang's résumé included horse rustling as well as the robbing of trains, banks, and mine payrolls. Between them they gave away a fortune in gold to friends, supporters, and even to strangers in need, establishing their reputation as latter-day Robin Hoods.

The image of a dashing, philanthropic band of outlaws did not sit well with authorities, who mustered teams of lawmen to go after them. The gang took to laying low through the winter months in **Brown's Hole** (now a wildife refuge; see overleaf), a broad river valley in remote northwest Colorado. Brown's Hole attracted a gathering of cowboys, fur-trappers, outlaws, and Indians, a self-made community with its own rules which made the perfect retreat for Butch and his cohorts. They were also known to visit (and get quite raucous in) the southern Wyoming towns of Baggs, Rock Springs, and Green River. Their saloon excesses were tolerated, though, because at the end of a spree they would meticulously account for every broken chair and bullet-hole, making generous restitution in gold. The gang, however, was eventually undone by their own vanity and love of a good time. During a visit to Fort Worth, Texas, five of them posed for a photograph in smart suits and derby hats, looking so dapper that the photographer proudly placed the photo in his shop window, where it was seen by a detective from the famous Pinkerton's agency.

Wearying of life on the run, Butch and Sundance sailed for **South America** in 1902 with **Etta Place**, the beautiful teacher with whom Sundance had fallen in love. They were soon cutting a dash in Argentina, Bolivia, and Peru, running a successful ranch and trying their hand at gold-mining, while robbing the occasional bank or train as well. The Hollywood version was true enough to this point, but Butch Cassidy did not die in a hail of bullets at the hands of Bolivian soldiers in 1909 as depicted in the film – although it seems that the Sundance Kid did.

Positive identification of the two men killed during the **shoot-out** was complicated by the damage done by hundreds of bullets and a lack of reliable witnesses. A number of Butch's friends in Rock Springs puzzled greatly over how he could have died in 1909 and still have shown up to go out drinking with them in 1920. A local mechanic even claimed to have repaired Butch's car in 1921, while the last say belongs to Josie Morris, an old girlfriend from Butch's Brown's Hole days; she insists that he came to see her on his return from South America, and claimed furthermore that Butch died an old man in Johnny, Nevada, some time during the 1940s.

a Ute horse-racing track, leading to the Ute attack. The government responded by forcing the removal of the Ute from the northwestern portion of Colorado – banishing them to a reservation south of Vernal, Utah – although to this day most of the confiscated land still remains uninhabited.

For a quick look at Meeker's history, check out the **White River Museum**, 565 Park St (mid-April to Nov Mon–Fri 9am–5pm; Dec to mid-April 11am–3pm; free), which displays the carriage used by President Theodore Roosevelt when he came hunting here. East of town is the start of the largely unpaved, but wide and well-graded **Flat Tops Trail Scenic Byway** on an eighty-mile route east to Yampa. It's a picturesque road through the largely pristine **White River National Forest**, which occupies a broad mesatop formed by molten lava and carved into shape by glaciers on gently rolling hills, now dotted with small lakes and smothered in stands of fir, spruce, and aspen. The road also accesses the **Flat Tops Wilderness Area**; see the box on p.305 for both details on Yampa's forest office and hiking opportunities in the area.

Practicalities

The **chamber of commerce** is at W Market and 7th (☎970/878-4492), though for more in-depth advice on the surrounding forests contact the **White River National Forest Ranger Station**, 361 7th St (☎970/878-4039). There's little in the way of accommodation here and the *Meeker Hotel*, 560 Main St (☎970/878-5255; ❸) a handsome, redbrick Victorian hotel, is the obvious place to stay. Its modest rooms have recently been renovated (some have private bath), and the lobby sums up the town: a large mural of the Meeker Massacre and over a dozen stuffed big-game trophy heads. **Campers** will find the convenient, but basic *Rimrock Campground* (☎970/878-4434; sites $12) beside the road just south of town at the junction of Hwy-64 and Hwy-13. But, if heading to the White River National Forest, you'd be better off camping in one of eight pleasant national forest campgrounds (mid-June to Oct). Twenty miles east of Meeker along CO-8 are the plush cabins of *Sleepy Cat Lodge and Restaurant* (☎970/878-4413; ❸), whose good **restaurant**, serving mainly heavy beef and chicken entrees (from around $12), is the most popular place to eat in the Meeker area. In Meeker itself, *The Bakery*, 265 6th St (☎970/878-5500), has particularly great fresh breads and pastries.

Dinosaur National Monument

The **DINOSAUR NATIONAL MONUMENT** straddles the border between Utah and Colorado in a remote area only conceivably visitable in your own vehicle. Divided into two separate sections, it was created to preserve a rock stratum in its Utah half, seven miles north of Jensen on Hwy-149, which has over the years provided brontosaurus skeletons and other astonishing remains to museums around the world. Uniquely, in the **Dinosaur Quarry** building, a tilted layer of sandstone has been painstakingly exposed to display an incredible three-dimensional jigsaw of fossilized dinosaur bones, left *in situ* for imaginative visitors to piece together.

The other half of the monument is a 25-mile drive north of the flyblown and unattractive little town of Dinosaur, Colorado, the site of the main **visitor center** (June–Aug daily 8am–4.30pm; Sept–May Mon–Fri 8am–4.30pm), which has video presentations and exhibits on the fossilized finds. It's free to get into the visitor center, but entrance to the other sections of Dinosaur National Monument costs $10 per vehicle. At the end of the road **Harpers Corner** provides a phenomenal view of the goosenecks of the Green and Yampa Rivers, approaching their confluence at imposing **Steamboat Rock**.

Travel details

Trains

Denver to: Granby (1 daily; 3hr 20min).

Granby to: Denver (1 daily; 3hr 40min).

Buses

Craig to: Denver (1 daily; 5hr 40min); Granby (1 daily; 3hr 40min); Hayden (1 daily; 25min); Hot Sulphur Springs (1 daily; 3hr); Kremmling (1 daily; 2hr 40min); Steamboat Springs (1 daily; 1hr 10min).

Denver to: Craig (2 daily; 5hr 40min); Fort Collins (3 daily direct; 1hr 15min); Granby (2 daily; 2hr); Hayden (2 daily; 5hr 20min); Hot Sulphur Springs (2 daily; 2hr 35min); Kremmling (2 daily; 3hr); Steamboat Springs (2 daily; 4hr 30min).

Fort Collins to: Denver (2 daily direct; 1hr 15min).

Flights

Denver to: Yampa Valley Regional Airport (Steamboat Springs); several United Airlines flights daily during winter, rest of year one flight daily.

United also has regular flights from several US hub cities to YVRA during winter (see "Steamboat Springs" p.296).

Northern Utah

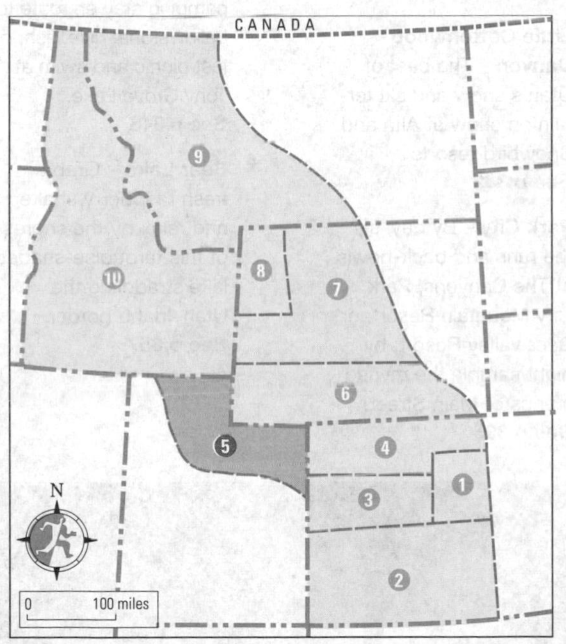

CHAPTER 5

Highlights

* **Temple Square** – The famous Mormon Tabernacle and the Mormon Church's multi-spired temple symbolize Salt Lake City's place as global center for the Church of Latter Day Saints. See p.322

* **Little Cottonwood Canyon** – The best of Utah's snow and ski terrain on show at Alta and Snowbird resorts. See p.332

* **Park City** – By day, ski the runs and back-bowls at The Canyons, Park City Mountain Resort, or Deer Valley Resort; by night sample the myriad menus of Main Street. See p.335

* **Sundance Film Festival** – Rub shoulders with movie royalty and the next wave of American cinema's brightest young things. See p.345

* **Logan Canyon** – An ideal spot for an overnight camping stay en route to Yellowstone; hike, fish, or just picnic and swim at Tony Grove Lake. See p.346

* **Bear Lake** – Grab a fresh raspberry shake and relax by the shores of this turquoise-shaded lake straddling the Utah–Idaho border. See p.357

5

Northern Utah

As the Rockies rumble north through Colorado and Wyoming, they poke an elbow westwards into Utah, which aside from a few top-notch ski resorts and alpine peaks, bears little resemblance to the other Rocky Mountain states. For evidence of this, look no further than its predominantly Mormon population and close historical and geographical ties with the Southwest. Still, as evidenced by the 2002 Salt Lake City Winter Olympics, much of **NORTHERN UTAH** is true Rocky Mountains territory. And while the global profile of this stunning mountain region may have risen a notch following the recent winter Games, summers in this part of Utah still offer uncrowded hiking, mountain-biking, whitewater rafting, fishing, and golfing. Snow-hounds, too, will be happy to know that the state's famous powder skiing – some of the very best in North America – continues to be served up with less fuss than in most of Colorado's ritzier resort towns.

Remote from European "civilization" until the mid 1880s, northern Utah was formerly populated by groups of indigenous Ute people, along with a scattering of wizened fur-trappers – who came to be known collectively as "the mountain men" (see box on p.402). Geographically associated more with the harsh southwestern climes of Nevada and Arizona than with the huge mountain range that was just beginning to be explored, it took a group suffering from religious persecution to summon up the determination to settle this part of the country. The first Mormons arrived in 1847, and made their home in

Accommodation price codes

All accommodation prices in this book have been coded using the symbols below. For **hotels**, **motels**, and **B&Bs**, rates are given for the least expensive double room in each establishment during peak season; variations are indicated where appropriate, including winter rates for all ski resorts. For **hostels**, we've given a specific price per bed; for **camping**, the overnight cost per site is given. For a full explanation see p.30 in Basics.

❶ up to $30	❹ $60–80	❼ $130–180
❷ $30–45	❺ $80–100	❽ $180–240
❸ $45–60	❻ $100–130	❾ over $240

**Note: Utah has a dizzying array of lodging taxes, and you may come across varieties of local bed tax or resort tax to go along with the usual state tax that is applied. These are most insidious at self-contained mountain resorts like Alta, Snowbird, Brighton and Solitude, where taxes may add as much as 25 percent to your roomrate. When booking a room at any Utah resort, always ask what the applicable taxes will amount to.*

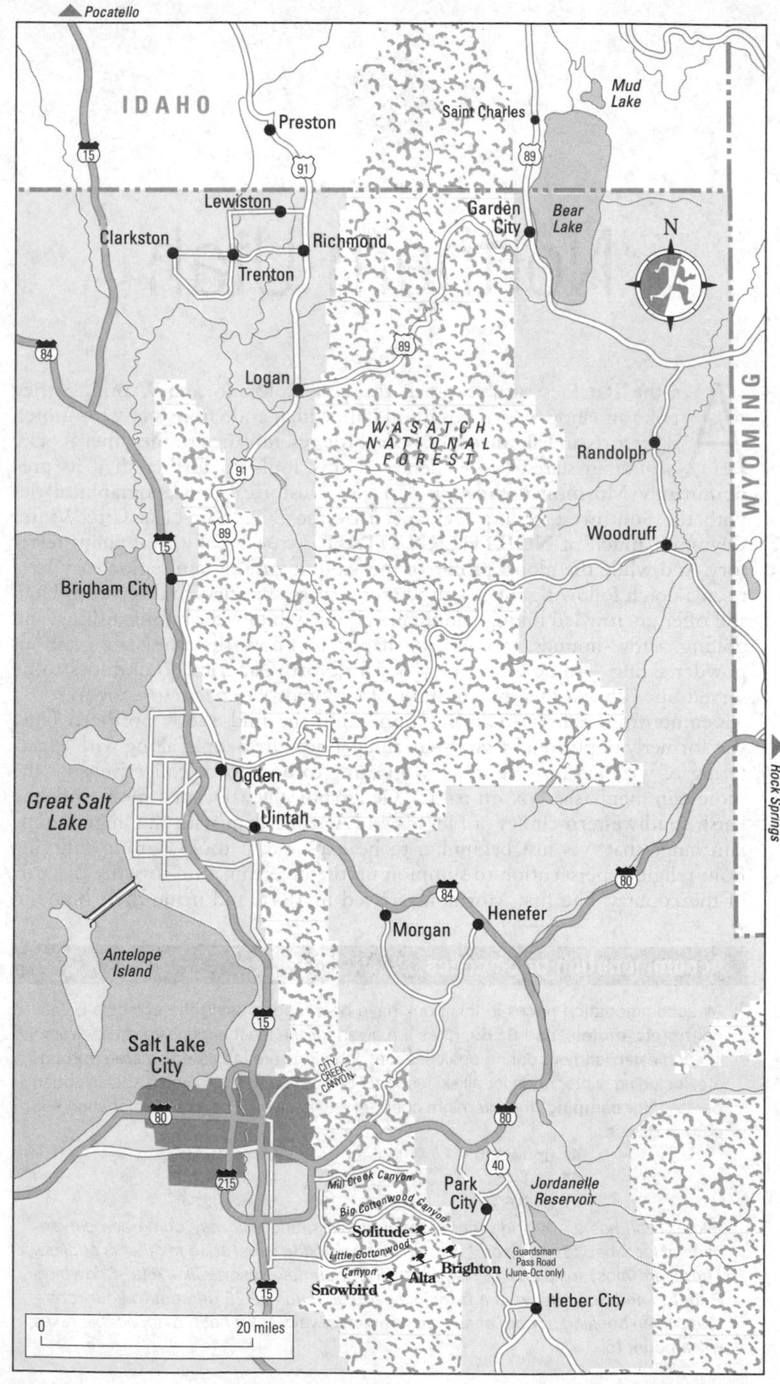
Pocatello
IDAHO
Preston
Saint Charles
Mud Lake
15
91
89
Lewiston
Garden City
Bear Lake
Clarkston
Richmond
Trenton
N
84
89
Logan
WASATCH NATIONAL FOREST
Randolph
WYOMING
91
89
15
Woodruff
Brigham City
Ogden
Great Salt Lake
Uintah
Rock Springs
80
84
Henefer
Morgan
Antelope Island
15
Salt Lake City
CITY CREEK CANYON
80
80
40
215
Mill Creek Canyon
Park City
Jordanelle Reservoir
Big Cottonwood Canyon
Solitude
Little Cottonwood Canyon
Brighton
Alta
Snowbird
Guardsman Pass Road (June-Oct only)
15
Heber City
0
20 miles

the Salt Lake Valley; today, three-quarters of the state's population resides in the 150-mile corridor between Salt Lake City and the Idaho border, on the western edge of the mountains known as the Wasatch Front.

Salt Lake City, the gateway for many visitors to the Rockies, is nestled at the base of the **Wasatch Mountains**. In winter, these are blanketed in the dry, light snow that draws skiers from all over the world to the low-key resorts of **Alta**, **Snowbird**, **Brighton**, and **Solitude**, as well as the more famous ones around **Park City**. The trails that serve skiers and snowboarders in winter give hikers access to alpine lakes and sweet-smelling stands of pines in the summer; mountain-bikers too can navigate the trails of the Wasatch canyons, or try the thrills of Park City's steep single-track trails via lift-served biking.

The **Great Salt Lake** itself is pretty much as its name suggests, huge and heavily salinated. Its shoreline doesn't warrant much of a visit, although the lake's **Antelope Island** does afford the opportunity to view a glorious sunset and the state's only bison herd. Further north, **Brigham City** is within reach of the pass in the Promontory Mountains where rail lines from the east met those from the west to complete the **first US trans-continental railway**. It's here that you pick up **I-89**, which winds its way north via **Logan** up to Yellowstone National Park eight hours away, the most scenic driving route between Salt Lake City and northern Wyoming. Not to be missed along this stretch are the wonderful hiking, fishing, and lazing about to be had in **Logan Canyon**, as well as some fine swimming in the impossibly blue waters of **Bear Lake**, which straddles the Utah/Idaho border.

Utah's drinking & smoking laws

Despite the Mormon church's influence, and largely because of increased tourism, there has been a relaxation of Utah's notoriously arcane **drinking laws**, and patrons of licensed restaurants can now purchase beer, wine, and mixed drinks. **Liquor stores** stock a limited range of wines and spirits, and you can also buy beer at most 24hr convenience stores – although the maximum alcohol content for all **beer** sold in Utah is 3.2 percent. One regulation that can be truly annoying, however, applies to going out to a **bar or nightclub** – for legal purposes, these are technically "private clubs" and you have to be a member to get in. You can join on the spot for a nominal **fee** (usually $5) that entitles the cardholder and up to five guests to two-weeks' membership. If you're with a group, only one of you need join, then sign everyone else in; alternatively, it's not unreasonable to ask the doorperson to find a member who will sign you in. It's difficult to predict just how strictly any individual proprietor will enforce the regulation, but in general it does get taken pretty seriously – a pain if you just feel like bar-hopping for an evening. On occasions when there's a cover-charge for a band or DJ, the membership fee is almost invariably absorbed by the cover-charge; if you're paying $10 to see a band, it's unlikely anyone will ask for an additional $5 membership. It's worth noting that **brewpubs** are exempt from the regulation as they invariably serve meals – as expected, they're a popular fixture in Salt Lake City and Park City.

Smokers may feel at more of a loss than those in search of a drink, as all of Utah's restaurants and quite a few hotels are completely nonsmoking. Many buildings even sport signs declaring that you may not smoke within 25 feet of the entrance.

Salt Lake City

Until the recent winter Olympics, the only thing that **SALT LAKE CITY** was really famous for was being the Mormon Church's spiritual and administrative headquarters. Yet beyond the boundaries of the church's Temple Square, Salt Lake feels much like other western US cities, its population increasingly drawn from different parts of the country (and Mexico) as people move to the mountains in search of a better quality of life. In fact, while the Mormon Church's global profile is undoubtedly at its highest here, the **Mormon population** now only makes up about half of the Salt Lake Valley's total of 780,000, compared with over seventy percent elsewhere in Utah. And, in 1999, voters even elected their first ever non-Mormon mayor, a clear shift in the balance of civic power.

In any case, the city has more going for it than just church institutions. Its setting is superb, towered over by the granite mountains of the **Wasatch Front**, whose canyons (see p.328) offer scenic alpine trails for hikers and bikers in summer, and unheralded ski areas that feature some of North America's best powder snow. And while there is a fundamental lack of things to do in the way of cultural diversions, besides perhaps attending a **Utah Jazz** NBA basketball game, the city's unhurried pace, together with the positive energy and lack of pretence of its people, can make for a surprisingly enjoyable experience.

That said, you may find the city most appealing simply as a gateway to the Rockies: it's an exceptionally convenient place from which to collect a rental car and head straight out onto an interstate highway for the drive north into Idaho or east to Colorado.

Arrival and information

Salt Lake City International Airport (ⓣ801/575-2400) is located just four miles west of downtown. Delta/SkyWest **flights** – both international and domestic – arrive at Terminal 2, while Terminal 1 is for everyone else. There is a Zions Bank **foreign exchange** counter in Terminal 2 (Mon–Fri 9am–5pm), and 24hr ATMs in both terminals.

A **cab** into town costs around $12; alternatively, take Utah Transit Authority (UTA) **bus** #50 or #150 (Mon–Fri every 30min 6.10am–6.50pm, Sat hourly 7.10am–6.20pm; evening service #150 Mon–Sat hourly 7.20–11.20pm; Sun #50 limited service; $1). The UTA stop is on Level 1 of the carpark across the road from the terminal buildings – go through the doors beside the parking cashier's booth, then turn right. **Shuttle vans** to downtown destinations are run by Express Shuttle (ⓣ801/596-1600 or 1-800/321-5554; $6–8), but almost all the downtown hotels offer free airport transfers.

The Greyhound **bus terminal** is located in the heart of downtown at 160 W South Temple (ⓣ801/355-9579 or 1-800/231-2222, ⓦwww.greyhound.com), while Amtrak **trains** pull in several blocks southwest of the city center at 600 W 340 S (ⓣ1-800/872-7245, ⓦwww.amtrak.com).

Visitor centers can be found downtown at 90 S West Temple in the Salt Palace Convention Center (Mon–Fri 8am–6pm, Sat & Sun 9am–5pm; ⓣ801/521-2822, ⓦwww.saltlake.org), or in Terminal 2 of the airport (daily 9am–6pm; ⓣ801/575-2660). For details on the rest of Utah, stop by the Utah Travel Council, across from the capitol at 300 N State St (Mon–Fri 8am–5pm, Sat & Sun 10am–5pm; ⓣ801/538-1900 or 1-800/200-1160, ⓦwww.utah.com).

Orientation and transport

Getting around Salt Lake City on foot is no problem, and the width of streets makes it even easier to negotiate **by car**; traffic is generally light and parking spaces plentiful. Streets are numbered in relation to Temple Square in a straightforward grid – thus the address 400 W 300 S is four blocks west and three blocks south of the square. This makes **orientation** easy enough, but with just seven of these huge city blocks roughly equal to a mile, you may want to avail yourself of the cheap and efficient UTA **bus and light rail** system. The light rail, or **TRAX** line, runs north–south between the Delta Center in downtown and a neighbourhood called Sandy, at about 9800 S; buy tickets from vending

Shuttle services to the mountain resorts

There are several **shuttle services** running between Salt Lake City Airport and the resorts of **Park City**, **Alta**, **Snowbird**, **Brighton**, and **Solitude** – all less than an hour's drive from the airport. Your choice of shuttle comes down to cost versus convenience; companies with a fleet of vans and frequent services charge more than the one-man operators, but the latter may pick up from the airport only once or twice a day. Expect to pay $20–25 one-way to the Wasatch canyons (most also offer a good deal on return-trip tickets for only a few more dollars) and $25–30 one-way to Park City. Best bets for the Wasatch Canyons are Canyon Transportation (ⓣ801/255-1841 or 1-800/255-1841, ⓦwww.canyontransportation.com) and Powder for the People (ⓣ435/649-6648 or 1-888/482-7547), while Express Shuttle (ⓣ801/596-1600 or 1-800/397-0773, ⓦwww.xpressshuttle.com) services the Park City resorts from the airport. Lewis Bros Stages (ⓣ877/491-8111, ⓦwww.lewis-bros.com) have frequent runs to all the resorts.

machines at TRAX stations. Individual bus and TRAX tickets cost $1 with free transfers good for two hours, including your return trip. All UTA services are **free** within the area bounded by North Temple, 400 W, 500 S and 200 E; if you plan to go beyond this narrow precinct several times during the day, it's well worth getting an **all-day pass** for $2. A Transit System map is available from tourist information offices (route and schedule information ⓣ801/287-4636).

Gray Line (ⓣ801/521-7060 or 1-800/309-2352) offers **bus tours** ranging from city jaunts to multiday trips, while AdvenTours (ⓣ801/288-2118 or 1-800/556-8884) covers more of the local area, with day-trips to Park City, the nearby Wasatch canyons and also Antelope Island (see p.326). To reach the best parts of the surrounding mountains under your own steam, however, you'll need a **car**; weekly rental of a compact sedan ranges from $200–300 (or around $40 per day). All the major rental companies are based near the airport (see "Listings" p.327), and run free shuttle buses to and from the airport terminals. **Bicycles** can be rented from several locations downtown (see "Listings" p.327) for $20–30 per day – UTA buses are equipped with external racks to carry bicycles.

Accommodation

Salt Lake City has a fine range of **accommodation**, including a couple of hostels, some luxurious downtown hotels, and the usual run of mid-range places near the airport and along the interstates. Unlike the nearby ski resorts, Salt Lake City hotels don't hike their prices in winter – which makes them a useful accommodation option **for skiers**. And while it remains to be seen what demand is like post-Olympics, it's likely that Salt Lake City will soon find itself heavily oversupplied with hotel rooms, a situation that should lead to plenty of discounted rates in coming years. **Campers** are best off staying in one of the two sites in beautiful Big Cottonwood Canyon (see p.330).

Hotels and motels

Brigham Street Inn 1135 E South Temple ⓣ801/364-4461 or 1-800/417-4461, ⓔbstreet@ecckids.com. This historic mansion is the city's most luxurious and peaceful B&B, thanks in large part to its location several blocks east of downtown toward the mountains. Each of the nine guestrooms has its own private bath – some have fireplaces too – and the breakfasts are beautifully presented. ❻

Deseret Inn 50 W 500 S ⓣ801/532-2900 or 1-800/359-2170. This downtown motor lodge is a real throwback to a bygone era; though far from smart its rooms are clean and comfortable, and the location is unbeatable for the price. ❷

Holiday Inn Airport 1659 W North Temple ⓣ801/533-9000 or 1-800/465-4329. Just about midway between downtown and the airport, this standard mid-range property includes a continental breakfast and airport transfers in the quite reasonable rates. ❺

Inn at Temple Square 71 W South Temple ⓣ801/531-1000 or 1-800/843-4668, ⓕ801/536-7272, ⓦwww.theinn.com. If you want to be close to Temple Square and can afford a slice of luxury, this is the place. An attractive, historic building built in 1930 and owned by the Mormon Church, the hotel is entirely nonsmoking. Rooms are large with deep carpeting and the bathrooms are enormous; a good buffet breakfast and airport shuttle are free. Enquire about weekend discounts. ❼

Hotel Monaco 15 W 200 S ⓣ801/595-0000 or 1-877/294-9710, ⓕ801/532-8500, ⓦwww.monaco-saltlakecity.com. The interior of this upscale boutique hotel, housed in a former bank, could fairly be described as "funky"; lime green ceilings, loud, striped wallpaper and contemporary furniture that betrays a North African-influenced Art Deco theme. The hotel's *Bambara* restaurant is also one of the city's best (see p.324). ❽

Motel 6 176 W 600 S ⓣ801/531-1252. Budget downtown motel that's handy for Amtrak. There's a small outdoor pool, and local calls are free. ❸

Peery Hotel 110 W Broadway (300 S) ⓣ801/521-4300 or 1-800/331-0073, ⓦwww.peeryhotel.com. This refurbished 1910 downtown landmark has small but characterful rooms with conservative furnishings alongside internet terminals in every room. The free hot buffet breakfast is not the best around, though it's still a value-added bonus. ❻

Shilo Inn 206 S West Temple ⓣ801/521-9500, ⓕ359-6527. Clean rooms in a central downtown tower– whose architecture – external elevator and huge neon sign – reeks of the early 1970s. Rooms are large and there's a pool, sauna, and gym onsite, along with free breakfasts and airport shuttles. Thirty percent discount on weekends, depending on availability. ❻

Travelodge – Temple Square 144 W North Temple ⓣ801/533-8200 or 1-800/255-3050. Most central and least expensive of the three local *Travelodges*; it's basic but clean and ideally located in relation to Temple Square. ❹

Hostels

Avenues HI Hostel 107 F St ⓣ801/359-3855, 1-888/884-4752, ⓕ801/532-0182, ⓦwww.hostels.com/ slchostel. Conveniently located five blocks east of Temple Square, this hostel has dorm beds and a few double rooms too. Unfortunately, its general untidiness and complete lack of atmosphere make it very much a last choice. Dorms $15.50; ❷

Ute Hostel 21 E Kelsey Ave ⓣ801/595-1645. Easily the better of Salt Lake City's two hostels, this small, private establishment, located a mile or so south of downtown, has dorm beds and a couple of double rooms, plus bike rental and a hot tub. You can't reserve a bed, but it's worth calling a day or two ahead to check whether they'll have room; just phone on arrival and someone will pick you up from the airport, Amtrak, or Greyhound. If you're driving or walking from downtown, head straight down State St past 1100 S and turn right into Kelsey Ave. Dorms $15; ❷.

The City

Of most interest to visitors are the buildings associated with the Mormon Church, and all of these are conveniently clustered together within a block of **Temple Square**; the only other major site of interest is the **Capitol Building**, located six blocks to the north.

The area southwest of Temple Square, site of the massive **Salt Palace** convention complex and the Delta Center (home of the Utah Jazz), continues to be transformed by the addition of new retail and apartment buildings, while the neighboring district of brick warehouses around the Union Pacific railroad tracks is quickly filling up with designer shops and art galleries. However, this is also where the city's emergency shelters and soup kitchens are located, so it remains a preserve of Utah's growing homeless population – particularly around Pioneer Park.

The moment you get below 700 S, the city becomes a wasteland of car dealers, gas stations, and fast-food joints. And unless you find yourself staying at the HI hostel (see above), it's not likely that you'll spend much time in the area to the northeast of downtown known as "the Avenues," a leafy residential neighborhood favored by Salt Lake City's professionals and academics.

Temple Square

The geographical and spiritual heart of Salt Lake City is the walled **Temple Square**, the world headquarters of the Mormon Church (or Church of Christ of Latter Day Saints – LDS). Its focus, the monumental **Temple** itself, was completed in 1893 after forty years of intensive labor. The multispired granite edifice rises to 210ft above the city – it's not the tallest building on the mainly flat skyline but, thanks to its crisply angular silhouette, it's just about the only interesting one. Only confirmed Mormons may enter the Temple, and even they do so only for the most sacred LDS rituals – marriage, baptisms, and "sealing," the joining of a family unit for eternity.

Wander through the gates of Temple Square and you'll swiftly be snapped up by one of the many waiting Mormons, and shepherded to join a free forty-minute **tour** of the various sites within. As well as being led past monuments to Mormon pioneers, you'll be ushered into the odd oblong shell of the **Mormon Tabernacle**. No images of any kind adorn its interior, home to the world-renowned Mormon Tabernacle Choir; a helper at the lectern laconically displays its remarkable acoustic properties by tearing up a newspaper and dropping a nail. There's free admission to both the choir's 9.30am Sunday broadcast and its rehearsals on Thursday evenings at 8pm.

The primary aim of the tours is to awaken your interest in the Mormon faith, but if you're simply taking a cursory interest in the city's **Mormon heritage**, time your tour to conclude with a screening of the film *Legacy*, in the northern visitor center (twice daily, 1pm & 7pm; free). This hour-long dramatization is surprisingly well executed, and tells the story of the travels and tribulations of Salt Lake City's pioneers. Combined with a stroll around the Museum of Church History and Art (see below), this should suffice to fill you in on the basics of the city's Mormon origins.

Around Temple Square

A block east of Temple Square along South Temple, the **Beehive House** (Mon–Sat 9.30am–4.30pm, Sun 10am–1pm; free) is a plain, white New England-style house, with wraparound verandas and green shutters. Erected in 1854 by church leader Brigham Young, it's now a small museum of Young's life, restored to the style of the period. Free twenty-minute tours, which you have to join to see much of the house, are given at least every half-hour.

The **Family History Library**, across West Temple from Temple Square (Mon 7.30am–6pm, Tues–Sat 7.30am–10pm; free), is intended to enable Mormons to trace their ancestors and then baptize them into the faith by proxy, but it's open to everyone. The world's most exhaustive genealogical library, it gives immediate access, through CD-ROMs and banks of computers, to birth and death records from over fifty countries, some dating back as much as five hundred years. If you're starting your search from scratch, however, you should begin at the **Family Search Center**, on the opposite side of the square in the **Joseph Smith Memorial Building**, 15 E South Temple (Mon–Sat 9am–9pm; free). All you need is a person's place of birth, a few approximate dates, and you're away; volunteers provide help if you need it, but leave you alone until you ask. The marbled and chandeliered lobby of this historic building is also worth a look if you're strolling by.

The Mormon Church

Worldwide, the **Church of Jesus Christ of Latter-Day Saints** (LDS) claims around nine million members. It is characterized by its emphasis on total obedience to church authority, the practice of tithing (giving up one-tenth of your income, usually to the church itself), the sanctity of the family unit, and a strict code of behavior that forbids the consumption of alcohol, tobacco, and even caffeine. Young church members are also expected to take on a missionary posting for at least one year. The church's two authoritative texts are the Bible and the Book of Mormon – the most controversial practice remains that of **polygamy**. Although the church formally forbid polygamy over a century ago, it is still known to be practised in Utah and in neighboring states. In fact, the Mormon Church suffered a hefty public relations body-blow in August, 2001, when LDS member Tom Green was sentenced to five-years' jail for polygamy; at the time, Green was living with his five wives and thirty children, and has also been ordered to repay $78,000 for welfare cheques fraudulently obtained.

The **Mormon Church** was founded in 1830 by **Joseph Smith**, a farmhand from Vermont. Smith claimed to have been visited by an angel five years earlier while he was living in Palmyra, New York; the angel, named Moroni, led Smith to a set of inscribed golden plates, which Smith translated into what would become the **Book of Mormon**. No one besides Joseph Smith would ever lay eyes on the plates, which were kept concealed behind a curtain in his house while he worked through his translations. The story they told was of an Israelite family that fled Jerusalem in 600 BC for a new "Promised Land." The patriarch, Lehi, had three sons, Nephi, Laman, and Lemuel; Nephi kept faith with God, while Laman and Lemuel threw in their lot with the heathen "Lamanites" – supposed ancestors of Native Americans. A classic good-versus-evil war waged for a thousand years between the Nephites and the Lamanites, until the Nephites were exterminated. The last survivor among them – Moroni, "son of Mormon" – buried the plates to ensure that their story would one day be told.

Pioneering folk rallied around Smith and his translations, and they headed west in wagon trains in search of a place to build a temple, around which they planned to settle and establish their own community. In 1838 they were camped in their thousands in Missouri, but were hounded on to Illinois, where the Mormon settlement of **Nauvoo** grew to become the largest city in that state by 1840, its population topping twenty-five thousand. But internal divisions resulted in Joseph Smith being jailed after he ordered the destruction of printing presses set up by a rival church. A group of vigilantes attacked the jailhouse, where Smith was shot and killed in 1844.

And so it was Smith's successor, **Brigham Young**, who would finally lead the Mormons on to the Salt Lake Valley in 1847. They immediately set about digging irrigation canals and diverting streams in an effort to subdue the harsh landscape and bend it to their agrarian way of life. Thanks to the sheer industry of the settlers, crops and orchards were soon established, while an unprecedented burst of environmental savvy saw them plant thousands of trees in the Salt Lake valley – the entire area today is a great deal more liveable as a result.

But with the successful creation of an independent Mormon community came **hostility** from the powers back East. Congress turned down Utah's first petition for statehood in 1850 – in part because the proposed name, Deseret, was a distinctly Mormon word meaning "honeybee" (the state symbol today is still a beehive). **Relations eased** when the Church realized in 1890 that it had better drop the practice of polygamy before being forced to do so. Utah finally became the **45th state of the US** on January 4, 1896, and more than a century later, around seventy percent of the state's 2.2 million-strong population are Mormons.

Next door to the library at 45 N West Temple, the **Museum of Church History and Art** (Mon–Fri 9am–9pm, Sat & Sun 10am–7pm; free) charts the rise of the Mormon faith in art and artifact – although the most interesting object is a three-dimensional map of the city as it was laid out in the late nineteenth century. Whatever your impressions of Mormonism, you may at least be encouraged by the religion's inclusiveness, evidenced here by the number of books in the shop here that tell the stories of Utah's women pioneers. There's also a tiny **cabin** rather oddly sandwiched between the Family History Library and the museum. On the unpredictable occasions when it's open, you get to view the usual re-created frontier-times living quarters; of more significance, however, is that it's one of only two surviving cabins built in 1847 – the year the first Mormon pioneers arrived in the Salt Lake valley.

Capitol Hill

Quite why the Mormons chose not to put their Temple on the gentle hill that stands above today's Temple Square is anyone's guess. As a result, when Utah was granted statehood in 1896, it was free to become the site of the imposing, domed **Utah State Capitol** (daily 8am–8pm; free guided tours Mon–Fri 9am–4pm). Along with the plaques and monuments you might expect, the corridors of power are packed full of earnest exhibits of great Utah moments. The basement area in particular holds a fine assortment of historical whatnots, ranging from mining dioramas to the eighteen-cylinder, 750-horsepower *Mormon Meteor*, raced by Ab Jenkins up to 200mph across the Bonneville Salt Flats in the 1950s. Directly opposite the Capitol building is another domed building, a quaint and attractive stone affair dating back to 1866. Formerly the city's **Council Hall**, which housed Utah's pre-statehood legislative assemblies, it was moved here, stone-by-stone, from its downtown location in 1963, and today is home to the Utah Travel Council.

Now called **Capitol Hill**, the neighborhood around the capitol holds some of Salt Lake City's grandest c.1900 homes, with dozens of ornate Victorian houses lining Main Street and Quince Street to the northwest. Walking tour maps of the district are available from the **Utah Heritage Foundation**, 485 North Canyon Rd (☎801/533-0858).

Eating

Though Salt Lake City has a perfectly good selection of **restaurants**, it lacks an atmospheric dining district. If you like to compare menus, the only downtown area with much potential is the block or two on either side of West Temple, south and east of the Salt Palace. Besides the usual **fast-food** emporiums, the city has its own chain, *Crown Burger* (300 W 118 N and also 377 E 200 S; Mon–Sat 10am–10.30pm), a step up from *McDonald's*. For general supplies, there's a huge Albertson's **supermarket** at 400 E 200 S (daily 6am–midnight; pharmacy Mon–Fri 9am–6pm, Sat 10am–5pm). For organic produce and wholefoods try Wild Oats at 645 E 400 S (Mon–Sat 7.30am–10pm, Sun 10am–8pm), while on Saturday mornings in summer, the transient park-dwellers are herded out of Pioneer Park to make way for a huge outdoor **farmer's market** (July–Oct).

Baba Afghan Restaurant 55 E 400 S ☎801/596-0786. Vegetarians and those with a hankering for something far removed from American chow will enjoy *Baba*'s Middle Eastern menu. Entrees $8–13, lunch specials daily. Closed Sun.

Bambara *Hotel Monaco*, 15 W 200 S ☎801/363-5454. With a different menu daily, this expensive restaurant features the city's most eclectic choice of dishes. A sample meal might include buffalo carpaccio as an appetizer, followed by either New Zealand elk or a steamy concoction of lobster, cockles, shrimp, mussels, and scallops called Portuguese Fisherman's Stew ($25). Like the hotel itself, the restaurant interior is a chic, post-Deco affair. Daily for breakfast and dinner; lunch Mon–Fri only.

Café Pierpont 122 W Pierpont Ave ☎801/364-1222. Large, downtown Mexican restaurant, with top-quality ceviche and gourmet dishes plus the usual standards, all competitively priced. Tasty specials include the Albuquerque chicken ($11) – breast fillet broiled over mesquite logs and topped with salsa verde, roasted chilis and cheese. The large chicken, beef, or shrimp fajitas, normally $13, go for $10 from 4–7pm. Lunch Mon–Fri only, dinner daily.

Café Trang 818 S Main St ☎801/539-1638. Although this Vietnamese/Chinese restaurant is pretty thoroughly Americanized, the food is excellent, and both the menu and the servings are enormous. Among the more authentic dishes are specialities made with crisp fried beancurd or flat noodles. Otherwise, a great standard is the Treasures in Love Nest ($8), a nest of crunchy noodles stuffed with seafood, pork strips, and crisp veggies. Daily for lunch and dinner; takeout also available. Reservations advised.

Lamb's Restaurant 169 S Main St ☎801/364-7166. This atmospheric diner, a city stalwart since 1939, dishes up great breakfasts that are best eaten at the long shiny counter. Excellent-value set meals are served throughout the day, while entrees such as steaks or chops run from $12 to $16. Closed Sun.

Market Street Grill 48 Market St ☎801/322-4668. This is Salt Lake City's effort at reproducing a dark New York-style bar and grill. Fresh seafood, especially oysters, plus steaks in all shapes and sizes, and good breakfasts too; $8 lunch specials, entrees $15–30. Mon–Sat 7am–11pm, Sun dinner only.

Mikado 67 W 100 S ☎801/328-0929. Among several sushi places in town, this one is better value than most (two-piece sushi plates $4–5) and very central. The combination plates for two or more are a good value. Mon–Sat for lunch and dinner.

Red Iguana 736 W North Temple. The finest inexpensive Mexican place in town and always crowded at lunch, so be prepared to wait for a table. Dishes include standards like burritos and enchiladas with deliciously subtle flavours, as well as excellent moles, a speciality of the Oaxaca region. Located a mile west of Temple Square. Most entrees under $10.

Rio Grande Café 270 S Rio Grande ☎801/364-3302. The food at this stylish Mexican cantina in the old Denver and Rio Grande railroad station is dependable, if not quite up to the standard of the *Red Iguana*. The trade-off is that it's closer to downtown – albeit in a slightly dodgy neighborhood – and the interior is a lot snazzier. The lunch specials are good value, and there's nothing on the menu over $9. Mon–Sat lunch and dinner, Sun dinner only.

Romano's Macaroni Grill 110 W Broadway (300 S) ☎801/521-3133. Lively, home-style Italian restaurant right in the heart of downtown. Big dishes of stuffed ravioli (made on the premises), veal, and daily fish specials are served up by cheerful waiters. The pizzas are good too. Entrees $9–16, desserts $5. Dinner daily.

Ruth's Diner 2100 Emigration Canyon Rd ☎801/582-5807. Good-value indoor and patio dining, often accompanied by live music, set in and around old railroad carriages in a narrow canyon three miles east of town. Wide selection of home-style roasts and chops, great salads and some of Utah's best breakfasts. Daily 8am–10pm.

Salt Lake Roasting Co. 320 E 400 S. This coffee-drinkers' den is a city favorite for its home-roasted arabica beans and an airy interior decked out with simple timber furniture and enormous coffee sacks. Light meals include vegetable-filled pastries and salads, and there's also a range of fruity deserts to go with the selection of international coffees. Mon–Sat 6.45am–midnight.

Drinking and nightlife

While nobody would claim that Salt Lake City is a swinging town, they don't roll up the sidewalks here when the sun goes down either. A couple of venues host visiting big-name bands, and at a few spots the locals can get downright rowdy. Most drinking venues are technically **private clubs** (see box on p.317), but there are also a handful of **brewpubs**, for which membership is not required. For **listings** of art, music, theatre, and club goings-on, pick up a copy of the free *City Weekly*; the monthly *Catalyst* (also free) is worth a look for its rundown of New Age shops and services and some of the more arty and "hippie" happenings. Both publications are distributed via racks at coffee shops, bars, and music stores and venues.

Bars and clubs

Dead Goat Saloon 165 S West Temple ☎801/328-4628. Raucous, semi-subterranean saloon, with live loud music most nights; emphasis is on blues and rock, but they're also known to host zydeco and acoustic bands. Cover $2–10.

Port O'Call 400 S West Temple ☎801/521-0589. A big, beery place spread over three floors and heaving on weekends, *Port O'Call* is a pretty good place to get amongst the locals to drink, dance, or shoot a game of pool. More a rowdy pub than a live-music venue, bands and DJs of variable quality nevertheless appear Wed–Sun.

Red Rock Brewing Company 200 W 254 S ☎801/521-7446. Award-winning beers plus a good-value menu makes this place a busy city favorite. Tasty bar-food includes Cajun fried shrimp, inexpensive wood-fired pizzas, and a fish-of-the-day special. Wait for a table near the broad windows at the front – the rear of the room feels a little pokey. 11am–midnight (till 1am Fri & Sat).

Squatters Pub 147 W Broadway ☎801/363-2739. Casual, friendly brewpub that offers a range of beers and several TV sets for sports enthusiasts. The menu includes all the pub basics like nachos, burgers, pasta, and salads, although it falls a little short of *Red Rock* for variety. 11am till late.

Zephyr Club 301 S West Temple ☎801/355-2582. Salt Lake's premier live-music club, hosting rock, pop, blues, and Country bands. There's a line-up of semi-famous names every month, so if you're hoping to catch a quality show, this is the first place you should look. Upmarket clientele, elegant decor, cover $5–20.

The Great Salt Lake

The **GREAT SALT LAKE**, in the barren desert northwest of Salt Lake City, is the last remnant of a 20,000-square-mile inland sea that once stretched into Idaho and Nevada. In the late nineteenth century, the lake's shores were lined with extravagant resorts, and steamboats and pleasure cruisers plied its waters. After years of mysterious decline, when enough of its contents evaporated to make it the world's second-saltiest body of water (after Israel's Dead Sea), it began equally mysteriously to refill in the 1980s. Today it's far higher than state planners ever bargained for, which has forced the raising of the adjacent I-80 interstate by several feet. Now roughly 75 miles long by 28 miles wide, the lake has no outlet, so water flowing in from the Bear, Weber and Jordan rivers steadily evaporates, leaving behind two million tons of salt each year – which contributes to a salt-extraction industry.

On the plus side, the lake's formerly abundant wildlife, and especially its **migratory birds**, have begun to reappear in numbers, although the place is still not especially attractive to humans. **Great Salt Lake State Park** (daily 8am–sunset), sixteen miles west of town on I-80, is the dingiest affair imaginable. It marks the site of the flamboyant 1890s Saltair pavilion, which closed down in 1968 when the waters receded, and was promptly destroyed by fire. A smaller version opened in 1983, just in time to be flooded out; it's now pretty decrepit and threadbare, but the **visitor center** (daily 9am–4pm) still gamely shows free videos of the lake, while gaudy railroad cars and a lake boat outside act as giftshops.

Antelope Island State Park

If you want to really enjoy a visit to the Great Salt Lake, a visit to **Antelope Island** is your best bet. The island terrain is dramatically different to that of the Salt Lake Valley, with clusters of red sand dunes, rocky ridges and even small depressions of stinky marshland. Besides the experience of floating in water so dense with minerals you can barely sink, the island affords views of glorious lake sunsets and is also home to the state's only wild **bison**; from the twelve animals introduced in 1893, the herd has grown to over five hundred.

Being the largest of the lake's eight islands – around fifteen miles long and five miles wide – Antelope Island was visited from time to time by nomadic tribes, but the first settlement was undertaken in 1849 by a resourceful and optimistic Mormon cattle rancher named Fielding Garr. The **Garr ranch house**, on the island's east coast, is now the oldest continually inhabited European dwelling in Utah. You can tour various parts of the ranch operations (summer daily 8am–6pm; free), but it's more rewarding to spend an hour or two exploring the surrounding barren, rocky landscape on **horseback** (ⓣ801/782-4946 to book a trail ride or hire a horse; $35 for 2–3hr), before dining cowboy-style at the ranch (bookings ⓣ801/776-6734).

To reach Antelope Island, drive twenty miles north of the city on I-15, then take exit 335 and head west to the island causeway; the toll is $7 per vehicle (bicycles $4). All **services** (apart from Garr Ranch) are clustered together at the island's northern end, including a **visitor center** (summer daily 10am–5pm; ⓣ801/595-4030), campgrounds (tent sites $12; reservations ⓣ801/773-2941), marina, picnic areas, toilets, and showers. To get out onto the lake, try Salt Island Adventures (ⓣ801/583-440, ⓦwww.gslcruises.com) for a **scenic cruise**; boats leave from the marina at the northern tip of the island (one-hour trip $12, dinner cruise $43).

Listings

American Express 175 S West Temple (Mon–Fri 9am–5pm; ⓣ801/328-9733).

Banks Zions First National at South Temple and Main St has a foreign exchange desk (Mon–Fri 9am–5.15pm); there are 24hr ATMs at several downtown locations.

Bike rental Guthries', 156 E 200 S (Mon–Fri 9.30am–7pm, Sat 9.30am–6pm; ⓣ801/363-3727); Utah Ski & Golf, 134 W 600 S (Mon–Fri 9.30am–6pm, Sat 10am–6pm; ⓣ801/355-9088); Wasatch Touring (Mon–Fri 9.30am–6pm, Sat 10am–6pm; ⓣ801/359-9361).

Bookshop Sam Weller's, 254 S Main St (Mon–Fri 9.30am–9pm, Sat 9.30am–7pm), has a huge selection of new and used books plus lots of maps and travel guides; also trades used books.

Car rental Advantage ⓣ801/531-1199 or 1-800/777-5500, ⓦwww.arac.com; Avis ⓣ801/575-2847 or 1-800/831-2847, ⓦwww.avis.com; Budget ⓣ801/575-2500 or 1-800/237-7251, ⓦwww.drivebudget.com; Dollar ⓣ801/575-2580 or 1-800/800-4000, ⓦwww.dollarcar.com; Enterprise airport ⓣ801/537-7433, downtown ⓣ801/534-1888 or 1-800/736-8222; Hertz ⓣ801/575-2683 or 1-800/654-3131, ⓦwww.hertz.com; Thrifty ⓣ801/265-6677 or 1-800/367-2277, ⓦwww.thrifty.com.

Climbing Rockreation, 2074 E 400 S ⓣ801/278-7473, has a huge indoor climbing wall and rents equipment too; this is also the place to get information and contacts for climbing in the nearby Wasatch canyons.

Hospital Salt Lake City Regional Hospital & Medical Center, 1050 E South Temple (ⓣ801/350-4111), has 24hr emergency care.

Internet access Salt Lake City Public Library, 209 E 500 S (Mon–Thurs 9am–9pm, Fri–Sat 9am–6pm, Sun 1–5pm; ⓣ801/524-8200; free).

Laundry Century, 910 W North Temple (daily 7am–11pm; ⓣ801/539-1513); Henrie's 223 E 300 S (Mon–Fri 7am–7pm, Sat 8am–6pm; ⓣ801/328-8789).

Outdoors and sporting equipment REI, 3285 E 3300 S (Mon–Fri 10am–9pm, Sat 9am–7pm, Sun 11am–6pm), large retailer carrying all manner of hiking, camping, and backcountry gear; Gart Sports, ZCMI Center, South Temple and Main St (Mon–Fri 10am–9pm, Sat 10am–7pm), for general sporting equipment including skis, snowboards, and golf clubs, plus sports footwear and hiking boots; Guthrie's, 156 E 200 S (Mon–Fri 9.30am–7pm, Sat 9.30am–6pm), is a long-established and centrally located bicycle dealer with a wide range of mountain bikes and equipment.

Pharmacy Broadway Pharmacy, 242 E 300 S (Mon–Fri 9am–9pm, Sat & Sun 9am–7pm; ⓣ801/363-3939); 24hr pharmacy information ⓣ801/553-7700.

Police 315 E 200 S ⓣ801/799-3100; emergencies ⓣ911.

Post office 230 W 200 S (Mon–Fri 8am–5.30pm, Sat 8am–1.30pm; ⓣ801/978-3001; zip code 84101); a smaller but more central branch is located on Level 2 of the ZCMI Center, across from Temple Square (Mon–Fri 8am–5.30pm, Sat 9.30am–5.30pm).

Swimming pool Steiner Aquatic Center, 645 S Guardsman Way, across from the University of

Utah at the base of the mountains (daily 6am–8/9pm; ☎801/583-9713; $3), has an indoor 25m pool and a superb outdoor 50m pool with a grassy area for sunbathing and free sun-lounges – call ahead to check there are no swim squads using the outdoor pool.

Taxi City Cab ☎801/363-5014; Ute Cab ☎801/359-7788; Yellow Cab ☎801/521-2100.

The Wasatch canyons

On the eastern edge of Salt Lake City, a series of narrow canyons snake their way into the imposing Wasatch mountains. Endowed with hiking trails, campgrounds, picnic areas, and ski resorts, they make up the prime Rocky Mountains playground for the people of Salt Lake City. In fact, the superb recreation opportunities on offer in the **WASATCH CANYONS** go a long way towards explaining why Salt Lake City is increasingly seen as a desirable "lifestyle" city across the US.

Closest to downtown, **City Creek** and **Mill Creek canyons** are visited mostly for their short trails and scenic picnic spots. Further away, though still under an hour's drive, are **Little Cottonwood and Big Cottonwood canyons**, the city's showpiece destinations offering fantastic hikes into glorious mountain environs, and four splendid **ski areas**, which have somehow remained relatively anonymous. With resort elevations topping out at between 10,000 and 11,000 feet, there are no really dense stands of trees to contend with, negating the need to cut trails all over the place; the effect is of a pleasingly natural-looking ski terrain that goes well with the best snow in the state.

For latest information on campsites and hiking trails in the Wasatch canyons, stop by the **Public Lands Information Center**, inside the REI store at 3285 E 3300 S, Salt Lake City (☎801/466-6411, Ⓦwww.fs.fed.us/wcnf/slrd). It's worth noting too that there are special usage conditions for some parts of the canyons, as they supply over sixty percent of the drinking water used by residents of the Salt Lake Valley. To keep the water here as clean as possible, the following prohibitions are strictly enforced: backcountry camping is not permitted within 200ft of any open water (lakes, streams, etc); pets are not allowed anywhere (not even in your car); and swimming is not allowed in lakes or streams.

Regular **UTA buses** run every day between 6.30am and 7.30pm from Salt Lake City to the Cottonwood canyons resorts during winter (services are less frequent in summer); from downtown, take the TRAX line to the station at 7200 S, then transfer to the Ski Bus for Brighton and Solitude, or the one for Alta and Snowbird. The fare is $1.75; phone ☎801/743-3882 for **schedule information**, or collect a timetable from tourist information. The trip takes around one hour.

City Creek Canyon and Mill Creek Canyon

City Creek Canyon is heavily used by local bikers, walkers and joggers, as the eight miles of paved Canyon Road begin just northeast of downtown beside Capitol Hill. A trailhead at the end of the road gives access to some pleasant enough hikes among wooded hills, but the more popular pursuit is having a **picnic** at one of the many roadside sites. Indeed, picnicking is so popular that sites often must be prebooked (☎801/483-6797). Bear in mind that during summer (June–Sept) the road is open to **bikers only** on odd calendar days, and to **motor vehicles only** on even days; a toll booth at the bottom of the canyon road controls traffic and collects $3 per motor vehicle. For bike routes and trails in the city area, pick up a free *Salt Lake City Bikeways Map* at the visitor center.

△ Alta, arguably the world's top powder skiing destination

Better hiking trails, featuring unbeatable views over the Salt Lake Valley, can be found in **Mill Creek Canyon**, entered at 3800 S Wasatch Blvd ($3 vehicle access **fee**; bicycles free). It's also a good choice for **mountain bikers**, though access is restricted on the south side of the canyon, which contains part of the Mount Olympus Wilderness area. A popular biker's run is the Pipeline trail, which runs parallel to the canyon road and so does not involve an exhausting climb – the 5.5-mile trail is best accessed from Rattlesnake Gulch, 1.5 miles into the canyon on your left.

One of the most popular hikes is up to the summit of 8300ft Grandeur Peak (2.8 miles one-way, elevation gain 2619ft); the trailhead is at the Church Fork picnic area, three miles in to the canyon on your right. Hikers who'd rather not risk tangling with mountain bikers should head for the Terraces picnic area, 4.5 miles into the canyon on the south side. A variety of trails lead from here into the Mount Olympus Wilderness, including a relaxed two-mile forest stroll to Elbow Fork and the more challenging Bowman Trail, which travels almost four miles up to Baker Pass (an elevation gain of over 3000ft), from where you can see Big Cottonwood Canyon.

Big Cottonwood Canyon

If you're going to visit just one of the Wasatch canyons – even for a short hike – it should be **BIG COTTONWOOD CANYON**. Less developed than Little Cottonwood and also unscarred by mining activities, it's just 35 minutes' drive from downtown Salt Lake City and thus a popular day destination for locals.

Of the two **ski resorts** in Big Cottonwood, **Brighton** has best taken advantage of its proximity to Salt Lake by becoming the local boarders' hill, tapping into the large population of school-age riders by providing cheap lift tickets. **Solitude**, meanwhile, could be fairly described as the most low-key place to ski in the Wasatch canyons. Near the latter is the Silver Lake Nordic Center, ground zero for day-hikers in the summer months (see box below).

From June to October, **Guardsman Pass Road**, which connects Big

Hiking and camping in Big Cottonwood Canyon

The Nordic Center at pretty Silver Lake, beside the Solitude ski resort, serves as an **information center** during summer (mid-May to Sept Wed–Sun 10am–7pm; ⓣ435/647-9071), dispensing free trail maps and advice to hikers and bikers. Every level of trail is accessible from the center, including a wheelchair-friendly boardwalk that circumnavigates Silver Lake itself in under a mile.

Most day-hikers head for the trails that intermingle with the ski-runs on the way up to Twin Lakes or Lake Solitude. The 1.25-mile hike to **Twin Lakes** – now merged as one behind a concrete dam – gains a strenuous 710ft in elevation while crisscrossing some of Solitude's ski runs. It's roughly the same distance again on to Twin Lakes Pass, a 9993ft perch with superb views down Little Cottonwood Canyon. The **Granite Lakes trail** also starts out from the south end of Twin Lakes, and ducks under the Millicent lift before following an almost level course for 1.5 miles to Lake Mary. Several summits nearby command grand views of the ski area and neighboring Little Cottonwood Canyon; a rough service road from the top of Millicent lift leads to the top of **Mount Millicent** (10,452ft) and on to **Mount Wolverine** (10,795ft), which is the highest peak in the Silver Lake area.

Two USFS **campgrounds** (ⓣ1-800/280-2267; $12) beside the canyon's highway have drinking water and toilets; *Spruces* is 9.7 miles into the canyon (June to mid-Oct; 97 sites) and *Redman* is a further three miles in (mid-June to Sept; 43 sites).

Cottonwood to Park City (see p.335), is open. There's is a pull-out just below the top of the pass on the Park City side where you can park your car and take a short, steep hike to fantastic views of the ski-lifts, canyon hiking trails, and some tiny but beautiful alpine lakes.

Solitude

With less people on the slopes than at nearby Brighton, **SOLITUDE** (Ⓣ801/534-1400 or 1-800/748-4754, Ⓦwww.skisolitude.com) lives up to its name, making it ideal for those learning to ski or board in pressure-free surroundings. It also has some decent accommodation – something Brighton cannot boast – so it's a good choice for families looking for a slopeside ski vacation in Big Cottonwood.

Solitude's **highest point** is 10,035ft, giving it a vertical drop just over 2000ft. The total **skiable area** of 1200 acres supports 63 **trails**, rated twenty percent beginner, fifty percent intermediate and thirty percent expert, serviced by seven **lifts**. The **ski terrain** is a tale of two distinct worlds. There's a collection of smooth, steep, groomed trails that are remarkably consistent in terms of the challenge they offer; most blacks feature few bumps and so are quite easy to ski. The alternate world of skiing Solitude is called **Honeycomb Canyon**, four hundred acres of backcountry adventure. Tiny, bumpy bowls open out sporadically into more open terrain, only to clam up again into a dodgem session among trees, bumps, rocks, and finally a narrow and sometimes icy road.

Solitude is proudly innovative with its renewable plastic card **lift tickets**. You can still get a regular day-pass ($39), but there's also the option of buying a specific number of lift rides instead; these can be paid for in increments of ten, up to a maximum of fifty, and may be used over a number of days and are entirely transferable. Thus you could purchase a twenty-ride card, ski a few runs in the morning before handing the card to a friend for the afternoon, and continue to use it the following day.

Practicalities

With lots of stone, wood, and pointy roofs, Solitude has somewhat of a European feel with its **accommodation** and amenities buildings. It's all very comfortable, and the village, though small for now, is cautiously expanding. At last count, there were three separate accommodation options, all managed by Solitude resort; call the resort line for all bookings. The 46-room *Inn at Solitude* features regular **hotel rooms** in the four-star range, with amenities such as heated outdoor pool and hot tub, fitness room, library, and even a small movie theatre; rates are $210 and don't include any meals. *Creekside at Solitude* and *Powderhorn Lodge* are both condo complexes, with configurations of one to three bedrooms; winter rates for a one-bedroom – which can accommodate up to four people – are $280–330.

Solitude Nordic Center

For pumping the lungs and working the legs, there's not much better than a day out on cross-country skis. The **Solitude Nordic Center** (Ⓣ801/536-5774), a couple of hundred yards east of the resort, is one of the best-appointed places on the Wasatch Front to do it. There are 20km of beautifully prepared tree-lined trails that cater for exponents of both classical and skating cross-country styles. Everything is on hand for the beginner too, with group workshops, private lessons, and equipment rental all available. A one-day trail pass costs $10, gear rental is another $12 and lessons and workshops run $35–40.

Solitude also boasts some proper **restaurants** – as opposed to the ubiquitous self-serve resort cafeteria – though none exudes much atmosphere. Your options are fine dining in *St. Bernard's*, family dining in *Creekside*, or the soups, sandwiches, and a mean chicken chili to accompany a cold microbrew in the *Thirsty Squirrel* pub. Of the on-mountain places for a bite to eat, the *Sunshine Grill* catches the sun at least until early afternoon and has a sociable "beach" scene going on most days.

Brighton

First of the Utah resorts to embrace the once-dreaded "shredders," **BRIGHTON** (Ⓣ801/532-4731 or 1-800/873-5512, Ⓦwww.skibrighton. com) has enjoyed the loyalty of a dedicated **snowboarding crowd** since the early 1990s. So while alpiners and telemarkers do take up a bit of slope space, this hill really belongs to the boarders, and the kind of ethos that has developed on the back of the boarding scene here is that getting down the hill is meant to be fun.

The resort's **highest point** is 10,500ft and the **vertical drop** is a tidy 1750ft. The **skiable area** of 850 acres is webbed with 66 **trails**, rated 21 percent beginner, 40 percent intermediate and 39 percent advanced, and the seven **chairlifts** include three quads. Standout features of the Brighton experience are the various **half-pipes and terrain parks** set up for boarders and the opportunities of backcountry exploration from the top of **Mount Millicent**. Of the groomed options, the central section below **Preston Peak** has a great mix of trails through dense stands of trees, while everything accessed from the **Great Western** quad-chair is pretty challenging intermediate-to-expert stuff, and allows for plenty of ducking and diving from trail-to-trail.

As the mountain keeps eighteen runs **open at night**, there's an array of lift tickets to choose from. Options include a 9am–4pm or 12.30–9pm session ($37), a 9am–9pm ticket for the highly motivated ($41), and a 4–9pm night jam (Mon–Sat only; $22). Those looking for a place to **learn to snowboard** should give Brighton due consideration, particularly as it offers a program called LTR (Learn To Ride), in which you start on a specially-designed learning board which helps in carving a turn.

Practicalities

Brighton is not terribly long on amenities. The only **accommodation** option is the twenty-room *Brighton Lodge* (Ⓣ801/532-4731), where a **double room** costs $110, and a **dorm bed** is $75, continental breakfast included. Though there's nothing very inspiring about it, the package deals on offer are good value; for example, for $300, it's possible to get four nights dorm accommodation (with breakfast) and four-days' lift tickets. Everything else on offer here – the ski-school, **equipment** shop, cafeteria-style restaurant, and *Molly Green's* **bar** – is housed in a single nearby building.

Little Cottonwood Canyon

About forty-minutes' southeast of downtown Salt Lake, **LITTLE COTTONWOOD CANYON** was first exploited over a century ago for its reserves of silver. At lower altitudes, much of the land is still owned by mining companies, and there is occasional speculation about this or that shaft being opened up and worked over one more time. However, Little Cottonwood can continue to pay its way without giving up further mineral resources, thanks to the presence of Utah's two finest ski areas, **Snowbird** and **Alta**. With around five hundred inches of snow arriving in the canyon year after year – often well into spring – there's little more that needs to be said to sell the Little Cottonwood ski experience to prospective winter visitors. In warmer months, the upper canyon remains visited thanks to some fairly strenuous **hikes** into broad alpine meadows, dotted with lakes carved out by shifting glaciers.

It's worth noting that **driving** can be treacherous up the steep and winding two-lane canyon road; don't take on heavy snow conditions without the appropriate vehicle and tires; for the latest road, weather, and ski conditions, tune your radio to 530 AM.

Snowbird

SNOWBIRD (Ⓣ1-800/640-2002, Ⓦwww.snowbird.com) was created in 1971 by millionaire mountaineer-adventurer **Dick Bass**, the first man to summit the highest peak on each of the seven continents. From the word go, it was conceived as a world-class winter resort, and the fact that the yearly US Freeskiing Nationals are held here is a good indication of what you should expect. Put simply, a gated double-black diamond here does not just imply a steep, off-trail descent – it means you're heading for a cliff or a vertical chute.

An aerial tram hauls you to the top of Hidden Peak, the resort's **highest point** at 11,000ft, giving a **vertical drop** of 2900ft to the base. There's nine **chairlifts** – two of which are high-speed quads – and 82 **trails** in all, rated 25 percent beginner, 35 percent intermediate and 40 percent advanced. Skilled boarders and skiers should not miss the newly opened **Mineral Basin** area, accessed via both the tram and Little Cloud chair. These five hundred acres of steep, wide-open terrain give an exhilarating 1400ft of vertical drop to a high speed quad chair that whisks you back to the top in four minutes flat.

A one-day **lift ticket** costs $56 for the aerial tram plus lifts, or $47 for the chair-lifts only; since you can reach the top of Hidden Peak without riding the tram – where you're packed in with your nose against the glass anyway – get the $47 lifts-only ticket. An even **cheaper option** is to buy your ticket in advance in Salt Lake City for $40; try Smith's Foods supermarkets, Gart Sports (see p.327), most ski-rental outlets, and major downtown hotels. If you'd like to ski Alta as well, the $68 combined ticket is the way to go. **Equipment rental** is available at *Cliff Lodge*, and the Snowbird Activity Center (Ⓣ801/933-2147) offers an introduction to ski and snowshoe **touring**, lift-served backcountry skiing day-tours and even mountaineering trips. Snowbird also has exceptional **child-care** facilities, if you've got little ones in tow.

Hiking in Little Cottonwood Canyon

Although Little Cottonwood ranks second to Big Cottonwood for hiking potential, there are still several **hikes** here that work especially well when combined with a lunch at one of its high-altitude lodges – from where you can best appreciate your route up while lazing on a sunny, slopeside deck.

The **White Pine trailhead**, 5.5 miles into the canyon, is the place to start; the parking area is on your right, just under a mile below Snowbird resort. The route in to **Red Pine Canyon** allows for several destination choices, starting at the canyon overlook (1.5 miles one-way; elevation gain 500ft), then on to Red Pine Lake (4.4 miles, elevation gain 1920ft), an uphill haul that'll really work your lungs. Branching off Red Pine trail after about two miles is the **Maybird Gulch** trail, which takes you to Maybird Lakes, a peaceful area to meander through pretty alpine meadows. To head instead towards **White Pine Lake**, you'll be taking a left-turn switchback about a mile from the trailhead and sticking to a rough service road; this too is a strenuous walk (four miles, elevation gain 2300ft).

Practicalities

Accommodations at Snowbird are expensive; there are no dorm beds available, and the five local lodgings – *The Inn*, *Iron Blosam Lodge*, *Lodge at Snowbird*, *Cliff Lodge*, and *Cliff Club Condominiums* – are all owned by Snowbird resort (Ⓣ801/947-8220 or 1-800/385-2002). The *Cliff Lodge*, whose interior is liberally adorned with exotic Oriental rugs, offers regular **hotel** rooms for around $300 during ski season (from $180 at other times); facilities include full spa, eucalyptus steam room, fitness room, and two outdoor pools and hot tubs. The rest are all **condo complexes** ($230–700), complete with standard resort facilities like saunas, hot tubs, restaurants, and lounges.

For **eating**, the *Lodge at Snowbird* and *Iron Blosam Lodge* both have dinner-only restaurants, while the Snowbird Center at the base of the lifts has a pizza joint, cafeteria, and family-style restaurant with moderate prices. Basic groceries are reasonable at General Gritts on the center's lower level, so if you're staying in a condo, you might consider putting together a square meal yourself. The *Cliff Lodge*'s *Aerie Restaurant* has a phenomenal all-you-can-eat skiers **breakfast buffet** for $10 and the lodge also boasts a sushi bar and Mexican cantina. There's little in the way of **entertainment** besides a leisurely aprés-ski drink at the lounge bars at *Iron Blosam Lodge* and *Lodge at Snowbird*. The *Aerie Lounge* at *Cliff Lodge* has a low-key jazz combo on Sunday evenings and occasional guest comedians, but if you're really up for a night out, head to downtown Salt Lake City.

Alta

The first lift carried skiers up the slopes of **ALTA** (Ⓣ801/359-1078, Ⓦwww.alta.com) in 1937, and the resort has done its best to remain enveloped in a time-warp ever since. The lodging is defiantly old-world, with not so much as an elevator to be seen, and the slopes are completely **snowboard free**.

The resort's **highest point** of 10,550ft leads to a **vertical drop** of some 2000ft. The 2200 skiable acres, serviced by eight lifts, are divided into 25 percent beginner, 40 percent intermediate and 35 percent advanced. As at Snowbird, Alta's snow and terrain leave no room for disappointment, though the backcountry options here are a tad less thrilling. Still, there are plenty of glorious off-piste black diamond runs, and lots of satisfying groomed blues as well. Beginners are likewise well off as the resort's northern base section is entirely made up of green trails.

An undeniable advantage to skiing at Alta is the deal on **lift tickets**. A full day runs just $35, and half-day passes are available for both morning (9.15am–1pm) and afternoon (1–4.30pm) for $27. There are no multiday tickets or dubious seasonal pricing fluctuations either, making the whole process fabulously simple. The one proviso is that Alta Resort maintains a **skier-limit** on the mountain. In practice this simply means you should call ahead during Christmas week and on any busy holiday weekend to check whether the mountain is "full" – which only really ever happens between 11am and 2pm. For $68, you can get a combined lift ticket that includes Snowbird as well; only bother once you've begun to tire of Alta's runs. With the exception of *Snowpine Lodge*, each of the lodges at Alta has an **equipment rental** shop, though it's cheaper to rent gear in Salt Lake City.

Practicalities

Where Alta shows its old-world character best is in its odd collection of five independent **lodges**, spaced evenly over half-a-mile in front of the ski hill. Predictably, they're all expensive, although four of them do offer **dorm beds**

– well worth considering, especially if you can arrange to get to the resort early in the day and squeeze in, say, three days skiing over a two-night stay. **Rates** for all lodges quoted below are for ski season; summer rates, if available, may be up to forty percent cheaper, though given the proximity to Salt Lake City, there's no especially compelling reason to stay overnight then.

Alta Lodge ⓣ801/742-3500 or 1-800/707-2582, ⓕ801/742-3504, ⓦwww.altalodge.com. For many longtime visitors to Alta, this lodge is still the original and the best. The place seems almost dowdy with its dark timber and lack of adornments throughout, but it has an air of quiet comfort and genteel leisure. The fifty-plus rooms range in size and features, although none has a television; communal amenities include a couple of saunas and hot tubs along with a cozy upstairs bar. Summer visitors should head to the Sunday brunch ($17), something of an institution and well worth setting aside a couple of leisurely hours for. Rates include breakfast and a three-course dinner; single $175–315, double $255–390, dorm $115. ❾

Alta Peruvian Lodge ⓣ801/742-3000 or 1-800/453-8488, ⓕ801/742-3007, ⓦwww.altaperuvian. citysearch.com. Rooms in this fifty-year-old rambling lodge run the gamut from dorms up to two-bedroom suites and chalets. Live bands visit the *Peruvian*'s bar on occasion, helping make it the closest thing to a lively drinking venue in the canyon. Per-person rates include breakfast, lunch and dinner, plus an Alta lift pass; room with shared bath $180, with private bath $215, dorm $140. ❽

Goldminer's Daughter ⓣ801/742-2300 or 1-800/453-4573, ⓦwww.alta.com/lodge/goldmine .html. Though the least aesthetically inspiring of Alta's lodges, *Goldminer's Daughter* is the most affordable and still right by the ski lifts. Rooms are similar to those of a slightly run-down motel, while dorms are simply standard rooms with four single beds crammed into them. There is, though, a small sauna and hot tub, and the property's most appealing feature, ideal for lunch, is its large sundeck. All rates are per person and include breakfast and dinner; single $144, double $110, dorms $94. ❻

Rustler Lodge ⓣ801/742-2200 or 1-888/532-2582, ⓕ801/742-3832, ⓦwww.rustlerlodge.com. The best choice for those who want modern hotel comforts and don't mind paying a bit extra for them. Rooms all have TV and phone, and other facilities include a large indoor pool, hot tub, and full fitness center. Dorm beds are available too; choose between the cheaper six-bed room with TV and bath, or a three-bed with shower, toilet, and sink. All rates include breakfast and dinner; doubles $326–398, dorms $108 or $118. ❾

Snowpine Lodge ⓣ801/742-2000, ⓕ742-2244, ⓦwww.skiutah.com/pages/snowpine.html. Staying at *Snowpine* feels like a cozy winter getaway with your extended family and there's typically a sociable gathering by a fireplace or around the lodge's lone television set. The cheaper rooms have shared bathroom facilities, and there are no telephones in rooms; dorms are imaginatively divided into small cubicles with two bunks and separate storage space in each, giving a communal ski-hostel experience with a modicum of privacy. Rates are per person and include breakfast and dinner; doubles $125–150, dorms $95. ❻

Park City

Despite Brigham Young's strictures against prospecting for precious metals – he feared a gentile "gold rush" – the first mining camp at **PARK CITY**, just thirty miles east of downtown Salt Lake City along I-80, was established in the late 1860s. In 1872, George Hearst laid the foundations of the Hearst media empire by paying $27,000 for a claim here that became the Ontario Silver Mine, worth $50 million. It turns out that Young was right to be fearful, as the town flourished on the backs of hard-drinking miners instead of hard-working Mormons; the 27 saloons that sprouted along Main Street simply left no room for any other kind of commercial endeavour. Today the town's population stands at 6900, and although the saloons number far fewer now, it's fair to say that the Mormon Church has never really managed to bring Park City to heel.

For many years engulfed by an ever-growing sprawl of new condos, factory outlet stores, and other developments, Park City became almost unrecognizable in the lead-up to the **2002 Winter Olympics**. Its restored Main Street now makes only token gestures towards mimicking the mountain mining community it used to be, with shops and restaurants striving to emulate upmarket ski resorts elsewhere in the Rockies. The beautiful people are no longer strangers to Park City either, thanks to the international profile of the Sundance Film Festival (see p.345).

Obviously, though, the ritzy shops and restaurants wouldn't exist if not for the town's glorious mountain environment. In summer there's decent **hiking** and phenomenal lift-served **mountain biking**. And winters here produce an **average snowfall** of 350 inches, with a miserly moisture content of around four percent. The three local ski areas – **Park City Mountain Resort**, **The Canyons** and **Deer Valley** – each has its own charms and quirks of character. There's no clear consensus over which is the best of the three, but fortunately all are close enough to try even on a short stay. Snowboarders, though, need a day less to decide as Deer Valley employs a **skiers only** policy. The **ski season** runs roughly mid-November to early April, and wilder backcountry **cat- and heli-skiing** options can be had through Park City Powder Cats (ⓣ435/649-6596, ⓦwww.pccats.com) and Park City Helicopters (ⓣ435/814-7248 or 1-888/261-3781).

Arrival, information, and transport

Downtown Park City – effectively just six small blocks on and around Main Street – remains out of sight until you're actually in it. Having turned off I-80 at Kimball Junction, you first must travel through five slightly depressing miles of fast-food restaurants and factory outlets on Hwy-248 to get to it. The upside, though, is that – apart from the ski hills and bike trails – all that need interest you in Park City is right here. Greyhound buses pull in beside *McDonald's*, five miles east of town at Kimball Junction.

Park City has two **visitor information** centers; the one downtown at 528 Main St (Mon–Sat 10am–7pm, Sun noon–6pm, except May & Oct Mon–Sat 11am–5pm only; ⓣ435/649-6104, ⓦwww.parkcityinfo.com) stands above the town's original jailhouse and doubles as an enjoyable museum of town history. The second, 750 Kearns Blvd at the junction with Park Avenue (daily 9am–6pm; ⓣ435/658-4541), is a more convenient place to stop and collect maps and parking information (the Park City parking guide is a must if staying on or near Main St) if arriving by car.

A free comprehensive **bus system** operates daily between 6am and 2.30am. The six routes are color-coded, and the easiest way to figure out which one you're after is to get a copy of the *Transit System Guide* (schedule information ⓣ435/615-5350) at a vistor center or on board a bus. The Canyons ski resort (see p.341 for transport to The Canyons) is not serviced by Park City Transit, but the other two ski areas are. A free **trolley** does a regular lap of Main Street, but the distance covered is so small that there's little value in it unless you're dead tired.

Accommodation

During the summer months, the town is generally only full for special events like the Jazz Festival, and at other times there may be room for bargaining a bit over the set rate. It's all bad news during ski season however, when **accommodation** rates nearly double. As all three ski areas are so close to town, there's no pressing need to stay slopeside. Of course, if you're looking to ski out the door to the lifts, the resorts each offer plenty of accommodation options. Regardless of where you bunk down, if you're with a group of four or more you'll almost certainly do better to **rent a condo**. Agents with a comprehen-

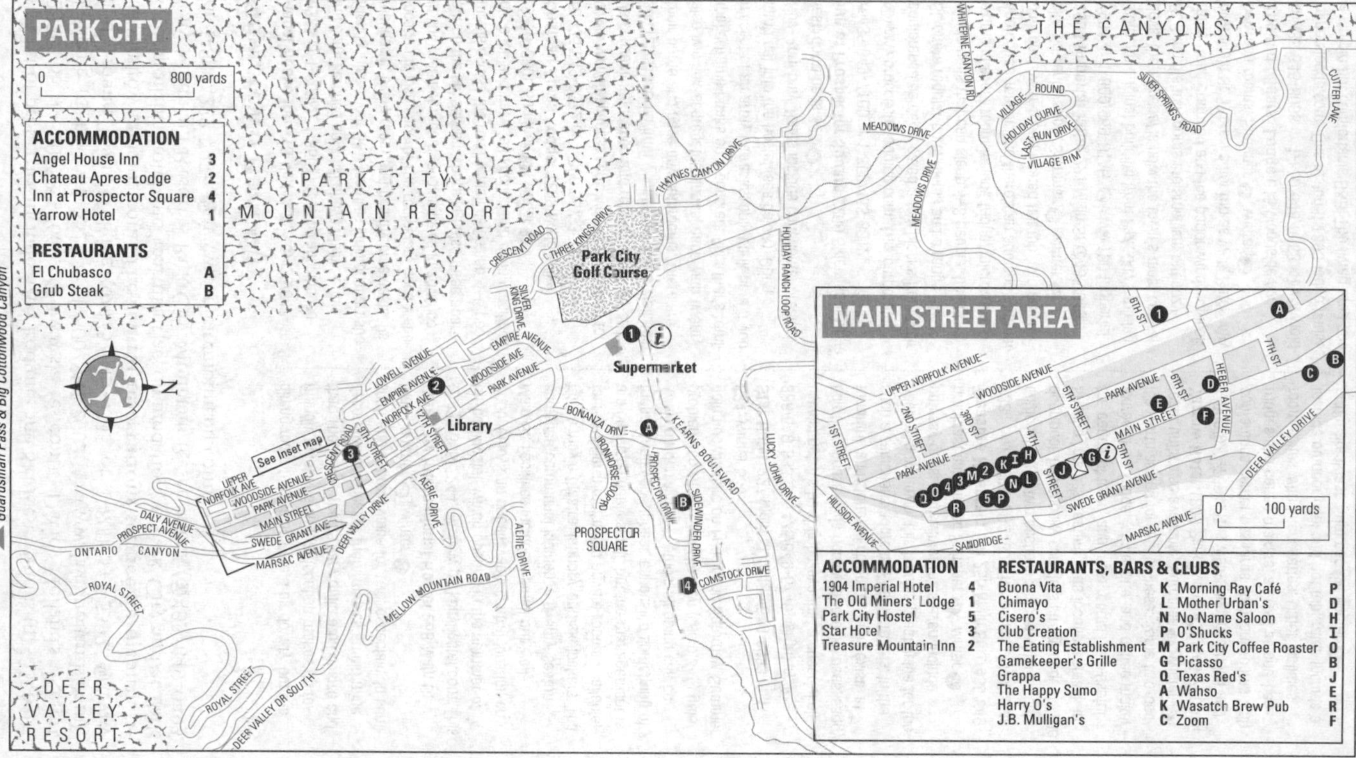
PARK CITY
0 800 yards
ACCOMMODATION
Angel House Inn 3
Chateau Apres Lodge 2
Inn at Prospector Square 4
Yarrow Hotel 1
RESTAURANTS
El Chubasco A
Grub Steak B
Guardsman Pass & Big Cottonwood Canyon
80 & Kimball Junction
PARK CITY MOUNTAIN RESORT
THE CANYONS
DEER VALLEY RESORT
Park City Golf Course
Supermarket
Library
PROSPECTOR SQUARE
See Inset map
N
CRESCENT ROAD
THREE KINGS DRIVE
THAYNES CANYON DRIVE
SILVER KING DRIVE
EMPIRE AVENUE
LOWELL AVENUE
WOODSIDE AVE
PARK AVENUE
NORFOLK AVE
12TH STREET
9TH STREET
UPPER NORFOLK AVE
WOODSIDE AVENUE
MAIN STREET
SWEDE GRANT AVE
MARSAC AVENUE
DEER VALLEY DRIVE
DALY AVENUE
PROSPECT AVENUE
ONTARIO CANYON
ROYAL STREET
DEER VALLEY DR SOUTH
MELLOW MOUNTAIN ROAD
AERIE DRIVE
BONANZA DRIVE
IRONHORSE LOOP RD
PROSPECTOR DRIVE
KEARNS BOULEVARD
SIDEWINDER DRIVE
COMSTOCK DRIVE
LUCKY JOHN DRIVE
HOLIDAY RANCH LOOP ROAD
MEADOWS DRIVE
WHITEPINE CANYON RD
VILLAGE ROUND
HOLIDAY CURVE
LAST RUN DRIVE
VILLAGE RIM
SILVER SPRINGS ROAD
CUTTER LANE
MAIN STREET AREA
UPPER NORFOLK AVENUE
WOODSIDE AVENUE
PARK AVENUE
MAIN STREET
SWEDE GRANT AVENUE
MARSAC AVENUE
DEER VALLEY DRIVE
HEBER AVENUE
HILLSIDE AVENUE
SANDRIDGE
1ST STREET
2ND STREET
3RD ST
4TH STREET
5TH STREET
5TH ST
6TH ST
7TH ST
0 100 yards
ACCOMMODATION
1904 Imperial Hotel 4
The Old Miners' Lodge 1
Park City Hostel 5
Star Hotel 3
Treasure Mountain Inn 2
RESTAURANTS, BARS & CLUBS
Buona Vita K
Chimayo L
Cisero's N
Club Creation P
The Eating Establishment M
Gamekeeper's Grille G
Grappa Q
The Happy Sumo A
Harry O's K
J.B. Mulligan's C
Morning Ray Café P
Mother Urban's D
No Name Saloon H
O'Shucks I
Park City Coffee Roaster O
Picasso B
Texas Red's J
Wahso E
Wasatch Brew Pub R
Zoom F

sive list of properties include AAA Lodging and Ski Reservations (Ⓣ435/649-2526 or 1-800/522-7669, Ⓦwww.ski-res.com), David Holland's Resort Lodging (Ⓣ435/645-3315 or 1-800/SKI-2002, Ⓦwww.davidhollands.com), and Around Town Lodging (Ⓣ435/645-9335 or 1-800/347-3392, Ⓦwww.aroundtownlodging.com). The **central reservations service** for the majority of available hotel and apartment accommodation in Park City and at Park City Mountain Resort is Park City Mountain Reservations (Ⓣ435/649-0493 or 1-800/222-7275, Ⓦwww.parkcitymountain.com).

Downtown Park City

Angel House Inn 713 Norfolk Ave Ⓣ435/647-0338 or 1-800/264-3501, Ⓦwww.angelhouse-inn.com. Perched on a hill above Main St, this friendly nine-room B&B features individual artistic touches in every room and healthy breakfasts. Its location is also superb. The rooms are good value in summer, but require booking well in advance during the ski season. There are also three apartments across the road, which can sleep 4–6 people each and have full kitchen and dining facilities ($230–330). Summer ❺, winter ❼

Chateau Apres Lodge, 1299 Norfolk Ave Ⓣ435/649-9372 or 1-800/357-3556, Ⓦwww.chateauapres.com. Worth considering for its convenient location and relatively low ski-season rates, but the drab double rooms are well past their prime and have tiny bathrooms. There are also two sex-segregated dorms, each with twenty metal-frame bunks on a concrete floor that's reminiscent of an army barracks; only book here if you can't get into the hostel (see below). Open Nov–April only. Rates include continental breakfast; dorm beds $28 ❺

Inn at Prospector Square 2200 Sidewinder Drive Ⓣ435/649-7100 or 1-800/453-3812, Ⓦwww.prospectorlodging.com. This corporate conference center, located a few blocks from Main St, offers regular hotel rooms and a range of condo units that can sleep 4–8 people. Useful extras in every room include fridge, microwave, and coffee-maker, and there's an outdoor summer-only pool, year-round heated hot tub, and an on-site ski-rental shop. Summer ❺, winter ❼.

1904 Imperial Hotel 221 Main St Ⓣ435/649-1904 or 1-800/669-UTAH, Ⓦwww.1904imperial.com. An original building from Park City's mining days, the *Imperial* is now the town's most central B&B inn. Its ten rooms are smallish, but cozy rather than cramped and the parlor windows look over Main St. There's a hot tub as well. Rates vary between rooms. Summer ❺, winter ❼

The Old Miners' Lodge 615 Woodside Ave Ⓣ435/645-8068 or 1-800/648-8068, Ⓦwww.oldminerslodge.com. This restored 1893 lodge houses a simple but comfortable B&B. The living area and dining room furnishings are a bit dowdy, but the friendly quiet and central location makes up for that. The twelve rooms vary quite a bit in size and decor; the smallest of them mimics an old mine shaft and is great value for two, especially in summer. Summer ❺, winter ❼

Park City International Hostel 268 Main St Ⓣ435/655-7244, Ⓦwww.parkcityhostel.com. This 68-bed hostel, which opened in the summer of 2000, enjoys an unbelievably central location on Main St. Facilities include a small but well-equipped communal kitchen, a twenty-seat in-house movie theatre, laundry, and ski lockers. The four-bed dorm rooms (no private rooms available) are understandably small, but the management is friendly and very upbeat, espousing something of a "ski hard, play hard" ethos; sleeping can be problematic when *Club Creation* (see p.344) gets going downstairs on Friday and Saturday. Summer $24, winter $30.

Star Hotel, 227 Main St Ⓣ435/649-8333 or 1-888/649-8333, Ⓕ435/649-5746, Ⓔgrixey@uswest.net. It's hard to believe that a cheerful old boarding-house-style hotel with creaky beds, saggy furniture, and cluttered common areas exists at such a salubrious address – yet here it is. In the heart of downtown, this hotel is great value for the unfussy guest, and winter rates even include breakfast and dinner. Summer ❹, winter ❼

Treasure Mountain Inn 255 Main St Ⓣ435/649-7334 or 1-800/344-2460. This broad, ugly Sixties edifice, built in two sections separated by an outdoor pool, has spooky corridors straight out of "The Shining." Its best feature is its location, smack in the center of town, and most rooms have useful extras like a fridge, kitchenette, and coffee maker – it's worth asking for one of these. Some two-bedroom units also available. Summer ❺, winter ❻

Yarrow Hotel 1800 Park Ave Ⓣ435/649-7000 or 1-800/927-7694. This well-appointed hotel and conference center has large standard rooms with fridges and coffee makers, as well as one-bedroom suites with kitchenettes. Other facilities include outdoor pool and hot tub; rates include a buffet breakfast. Summer ❻, winter ❼

Park City Mountain Resort

Marriott Mountainside Villas 1305 Lowell Ave ⓣ435/647-4000 or 1-800/845-5279. Recently opened, this resort, within walking distance of lifts, features both hotel rooms and "villas" along with all the usual expensive accoutrements like pools, hot-tubs, and a fitness center. Summer ❽, winter ❾

Shadow Ridge Resort 50 Shadow Ridge St ⓣ435/649-4300 or 1-800/451-3031, ⓦwww.shadowridgepc.com. A ski-vacation stalwart, offering a good range of small studio apartments through to one- and two-bedroom suites with full kitchen facilities, plus an outdoor pool, spa, sauna, and fitness center. Summer ❹, winter ❽

Snow Flower Condominiums 400 Silver King Drive ⓣ435/649-6400 or 1-800/852-3101. The complex contains plush, full-service condo complexes for two-to-ten people ($250–750); all feature kitchens, fireplaces, and hot tubs. Summer ❽, winter ❾

The Canyons

Grand Summit Resort Hotel ⓣ1-888/CANYONS, ⓕ435/649-7374. Five-star slopeside resort with superbly equipped hotel rooms and suites, and features that include a full range of fitness/spa facilities, indoor/outdoor heated pool and hot tubs, as well as exquisite dining at *The Cabin* restaurant (see p.343). A basic room goes for $330 during winter ($159 in summer). Summer ❼, winter ❾

Sundial Lodge Ski-in/Ski-out condominium lodge with both studio-style hotel rooms (winter $239/summer $129) and condos that sleep up to six people ($459/$349), plus two outdoor hot tubs with plunge pools. summer ❼, winter ❾

Deer Valley

Deer Valley Lodging ⓣ435/649-4040 or 1-800/453-3833, ⓕ435/647-3318, ⓦwww.deervalleylodging.com. Manages almost thirty lodges, townhouses and condo complexes clustered together in two distinct areas: Snow Park, near the chairlifts base, and Silver Lake Village, in the heart of the ski area almost halfway up the mountain. Because the properties are all high-end, they tend to be large and very comfortably appointed, with full-service kitchens, hot tubs, stone fireplaces, and mountain views, but there are not many one-bedroom places available – and even the smallest of these go for $340–400 per night in winter. For something approaching good value, a two-bedroom apartment or townhome which is set up to accommodate four adults might appeal at $400–600 per night. Summer ❼, winter ❾

Stein Eriksen Lodge ⓣ435/649-3700 or 1-800/453-1302, ⓦwww.steinlodge.com. The most salubrious address in Deer Valley's Silver Lake area, with award-winning restaurants, and basic necessities like hand-painted tiles in guestroom kitchens. Probably worth the money to anyone who can contemplate spending upwards of $700 a night. ❾

Park City Mountain Resort

Park City Mountain Resort (ⓣ435/649-0493 or 1-800/222-7275, ⓦwww.parkcitymountain.com) is home base for the **US Ski and Snowboard Teams**, and recently hosted the alpine giant slalom races and all the snowboarding events for the Salt Lake **Winter Olympics**. Still, it's actually less a domain for hardcore athletes than a family-oriented ski-resort, with huge areas of terrain particularly well-suited to intermediate enthusiasts – and it's often possible to access a variety of types of terrain from the same lift, ideal for a group that includes people of unequal abilities.

The **highest point** here is an even 10,000ft, giving a solid **vertical drop** of 3100ft. The overall **skiable terrain** of 3300 acres is served by fifteen **lifts** – including four six-passsenger chairs and one high-speed quad– and the network of one hundred **trails** is rated 18 percent beginner, 44 percent intermediate, and 38 percent expert. The groomed pistes offer variety enough for skiers and boarders of every disposition, and it's worth noting that while **McConkey's** and **Puma bowls** are studded with double-black diamonds on the trail map, they're really not too extreme. Further south, **Jupiter** and **Scott's bowls** are tougher going, best left to the experts. Freestyle riders have numer-

National Ability Center

One of Utah's most innovative organizations, the **National Ability Center** (PO Box 682799, Park City, UT 84068-2799; ⓣ435/649-3991, ⓕ658-3992, ⓦwww.nationalabilitycenter.org), is located at Park City Mountain Resort. The center runs programs year-round for **disabled outdoors enthusiasts** aged three to 75, with activities including skiing, snowboarding, snowshoeing, river rafting, fishing, cycling, water skiing, and horseback riding. Programs are available for people with physical, developmental and cognitive disabilities, and while costs are recovered through **program fees** (as well as donations and private grants), no one is denied participation due to inability to pay.

ous venues to catch air, including the **Sitka Super Park** and the **PayDay half-pipe**.

Pricing **lift tickets** is a bit problematic as the resort has a policy of "floating" ticket prices, with prices fluctuating between $30 and $60, based on demand. Prices, of course, are highest at peak holiday times. The usual multiday deals are available as well.

The Canyons

Situated four miles from downtown Park City, and formerly two separate ski areas, **THE CANYONS** (ⓣ435/649-5400 or 1-888/226-9667, ⓦwww.thecanyons.com) is the most ambitious project on the drawing board of the ferociously acquisitive American Skiing Company (ASC). When purchased in 1997, the resort's total ski area was 1400 acres; today that figure is around 4000 acres and counting, halfway through a five-year **expansion** plan that is expected to see The Canyons become one of North America's largest ski areas.

The **summit elevation** is 9990ft, with an impressive vertical drop of 3190ft. It would take several days to explore the resort's 134 **trails**, rated 14 percent beginner, 44 percent intermediate, and 42 percent expert and serviced by thirteen **lifts** and one high-speed **gondola**.

A quick appraisal of the trail map indicates a preponderance of blue runs, and also a density of trees. Though undeniably beautiful, the heavily forested narrow trails can lead to traffic jams on the most popular runs. Therefore, many stay off the trails altogether and head up to the backcountry bowls accessed via the **9990-Express chair**. **Experts** can find some real hair-raising dicing with trees and radical chutes from **Murdock Peak** at the southern edge of the ski area. Boarders can throw themselves about in a well-maintained **terrain park** that features some huge rails.

A one-day **lift ticket** costs $60, although as with Park City Mountain

Ski and snowboard rental

With well-stocked **equipment rental outlets** on location at each resort and others downtown, there's plenty of competition keeping rental rates at about the same levels of less salubrious ski towns. Expect to pay $18–25 for a day, while weekly rental packages vary greatly but will save you a good deal; both visitor centers usually carry brochures with rental rates and discount coupons. Downtown places with a good range of quality gear include; Destination Sports & Mountain Outfitters, who have three locations (738 Main St, Town Lift, and Park City Mountain Resort; ⓣ435/649-8092 or 1-800/247-6197); Jans Mountain Outfitters, 1600 Park Ave (ⓣ435/649-4949); and Cole Sport, 1615 Park Ave (ⓣ435/649-4806).

Resort, The Canyons is planning to introduce a system of flexible ticket prices based on demand. As the Park City Transit buses do not go to The Canyons, the resort runs its own free **shuttle service** (schedule information ⓣ435/649-5400) to and from downtown. If driving, much of the hassle is taken care of by the parking lot's **cabriolet gondola**, airborne buggies that zip you directly to the resort village.

Deer Valley

The reputation of **DEER VALLEY** (ⓣ435/649-1000 or 1-800/558-3337, ⓦwww.deervalley.com) as a vacation spot only for the rich has long preceded it, but, from a skier's perspective (boarding is not allowed) there are plenty of good reasons to spend at least a day here during a Park City visit. The resort is consistently rated North America's best for its food and lodging, and even more importantly the high standard of trail maintenance also sees it typically ranked in the various top-ten US ski resort lists. If you like to ski fast all day on broad, beautifully prepared pistes, you'll love the place. An added bonus is the culture of service that has always existed here, from the immaculate restrooms to slopes crawl-

Hiking, biking, and other Park City summer activities

Summer in Park City, like winter, revolves to a large extent around the ski resorts' chairlifts. Both the PayDay lift at Park City Mountain Resort (daily mid-June to early Sept, weekends only late May to mid-June and early Sept to mid-Oct; $8 single, $15 all day) and the Sterling lift at Deer Valley's Silver Lake (mid June to late Sept Wed–Sun; $9 single, $16 all day) give **hikers and bikers** access to trails among the ski runs and clapped-out mines high above town. The **alpine slide** toboggan run at Park City Mountain Resort, always a hit with kids, costs $8 per ride for adults and $2.50 for children. All you need before heading off for some high-altitude antics is the excellent *Park City Hiking & Biking Trail Map*, available free from visitor centers; several popular trails are marked and color-coded, with a brief description of each that includes distance and level of difficulty. Bikers after a real leg workout can take on steep trails like the **Sweeney Switchbacks**, but if your fitness and altitude acclimation are even a bit below par, then riding uphill into a ski area is not a great option. So long as you're geared up with a full-suspension bike, a good helmet, and a sense of adventure, it's hard to resist letting the chairlifts do the uphill work, while you spend the day whooping and hollering down the mountainside instead.

An excellent source of **information** on mountain-biking is **Bicycle Utah** (ⓣ435/649-8805, ⓦwww.bicycleutah.com), which produces a useful free annual vacation guide with suggested routes all over the state, plus lots of contacts for bike dealers and tour operators. While its main *raison d'etre* is the world-renowned slickrock biking around Moab in southern Utah, the organization actually makes its home in Park City. Two places with large selections of good rental bikes are Jans Mountain Outfitters, 1600 Park Ave (daily 9am–7pm; ⓣ435/649-4949) and Cole Sport, 1615 Park Ave (daily 8am–7pm; ⓣ435/649-4806), who both rent bikes for $25–35 per day.

All the other ski-town staples that keep people from going stir-crazy during the snow-free months are available in and around Park City, including **whitewater rafting** and **fly-fishing** on the nearby Provo and Weber rivers. Rafting trips cost $30–40 for a half-day of Class II and Class III rapids with High Country Tours (ⓣ435/645-7679). Information, gear and licenses for getting after some brown, rainbow, and native cutthroat trout is available from Park City Fly Shop, 2065 Sidewinder Drive (ⓣ435/645-8382). You can get an aerial view of the mountains on a **ballooning** joyflight with Park City Balloon Adventures (ⓣ435/645-8787 or 1-800/396-8787; $100 per hour), or make a sedate foray into the hills on **horseback** with Park City Stables (ⓣ435/645-7256 or 1-800/303-7256).

ing with mountain hosts who are there to give advice about trails and snow conditions and generally make you feel special. This used to translate to much higher prices (and probably kept most of the riffraff out), but **lift tickets** now cost $63 a day, only a couple of dollars more than at the neighboring resorts.

From the resort's **highest point** at 9570ft there's a **vertical drop** of 3000ft, and the total **skiable area** is 1750 acres. The 88 **trails** are broken down into 15 percent beginner, 50 percent intermediate, and 35 percent expert, and are serviced by nineteteen **lifts**, including a four-person gondola and eight quads. A theory worth exploring is that with its clientele of fairly conservative skiers and emphasis on trail-grooming, the **backcountry** gets ignored by the majority of visitors. Which might be enough to get your eyes riveted to the trail-map and its double-black diamond chutes and tree-runs off the **Empire Express** quad chair – or even to exert a little pressure on one of those helpful mountain hosts to tell you where the secret powder stashes are at. The **2002 Winter Olympics** committee bestowed further credibility upon Deer Valley when it assigned the prestigious slalom, aerial, and mogul ski events to the resort.

Eating

For many, exploring Park City's fine **restaurants** is an integral part of this town's vacation experience. Nowhere else in Utah is there so much to choose from, and with the pick of the restaurants lined up on Main Street, you can cruise for a bit and compare menus before settling in. That said, you will likely need a reservation to get a table at any of the more upmarket places listed below. One name that inevitably crops up in discussions of the best-of-the-best is dynamic chef-restaurateur Bill White, who owns and oversees three of the most popular and expensive restaurants in town: *Grappa*, *Chimayo*, and *Wahso*. Those on a really tight **budget** may want to load up at the Albertson's supermarket (see "Listings") and avoid eating out altogether. Most restaurants in Park City are **closed** for a few weeks during April–May and November.

Park City

Buona Vita 427 Main St ⓣ435/658-0999; delivery ⓣ649-6368. Any restaurant on Main St with entrees for less than $15 is worth jumping up and down about, and *Buona Vita* does have an appealing line-up of spaghettis, pizzas, and lasagnes in the $10–14 range.

Chimayo 368 Main St ⓣ435/649-6222. Bill White's attempt at "cutting-edge contemporary Southwestern cuisine" lives up to all three adjectives. Appetizers include a goat-cheese and mozzarrella chile relleno with a poblano and pumpkin-seed pesto. And the entrees, such as barbecued spare ribs with a chipotle and caramelized pineapple glaze ($30), are just as adventurous. Dinner only; winter daily, summer closed Mon.

The Eating Establishment 317 Main St ⓣ435/649-8284. A family-friendly menu starring babyback ribs, pasta primavera, breaded veal cutlets, and chicken-fried steak ($14–18). The breakfasts are old-school American; greasy, big, and popular with locals. Daily 8am–10pm.

El Chubasco 1890 Bonanza Drive ⓣ435/645-9114. Whether you're after a big plate of burritos or just a sanity check on the menu prices in Park City, this Mexican grill fits the bill. All the usuals – tacos, enchiladas, tamales, and moles – are in the $5–8 range. Lunch and dinner daily; takeout and delivery available.

Gamekeeper's Grille 508 Main St ⓣ435/647-0327. Exotic meat dishes like pan-seared ostrich medallions, grilled elk chops, and venison and pheasant accompany maple and pecan-crusted trout and a huge grilled T-bone steak on the *Gamekeeper's* menu. On par with the prices of Main St's other high-end restaurants.

Grappa 151 Main St ⓣ435/645-0636. The eldest of Bill White's superb Park City restaurants boasts the most satisfying and expensive Italian menu in town. Start with a grape and gorgonzola salad, and move onto cedar planked sea bass or scallopine of turkey saltimbocca style (entrees $26–36). Dinner only, reservations essential. Winter daily, summer closed Tues or Wed.

Grub Steak Prospector Square, 2200 Sidewinder Drive ☎ 435/649-8060. Reliably good steaks (served with baked potato), ribs, and even buffalo keep this restaurant popular with families. Prices, are a tad more than you might expect given its location well away from Main St; entrees run $16–30. Dinner daily, lunch Mon–Sat.

The Happy Sumo, 838 Park Ave ☎ 435/649-5522. One of several places where you can down raw fish in Park City. This is the pick for its location – central but tucked in just behind Main St where fewer tourists wander. Lunch and dinner Mon–Sat.

Morning Ray Café 268 Main St ☎ 435/649-5686. You may have to wait, but the basic breakfast menu of omelettes, bagels, and muffins is worth hanging about for. It's not especially cheap, however they do cook more "health-conscious" dishes than the *Eating Establishment* across the road. The lunch menu is wide-ranging and includes interesting salads, sandwiches, and vegetarian items. Daily 7am–midnight, and until 2am Fri & Sat.

Park City Coffee Roaster 221 Main St. With the popularity of the larger breakfast places on Main St, it's worth knowing about this tiny espresso bar with its own fresh-roasted coffees, slim selection of fresh muffins and pastries, plus a lone computer for internet access ($5 per hr). A second, larger version recently opened in a mall at 1300 Snow King Drive, at the junction of Park Ave and Kearns Blvd. Main St open daily 7am–6pm; mall location Mon–Sat 6am–4pm, Sun 7am–2pm.

Picasso 900 Main St ☎ 435/658-3030. Although this Spanish restaurant does have a full menu with lots of spiced and marinated meats and seafood, most come for an aprés-ski mix of drink and tapas at the bar. Tapas items $6–10, entrees $16–26. Live music Fri–Sat winter only. Dinner daily, closed Sun or Mon in summer.

Texas Red's 440 Main St. Get up to your elbows in ribs with spicy sauce ($15) at this amiable and affordable Main St joint. Daily 11.30am–10pm.

Wahso 577 Main St ☎ 435/615-0300. The third eatery in the Bill White stable is also where he's most likely to be found actually cooking. The menu is an adventurous marriage of French and Asian cuisine, and the wine list is mind-bendingly complete. The opulent interior features several intimate curtained booths, perfect for enjoying exquisite dishes like Chilean glazed sea bass and a spicy Sezchuan filet mignon (entrees $22–30). Dinner only, reservations essential. Winter daily, summer closed Sun–Mon.

Zoom 660 Main St ☎ 435/949-9108. This hip bar/restaurant's high-ceilinged interior is a creative mix of timber, copper, and glass wrapped around an open kitchen, where chefs toss about Thai BBQ shrimp, pastas, risottos, and flaming rib-eye steaks with deadly intent (entrees $17–22). Watching them work while tucking into a $10 burger or smoked turkey sandwich at the bar is worth every penny. Daily for lunch and dinner.

Park City Mountain Resort

Legends *Legacy Lodge*. This slopeside bar is superbly situated with huge windows looking straight onto skiers as they head down at day's end, and a relaxed mood with big chairs, a roaring fire, and usually a fairly unobtrusive acoustic duo; membership is required.

Pig Pen A rowdy aprés-ski venue one flight up in the resort plaza building behind the skating rink. They skirts the membership issue by serving up burgers and nachos, and have a pool table, foosball and even table-tennis, making for an ideal environment for a beery dissection of the day's events.

The Canyons

The Cabin *Grand Summit Resort Hotel* ☎ 435/615-8060. Swanky, expensive dining featuring a varied American West menu heavy on elaborate beef and lamb dishes (entrees $18–34) and boasting an extensive wine list.

Deer Valley

Café Mariposa *Silver Lake Lodge* ☎ 435/645-6715. A top-notch eating establishment where appetizers like dill cured salmon are $11, a Rocky Mountain rack of lamb costs $37 and a char-broiled yellowfin tuna steak $36, while the desserts come draped in all manner of dining awards. Tues–Sun 6–10pm.

McHenry's *Silver Lake Lodge* ☎ 435/645-6724. The quintessential ski-bum experience for its schmoozy deckchair "beach" vibe on a sunny winter's day – not to mention the best on-mountain burgers around ($8) and an excellent minestrone soup. Lunch daily, dinner Thurs–Mon only.

Drinking and nightlife

Park City holds itself up as quite the **nightlife** capital, which it undoubtedly is by Utah standards. There's nothing really wild going on, however, just a handful of pubs in which to get boisterous after a day in the mountains, and a club or two which host bands and DJs; Utah's club-membership requirements are enforced here as well (see box on p.317). With the exception of *Club Creation*, they're open every night in the busy summer and winter periods until at least 1am, while hours are less predictable when the town is quiet. For **listings** of upcoming events, check the weekly *Park Record* newspaper, or the **free** *Park City's E.A.R.*, a monthly entertainment rag.

Cisero's 306 Main St ⓣ435/649-5044. The basement bar of *Cisero's* Italian restaurant has a band or DJ playing at least a couple of nights a week. The house band is a basic blues-rock affair comprised of the owner and his friends, and there's a small dance floor and a couple of pool tables.

Club Creation 268 Main St ⓣ435/615-7588. Park City's hippest club for dance-fiends. Though unlicensed, which means no booze and those under 21 are welcome, it's open from midnight to 4 or 5am on Fridays and Saturdays only. The line-up stars reputable DJs and the cover is a hefty $20 – fair enough considering there's no bar. Guests of the *Park City International Hostel* (see p.338) get in free.

Harry O's 427 Main St ⓣ435/647-9494. The only place big enough to put on name bands and large Latin or funk combos, *Harry O's* is pretty well unchallenged as the town's "major" nightclub. There's little rhyme or reason to their line-up, and on any evening you might encounter a fourteen-piece ensemble or just about any species of DJ. Cover $5–20.

J.B. Mulligan's 804 Main St ⓣ435/658-0717. Though typically only hopping when there's a bluegrass, reggae, or rock band playing, *J.B.*'s is ideal for a beer and game of pool. Bands usually play three nights a week in winter, less regularly in summer. Cover $5–10.

Mother Urban's 625 Main St ⓣ435/615-7200. As befits a bar that hosts mainly jazz and original acoustic acts, this is a dark, subterranean room reached via a steep staircase. The musical vibe is usually a mellow one, although performers vary from angst-ridden singer-songwriters to superb New Orleans jazz/funk combos. There are also free big-screen movies on Monday nights in winter. Cover $5–10.

No Name Saloon 447 Main St. Formerly called the *Alamo*, and still mostly referred to by that name, *No Name* doesn't have bands or DJs, just a jukebox and lots of lively talking and drinking. There's a basic list of pub sandwiches, with occasional aprés-ski specials. Busy enough midweek, the place is packed to bursting on winter weekends with a mix of locals and visitors.

O'Shucks 427 Main St. There's no actual entertainment at *O'Shucks* beyond a couple of televisions and an occasional acoustic strummer/warbler, but if the young boarding-and-drinking crowd isn't at the *No Name Saloon*, they'll be here. Additional attractions are free peanuts and a decent garlic burger.

Wasatch Brew Pub 250 Main St. The moderately priced bar menu of sandwiches, steaks, burgers, salads, and even a sizeable rack of lamb is worth looking into, plus it ensures that this is one watering hole where you can get a decent microbrew without having to buy a membership. Ask if they're still serving "Wasatch 2002," a beer produced to mark the winter Olympics. It had a sticky legal run with the Olympics overlords – it's quite a story, and the little guy won (sort of). Daily 11am–midnight.

Park City festivals

Park City's roster of seasonal events is quite impressive, with several lively arts and music festivals run throughout the year. The headliner, of course, is the **Sundance Film Festival** (see opposite). Of the music events, the most worthwhile are the **Park City International Music Festival** (mid-July to mid-Aug; ⓣ435/649-5309, ⓦwww.pcmusicfestival.com), a month-long run of classical recitals, and the **International Jazz Festival** (held over a three-day weekend in mid-Aug; ⓣ435/649-2390). For detailed information contact the Park City Chamber of Commerce (ⓣ435/649-6100, ⓦwww.parkcityinfo.com).

Sundance Film Festival

The once maverick **Sundance Film Festival** (ⓣ435/328-3456, ⓦwww.sundance.org), noted for championing the work of independent American film-makers, celebrated its twentieth birthday in 2001 with its founder, **Robert Redford**, conspicuously absent. This may be a fair reflection of the fact that the festival has grown into the sort of establishment happening it once sought to undermine, with Hollywood dealmakers now as important as the film-makers themselves. However, every year still sees some unexpected gems emerge, and last-minute **tickets** can usually be had if you're prepared to stand in line and adopt a flexible attitude about which screenings to attend. Hotel rooms are much harder to come by, so the second half of January is not the most realistic time to try for a Park City ski vacation. An intriguing alternative is the **Slamdance Film Festival** (ⓣ323/466-1786, ⓦwww.slamdance.com), which started in 1994 in response to the increasingly mainstream look of Sundance; run over the same ten days in January, Slamdance showcases only first-time directors working with restricted budgets.

Listings

Banks Park City Bank, 820 Park Ave (Mon–Fri 9am–5pm, Sat 10am–4pm; ⓣ435/658-3730); Wells Fargo, 1776 Park Ave (Mon–Fri 9.30am–4.30pm, Sat 10am–4pm; ⓣ435/649-2384). The most centrally located 24hr ATM is the Bank One machine at 614 Main St.
Car rental All Resort (ⓣ435/649-3999); Avis (ⓣ435/649-7419); Budget (ⓣ435/645-7555); Enterprise (ⓣ435/655-7277).
Cross-country skiing The closest option to town is the Park City Golf Course (Nov–March 9am–6pm; ⓣ435/615-5858, ⓦwww.whitepinetouring.com; $10).
Internet access Park City Public Library, 1255 Park Ave (Mon–Thurs 10am–9pm, Fri–Sat 10am–6pm, Sun 1–5pm; ⓣ435/615-5600; free); Cyber Café & Art Gallery, 544 Main St (daily 8am–10pm; ⓣ435/940-0425; $5 per 30min).
Laundry Lost Sock, 1105 Iron Horse Drive (daily 8am–9pm; ⓣ435/647-9449).
Medical Center Snow Creek Emergency & Medical Center, 1600 Snow Creek Drive (Mon–Fri 9am–7pm, Sat–Sun 10am–6pm; ⓣ435/655-0055).
Pharmacy Albertson's, 1880 Park Ave (Mon–Fri 9am–9pm, Sat 9am–7pm, Sun 11am–5pm).
Police 445 Marsac St ⓣ435/645-5050; emergencies ⓣ911.
Post office 450 Main St (downtown), and 2100 Park Ave (hours and phone for both are: Mon–Fri 9am–5.30pm, Sat 9am–1pm; ⓣ1-800/275-8777).
Supermarket Albertson's, 1880 Park Ave (open 24hr).
Taxi Ace Cab Co. (ⓣ435/649-8294); Powder for the People (ⓣ435/649-6648).

North to Idaho

While Salt Lake City makes a convenient gateway destination to the entire Rocky Mountain region, connecting flights to smaller mountain towns tend to be expensive. They also negate the opportunity to travel through some glorious country en route to your ultimate destination. You should, therefore, consider driving on the **road north** from Salt Lake to Wyoming's Yellowstone and Grand Teton National Parks, one of the best in the west.

Brigham City

Nearly sixty miles north of Salt Lake City, and at the turnoff for I-89, **Brigham City** is a good place for a quick stop as, starting a mile or so east of town, the region's irresistible summer harvest of peaches, nectarines, and cherries are sold from carts dotted alongside I-89. Also east of town on I-89 is the *Maddox Ranch House*, no. 1900 (Tues–Sat 11am–9.30pm; ⓣ435/723-8545), a drive-in **diner** that's a genuine Utah institution. In operation for sixty years,

Golden Spike National Historic Site

On May 10, 1869, four symbolic spikes – two of them gold – were driven at a pass in Utah's Promontory mountains, linking the Union Pacific and Central Pacific railroads into the United State's **first trans-continental railway**, a moment of enormous social and economic significance. The site is marked today by a **visitor center**, 32 miles west of Brigham City on Hwy-13 (daily: May–Sept 8am–6pm; Oct–April 8am–4.30pm, ⓦwww.nps.gov/gosp; admission $7 per vehicle). Working replicas of the 1869 steam locomotives *Jupiter* and *119* are in operation May–Oct.

Maddox's serves up enormous buffalo steaks and burgers with mountains of cornbread and salad and a range of lethal cheesecakes (order your dessert "to go" and it's half-price). Folks really do drive from afar to eat here, so reserve ahead to avoid a likely thirty-minute wait for a table. Before continuing north, history and railroad buffs will want to take a brief detour east of Brigham City to the Golden Spike National Historic Site (see box above).

Logan and around

It's pretty uninspiring freeway driving from Salt Lake City to Brigham City, but the moment you leave the I-15 freeway for I-89 towards **LOGAN**, things take a turn for the better. The distinctive **Wellsville Mountains**, with the steepest incline of any mountains in the US, loom just to the west. It's a range more reminiscent of the European alps than the Rockies – indeed, it's easy to see how settlers from Switzerland saw this area as something close to home.Just north of the mountains and in the middle of the cool and green Cache Valley, Logan is a small Mormon town whose decent restaurants and hotels make it a good place to stop on your way to the national parks in Wyoming, or to base yourself while exploring the succession of **trailheads** that line I-89 as it runs through the picturesque **Logan Canyon**. The town makes for pleasant strolling, as there are plenty of green spaces about and even a classic old-time soda fountain (see "Practicalities", opposite); it's further enlivened by the presence of **Utah State University**, a largely agricultural school that numbers around 20,000 students. The only architectural sight of note is an impressive **Mormon Temple**, 175 N 300 E – you can't look inside unless you're an LDS church member, but visitors are welcome to walk the grounds.

Logan Canyon Scenic Byway

Logan Canyon Scenic Byway (I-89) begins just outside Logan at an altitude of 4700ft and runs for 37 miles through the Wasatch-Cache National Forest before topping out at 7800ft, a couple of miles above the western shore of Bear Lake (see opposite). Steep limestone walls, fields of wildflowers, and astonishing fall foliage in reds, yellows, and greens line the road, which can be driven in under an hour. But, it's worth spending at least half-a-day walking a trail or two, or simply driving up to Tony Grove Lake and unpacking a picnic basket.

If you plan to spend some time exploring, grab the free *Scenic Guide to Logan Canyon*, which explains the interpretive signs placed along the road, indicating trailheads, campsites, fishing spots, and points of interest. Two other useful free brochures, one listing fifteen **hiking trails**, the other nineteen **mountain- and road-bike trails**, are available from the information office (see opposite) and also from the USFS office at the mouth of the canyon at 1500 E I-89 (Mon–Fri 8am–5pm, Sat 10am–4pm; ⓣ435/755-3620). They also have info on hiking in the Wellsville Mountains, though this area is only for the hardy and well-prepared and lacks the variety found in Logan Canyon.

Logan Canyon hiking and camping

If you have plans to do a few hikes or to camp in the canyon, it's well worth stopping for a chat with rangers about trail and campground conditions. Highlights among the trails include those that start from **Tony Grove Lake**, which also has the most popular campground in the canyon. To reach Tony Grove Lake, turn left off I-89 nineteen miles north of Logan onto Tony Grove Road (Forest Road 003) and drive another seven miles to the lake and campground. Besides hiking or just mooching around the shoreline, people come here to picnic, fish, and even swim – though its elevation of 8050ft makes the lake a chilly proposition – and there's a boardwalk nature trail which follows the wildflower-speckled shoreline.

Peak-baggers can head out on the **Naomi Peak** (9980ft) trail from Tony Grove Lake for a three-mile hike (one-way) that gains almost 2000ft en route to spectacular views from the highest point in Cache Valley. Easier walks include the local favorite to picturesque **White Pine Lake**, a solid day's outing at nearly five miles one-way, but with only a modest gain in elevation. The 37 **campsites** at Tony Grove are often in demand, so it's worth booking one in advance through the USFS office. Riverside alternatives off I-89 include *Bridger* (ten sites), *Spring Hollow* (twelve sites) and *Guinavah-Malibu* (forty sites), all within ten miles of Logan; *Sunrise* (27 sites) is at the eastern end of the canyon in an elevated spot with views of Bear Lake. All have drinking water and toilet **facilities** but no showers (open May–Oct; reservations ⓣ1-800/280-2267; $10–12).

Logan practicalities

The Greyhound **bus** stop is at 2500 N 900 W (ⓣ435/752-4921). **Information** on the entire region can be had at the Bridgerland Visitor Information, 160 N Main St (Mon–Fri 8am–5pm; ⓣ435/752-2161 or 1-800/882-4433, ⓦwww.bridgerland.com).

Accommodations in town are dominated by mid-range chains, all of which offer standard amenities like a pool and/or hot tub, and whose rates include a basic breakfast of cereal, coffee, and pastries. Try the *Comfort Inn* (447 N Main St; ⓣ435/752-9141 or 1-800/228-5150; ④), or the slightly cheaper *Best Western Baugh Motel* (153 Main St (ⓣ435/752-5220 or 1-800/462-4154; ③). **Camping** is available at *Riverside RV/Campground*, 447 W 1700 S (ⓣ435/245-4469; $15).

Chinese cuisine features prominently among Logan's **restaurants**, and the best of the bunch is *Mandarin Garden*, 432 N Main St (ⓣ435/752-8384). Local favorite *Angie's*, 690 N Main St (daily 6am–10pm), has a no-frills diner menu, hearty servings, and cheap all-day breakfast specials ($3–4). *The Bluebird*, 19 N Main St, dates back to 1914 and boasts an original marble soda fountain. It's practically a must for an ice-cream soda, some wicked homemade chocolates, and to look at the bizarre mural depicting Logan's history from pioneer times through to a futuristic projection of what might yet come to pass.

Bear Lake

It's quite something when you crest the final hill at the eastern end of Logan Canyon and get a full view of **BEAR LAKE**. At around twenty miles long and eight miles wide, its waters are colored a stunning turquoise – the product of billions of limestone particles suspended in the water – making it very hard to resist a stop for the fine freshwater **swimming** to be had. Split pretty evenly between Utah and Idaho (see p.582 for the approach from Idaho), the lake gets plenty of attention from residents of both states coming to swim, water-ski, sail, fish, and lounge on its beaches.

Raspberry Days Festival

One inescapable aspect of a Bear Lake summer is the proliferation of raspberries. On the first weekend in August, Garden City hosts the **Raspberry Days Festival**, which celebrates the fruit through such happenings as a junior rodeo, the crowning of "Miss Raspberry," and copious amounts of arts and crafts. The raspberries really are fabulous, and you don't need to attend the festival to enjoy them. You can try a thick **raspberry shake** year-round at any one of Garden City's cafés, and raspberry jams and jellies are sold everywhere.

Garden City is the nearest thing to a town on the western shore, though it's basically a string of holiday cottages that straggle for several miles to the north and south. The two main recreation areas nearby, **Bear Lake Marina** and **Rendezvous Beach**, are both state parks and require a **fee** for day-use ($6). The former, located one mile north of Garden City, is the place for **boating activities** like water-skiing and sailing; water-sports craft including catamarans and jet-skis can be rented here. Rendezvous Beach, on the southwestern shore about eight miles south of Garden City, is a popular sandy spot perfect for swimming, sailing, and basking in the sun. If you just want to take a swim and would rather not pay, there's no problem with pulling over and diving in; cruise the stretch which starts two miles south of Garden City, ending just before Rendezvous Beach. **Fishing** from the shore or by boat is another popular pastime, and Bear Lake is known for trophy Bear Lake cutthroat trout and other native species, including the tiny Bonneville cisco. **Information** on the area is dispensed at a small visitor center on Hwy-30, just a few yards south of the junction with I-89 (May–Sept daily 10am–6pm).

If looking **to stay**, there are plenty of campsites with full facilities, including those at the *Rendezvous Beach* (136 sites; $13; open May–Sept) and *Bear Lake Marina* (13 sites; $13; open year-round); reservations for both of these can be made in advance (Ⓣ435/946-3343 or 1-800/322-3770). *Bear Lake KOA* is beside the marina and has a pool, mini-golf, a small store, and full laundry and shower facilities (Ⓣ435/946-3454; tent-sites $15, RVs $19, open May–Oct). For indoor accommodations, try *Bear Lake Motor Lodge*, beside the visitor center at 50 S Bear Lake Blvd (Ⓣ435/946-3271; ❹) or a lakeside condo at *Harbor Village Resort*, 900 N Bear Lake Blvd (Ⓣ435/946-3448 or 1-800/324-6840; one-bedroom ❺, two-bedroom ❼).

Travel details

Trains

Amtrak's California Zephyr travels through Colorado and Utah (departs daily from Salt Lake City heading west to California at around 4pm; departs daily heading east to Denver at around 4am).

Buses

Salt Lake City to: Brigham City (2 daily; 1hr 20min); Logan (2 daily; 1hr 50min); Park City (2 daily; 45min).

Southern Wyoming

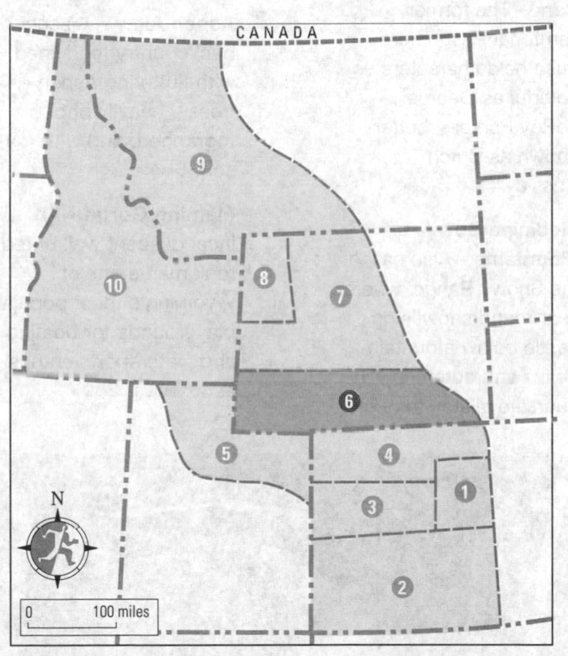

CHAPTER 6 Highlights

* **Frontier Days** – Cheyenne's premier annual event features the world's most prestigious outdoor rodeo – "the Daddy of 'em all." See p.357
* **Wyoming Territorial Park** – The former Territorial Prison here once held characters as colorful as George LeRoy Parker – better known as Butch Cassidy. See p.364
* **Medicine Bow Mountains** – Also called the Snowy Range, where year-round snowfields nestle below mountain peaks and outcrops of quartzite glisten throughout the summer. See p.365
* **Saratoga** – Sliced prettily in two by the North Platte River, this tiny spa resort is known for its healing hot springs. See p.367
* **Aspen Alley** – A scenic backcountry road lined with fluttering Aspen trees – heavily photographed, and with reason. See p.368
* **Flaming Gorge** – An incandescent wall of red rock marks one of Wyoming's most popular playgrounds for boating and watersports enthusiasts. See p.369

6

Southern Wyoming

The grassy plains of **SOUTHERN WYOMING** share little in common with the rest of the state. Indeed, its only in the central portions some thirty miles west of Laramie that you'll encounter any sort of mountainous region at all in the form of the **Snowy Range**, which rises briefly from the Medicine Bow National Forest. But while the natural features of this landscape may be less arresting than in other parts of the state, it's here that Wyoming's cultural and historical roots are most apparent. This is *the* classic cowboy country – the inspiration behind *Shane*, *The Virginian*, and countless other Western novels – where the state emblem of a hat-waving cowboy astride a bucking bronco comes alive at various rodeos, Country and Western dance halls and ubiquitous ranchwear stores. And while this may be one of the more populous areas in the US's ninth-largest state, cattle and pronghorn antelope still outnumber the local populace.

Besides the state's legislature, **Cheyenne** is home to a major military base and some of Wyoming's finest buildings, but its residents are proudest of their cowboy heritage – celebrated during the Frontier Days festival each July. The mantle of "cultural capital" goes to **Laramie**, which supports a young and energetic population thanks to the presence of the University of Wyoming, and has its own historical landmark in the Wyoming Territorial Prison and Old West Park. West of the Snowy Range, the spa resort town of **Saratoga** and the former mining and logging centers of **Encampment** and **Riverside** are quietly gathering momentum as tourist destinations, while savvy hikers and mountain bikers head for the starkly beautiful **Medicine Bow Mountains** or the shady forests of the **Sierra Madre** range. Heading west from here, I-80 crosses 125 miles of windy, dusty badlands before reaching the town of **Rock Springs** and the dramatic cliffs of **Flaming Gorge**, before heading for the Utah border and the next instalment of the Rocky Mountains.

Accommodation price codes

All accommodation prices in this book have been coded using the symbols below. For **hotels**, **motels**, and **B&Bs**, rates are given for the least expensive double room in each establishment during peak season; variations are indicated where appropriate, including winter rates for all ski resorts. For **hostels**, we've given a specific price per bed; for **camping**, the overnight cost per site is given. For a full explanation see p.30 in Basics.

❶ up to $30	❹ $60–80	❼ $130–180
❷ $30–45	❺ $80–100	❽ $180–240
❸ $45–60	❻ $100–130	❾ over $240

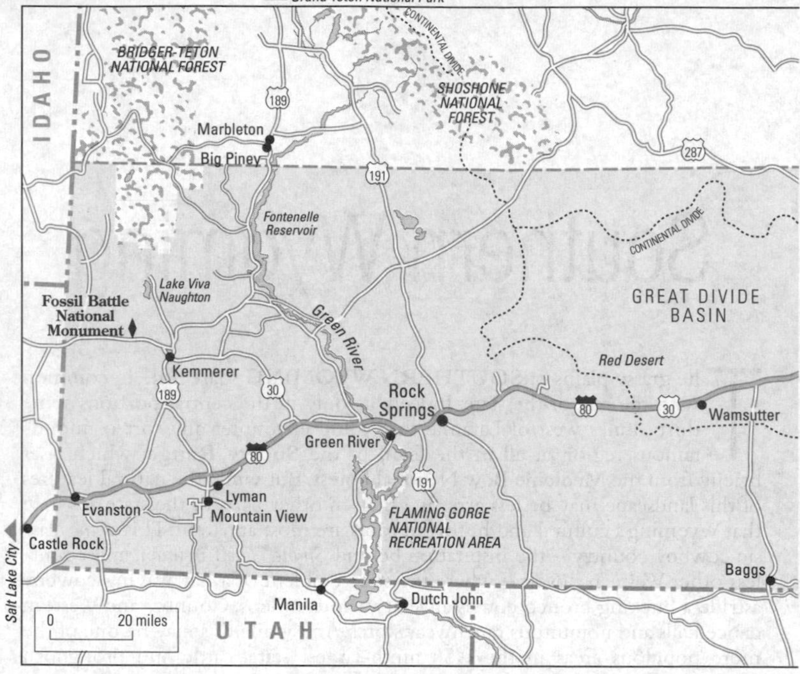

Some history

Wyoming has long been the "highway of the north," its relatively forgiving mountain passes favored by wagon-trains heading west along stretches of the Oregon and Mormon trails, into Utah's Salt Lake Valley and onto the Pacific Northwest. **Native American** tribes had for centuries crossed the same passes through to winter camps in Arizona, New Mexico, and Texas. and prior to the arrival of white pioneers their biggest problem was the fairly meager supply of buffalo in southern Wyoming, which often led to fierce intertribal wars over hunting grounds. However, Sioux, Cheyenne, and Blackfoot warriors still combined to inflict notable defeats on the US Army, before soldiers with better firepower managed to clear the way for pioneer settlement in the 1870s. Cattle folk by that time were already exploiting Wyoming's grazing conditions following two serendipitous events that combined to kick-start the ranching industry. In 1863, four years before the arrival of the Union Pacific railroad, a wagon-train was caught in a snowstorm near Cheyenne and its members, in order to out-ride the weather, were forced to leave their cattle to die. Returning next spring, the settlers were astonished to find the cattle alive and well; within two years ranchers were moving herds onto huge tracts of land in southeast Wyoming in anticipation of a railroad terminus being opened in Cheyenne. Sheep-farming homesteaders followed the lead of the cattlemen, and the two groups were soon engaged in violent **range wars** over grazing rights to the wiry grasslands.

Unlikely as it may seem, this rowdy, male-dominated territory was the first to grant women the vote in 1869 – a full half-century before the rest of the country. The practical reality was that the enfranchisement of women would

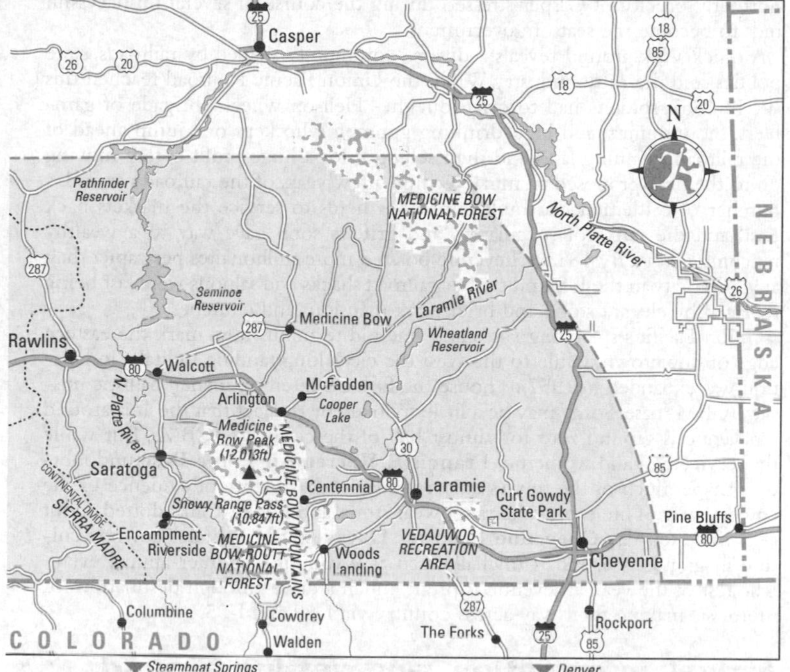

attract settlers and hasten statehood, which was in part dependent upon a minimum static population. But Wyoming's **suffragette movement** was not finished there, and in 1870 the country's first women jurors were appointed in Wyoming, twenty years before it became the 44th state of the union in 1890. Having been bestowed with the title, the "Equality State," it was just a matter of time before Wyoming elected the first female US governor too – Nellie Taylor Ross, in 1924.

In more recent times, Wyoming's diminishing oil industry has been overtaken by coal and natural gas extraction, bolstering the meat and livestock production on which Wyoming has traditionally relied. The paucity of major rivers and waterways to exploit for irrigation purposes seems to have put a lid on agricultural and population growth, and Wyoming's population is continuing to decline from its current total of around 460,000.

Cheyenne

The approach into **CHEYENNE**, dropping into a wide dip in the plains, leaves enduring memories for most travelers. With the snow-crested Rockies looming in the far distance and short, sun-bleached grass encircling the town, the sky suddenly appears gargantuan, dwarfing the outer suburbs and everything else below. Cheyenne is the nearest thing to a city that Wyoming has to offer, though with a population of just 54,000 it's not quite a bustling metropolis. For geographical and economic reasons it has always maintained closer ties with Omaha and Denver than with the rest of Wyoming – a point the more northerly oil city of Casper stressed during the course of several unsuccessful bids to become the seat of government.

A quick walk around reveals a diverse community shaped by railroads, state politics, and the cattle industry. When the Union Pacific Railroad reached this site in 1867, soldiers had to drive out the "Hell on wheels" brigade of gamblers, moonshiners, and hard-drinking gunmen who kept one jump ahead of the railroad, claiming land and then selling it for a huge profit before moving on to the next proposed terminal. Within a few years of the railroad's arrival, a number of cattlemen had built enormous herds to service the markets back East, and the ranks of speculators and grifters soon gave way to a wealthy ranching gentry. By 1883, Cheyenne boasted more millionaires per capita than any other city in the US, and timber railroad shacks and saloons were fast being replaced by elegant stone and brickwork mansions and churches.

Union Pacific's sprawling yards and fine old terminus now mark the eastern edge of downtown, while to the west the city's longstanding military installation was expanded in 1957 to house the first US intercontinental ballistic missile (ICBM) base. Some may be a little spooked by the fact that the area around Cheyenne is ground zero for almost half of the country's ICBMs. But while the servicemen and women of **Francis E. Warren Air Force Base** undoubtedly shape much of the town's culture today, there's plenty of evidence of the cowboy way of life too, as the ranchwear stores and honky-tonks dotted about attest. The ten-day **Cheyenne Frontier Days** festival celebrates cowboy culture in grand style, and is unchallenged as Wyoming's premier annual event. The rest of the year, Cheyenne is pretty much a drive-through destination for motorists making their way across country via I-80 and I-25.

Arrival, information, and getting around

While it is possible to fly in to Cheyenne's municipal **airport**, 200 E 8th Ave (Ⓣ307/634-7071) from Denver, it's not worth it as the drive over is under three hours long. A **shuttle** service between Cheyenne and DIA is provided by Armadillo Express (Ⓣ307/632-2223 or 1-888/256-2967; 5 daily; $28 one-way). Greyhound **buses** (Ⓣ307/634-7744) run east and west along I-80 and south to Denver, while Powder River buses (Ⓣ307/635-1327) travel through eastern Wyoming to Colorado and Montana. Both companies share the depot at 222 E Deming Drive, beside Central Avenue several blocks south of downtown.

The **visitor center**, 309 W Lincolnway (June–Aug daily 8am–6pm; rest of year Mon–Fri 8am–5pm; Ⓣ307/778-3133 or 1-800/426-5009, Ⓦwww.cheyenne.org), provides a free detailed map of the city. For information on tourism statewide, stop by the **Wyoming Travel Information Center**, perched at the windy highway junction of I-25 and College Drive, about four miles southwest of downtown (daily 8am–5pm; Ⓣ307/777-2883 or 1-800/225-5996).

If you're in Cheyenne without a car, your transport options are limited to the Cheyenne Transit Program **bus system** (Ⓣ307/637-6253; fare $1), which operates five routes around the city from roughly 6.30am until 6.30pm.

Accommodation

Cheyenne has plenty of cheap **motels** clustered near the various freeway exits, prominently on W Lincolnway between downtown and the junction with I-80. Bear in mind that Lincolnway follows the railway tracks, and it's likely you'll hear the rumblings of freight cars from your motel room. Downtown, there are few places of any note; best of the central options are a couple of very good **B&Bs**. If **camping**, *AB Camping* is closest to downtown at 1503 W

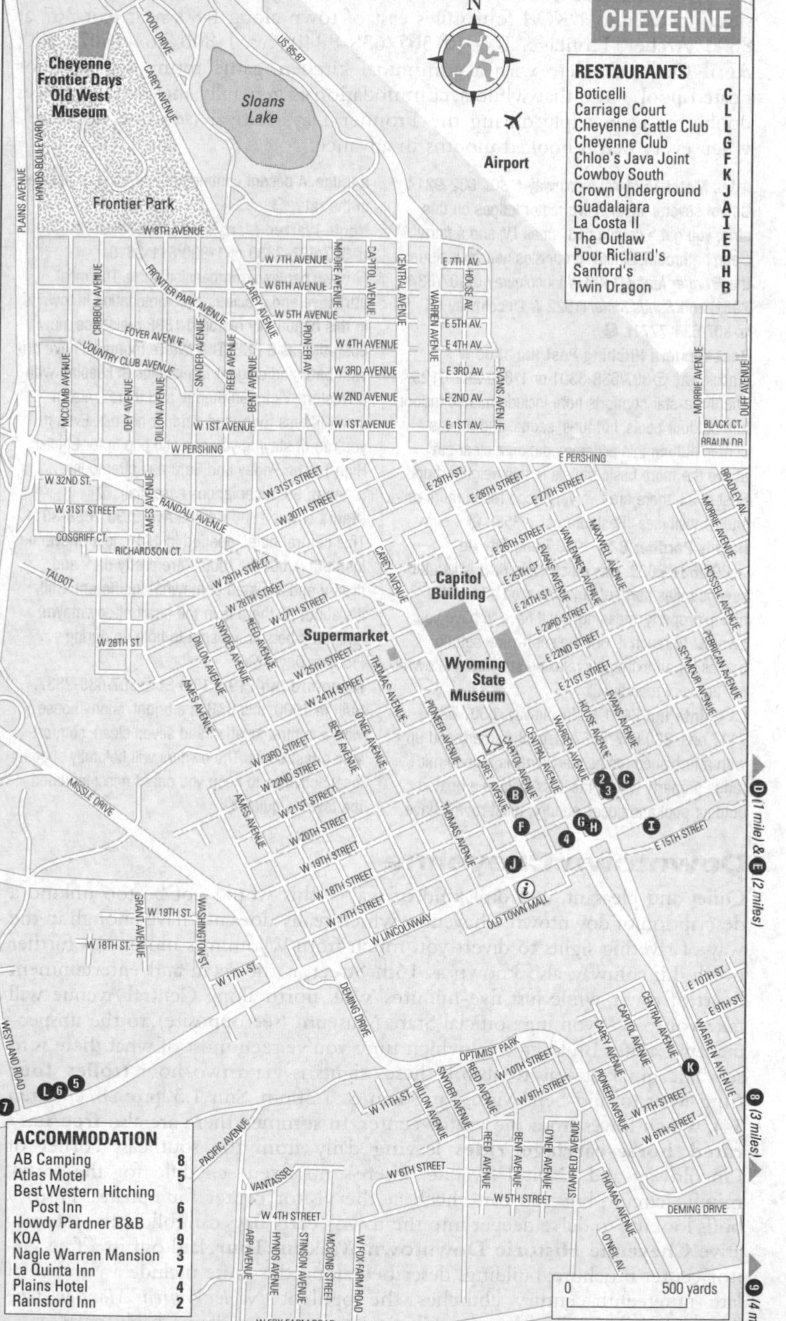
CHEYENNE
A (1 mile) & 1 (2 miles)
N
RESTAURANTS
Boticelli C
Carriage Court L
Cheyenne Cattle Club L
Cheyenne Club G
Chloe's Java Joint F
Cowboy South K
Crown Underground J
Guadalajara A
La Costa II I
The Outlaw E
Poor Richard's D
Sanford's H
Twin Dragon B
Cheyenne Frontier Days Old West Museum
Sloans Lake
Airport
Frontier Park
Capitol Building
Supermarket
Wyoming State Museum
US 85-87
POOL DRIVE
CAREY AVENUE
HYNDS BOULEVARD
PLAINS AVENUE
W 8TH AVENUE
W 7TH AVENUE
W 6TH AVENUE
W 5TH AVENUE
W 4TH AVENUE
W 3RD AVENUE
W 2ND AVENUE
W 1ST AVENUE
W PERSHING
E PERSHING
FRONTIER PARK AVENUE
FOYER AVENUE
COUNTRY CLUB AVENUE
CRIBBON AVENUE
MCCOMB AVENUE
DEY AVENUE
DILLON AVENUE
SNYDER AVENUE
REED AVENUE
BENT AVENUE
PIONEER AV.
MOORE AVENUE
CAPITOL AVENUE
CENTRAL AVENUE
WARREN AVENUE
HOUSE AV.
EVANS AVENUE
E 7TH AV.
E 5TH AV.
E 4TH AV.
E 3RD AV.
E 2ND AV.
E 1ST AV.
MORRIE AVENUE
DUFF AVENUE
BLACK CT.
BRAUN DR
W 32ND ST.
W 31ST STREET
COSGRIFF CT.
RICHARDSON CT.
RANDALL AVENUE
AMES AVENUE
TALBOT
W 31ST STREET
W 30TH STREET
W 29TH STREET
W 28TH STREET
W 27TH STREET
W 28TH ST.
W 25TH STREET
W 24TH STREET
W 23RD STREET
W 22ND STREET
W 21ST STREET
W 20TH STREET
W 19TH STREET
W 18TH STREET
W 17TH STREET
E 29TH ST.
E 28TH STREET
E 27TH STREET
E 26TH STREET
E 25TH CT
E 24TH ST.
E 23RD STREET
E 22ND STREET
E 21ST STREET
E 15TH STREET
VANLENNEN AVENUE
MAXWELL AVENUE
BRADLEY AV.
MORRIE AVENUE
ROSSELL AVENUE
SEYMOUR AVENUE
PEBRICAN AVENUE
THOMAS AVENUE
O'NEIL AVENUE
MISSLE DRIVE
OLD TOWN MALL
W LINCOLNWAY
W 19TH ST.
W 18TH ST.
W 17TH ST.
GRANT AVENUE
WASHINGTON ST.
WESTLAND ROAD
DEMING DRIVE
OPTIMIST PARK
W 11TH ST.
W 10TH STREET
W 9TH STREET
W 7TH STREET
W 6TH STREET
W 6TH STREET
W 5TH STREET
W 4TH STREET
W FOX FARM ROAD
E 10TH ST.
E 9TH ST.
PACIFIC AVENUE
VANTASSEL
ARP AVENUE
HYNDS AVENUE
STINSON AVENUE
MCCOMB STREET
W FOX FARM ROAD
STANFIELD AVENUE
O'NEIL AV.
DEMING DRIVE
D (1 mile) & E (2 miles)
8 (3 miles)
9 (4 miles)
Laramie (50 miles)
0 500 yards
ACCOMMODATION
AB Camping 8
Atlas Motel 5
Best Western Hitching Post Inn 6
Howdy Pardner B&B 1
KOA 9
Nagle Warren Mansion 3
La Quinta Inn 7
Plains Hotel 4
Rainsford Inn 2

College Drive (☎307/634-7035; $13; March–Oct), and it also has lots of RV sites. There's also a *KOA* four miles east of town along I-80, near exit 367 at 8800 Archer Frontage Rd (☎307/638-8840 or 1-800/562-1507; $20; April–Oct), complete with a communal kitchen, game room, and outdoor heated pool. Note that while accommodation is generally inexpensive, prices double or even triple during the Frontier Days festival (see box opposite), when every bed is booked months in advance.

Atlas Motel 1524 W Lincolnway ☎307/632-9214. One of several inexpensive motor lodges on this strip; you get a double bed, small TV, and a fairly clean bathroom. Similar properties nearby include the *Frontier Motel* (1400 W Lincolnway ☎307/634-7961) and *Sands Motel* (1022 W Lincolnway ☎307/634-7771). ❸

Best Western Hitching Post Inn 1700 W Lincolnway ☎307/638-3301 or 1-800/221-0125. The three-star comforts here include heated indoor and outdoor pools, hot tubs, sauna, and fitness center, putting this accommodation a clear cut above the more basic motels in this neighborhood. Best of all, there are two very good restaurants on-site as well (see "Restaurants" p.358). ❻

Howdy Pardner B&B 1920 Tranquility Rd ☎307/634-2822. This ranch-style B&B is located several miles north of downtown on a ten-acre hilltop property, meaning you'll have to have your own car to reach it. But the semi-rural setting makes for an extremely relaxing stay and the owners are very friendly. ❻

La Quinta Inn 2410 W Lincolnway ☎307/632-7117 or 1-800/687-6667. Recently smartened up with refurbished rooms, *La Quinta* is a good mid-range property whose facilities include a heated outdoor pool and guest laundry; most rooms have a fridge. A decent continental breakfast is included in the rate. ❹

Nagle Warren Mansion 222 E 17th St ☎307/637-3333 or 1-800/811-2610, Ⓦwww.naglewarrenmansion.com). The most attractive and gracious accommodation in town is in this beautifully restored 1888 residence, now operating as a B&B. The twelve rooms all have private bath and elegant furnishings in keeping with a Western-Victorian theme, and there's also a small fitness room and outdoor hot tub. Even if you're not staying you can still pop in for English High Tea on Friday and Saturday afternoons (3–4pm; $8; reservations essential). ❻

Plains Hotel 1600 Central Ave ☎307/638-3311. This central hotel, opened in 1911, is a Cheyenne institution, but the rooms are pretty dark and dreary and the staff somewhat indifferent. Still, it's about all there is in the heart of downtown and it's a boisterous spot to hole up during Frontier Days. ❸

Rainsford Inn 219 E 18th St ☎307/638-2337. Built in 1900, this B&B is a bright, sunny house with a central location and seven clean, comfortable guestrooms. The owners will helpfully suggest local activities to keep you out of mischief when the town is quiet. ❹

Downtown Cheyenne

Quiet and pleasant, in a dull kind of way – this would not be too unkind a description of downtown Cheyenne, which really does not have enough in the way of riveting sights to divert you much from Wyoming's mountains further north. Lincolnway, also known as 16th Street, is the retail and entertainment heart of town, while just five-minutes' walk north along Central Avenue will take you past Wyoming's official State Museum (see opposite), to the unspectacular Capitol Building – by which time you've seen most of what there is to see. The quickest way to absorb theses sights is via a two-hour **trolley tour** (mid-May to mid-Sept Mon–Sat 10am & 1.30pm, Sun 1.30pm; $8, children $4), which leaves from the visitor center. In summer, there are also **free narrated horse-carriage rides** leaving daily from the southeast corner of Lincolnway and Capitol Avenue. There's no fixed schedule for the forty-minute circuit, but you can check at the visitor center for updates. History buffs looking to delve deeper into the town's early days can follow the informative **Cheyenne Historic Downtown Walking Tour**, laid out in a free visitor center brochure; buildings described along the route include a number of late nineteenth-century churches, the opulent *Nagle Warren Mansion* (see "Accommodation") and even a Chevrolet showroom dating back to 1923.

The most easily identifiable landmark at the north end of downtown is the domed 1887 **Capitol Building**, at 24th Street and Capitol Avenue (Mon–Fri 8am–5pm; free). Though it doesn't exactly demand a visit, its central rotunda, with a smart marble floor overlooked by a blue-and-green stained-glass window from England, is worth a peak. As is the stuffed 3000-pound bison on display – a superb specimen of the official Wyoming state mammal. A block south, the **Wyoming State Museum**, 2301 Central Ave (Tues–Sat 9am–4.30pm; free), displays some Native American bits and pieces and dinosaur fossils, though the stars are some fabulous antique firearms, including a beautiful c.1880 pearl-handled Army Colt .38 revolver and a bizarre 1870 "Pocket Rifle" – still deadly despite its miniature scale.

The collection of Old West artifacts on display at the private **Nelson Museum of the West**, 1714 Carey Ave (June–Aug Mon–Sat 8am–5pm, Sept–May Mon–Fri 8am–noon & 1–5pm; $3), reflects the predilections of owner Robert L. Nelson. Big game trophies and elegant saddles dominate the museum, which also houses a number of Old West paintings and furnishings and some evocative Western movie posters as well.

There's little greenery around the city, so the **Cheyenne Botanic Gardens**, 710 Lions Park Drive (greenhouse open Mon–Fri 8.30am–4.30pm, Sat–Sun 11am–3.30pm; free), is a welcome spot to mooch about over a picnic lunch. The greenhouse, with its collection of exotic flora, vegetables, and cactii, is well tended and worth a brief look.

Like any cowboy town worth its salt, there's also a tacky **Old Cheyenne Gunfight**, 16th Street and Carey Avenue (May–Sept Mon–Fri 6pm, Sat "high noon"; free), in which hammy gunslingers do exactly what you'd expect them to do.

Cheyenne Frontier Days Old West Museum

The **Cheyenne Frontier Days Old West Museum**, 4501 N Carey Ave (Mon–Fri 9am–5pm, Sat & Sun 10am–5pm; $4), is where you can get in touch with the mood of the Frontier Days festival (see box, below). A video presentation makes clear what a hollerin' good time the festival is, but the pride of the exhibits is a collection of old carriages that are decked out once a year for the festival – these otherwise sit quiet in a huge room at the rear of the muse-

Cheyenne Frontier Days – the "Daddy of 'em all"

Forget the rest, this is the biggest and the best: **Cheyenne Frontier Days** (information and advance ticket sales ⓣ307/778-7222 or 1-800/227-6336, ⓦwww.cfdrodeo.com) is the largest annual event in Wyoming, and its showpiece is the most prestigious rodeo competition in the world, officially known as the "Daddy of 'em all." Held over ten days in late July, the festival attracts the very best bull- and bronc-riders and calf-ropers, competing for the coveted Frontier Days champion's silver belt-buckle. Also featured are nightly concerts by top Country performers, square dances, a chili cook-off, and a classic Western carnival with rides and games. Things only calm down at breakfast time – when thousands of free pancakes are served up to replenish sugar reserves – and during the four stately parades of antique horse-drawn carriages, traps, and buggies, which start out at 9.30am on Tuesday, Thursday, and on both Saturdays. The local top guns pitch in as well, with a team of US Air Force Thunderbirds putting on an aerial show on the first weekend.

In recent years visitor numbers have topped 300,000, so the only way to be sure of a bed in town during the festival is by reserving several months in advance; tickets to rodeo ($12–20) and concert events ($15–30) can be bought ahead of time too.

um. It's worth checking the place out, although a visit may serve to point out just how sedate the city is when the festival isn't on, and make you wish you'd timed your arrival to coincide with the annual rodeo frenzy.

Eating, drinking, and nightlife

No one is likely to try and sell you the idea that Cheyenne is any sort of culinary capital, but then you probably wouldn't expect them to either. Steaks and Mexican grub are the mainstays, but if you're not a passionate red-meat eater, you'll get along fine with some of the Italian, Chinese, and seafood **eating** options. **Drinking** and **nightlife** usually doesn't amount to much beyond a Country band or a DJ twirling a Top Forty playlist. If things get real slow, there's always the Lincoln Theatre (ⓣ307/637-7469), a cheap ($3) multiplex **movie theater** in the heart of downtown at 1615 Central Ave. There is also a **night rodeo** held at Terry Bison Ranch, ten miles south of town via I-25 and exit 2 (June–Aug Tues & Sat only; ⓣ307/634-4171; $6). It's an unashamed family-oriented tourist affair, where you can go for a chuckwagon dinner, a buffalo steak in *Senators Restaurant*, and an afternoon horseback ride before the show.

Restaurants

Boticelli 300 E 17th St ⓣ307/634-9700. A lavish 1883 Victorian home that now hosts a fine Italian kitchen which makes for one of the better dining experiences in town. Fresh pastas and salads perfectly complement classics such as *vitello alla Marsala* and *bistecca Toscana* (entrees $8–16), and the dessert menu includes spumoni and a fine tiramisu. Daily for lunch and dinner; reservations advised.

Carriage Court *Best Western Hitching Post Inn* ⓣ307/638-3301. With a menu boasting Alaskan king crab, sea bass, fresh oysters, and some creative salads, it's little wonder that many locals make this their top choice for a special dining occasion (entrees $14–34). Don't be put off by the motel address either – the dark-timbered interior is surprisingly stylish. Tues–Sat, dinner only.

Cheyenne Cattle Club *Best Western Hitching Post Inn* ⓣ307/633-3301. If the rowdy scene at *Sanford's* is not your thing and you don't mind the drive from town, then you might prefer a true-blue Wyoming steak ($14–20) from the highly regarded grill here. Dinner daily.

Chloe's Java Joint 1711 Carey Ave. Good coffee and fresh muffins are the staples of this tiny coffeehouse, but there are sandwiches, light lunches, and breakfast specials on offer too. Daily 7am–4.30pm.

Guadalajara 1745 Dell Range Rd ⓣ307/432-6803. Cuisine here is labeled "coastal Mexican," which translates to a strong seafood theme amongst the various chilis, fajitas, and chimichangas. Don't pass up the deep-fried ice-cream for dessert; it's crumbed with cinnamon, dropped into a tortilla bowl and doused in honey and whipped cream. Entrees $8–11; daily for lunch and dinner.

La Costa II 317 E Lincolnway ⓣ307/638-7372. In competition with *Guadalajara*, this Mexican place is the best in town. All the usual suspects appear on the menu at $8–12, and there's a fair range of beers from south of the border too. Daily for lunch and dinner.

Poor Richard's 2233 E Lincolnway ⓣ307/635-5114. Oysters, crab, soups, and salads, plus good-value beef and buffalo steaks (entrees $9–16) make up the menu at this bistro-restaurant. The lounge bar is a relaxing place for drinking too. Dinner daily, lunch Mon–Sat only.

Sanford's 115 E 17th St ⓣ307/778-2739. When it comes to trashy sporting paraphernalia and alligators-in-sunglasses hanging from the walls, *Sanford's* is pretty much the daddy of 'em all. Belly up to the bar for a monster steak ($16–22) and a beer in this lively brewpub which brings in a big college crowd most nights. Mon–Sat 11am–midnight, Sun 11am–10pm.

Twin Dragon 1809 Carey Ave ⓣ307/637-6622. The best Chinese place for miles has the standard Americanized menu: the servings are big (entrees $9–14) and the all-you-can-eat $6 lunch buffet is known to pack 'em in. Mon–Sat 11am–10pm, Sun 11am–9pm.

Bars and nightclubs

Cheyenne Club 1617 Capitol Ave ⓣ307/635-7777. At its worst, this club –the biggest downtown dance-space – can devolve into a parody of itself. But the mix of drunk Air Force personnel and rhythmically-challenged cowboys works out fine as long as you're drinking. The music is a pretty cheesy techno assault, peppered with a few Top Forty selections. Cover $1–2.

Cowboy South, 312 S Greeley Hwy ⓣ307/637-3800. Cheyenne's stronghold for all things Country and Western, and the town's premier beer-sodden meat-market during Frontier Days, is sadly bereft of line-dancing – in fact, Wyomingans insist that this unique feat of social engineering is really a posturing, Coloradan thing to do. Daily from 11am until late.

Crown Underground, 222 W 16th St ⓣ307/778-9202. This downstairs lounge bar features regular DJs despite the postage-stamp of a dance floor, and it's about as close to a hip evening destination as the city has to offer. There's a nice chill-out room with cushy sofas, plus some individual booths and a couple of bars. Cover $2–5.

The Outlaw, 3839 E Lincolnway ⓣ307/635-7552. This spit-and-sawdust cowboy saloon is old-school drinking territory, with pick-up trucks lined up outside and a pretty unreconstructed attitude towards females inside. Worth checking for live bands, mostly Country and blues. Daily from 11am until late.

Listings

Airlines United Express (ⓣ307/635-6623 or 1-800/241-6522), has several flights daily from Denver.

Banks Norwest, 1700 Capitol Ave (Mon–Fri 9am–5pm, Sat 9am–1pm) and American National, 1912 Capitol Ave (Mon–Fri 9am–4.30pm), have 24hr ATMs.

Car rental Advantage (ⓣ307/778-2889 or 1-800/777-5500), Avis (ⓣ307/632-9371 or 1-800/831-2847), Dollar (ⓣ307/632-2422 or 1 800/800-4000), Enterprise (ⓣ307/632-1907 or 1-800/325-8007), and Hertz (ⓣ307/634-2131 or 1-800/654-3131) are based at the airport; two downtown operators with cheaper deals and older cars are Affordable, 701 E Lincolnway (ⓣ307/634-5666 or 1-800/711-1564) and Price King, 1919 Westland Rd (ⓣ307/638-0688).

Internet access The Laramie County Public Library, 2800 Central Ave (Mon–Thurs 9am–6pm, Fri 10am–7pm, Sat 10am–4pm; free).

Laundry Sparkling Brites, 912 E Lincolnway (daily 7am–9pm; ⓣ307/635-6881); Lady Saver, 117 W 5th St (daily 7am–10pm; ⓣ307/632-2292).

Medical Center United Medical Center, 214 E 23rd St (ⓣ307/634-2273) has 24hr emergency care.

Outdoor wear Sierra Trading Post, 5025 Campstool Rd (daily 9am–6pm; ⓣ307/775-8050, ⓦwww.sierratradingpost.com), is an outlet retailer with discount deals on everything from ski clothing to hiking boots.

Pharmacy Walgreen's, cnr E Lincolnway and Converse Ave, is open 24hr.

Police 2020 Capitol Ave (ⓣ307/637-6525); emergencies ⓣ911.

Post office 2120 Capitol Ave (Mon–Fri 7.30am–5.30pm).

Sports equipment Gart Sports, 1400 Dell Range Blvd in Frontier Mall (Mon–Sat 9am–9pm, Sun 10am–6pm; ⓣ307/632-0712).

Supermarket Safeway, 2550 Pioneer Ave (Mon–Sat 6am–11pm, Sun 7am–10pm; no in-store pharmacy).

Taxi A-A Taxi (ⓣ307/634-6020); Checker Cab (ⓣ307/635-5555); Yellow Cab (ⓣ307/633-3333).

Western and cowboy gear Cheyenne Custom Cowboy, 216 W 17th St (Mon–Fri 8am–5.30pm, Sat 8am–4pm; ⓦwww.cowboyleather.com), has custom-made saddles, spurs, chaps, holsters, and other top-quality cowboy paraphernalia.

West to Laramie

The fifty-mile drive west from Cheyenne to Laramie is quickest via I-80, but **Hwy-210** (Happy Jack Rd), which runs parallel and just to the north, is worth taking for the better scenery. The highway undulates across familiar Wyoming grasslands and slices through plains studded with bizarrely shaped boulders and outcrops. Twenty-two miles before Laramie, the twin reservoirs at **Curt Gowdy State Park** (day-use fee $5, tent sites $9; ⓣ307/632-7946) appear on the south side of the highway. For **campers**, this may be the moment to decide whether to push on to a shadeless site in Laramie, or to spend the night in a clean, comfortable lakeside spot instead. During the day, the park is primarily a recreation spot for anglers and boating and water-skiing enthusiasts (no swimming allowed). Three of Wyoming's most impressive **ranch-style B&Bs** are also perched just off Hwy-210, all within a few miles of Curt Gowdy State Park: *Windy Hills Guest House*, 393 Happy Jack Rd (Ⓣ307/632-6423 or 1-877/946-3944, Ⓦwww.windyhillswyo.com; ❻), has two separate two-bedroom guesthouses as well as two suites in the main ranch house; *A. Drummond's Ranch*, 399 Happy Jack Rd (Ⓣ & Ⓕ307/634-6042; ❻), is set on a 120-acre property and has rooms with hot tubs and fireplaces; *Bit-O-Wyo*, 470 Happy Jack Rd (Ⓣ307/638-8340, www.bitowyo.com; May-Sept; ❺), offers six guestrooms in a log ranch house, and also stages Country and Western-themed dinner shows (mid-June until mid-Aug Fri & Sat only; $25).

Vedauwoo Recreation Area

The Arapaho word vedauwoo (pronounced vee-dah-voo) means "earthborn," and neatly describes the unique granite formations that mark this recreation and climbing area fifteen miles east of Laramie. Once a sacred site for young indigenous men seeking visions and enlightenment, the **Vedauwoo Recreation Area** now draws people who want to view the piled up mushroomed rock formations, hike around them, picnic beside them or just ride mountain bikes on the area trails. **Climbers** have the chance to master the rocks with some easy rock-scrambling, crack-climbing, or more technical assaults on faces which are dotted with worn knobs and hand-holds and some permanent bolts; the difficulty level varies from 5.0 to 5.14 and the highest formations rise to five hundred feet. Beginning just inside the pay-entrance to Vedauwoo is a trailhead which leads to the much-visited **Turtle Rock loop trail** (2.8 miles), allowing a circumnavigation of the area's landmark rock feature. Dispersed (free) **camping** is allowed, but there is a day-use fee of $3 to enter the recreation area and a fee of $7 to camp at one of the eleven USFS sites (open May–Sept only). To reach Vedauwoo from Happy Jack Road, turn south onto unsealed CO-700.

Laramie

The unassuming 27,000-strong college town of **LARAMIE** at first glance seems typical of rural Wyoming – a railroad hub beset by grassy plains and dusty winds. In fact, the biggest obstacle to enjoying a stop here is that it takes a couple of days to get any sort of feel for the place – less than ideal for people high-tailing it through town. A drive-through visit or an overnight stop reveals a rather barren town center, alleviated to some extent by the leafy university precinct. A stay of a couple of days may allow the chance to get elbow-to-elbow with fans at a university football game, or take in a little of the musical and theatrical talent regularly on show.

The town's name belongs to one **Jacques LaRamie**, a French fur-trapper who apparently fell foul of a group of Shoshone people and was killed in the early 1820s, and is not otherwise famous for anything else. The development of the town through the nineteenth century followed a familiar pattern. The earliest settlement on this site was Fort Sanders, established in 1866 to protect wagon trains; the arrival of the Union Pacific railroad two years later saw a population of five thousand sprout up virtually overnight, and it took another two or three years for an emerging civic body to weed out or kill off the worst

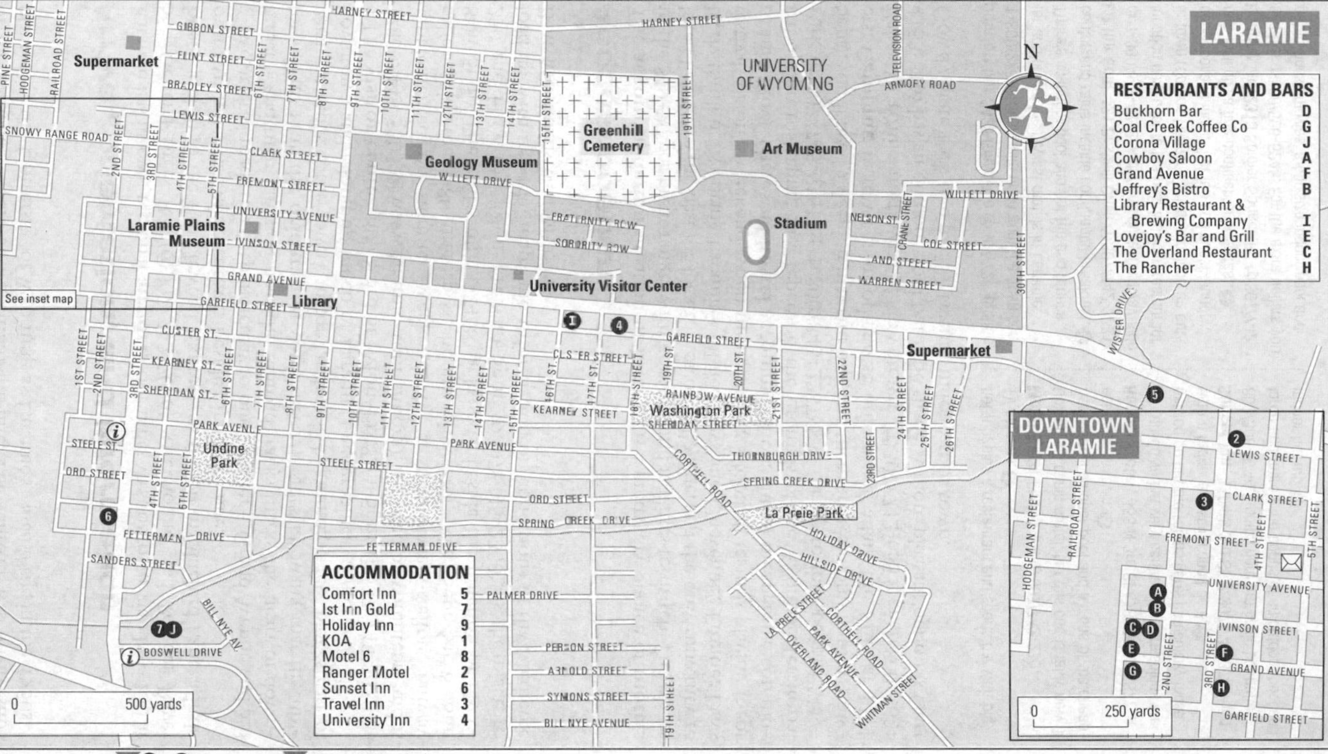
LARAMIE
RESTAURANTS AND BARS
Buckhorn Bar D
Coal Creek Coffee Co G
Corona Village J
Cowboy Saloon A
Grand Avenue F
Jeffrey's Bistro B
Library Restaurant & Brewing Company I
Lovejoy's Bar and Grill E
The Overland Restaurant C
The Rancher H
ACCOMMODATION
Comfort Inn 5
Ist Inn Gold 7
Holiday Inn 9
KOA 1
Motel 6 8
Ranger Motel 2
Sunset Inn 6
Travel Inn 3
University Inn 4
DOWNTOWN LARAMIE
1 (1 mile)
Wyoming Terratorial Park (1 milo)
8 & 9 (1/2 mile)
Cheyenne (50 miles)
See inset map
Supermarket
Laramie Plains Museum
Library
Geology Museum
Greenhill Cemetery
UNIVERSITY OF WYOMING
Art Museum
Stadium
University Visitor Center
Undine Park
Washington Park
La Preie Park
0 500 yards
0 250 yards
N

of the gambling rabble and gunmen-for-hire. The railroad was finally supplanted by the University of Wyoming as Laramie's *raison d'etre* in the 1950s.

Arrival, orientation, and information

Laramie has its own regional **airport**, four miles west of town via Hwy-130 at 555 General Brees Rd (ⓣ307/742-7006). Greyhound and Powder River **buses** pull in to the Tumbleweed Express gas station in Bluebird Lane, a little over two miles east of downtown beside Grand Avenue.

Two arterial roads run perpendicular to one another – Grand Avenue and 3rd Street – and their junction near the railroad tracks marks the heart of downtown. This is all the **orientation** you'll need, besides knowing that the university campus is the town's major landmark, beginning a few blocks east of downtown and taking up much of Laramie's geographical center.

The **visitor center**, 800 S 3rd St (Mon–Fri 8am–5pm; ⓣ307/745-7339 or 1-800/445-5303, ⓦwww.laramie-tourism.org), is staffed by volunteers and is supplemented on summer weekends by a small, bright-yellow railway caboose by the I-80 underpass, beside Hwy-287 (May–Sept Sat & Sun 8am–5pm). The USFS office, 2468 Jackson St beside the junction of Hwy-230 and Hwy-130 (Mon–Fri 8am-5pm; ⓣ307/745-2300), is the place to load up with free trail maps and information on conditions in the Medicine Bow Mountains west of town.

Accommodation

The **accommodation** situation in Laramie is a pretty dry choice of **motels** in the $40–90 per night range, with comfort and facilities to match. The places listed below are the best for location or overall value, and the only time they're likely to fill up is during Laramie's Jubilee Days and Cheyenne's Frontier Days festivals or on a weekend when the university's football team is playing (Sept to mid-Nov). There's no **hostel** accommodation, but an inexpensive communal option is sleeping in a tepee on the grounds of the Wyoming Territorial Park (ⓣ307/745-6161 or 1-800/845-2287; $30 for up to four people; May–Sept); you'll need a sleeping mat and bag, and there are restrooms but no showers. **Camping** in town is an otherwise uninspiring affair; the *KOA* at 1171 Baker St a mile northwest of downtown (ⓣ307/742-6553 or 1-800/562-4153; $16) has an outdoor pool but little shade. A more pleasant option is Curt Gowdy State Park (see p.359), twenty miles east of town.

Comfort Inn 3420 Grand Ave ⓣ307/721-8856 or 1-800/228-5150. A mile or so from the town center and one of the newest motels in Laramie. There's an indoor pool and hot tub and fitness center, and rates include continental breakfast. ❹

Ist Inn Gold 421 Boswell Drive ⓣ307/742-3721 or 1-800/642-4212. A dry and dusty highway-side location next-door to the best Mexican restaurant in town (*Corona Village*). Facilities include an outdoor pool and indoor hot tub and guest laundry; rate includes a fine continental breakfast. ❹

Holiday Inn 2313 Soldier Springs Rd ⓣ307/742-6611 or 1-800/526-5245. For the extra dollars you get in-house movies, a fair-size indoor pool and hot tub, plus a restaurant and sports bar with big TV screens. ❺

Motel 6 621 Plaza Lane ⓣ307/742-2307. Ubiquitous chain motel, but this one is fairly new, it has a small outdoor pool and it's one of the cheapest deals in town. ❸

Ranger Motel, 453 N 3rd St ⓣ307/742-6677. A bit run-down but very central; the furnishings are getting on but the rooms here, particularly those with a fridge, are still a good deal. ❸

Sunset Inn, 1104 S 3rd St ⓣ307/742-3741 or 1-800/308-3744. Rooms here are basic but quite large and there's the bonus of an outdoor pool and indoor hot tub. ❹

Travel Inn, 262 N 3rd St ☎307/745-4853 or 1-800/227-5430. Standard motel accommodation, but there's an outdoor pool and a basic continental breakfast is included. ❸

University Inn, 1720 Grand Ave ☎307/721-8855 or 1-800/869-9466. A nice leafy spot across from the university; the small, rather dark rooms all have fridge and TV. ❹

The town

At first glance, downtown Laramie feels slightly ramshackle and neglected, but this is because its nineteenth-century buildings have simply been preserved, without undergoing any sort of self-conscious Old West makeover. Perhaps that's because Laramie is a college town first and foremost, and behind downtown's Victorian facades lurk not souvenir shops but record stores, vegetarian cafés and secondhand bookshops. Helpful staff at the **university visitor center**, 1408 Ivinson Ave (Mon–Fri 8am–5pm; ☎307/766-4075), can tell you about current exhibits at the free university museums. The best is the **Geological Museum** (Mon–Fri 8am–5pm), home to some marvellous fossilized dinos, including one of only five apatosaurus (brontosaurus) skeletons displayed anywhere, the most complete specimen of allosaurus ever found, and a collection of fifty-million-year-old freshwater fossil fish. The **Art Museum** (summer Mon–Fri 10am–7pm, Sat 10am–5pm, Sun noon–5pm; rest of year Mon–Sat 10am–5pm) has nine galleries housing a series of changing exhibits throughout the year. The boisterous War Memorial Stadium on campus is where the University of Wyoming **football** team, the Cowboys, play their fall season. With no professional sports team to worship, the students and residents of Laramie vent their collective spleen in support of "the Pokes," as they're affectionately known (☎307/766-4850 or 1-800/922-9461, ⓦwww.wyomingathletics.com).

Besides campus area activities, Laramie's other notable sights are a trio of museums. The two biggest, the **Laramie Plains Museum** and **Wyoming Territorial Park** (see below for both), are must-sees for all visitors, while the third – the **Wyoming Children's Museum and Nature Center** – is strictly for the kids. Located at 412 S 2nd St (Tues–Fri 9am–5pm, Sat 10am–4pm; $2), it's a hands-on experience with gold panning, a crawl-through beaver lodge, and some live reptiles and turtles.

The biggest event of the summer is **Laramie Jubilee Days** (information and tickets ☎307/745-7339 or 1-800/445-5303), held over twelve days beginning on the Fourth of July. It follows the pattern of Cheyenne Frontier Days (see p.357) – albeit on a smaller scale – with rodeos, a carnival, country bands and square dances, barbecues and pancake breakfasts. The fireworks show is allegedly the biggest in Wyoming.

Laramie Plains Museum

The mansion which houses the **Laramie Plains Museum**, 603 Ivinson Ave (Mon–Sat 9am–6pm, Sun 1–4pm; tours $4), was built in 1892 by Laramie's most revered business, banking, and civic identity, **Edward Ivinson**. Having established his fortune as a timber-broker supplying railroad ties to the Union Pacific, Ivinson opened a bank in 1871 and then served for several years as Laramie's mayor – also making an unsuccessful run at becoming governor of Wyoming in 1892. His impressive Victorian stone mansion was deeded to an Episcopal missionary society in 1921 and it was run as a girl's school until 1958; the restored schoolhouse in the mansion's grounds is a feature of the hour-long tour. Since being saved from rats and squatters in the mid-1970s, the house has been partially rebuilt and decked out with superb period furnishings, crockery, century-old kitchen appliances – even the Ivinsons' fiftieth anniversary formal dress – and today provides a fascinating glimpse into Laramie's past.

Wyoming Territorial Prison and Old West Park

The centerpiece of the ambitious **Wyoming Territorial Prison and Old West Park**, west of town at 975 Snowy Range Rd (May–Sept daily 10am–6pm; ⓣ307/745-6161 or 1-800/845-2287; $6), is the old **prison** itself. Built in 1869, it was officially a "Territorial" prison because Wyoming did not achieve statehood until 1890. A touch overrestored, it now holds displays on the Old West and Wyoming's early women activists, as well as rooms that depict aspects of prison life. One not to be missed is the old dentist's office, complete with pedal-powered drill and a macabre box of silver teeth, while the original warden's office still looks suitably austere. Lining two of the stone walls are huge mugshots of ex-convicts, among them Butch Cassidy, who was incarcerated here for cattle-rustling (see box on p.310).

Besides the prison, the top attraction here is the **National U.S. Marshals Museum**, celebrating the exploits of the world's oldest federal law enforcement agency (1879) with a display of standard-issue firearms, old "Wanted" posters and even film clips of actors such as Ronald Reagan and John Wayne bringing the role of the U.S. Marshal to life. Also calling the park home is the **Horse Barn Dinner Theater** (June–Aug Wed–Sat 6–9pm; reservations required; $30), whose ensemble cast includes a mix of seasoned performers and talented local drama students and musicians.

Eating, drinking and nightlife

There's no sign of fine dining or Continental cuisine in Laramie, but you can **eat** well without spending a fortune thanks to the presence of thousands of hungry, cash-strapped students. The **drinking and nightlife** situation is totally dependent upon what the students are up to; when school is out the bars might as well be too, but during semester a slew of aspiring young musicians keep the evening venues rocking.

Restaurants

Coal Creek Coffee Co 110 Grand Ave. Laramie's best student coffee hangout, with fresh brews, excellent muffins, bagels, and light lunches, plus books and board games lying about. Mon–Fri 6am–10pm, Sat–Sun 6.30am–10pm.

Corona Village 421 Boswell Drive ⓣ307/721-0167. The finest of a handful of Mexican places in town; a bowl of *albondigas* soup, made with meatballs and vegetables, is a tasty filler at $4. Entrees are all in the $7–10 range – go for a chimichanga del mar, packed with seafood and veggies. Mon–Sat for lunch and dinner.

Grand Avenue 301 Grand Ave ⓣ307/721-2909. A cheery café serving pizza, pasta, soups, and salads. A large pizza loaded up with spicy Cajun chicken and green chilis goes for $15; salads are all $5–6, and large pasta entrees around $9. Tues–Sat 11am–9pm.

Jeffrey's Bistro 123 Ivinson Ave ⓣ307/742-7046. Great for vegetarian choices, including lasagna as well as salad and sandwich combos (entrees $6–10), and there are tasty desserts and pastries available at *Sara's Bakery* next door. Mon–Sat 11am–9pm; bakery Mon–Sat 7am–6pm.

Lovejoy's Bar and Grill 101 Grand Ave ⓣ307/745-0141. The big burgers, sandwiches, and specials like chicken pot pie and "Mom's Meatloaf" qualify *Lovejoy's* as an All-American eatery. The menu, though, still has its surprises, including fire-roasted chicken penne and portobello mushroom ravioli. Entrees $7–12; open daily for lunch and dinner.

The Overland Restaurant 100 Ivinson Ave ⓣ307/721-2800. A great all-day diner, with full ranch breakfasts and fresh cinnamon rolls to kick-start the day, a venison burger or Southwest chicken wrap ($6) for lunch and dinner deals, including soup or salad, like pork medallions and catfish creole (dinner entrees $8–16). Open daily.

The Rancher 309 S 3rd St ⓣ307/742-3141. This family feedbag is heaven for carnivores, with chicken fried steak ($8), huge half-pound beef burgers ($5–6), prime-rib and baby-back ribs the pick of the menu. Entrees $8–18; open daily for lunch and dinner.

Bars and nightclubs

Buckhorn Bar 114 Ivinson Ave ☎307/742-3554. The most reliable place to go for drinking and shooting pool, the *Buckhorn* also often hosts local college bands. Daily until late.

Cowboy Saloon 108 S 2nd St ☎307/721-3165. This cowboy bar can be a bit hit-or-miss; either you'll get a rollicking Country band and a boisterous crowd, or the place will resemble an empty barn with a forlorn publican in the middle. Hours variable, may be closed when school is out.

Library Restaurant & Brewing Company 1622 Grand Ave. Popular brewpub that's a good spot for a decent beer to go with a huge pub sandwich or burger ($5–7). Daily for lunch and dinner.

Listings

Airlines United Express (☎307/742-5296 or 1-800/241-6522).

Banks Ist Interstate, 221 Ivinson Ave and Community First, cnr 3rd St and Garfield Ave, have 24hr ATMs.

Car rental Avis (☎307/745-7156) and Dollar (☎307/742-8805) are based at the airport, while Enterprise (☎307/721-9876) and Price King (☎307/721-8811) have depots in town.

Hospital Ivinson Memorial Hospital, 255 N 30th St (☎307/742-2141) has 24hr emergency service.

Internet access The Albany County Library (Mon–Fri 9am–7pm, Sat 9am–5pm; ☎307/745-3365; free).

Laundry Spic & Span, 272 N 4th St (daily 7.30am–9pm).

Police Laramie Police Department, 620 Plaza Court (☎307/721-5313).

Post office 152 N 5th St (Mon–Fri 8am–5pm, Sat 9am–noon).

Supermarket Safeway in Gateway Plaza, 3rd St (daily 6am–11pm); Albertson's, Grand Ave and 30th St (24hr; pharmacy Mon–Fri 8am–7pm, Sat 9am–5pm).

Taxi Laramie Cab (☎307/745-8294).

The Medicine Bow Mountains

Just outside Laramie, **Hwy-130** (the Snowy Range Scenic Byway) dips into the huge wind-gouged bowl of Big Hollow and starts the steep climb up the **MEDICINE BOW MOUNTAINS**, one of Wyoming's most picturesque drives. These mountains are known as the Snowy Range for the year-round snowfields that nestle just below the peaks and for the outcrops of quartzite that glisten like snow throughout the summer. **Elevations** along this scenic byway range from 8100ft to 10,847ft over the 72-mile drive between Laramie in the east and Saratoga to the west. Overlooks at the top of the Snowy Range Pass (closed in winter) present picturesque alpine lakes and meadows, tight against steep mountain faces, and at lower levels there are plenty of good places to hike or pitch a tent. If your goal is further west of these mountains, you can bypass them altogether by sticking to I-80 towards Rawlins – indeed you have to go via I-80 in winter, as Hwy-130 will most likely be closed.

The name Medicine Bow derives from the practice of several Native American tribes, who would cut prized mountain mahogany from this region to make into fine **hunting bows**. The gatherings became more formalized until they were accompanied by ceremonies, which were explained to white people as "making medicine."

Centennial and around

From Laramie, the first point at which you can collect **information** on exploring the mountains is the USFS Centennial Visitor Center (May–Sept Tues–Sun 9am–4pm; ☎307/742-6023), on the north side of the highway five miles west of the tiny hamlet of **Centennial**. Either pick up the free *Snowy Range Trails* map with a good overview of the area's main trails, campgrounds and picnic areas, or the much more detailed USFS Medicine Bow National

Forest topographical map ($4) if you're planning on doing some backcountry exploring. If you'd like a roof over your head, you can **stay** in Centennial at the basic *Friendly Motel* (ⓣ307/742-6033; ❸), the classier *Brooklyn Lodge B&B* (ⓣ307/742-6916; ❻), or at *Snowy Mountain Lodge*, 3474 Hwy-130, seven miles west of Centennial (ⓣ307/742-7669, ⓦwww.snowymountainlodge. com; ❸), which has a range of simple cabins that sleep four-to-eight people. There are also plenty of campgrounds as well as good spots for free dispersed camping in the area (see box, below).

The Sugarloaf Recreation Area is also the place to go hiking; **mountain bikers**, though, have a few multiuse trails near Centennial to choose from. The Little Laramie trailhead, just north of the highway along Sand Lake Road, leads to a series of moderate loop trails, while the Barber Lake trail, accessed from the Green Mountain trailhead about two miles further west, is a challenging five-mile winding descent. You won't want to ride the return leg, so you'll need someone to collect you at Barber Lake.

Sugarloaf Recreation Area

The stark and often chilly beauty of the Snowy Range does not really become apparent until you reach **Sugarloaf Recreation Area**, roughly twenty miles on from Centennial ($3 day-use fee). Here, patches of snow and hard glittering quartzite can be seen clearly, making the peaks high above look especially forbidding. The weather in these alpine climes is notoriously unpredictable, and high-altitude hiking conditions prevail; take it slowly, drink lots of water, have waterproof gear on hand, and head down at the first sign of a storm rolling in. The hike to the top of **Medicine Bow Peak** (12,013ft) is an exhilarating one that rewards you with stunning alpine vistas and views south to Colorado. A six-mile loop takes you from the Lake Marie trailhead past Mirror Lake and Lookout Lake to the summit, from where you can head southwest along the rocky mountain ridge before a steep descent via the Medicine Bow Peak trail back down. The altitude gain is 1600ft and the last mile to the peak is a steep scramble over loose chunks of quartzite, so allow at least three hours for the hike with time to enjoy the view. A good one-way hike starts from the nearby **Lewis Lake trailhead** and heads east via Lost Lake and Telephone Lakes before dropping down to Brooklyn Lake campground (3.5 miles); ideally you need a designated driver to collect you, or alternatively hitch a ride back to your vehicle.

Camping in the Snowy Range

Attractive **camping** spots abound in the Snowy Range, from developed USFS sites to opportunities for free dispersed camping. At the western end of the range, a few miles beyond Lake Marie, is the signed turnoff to Silver Lake, which has a shady trail that circles the shore, as well as one of the best campgrounds (seventeen sites) in the range. Another mile beyond Silver Lake you can turn north onto CO-103 and pick from a number of good spots for free dispersed camping around Twin Lakes – your tent must be no closer than 200ft from any lake or river. Sugarloaf campground, at the recreation area by Libby Lake, is handy for hikers heading up to Medicine Bow Peak, but it's very popular so get in early. Exact dates vary seasonally, but the campgrounds are generally open from June or July until mid-Oct; the overnight cost per site is $10. The USFS office near Centennial (see above), or the Brush Creek Visitor Center, eight miles west of Silver Lake on Hwy-130 (May to mid-Oct Mon–Fri 9am–4pm), can supply a full list of sites, including four campgrounds that are within a mile of the Centennial USFS office.

The other requisite stop along this stretch of the highway is the **Libby Flats observation point**, half a mile west of Sugarloaf Recreation Area. The sweeping valley-forest panorama stretches clear to Colorado (free binoculars on site); there's also a short wildflower trail that attempts to showcase the native alpine flora, but it's a pretty scrappy affair.

Saratoga and around

Twelve miles beyond the western edge of the Medicine Bow Range, sleepy **SARATOGA** is a spa resort known for its healing hot springs. However, while the town is pleasant enough in its own right, cleft prettily in twain by the North Platte River, only a spin doctor could declare it a particularly desirable place to take the waters. Its landmark spa is the public **Hobo Hot Springs** on Walnut Avenue, an large outdoor pool fed by a 114°F spring; however, it's nestled in behind the town's noisy public swimming facility, and with its concrete surrounds does not really measure up to hot springs elsewhere in the Rockies. The only consolation is that it's free and accessible 24 hours a day. There are more hot springs across the river at the ritzy *Saratoga Inn* resort (see "Practicalities" below), but use of these is limited to guests only.

Apart from the springs, the other activities worth considering hereabouts are fly-fishing in the blue-ribbon trout waters in and around town and a stroll around the **Saratoga Museum**, 104 Constitution Ave at the southern edge of town (June–Aug Mon–Fri 1–5pm; free). Taking up the old Union Pacific railyard, the museum contains displays highlighting the area's logging and ranching history, while parked out front are an impressive old boxcar and caboose and an antique sheepherders wagon.

The North Platte River is renowned for excellent wild **trout fishing**, and with few dams anywhere along its course it's much favored by anglers as a "natural" waterway. Check with the USFS office (see below) about which stretches of river are open to the public, as some access points are on private land. Several outfitters in Saratoga run fishing and float trips ($70–120 per day), including Medicine Bow Drifters, 120 E Bridge St (Ⓣ307/326-8002), and Platte Valley Anglers, 112 S 1st St (Ⓣ307/326-5750).

Practicalities

The **chamber of commerce**, 115 W Bridge St (Mon–Fri 9am–5pm; Ⓣ307/326-8855), has an excellent free map of the town, worthwhile if you're here for a day or two. The **USFS office** is at the south entrance to town on Hwy-130 (summer Mon–Fri 7.30am–5pm; winter 7.30am–noon & 1–4.30pm; Ⓣ307/326-5258) and has free maps of trails in the Snowy Range.

Easily the best place to **stay** in Saratoga is the antique-furnished 1893 *Hotel Wolf*, 101 E Bridge Ave (Ⓣ307/326-5525; ❸), whose restaurant has very good grills plus a soup-and-salad bar (burgers $8, entrees around $17). Other central options are the *Sage & Sand Motel*, 311 S 1st St (Ⓣ307/326-8339; ❸), and *Silver Moon Motel*, 412 E Bridge St (Ⓣ307/326-5974; ❸), both of which offer rooms with kitchenettes. To sample Saratoga's finest hot springs, you'll need to fork out for the lodge-style luxury of the *Saratoga Inn*, 601 E Pic Pike Rd (Ⓣ307/326-5261, Ⓦwww.saratogainnresort.com; ❼), which has its own mineral pool and several smaller soaking tubs, as well as tennis, golf, and even a brewery. **Campers** can try *Deer Haven RV Park*, in town at 706 N 1st St (Ⓣ307/326-8746; $8), or head out to Saratoga Lakes, a mile-and-a-half north off Hwy-130; it's a quiet spot but there's no shade or showers (tent sites $7).

For **eating** choices apart from the *Hotel Wolf*, go for the subs, salads, and low-priced lunch specials at *Stumpy's*, 218 N 1st St. *Mom's Kitchen*, 402 S 1st St, is the top spot for breakfast, and *Bubba's Bar-B-Que*, 119 N River St, is a reliable franchise diner for steaks and ribs. The *Rustic Bar*, 124 E Bridge St, is a good spot for a beer and the occasional live band; alternatively, drive to the *Whistle Pig Saloon* near the USFS office at the south edge of town, which also has a sizeable menu of burgers and Mexican standards under $10. There's a Valley Foods **supermarket** beside the *Hacienda Motel* one mile south of the town center (Mon–Sat 7am–9pm; in-store pharmacy Mon–Fri 9am–5.30pm, Sat 10am–noon).

Encampment and Riverside

The tiny twin towns of **ENCAMPMENT** and **RIVERSIDE**, located barely a mile apart and eighteen miles south of Saratoga, were once the main settlements supporting a clutch of copper-mining camps in the shadow of the **Sierra Madre mountain range**. Hunters have long since been the dominant group to visit the area, but efforts to draw tourists interested in ghost towns, logging and mining history, and gorgeous fall foliage are beginning to pan out. A shared visitor **information** center sits on Hwy-70 between the two hamlets, and is staffed by volunteers at variable hours on weekdays during summer only. History buffs should stop in and collect a copy of the free basic sketch-map of area **ghost town** sites; these are dotted over some fifteen miles to the west of Encampment.

The **Grand Encampment Museum**, 807 Barnett Ave (June–Aug Mon–Sat 10am–5pm, Sun 1–5pm; free), is a fascinating traipse back to the turn of the last century, when a sixteen-mile aerial tramway (the world's longest) connected the copper mines to the huge Encampment copper smelter. You can see a small section of the tramway still standing, and among the impressive collection of buildings and exhibits are a well-preserved schoolhouse, a cabin with a brightly colored c.1900 linoleum floor and a fabulous two-story outhouse, built to provide access even under the deepest winter snows.

The stretch of Hwy-70 west of the towns through the Sierra Madres is renowned for the spectacular color of its aspen trees in fall. Anyone with a bent for photography should turn right after about fifteen miles onto CO-801 and drive the two-mile strip known as "**Aspen Alley**" – allegedly the most photographed piece of road in the entire state. It's also worth noting that another

Sierra Madre trails

Trails leading into the Sierra Madre range are less used than those in the Snowy Range because the altitude and scenery are less dramatic; there are also no loop trails among them, so you have to double back. However, the gentle elevations and quiet forest surrounds make for some pleasant walking, and are ideal for **cross-country skiing** too. A popular walk follows the Green Mountain River 2.5 miles to **Green Mountain Falls**; to reach the trailhead drive 5.5 miles west along Hwy-70 and then south on CO-550 for one-and-a-half miles. The **Huston Park Wilderness**, which straddles the Continental Divide just to the south of Hwy-70, takes in elevations up to 10,500 feet and offers greater variety in terrain and flora, with forests of spruce-firs and aspens opening onto alpine bogs higher up. There are a number of access points off unsealed roads west of Encampment; the USFS office in Encampment, 204 W 9th St (May–Oct Mon–Fri 7.30am–noon & 1–4.30pm; ⓣ307/327-5481) has free trail maps and can provide information on USFS campsites and dispersed camping opportunities.

well-maintained county road (#550) cuts south through the lush southern Sierra Madre on a scenic and shady fifty-mile mountain drive to Steamboat Springs (see p.296); #550 branches south from Hwy-70 38 miles west of Encampment/Riverside.

There's not much in the way of amenities to cater to the six hundred people who actually reside in Encampment and Riverside. **Camping** is free for up to three nights at the *City Trailer Park* in Encampment (no address, just follow the signs), while the *Lazy Acres Campground and Motel* (Ⓣ307/327-5968; tent sites $10; ❷) in Riverside has clean facilities and friendly owners. For fancier digs, go for a room at the *Old Depot B&B*, 201 1st St, Riverside (Ⓣ307/327-5277; ❹). The *Bear Trap* in Riverside has an extensive diner menu and hunter-size breakfasts, while the *Mangy Moose* next door is fine for a beer and a burger.

Southwest Wyoming

The long and monotonous drive across southern Wyoming on I-80 – the route also followed by the old train track – holds little to delight the eye. The largest town here, **Rock Springs**, is an unremarkable community 103 miles from the state's western border – and well on the way to the more appealing territory around Utah's Park City. It does, however, serve as a useful pit stop for visits to the **Flaming Gorge National Recreation Area**. Both **Rawlins** and **Fossil Butte National Monument** provide further limited distraction, though truth be told you're best off keeping the pedal firmly pressed down, continuing north toward Yellowstone or west to the mountains of Utah.

Rawlins and around

There would be little reason to stop at the tiny prairie town of **RAWLINS**, a hundred miles west of Laramie, but for one extraordinary sight: the **Wyoming Frontier Prison**, 5th and Walnut (hourly tours 8.30am–5.30pm June–Aug; by reservation only the rest of the year; Ⓣ307/324-4422; $4.25). In service until 1981, this huge, creepy jail with dark, neglected cells, peeling walls, and echoing corridors is as different from Laramie's Wyoming Territorial Park (see p.364) as it is possible to be. While the whole experience is troubling – not least due to the fascinating life stories and anecdotes told with aplomb by the

Flaming Gorge

It took a major controversy in the 1950s to spare the Green and Yampa confluence from submergence by a new dam. **Flaming Gorge**, starting just south of Rock Springs, was not so lucky; the damming of the Green River's Red Canyon in 1964 has turned it into a National Recreation Area, another "splendid recreational playground" for water-sports enthusiasts and anglers.

Ambivalence about its creation can't obscure its continuing beauty, which can be appreciated from various points on the loop drive that circles the canyon. The Gorge itself is an incandescent wall of red rock named by John Wesley Powell and best seen from the Antelope Flat marina-cum-campground on the eastern side just over the Utah border. The other sights of interest are also on the Utah side, including the Red Canyon Visitor Center (summer daily 10am–4pm), with a dramatic overlook and attractive nearby campground (the actual dam is not all that exciting). There are plenty of other campgrounds in the area too; stop in at Flaming Gorge National Recreation Area headquarters, at the junction of Hwy-43 and Hwy-44 (daily 8am–4.30pm; Ⓣ435/784-3445) for further information.

exceptional guides – the darkest moment comes as the gas chamber (in use from 1937 until 1965) is revealed.

Just to the west of town, the Continental Divide briefly splits into two in the **Great Divide Basin**. In theory, rain that falls here remains here, unable to flow towards either ocean – unfortunately virtually none does stay, and the brick-red hell of the **Red Desert** stretches implacably away to the horizon.

Fossil Butte National Monument

Roughly eighty miles northwest of Rock Springs – and reached by turning north from I-80 just west of the "world's largest service station" at Little America – **Fossil Butte National Monument** preserves a fossilized cross-section of the fish population of a fifty-million-year-old lake. From a distance, you can clearly see the relevant pale-limestone strata on the flat-topped Butte itself, but the various trails turn out to show you less than the displays at the **visitor center** (daily: June–Aug 8am–7pm; Sept–May 8am–5pm; ⓣ307/877-4455; free).

Travel details

Flights

There are regular daily United Express flights between Cheyenne and Denver, Colorado.

Buses

Three services daily connect Cheyenne with towns further west along I-80 and also with Denver, Colorado. Approximate travel times are: Laramie (1hr), Rock Springs (4hr 30min), Denver (3hr 20min).

Central and northern Wyoming

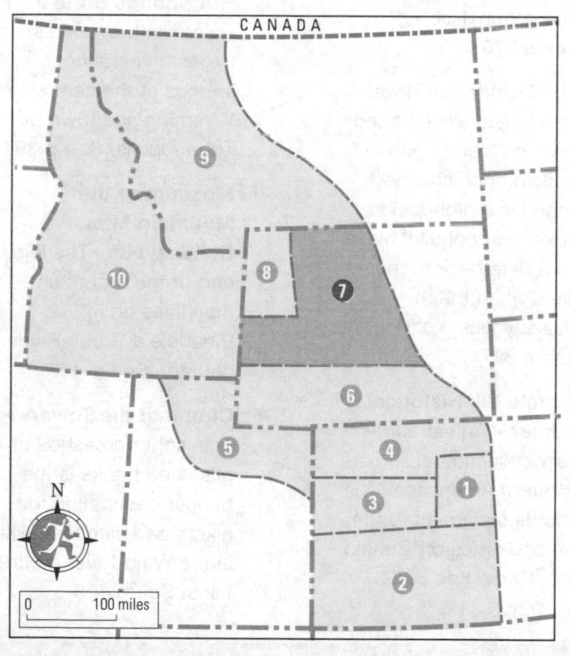

CHAPTER 7

Highlights

- **Devils Tower** – Designated as the country's first national monument in 1906, it took Steven Spielberg's inspired use of it in *Close Encounters of the Third Kind* to make this eerie volcanic outcrop a true national icon. See p.376

- **The Occidental Hotel** – This beautifully restored classic Western pub in Buffalo once changed hands in a high-stakes poker game; bullet holes here date back to the days when Butch Cassidy was a patron. See p.327

- **Buffalo Bill Historical Center** – An extraordinary collection of Western Americana stands testament to the life and times of "Buffalo Bill" Cody. See p.383

- **Wind River Indian Reservation** – Witness the celebratory side of Shoshone or Arapaho culture at a powwow, and visit the gravesites of Chief Washakie and Sacagawea. See p.389

- **Hot Springs State Park** – Soak in the world's largest mineral hot springs at the central Wyoming spa town of Thermopolis. See p.391

- **Museum of the Mountain Man Rendezvous** –The legend of the mountain man lives on in Pinedale's Green River country. See p.403

- **Cirque of the Towers** – This tight horseshoe of glaciated peaks is the banner destination for hikers and climbers alike in the Wind River mountains. See p.405

7

Central and northern Wyoming

For many, following a driving route through **NORTHERN AND CENTRAL WYOMING** is a case of searching out the fastest road to Yellowstone and then leaning on the gas pedal. But even a brief scan of a state map shows up some promising mountainous bulges that, though lacking the global acclaim of the national parks in the far northwest, actually lose little by comparison. Without doubt the highlight of the region is the stunning **Wind River Mountain Range**, widely considered Wyoming's most scenic and challenging backcountry area for hiking, climbing, and angling – bar none. Flanked by a trio of friendly towns in **Lander**, **Dubois**, and **Pinedale**, the Wind Rivers are also home to large populations of Shoshone and Arapaho people, who have lived in central Wyoming for many hundreds of years.

Perhaps the most appealing aspect of travel through this region is the sheer variety of cultures and communities you come across, in concert with the rapidly changing nature of the landscape itself. From the greenly forested **Bighorn Mountains** to the grassy flatlands and dry, windy buttes of the **Wind River Indian Reservation**, the terrain does not stay the same for long. And most towns hereabouts have managed to shape an identity that takes a little from both the prairie-range cowboy culture of southern Wyoming and the wild embrace between tourism and nature that defines the communities around Yellowstone and the Grand Tetons. East of the Bighorns the town of **Buffalo** could hardly be more relaxed and pleasant, while the hot springs of **Thermopolis** literally add an effervescence that belies the somewhat staid

Accommodation price codes

All accommodation prices in this book have been coded using the symbols below. For **hotels**, **motels**, and **B&Bs**, rates are given for the least expensive double room in each establishment. Seasonal variations are indicated where appropriate, and for all ski resorts. For **hostels**, the actual price per bed is given; for **camping**, the cost per site is given. For a full explanation see p.30 in Basics.

❶ up to $30	❹ $60–80	❼ $130–180
❷ $30–45	❺ $80–100	❽ $180–240
❸ $45–60	❻ $100–130	❾ over $240

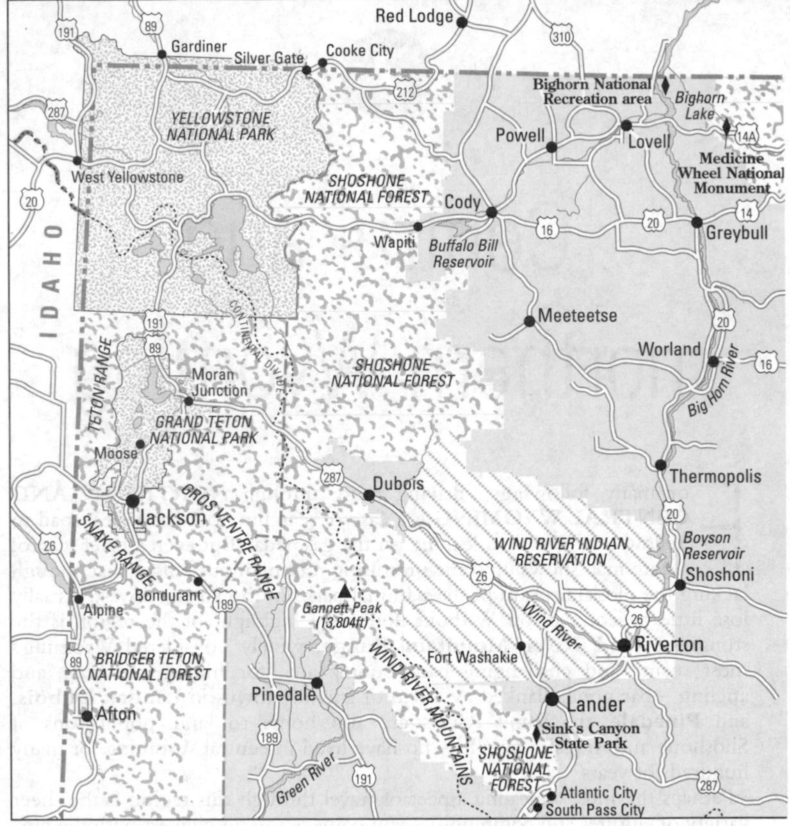

outlook of its residents. Even the town of **Cody**, whose existence should be defined simply by its role as the eastern gateway for visitors to Yellowstone, wears the multihued stamp of the famous Buffalo Bill, an Old West legend who was part horseman, part showman, and all entrepreneur.

Bighorn country

Most of central Wyoming flattens out into a dry and windy landscape dotted with tiny towns and mining operations, and does not warrant any of your attention; indeed, you have to drive all the way north to the charming town of **Buffalo** before you're within shouting distance of some proper hills and forests once more. It's here that the massive and heavily wooded **Bighorn Mountains** soar abruptly from the plains to over 9000ft, before subsiding on the western side into the wide expanse of the **Bighorn Basin**.

Two scenic byways cut across the northern Bighorns on the route west towards Yellowstone National Park: US-14 (Bighorn Scenic Byway) and US-14A (Medicine Wheel Passage Scenic Byway) are both accessed from I-90

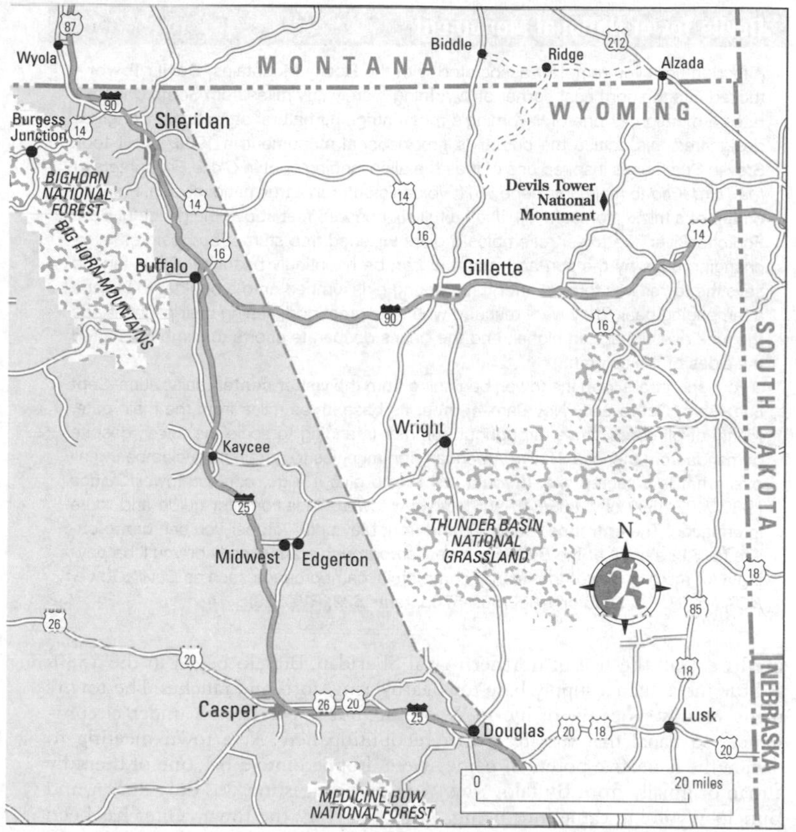

some thirteen miles north of the unremarkable town of Sheridan. At the point where the road splits at Burgess Junction, your options are to turn south with US-14 and follow the straightest route on to Cody, or to take the slightly longer journey via US-14A, with more spectacular sights on the western side of the range. This alternate highway edges its way up Medicine Mountain, on whose windswept western peak the mysterious **Medicine Wheel** – the largest such stone monument still intact – stands protected behind a wire fence.

The route down the western side of this scenic byway, which also crosses the steep river canyon of **Bighorn Canyon National Recreation Area**, has gradients of ten to twenty percent and three massive runaway truck ramps. Tight hairpin bends keep the driver's eyes off the magnificent overlooks, but the best view comes near the bottom, when the road lets you out into the Bighorn Basin. This ultraflat, sparsely vegetated valley, walled in by mighty mountains on three sides and ragged foothills to the north, can strike you as a land that time forgot.

Buffalo

Of the two eastern gateway towns to the Bighorns, **BUFFALO** (pop. 3700) – snuggled amongst the range's southeastern foothills – is by far the more appeal-

Devils Tower National Monument

Although not even remotely associated with the Rocky Mountains, **Devils Tower** – tucked into the northeast corner of Wyoming, barely fifty miles from South Dakota – rates a mention as one of Wyoming's most intriguing natural attractions. Congress designated this edifice the country's first national monument in 1906, but it took Steven Spielberg's inspired use of it as the alien landing spot in *Close Encounters of the Third Kind* to make this eerie 867ft volcanic outcrop a true national icon. Plonked on top of a thickly forested hill, itself a full six hundred feet above the peaceful Belle Fourche River, the tower resembles a giant wizened tree stump; but, painted ever-changing hues by the sun and moon, it can be hauntingly beautiful. Sioux legend says the tower was formed after three young girls jumped onto a boulder to escape a rampaging bear. They were rescued when the great god, seeing their plight, made the rock rise higher and higher, and the bear's desperate efforts to climb up scored the sides of the column.

Four short trails loop the tower, beginning from the **visitor center** (daily: June–Sept 8am–8pm, Oct to early Nov 9am–4pm) at its base, three miles from the main gate. Plenty of **climbers** arrive throughout summer intending to scale the tower, despite demands from the local Native American communities to refrain from clambering all over what is a sacred site. If you'd still like to give it a go, contact Tower Guides (ⓣ307/467-5589 or 1-888/345-9061, ⓦwww.towerguides.com) for guide and route information. The **entrance fee** is $8, and from May until October you can **camp** on-site for $12 a night at the *Belle Fourche Campground* – arrive early or you'll be paying a lot more at one of the nearby commercial campgrounds such as *Devil's Tower KOA* (ⓣ307/467-5395 or 1-800/562-5785; tents $22, RVs $28).

ing base. Half the size of northern rival Sheridan, Buffalo began in the 1880s as little more than a supply base for nearby army forts and ranches. The town's name sounds evocative of life in Wyoming, but it was chosen under circumstances so banal that they're worth recounting here. At a town meeting to decide the issue, five potential names were dropped into a hat, one of them by a man originally from Buffalo, New York. His suggestion was duly drawn, and Buffalo, Wyoming came into being. In recent years, the town center has been spruced up in honor of the small number of tourists who do make it to this part of the state. Happily, Buffalo still gets along at a relaxed place, and remains surprisingly unaffected by the bustle of the nearby I-90/I-25 intersection.

Arrival, information, and accommodation

Powder River **buses** stop at Just Gone Fishing, at the corner of Fort (Hwy-16) and Spruce streets, about a mile west of downtown. Pick up information from the **visitor center**, 55 N Main St (mid-May to mid-Sept Mon–Fri 8am–6pm, Sat & Sun 10am–6pm; rest of year Mon–Fri 8am–5pm; ⓣ307/684-5544 or 1-800/227-5122, ⓦwww.buffalowyoming.org). For all information and maps for hiking, cross-country skiing and even snowmobiling in the Bighorns, check with the **USFS office** at 1425 Fort St (Mon–Fri 8am–4.30pm, summer also Sat 8am–4.30pm; ⓣ307/684-1100).

The only time you'll need to make **accommodation** reservations in town is during the main hunting season (Oct–Nov), though booking ahead in June–August is a good idea if you've got your heart set on a particular establishment. In addition to the in-town places reviewed below, you can find a series of mid-range chain motels (❹) east of town along Hwy-16. There's not too much between Buffalo's **campgrounds** – also dotted along Hwy-16 east of town – in terms of cost and facilities (tent sites $14–16, RVs $21–23). *Indian*

Campground (☎307/684-9601) is closest to town, just west of the I-25 underpass; a *KOA* (☎307/684-5423 or 1-800/562-5403) and *Deer Park* (☎307/684-5722 or 1-800/222-9960) are about a mile further east. Facilities at each include pool, laundry, and small general store; open roughly April–Oct.

Arrowhead Motel 749 Fort St (Hwy-16 W) ☎307/684-9453 or 1-800/824-1719. Rooms are small and a bit dreary, but they're cheap and clean and some have kitchenettes. ❷

Big Horn Motel 209 N Main St ☎307/684-7822 or 1-800/936-7822. Friendly and well-managed motel that's also one of the most central on the main drag. The recently remodeled rooms feature queen-size beds. ❹

Blue Gables Motel 662 N Main St ☎307/684-2574 or 1-800/684-2574. This motel, a half-mile north of the town center, features pleasant individual log cabins, some with fridge and/or microwave; there's an outdoor pool as well. ❸

Clear Creek Bed & Breakfast 330 S Main St ☎307/684-2317 or 1-888/865-6789, ⓦwww.clearcreekbb.com. This historic B&B, built in 1883 and located three blocks south of the downtown district, has four homey guestrooms (two with private bath), a living area with TV and stereo, and a wide, wrapround veranda that is ideal for whiling the afternoon away. ❹

Mansion House Motel 313 N Main St ☎307/684-2218 or 1-888/455-9202. Rooms in the elegant *Mansion House* are large and feature home-style furnishings like Native American prints and cowboy bits-and-pieces; they represent excellent value, especially in comparison with the cheaper motel units (❸) across the parking lot, which are less attractive although perfectly adequate. There's an indoor hot tub and a basic breakfast of juice, coffee, and muffins is included in the rate. ❹

Mountain View Motel and Campground 585 Fort St (Hwy-16 W) ☎307/684-2881. Tidy, faux log-interior cabins and tent sites ($15) in a quiet, shady area. Cabins have queen beds and private bath (larger family units also have kitchenettes), while communal facilities for campers include clean showers and laundry plus picnic tables. ❸

Z-Bar Motel 626 Fort St (Hwy-16 W) ☎307/684-5535 or 1-888/313-1227. These tidy log cabins are nestled in a shady spot a half-mile west of downtown. Each has either a king or queen bed and a fridge, and some have kitchenettes. Ask for one of the larger cabins, most of which also have a proper bathtub and come at no extra charge. ❸

The Town

A brief perambulation about Main Street will take you past a few of the town's most venerable buildings, but besides some pleasant cafés and such, the only two places where you might usefully while away some time indoors are a museum and a grand old pub. Summer visitors, however, would do well to extend their stroll beyond Main Street and mosey over to the large and free public outdoor **swimming pool** in Washington Park at the southwest end of town (summer daily 11am–6pm).

Downtown's major landmark is the wonderful **Occidental Hotel**, whose plain saloon-storefront facade gives little hint of the ambitious restoration being carried out within. The hotel – which allegedly once changed hands in a high-stakes poker game – was in continuous operation from 1910 until 1975, but then sat dormant until 1997, when new owners arrived to save the building from rack and ruin. Today the *Occidental*'s saloon boasts a replica ornate copper ceiling and an original 1894 "bank billiards" table (no pockets). The lobby is redolent of the hotel's 1930s heyday, and much of the ground floor functions as an unofficial town **museum** (May–Sept Mon–Sat 10am–5pm; ring doorbell for admittance; ☎307/684-8844 for appointment Oct–April; $2), exhibiting pieces of period furniture as well as photos depicting life in Buffalo during the late nineteenth century.

A couple of blocks north, the **Jim Gatchell Museum**, 100 Fort St (June–Aug daily 9am–7pm; May, Sept & Oct Mon–Fri 9am–5pm; $2), is stacked full of Old West curiosities pertaining to soldiers, ranchers, and Native Americans. The collection is such an eclectic jumble that highlights depend

Johnson County Cattle War

Without doubt the most polarizing events in Johnson County were the so-called **cattle wars** that pitted big cattle barons against small independent graziers in a tussle for control of rich prairie lands. The big ranchers operated as a sort of collective, running vast herds across thousands of acres to which they claimed exclusive grazing rights. A number of smaller graziers begged to differ, especially as the winter of 1886–87 went from bad to worse, and they took to poaching cattle from the bigger branded herds. The situation escalated and in early 1892 the cattle barons got together and hired fifty **Texas Rangers** to sort out the homesteaders once and for all. The first major confrontation took place at the Kaycee Ranch, fifty miles south of Buffalo, where small-time cattlemen Nate Champion and Nick Ray were captured and hanged; word spread quickly among the other homesteaders, who formed an ad hoc army of almost four hundred men to go after the Texans. The hired guns took refuge at the T.A. Ranch near Buffalo, where they held out for three days, swearing to die on their feet with rifles blazing. Troops of the 6th US Cavalry finally rode in on April 13 and broke the seige; there was no last-ditch battle and none of the participants ever stood trial, but almost every citizen chose a side, and the resulting community divide remained for several generations.

entirely on your own predilections; there's plenty by way of Native American oddments, including some attractive moccasins of Shoshone and Arapaho design, while the two c.1900 cash registers and an even older safe are worth a close up look as well. And you may find it difficult to view the exhibit of "Frontier Hide Clothing" without coveting a buffalo coat or a natty pair of blond angora chaps. There's also a handy diorama which sets the scene of the Johnson County Cattle War (see box above).

Fort Phil Kearney

The remains of **Fort Phil Kearney**, one of the bloodiest of the Western army forts, stand seventeen miles north of Buffalo, off I-90, on Hwy-193. Only operative from 1866 to 1868, it was repeatedly stormed by Sioux, Apache, and Cheyenne, and destroyed by jubilant Sioux when finally abandoned in 1868. A **museum** beside the site of the partially rebuilt fort (mid-May to Sept daily 8am–6pm; April to mid-May & Oct–Nov Wed–Sun noon–4pm; $2) tells the story of the 1866 **Fetterman Massacre**, when Captain William Fetterman (who bragged that with eighty men he could whip any amount of Indians in battle) ignored strict orders and was lured into the path of over a thousand Sioux warriors. Fetterman and his eighty soldiers were killed, the first US Army defeat ever to leave no survivors.

Eating and drinking

Far and away the best place for a **drink** is the *Occidental Hotel* (see overleaf); bar-staff will point out bullet-holes in the walls and ceiling from the days when outlaw Butch Cassidy (see p.310) was an occasional patron. For **eating**, try the *Sagewood Cafe*, 15 N Main St (Mon–Sat 11am–3pm), which has fine soups, sandwiches, and fresh-baked brownies; the *Stagecoach Inn*, 845 Fort St, has inexpensive all-you-can-eat deals, including a $7 buffet lunch and $2 pancake breakfast. At the top end is the *Winchester Steakhouse*, 117 Hwy-16 E (☎307/684-8636; dinner only Mon–Sat), busy serving excellent prime rib and seafood at fairly expensive prices. If camping, you can stock up at the IGA **supermarket**, three blocks west of downtown along Hwy-16 W (daily 7am–9pm).

The Bighorn mountains

Besides being the more attractive of the towns that border the mountains, Buffalo is also handiest to the best hiking and camping in the Bighorn National Forest. Occupying much of the central Bighorn range is the 295-square-mile **Cloud Peak Wilderness** – a forested playground for those who take the time to do some hiking or angling. For winter visitors there are groomed trails ideal for **cross-country skiing** too, notably around Willow Park and Meadowlark Lake, about ten miles east of Tensleep on US-16, and also **Sibley Lake** just east of Burgess Junction on US-14.

Bighorn Canyon National Recreation Area

Before US-14A gets to Lovell, Hwy-37 turns north to the **Bighorn Canyon National Recreation Area** (fee $5 per vehicle; camping is free), an unexpected red-rock wilderness straddling the border between Wyoming and Montana. No road runs the full length of the canyon, which since being flooded by the 525ft Yellowtail Dam (only accessible from Montana) has become primarily the preserve of watersports enthusiasts. In summer, **boat tours** leave from Horseshoe Bend, at the north end of Bighorn Lake. The Horseshoe Bend marina (☎307/548-7230) rents out assorted equipment, and a shadeless beach of red sand offers swimming in the most bizarre of settings; there's a developed **campground** here too (drinking water, toilets, picnic tables) but the sites are all pretty rocky. The Devil's Canyon overlook, just off Hwy-37 three miles over the border into Montana, affords landlubbers an opportunity to gauge the knee-knocking 1000ft-plus drop into the abyss. The **Bighorn Canyon Visitor Center**, just east of Lovell on US-14A (daily 8.30am–5pm, slightly

Hiking in the Bighorns

The most useful trailheads close to Buffalo are at Hunter, sixteen miles west of town (take the turnoff onto Forest Road 19 from US-16), and Circle Park (two miles further on US-16, then turn onto Forest Road 20). From the **Hunter trailhead**, it's seven miles one-way to the Seven Brothers, a string of lakes that are popular sites for fishing or lazing about over a picnic. From **Circle Park**, there's an easy seven-mile day-hike loop that passes several en route. The main route in to 13,175ft **Cloud Peak** itself – whose summit is often beset by clouds – starts from the **West Tensleep Lake trailhead**, reached via Forest Road 27 (turn north off US-16 at Meadowlark Lake, ten miles east of Tensleep). The trip to the summit and back takes the best part of three days, and most pitch a tent at **Mistymoon Lake** on the way in and again on the way out. The nontechnical route to the summit is via the southwest ridge; you should collect a detailed description from a local USFS office (see below). A slightly longer approach is to hike first to Seven Brothers from the Hunter trailhead and on to Mistymoon Lake from there.

Backcountry permits are not required to camp in the Cloud Peak Wilderness, but every hiker and camper must **register** before setting out (you'll find registration forms in boxes at the trailheads and at USFS offices). There are a number of developed USFS **campgrounds** dotted around the edge of the Cloud Peak Wilderness too, and most have drinking water, pit toilets, and fire grates ($8–10 per night); useful sites for access to hiking trails include *Sitting Bull* (43 sites), *Island Park* (ten sites), *Deer Park* (seven sites), and *West Tensleep Lake* (ten sites), all of which are along the route to the West Tensleep Lake trailhead, while *Circle Park* (ten sites), *South Fork* (fifteen sites) and *Middle Fork* (ten sites) are handy to the Circle Park and Hunter trailheads. For all information and maps in the Bighorns, check with the USFS office in Buffalo (see p.376) or in Sheridan at 1969 S Sheridan Ave (Mon–Fri 8am–5pm; ☎307/674-2600).

Medicine Wheel National Historic Landmark

Local Native American legends offer few clues as to the original purpose of the **Medicine Wheel**, an arrangement of flat stones laid out with 28 spokes about 80 feet long, for a total circumference of 245ft. Revered as a sacred site by various indigenous people, including Shoshone, Arapaho, Cheyenne and Crow, the "wheel" was perhaps originally part of a sun-worship ritual, or perhaps even related to theories of astronomy.

Constructed between 1200 AD and 1700 AD, accounts of its design published in 1885 mention a series of small huts, each one positioned at the end of a spoke, which may have functioned as sanctuaries for prayer and meditation. Today, the wheel features in a range of ceremonies, and there are often tribute items such as feathers, bells, herbs, and flowers adorning the fence that surrounds the site. USFS officers are on hand daily from mid-June to mid-October (8am–6pm) to keep an eye on things; an attitude in keeping with a visit to any other place of worship is appropriate here. During religious ceremonies, the site may be closed to the public; otherwise it's accessible year-round – though the road leading to it is usually snowed in from November to May.

To reach Medicine Wheel National Historic Landmark, turn north off I-14 "Alt" about 27 miles east of the town of Lovell, onto the signposted, unsealed road (Hwy-12). Leave your car at the parking lot and **hike** the last mile-and-a-half to the site.

longer hours during summer; (Ⓣ307/548-2251), displays a 3-D map of the canyon and runs videos on the Pryor Mountain Wild Horse Range, the Medicine Wheel, and the canyon itself.

An added curiosity in the Bighorn Canyon area is the **Pryor Mountain Wild Horse Range**, effectively a 47,000-acre protection zone for a herd of about 120 feral horses. With luck you might see a free-spirited mustang or two somewhere near the road north of Horsehoe Bend; you could even take one home, as part of the BLM management strategy for the size of the herd (Ⓦwww.adoptahorse.blm.gov).

Cody

CODY, which sits alongside the North Fork of the Shoshone River some 52 miles east of Yellowstone, was the brainchild of investors who in 1896 persuaded William "Buffalo Bill" Cody to get involved in their development company knowing his approval would attract homesteaders and visitors alike. Being at the western end of the dry Bighorn Basin, it was always clear that Cody would need a significant irrigation source if the town was to grow into a center of agriculture and a gateway for tourism to Yellowstone National Park. Bill Cody was probably the only person who could have drawn the support and funding for the dam and reservoir that today bear his name, so the town, whose population is closing on 9000, really does owe its existence to the man. It's hardly surprising then that Cody's other famous son – the painter **Jackson Pollock** – remains vastly overshadowed by the spectre of Buffalo Bill.

During summer, tourism is big business, but underneath all the Buffalo Bill-linked attractions and paraphernalia, Cody manages to retain the feel of a rural Western settlement. As a base for visiting Yellowstone, it's more relaxed and low-key than Jackson – which is about the same distance away from the park. The priority for the vast majority of visitors to Cody is a visit to the **Buffalo Bill Historical Center**, before hightailing it across the Wapiti Valley to Yellowstone.

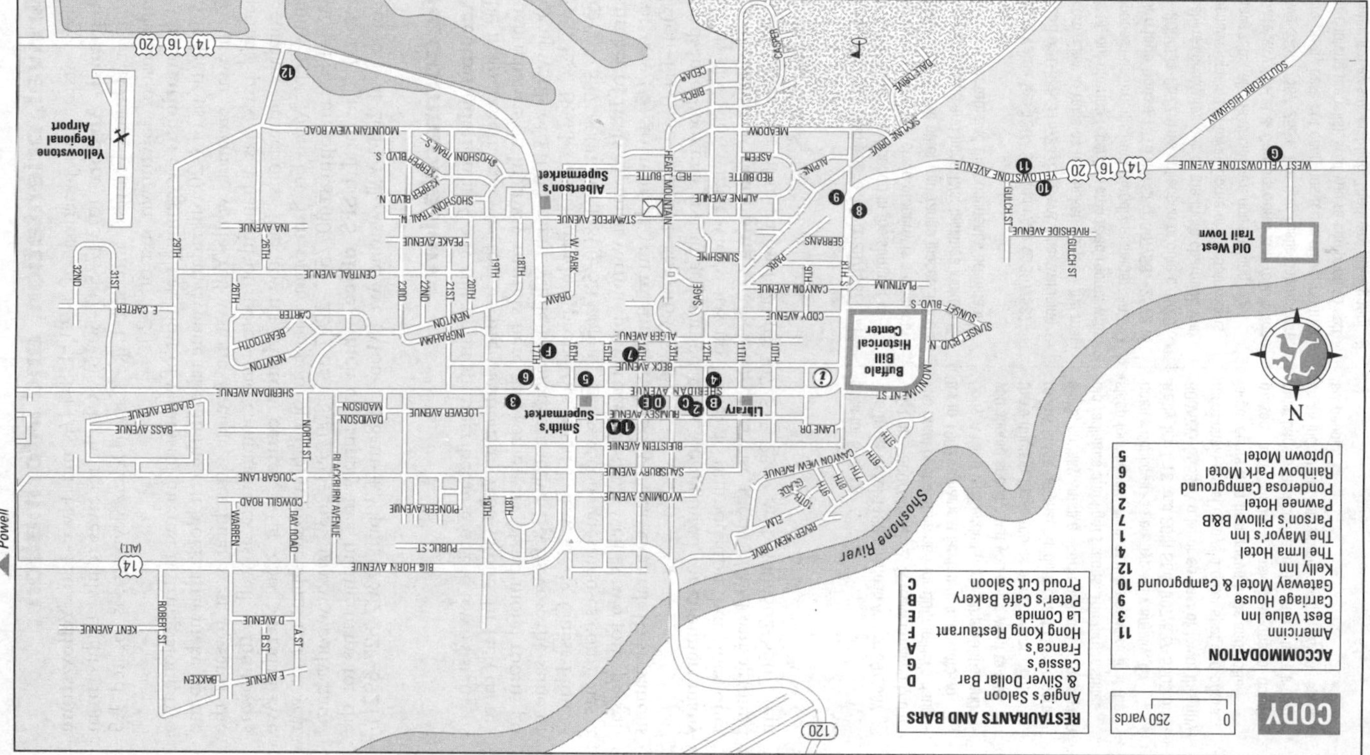
CODY
0 250 yards
ACCOMMODATION
Americinn 11
Best Value Inn 3
Carriage House 9
Gateway Motel & Campground 10
Kelly Inn 12
The Irma Hotel 4
The Mayor's Inn 1
Parson's Pillow B&B 7
Pawnee Hotel 2
Ponderosa Campground 8
Rainbow Park Motel 6
Uptown Motel 5
RESTAURANTS AND BARS
Angie's Saloon & Silver Dollar Bar D
Cassie's G
Franca's A
Hong Kong Restaurant F
La Comida E
Peter's Café Bakery B
Proud Cut Saloon C
Powell
Yellowstone Park (east entrance)
Yellowstone Regional Airport
Buffalo Bill Historical Center
Old West Trail Town
Smith's Supermarket
Albertson's Supermarket
Library
Shoshone River
SOUTHFORK HIGHWAY
WEST YELLOWSTONE AVENUE
YELLOWSTONE AVENUE
SKYLINE DRIVE
BIG HORN AVENUE
SHERIDAN AVENUE
MOUNTAIN VIEW ROAD
CENTRAL AVENUE
STAMPEDE AVENUE
CANYON AVENUE
CODY AVENUE
ALGER AVENUE
BECK AVENUE
RUMSEY AVENUE
BLEISTEIN AVENUE
SALSBURY AVENUE
WYOMING AVENUE
LOEWER AVENUE
PIONEER AVENUE
MONUMENT ST
RIVERSIDE AVENUE
GULCH ST
MEADOW
ALPINE AVENUE
RED BUTTE
HEART MOUNTAIN
SUNSHINE
SAGE
GERRANS
PLATINUM
CASPER
DALE DRIVE
BIRCH
CEDAR
LANE DR.
CANYON VIEW AVENUE
RIVER VIEW DRIVE
ELM
KENT AVENUE
ROBERT ST
BAKKEN
E AVENUE
D AVENUE
A ST
B ST
WARREN
DAY ROAD
COWGILL ROAD
COUGAR LANE
NORTH ST
BLACKBURN AVENUE
DAVIDSON
MADISON
BASS AVENUE
GLACIER AVENUE
PUBLIC ST
INA AVENUE
PEAKE AVENUE
NEWTON
INGRAHAM
BEARTOOTH
CARTER
E. CARTER
W. PARK
DRAW
SHOSHONI TRAIL N.
SHOSHONI TRAIL S.
KERPER BLVD. N.
KERPER BLVD. S.
SUNSET BLVD. N.
SUNSET BLVD. S.
14 16 20
14 (ALT)
120

Arrival, orientation, and information

Cody sits at the junction of I-20, US-14A and Hwy-120. **Yellowstone Regional Airport** (ⓣ307/587-5096), which receives daily flights from Denver (United Express) and Salt Lake City (Delta/Skywest), is located 1.5 miles east of downtown, just off I-20.

Orientation is easy enough as most of what is of interest is strung along two main sections of I-20: Sheridan Avenue takes in the ten blocks that make up the downtown precinct, while Yellowstone Avenue, stretching west towards the national park, has a handful of motels and campgrounds as well as the town's secondary attractions. The town's **visitor center** is at 836 Sheridan Ave (June–Sept Mon–Fri 8am–6pm, Sat 9am–6pm, Sun 10am–3pm; rest of year Mon–Fri 8am–5pm; ⓣ307/587-2297 or 1-800/393-2639, ⓦwww.codychamber.org). The local **USFS office**, which can supply free hiking maps for the region, is at 203A Yellowstone Ave (Mon–Fri 8am–4.30pm; ⓣ307/527-6921).

Accommodation

Accommodation in Cody fills up in summer because of the town's status as the main eastern gateway for driving vacations to Yellowstone. In fact, there's such reliance on highway **motels** here that some very bland motel rooms go for upwards of $100 a night, while far more attractive **B&Bs** cost the same or even less. Besides the individual properties listed below, Cody Guest Houses (ⓣ307/587-6000 or 1-800/587-6560, ⓦwww.codyguesthouses.com) has a number of B&B rooms at various properties (6–8) as well as two four-person cottages (7) to rent. If you're stuck, call Cody Area Central Reservations (Mon–Fri 9am–5pm; ⓣ1-888/468-6996).

Advance bookings for all accommodations are required for summer; many places close for winter. Cody has no hostel accommodation, but does offer excellent in-town **camping** (see below); otherwise, Cody's *KOA* campground is 2.5 miles east of town on I-20 (ⓣ307/587-2369 or 1-800/562-8507; tent sites $21, RVs $29).

Americinn 508 Yellowstone Ave ⓣ307/587-7716 or 1-800/634-3444. Opened in the summer of 2000, this three-star chain property is a clear cut above most of the other mid-range places. Rooms have king beds and huge TVs; facilities include pool and hot tub, and the continental breakfast is free. 6

Best Value Inn 1807 Sheridan Ave ⓣ307/587-4258 or 1-888/315-2378, ⓦwww.bestvalueinn.com. Easy to miss as it's tucked back off the main drag, but offering recently remodeled rooms with spotless bathrooms, and friendly management. 3

Carriage House 1816 8th St ⓣ307/587-2572 or 1-800/531-2572. This collection of cute c.1920 cabins constitutes one of the more charming inexpensive options in town. Some of the bathrooms have tubs; all the cabins are nonsmoking. 4

Gateway Motel & Campground 203 Yellowstone Ave ⓣ307/587-2561. The tiny, rustic cabins here are pretty bare but each has a gas stove (no fridge or cooking utensils), so if you're equipped to self-cater, it may suit just fine. There are grassy tent sites for $12. 2

The Irma Hotel 1192 Sheridan Ave ⓣ307/587-4221 or 1-800/745-4762, ⓦwww.irmahotel.com. The hotel built and named for Buffalo Bill's daughter in 1902 remains a landmark in downtown Cody. A wing was added during the 1980s, and you should specify that you don't want to stay there (though these rooms are cheaper; 4); rooms in the original building boast classic corner sinks, chunky antique wardrobes and some stylish old radiators and light fittings. The larger suites sleep four people. Nonsmokers beware that the hotel's public areas are typically smoky. 5

Kelly Inn I-16 and 26th St ⓣ307/527-5505 or 1-800/635-3559. A mile or so east of town, this fifty-room chain motel enjoys a quiet spot and offers large rooms with firm queen beds and coffeemakers, and includes a basic breakfast of doughnuts, bagels, and coffee in the rate. There's also a small indoor hot tub. Family rooms (7) sleep up to six people. 6

The Mayor's Inn 1413 Rumsey Ave ☎307/587-8004. Constructed in 1909, the inn was moved here piece-by-piece from its original Sheridan Ave location in the mid-1990s, to be lovingly restored as a B&B; furnishings include pieces salvaged from houses around Cody, as well as from the *Irma Hotel*. The three guestrooms have luxury touches like fluffy robes and bubble-jet tubs in each bathroom. Rates often negotiable for stays of three nights or more. ⑥

Parson's Pillow B&B 1202 14th St ☎307/587-2382 or1-800/377-2348. Built in 1902, this quaint little B&B was originally a Methodist-Episcopal church and the current owners replaced the missing bell tower and steeple in 1996. The four guestrooms each feature their own distinct bathroom touches including an antique clawfoot tub or an oak-framed "prairie tub." Rates for stays of three nights or more are often negotiable. ⑤

Pawnee Hotel 1032 12th St ☎307/587-2239. This two-story c.1900 hotel has 22 somewhat dark and gloomy rooms, but the location is unbeatable, it's all nonsmoking and you just might prefer it to a bland highway motel. Best of the rooms feature full-size clawfoot bathtubs. ③

Ponderosa Campground 1815 Yellowstone Ave ☎307/587-9203. The best camping in Cody, friendly and well-run, with exceptionally clean shower and toilet facilities. There's also a general store, laundry, and games room. Options include a basic tent site ($15), a tepee (sleeping mat and bag required; $20), or camper-cabin ($34); go for a site in the "rustic tenting" area, which is below the main campground and right beside the Shoshone River. Open May to mid-Oct.

Rainbow Park Motel 1136 17th St ☎307/587-6251 or 1-800/341-8000. A basic motor court with the bonus of a grassy area in the center of the parking lot; rooms are not flash but perfectly clean and functional. ③

Uptown Motel 1562 Sheridan Ave ☎307/587-4245. This old-fashioned motel does not look like much from the road, but the rooms are surprisingly bright and clean, and some have kitchenettes. ③

The town and around

Cody's main thoroughfare, **Sheridan Avenue**, is wide enough for a couple of wagon teams at least, but really there's little else to evoke the feel of the Old West. Even the historic **Irma Hotel** fails to inspire as part of the streetscape, despite its connections to Buffalo Bill. Native American arts, crafts, and jewelry feature heavily among the stores along the main drag, and there's a huge shop which sells every conceivable variation on the cowboy hat – although in presentation and price, it's clearly aimed at cowboys from LA and London, rather than northwest Wyoming.

The hokey **gunfight**, a staple of Western towns like Cody, is quite a production with up to twelve participants shooting off their mouths and guns to entertain the crowds; it kicks off at the *Irma Hotel* at 6pm Monday to Saturday throughout summer. The town's biggest annual festival is the **Cody Stampede**, held July 1–4 (☎307/587-5155 or 1-800/207-0744), which features parades, street performances, fireworks, and of course, a huge rodeo. Smaller though still popular is Cody's **night rodeo** (June–Aug nightly 8.30pm; ☎307/587-5155 or 1-800/207-0744; $10–12), which takes place at the western edge of town at 421 W Yellowstone Ave.

Buffalo Bill Historical Center

The nation's most comprehensive collection of Western Americana, Cody's giant **Buffalo Bill Historical Center** at 720 Sheridan Ave, comprises four distinct museums (June to mid-Sept daily 7am–8pm; mid-Sept to Oct daily 8am–5pm; Nov–March Tues–Sat 10am–3pm; April daily 10am–5pm; May daily 8am–8pm; ☎307/587-4771; $10); keep your ticket for a free return visit the following day, as there's a lot to get through.

Artifacts from William Cody's various careers, such as guns, gifts from European heads of state, billboards, clothes, and dime novels, help the **Buffalo Bill Museum** to chronicle the years of the Pony Express, Civil War, Indian Wars, and Wild West shows. Among the showier highlights are a number of ornate **saddles** of tooled leather with silver trim – check out the "Parade Saddle," detailed in gold and sterling silver, made by Edward Bahlin, Hollywood's former master of the over-the-top cowboy fashion statement. It's interesting, too, to see the contrast between some of the **photos** of Buffalo Bill on display; in one he looks like an overdressed and overweight dandy, while in another he's in classic mounted pose, cutting a dash with a leather gauntlet in hand, experience and gravitas etched into his weathered face.

The lives of western Native Americans are celebrated in the **Plains Indian Museum**. Many of the ceremonial garments are in stunning condition; one prize exhibit is a brightly decorated shirt which belonged to Red Cloud, a Lakota Sioux chief who visited Washington several times during the 1870s to petition for peace on behalf of his people. A superb bear-claw necklace is another standout, dramatically evocative of what a bear is equipped to do in a fight. The museum's permanent historical collection is given a tragic note by the display of Ghost Dance shirts. In the late 1880s, the religious revelation of the Paiute prophet Wovoka swept the western tribes. He declared that ritual purification through song and dance would hasten the day when all whites would be buried by a heaven-sent fall of soil, and their dead warriors, along with huge herds of buffalo, would return to the Plains. The US Army condemned Ghost Dances as unacceptable shows of resistance, and mobilized troops to disrupt ceremonies.

Buffalo Bill

The much-mythologized exploits of **William Frederick "Buffalo Bill" Cody**, born in Iowa in 1846, began at the age of just eleven, when the murder of his father forced him to take a job as an army dispatch rider. An early escape from ambush brought Cody fame as the "Youngest Indian Slayer of the Plains"; four years later, he became the youngest rider on the legendary **Pony Express**. After a stint fighting for the Union, Cody found work – and a lifelong nickname – supplying buffalo meat to workers laying the transcontinental railroad. He killed over 4200 in just eighteen months, before rejoining the army in 1868 as its chief scout. In the next decade, when the **Plains Indian Wars** were at their peak, he earned a Congressional Medal of Honor and a remarkable record of never losing any troops in ambushes. Among battles in which he took part was the 1877 encounter with Sioux forces when he killed – and scalped – Chief Yellow Hand.

By the late 1870s, exaggerated accounts of Cody's adventures were appearing back East in the "dime novels" of Ned Buntline, and with the Indian Wars all but over he took to guiding Yankee and European gentry on buffalo hunts. He referred to the vacationers as "dudes," and called his camps "dude ranches." The theatrical productions he laid on for his rich guests developed into the world-famous **Wild West Show**. First staged in 1883, these spectacular outdoor carnivals usually consisted of a re-enactment of an Indian battle such as Custer's Last Stand, featuring Sioux who had been present at Little Bighorn, trick riders, buffalo, clowns, and a shooting and riding exhibition by the man himself. The show spent ten of its thirty years in Europe, where, dressed in the finest silks and sporting a well-groomed goatee, Cody stayed in the grandest hotels and dined with heads of state; Queen Victoria was so enthusiastic in her admiration that rumors circulated of an affair between them.

In later life, a mellowing Cody played down his past activities, to the point of urging the government to respect all Native American treaties and put an end to the wanton slaughter of buffalo and game. Although the Wild West Show was reckoned to have brought in as much as one million dollars per year, his many investments failed badly, and, in January 1915, a penniless 69-year-old Buffalo Bill died at his sister's home in Denver. His grave can be found atop Lookout Mountain, outside Golden, Colorado (see p.85).

In the beautifully laid-out **Whitney Gallery of Western Art**, the contrasting styles of Frederic Remington and Charles M Russell command the most attention. The propagandist Remington dwells on conflict, depicting the Indian as a savage in the path of progress, while Russell's work shows a consistent respect for native life.

For something altogether different, a quick round of the **Cody Firearms Museum** is worthwhile for a look at some of the superbly crafted rifles, pistols, and revolvers – particularly those made through the course of the nineteenth century, when manufacturers strove to outdo each other with their designs. There are around 4200 pieces in all, including European rifles and pistols and the largest collection of US firearms in the world.

Old Trail Town

Although it's a pretty random collection of old log cabins salvaged from all over the region, **Old Trail Town**, 1831 DeMaris Drive (mid-May to mid-Sept daily 9am–6pm; $5), makes for a handy one-stop viewing of a little frontier culture. The 25 buildings date between 1879 and 1901, and include a re-created general store, trapper's cabin, and blacksmith's shop. Photographs in the buffalo hunter's cabin give some idea of the scale of the infamous buffalo slaughter, with piles of hides depicted, as well as some of the hapless beasts being skinned. In Curley's Cabin there are some surprisingly good pictures of Curley, the Crow Indian scout and acolyte of Custer's who survived the battle of Little Bighorn; don't miss the fantastically grim hearse in the Museum of the Old West.

At the western end of Old Trail Town you'll find a memorial to the mountain men of the fur-trapping era (see box on p.402), and a number of gravesites of various trappers and buffalo hunters. Among them is the grave of the infamous John (Jeremiah) "Liver Eating" Johnston (see p.481) and also that of William Garlow Cody (1913–92), grandson of Buffalo Bill.

Buffalo Bill State Park

The main feature of **Buffalo Bill State Park**, six miles west of Cody along I-20, is the Buffalo Bill Dam and Reservoir and its **visitor center** (May–Sept daily 8am–8pm; ⓣ307/527-6076). Construction on the dam spanned five years from 1904 to 1909, and on completion, it was the highest in the world at 325 feet. Additions in 1993 raised its height to 353 feet, and doubled its capacity. Besides providing water for the residents of Cody and other towns in the Bighorn Basin, the reservoir is popular for fishing and boating. Two state park **campgrounds**, North Shore Bay and North Fork, cost $9 per night for a bare and windswept site (the reservoir is ideal for windsurfing and kite-surfing; day-use costs $5.

Outdoor activities and national park tours

Apart from the dam and reservoir, your outdoors pursuits will likely be about moving on to the national park, or perhaps trying a whitewater expedition closer to town. There's fine **rafting** (half-day around $45) on the North Fork of the Shoshone River, and also gentler sightseeing **float trips** (2–3hr around $20); wildlife including elk and bighorn sheep can often be seen from the river. Try Red Canyon, 1374 Sheridan Ave (ⓣ307/587-6988 or 1-800/293-0148), River Runners, 1491 Sheridan Ave (ⓣ307/527-7238 or 1-800/535-7238), or Wyoming River Trips, 233 Yellowstone Ave (ⓣ307/587-6661 or 1-800/586-6661). **Fishing** enthusiasts can check in with North Fork Anglers, 1438 Sheridan Ave (ⓣ307/527-7274), for gear or to join a guided trip on the North or South Fork of the Shoshsone or one of several great trout-fishing spots inside Yellowstone ($80–130 per day).

Tours of Yellowstone start with a basic day-trip around either the park's north or south loop roads; Yellowstone Tours (ⓣ307/527-3677 or 1-800/442-3682) offers day-trips from $60 (plus $10 park entrance fee) as well as multi-day outings; Grub Steak Expeditions (ⓣ307/527-6316 or 1-800/527-6316) takes mostly small groups for a more in-depth park experience, with the per person price dependent on the size of the group.

Eating, drinking, and nightlife

For a town that sees over one million visitors pass through each summer, Cody is hardly overendowed with interesting **restaurants**. A good steak is easy to find, but the options beyond that are fairly limited; most of the major fast-food chains are represented, however. Those heading on to Yellowstone should definitely stock up at one of the big supermarkets (see Listings, opposite). Cody's **pubs** are pretty basic watering holes, although having a beer at *Irma's* famous bar (see below) is a requisite for any visitor. During summer a variety of bands do come through town, but entertainment is otherwise limited to a little old-school boot-scooting or a game of pool.

Restaurants

Franca's 1421 Rumsey Ave ⓣ307/587-5354. The Italian set-menu changes daily, and includes antipasto, appetizer, entree, and salad; a couple regular selections are veal tenderloin and fresh halibut with sautéed red peppers. One of Cody's best restaurants. Open for dinner only Wed–Sun ($25–30); reservations essential.

Hong Kong Restaurant 1201 17th St ⓣ307/587-6420. You get the usual Americanized Chinese selections here, but they're all pretty good and good value too (entrees $8–13). Daily for lunch and dinner plus brunch (a dim sum of sorts) on Sundays.

Irma's *Irma Hotel* ⓣ307/587-4221. A good spot for a slab of prime rib for dinner, and the breakfast and lunch buffets are great for filling up on a range of dishes (both $6.95); the selection is expanded for Sunday brunch ($8.95) to include roasts, hot veggies, plus plenty of salads and desserts. Take heed, though, that the dining area and the bar are often smoky.

La Comida 1385 Sheridan Ave ⓣ307/587-9556. Good-value Mexican standards but also some nice light selections such as *pechuga* salad (bites of chicken in cream and green chilis over leafy greens). The white-chocolate almond cheesecake ($4) is a winner too. Entrees $7–12. Daily for lunch and dinner.

Peter's Cafe Bakery 1191 Sheridan Ave. A cheerful place for a full breakfast as well as bagels, muffins and a range of coffees. Mon–Sat 6.45am–7.15pm, Sun 6.45am–3.30pm.

Proud Cut Saloon 1227 Sheridan Ave ⓣ307/587-7343. A local favorite for big lunchtime burgers ($6–8) and even bigger dinnertime steaks ($14–24) but the service is disorganized and slow. Daily for lunch and dinner; the bar is not a bad place for an afternoon drink.

Tuscany Italian Pasta Lounge 1244 Sheridan Ave ⓣ307/527-7744. A new addition to downtown dining in Cody serving up some good Italian classics including minestrone, lasagna, and gnocchi, besides fishy appetizers that include smoked trout, scampi, and scallops (entrees $10–18). Daily 11am–10pm.

Bars and pubs

Angie's Saloon & Silver Dollar Bar 1313 Sheridan Ave ⓣ307/587-3554. This should be the first place you check for live music – mostly rock, and definitely for those who would not be seen dead in *Cassie's*. Otherwise it's the scene of some lively talking, drinking, and shooting pool.

Cassie's 214 Yellowstone Ave ⓣ307/527-5500. You may need a cowboy hat to really feel comfortable at *Cassie's*, but for a Wyoming cultural experience this is a good bet. Entertainment ranges from line-dancing classes to Country and Country-rock bands, and there are pool tables too. You can settle in for a full evening here including dinner, but the meaty menu, while pretty good, is surprisingly expensive (entrees $14–30). There are regular weekday lunch specials too.

Silver Saddle Saloon in the *Irma Hotel*. The *Irma's* most famous feature is its gorgeous imported European cherrywood bar, which at $100,000 reputedly cost twenty grand more than the hotel itself. Happy hour (5–7pm) pulls in a fair mix of locals and tourists.

Listings

Airlines Sky West/Delta ⓣ307/587-9740 or 1-800/453-9417; United Express ⓣ307/587-7683 or 1-800/241-6522.
Banks Community First, Sheridan Ave and 11th St and Shoshone First, Sheridan and 14th, have 24hr ATMs.
Car rental Avis ⓣ307/587-5792, Budget ⓣ307/587-6066, Hertz ⓣ307/587-2914, and Thrifty ⓣ307/587-8855 have depots at the airport.
Hospital West Park Hospital, 707 Sheridan Ave ⓣ307/527-7501, has 24hr emergency care.
Internet access Park County Library, 1057 Sheridan Ave (Mon & Thurs noon–5.30pm & 7–9pm, Tues, Wed & Fri 10am–5.30pm, Sat 10am–1pm; free).
Laundry Skippy's, 728 Yellowstone Ave (ⓣ307/527-6001; open 24hr).
Police 1131 11th St ⓣ307/527-8700; emergencies ⓣ911.
Post office 1301 Stampede Ave (Mon–Fri 8am–5.30pm, Sat 9am–noon).
Supermarket Albertson's, 1825 17th St (daily 5am–midnight; pharmacy hours Mon–Fri 9am–8pm, Sat 9am–6pm, Sun 10am–4pm); Smith's, 1526 Rumsey St (daily 6am–midnight; no in-store pharmacy).

Cody to Yellowstone – the Wapiti Valley

The drive west from Cody to Yellowstone National Park is a superb preparation for the splendors of the park itself. It begins by skirting the Buffalo Bill Dam and Reservoir, then runs alongside the Shoshone River through the open **Wapiti Valley**, the heart of Wyoming's "beef country," before climbing through the rugged mountains to Sylvan Pass (8,559ft). This stretch of I-20, known as the **Buffalo Bill Cody Scenic Byway**, is a busy two-lane affair, so slowing down to look for wildlife and such is very unwise. Use pull-outs to admire the scenery and spot beasts such as bighorn sheep, pronghorn antelope, and mule deer; there is also a fair amount of grizzly activity on the south side of the highway. Check in at the Wapiti Valley Visitors Center, 29 miles west of Cody (June–Aug Mon–Fri 8am–8pm, Sat–Sun 8.30am 5pm; ⓣ307/587-3925), for the latest spotting information. Be sure also to stop at the pull-out a couple of miles further west to marvel at an extraordinary rock formation known as the "**Holy City**" – its silhouette supposedly mirrors that of the city of Jerusalem.

Other than in the busiest period (July–Aug), not many people stop overnight en-route to the park, although there are some very pleasant places to do so; some of the **campgrounds** and **lodges** are within a few miles of the park's east entrance, and are worth considering as a base. *Elephant Head Lodge*, ten miles east of Yellowstone (ⓣ307/587-3980, ⓦwww.elephantheadlodge.com; ⑤), has cabins for two-to-eight people, all en-suite, as well as a restaurant and activities like horseback riding; *Absaroka Mountain Lodge*, twelve miles east of Yellowstone (ⓣ307/587-3963, ⓦwww.absarokamtlodge.com; ⑤), offers similar amenities. Most of the USFS campgrounds along I-20 are on the south side of the highway, and have drinking water, vault toilets, fire rings, and essential bear-proof storage bins and are usually open May to early October. The three closest campgrounds to the park are *Three Mile* (3 miles; 33 sites), *Eagle Creek* (7 miles; 20 sites), and *Newton Creek* (14 miles; 31 sites); each costs $9 per night. There are several **hiking trails** that follow trout streams into the Absaroka Wilderness on the north side of the highway, and also the Washakie Wilderness on the south side; for information and maps, visit the USFS office in Cody (see p.382) or the Wapiti Valley Visitors Center (see above). The map you'll need is the *Shoshone National Forest – North Half* ($6).

△ Highway-side mailboxes near Devils Tower

Wind River country

Were it not for the Grand Tetons and Yellowstone just up the road, the **Wind River Mountains** would undoubtedly constitute one of the most visited and valued national parks in the US. Easily Wyoming's longest and highest range, the Wind Rivers boast at least forty mountains topping 13,000ft – including the state's highest, the 13,804ft Gannet Peak – as well as 150 glaciers and three huge Wilderness Areas (Bridger, Fitzpatrick, and Popo Agie). No roads cross the mountains, but there are some great bases from which to explore them, including **Pinedale** from the west, and **Lander** or **Dubois** from the east. The mountains give way to grassy hills and flattop buttes to the east of the range, where large populations of Shoshone and Arapaho people make their home on the **Wind River Indian Reservation**. North of here, at the point where the Wind River becomes the Bighorn River, hikers get to ease any aches and pains at the distinctive spa town of **Thermopolis**.

Wind River Indian Reservation

The **WIND RIVER INDIAN RESERVATION** occupies a large (and largely forgotten) swath of west central Wyoming, overshadowed by the high snowcapped peaks to the west and south. It is the only Indian reservation in Wyoming, and extends roughly seventy miles from the natural spa town of Thermopolis in the east through arid grasslands and uranium-rich badlands to Dubois in the west. At its heart are the rich fishing grounds of the cottonwood-lined Wind River itself. The reservation was created in 1863 as a permanent home for the Eastern Shoshone, but due to US government imposition, it soon came to accommodate the Northern Arapaho as well; these days, the Arapaho account for more than double the Shoshone population. In all, nearly eight thousand Native Americans now live on the 3600-square-mile reservation.

Not surprisingly, the land set aside by the government does not represent the very best of Wyoming – being largely dry, grassy plains – and on occasion, mining and other development has taken precedence over native title, resulting in the "reclaiming" of thousands of acres for minimal compensation. However, the reservation does operate with a large degree of autonomy, running its own taxation system and public infrastructure, funded largely by royalties received for oil and gas extraction on reservation land.

The main reasons for visiting the reservation are to witness the celebratory side of Shoshone or Arapaho culture at one of the **powwows** held regularly throughout the year, and to visit the gravesites of revered **Chief Washakie** and supposedly that of **Sacagawea** (see box, overleaf). Both gravesites are near the town of Fort Washakie, fifteen miles north of Lander along Hwy-287. The **Shoshone Tribal Cultural Center**, 31 Black Cole St, Fort Washakie (Mon–Fri 8am–5pm; ⓣ307/332-9106), dispenses a small map indicating their locations. Information and dates for upcoming powwows, which feature traditional singing, costume, and dance, are available from the cultural center too, or through the visitor information office in Lander (see p.394). Lander is also the handiest place to stay in relation to Fort Washakie; **transport by bus** around the reservation is provided by the Wind River Transportation Authority (ⓣ307/856-7118 or 1-800/439-7118), and the nearest Powder River bus stop is in the town of Shoshoni, about fifty miles east of Fort Washakie.

A somewhat underutilized reservation resource are its rivers and lakes, which regularly yield enormous brown, brook, and rainbow trout. The cost of the **special license** to fish on the reservation is somewhat prohibitive ($25 per day, $65

Chief Washakie and Sacagawea

Rightly revered as one of the great statesmen of the nineteenth century, **Chief Washakie** was born in 1798 and went on to lead the Shoshone people through sixty years of tumultuous relations between native and white Americans. Having befriended legendary mountain man Jim Bridger in the 1830s, Chief Washakie became fluent in English and quickly realized the folly of trying to stem the tide of white settlers via endless confrontation. Instead he set about establishing coalitions with the whites – in the process almost certainly saving his own people from being overrun by larger tribes of Sioux and Arapaho. This ability to galvanize his own people towards peaceful resolutions, even while facing his enemies unflinchingly, sees him revered today as the greatest Shoshone warrior of all. Chief Washakie's integrity as a statesman and negotiator was further recognized upon his death in 1900, when he was accorded a full US military funeral – the only Native American chief to receive that honor.

Amost as famous a figure in Shoshone history is **Sacagawea** – whose name translates as "Bird Woman" – a young woman who found accidental fame through her participation in the expedition of Lewis and Clark. A number of details of her story remain up for dispute, including whether she is in fact buried on the Wind River Indian Reservation. The story goes that she was abducted as a child by the Minnetaree tribe and sold as a bride to a French-Canadian fur-trapper named named **Charbonneau**; Sacagawea was probably about eighteen years old when she and her husband met Lewis and Clark in North Dakota in the winter of 1804, where they were asked to join the party. Sacagawea would become invaluable to the explorers over the next two years for her ability to speak English, French, and the Shoshone language. She was able to negotiate not only safe passage with the Shoshone, but also to successfully petition them for supplies and fresh horses, without which the expedition would certainly have foundered. If indeed it is Sacagawea buried on the reservation, then she also assisted Chief Washakie in negotiations that helped establish a permanent home for the Shoshone in Wyoming. Since her death on April 9, 1884, her status as a folk hero has steadily grown, and in 2000 she was finally honored by the US government, which minted the new **one-dollar coin** with a (theoretical) likeness of the young Sacagawea on one side.

per week, plus an additional $5 "recreation stamp"), and good **fishing spots** hard to reach, but committed anglers consider the effort worthwhile when they land a 24-inch trout. For information and permits – also available from sporting goods retailers in Lander and Dubois – and advice on getting to the best spots (ask about Bull Lake Creek) contact the reservation's Fish and Game Office (ⓣ307/332-7207). Note too that a fishing license is required for any backcountry visit on the reservation, whether you're actually fishing or not.

Thermopolis

Hugging the western shore of the Bighorn River at the northeastern edge of Wyoming's Wind River region, **THERMOPOLIS** boasts the **world's largest mineral hot springs** – which today constitute one of the most visited state parks anywhere in the Rocky Mountains. The town is really not on the way to anywhere much else, but it is definitely worth a detour to anyone hankering for a bit of medicinal soaking. People come to Thermopolis from all over the world to dunk themselves in the mineral pools and the local population of 3200 could probably live well enough off these visits alone. The region is further endowed, though, with some of Wyoming's most promising **dinosaur fossil beds**, as well as a museum that displays the more interesting finds.

Information and accommodation

The **visitor center**, 700 Broadway (May–Sept Mon–Sat 8am–5pm, Oct–April Mon–Sat 9am–4pm; ⓣ307/864-3192 or 1-800/786-6772), is situated a block west of 6th Street, which is I-20 as it runs north–south through the town center. The center dispenses **information** as well as a free combined town map, dining and accommodation guide, and is also home to the Hot Springs Historical Museum (see below).

During summer, **accommodation** reservations are a good idea; things quieten down considerably from mid-September, and rates may be as much as thirty-percent lower between October and April. If your visit is primarily about taking the waters, you should consider staying at one of the hotels inside the state park; the surrounds are green and pleasant, and you'll be within shouting distance of all the hot springs.

Best Western Moonlighter 600 Broadway ⓣ307/864-2321 or 1-800/528-1234. Rooms here are a little drab but the bathrooms are spotless and the place is perfectly adequate for a night or two; plus it's located right in the middle of town, by the only traffic lights in Thermopolis. ④

Cactus Inn 605 South St ⓣ307/864-3155 or 1-877/621-7811, ⓦwww.cactusinn.com. This basic motor lodge is worth a mention for its central location and value rates; rooms have fridges and microwaves and there are suites with kitchenettes for a few dollars more. ③

Fountain of Youth RV Park 250 N I-20, two miles north of town ⓣ307/864-3265. Although it's a little pricey for a campground in these parts, you might be happy to pay the extra for access to the park's hot mineral pool, which at 235 feet by 72 feet is the largest in Wyoming. RV and tent sites $22.

Grandview RV Park 122 S I-20 ⓣ307/864-3463. Just a half-mile south of the town center, this campground has clean facilities and a guest laundry too. RV sites $16, tents $13, showers for nonguests $3.

Holiday Inn of the Waters Hot Springs State Park ⓣ307/864-3131, ⓦwww.holidayinnthermopolis.com. One of the stranger lodging properties in Wyoming, this Holiday Inn has been decked out with the spoils of numerous safari trips undertaken by its owner – the walls are studded with an extraordinary array of wildlife. Facilities include a fitness room, pool, and an excellent outdoor mineral hot tub; the hotel's *Safari Club* offers decent meals and a pleasant bar area too (see "Eating and drinking", overleaf) ⑥

Quality Inn Plaza Hotel Hot Springs State Park ⓣ307/864-2939 or 1-888/919-9009. Built in the 1930s and thoroughly refurbished in 1999, the *Plaza* is the pick of the hotels for its springs-side location, peaceful surrounds and excellent facilities. There's a private mineral spa for guests, and a continental breakfast is included in the rate. ⑤

Roundtop Mountain Motel 412 N 6th St ⓣ307/864-3126 or 1-800/584-9126, ⓦwww.roundtopmotel.com. A quiet and friendly motor lodge with small standard motel rooms along with some larger freestanding log cabins (⑤) that are equipped with kitchenettes. Also within walking distance of the hot springs. ④

The town and Hot Springs State Park

Before heading off to the Hot Springs State Park on the northeast edge of town, stop in at the **Hot Springs Historical Museum**, inside the visitor center at 700 Broadway (June–Aug Mon–Sat 8am–5pm, Sun noon–4pm; rest of year Mon–Sat 9am–4pm; $3). The museum sports the usual exhibits devoted to ranching life and the Old West, as well as a collection of Native American artifacts, the most notable of which is an elk hide painted by Chief Washakie (see box, opposite).

A mile or so east of downtown (follow the signs) an altogether different kind of history is being slowly revealed at the **Wyoming Dinosaur Center** (daily: June–Aug 8am–8pm; rest of year 10am–5pm; $6, $12 including tour of the dig site; ⓣ307/864-2997, ⓦwww.wyodino.org;). Opened in 1995, it functions as both a museum and research center for the thousands of dinosaur bones uncovered nearby each year. Exhibits include several partial skeletons as well as

"Morris," a complete, sixty-foot-long camarasaurus (a gigantic, long-necked herbivorous dinosaur). Tours of the current dig site can also be had, where excavators have already uncovered enough stegosaurus bits, allosaurus teeth, diplodocus vertebrae and the like to suggest they're working in what was once a feeding ground for huge predators like allosaurus and T-Rex. The museum laboratory is of interest too, as it's open to public view (behind glass) and you can watch bones being cleaned and prepared for display.

Until 1896, the area encompassing **Hot Springs State Park** (free) was part of the Wind River Indian Reservation. A treaty signed that year by Chief Washakie saw the US government assume ownership of a ten-square-mile parcel of land that included the springs, for a payment of $60,000. Chief Washakie had stipulated in the treaty that a section of the springs should remain freely accessible to all people, and his legacy became known as the "Gift of the Waters." You can collect a map of the site at park headquarters, 220 Park St (Mon–Fri 7.30am–4pm; ⓣ307/864-2176), but all of the springs are within a hundred yards or so of each other, so you shouldn't have any problem finding them. The dominant feature of the park is the sculpted mineral terraces of **Big Spring**; the 135°F water bubbles up from underground and flows out at around 2600 gallons per minute, making this the world's largest mineral hot spring. You can soak in the waters – renowned for their healing properties – at the **State Bath House** (Mon–Sat 8am–5.30pm, Sun noon–5.30pm; 20min time limit; free), or try the waterslides and hot pools at two commercial complexes nearby. **Star Plunge** (daily 9am–9pm; $8) takes its name from its five-hundred-foot waterslide, and it has a large, hot mineral pool with diving board as well as a steam room and three hot tubs. **Hellie's Tepee Spa** (daily 9am–9pm; $8) has probably the nicest collection of plunge pools and hot tubs, along with sauna and weight room. Towels are available for rent at all three places ($2); keep in mind that you'll want to soap up and shower off within an hour or so afterwards, as the minerals can leave you with itchy skin.

A somewhat *au naturelle* alternative is to hop right into the river beside the boat-ramp directly behind Hellie's Tepee Spa; this is where the collected run-off from the springs trickles down into the river via a shallow ravine. It's also worth driving a few hundred yards along the highway as it runs north of the park for a view back over the terraces and steaming pools; keep an eye out for the small bison herd which grazes around the park's northeast corner.

Eating and drinking

When it's time to **eat**, *Li'l Wrangler,* 800 Shoshone St, at the south end of town (daily 6am–10pm), is a nondescript but popular diner offering burgers, steaks, and big breakfasts. For a more expensive seafood or steak dinner in stylish surrounds, try the *Legion Supper Club* (ⓣ307/864-3918), at the golf course two miles north of town via 7th Street. The *Safari Club Restaurant & Lounge* (ⓣ307/864-3131), inside the *Holiday Inn*, has a reliable mid-priced menu of pastas, fish, chicken, buffalo, and such along with a decent salad bar. The largest **supermarket** in town is Don's IGA, 225 S 4th St (daily 8am–9pm). There are no standout places to go for a **drink**: the *Safari Club*'s lounge bar is low-lit and relaxed and offers early evening happy hour drinks on weekdays; in town, *One-Eyed Jack's*, 633 Broadway, may be either subdued or overrun with bikers.

Lander and around

Occupying a prime location for forays into both the Wind River Mountains and the Wind River Indian Reservation, the prosperous and friendly town of **LANDER** heads the list of towns to visit if exploring this neck of the

Wyoming woods. The earliest settlement at this site, which straddles the Popo Agie River (pronounced "po-po-zsa'), was Camp Augur – a small military post established in 1869 to protect the reservation's Shoshone people from incursions by warring tribes and opportunistic gold prospectors. The town's population was bolstered over the following couple of decades as mines in the nearby South Pass City and Atlantic City areas played out, forcing miners to look for steadier work. The railroad arrived in 1906 with less dramatic economic and social consequences than elsewhere in Wyoming, largely because the first wave of miners had already passed, and it would be another sixty years before iron ore was discovered and mined forty miles away. In 1972 the freight trains stopped arriving altogether, and the last of the mining operations ceased in the early 1980s.

Today, Lander's population of around 7500 is steadily embracing tourism of the Wind River region, but with a strong emphasis on responsible use of the mountain environment – driven in large part by the presence of the **National Outdoor Leadership School** (NOLS). Happy-but-exhausted climbers and hikers are a common sight in the cheerful cafés and bars along the main drag, while the leafier blocks on the south side of town are becoming highly sought-

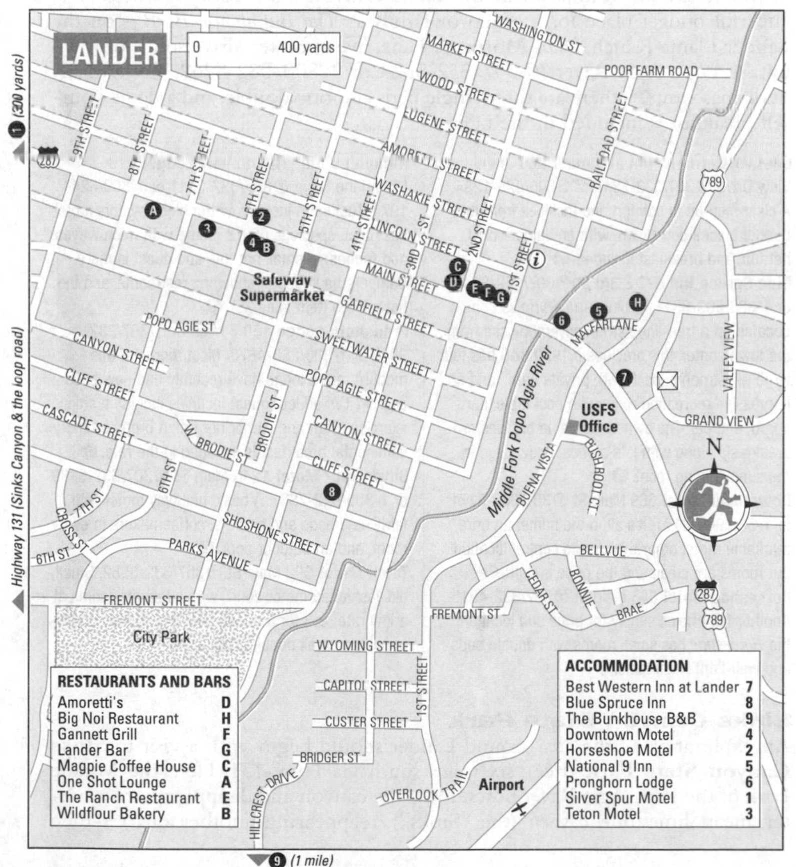

after real estate for active young families moving into the area. **Sinks Canyon State Park** provides a neighborhood playground for easy-to-moderate hiking, biking and even climbing – it's just a few miles down the road.

Arrival, information and accommodation

Due to lack of use, the regional bus routes serving Lander were cancelled in 2001; call the Wind River Transportation Authority (WRTA; ⓣ307/856-7118 or 1-800/439-7118) for an update. The **chamber of commerce**, 160 N 1st St (Mon–Fri 9am–5pm, extended hours June–Aug; ⓣ307/332-3892 or 1-800/433-0662, ⓦwww.landerchamber.org), has information and brochures for every driving route and backcountry outfitter around. For more on nearby hiking and camping options, visit the **USFS office**, 333 S Hwy-789 (Mon–Fri 8am–5pm; ⓣ307/332-5460).

Finding decent **accommodation** in Lander is not too difficult, and the only occasions that put a little pressure on available rooms are two summer festivals. There are several budget **motels** clustered together in the town center, and you can even **camp for free** in City Park, 405 Fremont St (May–Sept, three-night maximum stay; ⓣ307/332-4647), where you have access to fire grates, restrooms, and drinking water (showers available at the public pool, 450 S 9th St); there are also campsites in the Sinks Canyon State Park (see below). A cheerful budget place for a group or family is *The Bunhkouse B&B* – on the Lander Llama Ranch, 2024 Mortimer Lane, five-minutes' drive south of town by the Popo Agie River (ⓣ307/332-5624 or 1-800/582-5262, ⓦwww.landerllama.com; ④); there are three single beds and one double, and a do-it-yourself breakfast is included in the rate.

Best Western The Inn at Lander 260 Grand View Drive ⓣ307/332-2847 or 1-800/528-1234. A clear step up in comfort and facilities from the budget places downtown, with an outdoor pool, hot tub, and breakfast included. ⑤

Blue Spruce Inn 677 S 3rd St ⓣ307/332-8253 or 1-888/503-3311, ⓔbluespruce@rmisp.com. Located on a tree-lined street several blocks from the town center, this gracious c.1920 B&B has four large guestrooms (each with private bath), and an impressive recreation room with pool table, dartboard, and bar. The owners serve up big Western breakfasts along with lots of local knowledge in the sunny dining room. ⑤

Downtown Motel 569 Main St ⓣ307/332-3171 or 1-800/900-3171. It's all in the name; an unremarkable motel other than for its central location, but rooms are clean and the price is right. ②

Horseshoe Motel 685 Main St ⓣ307/332-4915. Another fair choice simply for price and location, the *Horseshoe* has small rooms with double beds and well-kept bathrooms. ②

National 9 Inn (The Holiday Lodge) 210 McFarlane Drive ⓣ307/332-2511 or 1-800/624-1974. Tucked in just below the highway, this motel has quiet, spacious rooms (some with microwaves and fridges), a small hot tub, and guest laundry. Campers have use of showers, restrooms, and the hot tub too (tent sites $5). ③

Pronghorn Lodge 150 E Main St ⓣ307/332-3940 or 1-800/283-4678. Most rooms at this modern motor lodge have recently had new beds and big TVs added; guest facilities include a small exercise room and indoor hot tub. A pretty ordinary continental breakfast is included in the rate. ④

Silver Spur Motel 1240 Main St ⓣ307/332-5189 or 1-800/922-7831. A basic highway motel with fairly new beds and carpets, coffeemakers in every room, and an outdoor pool. ③

Teton Motel 592 Main St ⓣ307/332-3582. Small, old-fashioned motor court, with adequate rooms at a low rate; ask for a queen bed, or you may end up with a small double instead. ②

Sinks Canyon State Park

An exploration of the area around Lander should begin with a visit to **Sinks Canyon State Park** (free), six miles south via Hwy-131. Here the Middle Fork of the Popo Agie River flows down the canyon and disappears into a subterranean limestone cavern (the "Sinks"), reappearing another quarter-mile

National Outdoor Leadership School (NOLS)

The local institution of which Lander residents are most proud is without doubt the **National Outdoor Leadership School (NOLS)**, a nonprofit organization that is unchallenged as the premier educator in outdoor skills and leadership in the US. Established in 1965 by mountaineer Paul Petzoldt, the school has seen over 50,000 students pass through its courses in backpacking, climbing, mountaineering, horsepacking, kayaking, sailing, and canoeing. Its stated aim is to have people develop leadership and self-reliance while learning to respect and protect the planet's wilderness.

Courses vary from backcountry trips of a few days to fully accredited training for instructors, which may take months or even years. Along with trips in the Rocky Mountains region, NOLS offers courses in Mexico, Argentina, India, and Australia. For all information or to receive a course catalog, contact the office at 288 Main St (Ⓣ307/332-5300, Ⓦwww.nols.edu).

below in a calm pool (the "Rise"). The water takes over two hours to travel the relatively short distance, but there are only guesses as to why. There's usually a gathering of up to one hundred big, healthy-looking rainbow trout in the waters of the Rise, swimming lazily about – fishing in the Rise is forbidden, and these trout have clearly never experienced any threat to their survival.

You'll find interpretive signs at each of the sites and a summer-only **visitor center** at the Sinks (daily 9am–7pm); a free brochure details the workings of the Sinks and the Rise, and also identifies some of the flora and fauna to be found in the canyon. Two roadside state park **campgrounds** close by are *Sawmill*, one mile north of the Sinks, and *Popo Agie*, one mile to the south; both have basic toilets, drinking water, tables, and fire grates ($9).

A popular and easy **hike** in the canyon goes up to **Popo Agie Falls** – a 1.5-mile walk with a 600ft gain in elevation. The trail begins beside the Bruce Picnic Area, about a mile further into the canyon past the Sinks; the lower section travels through aspen stands and wildflower clusters before the terrain becomes progressively more barren and rocky. Crossing a wooden bridge, you get a view of the upper section of the falls, and if you cross two more bridges to the end of the trail you'll view all the sections of the falls as the water-flow tumbles, collects itself, and then tumbles again. All of the trails off Sinks Canyon Road are open to **mountain bikers** as well. The Middle Fork trail, which begins at the end of the canyon just past the Bruce Picnic Area, is a popular moderate ride; the trail proceeds directly west for five miles, to the junction with the Sheep Bridge Trail. If you turn left (south) here, it's a far more technical and demanding ride to the Sheep Bridge trailhead, where you rejoin the loop road for the seven miles of gravel switchbacks back to the Middle Fork trailhead. Freewheel Ski & Cycle, 378 Main St (Mon–Sat 9am–6pm; Ⓣ307/332-6616), is the place to hire a mountain bike ($20 per day) and get tips on trails and conditions; during winter you can also hire **cross-country skis** and **snowshoes** here.

Climbing, fishing, and local outfitters

Lander draws **climbers** from around the world to the boulders and south-facing dolomite walls (these gather thermal heat and so allow for comfortable climbing conditions in the fall and even early winter months) in Sinks Canyon, and to the limestone walls at legendary **Wild Iris**. There are at least 150 established routes at Wild Iris, many lined with permanent pins and bolts. An excellent contact point for information, gear, and even drumming-up climbing partners is Wild Iris Mountain Sports, 333 Main St (Mon–Sat 9am–7pm, Sun 10am–5pm; ⓣ307/332-4541, ⓦwww.wildirisclimbing.com). The driving route in to Wild Iris is not well marked; take Hwy-28 south from Lander for 29 miles, then turn right onto County Road 326, which forks after a mile or so – take the right fork, County Road 327, up to the parking area and trailhead. You can't camp at Wild Iris, and the nearest serviced campgrounds are those near Atlantic City, over on the east side of the highway (see p.398).

Fishing almost anywhere in the Wind River region is likely to be a rewarding experience, and some anglers choose to try their luck along the Popo Agie just to the north of town. But if bagging a trout or two is a serious mission, think about taking a pack trip into the mountains (see below), where you'll come upon countless alpine lakes and streams – many seldom pillaged by fisherfolk. For gear and advice, stop by The Good Place, 155 W Main St (Mon–Sat 8.30am–5pm; ⓣ307/332-3158), which issues fishing permits – including the license to fish on the Wind River Indian Reservation (see p.389) – and has an excellent selection of topographic trail maps.

With all the enticing backcountry exploration available from Lander, it's little wonder that several **outfitters** run trips into the mountains – and they employ almost every type of conveyance to do so. You can book yourself on to a horsepacking trip, head off with a team of llamas, or even a gaggle of goats; expect to pay $110–150 per day. Well-reputed operators include: Lander Llama Company (ⓣ307/332-5624 or 1-800/582-5262, ⓦwww.landerllama.com); Wind River

Hiking in the southern Wind River Mountains

With so many routes and possible backcountry itineraries, it's worth collecting the eight-page *Shoshone National Forest* handout from the USFS office in Lander, and also investing in the *Shoshone National Forest – South Half* map ($6) before you set off into the **southern Wind River Mountains.**

The **major trailheads** near Lander, from north to south, are **Bears Ears**, **Smith Lake**, **Middle Fork**, and **Sheep Bridge Roaring Fork**. The banner destination in the Wind River mountains is the **Cirque of the Towers** – a stunning cluster of peaks forming an imposing semicircle around Lonesome Lake. During summer, there's always quite a collection of tents and numerous hikers dotted about this lake, as well as climbers tackling peaks such as Wolf's Head (12,163ft), Shark's Nose (12,229ft), Bollinger (12,232ft), and Pylon (12,378ft). Hiking in to the cirque from the east side takes longer than from trailheads near Pinedale in the west (see p.405), but the terrain on this side is less rocky and barren and you're also spared crossing some exhausting mountain passes. The shortest route to the cirque starts from the **Smith Lake trailhead** (heading south and then west along the North Fork trail); it's a fourteen-mile haul one-way, and if you want to explore along the way, it means setting aside three days at least. It's also important to check trail conditions at the USFS office in Lander before you set out, largely because the trail crosses the Popo Agie River in four places and at times the river may be impassable – it's typically at its peak during late spring and early summer.

For hard-earned but spectacular mountain vistas, a two- or three-day trip to **Valentine Lake** (10.5 miles, elevation gain 2680ft) or beyond to **Washakie Lake** (13.2 miles, elevation gain 3080ft) from the Bears Ears trailhead also guarantees a fair degree of solitude. Along the way you can hike to the top of **Mt Chauvenet** (12,250ft), from where you get a breathtaking 360-degree panorama of the Wind River mountain range. Easier day and overnight trips include the walk from Fiddler Lake to Christina Lake, and several possible loop hikes which incorporate the Sheep Bridge and Stough Creek Lakes trail; the **Stough Creek Basin** is classic alpine stuff, with flower-flecked meadows punctuated by lakes and stands of firs and pines.

Pack Goats (☎307/332-3328, Ⓦwww.goatpacking.com); and Rocky Mountain Horseback Adventures (☎307/332-8535 or 1-800/408-9149).

Eating, drinking, and entertainment

There's not much by way of exotic **places to eat** in Lander, but the usual meaty Wyoming grills are good ones and there are one or two places that add a little international flavor. Between the supermarket and the town's excellent bakery you can prepare your own edibles for a day or two out in the mountains, and as a last resort, the dreaded golden arches stand sentinel at the eastern entrance to town. The town's best **drinking** venue is the *Lander Bar*, connected to the *Gannett Grill* at 126 Main St (see below), and which features live bands on occasion during summer. The *One Shot Lounge*, 695 Main St, has a pool table, but the bar here is pretty quiet unless there's a hunting crowd in town.

Two summer events do raise the pulse in this otherwise relaxed community: the **International Climber's Festival**, held over five days in early July (☎307/332-8662, Ⓦwww.climbersfestival.org), features climbing competitions, demonstrations, slide presentations, and social events; and the **Lander Wyoming Jazz Festival**, held on Labor Day weekend (☎1-800/433-0662, Ⓦwww.landerjazz.com), which has hosted appearances from the Beale Street Jazz Band among other notables.

Amoretti's 202 Main St ☎307/335-8500. You may have to tidy up after a few days in the mountains before settling in for a meal in the stylish surrounds at *Amoretti's*. Try classic soups like gazpacho and minestrone ($4) or some green-lip mussels ($7) to start, followed by *ossobuco alla milanese* or filet *sangiovese* (entrees $12–20); the wine list is unusually stimulating for a Wyoming restaurant too. Daily for dinner only.

Big Noi Restaurant 8125 Hwy-789 ☎307/332-3102. In a commendable attempt to be all things to all people, this kitchen dishes up Thai standards like beef in a peanut-red-curry sauce and Pad Thai ($8–10), along with fried chicken, linguine, and rib-eye steak. It's all pretty good, but you might as well stick with the Thai dishes. Dinner daily; take-away and delivery also available.

Gannett Grill 126 Main St ☎307/332-8228. Rub shoulders with the largely local crowd while tucking in to a moderately priced burger, pizza, or monster salad and sampling a microbrew; beery evenings in summer can get pretty lively. Daily for lunch and dinner.

Magpie Coffee House 159 N 2nd St. A cheery little place for coffee, light breakfasts, lunches, and, most vitally, dessert – all inexpensive. Mon–Sat 7am–4pm.

The Ranch Restaurant 148 Main St. You could conceivably take care of all your daily caloric requirements at the *Ranch*: breakfast specials include $3 for eggs, bacon, hash browns, and toast, good lunch options are the burgers and chicken sandwiches, while most nights there's an all-you-can-eat deal on barbecue ribs or similar fare. This is also the site of the Popo Agie Brewing Co., so you'll have a handful of good beers to try as well. Mon–Sat 8am–11pm, Sun 9am–1pm.

Wildflour Bakery 545 Main St. You can get some interesting breads and far-out bagels (swiss-chive, cranberry-orange) here, along with muffins, cookies, and a decent cup of coffee. Open Mon–Fri 7am–5pm, Sat 7am–3pm.

Atlantic City and South Pass City

An interesting piece of Wyoming history has been preserved in the mining towns of **Atlantic City** and **South Pass City**, located within four miles of each other roughly forty-minutes' drive south of Lander via Hwy-28. Atlantic City remains a going concern as a town today, and still sees its share of tourists through the summer, and hunters through the fall. An unmissable landmark is the 1893 **Atlantic City Mercantile** (daily 11am until late) – a classic saloon where rowdy sessions around the piano are not unknown on summer weekends. The town otherwise feels like an all-but-deserted mining village, its clutch of nineteenth-century stone and timber buildings kept upright thanks to the population of fifty or so people who still inhabit some of them. The **Gatrix Cabin** is thought to

The Atlantic and South Pass cities loop

The twin former mining towns of Atlantic City and South Pass City can also be reached on a popular seventy-mile driving **loop** that runs south from Lander along Hwy-131 into Sinks Canyon and on to picturesque **Louis Lake**, before reaching the mining towns and linking with Hwy-28 back to Lander. The *Resort at Louis Lake*, 1811 Louis Lake Rd, 28 miles from Lander (ⓣ307/332-5549 or 1-888/422-2246, ⓦwww.louislake.com), hires out recreation gear as diverse as canoes, horses, and snowmobiles; the rustic cabins all have great beds, linen, wood-burning stoves, and simple kitchens, and share communal bathroom facilities. Cabins sleep from two (❹) right up to eight people (❼); tent sites cost $15. Otherwise, there are three USFS **campgrounds** (all $6) with lakeside addresses that appear in the following order as you drive from Lander along the loop: *Worthen Meadows* (16 miles; 28 sites), *Fiddlers Lake* (23 miles; 13 sites) and *Louis Lake* (28 miles; 9 sites) – each has toilets, drinking water, tables, and fire grates.

be the oldest of the lot, built around 1860, while the log-built **St Andrews Episcopal Church** has been used for Sunday services since 1913.

An evening out at "the Merc" is recommended for a fine steak **dinner**; call ahead for dinner reservations and to check whether there's a band or piano player on (restaurant open May–Sept Thurs–Sun, Dec–April Fri–Sat; ⓣ307/332-5143 or 1-888/257-0215). If things really get going, you might decide to **stay the night**, either in one of the A-frame cabins beside the saloon (summer only; ❸), or at the cozy *Miner's Delight* B&B (ⓣ307/332-0248), which has two rooms with private bath (❺) and four log cabins with shared facilities (❹). There are also two BLM **campgrounds** near Atlantic City, handy as a base for the Wild Iris climbing area (see p.395): *Atlantic City* (June–Oct; 18 sites; $6) and *Big Atlantic Gulch* (June–Oct; 8 sites; $6) are both off County Road 237, and have toilets, drinking water, tables, and fire grates.

There's really not much left of South Pass City, which had three hundred buildings during the height of the mining boom in the 1860s. Today just thirty remain, painted up, decked out with furnishings salvaged from nineteenth-century homes and businesses, and designated as the **South Pass City State Historic Site** (mid-May to Sept daily 9am–6pm; $2). A brochure details the history of each of the restored buildings and, typically for a mining town, saloons feature prominently, including the *Miners Exchange Saloon*, run by the multitasking John Swingle, also a county commissioner, building contractor, stable owner, and undertaker.

Dubois

The former logging town of **DUBOIS** ("Dew-boys"), squeezed into the northern tip of the Wind River valley as the mountains begin in earnest, began life as a major provider of railroad ties, and its economy was driven by the timber industry for the entire century 1887–1987. But proximity to the Wind River Mountains, Yellowstone National Park, and superb fishing in the Wind River itself have since ensured a prosperous transition from timber to tourism for the 1100 residents of Dubois. The town now makes an affordable and relaxed base for getting into the mountains, hooking a trout, or even uncovering some of the mysterious ways of one of the Rockies' most majestic creatures at the **National Bighorn Sheep Center**.

Arrival, information, and accommodation

As in Lander, the regional bus routes run by the Wind River Transportation Authority (WRTA; ⓣ307/856-7118 or 1-800/856-7118) have recently been cancelled; they may begin again, so call for an update. The **chamber of commerce** operates a rather hard to spot information office, 616 W Ramshorn (June–Aug Mon–Sat 9am–7pm, Sun noon–5pm; rest of year Mon–Fri 9am–5pm; ⓣ307/455-2556 or 1-800/645-6233); it's in a tiny hut beside the Food Town supermarket. The **USFS office** is at 1403 W Ramshorn, at the west end of town (Mon–Fri 8am–5pm; ⓣ307/455-2466).

Positioned 82 miles southeast of Yellowstone, Dubois comes into the reckoning as a base for seeing the park, so the town's **accommodation** can get stretched during July and August. However, it remains a cheaper option than Jackson, and as long as you call at least a few days in advance it's likely that you'll find a room. This is also an excellent place to try a slice of ranching life at a Wyoming guest (dude) ranch; several fine ranches in the area offer packages that include all meals and accommodation as well as activities such as fishing and horse riding. A comprehensive list of properties can be found at ⓦwww.ranchweb.com.

Bald Mountain Inn 1349 W Ramshorn St ⓣ307/455-2844 or 1-800/682-9323. Perched above the river at the west end of town beside the USFS office, the *Bald Mountain Inn* has a range of comfortable rooms, some of which have kitchenettes and even fireplaces. ❸

Branding Iron Inn 401 W Ramshorn St ⓣ307/455-2893 or 1-888/651-9378, ⓔbrandingiron@wyoming.com. These riverside log-built cabins, which date back to the 1940s, have been modernized without losing their rustic charm; some now have kitchenettes. The friendly owners are a fountain of knowledge on local hikes and activities. ❸

Brooks Lake Lodge Brooks Lake Rd, 26 miles northwest of Dubois ⓣ307/455-2121, ⓦwww.brookslakelodge.com. The guestrooms in the c.1922 lodge building are complemented by six log cabins, and all are decked out with beautifully finished lodgepole-pine furniture. The hefty rates ($380–420) include all meals as well as activities including horseback riding, canoeing, and fishing, and the lodge has its own bar-restaurant and a communal hot tub. Open for two separate seasons, July–Sept & late Dec through March. ❾

Circle-Up Camper Court 225 W Welty St ⓣ307/455-2238. The most central campground is also the best for its riverside location and range of accommodation. Besides tent and RV sites, you could stay in a tepee ($20), although the basic camper cabins, each of which has two double bunk beds but nothing else, are better value at $25. Facilities here include indoor pool and recreation room with pool table, plus there are clean bathrooms and a guest laundry. RV sites $20, tent sites $15.

Stagecoach Motor Inn 103 Ramshorn St ⓣ307/455-2303 or 1-800/455-5090. Smack in the middle of town, the *Stagecoach* is the largest motel in town and worth checking when rooms are scarce. The rooms have been refurbished in recent years, but the decor is still pretty uninspiring; however, the large outdoor pool may prove adequate compensation. ❸

T Cross Ranch fifteen miles north of town via Horse Creek Rd ⓣ307/455-2206, ⓦwww.ranchweb.com/tcross. Though the Dubois area is studded with dude ranches, the *T Cross* is worthy of special mention for its secluded riverside location, excellent fishing and horse riding, and peerless hospitality. During July and August a week's minimum stay may be required (around $600 per person). ❽

Trail's End Motel 511 W Ramshorn St ⓣ307/455-2540 or 1-888/455-6660, ⓔtrailsend@wyoming.com. This riverside log-built motel has small but nicely furnished rooms, each with fridge and microwave; for a few extra dollars you can get one with its own deck over the Wind River itself. ❸

Twin Pines Lodge and Cabins 218 Ramshorn St ⓣ307/455-2600 or 1-800/550-6332, ⓔtwinpines@wyoming.com. The beautiful 1934 log-built lodge and cabins have retained all of their cozy charm, despite being brought up to date with modern bathrooms and TVs with VCRs – a huge selection of videos is freely available. The cabins can accommodate up to six people (❹–❺), while the lodge rooms all have queen-size beds; a continental breakfast is included in the rate. ❹

Wind River Motel 519 W Ramshorn St ☎307/455-2611 or 1-877/455-2621. One of the more basic motels in town (no phone in rooms), but it's very clean, the management friendly and the price is hard to beat. Closed in winter. ❷

The town

Driving right through Dubois, one would probably think little of the place, but its riverside location and backdrop of rocky hills conspire to create an attractive setting. The town itself does not boast any particular sights apart from the Bighorn Sheep Center (see below), although there is a small museum which may warrant a little of your time; the **Wind River Historical Center**, 900 W Ramshorn (May–Sept daily 9am–5pm; $1), consists of seven log cabins, each one evocative of a different aspect of life in the Wind River region. The nineteenth-century schoolhouse and bunkhouse are appropriately decked out, but the saddle-shop is of most interest for its display of the various styles of saddle over the past two centuries; check out the gruesome-looking "permanent wave" hairdresser's machine inside the homestead cabin too.

Opened in 1993, the **National Bighorn Sheep Center**, 907 W Ramshorn St (daily: June–Aug 9am–8pm; rest of year 9am–5pm; ☎307/455-3429, Ⓦwww.bighorn.org; $2), is a highly contemporary exhibit, boasting interactive displays that provide a unique insight into the lives of these extraordinary high-country dwellers. There's some riveting video footage of the fall rut, when the big males literally lock horns, but most fascinating are the various mounted heads of bighorns from as far afield as Iran, Syria, Mongolia, and Mexico – it's quite something to see the stark differences between the species.

It's no coincidence that Dubois was chosen as the home for this exhibit – the area is still home to the biggest herd of bighorn sheep in the Lower 48. The **Whiskey Basin Wildlife Habitat Area** is prime grazing habitat for almost one thousand bighorns, which show up in numbers to feed during the winter months. You can view the sheep independently by simply driving out to the Torrey Valley (turn onto Fish Hatchery Rd, roughly 4.5 miles east of town, and then onto Trail Lake Rd, and follow the signs). There are strict rules about observing the bighorns, as they're easily stressed if approached or startled by noise – to photograph them you'll need a hefty zoom lens. You may have a better viewing and photographing experience on one of the **winter tours** run by the National Bighorn Sheep Center (about 5hr, departing 9am; $20); these are run from November through March and generally require booking in advance. If you are going it alone, it's worth collecting the *Wildlife Tour* brochure at the Bighorn Sheep Center; it traces the driving route and the best viewing spots in the Whiskey Basin area.

Outdoor activities

There's no store in town that rents out fishing gear, but Whiskey Mountain Tackle, 1418 Warm Springs Drive at the west end of town (daily 8am–5pm; ☎307/455-2587), can at least sell you a basic **fly-fishing** rig for around $50, and give you some hints on local spots and conditions.

The USFS office (see overleaf) has some basic **free trail maps** of area hikes (see box, opposite), but if you're going to get into the backcountry for a day or two you'll need the detailed *Shoshone National Forest* map ($6). It's worth stopping in here anyway for an eyeful of a stunning (stuffed) gray wolf – the alpha male of the Washakie wolf pack, shot in October 1997 for poaching livestock.

Hiking the northern Wind River Mountains

There are several popular **hiking trails** within a few miles or so of town, none more so than those in the scenic **Brooks Lake** area. To reach the lake, drive 23 miles west of Dubois along I-26/287, and then turn north onto Brooks Lake Road; the lake itself is backed by some dramatic cliff-faces, and it attracts picnickers, boaters and groups on horseback as well as hikers. A pleasant walk takes you past Brooks Lake and then through a stretch of pine forest to the astonishingly green **Jade Lakes** and covers about 2.5 miles one-way. There are also two USFS **campgrounds** at Brooks Lake, *Pinnacles* (21 sites; $8) and *Brooks Lake* (13 sites; $8); both have drinking water, toilets, tables, and fire grates, and are generally open from late June through September.

Backcountry enthusiasts might well be tempted to tackle the **Glacier Trail**, which begins from the Trail Lake trailhead; follow the directions given for the Whiskey Basin Wildlife Habitat, and continue on past Torrey Lake to the trailhead. The Glacier Trail cuts 25 miles into the Fitzpatrick Wilderness south of Dubois, and gets you into the heart of the Wind River range, winding its way past scenic lakes to the base of Gannett Peak, the highest mountain in Wyoming (13,804ft). As the mountain is beset by glaciers, routes to the summit demand technical skills and equipment and you should check on conditions with the USFS office or consider joining a group of summiteers (contact Exum Mountain Guides in Jackson; see p.442). Pack a rod to try the excellent trout lakes and streams along the way.

An alternative area worth exploring is along **Horse Creek** north of town; there are two USFS **campgrounds** with toilets, drinking water, and fire grates which make good bases for fishing and hiking. The first is *Horse Creek* (twelve miles along Horse Creek Rd; 9 sites; June–Oct; $6), and the second is *Double Cabin* (29 miles along Horse Creek Rd, then turn onto Wiggins Fork Rd; 15 sites; June–Sept; $6). Driving right in to *Double Cabin* puts you deep in the backcountry, where there's excellent fishing in the Wiggins Fork River. It's worth noting that you are in **grizzly country**; special safety rules apply when hiking or camping (see box on p.550).

Eating, drinking, and entertainment

The only evening **entertainment** in Dubois is watching country crooners in classic Western bars such as the *Rustic Pine Steakhouse & Bar*, 119 E Ramshorn St (☎307/455-2772); the steakhouse's moderately priced menu includes excellent prime rib and Alaskan salmon, while the bar features Country bands on Friday and Saturday nights during summer. The *Hang-Out*, 8 Stalnaker St (☎307/455-3800), is good for sandwiches, soup, and coffee, while the *Cavallo Creek Grille*, 112 E Ramshorn (☎307/455-3979), has a short but promising menu of classic pasta dishes, one or two beef entrees, and a decent wine list. The *Cowboy Cafe*, 115 E Ramshorn, is Dubois' requisite old-school diner – a full breakfast here will keep you quiet for some time. You'll also find a Food Town **supermarket** at 610 W Ramshorn St.

Pinedale and around

On the western side of the Wind River range, tiny well-to-do **PINEDALE** on I-191 is fast becoming an alternative base for visiting Yellowstone National Park – though at 120 miles to the park's southern edge, it's not a terribly realistic day-trip. Once a major logging center, Pinedale now attracts second-homeowners and retirees, and continues to have something of an ambivalent attitude to tourism. In short, while a party of hikers emerging from the mountains is a common occurrence and roundly approved of in Lander, folks in

Pinedale still seem to find the sight of happy hikers returning from the backcountry just a bit weird.

Pinedale is otherwise notable as being the spiritual home of the mountain man; in 1824, explorer Jedediah Smith and a small party of fur-trappers made a foray into the area around Green River and its tributaries near present-day Pinedale, and found themselves in the richest beaver waters they had ever seen. For the next sixteen years, this area would be the center of the trade in beaver pelts, and would spawn the legend of the Mountain Man Rendezvous (see box, below).

Downtown can be roughly defined as the seven or eight blocks of I-191 (referred to as Pine St as it runs through Pinedale) between the bridge which crosses Pine Creek and the turnoff onto Fremont Lake Road. The town's only must-see attraction is the Museum of the Mountain Man (see opposite).

Information and accommodation

The Pinedale **visitor center**, 32 E Pine St (April–Oct Mon–Fri 9am–6pm, rest of year Mon–Fri 10am–2pm; ☎307/367-2242), has a free town map, worth having if you're here for a day or two. The **USFS office**, loaded with hiking maps, is at 29 Fremont Lake Rd (June–Aug Mon–Sat 8am–5pm, rest of year Mon–Fri 8am–5pm; ☎307/367-4326).

In Pinedale itself, there is a fair range of **accommodation** from mid-range motels to B&Bs and also a privately run campground. Prices are pretty stable throughout the year, although with each summer season more and more people seem willing to base themselves here and take on a 250-miles-plus round-trip day-excursion to Yellowstone; thus you might find a bit of pressure on rates

The Mountain Man Rendezvous

There's no doubt that the **Mountain Man Rendezvous**, though a short-lived phenomenon, represents one of the most extraordinary social and entrepreneurial gatherings in US history. Begun in 1825 simply as a meeting between fur-trappers and traders, it became an annual event that grew to include all manner of adventurers and explorers who were then eking out a living in the harsh, lonely environs of the Rocky Mountains. Significantly, the survival of these men depended largely upon the goodwill of the indigenous people in whose country they were essentially guests. Thousands of Native Americans took part in the rendezvous, in a show of interdependence that has perhaps not been replicated in the country since.

In the early days of the **beaver trade** – which boomed in the early 1800s as beaver pelt hats became the epitome of fashion in Europe – most trappers worked alone or with one partner, disappearing into the mountains for the winter and spring months, when the beavers' fur was at its most thick and lush. They would emerge in the summer with as many as 150 pelts, bushy beards, and tall tales of survival against the odds. Many of the mountain men learned the local languages, and several of them married indigenous women; it wasn't long before even the army began to look to the trappers for help in guiding wagon-trains over treacherous mountain passes, negotiating safe passage with local tribes along the way.

The first rendezvous was held just west of the Green River by the Wyoming–Utah border, arranged by a fur trader in order to collect pelts and resupply several trappers. It lasted barely a day but in subsequent years as many as five hundred trappers and explorers and three thousand Native Americans gathered in a single river valley for up to three weeks, trading, drinking, gambling, fighting, and sharing stories. By the mid-1830s, the fashion for beaver hats was in decline, and the last rendezvous was held in 1840. In all just sixteen Mountain Man Rendezvous were held, a number of them at sites along the Green River close to downtown Pinedale, where their legacy is recalled at the Museum of the Mountain Man.

and available rooms during July and August. An appealing option is to stay a few miles out of town at one of two lakeside resorts, which offer swimming and boating and lots of peace and quiet (see "Fremont Lake and Elkhart Park", overleaf).

Best Western Pinedale Inn 850 W Pine St ☎307/367-6869 or 1-800/528-1234. This modern motel outstrips its smaller rivals for facilities, with an indoor pool, hot tub, and fitness center; a free continental breakfast is included too. ❻

The Chambers House 111 W Magnolia St ☎307/367-2168 or 1-800/567-2168, Ⓦwww.chambershouse.com. Situated one block north of the town center, this renovated 1933 log-built B&B has five guestrooms of various sizes – two with private bath. A big ranch-style breakfast is served in the formal dining room, and there's a guest sitting room with fireplace but no TV – ideal for retiring to with a good book. ❹

Log Cabin Motel 49 E Magnolia St ☎307/367-4579. These c.1929 log cabins have been thoroughly refurbished and are far more atmospheric than most of the standard motels in town. The larger cabins each have two bedrooms and a small kitchenette, and can accommodate four adults. Open May–Sept. ❹

Pinedale Campground 204 Jackson Ave ☎307/367-45550. Situated two blocks south of Pine St along Jackson Ave, this campground has adequate shower and toilet facilities but it's a shadeless area that can be extremely hot for tenting in midsummer. Tent sites $11, RVs $18.

Wagon Wheel Motel 407 S Hwy-191 ☎307/367-2871. Everything about this modest-looking motor lodge is just a bit more expansive than the other motels in town; the rooms are bigger, most have queen beds, and even the parking lot is huge. ❹

Window on the Winds 10151 Hwy-191 ☎307/367-2600 or 1-888/367-1345, Ⓦwww.windowonwinds.com. Located one mile north of town, this lively family-run B&B has four guestrooms, two with private bath, and all have queen-size lodgepole-pine beds. The communal living room has a TV and small library, and there's an indoor hot tub too. ❺

The Museum of the Mountain Man

The excellent **Museum of the Mountain Man**, 700 E Hennick Rd, just off Fremont Lake Road at the east end of town (May–Sept daily 10am–6pm; Oct daily 10am–noon & 1–3pm; rest of year by appointment only; ☎307/367-4102, Ⓦwww.museumofthemountainman.com; $4), commemorates the way of life of the so-called mountain men, and the era of the Mountain Man Rendezvous (see box, opposite). A video presentation talks you through the early history of the fur-trade – essential viewing to get a grasp of the barely credible lives led by these intrepid adventurers. Hats and other products made from beaver fur are displayed, alongside several of the firearms favored by the fur-trappers – including an example of the famous Henry rifle. The prize piece, however, is a c.1853 rifle owned by legendary explorer and mountain man Jim Bridger. There is a wide-ranging collection of Indian artifacts, clothing, weapons and implements too, while the museum's lower level houses exhibits on the history of Sublette County.

White Pine Ski Area

The low-key **White Pine Ski Area**, eleven miles from Pinedale via Fremont Lake Road and in the Bridger-Teton National Forest (☎307/367-6606, Ⓦwww.whitepine-ski.com), enjoys a quiet, almost isolated forest location, and may be well worth a look if you're visiting this area during the winter. With **annual snowfall** of around 300 inches, and a **peak elevation** of 9500ft (dropping 1100 feet to the two chairlifts), it's a modest ski hill, but one with ambitious plans for the coming winters. Already a new day-lodge has opened, complete with bar-restaurant, ski-school, and equipment hire, and there are plans to open up more terrain and add accommodation facilities in the near future. **Lift tickets** cost just $24 per day, and there are a number of **Nordic ski trails** that branch out from the lodge area too.

Fremont Lake and Elkhart Park

To get a bood look at the biggest peaks in the state, drive the sixteen-mile road that winds east from Pinedale past **Fremont Lake** – whose 22-mile shoreline offers swimming at the southern end, and is great for boating and fishing. Several lookouts along this route have awe-inspiring views out to the Wind Rivers' mightiest peaks, justifying the road's **Skyline Drive** sobriquet. The road ends at **Elkhart Park**, where you'll find the *Trails End* USFS campground (8 sites; $7).

At the southern end of Fremont Lake is *Lakeside Lodge Resort and Marina* (Ⓣ307/367-2221, Ⓦwww.lakesidelodge.com); the resort has eight brand new cabins with two queen beds, fireplace, and own bath (❻) as well as six rustic cabins which share a communal shower and toilet block (❹), plus a highly regarded bar-restaurant. *Half Moon Lake Resort*, located nine miles along Fremont Lake Road (open May–Oct; Ⓣ307/367-6373, Ⓦwww.halfmoonlake.com; rates $25 higher June–Aug; ❻) offers several four- to eight-person cabins, each with its own elevated perch among the trees above the lake. Cabins are equipped with fridge, microwave, and coffee-maker, and the resort has its own restaurant (see "Eating and drinking", below), as well as various boats and horses for hire.

Local outfitters

Elk Ridge Outfitters Ⓣ307/367-2553. Specializes in hunting trips for everything from deer to mountain lion, from its base lodge near the Green River Lakes.

The Great Outdoor Shop, 332 W Pine St Ⓣ307/367-2440. Sells fishing licenses and runs float trips; will also rent you a fly-fishing rig for around $15 a day.

Green River Outfitters Ⓣ307/367-2416, Ⓦwww.greenriveroutfitters.com. Does horse-riding trips, from one-day ($120 includes a cookout) and overnight ($180) to pack trips from 3–10 days into the Winds.

Two Rivers Emporium Ⓣ307/367-4131, Ⓦwww.2rivers.net. Offers guided fly-fishing trips from around $150 per person per day.

Eating and drinking

While you can get a good steak, burger, takeout Mexican or pizza, the best of Pinedale **dining** is undoubtedly a lakeside table for some fresh fish and a chilled bottle of wine. Any one of the three **saloons** in town – *Calamity Jane's World Famous Corral Bar*, *The Cowboy* and *Stockman's* – may have a live Country or blues band or just general rowdiness from a mob of cowboys. Fortunately they're all within hollering distance of one another in the center of town.

Half Moon Lake Resort nine miles northeast of Pinedale along Fremont Lake Rd Ⓣ307/367-6373. Thanks in part to a beautiful lakeside setting, the resort is the premier choice for locals wanting to dine out in style. The menu features swordfish, king crab, lobster, and ginger salmon (entrees $18–30). Dinner only; reservations essential.

LaVoie 406 W Pine St. Usually the most laid-back place for a drink in town, the interior here has lounge chairs and lots of polished timber. On offer are some decent microbrews, a pool table, a basic pub menu, and usually less cigarette smoke than the other drinking venues.

McGregor's Pub 21 N Franklin Ave Ⓣ307/367-4443. While the menu does have a dozen different cuts of beef ($18–22), plus Alaskan halibut ($19) and various pastas, it comes in second to *Half Moon Lake Resort* in the moderate-to-expensive dining category. During summer, try and reserve a patio table. Lunch and dinner daily.

Patio Grill 35 W Pine St Ⓣ307/367-4611. Along with good burgers, a fine chicken-breast salad, and some homemade pies, the *Patio Grill* also offers all sorts of cooked breakfasts. On a cold day, the excellent chili will really hit the spot, and the roast dinner includes soup, bread, and butter ($12). Open daily for breakfast and lunch only.

Hiking the western Wind River Mountains

From Elkhart Park, trails lead past beautiful **Seneca Lake** and along rugged Indian Pass to the glaciers and 13,000ft peaks of the Continental Divide. **The Pole Creek Trail** links with the **Seneca Lake Trail** and then the **Indian Pass Trail** into some of the most scenic country in this part of the Winds. Many people hiking this route pitch a tent overnight at **Island Lake** (at eleven miles from the trailhead it's a handy distance for a solid day-hike) before heading up into the stunning, wildflower bedecked **Titcomb Basin** – bounded by majestic, glaciated peaks to the north and east. It's around fourteen miles from the trailhead at Elkhart Park to Titcomb Basin, and with all the pristine lakes and creeks along the route in which to cool your feet, you can easily construct your own three- or four-day itinerary. In summer particularly you may find the campsites around Island Lake in heavy use, in which case it's worth pushing on another mile or so northeast to the beautiful and peaceful Indian Basin. For a day-hike from Elkhart Park, take the Pole Creek Trail 4.3 miles to a lookout known as **Photographer's Point** (10,095ft) for a view out to the jagged peaks of the Continental Divide and several deep blue lakes below.

A couple of major trailheads north of Pinedale lead in to the **Green River Lakes** area, which offers less demanding hiking terrain than that closer to the Continental Divide. Hwy-352 leaves I-191 seven miles west of town and takes you sixteen miles north to campgrounds and a trailhead by the **New Fork Lakes**. Here you can take a leisurely hike to a sandy beach at its northeast corner, or take on something more ambitious, such as the twelve-mile trip along the **New Fork Trail** in to **Lozier Lakes**; the basin here erupts with wildflowers each spring. The two **USFS campgrounds** by the New Fork Lakes are *New Fork Lake* (15 sites, toilets, no drinking water; $4) and *Narrows* (19 sites, toilets, drinking water; $6). The drive to the *Green River Lakes* campground (37 sites; $7) and trailhead is along almost twenty miles of unsealed road once you go past the turnoff to New Fork Lakes. Again there are numerous trail options; the six-mile walk to **Slide Lake** is a popular day-trip as it takes in the cascades of Slide Creek Falls along the way.

The shorter but more challenging approach to the spectacular **Cirque of the Towers** (see also box on p.396) is from this side of the mountains. The trail begins at the **Big Sandy trailhead** and campground (12 sites, toilets, no drinking water; $4), reached via a convoluted series of backroads beginning at the town of Boulder, twelve miles south of Pinedale. Here you turn east onto Hwy-353 and drive twenty miles to Big Sandy Junction; turn left and drive nine miles on a dirt road to an intersection with "Muddy Speedway"; turn left again and drive 7.5 miles to Big Sandy Entrance, marked the "Dutch Joe Guard Station" sign. Turn left once more and drive past turnoffs to Dutch Joe and Big Sandy Lodge before reaching the campground, 46 miles from Boulder.

There are numerous hiking options once you leave Big Sandy Trail at **Big Sandy Lake**, just under six miles from the trailhead. At 1.1 miles and 2.6 miles further on respectively, **Clear Lake** and **Deep Lake** are popular diversions, sunk dramatically in to the bottom of an austere, rocky basin beset by peaks and crags. The jagged peaks, lush meadows, and snow-fed lakes of the Cirque of the Towers rightly attract thousands of hikers every year, but the 8.6-mile trek from the trailhead is a real up-and-down slog, with an elevation gain of 2120ft.

The USFS office (see p.402) can provide information on the various hiking routes, and sells the essential Bridger-Teton National Forest map ($6).

Stockman's Steak Pub 117 W Pine St ⓣ307/367-4563. The dining room is brighter and more pleasant than the attached saloon, and the menu is a family-friendly mix of burgers, pastas, and even roast lamb (entrees $9–18); the huge salad bar is a real bonus. Daily for lunch and dinner.

Taqueria Del Gallo 650 W Pine St ⓣ307/367-6265. The best bet for food on the run, as Pinedale is thus far mercifully free of the big fast-food chains. The tacos and burritos are pretty good

($3–4), while the Super Burrito ($5.50) is loaded with beans, salad and salsa plus beef or chicken, and makes a full meal. Call ahead to order a custom-built pizza (small $7, large $15). Daily 11am–9pm.

Wrangler Cafe 905 W Pine St ⓣ307/367-4233. This cheerful diner serves up inexpensive and big roast dinners, chicken-fried steak, and the like, teamed with a pretty good salad bar. There's a huge selection of fresh pies on offer too, and at breakfast you can get coffee and a cinnamon roll for around $2. One downside is that the low-ceilinged place can get very smoky. Daily for breakfast, lunch, and dinner.

Travel details

Buses

Buffalo to: Billings (2 daily; 3hr); Cheyenne (2 daily; 6hr 30min).

Shoshoni to: Douglas (1 daily; 3hr).

8

Yellowstone and the Tetons

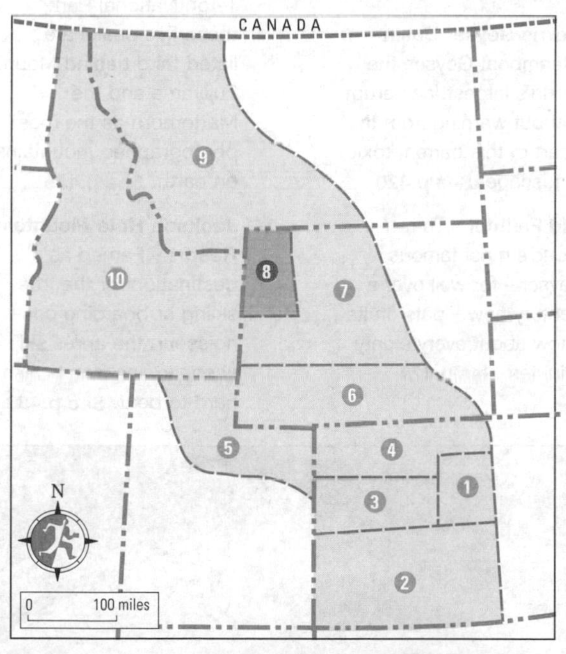

CHAPTER 8

Highlights

* **The Lamar Valley** – Prosaically referred to as "North America's Serengeti" for its abundant wildlife, the valley is home to predators such as grizzlies, wolves, and coyotes and their prey. See p.420

* **Norris Geyser Basin** – Steamboat Geyser, the world's largest, can erupt without warning from the heart of this barren, toxic landscape. See p.420

* **Old Faithful** – The world's most famous geyser – for well over a century now – puts on its show about every eighty minutes. See p.420

* **Artist Point** – Arrive early to beat the crowds and get the best light conditions for this, the park's quintessential photo opportunity. See p.423

* **The Tetons** – The standout feature of Grand Teton National Park, these five peaks are listed third behind Mount Fujiyama and the Matterhorn as the most photographed mountains on earth. See p.439

* **Jackson Hole Mountain Resort** – Famed as a destination for the true skiing or boarding connoisseur; the aprés ski scene in Jackson is also hard to beat. See p.450

Yellowstone and the Tetons

For many of the millions of people who visit the Rocky Mountains each year, a single, narrow corridor in far northwest Wyoming will be their primary goal – and with very good reason. Tucked in against the state's borders with Montana and Idaho is the world's oldest, and arguably most famous national park. And as if the bizarre geothermal features and extraordinary concentration of wildlife in **Yellowstone National Park** aren't enough to bring in the crowds, the unbelievably photogenic peaks and scenic hiking trails of **Grand Teton National Park** are literally just down the road. Add to that the broad river basin of **Jackson Hole**, where one can float or fish the Snake River in summer and take on the awe-inspiring ski terrain of **Jackson Hole Mountain Resort** in winter, and there's no doubt one could profitably devote an entire Rockies vacation to just this neighborhood alone.

Yellowstone National Park

Around three-and-a-half million visitors each year come to **YELLOWSTONE NATIONAL PARK**, the largest national park in the lower 48 states, to glory in its magnificent mountain scenery and abundant wildlife, and above all to witness geothermal phenomena on a unique scale. Measuring roughly sixty by fifty miles, Yellowstone more than lives up to all the hype that surrounds it, combining the glorious colors of the Grand Canyon of the Yellowstone River, limpid Yellowstone Lake and rainbow-hued hot springs, along with the sounds of subterranean rumblings, belching mudpots, steam hissing from the mountainsides, and of course the spectacular geysers. All of which would be more than enough to justify its status as the country's premier national park, but Yellowstone is further blessed with an astonishing array of wildlife that includes bison, moose, elk, mountain lions, wolves, grizzlies, and coyotes.

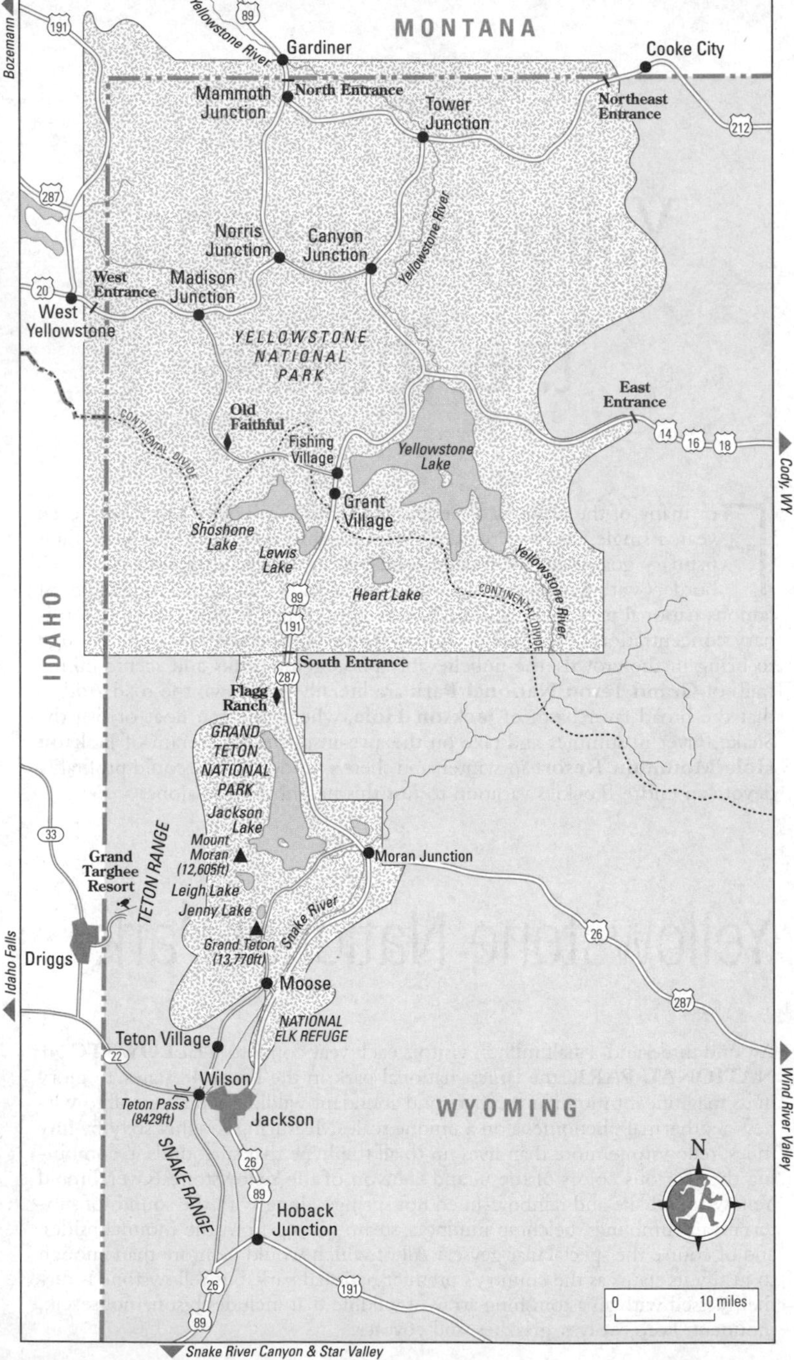
Livingston
Bozemann
MONTANA
Yellowstone River
89
191
Gardiner
Cooke City
North Entrance
Mammoth Junction
Tower Junction
Northeast Entrance
212
287
Yellowstone River
Norris Junction
Canyon Junction
8
West Entrance
Madison Junction
20
West Yellowstone
YELLOWSTONE NATIONAL PARK
East Entrance
Old Faithful
CONTINENTAL DIVIDE
Fishing Village
Yellowstone Lake
14
16
18
Cody, WY
Grant Village
Shoshone Lake
Lewis Lake
Yellowstone River
Heart Lake
CONTINENTAL DIVIDE
89
191
IDAHO
South Entrance
287
Flagg Ranch
GRAND TETON NATIONAL PARK
Jackson Lake
33
TETON RANGE
Mount Moran (12,605ft)
Moran Junction
Grand Targhee Resort
Leigh Lake
Jenny Lake
Snake River
26
Grand Teton (13,770ft)
Idaho Falls
Driggs
Moose
287
NATIONAL ELK REFUGE
Teton Village
22
Wind River Valley
Wilson
Teton Pass (8429ft)
WYOMING
Jackson
SNAKE RANGE
26
N
89
Hoback Junction
26
191
0
10 miles
89
Snake River Canyon & Star Valley

Accommodation price codes

All accommodation prices in this book have been coded using the symbols below. For **hotels**, **motels**, and **B&Bs**, rates are given for the least expensive double room in each establishment during peak season; variations are indicated where appropriate, including winter rates for all ski resorts. For **hostels**, the actual price per bed is given; for **camping**, the overnight cost per site is given. For a full explanation see p.30 in Basics.

❶ up to $30	❹ $60–80	❼ $130–180
❷ $30–45	❺ $80–100	❽ $180–240
❸ $45–60	❻ $100–130	❾ over $240

The park's popularity is its Achilles heel, both from the point of view of the enjoyment of the visitor and the pressure put on the environment by so much human traffic. If you visit during high summer (June–Aug) be prepared for hordes of tourists – notably Americans on vacation in huge RVs – but if you let yourself get frustrated by it all, you'll be missing something very special. The **best time to visit** is during the fall (late Aug to Sept) when the foliage is turning to blinding shades of red and gold, and animals become more active as the heat of summer fades. The key to appreciating the park is to take your time, and to plan carefully; it's possible to take in the major sights in three days, but if you'd prefer to include some leisurely exploration and a hike or two, you'll need five days at least. Take into account that, while there are certainly some rewarding hikes in Yellowstone, the consensus view is that the best of the hiking in northern Wyoming is in the Tetons and the Wind River Mountains – if you have limited time, you may want to leave your hiking for either of those areas.

Note that most entrances and roads in the park are **open** from early May to October only. The only year-round access point is the North Entrance at Gardiner, and the only road that remains open to wheeled vehicles all winter is the road from Gardiner via Mammoth Hot Springs to Cooke City near the Northeast Entrance. Travel east of Cooke City on the Beartooth Highway is not possible in the winter months. Bear in mind that if you plan to visit **in winter** from a southern gateway such as Jackson, you're in for a day-long drive on icy roads through Idaho and on up to Bozeman in Montana to link up with the road to Gardiner. For more detailed information on the park's road schedule see Ⓦwww.nps.gov/yell/planvisit/orientation/travel/roadopen.htm.

Some history

Although Native Americans had long hunted in what is now Yellowstone National Park, they were decimated by disease by the time the first white man, **John Colter**, arrived in 1807. A veteran of the Lewis and Clark expedition, his account of the exploding geysers and seething cauldrons of "Colter's Hell" was widely ridiculed. However, as ever more trappers, scouts, and prospectors hit upon Yellowstone, the government eventually sent out survey teams in 1870. Just two years later, Yellowstone was set aside as the **world's first national park**, in part to ensure that its assets were not entirely stripped by hunters, miners, and lumber companies.

At first, management of the park was beset by problems, with Congress devoting enthusiasm but little funding towards its protection. Irresponsible tourists stuck soap down the geysers, ruining the intricate plumbing, and bandits preyed on stagecoaches carrying rich excursionists. Congress took the park out of civilian hands in 1886, and put the army in charge. By the time they handed over

A geothermal wonderland

Yellowstone National Park centers on a 7500ft-high plateau, created by a vast volcanic eruption which occurred around 600,000 years ago. A huge underground chamber disgorged 250 cubic miles of molten rock, and then promptly collapsed upon itself, creating the Yellowstone **caldera**; its rim measures about 47 miles by 28 miles at its broadest. Into it are crammed more than half the world's geysers, plus thousands of fumaroles jetting plumes of steam, mud pots gurgling with acid-dissolved muds and clays, and hot springs. Most of the park's geothermal features sit within the caldera – as does much of Yellowstone Lake – but there is plenty of peripheral volcanic activity as well, as evidenced by the Norris Geyser basin and Mammoth Hot Springs, both of which are outside the caldera boundary.

The park's **geysers** erupt when superheated groundwater rising towards the surface gets constricted by fissures and narrow channels, and the bubbles that form literally blow the water through vents at the top. Yellowstone has at least three hundred geysers, appearing in two basic forms: **fountain geysers**, which bubble up into a pool and then shoot water all over the place before subsiding, and **cone geysers**, which shoot a single jet upwards through a cone or nozzle formation, created through a steady accumulation of mineral deposits.

Some of the park's most visually splendid features are its **hot springs**, which, like geysers, are sourced from underground by boiling water. The most distinctive feature of the hot springs is the amazing range of colors they exhibit, from aquamarine blues to fiery reds and oranges; this is caused by the brightly colored algae and bacteria that thrive in them, and each color indicates a specific temperature range. Green and brown indicate cooler water, while oranges and yellows indicate hotter water (in water hotter than 165°F visible organisms cannot survive).

The other features you'll see are **mudpots**, which are simply hot springs that are highly acidic, and so continually break down the surrounding rock into muddy clay, and **fumaroles**, which are hot springs that are short of water, so have to be content with hissing steam through their underground fissures.

to the newly created National Park Service in 1917, the ascendancy of the automobile in Yellowstone had begun, and visitor numbers began to boom.

The conflict between tourism and wilderness **preservation** has raged ever since. The elimination of predators such as mountain lions and wolves allowed the elk herd to grow unsupportably large; the former policy of permitting bears to feed from tourist scraps resulted in maulings. Most of these issues have since been addressed, but ecologists now warn that the park cannot stand alone as some pristine paradise, and must be seen as part of a much larger "Greater Yellowstone Ecosystem"; this notional ecosystem encompasses Yellowstone, the Tetons, the Snake River Valley south of Jackson to just over the Idaho border, and the northern Wind River Mountains.

The largest recent event to bring Yellowstone's environmental policies into focus was the series of **fires** that razed 36 percent of the park in 1988. Park authorities insisted the burn was a natural part of the forest's ecocycle, clearing out 200-year-old trees to make way for new growth, but the sight of the country's flagship national park in flames was seen by some as a public relations disaster. The aftermath did indeed see a burst of new growth, and the scarred mountainsides have been steadily recovering since.

Approaches to Yellowstone

The park occupies the far northwest corner of Wyoming, overlapping slightly into Idaho and Montana. Two of the park's **five entrances** are in Wyoming, via I-14/16/20 to the east (East Entrance) and I-89/191/189 to the south (South

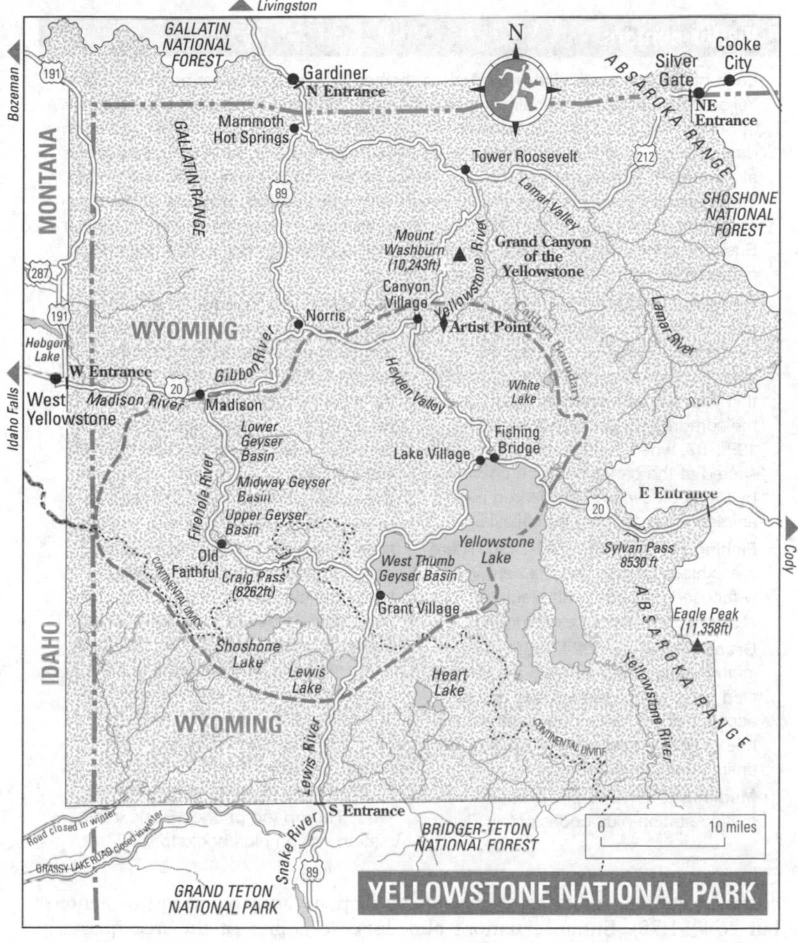

Entrance); to reach the South Entrance from Jackson – a distance of 57 miles – you drive through Grand Teton National Park (the entrance fee of $20 covers both national parks). Driving distance from Cody to the East Entrance is 53 miles. The other three entrances are all in Montana, via the gateway towns of **West Yellowstone** to the west (West Entrance), **Gardiner** to the north (North Entrance), and **Cooke City** to the northeast (Northeast Entrance); for further details of the gateway towns, see the relevant headings later in this chapter.

Information and getting around

Admission – $20 per car ($10 for pedestrians or cyclists) – is good for seven days, and includes entry to the Grand Teton park; keep your receipt to be able to leave and re-enter the park during this period. An annual pass for entry to the two parks costs $40. On arrival you'll be given a **free park map** at the

Visitor centers

Each of the **five main visitor centers** is themed around a different aspect of life in Yellowstone. All are open daily in summer (June–Aug 8am–7pm), plus shorter hours in September and October (9am–6pm); the Old Faithful visitor center is also open during winter (mid-Dec to mid-March daily 9am–5pm), while the park headquarters at Mammoth Hot Springs is the only visitor center that remains open year-round. There are also two supplemental summer-only **information stations** at Madison and West Thumb (both daily 9am–5pm), as well as a **museum** at Norris Geyser Basin that includes an exhibit on geothermal features (summer daily 8am–7pm; museum hours 9am–6pm; ⓣ307/344-2812).

Canyon ⓣ307/242-2550. Bison are the stars of the show at Canyon visitor center; two things not to miss are video footage of foolhardy tourists getting charged and gored by bison, and the sombre account of the winter of 1996–97, when 1800 bison were massacred at the park's northern boundary by livestock owners who feared the animals were carrying brucellosis.

Fishing Bridge ⓣ307/242-2450. There are exhibits on park wildlife here, mainly focused on birds, with plenty of stuffed specimens to examine.

Grant Village ⓣ307/242-2650. The infamous park fires of 1988 are chronicled here, with video footage and an account of the fierce debate about the role of fire in regeneration that has not entirely subsided since.

Madison ⓣ307/344-2821. Basic information station plus bookstore.

Mammoth Hot Springs ⓣ307/344-2263. This is the official park headquarters, where the theme is "natural and human history"; exhibits and videos trace the history of the park, from the earliest tourist expeditions through the army's 32 years in control and the NPS years since.

Old Faithful ⓣ307/545-2750. Not surprisingly, this center runs lots of short films on geyser behavior as well as general park features and geology. Given the number of people who come through the place, it's hopelessly inadequate in terms of space and facilities – an ambitious new center is planned, but probably won't open before 2004 at the earliest. Check the board here for predicted eruption times for the following geysers: Old Faithful, Castle, Daisy, Riverside, and Great Fountain.

West Thumb (no phone). Basic information station plus bookstore.

entrance station (additional copies of the map are available at visitor centers, but cost $1.75). Entrance stations also dispense copies of the free quarterly *Yellowstone Today*, the official park newssheet; it lists activities such as free ranger-led talks and campfire programs, and also has a useful directory of park services, as well as advice on fishing and wildlife watching.

Information is provided at five main visitor centers (see box, above), each of which stocks plenty of trail maps and a wide range of books. The most useful things you'll need to collect are the free maps of popular day-hikes and the various trail guides (50¢) that provide an overview of each of the major geothermal sites – these guides are also available at the sites themselves.

Details of ranger talks and an online version of *Yellowstone Today* are also posted on the comprehensive NPS **website** ⓦwww.nps.gov/yell, which also has plenty of information on activities and services within the park. You can tune in to 1610 AM for weather information.

Maps and books

The park **map** supplied upon entry is all you really need if you're just driving about the park and stopping off to enjoy a few short trails, but if you're plan-

Park services

You can find **ATMs** at *Old Faithful Inn* and *Old Faithful Snow Lodge*, *Lake Yellowstone Hotel*, *Mammoth Hot Springs Hotel*, and *Canyon Lodge*, as well as inside general stores at Fishing Bridge, Grant Village, Mammoth Hot Springs, Old Faithful, and Canyon.

The park's only year-round **post office** is at Mammoth Hot Springs, while there are seasonal offices (May–Sept/Oct) at Canyon, Grant, and Lake villages as well as at Old Faithful.

Medical services are available at clinics at Mammoth Hot Springs (year-round Mon–Fri 8.30am–1pm & 2–5pm; ⓣ307/344-7965), Old Faithful (mid-May to mid-Oct daily 8.30am–5pm; ⓣ307/545-7325), and Lake Hospital, near *Lake Yellowstone Hotel* (mid-May to mid-Sept; clinic daily 8.30am–8.30pm, 24hr emergency service available; ⓣ307/242-7241).

Supplies – including gas, groceries, snacks, drinks, film, and souvenirs – are available from stores at Old Faithful, Lake Yellowstone, Mammoth Hot Springs, and Fishing Bridge, as well as Canyon, Grant, and Roosevelt villages.

ning on venturing out into the backcountry, it's worth investing in a more detailed map (see "Hiking in Yellowstone" box on p.424 for more details).

Many **books** on sale at the vistor centers are published or distributed by the Yellowstone Association, a nonprofit organization that helps fund research and education projects within the park. You can order from their catalogue online (Ⓦwww.yellowstoneassociation.org). There has been plenty written about the park overall. *The Geysers of Yellowstone*, by T. Scott Bryan (University Press of Colorado), presents an exhaustive description of the formation, physical characteristics and eruption patterns of the park's most famous features in a scholarly yet exceptionally readable work. A short-and-sweet round-up of the park's **geology** is *Interpreting the Landscape – Recent and Ongoing Geology of Grand Teton and Yellowstone National Parks*, by John Good and Kenneth Pierce (Grand Teton Natural History Assoc). The definitive **park history** is *The Yellowstone Story*, by Aubrey L. Haines (University Press of Colorado): Volume I begins in ancient times, when the only inhabitants were indigenous hunter-gatherers, through to the 1880s when the park first experienced tourism; Volume II covers the period when the park was under military administration, on through the post-World War II tourism boom and developments since. A popular offbeat read is *Death and Yellowstone – Accidents and Foolhardiness in the First National Park*, by Lee H. Whitely (Court Wayne Press), featuring mishaps and near escapes, drownings and bear stories.

Getting around

There is no public transport within the park, and bus companies can only get you as far as West Yellowstone (on the park's western border), Bozeman (90 miles), Jackson (57 miles east), and Cody (53 miles south). While you can join **tours** from the various gateway towns and park villages (see box, overleaf), it's definitely best to have your own vehicle.

You can get **gas** at each of the five main villages – Old Faithful, West Thumb, and Lake Village/Bridge Bay on the south loop; Mammoth Hot Springs and Canyon Village on the north – as well as at Flagg Ranch near the south entrance and Tower-Roosevelt on the north loop road; it costs around five cents a gallon more than in nearby towns. Roads are fairly narrow and drivers tend to be inattentive as they're busy looking out for wildlife, so it's no place to be trying to **cycle** around.

Tours of the park

AmFac (Ⓣ307/344-7311, Ⓦwww.travelyellowstone.com) runs several day-tours which depart from the park villages ($28–35); the rather ambitious "Yellowstone in a Day" outing ($35) takes about eleven hours. In the winter AmFac runs snowcoach tours of the park from West Yellowstone, Flagg Ranch at the southern entrance, Old Faithful, and Mammoth Hot Springs.

Buffalo Bus Touring Company, 420 Yellowstone Ave, West Yellowstone (Ⓣ406/646-9564 or 1-800/426-7669, Ⓦwww.yellowstonevacations.com), offer tours of the park from West Yellowstone and will pick up and drop off at your motel or campsite. Tours of one loop run $38; both loops $70.

Gray Line, West Yellowstone (Ⓣ406/646-9374), offers bus tours through the park for around $40. They have two options, starting from the *Stagecoach Inn*, 209 Madison Ave, West Yellowstone: the "Upper Loop Adventure" runs Monday, Tuesday, Thursday, and Saturday past Mammoth Hot Springs and Dunraven Pass in the north of the park; and the "Lower Loop Adventure" runs daily trips to Old Faithful, Yellowstone Lake, and the Grand Canyon of the Yellowstone.

Yellowstone Alpine Guides, West Yellowstone (Ⓣ406/646-9591), offers full-day winter snowcoach tours to Old Faithful ($89) and the Grand Canyon of the Yellowstone ($89). These incorporate walking and/or cross-country skiing around the Old Faithful region.

Accommodation

All **accommodation** within the park is run by AmFac Parks and Resorts (Ⓣ307/344-7311, Ⓦwww.travelyellowstone.com). **Reservations**, strongly recommended from June through September, are essential over public holiday weekends. Prices beyond the park boundaries are a little lower, but staying inside can be wonderfully relaxing; none of the rooms at the various hotels, lodges, and cabins has a TV, and few après-hike revelers stay up past midnight. Each of the five villages in the park has a lodge building offering dining facilities and other services (see box, overleaf).

AmFac also operates twelve **campgrounds** in Yellowstone, including one for RVs only. Of these campgrounds, seven operate on a first-come, first-served basis; you have to arrive early in the day to get a site during June–August as most are full by 11am. The remaining five campgrounds – *Bridge Bay*, *Canyon*, *Fishing Bridge*, *Grant Village*, and *Madison* – accept **reservations** (Ⓣ307/344-7311, same-day reservations Ⓣ307/344-7901, Ⓦwww.travelyellowstone.com). All campgrounds have toilet facilities, but there are showers only where indicated (these cost $3.50, including towel and soap). RV owners should note that generators are not allowed at the following campgrounds: *Indian Creek*, *Pebble Creek*, *Slough Creek*, and *Tower Fall*.

The alternative to staying at the established campgrounds is to camp in the **backcountry**, though you'll need a permit for this – see the box on p.424 for more details.

Hotels and cabins

Canyon Lodge and Cabins Located half a mile from the Grand Canyon of the Yellowstone, the collection of cabins here represents some of the least inspiring accommodation in the park. Rooms in the two hotel-lodge buildings are far more appealing, and each has its own bathroom, phone and coffee-maker; some of the older cabins may soon be demolished to make way for a third hotel-lodge. Open June to mid-Sept. Rooms ⑤, cabins ③

Grant Village This development – the southern-most accommodation in the park – has borne plenty of criticism for its lack of any style, or empathy with its surroundings. Accommodation is in cramped motel-style rooms, each with own bath, in a dreary brown building on the southwest shore of Yellowstone Lake. Open mid-May to Sept. ❺

Lake Yellowstone Hotel and Cabins Rooms in this grand colonial-style hotel are quite small but comfortable and decked out in light, cheery colors. The entire hotel is bright and airy inside, and the "Sun Room," which looks directly over the lake, is a fine place for an evening drink. The 100-odd cabins out front are uninspiring shadeless boxes, though each has its own bathroom plus two double beds. Open mid-May to Sept. Rooms ❺, cabins ❹

Lake Yellowstone Lodge and Cabins Just along the lakeshore from the *Lake Yellowstone Hotel* are 186 cabins all with own bath (none have actual lakeside locations), lined up behind the grand log-built *Lake Yellowstone Lodge*, which features a dining room, gift shop, guest laundry and two huge roaring fires; the lake-facing deck is a serene place to curl up with a book. There's a stark trade-off in your choice of cabins, as those handiest to the lodge are shadeless, while those back towards the forest (sections H and J) are larger and enjoy more peaceful surrounds; the cheapest cabins have one double bed, others have two doubles and can accommodate four people. Open mid-May to Sept. ❹

Mammoth Hot Springs Hotel & Cabins The exterior of this 1930s hotel, which is right at the north end of the park, is sprucer than the rather dreary rooms inside. The cheapest of the rooms and cabins have shared bath, those with their own bathroom cost a little more. Many people actually prefer to stay in one of the cabins for a little extra privacy; a number of elk often snooze the afternoon away on the grassy areas out front. Open May to mid-Oct & mid-Dec to early March. Rooms ❹, cabins ❸

Old Faithful Inn and Cabins At least one night at Old Faithful is really a must, ideally in a rustic room (some have own bath) at the amazing 1903 *Old Faithful Inn* – said to be the world's largest log building. Rooms in the newer annex are pretty standard motel-style ones, and there are also a number of cabins with and without private bathroom – but you'll need to book a couple of months in advance for any room at all during June–August. Note that 2004 marks the centennial of *Old Faithful Inn*, and it may be necessary to make reservations for that summer a year in advance. Open May to mid-Oct. Rooms ❺, cabins ❷

Old Faithful Snow Lodge and Cabins Along with *Mammoth Hot Springs Hotel*, the *Snow Lodge and Cabins* provide the only accommodation open in the winter. Built in 1998, the lodge has a modern hotel feel about it, while the en-suite cabins are pretty basic but well sealed against the cold. Open May to mid-Oct & mid-Dec to early March. Rooms ❺, cabins ❺

Roosevelt Lodge Cabins These 82 rustic cabins in the north of the park are situated well away from the most popular places to stay, and this accounts for much of their appeal. The lodge building has a restaurant, bar, gift shop, and log-fire, and there are rocking chairs on the outside deck. The most basic of the cabins are not much more than wooden shelters with two beds and a wood-stove. All cabins share communal bathroom facilities, although the most expensive have their own shower. Open mid-June to mid-Sept. ❷

Campgrounds

Bridge Bay 3 miles south of Lake Village. Open area with very little shade; the further back you go towards the forest, the more shade there is and you may even find a site high enough for a lake view. Handy to the lake's main marina, so ideal for anglers and boating enthusiasts. Nearest pay showers and coin laundry are four miles away at *Fishing Bridge Campground* (see below). Open late May to mid-Sept. 430 sites; tents $15, RVs $23.

Canyon Beside Canyon Village. This has the most tent-only sites, largely because it's densely forested and thus not well-suited to RVs. Close to the most photographed view in the park, at the south end of the Grand Canyon of the Yellowstone. Restaurants, gas, store, pay showers, and coin laundry. Open June to mid-Sept. 272 sites; tents $15, RVs $23.

Fishing Bridge Just east of the bridge itself, this campground is for RVs only, due to frequent bear activity in the area; reservations essential. Full electrical hookup available, pay showers and coin laundry, gas, and store. Open mid-May to Sept. 340 sites; $27.

Grant Village In contrast to rooms at the lodge building, the campsites here are very appealing, tree-shaded and close to the lakeshore. Restaurants, gas, store, pay showers, and coin laundry. Open mid-June to Sept. 425 sites; tents $15, RVs $23.

Indian Creek 8 miles south of Mammoth Junction on the north loop. Quiet sites in a lightly-wooded forest. Open mid-June to mid-Sept. 75 sites; tents $10, RVs $23.

Lewis Lake 10 miles from the southern park entrance beside the lake. Plenty of quiet and shade, with the bonus of easy access to Lewis Lake; this is the southernmost of the park's campgrounds. Open late June to Oct. 85 sites; tents $10, RVs $23.

Madison Beside Madison Junction on the south loop. Situated near the junction of the Madison and Firehole rivers, this campground is popular with anglers. No showers or laundry. Open May–Oct. 280 sites; tents $15, RVs $23.

Mammoth At the bottom of the windy road below Mammoth Hot Springs. This dry and dusty sage-brush plot sits right beside the road, and is only worth considering as a last resort, or for camping in winter. Open year-round. 85 sites; tents $12, RVs $23.

Norris Just north of Norris Junction on the north loop. Pleasant forested sites elevated above the Gibbon River. Open mid-May to Sept. 116 sites; tents $12, RVs $23.

Pebble Creek Creekside but still near the road, at the eastern end of the Lamar Valley. Popular spot for hikers heading into the backcountry, as a selection of fine trails is accessible from here. Open June–Sept. 32 sites; tents $10, RVs $23.

Slough Creek 2.5 miles north of the main road through the Lamar Valley. Ideal location beside the creek, with handy access to some great back-country hikes. Open late May to Oct. 29 sites; tents $10, RVs $23.

Tower Fall Across the road from Tower Falls near Tower-Roosevelt Junction. Close to wildlife viewing spots in the Lamar Valley; "civilization," in the form of *Roosevelt Lodge* and its amenities, is barely three miles away. Open mid-May to Sept. 32 sites; tents $10, RVs $23.

Eating and drinking

Snack bars and restaurants inside the park aren't cheap, but given where you are, they're not hideously expensive either. The seven **general stores** (see box on p.415) stock moderately priced groceries including canned goods, cereal, booze, fruit, fresh bread, milk, and ice. Campers should ideally stock up before arriving in the park, at a supermarket in one of the gateway towns or in Jackson or Cody. For details on eating options in the nearby towns of West Yellowstone, Gardiner, and Cooke City, see the individual town accounts later in this chapter.

Besides the do-it-yourself approach, there are three options for eating in the park: sandwiches and drinks from one of the general stores; a basic feed at one of the self-serve park cafeterias; or a full-blown meal at one of the park's restaurants. There's not a lot of menu variation among the **restaurants**, which are located at *Old Faithful Inn*, *Old Faithful Snow Lodge*, *Roosevelt Lodge*, *Lake Yellowstone Hotel*, *Mammoth Hot Springs Hotel*, *Canyon Lodge* and *Grant Village*; however, *Old Faithful Inn* and *Lake Yellowstone Hotel* are the clear standouts for location, mood, and ambience. Entrees ($14–22) run from salmon and steak to roast dinners and lighter choices such as burgers or Caesar salads ($8), with desserts ($4–5) and a basic range of beers and wines available too. Note that **dinner reservations** are required during summer at *Old Faithful Inn* (ⓣ307/545-4999), *Lake Yellowstone Hotel* (ⓣ307/242-3899), and *Grant Village* (ⓣ307/242-3499); you won't get a table without one. The restaurants are open for lunch and **breakfast** too; they usually offer a breakfast buffet that includes fresh fruit, cereals, pastries, and standard cooked breakfast items, all for around $7.

Cafeterias, found at *Old Faithful Lodge*, *Canyon Lodge* and *Lake Yellowstone Lodge*, have basic but filling meals ($5–8), plus sandwiches, drinks, and ice cream; the bakery at *Old Faithful Lodge* is a good choice for a cheap breakfast on the run – there are fresh muffins, cookies, and cinnamon rolls.

The best places for a **drink** are the bar at *Old Faithful Inn* or in *Lake Yellowstone Hotel*'s colonial-style "Sun Room"; the bar at *Canyon Lodge* is relaxed and quiet but has very little charm.

Exploring the park

Yellowstone could be fairly described as Mother Nature's theme park, with one jaw-dropping sight after another, all of them labeled and signposted within a few hundred yards of the 142-mile figure-of-eight **Loop Road**. In fact, unlike national parks elsewhere in the country, Yellowstone really can be treated like one large tourist attraction; you can simply drive from one sight to the next, walk around, take some pictures and drive on. This would normally be the way to miss out on really experiencing a national park, but in the case of Yellowstone, it's a perfectly legitimate way to see the best that it has to offer. Of course, it's this easy accessibility to so many astonishing natural wonders that makes the place so popular; Yellowstone is ideally suited to families and those whose physical capabilities would restrict them from spending days hiking about in the mountains. At the same time, and precisely because the vast majority of visitors never leave the loop road, there are great rewards for people who do venture into the wilds.

The **speed limit** is a radar-enforced 45mph; traffic and unpredictable hazards like "bison-jams" make journey times hard to predict.

North loop and Lamar Valley

The highlights of the north loop and its branch road which runs towards the Northeast Entrance are two major geothermal sites – **Mammoth Hot Springs** and **Norris Geyser Basin** and the park's most prodigious wildlife habitat, the **Lamar Valley**. The north loop itself covers seventy miles, and it's a further 29 miles from Tower-Roosevelt Junction through the Lamar Valley to the northeast park entrance.

Mammoth Hot Springs and Tower-Roosevelt

At **Mammoth Hot Springs**, at the northern tip of the Loop Road, terraces of barnacle-like deposits cascade down a vapor-shrouded mountainside. Tinted a marvelous array of grays, greens, yellows, browns, and oranges by various kinds of algae, they are composed of travertine, a form of limestone which, having been dissolved and carried to the surface by boiling water, is deposited as tier upon tier of steaming stone. The springs lack the drama of the more explosive features of the geyser basins, but there is nothing else in the park that looks quite like this arrangement of **sculpted terraces**, and groups of elk often provide a curious photo opportunity as they bask in the middle of them. It takes around ninety minutes to stroll the two sections of boardwalk which traverse the Upper and Lower terraces.

The main landmark of **Tower-Roosevelt**, east of Mammoth Hot Springs, is **Mount Washburn**, one of the park's highest peaks (10,243ft), whose lookout tower can be reached by an enjoyable all-day hike or a grueling cycle ride (almost seven miles round-trip) along a rough road starting fourteen miles south of Tower-Roosevelt Junction. A far less demanding trail begins just two miles south of the junction and leads down to the spray-drenched base of **Tower Fall**; it's only a mile or so round-trip, and the best view is from the bottom, not the top. A half-mile north of the falls is the **Calcite Springs** overlook, from where you get a clear view of spookily steaming cliff-faces on the far side of the river canyon.

Lamar Valley

From Tower Junction, I-212 wanders away east through the meadows of serene **Lamar Valley**, towards the ice-packed peaks of the Beartooth Mountains. Prosaically referred to as "North America's Serengheti" because of its **abundant wildlife**, the valley is carpeted in sagebrush and grasslands and is the scene of a daily life-and-death struggle between predators (grizzlies, wolves, coyotes, mountain lion) and their prey (elk, bison, deer). There are no major sights as such, but every day around sunset and sunrise, people gather at the various roadside pull-outs between Slough Creek and Pebble Creek with their folding chairs, thermos flasks, and binoculars, patiently waiting for a bear to lumber out of the forest, or a wolf pack to gallop into view in hot pursuit of a hapless elk.

The valley is also home to the park's premier research and education facility, the **Yellowstone Institute** (Ⓣ307/344-2293, Ⓦwww.yellowstoneassociation.org), the base for a range of naturalist-led **field trips**, seminars, and expeditions including wildlife-watching, geology, and environmental education. Check the association's website for a full list of activities and fees.

Norris Geyser Basin

At the southern end of the north loop, **Norris Geyser Basin** is comprised of two sections, Porcelain Basin and Back Basin, and makes a dramatic contrast with the pretty settings of most of the park's other geyser basins. In this pallid, toxic landscape it's easy to imagine billions of amoeba and protozoa marshalling their forces, before crawling forth from the primeval slime to kick-start life on earth. In amongst the clumps of dead trees are the iridescent Cistern and Emerald springs, and the famous **Steamboat Geyser**, the world's tallest (on the rare occasions that it does decide to blow). Allegedly capable of forcing near-boiling water over 300ft into the air, Steamboat did favor a couple of lucky early-morning visitors with a millennium show on May 2, 2000; its closest previous eruption was way back on October 2, 1991, so you may not wish to sit and wait for the next one. Meantime it tantalizes the crowds with lesser bursts of ten to forty feet a couple of times a day. The basin's **Echinus Geyser** is the largest acid-water geyser known; every 35 to 75 minutes it spews crowd-pleasing, vinegary eruptions of forty to sixty feet. A number of elk roam Norris Basin too and, as always, a measure of respect is in order as they can be aggressive.

South loop

The highlights of the 86-mile south loop include the park's marquee attraction, **Old Faithful** geyser, along with a number of other, equally spectacular geothermal wonders. **Yellowstone Lake** itself is a serene sight, and the view across it from beside the gorgeous pools of the **West Thumb Geyser Basin** is not to be missed. The view from **Artist Point**, at the south end of the **Grand Canyon of the Yellowstone**, is the park's most photographed scene for very good reasons; there are in fact very few sights on the south loop which are not "A-list" attractions – try and give this region the minimum two days it deserves.

Old Faithful and around

For well over a century, the dependable **Old Faithful** has been the most popular geyser in the park, erupting more frequently than any of its higher or larger rivals. As a result, a half-moon of concentric benches now surround it at a respectful distance on the side away from the Firehole River. On average, it

Winter in Yellowstone

Blanketed in four feet of snow between November and April, Yellowstone takes on a whole new appearance in **winter**: a silent and bizarre world where waterfalls freeze in mid-plunge, geysers blast towering plumes of steam and water into the cold air, and buffalo, beards matted with ice, stand around in huddles. Only the road from Gardiner to Cooke City via Mammoth Hot Springs is kept open (the Beartooth Highway east of Cooke City is closed), and **accommodation** is limited to the *Mammoth Hot Springs Hotel* and the *Old Faithful Snow Lodge* – with the latter usually only accessible by snowcoach or snowmobile. Popular winter **activities** run from both locations are snowshoeing and cross-country skiing and wildlife-watching tours; equipment rental is also available.

Snowcoach **tours** of the park are run by AmFac and Yellowstone Alpine Tours (see box on p.416). **Snowmobile** rental, generally cheapest in West Yellowstone, costs around $130 a day (see box on p.430 for West Yellowstone rental outfits). Several companies in Jackson run snowmobile tours of Yellowstone, from one to five days: try Old Faithful Snowmobile Tours (☎307/733-9767 or 1-800/253-7130) or Jackson Hole Snowmobile Tours (☎307/733-6850 or 1-800/633-1733). Much cheaper and less invasive is **cross-country skiing**; several miles of groomed trails explore the park's west side (see box on p.431).

Wildlife watching during winter is a unique experience; elk, deer, and bison scratch out a parlous living among whatever vegetation they can reach beneath the snow. They tend to gather at warm thermal and riverside locations where the snow never quite takes hold, although you'll also see **bison** putting their massive foreheads to use as snow shovels, clearing a way to the greenery buried underneath. Of the predators, the **grizzlies** are smart enough to curl up and wait out the winter months, while **coyotes** have developed the dangerous habit of wandering the roadsides begging for scraps from motorists. Meanwhile, the **wolves and mountain lions** really come into their own, taking down the weakest of the grazing animals the moment they falter. Winter **wolf-watching trips** are among the most popular activities run by the Yellowstone Institute (see opposite).

At the time of writing, it appears likely that snowmobiles will be phased out from the park by 2004, unless significant modifications are made to reduce noise and fuel emissions. If and when the machines are banned, this will greatly limit the possibilities for travel within the park, and may impact on winter accommodation and services at Old Faithful and Flagg Ranch.

"performs" for the expectant crowds every 78 minutes, with a minimum gap of half an hour and a maximum of two hours; approximate schedules are displayed in the visitor center and in the lobby of the inn. The first sign of activity is a soft hissing as water splashes repeatedly over the rim. After several minutes, a column of water shoots to a height of 100 to 180 feet, the geyser spurting out a total of 11,000 gallons.

Two miles of boardwalks lead from Old Faithful to dozens of other geysers in the Upper Basin. Check the predicted times when **Grand Geyser** is due to explode – they're usually posted on a board near the geyser itself. This colossus blows on average just twice a day, for twelve to twenty minutes, in a series of four powerful bursts that climb to 200ft. Other favorites of the Old Faithful area are **Castle Geyser** and **Giant Geyser**, both of which erupt infrequently and are thus hard to predict. When they do explode however, each may throw jets over two hundred feet into the air, so some people pack a lunch and settle in to wait for the show to begin. If you're hoping to **photograph the geysers**, including Old Faithful, you may only have one chance; position yourself upwind, otherwise you'll be photographing a big cloud of steam instead of the actual water spout. In this area too are a number of pretty hot springs, with **Morning Glory Pool** the most beautiful – it's well worth the twenty-minute walk from Old Faithful to savor the color in the pool's yellow-orange outer rings and mesmerizing blue depths.

Biscuit Basin, a short drive north of Old Faithful, is named for "biscuits" of rock that were blown from around **Sapphire Pool** following an earthquake in 1959 (see p.474). Sapphire Pool certainly lives up to its name, and the nearby **Black Sand Basin** has its own distinct charms; here a plateau of volcanic black sand is split by gurgling Iron Spring Creek. Attractions include three very pretty hot pools, including the gorgeous **Sunset Lake**, whose central geyser sends waves lapping constantly onto vermilion shores, and **Cliff Geyser**, which occupies an impossibly picturesque position and looks like the perfect six-person creekside hot tub. You can walk or even cycle along paved paths about a mile from the Old Faithful area to Biscuit Basin and Black Sand Basin.

Along the Firehole River: Old Faithful to Madison

About four miles north of Old Faithful is the **Midway Geyser Basin**, where **Excelsior Geyser** – now mostly a big, bubbling crater – constantly disgorges thousands of gallons of superheated water into the Firehole River below. One of the park's more eccentric geysers, Excelsior erupted regularly until the late 1880s, and then went inexplicably quiet until 1985, when it blew its stack continuously for two days. Based on the impressive photograph on display at the site, you would not want to be standing on the boardwalk the next time it does go off. Another highlight here is the park's largest hot spring, **Grand Prismatic Spring** – named for its amazing spectrum of rich colors, from royal blue through to fiery orange.

About two miles north of Midway Geyser Basin you can take a short detour along the one-way (northbound) **Firehole Lake Drive**, which travels past **Great Fountain Geyser**, whose eruptions may come as often as every ten hours. Bursts can go to two hundred feet, and the circular tabletop of accumulated minerals which skirts the geyser pot creates an appealing stage for a steamy show. Firehole Lake itself spills its waters into neighboring Hot Lake.

At the northern end of the drive you'll find the **Fountain Paint Pot Nature Trail**, which, though fairly small, offers a grab-bag of every type of geothermal feature found in the park. The paint pot itself is aptly named, a bubbling mixture of clay minerals and particles of silica that just needs a good stir to blend the streaks of orange and red into the dominant heavy cream color. There are two pretty pools, Silex and Leather, a couple of hissing fumaroles, and a small cluster of geysers which erupt frequently if not terribly spectacularly. The enigmatic "Red Spouter" is sometimes a fumarole, sometimes a dirty, bubbling pool and sometimes a mudpot, depending on its supply of water.

Another two-mile spur road, **Firehole Canyon Drive**, runs one-way (southbound) from just below Madison Junction. You can stop at the overlook of **Firehole Falls**, where whitewater surges through a narrows in the canyon. This is also one of the few places you can **swim** in the park – a huge relief on a hot summer's day.

The Grand Canyon of the Yellowstone

The Yellowstone River roars and tumbles for 24 miles between the sheer golden-hued cliffs of the **Grand Canyon of the Yellowstone**, whose width varies between 1500 and 4000 feet and its depth between 800 and 1200 feet; almost the entire length of the canyon actually runs parallel to the road between

Canyon Village and Tower-Roosevelt on the north loop, but you're too far from the canyon to get any decent views. The best viewpoints are clustered together just below Canyon Village. The most visited is **Artist Point**, and the moment you glimpse the impossibly perfect waterfalls, juxtaposed with sheer canyon walls fired with streaks of orange and red, the origins of the name will be only too clear. Artists are indeed out in force every day, laying claim to the best vantage points above what must be the most reproduced painting subject in North America.

The 2.5-mile North Rim Drive, which runs one-way (south) from Canyon Village, provides access to several overlooks on the north side of the canyon; you can simply park and take in the view, but it's well worth getting right down to the falls themselves. A short trail leads to the **Brink of Lower Falls** (a steep ten-minute walk), from where you can see close up the awesome power of the 2,245,000 gallons of water which go over every minute, and watch the thunderous 308ft falls making short work (geologically speaking) of the rock walls below. A spur road also goes to the Brink of Upper Falls, from where you can walk two hundred meters for a closer look at the 109ft **Upper Falls**. On the south rim, **Uncle Tom's Trail** descends steeply down into the canyon to a gently vibrating, spray-covered platform right in the face of Lower Falls.

Mud Volcano and around

You will probably already have visited a geyser basin or two before you arrive at **Mud Volcano**, and if you thought the geysers' outpouring of sulphurous gases was an olfactory experience, you're in for a real treat here. The key to these features' difference from the geysers and hot springs is a higher level of acidity, constantly at work breaking down rock into clay mud. This collection of mudpots and cauldrons make up the moodiest and ugliest of the park's thermal regions; a one-mile boardwalk winds through gurgling pools of sickly brown and yellow mud, past trees that have been steamed to death, to the bleak, barren shores of **Sour Lake** – the perfect set for a horror movie. Joining a free ranger-led tour here gives you the chance to get off the boardwalk and into the backcountry, where the **Big Gumper**, which blew into existence in the 1970s, bubbles with big gray globs of smelly mud. Across the road from Mud Volcano is a single, isolated feature simply called **Sulphur Cauldron**. It won't surprise you to learn that this sickly yellow arrowhead-shaped bubbling pool is thought to be the most acidic in the entire park. Groups of bison often congregate in the Mud Volcano area, and bison-jams may hold up traffic for some minutes.

Yellowstone Lake and the Yellowstone River

North America's largest alpine lake, the deep and (usually) deceptively calm **Yellowstone Lake** fills the eastern half of the Yellowstone caldera, its shoreline measuring 110 miles. At 7733ft above sea level it's high enough to be frozen for half the year, but in summer it's popular with tourists taking cruises (1hr; $8.75), in rowboats ($6 per hour), and on guided fishing expeditions ($55 per hour for a boat which can carry up to six people). Boat tours leave from the Bridge Bay Marina at **Fishing Bridge**.

The **Yellowstone River** itself winds its way through **Hayden Valley**, a wide open plain that makes for an especially arresting sight in fall – carpeted in red and gold and speckled with thousands of grazing bison. About three miles north of Fishing Bridge is the **Le Hardy Rapids**, one of the most animated stretches of water along the Yellowstone. A short boardwalk follows the riverbank, and during June and July you may see cutthroat trout leaping upstream on their way to spawn. There's no fishing allowed in the area of the rapids themselves, but the river on either side is very popular with anglers.

West Thumb Geyser Basin

Although it can't boast the explosiveness of the geysers in the Old Faithful area, **West Thumb Geyser Basin**, north of Grant Village, is still spectacular as it's perched right on the edge of Yellowstone Lake. A couple of hot pools empty right into the tranquil waters and fizz away into nothing, and it's easy to see

Hiking in Yellowstone

While there are certainly some rewarding **hikes** in Yellowstone, the best of the hiking in northern Wyoming is in the less-visited Tetons and Wind River Mountains – if you have limited time, you may want to leave your hiking for either of those areas. That said, seeing as the vast majority of visitors never leave the loop road, the one thousand-plus miles of trails here can be surprisingly secluded, and the chances of spotting wildlife are nearly guaranteed.

There are plenty of free **trail maps** available at visitor centers that provide a basic sketch of recommended day-hikes, as well as a Trails Illustrated basic trail map for the entire park ($2.95); if you're planning further exploration of the backcountry, it's worth investing in the American Adventures Association map, which splits the park into two halves (north and south; $3.95 each), while a 1:168,500 Trails Illustrated topography map of the park costs $9.95.

To **camp in the backcountry** you need a permit, free from visitor centers, information stations, and ranger stations; these can be collected no earlier than 48 hours in advance of your camping trip. There are around three hundred designated backcountry sites, and as relatively few people venture off the main roads, it's rarely a problem to get a reservation. However, for the most popular sites around Yellowstone Lake and the northern half of the Lamar Valley, you may want to make reservations in advance; these cost $15, and are made by post (Backcountry Office, PO Box 168, Yellowstone National Park, WY 82190). All permits must be collected in person and there's a mandatory half-hour video on backcountry safety. This is bear country, and safety measures for hiking and camping should be observed (see p.550).

Day-hikes

Among a number of day-hikes which lead to views of Lake Yellowstone, the **Elephant Back Mountain** trail is probably the most popular. The trailhead is a mile south of Fishing Bridge Junction – easy walking distance from the *Lake Yellowstone Hotel*. The three miles round-trip through pine forest make for a fairly short and moderate loop-hike, but it's worth setting aside a few hours so you can bask in the sun and the lake view from a rocky outcrop while tucking into a picnic lunch.

The trek to the top of **Mount Washburn** (10,243ft) features at or near the top of most rangers' picks of the park's best day-hikes (approx. 4hr). Two trailheads along the Canyon–Tower road (Chittenden Rd and Dunraven Pass, both with parking areas) each lead to a strenuous three-mile series of switchbacks to the summit (elevation gain 1500ft), where you'll find an enclosed observation area with telescope to maximize the views. The fragile tundra up top supports alpine flowers, pikas, and marmots, and is frequented by bighorn sheep during summer; bear in mind you'll be exposed to sometimes chilly winds, sun, and possibly lightning storms.

The Lamar Valley in the park's northeast is far from the major geothermal sites, so a day's hiking here is well worth considering as a break from the summer crowds. Begin by driving to the *Slough Creek* campground; pick up the **Slough Creek** trail a few hundred yards south of the campground, which follows an historic wagon trail

why early tourists would have made use of the so-called **Fishing Cone** by cooking fresh-caught fish in its boiling waters. The boardwalk, under a mile long, takes you past a string of pools and springs and around the lake's edge. The stunning 53ft deep **Abyss Pool** and nearby **Black Pool** (actually a deep azure blue) are the standout features, and while there have been no regular geyser eruptions in recent years, the collection of otherworldly-colors and the stunning lake vista make this basin unmissable – try for a late afternoon visit to skip the crowds and catch a breathtaking sunset over the lake.

north through fir forest and several pretty meadows. It's an up-and-back hike, so the distance is up to you; It's two miles to the first meadow, where the trail meets the creek, and five miles to the second (one-way). This is a popular day-trip for anglers, and moose may be seen along the way.

There's plenty to look at in the course of following the **Yellowstone River Picnic Area** loop trail, which skirts the east rim of the Grand Canyon of the Yellowstone for almost half of its 3.7 miles (the trailhead is 1.25 miles northeast of Tower Junction). Besides views of the river including the "Narrows of the Yellowstone," there are occasional bighorn sheep sightings along the precipitous cliffsides.

Multiday hikes

One of the first places that grabs the attention of long-haul hikers as they pore over the park map is **Shoshone Lake**; far enough from the roads to be tantalizing but close enough to hike to inside of a day, this is the largest lake in the Lower 48 that doesn't have any direct access by road. The quickest way to reach it is via the DeLacy Creek trail (three miles one-way), which begins to the north of the lake on the road between Old Faithful and West Thumb. The 22-mile trail which then circumnavigates the lake wanders away from its shore at various points, and has a number of designated backcountry campsites (advance reservations advised in summer; see above for details). The Shoshone Geyser Basin, with its collection of pools, small geysers, and mudpots, is by the far western edge of the lake.

It's important to be bear-aware during any extended venture among the trails to the north of the **Lamar Valley**. One of the easier ways to tackle a long hike here is to start out at the Warm Creek Picnic Area (a mile-and-a-half west of the northeast entrance station), and hoof it up a steep 1200 feet in 1.6 miles to get straight into the high country. From there you'll be heading westward and largely downhill, across **Pebble Creek** – which can be tricky to ford when the water level is up in spring and early summer – and onto the **Bliss Pass** trail, which heads west to link with the Slough Creek trail. For a comfortable two-day trip you may choose to turn south back down to the road via the Pebble Creek trail, while the full distance from the Warm Creek Picnic Area all the way to the *Slough Creek* campground (around twenty miles) can be strung out into a lazy three days.

To the northwest of the Lamar Valley, a trail through the **Black Canyon of the Yellowstone** makes for another memorable overnight hike. With several riverside backcountry sites strung along the trail, which mostly follows the Yellowstone River from the Black Creek trailhead to Gardiner in Montana, it's best to stretch the reasonably strenuous one-way fifteen-mile hike into a two-day journey. Though there are few geothermal features, the trip takes in nearly all of the park's different landscapes, from high plains to deep forests and river valleys. The last four miles then heads through a semi-desert environment, surrounded by beautiful "painted" canyon walls on both sides; stock up on water before entering this portion of the hike and also keep a look out for rattlesnakes (see box on p.259 for more on rattlers).

△ Mammoth Hot Springs in Yellowstone National Park

Fishing and boating in Yellowstone

If you plan on doing some angling in the park, you'll need a special Yellowstone **fishing permit**, available at visitor centers and general stores ($10 for ten days, $20 for the season); a regular Wyoming state fishing license isn't required. The **fishing season** runs roughly from June through October, although this varies at some locations. Read the free *Fishing Regulations* brochure for specific details on restricted areas, catch limits and other conditions. A special fishing regime is in force for Yellowstone Lake, where exotic **lake trout** are endangering the survival of the native cutthroat species; in essence, you must release any cutthroat trout you catch, but keep every lake trout you haul out.

Boating permits are required for all water craft in Yellowstone (even float tubes): these cost $10 per week ($20 per year) for motorized craft and $5 per week ($10 per year) for nonmotorized. Check the *Boating Regulations* brochure for details on which craft are allowed where and for locations to purchase boating permits.

Wildlife

Besides the geothermal wonders, people are drawn to Yellowstone for the opportunity to see many different kinds of **wildlife**. And while many animals are undoubtedly well used to being inundated with humans and their noisy motor vehicles, there are also some that remain reclusive and have little contact with people at all. Grazing animals that you will almost certainly encounter – probably without leaving your car – include **elk** (population 20,000), **bison** (population 2000), **mule-deer** (population 2500), and **coyotes** (common). **Moose** (population 500) are less frequently spotted along marshy riverbanks not far from the roads. The major predators at large within the park include the gray wolf, mountain lion, and grizzly bear. If you're keen to observe these more sought-after animals, there are various hotspots around the park where sightings are more likely: **grizzlies** (population 300–600) can be spotted in the open meadows of the Lamar and Hayden valleys, the Fishing Bridge area, and the east side of the road below Tower Fall; **wolves** (population around 200 but growing steadily) can be found in the Lamar Valley, on either side of the Lamar River and Soda Butte Creek; extremely rare sightings of **mountain lions** (population unknown but probably fewer than twenty) occur along the road at the eastern end of the Lamar Valley; while **bighorn sheep** (population around 250) can be found on the cliffs just north of Tower Fall, along the Gardner River south of *Indian Creek* campground, and on Mount Washburn.

There are a few **safety issues** with regard to contact with animals, most of which amount to using common sense – if an animal is reacting to your presence, then you're too close. Bison and elk get agitated when approached, and are known to behave aggressively towards humans. Every year several tourists are trampled and gored by irate **bison** – usually while doing something stupid like trying to photograph one from six feet away. Always give bison a wide berth (at least fifty feet); if an **elk** appears unsettled by your presence, back away slowly. Most people know well enough not to feed any animal; **coyotes** try to beg food from motorists, and end up being run over accidentally or shot by park rangers. You can find specific information elsewhere in this book on safety and behaviour with regard to **bears** (see p.550) and **mountain lions** (see p.286). A free brochure, available at visitor centers, lists the park's mammals and their approximate numbers, and also briefly describes their usual habitat.

The wolves of Yellowstone

The last native **Yellowstone gray wolf** was shot and killed by park rangers in 1922, during an extermination program that predated the notion of an ecosystem in which all species are interdependent. Debate raged for years over the possibility of reintroducing wolves to this area, especially as it became clear the predator–prey balance was getting out of hand. Finally, in 1995, despite opposition from cattle ranchers, fourteen gray wolves were captured in Alberta, Canada, and released into Yellowstone's Lamar Valley. Today there are as many as two hundred wolves roaming the Greater Yellowstone area in at least fifteen different packs. Their reintroduction has been a spectacular success, and management of issues such as livestock protection and the (illegal) poaching of wolves has so far proven effective. Most importantly, there are now significant numbers of these marvelous predators doing their job of taking out the sick, old, and weak among the park's large ungulates, while wolf-watching has made a fascinating addition to the Yellowstone experience.

The gateway towns

Despite the fact that only a small part of Yellowstone lies within Montana, three of the park's major gateway towns are all within the Big Sky state. On the northwest side of the park is **West Yellowstone**, the biggest and brashest of the entrances. On the north side are **Gardiner**, good for access from Bozeman and the only entrance that's open year-round to vehicles, and **Cooke City**, dramatically reached via the Beartooth Highway (see box on p.485).

West Yellowstone

Located at the junction of US-287 and US-20, **WEST YELLOWSTONE** is a busy, commercialized grid of streets where chain restaurants and motels, souvenir shops and outfitters vie for your business. In summer the town overflows with tourists, bikers on Harleys, even hot rod conventions, and in winter it becomes a haven for snowmobilers. Although it's not a particularly relaxing place, it makes a handy stopover on your way to or from the park and is a good spot to stock up on supplies – there are even one or two points of interest around town if you have a spare hour or two.

Tourism has been a major source of income to the area since the first tourist stagecoaches made the arduous journey from Virginia City to the national park in 1881. In 1907 the town (then called Riverside) became an official park entrance, and the following year the Union Pacific Railroad opened a depot here, allowing tourists to access the national park on the *Yellowstone Special*. That same year the town was renamed Yellowstone (it only became West Yellowstone in 1920 to avoid confusion with the park). Tourists were provided for by *Murray's Yellowstone Hotel* (now the *Madison Motel*) and a general store operated by Sam and Ida Eagle that today still trades under the name of Eagle's. With the development of the highway from Bozeman in the 1920s, more tourists began to arrive in motor coaches or their own cars, and the train service was discontinued in 1960.

Arrival and information

During the summer, you can fly into West Yellowstone Airport with Skywest Airlines (☎406/646-7351 or 1-800/453-9417), although it may be more convenient to fly instead to Bozeman, which has more daily services, and take the

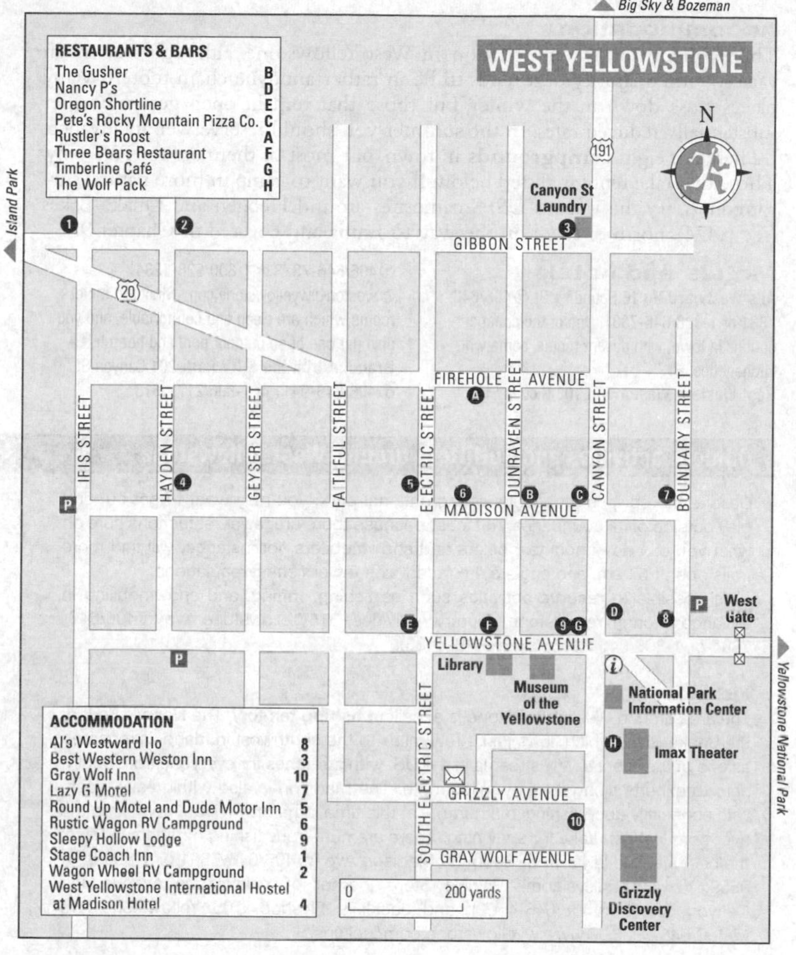

bus for the two-hour journey to the park with either 4x4 Stage Inc. (Ⓣ406/338-6404 or 1-800/517-8243), Karst Stages Inc. (Ⓣ406/586-8567 or 1-800/845-2778), or Greyhound (Ⓣ1-800/231-2222).

There are two sources of **information** about the region: the West Yellowstone Chamber of Commerce in Grizzly Park on Canyon Avenue (daily 8am–5pm; Ⓣ406/646-7701, Ⓦwww.yellowstonechamber.com); and, next door, the Yellowstone National Park West Entrance Information Station (daily: June–Aug 8am–8pm; rest of year 9am–6pm; Ⓣ406/646-7332), which has more park-specific information, including useful maps. Several local operators run **tours** of the park (see box on p.416).

The **post office** is on Electric Street, and you can check your **email** at the library at 100 Yellowstone Ave. If you're coming in from a few days out in the wilds you can clean up yourself and your clothes at Canyon Street Laundry, 312 Canyon St, which also has showers.

Accommodation

There's plenty of accommodation in West Yellowstone, although not much variety – the majority of it tends to be in rather anodyne chain motels. Many places close down in the winter, but those that remain open generally offer substantially reduced rates. In the summer you should reserve well in advance.

There are eight **campgrounds** in town, but most of them are for RVs only. Those that take tents are listed below. If you want to camp in more natural surroundings, try the various USFS campsites around Hebgen and Quake Lakes (see p.474), north of town on the way to Ennis and covered in Chapter 9.

Motels and hotels

Al's Westward Ho 16 Boundary St ⓣ406/646-7331 or 1-888/646-7331. One of the cheaper options in town, with decent rooms, some with kitchenettes. ③

Best Western Weston Inn 103 Gibbon St ⓣ406/646-7373 or 1-800/528-1234, ⓔweston@wyellowstone.com. Standard motel rooms which are clean and comfortable, and you also get use of an outdoor pool and hot tub. ⑤

Brandin' Iron Inn & RV Park 201 Canyon St ⓣ406/646-9411 or 1-800/217-4613,

Outdoor activities and outfitters around West Yellowstone

Despite the obvious attractions of the national park, you may want to get out and play outside of its boundaries, not least because there are fewer restrictions here on what you can do – mountain bikers and snowmobilers, for instance, will find more trails open to them, and anglers are faced with fewer fishing regulations.

It's possible to **reserve** activities such as fishing, rafting, and snowmobiling in advance through Yellowstone Country Activities, 315 Yellowstone Ave (ⓣ406/646-7365 or 1-800/646-7365, ⓕ406/646-4433).

Fishing

The area around West Yellowstone is excellent **fishing** territory. The Henry's Fork of the Snake River, which flows just a few miles to the southwest in Idaho, is regarded as one of the finest dry fly streams in the US, with stretches for everyone from beginners to experts along its sixty-mile length. The Madison is also within easy reach, with especially good fishing in autumn – at this time large brown trout come into the river from Hebgen Lake for spawning. There are numerous fishing outfitters in town; the best are Bud Lily's Trout Shop, 39 Madison Ave (ⓣ406/646-7801 or 1-800/854-9559, ⓦwww.budlilys.com); Eagle's Store, corner of Yellowstone Avenue and Canyon Street (ⓣ406/646-4502); and Jacklin's Flyshop, 105 Yellowstone Ave (ⓣ406/646-7336, ⓦwww.wyellowstone.com/jacklins).

Horseback riding

There are good routes for **horseback riding** north of town at Whit's Lake Road trailhead on US-287, about ten miles from town, and two miles further on at Red Canyon Road, which opens up to give great views of the mountains of the Madison Range. Local outfitters include Diamond P Ranch, 2865 Targhee Pass Hwy (ⓣ406/646-7246), and Parade Rest Guest Ranch, ten miles west of town at 7979 Grayling Creek (ⓣ406/646-7217 or 1-800/753-5934, ⓔparaderest@wyellowstone.com). Look at spending around $60 for a four-hour trail ride and $150 per night for accommodation packages.

Mountain biking

Mountain bikers will find some good trails on old logging roads and technical single-track close to West Yellowstone. The eighteen-mile Rendezvous Trail System starts from Geyser Street on the south side of town and is especially popular with a mix of rolling terrain and steeper ascents and descents. More details, including trail maps, are available from Free Heel & Wheel, 40 Yellowstone Ave (ⓣ406/646-7744,

Ⓔ info@brandiniron.com. Pleasant rooms with refrigerators and HBO, and guest hot tubs. 5

Gray Wolf Inn 250 S Canyon St Ⓣ406/646-0000 or 1-800/852-8602, Ⓔ graywolf@graywolf-inn.com. One of the newer motels in town, with spacious, comfortable rooms, free continental breakfast, plus pool and spa. Open year-round and convenient for the IMAX theater. 5

Lazy G Motel 123 Hayden St Ⓣ406/646-7586, Ⓔ LAZYG@wyellowstone.com. Good-value if pretty basic rooms, some with kitchenettes for $10 extra. 4

Round Up Motel and Dude Motor Inn 3 Madison Ave Ⓣ406/646-7301 or 1-800/833-7669, Ⓔ roundup@wyellowstone.com. Located in one of the quieter parts of town but only a block from all the action, the rooms here are clean and well maintained, and some have two bedrooms and kitchenettes. 4

Sleepy Hollow Lodge 124 Electric St Ⓣ406/646-7707, Ⓔ sleepyhollow@wyellowstone.com. Attractive log cabins with fully equipped kitchens and a free continental breakfast, plus a fly-tying bench for anglers. Good value. 4

Stage Coach Inn 209 Madison Ave Ⓣ406/646-7381 or 1-800/842-2882, Ⓔ sci@wyellowstone.com. One of the town's oldest and most historic buildings, with comfortable rooms, an attractive lobby and reading area, a hot tub and sauna, and a good restaurant. Open year-round and there are some great off-season deals, with rooms for under $40. 5

Ⓔ freeheel@wyellowstone.com), and Yellowstone Bicycles, 132 Madison Ave (Ⓣ406/646-7815), who also rent bikes for around $30 per day.

Cross-country skiing

Along with snowmobiling (see below), **cross-country skiing** is the prime winter activity in and around West Yellowstone. Cross-country skiers will find some of the best trails in the US around West Yellowstone, which is the base for the US Ski and Biathlon Team's Fall Training Camp. The Rendezvous Trail System is the big attraction, with over thirty miles of groomed trails that start on the south side of town on Geyser Street. A trail pass costs $3 (contact the chamber of commerce), and Bud Lily's Trout Shop (see "Fishing," opposite) rents out cross-country skis and snowshoes for around $15 per day.

Snowmobiling

Snowmobiles have become a fixture in West Yellowstone and the national park in winter, albeit a somewhat smelly and noisy one. At the time of writing, pollution from the machines had become such a problem – with rangers at the West Yellowstone park entrance complaining of health problems from ingesting two-stroke engine fumes – that serious consideration is being given to banning snowmobiles from the park entirely by 2004.

There are hundreds of miles of **trails** leading from the town into Montana, Idaho, and Wyoming, varying from steep expert trails such as the ten-mile Lionhead Loop to flatter, less demanding routes such as the Lower Loop Road through the national park where you may get close to wildlife such as moose and bison. Another popular trail from West Yellowstone is Two Top, the first designated snowmobile trail in the US. The trail takes around three hours to complete, although there are additional loops that can shorten or lengthen the ride. The trail begins just west of town and climbs up past several "play areas" to the Continental Divide from where there are magnificent views of Montana, Idaho, and Wyoming.

There are almost as many snowmobile **rental outfits** around West Yellowstone as there are miles of trails; among these are Alpine West, 300 Hayden St (Ⓣ406/646-9883 or 1-800/858-9224, Ⓔ kate@avicom.net), Rendezvous Snowmobile Rentals Inc., 415 Yellowstone Ave (Ⓣ406/646-9564 or 1-800/426-7669, Ⓦ www.yellowstonevacations.com), and Yellowstone Arctic/Yamaha, 208 Electric Ave (Ⓣ406/646-9636, Ⓔ arcticyamaha@montana.net).

Hostel and campgrounds

Rustic Wagon RV Campground 634 Hwy-20 West ⓣ406/646-7387, ⓦwww.wyellowstone.com/rusticwagon. On the west side of town and popular with families, there are 36 RV sites ($25) and nine tent sites ($15) here. Facilities include showers and laundry.

Wagon Wheel RV Campground 480 Gibbon Ave ⓣ406/646-7872, ⓦwww.wyellowstone.com/wagonwheel. Located in town so not exactly a wilderness experience although it's still a pleasant woodsy environment; there are 32 RV sites ($25) and just six tent sites ($15). Facilities include showers and laundry.

West Yellowstone International Hostel at Madison Hotel 139 Yellowstone Ave ⓣ406/746-7745 or 1-800/838-7745. A real boon for budget travelers, this is one of the very few hostels in Montana. The attractive log-hewn building dates back to 1912 and has rooms with bunks for up to four people ($20 each) and private rooms for around $50. Open late May to early Oct.

Yellowstone Park KOA six miles west of town on US-20 ⓣ406/646-7606 or 1-800/562-7591. A large campground in a pleasant enough setting with mountain views, but passing traffic can be an annoyance. Facilities include a pool, hot tub, and evening barbecue. Rates are high – around $35 for a RV, $20 for a tent.

The town and around

West Yellowstone is small enough to wander around quite easily, although peak-season crowds lead to a certain amount of ducking and weaving on the streets. One of the town's biggest visitor attractions is the **Grizzly Discovery Center**, on 201 S Canyon St (daily 8.30am–8.30pm; $7; ⓦwww.grizzlydiscoveryctr.com), the one place around Yellowstone National Park where you're guaranteed to see grizzly bears. The center houses "problem" grizzlies and non-native Kodiak bears that may have injured humans or be addicted to raiding garbage cans and thus cannot live safely in the wild. There's also a small gray wolf pack, all of whom have been born in captivity. Though it's rather sad seeing these animals hemmed in by fences, proponents of the center rightfully argue that the only other option is to have them put down. You can get up to within a few feet of the bears and wolves, and the center has some good interpretive material on the animals, including useful advice on how to tell the difference between a black bear and a grizzly.

Next door is the **Yellowstone IMAX Theater** (daily: May–Sept 9am–9pm; Oct–April 1–9pm; $10; ⓣ406/646-4100), which has regular on-the-hour showings of spectacular movies featuring the national park and various unrelated outdoor adventures such as the ascent of Everest – all projected on to a six-story screen. Around the corner on Yellowstone Avenue, the **Museum of the Yellowstone** (daily 8am–9pm; $5) has a good introduction to the natural history of the park, including three impressively large stuffed bison, and a good bookshop.

Eating and drinking

The Gusher Cnr Madison Ave and Dunraven St ⓣ406/646-9050. Good range of pizzas, sandwiches, burgers and vegetarian dishes, plus free delivery.

Nancy P's 29 Canyon St ⓣ406/646-9737. A popular breakfast spot and a good place to relax with a coffee and pastry.

Oregon Shortline In *West Yellowstone Conference Hotel*, 315 Yellowstone Ave ⓣ406/646-7365. Upmarket dining with a local touch – bison, elk, and mountain trout are on the menu, which will set you back $15–22. Check out the perfectly preserved 1903 rail car next to the restaurant before you dine.

Pete's Rocky Mountain Pizza Co. 104 Canyon St, Canyon Square Mall ⓣ406/646-7820. Busy restaurant popular with families, with a varied menu plus build-your-own pizzas.

Rustler's Roost 234 Firehole Ave ⓣ406/646-7622. Another good spot if you want to dine on local wild game, including elk and bison. Also open for breakfast. Dinners start at around $15.

Three Bears Restaurant 215 Yellowstone Ave ⓣ406/646-7811. Popular restaurant with a cozy log interior and interesting old black-and-white photos and artifacts around the walls. Good range of American cuisine – save room for the Apple Brown Betty á la Mode dessert – and dinner shouldn't cost more than $20. Open for breakfast (from 6.30am) and dinner, but not lunch.

Timberline Café 135 Yellowstone Ave ⓣ406/646-9349. The *Timberline* has been around since the early 1900s and specializes in home-made soups, pies, and pastries in a friendly rustic environment. Also open for breakfast from 6.30am.

The Wolf Pack 111 S Canyon St ⓣ406/646-PACK. West Yellowstone's own brewing company, with a good range of traditionally brewed beers. A convenient spot to stop off for a quick drink after you've been to the IMAX or Grizzly Discovery Center.

Gardiner

The only national park access point open year-round, the small town of **GARDINER** has been making a living from Yellowstone visitors for over a hundred years, managing to avoid the tackiness of West Yellowstone, Montana's most popular park access point. The town, located at the southern end of the Paradise Valley, still has a faint whiff of the frontier about it, and there's an air of excitement over the proximity of the world's oldest national park that is lost amidst the commercialization of West Yellowstone.

Several **outfitters** in town can sort you out for trips into the park (see box on p.416), but bear in mind if you're here to raft, kayak, or mountain bike you won't be allowed in the park – for details of both activities to the north of here in the Paradise Valley see p.479.

Gardiner is split in two by the Yellowstone River, which flows from east to west through town. The north side is dominated by a strip of motels and tourist facilities along US-89 – known as Scott Street as it runs through town parallel to the river, and then 2nd Street once it turns south and crosses the Yellowstone Bridge to the south side of town. This southern side is older and more attractive, with elk and deer occasionally to be seen grazing in local gardens. The main thoroughfare, Park Street, makes for a short but enjoyable stroll. At its western end the **Roosevelt Arch** is the town's most interesting historical feature, marking the entrance to the park and dedicated in 1903 by President Teddy Roosevelt in front of 5000 people.

You'll find tourist **information** on the national park at the Gardiner Chamber of Commerce, corner Main and 3rd streets (Mon–Fri 9am–5pm, opens noon in winter; ⓣ406/848-7971, ⓦwww.gardinerchamber.com); for outdoor recreation information contact USFS Gallatin National Forest Gardiner District Office on Scott Street (Mon–Fri 8am–5pm; ⓣ406/848-7375). The **post office** is on Main Street between 2nd and 3rd streets, and **internet access** is available for a small charge from Gardiner Hardware, W Main Street at 3rd Street S (ⓣ406/848-7977). If you're about in mid-June you may catch the small-scale **Gardiner Rodeo**, often attended by some of the better rodeo riders.

Gardiner outfitters

North Yellowstone Outfitters 172 Jardine Rd ⓣ406/848-7651. Hiking, horseback riding, and hunting trips into and around Yellowstone National Park.

Park's Fly Shop, 2nd Street between Stone and Main ⓣ406/848-7314. The place for anglers to head for – they have a free fishing map of Yellowstone National Park and the Gallatin and Missouri rivers and organize guided trips. In winter they also rent cross-country skis for the park's excellent trails.

Wilderness Connection 21 Shooting Star Trail ⓣ406/848-7651. Hiking, horseback riding, and hunting trips into the park.

Accommodation

Gardiner has a lot of choice in terms of **accommodation**, but it can be booked up in summer, so it pays to make reservations. Scott Street is the main strip for chain motels such as *Motel 6* and *Super 8*, but even their prices are not especially cheap ($80–100). There are numerous USFS **campgrounds** in the area, full details of which are available from the Gardiner District Office (see overleaf); the office also has details on cabins, which are very basic but cost as little as $20 per night.

Motels and hotels

Absaroka Lodge US-89 at the Yellowstone River Bridge ⓣ406/848-7414 or 1-800/755-7414. Located in a great position overlooking the river on the north side of Yellowstone Bridge. Pleasant, modern rooms with queen beds and good views of the north edge of the park. ⑥

Best Western by Mammoth Hot Springs on US-89 south of town ⓣ406/848-7311 or 1-800/828-9080, ⓦwww.bestwestern.com/mammothhotsprings. One of the more upmarket options, with spacious, comfortable rooms with good river and mountain views, a large indoor pool, hot tub, sauna and cable TV, plus restaurant, lounge, and casino. You can also book rafting, hiking, and fishing trips here. ⑤

Cabin by the River 1049 US-89 S ⓣ406/848-2223, ⓔriver1@gomontana.com. A secluded country cabin on the banks of the Yellowstone ten minutes out of town. ⑥

Hillcrest Cottages 200 Scott St ⓣ406/848-7353. Comfortable cottages with kitchenettes. Good value, especially the larger ones which will accommodate up to six people. ④

Town Café and Motel cnr of E Park St and S 2nd St ⓣ406/848-7322. Eleven recently remodeled rooms which are comfortable and not too pricey. Decent café and restaurant attached (see below). ④

Yellowstone Inn cnr Main and 2nd St ⓣ406/848-7000. An attractive Victorian-style building with cozy rooms. Particularly good value in the off-season, when there are twenty-percent discounts. ④

Yellowstone Village Inn cnr Main and 2nd St ⓣ406/848-7417 or 1-800/228-8158, ⓦwww.yellowstoneVinn.com. Forty basic but clean and comfortable rooms, with kitchen suites. There's also an indoor pool, and horseback riding, fishing, and rafting can be organized for you. ⑤

Campgrounds

Eagle Creek Campground Jardine Rd, two miles north of Gardiner. Pleasant but basic USFS site, with pitches costing $7 per night; open all year, no hookups.

Rocky Mountain Campground Jardine Rd, half a mile north of Gardiner ⓣ406/848-7251. Busy campground with good grassy sites ($18) with fine views, and a store, laundry, and hot showers. It also caters for RVs ($24) and has tent cabins for around $25 per night.

Eating and drinking

High Country Espresso Cecil's Building, Park St ⓣ406/848-7707. A good place to get your daily caffeine fix as they have a wide selection of coffees plus sodas and fruit smoothies.

Helen's Corral Drive Inn south side of US-89, half mile west of 2nd St bridge ⓣ 406/848-7627. This unassuming burger stand with picnic tables out front makes for the perfect reward after days in the backcountry. The legendary burgers are huge, juicy, and delicious, and the thick milkshakes impossible to pass up.

Sawtooth Deli 220 W Park St ⓣ406/848-7600. Good hot and cold sandwiches and salads, plus vegetarian specials, and there's an outdoor patio for dining and a nightly barbecue pit.

Town Café Park St ⓣ406/848-7322. Lively and friendly place serving good, filling breakfasts. Upstairs the *Town Loft*, which overlooks the Yellowstone River, serves up decent steaks.

Cooke City

On the northeast edge of the national park, the one-street town of **COOKE CITY** (7651ft) is accessible all year round from the west (the road through the national park from Gardiner is kept plowed all winter); however, the spectacular Beartooth Highway to the east is impassable from mid-October to late May. The national park landscape to Cooke City's west is complemented by the Absaroka-Beartooth Wilderness to the north, which also provides fantastic recreational competition (see p.480).

You can pick up supplies for backpacking in the park here, and there are a number of **outfitters** who run guiding and hunting services (the latter outside of Yellowstone), including Beartooth Plateau Outfitters (ⓣ406/838-2328) and Skyline Guide Services (ⓣ406/838-2380 in summer, ⓣ406/664-3187 in winter); the Cooke City Bike Shack (ⓣ406/838-2412) is a friendly source of advice and gear for mountain biking (outside the park), hiking, and skiing in the park and the wilderness area.

There are a limited number of places to **stay** in the town. Best choices include *Hoosier's Motel* (ⓣ406/838-2241; ③), which also has the popular *Hoosier's Bar*; the good-value *High Country Motel* (ⓣ406/838-2271; ②); and the more upmarket *Soda Butte Lodge* (ⓣ406/838-2251 or 1-800/527-6462; ④), which has the luxury of some more-expensive hot-tub suites. The *Yellowstone Yurt Hostel* is at the west end of town, three block north off Main Street (ⓣ406/586-4659 or 1-800/364-6242), and offers the rare chance to sleep in a large yurt equipped with cooking facilities and showers for only $14 a night. You can also camp just east of town at one of three no-frills USFS **campgrounds** off the Beartoooth Highway: *Colter*, *Chief Joseph*, and *Soda Butte*.

After a day out, enjoy the view with a coffee and cake from the porch of the *Beartooth Café* (ⓣ406/838-2475), or grab a basic but tasty evening meal at *Joan and Bill's* (ⓣ406/838-2280), both on the main drag. If you want to cook for yourself or pick up any other supplies, take a wander around the characterful and historic Cooke City Store.

Grand Teton National Park and Jackson Hole

The classic triangular peaks of **Grand Teton National Park**, which stretches for fifty miles from just north of the town of Jackson, are far more dramatic than the mountains of its neighbor, Yellowstone. Though not especially high or extensive by Rocky Mountain standards, these sheer-faced cliffs make a magnificent spectacle, rising abruptly to tower 7000ft above the valley floor. A string of gem-like lakes is set tight at the foot of the mountains; beyond them lies the broad, sagebrush-covered **Jackson Hole** river basin, broken by broad and winding Snake River. The town of Jackson itself is the busiest base for summer tourism in the vicinity of the Tetons and Yellowstone, and is also home to one of the Rockies' most challenging ski hills, **Jackson Hole Mountain Resort**.

Grand Teton National Park

The Shoshone people knew these mountains as the *Teewinot* ("many pinnacles"), but the name *les trois tetons* (literally "the three breasts") was bestowed in the 1830s by French-Canadian fur-trappers, who presumably had not seen any females for quite some time. After Congress created **GRAND TETON NATIONAL PARK** in 1929, it took another 21 years of legal wrangling for Grand Teton to reach its current size – local ranchers protested that the economy of Jackson Hole would be ruined if any further land was surrendered to tourism. The original designation included only the Teton mountains themselves and the cluster of lakes at their feet, and it's likely that nothing would have changed had not **John D Rockefeller Jr** taken a personal interest in the area; he bought up some 56 square miles of Jackson Hole and presented it to the government for free. Commercial aspirations were clearly not entirely absent from his thought processes, however, as his one condition was that the Grand Teton Lodge Company, which he then owned, would be the exclusive operator of park concessions.

Today the park encompasses 485 square miles, and hosts around four million visitors per year. Many come simply to view the awe-inspiring Tetons – listed third behind Mount Fujiyama and the Matterhorn as the most photographed mountains on earth – or to do a little hiking, fishing, boating, and wildlife-watching. For hardy hikers and climbing enthusiasts, however, the Tetons provide scenery and challenges which exceed those of neighboring Yellowstone.

Arrival and information

There are only **two entrance stations**, one at the southern end of the park at **Moose** and the other at **Moran Junction**, on the park's eastern edge. The 26-mile stretch of I-26/89/191 that connects the two technically runs through the park, but you can use this road without going through an entrance station or paying for a permit. The third point of entry is at the north end of the park, **via Yellowstone**; there is no entrance station for Grand Teton here, but you can collect a park map and information nearby at Flagg Ranch (see box below). A free park map is available at entrance stations and visitor centers, and the free *Teewinot* newspaper gives details on camping, wildlife, park services,

Visitor centers

The park's **three visitor centers** are located – from south to north – at Moose, Jenny Lake, and Colter Bay; there is also a supplemental information station in the far north of the park at Flagg Ranch, and a museum at Colter Bay.

Moose, the park's southern entrance and official park headquarters (daily: June to early Sept 8am–7pm; rest of year 8am–5pm; ☎307/739-3399).

Jenny Lake, on the east shore of Jenny Lake eight miles north of the southern park entrance (daily: June–Aug 8am–7pm; Sept 8am–5pm; ☎307/739-3343).

Colter Bay, on the east shore of Jackson Lake (daily: mid-May to late May 8am–5pm; late May to early June 8am–7pm; early June to Aug 8am–8pm; Sept 8am–5pm; ☎307/739-3594). The **Indian Arts Museum** here (daily: summer 8am–8pm; spring & fall 8am–5pm; free) has an impressive display of Native American art and craftwork. There are usually some exquisite items of art and jewelry for sale too, made by various indigenous guest artists.

Flagg Ranch Information Station, in the far north of the park near the southern entrance to Yellowstone (June to early Sept daily 9am–6pm).

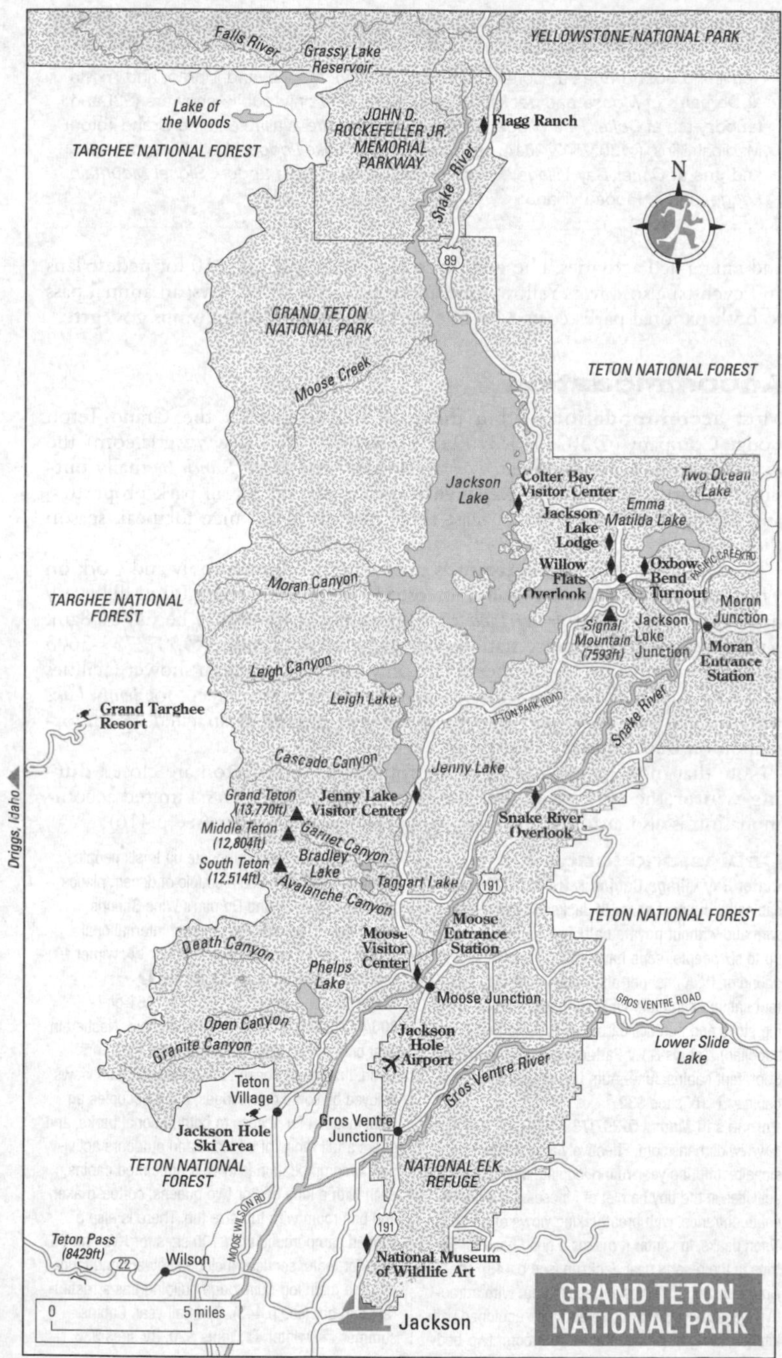
Falls River
Grassy Lake Reservoir
YELLOWSTONE NATIONAL PARK
Lake of the Woods
JOHN D. ROCKEFELLER JR. MEMORIAL PARKWAY
Flagg Ranch
TARGHEE NATIONAL FOREST
N
Snake River
89
GRAND TETON NATIONAL PARK
TETON NATIONAL FOREST
Moose Creek
Jackson Lake
Colter Bay Visitor Center
Two Ocean Lake
Emma Matilda Lake
Jackson Lake Lodge
Willow Flats Overlook
Oxbow Bend Turnout
PACIFIC CREEK RD
Moran Canyon
TARGHEE NATIONAL FOREST
Signal Mountain (7593ft)
Jackson Lake Junction
Moran Junction
Moran Entrance Station
Leigh Canyon
Leigh Lake
TETON PARK ROAD
Snake River
Grand Targhee Resort
Cascade Canyon
Jenny Lake
Driggs, Idaho
Grand Teton (13,770ft)
Jenny Lake Visitor Center
Middle Teton (12,804ft)
Garnet Canyon
Snake River Overlook
South Teton (12,514ft)
Bradley Lake
Taggart Lake
Avalanche Canyon
191
TETON NATIONAL FOREST
Death Canyon
Moose Visitor Center
Moose Entrance Station
Phelps Lake
Moose Junction
GROS VENTRE ROAD
Open Canyon
Jackson Hole Airport
Granite Canyon
Lower Slide Lake
Gros Ventre River
Teton Village
Jackson Hole Ski Area
Gros Ventre Junction
TETON NATIONAL FOREST
NATIONAL ELK REFUGE
MOOSE WILSON RD
191
Teton Pass (8429ft)
22
Wilson
National Museum of Wildlife Art
0
5 miles
Jackson
GRAND TETON NATIONAL PARK

Park services

You'll find **post offices** at Colter Bay (summer only), Moose, and Moran, and **ATMs** at *Dornan's in Moose* and *Jackson Lake Lodge*. The only public showers ($2) and **laundry** are at *Colter Bay Village*. **Medical services** are available at the Grand Teton Medical Clinic (Ⓣ307/543-2514) opposite *Jackson Lake Lodge*. You'll find **groceries** and **gas** at *Colter Bay Village*, *Flagg Ranch*, *Jackson Lake Lodge*, *Signal Mountain Lodge*, and in Moose Village.

and ranger-led activities. The **entrance fee** of $20 per car ($10 for pedestrians and cyclists) also covers Yellowstone and is good for seven days; an annual pass to both national parks costs $40. The park's **website** is Ⓦwww.nps.gov/grte.

Accommodation

Most **accommodation** within the park is managed by the Grand Teton Lodge Company (Ⓣ307/543-3100 or 1-800/628-9988, Ⓦwww.gtlc.com); the exceptions are *Signal Mountain Lodge*, *Dornan's*, and *Flagg Ranch* (actually outside the park's boundaries). **Reservations** are advised for all park properties, and ideally should be made at least three months in advance for peak season (July–Aug).

The park's five NPS **campgrounds** operate in the summer only and work on a first-come, first-served basis; all sites cost $12 per night. Campgrounds fill every day in July and August; *Jenny Lake* is the most popular and may be full by 8am. Visitor centers and entrance stations can advise on availability (Ⓣ307/739-3603 recorded information for campers). The only campground with shower facilities ($2) is *Colter Bay*, and the maximum stay is fourteen nights, except for *Jenny Lake* (seven nights). In addition, *Flagg Ranch* has a campground attached. For information on **backcountry camping**, see p.440.

Note that most lodges and all campgrounds in Grand Teton are closed **during winter**; the only exceptions are *Flagg Ranch* and *Dornan's*. Limited accommodation is also available in Yellowstone throughout winter (see p.416).

Cabins and lodges

Colter Bay Village Cabins & RV Park 208 log cabins by the east shore of Jackson Lake, both with and without private bath, and some sleeping up to six people; none have kitchen facilities, phone or TV. A cheaper alternative is to stay in a tent cabin; each has four bunk beds, a wood-burning stove and outdoor barbecue grill (no bed-linen supplied). Cabins & RV Park open late May to late Sept, tent cabins June–Aug. Log cabins ❹, tent cabins ❷, RV sites $32

Dornan's in Moose Ⓣ307/733-2522, Ⓦwww.dornans.com. Effectively a park concessionaire, offering year-round lodging, dining, and activities in the tiny hamlet of Moose by the park's south entrance, with breathtaking views of the main Teton peaks. In winter it makes a good base for ski trips to the resorts near Jackson (see p.443). The *Spur Ranch Log Cabins* are decked out with attractive lodgepole-pine furniture and fully-equipped with kitchen, living area, and private bathroom; two-bedroom cabins can accommodate up to six people. Other amenities include a couple of decent places to eat (see p.443), and Dornan's Wine Shoppe, which has an astounding range of international wines. Open all year. Cabins summer ❼, winter ❻; two-bed cabins summer ❽, winter ❼

Flagg Ranch Resort Ⓣ307/543-2861 or 1-800/443-2311, Ⓦwww.flaggranch.com. Nestled in light pine forest at the northern edge of Grand Teton, this resort doesn't have the mountain views enjoyed by some park lodges, but it occupies an ideal location for access to both national parks, and offers a full range of services and outdoors activities. Accommodation is in well-appointed cabins, each with a king bed or two queens, coffee-maker, and bathroom with full-size tub. There is also a shaded campground with 100 sites for RVs and 75 sites for tents; services include showers and laundry. The main log-built lodge building has a restaurant and bar (see p.443). Open all year. Cabins summer ❼, winter ❻; tents $20, RV sites $33

Jackson Lake Lodge This lodge, just north of Jackson Lake Junction, enjoys a peerless view of the Tetons from above the marshy expanse of Willow Flats, which is prime moose habitat. The 37 rooms in the lodge building are quite large and have two comfortable double beds plus private bath; there are also 348 "cottage rooms," which have similar amenities. The extra cost for a room facing the mountains is well worth it. Open mid-May to mid-Oct. Cottages 7, lodge rooms 6

Jenny Lake Lodge ☎307/733-4647. This is the park's premium lodging and dining property, boasting 37 luxury log cabins – each with its own bathroom and a huge pine bed – a quarter-mile from the north shore of the lake. The rate ($400) includes breakfast and dinner (see also "Eating" on p.443). Open June to early Oct. 9

Signal Mountain Lodge and Cabins ☎307/543-2831, ⓦwww.signalmountainlodge.com. Set on the southeast shore of Jackson Lake, this lodge offers bland motel-style units with two double beds, bathroom, and fridge, or much nicer rustic log cabins with two doubles plus private bath. There are also some larger rooms with a king bed plus sofa bed and kitchenette, and family bungalows which accommodate up to five people; note that none of the kitchens are equipped with crockery or utensils. Open mid-May to mid-Oct. Log cabins 5, motel units 6, family bungalows 8

Campgrounds

Colter Bay 350 shaded sites along the Jackson Lake shore, and a separate RV park. Facilities available at Colter Bay Village include store, marina, and restaurants. Fills by noon in summer. Open mid-May to mid-Sept.

Gros Ventre 360 sites alongside the Gros Ventre River in the southeast corner of the park, just eight miles from Jackson. This dry, sagebrush covered area has around 100 tent-only sites, but its large sites are ideal for big RVs, a fact that keeps most campers away. The location is not terribly handy to anything in the park either, so it's always the last to fill – if it does at all. Open May to mid-Oct.

Jenny Lake 49 tent-only sites near the south shore of the lake. Very popular because of the absence of RVs and proximity to some of the most popular hiking trails in the park; fills by 8am most days during summer. Open mid-May to mid-Sept.

Lizard Creek 60 sites on a small peninsula at the north end of Jackson Lake. This relatively secluded spot has shaded sites with great views down the lake. Fills by 2pm in summer. Open early June to early Sept.

Signal Mountain 86 sites by *Signal Mountain Lodge*, on the southeast shore of Jackson Lake. This is a great lakeside location and there's a fair amount of shade; arrive early to grab a site with lake views. Facilities at the nearby lodge include gas, groceries, bar, and restaurants. Fills by 10am in summer. Open mid-May to early Oct.

Exploring the park

The Teton mountains themselves are so much the dominant feature of the park that it's as well to be able to identify them before you do too much else. While the mountains now known collectively as the Teton Range actually comprise twelve main peaks, there are five clearly dominant summits (amongst them *les trois tetons*); in order from south to north, these are **Nez Perce** (11,901ft), **Middle Teton** (12,804ft), **Grand Teton** (13,770ft), naturally the tallest of the bunch, **Mount Owen** (12,928ft), and **Teewinot Mountain** (12,325ft).

There is no public transport within the park, and you'll ideally want a car to get around. No road crosses the Tetons inside the park boundary, but those that run along their eastern flank were designed with an eye to the mountains, affording stunning views at every turn. For the classic photograph of the Tetons, an hour or two past sunrise is best; the **Snake River Overlook**, roughly halfway between Moose and Moran Junction, is generally considered the top spot. **Willow Flats Overlook**, just south of *Jackson Lake Lodge*, is another beauty, as is the viewing deck at the lodge itself. Towards Moran Junction is the **Oxbow Bend** turn-out, another excellent position; the view from here is dominated by Teewinot Mountain, while the nobbly pinnacle of Grand Teton is just visible to your far left. Oxbow Bend is also a pretty spot to take out your folding chair and binoculars and settle in to watch for beaver, moose, and bird activity early or late in the day. Another popular drive is to the top of the five-mile **Signal Mountain Summit Road**, 800ft above the valley floor, for a panoramic view. The five-mile **Jenny Lake Scenic Loop** is one-way southbound from String Lake at the north end of Jenny Lake (it's two-way northbound), and affords tantalizing glimpses through the trees of the mountains towering above the lake's southwest shore.

Hiking and other outdoors activities

There's only so long that you can – or indeed should – just stand and gaze at the Tetons in slack-jawed wonder; this range is one of the most inspiring places to **hike** and **climb** in the country, and there are easy, moderate, and strenuous routes to take you right into the mountains. And if you're not inclined towards exertion under your own power, there are numerous other means of getting off the road and taking in this awesome terrain from up-close – whether on a Snake River float-trip, a fishing expedition, or aboard a four-legged conveyance.

Grand Teton Lodge Company (Ⓣ307/543-3100 or 1-800/628-9988, Ⓦwww.gtlc.com) offers a range of summer activities, including **float-trips** on the Snake River (3hr; $38), **horseback riding** from *Jackson Lake Lodge* and Colter Bay Village (2hr; $35), and **scenic cruises** (1hr) – which leave from Colter Bay Marina ($14). A half-day **bus tour** of Grand Teton costs $25. A number of operators in Jackson also run float and fishing trips inside the park (see p.449 for details), and you can rent canoes, rowboats, and motorboats at Colter Bay and Signal Mountain marinas. *Dornan's in Moose* can also arrange canoe and kayak rental ($35), while *Flagg Ranch Resort* offers a variety of activities including float trips on the Snake River (2.5hr; $25), horseback riding (2hr; $25), and day-trips by coach through Grand Teton or Yellowstone ($55).

The **shuttle boat** across Jenny Lake (June–Aug daily 8am–6pm; $5 round-trip) is a perennial park favorite, particularly combined with a hike up to Inspiration Point on the west side of the lake; the boat runs every twenty minutes, and is in highest demand from around 4 to 6pm, when everyone heads home for the day. Anglers can collect a copy of the free park **fishing** guide, which details catch limits and seasonal restrictions; a regular Wyoming fishing license is required, available at Moose Village general store, Colter Bay Marina, and *Signal Mountain Lodge*.

On the flat roads of Jackson Hole, **cycling** is a breeze; bike rental is available inside the park at *Dornan's in Moose* ($25–28 per day) or in Jackson (see p.449). Teton Mountain Bike Tours, based in Jackson (Ⓣ307/733-0712 or 1-800/733-0788), runs half-day tours ($45–55).

In **winter**, all hiking trails are open to cross-country **skiers**, while **snowmobiles** can be rented from Grand Teton Park Snowmobile Rental (Ⓣ307/733-1980 or 1-800/563-6469; $120 per day, $80 per half-day) and *Flagg Ranch Resort*, a popular base for snowmobilers ($140 per day single, $195 double), or from outlets in Jackson.

Hiking and backcountry camping

The Teton mountains are purpose-designed for hiking – a tight clutch of stunning peaks, ribbed with canyons that shelter picturesque creeks and bird-filled forests. Hikers should pick up the free *Day Hikes* brochure, which briefly describes fifteen hikes with their distances and levels of difficulty, as well as the more detailed free **trail guides** for areas including Cascade Canyon, Colter Bay, Jenny Lake, and Taggart and Bradley Lakes. If you're planning on doing any longer hikes, it's worth investing in a more detailed map of the area. Good topographic **maps** available at visitor centers include the Trails Illustrated map of the entire park (1:78,000) and the Earthwalk Press *Hiking Map and Guide* (1:48,000), which covers only the southern half, where most people do their hiking. *Jackson Hole Hikes*, by Rebecca Woods (White Willow Publishing) has highly readable descriptions and basic trail maps for hikes in Grand Teton National Park and elsewhere in Jackson Hole.

For **backcountry camping**, you need a permit, available free from the Moose and Colter Bay visitor centers and the Jenny Lake Ranger Station, near the Jenny Lake Visitor Center. To reserve in advance ($15) from January–May 15, write to the Permits Office, GTNP, PO Drawer 170, Moose, WY 83012 (still need to collect permit in person); call ☎307/739-3309 for more details.

As ever, respect for the environment and the elements is your best means of avoiding **backcountry hazards** while hiking. Warm and waterproof clothing are the basics, in case of a cold change, rain or snow, and you should have plenty of drinking water (or a means to purify water from mountain creeks); for detailed information on hiking safety, see p.50.

Encounters with animals are always a bonus on any hiking trip, and among those you may well see are elk and mule-deer – although the higher into the mountains you go, the less forage there is and so their numbers tend to dwindle. With luck you may have a surprise encounter, even at higher elevations, with a moose or two or even a bear. Moose are known to wade along the creekbeds that run through Cascade and Paintbrush canyons. Bears are seldom seen, although there are a small number of both black and grizzly bears at large in the park; as a general rule, black bears stick to the lowlands, while grizzlies – of which there are few – might be found in the higher reaches, about the Teton Crest Trail. For detailed information on bear encounters, see box on p.560.

One factor more likely to give pause to hikers is the park's **hunting season** for elk (roughly mid-Oct through Nov); reflecting the shortage of large predators in Grand Teton, the park opens sections of the grassy lowlands alongside the Snake River between Moose and Moran Junction, and also further north towards Flagg Ranch, to hunters. Assuming that a bright orange vest is not part of your regular hiking apparel, it's best to avoid these areas when the shooters are about.

Day-hikes

The most popular trails are those that start from **Jenny Lake**; one easy walk from here goes north along the sandy beaches of **Leigh Lake**, where the imposing 12,605ft Mount Moran bursts out dramatically from the lakeshores. People who only do one hike while visiting the park invariably follow the two miles of trail around the south and west shores of Jenny Lake to **Hidden Falls**. This lakeside stroll is very pretty and shaded, and you can keep an eye out for trout sheltering in rocky shallows. There's no elevation gain until the last few hundred yards up to the falls, so this is a very accessible hike; an even more leisurely alternative is to take the shuttle boat (see opposite) across the lake, and walk the remaining 800 yards to the falls. If you've come this far, hoof it up another 500ft to **Inspiration Point** for a glorious view over the lake and across to Jackson Hole. For the more adventurous, a further nine miles of rocky trail leads on from Hidden Falls through **Cascade Canyon** to breathtaking **Lake Solitude**, whose surrounds are carpeted with wildflowers until late summer. Cascade Creek along the bottom of the canyon is also a favorite haunt for moose, and this entire canyon trail runs alongside the imposing edifices of Mount Owen and Teewinot Mountain.

Another strenuous hike, and an excellent way to reach treeline in a short distance, is the five-mile trail from **Lupine Meadows**, just south of Jenny Lake, which skirts small glacial pools like Amphitheater and Surprise lakes. This route takes you towards the Grand Teton itself, and is often peppered with people geared up with climbing equipment; the three miles of switchbacks up to Surprise Lake gain about 2600ft in elevation, so it's not for the faint-hearted.

Multi-day hikes

Among the choices for longer excursions into the Tetons, the **Cascade Canyon-Paintbrush Canyon loop**, for a total distance of almost twenty miles, can be done over two or three days, with some excellent backcountry campsites to choose from along the north fork of Cascade Creek and around Holly Lake.

A section of this loop also forms part of the **Teton Crest Trail**, which provides a huge challenge for the few hundred hardy souls who take it on every summer. This trail runs the length of the Tetons, for a distance of 38.6 miles through the most photogenic mountain range in North America. Most hikers start at the southern end, from the Coal Creek trailhead on the west side of Teton Pass; the trail winds in and out of Grand Teton National Park, and bypasses several clusters of jewel-like alpine lakes and through moose, deer, and beaver habitat. At a comfortable pace it takes five days (four nights) to walk the entire trail, but you can also join it at several points within the national park, including Death Canyon west of Moose, and Cascade and Paintbrush canyons further north.

Climbing in the Tetons

The sight of the Tetons is enough to get many nonclimbers thinking about roping up and having a go, and indeed it is a five-star destination for **climbing** enthusiasts from all over the world. The goal for most is of course the summit of the **Grand Teton** – at 13,770ft, the second-highest mountain in Wyoming. This is a technical climb, requiring the appropriate equipment and expertise, although it is also possible to do the climb as part of an introductory **climbing course**. Two well-regarded places that offer climbing instruction are Exum Mountain Guides, based at Moose (Ⓣ307/733-2297, Ⓦwww.exumguides.com), and Jackson Hole Mountain Guides, 165 N Glenwood St, Jackson (Ⓣ307/733-4979 or 1-800/239-7642, Ⓦwww.jhmg.com). The most popular basic climbing courses run over four days and culminate in an ascent of the Grand Teton ($850); those with climbing experience can join a two-day expedition ($380).

The route to the top of **Middle Teton** (12,798ft) is nontechnical but there's a fair amount of scrambling to be done. Overnight bases for access to these mountains are the backcountry campsites in **Garnet Canyon** (see overleaf for more information about backcountry camping). From June through September, climbers should collect free permits for any trip involving technical climbing from the **Jenny Lake Ranger Station** (daily June–Sept 8am–6pm; Ⓣ307/739-3343) near the Jenny Lake Visitor Center (see box on p.436); this should in any case be your first stop for information and advice on routes and conditions (note that snow may persist until Aug on some passes). At other times, permits are available at the Moose Visitor Center. Climbing permits are no longer required for day-climbs, and climbers on day-trips should therefore leave an itinerary with a friend.

Climber's Ranch, on Teton Park Road (Ⓣ307/733-7271; mid-June to mid-Sept), has basic bunk **accommodation** for climbers, plus showers and cooking facilities, for $7 per night.

Eating and drinking

The park **restaurants** are good but a little pricey; campers should stock up at a supermarket in Jackson before entering Grand Teton. The best places for a civilized evening **drink** with mountain views are *Jackson Lake Lodge* and *Signal Mountain Lodge* (see below).

Colter Bay Village Choices here are the *John Colter Chuckwagon* for moderately-priced breakfast, lunch, and dinner buffet meals, or the *John Colter Cafe Court Pizza & Deli* for a sandwich, pizza, salad, or even a whole roast chicken.

Dornan's in Moose The *Spur Bar plus Pizza & Pasta Co* has high ceilings and a cheery, casual aprés-hike/ski/whatever bar crowd, along with pasta dishes for around $10, and pizzas for $9–12, while the summer-only *Original Moose Chuckwagon* is good for huge prime-rib dinners ($15) and pancake breakfasts.

Flagg Ranch Resort The main lodge building has a smart but cozy restaurant and bar with fireplace; dinner entrees are $10–17, there's a full breakfast menu too, and sandwiches, burgers, and salads for lunch ($5–8).

Jackson Lake Lodge ⓣ307/543-2811. The lodge's *Mural Room* is aptly named for its huge picture-window looking straight at the Tetons. The menu is an expensive array of meat and seafood dishes (entrees $16–30); cheaper lunch items include sandwiches and salads, and there is a superb breakfast buffet daily which features Belgian waffles. Next door is the *Pioneer Grill*, a counter-and-stools diner affair, with inexpensive food (burgers and such $6–8), but no view. Prime spot for an evening drink is the *Blue Heron Lounge*, where you can recline in comfortable chairs and watch the ever-changing blues, grays, purples, and warm pinks of Mount Moran. Reservations advised for the *Mural Room*.

Jenny Lake Lodge ⓣ307/733-4647. This is the park's finest dining, with a top-notch fixed-price menu for breakfast and dinner plus an à la carte menu at lunch (dinner around $45 per person); Sunday evenings feature a huge buffet dinner. Jacket and tie "preferred." Reservations essential.

Signal Mountain Lodge ⓣ307/543-2831. The food here is a bit fancy and none-too-cheap, but the mountain views should ease the pain when the bill arrives. The dinner-only *Peaks Restaurant* has lake and mountain views and a menu which includes elk medallions, Thai chicken, and salmon (entrees $16–24). The *Trapper Grill* has tasty breakfast items like buffalo sausage, fresh trout, and a range of omelettes, all in the $6–8 range; lunch is the standard range of burgers, salads, and so on ($5–8). The lodge's *Deadman's Bar* has great views too, and the lakeside deck is perfect on a summer's day.

Jackson Hole

Named for renowned fur-trapper and mountain man Davey Jackson in 1829, **Jackson Hole** is simply a broad river basin, hemmed in by the Gros Ventre mountains to the east, the Snake Range to the west and the Tetons to the north; it measures 48 miles north-to-south and between five and ten miles across. In the nineteenth century, "Hole" was a noun often employed to describe this type of geographic feature, and indeed the Rockies was once peppered with "Holes." The term fell from favor once its derogatory connotations outdistanced the descriptiveness of the term, but in northwest Wyoming it has hung grimly on. Unkind visitors to the town of **JACKSON**, tucked in at the south end of Jackson Hole, are known to remark that the word "hole" now neatly encapsulates the mash of cowboy/ski-bum/billionaire/vacationer cultures upon which the town has grown - its current population is around 6000.

Today Jackson Hole encompasses the communities of Jackson, **Wilson**, and **Teton Village**, as well as a fair chunk of Grand Teton National Park. The actual town of Jackson sits just east of the gorgeous Snake River, ten miles south of the entrance to Grand Teton National Park and 57 miles south of Yellowstone's southern entance. Jackson's in-town ski-hill is **Snow King**, while the more famous **Jackson Hole Mountain Resort** is roughly fifteen-minutes' drive northwest of town – Teton Village is simply the cluster of accommodation and services that go with the resort. A third ski area, **Grand Targhee**, can be visited from Jackson too, as it's about an hour's drive away near the Idaho border (see Idaho chapter, p.585). The tiny hamlet of Wilson, five miles west of Jackson, is of little interest apart from a notable bar-nightclub and an excellent restaurant.

Jackson is often mentioned in the same breath as Aspen, Colorado, but it's a somewhat erroneous comparison as the only things the two really have in common are heart-stopping real estate prices and great skiing. Think of Aspen as a place where parading about town in a floor-length mink coat is quite acceptable; in Jackson, the millionaires like to dress and act like regular folk, and in the main live in relative seclusion on ranches several miles from the town itself. But there's no mistaking the pulling power of this area for the rich and famous, evident in the daily line-up of private Lear Jets on the airport runway.

Arrival, information, and getting around

Jackson Hole's **airport** is actually within the national park, eight miles to the north of Jackson; it's linked to town by All-Star Transportation **shuttle service** (ⓣ307/733-2888; $8 one-way), while the regular **taxi** fare is around $20. There are regular **flights** to Jackson from Salt Lake City with Delta, and from Denver with United Express; these are uniformly more expensive than flying in to Salt Lake City and taking a shuttle van from there. Jackson Hole Express (ⓣ307/733-1719 or 1-800/652-9510) operates two direct **shuttle services** daily between the international airport in **Salt Lake City** and Jackson (around 5hr; $47 one-way); pickup and dropoff in Jackson is at the MiniMart beside *Burger King* on W Broadway.

Jackson's excellent **Wyoming Information Center**, 532 N Cache St (daily: May–Sept 8am–7.30pm; rest of year 9am–5pm; ⓣ307/733-3316, ⓦwww.jacksonholechamber.com), has an ATM, restrooms, and tons of information on the area. Nearby, the **Bridger-Teton National Forest Headquarters**, 340 N Cache St (Mon–Fri 8am–4.30pm; ⓣ307/739-5500), has details of hiking and camping in the Gros Ventre mountains to the east – there are usually one or two rangers on hand at the Wyoming Information Center during summer however, so you should check there first.

Transport around Jackson Hole is provided by START buses (ⓣ307/733-4521, ⓦwww.startbus.com), which operates three color-coded routes, roughly 6.30am to 10pm daily. It's a good idea to grab a timetable on board or from the information center as services vary seasonally; rides within the town of Jackson are free, to Teton Village is $2 one-way, to the Museum of Wildlife Art and the Elk Refuge costs $1.

Shuttle services and tours to the national parks and ski areas

AllTrans (ⓣ307/733-3135) runs daily shuttles during winter from Jackson to Flagg Ranch, by the south entrance to Yellowstone ($35 one-way, $58 round-trip); from here you need to take either a snowmobile or snowcoach to reach Old Faithful.

Grand Teton Lodge Company (ⓣ307/733-2811) operates various services from Jackson and the airport to its properties in Grand Teton National Park.

Gray Line, 330 N Glenwood St (ⓣ307/733-4325), will pick you up at your hotel and whisk you through either Grand Teton National Park (8hr; $60) or Yellowstone (11hr; $65) on a brisk one-day drive.

Targhee Express (ⓣ307/734-9754) does the ski season run to Grand Targhee Resort ($20 round-trip); a $56 transport-plus-liftpass saves you around $8.

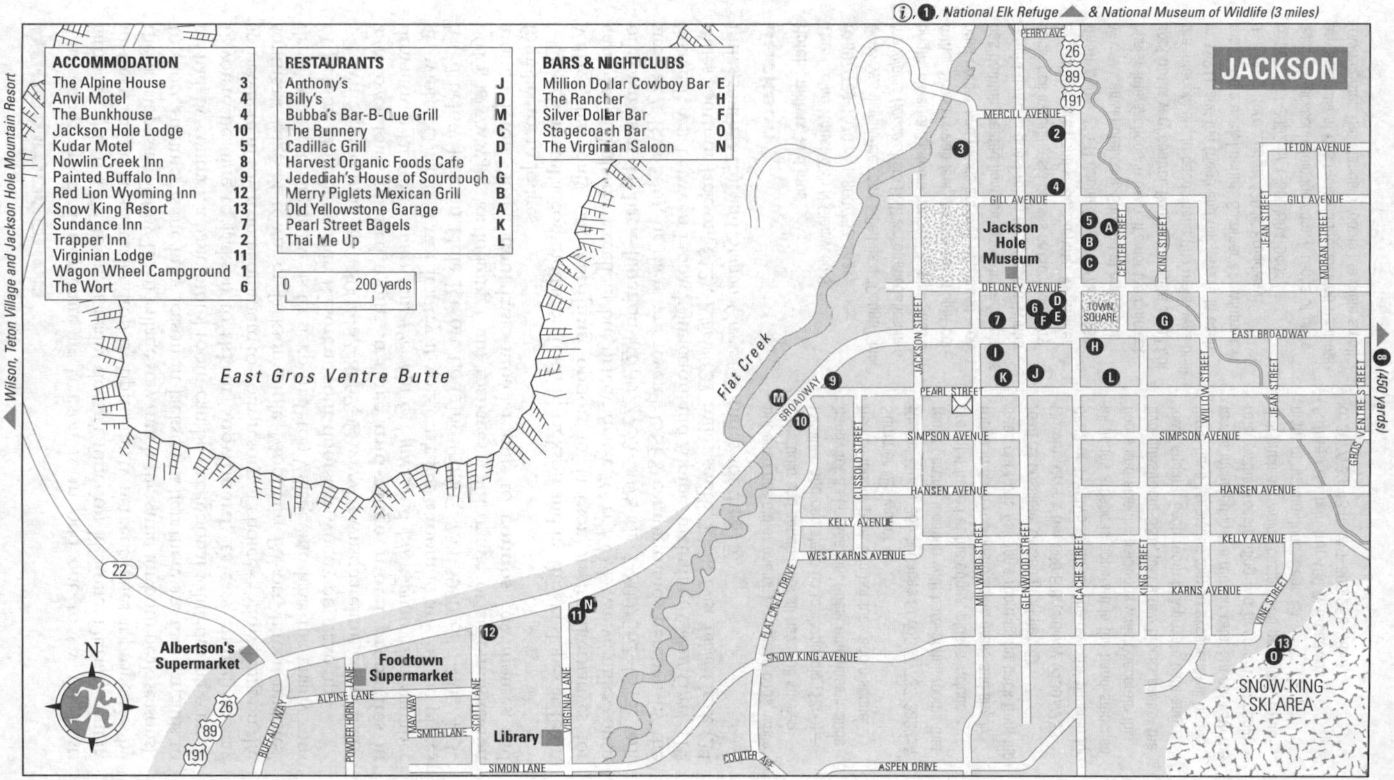

JACKSON

ACCOMMODATION

The Alpine House	3
Anvil Motel	4
The Bunkhouse	4
Jackson Hole Lodge	10
Kudar Motel	5
Nowlin Creek Inn	8
Painted Buffalo Inn	9
Red Lion Wyoming Inn	12
Snow King Resort	13
Sundance Inn	7
Trapper Inn	2
Virginian Lodge	11
Wagon Wheel Campground	1
The Wort	6

RESTAURANTS

Anthony's	J
Billy's	D
Bubba's Bar-B-Cue Grill	M
The Bunnery	C
Cadillac Grill	D
Harvest Organic Foods Cafe	I
Jedediah's House of Sourdough	G
Merry Piglets Mexican Grill	B
Old Yellowstone Garage	A
Pearl Street Bagels	K
Thai Me Up	L

BARS & NIGHTCLUBS

Million Dollar Cowboy Bar	E
The Rancher	H
Silver Dollar Bar	F
Stagecoach Bar	O
The Virginian Saloon	N

0 200 yards

Wilson, Teton Village and Jackson Hole Mountain Resort
(i), 1, National Elk Refuge & National Museum of Wildlife (3 miles)
8 (450 yards)
East Gros Ventre Butte
Flat Creek
Jackson Hole Museum
Town Square
Albertson's Supermarket
Foodtown Supermarket
Library
Snow King Ski Area
Perry Ave
Mercill Avenue
Gill Avenue
Deloney Avenue
East Broadway
Broadway
Pearl Street
Simpson Avenue
Hansen Avenue
Kelly Avenue
West Karns Avenue
Karns Avenue
Snow King Avenue
Flat Creek Drive
Coulter Ave
Aspen Drive
Teton Avenue
Jackson Street
Clissold Street
Millward Street
Glenwood Street
Cache Street
Center Street
King Street
Willow Street
Jean Street
Moran Street
Gros Ventre Street
Vine Street
Buffalo Way
Alpine Lane
Powder Horn Lane
May Way
Smith Lane
Scott Lane
Virginia Lane
Simon Lane
22
26
89
191

Accommodation

The **accommodation** picture in Jackson is an odd one to say the least: although this is a ski-town, it really doesn't function like one. During winter, in-town room rates actually drop by up to thirty percent (rates at properties by the ski slopes in nearby Teton Village stay much the same for both peak seasons). In short, summer is the busy season in Jackson, when there are few bargains to be had; by contrast, a basic motel room can be exceptional value during winter. If you're heading to Jackson to **ski or snowboard**, it's easy enough to stay somewhere in town and commute to your resort of choice – Snow King on the southeast edge of town, or Jackson Hole Mountain Resort, fifteen-minutes' drive away; the alternative is to sleep in Teton Village and have the gnarly runs of Jackson Hole Mountain Resort at your doorstep when you wake up.

Town Square Inns (Ⓣ1-800/483-8667, Ⓦwww.townsquareinns.com), manages over four hundred rooms in three **mid-range motel properties** in downtown Jackson (*Antler Inn*, *49er Inn & Suites*, and *Elk Country Inn*; summer ❹, winter ❸), and is worth a try if you can't get a room at any of the places listed below. Jackson Hole Resort Lodging (Ⓣ307/733-3990 or 1-800/443-8613, Ⓦwww.jhresortlodging.com) manages a full range of accommodation around Teton Village, from basic motel rooms to **condos**, townhouses, and four-bedroom lodges.

There's **hostel** accommodation both in Jackson and by the ski slopes at Teton Village, but only one **camping** option in Jackson itself. Alternatives for campers include the excellent but pricey *Snake River KOA*, twelve miles south of town near Hoback Junction (Ⓣ307/733-7078 or 1-800/562-1878; tent sites $27, RVs $36); or there are several USFS campgrounds perched by the Snake River between Hoback Junction and Alpine, including *Cabin Creek* (19 miles south of Jackson; $12), *Elbow* (22 miles south; $15), *East Table Creek* (24 miles south; $15), and *Station Creek* (25 miles south; $15).

Jackson

Hotels, motels, and inns

The Alpine House 285 N Glenwood St Ⓣ307/739-1570 or 1-800/753-1421, Ⓦwww.alpinehouse.com. Billed as a "Country Inn," the *Alpine House* offers B&B accommodation in a bright, cheerful 21-room house. The place has a rather Scandinavian feel, decked out in light-colored timber, and rooms are well-appointed – each has bathtub, heated floor and some have fireplaces – right down to guest robes and slippers. Winter packages including ski passes or cross-country expeditions are good value. Summer ❼, winter ❻

Anvil Motel 215 N Cache St Ⓣ307/733-3668, Ⓦwww.anvilmotel.com. Situated at one of the busier intersections in town, it's not the quietest spot but is very central. Rooms are quite small but the interiors are in good shape (the motel was built in 1991), and the fridge and microwave in each room are a useful bonus. Summer ❺, winter ❸

Jackson Hole Lodge 420 W Broadway Ⓣ307/733-2992 or 1-800/604-9404, Ⓦwww.jacksonholelodge.com. A range of units are available at this motel-lodge, located near the town center. The standard rooms are quite small but each has either one or two queen beds, while the studio and condo units all have full kitchen facilities and can sleep up to six people ($250) – handy for a ski vacation. Guest amenities include heated indoor pool, two hot tubs and a sauna. Summer ❻, winter ❺

Kudar Motel 260 N Cache St Ⓣ307/733-2823. A really central location with bare-bones rooms that are a bit frayed at the edges; pluses include a fridge in each room and some grass and shady trees out front. Ask for a room as far back from the road as possible. Closed in winter. ❹

Nowlin Creek Inn 660 E Broadway Ⓣ307/733-0882 or 1-800/533-0882. The owners' passion for all things artistic is apparent in the hand-stenciled floors and eclectic paintings which decorate this five-guestroom B&B, just a few blocks east of the town square. Each room has private bath and three have fireplaces too; an excellent full breakfast is included in the regular rate, but not with the rate for the freestanding two-bedroom log cabin (full kitchen), which costs $250 per night. Three-night minimum June–Sept. ❼

Painted Buffalo Inn 400 W Broadway Ⓣ307/733-4340 or 1-800/288-3866,

ⓦ www.paintedbuffalo.com. Among the newest and largest motels in the town center, the *Painted Buffalo* has facilities and rates a cut above some of its neighbors. The 140 rooms have one or two queen beds, there's a large heated indoor pool and an on-site coffee shop which offers sandwiches and baked goodies. Excellent value during ski season. Summer ⑥, winter ④

Red Lion Wyoming Inn of Jackson 930 W Broadway ⓣ 307/734-0035 or 1-800/844-0035, ⓦ www.wyoming-inn.com. One of the best in the upper mid-range market, the *Red Lion* is completely nonsmoking, and offers free extras including continental breakfast, laundry, and even internet access. There are coffee-makers in each of the 73 guestrooms, and suites all have a gas fireplace and hot tub; a huge log fireplace gives the lobby a cozy lodge feel too. Summer ⑧, winter ⑦

Snow King Resort ⓣ 307/733-5200 or 1-800/522-5464, ⓦ www.snowking.com. The rooms at this slopeside resort are large and were fully renovated in 2000; most have either one king or two queen beds, and there are also two, three, and four-bed condos available ($240). Guest facilities include an outdoor heated pool, two hot tubs, fitness center, and sauna, as well as on-site services such as ski equipment rental, gift shop, laundry, and hairdresser. ⑧

Sundance Inn 135 W Broadway ⓣ 307/733-3444 or 1-888/478-6326, ⓦ www.sundanceinnjackson.com. Small, basic motel rooms at an an unbeatable location; the owners are friendly and helpful, and there's a free continental breakfast included as well as a "social hour" (5–6pm) for hot drinks and homemade cookies. Summer ⑤, winter ④

Trapper Inn 235 N Cache St ⓣ 307/733-2648 or 1-800/341-8000. Central motel whose rooms have queen or king-size beds (some with fridge) and amenities including small indoor and outdoor hot tubs and a guest laundry. Great value in winter. Summer ⑥ winter ④

Virginian Lodge 750 W Broadway ⓣ 307/733-2792 or 1-800/262-4999. The 170 rooms are pretty basic but complemented by a big outdoor pool and hot tub which sits in the middle of a grass-covered courtyard. Ask for a room which faces the grass – the alternative is the asphalt parking lot. There's a family-style restaurant on-site, a saloon, liquor store, and guest laundry too. Best value during summer, this is one of the few motels to raise its rates in winter. Summer ③, winter ⑤

Wolf Moon Inn 285 N Cache St ⓣ 307/733-2287 or 1-800/964-2387. A central location plus large rooms with queen beds – some with fridges and microwaves – is reason enough to consider the place; a ski group could get extra value from the motel's largest rooms (winter ⑤), which have three queen beds. Summer ⑤, winter ③

The Wort Hotel 50 N Glenwood St ⓣ 307/733-2190 or 1-800/322-2727, ⓦ www.worthotel.com. Built in 1941, this is Jackson's most venerable high-end property, combining old-world style with modern facilities that include two large hot tubs, a grill-bistro and an attractive bar (see "Eating and drinking", p.452). Rooms are furnished with enormous lodgepole-pine beds and big TVs, and bathrooms have full-size tubs too. Summer ⑧, winter ⑦

Hostel and campgrounds

The Bunkhouse In the *Anvil Motel*, 215 N Cache St ⓣ 307/733-3668. There's little joy about this windowless bunker below the motel reception area; kitchen facilities amount to a lone microwave oven and two fridges, there's no cooktop and no utensils and the 22 beds are clustered haphazardly into one big dorm space. On the upside, the lounge/TV area is spacious, bathroom facilities are clean and well-maintained and there's a guest laundry. The rate is the same year-round, making it poor value in winter when there are plenty of cheap motel rooms to be had. $22.

Wagon Wheel Campground 525 N Cache St, behind the *Wagon Wheel Motel* ⓣ 307/733-4588. This is about the only spot to pitch a tent in Jackson itself – beside Flat Creek and a ten-minute walk north of the town square. Basic toilet and shower facilities and not much shade. $16.

Teton Village

Hotels, motels, and inns

The Alpenhof Lodge ⓣ 307/733-3242 or 1-800/732-3244, ⓦ www.alpenhoflodge.com. Classic Tyrolean lodge which offers 42 handsomely appointed guestrooms, some with fireplaces and balconies. Amenities include a heated outdoor pool and hot tub, sauna, ski shop, and laundry. There's a casual bistro as well as the *Alpenhof Dining Room* (see "Eating and drinking," p.453). Summer ⑥, winter ⑦

Best Western The Inn at Jackson Hole 3345 McCollister Drive ⓣ 307/733-2311 or 1-800/842-7666, ⓦ www.innatjh.com. Standard three-star chain motel accommodation, offering mid-size rooms with either one queen bed or two doubles. The village's only sushi restaurant is here too. Summer ⑦, winter ⑥

Best Western The Lodge at Jackson Hole 80 Scott Lane ⓣ 307/739-9703 or 1-800/458-3866, ⓦ www.lodgeatjh.com. Slightly more upmarket than the neighboring *Inn at Jackson Hole*, the lodge has standard rooms with two queen beds and deluxe rooms with king bed, kitchenette, and fireplace. Summer ❽, winter ❻

Renaissance Resort and Spa 3245 W McCollister Drive ⓣ307/733-3657, ⓕ733-9543, ⓦwww.renaissancehotels.com. This five-star resort hotel has all the usual top-end amenities including bar, restaurant, sauna, and hot tub, and has recently added a number of new condos; its range of rooms can now accommodate from two to eight people. Summer ❾ ($280), winter ❽

Hostel and campground

Hostel X ⓣ307/733-3415, ⓦwww.hostelx.com. Excellent slopeside hostel accommodation, with amenities including lounge with fireplace, TV and games room, ski lockers and storage, microwave oven, free tea and coffee but no kitchen. During summer dorm beds can be reserved individually, but in winter each four-bunk room is rented as a unit, and usually requires a five-night minimum stay. Summer: dorm bed $19, four-bed room $55, double room $45. Winter: four-bed room $61, double room $48.

Teton Village KOA ⓣ307/733-5354 or 1-800/562-9043. Halfway between Jackson and Teton Village, this campground offers some decent shady sites, all the usual facilities plus a games room, but it's not budget camping by any means. Tent sites $26, RVs $36.

Jackson and around

To describe Jackson as an anachronism in the cowboy state of Wyoming is to put the situation mildly; art galleries, restaurants, flashy boutiques, and gift stores dominate retail spaces, and it's fair to say that not everyone who visits is terribly enamored of the moneyed-vacation culture upon which the town thrives, notably during summer. Oddly, however, much of the residential neighborhood – between Pearl Avenue and Snow King Resort – still consists largely of downmarket timber cottages, betraying little evidence of the vast fortunes which are tied up in Jackson real estate.

The main street (I-26 and I-191) running east–west through Jackson is Broadway, while Cache Street is the north–south divide; most of the bars, restaurants and services are within four blocks of the junction of these two streets. The **center of town** is marked by a tree-shaded square, which has an arch of tangled elk antlers at each corner; on summer evenings, an amateurish **shoot-out** is staged here (Mon–Sat 6.30pm; free). For a couple of blocks on all sides of the square there are Old West-style boardwalks lining streets filled with art galleries and eateries. The obligatory Old West exhibit space is the **Jackson Hole Museum**, 105 N Glenwood St (June–Sept Mon–Sat 9.30am–6pm, Sun 10am–5pm; $3), which houses an unexciting collection of Indian and mountain man artifacts such as arrowheads and basic tools; best is a small display of antique pistols. One of the curators also conducts hour-long **walking tours** of downtown Jackson three mornings a week in summer (10am; $2).

Far more appealing is the **National Museum of Wildlife Art**, three miles north of town via I-89 at 2820 Rungius Rd (summer daily 8am–5pm; winter daily 9am–5pm; spring and fall Mon–Sat 9am–5pm & Sun 1–5pm; $6). Founded in 1987 with a prestigious private collection of wildlife art, the museum is well supported by a wildlife- and art-loving community. Featured artists include John J. Audubon, Albert Bierstadt, George Catlin, Pablo Picasso, Carl Rungius and Charlie Russell. Of note too are several bronze sculptures of wild animals in animated poses, and a permanent exhibit that documents the travails of the American bison.

These artists would no doubt be inspired by scenes at the **National Elk Refuge**, which the museum overlooks (ⓣ307/733-9212). Established in 1912, the refuge protects nearly 25,000 acres of prime winter habitat, used by some 10,000 elk that roam Jackson Hole and the Greater Yellowstone area. The animals have literally had to be kept alive through the winter months ever since the town's expansion left them cut off from vital winter feeding areas. Today, forage vegetation is seeded and cultivated on the refuge, and during the harshest months up to thirty tons of alfalfa pellets are fed to the animals each day. From mid-December until early April you can take a **sleigh ride** ($12) onto the refuge to feed the elk and photograph them close up; rides leave from the National Museum of Wildlife Art – a combined museum-and-sleigh-ride ticket is good value at $15.

Summer activities

Summer visitors can enjoy **chairlift** rides up 7751ft Snow King Mountain from Snow King Avenue (mid-May to early Sept; $7 or $10 including lunch at the *Panorama* restaurant), descending by hiking, cycling, or the thrilling 2500ft **Alpine Slide** ($6 a go). Out at **Teton Village**, the aerial tram provides a scary enough vista to make some people think twice about a return visit for the ski season (daily: June–Aug 9am–7pm; May & Sept 9am–5pm; $16); you can hike a trail or two while you're up top, but in truth it's all pretty barren terrain so the payoff is really the incredible view over the Snake River Valley.

Mountain bikes can be rented ($25–30) from Teton Cycle Works, 175 N Glenwood St (☎307/733-4386), or from Hoback Sports, 40 S Millward St (☎307/733-5335); the latter also runs guided bike tours in the Jackson Hole area for $55 including equipment, and sells the useful *Jackson Hole Ride Guide* ($4), a map of local bike trails. Teton Mountain Bike tours take biking road trips into Grand Teton National Park (see p.440).

The Snake River offers lots of good spots to try your hand at **fly-fishing**, and you can have a guided day out angling or float-fishing with Jack Dennis Fishing Trips (☎307/733-3270), or Westbank Anglers (☎307/733-6483 or 1-800/922-3474) for $120–180; you can also get local tips and hire fishing gear, including waders, at Jack Dennis' Outdoor Shop, 50 E Broadway.

Those who fancy riding **horses** can go for a pretty-traditional nose-to-tail trail ride from Teton Village with Jackson Hole Trail Rides based at Teton Village (☎307/733-6992; half-day $50, full-day $80), or join a customized group outing at Mill Iron Ranch, ten miles south of Jackson near Hoback Junction (☎307/733-6390), or Goosewing Ranch, about thirty miles northeast in the Bridger-Teton National Forest (☎307/733-5251 or 1-888/733-5251); itineraries can include a cowboy cookout and even fly-fishing, and cost $80–120 for a full day.

Trips on the Snake River

Literally dozens of companies in Jackson offer **float trips** on the Snake River, and there's no doubt that floating along while gazing up at the magnificent Tetons is the quintessential Jackson summer experience (half-day trips cost around $35). The Snake River becomes a bit more rambunctious further south, and **whitewater rafting** companies work the section between Hoback Junction and Alpine, where the Snake River Canyon constricts the river into producing mostly Class III rapids (half-day around $35, full-day around $60). Among the longtime reliable operators for both float and rafting trips are: Barker-Ewing, 45 W Broadway ☎307/733-1000 or 1-800/448-4202; Dave Hansen Whitewater, 455 N Cache St ☎307/733-6295 or 1-800/732-6295; and Lone Eagle, 455 W Broadway ☎307/733-1090 or 1-800/321-3800 (offers budget half-day rafting trips for $26, with no transport included).

Another alternative to getting onto the river is in a **kayak** or **canoe**; Snake River Kayak & Canoe School, 365 N Cache St (☎307/734-6745 or 1-800/529-2501), and Jackson Hole Kayak School, 1033 W Broadway (☎307/733-2471 or 1-800/733-2471), both offer instruction (from around $130) and river trips (from around $45).

Winter activities

There could hardly be more contrast between the **three ski resorts** in this region of the state: **Snow King** is Jackson's family-friendly hill, also lit for night-skiing, while **Jackson Hole Mountain Resort** is a massive mountain with a huge vertical drop and terrain best suited to upper intermediate-to-extreme downhillers. Odd one out is **Grand Targhee** (covered on p.585 in the Idaho chapter) on the west side of the Teton range near the Idaho border, which has minimal developments and mind-boggling snow statistics. There's no reason not to try out all three, although for many visitors the choice is so clear-cut that they simply pick the one which suits them best and then stick with it.

You can buy, rent, and demo **ski and snowboard equipment** at the resorts themselves, but you'll get a better deal on rentals – especially for multiday hire – in Jackson. Try Hoback Sports, 40 S Millward St (Ⓣ307/733-5335); The Edge Sports, 490 W Broadway (Ⓣ307/734-3916); or Boardroom of Jackson Hole, 245 W Pearl St (Ⓣ307/733-8327).

Jackson Hole Mountain Resort

Famed around the world as a destination for the true skiing or boarding connoisseur, **JACKSON HOLE MOUNTAIN RESORT** (Ⓣ307/733-2292 or 1-888/333-7766, Ⓦwww.jacksonhole.com), situated twelve miles northwest of Jackson via Hwy-390 (Teton Village Rd), deserves the accolades. The largest of its two peaks, Rendezvous Mountain, is the venue of choice for many of North America's sponsored skiers and boarders, who wage a constant war with the exceptionally challenging chutes, drop-offs, and couloirs that have made the resort famous.

The average **annual snowfall** is 402 inches, the **peak elevation** is 10,450ft and the **vertical drop** a giddying 4139ft. The total **skiable area** of 2500 acres is marked with 76 **trails** designated ten percent beginner, forty percent intermediate, and fifty percent advanced. Besides the eight **chairlifts** there's an eight-person gondola and a 63-passenger aerial tram. **Lift tickets** cost $56 per day, with slight savings for multiday passes.

Skiing Teton Pass

Driving on Hwy-22 over **Teton Pass** (8429ft), just west of Wilson, in winter you can't help but notice that the roadside pull-out resembles a parking lot, with upwards of fifty cars squeezed into it at any one time. The fabulous backcountry tree-skiing and boarding and deep powder stashes accessible from here are no secret, but it's important to be properly prepared if you've decided to head out into the wilds. Just to the north of the parking area is a clearly visible boot track up Mount Glory; it's a steady fifty-minute hike to the top, from where you can head down Glory Bowl to the east, Twin Slides to the south, and Calvert's Ridge to the west – each of which leads straight back down to Hwy-22. South of the parking lot is Pass Ridge, which takes you into Telemark Bowl, the most accessible and most heavily used bowl around Teton Pass. It's best not to explore much beyond these areas – which are visible from the road – without the benefit of a little local guidance; in any event you should carry the appropriate **safety equipment** and know how to use it (the basics are an emergency transceiver, a shovel, and probe), and ski or ride with at least one partner. Check the **avalanche hotline** for the latest conditions (Ⓣ307/733-2664, Ⓦwww.untracked.com/forecast). Rendezvous Ski Tours (Ⓣ307/787-2906) give guided **tours** of Teton Pass.

The only place you can really stay out of trouble is on **Apres Vous Mountain**, which is crisscrossed with blue and green runs and only drops 2100 vertical feet; the lifts are rarely ever crowded. There are blue runs on **Rendezvous Mountain** as well, but these all make huge lateral traverses across much gnarlier runs. For advanced skiers and boarders, the only limits on exploring the terrain on Rendezvous are your daring and the amount of snow cover. From the top of the tram you can traverse right and duck through a gate into Cody Bowl and Rock Springs Bowl, or stay in-bounds and take on a steep mogul run or two beneath the Thunder quad chair. Almost everyone pauses for a peek at the infamous **Corbet's Couloir** too, where hundreds of people inexplicably throw themselves in every year and take their chances.

For a guided expedition into the **backcountry** of the ski area, contact Jackson Hole Guide Service (☎307/739-2663); even finer snow can be reached with High Mountain Heli-Skiing (☎307/733-3274). There are trails for **cross-country skiers** beside Teton Village at Jackson Hole Nordic Center (☎307/739-2629; day-pass $8, equipment rental available). Four equipment shops in Teton Village rent and sell ski and snowboard gear.

Snow King Resort

Generally thought of as Jackson's family-friendly ski resort thanks to its convenient in-town location and cheap lift tickets, **SNOW KING RESORT** (☎307/733-5200 or 1-800/522-5464, ⓦwww.snowking.com) also offers the fun of skiing, boarding, and tubing at night under lights. With a **peak elevation** of just 7808ft the annual snowfall statistics here are probably less than staggering (the resort does not publish any actual figures), but as there is near-constant snowmaking on more than a quarter of the 400 acres of **skiable terrain**, patchy snow is not likely to cramp anyone's style. Don't be fooled by Snow King's somewhat modest reputation however; the trails on which you negotiate the **vertical drop** of 1571ft are steep and very narrow in places, a fact borne out by their designation as 15 percent beginner, 25 percent intermediate, and 60 percent advanced – served by five **chairlift**s and a surface tow. The runs from the top of the Summit chairlift are almost all double-black diamonds, steep and skinny with plenty of trees on all sides – a no-go zone for beginners. Boarders get to cut loose in a 300ft **half-pipe** and there's a **terrain park** too, both lit at night. **Lift tickets** cost $30 per day, night skiing costs $14 (Tues–Sat 4–8pm) and tubing is $6. It's also worth considering the ski season packages on offer at the *Snow King Resort* lodge (see p.447), especially as some include lift passes for all three ski areas.

Eating, drinking, and nightlife

Having to cater for jet-set ranch owners and the town's well-heeled tourists while not forgetting the locals who still have to work for a living, Jackson's **restaurants** are increasingly positioning themselves to cater to one group or the other. As a result, there are a handful of stolid, good-value family favorites and plenty of high-end eateries, with not too much in between. The year-round tourist trade makes Jackson Wyoming's liveliest **nightlife** community, but you need to know what's happening on which night as people tend to pack in to one or two places and abandon the rest completely. Check the free *Jackson Hole Daily* – readily available from vendors and newsstands – for details on bands, clubs, and also dining specials.

Jackson

Restaurants

Anthony's 62 S Glenwood St ☎307/733-3717. Imaginative Italian entrees at pretty fair prices by Jackson standards (entrees $15–20). Lots of pastas and veal items go well with the solid wine list, and dinners include soup, salad, and garlic bread. Daily for dinner only.

Atrium At the *Snow King Resort* ☎307/733-5200. Large, light, and airy restaurant serving breakfast, lunch, and dinner at moderate prices; the breakfast buffet is a huge spread for $9.

Billy's 55 N Cache St. A cheery place to sit on a barstool and tuck in to an enormous cheeseburger ($5 including fries); all the shiny steel and mirrors contrive to effect a polished-up Fifties diner. Daily for lunch and dinner.

Bubba's Bar-B-Que Grill 515 W Broadway. This is the best place in town to fill up on stupendous barbecued babyback ribs (full rack $13), sandwiches, burgers, steaks, and such – all great value. It's also the premier locals' breakfast venue, and you can expect to wait at least half an hour for a table on weekend mornings. A huge omelette with grits, biscuits, and coffee is around $5; the double stack of plate-size blueberry pancakes is another top choice at $3. Daily 7am–9pm.

The Bunnery 130 N Cache St. This bakery-cum-cafe is at its best for breakfast and lunch, with lots of fresh baked cakes and pies, good espresso, and daily vegetarian specials like veggie quesadilla and mushroom melts. Open daily: summer 7am–3pm & 5–9pm; winter 7am–2pm.

Cadillac Grill 55 N Cache St ☎307/733-3279. Fancy Art Deco restaurant on the main square. Huge burgers, but also buffalo, wild boar, caribou, antelope, and seafood entrees for $12–20. Reservations recommended. Daily for lunch and dinner.

Harvest Organic Foods Cafe 130 W Broadway. Earnest healthfood store with a veggie food counter: burgers, tofu, baked goods, chili, gourmet sandwiches, and fruit smoothies – to eat in or to go. Open daily: summer 7am–8pm; winter 8am–6pm.

Jedediah's House of Sourdough 135 E Broadway. Although justly famed for its sourdough pancakes, the casual and inexpensive *Jedediah's* also does salads, burgers, and fish dinners. Open daily in summer for breakfast, lunch, and dinner; winter for breakfast and lunch only.

Merry Piglets Mexican Grill 160 N Cache ☎307/733-2966. Reliable and inexpensive Mexican entrees ($9–12) go nicely with the restaurant's famed margaritas, which you can get by the "half-yard." Daily for lunch and dinner; takeaway also available.

Nora's Fish Creek Inn 5600 W Hwy-22, in the nearby hamlet of Wilson ☎307/733-8288. Incredibly popular locals' spot for a huge, leisurely breakfast of pancakes, eggs, or an omelette with all the trimmings. Lunch and dinner menu features great prime rib, salmon, and trout along with homemade desserts. Prices are moderate. Reservations advised especially on weekends.

Old Yellowstone Garage 175 Center St ☎307/734-6161. One of Jackson's finest restaurants, offering flawless service and a (brief) Northern Italian-themed menu which changes daily; items might include rare elk tenderloin and roasted sweet pepper risotto (entrees $22–28). On Sunday night the menu is ditched altogether in favor of an all-you-can-eat pizza extravaganza ($10). Reservations advised. Dinner only Tues–Sun.

Pearl Street Bagels 145 W Pearl Ave. It's all in the name – a plethora of fresh and tasty bagels, from tomato-herb to cinnamon-raisin. Daily 6.30am–6pm.

Thai Me Up 75 E Pearl St ☎307/733-0005. Red, green, and yellow curries feature alongside lots of interesting seafood variations as well as noodle dishes (entrees $12–16) at Jackson's only Thai restaurant. The interior is modern but warm colors save it from being too stark; the food is fresh and well-presented and the service pretty quick too. Takeaway and delivery also available. Open daily for dinner.

Bars and nightclubs

Million Dollar Cowboy Bar 25 N Cache Drive ☎307/733-2207. Cheesy it may be, but everyone who visits Jackson at least ducks in to this hugely touristy Western-themed watering hole, to sit on one of the saddles at the bar, get out on the dance floor with the other self-conscious tourists, or even indulge in a little drunken karaoke. There are also four pool tables. Cover most nights $5. Daily noon until late.

The Rancher 20 E Broadway. There's nothing remotely stylish about this upstairs pool den, but it's the drinking venue of choice for a mostly young local crowd; roll up for Tuesday night's "Town Meeting," which features dollar drinks. Daily until late.

The Shady Lady Saloon At the *Snow King Resort* ☎307/733-5200. Disco fever hits this bar/nightclub every Sunday night, and the place is well set-up for the live bands and DJs that play on other nights too. Cover charge varies. Daily until late.

Silver Dollar Bar In the *Wort Hotel*, 50 N Glenwood St. This is the closest thing to an upscale bar in town, but it's still pretty relaxed and casual; hosts mellow Country bands, singers, and piano players of variable quality. The silver dollars embedded in the bar-top number 2032. No cover charge.

Stagecoach Bar 5755 W Hwy-22, in the nearby hamlet of Wilson ⓣ307/733-4407. Worth the drive for its renowned Thursday "disco night" – for which you're encouraged to dress up – the *Stagecoach* sometimes hosts bands and big crowds on Sundays too. Call ahead to check what's happening.

The Virginian Saloon 750 W Broadway. Just your basic watering hole, but a good place to retire to for happy hour (4–7pm) and watch a game on the big-screen TV. Daily from noon until 11pm or midnight.

Teton Village

Alpenhof Dining Room In the *Alpenhof Lodge* ⓣ307/733-3462. The village's only fine-dining restaurant, with a menu including Western exotica such as caribou, venison, buffalo, and elk (entrees $25–35). Meals at the lodge's bistro are more moderately priced, and a large log fire lends a warm and cheerful ambience to proceedings. Reservations advised.

The Mangy Moose ⓣ307/733-9779. The *Moose* is Jackson Hole's legendary ski-bum hangout, famed for its aprés-ski sessions which segue into rowdy evenings of live rock or reggae. The bustling upstairs dining-room does decent basic fare like burgers, chicken, pasta, and a salad bar; the *Moose's Belly* downstairs dishes up a pretty ordinary $7 skiers breakfast buffet. Cover charge for live bands $5–10. Open daily from 11am until late.

Masa Sushi In the *Best Western The Lodge at Jackson Hole* ⓣ307/733-2311. Standard sushi and sashimi menu in this cozy upstairs nook – makes a great change from buffalo burgers and the like. Prices are not far above normal either (two-piece sushi plates $3–4), with selection platters for two pretty good value. Reservations advised. Closed Mon.

Listings

Airlines Delta ⓣ307/733-7920; United Express ⓘ1-800/241-6522.

Banks Foreign exchange and 24-hour ATM access is available at Jackson State Bank, cnr Center St and Deloney Ave. Other ATMs include Bank of Jackson Hole, cnr Cache St and Broadway, and Community First, cnr Glenwood St and Pearl Ave.

Car rental Alamo ⓣ307/733-0671, Avis ⓣ307/733-3422, Budget ⓣ307/733-2206, and Hertz ⓣ307/733-2272 are based at the airport; in town you'll find Eagle ⓣ307/739-9999, National ⓣ307/733-0735, and Thrifty ⓣ307/739-9300.

Hospital St John's, 625 E Broadway ⓣ307/733-3636, has 24-hour emergency care.

Internet access Teton County Library, 125 Virginian Lane (Mon–Thurs 10am–9pm, Fri 10am–5.30pm, Sat 10am–5pm, Sun 1–5pm; ⓣ307/733-2164) has computers which are free of charge and in high demand, but you can phone the day before to reserve a terminal. Alternatively try *Cyber City Cafe*, 265 W Broadway (daily 10am–8pm; ⓣ307/734-2582; $12 per hr).

Laundry Soap Opera, 835 W Broadway (daily 8am–9pm; ⓣ307/733-5584).

Outdoors equipment Gart Sports, 455 W Broadway (Mon–Sat 9am–8pm, Sun 9am–6pm; ⓣ307/733-4449), is one of the country's biggest retailers of outdoors and sporting gear, clothing and footwear.

Pharmacy Inside Albertson's supermarket (see below).

Post office 220 W Pearl Ave (Mon–Fri 7.30am–6pm).

Supermarket Albertson's, at the junction of Broadway and Hwy-22 (daily 6am–midnight; pharmacy hours Mon–Fri 9am–9pm, Sat 9am–7pm, Sun 10am–4pm); Foodtown, in Powderhorn Mall, 970 W Broadway (daily 7am–11pm).

Taxis All-Star ⓣ307/733-2888; AllTrans ⓣ307/733-3135.

Travel details

Flights

Daily services to Jackson from Denver (United Express) and Salt Lake City (Delta).

Buses

Jackson to: Salt Lake City (2 daily; 5hr).

West Yellowstone to: Bozeman (several daily; 2hr).

Montana

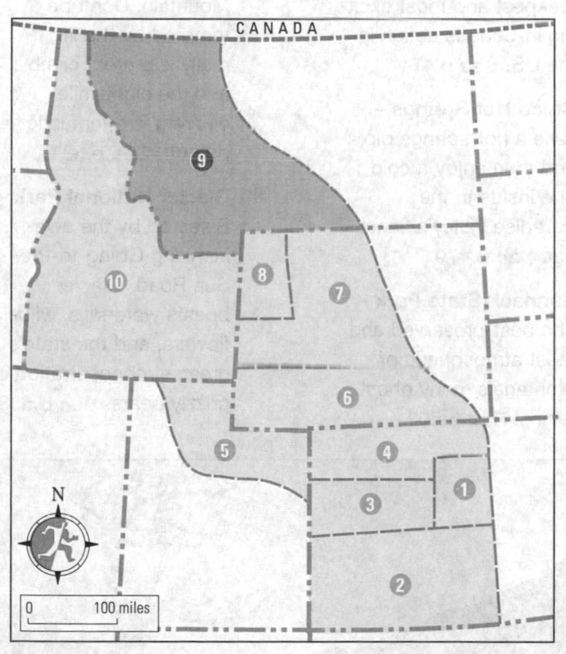

CHAPTER 9

Highlights

* **Bozeman** – Home to both the worthwhile Museum of the Rockies and a vibrant mix of students and outdoor enthusiasts. See p.461
* **Big Sky Resort** – Ski and board some of the steepest and most exciting in-bounds action in the US. See p.471
* **Chico Hot Springs** – Take a hot-springs dip and then enjoy a cold one inside in the Paradise Valley's finest bar. See p.479
* **Bannack State Park** – The best-preserved and most atmospheric of Montana's many ghost towns. See p.503
* **Missoula** – One of the Rockies' coolest towns, with great bars and restaurants and an atmosphere that inspires lingering. See p.513
* **Big Mountain** – Mountain bike up Big Mountain. Don't be tempted by the lift, it really is a great climb, and the eight-mile descent is a fantastic pay-off. See p.537
* **Glacier National Park** – Bisected by the awe-inspiring Going-to-the-Sun Road, Glacier boasts waterfalls, wildflowers, and the state's greatest concentration of grizzly bears. See p.538

Montana

MONTANA is Big Sky country. The nickname is no empty cliche: the entire state is blessed with a huge blue roof that both dwarfs the beautiful countryside and complements it perfectly. The US Rocky Mountains find their northernmost limits in the western portion of the state, an area of snowcapped summits, turbulent rivers, spectacular glacial valleys, heavily wooded forests, and sparkling blue lakes, at their most dramatic in **Glacier National Park**, in the far north. The eastern side of the state is more or less prairieland, and thus beyond the scope of this book.

Preconceptions of a desolate land populated by cowpokes are soon shattered: each of Montana's small cities has its own proud identity. The university and sawmill community of **Missoula**, for example, possesses a high-culture feel absent from the heavily Irish, copper-mining town and union stronghold of **Butte**, while state capital **Helena** still harks back to its prosperous gold mining years. And **Bozeman**, only ninety miles north of Yellowstone National Park, is a buzzing university town that's perhaps the best place to begin a tour of the state.

The fur trappers and gold miners who were the first whites to brave this inhospitable terrain soon moved on, but as white settlers invaded Native American hunting grounds, conflict was inevitable. A key plank of army strategy was to starve the Native Americans into submission: "For the sake of a lasting peace let them [professional hunters] kill, skin and sell until the buffalo are exterminated. Then your prairies can be covered by the speckled cow and the festive cowboy," declared General Philip Sheridan. By the late 1870s the buffalo were almost gone, and most of Montana had been cleared for settlement.

Accommodation price codes

All accommodation prices in this book have been coded using the symbols below. For **hotels, motels**, and **B&Bs**, rates are given for the least expensive double room in each establishment during peak season; variations are indicated where appropriate, including winter rates for all ski resorts. For **hostels**, the actual price per bed is given; for **camping**, the overnight cost per site is given. For a full explanation see p.30 in Basics.

➊ up to $30	➍ $60–80	➐ $130–180
➋ $30–45	➎ $80–100	➑ $180–240
➌ $45–60	➏ $100–130	➒ over $240

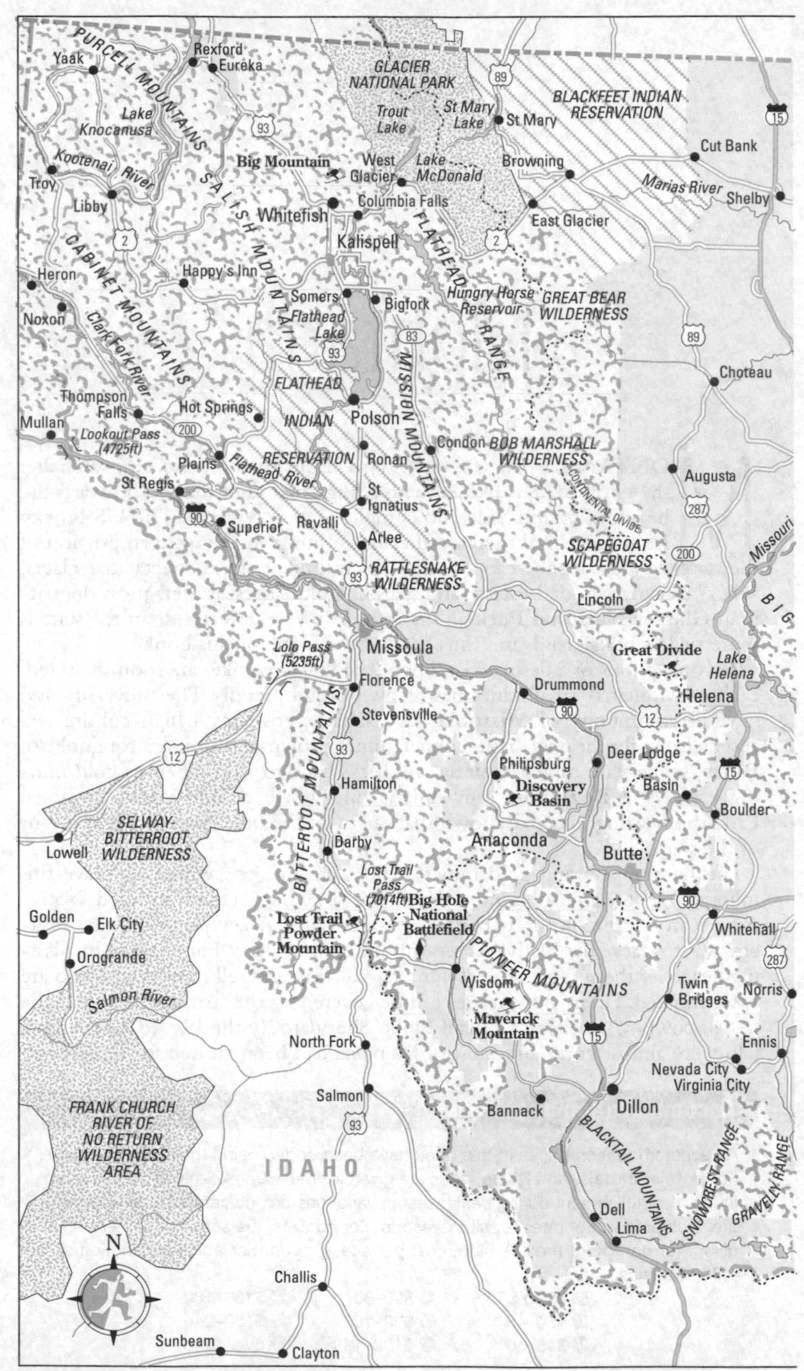
PURCELL MOUNTAINS
Yaak
Rexford
Eureka
GLACIER NATIONAL PARK
BLACKFEET INDIAN RESERVATION
Lake Knocanusa
Trout Lake
St Mary Lake
St Mary
Cut Bank
Kootenai River
Troy
Libby
Big Mountain
West Glacier
Lake McDonald
Browning
Marias River
Shelby
SALISH MOUNTAINS
Whitefish
Columbia Falls
FLATHEAD RANGE
East Glacier
Kalispell
CABINET MOUNTAINS
Heron
Happy's Inn
Somers
Bigfork
Hungry Horse Reservoir
GREAT BEAR WILDERNESS
Noxon
Clark Fork River
Flathead Lake
MISSION MOUNTAINS
Choteau
FLATHEAD
INDIAN
RESERVATION
Thompson Falls
Hot Springs
Polson
Mullan
Lookout Pass (4725ft)
Condon
BOB MARSHALL WILDERNESS
Plains
Ronan
Augusta
Flathead River
CONTINENTAL DIVIDE
St Regis
St Ignatius
Superior
Ravalli
Arlee
SCAPEGOAT WILDERNESS
Missouri
RATTLESNAKE WILDERNESS
Lincoln
BIG
Missoula
Lolo Pass (5235ft)
Great Divide
Lake Helena
Florence
Drummond
Helena
BITTERROOT MOUNTAINS
Stevensville
Deer Lodge
Philipsburg
Discovery Basin
Basin
Hamilton
Boulder
SELWAY-BITTERROOT WILDERNESS
Lowell
Anaconda
Darby
Butte
Lost Trail Pass (7014ft)
Big Hole National Battlefield
Lost Trail Powder Mountain
Whitehall
Golden
Elk City
Orogrande
PIONEER MOUNTAINS
Wisdom
Twin Bridges
Norris
Salmon River
Maverick Mountain
North Fork
Ennis
Nevada City
Virginia City
Salmon
Dillon
Bannack
FRANK CHURCH RIVER OF NO RETURN WILDERNESS AREA
BLACKTAIL MOUNTAINS
SNOWCREST RANGE
GRAVELLY RANGE
IDAHO
Dell
Lima
N
Challis
Sunbeam
Clayton

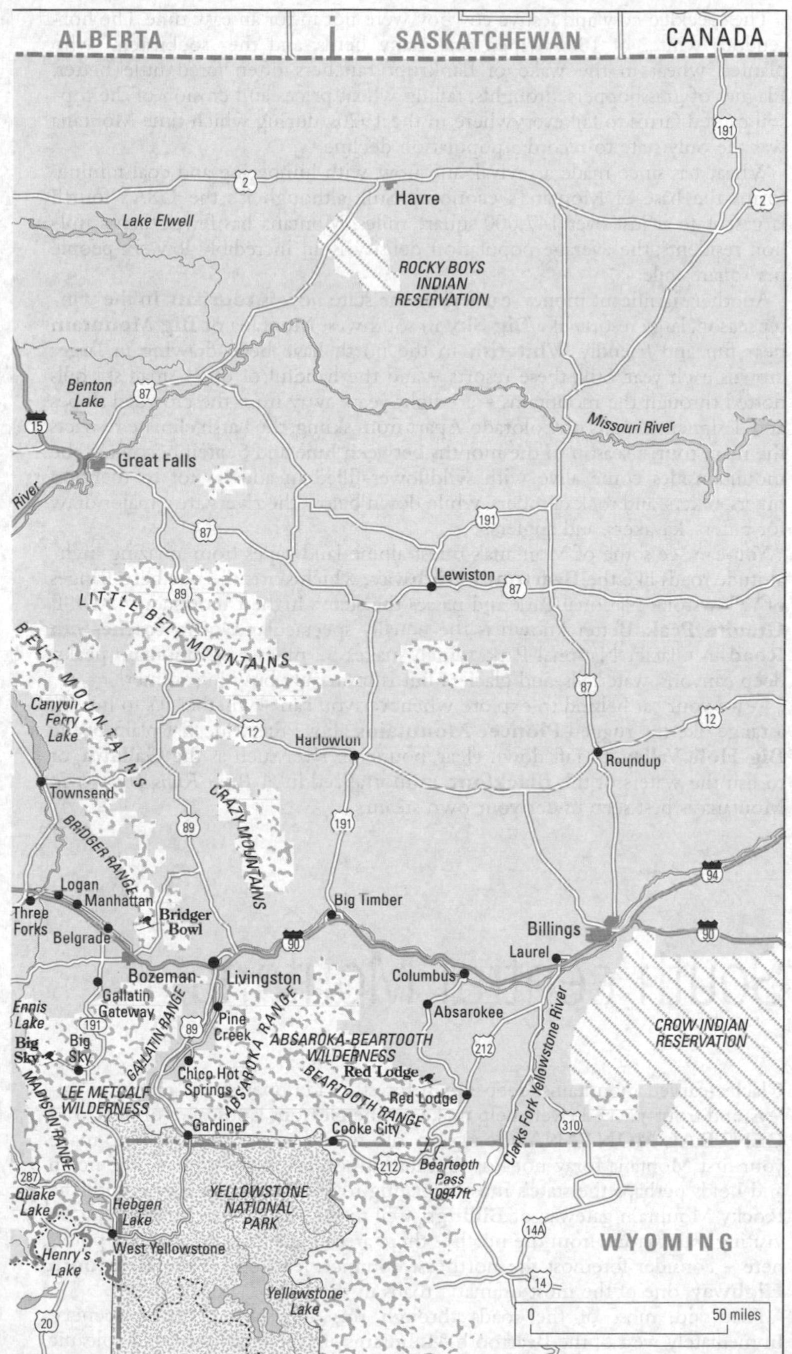
ALBERTA
SASKATCHEWAN
CANADA
Havre
Lake Elwell
ROCKY BOYS
INDIAN
RESERVATION
Benton
Lake
Missouri River
Great Falls
River
Lewiston
LITTLE BELT MOUNTAINS
BELT MOUNTAINS
Canyon
Ferry
Lake
Harlowton
Roundup
Townsend
CRAZY MOUNTAINS
BRIDGER RANGE
Logan
Manhattan
Three
Forks
Belgrade
Bridger
Bowl
Big Timber
Billings
Laurel
Bozeman
Livingston
Columbus
Gallatin
Gateway
Absarokee
Ennis
Lake
GALLATIN RANGE
Pine
Creek
ABSAROKA RANGE
ABSAROKA-BEARTOOTH
WILDERNESS
CROW INDIAN
RESERVATION
Big
Sky
Big
Sky
Chico Hot
Springs
Red Lodge
BEARTOOTH RANGE
Red Lodge
Clarks Fork Yellowstone River
MADISON RANGE
LEE METCALF
WILDERNESS
ABSAROKA RANGE
Gardiner
Cooke City
Beartooth
Pass
10947ft
Quake
Lake
Hebgen
Lake
YELLOWSTONE
NATIONAL
PARK
West Yellowstone
WYOMING
Henry's
Lake
Yellowstone
Lake
0
50 miles
2
2
191
15
87
87
191
87
89
87
12
12
89
191
94
90
90
191
89
212
310
212
287
14A
14
20

The speckled cow and festive cowboy were not in for an easy time. The horrendous winter of 1886 wiped out many herds, and the "sodbusters" who planted wheat in the wake of bankrupt ranchers often fared little better. Plagues of grasshoppers, droughts, falling wheat prices and erosion of the topsoil caused farms to fail everywhere in the 1920s, during which time Montana was the only state to record a population decline.

Wheat has since made a revival, and now, with lumbering and coal mining, forms the base of Montana's economy. Still, although it's the USA's fourth largest state at just over 147,000 square miles, Montana has fewer than a million residents; the average population density is an incredibly low six people per square mile.

Another significant money-earner for the state now is **tourism**. In the winter season, large resorts like **Big Sky** in southwest Montana or **Big Mountain** near fun and friendly **Whitefish** in the north have been drawing in larger crowds each year. Still, these resorts – and the handful of other small ski hills dotted through the mountains – are light years away from the crowded slopes and designer ski-suits of Colorado. Apart from skiing, the harsh climate restricts the main tourist season to the months between June and September, when the mountainsides come alive with wildflower-filled meadows, not to mention hikers, bikers, and rock climbers, while down below the rivers are a major draw for rafters, kayakers, and anglers.

You can see some of Montana's finest alpine landscapes from amazing high-altitude roads like the **Beartooth Highway**, which skirts the northern fringes of Yellowstone National Park and passes the state's highest mountain, 12,799ft **Granite Peak**. Better known is the equally spectacular **Going-to-the-Sun Road** in Glacier National Park, which snakes 52 miles past mountain peaks, deep canyons, waterfalls, and glaciers but is invariably busy in summer.

Leave your car behind to explore whenever you can – whether it's to hike in a range like the rugged **Pioneer Mountains** above the wide, flat plain of the **Big Hole Valley**, to raft down clear, bouncing river such as the **Gallatin**, or to fish the waters of the **Blackfoot**, immortalized in *A River Runs Through It*, Montana is best seen under your own steam.

South central Montana

Glacier-carved mountains, deep-green forests, wide open cattle ranching valleys, and trout-packed rivers help make up the glorious landscapes of **SOUTH CENTRAL MONTANA**, the region into which you're quite likely to make your first Montana foray, not least because it borders Yellowstone to the north and holds perhaps the state's most engaging town, **Bozeman**, along with the Rocky Mountain gateway of **Billings**, well to the east. If you are planning on visiting Yellowstone from the north – there are no less than three access points here – consider foremost the northeast entrance, reached via the **Beartooth Highway**, one of the most dramatic roads in the US.

That said, most of the roads through this area pass dramatic scenery. Immediately west of the Beartooth Mountains are the heavily eroded volcanic peaks of the Absaroka Range, separated in turn as you travel west from the Madison and Gallatin ranges. In the latter, you'll find some of the best skiing in the Rockies on **Lone Mountain** at the **Big Sky Resort**. Between these ranges, and futher west, run the headwaters of the **Missouri River** – the **Jefferson**, the **Gallatin**, and the **Madison**, all of which are famed for their trout fishing. Towns such as **Ennis** and **Three Forks** along the riverside rely heavily on anglers for their livelihood.

The **Yellowstone River**, though, is the mightiest of these, flowing north from the national park up the **Paradise Valley** and through the old railroad town of **Livingston** before heading east across the state.

Bozeman and around

Pretty, tree-lined **BOZEMAN**, which has grown over the last century on a steady diet of tourism, agriculture, and education, is one of the finest mid-sized towns in the Rockies. Founded by farmers in 1863, it's the only sizeable town in Montana not to owe its roots to mining, railroading, or lumbering. The smart-looking storefronts along the busy and attractive Main Street make for good aimless wandering, and the student's attending the town's **Montana State University (MSU)** ensure that the nightlife remains lively.

Though Bozeman has seen a fairly explosive build up on its outskirts over the past few decades, it has managed to keep its lively, **historic downtown** core intact. Here you'll find one of the state's finest collections of bars and restaurants, as well as galleries featuring local artists and plenty of fine sporting goods stores and outfitters. A short fifteen-minute walk south from the main drag of Main Street through leafy neighborhood side streets is MSU's verdant campus, home to the excellent **Museum of the Rockies**.

Despite these urban attractions, it's Bozeman's superb location and attendant year-round recreational opportunities that have put it on the map. The region, which Lewis and Clark passed through on their epic journey to the Pacific, is within spitting distance of a whole heap of mountain ranges which the Corps of Discovery looked upon rather less favorably than do today's locals. Right on Bozeman's southern doorstep is **Hyalite Canyon**, crammed with hiking and biking trails and good climbing routes. Twenty-minute's drive north of town is the **Bridger Range**, named after legendary mountain man Jim Bridger and home to **Bridger Bowl Ski Area**.

Arrival, information, and getting around

Eight miles north of town, Bozeman's small **Gallatin Airport** (ⓣ406/388-6632), with flights arriving from Salt Lake City, Denver, Portland, and Seattle, is mostly used for get-there-quick trips to both Yellowstone National Park and the Big Sky ski resort, both within ninety miles to the south. A taxi downtown will cost you around $12. In town, the Greyhound **bus** terminal is at 625 N 7th Ave (ⓣ406/587-3110). Karst Stages (ⓣ406/586-8567), with summer trips out to Big Sky and West Yellowstone, and regional Rimrock Trailways (ⓣ406/549-2339 or 1-800/255-7655), which runs west along I-90 to Seattle and east to Minneapolis, both use this terminal as well.

The Bozeman **chamber of commerce**, north of downtown at 1001 N 7th (Mon–Fri 9am–5pm; ⓣ406/586-5421 or 1-800/228-4224, ⓦwww.bozeman-chamber.com), has good maps and the useful *Bozeman Area Visitors Guide*. The more accessible Downtown Bozeman Association Visitor Center, 224 E Main

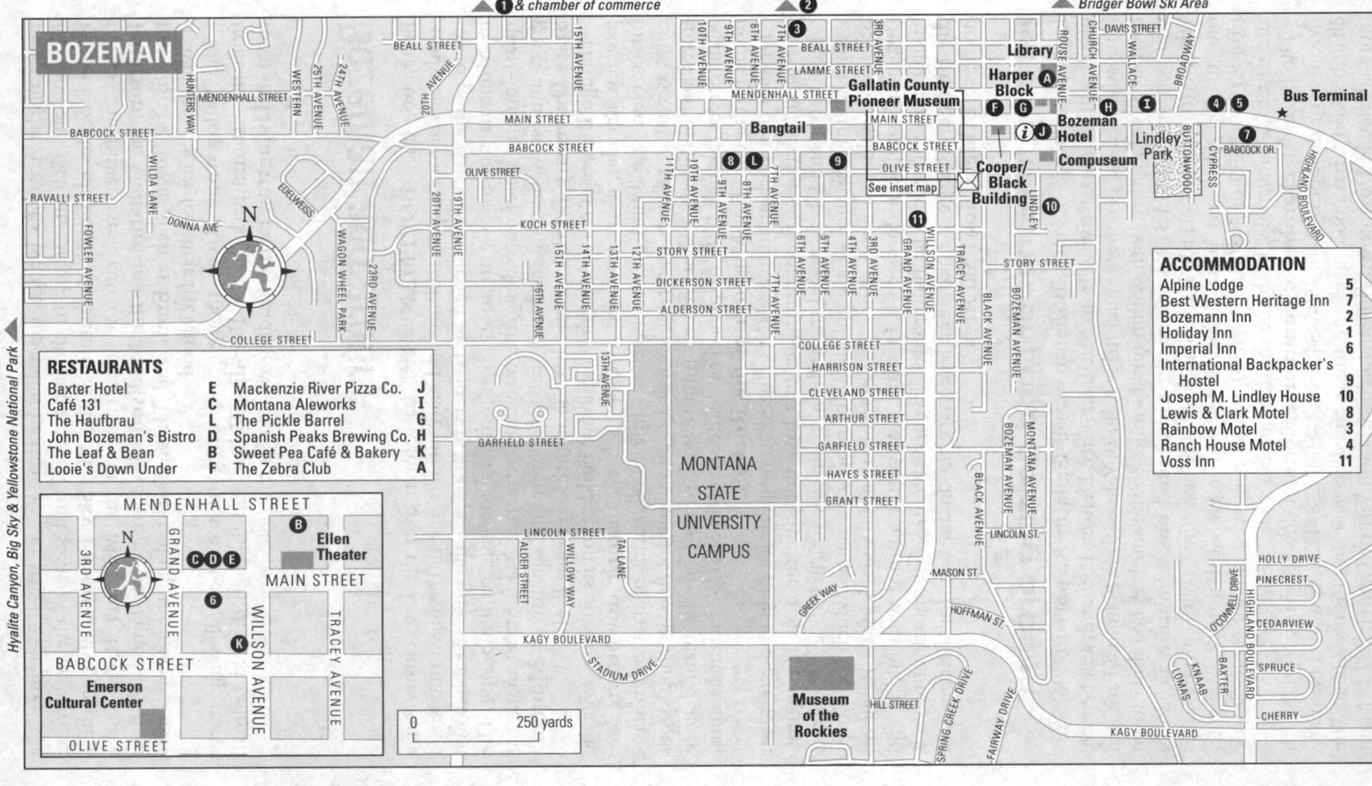
BOZEMAN
& chamber of commerce
Bridger Bowl Ski Area
Hyalite Canyon, Big Sky & Yellowstone National Park
Library
Harper Block
Gallatin County Pioneer Museum
Bangtail
Bozeman Hotel
Compuseum
Lindley Park
Cooper/ Black Building
Bus Terminal
See inset map
MONTANA STATE UNIVERSITY CAMPUS
Museum of the Rockies
Ellen Theater
Emerson Cultural Center
0 250 yards
RESTAURANTS
Baxter Hotel E
Café 131 C
The Haufbrau L
John Bozeman's Bistro D
The Leaf & Bean B
Looie's Down Under F
Mackenzie River Pizza Co. J
Montana Aleworks I
The Pickle Barrel G
Spanish Peaks Brewing Co. H
Sweet Pea Café & Bakery K
The Zebra Club A
ACCOMMODATION
Alpine Lodge 5
Best Western Heritage Inn 7
Bozemann Inn 2
Holiday Inn 1
Imperial Inn 6
International Backpacker's Hostel 9
Joseph M. Lindley House 10
Lewis & Clark Motel 8
Rainbow Motel 3
Ranch House Motel 4
Voss Inn 11

Gateway to Yellowstone

Tourism first took off in Bozeman in the early 1900s, when the Northern Pacific began promoting Yellowstone National Park. In order to house these tourists, the red-tile roofed **Gallatin Gateway Inn** (ⓣ406/763-4672 or 1-800/676-3522; ⑤), fifteen miles southwest of town on US-191, was constructed in 1927. One of the grandest railroad hotels in the West, it became quite literally a gateway to Yellowstone, visitors traveling here by train and then transferring to motor coaches to head into the park.

With the eventual decline in rail passengers, the venerable old hotel hit hard times, becoming amongst other things a Country and Western bar, and, unbelievably, a mud wrestling venue before it went through several years of restoration in the Nineties. The inn once again reflects its original style and class, featuring Polynesian mahogany woodwork, high arched windows, and attractive cream-colored stucco walls. Though small, the stylish rooms are all individually decorated, and are particularly good value in winter. The inn also has a tennis court, hot tub, and swimming pool. If not a guest, you can still stop in to eat at the onsite **restaurant**, one of the finest in the Bozeman area. Featuring fresh local meats and produce, highlights of the rotating contemporary American menu include a fine grilled rack of lamb, smoked trout, and a Montana morel mushroom risotto; expect to pay $20–25 per entree.

St (ⓣ406/586-4008, ⓦwww.historicbozeman.com), has more of the same and also allows limited free internet access. For recreational information, head to the **Bozeman Ranger District Office**, 3710 Fallon St, Suite C (Mon–Fri 8am–5pm; ⓣ406/522-2520, ⓦwww.fs.fed.us/ri/gallatin), four miles east of downtown on Hwy-191.

Accommodation

Bozeman has a wide range of **accommodation** to suit most budgets – including a handful of memorable **B&Bs** – and much of it is within easy reach of downtown. There are also the usual chain motels close to I-90, many of which offer cut-rate deals in the off-season. In winter, some of the places listed below offer special Bridger Bowl Ski Area (see p.467) packages, which can be great bargains – call the mountain (ⓣ406/587-2111) for details.

If roughing it, there are a handful of **campgrounds** within a couple miles of downtown. A more inspired choice, though, is one of the Forest Service **cabins** hidden in the surrounding mountains (see p.471), which provide very basic accommodation and a whole lot of solitude for around $20–30 per night – contact the Bozeman Ranger District for full details (see above).

Hotels, motels, and a hostel

Alpine Lodge 1017 E Main St ⓣ406/586-0356 or 1-888/922-5746, ⓦwww.alpine-lodge.com. Well located for downtown and recently remodeled on an appropriately alpine theme, the *Alpine Lodge* has a selection of attractive individual cottages with kitchens and motel rooms. Nonsmoking. ④

Best Western Heritage Inn 1200 E Main St ⓣ406/586-8534 or 1-800/877-1094. Large rooms with king or queen beds, a hot tub, fitness room, and free breakfasts, plus a location within easy reach of downtown make this chain accommodation relatively good value. ④

Bozeman Inn 1235 N 7th Ave ⓣ406/587-3176 or 1-800/648-7515. Convenient for I-90's exit 306, the spacious, fairly priced rooms come with comfy queen- or king-size beds. Facilities include hot tub, sauna, outdoor pool, nonsmoking rooms, and free continental breakfast. Rates often lowered in winter. ④

Holiday Inn 5 Baxter Lane ⓣ406/587-4561 or 1-800/366/5101, ⓕ406/587-4413, ⓦwww.bzn-holinn.com. Off of I-90, this above-average *Holiday*

Inn has large, well-equipped rooms, a large indoor pool, hot tub and exercise room, fireside guest lounge, restaurant, and free airport shuttle. ⑤

Imperial Inn 122 W Main St ⓣ406/587-4481 or 1-800/541-7423. With a great downtown location, the friendly *Imperial Inn* has clean and comfortable rooms and is not too hard on the budget (it has cheaper off-season rates), making it a good bet if you want to be close to the action downtown. ④

International Backpacker's Hostel 405 W Olive St ⓣ406/586-4659. A rare find in this part of the world, the hostel has bunks for $15 per night and facilities include a kitchen and laundry. A good place to meet fellow travelers and maybe pick up a ride for your onward journey.

Lewis & Clark Motel 824 W Main St ⓣ406/586-3341 or 1-800/332-7666. You can't miss the classic American motel lines of the *Lewis & Clark* on the west side of downtown, close to the MSU campus. It can be a little noisy as it's on the main strip, but the rooms are perfectly adequate and you also get a pool, hot tub, sauna, and sun deck. Rates drop considerably in the off-season. ④

Rainbow Motel 510 N 7th Ave ⓣ406/587-4201. Located within easy reach of both downtown and MSU campus, the *Rainbow* provides quite plain but perfectly adequate accommodation, and also has an outdoor pool and free continental breakfast. ④

Ranch House Motel 1201 E Main St ⓣ406/587-4278. Nothing fancy but the rooms are clean and economical, and it's within walking distance of downtown, with easy access to the freeway. ③

B&Bs

Howler's Inn 3185 Jackson Creek Rd ⓣ406/586-0304 or 1-888/469-5377, ⓦwww.howlersinn.com. This one-of-a-kind accommodation is a combined B&B and wolf sanctuary combined set in Bridger Canyon, three miles off I-90. Besides howling wolves, you also get great mountain views and large rooms with private baths, a shared sauna and hot tub, and workout room, all in a beautiful log and stone home. The wolves, which for various reasons cannot be released into the wild, are kept in a three-acre enclosure. ⑤

Joseph M. Lindley House 202 Lindley Place ⓣ406/587-8403 or 1-800/787-8404, ⓔlindley@avicom.net. This charming Victorian manor house, built in 1889, retains original features like antique beds that are augmented by modern amenities including a hot tub and sauna. Good access to downtown. ⑤

Silver Forest Inn 15325 Bridger Canyon Rd ⓣ406/586-1882 or 1-888/835-5970, ⓦwww.silverforestinn.com. Listed on the National Historic Register, this log-hewn B&B sits in the forest a mile below Bridger Bowl Ski Area. Built as an artist's retreat in 1932, it has six attractive guestrooms, a sun deck with a hot tub, and great mountain views, and equally good breakfasts. ⑥

Voss Inn 319 S Willson Ave ⓣ406/587-0982, ⓕ585-2964, ⓦwww.bozeman-vossinn.com. Six antique-decorated rooms, each with private bath, in a lovely 1883 home on a leafy side street just a two-minute walk from downtown. Fantastic breakfasts can be eaten in room or in the period lounge. Airport pick-up service also offered. ⑥

Campgrounds

Bear Canyon Campground ⓣ406/587-1575. Located only three miles east of Bozeman off I-90's exit 313, tent sites here cost $10 per night (seventh night free if you pay in advance). Open May–Oct, extras include a heated pool, store, and laundry.

Bozeman Hot Springs KOA ⓣ406/587-3030. Not too convenient for town unless you have a car – it's eight miles south of town on US-191 – and the location is rather drab. There are, though, excellent hot springs facilities (see opposite). Campsite fees are $24, RVs $32. Open year-round.

Hyalite Canyon Recreation Area Located south of town on Hyalite Canyon Rd, this recreation area has three campgrounds for $7 per night spread out between ten and eighteen miles south of downtown – the scenery gets better the further south you go.

The town

Downtown Bozeman is centered on Main Street, a throughway where Bozeman's eclectic mix of students, creative-types, business professionals, and outdoor adventurers rub shoulders. Most of the action takes place in its immediate environs between 10th Avenue to the west and Church Avenue to the east, a stretch which holds a nice mix of bookstores, sporting goods stores, restaurants, and art galleries, in addition to some fine historic buildings, such as the **Harper Block**, 237 E Main St, an elaborate little blacksmith's shop from 1873, and the elegant 1919 Neoclassical **Ellen Theater** at 17 W Main St, one of the best-preserved movie houses in the Rockies.

Equally interesting is the nearby **Gallatin County Pioneers Museum**, 317 W Main St (June–Sept Mon–Fri 10am–4.30pm, Sat 1–4pm; Oct–May Mon–Fri 11am–4pm, Sat 1–4pm; free). Located beside the Art Deco county courthouse, it's an amusing diversion, crammed with everything from the town's old gallows to a selection of weapons confiscated from resident inmates when this was the town jail. There's also a small display on Helena boy Gary Cooper, featuring cartoons he drew before hightailing it to Hollywood. South of Main Street is the unique **Compuseum**, 234 E Babcock St. (June–Aug Mon–Sun 10am–4pm; Sept–May Tues–Wed & Fri–Sat noon–4pm; $3; Ⓦwww.compuseum.org), with a small but absorbing exhibit on computing technology from the abacus to far more modern advances.

The Museum of the Rockies

Bozeman's must-see attraction is the **Museum of the Rockies**, on the southeast side of the MSU campus at 600 W Kagy Blvd (June–Aug daily 8am–8pm; Sept–May Mon–Sat 9am–5pm, Sun 12.30–5pm; $7, combined museum and planetarium ticket $9). Famed for its dinosaur collection, which includes a fearsome looking T. Rex skull excavated in eastern Montana in 1990, the overall theme is the history of Montana through geological time to the present. Give yourself a half-day at least to see the well-presented exhibits, highlights of which are the "Mammoths and the Great Ice Age" exhibition, the dino bones, and exhibits on Native American culture, including a furnished and beautifully decorated tepee. The pioneer era is brought to life directly outside the museum in a "Living History Farm," where staff members in period costume depict life on a homestead. On a much different note, the museum's **Taylor Planetarium** holds regular shows each day on the life of planets, stars, and the universe.

Bozeman Hot Springs

Traditionally used by Native Americans and now one of the more popular local relaxation spots is **Bozeman Hot Springs** (Ⓣ406/586-6492), off Hwy 191 eight miles west of town. Tastefully refurbished, the springs have seven pools with temperatures from 50°F to 104°F, and a sauna and steam room. As it's open until 10pm most days and midnight on Saturday, this is a good place to wind down after a day out in the local mountains. Rates are $5.50, with reductions if staying at the KOA site alongside (see opposite).

Summer activities

The most popular spot with locals looking for some outdoor action is **Hyalite Canyon**, but with so many mountain ranges within easy reach of the city, plus lift-served hiking and biking at Big Sky to the south, and Yellowstone National Park just beyond, you're really spoilt for choice.

Hiking, biking, and horseback riding

The **Bridger Range** beckons from the immediate north, and in their foothills you'll find the appropriately named twenty-mile one-way **Foothills trail**, accessed from Hwy-86 (Bridger Canyon Rd) four miles north of town at the "M" picnic area. As soon as you set out, fine views of the mountains open up, and with over 2600ft of ascent on the route these get ever more impressive the further you go. A shorter hike here is the four-mile round-trip **Sacajawea Peak trail**, although it involves 2000ft of stiff climbing – the payoff is magnificent views of the landscape for miles in all directions. The trailhead is reached from town via a 24-mile drive along Hwy-86 to Forest Road 24, where you turn west and drive another seven miles to the trailhead at the *Fairy Lake Campground*.

There are several good trails in **Hyalite Canyon**, an attractive region of waterfalls and hanging valleys that includes the 200-acre Hyalite Reservoir. To reach the canyon, take the thirty-minute drive south of Bozeman along 19th Avenue for seven miles to Hyalite Canyon Road. Next to Hyalite Dam is Blackmore Recreation Area, from where a hard ten-mile round-trip hike on the **Blackmore trail** will take you up Mount Blackmore (10,154ft). In Hyalite Canyon, mountain bikers will enjoy the thirteen-mile **History Rock Loop**, which includes three miles of wild single-track, some lung bursting climbing and great views of the Bridgers. Four miles south of Hyalite Reservoir, the tough, nine mile **Emerald Lake Loop** also has some superb single-track through beautiful alpine scenery along with the chance to spot wildlife including mountain goats. The best source for local routes is *Mountain Biking Bozeman* by Will Harman (Falcon Books), although most bike and outdoor stores will have information on the local riding too.

For a more traditional way of riding through the mountains, head northeast of Bozeman to Manhattan and the Gallatin River Ranch, 3200 Nixon Gulch Rd (Ⓣ406/284-3782 or 1-800/232-3295, Ⓦwww.gallatinriverranch.com), where you can arrange to get out on **horseback** amongst stunning canyon and ridgetop scenery. Rides are from one hour ($25) to a full day ($125), with breakfast, dinner, and moonlight expeditions also available.

Fishing and rafting

Though the **fly-fishing** in Bozeman itself isn't that great, many visitors use the town as a base for the superb fishing available on the Gallatin River to the south, on the Yellowstone River in the Paradise Valley to the southeast, and on the Madison River to the southwest. There are several angling outfitters in and around Bozeman, the best being The River's Edge, 2012 N 7th Ave (Ⓣ406/586-5373), which has a free map of local fishing spots, provides licences and arranges guided trips for around $210 per day. Downtown, try the Bozeman Angler, 23 E Main (Ⓣ406/587-9111 or 1-800/886-9111, Ⓦwww.bozemanangler.com), which provides much the same service.

The same rivers that make for such fine fishing also make for a worthwhile float. **Rafts** and **kayaks** can be hired from Montana Whitewater (Ⓣ406/763-4465 or 1-800/799-4465, Ⓦwww.montanawhitewater.com), based twelve

Local outfitters

Bangtail 500 W Main St Ⓣ406/587-4905. The best source in town for cross-country skiing and telemarking gear and information. In summer, mountain biking takes over, with rental from $20 per day for a front-suspension machine.

Barrel Mountaineering 240 E Main St Ⓣ406/582-1335, Ⓦwww.barrelmountaineering.com. This climbing shop has a knowledgeable staff, great selection of climbing, hiking, and backpacking gear and maps and guidebooks, and a very useful log book of local climbing routes started by the late, great Alex Lowe that's updated regularly.

Summit Bike, Ski & Skate Shop 26 S Grand Ave Ⓣ406/587-1064. Provides bike specific information and advice on where to ride off road; also the place to go for backcountry skiing advice in winter.

World Boards 601 W Main Ⓣ406/587-1707. The spot in town for boarders and skaters, with board rental $30 per day, down to $15 for five days or more.

miles south of Bozeman on Hwy-191, who also offer half-day and full-day trips on the Gallatin and Yellowstone rivers from around $40. Also headquartered in the Bozeman area is the Yellowstone Safari Company (Ⓣ406/586-1155, Ⓦwww.yellowstonesafari.com), who provide original, anecdote-filled Lewis and Clark themed float-trips down the Jefferson, Missouri, and Yellowstone rivers from around $150 per person (including lunch). Run by local biologist Ken Sinay, the company also runs well-organized animal safaris into Yellowstone National Park; check website for full details.

Winter activities

Winter around Bozeman is as much fun, if not more, than summer, with locals using their cold weather toys from November through April or May. Though the massive Big Sky resort (see p.471) is only an hour's drive south, many locals prefer the smaller, more personable **Bridger Bowl** (see below). The menu of winter activities extends well beyond downhill action, and **cross-country skiers** have several fine options, including the Gallagator Linear in town, an easy two-mile trail that starts at S Church Avenue and Storey Street. At Bohart Ranch (Ⓣ406/586-9070), sixteen miles north of Bozeman on Hwy-86 in Bridger Canyon, there are over twenty miles of picturesque mountain trails suited to all levels of ability; rates are $8 and rentals are available for around $10 per day. Hyalite Canyon (see opposite) also has several cross-country and snowshoe loops and is also one of the best, most accessible **ice-climbing** areas in the Rockies; stop by Barrel Mountaineering (see box, opposite) for more information.

Bridger Bowl Ski Area

Though the **Bridger Bowl Ski Area** (Ⓣ406/587-2111 or 1-800/223-9609, snow report Ⓣ406/586-2389, Ⓦwww.bridgerbowl.com), twenty minutes north of town on Hwy-86, has a reputation for being an extreme skier's haven, ordinary mortals can also have a great time here. Over fifty percent of the hill is rated suitable for beginners or intermediates, but **The Ridge**, towering above the main slopes, is where the experts go to play. Accessed via a steep 500ft hike, you'll need to sign in with ski patrol and have an avalanche transceiver, shovel, and partner to ski or board it. Those with a bit less experience should head for the black diamonds in the North Bowl or the double-blacks beneath The Nose, while intermediates will have a blast on steep Emil's Mile and on several beautiful cruisers through the open glades. Pretty much everything on the lower mountain is suitable for newbies.

Typically open by early December, the 1240 skiable acres are serviced by seven **lifts** that access some 2000ft of **vertical drop** from a top elevation of 8700ft. The most notable number though is the **average snowfall** – some 350 inches a year. The best time to visit Bridger is weekdays when the town's snow-mad students are locked up in college and the runs are uncrowded. Refreshingly in the increasingly corporate world of ski resorts, Bridger Bowl is run as a private, nonprofit ski area; consequently, a **lift ticket** costs only $34 and rental packages start at under $20. Getting to the mountain without a car can be tricky, though on weekends and holidays the Bridger Bowl Ski Bus ($5; Ⓣ406/586-8567) leaves from various locations in Bozeman from 8am. There are no places to stay on the hill, but if looking for a meal there are several options, including the basic *Jim Bridger Lodge* in the base area and the elegant mid-mountain *Deer Park Chalet* – a filling lunch here will set you back around $10–12.

Eating, drinking, and nightlife

Whatever your tastes or budget, Bozeman can more than likely meet your requirements in style – from coffee shops and live music venues to upmarket **restaurants** and cool brewpubs, there's as wide and entertaining a range of dining and drinking options here as any other city in Montana. The best **bars** and restaurants are located on or close to the downtown stretch of Main Street, making it easy to drift from one to the other over an evening, and there tends to be quite a mix of clientele in most places.

Cafés and restaurants

The Baxter 105 W Main St ⓣ406/586-1314. Great Neoclassical and Art Deco features make the recently renovated 1929 *Baxter* one of the most stylish casual dining venues in town. You can get good steaks and seafood in the *Baxter Grill*, and breakfast, lunch, and dinner indoors or out at the *Bacchus Café* – check out the portobello mushroom burger ($6.95) or the buffalo burger ($7.95). Also in the same building is the *Robin Bar*, a lively evening spot which serves fine pub food along with entertainment that can vary from excellent local jazz bands to heinous but hilarious karaoke nights. Look out for their happy hour from 5–7pm Sun–Thurs.

Café 131 131 W Main St ⓣ406/587-5100. A popular coffee shop with a good range of caffeine-rich beverages along with pastries, where you can kick back and read the free magazines, although it gets busy around lunchtime when locals call in for tasty and filling sandwiches and soups.

John Bozeman's Bistro 125 W Main St ⓣ406/587-4100. One of Bozeman's most sophisticated restaurants, with an eclectic menu featuring fresh fish cooked in different regional styles, good stir fries and local wild game – try the tasty Cajun-style bison steak. Lunch comes in at around $10, dinner $20 and up. They also have a good wine cellar. Closed Sun & Mon.

The Leaf & Bean 35 W Main St ⓣ406/587-1580. A fine selection of coffee, teas, microbrews, and pastries are served up amongst local art in this friendly coffeehouse, which stays open well into the evening. There's also a couple of pool tables and live music on weekends.

Looie's Down Under 101 E Main St ⓣ406/522-8814. Fine dining featuring American and European-style menus and a sushi bar. Tasty appetizers include fried shrimp or smoked trout ($8–10), and good entrees include rack of lamb and Alaskan halibut for $20–25. The wine list is extensive and there's live music on Saturday nights and a good-value Sunday lunch buffet.

Mackenzie River Pizza Company 232 E Main St ⓣ406/587-0055. An excellent selection of gourmet pizzas, including local specials like the trout pizza, massive sandwiches, and great salads. A wide array of Montana microbrews and fine wines round out the menu.

The Pickle Barrel 209 E Main St ⓣ406/582-0020. A popular Bozeman eatery (so expect queues at lunchtime), the *Pickle Barrel* serves up huge and tasty subs like the "American," featuring salami, bologna, and Monterey jack cheese, or the gut-busting "Ken's Special," stuffed with ham, turkey, pepperoni, Monterey jack, and Swiss cheese. There's a second location at 809 W College (ⓣ406/587-2411).

Sweet Pea Café & Bakery 19 S Willson ⓣ406/586-8200. Well-known for their breads, pastries, and sweets, the *Sweet Pea* is open for breakfast through to dinner every day except Sun and Mon. A fine entree is the seared bacon wrapped tenderloin with a Merlot demiglaze, served with Roquefort gratin of potatoes, although it's pricey at $28. Other entrees are cheaper at around $20. Reservations are recommended.

Brewpubs and bars

The Haufbrau 22 S 8th Ave. About as basic as it comes, the *Haufbrau* is a popular student hangout where the beer comes in plastic glasses and the regular live music is downright gritty – like much of the clientele. Pints come in at only $1.50, pitchers an even more economical $6.

Montana Aleworks 611 E Main St ⓣ406/587-7700. One of the best bars in Montana, located in the former Little Montana Transport building, a large railroad warehouse that has been superbly renovated and has plenty of room for eight pool tables, a snooker table, a large and busy central bar, and a pleasant dining area. There are over forty microbrews on tap, and excellent pub food is available with great standbys like fish and chips, ribs, and burgers from $8 up. There's also a deck for year-round outside dining, and $2 pints from 4–6pm.

Spanish Peaks Brewing Co. Main and Church Sts ⓣ406/585-2296. Located in a two-story building with a contemporary architectural feel featuring plenty of steel and glass, *Spanish Peaks* produces four different brews (lager, pale ale,

Black Dog, and honey raspberry) and various seasonal selections. Good food is also available, with entrees from $15–24 – appetizing options include the pork chop, Atlantic salmon, and shrimp creole fettuccini.

Stacy's 300 Mill St, Gallatin Gateway ☎406/763-4425. Situated fifteen miles southwest of town down US-191 a few hundred yards south of the *Gallatin Gateway Inn* (see p.463), this authentic, no-frills Montana cowboy bar is worth checking out for great C&W music and to see the local cowboys strut their stuff on the dance floor. Look out for a neon sign outside the bar, which actually says "Old Faithful."

The Zebra Cocktail Lounge 321 E Main St ☎406/585-8851. One of the most happening bars in town, with a good mix of younger clientele, especially students, particularly on Wed–Sat nights when there's DJs and live music, often featuring local indie bands.

Listings

Bookstore Vargo's Books, 6 W Main St (☎406/587-5383).

Deli/Food Store Community Food Co-op, 908 W Main St.

Hospital Bozeman Deaconess Hospital, 916 Highland Blvd (☎406/585-5000).

Internet Access is available free (with half an hour maximum computer time) at the Bozeman Public Library, 220 E Lamme St (☎406/586-4787).

Laundry East Main Laundry, 536 E Main St.

Post office The main post office is on Baxter St, between Tracy and Black aves.

Big Sky and the Gallatin Valley

Once past the celebrated *Gallatin Gateway Inn* (see p.163) fifteen miles south of Bozeman, US-191 emerges from flat plains into the twisting **Gallatin Valley** en route to Yellowstone National Park. Following the fast-moving, clear waters of the Gallatin River, the highway is framed on either side by steep crags and forested hillsides rising to the Gallatin Range to the east and the Madison Range to the west (including the Spanish Peaks, a popular hiking and back-country skiing destination). The highway was constructed in 1911, and ever since has been a major artery for travelers to Yellowstone who can get a preview of what to expect in the park en route as moose and mountain sheep are often spotted along the road Also commonly seen are the fishermen and rafters that flock to the river.

One sight you certainly won't miss is the magnificent **Lone Mountain**, an 11,166ft pyramid of snow and rock that dominates the western skyline an hour south of Bozeman and sits above the resort of **Big Sky**. Montana's biggest destination resort, the ever-expanding Big Sky is home to some of the finest advanced and expert skiing terrain in North America, as well as a selection of Montana's best upmarket restaurants and lodges.

Orientation and information

You won't get lost traveling down the Gallatin Valley since the only major road is US-191, with just the occasional turnoff into the mountains either side. One turnoff you won't want to miss is Hwy-64 leading west to Big Sky, some 45 miles south of Bozeman. At the turnoff, look out for the unostentatious **Soldier's Chapel**, a small log building which commemorates Montana soldiers who died in World War II. If you have time, step inside to see the window behind the altar that perfectly frames Lone Mountain's peak.

On the eight-mile drive up to Big Sky's **Mountain Village**, you'll pass the small settlements of **Meadow Village**, a couple of miles after the turnoff, and **West Fork Meadows**, about four miles further up the road. Both are recent additions to the landscape, built to cater exclusively for the tourist trade, and have regular **shuttle services** to and from Big Sky.

For more information contact the **chamber of commerce** in West Fork Meadows (Mon–Fri 9am–5pm, Sat 10am–4pm; Ⓣ406/995-3000 or 1-800/943-4111, Ⓦwww.bigskychamber.com), or check out the free *Lone Peak Lookout* newspaper for listings and events.

Accommodation

Where you choose **to stay** depends largely on the season. In winter, try to get accommodation in Meadow Village if you can afford it as it saves the drive up to the ski hill, which can be a hassle after heavy snow. Most of the accommodation here is run by the resort (Ⓣ1-800/548-4486, Ⓦwww.bigskyresort.com) – where no phone number is given below, contact this number. In summer, however, accommodation options lower down the mountain are worth considering for their proximity to the river and the numerous hiking trails along the Gallatin Valley. Many of the hotels in the area offer special winter ski packages, which are excellent value and can effectively enable you to ski for free.

Mountain Village

Huntley Lodge The resort's original hotel has received a recent facelift, sprucing up the still rather drab rooms a notch. The facilities, though, are excellent, and include a swimming pool, hot tubs, workout room, and the popular *Chet's Bar and Grill* (see "Eating and drinking," p.473). Rates include a very good free buffet breakfast, and ski-and-stay packages help cut the cost. ❼

Moonlight Basin Lodge 1 Mountain Loop Rd Ⓣ406/995-7700, Ⓦwww.moonlightspa.com. Located at the base of Powder River Run a mile west of Meadow Village, this sumptuously designed hotel is an attractive combination of timber and river rock. Rooms are just as beautifully decorated and will have you basking in the lap of luxury. Facilities include the excellent *Timbers* restaurant (see "Eating and drinking," p.474), a workout room, heated outdoor pool, and the Moonlight Spa, where you can get a great après-ski massage. ❽

Shoshone Condominium Hotel Ski-in, ski-out suites with private bedrooms, full kitchens, gas fireplaces, and balconies, plus access to *Huntley Lodge*'s health club, sauna, steam room, and lap pool. In summer a four-person condo can be had for little more than $200 per night. ❽

Summit at Big Sky Opened in 2000, the *Summit* features large, elegant rooms, most with good mountain views along with wet bars, small kitchens, fireplaces, and large tubs. There is also a workout room and an onsite spa. ❽

Off the mountain

Best Western Bucks T-4 US-191, less than a mile south of the Big Sky turnoff Ⓣ406/995-4111 or 1-800/822-448, Ⓦwww.buckst4.com. *Bucks*, a former hunting lodge, exudes far more personality than most Best Westerns. Though rooms are standard – comfortable queen beds, TV, coffeemaker – the common areas are anything but, including a pleasant lobby with fireplace, large country hall hosting the occasional concert and a highly recommended restaurant (see "Eating and drinking," p.474). Rates include a complimentary buffet breakfast. ❺

Big EZ Lodge 7000 Beaver Creek Rd Ⓣ406/995-7000 or 1-800/244-3299, Ⓦwww.bigezlodge.com. Located high above Meadow Village and a winding half-hour drive from Lone Mountain, the lodge, originally designed as the owner's personal residence, features thirteen art-filled suites, breathtaking views, and a guest's-only gourmet dining room. Eighteen-hole putting course, stocked trout ponds, and a huge outdoor hot tub round out the expensive ($300 per night and up), but worthwhile package. ❾

Golden Eagle Lodge Meadow Village Ⓣ406/9950-4800 or 1-800/548-4488. Well located for the shops in Meadow Village, the *Golden Eagle* has a range of relatively plain but perfectly adequate studios and condos, the more opulent having extras such as hot tubs, and there's also a full restaurant and bar onsite. ❺

Rainbow Ranch Lodge US-191, five miles south of Big Sky turnoff Ⓣ406/995-4132. A dozen attractive, individually decorated rooms only a few steps from the Gallatin River. There's an outdoor hot tub, Western-style lounge featuring a roaring fireplace and overstuffed leather couches, and a very fine restaurant and wine cellar (see "Eating and drinking," p.474). ❼

River Rock Lodge Westfork Meadows Ⓣ406/995-2295 or 1-800/995-9966. Fine lodging

Cabins and campsites in the Gallatin Valley

If you're looking to rough it, there are plenty of choices in the Gallatin Valley. On top of the typical range of **campsites**, the USFS manages a sprinkling of backcountry **cabins** in the region. These can be rented for $30 per night through the Bozeman Ranger Station (see p.463); a selection of the best is listed below. All are equipped with wood stoves, tables, cots or bunk beds, and axes; some have pots and pans. Potable water is not always available, and use is generally restricted to five consecutive nights. Some cabins you can drive to, others require a hike.

Also remember that regardless of whether you're in a tent or a cabin this is **bear** country and all appropriate precautions should be taken; see p.550 for more on avoiding an unpleasant encounter.

Cabins

Little Bear Cabin Thirteen miles south of Gallatin Gateway – turn east off US-191 on Little Bear and Big Bear roads into rolling, forested hills. The cabin is accessible by car in summer and sleeps four. In winter it's ten miles by ski or snowmobile.

Spanish Creek Cabin Eight miles from US-191 on Spanish Creek Rd at the north end of the Gallatin Valley. Cabin with good views of the Spanish Peaks and sleeps four people. In winter, it's 3.5 miles by ski or snowmobile to the cabin.

Windy Pass Cabin Nine miles from US-191 via the Portal Creek Rd and Windy Pass trail, with views across to Lone Mountain. Sleeps four. From the trailhead it's a stiff 2.5-mile hike, climbing 1300ft.

Yellow Mule Cabin Southwest of Big Sky, approximately fourteen miles from US-191 via Buck Creek Ridge Rd and Buck Creek Ridge Trail #10. It's an eight-mile hike from the trailhead, or in winter fourteen miles on skis or snowmobile. This is a good base from which to explore the remote southern mountains of the Lee Metcalf Wilderness. Sleeps two ($20).

Campgrounds

Greek Creek Thirty-one miles south of Bozeman on US-191. One of the best spots if fishing the Gallatin. The shady campground has toilets, water, and fourteen sites ($9).

Red Cliff Forty-eight miles south of Bozeman on US-191. Also well placed for fishing the Gallatin as well as for accessing local hiking trails. There are 68 sites ($9), with water and toilets.

Spire Rock Twenty-six miles south of Bozeman on US-191, then east on Squaw Creek Rd #132 for two more miles. A scenic location beneath the mountains and beside Squaw Creek. There are ten sites ($6); toilets but no water.

Swan Creek Thirty-two miles south of Bozeman on US-191 then east on Swan Creek Rd #186 for one mile. A lovely creekside location with 11 sites ($9), water and toilets, and good fishing and hiking trails close by.

choice with attractive Western-style rooms featuring queen beds complete with down comforter and snug wool blankets, minibar, and coffeemaker. Rates are reduced in the off-season. ❻

The 320 Ranch US-191, about a dozen miles south of the Big Sky turnoff ☎406/995-4283 or 1-800/243-0320. In business for a hundred years, accommodation is in cozy rustic log cabins; the larger ones have kitchenettes, although if you don't want to cook there's a good onsite restaurant. Activities such as fishing and cross-country skiing can be organized through the ranch. ❺

Big Sky Resort

Quite often, the massive, relatively uncrowded **Big Sky Resort** boasts the first skiable snow in the Rockies. The resort was the brainchild of American newscaster Chet Huntley, who, with other major investors bought a huge chunk of

Lone Mountain in 1969 with the aim of developing a mountain resort in harmony with its surroundings. After the current owner Boyne Developments took over, these developments have continued apace, but for now nature still holds the upper hand at the rugged and wild ski hill where moose and bear spotting are not unheard of.

The resort is divided into three mountains (Lone Mountain 11,166ft, Andesite Mountain 8800ft, and Flat Iron Mountain 8092ft) with 3600 **skiable acres**, a huge 4350ft of **vertical drop**, and a longest run of some six miles (Liberty Bowl to Base Area). The 122 named runs are serviced by fourteen lifts, four surface tows, and the thrilling fifteen-passenger Lone Mountain Tram, which heads up to the summit of Lone Mountain coming within an arm's breadth of the mountain's vertiginous crags. The **annual snowfall** is a mighty 400 inches, and the resort can open as early as October (weekends only), though the official season lasts from mid-November to mid-April. **Night skiing** is also available from around Christmas to mid-March.

Beginners may feel a little left out here; green runs make up only ten percent of the mountain, while 47 percent are intermediate blues and the rest are designated blacks. Of the few beginner's runs, Mr K and Morning Star between the trees are open and inviting. Intermediates will love cruisers such as Madison Avenue and Elk Park Ridge on Andesite Mountain for their reasonably challenging pitch and wide-open feel. Advanced skiers, of course, have a huge range of options, from the bumps of Snake Pit and Mad Wolf on Andesite to the big bowl beneath Turkey Traverse or the double-blacks beneath the aptly named Challenger Lift. Experts will want to take on the challenge of the fantastically steep double-black runs on Lone Peak – true experts may be tempted by the **Big Couloir**, a 45-degree slope that requires you to sign in with ski patrol and have a partner and avalanche rescue gear. Freestyle riders will want to head over to Andesite Mountain, where there's a **terrain park** and **half-pipe**.

Lift tickets are around $55, with slight discounts on multiday purchases. Facilities include *The Dugout* on Andesite Mountain, which does good barbecues, and several restaurants and ski and board rental shops in the Mountain Village. If renting, try Lone Mountain Sports in the Arrowhead Mall (Ⓣ406/995-4471) – expect to pay around $30 a day for skis or board rental. If you're staying down below, there's a free **shuttle** bus between the villages from 7am–11pm.

Cross country skiers will find over thirty miles of some of the best trails in the state at Lone Mountain Ranch, a couple of miles down Hwy-63 from Mountain Village, with lift passes costing $10 a day, and ski rental available from around $15. Check out the ranch's great bar and restaurant after your exertions.

Summers around the resort are very laid-back, with most business coming in from corporate conventions. Still, there's good hiking to be had up and down Lone Mountain, and the gondola gives access to great views and a range of marked **hiking** and biking trails (daily 9.30am–4.30pm June–Oct; $20 day-pass). **Mountain bikers** will find trails varying from winding fire roads to technical single track. Bikes can be rented in Mountain Village for around $30 per day.

The Gallatin Valley

Despite the fact that US-191 follows nearly every twist and turn of the **GALLATIN VALLEY** and its eponymous river, this detracts very little from the beauty of one of Montana's finest fly-fishing regions and the filming location for much of *A River Runs Through It*. But keep your eyes glued to the road when driving as this is reputedly one of the most dangerous stretches of highway in the state.

In summer, **whitewater** enthusiasts will find plenty of challenges on the river here – stretches such as the "Mad Mile" on its upper reaches have plenty of Class IV–V rapids. One of the best local guides is Geyser Whitewater Expeditions, located due south of the Big Sky turnoff (☎406/995-4989), with trips ranging from an easy half-day float down a meandering Class I section of the Gallatin ($40) to a strenuous full-day voyage that takes in rapids up to Class IV ($77). **Anglers** can pretty much pull off the road anywhere to access quality fishing; specific access points include *Greek Creek* and *Red Cliff* campgrounds (see box, p.471). Boat fishing is prohibited, and the trout season runs from April to late October. One of the best local outfitters is Gallatin River Guides in Big Sky (☎406/995-2290).

With spectacular mountain ranges either side of the Gallatin Valley and 25 peaks over 10,000ft in the Gallatin Range alone, this is not an area short of great **hiking** and **climbing** opportunities. Good maps of the region are available from the ranger station in Bozeman or Big Sky Chamber of Commerce. One of the most popular spots to forage about in is the **Lee Metcalf Wilderness Area**, which runs west of the valley along much of the Madison Range. Within the wilderness area are the **Spanish Peaks**, laced with some unforgettable hiking trails, although their height means the upper reaches are still covered in snow until July. A good access point for the Spanish Peaks is at USFS *Spanish Creek Campground*, signposted to the west of US-191 some 7.5 miles south of Bozeman. From the campground, a 23-mile loop trail alongside the South Fork Spanish Creek takes you beneath a whole range of 10,000ft peaks and past sparkling blue alpine lakes; you'll need to camp out for at least one night. A shorter hike is the nine-mile round trip **Lizard Lakes trail**, which passes bizarrely shaped rock outcrops (including the appropriately named Sphinx Mountain) and provides great views of the Gallatin and Madison ranges as well as several places from which to fish. To reach the trailhead, head sixteen miles south of the Big Sky turnoff and west onto Taylor Fork Road (FR134); after eight miles, turn right onto Cache Creek Road (FR134) and follow it for three miles to the trailhead.

Eating and drinking

One thing you won't go short on around Big Sky is good food – there's a wide selection of fine dining spots both on the mountain, in the villages below, and strung out along the Gallatin Valley, from high-end, sophisticated **restaurants** to beer-swilling true-grit Western **bars**. A few of the bars and restaurants on the mountain stay open year-round, but be warned that in summer things are rather dead. If you're catering for yourself, check out the well-stocked Hungry Moose Market & Deli, 11 Skywood Rd (☎406/995-3045).

Mountain Village

Chet's Bar & Grill ☎406/995-5784. Located in *Huntley Lodge* and generally busy immediately after the lifts close thanks to a happy hour that includes nightly entertainment. If you stay around after happy hour try the delicious smoked pheasant quesadilla appetizer, or the char-grilled buffalo strip steak main. Appetizers average $8–10, entrees $15 up.

Mountain Top Pizza Mountain Mall ☎406/995-4646. Good pizzas served from lunchtime onwards. Expect to pay around $14 for a large with a few toppings; free delivery.

M.R. Hummers Mountain Mall ☎406/995-4343. One of the most popular après-ski spots in the village, with great baby back ribs to go with your beer, and filling sandwiches for under $10.

Sundog Café ☎406/996-2439. Located right beside the lift ticket booths, the *Sundog* is a convenient place to stop off for a quick breakfast before you hit the mountain or for a midday break, with a tasty range of soups, chili, sandwiches, wraps, and baked goods, plus great coffee. Expect to pay around $7–10 for a decent lunch.

Timbers at Moonlight Basin Lodge 1 Mountain Loop Rd ⓣ406/995-7777. Though you can ski up to the bar and deli here for lunch, its best for dinner at the magnificent *Timbers Restaurant*, home to a massive stone fireplace. Highlights of the menu include the tenderloin of Montana beef topped with wild mushrooms, a sautéed Michigan venison loin, and Alaskan cod and chips. Entrees average around $25.

Off the mountain

Allgood's Bar & Grill Meadow Village ⓣ406/995-2750. Attracting a younger crowd, this bar and grill specializes in barbecued ribs and chicken ($12–14)and is also open for breakfasts (omelettes $6–8). The lively bar has a pool table, darts, and poker.

Blue Moon Bakery Meadow Village ⓣ406/995-2305. Good coffee and fresh-baked bagels and pastries make this a great breakfast stop on the way up Lone Mountain. During the lunch and dinner hours, the menu expands to include pizzas, pastas, salads, and sandwiches.

Bucks T-4 US-191, less than a mile south of Big Sky turnoff ⓣ406/995-4111. Probably the only Best Western restaurant featured in *Gourmet* and *Wine Spectator* magazines, *Bucks* specializes in imaginatively prepared exotic and local game. Stand-out entrees include the grilled New Zealand red deer in a port wine sauce and the pan-seared elk chop. Mains run from $20 to $35, and reservations are essential.

The Corral US-191, five miles south of Big Sky turnoff ⓣ406/995-4249. Open for breakfast from 7am, but it's the prime rib ($10 or $20 portions), local rainbow trout and Pacific halibut and salmon ($13–20) for lunch or dinner that make *The Corral* worth a visit. Also the place to come for a brew in a genuine Western roadhouse atmosphere.

Lone Mountain Ranch and Dining Lodge between Meadow and Mountain Villages ⓣ406/995-2782. Classic ranch-style cuisine, including Montana beef, local game, and poultry, plus seafood and vegetarian option in a stylish and intimate nonsmoking log lodge environment. Also does hearty buffet lunches and a chuckwagon dinner every Saturday night. Reservations required.

Rainbow Ranch Lodge US-191, five miles south of Big Sky turnoff ⓣ406/995-4132. Expensive, but mains like cinnamon-cured pork chops on a bed of sweet potato hash ($23) and fine starters like lobster and rabbit ravioli ($10) make dinner here well worth the splurge. Ask to see the Bacchus Room, an extraordinary 10,000-bottle wine cellar complete with "weeping walls."

Quake Lake

It's a delightful drive down US-191 between thickly timbered hillsides to the turnoff on US-287 to **Hebgen Lake**, just a few miles before West Yellowstone (see p.428). The lake, circled by aspen groves, sits east of **Quake Lake** – a cursory glance at the dead trees poking above the surface of the latter indicates that it's no ordinary lake. Indeed, there wasn't even a lake here until August 17, 1959, when an **earthquake** measuring 7.1 on the Richter Scale released a vast slide of rock, damming the Madison River Canyon. Twenty-eight people camping in the area were killed, and Hebgen Lake's north shore dropped by eighteen feet causing a tidal wave to race down the lake and sweep over Hebgen Dam, which miraculously held under the pressure. The incident is remembered at the **Madison River Canyon Earthquake Area Visitor Center** on US-287 at the west end of Quake Lake (June–Aug daily 9am–6pm; ⓣ406/646-7369), from where there's also a good view of the scene.

The Madison River Valley: Three Forks and Ennis

West from Bozeman, I-90 skirts past the unremarkable towns of Belgrade and Manhattan before coming to small **THREE FORKS**, located near the confluence of the three rivers that form the mighty **Missouri River**. Lewis and Clark canoed through this area in 1805, naming the rivers after their benefactors – the US President (**Jefferson**), the Secretary of the Treasury (**Gallatin**) and the Secretary of State (**Madison**) – and noted that they marked "an essential point in the geography of this western part of the continent." A more exciting episode occurred here three years later, when **John Colter**, a veteran of the Lewis and Clark expedition and the first person to describe Yellowstone (see p.411), was captured by a party of Blackfoot Indians while trapping for beaver along the rivers' edge. After killing his partner John Potts, they stripped Colter naked and made him run for his life, giving him a sporting 300-yard start before sending a party of braves in pursuit – Colter's scalp was the "prize" for whomever caught him. After four miles only one warrior had managed to keep up with Colter, who bravely turned on his pursuer and fought him to the death, then hid under a driftwood snag on the Madison River. The remaining braves eventually gave up their search, leaving Colter to tramp barefoot for the next eleven days to a fort on the Big Horn River, 250 miles away, carrying only a blanket and spear that he'd taken from the Blackfoot he killed.

More tales of derring-do are told at the **Missouri Headwaters State Park** (open year-round sunrise–sunset; $5 per vehicle; ⓣ406/994-4042), a well signposted drive three miles east of Three Forks. Here, along the 1.5-mile length of the park abutting the rivers, you'll find panels filled with useful details on Lewis and Clark and local flora and fauna, as well as a swimming area, boat dock, and 23-site **campground** ($12) with pit toilets, fire rings, and picnic tables. There are also a couple of old buildings transplanted from now-abandoned Gallatin City and some poorly preserved pictographs, though time is better spent looking out for the ospreys, herons, and golden eagles that live locally.

There's more to be seen at the **Lewis and Clark Caverns State Park**, seventeen miles west of Three Forks on Hwy-2 (May–Sept daily 9am–5pm; $6; ⓣ406/287-3541). Any connection to Lewis and Clark is tenuous (the caverns were discovered forty years after they passed by); instead the regular two-hour guided tours let you discover weirdly shaped and beautifully colored limestone formations, along with passageways as long as 3000ft, making this the third-largest known cavern in the US. If you go, bring a fleece; the caverns remain at 50°F year-round.

Ennis and around

South of Three Forks, US-287 winds through the wide ranching valley of the Madison, bounded on the northwest by the wild 10,000ft Tobacco Root Mountains and on the east by the bulky 11,000ft summits of the Madison Range, eventually rolling in to the cheery little town of **ENNIS**, some 55 miles away. Originally a supply town for the gold-mining towns of Virginia City and Nevada City, the town is now a focal point for anglers (see box, overleaf). But even if you've can't tell the difference between a rainbow and a brownie, Ennis' Main Street is worth checking out for its appealing cowboy atmosphere and collection of unassuming, Western-style buildings housing an assortment of outfitters, bars, and restaurants. North of town, **Ennis Lake** makes for pleasant swimming in summer.

Practicalities

Ennis' **visitor center**, at the east of the town's short Main Street (Mon–Fri 9am–5pm; ⓣ406/692-7244), can help with fishing permits, as can the **ranger station** just west of town at 5 Forest Service Rd (Mon–Fri 8am–5pm ⓣ406/682-4253). If looking to **stay the night**, the prime options are the motels strung along US-287 north and south of town; in summer, you'll need to book in advance as they tend to fill quickly. On the north side of town, the

Fishing the Madison

The stretch of the Madison River between Ennis and Quake Lake is one of Montana's best **fly-fishing** areas, and there are numerous free access sites indicated by brown-and-white signs along US-287. The stretch of river between Varney Bridge in the small town of Cameron eleven miles south of Ennis, to Hebgen Lake, some forty miles south again, is open year round.

The most likely catch will be rainbow or brown trout, although there is also Arctic grayling and whitefish. Two of the best **outfitters** out of Ennis are Madison River Fishing Company,109 Main St (Ⓣ406/682-4293 or 1-800/227-7127), and The Tackle Shop, 127 Main St (Ⓣ 406/682-4263). Guiding rates start at around $150 per half-day for two people, $250 per full day, including lunch.

Sportsman's Lodge, 310 US-287 N (Ⓣ406/682-4242; ④), has comfortable non-smoking motel rooms and rustic cabin units set amongst attractively landscaped grounds. In town, the convenient *Fan Mountain Inn*, 204 N Main St (Ⓣ406/682-4424; ③), has plain but clean cabins. A more upmarket local choice is the *T Lazy B Ranch* (Ⓣ406/682-7288; ⑦), eight miles east on Jack Creek Road. Built in the 1930s, the ranch caters mainly to anglers and has three snug cabins with a shared bathhouse. If **camping**, *Camper Corner*, corner US-287 and Country Road 287 (Ⓣ406/682-4514), is within walking distance of town, and has ten tent sites ($15), twenty RV spots ($22), showers, and a laundry.

A reasonable selection of **eateries** line Main Street, including *Yesterday's Restaurant*, 124 Main St (Ⓣ406/682-4246), a friendly spot serving steaks, omelettes, and burgers where lunch will cost around $8–10. The *Continental Divide*, 315 E Main St (Ⓣ406/682-7600), is a bit fancier and serves worthy steaks for around $20. Good for a **drink**, the *Silver Dollar Saloon*, 133 Main St (Ⓣ406/682-7320), offers the best chance to mingle with gregarious, unpretentious locals.

Virginia and Nevada cities

West of Ennis on US-287 towards Dillon stand the marvellously preserved gold-rush towns of **Virginia City**, thirteen miles on, and **Nevada City**, 1.5 miles further west. If they have a familiar look it's probably because you've seen them in Hollywood westerns like *Missouri Breaks* or *Little Big Man*. In 1863, a couple of prospectors looking for enough gold to buy some tobacco struck a solid vein at nearby **Alder Gulch**. In the usual way, within a year some 10,000 people struck with gold fever were living and working in a fourteen-mile stretch centered on these two towns.

Today, Virginia City's main and pretty much only drag is Wallace Street (US-287), which has a fine collection of 1860–70s boomtown buildings as well as two decent theaters. Among the best are the imposing **Montana Post Building**, which published the state's first newspaper and has a display of printing equipment, and the atmospheric **Thompson-Hickman Memorial Museum** (daily June–Aug 9am–5pm; free), worth stepping into to see the club foot that gave outlaw "Clubfoot George" his nickname. Also of interest is **Boothill Cemetery**, a short walk above town, where criminals hung by the Montana Vigilante movement are buried (see p.504). The biggest draw on summer evenings is the splendid **Opera House**, where the Virginia City Players perform over-the-top period pieces and comedies ($10; Ⓣ406/843-5377); the Brewery Follies Players give colorful vaudeville performances in Montana's first brewery, the restored **H.S. Gilbert Brewery** ($8; Ⓣ406/843-5314), where you can indeed get a drink.

You can make the 1.5-mile journey west to one-street Nevada City on the steam-powered **Alder Gulch Short Line Railroad** (daily June–Aug 9am–5pm; $5; ⓣ406/843-5382). The price of this also includes admission to a fine railroad museum in the center of Nevada City, which displays an observation car used by President Calvin Coolidge. There's nothing especially worth staying over for in Nevada City, though the collection of late nineteenth-century buildings – restored to match an 1885 photograph of the town – is worth a look. If you do stay over, consider the *Nevada City Hotel and Cabins* (ⓣ406/843-5377 or 1-800/648-7588; ❸), an old-fashioned log hotel with more than a whiff of authenticity, both in its rooms and cabins.

Livingston and the Paradise Valley

LIVINGSTON, 35 miles east of Bozeman on I-90, developed as a tough, hard-drinking frontier town where the locals included the infamous prostitute Calamity Jane, once described as having "the build of a blacksmith, the vocabulary of a mule skinner and the tender heart of a priest." With the arrival of the Northern Pacific in the late 1880s the town was well placed as a gateway for the newly created **Yellowstone National Park**, and park tourism has been an important source of income since.

Many of Livingston's buildings are on the National Historic Register, and despite the restoration of some to galleries, restaurants, and the like there's still an authentic Old West feel to the town's architecture. This pleasing combination of old and new has led to Livingston becoming quite a hip hangout for artists, writers and outdoor types.

Flowing through the center of town from the lovely **Paradise Valley** to the south, the Yellowstone River heads northeast from Livingston past the Crazy Mountain and across the flat, brown Montana Plains.

Arrival, information, and accommodation

Greyhound **buses** pull in at the depot on 107 W Park St (ⓣ406/222-2231), by the *Guest House Motel*. Rimrock Stages (ⓣ1-800/255-7655) also leave from here, with a daily service to Billings, Helena, and Missoula. The town's **chamber of commerce**, in the former railroad crew quarters of the Burlington Northern Railroad, which also used to run through the town, are at 303 E Park St (June–Aug Mon–Fri 8am–6pm, Sat–Sun 10am–2pm; ⓣ406/222-0850, ⓦwww.livingston-chamber.com), and is a good spot to pick up information on activities in the Paradise Valley.

Though you'll most likely be just passing through on the way to or from Yellowstone, there's a reasonably varied selection of **accommodation** should you choose to stay the night. If looking to **camp**, you're better off heading down the Paradise Valley (see overleaf).

Best Western Yellowstone Inn 1515 W Park St ⓣ406/222-6110 or 1-800/826-1214. Standard mid-range motel rooms with perks that include a heated indoor pool, lounge, and restaurant. ❺

Budget Host Parkway Motel 1124 W Park St ⓣ406/222-3480 or 1-800/727-7217. Decent-sized rooms and easy access to the highways make this a good bet if you're just passing through. There's also a restaurant, heated pool, and in-room coffeemakers. ❹

Econo Lodge 111 Rogers Lane (ⓣ406/222-0555 or 1-800/553-2666). The newest motel in town has spacious rooms featuring king-size beds, free continental breakfast, and cable TV. There's also an indoor pool and hot tub. ❹

The Guest House Motel 105 W Park St ⓣ406/222-1460 or 1-888/222-1460. Plain but economical accommodation convenient for downtown and the bus stop. The rooms are plain but clean, and have air conditioning and cable TV, and there's a guest lounge. ❸

The Main Motel 130 North F St ☎406/222-8103. The cheapest place in town. You get what you pay for – rooms are plain and the atmosphere smoky – however it is within walking distance of downtown. ❷

Murray Cabin 201 W Park St ☎406/222-1350. The most atmospheric lodging in town, the *Murray* is a prototypical Western inn. Both the rooms and public spaces are done up in a traditional period decor, and there's also the luxury of a rooftop hot tub – something Calamity Jane would have undoubtedly adored. Movie director Sam Peckinpah lived and caroused in a suite here in the 70s. ❸

The town

Livingston's atmospheric **downtown** is easy to wander around, with a fine selection of Western architecture and such interesting little foibles as cigarette advertisements etched into the paving stones outside the Empire Cinema (corner of 2nd and Callender streets). Perhaps a bit odd for a railroad town, there's a number of **galleries** here; two worth checking are Visions West Gallery, 108 S Main St, which has a good selection of Western-themed artwork, and Chatham Fine Art, 120 N Main (☎406/222-1566), featuring the landscapes of Russell Chatham, the town's best-known artist.

Immediately obvious in the middle of town is the 1902 **Livingston Depot Center**, 200 W Park St (June to mid-Oct Mon–Sat 9am–5pm, Sun 1–5pm, rest of the year Thurs–Sun 1–5pm; $3), built in an attractive Italian villa-style for the Northern Pacific. Besides the expected collection of railroad artifacts, there's also an enjoyable Western art collection featuring works by Charles Russell, Frederick Remington, and Thomas Moran. Across the tracks to the north is the **Yellowstone Gateway Museum**, 118 W Chinook St (June–Aug daily 10am–8pm; $3), easily spotted as there's an 1889 Northern Pacific railroad carriage parked outside. The small collection inside is fairly rote, though mountain bikers will be fascinated by the full-suspension bike on display – it dates back one hundred years. Just a few blocks east of the Depot Center is the **Natural History Exhibit Hall**, 120 E Park St (June–Sept daily 10am–6pm, Oct–May Thurs–Sun noon–5pm; $4), which has some good dinosaur exhibits.

If you're here to cast a line in the local rivers check out the **International Fly Fishing Center**, 215 E Lewis St (May–Sept daily 10am–6pm; $3), which displays thousands of flies, fly rods, and fishing accessories, has an aquarium, and offers free fly-casting lessons every Tuesday and Thursday evening.

Eating and drinking

Livingston's downtown streets are lined with **eateries**. One of the best is the *Livingston Bar and Grille*, 130 N Main St (☎406/222-7909), where local ranchers and ladies of ill-repute used to once raise hell – today, things are far more refined and entrees ($20) include fresh fish, rabbit, and juicy steaks. More in keeping with the railroad side of town life is *Martin's Restaurant*, 108 Park St (☎406/222-2311), which serves up no-frills diner-style food 24-hours a day. If you're in a rush, the *Pickle Barrel* at 113 W Park St (☎406/222-5469) has a large range of huge sandwiches, and for good-value, filling breakfasts check out *Pinky's* on the corner of Park and B streets (☎406/222-0668).

The Paradise Valley

From Livingston, the **Paradise Valley** narrows as it becomes squeezed between the **Absaroka Mountains** and the **Gallatin Range** on its way to the north entrance of Yellowstone National Park (see Chapter 8). This was the first access route to the park and is still one of the most popular, though activities in the valley itself are increasingly causing folks to stick around for a day or two instead of zipping straight through. The Yellowstone River flowing along its floor is the longest undammed river in the lower 48, running some 680 miles east to join the Missouri in North Dakota. Its route here is paralleled by two roads, US-89 and the less travelled East River Road (Hwy-541), which is considerably narrower but gives you a better feel for the valley and landscape.

There are few settlements of any real size in the valley until you reach the national park gateway town of Gardiner (see p.433). Much of the land is taken up by large ranches – many the second homes of Hollywood stars – as well as the compound of the **Church Universal and Triumphant**, whose retired leader Elizabeth Claire Prophet has unsuccessfully predicted Armageddon several times. Twelve miles south of Livingston on East River Road, the bucolic little settlement of **Pine Creek** makes a good pull off to gander at the huge peaks of Elephant Head Mountain and Mount Delano looking down from the Absarokas to the east. Here you'll find archetypal log cabins to rent at the *Pine Creek Store and Lodge* (Ⓣ406/222-3628 or 1-800/746-3990; ❹).

Ten miles south, the low-key resort of **Chico Hot Springs** (Ⓣ406/333-4933 or 1-800/468-9232; ❺) pulls people in to take the waters ($5 non-guests); the attendant main lodge, built in 1900, is suitably decked out in antiques and has three floors of small, but atmospheric rooms. Several other more-expensive accommodation options – including fully equipped cabins and even houses – are on offer, as is the valley's finest **restaurant**, featuring a delicious pine-nut crusted halibut ($24) and a renowned beef Wellington for two ($50). The poolside **bar**, a classic honky-tonk, is well worth a visit.

Outdoor activities

Though often dry and dusty due to drought conditions, the Paradise Valley does offer up a wide array of **outdoor activities**. The Yellowstone River here is yet another prime local fly-fishing area, usually at its best from June to October. It's also popular with rafters; based in Gardiner, the Yellowstone Rafting Company (Ⓣ1-800/858-7781, Ⓦwww.yellowstoneraft.com) offers both half-day ($30) and full-day ($55) excursions.

One of the best overnight hikes here leads up to the foothills of the somewhat forbidding **Mount Cowen**, at 11,206ft the highest point in the Absarokas. It's a tough eighteen-mile round-trip that starts easily enough on Trail 51 before turning north on to Upper Sage Creek Trail (#48) to climb relentlessly for over 3000ft to Elbow Lake; there are backcountry campsites at the lake. To get to the trailhead turn east onto Mill Creek Road (Forest Road 486) off US-89 about twenty miles south of Livingston; after eleven miles turn northeast onto Forest Road 3280 and drive a final mile to the trailhead. To explore the Gallatin Range on the valley's west side, check out the **Big Creek trailhead**, on the west side of US-89 about thirty miles south of Livingston and up Big Creek Road, where there is access to several trails leading up to alpine lakes and high mountain country.

Though no trails are specifically marked for **mountain biking**, any route outside the Absaroka-Beartooth Wilderness is open to bikers, and there's a good network of logging and forest service roads in both ranges. For advice on the best riding, stop by Timber Trails in Livingston, 309 W Park St (Ⓣ406/222-9550).

Whether hiking or biking, it pays to be aware that you're in prime **rattlesnake** country; see the box on p.259 for details on what to do should you stumble across one.

Red Lodge and the Absaroka-Beartooth Wilderness

The brooding mass of the Absaroka Range, and to the east the smaller but more rugged alpine landscape of the Beartooth Range make up the 1475-square-mile **ABSAROKA-BEARTOOTH WILDERNESS**. Much of the wilderness area can be viewed on the spectacular 10,000ft-high **Beartooth Highway**, one of the most scenic drives in the country. This alone is reason enough to visit the region, but mountaineers and hikers will also be drawn by Montana's highest mountain, rugged **Granite Peak** (12,799ft), which rises above a series of wind-scoured tundra plateaus and alpine meadows incised by steep canyons.

Located to the east of the wilderness area is the relatively unknown **RED LODGE** ski and summer resort, where you'll find some of the best skiing in Montana and a fine range of summer hiking and biking. Indeed, apart from the Beartooth Highway, your best bet here is to leave the car and head off under your own steam as the mountains, alpine lakes, forests, and rivers of this region are some of the most scenic in the state.

Exploring the Absaroka-Beartooth Wilderness

If you're thinking about taking a backpacking trip into the northern reaches of Yellowstone National Park, consider instead tackling a trip in the **Absaroka-Beartooth Wilderness**. More secluded and with better vistas, there's a solid network of trails here that lead up through silent timbered mountainsides and alpine meadows that erupt with bright wildflowers during the brief six-week July and August growing season. Above the treeline, it's a harsh but beautiful high-alpine landscape that can see snow at any time of year. These tundra plateaus are particularly fragile environments, so be sure to stay on the trails at all times.

The best **access points** into the Absaroka Range are from a series of county roads to the northwest of Red Lodge, from Hwy-298 south of Big Timber, and from the Paradise Valley south of Livingston. The Beartooths are best accessed from Hwy-78/US-212, both of which pass through Red Lodge.

An excellent multiday backpacking adventure in the Absarokas is the 28-mile round trip to **Lake Pinchot**, which takes you up to almost 10,000ft, past several trout-filled alpine lakes and beneath Mount Douglas and Chalice Peak, both over 11,000ft high. The trailhead is located fifty miles south of Big Timber at the end of Boulder River Road (Forest Road 298), from where you take Trail 27 and climb gradually up for two miles alongside the East Fork of the Boulder River to Trail 28. Turn left onto this and continue uphill for another twelve miles all the way to Lake Pinchot, a lovely spot to camp. You return on Upside Down Creek Trail (#26).

If you only have time for a day-hike, try the flat six-mile round trip to **Rock Island Lake**. At 8000ft, this is a great introduction to the area and there are several other fine trails from the lake if you decide to stay out in the wilds a little longer. The trailhead is reached from US-212 ten miles east of Cooke City, where you turn north onto Forest Road 306 for about one mile to Trail 3. Follow Trail 3 past Kersey Lake to Trail 566, which takes you to the convoluted shoreline of Rock Island Lake beneath craggy mountaintops.

More adventurous hikers may want to check out **Granite Peak**, visited on a tough 21-mile round-trip hike to the base of the mountain. The hike to "base camp" involves 5000ft of ascent; the actual summit is about another 1300ft up and should only be attempted by experienced climbers. To get to the trailhead drive south through the town of Fishtail (just over thirty miles northwest of Red Lodge) for a mile then turn south on West Rosebud Road from where you follow signs to West Rosebud Lake and the trailhead at Mystic Dam Power Station. Follow Trail 9 then Trail 17 (Phantom Creek trail) which will take you to within striking distance of Granite Peak and some awesome views east over the Montana Plains.

For more information on trails within the wilderness area, call in at the Beartooth Ranger Station in Red Lodge (see p.483).

Red Lodge and around

On the eastern edge of the Absaroka-Beartooth Wilderness, stunningly situated **RED LODGE** is not unlike Aspen, Colorado before the big money moved in, though a similar trend has started here, and how long it will continue to keep its friendly, down-home feel is open to conjecture. For now, Red Lodge remains a fine base for the **Red Lodge Mountain Ski Area** and for heading into the nearby wilds. Plus, it's the last pit stop for those heading onto the spectacular **Beartooth Highway** (see box p.485).

The town developed towards the end of the ninteenth century, first as a center for ranching and farming and then as a mining locale after the discovery of coal on the plains to the north. Miners from all over the world, particularly Finland and Italy, came here in search of wealth, and with the construction of a railroad depot by Northern Pacific in 1889 Red Lodge's future seemed secure. All the same, it was still a genuine Wild West frontier town, attracting some of the West's most colorful characters – Buffalo Bill, "Liver Eating" Johnson (see box, below), Calamity Jane, and the Sundance Kid all did their thing here at some point.

"Liver Eating" Johnson

Red Lodge attracted its share of Wild West characters in its early days, perhaps the most colorful being **John "Liver Eating" Johnson**, inspiration for Robert Redford's movie *Jeremiah Johnson*.

Johnson moved to Red Lodge in 1894 to become the town's long arm of the law after a notorious career as a whaler, Indian fighter, cavalry rider, and scout. By this time he had already acquired his bizarre nickname, and numerous tales circulated over how it was earned. Some claimed he killed, scalped, and ate the livers of some Crow Indians who had killed his wife, while others argued he had ripped open a calf in a fight with some Sioux and eaten its liver. Still more said it came from a simple boast, Johnson claiming he'd eat the liver of any Indian who gave him trouble.

The truth, it seems, is somewhere in between. According to Johnson, it all began with a fight with a Sioux warrior that was witnessed by a man named Ross. Said Johnson: "I was all over blood and I had the liver on my knife, but I didn't eat none of it. The liver coming out was unintentional on my part. But Ross he vowed 'twas so and I never got rid of the name."

His appetite for liver may have been exaggerated, but Johnson, like any good frontiersman, enjoyed his meat. He supposedly ate thirteen buffalo over a single winter, and is said to have consumed as much as six pounds of meat at a single sitting.

△ Life in the Big Hole Valley

Arrival, information, and accommodation

US-212 (Broadway Ave) runs north–south through the town, before becoming the Beartooth Highway on it's way to Yellowstone National Park. Cody Bus Lines (T 406/446-2304 or 1-800/733-2304) **buses** running between nearby Billings and Cody, Wyoming pull off this road at the south end of town. The **chamber of commerce** is at 601 N Broadway Ave (Mon–Sat 9am–5pm, reduced hours in winter; T 406/446-1718, W www.redlodge.com), but for information on the Absaroka-Beartooth Wilderness Area and the Beartooth Highway, head instead for the **Beartooth Ranger Station**, three miles south of town on US-212 (Mon–Fri 8am–4.30pm; T 406/446-2103).

Most of the **accommodation** in Red Lodge is conveniently situated on Broadway, thus putting the town's bars and restaurants within easy walking distance. If **camping**, the closest option is *Perry's RV Park and Campground* (T 406/446-2722; $10 tent, $14 full hookup), two miles south on US-212 with shady sites and good views of the Beartooths. In the opposite direction, four miles north on US-212, is the local *KOA* (T 406/446-2364; $18, $31 full hookup), where most sites have a pleasant creekside location. Rougher USFS sites are scattered throughout the Beartooths nearby; contact the Beartooth Ranger Station (see above) for details.

Bear Bordeaux 302 S Broadway T 406/446-4408. A lovingly decorated downtown B&B with bright, colorful rooms that have great mountain views. There's a hot tub, filling breakfasts, and an enormous video library (each room has a VCR). 4

Chateau Rouge 1505 S Broadway T 406/446-1601 or 1-800/926-1601, W www.chateaurouge.com. Spacious but cozy alpine-style one-room studios with kitchenettes and queen beds, and two-floor, two-bedroom condo apartments with kitchens and fireplaces which can sleep four (or more at a squeeze). There's also an indoor pool, hot tub, and a free continental breakfast. 5

Comfort Inn 612 N Broadway T 1-888/733-4661. Decent-sized rooms with cable TV and dataports. Extras include a free continental breakfast, indoor pool, hot tub, and guest laundry, although you still get pretty much the standard chain motel atmosphere. Located at the south end of town within walking distance of downtown. 5

The Pollard Hotel 2 N Broadway T 406/446-0001 or 1-800/678-8946, W www.pollardhotel.com. Built back in 1893, this is one of Montana's finest and most historic hotels. Red Lodge's first brick building, local heroes like Buffalo Bill and Frederick Remington used to spend the night here before the hotel fell into disrepair. Renovated in the early 1990s to high standard, extras include bathrobes, private balconies, and good mountain views from some of the rooms. The lounge and bar – roaring fire, oak panelling, and worn leather chairs – are pure Montana class. *Greenlee's*, the hotel's restaurant, is also excellent (see p.485). 5

Red Lodge Inn 811 S Broadway T 406/446-2030. Plain but clean rooms within walking distance of downtown. There's also an indoor pool. 4

Rock Creek Resort five miles south of town on US-212 T 406/446-1111 or 1-800/667-1119. At Red Lodge's fanciest resort, you can choose between staying in log-and-stone lodges or in condos set amongst private grounds. Heaps of facilities including a restaurant, indoor pool, health club, tennis, and horseback riding and mountain biking. Decent ski packages are often offered. 6

Willows Inn 224 S Platt Ave T 406/446-3913. A Victorian B&B with five attractive rooms decorated with period furniture, located one block east of Broadway. There are also three six-person guest cottages with kitchens on the same lot for similar rates. 5

Yodeler Motel 601 S Broadway T 406/446-1435, W www.yodelermotel.com. Clean, comfortable rooms in an alpine-style building, within walking distance of downtown. A large outdoor hot tub, dataports, and cable TV add value. 4

The town

The **downtown** area of Red Lodge, small but full of character, is anchored by the redbrick *Pollard Hotel*, where guests back in 1897 watched the Sundance Kid and cronies rob the bank across the street. Many visitors spend their time strolling in and out of the town's many galleries, most of which feature the expected range of wildlife photography and Native American works. Not a gallery as such, but well worth a visit for the wide selection of Native American rugs, blankets, and jewelry, is Outpost, 119 Broadway (Ⓣ406/446-3222).

If you're not into shopping, check out the **Peaks to Plains Museum**, located in the 1909 Labor Temple at the north end of town (June–Aug daily 10am–6pm; $3). Exhibits including a collection of cowboy and rodeo memorabilia, dozens of antique guns, a restored 1890s Yellowstone National Park touring coach and costumes from the early fur trade. Nearby, the **Beartooth Nature Center**, 900 N Bonner Ave (June–Aug 10am–5.30pm; rest of year 10am–2pm; $4), cares for native animals unable to be returned to the wild, and helps support the costs by allowing the public in to view them. Wolves, black bears, moose, and mountain lions may be present, and there's also a small petting zoo for children featuring domesticated animals.

Red Lodge Mountain Resort

Six miles above town, **Red Lodge Mountain Resort** (Ⓣ406/446-2610, snow report Ⓣ406/446-2610, Ⓦwww.redlodgemountain.com) is on the cusp of major discovery. The combination of dry Montana powder, uncrowded and challenging runs, and superb panoramas across rugged mountains to the west and the slate-flat plains to the east are the reason why. And a **snowmaking** system that covers forty percent of marked trails keeps things running smoothly when Mother Nature doesn't feel like helping out.

Spread over two mountains, there's a total of seven **chairlifts** accessing 1600 acres of terrain broken down as 15 percent beginner, 55 percent intermediate, and 30 percent expert. The highest mountain, Grizzly Peak (9416ft), allows for a maximum **vertical drop** of 2400ft and has a network of 45 trails that vary from easy greens like Turnpike to lovely cruisers such as Barriers, which provides some fine views back down towards the town. There's also a series of more demanding blacks, including the vicious moguls on Upper Continental, as well as the double-black tree skiing on East Parks. On Nichols Peak (9390ft), which tends to hold better snow (**average snowfall** for the resort is 250 inches per year), you'll find mainly blacks and double-black – True Grit is one of the steepest runs in the region – although intermediates enjoy the reasonably strenuous Latigo and Meeteetse Trail runs. Snowboarders are also well catered for – this was the first mountain in Montana to allow snowboarders on the slopes, way back in 1983 – with two well-designed **terrain parks**.

Lift tickets cost $36, and on-mountain facilities include the airy Midway Chalet, halfway up Grizzly Peak, and the homely *Willow Creek Saloon* at the base. There's also a gear and rental shop here, but no lodging options as of now; try your luck back in town.

Eating, drinking, and entertainment

As with accommodation, the majority of Red Lodge's **restaurants** and **bars** are strung along Broadway Avenue, which makes for a fairly lively scene in the evenings. Still, the only time the town really goes off is at holiday weekends or during one of its **festivals**. In late July and early August, the **Mountain Man Festival** sees an 1840s trading camp set up close to the town. Admission is $3, though dressing in your best fur trade-era outfit will get you in free. More unique is March's **National Ski-Joring Finals**, in which competitors on skis are pulled by galloping horses around a course.

The Beartooth Highway

Red Lodge faced extinction in 1924, when its largest coal mine closed, but its future was secured by the construction of the 65-mile **Beartooth Scenic Highway** to Cooke City at the northeastern entrance to Yellowstone National Park. Other roads in the Rockies may be higher, but none gives quite such a top-of-the-world feeling as this succession of tight switchbacks, steep grades, and exciting overlooks. Even in summer, the springy tundra turf of the 10,940ft **Beartooth Pass** is covered with snow that (due to algae) turns pink when crushed. All around are gem-like tarns, deeply gouged granite walls, stretches of scree, and huge blocks of roadside ice. Several pull outs along the way allow you to view the sights without the risk of driving off the road.

The highway is only **open** late May through October, and a detailed map of the route that also indicates a number of hiking trails along the way is available from Beartooth Ranger Station (see p.483). Early in the season you can also access thousands of acres of "corn snow" from the road for some fun backcountry skiing.

Bear Creek Saloon seven miles east on Hwy-308 ⓣ406/446-3481. Any bar that has pig racing through the summer as well as Montana's first "velcro wall" has got to be worth a visit. Decent bar food (charbroiled steaks, burgers, seafood, and chicken breast sandwiches) and a good-natured, beer-swilling atmosphere make for a memorable experience.

Bogart's 11 S Broadway ⓣ406/446-1784. A family restaurant serving a wide range of sandwiches, complemented by good pizzas and Mexican food, for around $10–12 per head. Nonsmoking.

Greenlea's *Pollard Hotel* ⓣ406/446-0001. The classiest dining downtown, *Greenlea's* features wood-grilled steaks, a fine wild mushroom risotto, delicious fresh-baked breads, and superb desserts, plus a lengthy wine list. Entrees will set you back around $25.

P.D. McKinney's 407 S Broadway ⓣ406/446-1250. It doesn't look too stylish from outside, but you can get a good-value filling breakfast or diner-style lunch here – try the breakfast omelettes which should keep you going for most of the day.

Red Box Car Drive-In 1300 S Broadway ⓣ406/446-2152. Heading south out of town, you can't miss the colorful red box car that serves as a summer-only burgers and fries joint. You can also eat in the pleasant surroundings alongside adjacent Rock Creek.

Red Lodge Pizza Company 123 S Broadway ⓣ406/446-3933. A great combination pizzeria and brewhouse with one of the largest ranges of beers in town. On Mondays and Tuesdays there's an eat-all-you-can salad and pizza bar for $7.95; the rest of the week expect to pay $11.95 upwards for a large pizza. Nonsmoking.

Snow Creek Saloon 124 S Broadway. This always-busy bar is a popular après-ski joint with locals and visitors alike, making for a fine and unostentatious place to sink a beer.

Billings

A gateway to the Rockies, **BILLINGS**, is Montana's largest city and very much a working town servicing the surrounding beef and wheat ranches. Though the Rocky Mountains to the west are visible on a clear day, it's far from a mountain town, and has a rather bland, urban feel. That said, the Yellowstone River and a four-hundred-foot-high sandstone bluff known as the **Rimrocks** that looms over the north side of town provide echoes of the nearby mountains.

Billings was established in the early 1880s as a base for the construction of the Northern Pacific Railroad, developing further along with the local agricultural industry and banking (several large banks have their headquarters in Billings). The recent refurbishment and gentrification of the old downtown area along **Montana Avenue** and beside the railroad tracks has resulted in a surprisingly

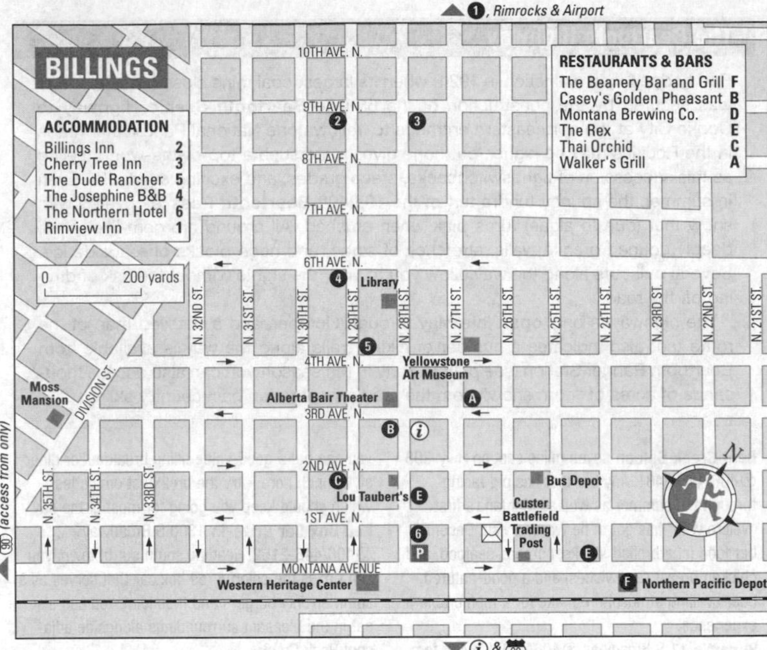

vibrant strip of galleries, bars, and restaurants. So while most travelers are likely to pass quickly through on their way to or from Yellowstone National Park, there's definitely enough here to keep you occupied for a day or so.

Arrival, information, and accommodation

Billings **Logan Field Airport**, the largest in Montana, is two miles north of town at the top of the Rimrocks. The city is also well served by **buses**, with Greyhound, Rimrock Stages, and Powder River Transportation operating from the station at 2502 1st Ave N (ⓣ406/245-5116). Between them they provide daily services to all of Montana's major cities, as well as Seattle and Denver. MET (ⓣ406/657-8218) provides a bus service within the city. Information is available from the **visitor center**, 815 S 27th St (ⓣ406/252-4016 or 1-800/735-2635) – it's half a mile north of Exit 450 on I-90 (look out for the "Cattle Drive Monument" outside).

Though there's the expected strip of **hotels** and **motels** alongside I-90, you'll find more variety and character in the lodgings available downtown. **Campers** should head to the *Billings KOA*, a half a mile south of I-90, which has shady sites ($17) in an attractive spot beside the Yellowstone River. This was America's first KOA and the facilities include a store, outdoor pool, laundry, and mini-golf course.

Billings Inn 880 N 29th ⓣ406/252-6800. Basic, clean nonsmoking rooms within four blocks of downtown with extras including a free continental breakfast, pool, guest laundry, and disabled access. ③

Cherry Tree Inn 823 N Broadway ⓣ405/252-5603 or 1-800/237-5882. Within walking distance of downtown with small but comfortable nonsmoking rooms, free continental breakfast and disabled access. ③

The Dude Rancher 415 N 29th St ⓣ406/259-5561 or 1-800/221-3302. Something of a Billings institution and dating back to the 1940s, the *Dude Rancher* is a bright and cheerful motel with a strong Western theme. The nonsmoking rooms are nicely furnished with old ranch-style furniture and there's a good coffee shop and restaurant. ③

The Josephine 514 N 29th St ⓣ406/248-5898. Beautifully maintained Victorian B&B with friendly owners and five elegant rooms featuring period furniture, some with bathrooms. There's an attractive wrapround porch, breakfasts are excellent, and it's also within walking distance of downtown. ④

The Radisson Northern Hotel 19 N 28th St ⓣ406/245-5121 or 1-800/333 3333. A venerable Billings institution, the *Northern* was built in the early 1900s and still retains plenty of character despite being damaged by fire in the 1940s, with large, quiet rooms featuring queen beds, coffee makers and cable TV. The hotel also has a guest hot tub. ④

Rimview Inn 1025 N 27th St ⓣ406/248-2622 or 1-800/551-1418. Located just below the Rimrocks on the north side of town and convenient for the airport. The nonsmoking rooms are spacious, and some have full kitchens. A free continental breakfast is included. ③

War Bonnet Inn 2612 Belknap Ave ⓣ406/248-7761 or 1-888/242-6023. One of the better motels off of I-90, with good-value large, bright rooms, a decent restaurant and lounge, and a pool and hot tub. ③

The town

The **Billings Historic District** has recently seen something of a renaissance and holds an interesting and eclectic selection of galleries, bars and shops. One of the best galleries is the friendly Custer Battlefield Trading Post, 2519 Montana Ave (ⓣ406/256-1876), which has an excellent collection of Western and Native American artwork. There are several other galleries along the same block; you can visit them all on a **Downtown Artwalk** (ⓣ406/252-0122; run from 5–9pm on the first Friday of Feb, May, Aug, Oct, and Dec). Also on Montana Avenue is the **Western Heritage Center**, 2822 Montana Ave (Tues–Sat 10am–5pm, closed Jan; free), which houses an interesting collection of exhibits relating to the cultural history of the Yellowstone Valley from the original Native American residents to later settlers from countries as varied as China and Germany. A few blocks northeast along Montana Avenue is the attractive **Northern Pacific Depot**, 2314 Montana Ave, which now houses the *Beanery Bar and Grill* (see p.489). The depot was built in 1909, and by 1914 it had tracks extending in ten directions, with nearly thirty passenger trains a day pulling in.

Just north of Montana Ave is the excellent Lou Taubert Western store, 123 N Broadway (ⓣ406/245-2248 or 1-800/871-9929), where you'll find a massive selection of cowboy wear from hats down to boots. North again a few blocks is the **Yellowstone Art Museum**, 401 N 27th St (Tues–Sat 10am–5pm, Sun noon–5pm; $5; ⓦwww.yellowstone.artmuseum.org). Partly housed in the town's 1910 jail, highlights of the permanent collection include an absorbing display of book illustrations, paintings, and posters by cowboy illustrator Will James.

Another old town building, the **Moss Mansion Historical House Museum** at 914 Division St (tours 1–3pm daily, appointments required outside of summer; $6; ⓣ406/256-5100), has been maintained in almost the same state as when it was built in 1903 by RJ Hardenbergh, who also designed New York's *Waldorf Astoria*. The 28-room red-sandstone building contains a mix of European-influenced architectural styles.

A drive, bike or hike up to the **Rimrocks** is well worth it for the marvellous views of the city and the mountains to the west. The **Black Otter trail** along the edge of the escarpment takes you past the grave of frontiersman Yellowstone Kelly and then down to the base of the escarpment to **Boothill Cemetery**, a mile or so to the east. The cemetery holds the grave of "Muggins" Taylor, the man who brought news of General Custer's defeat at nearby Little Bighorn.

The Battle of the Little Bighorn

An hour's drive east of Billings is the **Little Bighorn National Monument** (June–Aug daily 8am–8pm; rest of the year 8am–4.30pm; $10), the site where George Armstrong Custer and his men of the 7th Cavalry were defeated in June of 1876 by a band of up to 2000 Cheyenne and Lakota warriors. The monument consists of both the battlefield and a well-presented visitor center, which holds interesting items like Custer's notebooks and uniform, a fine diorama of the battle site, and superb maps and interpretations of the battle. You can also take a four-mile **car tour** of the battlefield – if you can, do it in the off-season when there are fewer visitors about to get a better feel for the melancholy air of the place. The sites where 7th Cavalry soldiers fell are marked by small white headstones, and it's chilling to see the way they're often grouped in twos and threes as they retreated unsuccessfully from their attackers.

The **Battle of the Little Bighorn** was part of a larger war as the Northern Plains Indian made one last attempt to preserve their culture from the advance of white settlers in search of gold and land. By the mid-1870s, the Lakota, Cheyenne, and other tribes were beginning to revolt against this intrusion, coming out of their reservations to raid settlers and travelers on the edge of their territory. The Commission of Indian Affairs ordered them to return to their reservations by January 31, 1876 or the military would be sent in. The Indians disregarded the warning, leading to a series of skirmishes that eventually resulted in the 600 men of the 7th Cavalry, led by Custer, being ordered to search out a large Cheyenne–Lakota force encamped in the Little Bighorn area.

Custer located their camp early in the morning of June 25, and divided his regiment into three battalions (under himself, Maj. Marcus A. Reno and Capt Frederick W. Benteen). One group was sent to scout bluffs to the south while the other two columns approached the camp in the Little Bighorn Valley.

Reno's battalion was eventually forced to retreat and join forces with Benteen's, both of whom then became pinned down for over a day by the Indians. Meanwhile Custer and his men, whose precise movements have never been determined, had been in a fierce battle to the death on a low hill to the north. Here Custer was surrounded and his command was gradually destroyed – Northern Cheyenne **Chief Two Moon** described afterwards how "we circled all around him…swirling like water round a stone. We shoot, we ride fast, we shoot again. Soldiers drop and horses fall on them."

Around 210 men died with Custer, and a further 53 were lost in the skirmishes to the south. The Indians lost around 100 men, but although they won the battle they inevitably lost the war – within a few years most of them had returned to the reservations, their traditional way of life gone forever.

Some thirty miles to the northeast of Billings off I-94 is **Pompey's Pillar**, in itself a relatively unremarkable pillar of rock, but one that was designated a national monument in 2001. This is because William Clark of the Lewis and Clark expedition etched his name into it on July 25, 1806 – the only concrete sign of the expedition's passing along the whole of their trail. A wooden walkway leads to the rock from the BLM visitor center at the site (8am–8pm). The rock was named after the infant Sacajawea (see p.390).

Eating, drinking, and entertainment

Befitting of the largest city in the state, Billings has a varied and lively selection of entertainment, from jazz **bars** and ethnic **restaurants** to good ol' steakhouses. If you're looking for decent live theater, a good bet is the **Alberta Bair Theatre**, 2801 3rd Ave N (☎406/256-6052), which has regular performances featuring either touring professional companies or the Billings Symphony

Orchestra. In October, the **Northern International Livestock Exposition (NILE)** includes five nights of rodeo at Billings MetraPark on the northeast side of town; call ⓣ406/256-2422 for exact dates and tickets.

The Beanery Bar and Grill 2314 Montana Ave ⓣ406/896-9200. The original dining hall of the Northern Pacific Depot, this beautifully restored restaurant is well worth a visit for lunch, dinner, or just a quick microbrew at the bar. Entrees run $15 up, with crab cakes being one of the specialties, plus there are great desserts, a wide range of beers and wine, and free ski movies on Wed evenings in winter.

Casey's Golden Pheasant 222 N Broadway ⓣ406/256-5200. One of the busiest bars in town, especially at weekends when a varied array of customers gather around the splendid 1870 mahogany bar to throw back the beers. There's live music every night, and a casino and pool tables.

Montana Brewing Company 113 N Broadway ⓣ406/252-9200. An inviting bar with a pretty mixed clientele and plenty of atmosphere, the *Montana Brewing Co* produces its own range of beers and tasty pub food including wood-fired pizza, pastas, and burgers for under $10.

The Rex 2401 Montana Ave ⓣ406/245-7477. A classic old hotel that has been lovingly refurbished and serves up an appetizing range of dishes including aged Montana beef, fish, and game. Entrees vary from $15–20.

Thai Orchid 2926 2nd Ave N ⓣ406/256-2206. The Thai Orchid is one of the best ethnic restaurants in town with particularly good vegetarian dishes. Entrees come in at around $15.

Walker's Grill Chamber Building, 301 N 27th St ⓣ406/245-9291. A sophisticated bistro with a menu that includes roast lamb, fresh fish, and pizza, alongside a good wine list to round off your choice. An entree will set you back around $15.

Gold Country

The southwest corner of Montana is touted by info centers as **Gold Country**, harkening back to the 1860s when veins were struck in evocatively named sites like **Last Chance Gulch** (now the state capital of Helena) and **Grasshopper Creek**, some fifty years after Lewis and Clark passed through and twenty years after missionaries established the first permanent white settlements in the Bitterroot Valley.

Gold wasn't all to be found: one of the world's richest reserves of **copper** was discovered at **Butte**, and the neighboring town of Anaconda was developed to smelt the stuff. Not too long after, ranching became an important source of revenue, which was no bad thing considering that the boom-and-bust nature of the mines would eventually run its cycle, with only Butte and Helena growing into substantial permanent settlements. Though now perhaps shadows of their former rambunctious selves, these very different towns are worth at least a day or two of exploration, with some fine cultural and historical sights and the best array of eating and accommodation options in the area. Neither is far from decent outdoor opportunities either, though you might be better off heading down to the **Big Hole Valley** in the south or **Bitterroot Valley** in the west, along the Idaho border, for hiking, backpacking, and other such activities. **Dillon** is the best base for the former, **Hamilton** the latter.

Despite all the digging that took place around these parts, the landscape – stretching from the Garnet Range in the north down through various dramatic mountains, valleys, canyons, and passes until reaching the Idaho border – has not changed all that much, and it can still take some patience and time to navigate; the scenic rewards are, however, well worth it. I-15 is the major north–south route through the area, but try to get off it to explore the magnificent backcountry.

Helena and around

In 1863, four disheartened miners from Georgia (ever after known as the "Four Georgians") made one last attempt to discover gold before heading back home. As luck would have it, they hit paydirt at Prickly Pear Creek, aptly naming the wild community that sprung up around their claim Last Chance Gulch. The evolving town soon went on to become the more demurely monikored **HELENA**, which remained equally boisterous – a popular saying of the time went "In pronouncing the name, understand me well, strong emphasis should be laid on the Hel."

By 1875, Helena and it's population of 4000 took over the helm of territorial capital from Virginia City to the southwest. More than just a mining camp, it was also a major supply center, a position that was cemented after the arrival of the Northern Pacific in 1883. By this time gold and the supply trade had produced more millionaires per capita in Helena than any other city in the US, helping it become state capital in 1894.

Today, the original core of the town, Last Chance Gulch, is a winding pedestrian thoroughfare that helps keep this elegant and pleasantly laid out city an attractive place to visit. And, with a location sandwiched between the Continental Divide, rising to over 7000ft to the west, and the 9000ft Big Belt Mountains to the east, there's plenty to do outside of it as well, from hiking around Mount Helena to fishing on the **Missouri River** and skiing at **Great Divide Ski Area**.

Arrival, information, and getting around

The **Helena Regional Airport** (☎406/442-2821), served by Big Sky, Delta, Sky West, and Horizon, is a few miles northeast of town off I-15. Intermountain and Rimrock (which links with Greyhound) **buses** pull in at the depot on 3122 Prospect Ave (☎406/442-5860) well to the east of downtown. If looking to **rent a car**, try Budget, 1930 N Main (☎406/442-7011).

The **chamber of commerce**, 225 Cruse Ave (Mon 9am–5pm, Tues–Fri 8am–5pm; ☎406/442-4120), produces a small free visitor guide, though the free *Lively Times*, available all over the city, is better for up-to-date listings. Information and maps on local hiking trails and camping are available from the **Helena National Forest Ranger Station**, 2001 Poplar St (☎406/449-5490).

An easy way to the town's major sites is with **Last Chance Tours** (daily May–Sept; $5; ☎1-888/423-1023), who provide hour-long narrated tours in an open-air imitation steam train; hop on outside the Montana Historical Society on the corner of 6th Avenue and Roberts Street.

Accommodation

If you can afford it, stay in one of the city's B&Bs, which provide a nice taste of the Old West. Otherwise Helena has an excellent, if not necessarily inspiring, selection of chain motels close to the city center. The best local **campsite** is the *Helena Campground and RV Park*, 5820 N Montana Ave (☎406/458-4714), situated about four miles north of town with shaded sites, pool and hot tub, showers, laundry, and general store (tents $16, full hookup $22).

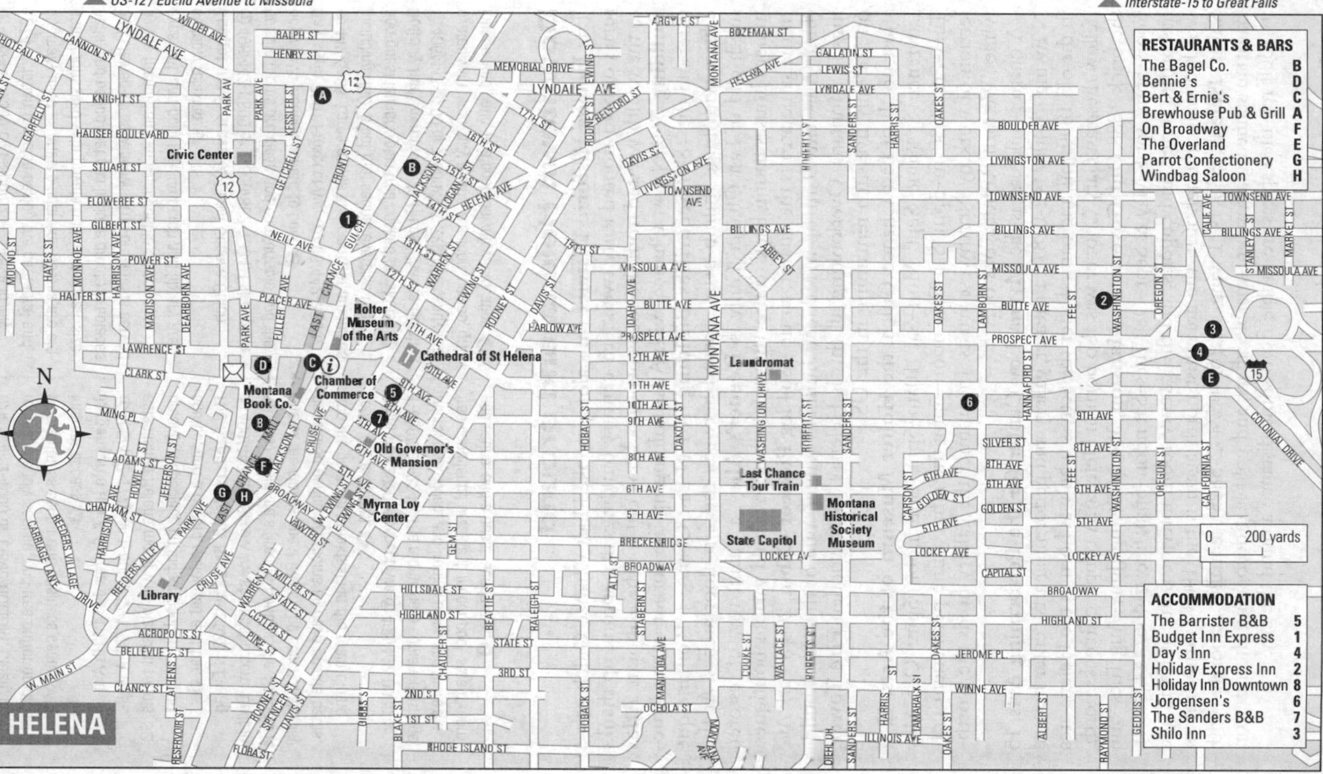
HELENA
US-12 / Euclid Avenue to Missoula
Interstate-15 to Great Falls
Interstate-15 to Butte
Mount Helena
Library
Civic Center
Montana Book Co.
Chamber of Commerce
Holter Museum of the Arts
Cathedral of St Helena
Old Governor's Mansion
Myrna Loy Center
Laundromat
Last Chance Tour Train
State Capitol
Montana Historical Society Museum
0 200 yards
RESTAURANTS & BARS
The Bagel Co. B
Bennie's D
Bert & Ernie's C
Brewhouse Pub & Grill A
On Broadway F
The Overland E
Parrot Confectionery G
Windbag Saloon H
ACCOMMODATION
The Barrister B&B 5
Budget Inn Express 1
Day's Inn 4
Holiday Express Inn 2
Holiday Inn Downtown 8
Jorgensen's 6
The Sanders B&B 7
Shilo Inn 3

The Barrister Bed & Breakfast 416 N Ewing ⓣ406/443-7330 or 1-800/823-1148. A lovely 1874 Victorian mansion beside the cathedral and originally used as priest's quarters. Rooms are elegantly furnished with private bath and queen-size beds, and period features include ornate fireplaces and stained-glass windows. The breakfasts served by the friendly and knowledgeable owner are excellent, and both the sun porch and library are suitably relaxing. ⑤

Budget Inn Express 524 Last Chance Gulch ⓣ406/442-0600 or 1-800/862-1334. Fairly plain, but the rooms are clean and comfortable and the downtown location is hard to beat. ③

Day's Inn 2001 Prospect Ave ⓣ406/442-3280, ⓕ442-3108. Large rooms and plenty of amenities including HBO, a hot tub, sauna, exercise room, and guest laundry, plus free cooked breakfast. ④

Holiday Inn Downtown 22 N Last Chance Gulch ⓣ406/443-2200 or 1-800/332-2290. Recently renovated with large, airy rooms, a saloon, casino, grill, lounge, and patio, in a good downtown location. ⑤

Holiday Inn Express 701 Washington St ⓣ406/449-4000 or 1-800/HOLIDAY. Clean, plain rooms, friendly service, and free buffet breakfast, plus a fitness center and business center with internet access. ④

Jorgensen's Inn & Suites 1714 11th Ave ⓣ406/442-1770 or 1-800/272-1770. A well-established Helena motel with pleasant rooms, $2 breakfast specials, an indoor pool, free airport shuttle, and a decent restaurant and bar. ④

The Sanders Bed & Breakfast 328 N Ewing ⓣ406/442-3309, ⓦwww.sandersbb.com. Built in 1875 by Montana's first US Senator, the *Sanders* is one of the state's finest B&Bs. The seven tastefully decorated period bedrooms all have private baths, and the gourmet breakfasts in the main dining room are excellent. ⑤

Shilo Inn 2020 Prospect Ave ⓣ406/442-0320 or 1-800/222-2244. The rooms here come with fridge, microwave, video, and ironing units, and there's a free continental breakfast, indoor pool, steam room and sauna, and a guest laundromat. ④

Downtown Helena and around

The **Helena Historic District** runs along crooked Last Chance Gulch past a series of bold-fronted early twentieth-century buildings that sprung up thanks to the wealth wrested from the rocks beneath. Look out for the elaborate **Atlas Building**, 7–9 N Last Chance, with Atlas holding up the corner of the structure; and the 1886 **Securities Building**, 101 N Last Chance, a Romanesque edifice with huge thumb-prints carved between the first-floor arches. At the south end of Last Chance Gully is **Reeder's Alley**, a quaint row of restored miner's houses dating back to the 1860s–80s that now hold various boutiques. In the same area is the quaint, rustic 1864 log **Pioneer Cabin**, 208 S Park Ave (June–Aug daily 9am–5pm, reduced hours in winter) one of the oldest buildings in Montana. Overlooking all this is Helena's 1876 wooden **Fire Tower**, one of only five such remaining in the US.

Just north of Last Chance Gulch, the **Holter Museum of the Arts**, 12 E Lawrence St (June–Sept Mon–Sat 10am–5pm, Sun noon–5pm; Oct–May Tues-Fri 11.30am–5pm, Sat–Sun noon–5pm; free), has a fine permanent collection of work by Northwest artists. In summer the gallery holds the worthwhile "Western Rendezvous of Art."

A quarter-mile east is the **Myrna Loy Center for the Performing Arts**, 15 N Ewing (ⓣ406/442-0287), a theater, gallery, and performing arts center housed in the old 1890s jail, and named after the actress who was born in the Helena area (fellow thespian Gary Cooper was also born in Helena). A couple of blocks north, the brick 1888 **Old Governor's Mansion**, 304 N Ewing (June–Aug Tues–Sun noon–5pm; April–May & Sept–Dec Tues–Sat noon–5pm; free; ⓣ406/444-2694), has ornate turrets and cupolas, and the twenty-room interior is just as florid and worth a walk through if in the area. Just north again is the 1908 **Cathedral of Saint Helena**, 530 N Ewing St (ⓣ406/442-5825), equally elaborate with Bavarian stained glass, white-marble altars, and gold leaf decorating the interior; its 230ft red-tiled spires are visible from some distance around the city.

East of downtown

A pleasant fifteen-minute walk east from downtown through leafy suburbs leads to the steps of the impressive **Montana State Capitol** (free **tours** on the hour Mon–Sat 10am–4pm, Sun 11am–3pm; ☎406/444-4789), on 6th Avenue between Montana Avenue and Roberts Street. While the Greek Neoclassical exterior, dominated by a 165ft-high copper-clad dome is impressive enough, it's the interior that makes this arguably Montana's most memorable edifice. Amongst the many stained-glass windows and large murals inside is Charles Russell's wonderfully evocative *Lewis and Clark Meeting the Flathead Indians at Ross' Hole*, along with six canvases by Edgar S. Paxson depicting various periods in Montana's history. Also worth noting is the statue of Jeanette Rankin, the first woman to be elected to Congress and the only person to vote against entering both world wars.

Opposite the capitol building is the excellent **Montana Historical Society Museum**, 225 N Roberts (June–Aug Mon–Fri 8am–6pm, Sat–Sun 9am–5pm; rest of year Mon–Fri 8am–5pm, Sat 9am–5pm; free). Exhibits include a major collection of work by Western artist Charles Russell, fascinating drawings by Karl Bodmer recording a trip along the Missouri in 1833, and some fine Native American artifacts, including a huge (and heavy) buffalo skin cape that you can try on.

Mount Helena City Park

Overlooking the city from the southwest, Mount Helena (5468ft) is the central feature of the large **Mount Helena City Park**, where wooded slopes lead up to a craggy summit. A series of well-marked trails, accessed via Reeder's Alley, take you to the summit viewpoint, giving glorious views of the city, the Big Belt Mountains to the east and the Helena National Forest to the south and west. The most direct route up is the 1906 Trail (two-mile round-trip) following the base of limestone cliffs along the north side of the mountain before veering south to climb steeply to the peak. Once on the summit, you can follow the rocky Hogback Trail south along the Hogback Ridge for fine panoramas in all directions. The Prospect Shaft Trail (1.5 miles one-way) twists and turns back down the mountain from the Hogback Trail, past some old mine shafts and through the southeast corner of the park. Trail 373 (5.5 miles one-way) heads southwest off the 1906 Trail for a fine ridge walk to the suburb of Park City – if you can arrange a shuttle to collect you from the end of the hike, this makes for a good half-day tramp.

Eating and drinking

Helena is no longer the hell-raising town it once was and it's generally pretty quiet on the streets at night. Still, even though there may not be the same buzz as in nearby Missoula or Bozeman, there are some **bars** and **restaurants** worth hunting down, especially in the downtown area.

The Bagel Co. 735 N Last Chance Gulch ☎406/449-6000. A friendly spot for bagels and coffee, open from 6am (Sun 7am).

Benny's 305 Fuller Ave ☎406/443-0105. Good soups, sandwiches, and light meals ($5–10) dished out in one of the town's most popular eateries.

Bert & Ernie's 361 N Last Chance Gulch ☎406/443-5680. A welcoming and easy-going nonsmoking bar where you can get filling sandwiches, and good burgers and pasta for $10–12.

The Brewhouse Pub & Grill 939 Getchell St ☎406/457-9390. The *Brewhouse* is famed locally for its tasty Sleeping Giant beer, named after a nearby mountain. The bar food is also worth a stab.

On Broadway 106 Broadway ☎406/443-1929. Not far from Last Chance Gulch, this is Helena's finest Italian restaurant. The somewhat plain decor may not bowl you over, but the excellent seafood dishes – especially the clam sauce – and above-average Italian meat dishes should. Entrees run $10–18.

The Overland 2250 11th Ave ⓣ406/449-2635. A popular restaurant for both lunch and dinner, well situated for the motel strip. A thick steak will set you back around $12–15.

Parrot Confectionery 42 Last Chance Gulch ⓣ406/442-1470. A genuine taste of the old days, the *Parrot* has been serving various ice-cream concoctions since 1935 and still has much of the original decor. Also sells Helena's best chocolates.

Windbag Saloon 19 S Last Chance Gulch ⓣ406/443-9669. Fresh fish, filling pastas, and excellent burgers for $10–15, plus a good selection of beers, all served up in what was "Big Dorothy's" brothel until 1973. The "windbags" were presumably (and no doubt still are) the politicians doing business at the nearby State Capitol. Reservations recommended.

Around Helena

Once you've exhausted the possibilities in town, Helena has several prime outdoor recreation areas nearby. In winter, head for the Great Divide Ski Area (see opposite), a fun local hill. At other times, make a break for the **Gates of the Mountains Wilderness Area**, eighteen miles north on I-15/US-287 and named after a spectacular 1000ft-deep limestone canyon through which flows the Missouri River. Upon discovering the canyon in 1805 Meriwether Lewis called these "the most remarkable cliffs that we have yet seen." The best way to view the canyon is via a two-hour **boat tour** ($8.50) – such tours have been operating here since 1886 – on which bighorn sheep, mountain goats, and even black bears are regularly spotted, while eagles, ospreys, and falcons wheel in the skies above. The boat landing is reached from the Gates of the Mountains exit on I-15/US-287 – simply drive two miles to the end of the road. For more details on tours and schedules, contact Gates of the Mountains Inc. (ⓣ406/858-5241, ⓦwww.gatesofthemountains.com).

Holter Lake, 43 miles northeast of Helena on I-15/US-287, is the most attractive of Helena's popular Missouri River reservoirs and a popular watersports venue. The Gates of the Mountains lie just behind the dam, and there are three USFS campgrounds ($8) on the east shore. The popular two-mile round-trip **Refrigerator Canyon Trail** into the Gates of the Mountains starts from a trailhead at Beaver Creek Road to the east of the lake – the canyon is so named because it's always several degrees cooler here than in the surrounding countryside. To reach the trailhead, take Hwy-280 from Helena for about twenty miles to tiny York, then head for equally small Nelson, where you turn right onto Beaver Creek Road and drive for five miles to the well-marked trailhead.

Closer to town and therefore much busier is **Hauser Lake**, another Missouri River reservoir, located only eleven miles north of Helena via Hwy-280 (York Rd). It's renowned for its kokanee fishing (the state record was hauled out here) and also as a viewing area for bald eagles. Just east of the lake you can try your hand at **sapphire mining** at Eldorado Sapphire Mine, 6240 Nelson Rd (ⓣ406/442-7960) – it's $25 to sift through a bucket of gravel that is almost certain to contain some rough gemstones. If you want to stay at Hauser Lake,

Local outfitters

Base Camp Outdoor Gear 333 Last Chance Gulch ⓣ406/443-5360. A good place to ask about local hiking trails as well as to stock up on new gear.

Cross Currents 326 N Jackson ⓣ406/449-2292. An excellent selection of fly-fishing gear; also organize guided angling trips.

Great Divide Cyclery 336 N Jackson ⓣ406/443-5188. This one-stop shop for bikers has a wide range of bikes and gear and can also provide bike rental for around $30 per day along with advice on the best local trails.

The Lakeside Resort, 5295 York Rd (⑦406/227-6076), has RV sites ($20) and tent sites ($12) along with a wide range of facilities that include boat slips, swimming areas and a busy restaurant.

Great Divide Ski Area

The uncrowded **Great Divide Ski Area** (⑦406/449-3746, snow report ⑦406/447-1310, ⓦwww.greatdividemontana.com), 22 miles northwest of Helena off Hwy-279, has eighty marked trails set in four open bowls covering over 1000 acres of terrain. It's not interested in glitz and glam, as attested by the four endearing if rather ancient double chairs, but affordable **lift tickets** ($24) and an average yearly snowfall of around 150 inches combine to make this quite a hidden gem.

Although the **vertical drop** is a modest 1500ft, there are plenty of challenging runs; the terrain is broken down into only 15 percent beginner and 30 percent intermediate, with the rest designated advanced terrain. The latter group will revel in black runs like the steep Big Open along with Puma and Earthquake in Rawhide Gulch, while intermediates should check out the blues on Mount Belmont – Snowfield and Belmont Bowl are a good start. Beginners will enjoy the easy greens of Meadow Mountain before moving up to more challenging trails off the Good Luck lift. As far as practicalities go, there's an unpretentious bar/restaurant at the base along with a small shop and rental service. On weekends and holidays, the mountain is served by **bus** (departs 8.40am; $5 round-trip; ⑦406/442-5654) from downtown Helena.

Butte and around

The mining activities of the mid-nineteenth century, in which silver, sapphires, and in particular phenomenal copper deposits were unearthed, are quite apparent around **Butte** and the copper smelting town of **Anaconda**, 26 miles to the west. Still, large areas of this wild mountainous region have escaped relatively unscathed, making for a fine area to hike, bike, ski, and otherwise enjoy yourself.

Besides approaching the town from Helena in the north on I-15 and Bozeman in the west on I-90, you can also access the Butte area on the **Pintler Scenic Byway** (Hwy-1). From Butte, this memorable detour heads west through Anaconda, climbing up between the Flint Creek and Sapphire Mountain ranges and past busy **Georgetown Lake** and the excellent **Discovery Basin Ski Area**, then down to the charming old mining town of **Philipsburg**.

Butte

A historic marker at a turn-out on I-15 to the northwest of **BUTTE** says it all about the town's wild past – "She was a bold, unashamed, rootin', tootin', hell-roarin' camp in days gone by and still drinks her liquor straight." Today, Evel Knievel's home town is still recovering from the hangover. Butte sits at an elevation of 5755ft on steep, almost treeless hillsides where massive black headframes of long-abandoned pits soar up among paint-bare homes, stark grey business premises, and a ring of surface workings, dirty yellow slag heaps and the massive toxic pool of **Berkeley Pit**, once the largest open-cast working in the US. Yet despite the less than attractive picture this description paints, it's an oddly compelling landscape, best appreciated at dusk, when the golden-pink light casts a glow on the mine-scoured hillsides, and the old neon signs illuminate uptown's historic brick buildings.

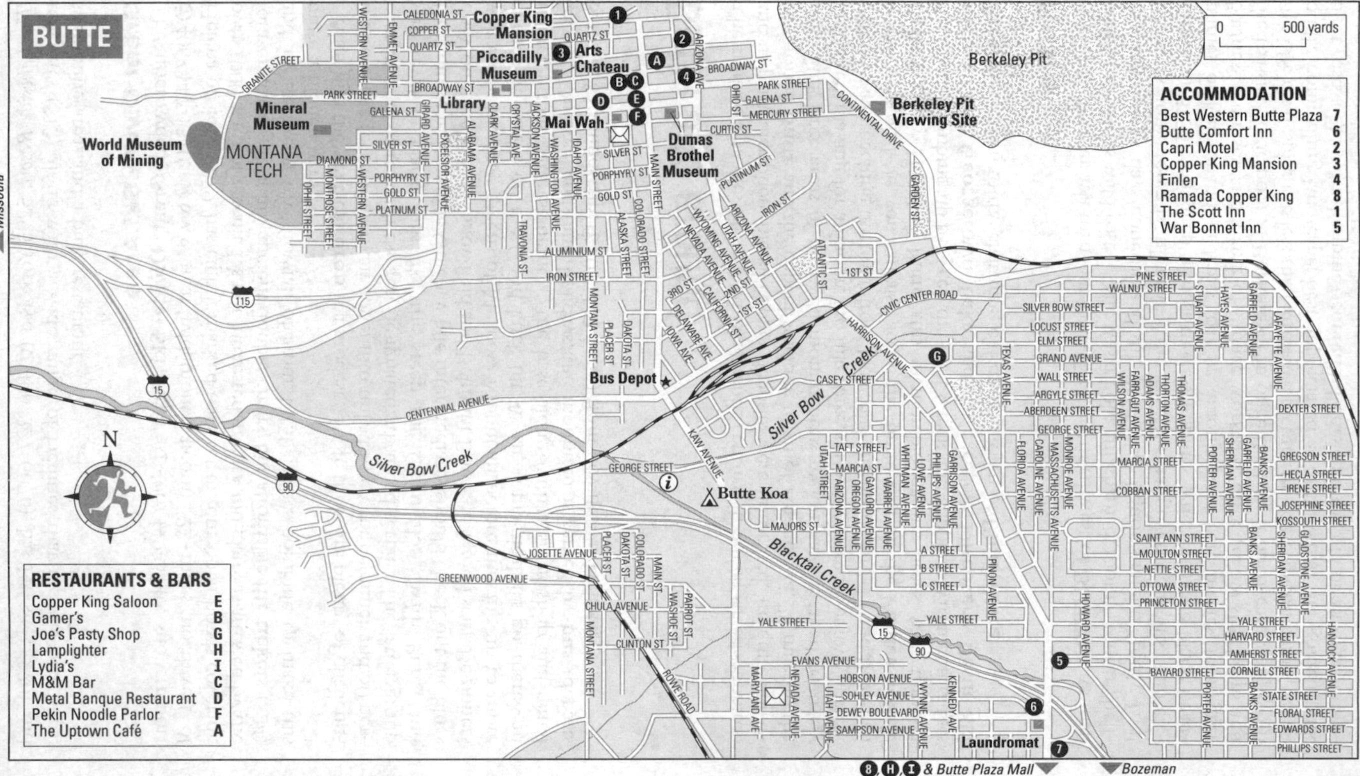
BUTTE
0 500 yards
Berkeley Pit
Berkeley Pit Viewing Site
Copper King Mansion
Arts Chateau
Piccadilly Museum
Library
Mai Wah
Dumas Brothel Museum
Mineral Museum
World Museum of Mining
MONTANA TECH
Bus Depot
Butte Koa
Silver Bow Creek
Blacktail Creek
Laundromat
Missoula
Bozeman
8, H, I & Butte Plaza Mall
N
ACCOMMODATION
Best Western Butte Plaza 7
Butte Comfort Inn 6
Capri Motel 2
Copper King Mansion 3
Finlen 4
Ramada Copper King 8
The Scott Inn 1
War Bonnet Inn 5
RESTAURANTS & BARS
Copper King Saloon E
Gamer's B
Joe's Pasty Shop G
Lamplighter H
Lydia's I
M&M Bar C
Metal Banque Restaurant D
Pekin Noodle Parlor F
The Uptown Café A

A short history of Butte

Once known as 'the richest hill on Earth' for it's immense silver and copper deposits (estimated to have totalled $22 billion by the 1980s), Butte developed after miners discovered gold (and later silver) here in the 1860s. Entrepreneurs such as **William Clark** and **Marcus Daly** moved in to develop the mines, and immediately realized the potential for mining the huge local copper deposits as well. Daly's **Anaconda Mine**, purchased in 1880, became one of the world's major copper producers. The town of Anaconda, also built by Daly, became the site for a huge smelter.

Miners from around the world poured into Butte, increasing the population from 250 in 1870 to 22,000 by 1885, and leading to the colorful multiethnic community for which Butte has been known ever since. The Irish in particular were well represented and the town has the most exuberant **St Patrick's Day** celebration in the Rockies, while pasties, introduced to the area by Cornish miners, are still a popular local dish. But Butte was a hideous place to live and work – air pollution from the mines, smelters, and dwellings was so bad that trees were unable to grow and street lights had to be left on 24 hours a day.

From its early days, Butte was also a union stronghold in the anti-union West. Miners used their collective strength to obtain a minimum wage and eight-hour days, and it became impossible to get work without a union card. Such confidence bred radicalism, and Butte sent the largest delegation to the founding convention of the International Workers of the World (known as "Wobblies") in 1906. But the eventual consolidation of mining operations under the huge Anaconda Company in the early twentieth century led to inter-union rivalry and violence, including the lynching of IWW organizer Frank Lynch in 1917, an event fictionalized in Dashiel Hammots' *Red Harvest*. The same year, the town also saw the death of 168 men in a fire at the Speculator Mine. Butte's days were numbered with the falling price of copper in the Great Depression, and from 1955 to 1982 the Anaconda Company excavated the Berkeley Pit (see p.499) as a more cost-effective and less labor-intensive means of mining; by 1983, the last major mine had closed.

Arrival, information, and accommodation

Greyhound and Intermountain Transit **buses** drop off at the Greyhound depot (Ⓣ406/723-3287) at 101 E Front St, with daily services to Dillon ($11 one-way), Helena ($11 one-way), Missoula ($12 one-way), Bozeman ($14 one-way) and Billings ($31 one-way). If you only have a short time in town, hop on one of the good ninety-minute **trolley tours** of the town on Old No. 1, a replica of an open electric trolley (9am, 11.00am, 1.30pm, 3.30pm; $5). The trolley leaves from the **chamber of commerce**, 1000 George St (May–Aug daily 8am–8pm; Sept–Oct daily 8am–5pm; Nov–April Mon–Fri 9am–5pm; Ⓣ406/723-3177, Ⓦwww.butteinfo.org), which has fascinating old black-and-white photographs of Butte.

Driving into Butte you can't miss the string of chain **motels** along Harrison Avenue to the south of the historic "uptown" district. If you want convenience, these are a good bet – if you want something with more character the limited options in the historic district are better. If **camping**, the *Butte KOA*, 1601 Kaw Ave (Ⓣ406/782-8080 or 1-800/562-8089), is located two blocks north of town off I-90's exit 126. It isn't the most attractive place to bed down, but it's reasonably close to town and has a wide range of facilities including a laundry, showers, pool, and store (tents $16, full hookup $25).

Best Western Butte Plaza 2900 Harrison Ave Ⓣ406/494-3500 or 1-800/543-5814. Large rooms, an excellent pool, steam room, and gym, and generous continental breakfast make this chain lodging a pretty good deal. ❺

Butte Comfort Inn 2777 Harrison Ave Ⓣ406/494-8850 or 1-800/442-4667. One of the largest motels in town, the *Comfort Inn* has well-kept if uninspired rooms and plenty of facilities including a restaurant, indoor pool, hot tub, fitness room, and large breakfasts. ④

Capri Motel 220 N Wyoming ⓣ406/723-4391 or 1-800/342-2774. Pleasant but basic accommodation in one of Butte's older motels, with the advantage of being in the historic part of town. There's also a laundry, most useful if you're just in from the backcountry, and free continental breakfast. ④

Copper King Mansion 219 W Granite ⓣ406/782-7580. Over 100 years old, this beautiful Victorian mansion was built for William Clark, and has four rooms, two with private bath, two shared. Actually a museum in the daytime (see below), so bear in mind that you'll have strangers wandering in and out of your room if you stay here and will need to secure your belongings. ④

Finlen Hotel and Motor Inn 100 E Broadway ⓣ406/723-5461 or 1-800/729-5461. You have a choice of rooms here, either in the old 1920s hotel where the period rooms have plenty of atmosphere, or in the less appealing but more modern annex. ③

Ramada Copper King 4655 Harrison Ave ⓣ406/494-6666 or 1-800/332-8600. Large, standard chain-motel rooms with lots of facilities including a restaurant and lounge, indoor pool, hot tub, sauna, fitness room, indoor tennis courts, and guest laundry. ⑤

The Scott Inn 15 W Copper ⓣ406/723-7030 or 1-800/844-2952. A renovated miner's boarding house built in 1887, this B&B has been skilfully renovated and each of the attractive period rooms has a private bath. ⑤

War Bonnet Inn 2100 Cornell Ave ⓣ406/494-7800 or 1-800/443-1806. Another large chain motel with well-furnished rooms and guest pool, hot tub, and fitness room plus a restaurant and lounge. ⑤

The town

The buildings in the historic district make up one of the largest National Register of Historic Landmark Districts in the country, with many sporting silver plaques relating their history. Start at the **Copper King Mansion**, 219 W Granite (May–Sept daily 9am–4pm; $5; winter tours by appointment; ⓣ406/723-7211), built for self-made mining millionaire and "Copper King" William Clark between 1884–88. The 35 rooms were constructed by the finest craftsmen in the state and contain such features as hand-carved illustrative panels in the oak staircase, Tiffany-style stained-glass windows and frescoed ceilings. The mansion also operates as a B&B (see above). Next door is the Italianate **Leonard Hotel**, said to have been built by Marcus Daly to obstruct Clark's view.

A block south, Clark's son Charles built himself an equally opulent home in 1898 at what is now the **Arts Chateau**, 321 W Broadway (May–Sept Tues–Sat 10am–5pm, Sun noon–5pm; rest of year Tues–Sat 11am–4pm; $3; ⓣ406/723-7600). Constructed as a vague representation of a French chateau, the ornate brick and sandstone structure contains a freestanding spiral staircase, hand painted wallpaper and a redwood-paneled fourth-floor ballroom. The first and second floors house art galleries, though the house itself is really the star attraction.

At the other end of the cultural spectrum is the **Dumas Brothel Museum**, 45 E Mercury (May–Sept daily 9am–5pm; tours $3.50; ⓣ406/782-3808, ⓦwww.dumasbrothel.com). The Dumas was designed and built as a brothel in 1890 and was in business until 1982. It's the only surviving building in what was once a thriving red-light district, and the guided tour gives you a good insight into what life was like for the occupants and their clients during Butte's heyday. The tour takes in the building's underground "bedrooms", accessible through tunnels that connected with the uptown business district.

Just down the road is the **Mai Wah**, 17 W Mercury (June–Aug Tues–Sat 11am–3pm; free; ⓣ406/723-3177), an old noodle parlor with a display focusing on the history of Butte's large Chinese community. At the end of the nineteenth century, the narrow strip between Mercury and Galena streets was known as China Alley, the heart of a 600-strong community; by the 1940s widespread racism had reduced the community to just a few families. The museum here has a small, intriguing collection of photos, cooking implements, kites, fireworks, menus, and books.

Butte's mining museums

One of Butte's biggest and best visitor attractions is the **World Museum of Mining** (May–Oct daily 9am–6pm; $4; ☎406/723-7211) on Butte Hill overlooking the west side of town at the Montana Tech campus. Although the "world" bit of the title is more that a little misleading, this is nevertheless an excellent collection of memorabilia from Butte's boom years including mine cages, ore wagons, and a 1928 La Salle armored pay car riddled with bullet holes. The site also features **Hell Roarin' Gulch**, a 35-building re-creation of an 1889 mining camp with cobbled streets complete with saloon, bordello, church, schoolhouse, and Chinese laundry. Evidence of Butte's diverse ethnic background can be seen in such items as a "No Smoking" sign in seventeen different languages.

Also on the Montana Tech campus is the **Mineral Museum** (June–Aug daily 9am–6pm; rest of year Mon–Fri 9am–4pm; free), which has a stunning collection of minerals and gemstones, including two impressive local finds – a 27.5-ounce gold nugget and a 400-pound quartz crystal.

The Berkeley Pit

The gigantic **Berkeley Pit** (☎406/723-3177; free), just east of the historic district on Continental Drive, was started in 1955 and operated until 1982, and was at one time the largest truck-operated open-pit mine in the US, with almost 1.5 billion tons of material ripped out of the ground. The resultant hole, viewed from a platform off Continental Drive, is 7000ft long, 5600ft wide and 1600ft deep, and the cobalt blue water that now fills it to a depth of 800ft is some of the most toxic in the US.

This groundwater rose through several thousand miles of interconnected mine shafts that had been burrowed into Butte Hill to the west and seeped into the pit after mining ceased. Since 1996 pumping has started again at the site to prevent surface water flows from entering the pit, and to stop the water within entering groundwater flows – over 2.5 million gallons a day are extracted. Meanwhile, the pit's owners are working with the US Environmental Protection Agency and state agencies to develop a method of treating the water, which is so toxic that birds have to be prevented from landing on it.

Our Lady of the Rockies

An unmissable feature of the landscape around Butte is **Our Lady of the Rockies**, a 90ft steel statue of a Madonna-like figure that is the second tallest in the US after the Statue of Liberty. It sits on top of an 8150ft ridge and is illuminated at night; despite its semi-religious overtones, the statue, constructed in 1985, is said to represent all women. You can only visit the statue from bus tours leaving from the Butte Plaza Mall, 3100 Harrison Ave ($10; three hours round-trip; ☎406/782-1221), which allows you to also enter and climb to the top, from where there are stupendous views to the south and west.

Eating and drinking

Butte's **bar** history is as colorful at its cultural background. In its prime, the town's drinking dens throbbed with action 24 hours a day – the former *Atlantic Bar* alone stretched a full block and its fifteen bartenders are said to have served 12,000 beers on Saturday nights. The town's bars are no longer the hectic saloons they were a hundred years ago, but they still have plenty of grit and character. As far as eating goes, Butte is especially proud of its "traditional" dish, the **pastie**, a meat and potato pie brought by miners from Cornwall; one of the best places to get one is Joe's Pasty Shop, 1641 Grande Ave (☎406/723-9071).

The Copper King Saloon 1000 S Montana St ☎406/723-9283. A lively and unpretentious bar that makes for one of Butte's most authentic saloons.

Gamer's 15 W Park St ☎406/723-9083. Pretty basic and very unassuming, and popular with locals for breakfast and lunch, *Gamer's* also does good pasties.

Lamplighter 1800 Meadowlark Ave ☎406/494-9910. A mix of American and English here in the form of good steaks and prime rib with, if you feel the need, Yorkshire pudding. Expect to pay around $10–12 for a good meal.

Lydia's Five Mile and Harrison Ave ☎406/494-2000. A mile or so south of downtown, *Lydia's* is a no-smoking restaurant renowned for Italian food in a romantic, old fashioned setting. A good pasta dish won't set you back more than $15.

M&M Bar 9 Main St ☎406/723-7612. Probably the best-known bar in the region, the *M&M* has a 24-hour café serving the cheapest grease-laden breakfasts in town, a casino, and a clientele who can drink you under the table. It's also a focal point for the town's St Patrick's Day parade, when an incredible 40,000 customers are said to pass through.

Metal's Banque Restaurant Park and Main streets ☎406/723-6160. Tasty, good-value Tex-Mex, pasta, and steaks served in a converted and atmospheric old bank vault, complete with an enormous metal safe. Expect to pay around $15–20 for an entree, and check out the restaurant's own good beers.

Pekin Noodle Parlor 117 S Main St ☎406/782-2217. A classic Chinese diner with very basic and rather greasy food served in individual dining cabins – you go here for the atmosphere as much as the food.

The Uptown Café 47 E Broadway ☎406/723-4735. Relatively upscale but informal dining in nonsmoking suroundings, the *Uptown* serves good-value fixed five-course meals for $15–20 and is particularly strong on Mediterranean-style seafood.

Anaconda

Sitting beneath the massive bulk of Mount Haggin (10,598ft) and other similarly lofty peaks, **ANACONDA's** location is betrayed for miles around by the massive 585ft smokestack of the disused **Washoe Smelter** perched above town – it's the largest freestanding masonry structure on the planet and a vivid reminder of Anaconda's aluminum producing past. In 1883 Marcus Daly chose the area to build a copper smelter for the vast reserves of the ore he was extracting around Butte. Daly wanted to name the town "Copperopolis"; amazingly Montana already had a town with that name. To bring copper ore here, Daly also built the Butte, Anaconda and Pacific Railway, and then went on to lobby for Anaconda to become the state capital before his business rival William Clark succeeded in pushing Helena through in 1894.

Highlights of the downtown area include the brick and granite **City Hall**, 401 E Commercial St, now home to the **Copper Village Museum and Arts Center** (daily Mon–Fri 9am–5pm; free) which has exhibits on the smelting process. The beautiful 1936 **Washoe Theater**, 305 Main St, is also worth a look for its preserved Art Deco interior, a riot of murals and silver, copper, and gold leaf ornamentation; movies still show here nightly.

There's not much reason to spend the night in town, but if hungry look out for *Donivan's*, 211 E Park Ave (☎406/563-6241), a busy restaurant with a big choice of good-value diner-style meals varying from omelettes to steaks.

Georgetown Lake and Discovery Basin

Driving west from Anaconda on the Pintler Scenic Highway, the road climbs gradually up alongside Warm Springs Creek to **Georgetown Lake**, set beneath the Flint Creek Range and the Discovery Basin Ski Area (see opposite). The lake is busy year-round, with boaters and windsurfers sharing the waters in summer and fishermen cutting through the ice in winter. If you'd like to be part of the action, consider staying at *Seven Gables Resort*, 18 S Hauser (ⓣ406/563-5072 or 1-800/472-6940; ❸), just along the turnoff to the ski area. This rustic resort has clean, basic rooms and a great bar serving filling bar meals – it's known by locals as "The Trap" for its ability to keep you there far longer than intended. **Camping** options include *Denton's Point KOA* (ⓣ406/563-3402) on South Shore Road, which has a good lakeside location with a marina, bar and restaurant (tent sites $15), or more secluded USFS sites ($7) on the west side of the lake at *Sandy Beach* and *Piney Point*.

One of Montana's lesser-known ski areas, **Discovery Basin** (ⓣ406/563-2184, ⓦwww.skidiscovery.com) is also one of the state's most challenging. Though easily accessible from Missoula, Butte, and Helena, lift lines are a rare sight and there's a good mix of terrain, making it popular with families. There are forty trails in total, with the steepest of the bunch located on the challenging back side of the hill; indeed, this is some of the trickiest in bound skiing in the state. In total, the mountain offers 360 acres of terrain and a vertical drop of 1300ft, accessed by four chairlifts. **Lift tickets** are $24 and there's a good, no-frills lodge at the base of the mountain where you can also rent gear.

Philipsburg

The attractive mining town of **PHILIPSBURG**, set in the jagged Flint Creek Range around fifty miles northwest of Butte, developed after the discovery of silver in 1866. Virtually every property on Broadway, the short Old West-style main strip, is in the National Register of Historic Places. Amongst the finest of the bunch are the pastel-painted **Walker Commercial Company Building**, built in the 1890s and the timber-built **Hynes House**, an 1880 boarding house. Pick up the free walking tour map of the town at the **Granite County Museum and Cultural Center**, 155 Sansome St (summer daily 10am–5pm; free), where you'll also find the **Ghost Town Hall of Fame**. Displays include replicas of a silver mine adit and a miner's cabin, plus an excellent array of old black-and-white photographs of mining towns.

Another worthwhile town attraction is the **Sapphire Gallery**, 115 E Broadway (daily: summer 9am–6pm; rest of year 10am–5pm; ⓣ406/859-3236 or 1-800/525-0169, ⓦwww.sapphire-gallery.com), which has a fine collection of locally mined sapphires; for $25 you can buy a bag of gravel and sieve for your own. The store offers a service cutting and mounting any stones you find, giving you a unique Montana souvenir. Next door, the equally popular **Sweet Palace** (daily except Sat: summer 9am–6pm; rest of year 11am–6pm) is a beautifully restored Victorian confectionery store which stocks over four hundred kinds of candy and makes its own fudge, chocolate, and taffy.

There isn't a huge range of **accommodation** in town; *The Inn at Philipsburg*, 915 W Broadway (ⓣ406/859-3959, ⓦwww.theinn-philipsburg.com; ❸) is one of the best options, with spacious motel rooms and an RV park for around $20. Two good B&Bs are the *Blue Heron B&B* (ⓣ406/859-3856, ⓦwww.blueheronmt.com; ❹), a refurbished miner's boarding house, and the *Big Horn B&B*, 33 Lower Rock Creek (ⓣ406/859-3109; ❺), with an attractive riverside location that's a reliable fishing spot. If looking to **eat**, *The Rendezvous*, 204 E Broadway (ⓣ406/859-3529), does sturdy Southwestern-style food and has fine espresso drinks, while just across the road *The Gallery*, 127 E Broadway (ⓣ406/859-3534), doles out tasty breakfasts and also has a good selection of homemade soups and sandwiches.

The ranch life

Situated at the north end of the rather dull town of Deer Lodge some thirty miles northwest of Butte is the **Grant-Kohrs Ranch National Historic Site** (daily: June–Aug 9am–5.30pm; rest of year 9am–4.30pm; $5 summer, free rest of the year; ⓣ406/846-3388), built in 1862 by Canadian rancher **Johnny Grant** and sold in 1866 to German immigrant **Conrad Kohrs**. Kohrs, working with his wife Augusta and partner and half-brother John Bielenberg, developed the ranch into one of the most prosperous in Montana. At one point, it was the base of operations for herds of cattle on various ranches that covered more than a million acres of land in the US and Canada and by the late nineteenth century Kohrs was shipping 8000–10,000 cattle to market each year. However, by the beginning of World War I homesteaders had fenced in much of the open range, forcing Kohrs and Bielenberg to sell off all but the 1500 acres or so around Deer Lodge.

The ranch was set aside as a National Historic Site in 1972, and a tour of the grounds allows you to see what a working ranch from the peak of the ranching and cowboy era looked like. On display is the lovely old two-story wooden ranch house, complete with fine furnishings shipped in from the East Coast by steamboat, the spartan bunkhouse where the ranch cowboys lived, and various animal barns and stables complete with old tools and equipment. Cattle still graze the land, and there are frequent demonstrations of ranch work.

If you have the time, the **Old Montana Prison Complex** (daily: June–Aug 8am–9pm; rest of year 9am–5pm; $8; ⓣ406/846-3111) in Deer Lodge is also worth a visit. Items on display include the "Galloping Gallows," used for executions outside the prison, some evil looking homemade knives confiscated from prisoners, concrete-soled shoes designed to prevent escape attempts, and the handcuffs worn by Lee Harvey Oswald when he was shot. Next to the prison, the associated auto museum has an excellent collection of veteran and vintage cars.

Dillon and around

The outskirts of friendly **DILLON** (pop. 4001) reflect its livelihood, with farm suppliers and lumber companies lining the streets. A railroad runs right through the town center, where there are some grand old bars such as the *Metlen Hotel*, and leafy residential streets lined with elegant Victorian homes fringe the downtown area. Though easily viewed in a morning, Dillon is also worth considering as a laid-back base for activities in the surrounding countryside, which include skiing at the nearby **Maverick Mountain** or exploring **Bannack State Park**, home to one of the best-preserved ghost towns in the Rockies.

Arrival, information, and accommodation

Daily Rimrock Trailways (ⓣ406/683-2344) **buses** from Butte and Idaho Falls pull in at 17 E Bannack St. Information, including a walking-tour map of the town, is available from the **visitor center** in the old Union Pacific Railroad Depot, 125 S Montana St (Mon–Fri 9am–5pm; ⓣ406/683-5511). For camping and hiking advice on the surrounding Beaverhead National Forest head to the **USFS Office** at 420 Barrett St (ⓣ406/683-3900).

The strip of chain motels along N Montana Street offer plentiful and affordable **accommodation**, but if your budget allows it go for a more traditional guesthouse or inn in the suburbs or outskirts. The closest spot for **campers** is the *Dillon KOA*, 735 W Park St (ⓣ406/683-2749), which has thirty tent sites

($18) and 68 RV sites ($25) in a pleasant riverside location just west of town, with a pool, fishing access, and showers. For something a bit more rugged, head thirteen miles north of town along Hwy-73 to the *Grasshopper Campground*, which has twenty-odd sites ($8) along with toilets, water, and fishing access. Three miles north is the similar *Price Creek Campground*.

Beaverhead Rock Ranch Guest Houses 4325 Old Stage Rd ⓣ406/683-2126 or 1-800/338-0061 ⓦwww.fishingcabins.com. Just to the southwest of town of I-15's exit 56, options here include a fully modernized 1917 log farmhouse or an attractive, renovated century-old log cabin in an idyllic setting beside the Beaverhead River. ❺

Best Western Paradise Inn 650 N Montana St ⓣ406/683-4214 or 1-800/528-1234. One of the biggest and smartest motels in town, with large rooms and good facilities including a restaurant, lounge and indoor pool and hot tub. ❹

Centennial Inn 122 S Washington St ⓣ406/683-4454. A beautiful 1905 Queen Anne-style house with four very cozy and tastefully decorated rooms, each with a private bath and period furniture. The friendly owners are descendants of Montana pioneer families and have some great family stories from the old days; breakfasts here are superb. Dinners are also available on request. Rates are cheaper off-season. ❺

Sacajawea Motel 775 N Montana St ⓣ406/683-2381. The *Sacajawea* has plain but very good-value rooms, some with kitchenettes for a few dollars more. It's a short walk from downtown and close to the town's cinema. ❷

Sundowner Motel 500 N Montana St ⓣ406/683-2375 or 1-800/524-9746. Within walking distance of downtown, the rooms here are clean, and comfortable with queen beds and coffee-making facilities, and you also get free morning coffee and doughnuts. ❸

The town

The first port of call on your tour of Dillon should be the cheerful **Beaverhead County Museum**, 15 S Montana (June–Aug Mon–Fri 10am–8pm, Sat–Sun 1–5pm; rest of year Mon–Fri 10am–5pm; free). Besides the expected Native American and pioneer exhibits, there's also an eclectic jumble of items that includes a huge Kodiak bear (not native to the region) and, bizarrely, a stuffed two-headed calf and one-eyed lamb – you decide if they're real. Across the rail-tracks from here is the Gothic, down-at-the-heels **Metlen Hotel** (ⓣ406/683-2335), built in 1897 with no expense spared; the main staircase in the once grand interior was actually built in and shipped from Wales. The hotel has seen better days, but its cozy back bar is still full of life and open for drinking and poker most nights, and you can also stay in the characterful but very basic rooms for $15–25 per night. If you're looking for some new outdoor gear, it's worth noting that there's a **Patagonia Outlet Store** on 34 N Idaho St (ⓣ406/683-2580) – it's one of the company's few outlet stores in the US.

Bannack State Park

Home of cutthroats and ne'er do wells and one of the richest gold towns in US history, **Bannack State Park** (daily: June–Aug 7am–9pm; rest of year 8am–5pm; $3 per vehicle, camping $12; ⓣ406/834-3413) is centered on an authentic ghost town that hasn't been overly dolled up for the tourist trade. Located in a secluded spot 6000ft up in the mountains and 26 miles southwest of Dillon off Hwy-278, it's very easy to imagine life here in the 1860s when over 3000 people lived and worked in the area.

The town sits on Grasshopper Creek, where the first major gold strike in Montana occurred in July 1862; within a year thousands of miners had rushed here to try their luck. By 1864 Bannack – named after the local native Bannock tribe – was big enough to be made territorial capital, although this honor hop-scotched from Virginia City to Helena soon after. More than fifty log and frame buildings from these wild times sit amongst the sagebrush and

3-7-77

Bannack really was the Wild West writ small, with classic tales like that of **Sherrif Henry Plummer** and the **Vigilantes**. Plummer was the town sheriff in 1862–63, but despite his badge he organized a group of 25 into a gang that called themselves "The Innocents." These not so innocent bandits went around robbing local gold camps, murdering just about anyone who got in the way – they're thought to have killed upwards of 100 people. Strangely, they left the "secret" number 3-7-77 attached to their victims, the relevance of which has yet to be reasonably explained to this day. Once the citizens of Bannack began to suspect their own sheriff of organizing these nefarious activities a Vigilante Committee was organized to track down the gang, eventually cornering Plummer and hanging him from gallows that he himself, as sheriff, had erected. In all, at least 22 gang members were dispatched by the Vigilantes – and as the ultimate irony the Vigilantes marked them with 3-7-77 after their deaths.

But the mystery of the 3-7-77 didn't end there. If you happen across a Montana Highway Patrol officer – or just get pulled over – check their badges and you'll see they bear those same numbers. They adopted this in 1935, apparently because the placing of those numbers on the "bad guys" by the Vigilantes was the first form of real justice in the state.

greasewood, and an informative visitors booklet ($2) is available at the entrance. Highlights include the **Hotel Meade**, originally the county courthouse and now boasting several decades of graffiti on the walls – citizens of the town took refuge here when the Nez Percé Indians camped nearby after the Battle of the Big Hole in 1877. The **Masonic Lodge and Schoolhouse** is another imposing and ornate building, still used occasionally by Masons, and **Bachelor's Row** is a tight line of log shacks beside the creek where miners lived on top of their claim (the creek would freeze over in winter, bringing a halt to operations). Look out to the eastern outskirts of the town for the old gallows – although these aren't the originals, this is the site were outlaw sheriff Henry Plummer was swung in 1863 (see above).

Outdoor activities

Before heading out to explore the mountains around Dillon, you should first head for the USFS office (see p.502) for advice and trail maps as the ranges here are isolated and you're generally on your own even when you're on the beaten track, let alone off it. For good mountain views and the chance to camp overnight amongst fine alpine scenery without too long a trek try hiking the **Agnes Lake Trail**, a moderately strenuous but short 4.5-mile round-trip. The first 1.5 miles of the trail is a steep 1000ft climb to Agnes Lake through dense forest, after which it eases off and continues to Rainbow Lake. The views get ever better as you climb higher, and you can camp beside either lake. To get to the trailhead take I-15 north of Dillon for 22 miles, turn off on the Glen exit and follow signs west for eight miles up Rock Creek to *Brownes Lake Campground* – the trailhead is on the south side of the campground.

Fishing in and around the Beaverhead Valley is angling at its best – wide-open high-country vistas, clean bubbling waters, and plenty of fish to test your skills. The **Beaverhead River**, flowing through Dillon, originates at the **Clark Canyon Reservoir** in the Tendoy Mountains to the south, and the continual water level provided by the dam helps maintain quality stocks of brown and rainbow trout. The river is divided into upper and lower portions by the

Maverick Mountain and Elkhorn Hot Springs

A 45-minute drive northwest of Dillon along the Pioneer Mountain Scenic Byway (Hwy-73 – turn north off Hwy-278 midway between Dillon and Jackson) is the low key **Maverick Mountain Ski Area** (Thurs–Sun 9.30am–4pm; ⓣ406/834-3454, ⓦwww.beaverhead.com/maverick). Only one chair and one T-bar serve the mountain's eighteen runs, but if you're around after a good snowfall the vertical drop of 2120ft allows for some fun runs. Being pretty steep on the whole, it's not great for beginners – about eighty percent of the mountain is split evenly between blue and black runs. Lift tickets are $20, half that on Thursday and Friday. When you're all exhausted from the skiing, head for **Elkhorn Hot Springs** (ⓣ406/834-3434 or 1-800/722-8978; ③) below the mountain on Hwy-73. There are two stone-lined hot pools where you can ease away your aches while gazing up at the Pioneers, and you can stay over in one of the rustic cabins set amongst the pines, or cozy rooms in the lodge itself.

Barrett Station Diversion Dam some eight miles south of Dillon; the upper river is better for float fishing, the lower for canoe or wader fishing. The Clark Canyon Reservoir also has excellent fishing for rainbow and brown trout and ling, recommended for both their large size and great taste, and you can go ice-fishing here in winter. Two of the best local **outfitters** are Tom Smith's Backcountry Angler, 426 S Atlantic St (ⓣ406/683-3462), and Watershed Fly Fishing Adventures, 610 N Montana St (ⓣ406/683-6660, ⓦwww.watershedadventures.com). Full-day guided trips start from around $300 for one person, $325 for two.

Eating and drinking

Blacktail Station 26 S Ave (ⓣ406/683-6611). Often busy, the *Blacktail* is a reasonably vibrant spot for tasty steaks and pasta at reasonable prices.

Lion's Den 725 N Montana (ⓣ406/683-2051). Large steak, prime rib, and seafood dishes for under $15, or hot sandwiches for around $7. With a pool table, bar, and poker machine and dancing some nights if you're in luck you could have quite a lively night here.

Longhorn Saloon & Grill 8 N Montana (ⓣ406/683-6839). Filling all-day breakfasts and value-for-money lunch and dinner specials daily.

Metlen Hotel S Railroad Ave (ⓣ406/683-2335) Another good breakfast stop, or in the evenings a great place to meet real cowboys and cowgirls while enjoying a beer and tasty and plentiful pub food.

Papa T's 10 N Montana (ⓣ406/684-6432). The best pizzas in town, with a large for $12–14, and good burgers and vegetarian dishes, plus a busy bar. *Papa T's* also does a delivery service and occasionally features live music.

The Red Rock Lakes National Wildlife Refuge

After leaving Dillon, I-15 climbs gradually up towards the Continental Divide and the border with Idaho, 64 miles south at Monida Pass. Flanked by the remote mountains of the Tendoy and Snowcrest ranges, the most notable detour en route is the **Red Rock Lakes National Wildlife Refuge** (daily: dawn–dusk; ⓣ406/276-3536; free), encircled by the smooth peaks of the Centennial Mountains rising up to almost 10,000 feet. To reach the lakes, head east on unpaved Hwy-509, located just before the state border, for nearly thirty miles. The lakes are home to several hundred **trumpeter swans**, North America's largest waterfowl with a wingspan of up to eight feet, and once though to be extinct. There's also plenty of other wildlife in this unspoiled corner, including sandhill cranes, blue herons, moose, deer, elk, and antelope. You can fish on the lakes, and canoe on the various creeks that connect them, and there are two free primitive campgrounds as well.

The Big Hole Valley

The sheer size of the **BIG HOLE VALLEY** and the mountains on either side are what will linger in your memory long after you've travelled through it. Mirror flat and 35 miles wide at its broadest, the valley is hemmed in on the southeast by the remote 9000ft Pioneer Mountains, while at the head of the valley is the 10,000ft Bitterroot Range, along which runs the Continental Divide.

Exploring the Big Hole Valley

You can access the Big Hole by various routes from Dillon (or Butte to the northeast), but by far the best is via the turnoff from I-15 onto Hwy-43 some forty miles north of Dillon – this route allows you to enjoy the entire length of the valley. Before you start the eighty-mile drive up to the head of the Big Hole though, consider checking out the bizarre white-granite rock formations of the **Humbug Spires Primitive Area**, accessed from a trailhead three miles east of the Moose Creek interchange on I-15, about halfway between Dillon and Butte. The needle-like spires are the result of intense faulting and fracturing of granite extrusions, and some of them rise 600ft above the surrounding forests. There are some short day-hikes into this 7000-acre preserve, through stands of old growth Douglas fir, as well as a number of good rock-climbing routes on the spires themselves.

By the time you reach the one-street settlement of **Wise River**, twelve miles from the I-15 intersection, rolling, timbered mountains and rocky crags soar above the wide, pancake-flat valley bottom. Pick up **information** on the Big Hole region from the Wise River Ranger District Office on Hwy-43 on the south side of town (Mon–Fri 8am–4.30pm; ⓣ406/832-3178). Between here and **Wisdom**, a small crossroads ranching community set amongst open sagebrush plains, the valley narrows again and there are a number of good fishing spots (see box opposite). Hwy-278 runs south from Wisdom to the tiny community of **Jackson Hot Springs**, where you can soak in the hot pool at *Jackson Hot Springs Lodge* ($5; ⓣ406/834-3151). There are rustic motel rooms (❹) and cabins (❷) to rent at the springs if you want to hang around. If you continue south on Hwy-278, you'll roll over Big Hole Pass (7360ft) and back down to Dillon.

Back at Wisdom, Hwy-43 heads west up pine-clad mountains to Chief Joseph Pass (7264ft) and into Idaho. Just before the border is the **Big Hole National Battlefield**. Chief Joseph of the Nez Percé and 800 tribal members camped here on their 1800-mile exodus from their tribal lands in northeast Oregon and central Idaho to Canada while being pursued by the US Army in August 1877 (see p.629). At dawn on August 9, they were attacked by the US cavalry, who indiscriminately gunned down men, women, and children. The Nez Percé defended their position for a day, with both sides sustaining heavy casualties, before fleeing east to be forced to surrender two months later just a few miles short of sanctuary in Canada. There's an informative **visitor center** (daily: June–Aug 8am–8pm; rest of year 8am–5pm; $5 per vehicle; ⓣ406/689-3155) with audiovisual displays describing the battle, weapons recovered from the battlefield, and a small store. At the battlefield there are trails to the Nez Percé camp and the point where the Nez Percé captured the cavalry's howitzer, from where there are fine views over the Big Hole Valley.

Camping and outdoor activities in the Big Hole Valley

It should come as no surprise to find that there are plenty of marked hiking trails and some fine cross-country skiing trails in winter that allow you to get out and explore the inspiring scenery of the Big Hole Valley. Of course, being that this is Montana, there's also some excellent fishing to be had.

To the south of **Wise River** along Hwy-73 is the trailhead for the 6.5-mile **Gold Creek Trail** (Trail #152), found a half-mile south of Gold Creek and Maurice Cemetery. There are some steep climbs involved in this hike that takes you through wildflower meadows and sagebrush hillsides before climbing to look down on Gold Creek and across the Pioneer Mountains. A longer hike in the Wisdom area is the **Sand Lake/Lily Lake Trail (Trail #380)**, an eleven-mile tramp up into the Pioneer Mountains that gives access to Sand Lake after eight miles and Lily Lake a further three miles on. At Sand Lake backpackers can join the 35-mile **Pioneer Loop National Recreation Trail** which travels along the spine of the West Pioneer Mountains past several alpine lakes, and has marvellous views over the Big Hole region. The Sand Lake/Lily Lake trail starts one mile west of *Steel Lake Campground* which is 5.5 miles east of Wisdom on Steel Lake Road.

Anglers on the Big Hole River may pull in rainbow, cutthroat, and brown trout (the latter of which can get very large in the river's lower reaches), while the upper Big Hole River has the last holdings of Arctic grayling in the lower 48 (strict catch and release only). For details of what's biting when and where, contact Pioneer Outfitters, 400 Alder Creek Rd, Wise River (⑦406/832-3128 or 1-800/290-5393).

In winter, there are several ungroomed **cross-country ski trails** in the Wise River area, maps of which are available from the Wise River Ranger District Office (see opposite); there's also fifteen miles of well-groomed trails at the **Chief Joseph Cross Country Trails System**, 28 miles west of Wisdom on Hwy-43.

Campgrounds

There are a huge number of campsites in the Big Hole Valley, and if you're on public land you can literally just pull off the road and set up camp. In the **Wise River** area, *Boulder Creek* campground ($8) has a dozen units, water, and local fishing and is in a great setting in the Pioneer Mountains thirteen miles south of Wise River on Hwy-73. In the **Wisdom** area some great lakeside camping is available on the eastern slopes of the Bitterroots. *Miner Lake* ($7 per night) has eighteen sites, a boat launch, and water (from 0.5 miles south of Jackson take CO-182 west for 6.75 miles, then west for 3.25 miles on Forest Road 182); *Mussigbrod Lake* (free) has ten sites, a boat launch, and water (one mile west of Wisdom on Hwy-43 take Lower North Fork Rd for 7.5 miles then Forest Road 573 for ten miles); and *Twin Lakes* ($7) in the Bitterroots has 21 sites, a boat launch, and water (travel seven miles south of Wisdom on Hwy-278 then take Briston Lane Rd for seven miles, then Forest Road 945 for five miles and finally Forest Road 183 for five miles).

The Bitterroot Valley

Though home to none of Montana's major cities, the **BITTERROOT VALLEY** witnessed three of the most formative events in Montana's pioneer history. In 1805, the local Salish Indians assisted Lewis and Clark as they passed down the valley then over "the most terrible mountains" at **Lolo Pass** to the west of present-day Missoula. Over three decades later in 1841, Jesuit Father Pierre Jean de Smet established the first permanent white settlement in Montana at the **St Mary's Mission**, near what is now **Stevensville**. And not far from here Major John Owen made the first gold find in Montana in 1852, laconically recorded

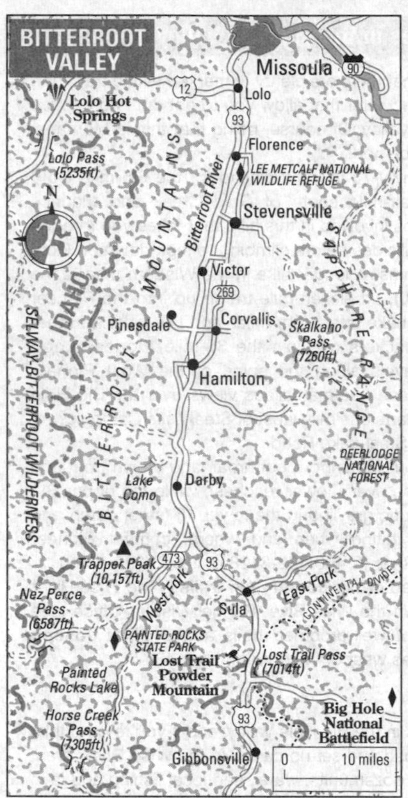

in his diary – "Sunday 15 [Feb] – Gold Hunting found some." It was not gold that helped the Bitterroot develop though, but agriculture on the fertile valley which boomed in the 1860s – indeed, the Salish were moved out to the Flathead Indian Reservation in the Mission Valley, north of Missoula, to make room for white settlers.

Lost Trail Pass north to Darby

There can be few more dramatic entrances to any US state than the drive from Idaho over Lost Trail Pass (7014ft) and into the Bitterroot Valley. From the top of the pass, Hwy-43 shoots off east past the Big Hole National Battlefield (see p.506), while US-93 winds north past **Lost Trail Powder Mountain** (Ⓣ406/821-3211, Ⓦwww.losttrail.com) and gradually down through fir, larch, and ponderosa pine forests between towering mountain peaks that are still relatively unexplored. The ski area has only 23 runs over 800 acres, but if you get here on a Thursday morning (the mountain is only open Thurs–Sun; $20) the chances of getting deep, untracked powder are good – especially as the mountain receives 300 inches of snow annually. The top elevation is 7800ft, with a **vertical** of 1200ft, and runs break down as twenty percent beginner, sixty percent intermediate, and twenty percent advanced. There's a small lodge and rental facilities at the base.

Six miles south of Lost Trail Pass, tucked beneath the Bitterroots, is **Lost Trail Hot Springs Resort** (Ⓣ406/821-3574 or 1-800/825-3574), where there are plain but cozy motel rooms (❸), more upmarket log cabins (❹), and, of course, hot springs. Set in a grove of trees, the springs are enclosed in a man-made pool that is open to the public year-round (June 15–Aug daily 8am–10pm; closed Mon–Tues rest of the year; $5). The resort also has a bar and restaurant that is open for meals all day long ranging from good-value charbroiled chicken sandwiches ($5) to huge 16oz T-bone steaks ($14). Reservations are advised.

Continuing north on US-93, look out for the Hwy-473 turnoff a few miles north of the small hamlet of **Sula**. This well-maintained two-lane road leads into the heart of the Bitterroots and the pictograph-rich area of **Painted Rocks State Park** (free) and **Painted Rocks Lake**, which has some pleasant, easy hikes beside the shore. Just to the south of the lake along West Fork Road is the 1899 **Alta Ranger Station**, reputedly the first forest ranger station built in the US at the site of what was then a 500-man gold camp. The one-room log building is no longer in use, but you can peek in through the windows and imagine the isolation of being based here a century ago.

Between mileposts 20 and 21 on US-93 north of Sula, look out for a ponderosa pine decorated with brightly colored strips of cloth, bunches of herbs, and feathers. This is the native Salish's sacred **Medicine Tree**, upon which offerings are left to the spirit Coyote, said to have destroyed a wicked mountain sheep at this spot. Continuing north, you come to the bustling little town of **DARBY** (pop. 629), 44 miles on from the Lost Trail Pass. The town lives off a slightly mismatched combination of logging, farming, and tourism, and its Main Street is lined with antiques stores along with the small **Pioneer Museum** (June–Aug daily 9am–5pm; free). Housed in a century-old refurbished log cabin moved from nearby Tin Cup Creek, the museum features a trapper's cabin complete with bearskin rug and traps on the wall, but the 1930s **Darby Ranger Station** (daily 9am–5pm; ⓣ406/821-3913) on Main Street is of as much interest for its displays of Forest Service memorabilia, as well as for advice and maps on the surrounding forests. If you're looking to **stay over**, you can't miss the rather brash but friendly *Bud & Shirley's Motel* (ⓣ406/821-3401; ❸) on the corner of Main Street and Missoula Avenue. Rooms here are clean and comfortable, but an even better bet for budget travelers is the *Wilderness Motel* at the south end of Main Street (ⓣ406/821-3405; ❷), which has motel rooms with kitchens and queen-sized beds, along with tent ($5) and RV sites ($15).

Hamilton

By the time you reach **HAMILTON**, the Bitterroot Valley has opened out and the wider valley floor doesn't have the drama of the canyon further south. The town's characterless outskirts don't help much either, however they give way to a neat town center designed to be a "model town" in 1890 by Copper King Marcus Daly after he had his mansion built nearby (see below). Daly was attracted to the valley by both its beauty and the more pragmatic fact that it contained abundant supplies of the timber he needed for his mining and smelting operations in Butte and Anaconda. This was a company town, with most of the residents working for Daly, living in his homes, and shopping at his stores.

Wandering around the town, it's hard to miss the brick and masonry Romanesque-style **Ravalli County Courthouse**, 205 Bedford St, which features a copper cupola and is now home to the **Ravalli County Museum** (June–Aug Mon–Fri 10am–4pm, Sun 2.30–5pm; rest of year Mon, Wed, Fri 1–4pm, Sun 2.30–5pm; free). Surprisingly, a worthwhile exhibit on wood ticks is inside; the local Rocky Mountain Laboratories discovered the cure for Rocky Mountain spotted fever, transmitted by ticks endemic to the region and which, although not fatal, can debilitate both humans and livestock. The town's main attraction is, however, the Georgian revival-style **Marcus Daly Mansion**, a couple of miles south on Hwy-269 (April 15–Oct 15 daily 11am–4pm; tours on the hour; $5). Built in 1890, it was part of Daly's 22,500-acre Bitterroot Stock Farm, where he bred prize racehorses. The grand and opulent pile, set in fifty pleasingly landscaped acres, has 42 rooms, including an amazing 24 bathrooms. Much of the original furniture and fittings remain, adding to the atmosphere.

Practicalities

The only public transport into Hamilton is on the CART service (ⓣ208/756-2191) between Missoula and Salmon, which operates twice a day on Tuesday, Wednesday and Friday. The **chamber of commerce** is at 105 E Main St

(June–Aug daily 8am–6pm; rest of year Mon–Fri 8am–5pm; ⓣ406/363-2400, ⓦwww.bvchamber.com), and the local **USFS Ranger Office** is at 1810 N 1st St (daily Mon–Fri 8am–5pm; ⓣ406/363-2400). **Accommodation** choices in town include two good-value downtown motels; the *City Center Motel*, 415 Main St (ⓣ406/363-1651; ❷), which has plain but comfortable rooms (some with kitchenettes), and *Deffy's Motel*, 321 S 1st St (ⓣ406/363-1244; ❸), with queen beds and an indoor hot tub. If **camping**, check out *Angler's Roost*, 815 Hwy-93 S (ⓣ406/363-1268), beside the Bitterroot River; tent sites and full hookups run $16 per night, and extras include showers, laundry, and a well-stocked store.

Hamilton has a good choice of **restaurants** and **bars**, including *A Place to Ponder*, 166 S 2nd St (ⓣ406/363-0080), featuring home-baked pastries and tasty soups and sandwiches. Up the road, *Nap's Grill*, 220 N 2nd St (ⓣ406/363-0136), has good-value burgers and steaks – burger, fries, and a soda costs under $7. For dinner, check out the *Banque Club*, 225 W Main St (ⓣ406/363-1955), a busy bar/restaurant set in an old bank, where the beef tenderloin with mushroom and brandy sauce ($22) is recommended.

The Eastside Highway

From Hamilton, it's far more pleasant to get off Hwy-93 to take the quieter and more scenic Eastside Highway (Hwy-269) north up towards Missoula. In the pleasant little town of **Stevensville**, you'll find **Saint Mary's Mission**, W 4th St (Wed–Sat 10am–5pm, Sun 10am–2pm; $3; ⓣ406/777-5734).

Outdoor activities and outfitters in the Bitterroot Valley

There are a vast number of trails in the Bitterroots leading into the wild heart of some of Montana's most beautiful mountain landscapes. Undoubtedly one of the oldest is at Lost Trail Hot Springs, where you can follow the **Nee-Me-Poo Trail** along the route of the Nez Percé on their flight from the US Army in 1877 (see p.629). The six-mile hike takes you through ponderosa pine forest up to Gibbons Pass on the Continental Divide, from where there are good views down the Bitterroot Valley.

One of the best day-hikes is the challenging twelve-mile round trip up to the craggy summit of **Trapper Peak**, at 10,157ft the highest mountain in the Bitterroots. You climb a tough 4000ft in six miles, but the views from the summit are sensational. To get to the trailhead turn off US-93 some five miles south of Darby onto Forest Road 473 for nine miles, then turn west on Forest Road 5630A for seven miles of gravel switchbacks to the trailhead. Follow Trail 133 as it climbs steeply for two miles, then eases off a little before eventually emerging from timber into a harsh landscape of exposed granite peaks, where you should follow the obvious cairns to the summit. Be prepared for snow at any time of year up top.

Close to Hamilton is a relatively easy eight-mile round-trip hike to the popular **Canyon Falls**. To reach the trailhead take Bowman Road west off US-93 two miles north of Hamilton until it intersects with Forest Road 735, which you follow west to the trailhead at Canyon Creek. From here Trail 525 is a steady climb along the side of the creek to Canyon Falls, a series of cataracts falling around 200ft – a good time to visit is May or June when snowmelt makes the falls more spectacular.

To see the less-frequented **Sapphire Mountains** on the east side of the Bitterroot Valley, try the moderately strenuous ten-mile round-trip to **Dome Shaped Mountain** (8656ft). To get to the trailhead you take Skalkaho Road (Forest Road 38) east off US-93 three miles south of Hamilton, past Skalkaho Falls and over the 7260ft Skalkaho Pass (the drive itself is a minor adventure). Two miles on the east side of the pass on Forest Road 78578 is *Crystal Creek Campground*, with the trailhead just to the northwest. The route follows Forest Road 78578 for half-a-mile, then becomes Trail 10 as

Established in 1866, this pretty one-room timber church with belfry is the oldest in Montana, and twee interior features such as the wood-burning stove help retain its character. The church was actually constructed from materials used in an earlier mission of the same name, built close by in 1841 to convert members of the Flathead tribe to Christianity.

Four miles north of Stevensville is the 2800-acre **Lee Metcalf National Wildlife Reserve** (dawn–dusk; free) ⓣ406/777-5552). Well signposted off Hwy-269, it's well worth visiting as you can both drive and hike through to spot birdlife such as ospreys, tundra swans, and heron; larger animals that may also be seen include coyote, deer, and fox.

From Florence a few miles north, it's pretty much a straight shot through Lolo (see below) to Missoula 24 miles away.

West on US-12 to Lolo Pass

Lolo, an untidy rash of gas stations and stores, is at the crossroads of US-93 and US-12. From the latter, it's a lovely 33-mile drive up into the Bitterroot Mountains to Lolo Pass (5235ft) at the Idaho border. This is the route followed by Lewis and Clark as they made a second, and ultimately successful attempt to cross the Continental Divide in 1805. About five miles before the pass, you'll come across **Lolo Hot Springs** ($6; ⓣ406/273-22909, ⓦwww.lolohotsprings.net), another place to take the waters, either in an outdoor swimming pool (94°F) or a steaming indoor soaking tub (104°F). Accommodation

it passes gradually up through meadows to become Trail 313 to the grassy summit of Dome Shaped Mountain. Note that the trail can be difficult to follow in the later stages.

Fishing

Anglers will find good sport on the **Bitterroot River**, with numerous signposted fishing access points off US-93. Both the Bitterroot and it's tributaries have healthy populations of rainbow, cutthroat, and brook trout, with the biggest numbers found in the fast moving waters in the south of the valley. The mountain lakes on the west side of the valley are also worth a visit for their trout. The biggest and best known of these is **Lake Como**, in a splendid setting beneath high mountain peaks, but it can be noisy here from speedboats and jet skis. **Painted Rocks Lake** to the south (see p.508) is quieter and the fishing here is often better than Lake Como.

Local outfitters

Bitterroot Anglers 4039 Hwy-93 N, Suite B, Stevensville ⓣ406/777-5667. All flies cost $1.75 each here, and the guides have over twenty years experience of local waters.

Fly Fishing Always 668 Foley Lane, Hamilton ⓣ406/363-0943, ⓦwww.cybernet1.com/flyfishingalways. Full-day guided fly-fishing on the Bitterroot River from around $300 for two people including lunch.

Pipestone Mountaineering 315 W Main St, Hamilton ⓣ406/363-3855. Open seven days a week, this is a good spot to pick up maps and guides, rent backpacking gear, and get local trail advice.

Trapper Creek Lodge 158 Trapper Rd (along West Fork Rd) Darby ⓣ406/821-4970 or 1-888/821-4970. A well-established business offering hunting, fishing, and horseback trips in the Bitterroots; they also have attractive guest cabins from $65 per day.

Two Bears Outfitters 505 Camas Creek Loop, Hamilton ⓣ406/375-0070, ⓦwww.elkoutfitters.com. Two Bears offer wilderness pack trips from $200 per person per day and horseback forest trails rides from $80 per day.

Rooms with a view

The majority of properties run by the USFS were built in the first half of the twentieth century as **lookout cabins** and **towers**, **guard stations**, or **work centers** in remote forest and mountain locations. In recent years, their official use has declined, leading the USFS to begin renting them out to those wanting to get as far away from it all as possible.

The often primitive cabins come with bunks (but not necessarily mattresses), stove, propane cooker, tables, and chairs; the chemical toilet may be over 100 yards away and you'll need to bring your own drinking water and chop your own firewood (and leave some ready for the next guest). The cheapest, four-person cabins cost around $20 per night; an eight-person unit costs $50–60 per night. Accessibility varies – you can drive to some cabins, others are only reached after a long hike or ski. A typical cabin is **West Fork Butte** to the south of Lolo Hot Springs. The 14ft x 14ft timber cabin is perched on top of bare rock slabs and fastened to the ground with steel hawsers bolted into the rock – presumably to prevent it from being blown halfway to Chicago in a big storm. Furnishings consist of two squeaky bunks, a stove, a cooker, and a chair, but the view is priceless. Through huge wall-to-wall windows, you can see across the endless blue ridges of the Selway-Bitterroot Wilderness Area, rolling west into Idaho, snow patches still visible on the summits even in mid-July. There's not a road or a building visible in any direction.

For **general information** on staying in USFS cabins and lookout towers throughout the Rocky Mountain region contact USDA Forest Service, Recreation, Heritage and Wilderness Resources, PO Box 96090, Washington, DC 20090-6090, USA (Ⓣ202/205-1706, Ⓦwww.fsfed.us/ (check under "Recreation"). For information on cabins in the Bitterroot and Lolo Pass area call Bitterroot National Forest (Ⓣ406/363-7161) or Lolo National Forest (Ⓣ406/329-3750).

is available in pleasant motel rooms (❸) or tepees (❶), plus there are tent sites for $13 and full hookups for $19; there's also a restaurant and a friendly bar. At **Lolo Pass**, a sign commemorates its crossing by both Lewis and Clark and the Nez Percé. It's an interesting juxtaposition since the former were opening up the land to the east for the descendants of white pioneers responsible for driving the latter back over the mountains and out of their homeland seventy years later. The **Lolo Pass Visitor Center** is situated just over the border in Idaho (see p.634), and is a popular base for cross-country skiing. There's also some excellent hiking up here around the Continental Divide – see p.636 for some suggested trails that can be accessed from I-90 to the north. Also, don't forget to turn your watch back an hour to Pacific Standard Time as you cross the border.

Glacier National Park and the northwest

Northwest Montana is fairly dominated by the glorious alpine meadows and tightly packed peaks of **Glacier National Park**, right up against the Canadian border. That's where many head straight for, and to an extent rightly so – the main road through is one of the most spellbinding drives in the Rockies, if not the States, and the hikes, once you're off the road, equally intoxicating. Nevertheless, there's much to be found in the rest of the region, even if most of it is also of the wilderness variety, and thus perhaps slightly diminished in comparison.

The region's biggest settlement, **Missoula**, is a likeable college town, and right on the doorstep of the **Mission Valley** to the north, home to abundant wildlife at the National Bison Range and some wildfowl refuges. Massive **Flathead Lake**, north of the valley, gets plenty of visitors for its wealth of outdoor activities, namely fishing, swimming, and camping around its shores. **Whitefish** and **Kalispell**, further up, are useful bases for the nearby mountain exploration – the ski resort of **Big Mountain**, with its tough terrain and plentiful snow, is within spitting distance of Whitefish – and interesting enough towns in themselves. East of here is the **Seeley-Swan Valley** and **Bob Marshall Wilderness Area**, continuing the theme of the great outdoors and, pointedly, **grizzly bear country**. In the far northwest corner, there's not too much happening save for remote mountain areas and one-horse lumber towns.

Accommodation price codes

All accommodation prices in this book have been coded using the symbols below. For **hotels**, **motels**, and **B&Bs**, rates are given for the least expensive double room in each establishment during peak season; variations are indicated where appropriate, including winter rates for all ski resorts. For **hostels**, the actual price per bed is given; for **camping**, the overnight cost per site is given. For a full explanation see p.30 in Basics.

- ❶ up to $30
- ❷ $30–45
- ❸ $45–60
- ❹ $60–80
- ❺ $80–100
- ❻ $100–130
- ❼ $130–180
- ❽ $180–240
- ❾ over $240

Missoula

Blue-collar and academic cultures converge in **MISSOULA** to produce one of the most vibrant and friendly small towns in the country. It's a town of contrasting faces – truck sales yards and bookstores, continental cafés and gun shops – surrounded by mountains, forests, and rivers which make for fine outdoor playgrounds. Amongst these are challenging **Montana Snowbowl Ski Area** to the northwest of town, and only a few minutes drive north of downtown the **Rattlesnake National Recreation Area and Wilderness**.

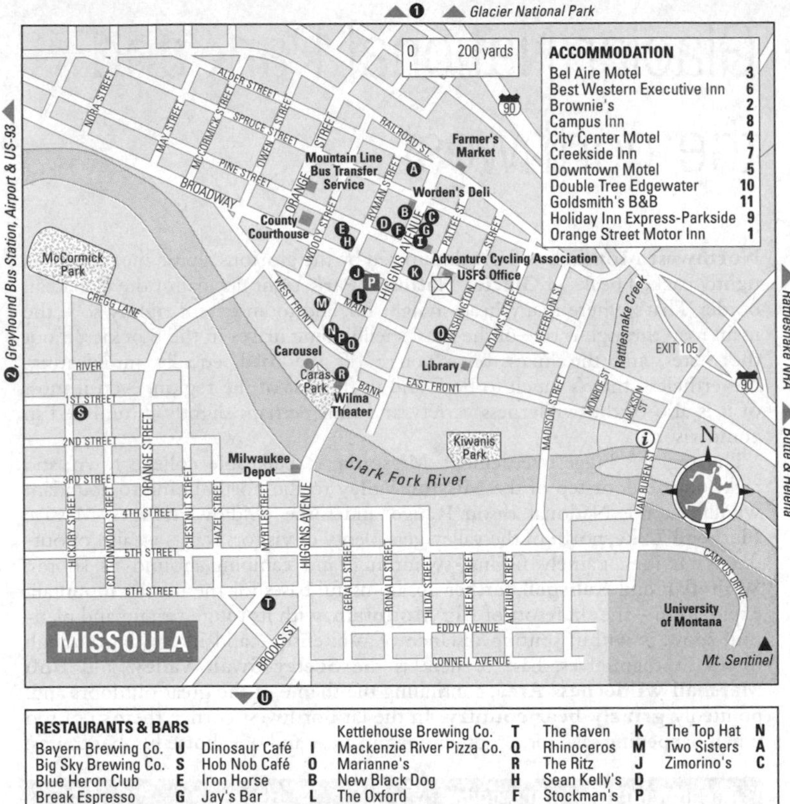

Arrival, information, and getting around

As one of the state's major urban centers, getting to and from Missoula is rarely a problem. The town has **bus services** operated by Greyhound, Rimrock, and Intermountain Express from the bus depot a mile west of downtown at 1660 W Broadway (ⓣ406/549-2339), from which there are daily services to Helena, Butte, Bozeman, Billings, and Kalispell/Whitefish. If you're coming in by **air**, the Johnson-Bell County Airport (ⓣ406/728-4381) is five miles west of downtown on I-90, with Delta, Horizon, Northwest, and Big Sky offering services throughout the northwest. Yellow Cab **taxis** (ⓣ406/543-6644) cost around $10 to get downtown, though the local bus line (see below) services the airport as well. The best bet for **car rental** is with Enterprise (ⓣ406/721-1888) or Thrifty (ⓣ406/542-8459) in town, who have a pick-up service from the airport.

The helpful **chamber of commerce** is next to the Missoula Grizzlies stadium at 825 E Front St (ⓣ406/543-6623, ⓦwww.missoulachamber.com). For outdoor advice call in at the regional **USFS office** downtown at 340 N Pattee (Mon–Fri 8am–4.30pm; ⓣ406/329-3511). For **listings** and current events, the free *Independent* newspaper is good, while the *Missoulian* newspaper features a detailed entertainment section each Friday.

Missoula by bike

Missoula has enjoyed close ties with **cycling** as far back as 1896, when it became home to the 25th Infantry Bicycle Corps, founded to test the military potential of bikes as a means of transporting troops in mountainous regions. The bike corps was tested with a 1900-mile ride from Missoula to St Louis over rough ground and poor trails – the journey took 41 days and the troops returned home by train. Soon after, the army decided that cycling soldiers were not a viable proposition.

More recently, the excellent **Adventure Cycling Association**, 150 E Pine St (Ⓣ406/721-1776, Ⓦwww.adventurecycling.org), has set up its national headquarters in town. Call in at their friendly offices for advice on everything from the best bike stores to good places to ride.

Within the city, Mountain Line **buses** (Ⓣ406/721-3333, Ⓦwww.mountainline.com) runs regular and extensive services from around 7am–6pm for a flat rate of 85 cents, including a service to the airport. Also look out for the free **trolley** (Ⓣ406/721-3333) running between downtown and the university.

Accommodation

As you might expect of Montana's second-largest city, **accommodation** in Missoula is plentiful and varied, with good-value motels clustered downtown on Broadway. The only place you can camp in Missoula is at the suburban *Missoula KOA* (Ⓣ406/549-0881), three miles west of downtown at 3695 Tina Ave (take exit 101 off I-90), which has a pool, hot tub, laundry, and even a petting zoo for kids. Tents sites cost $18, full hookups $25.

Bel Aire Motel 300 E Broadway Ⓣ406/543-3818. Well located for both downtown and the university, the *Bel Aire* has bright, pleasant rooms and facilities include kitchenettes, an indoor pool, hot tub, fitness rooms, and guest laundry. ④

Best Western Executive Inn 210 E Main Ⓣ406/543-7221 or 1-800/528-1234, Ⓕ406/543-7225. Large, spacious rooms with queen beds, cable TV, and fridges, plus a decent restaurant and indoor pool. ④

Best Western Grant Creek Inn I-90 and Reserve St exit Ⓣ406/543-0700 or 1-888/543-700. About three miles west of town off I-90, the *Grant Creek Inn* is well located for accessing Snowbowl Ski Area. The rooms are large and comfortable, and facilities include a pool and hot tub. ④

Brownie's Plus Motel 1540 W Broadway Ⓣ406/543-6614 or 1-800/543-6614. Convenient for the bus station, *Brownie's* has clean, plain rooms and is good value, although it's a bit of a hike from downtown. ③

Campus Inn 744 E Broadway Ⓣ406/549-5134 or 1-800/232-8013. Pretty standard motel rooms alongside busy Broadway, with free continental breakfast, outdoor pool and hot tub, and disabled access. ③

City Center Motel 338 E Broadway Ⓣ406/543-3193. One of the cheapest lodgings in town, the rooms are rather old and basic, but clean, and within a couple of minutes walk of downtown. ②

Creekside Inn 630 E Broadway Ⓣ406/549-2387 or 1-800/551-2387. Well-kept rooms in a non-smoking establishment situated midway between downtown and the university, with a pool for cooling off in summer. ④

Double Tree Hotel Edgewater 100 Madison St Ⓣ406/728-3100 or 1-800/547-8010, Ⓕ406/723-2530. One of the finest hotels in town, the *Double Tree* is in a fairly quiet, attractive location on the Clark Fork and close to the campus. The large rooms have queen beds, cable TV, and coffee-makers, and facilities include a good restaurant, pool, and hot tub. ⑤

Downtown Motel 502 E Broadway Ⓣ406/549-5191 or 1-800/303-5191, Ⓕ406/543-9479. One of the best budget choices in the downtown area, the nonsmoking rooms are old and nothing fancy, but the location is hard to beat. ②

Goldsmith's Inn 809 E Front St Ⓣ406/721-6732. The best established B&B in town, the 1911 *Goldsmith's* has seven beautifully appointed rooms with Victorian-style beds and furniture, fireplaces, reading nooks, and private baths. In summer you can enjoy an excellent breakfast on the deck overlooking the Clark Fork. ⑤

Holiday Inn Express – Parkside 200 S Pattee ⓣ406/549-7600 or 1-800/465-4329. The more convenient of the two *Holiday Inns* in town (the other is on E Broadway), just a couple of minutes walk from downtown. Rooms are spacious with queen beds, TV, and coffee-making facilities, and there's a restaurant, pool, and hot tub. ❹

Orange Street Budget Motor Inn 801 N Orange ⓣ406/721-3610 or 1-800/328-0801, ⓕ406/721-8875. A good bet if you're coming in from I-90 exit 104 on the north side of town, but also within easy reach of downtown, the rooms are standard motel fare but comfortable enough, and included in the price are a free continental breakfast and use of an exercise room. ❸

The city

Both **downtown** and the **university campus** have an understated stylishness to them, though neither is especially stocked with cultural attractions – more a buzz from the mix of people and the fine selection of venues in which they hang out: coffeehouses, bars, restaurants, and the like. Downtown is roughly bounded by the Clark Fork to the south, Alder Street to the north, Woody Street to the west, and Washington Street to the east, and you can begin a tour of it pretty much anywhere. You'll find a number of attractive older buildings in the downtown area, such as the exuberant 1889 **Higgins Block**, 202 N Higgins, which features Queen Anne-style commercial architecture and the 1901 Renaissance Revival-style **Northern Pacific Depot** (no longer in operation) on the same street. However, they're rather staid compared to the delightful **Carousel for Missoula**, beside the river in Caras Park (daily: June–Aug 11am–7pm; Sept–May 11am–5.30pm; $1). The only hand-carved carousel to be built west of the Mississippi since the 1930s, it comes complete with melodious band organ and attracts kids of all ages; the park itself is also a cheery place to hang out on a sunny afternoon.

From Caras Park, it's a ten-minute stroll east along the riverbank to the grassy campus of the **University of Montana** and its attractive 1899 University Hall – its elegant central tower houses a carillon that gives a fifteen-minute recital at midday. A good deal of Missoula's lively atmosphere emanates from the 10,000 students that go here, and it's also given the town something of a literary reputation – Wallace Stegner and Ivan Doig are just two of the acclaimed writers to have graduated from the university's creative writing school. For a quick workout from the campus, try the steep switchback footpath up to the concrete "M" on **Mount Sentinel**, directly above the university. The stiff hike will take you about forty minutes and the marvellous views of the city and beyond are well worth it.

Two of Missoula's finest attractions are actually located a short drive out of the downtown core. Closest is the **Rocky Mountain Elk Foundation Wildlife Visitor Center**, two miles northwest of town at 2291 W Broadway (June–Aug daily 8.30am–8.30pm; rest of year Mon–Fri 8.30am–5pm, Sat–Sun 11am–4pm; free). Though there are no live elk, you will find a fantastic display of world record elk racks (antlers), and a good diorama of various other Rocky Mountain critters including grizzly bear and wolf, alongside exhibitions on the preservation of elk habitats. Further northwest out of town is one of the most interesting visitor attractions in Montana, the **Smokejumper Center** (June–Aug daily 10am–5pm; free; ⓣ406/329-4934), at Johnson Bell Airport on US-93. Exhibits include a reconstructed forest lookout tower, equipment used by smokejumpers, and some thrilling and informative video footage on the history of smokejumping and what's actually involved in leaping out of a plane to extinguish an otherwise inaccessible wildfire. If you visit while the frequent summer wildfires are burning in the region's forests you may well see the jumpers heading out or returning to base, when there's a real air of drama and excitement about the place.

Eating and drinking

Missoula's compact downtown is perfectly designed for **eating out** and then moving on for an evening of **bar** hopping. From microbreweries (see box, overleaf) to cowboy saloons, there's more than enough variety to allow you to visit a different drinking establishment every night of your stay. Indeed, author James Crumley wasn't far off the mark when he wrote that Missoula is a "town with the best bars in a state of great bars."

Restaurants and cafés

Break Espresso 432 N Higgins St ⓣ406/728-7300. A late opening coffee shop popular with students and bookish types.

Dinosaur Café 428 N Higgins St ⓣ406/549-2940. One of the more gritty and atmospheric haunts in Missoula, where the smoke hangs heavy in the air and you can get tasty traditional Cajun food, burgers, steaks, and chicken for under $10 per head.

Hob Nob Café 208 E Main St ⓣ406/542-3188. A quaint spot in the back of the Union Club where the fare includes good organic produce and homemade breads and desserts.

MacKenzie River Pizza Co 137 W Front St ⓣ406/721-0077 Design your own pizza for under $15 and dine either in the rustic interior or on the deck within sight of the river.

Marianne's at the Wilma 131 S Higgins St ⓣ406/728-8549. Located in the 1921 Wilma Building, listed in the National Register of Historic Buildings, *Marianne's* is open from 7am and for lunch and dinner, with some fine seasonal menus featuring dishes such as smoked duck terrine and Chilean sea bass. There's live jazz in the evenings as well. Expect to pay $15–25 for dinner.

New Black Dog 138 W Broadway ⓣ406/542-1138. A good laid-back vegetarian venue, with live music on Wednesday night and $6 pitchers of microbrew on Thursday.

The Raven 130 E Broadway ⓣ406/829-8188. Comfortable sofas and chairs, fine coffee and pastries, breakfast for around $7, and a top jukebox make the *Raven* one of the best hangouts in Missoula.

Two Sisters 127 W Alder St ⓣ406/327-8438. *Two Sisters* has a colorful, hippieish atmosphere but the menu, which changes seasonally, is anything but lentils and rice. Try the fresh smoked salmon, rib-eye steaks or New York strips, all from around $20 and served with organic greens. There's also a fine selection of vegetarian dishes and great desserts.

Zimorino's Red Pies over Montana 424 N Higgins ⓣ406/549-7434. One of the best Italian restaurants in town, where the delicious creamy pasta – served with lashings of garlic, olive oil, and parmesan cheese plus garlic bread and salad – is a great deal at under $9. The wine and beer list is also extensive and the service is warm and friendly.

Bars and clubs

The Blue Heron Club 140 W Pine ⓣ406/543-2525. Missoula's newest and hippest live music venue; manages to pull in the best of the local and regional rock scene in cool and comfortable surroundings.

Iron Horse Brew Pub 501 N Higgins ⓣ406/728-8866. A lively bar with a very mixed clientele from students and visitors to sawmill workers hanging around the pool tables or lounging outside in summer. They also serve plain pub grub.

Jay's Bar 119 W Main ⓣ406/728-9915. If you like live music fast and furious and played in a grungy atmosphere, this is your spot.

The Oxford Saloon 337 N Higgins ⓣ406/549-0117. You haven't visited Missoula until you've had a drink and meal in the *Oxford*. Known for such delicacies as brains and eggs, this is a no-frills 24-hour booze can that feels more 1950s than twenty-first century. The clientele has as much character as the saloon as well.

Rhinoceros 158 Ryman ⓣ406/721-6061. A great bar serving over fifty beers from around the world to a lively mix of students to outdoor types. Friendly, easy-going bar staff round out a top place to down a few cold ones.

The Ritz Lounge 208 Ryman ⓣ406/721-6061. One of Missoula's best-established live music venues, competing with the *Blue Heron* for the better local up-and-coming rock and indie bands.

Sean Kelly's Brew Pub 130 W Pine ⓣ406/542-1471. One of the friendliest bars in town with a mix of Irish/English style decor and atmosphere, and a fine range of beers and whiskies, plus live jazz, blues, or Celtic music most nights.

Stockman's 125 W Front St. Not the most sophisticated joint in town – the sign out front reads "Liquor up front, poker in the rear" – but the eclectic mix of cattle ranchers, cowboys, and students ensure that this busy 1940s gambling and pool bar has plenty of life.

The Top Hat 134 W Front. Another nice old-fashioned bar, which also features regular live music, particularly blues bands. The lighting is low to the point of being dingy, but this adds to the distinctly relaxed atmosphere.

Missoula's microbreweries

All of the breweries below have tasting rooms where the beer is free – within reason.

Bayern Brewing Co 2600 S 3rd West St (Mon–Tues noon–6pm, Wed–Sat noon–8pm, Sun noon–5pm; ☎406/721-1482). Bayern produce light, German-style lagers, with three perennials and seven seasonal brews, including Pilsener and the popular Oktoberfest.

Big Sky Brewing Co 120A Hickory St (Mon–Fri 11am–6pm, Sat noon–5pm; ☎406/549-2777). Montana's best-known brewery and producer of the famous Moose Drool Ale, along with several others such as the Scape Goat, based on English-style brewing techniques using genuine Kentish hops. There's also a shop here with some fine logo wear.

Kettlehouse Brewing Co 602 Myrtle St (Mon–Thurs 3–9pm, Fri–Sat noon–9pm; ☎406/728-1660). A small locally owned brewery and tap room using mostly Montana grown barley for their distillations. There are up to ten different beers served, including Olde Bong Water, an obvious favorite of the local student crowd.

Entertainment and festivals

Missoula attracts its fair share of reasonably big names and events and there's usually some sort of shindig going on over the summer months. Much of the action is centered on the **Wilma Theatre**, 131 S Higgins (☎406/728-2521), which plays movies, hosts live theater and the occasional rock band, and is also home to the Missoula Symphony Orchestra. If you're in town in April, don't miss the acclaimed **International Wildlife Film Festival** (☎406/728-9380), which offers a chance to view top-notch wildlife films from around the world from the likes of the BBC and National Geographic.

Outdoor activities around Missoula

Some fantastic outdoor playgrounds are within easy driving distance of Missoula, from the Bitterroot Mountains, easily accessed from the **Bitterroot Valley** (see p.507) only 25 miles south to the magnificent **Bob Marshall Wilderness Area** (see p.529) around sixty miles northeast. Even closer, there's the challenging **Snowbowl Ski Area** only twelve miles out of town (see box, opposite), or for year-round outdoor action, the 61,000-acre **Rattlesnake National Recreation Area and Wilderness** – actually devoid of the poisonous snake – ten minutes drive north of downtown.

To get to the Rattlesnake area, take Van Buren north, then Rattlesnake Drive, which leads you to the main trailhead off Rattlesnake Creek (easily accessed from Rattlesnake Drive), where there's an excellent system of trails. The main area, where you can hike, mountain bike, and horseback ride, is in the "South Zone" where the well-marked **Sawmill-Curry Trail System** takes you up towards Curry Peak (5040ft), from where there are inspiring views of the surrounding mountain and forests and the Clark Fork Valley. These trails are used by **cross-country skiers** and **snowshoers** in winter. A longish hike here that makes for a good overnight trip is the twenty-mile round trip to **Stuart Peak** (7960ft), which takes you into a beautiful landscape of alpine lakes and fine mountain views. The hike starts from a well-marked trailhead at the mouth of Sawmill Gulch, accessed from Rattlesnake Drive and follows the gradual ascent of Spring Gulch Trail to below the summit. This is also popular with **mountain bikers** and **horseback riders** who can make the ride longer by connnecting with Forest Road 99 at the top of the trail.

Local outfitters

The Bike Doctor 420 N Higgins St ⓣ406/721-5357. A cool and friendly bike shop with a good range of equipment and a good repair service, plus rental bikes from around $30 per day.

Board of Missoula 624 S Higgins St ⓣ406/721-7774. Missoula's best stop for snowboard gear and clothing.

Gull Ski Shop, 2601 W Broadway ⓣ406/541-2728. A huge range of ski equipment and clothing (often with some good sale items) and a fast, efficient tuning and repair service.

The Kingfisher 927 E Broadway ⓣ406/721-6141. One of Missoula's finest fishing stores and guide services, with full-day float trips from $300 and wading trips from $250, including streamside lunches.

Montana River Guides 210 Red Fox Rd ⓣ406/273-4718, 1-800/381-RAFT. Guided rafting trips on the Clark Fork at Alberton Gorge and the Blackfoot River. Expect to pay around $70 for a day on the Clark Fork and upwards of $150 for an overnight trip down the Blackfoot.

Pipestone Mountaineering 101 S Higgins St ⓣ406/721-1670. A well-stocked store with gear for hiking, camping, cross-country and telemark skiing, and kayaking, plus a good range of local trail maps and advice.

The Trailhead corner Higgins and Pine ⓣ406/543-6966. The Trailhead has a great range of backpacking gear and also rents out backpacking equipment.

The actual wilderness area is to the north of the recreation area, and the further you travel into it the better your chances of spotting wildlife, including elk, coyote, black bear, moose, and mountain lions. Mountain bikers should bear in mind that this area is not accessible to them. Here, try the easy seven-mile **Boulder Lake Trail** (Trail 333). From the trailhead, the path moves across gentle ground then climbs gradually before a final descent to pristine Boulder Lake. Before you drop down to the lake take the short detour to your right up to the old fire lookout on Boulder Point for fine views north to the Mission Mountains. To reach the trailhead, drive east out of Missoula on Hwy-200 to Bonner, then northwest on Gold Creek Road (Forest Road 126) for six miles, after which head west on Forest Road 2103 until a left fork onto Forest Road 4323 takes you to the West Fork of Gold Creek Trailhead.

For more detailed information contact the downtown USFS office (see p.514).

Skiing in Missoula

Of Missoula's two ski hills, the 905-acre **Montana Snowbowl** (ⓣ406/549-9777, snow report ⓣ406/549-9696, ⓦwww.montanasnowbowl.com; $30) is easily the largest and also home to some challenging skiing and boarding. Located twelve miles northwest of town off I-90 at the Reserve Street exit, it can get pretty busy at weekends, when a free shuttle bus (ⓣ406/549-9777) leaves from various locations in Missoula. From a highest point of 7600ft, there's a very respectable vertical of 2600ft and a ski area of 1200 acres. Despite the lack of beginner runs, access to what there are is well thought out, with Second Thought, wending its way gently between trees, being a good start. Intermediates will find that Longhorn and Grandstand have sustained steepish pitches, and advanced skiers and boarders will enjoy the challenges of East Bowls below Big Sky Mountain, the bumps on Grizzly Chute and Angel Face, and the 500 acres of tree skiing. Experts should check with ski patrol for details on the best backcountry action.

Missoula's other ski hill, **Marshall Mountain** (ⓣ406/258-6000), is seven miles east of town and very family/beginner oriented. Still, there is some 2000ft of veritcal to play with, and **lift tickets** are an economical $19; you can also get two- and four-hour tickets ($6/$12). The hill is open 9am–9pm every day except Sunday (9am–4pm).

Listings

Internet Sip-N-Surf, 821 S Higgins, just on the south side of the river, provides a half-hour of computer time for $1 with any espresso drink, and is open Mon–Fri 7am–2am, Sat–Sun 10am–2am. See also library below.

Laundry The two most convenient for the downtown/campus area are Sparkle Laundry, 821 S Higgins and the Dry Cleaning and Laundry Shoppe, 700 S Higgins (☎406/728-7245).

Library Check your email at the public library at 301 E Main (☎406/721-2810), where you can get thirty minutes of free internet access time, although you'll probably have to queue.

Post Office The downtown Hellgate Station Post Office is at 200 E Broadway (☎406/329-3105), and the Main Office (for general delivery) is at 1100 W Kent (☎406/329-2200).

Supermarket Worden's Market, 451 N Higgins (☎406/549-1293), is a Missoula institution, with an excellent deli, great wine and beer selection, even a small sidewalk dining area.

East of Missoula: the Blackfoot Valley and beyond

Running east from Missoula and south of the Bob Marshall and Scapegoat wilderness areas, the **Blackfoot Valley** was immortalized in Norman Maclean's classic novel *A River Runs Through It* as a pristine landscape of gurgling rivers and streams, open meadows, and forest draped mountains. However, both the presence of busy Hwy-200, which follows the course of the Blackfoot River and connects Missoula with Helena, and the clear-cut felling of many of the hillsides has left scars on the landscape. All the same, **anglers** in particular will enjoy the journey along the valley as the Blackfoot and its tributaries offer some delightful fishing for brown, rainbow, cutthroat, and bull trout (catch-and-release only for the latter two) – look out for the brown-and-white highway signs indicating fishing access points.

To the north of the Blackfoot Valley's eastern end is the **Rocky Mountain Front**, a dramatic point where Montana's vast plains and mountain regions converge. The front is also home to a couple of small towns that give good access to the eastern side of the Bob Marshall Wilderness.

Exploring the Blackfoot Valley

A little over twenty miles east of Missoula on Hwy-200 is the first notable **BLACKFOOT VALLEY** attraction, the well-preserved ghost town of **Garnet**. The gravel turnoff leading to the town can be tricky, especially in winter, when 4WD is advisable, though the old gold mining town still has enough 100-year-old-plus buildings standing to be worth a quick visit. A number of log buildings have been preserved and two of them can be rented in winter as bases for **cross-country skiing** and **snowshoeing** – call the BLM ☎406/329-3914 for details. There's also an easy half-mile **hike** that climbs up from the town and gives good views over the surrounding Garnet Range.

Another twenty of so miles east is bucolic **Ovando**, most notable for *Trixi's Antler Bar* which you can't miss on the south side of Hwy-200. Don't let the rather macho collection of pickups and bikes outside scare you off as inside you'll find it's a friendly introduction to a "traditional" Western bar. The final place of note along the valley is the rustic little town of **Lincoln**, its pleasant tree-lined main street set beneath thickly timbered hills and mountains. Though it makes a good base for entering the Bob Marshall Wilderness Area to the north (see p.529), Lincoln is better known as the one-time home of the Unabomber Ted Kaczynski, arrested here in 1996. On a more positive note, the town is also the home of Doug Swingley, the only man ever to win four Iditarod sled dog races; you can have a go at **dog sledding** yourself in winter at Montana Mush in Lincoln (☎406/362-4988) for around $30 an hour. Along Hwy-200, the town's main drag, you'll find a supermarket, a couple of outfitters and the friendly *Lost Woodsman Coffee House & Gallery*, which has a homely timbered interior and serves excellent coffee, cakes, sandwiches, and microbrews.

If you're heading onwards to Helena, consider taking the scenic route from here on the mostly unpaved road over **Stemple Pass** (6376ft) which heads south from the center of town and gives you good views across the surrounding Helena National Forest. It's kept open through the winter since there are a number of **cross-country ski trails** running off the pass. Ideally it should be tackled in a 4WD, and in summer it won't take you much longer than the paved road as it's more direct.

The Rocky Mountain Front

Along the **ROCKY MOUNTAIN FRONT**, the mountains suddenly burst up from the plains in an awe-inspiring 1000ft-high, 100-mile-long wall. To the east lies flat, monotonous rangeland given over to natural gas extraction, missile sites, and cattle raising; to the west is a tangled mass of mountains, forests, rivers, and lakes. This is a climatic transition zone, with Chinook winds sweeping east off the Front in winter to bring considerably warmer conditions to the region, meaning it may well be snow-free in early spring, giving earlier access to the mountains for fair-weather hikers.

The only real reason to stick around in the Front's two main towns of **Choteau** and **Augusta**, both strung along Hwy-287, is that they have good access to the Bob Marshall Wilderness to the west (see p.529). Still, tiny Augusta, at the southeast end of the Front, is an attractive town with Western-style architecture and raised sidewalks, and if you choose to stay head for the woodsy *Bunkhouse Inn*, 122 Main St (☎406/562-3387; ❷) where the clean and basic rooms have shared bathrooms. If **camping**, head west out of town from **Augusta Information Station** (☎406/562-3247), a useful source for local information and trail maps, on Manix Street, to the Gibson Reservoir. Here you can camp in a fine location beneath the Front and above the reservoir at *Mortimer Campground* ($7), from where there's a trail into the Bob Marshall Wilderness.

Twenty-six miles northwest of Augusta on US-287, Choteau is an unremarkable ranching town in an area with a remarkable prehistory. In the 1970s, fossilized dinosaur eggs of the species *maiasauras* were discovered at **Egg Mountain** to the south, which apparently proved that dinosaurs were not the cold-blooded killers of myth but actually raised and tended to their offspring. Informative exhibits on this can be found in the **Old Trail Museum**, 823 N Main (May–Sept daily 10am–5pm; free), although they don't compare to the larger exhibits in Bozeman's Museum of the Rockies (see p.465). You can also visit Egg Mountain and take a tour of the 80-million-year-old rock formation where the eggs were found (July–Aug daily 2pm; check with museum to ensure the tour is running). Choteau's other claim to fame is that it was the home of novelist A.B. Guthrie, author of the novel *The Big Sky*, from which Montana derives its evocative nickname; see p.683 on Contexts for a review.

The Mission Valley

Directly north of Missoula on US-93 is the beautiful farming and ranching country of the **MISSION VALLEY**, stretching some thirty miles north to Flathead Lake, with the steep slopes of the jagged Mission Mountains thrusting up in the east. Much of the valley falls within the **Flathead Indian Reservation**, which covers some 1.2 million acres and is home to around 3800 members of the **Salish** and **Kootenai** tribes. The Salish originally resided in the Bitterroot Valley south of Missoula, where they had good relations with white settlers. Indeed, they even offered to defend them if need be against the Nez Percé, who passed through the region in 1877 while fleeing from the US Cavalry (see p.629).

Under pressure from white settlers, the government relocated the Salish in the latter part of the nineteenth century to the present-day reservation. However, non-natives continued to move into the area throughout the twentieth century, so that now only twenty percent of the population within the Flathead Reservation is actually Native American.

If you're looking to do some hiking or fishing on the reservation, head for the 93,000-acre **Mission Mountains Tribal Wilderness** area, the nation's first wilderness preserve on tribal lands. Located on the west side of the Mission Range, you must have a permit for hiking and camping ($6 for three days) and for fishing ($18 – this also includes the southern half of Flathead Lake), available at local sporting goods stores. For more information call the Tribal Recreation Department on ⓣ406/675-2700 ext 356.

Exploring the valley

A few miles northwest of Missoula on I-90, US-93/Hwy-200 branches north and enters the Flathead Reservation at the unremarkable little town of Evaro. Up next is another small town, **Arlee,** worth calling in at during the renowned (and free) **Fourth of July Pow Wow**. The booths selling Native American crafts in the huge encampment of tepees and tents are worth browsing, but it's the impressive displays of traditional dancing and drumming that pull in the crowds.

Five miles north again on US-93 stands the settlement of **St. Ignatius**, founded in 1854 by Jesuit missionaries, and home to the second Catholic mission in Montana. The mission is located west of the highway, and though one of the original log building remains, it's the 1891 redbrick church built alongside that's most worth a look; inside are vivid if unsophisticated frescoes and murals depicting New Testament scenes, painted by the mission cook Brother Joseph Carignano. For **information** on the reservation and around, stop in at Doug Allen's Trading Post (ⓣ406/745-2951) on US-93 to the west of here. Next door there's also the plain but clean *Lodgepole Motel* (ⓣ406/745-9192; ③). Cheaper lodging is available at the *Hostel of the Rockies-St. Ignatius* (ⓣ406/745-3959, ⓦwww.camp-hostel.com/) at the north end of town. Here you can stay in the unusual "Earthship," a partially subterranean bunkhouse constructed of tires, concrete, and cans, for around $12, or pitch a tent ($10; RVs $20).

Though there's a small herd of bison – not buffalo (see box, opposite) – in a paddock close by Doug Allen's Trading Post, save your film to take snaps of the 500 or so that roam freely at the nearby 18,500-acre **National Bison Range** (daily: mid-May to late Oct 8am–8pm; rest of year 8am–4.30pm; $5; ⓣ406/644-2211). To reach the preserve, head south back down US-93 for five miles and then west at the junction with Hwy-212 for about ten miles to the

Bison: what's in a name?

Though **bison** and **buffalo** are often used interchangeably, technically speaking what you'll see throughout the Rockies is a bison. A true buffalo is the water buffalo of Asia or the Cape buffalo of Africa. An amazingly large animal, Bison bulls can weigh up to 2000 pounds, with heavy horns on a huge head, supported by the thick hump of muscle above their shoulders. Their coats are thick and shaggy, even in summer, and in winter they insulate the animal so well that snow settling on their backs doesn't melt. Cows are half the weight of bulls, with smaller horns that may almost meet in the middle, a smaller hump and a smoother coat. Although males are generally the more aggressive, cows can also be dangerous – especially when they have a calf by their side. In either case these are not creatures to mess with, since they can run as fast as a horse when the mood takes them, so give them plenty of space when viewing.

main entrance at Moiese. There's a visitor center here, but the main attraction is the range's three roads, on which you can see the animals in their natural habitat. There are also two short trails from which, besides bison, you may also spot elk, deer, pronghorn antelope, black bear, coyote, and bald eagles. Interestingly, the range owes its start to a Pend d'Oreille Indian named **Walking Coyote**, who brought five orphaned bison here from the plains in 1873. Within a few years, a dozen more bison had been born and he sold them to a pair of ranchers, Michael Pablo and Charles Allard. At this time there were fewer than 1000 bison left in all of North America, and both ranchers succeeded in increasing the size of their herds. Allard eventually sold his bison to Charles Conrad in Kalispell, while Pablo sold his to Canada after the US government showed no interest in purchasing them. The outcry that followed this exportation of one of the last large herds of bison left led to the establishment of this reserve (using Conrad's animals as the nucleus) as well as two others between 1907-09.

North of the range, in **Charlo** (off US-93 on Hwy-212), is the *Branding Iron Bar & Grill* (Ⓣ406/644-9130), famed for hosting the annual **Mission Mountain Testicle Festival** in early June, a raucous affair that combines the consumption of Rocky Mountain oysters with live bands. Things are rather quieter during the rest of the year, but it's still worth popping in for a cool one in down-home surroundings.

Continuing north along US-93 from St. Ignatius you pass **Ninepipe** and **Pablo Reservoirs**, both National Wildlife Refuges that between them cover 4500 acres of water, marsh, and wild-grass habitats that support upwards of 100,000 birds in the fall. There's decent fishing on both lakes; tribal permits are available from sporting goods stores. At the Ninepipe Refuge, you'll also find the small **Ninepipe Museum of Early Montana** (hours vary; $4; Ⓣ406/644-3435), featuring a small but very fine collection of Native American artifacts including some beautiful beadwork, along with a huge stuffed grizzly.

If you're interested in Salish and Kootenai culture, take time to stop off in **Pablo** (five miles north of Ronan on US-93) to view the **Sqelix'u AqtAmak nik Cultural Center** (April–Sept daily 9am–9pm; Oct–March Mon–Fri 9am–5pm; Ⓣ406/675-0610). Fortunately it's known locally as "The People's Center," and inside there are some well-presented exhibitions focusing on Salish and Kootenai culture and a fine store selling books and artwork.

Flathead Lake and around

The rippling waters of **FLATHEAD LAKE** make up the biggest natural body of freshwater west of the Mississippi – 28 miles in length, up to eight miles wide and over 300 feet deep. The Mission Mountains rise dramatically up from the lake's eastern shore, and when they're snow covered, the view of the lake and mountains is a particularly fine sight. The lake is abuzz with activity in summer as people head here to swim, boat, water ski, jet ski, and generally goof off. There are several campgrounds around the lakeshores, and the lake's biggest town of **Polson** on the south shore is the best base, with some decent shops, bars, and restaurants, all making for an agreeable place to hang out for a day or two. At the north end of the lake is the almost unbearably twee **Bigfork**, situated on a pretty bay where the Swan River flows into the lake. Self-consciously rustic and festooned with art galleries and boutiques, Bigfork feels more like northern California than northwest Montana.

Polson

Developed in the early twentieth century, **POLSON's** great attraction is its lakeside location, nicely set off by a number of pleasant parks along the shore that are popular places to hang out and swim in summer. Though getting on Flathead Lake should be your first goal (see box, opposite), there are a couple of museums here worth checking out if the weather turns sour. The **Miracle of America Museum**, on US-93 just south of the junction with Hwy-35 (daily: Mon–Sat 8am–8pm; $3), has a huge assortment of exhibits celebrating all things American. Among the more eclectic are an "antique" snowmobile and a remarkable sheep-powered treadmill; more traditional exhibits include a furnished trapper's cabin, part of a large 26-building pioneer village. Equally jumbled is the **Polson-Flathead Historical Museum**, 704 Main St (June–Aug Mon–Fri 9am– 6pm, Sun noon–6pm; $2), stuffed to the gills with bits of everything, including Calamity Jane's saddle and a seven-foot sturgeon caught in Flathead Lake in 1955.

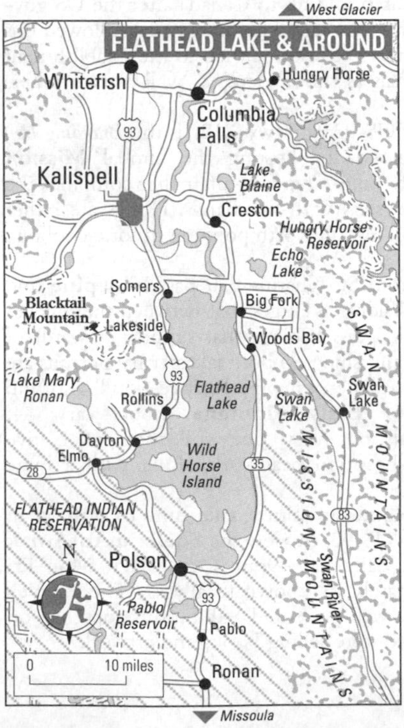

Practicalities

If looking for other things to do around town, call in at **the chamber of commerce** at 302 Main St (Mon–Fri 9am– 5pm; ⓣ406/883-5969, ⓦwww.polsonchamber.com); for outdoor-specific information try Bear Dance, 13 2nd Ave E (ⓣ406/883-1700), which has a good range of maps and guidebooks as well as a wide

Getting onto Flathead Lake

Flathead Lake comes alive in summer, with brightly-colored sailboats plying the waters and kids of all ages splashing about in rowboats, kayaks, and canoes or just swimming from the various beaches. You can **get out onto the lake** at various spots along its shores. The most grandiose option is the fifty-passenger *KwaTaqNuk Princess* (☎406/883-2448) which sails from *KwaTaqNuk Resort*'s marina, just off US-93 in Polson, on three-hour trips daily through the summer, departing at 1.30pm ($20). These head around Wild Horse Island and Bird Island. There are also ninety-minute cruises departing at 10.30am and 7.30pm ($13/$6). Up in Bigfork, groups of up to nine people can rent skippered charter boats for private scenic cruises for $225 half-day, $350 full day from Pointer Scenic Cruises (☎406/837-5617).

Flathead Boat Rentals (☎406/883-3900 or 1-800/358-8046) operate out of both the *KwaTaqNuk Resort*'s marina and Somers Bay and rent out canoes, pedal boats, jet skis, ski boats, and fishing boats. In Bigfork, similar craft are also available from *Marina Cay Resort* (☎406/837-5861) and *Bayview Resort and Marina* (☎406/837-4843). Average half-day rental prices are **paddle boats** $50; **fishing boats** $85; **ski boats** $200; **jet skis** $150; **canoes** $50. A fun way to see the lake is by paddling along all or part of the thirty-mile **Flathead Lake Marine Trail** – call at the Bear Dance (see Polson's "Practicalities") for full details. Bear Dance also rent out sea kayaks for $30 half-day/$50 day.

range of equipment. Of the **motels** in town, the lakeside *Best Western KwaTaqNuq Resort* (☎406/883-3636 or 1-800/882-6363; ⑤) is the biggest and plushest, owned by the Confederated Salish and Kootenai Tribes. Rooms inside are well-appointed and facilities include indoor and outdoor pools, a hot tub, restaurants, and watercraft hire (see box, above). One of the few **B&Bs** in town is the friendly *Swan Hill Bed & Breakfast*, 460 King's Point (☎406/883-5292 or 1-800/537-9489; ⑤), a modern redwood home set in secluded wooded grounds above the lake four miles to the north of Polson. Options include three queen rooms and one twin bedroom with private baths, along with a hot-tub suite; there's an indoor pool, sauna, and large sunny decks from where you should spot deer – and maybe even black bears. For **camping** close to town, the *Polson/Flathead Lake KOA*, a mile north on US-93, is a good bet. Overlooking the lake, tent sites run $16, RV sites $20 and there's a swimming pool, sauna, store, and laundry.

If you're **eating** out, one of the best choices is the *Rancho Deluxe Supper Club*, 602 6th St W (☎406/883-2300), overlooking the Flathead River. The restaurant does good steaks, pastas, and pizzas for around $10–15 – reservations are advised. In the middle of town, check out the popular *Watusi Café*, 318 Main St (☎406/883-6200), for tasty soups and sandwiches, for under $10, while just along the road is the attractive *Old Mill Place*, no. 501 (☎406/892-1490), where you can enjoy breakfast bagels, sandwiches, and ice cream on a sunny deck.

The western shore

US-93 winds along the lake's undulating western shoreline, offering wonderful views east to the Mission Mountains at just about every point. Just north of Polson, the conical **Wild Horse Island** rises up from the waters. It's home to not just wild horses but also bighorn sheep, ospreys, and bald eagles. You can rent a boat out to the day-use only island from Big Arm Resort and Marina (☎406/849-5622) for around $30 per day, and there's also a busy campground here ($11) and a small grocery store. The resort is thirteen miles north of Polson on US-93.

On the northwest shore, the pleasingly located small town of **Lakeside** marks the turnoff for the half-hour drive to the Blacktail Ski Area (see below). A few miles north, tucked into the northwest corner of Flathead Lake, is the old lumber town of **Somers**. Though a good place to pull over to spot osprey soaring over the lake, the town is most notable for a fine B&B and a pair of good restaurants, all good choices if you value peace over the hubbub of nearby Bigfork (see below). The *Osprey Inn*, about a mile south of town at 5557 US-93 (Ⓣ406/857-2042 or 1-800/258-2042; ❻), has a superb waterside location and three attractive guestrooms. There are canoes and a rowing shell for guest's use, plus a hot tub and a picturesque deck for breakfast. Within walking distance of the inn is the lakeside *Montana Grill* (Ⓣ406/857-3889), one of the best restaurants in the area. Check out the fresh mesquite-grilled fish or the juicy steaks, served up in a relaxed, easy-going atmosphere with superb lake and mountain views from the dining room. Look at paying $20–25 for dinner. Somewhat less pricey is *Tiebecker's Pub and Eatery*, 75 Somers Rd (Ⓣ406/857-3335), located in the atmospheric Victorian Somers Lumber Co. building. The menu here has an Italian flavor and a dinner will set you back around $15.

Blacktail Mountain Ski Area

Fourteen miles inland from Lakeside is the small **Blacktail Mountain Ski Area** (Dec–April Wed–Sun 9.30am–4.30pm and holidays; Ⓣ406/844-0999, Ⓦwww.blacktailmountain.com), where the mountain's northern exposure means that it sometimes has better snow than its larger neighbor Big Mountain. Either way, great views across Flathead Lake to the Mission and Whitefish Ranges are guaranteed. Average annual snowfall is 250 inches, and the mountain has 1440ft of vertical drop from a summit of 6676ft. There are 24 runs, served by three chairs and a tow. The breakdown of the runs is fifteen percent beginner, seventy percent intermediate, and fifteen percent advanced, plus there's a fun terrain park and a recently developed thirty-acre glade skiing area. There's a lodge at the top of the mountain with a lounge, two restaurants, rental, and day-care facilities. Lift tickets are a reasonable $25. There's also a system of **cross-country ski trails** below the mountain, but only the easiest trails are groomed.

The eastern shore

The quickest way of getting to the north end of Flathead Lake is along Hwy-35 beside the lake's eastern shore. In the southern reaches the steep, heavily timbered slopes of the Mission Mountains rise dramatically up from the lakeside. Cherry orchards crowd the narrow valley floor, making any drive through here in spring when the trees are in blossom particularly worthwhile.

There are few settlements of any size between Polson and Big Fork along the east shore, but there are a few **campgrounds**, though they're no secret and can be noisy in summer. At the southeastern end of the lake is the **Finley Point State Recreation Area**, four miles east of Hwy-35 and set amongst cherry, pine, and fir trees on Finley Point. Camping here costs $11, and there's a $4 day-use fee allowing you to hike around the promontory and swim off the beaches. Midway up the east shore is the picturesque Yellow Bay State Recreation Area which is a good spot for swimming and camping ($11).

Bigfork

Quaint **Bigfork**, located at the north end of Flathead Lake, has a fine Christmas lights display which brings color to the town in the depths of winter, but it really comes alive during the warmer summer months. Indeed, the population of around 3000 easily doubles during the high season thanks to the town's vice-like embrace of tourism. Though watersports play a part, an equally big draw is the chichi atmosphere engendered by art galleries (there are fourteen in just a few blocks of the small downtown area) and upmarket restaurants and boutiques within spitting distance of the Mission and Swan Ranges.

The small downtown area is centered on Electric Avenue, with the Swan River flowing just to the south and east and opening up into a wide and busy bay in the lake's northeast corner. Most of the **galleries** are here, as is the **Bigfork Art & Cultural Center**, no. 525 (daily 9am–5pm; free; ⓣ406/837-6927), which exhibits the work of Montana artists and has a decent gift shop featuring work by artists and craftspeople from around the state. The town is also known for the productions of the **Bigfork Summer Playhouse** (ⓣ406/837-4886) 526 Electric Ave, a number of whose actors have gone on to play on Broadway. Tickets for shows (which are generally classic Broadway musicals and run Mon–Sat evenings throughout the summer) cost around $20.

If you're looking to escape the slightly precious atmosphere, head for either the lake or the nearby Jewel Basin (see box, below). If you choose the former, you can hang out and swim at **Wayfarers State Park** ($4; shady camping sites $8) a quarter-mile south of town, or head out onto the water using a local rental outfit (see box p.525). For maps and advice on local hiking, biking, and camping visit the **Flathead National Forest Office** off Holt Drive (ⓣ406/837-7500).

If **staying over**, the best choice around is the *Coyote Roadhouse Inn*, seven miles east on the Swan River at 603 Three Eagle Lane (ⓣ406/837-4250; ❻). Here you'll find six large, opulently furnished suites, two with hot tubs, along with fine Italian cuisine at the inn's *Roadhouse Restaurant*. A cheaper option is the *Bigfork Timber Motel*, 8540 Hwy-35 (ⓣ406/837-6200 or 1-800/821-4546; ❹), with forty well-appointed rooms and a hot tub and sauna. Bigfork is known for having some of the best **restaurants** in Montana. For a casual lunchtime atmosphere, try the outside deck at the *Village Well*, River Street

Hiking in the Jewel Basin

The **Jewel Basin Hiking Area** just northeast of Bigfork is a designated backcountry hiking area of over 15,000 acres, sprinkled with nearly thirty clear alpine lakes, fresh mountain streams, densely timbered slopes, and craggy peaks rising to over 7000 feet. All of this is connected by over thirty miles of easily accessible hiking trails, which in winter can also be used for cross-country skiing and snowshoeing. One of the most popular trails leads to **Crater Lake**, a twelve-mile round trip from the main parking lot, well marked from Forest Road 5392 to the northeast of Echo Lake, itself northeast of Big Fork off Hwy-83. The route climbs around 1000 feet and skirts through wildflower meadows beneath Mount Aeneas (7528ft) along Trail 68 then Trail 7, passing Birch Lake and Squaw Lake before heading through thick forest and meadows down to the rocky basin of Crater Lake. There's a free USFS campsite here, but be aware that black and grizzly bears are known to inhabit the area. Anglers should also note that the lakes here make for some of the finest high-mountain **fishing** in the region.

To get to Jewel Basin from Bigfork take Hwy-83 east out of town for two miles, turn north onto Echo Lake Road then after two miles turn right on Jewel Basin Road (Forest Road 5392) for the seven-mile drive to the trailheads. You can also access the area from Hungry Horse Reservoir to the northeast from West Side South Fork Road (Forest Road 895) from Hungry Horse Dam. To obtain a map of the Jewel Basin Hiking Area ($2), stop by the USFS office in Bigfork (see above).

(☎406/837-5251), where you'll find good pizza and sandwiches for $7–15. For dinner, the *Showthyme Restaurant*, 548 Electric Ave (☎406/837-0707), is set in an old bank next to the Playhouse and has a wide range of pasta, steak, and chicken dishes for around $15.

The Seeley-Swan Valley and Bob Marshall Wilderness Area

The stunning **Seeley-Swan Valley**, hemmed in by the 9000ft Swan Range and the equally lofty Mission Mountains, is bisected by Hwy-83, which runs its ninety-mile length from Bigfork in the north to the Blackfoot Valley in the south. In the valley, a string of lakes that are important wildfowl habitats are connected by the Swan and Clearwater rivers, giving anglers and canoeists plenty to go at. The **Bob Marshall Wilderness Area** in the Swan Range and the **Mission Mountains Wilderness** to the west safeguard alpine landscapes that are easily accessed off Hwy-83, yet all but the most popular trails remain quite lightly used. Indeed, if the better-known Glacier National Park to the north seems too busy, these two regions are worth considering as alternative hiking and backpacking venues.

Exploring the Seeley-Swan Valley

Heading south on Hwy-83 from Bigfork, with the bulky western front of the Swan Range bearing down above your left shoulder, you'll soon come across **Swan Lake**. At its north end the well-signposted **Swan River National Wildlife Refuge**, worth the time to tread gently along the refuge's trails, carefully looking out for a whole heap of wildlife that ranges from Canada geese to bald eagles and elk to moose. There's also a USFS campground ($7) at Swan Lake Recreation Area on the east side of Hwy-83 which has a pleasant swimming beach.

Some 35 miles further south sits **Holland Lake**, a popular access point for the Bob Marshall Wilderness (see opposite). The lake alone is worth a visit for its impressive alpine surroundings, and there's a busy and attractive USFS campground here ($11). Indoor accommodation is available at the rough-hewn but charming seventy-year-old *Holland Lake Lodge* (☎406/754-2282 or 1-800/648-8858, ⓦwww.hollandlakelodge.com; ❺), which offers both very basic rooms and cabins in a lovely lakefront setting, and also serves excellent lunch and dinner. The lodge rents out canoes ($5 per hour) and has cross-country ski and snowmobile trails in winter.

Continuing south down Hwy-83, you'll see a chain of small, pretty lakes on your west before arriving at the woodsy one-street town of **Seeley Lake**, sitting on the southeast shore of its eponymous lake. As the largest town in the valley, it's a good place to stock up on supplies and information before heading into the nearby wilds. For maps and general outdoor advice, stop by the **Seeley Lake Ranger Station**, three miles north of town on Hwy-83 (Mon–Fri 8am–5pm; ☎406/677-2233), where there's a frightening-looking stuffed grizzly to greet you at the entrance. The valley's only supermarket is Wold's Valley Market (☎406/677-2121), located on Hwy-83 at the south end of town. To see the best of Seeley Lake's watery world, paddle the 3.5-mile **Clearwater Canoe Trail** which is accessed four miles north of town and meanders gently along, allowing close-up views of the rich wildfowl populations. It's an easy one-mile hike back to the put-in from the end of the trail, and canoes can be rented from All Sports Rentals (Ⓣ406/677-6050) downtown. **Anglers** will find bass and rainbow trout in Seeley Lake, and Salmon Lake to the south is good for both kokanee salmon as well as trout.

Mission Mountains Wilderness Area

To the northwest of Seeley Lake is the 73,000-acre **Mission Mountains Wilderness Area**, an untamed landscape of snowcapped mountains, small glaciers, alpine lakes, and thick forests of pine, larch, fir, and cedar. It's also an important wildlife habitat, home to all of the northern Rockies' usual suspects – black and grizzly bears, elk and deer, mountain goat and lion, and a few gray wolves. The area borders in the west on the Mission Mountains Tribal Wilderness, for which a $6 permit must be acquired (see p.522).

This region is relatively lightly used – indeed, it wasn't even mapped until 1922 – and there are around 45 miles of maintained **trails** here, mostly used by backpackers rather than horsepackers on account of their generally steep and rugged nature. The southern area is the steepest and most visited corner, with the easiest **access** located six miles south of the hamlet of Condon, mid-way between Swan Lake and Seeley Lake – head west off Hwy-83 along Kraft Creek Road (Forest Road 561), at the end of which is the head of Trail 690. From here, you can take an easy 2.5-mile round-trip hike up to **Glacier Lake**, periodically stocked with cutthroat trout, for fine views of the region's jagged peaks. A more strenuous option is the eighteen-mile round trip to the beautiful **Mollman Lakes**, though it involves hacking your way along poorly maintained trails through grizzly country – compass and map-reading skills are a must. The unmarked trailhead is at the end of Forest Road 10291 off Hwy-83 to the south of Swan Lake, and follows trails 300 and 301. Stop by the Seeley Lake Ranger Station (see opposite) to pick up the essential wilderness area map ($3).

The Bob Marshall Wilderness Area

The **BOB MARSHALL WILDERNESS AREA** is an almost perfectly preserved mountain ecosystem, a remote landscape that holds all of natural Montana's greatest hits – coniferous forests, clear alpine lakes, cascading waterfalls, and brightly colored wildflower meadows. It's also home to every species of mammal indigenous to the northern Rockies other than bison and woodland caribou, and there's as good a chance here as anywhere in Montana of spotting black and grizzly bears, mountain goats, bighorn sheep, and elk. Adjoining the "Bob" to the north is the **Great Bear Wilderness Area**, which runs to the southern boundary of Glacier National Park, while to the south is the **Scapegoat Wilderness**, extending as far as Hwy-200. Running sixty miles along the Continental Divide, between them they make up the second-largest wilderness area in the lower 48 at a massive 1.5 million acres in size, second only to Idaho's Frank Church-River of No Return Wilderness.

The entire area is interwoven by over 3200 miles of **trails** (see box, overleaf), creating a haven for backpackers, horsepackers, and, in the fall, hunters. The trails become less managed as you get deeper into the wilderness, and some of the more easily accessed trails show signs of overuse, so if you can, literally, try and get off the beaten path. As a wilderness area, all vehicles are prohibited.

For more **information** on the Bob Marshall Wilderness contact Seeley Lake Ranger Station (see opposite), Hungry Horse Ranger Station, Hwy-2, Hungry Horse (Ⓣ406/387-3000), or the Rocky Mountain Ranger District, 1102 Main Ave NW, Choteau (Ⓣ406/466-5341).

Accessing the "Bob"

You don't need a permit to hike or camp in the wilderness area unless you're hunting or fishing. There are no designated pitches, and **backcountry camping** is limited to fourteen days at the same site. It goes without saying that

Hiking in the Bob Marshall Wilderness Area

You can't hope to see more than a fraction of the vast terrain that makes up the "Bob" unless you plan on **hiking** for several weeks. While that's not feasible for most, all of the hikes described below can be continued into the wilderness area on connecting trails if you have the time.

Sapphire Lake Trail twelve-mile round trip. A popular and marvelously varied hike just outside the western edge of the "Bob" that passes waterfalls thundering down the steep slopes of the Swan Range, follows the shores of deep-blue alpine lakes, and gives spectacular mountain views. The trailhead is at the north end of Holland Lake, some 24 miles northeast of Seeley Lake, and follows trails 415 and 35 out and trails 110, 42, and 415 back. This can be made into an easy overnight trip by camping at Sapphire Lake, but be prepared for the mosquitoes.

Heart Lake eight-mile round trip. At the southern end of the wilderness area is this very popular and relatively easy hike on Trail 481 leading past Lone Mountain (6773ft) to the shores of picturesque Heart Lake. The trailhead is along Copper Creek Road (Forest Road 330), five miles east of Lincoln, then after around eight miles turn right on Forest Road 1882 to Indian Meadows Trailhead.

Mount Wright five-mile round trip. On the east side of the Bob Marshall Wilderness, the quite strenuous hike (3500 feet of ascent) on Trail 169 up 8855ft Mt Wright provides stunning views that take in Glacier, the Scapegoat Wilderness, and the plains to the east. Head four miles north of Choteau on Hwy-89 to Forest Road 144, which you then follow west for 25 miles to the trailhead located just past the West Fork Ranger Station.

South Fork Trail twelve-mile round trip. This six-mile steep climb up to Prairie Reef is worthwhile for the fantastic views of the 100ft Chinese Wall, and it also takes you deep into the wildlife-rich Sun River Game Preserve. To get to the trailhead head west out of Augusta on Manix Street to Gibson Reservoir – the trail starts from the reservoir's west end.

Great Northern Mountain eight-mile round trip. The Great Bear Wilderness can be accessed on a truly spectacular eight-mile hike up Great Northern (8705ft). You need to be comfortable scrambling along exposed mountain ridges to enjoy this route, which climbs up above the timberline and small Stanton Glacier to give fantastic views north towards Glacier National Park. To reach the trailhead drive from Hungry Horse on the East Side Hungry Horse Reservoir Road for about nine miles to the Emery Bay turnoff, where you turn east on Forest Road 1048 for half a mile; park up at Hungry Horse Creek. From here you follow a primitive trail through dense undergrowth and huckleberry patches (beware of bears) before emerging onto the left-hand ridge up Great Northern, following cairns to the summit.

Horsepacking

Horsepacking is a popular way of seeing the Bob Marshall Wilderness, and there are several outfitters close by that will either guide you or rent out horses. Prices are generally around $200 per day for guided trips. A good choice is *White Tail Ranch Outfitters* in the hamlet of Ovando (see p.520; ⓣ406/793-5666 or 1-800/987-5666), which is good for accessing the south end of the Scapegoat/"Bob." An alternative to horses is llama packing – try this with *Great Northern Llama Co.*, 600 Blackmer Lane, Columbia Falls (ⓣ406/755-9044, ⓦwww.gnllama.com). They charge around $185 per person per day for a standard four-day trip.

backpackers should practice a "Leave no Trace" policy; for more details on backcountry camping see p.50. But while you don't need a permit, you'll most definitely need a good **map**. Those entering the area from the east should get hold of the USGS *Lewis and Clark National Forest – Rocky Mountain Division* map; hikers coming in from any other direction need the USGS *Bob Marshall, Great Bear and Scapegoat Wilderness Complex*. Each cost $6 and can be bought at most local bookstores, outfitters, and ranger stations.

If heading in from the wilderness area's **west** side, the easiest access is from Pyramid Pass near Seeley Lake, from where a trailhead leads to the headwaters of the South Fork of the Flathead. This is reached along Cottonwood Lakes Road (to the north of town) then left onto Morrel Road for six miles, and right onto Pyramid Pass Road for six miles to the trailhead. You can also enter from Holland Lake (see p.528) via Gordon Pass. Both these approach routes are steep hikes.

From the **east** the best access – and along gentler gradients than the west side – is from Benchmark Trailhead to the west of Augusta, or just north of this from Gibson Reservoir. The approaches here give excellent views of the **Chinese Wall**, a 1000ft-high, 22-mile-long limestone escarpment. From Choteau, you can enter the wilderness from the trailhead at the end of South Fork Road, which is accessed from a turnoff on Hwy-89 four miles north of town.

On the area's **northern** side, there are trailheads into the Great Bear Wilderness from the Spotted Bear Ranger Station at the south end of Hungry Horse Reservoir. Finally, from the **south** you can access the Scapegoat Wilderness from trailheads off Hwy-200, the easiest being from Heart Lake, reached from Indian Meadows Trailhead along Forest Road 330, a few miles north of Lincoln (see p.520).

Kalispell

The biggest town north of Missoula and a commercial hub for the surrounding region, busy **KALISPELL** (pop. c. 17,000) is situated eight miles north of Flathead Lake and is a popular base for approaching Glacier National Park. Neither Kalispell nor its location are as pretty as smaller Whitefish (see p.534) to the north though, and the constant flow of traffic through the center of town along with a bland strip of hotels, gas stations and car dealers either side of downtown add nothing to the appeal.

The town was settled by entrepreneur Charles Conrad with his Blackfoot wife in 1891 at the same time as the arrival of the Great Northern Railroad. Prior to this, local communications had been via steamboats on Flathead Lake to the south – once the railway arrived, the town they served, Demersville, simply upped and moved four miles east to the rail tracks and became Kalispell. Conrad's time in the town is remembered at the 1895 **Conrad Mansion**, 330 Woodland Ave (May 15–Oct 15 daily 9am–8pm; $7; ⓣ406/755-2166). The architectural style is similar to that of the Glacier Park lodges, and guides in period clothing offer one-hour tours of the 26-room house. Highlights include colorful Tiffany windows, ornate sleigh-style beds and marble bathrooms, and, rare at the time, an elevator and intercom system.

Many of the buildings along Main Street, such as the *Kalispell Grand Hotel*, were erected around the same time as Conrad Mansion and have attractive early twentieth-century facades. A good number are now occupied by a mixed bag of art galleries and antique shops, but one place for art where quality is guaran-

△ A large bull elk "bugles" for a potential mate

Local outfitters

Bike Rite 110 E Idaho ⓣ406/756-0053. Mountain-bike sales and rental plus good local trail knowledge. Bike rental starts at around $25 a day.

Rocky Mountain Outfitters 135 Main St ⓣ406/752-2446. A good selection of quality outdoor and camping equipment.

Sportsman & Skihaus corner of US-2 and US-93 ⓣ406/755-6484. Open seven days a week and stocks a comprehensive selection of camping, fishing, skiing, and kayaking gear.

teed is the **Hockaday Center for the Arts**, 2nd Avenue E and 3rd Street E (Tues and Thurs–Sat 10am–5pm, Wed 10am–8pm; free; ⓣ406/755-5268). The center is renowned for contemporary work by local artists and for an excellent exhibit of modern expressionism featuring work by giants such as Willem de Kooning and Jackson Pollock – along with a canvas by actor Robert DeNiro.

Arrival, information, and accommodation

Intermountain Transport (ⓣ406/705-4011) operates a daily **bus** service to and from Whitefish, Missoula, Helena, Bozeman, and Seattle from the depot at 15 13th St E. You can get information on the limited number of local attractions from the **chamber of commerce** on the corner of Main and Center streets (ⓣ406/752-6166). For information on the Bob Marshall Wilderness, call in at the Flathead National Forest Headquarters, 1935 3rd Ave E (Mon–Fri 8am–4.30pm; ⓣ406/752-6956) to the south of downtown.

As a base for getting out into the surrounding mountains, Kalispell has a decent selection of reasonably priced accommodation. However, the proximity to Glacier can mean these fill quickly in summer, so it's wise to make reservations. The town's busy **campgrounds** are RV-oriented and probably won't appeal much to tent campers. One mile east of town on Hwy-35 is the *Glacier Pines RV Campground* (ⓣ406/752-2760), with 75 tent sites ($13) plus RV sites for $19. Just east of the junction of US-2 and US-93 is the *Greenwood Village Campground* (ⓣ406/257-7719), with both tent sites ($13) and RV sites ($20) in a rather drab location.

Hotels and motels

Aero Inn 1830 US-93 S ⓣ406/755-3798 or 1-800/843-6114, ⓦwww.aeroinn.com. Reasonable value motel rooms with queen beds, some with kitchenettes, plus free continental breakfast, indoor pool, sauna, and hot tub. ④

Cavanaugh's West Coast Kalispell Center 20 N Main St ⓣ406/752-6660 or 1-800/843-4667. One of the best-appointed hotels in town with fair-sized rooms and queen beds plus a restaurant, indoor pool, sauna, and hot tub. It's usually busy with tour groups so reservations are recommended. ⑥

Hilltop Inn 801 E Idaho St ⓣ406/755-4455. Clean, comfortable, reasonably good-value rooms with queen beds, convenient for US-2 and Hwy-35 but also close to parkland and within walking distance of downtown. ③

Kalispell Grand Hotel 100 Main St ⓣ406/755-8100 or 1-800/858-7422. A characterful refurbished 1909 hotel, which has kept much of its original decor except in the rooms – however, these have been very nicely refurbished and are large and airy with queen beds and quite luxurious bathrooms. Extras include free continental breakfast. The hotel also has a casino, two restaurants, and a beautiful old lounge. ⑤

Motel 6 1540 US-93 S ⓣ406/752-6355. Located at the south end of town this is one of the best budget options in town. Recently renovated with large, bright rooms with queen beds, TV, and coffee-making, plus a heated outdoor pool. ③

Eating and drinking

Café Max 121 Main St ☎406/755-7687. One of the best restaurants in town with a fine and ever-changing range of game dishes, seafood, and very good veal from around $18, plus superb desserts, all served in an elegant and intimate atmosphere.

DG Barley's Brewhouse & Grill corner of US-2 and US-93 ☎406/756-2222. A large, bright and busy bar and restaurant serving a wide range of microbrews and wines along with tasty ribs, steak and pizzas. There's also a gambling lounge.

Montana Coffee Traders 326 W Center St ☎406/756-2326. The best place in town for simple sandwiches or for a pastry and cup of coffee.

Sawbuck Saloon, Casino and Restaurant 1301 US-93 S ☎406/755-4778. Open for breakfast, lunch and dinner, and serving good steaks and better burgers from $10 up in a lively if not very sophisticated atmosphere (there are 23 TVs in the place). Happy hour is from 4.30–6.30pm, and the *Sawbuck* is convenient if you're lodging on the south side of town.

Whitefish

WHITEFISH is easily one of the coolest towns in the Rockies. Set beside **Whitefish Lake** and near **Big Mountain**, one of Montana's finest ski resorts, not to mention Glacier National Park only twenty-five miles away, the attractive Western-style downtown area bustles with a young, outdoor-oriented population. Little wonder then that this former logging town is rapidly becoming one of the most desirable places in the state to relocate, and the rising prices of everything from property to dining out reflect this.

There was no permanent white settlement in this area until 1883, prior to which fur trappers and loggers had passed through the region only on occasion. Things took off with the arrival in 1894 of the Great Northern Railway, and the town developed so quickly that the streets remained spiked with tree stumps where the original forest had been quickly cut down – hence it's early nickname of "Stumptown."

Arrival and information

Whitefish sits astride US-93, which rolls into town from Kalispell thirteen miles south. Rimrock Bus Service (☎406/862-6700) operate a daily **bus** service to and from Kalispell and Missoula from Your C-Stop gas station, 403 2nd St. Glacier Park International **Airport** (☎406/257-9994) is midway between Kalispell and Whitefish on US-2 and is served by Big Sky, Delta, Horizon, and United Express. Note that the "international" tag only comes from the fact that you can fly to Canada from here. The airport **shuttle** (☎406/752-2842) costs $15 to both Kalispell and Whitefish.

Amtrak's Empire Builder **train** service operates from the picturesque depot at the north end of Central Avenue (☎406/862-2268), the busiest stop between Seattle and Minneapolis. It has a service to Chicago in the east (arriving 9.20pm) and Portland in the west (arriving 7.15am). The latter stops off in West Glacier in Glacier National Park ($15 round-trip) and leaves daily at 7.35am.

Information is available from the **chamber of commerce** (June–Aug Mon–Fri 8am–6pm; rest of year 9am–5.30pm; ☎406/862-3501 or 1-877/862-3548), located in the Whitefish Mountain Mall to the south of town on US-93, and from a small counter in the railway depot (see above). The **Tally Lake Ranger Station** (Mon–Fri 8am–4.30pm; ☎406/862-2508), one mile west of town on US-93, is the best source of information on outdoor recreation.

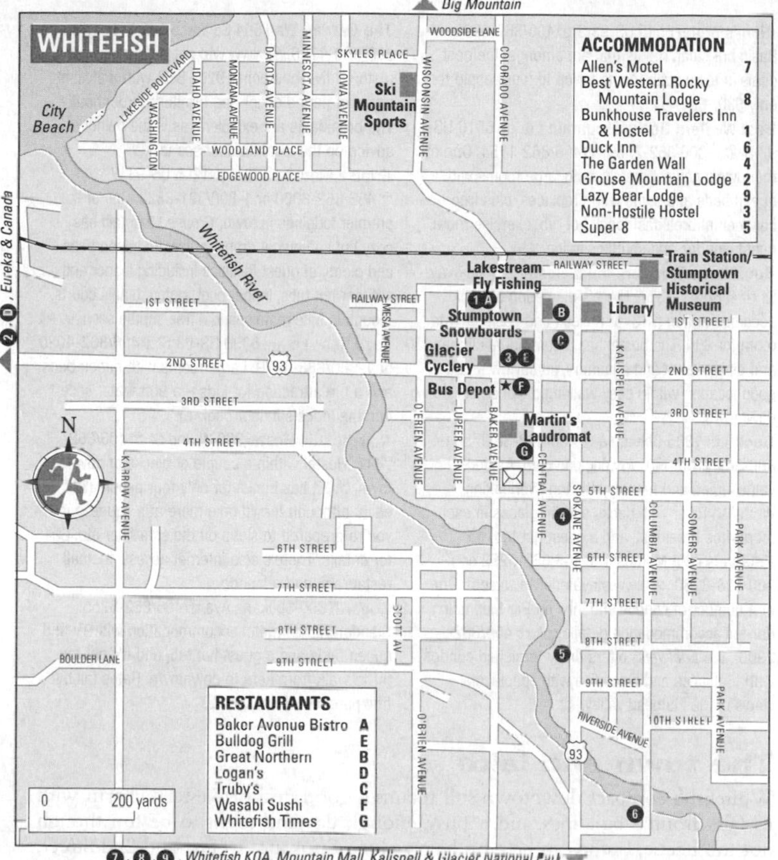

Accommodation

Because of the town's popularity, **hotel** and **motel** rooms can fill up quickly. Making matters worse, there's relatively little accommodation in the downtown area of town – most is to the south on US-93, so be prepared to walk or drive into town unless you book far in advance. A bright spot though is the town's **hostel** scene; a rare commodity in Montana, Whitefish has two of them.

There are no **campgrounds** within walking distance of downtown, and as with everything else they tend to fill up quickly, so reservations are recommended. The closest are at **Whitefish Lake State Park** ($4 day-use fee), two miles west of town on US-93. The sites ($11) here can be noisy (trains run close to the campground) and facilities are fairly basic – toilets, water, a swimming beach, and boat launch – but overall it's a friendly place. Four miles south of town on US-93 is the *Whitefish KOA* (☎406/862-4242 or 1-800/562-8734), where there are fifteen wooded tent sites ($18) and RV sites ($25) along with a store, hot showers, laundry, and popular evening barbecues.

Allen's Motel 6540 US-93 S ⓣ406/862-3995. Basic but clean rooms that are amongst the best deals in town, with rooms for up to four people for only $80. ❹

Best Western Rocky Mountain Lodge 6510 US-93 S ⓣ1-800/862-2569, ⓕ406/862-1154. One of the town's newest motels, with large rooms with queen beds and some with fireplaces, plus free continental breakfast, pool, hot tub, exercise room, guest laundry, and shuttle service. ❻

Bunkhouse Travelers Inn & Hostel 217 Railway St ⓣ406/862-3377. There's the option of bunk accommodation ($13) or a clean and basic private room for $30. The hostel has a communal kitchen and dining room and a laundry, no curfew and a good location within easy walking distance of downtown.

Duck Inn 1305 Columbia ⓣ406/862-3825 or 1-800/344-2377, ⓦwww.duckinn.com. A good-value, quiet, and friendly little inn overlooking Whitefish River with decks and fireplaces in each room, free breakfast, and a guest hot tub. ❹

Edelweiss Big Mountain ⓣ406/862-5252 or 1-800/228-8260, ⓦwww.stayatedelweiss.com. One of a number of condos and inns on Big Mountain (for full accommodation details call ⓣ406/862-2900), the *Edelweiss* offers finely furnished condos with fireplaces and balconies with spectacular views of the Flathead Valley. ❻

The Garden Wall 504 Spokane Ave ⓣ1-888/530-1700, ⓦwww.wtp.net/go/gardenwall. A restored five-bedroom 1920s B&B with a stylish range of period decor and furniture throughout. The breakfasts are excellent, as is the owner's advice on the local outdoor scene. ❺

Grouse Mountain Lodge 1205 US-93 W ⓣ406/862-3000 or 1-800/321-8822. One of the premier lodgings in town, *Grouse Mountain* has cozy but somewhat drab rooms with queen beds and plenty of guest facilities including indoor and outdoor hot tubs, indoor pool, sauna, tennis courts, mountain bike rentals, and a free shuttle service. ❼

Lazy Bear Lodge 6390 US-93 S ⓣ406/862-4020 or 1-800/888-4479. Large rooms with queen beds and a big attraction for kids – a 90ft water slide into the lodge's indoor pool. ❹

Non-Hostile Hostel 300 W 2nd St ⓣ406/862-7447. Hostel within a couple of blocks of downtown, but it has bunks for only four people ($15 each) although they'll take more at a squeeze if you're prepared to sleep on the sofa/floor etc. Call for details. There's also internet access, a small restaurant, and a laundry.

Super 8 800 Spokane Ave ⓣ406/862-8255. Standard chain motel accommodation with TV and queen beds and a guest hot tub, and it's not too far to walk from here to downtown. Rates fall by fifty percent off-season. ❺

The town and lake

Whitefish's compact downtown still retains a good deal of Western charm with its false-fronted buildings, and is busy enough day and night to be fun though not too hectic. Traffic can be a bit heavy along Spokane Avenue and 2nd Street, and there's a constant movement of freight trains through the town, but this adds to the buzz rather than detracts. At the north end of downtown, take a few minutes out to peek around the **Stumptown Historical Museum** (daily 9am–5pm; free), set in the elegant 1927 Great Northern depot. Inside are some fascinating black-and-white photos of the railway, Whitefish, and Big Mountain's early days. Just south of here on Central Avenue is the contemporary glass and stainless steel facade of the **Great Northern Brewing Co.** (Mon–Fri: winter 3–7pm; summer noon–6pm; ⓣ406/863-1000), where you can sample the wares for free – check out the award-winning Black Star Golden Lager or the smooth Snow Ghost Winter Lager, brewed with a touch of chocolate malt.

Beyond an understated **Frank Lloyd Wright**-designed office building between 3rd and 4th streets on Central Avenue, there are few other sites worth visiting. This won't worry most, though, as this is first and foremost a town to base yourself for outdoor action. The closest spot to do so is **Whitefish Lake**, which offers a chance to cool off in summer, when it's alive with the activity of swimmers and canoeists close to shore and boaters and wakeboarders out in deeper waters. Sandy **City Beach** at the south end of the lake, and less than five-minute's drive northeast of downtown, is the most accessible stretch of lakeshore – there are diving pontoons just offshore and lifeguards as well. The busy **Whitefish Lake State Recreation Area** ($4) four miles west of town and set amongst pines that come down to the water's edge is also worth a call, and there's a boat launch here if you want to head out to a quiet nook on the lake somewhere. You can **rent** watercraft from Whitefish Lake Lodge, 1400 Wisconsin Ave (Ⓣ1-800/735-8869); ski boats go for $70 an hour, jet skis are $52, fishing boats $35 (two hours), sea kayaks $15, and canoes $12. The best **fishing** on the lake is for whitefish, mackinaw, and cutthroat trout.

Big Mountain Ski and Summer Resort

Big Mountain (Ⓣ406/862-1900, snow report Ⓣ406/862-SNOW, Ⓦwww.skiwhitefish.com) is by far northern Montana's biggest and best year-round mountain resort. Even if you don't intend to ski, hike, or bike here, consider taking the twenty-minute drive up from town to enjoy the lift-assisted visit to 7000ft Summit House – the views of the Flathead Valley and the rugged peaks of Glacier National Park are nothing short of magnificent.

In winter, the mountain averages 335 inches of snow, blanketing some 3000 acres of skiable terrain with a maximum vertical drop of 2500ft. Eight chairlifts and three surface tows access nearly eighty marked runs (broken down as 25 percent beginner, 50 percent intermediate, and 25 percent advanced) and there's also a half-pipe, boardercross run, and freestyle jumping area to go at. Beginners will enjoy the long and winding Home Again or the more challenging traverse of Russ's Street; good intermediate runs include the wide Inspiration and Goat Haunt on the North Side of the mountain. Advanced skiers and boarders should seek out Schmidt's Chutes, running through the trees, and the experts will revel in the steep launch into Bighorn on the North Side. Other attractions in winter include lift-serviced **tubing** and over ten miles of **cross-country skiing** at Big Mountain Nordic Center, just below the main parking lot (Ⓣ406/862-2946; $5).

Lift tickets cost $44, and there's night skiing ($12) until 9pm Wednesday through Saturday. Ski and board rentals and lessons are available from the base of the mountain, and there's a daily shuttle service to and from Whitefish which runs from 7am–10pm. Facilities on the mountain are excellent – there are ten restaurants and bars, the most popular being the *Hell Roaring Saloon* (Ⓣ406/862-6364) which has a good range of beers and decent pub grub dinners for around $10–15.

In **summer**, the Glacier Chaser lift ($12.75 one-way/$17.75 full day) remains open allowing access to twenty miles of **mountain bike** and **hiking** trails. The bike routes incorporate some brilliant trails, including a great eight-mile single-track climb to the summit designed with a gentle gradient that allows you to ride it all the way, and the descent back down is as good as it gets. Full-suspension bikes can be rented on the mountain from $35 a day.

Eating and drinking

Whitefish is the best small town in Montana for **eating** and **drinking**, with a wide range of restaurants and bars packed into the downtown area. Be warned, though, that most places are busy, especially at weekends and holidays, so you may need to reserve a table.

Baker Ave Bistro 10 Baker Ave Ⓣ406/862-6383. A popular breakfast spot for bagels, omelettes, and coffee before heading up to Big Mountain.

Bulldog Grill 144 Central Ave Ⓣ406/862-5601. A friendly atmosphere, fine local beers and large, filling burgers make this a good place to hang out if you're not looking for anything sophisticated – both the male and female bathrooms contain a large collection of centerfolds.

Great Northern Bar & Grill 27 Central Ave Ⓣ406/862-2816. A great place to meet folks out to have a good time and drink plenty of beer. A

Local outfitters

Glacier Cyclery 336 E 2nd St ⓣ406/862-6446. An excellent bike shop where you can get maps of local mountain-bike trails and join the Monday night rides which depart from the store at 6.30pm. They also rent bikes from around $25 per day.

Lakestream Fly Fishing Shop 15 Central Ave ⓣ406/862-1298. A wide range of fishing gear plus guided trips, instruction and fly-tying classes.

Montana Adventure Company, 1205 US-93 W (ⓣ1-877/723-0742, ⓦwww.montansfinest.com. Guided whitewater rafting, trail rides, boat cruises, fishing, cross-country skiing, and dog sledding in and around Glacier National Park.

The Runner Up 550 E 1st St. If money's tight, this store has a wide range of well-maintained secondhand outdoor gear ranging from skis to kayaks.

Snowfrog, 903 Wisconsin Ave ⓣ406/862-7547. Usefully located en route to Big Mountain, you'll find a good range of ski equipment for sale or rent here.

Stumptown Snowboards 128 Central Ave ⓣ406/862-0955. The standard self-consciously cool board shop with a good range of gear for sale and rental.

boisterous setting, good-value bar food, ping-pong tables, and bands at weekends ensure you can easily end up here a lot longer than planned. If you're on a budget call in for the 4–6pm happy hour.

Logan's Bar & Grill *Grouse Mountain Lodge*, 1205 US-93 W ⓣ406/862-3000. One of the finest restaurants in town offering contemporary regional fare such as peppercorn-crusted elk carpaccio and seared salmon fillet, served up in a cozy mountain lodge setting. An entree costs around $20.

Truby's 115 Central Ave ⓣ406/862-4979. The best wood-fired pizzas in town along with a warm and welcoming atmosphere ensure that it can be hard to get a table at *Truby's*. There's a shady deck alongside, and the bar staff are a great source of information on the local outdoor scene.

Wasabi Sushi Bar 419 2nd St E ⓣ406/863-9283. Reservations are recommended at this popular sushi bar which serves traditional sushi and teriyaki-style kebabs, sashimi, and tempura.

Whitefish Lake Restaurant ⓣ406/862-5285. Situated at Whitefish Lake Golf Club on US-93 west of town, this is one of the more upmarket restaurants in town with especially good seafood and prime rib. Expect to pay around $20–25 for an entree.

Whitefish Times 344 Central Ave ⓣ406/862-2444. Coffee and cakes in wonderfully relaxing surroundings, where you can lounge on a sofa and read from the wide range of complimentary magazines and newspapers.

Glacier National Park

Two thousand lakes and a thousand miles of rivers, threading between thick forests and glorious meadows, weave a blue-and-green carpet below the alpine heights of **GLACIER NATIONAL PARK** – a haven for bighorn sheep, mountain goats, black bears and threatened grizzlies, wolves, and mountain lions. Though the park still holds fifty small glaciers, its name comes from the fact that these immense valleys were carved by huge flows of ice, millennia ago. Crisp air, freezing waterfalls, and year-round snow combine to give the impression of being very close to the Arctic Circle; in fact, the latitude here, even near as it is to Canada, is lower than that of London.

The star attraction is the spectacular **Going-to-the-Sun Road**, which has had thrown at it nearly every accolade in the book, and still comes out looking good. It weaves past many of Montana's – if not the country's – more breathtaking viewpoints en route between the gateway towns of **West Glacier** and **St Mary**. Just driving the road is not sufficient, however. With so much to

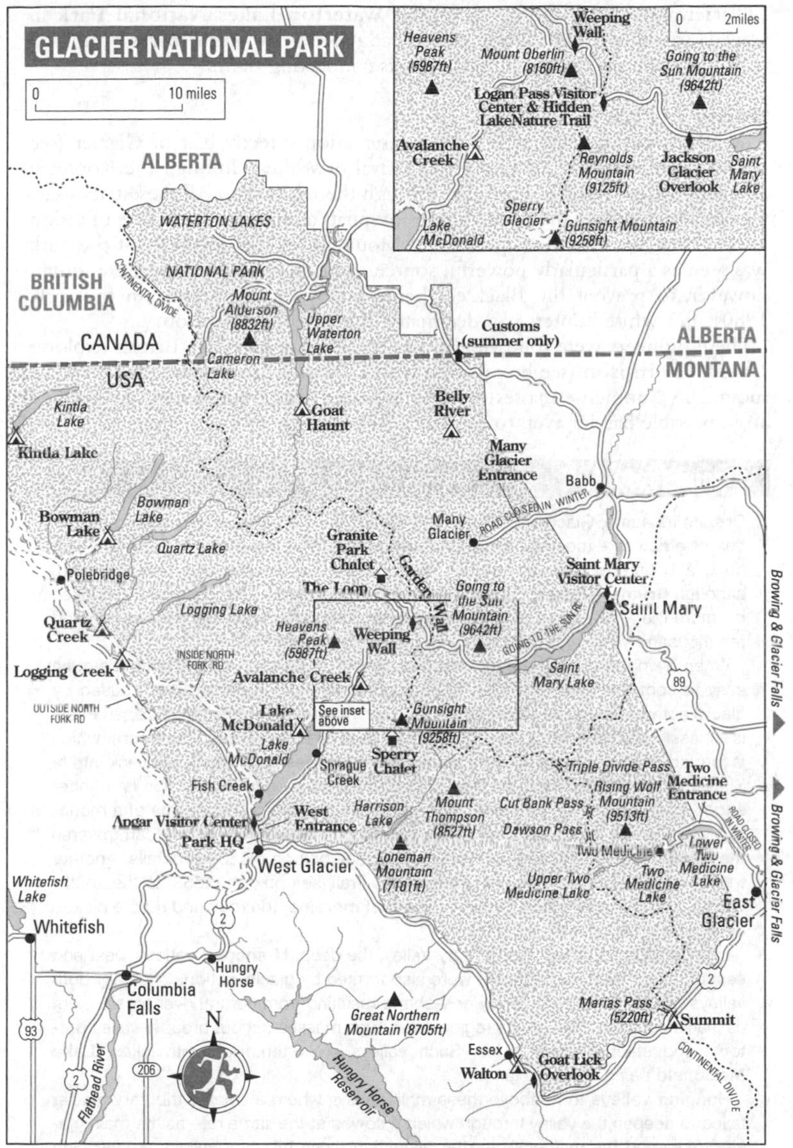

see, you've got to get out for at least a day's exploration on foot and amble along at least a portion of the seven hundred plus miles of **hiking trails** weaving through the park. If you can handle the crowds, there is no better place in the state for a hike. **Many Glacier** and the more isolated **Polebridge**, both located off the Going-to-the-Sun, are also worth a look, as is a boat tour on one of the park's larger lakes.

Glacier also adjoins the much smaller **Waterton Lakes National Park** in Canada (see box p.544); although you can move between the parks on hiking trails, there are no roads within the parks connecting them.

Some history

The **Blackfeet** Indians, who have a reservation directly east of Glacier (see p.549), dominated the area until the arrival of whites, although the Kootenai and Salish tribes lived and traveled through the region too. All these tribes saw Glacier's high mountains as the homes of spirits and used it as the site of vision quests – the huge anvil-shaped Chief Mountain in the northeast of the park was seen as a particularly powerful source of medicine. Not powerful enough, however, to prevent the Blackfeet being hit by serious famine in the early 1880s after white hunters had decimated the buffalo population.

These pioneers were following in the footsteps of men like British explorer **David Thompson** (see box p.652), who a century before described how the mountains' "immense masses of snow appeared above the clouds, and formed an impassable barrier even to the Eagle." The presence of this "impassable bar-

Glacial features

Despite its name, Glacier National Park doesn't have a particularly inspiring collection of **glaciers** – most are small and rather grubby in summer when layered with dust, and unfortunately are getting even smaller as a result of global warming, although **Grinnel Glacier** is nevertheless still impressive and accessible to any hiker. It's more the after-effects of glacial actions occurring here between two million and ten thousand years ago that has given the park its name.

When hiking through the park or driving along Going-to-the-Sun Road, it's quite easy to spot textbook examples of geological and landscape features caused by glacial activity. Reynolds Mountain (9125ft) for instance, to the south of Logan Pass, is a classic **glacial horn**, a pyramid-shaped peak like the famous Matterhorn, which is formed as two or more glaciers at the mountain's base erode and eat back into it. Similar erosive activity formed the Garden Wall near Logan Pass – this is a knife-edged divide known as an **arete**, formed by two glaciers on either side of a mountain which scour away until only a thin, precipitous ridge remains. You can traverse the Garden Wall on the superb Highline Trail; see box on p.553 for details. Another trail past glacial deposits is the Hidden Lake Trail (see box on p.553) to the southwest of Logan Pass, which follows a swath of **moraine**, the rock and rubble picked up and later deposited by a glacier.

Lake McDonald Valley and St Mary Valley, the deep, **U-shaped valleys** west and east of Logan Pass respectively, were also formed by glacial action. Originally both valleys would have had a narrower V-shape resulting from natural river erosion, but as glaciers moved through the region, their huge masses cut out broader valley bottoms and steeper valley sides. Such valleys are often filled with lakes, **Lake McDonald** being a good example.

Hanging valleys form above these main valleys where a smaller tributary glacier failed to deepen the valley through which it flowed at the same rate as the main glacier deepened the main valley. After glaciation these tributary valleys are left high above the main valley floor, and any drainage they possess flows into the main valley as a waterfall, such as at **Bird Woman Falls** along the Going-to-the-Sun Road.

At the head of many U-shaped valleys – for example, that which holds Many Glacier – are **cirques,** huge amphitheaters hollowed out by glacial action. These often hold **tarns** (a small lake), commonly dammed by deposits of glacial moraine and often a milky-blue color typical of glaciated areas, caused by the refraction of sunlight off suspended sediments transported there by glacial meltwater.

rier" meant that it was not until the railroads started pushing west in the late nineteenth century that whites moved into the region.

Most of those coming in on the railroad expended their energy in marginally successful efforts to find gold, copper, and oil in the mountains. Meanwhile **George Bird Grinnel**, the influential editor of *Forest and Stream* and founder of the Audubon Society, was lobbying to have the region designated a national park – successfully so, for in 1910 President Taft signed the bill creating the country's tenth national park. Jumping at the money-making opportunities, the Great Northern encouraged tourists to visit on their **Empire Builder** service, which called in at stations in East Glacier, Essex, and West Glacier. The company also built an array of lodges and campgrounds between 1910–17 to house these visitors, few of which are still standing. All the accommodations were located a day's horseback ride apart, which remained the standard means of discovering Glacier until the completion of the **Going-to-the-Sun Road** in 1932. The same year Glacier and Waterton Lakes National Park (the latter of which had been protected by the Canadian Government since 1895) were designated **Waterton-Glacier International Peace Park** following petitions from Rotary clubs in both countries.

In the intervening years, despite ever more visitors (at present almost three million annually to both parks combined), Glacier has generally not come under the pressure of better-known parks such as Yellowstone. It's still the only place in the lower 48 where grizzlies, wolves, and mountain lions have maintained a continuous existence. Indeed, such is the importance of the region in terms of landscape, culture, and ecology that in 1995 it was designated a World Heritage Site.

Arrival

Glacier National Park is **open** year-round; however, from November to May or June, most roads are closed to car traffic due to snow. This includes the central section of Going-to-the-Sun Road, the only paved road through the park. The park's main **entrances** are West Glacier on the west side and St Mary on the east, at either end of Going-to-the-Sun Road. You can also enter the park at Camas Creek off the Outside North Fork Road to the north of Apgar; at Polebridge off the Outside North Fork Road; at Two Medicine off Hwy-49 which runs off US-89 north of East Glacier; at Cut Bank off US-89; and at Many Glacier off US-89.

While the majority of visitors arrive by car, Glacier National Park is one of the few national parks also easily reached by **train**. Amtrak's Empire Builder, traveling between Chicago and Seattle, calls in at East Glacier (Glacier Park Station; summer only) and West Glacier (Belton Station); eastbound trains arrive at around 8am (it's thirty minutes between stations), westbound trains at around 8pm. In between the two is Essex, where the train will stop only on request. The nearest **airport** is Glacier International, twenty miles to the southeast at Kalispell (see p.531).

In addition, **Glacier Park, Inc (GPI)** (Ⓣ406/226-5666 Ⓦwww.glacierparkinc.com), the official park concessionaire, operates shuttles to Glacier from Kalispell and Great Falls; Flathead Glacier Transportation (Ⓣ1-800/829-7039) in Kalispell also run a shuttle service.

Getting around

Getting around the park on your own is straightforward enough, although with only one road through Glacier there's a limit to what you can see by vehicle only. Roads in and around the park are invariably busy in summer, espe-

Park practicalities

ATMs There are ATMs in the lodges at the *St Mary*, *Lake McDonald*, and *Glacier Park* lodges, as well as at the *Many Glacier Hotel* and the Cedar Tree Deli in Apgar.

Laundry and showers In West Glacier, both the *Glacier Campground* and *West Glacier KOA* have laundry and shower facilities. Around East Glacier, head for the *Firebrand Campground*, while near St Mary the *Swiftcurrent Motor Inn* is your best bet.

Medical attention There are no medical facilities in the park – call a park ranger at park headquarters (☎406/888-7800) in an emergency.

Post Office There's a post office in both West Glacier and East Glacier, behind the Glacier Trading Co. on the east side of US-2. In St Mary, you can buy stamps and post mail in *St Mary Lodge*.

Supplies There are grocery stores in St Mary and Apgar Village, as well as smaller supply stores in the *Rising Sun Motor Inn, Swiftcurrent Motor Inn*, and *Lake McDonald Lodge*.

Weather Glacier's mountains create their own **climate**, and the west side of the Continental Divide receives more rainfall/snow than the east, which is sunnier, but windier. Summertime temperatures at lower elevations like West Glacier average in the high seventies, while overnight lows hover around the upper 40°F's. Expect to find temperatures ten to fifteen degrees lower at higher altitudes, and if hiking in the mountains be prepared for snow even at the height of summer. Glacier has prodigious snowfalls – along the Continental Divide it can reach as much as eighty feet per year.

cially the Going-to-the-Sun Road where roadside parking places and viewpoints may be full. If at all possible, try and do your driving early in the morning to avoid the worst of the crowds. Vehicle **size restrictions** are also enforced; see box on p.548.

If you'd rather let someone else do the worrying, freeing you to gawk all you'd like, GPI (see overleaf) operates various **bus tours** in the park. The most unique are those run in the park's original motor transport, bright red 1930s roll top **"jammer" buses** – so named because the drivers had to jam the gears into position. Seventeen of these buses have recently been converted to environmentally friendly propane gas engines. Tours are run from Lake McDonald, East Glacier, Many Glacier, and Waterton by GPI – as an example of prices, the 2.5-hour tour from Lake McDonald to Logan Pass and back costs $21. They also run a service between park lodges and between East Glacier, West Glacier, St Mary, and Waterton; shuttle rates are $8 from any points between Logan Pass and West Glacier; $8 from any points between Logan Pass and the East Entrance at St Mary; $17 for a one-way trip from St Mary to West Glacier. The final GPI service is the **Hikers Shuttle** (July to early Sept daily 7.30am–8pm) along Going-to-the-Sun Road, with drop-offs at trailheads along the route. Examples of rates (from St Mary) are Siyeh Bend ($13), Logan Pass ($17), and The Loop ($20).

You can also see Glacier via a **helicopter tour**, an exciting and expensive way to take in the park's tremendous landscapes. Rates start at around $90 per person for a half-hour trip with Kruger Helipcop-Tours (☎406/387-4565 or 1-800/220-6565), located one mile west of West Glacier on US-2.

Information

For a private vehicle, the park **entrance fee** is $10, valid for a week; motorcyclists, cyclists, and hikers pay $5. Keep your receipt to allow for re-entry to

Visitor centers and ranger stations

The park's **visitor centers** are aimed more at the general visitor, selling books and gifts as well as dispensing advice – **ranger stations** are the better choice for specific recreation information such as hiking, camping, and bear sightings.

Glacier National Park Headquarters on US-2 to Apgar, West Glacier, MT 59936 (year round Mon–Fri 8am–4.30pm; ⓣ406/888-7800). The headquarters can supply useful visitor information by post in advance of your visit and has stacks of information and advice if you want to call in person. It's convenient if you're taking the Going-to-the-Sun Road from West Glacier.

Apgar Visitor Center (late May to late June & early Sept to end Oct daily 8am–4.30pm; late June to early Sept 8am–8pm; ⓣ406/888-7939). Located near the foot of Lake McDonald and well signposted, this is one of the busiest and best of the visitor centers, with exhibits on the park's flora and fauna and information on weather, road, and camping conditions for the whole park. You can also book onto a wide range of regular ranger-led activities from hikes to campfire talks here. The center has a café, and also issues backcountry permits.

Logan Pass Visitor Center (early June to mid-Oct; various hours, but always open at least 10am–4pm daily; no phone service). Located at the top of Logan Pass on Going-to-the-Sun Road, there are good displays here on the natural history of the park, regular ranger talks and activities and a very good bookstore.

Many Glacier Ranger Station (daily: late May to late June & early Sept to late Sept 8am–4.30pm; late June to early Sept 8am–6pm; ⓣ406/732-7750). Located next to *Many Glacier* campground, this is an essential stop for information on natural history, geology, bears, trail and weather conditions before you head into the surrounding mountains, and there are ranger-led activities throughout the summer. Also issues backcountry permits.

Polebridge Ranger Station Outer North Fork Rd, Polebridge (late May to mid-Sept daily 9am–5pm; ⓣ406/888-5416). Only worth stopping in if you're planning on heading into the backcountry here in the least-visited corner of Glacier. Also issues backcountry permits.

St Mary Visitor Center (late May to mid-June & Sept to mid-Oct daily 8am–5pm; mid-June to early Sept daily 8am–9pm; ⓣ406/732-7750). Located at the north end of St Mary Lake off Going-to-the-Sun Road, rangers here provide talks and guided hikes and there's a good selection of books and maps, plus a café. Also issues backcountry permits.

Two Medicine Ranger Station (late May to mid Sept 9am–5pm; ⓣ406/226-4484). Situated at the northeast end of Two Medicine Lake, there's a handy snack bar here, and you can also book boat tours on Two Medicine Lake. Also issues backcountry permits.

the park during that period. An annual pass costs $20, though if you plan on visiting any other national parks throughout the year fork out an additional $30 and get a National Parks Pass instead. Upon arrival, you'll be given a free park **map**.

For general **information** before arriving, log onto the park's useful website (ⓦwww.nps.gov/glac/home.htm) or call ⓣ406/888-7800. Once at the park, more in-depth information is given out at several different **visitor centers** and **ranger stations** (see box, above), all of which have a wide array of free hiking maps; many have cafés and backcountry permit desks as well. Two useful free visitor **publications** are the *Waterton-Glacier Guide* newspaper, and the small, glossy *Glacier National Park Guide*, good for additional information on natural history and listings of park-related events and interpretation programs.

Waterton Lakes National Park

At the US/Canadian border, Glacier adjoins the much smaller **Waterton Lakes National Park**, the two parks together being known as the Waterton-Glacier International Peace Park. Though they share a name, the parks operate their own fees and regulations, and you have to drive through St Mary on the east side of Glacier and pass Canadian customs before entering Waterton, where the fee is CAN$4 per person or CAN$8 per group in a vehicle. Waterton tends to be less visited than Glacier, so the only pressing reason to head on over is if you're looking for complete solitude. For **information** on Waterton Lakes National Park, contact the Waterton Lakes Visitor Reception Center (daily mid-May to early Sept 8am–6pm (9pm mid-summer), variable hours until mid-Oct; ⓣ403/859-5133, ⓦwww.parkscanada.pch.gc.ca/waterton) in Waterton.

Accommodation

Accommodation in and around the park varies enormously. The gateway towns of West Glacier, East Glacier, and St Mary hold a mix of modern hotels and motels, some cheaper hostels and campgrounds, while the park itself is home to more campgrounds and the historic and atmospheric national park lodges. If you're budget allows it, try and spend at least a night here in one of the national park lodges. In summer, all forms of accommodations are busy, so if you haven't reserved far in advance, you'll most likely have to stay in nearby Whitefish (see p.534) or Kalispell (see p.531). In winter, many of the lodgings shutter up.

The majority of hotel accommodation in the park is operated by Glacier Park, Inc (GPI; ⓣ406/756-2444, ⓦwww.glacierparkinc.com), including the *Village Inn Motel*, *Lake McDonald Lodge*, *Rising Sun Inn*, *Swiftcurrent Inn*, and *Many Glacier Lodge*.

Without exception, Glacier's selection of campgrounds are superbly located. The NPS operates thirteen **campgrounds** in the park, only two of which – *Fish Creek* and *St Mary* – can be reserved in advance (ⓣ1-800/365-2267, ⓦwww.reservations.nps.gov). For details on availability at the other sites, which are first-come, first-serve, call ⓣ406/888-7800. In **winter**, all sites are open for primitive camping (fees average around $6) apart from *Avalanche*, *Cut Bank*, *Rising Sun*, and *Sprague Creek*. Where hiker/biker sites are indicated, a limited number of sites are reserved until 9pm for cyclists, motorcyclists, and hikers. These sites are shared, cost $3 per person, and have a capacity of eight. Utility hookups are not provided at sites within the park. For information on **backcountry camping** see box on p.552.

West Glacier and around

Hotels and cabins

Apgar Village Inn ⓣ406/888-5484. Situated at the southern end of Lake McDonald, this motel-style lodge is well-located for the lake, Apgar Visitor Center and Going-to-the-Sun Road. The lodge has plain but comfortable motel rooms, some with kitchenettes, and all rooms have TV and showers. ❺

Belton Chalet US-2 E, West Glacier ⓣ406/888-5000 or 1-888/235-8665, ⓦwww.beltonchalet.com. This beautifully restored 1910 chalet was built by Great Northern and offers tastefully appointed rooms with period furniture and no phones or TV to disturb you. The rustic atmosphere and stone and timber interior give a real feeling for how it would have been to take a vacation in Glacier in 1910. There's also a very good grill and taproom on site. ❻

Glacier Highland Resort Motel ⓣ406/888-5311 or 1-800/831-7101. Situated off US-2 at the park's west entrance, the rooms here are pleasantly furnished but not especially good value, although rates drop outside of summer. ❺

Granite Park Chalet early July to mid-Sept ⓣ406/387-5555, ⓦwww.glacierguides.com.

Located north of The Loop on Going-to-the-Sun Road and perched on a rocky outcrop at the north end of The Garden Wall, *Granite Park Chalet* can only be reached by hiking – four trails lead to the chalet, the most popular of which is the magnificent seven-mile Highline Trail (see box p.553). The rustic accommodation includes beds, an optional bed linen service, a common kitchen, and a dining room with spectacular views of 8987ft Heaven's Peak. You need to bring sleeping bag, water, food, and cooking utensils. ❹

Lake McDonald Lodge ⓣ406/888-5431. Located at the northeastern end of Lake McDonald, this wonderfully atmospheric old hunting lodge dates back to the early 1900s, and features a huge lobby with gigantic timber supports and a selection of local wildlife trophies. The pictographs decorating the massive stone fireplace are said to have been drawn by Western artist Charles M. Russell. Unfortunately the lodge rooms (❼) are quite plain and don't have the charm of the rest of the lodge; the cheaper motel rooms (❺) are better value, as are the cabins (❺) next to the lodge. ❺

Sperry Chalet early July to mid-Sept; ⓣ406/387-5654, ⓦwww.ptinet.net/sperrychalet. Built in 1914 by Great Northern and extensively refurbished recently, *Sperry Chalet* can only be reached by hiking in as it's located 6.5 miles between *Lake McDonald Lodge* and Logan Pass. Very basic dorm-style lodging is provided here, plus breakfast and lunch, with private rooms for an extra $50. The facilities are very rustic and include outhouses, but the chance to sleep in the wilds in relative comfort is what you're paying for. ❽

Village Inn Apgar Village ⓣ406/888-5632. At the south end of the lake, the modern motel-style rooms have good views across the lake and mountains, but are rather plain and not the greatest value. Some rooms have kitchenettes, for which you have to pay around $30 more. ❺

Campgrounds

Apgar At the southwest end of Lake McDonald, this is the busiest campground in Glacier and not the place to head for if you want peace and quiet. Facilities include flush toilets and a disposal station, and primitive camping is allowed here for free out of season. Hiker/biker sites are also available. Open early May to mid-Oct. 191 sites; $14.

Avalanche Located near to some good, easy hiking, and has hiker/biker sites which are convenient for cyclists wanting to get over Going-to-the-Sun Rd before the 11am cut off. Facilities include flush toilets. Open mid-June to early-Sept. 87 sites; $14.

Firebrand Campground Lindhe Ave, East Glacier ⓣ406/226-5573. The big draw at this private campground are good washroom, shower, and laundry facilities – the sites are not that attractive themselves, but the views of the mountains are good. Open June to early Sept. 10 tent sites ($13), 30 RV sites ($20).

Fish Creek Located on the north shore of Lake McDonald and within easy reach of Apgar Village, the sites at *Fish Creek* include two hiker/biker sites, flush toilets, and a trash disposal system. Despite it's size it's possible to find relatively secluded sites here. Open June to early–Sept. 180 sites; $17.

Sprague Creek On the shores of Lake McDonald, sites here include two hiker/biker sites. Facilities include flush toilets. This is a good site for cyclists heading over Going-to-the-Sun Rd. Open mid-May to late Sept. 25 sites; $14.

West Glacier KOA ⓣ406/387-5341. Located 2.5 miles east of West Glacier on US-2, this busy campground has a wide array of facilities including a heated pool and two hot tubs and nightly barbecues, a store, and laundry, and there are cabins ($55). Open mid-May to mid-Sept. 42 tent sites ($22),100 RV sites ($30).

East Glacier and around

Hotels, cabins and hostels

Backpacker's Inn behind *Serrano's Restaurant*, Dawson Ave, East Glacier ⓣ406/862-5600. Has two single-sex and one coed dorm, all of which are simple and basic but good value at $10 ($12 if you need a sleeping bag). Note that there's no kitchen here.

East Glacier Motel Hwy-49, East Glacier ⓣ406/226-5593. Bright and comfortable motel rooms (❻) and attractive cottages alongside (❺), with rates that fall off markedly outside peak period. ❺

Glacier Park Lodge East Glacier ⓣ406/226-5551. Built between 1912–14, this is a terrific place to stay with simple but elegant and comfortable rooms, a cozy lobby lined with enormous Douglas fir pillars, a veranda with mountain views, a swimming pool and nine-hole golf course, and a very good restaurant. ❻

HI-Brownie's Hostel 1020 Hwy-49, East Glacier ⓣ406/226-4426. *Brownie's* is a popular spot for budget travelers, with single-sex eight-bed dorms ($12) and private double rooms ($20), and a friendly, vibrant atmosphere. It's above Brownie's Grocery and Deli, has a good common room stacked with books and records, and a clean kitchen, and is a good place to meet fellow outdoor-types.

Sears Motel Hwy-49, East Glacier ☎406/226-4432. Good-value accommodation in cabins with cable TV, there's also a tent ($11) and RV ($18) campground alongside – this is a good bet if you don't want a hostel but can't afford the park's lodge accommodation. ❸

Campgrounds

Two Medicine Set in a lovely lakeside location beneath Rising Wolf Mountain (9513ft) this is a good base for exploring Two Medicine Lake (there are boat trips from here) and the surrounding peaks, although it can get quite busy. Facilities include a camp store, evening campfire presentations by park naturalists and Blackfeet tribe members, hiker/biker sites, and flush toilets; sites are available out of season. Open end May to mid-Sept, but available for primitive camping in winter. 99 sites; $14.

St Mary, Many Glacier, and around

Hotels and cabins

Many Glacier Hotel Many Glacier ☎406/732-4411. The largest lodge in the park, the Swiss-style, 211-room *Many Glacier Hotel* has a great location, tucked beneath the glacier after which it's named and on the shores of Swiftcurrent Lake. The rooms are rather plain in comparison to the overall grandness of the lodge, but the surroundings are the major attraction here and this makes a fine base for exploring them. The lodge also has a restaurant, and offers boat and horseback tours. ❻

Rising Sun Motor Inn Going-to-the-Sun Rd ☎406/732-5532. Six miles east of St Mary on the north shore of St Mary Lake, the *Rising Sun* has rather drab motel rooms and cabins which are not particularly good value, but the lakeside location beneath dramatic mountain walls is splendid. There's also a restaurant here serving breakfast, lunch, and dinner. ❺

St Mary Lodge & Resort St Mary Village ☎406/732-4431 or 1-800/732-9265. An attractive lodge with sumptuous rooms, each with a balcony that overlooks the park. There's also a guest hot tub. Not cheap but worth the money, and although located just outside the park you're still within easy driving distance of all the major attractions on this side of Glacier. ❽

Swiftcurrent Motor Inn Many Glacier ☎406/732-5531. Located close to *Many Glacier Hotel*, this motel has rather uninspiring rooms and cabins that rely on the impressive surroundings to attract you. A better budget choice are the associated *Swiftcurrent Cottages* (❸) which are rather basic (no toilets or kitchens) but quite still cozy in an old-fashioned sort of way. The inn also has a restaurant. ❺

Campgrounds

Cut Bank Located on the east side of the park and well-placed for hiking to Triple Divide Peak and Pass. The campground is accessible only by dirt road. Open end May to mid-Sept. 19 sites; $12.

Many Glacier A relatively large campground that's typically busy due to its location in the heart of some fine hiking territory. Facilities include hiker/biker sites and flush toilets. Open late May to late Sept but available in winter for primitive camping. 110 sites; $14.

Rising Sun On the north shore of St Mary Lake with good mountain views, facilities include hiker/biker sites, flush toilets, and disposal units, and there are pay showers in the nearby *Rising Sun Motor Inn*. Open late May to late Sept. 82 sites; $14.

St Mary Large campground and not especially attractive by Glacier standards, with rather exposed, unshaded sites. However, it is convenient for St Mary Village and Going-to-the-Sun Rd. Facilities include hiker/biker sites, flush toilets, and disposal units, and sites are available out of season. Open late May to mid-Sept but available in winter for primitive camping. 148 sites; $17.

Polebridge and around

Cabins and hostels

North Fork Hostel and Square Peg Ranch 80 Beaver Drive, Polebridge ☎406/888-5241. A friendly hostel – the owners offer free use of cross-country skis, snowshoes, mountain bikes, and canoes – and a good place to meet fellow outdoor folk. Bunk beds are $15 per night (bring your own sleeping bag) and other accommodation options include small log cabins out back for $30 per night. Power for the hostel and cabins is courtesy of kerosene or propane and you should bring a flashlight for getting around at night. Wood stoves provide the heat. Reservations are recommended, and if you don't have your own transport they'll pick you up from the Amtrak station at West Glacier for $25.

Polebridge Mercantile ☎406/888-5105. Adjacent to the *Square Peg*, the rustic cabins here go from $35 per night, and have basic furnishings, wood stoves, propane lights, and outhouses – you'll need your own sleeping bag, cooking utensils, flashlight, and water container. The old "Merc" can also provide essential supplies. ❷

Campgrounds

Bowman Lake One of the most remote campgrounds in the park, along a dirt road to the northeast of Polebridge. There are some good hiking trails from the campground. Open mid-May to mid-Sept, available for primitive camping in winter. 48 sites; $12.

Kintla Lake A small and secluded primitive campground in the northwest corner of Glacier, reached along a dirt road. Open mid-May to mid-Sept, available for primitive camping in winter. 13 sites; $12.

Logging Creek A small, rather primitive site just southeast of Polebridge on the Inside North Fork Rd. Open July to early Sept, available for primitive camping in winter. 8 sites; $12.

Quartz Creek Located just northwest of *Logging Creek* campground on the Inside North Fork Rd, this is a small, secluded primitive campground. Open July to early Sept, available for primitive camping in winter. 7 sites; $12.

Exploring the park

The only highway through Glacier is the truly spectacular **Going-to-the-Sun** road, which manages to pull off an admirable job of showing off many of the park's scenic highlights. There are also plenty of trailheads along the way where you can get out and hike into the heart of Glacier, although the trails from here will invariably be busy due to ease of access. Other road access to the park is limited to a few roads pushing into the eastern and western sides, but by driving to the trailheads at the end of these you can head out into the wilds on hikes which vary from easy half-day strolls to major backcountry expeditions.

You can see more of Glacier on **boat trips** plying lakes McDonald, St Mary, and Two Medicine, or by **rafting** down the North or Middle Fork of the Flathead on the western and southern boundaries. In **winter**, when Glacier is perhaps at it's most dramatic, cross-country ski and snowshoe trails will take you into a far quieter landscape than in summer.

Whether driving, hiking, or floating, you are almost certain to come across some of the park's plentiful **wildlife**. Look out in particular for mountain goats and bighorn sheep perched high up on cliffs. Bears are also common – keep a look out for both grizzlies and black bears in order to avoid them as much as gawk at them (see box on p.550).

Going-to-the-Sun Road

Opened in 1932, the **GOING-TO-THE-SUN ROAD** continues to be an engineering marvel – few, if any, highways in the US can compare with it for sheer drama and scenery. Driving the road creates the illusion that you'll be climbing forever – after a stealthy ascent of the foothills, when the road appears to be heading straight into huge bare mountains that fill the entire windscreen, each successive hairpin confronts you with a new wall of rock and snow. However, the road is far from a secret, and during the busiest times in summer you should give yourself several hours to complete the 52 miles between West Glacier and St Mary.

Due to Glacier's tremendous snowfalls, the road is **closed** for around half the year (see box, overleaf). That it opens as early as May is only thanks to continuous round-the-clock work by park service personnel to clear snow drifts as deep as 70 feet. This can be dangerous work – in 1953 two park employees were killed and one seriously injured by an avalanche across the road five miles below Logan Pass. For details of **shuttle services** along Going-to-the-Sun Road see "Getting around" on p.541.

Once beyond West Glacier and Lake McDonald (see overleaf), the road begins to climb in earnest. Rounding **The Loop**, where the road arcs northwest into the bosom of the mountains, you come to a series of trailheads, including that to **Granite Chalet**. Snowmelt from waterfalls gushes over the road, spilling over the sheer drops on the other side, and one of the many lookouts allows you a

Road Restrictions on Going-to-the-Sun Road

Though three lower portions of **Going-to-the-Sun Road** remain open year round, at higher elevations the road is closed from the third Monday in October until late May or early June. You can ski or snowshoe along the snowed-in sections during the winter.

To help reduce congestion on the narrow road, vehicle and vehicle combinations longer than 21ft (including bumpers) and wider than 8ft (including mirrors) are prohibited between *Avalanche Campground* (west side) and the Sun Point parking area (east side). The **speed** limited is 45mph unless otherwise indicated.

There are **bicycle restrictions** from June 15 through Labor Day. From Apgar Village to the *Sprague Creek Campground*, bicycles are prohibited in both directions from 11am–4pm, and from Logan Creek to Logan Pass eastbound (uphill) traffic is also prohibited between 11am–4pm. It takes about 45 minutes to ride from Sprague Creek to Logan Creek and about three hours from Logan Creek to Logan Pass.

view south to **Bird Woman Falls**, which plummets almost 500ft from a hanging valley between Mount Oberlin and Mount Cannon.

The winding route nudges past the huge crenellated cliffs of the **Garden Wall** and over the Continental Divide at **Logan Pass** (6646ft), where wildflowers bloom in an alpine tundra landscape. There's a large parking lot at the visitor center here (see p.543), though it's normally full by midday in July and August so plan accordingly. From the pass, a short hike leads to **Hidden Lake**, the biggest of Glacier's alpine tarns, or you can take the longer **Highline Trail**, which runs north along the timberline and beneath the Garden Wall, with awe-inspiring mountain views. See the box p.552 for full details of both hikes.

As you head east down from the heights, the road passes through the dank **East Side Tunnel** and across a savage alpine landscape of wind-blasted firs and frost-shattered crags, and four miles on there's an overlook at **Jackson Glacier**, one of the few glaciers visible from the roadside. Towards St Mary Lake, the giant crags of peaks such as **Mount Logan** and red-tinted **Red Eagle Mountain** reassert their authority over the landscape and are often reflected in the tranquil waters of the lake. Once you arrive in St Mary (see opposite for a full description of this area), it's worth driving another five miles southeast on US-89 for tremendous views over the start of the Great Plains, which stretch 1600 miles east to Chicago.

West Glacier to Lake McDonald

The main west entrance to Glacier takes you through the busy and commercialized **West Glacier** where the park headquarters (see p.543) are a good source of information, but the somewhat glitzy tourist atmosphere is unlikely to encourage you to hang around for long. Instead, stock up on any last-minute supplies and jump on to the beginning of the Going-to-the-Sun Road.

From West Glacier, it's only a few miles north to the magnificent **Lake McDonald**. Ten miles long, two miles wide, and 400 feet deep, its dark blue waters lie in a steep U-shaped valley, surrounded on all sides by dense forests that, dotted with red cedar, feel more like the Pacific Northwest than the Rockies. Strikingly, the huge mountains here rise some 5000 feet above the waters of the lake's northeastern shores, and it's easy to see why the Kootenai, who called the lake "Dancing Sacred Lake," were inspired to perform sacred ceremonies on its shores.

At the lake's southern end is **Apgar Village**, like West Glacier a busy spot but more pleasant due to the lake and mountain setting. Though completely inside the park, portions of the village are still privately owned, as evidenced by a selection of gift shops. Here you'll also find the Apgar Visitor Center (see p.543) and just to the north, *Fish Creek*, one of the most popular campgrounds in the park and open year round (see p.545).

From Lake McDonald, most people take Going-to-the-Sun Road up into the mountains, though you can also head north on **Camas Road** and **Inside North Fork Road** to Polebridge in the park's secluded northwest corner (see p.552).

St Mary, Many Glacier, and the northeast corner

At the opposite end of the Going-to-the-Sun Road from West Glacier is the small and unremarkable town of **St Mary**, also at the US-89 junction, ensuring that it's nearly always awash with both traffic and tourists. Although rather bland, it's a good base for exploring the eastern side of Glacier, and home to the useful St Mary Visitor Center (see p.543). A few miles east of town, one hour boat tours ($11) of **St Mary Lake** leave from the dock across from the Rising Sun Complex on the lake's north shore. The best of the bunch is the scenic 7pm sunset cruise, when the lake takes on a range of pink, red, and mauve pastel shades.

Nine miles north of St Mary on US-89 stands **Many Glacier**. Many Glacier is not a town as such but a bustling collection of lodges and campgrounds clustered around **Swiftcurrent Lake**. Like St Mary and West Glacier, it's a hive of activity in high season, with day-trippers and hikers enjoying some of the most popular trails in the park, making it difficult to really get away from the madding crowds unless you head way out into the backcountry. Even so, the mountain scenery here is some of the park's best, from the placid deep-blue waters of **Lake Sherburne** up through a verdant carpet of forest to raw-boned mountain peaks, and retreating glaciers clinging to hollows from which snow encrusted crags rise above. There are healthy black and grizzly bear populations here, so keep your eyes open on the trails. You may also get to see deer, mountain goats, bighorn sheep, and marmots, while much more reclusive residents include mountain lions and wolves.

It's only reasonable to expect to see a **glacier** in Glacier National Park, and in this quarter of the park there are several. The most accessible is **Grinnell Glacier**, which you access on an eleven-mile round-trip trail from *Many Glacier Hotel* (see box p.546) or a shorter seven-mile round-trip if you take the shortcut by boat across Swiftcurrent and Josephine lakes ($7). Don't expect a huge wall of blue ice – it's more of a pocket-handkerchief of compressed snow and ice rolling down banded black cliffs into Grinnell Lake.

East Glacier and Two Medicine Region

This, the southest corner of Glacier, is where you'll find the park's strongest Native American presence. Indeed, the essentially one-street town of **East Glacier**, the park's southeastern gateway and easily accessed from the east on US-2, is within the **Blackfeet Reservation**. This was a popular entrance point to Glacier for early visitors, who would stay at the town's imposing *Glacier Park Lodge* (see p.545) after disembarking from the train. With the completion of the Going-to-the-Sun Road in 1931, though, visitor numbers fell dramatically, which has helped East Glacier retain a more gritty, Western feel than West Glacier, and it's noticeably less commercialized.

The scenery here is at its best around the deep, glacier-scoured valleys, crashing waterfalls, and 9000ft peaks of **Two Medicine Lake**, and if you're looking for alpine solitude this is a good spot to head. Driving north from East Glacier on Hwy-49 along the park's eastern boundary, turn-outs allow you to pull over and view the amazing transition in the landscape as the plains to the east suddenly come up against the Rockies, thrusting thousands of feet up into Montana's intense blue skies.

Essex and Glaciers southern edge

The southern edge of Glacier can only be accessed from trailheads off US-2, which meanders southeast from West Glacier above the Middle Fork of the Flathead, along which you'll invariably see rafters splashing their way downstream. It also follows the railroad line as it wends its way down from Marias Pass (5220ft) to the east. The highway here over the pass wasn't completed until 1930, prior to which cars were loaded onto trains either side of the pass and shipped over.

The most obvious stopover is the elegant, half-timbered *Izaak Walton Inn* at **Essex** (Ⓣ406/888-5700, Ⓦwww.izaakwaltoninn.com; ⑥), thirty miles south-

Bear encounters

Two types of **bears** roam the Rockies – black bears and grizzlies – and you don't want to meet either up close. They're at their most common around Glacier National Park, which has the largest concentration of grizzlies in the lower 48 – though elsewhere in the Rockies it pays to know what to do if you encounter either species. In the national park, sightings are monitored and posted at park centers, and the risks of running into a bear are pretty low on heavily tramped trails. Regardless, it's still essential when hiking and camping to be vigilant, obey basic rules, know the difference between a black bear and a grizzly (the latter are bigger and have a humped neck), know how to avoid dangerous encounters, and understand what to do if confronted or attacked.

Popular misconceptions about bears abound – that they can't climb trees, for example (they can, and very quickly) – so it's worth picking up the national park services' free bear country leaflets, which cut through the confusion and lay out some occasionally eye-opening procedures.

Be prepared, and if you don't want to be attacked, follow the **cardinal rules**: store food and garbage properly, make sure bears know you're there, don't approach or feed them, and, if you find yourself approached by one, don't scream and don't run. When hiking, walk in a group – bears rarely attack more than four in a group – and make noise, lots of it, as you traverse the wilderness; bears are most threatened if surprised, so warning of your approach will give them time to leave the area. Many people shout, rattle cans with stones in or carry a whistle; be warned, the widely touted hand-held, tinkling bells are not loud enough. Be especially alert and noisy when close to streams, in tall vegetation, crossing avalanche slopes or when traveling into the wind, as your scent won't carry to warn bears of your approach: move straight away from dead animals and berry patches, which are important food sources. Watch for bear signs – get out quick if you see fresh tracks, diggings, and droppings – and keep in the open as much as possible.

Camp away from rushing water, paths, and animal trails, and keep the site scrupulously clean, leaving nothing hanging around in the open. Lock food and rubbish in a car, or hang it well away from a tent between two trees at least 4m above ground (many campgrounds have bear poles or steel food boxes). Take all rubbish away – don't bury it (bears'll just dig it up) and certainly don't store it in or near the tent. Avoid smelly foods, all fresh, dried, or tinned meat and fish, and never store food, cook or eat in or near the tent – lingering smells may invite unwanted nocturnal visits. Aim to cook at least 150 yards downwind of the tent: freeze-dried meals and plastic-bag-sealed food is best. Likewise, keep food off clothes and sleeping bags, and sleep in clean clothes at night. Bears have an acute sense of smell, so avoid *anything* strongly scented – cosmetics, deodorant, shampoo, gel, lip balm, insect repellents, toothpaste, sun screen. Bears can be attracted to women during men-

east of West Glacier. Built in 1939 by the Great Northern to house railroad workers, the hotel is named after English author and angler Sir Izaak Walton. It's surrounded by excellent trout fishing and over eighteen miles of groomed cross-country ski trails (see p.554) – those outside the park revert to mountain-bike trails in summer. The Empire Builder train service stops here on request. The inn has cozy, atmospheric rooms and four small converted cabooses that sleep four and have kitchenettes ($525 for three nights). Even if you're not staying here it's worth calling in to check out the lobby with its welcoming log fire, or for a drink in the hotel bar.

Just to the south of Essex is the **Goat Lick Overlook**, a short walk off the highway where you can watch mountain goats slurping away at salt seeping out of cliffs.

struation, so dispose of tampons in an airtight container; they're also attracted by the smell of sex, so watch what you do in your tent if you don't want a rather drastic coitus interruptus.

Bears are unpredictable, and experts simply can't agree on best tactics: there's no guaranteed life-saving way of coping with an aggressive bear. Calm behavior, however, has proved to be the most successful strategy in preventing an attack after an encounter. Bears don't actually want to attack; they simply want to know you're not a threat. Mothers with cubs are particularly dangerous and prone to suspicion. A bear moving towards you can be considered to have it in for you, other signs being whoofing noises, snapping jaws, and the head down and ears back. A bear raised on its hind legs and sniffing is trying to identify you: if it does it frequently, though, it's getting agitated; ideally, on first encounter you want first to stand stock still, never engage in direct eye contact (perceived as aggressive by the bear) and – absurd as it sounds – start speaking to it in low tones. Whatever you do, don't run, which simply sets off an almost inevitable predator–prey response in the bear (a bear can manage 35mph – easily faster the fastest Olympic sprinter); instead, back away quietly and slowly at the first encounter, speaking gently all the while to the bear. If the backing off seems to be working, then make a wide detour, leave the area or wait for the bear to do so – and always leave it an escape route. If things still look ominous, set your pack gently on the ground as a distraction as you continue to back away.

If **attacked**, things are truly grim, and quack tactics are unlikely to help you. With grizzlies, playing dead – curling up in a ball, protecting face, neck and abdomen – may be effective. Fighting back will only increase the ferocity of a grizzly attack, and there's no way you're going to win. Keep your elbows in to prevent the bear rolling you over, and be prepared to keep the position for a long time until the bear gets bored. You may get one good cuff and a few minutes' attention and that's it – injuries may still be severe but you'll probably live. With a black bear the playing dead routine won't wash, though they're not as aggressive as grizzlies, and a good bop to the nose or sufficient frenzy on your part will sometimes send a black bear running: it's worth a try. Don't play dead with either species if the bear stalks or attacks while you're sleeping: this is more dangerous, as bears are often after food. Instead, try and get away or intimidate – people who have survived such attacks have often had a brave companion who has attacked the bear in return with something big and heavy.

Chemical repellents – know as **bear spray** – are available, but of unproven efficacy, and in a breeze you're likely to miss or catch the spray yourself. If this all sounds too scary to make you even contemplate walking or camping, remember that attacks are very rare – consider the number of people out there hiking compared to the rarity with which you hear of attacks and you'll get a realistic view of the threat.

Polebridge and the northwest corner

The park's northwest corner is one of its least explored regions, where the clear waters of the North Fork of the Flathead River wend in and out of the park's northwest boundary (the Canadian border). Unfortunately a good deal of this area was burnt by wildfires in 2001, but even this can't detract from the marvellous views east to the high mountains of the Livingston Range, along which runs the Continental Divide.

The small and atmospheric settlement of **Polebridge** sits just outside the park along the bumpy, partially paved Inside North Fork Road from Apgar (see p.548). The town is a quaint collection of timber buildings and dirt streets with a grass-roots vibe and strong environmentalist leanings – the residents are strongly opposed to most plans for further development, whether it be road

Hiking and backcountry camping in Glacier National Park

With around 730 miles of **trails** to choose from, Glacier caters well for everyone from multiday backpackers to enthusiastic coach potatoes – indeed, even the busiest and easiest hikes allow you access to some of the finest scenery. However, in summer the more popular trails around Lake McDonald, Many Glacier, and along Going-to-the-Sun Road can get absurdly busy, to the point of actually having to wait in line. At these times, make a break for less-visited areas of the park such as the northwest corner if you're looking for a true backcountry experience. The best **map** for all hikers is the USGS *Topographic Map of Glacier National Park* (1:100,000) which costs $7. Remember when planning your hike that GPI offers a hiker's **shuttle** service (see p.542), meaning not all trips need to be planned as round-trip.

A permit, available for a maximum of six nights, is required if you're planning on **camping in the backcountry**. These cost $4 per person per night and are available from most ranger stations (see box on p.543). You must camp in one of the sixty or so designated backcountry sites, and only those closest to roads and park entrances are likely to require a reservation. Reservations for more than 24 hours in advance are available at Apgar, St Mary, and by mail for a $20 reservation fee from Glacier National Park – Backcountry Permits, West Glacier, MT 59936 (Ⓣ406/888-7800). More information on backcountry camping and hiking is available on the Glacier National Park website (Ⓦwww.nps.gov/glac/home.htm), including an incredibly useful pdf file that can be downloaded for free.

The one thing that can't be stated too much about Glacier is that this is grizzly and black **bear country**, and you need to keep this in mind at all times. For detailed advice on hiking and camping in bear country, see the box on p.550.

Unless otherwise noted, the distances for the following hikes are all round-trip:

Avalanche Lake Trail four miles. This easy hike has only 500ft of ascent, and begins at *Avalanche Creek Campground* on Going-to-the-Sun Rd, where parking can be tight. The trail wends its way through Pacific Northwest rainforests, with good views of the deeply incised Avalanche Creek. From the trail end at the lake in early summer you can watch in safety as avalanches roll down off Little Matterhorn, Bearhat Mountain, and Mount Cannon.

Cracker Lake Trail twelve miles. This moderately strenuous hike has 1400ft of ascent and makes a long half-day out, or a more relaxed full day, but it can be busy. The trail starts from *Many Glacier Hotel*, up through steep-sided Canyon Creek Canyon to Cracker Lake, with truly magnificent views, including Mount Siyeh towering 4000ft above.

Grinnell Glacier six miles, or four miles from boat dock at head of Lake Josephine. The longer trail, which starts from Swiftcurrent Picnic Area above Many Glacier, is pretty strenuous with 2800ft of ascent. From the trail-head, follow the west shore of Swiftcurrent Lake then cross to the

building, logging, mineral exploration, or town expansion. The *North Fork Hostel* here (see p.546) is a great base if you want to kick back and enjoy some quiet daytime hiking and mellow evenings in the adjacent *Northern Lights Saloon* (see p. 555).

From Polebridge, the Inside North Fork Road heads north to end at pretty **Kintla Lake**, set beneath Kintla Peak (10,101ft). Equally attractive is **Bowman Lake**, a six-mile drive northeast of Polebridge. The quiet woods and lakeshore in both areas are home to a wide variety of wildlife including moose, bears, mountain lions, and wolves.

Note that in winter, the North Fork Road is closed, and you'll need to use the Outside North Fork Road from Columbia Falls or Blankenship Road off US-2 to the south of West Glacier.

north shore of Lake Josephine – halfway along the lake you begin to climb steadily up to Grinnell Glacier, where icebergs bob in the small tarn beneath the glacier. Craggy mountain peaks and the massive Garden Wall arete tower above you at this point.

Hidden Lake Overlook two miles. If you're pushed for time and you're driving the Going-to-the-Sun Rd, try this short, easy (but invariably busy) hike. From the trailhead at the Logan Pass Visitor Center, the trail passes through alpine meadows often strewn with wildflowers in midsummer and protected by a boardwalk, beneath towering peaks such as Mount Oberlin (8180ft) and Reynolds Mountain (9125ft). The trail ends at a superb overlook hundreds of feet above Hidden Lake.

Highline Trail fifteen miles one-way. The Highline Trail teeters along the west side of the Garden Wall with marvellous views of the mountains, waterfalls, and lakes of the west side of Glacier, plus a chance to call in at Granite Park Chalet for lunch or even overnight (see p.544). The trail starts at the Logan Pass Visitor Center and edges up above the valley floor (there are handholds for the less confident) past Haystack Butte and to the chalet, then over Swiftcurrent Pass and east steeply down to Many Glacier, from where you'll need to shuttle back to your start point. Note that this trail can be busy – the earlier you start the better.

Iceberg Lake ten miles. This is a moderately strenuous hike with around 1000ft of ascent. The trail starts from the parking lot behind *Swiftcurrent Motel* and climbs gently upwards through wildflower meadows and forest to the aptly named Iceberg Lake, strewn with huge chunks of ice.

Pitamakan and Dawson Passes nineteen miles. This is a hard hike taking in around 3000ft of ascent, best done as an overnight backpacking trip. From the trailhead at Pray Lake, just below Two Medicine Lake, you climb north beneath 9513ft Rising Wolf Mountain, along the side of Dry Fork Creek (which is anything but) to Oldman Lake. The trail continues upwards to Pitamakan Pass, then over the Continental Divide and south to Dawson Pass, where you cross back over the divide again and descend steeply to No Name Lake beneath the sheer walls of Pumpelly Pillar. Then the trails lead back along the north shore of Two Medicine Lake to the start. A superb high mountain experience.

Red Eagle Lake Trail fifteen miles. Despite its length this old buffalo-hunters' trail has only 200ft of ascent. From St Mary Ranger Station the trail meanders past the south shore of St Mary Lake to Red Eagle Lake where you can camp overnight.

Swiftcurrent Lake Trail three miles. A great chance to enjoy glacier views without any major effort, this easy, level loop around Swiftcurrent Lake gives you sight of Grinnell and Salamander Glaciers and 9553ft Mt Gould. The trailhead is at the Many Glacier Picnic Area.

Outdoor activities in Glacier

Although most people come to Glacier for its superb hiking (see box on p.552), there are plenty of other oútdoor options in the park. The original way to see Glacier was on lodge-to-lodge **horseback trips**, and guided horseback rides around the park are still possible with Rawhide Trail Rides, located near West Glacier (ⓣ1-800/388-5727), the Lake McDonald Corral (ⓣ406/888-5121), and Many Glacier Corral (ⓣ406/732-4203). Look to pay around $50 for a half-day ride.

Out of West Glacier, both the Glacier Raft Company (ⓣ1-800/235-6781, ⓦwww.glacierraftco.com) and Glacier Whitewater (ⓣ1-800/700-7056, ⓦwww.riverwild.com) offer relaxed Class II/III **whitewater rafting** trips down the Middle and North Forks of the Flathead on the western and southern park boundaries; expect to pay $40 for a half-day trip. Another water-based option is to get out onto some of the park's lakes under your own steam – rental of **canoes**, **kayaks**, **rowboats**, and small **motor boats** is available at Lake McDonald, Two Medicine Lake, and Many Glacier Lake (not motor boats) – contact Glacier Park Boat Co. (ⓣ406/226-4467) for details. Canoes and rowboats cost around $5 an hour, motorboats $15 an hour.

Anglers can fish without a permit on the park's lakes and on the Middle and North Fork of the Flathead within Glacier (outside the park a Montana state permit is required). The lakes tend to be better than the rivers though, with Bowman Lake, Lake McDonald, and Glenns Lake being amongst the best for cutthroat, brook trout, kokanee, and Arctic grayling, and boat fishing usually gives the best catches.

If Glacier's lakes and mountains are too busy for you in summer, try visiting in winter for some fine **cross-country skiing** and **snowshoeing**. The Going-to-the-Sun Road is kept open as far as the northeast end of Lake McDonald, from where trailheads lead off in many directions. All the park's hiking trails are also accessible for cross-country skiing and snowshoeing. Relatively easily accessible trails include the 11.6-mile round trip to Avalanche Picnic Area at the upper end of Lake McDonald, which has good views of McDonald Creek and the mountains of the McDonald Valley, and the six-mile Autumn Creek Trail at Marias Pass, which again has beautiful mountain views.

Eating and drinking

The **restaurants** in Glacier and its gateway towns are not always that inspiring – although there are some exceptions – and they're quite pricey. Everyone seems pretty much too tired out after a day spent foraging about for there to be much of a **nightlife** scene in and around the park – if you need a night on the town, head over to nearby Whitefish (see p.534). Campers should stock up on supplies at a supermarket in one of the park's gateway towns, or better yet stop even further out in Kalispell or Whitefish where the markets are even cheaper.

West Glacier and around

Belton Chalet Grill and Dining Room US-2 E ⓣ406/888-5000. One of the best dining options around Glacier, the recently refurbished chalet takes you back to the Great Northern chalet's 1920s glory days. The original dining room has marvelous views of the surrounding forests and mountains, as does the large deck – try the grilled pork chops rolled in cracked peppercorn and grilled ($19). The adjacent Taproom has a large selection of Montana microbrews and is an especially cozy spot in winter when you can sit by the log fire and watch the trains passing just outside.

Eddie's Restaurant Apgar Village. Located at the southwest end of Lake McDonald, *Eddie's* does good-value buttermilk pancakes, apple pies, and huckleberry shakes, plus a nice pan-fried trout for dinner ($15), served up in unpretentious surroundings at the foot of the lake.

River Bend Restaurant 200 Going-to-the-Sun Rd, Apgar Village ☎406/888-5403. A good spot for a filling breakfast before heading out into the wilds.

Russell's Fireside Dining Rooms *Lake McDonald Lodge* ☎406/888-5431. The hunting lodge theme here is nicely done with huge rough-hewn beams and hunting trophies lining the walls, but it's not cheap – the specialty is game dishes, each of which will set you back over $20. However, you can pick up a salad or chili for around $10.

East Glacier and around

Great Northern Steak and Rib House *Glacier Park Lodge* ☎406/226-5551. One of the best restaurants in the park complete with an impressive lodge-style timber interior. The menu has a Western-theme consisting of beef, barbecued ribs, chicken, and fish entrees from $20 up. There's also a full breakfast buffet from 6.30am.

Serrano's 29 Dawson Ave (mid-April to mid-Oct) ☎406/229-9392. Serves delicious Mexican food and microbrews, and a great margarita. You can get a filling meal here for under $12, meaning it's nearly always busy.

Whistlestop Restaurant 1020 Hwy-49 ☎406/226-4426. Excellent barbecue chicken and ribs for $10 up, tasty breakfast omelettes and great homemade desserts, plus a bustling and friendly atmosphere make this one of the best bets if you're on a budget. *Brownie's* in the same building does an excellent range of home-baked breads, bagels and pastries, deli sandwiches, and ice cream.

St Mary, Many Glacier, and around

Italian Gardens Ristorante *Swiftcurrent Motor Inn*, Many Glacier ☎406/732-5531. If you're into pizza or pasta this is the spot. A large pizza goes for around $13 and the setting is relaxed and informal; if you're setting out early breakfast is available from 6.30am.

Johnson's St Mary ☎406/732-5565. Located at the north end of town on US-89, *Johnson's* does filling, no-frills home-cooked meals varying from burgers and fries to pies and pastries – $10 should see you full to busting.

Ptarmigan Dining Room *Many Glacier Hotel* ☎406/732-4411. Swiss-themed decor and great lakeside views add to the ambience of the *Ptarmigan* although the menu tends to be fairly standard and not especially cheap – an entree will set you back $20 up.

Two Sisters Café Hwy-89, Babb ☎406/732-5535. Located four miles north of St Mary, the bright and friendly *Two Sisters* is worth the drive just to check out the "Aliens Welcome" sign on the roof. The food is also top notch, with breakfasts for around $6, lunch $10, and dinner $15. Highlights of the menu include chicken-fried steak ($12) and St Mary Lake whitefish ($14).

Polebridge

Northern Lights Saloon 80 Beaver Drive, Polebridge ☎406/888-5241. Smack in the middle of the village and the focal point of social life here. A great place to eat excellent pub grub – the burgers are especially good – sink a few cold ones and join in the Friday evening volleyball games on the grass outside.

The northwest corner

Montana's isolated upper **northwest corner**, wedged between US-93, Glacier National Park, and the Idaho and Canadian borders, is the least explored part of the state. The dense forests and wild mountain ranges have more of a Pacific Northwest feel about them, and have always been difficult to travel through, though for most of the twentieth century logging companies did their best to remove as much timber as possible from the region. It would be folly to come all this way for recreation and exploration rather than opt for nearby Glacier or Whitefish (or Sandpoint in Idaho which is equally close, see p.645), but for low-key towns such as **Eureka** and untrammelled wilderness like that of the **Cabinet** and **Purcell mountains**, you could do worse.

Eureka and Lake Koocanusa

The pleasant small town of **EUREKA**, some 50 miles northwest of Whitefish, makes for a decent stopover for travelers en route to or from Canada, with atmospheric Victorian buildings lining its main strip, Dewey Street (US-93), and housing bookstores, gift stores, and coffee shops. Similar structures are collected in the slightly ramshackle **Tobacco Valley Historic Village** (call for opening times ⓣ406/296-2514) at the south end of town, made up of old buildings salvaged from the village of Rexford to the northwest.

Call in for a coffee and pastry at the *Sunflower Bakery and Coffeehouse* on Dewey Street, or lunch or dinner at the popular *Dewey Street Diner* (ⓣ406/296-2197) in the center of town. If for some reason you need to **stay** overnight, try *Creek Side Motel*, 1333 Hwy-93 N (ⓣ406/296-2361; ❸), which has good-value, clean rooms plus RV and tent sites for around $15. If you head north out of town you pass the Eureka Ranger Station, 1299 US-93 (ⓣ406/296-2536), the best source of information on hiking in the region, then a little further on you have the choice of turning west onto Hwy-37 or continuing north for seven miles to the **Canadian border** (open 24 hours).

Hwy-37 takes you alongside the sparkling blue waters of ninety-mile-long **Lake Koocanusa** (for *Koo*tenai, *Can*ada, *USA*), of which almost half lies in nearby British Columbia. The lake is the result of damming the Kootenai River, an act quite harmful to wildlife habitats downstream. However, that hasn't stopped it from becoming a popular recreational site, with plenty of folks coming to fish or boat, or take advantage of the hiking and cross-country ski trails around **Libby Dam** at the south end. The dam's **visitor center** (June–Aug daily 9.30am–6pm; ⓣ406/293-5577) has some well-presented if somewhat self-serving displays, as well as the requisite info on what to do in the area.

Libby

Although in a fine setting beneath the forested slopes of the Purcell and Cabinet mountains, the no-nonsense lumber town of **LIBBY**, at the junction of US-2 and Hwy-37, isn't given over to tourism and has little to hold most travelers. Around half the town is employed by the Stinson Logging Company, and with the decline in logging the kind of views most travelers hold on forest conservation doesn't always go down well with the locals.

The heyday of logging and mining times is recalled in the **Heritage Museum**, 1367 US-2 E (June–Aug daily 10am–6pm; free), which has fairly standard exhibits of logging and mining equipment including a logger's cookhouse and miner's cabin. Otherwise, the only thing that might detain you are a few decent **bars** and **restaurants**. *Beck's Montana Café*, 2425 US-2 W (ⓣ406/293-6687), is good for breakfast, with excellent huckleberry pancakes, while lunch or dinner can be had at the friendly *Hidden Chapel*, 1207 Utah Ave (ⓣ406/293-3129), where the menu includes fairly standard steak, seafood, and

Turner Mountain

Unpretentious **Turner Mountain** (Fri–Sun; ⓣ406/293-4317, ⓦwww.libby.org/ski-turner), twenty miles north of Libby on Hwy-57, is very much a mountain for experienced skiers and boarders. A full seventy percent of its runs are marked off for advanced, twenty percent intermediate, and a measly ten percent for beginners; 75 percent of the runs are also ungroomed. The mountain receives 250 inches of **annual snowfall** and has a pretty modest high point of 5952ft, below which is a respectable 2110ft of **vertical**; it also claims to have the longest T-bar in the world (1.1 miles in length) – snowboarders in particular should note that this is the only lift on the mountain. There's a snack bar and ski and board rental at the base, but not much else. Lift tickets are $19.

chicken dishes – expect to pay around $20. About seven miles north of town on Hwy-567 is the rustic and lively *Red Dog Saloon*, where the pizzas are the best in the area and the locals are friendly, although the bar staff can be pretty sullen. It's a good spot to bike to on a summer evening or stop off after skiing Turner Mountain (see box, opposite). For information on hiking, camping, and local trails, contact **Kootenai National Forest Office** on the west side of town at 1101 US-2 W (☎406/293-6211).

North of Libby: Yaak

About an hour north of Libby on CO-567 is tiny **YAAK**, set in the valley of the same name. The town has little to offer, save its perch on the edge of some terrific backcountry wilderness, full of moose, wolves, and grizzlies. The timber industry, the USFS, and the Sterling Mining Company have for decades extracted timber and minerals from the Yaak Valley to the detriment of the environment, with clear-cut operations in particular having destroyed or damaged watersheds and wildlife. If you decide to spend time here exploring what remains of the wilderness – and there's thankfully still a lot of it – there are small primitive **campgrounds** along the Yaak River Road (Forest Road 68), which links Yaak with US-2 to the southeast. There are seven sites at *Yaak Falls Campground* and another twelve at *Pete Creek Campground* (the nicest of the two) northwest of Yaak along Forest Road 92. Expect to pay $5-12. Maybe the best reason to come all this way is to grab a beer at the *Dirty Shame Saloon* (☎406/295-5439) at the junction of County Road 567 and 508 in town. Even if you're put off by the sign on the door advising you to turn in your firearms at the bar, you should find the folks friendly, the beer cold, the food good, and the rustic log-hewn interior warm and inviting.

West on US-2 to Idaho

US-2 runs west from Libby along the bank of the Kootenai River (the setting for parts of the Meryl Streep movie *The River Wild*); five miles on, you come to the **Kootenai Falls**, which drop 200 feet in a series of powerful turquoise cascades. These are the largest undammed falls in the northern Rockies, and a short trail from a roadside parking area takes you to the spray-blasted edge and across a wobbling suspension bridge above the falls.

About another ten miles west is the small town of **TROY**, which at 1892ft is the lowest point in Montana. You'll likely pass straight through, though if you're interested in floating sections of the Kootenai, you can try your luck with local outfitter Cabinet Mountain Adventures (☎1-800/201-7238), whose rates are $85 per day. If you need **accommodation**, the best choices are the *Holiday Motel*, 218 E Missoula (☎406/295-4117; ❸), or the *Ranch Motel*, 914 E Missoula (☎406/295-4332; ❸), both of which offer plain but adequate rooms. For **food** the rustic *Silver Spur* on US-2 W (☎406/295-9937) offers standard American cuisine.

Bull River Road to Thompson Falls

The former Indian trail of **Bull River Road** (Hwy-56) runs south for 35 miles from just below Troy, following the tumbling waters of the Bull River before joining Hwy-200 forty miles north of Thompson Falls.

On the east of both roads is the Cabinet Mountains Wilderness where there are numerous good hiking trails along the open mountain ridges and thickly forested valleys. If you don't have time to explore this inspirational landscape

Hiking in the northwest corner

It helps to like trees when you're **hiking** in the northwest corner, because you'll be spending most of your time slogging through and beside them until you get to higher ground. You'll also need to be especially **bear aware** as this is both grizzly and black bear territory. The following are some of the best hikes in the area, starting from the north near Eureka and heading down towards the Libby region:

Ten Lakes. The Ten Lakes Scenic Area is a region of alpine lakes and magnificent mountain views, which has several excellent trails within easy reach of Eureka. To get there turn off US-93 ten miles south of Eureka at Grave Creek (Forest Road 114) and follow the road to Forest Road 319 and its end about 25 miles from US-93. Here you'll find the trailhead for the 1000ft, two-mile ascent to Bluebird Lake, where you can join the Highline Trail (339) to make a multiday loop either north or south (contact Eureka Ranger Station (see p.556) for detailed maps).

Fish Lakes Canyon. Twelve-mile round trip. This hike feels more remote than it actually is and gives you a chance to experience the wild landscapes of the Yaak Valley as you trek along a narrow, rocky canyon laced with glassy lakes and larch and cedar forests. To reach the trailhead drive south from Yaak on Yaak River Rd (FR 68) for four miles then left on Vinal Lake Rd (FR 746) for 6.1 miles to the trailhead. From here it's a pretty easy six-mile hike with only 600ft of ascent to Upper Fish Lake.

Leigh Lake. Three-mile round trip. Although short there's 1000ft of climbing on this fine hike which takes you into the Cabinet Mountains Wilderness and beneath 8712ft Snowshoe Peak, the highest mountain in the region (which can also be climbed via this trail). To reach the trailhead drive south for 7.7 miles from Libby on US-2 then turn west on Bear Creek Rd (FR 278), then right on Big Cherry Creek Rd (FR 867) following signs for Leigh Lake, the trailhead being a further nine miles. The last two miles are rough and require a 4WD, so you may need to include this to make a longer but no less pleasant hike.

in detail, you can get a good feel for it by pulling over at **Ross Creek Cedar Grove** just south of Bull Lake and four miles down a steep gravel road. The western red cedars here make up a Pacific rainforest environment, rare in Montana, which can be accessed on a short interpretive hike. In winter there's a gorgeous cross-country ski trail through the trees.

Named after the intrepid Welsh explorer David Thompson (see box p.652) who established a fur trading post called Saleesh House here in 1808, unremarkable **THOMPSON FALLS** has in fact no falls at all to attract you, these having been dammed in 1916 to create a glassy lake. As a result, consider stopping only as a rest between Missoula and Sandpoint, Idaho; if for some reason you need to **stay**, try good-value *Rimrock Lodge*, just west of town on Hwy-200 (Ⓣ406/827-3536; ③), on a nice riverside location and with bright, neat rooms; it also has a decent **restaurant**.

Just east of Thompson Falls on Hwy-200, the **KooKooSint Mountain Sheep Viewing Area** affords one of your better opportunities to see a true Rocky Mountain patriarch. A full-grown bighorn male may average 40 inches at the shoulder and weigh as much as 350 pounds, and his huge curved horns grow up to 50 inches long. These are used for battering opponents during the early winter mating season, when they'll literally clash head on in bone shaking battles for a harem. Your best chance of seeing bighorns at KooKooSint is in spring or early winter. KooKooSint, incidentally, was the name the Flathead Indian gave David Thompson, literally "Man Who Looks at Stars," presumably from his use of the heavens for navigation.

Travel details

Trains

Whitefish to: Chicago IL (1 daily; 32hr 30min); East Glacier Park (1 daily; 1hr); Sandpoint, ID (1 daily; 2hr 30min); Seattle, WA (1 daily; 13hrs); West Glacier (1 daily; 30mins).

Buses

(All Greyhound unless otherwise stated)

Billings to: Bozeman (3 daily; 3hr 15min); Butte (3 daily; 5hr 30min); Helena (2 daily; 7hr); Missoula (3 daily; 8–9hr).

Bozeman to: Billings (3 daily; 3hr 15min); Butte (3 daily; 2hrs); Helena (2 daily; 3hr 30min–4hr); Idaho Falls (2 daily; 6hr); Missoula (4 daily; 5hrs).

Butte to: Billings (3 daily; 5hr 30min; Greyhound and Rimrock Trailways); Bozeman (3 daily; 2 hr); Idaho Falls (2 daily; 3hr 20min); Missoula (3 daily; 2–3hr).

Helena to: Billings (1 daily; 7hr; Rimrock Trailways); Bozeman (2 daily; 3hr 30min–4hr); Missoula (1 daily; 5hr 30min).

Missoula to: Billings (3 daily; 8–9hr); Bozeman (4 daily; 5hr); Butte (3 daily; 2hr 15min–3hr 30min); Coeur d'Alene, ID (3 daily; 4hr); Great Falls (2 daily; 6–7hr); Helena (2 daily; 4–5hr); Idaho Falls (2 daily; 8hr); Salmon, ID (1 daily Tues, Wed, Thurs; 3hr 30min; CART).

10

Idaho

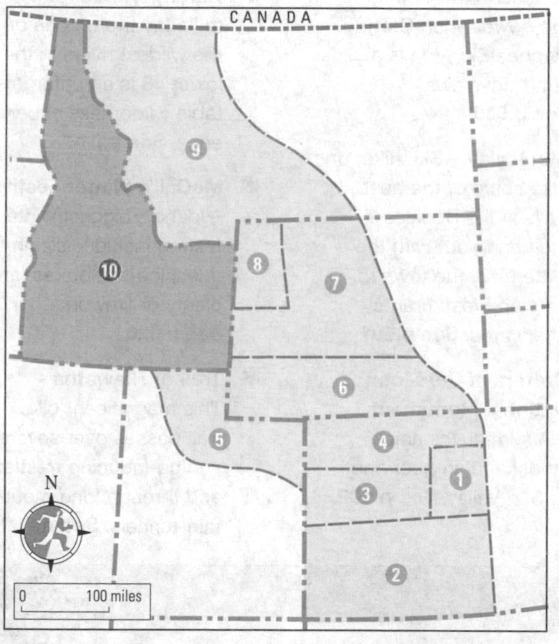

CHAPTER 10 **Highlights**

* **Boise** – Attractive and full of green spaces, Idaho's surprisingly diverse state capital makes for a fine base. See p.567
* **Driggs** – Home to some superb outdoor action in summer and in winter the powder-rich Grand Targhee Ski Area is a short drive away. See p.585
* **Sun Valley** – Ski, hike, or bike some of the best trails in the Rockies – then hang out with the glitterati in the town's bars and restaurants afterwards. See p.591
* **Craters of the Moon National Monument** – A surreal volcanic landscape an hour south of Sun Valley. See p.602
* **Sawtooth National Recreation Area** – Backpack among the spectacular Sawtooth Mountains, and call in at Stanley when you get back to civilization. See p.604
* **Rafting the Salmon** – A multiday trip on one of the wildest rivers in the lower 48 is an unforgettable wilderness experience. See p.616
* **McCall's Winter Festival** – Idaho's biggest winter festival includes sleigh rides, ice-sculptures, and plenty of fireworks. See p.620
* **Trail of Hiawatha** – This magnificent bike trail passes over several vertigo-inducing trestles and through long mountain-tunnels. See p.660

10

Idaho

The least visited of the Rocky Mountain states, rugged **IDAHO** was also the last of the lower 48 to be penetrated by whites, and is second only to Alaska in its sheer scale of barely explored **wilderness** areas. Though much of its scenery deserves national park status, its citizens have long been suspicious of encroachment by federal government and tourism alike, happy to let the rest of the nation believe that the only thing the state had to offer was massive mounds of potatoes.

In 1805, **Lewis and Clark** declared central Idaho's bewildering labyrinth of razor-edge peaks and wild waterways to be the most difficult leg of their mammoth journey from St Louis to the Pacific. Only their Shoshone guides enabled them to get through; to this day, there is no east–west road across the heart of the state. Reports of abundant wildlife attracted the usual legions of itinerant trappers, but the gold rush of the 1860s and white pressure for land is what truly hastened the violent end of traditional life here. Four hundred Shoshone men, women, and children were killed along the Bear River in 1863, the Nez Percé were driven out, and by the end of the 1870s the "Indian problem" had been eradicated.

Over a century later, Idaho's continued lack of major urban centers (the pleasant state capital **Boise** in the southeast the only real exception) makes it very much a destination for outdoors enthusiasts. Natural wonders in its five-hundred-mile stretch include **Hell's Canyon**, America's deepest river gorge, the dramatic **Sawtooth National Recreation Area** and the black, barren **Craters of the Moon National Monument**. Beyond these, **hikers** and **backpackers** have the choice of no fewer than 81 mountain ranges, interspersed with virgin forest and lava plateau, while the mighty **Snake** and **Salmon** rivers offer endless opportunities for **fishing** and **whitewater rafting**.

In winter, the trails cutting through Idaho's wilds, including the massive **Frank Church-River of No Return Wilderness Area** and idyllic **Priest Lake** region up near the Canadian border, are tailor made for secluded **cross-country skiing** and **snowshoeing**. No area, though, gets as much attention when the snow falls as the famed **Sun Valley** region, with its high-society resort aura and high-priced real estate. More down to earth – though no less worthwhile – resort towns pepper the rest of the state, including **McCall**, parked alongside the glinting blue waters of **Payette Lake** a two-hour drive north of Boise, and **Coeur d'Alene** and **Sandpoint**, two more amiable lakeside towns tucked away in Idaho's forested Panhandle.

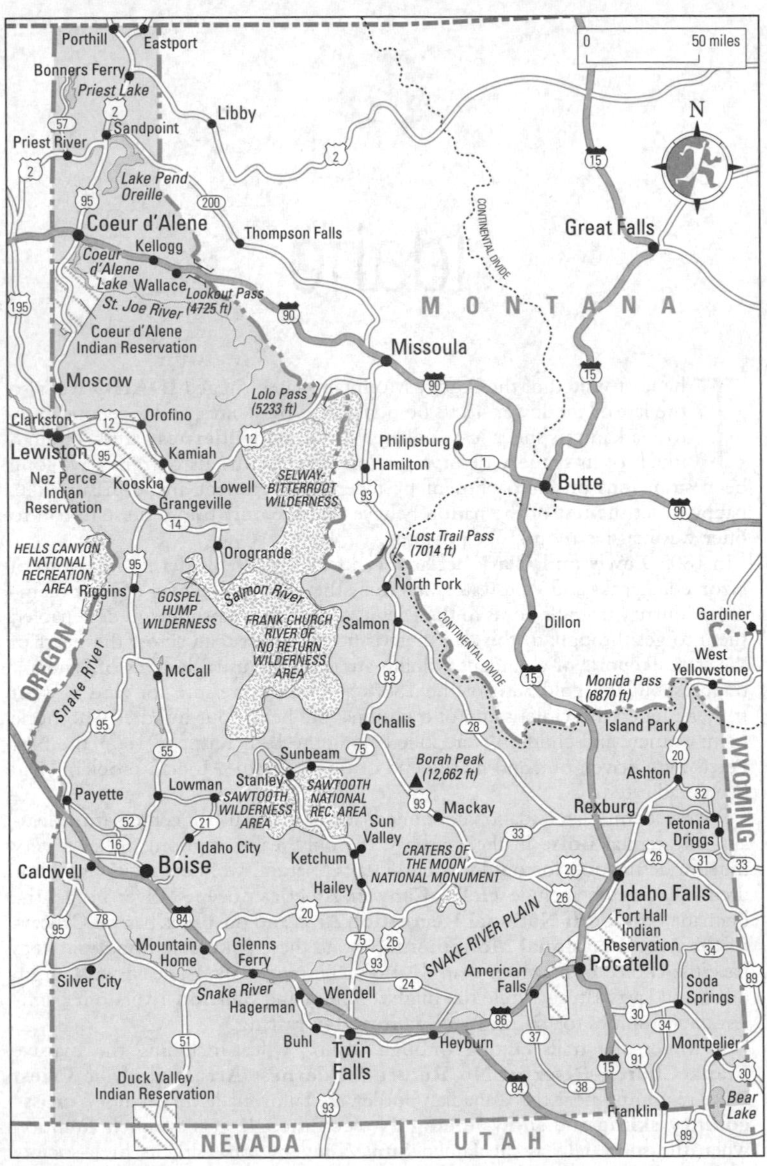
0
50 miles
N
Porthill
Eastport
Bonners Ferry
Priest Lake
Libby
Sandpoint
Priest River
Lake Pend Oreille
Coeur d'Alene
Kellogg
Thompson Falls
Coeur d'Alene Lake
Wallace
Lookout Pass (4725 ft)
St. Joe River
Coeur d'Alene Indian Reservation
CONTINENTAL DIVIDE
Great Falls
MONTANA
Missoula
Moscow
Lolo Pass (5233 ft)
Clarkston
Orofino
Lewiston
Kamiah
Philipsburg
Hamilton
Nez Perce Indian Reservation
Kooskia
Lowell
SELWAY-BITTERROOT WILDERNESS
Butte
Grangeville
Lost Trail Pass (7014 ft)
HELLS CANYON NATIONAL RECREATION AREA
Orogrande
Riggins
North Fork
GOSPEL HUMP WILDERNESS
Salmon River
FRANK CHURCH RIVER OF NO RETURN WILDERNESS AREA
Salmon
Dillon
Gardiner
OREGON
Snake River
McCall
West Yellowstone
Monida Pass (6870 ft)
Challis
Island Park
WYOMING
Sunbeam
Borah Peak (12,662 ft)
Ashton
Stanley
SAWTOOTH NATIONAL REC. AREA
Lowman
SAWTOOTH WILDERNESS AREA
Payette
Mackay
Rexburg
Tetonia
Driggs
Sun Valley
Idaho City
CRATERS OF THE MOON NATIONAL MONUMENT
Ketchum
Caldwell
Boise
Hailey
Idaho Falls
Fort Hall Indian Reservation
SNAKE RIVER PLAIN
Mountain Home
Glenns Ferry
Pocatello
American Falls
Soda Springs
Silver City
Snake River
Wendell
Hagerman
Montpelier
Buhl
Twin Falls
Heyburn
Duck Valley Indian Reservation
Bear Lake
Franklin
NEVADA
UTAH

Southern Idaho

Southern Idaho is home to the state's largest cities, including the vibrant capital of **Boise**, and is the center of its agricultural industry, with acre after acre of Idaho's famous **potatoes**. Though not as mountainous as the rest of the state, there are still plenty of memorably scenic areas to explore – just be prepared to drive through some monotonous landscapes of irrigated fields along the away.

The defining geographical feature is the huge sweep of the **Snake River Plain**. Before hitting the plains though, the Snake River, the country's sixth longest, runs west from Wyoming into picturesque southeast Idaho. Perhaps the most pleasing portion of southern Idaho, it's an inspiring landscape of rocky cliffs and waterfalls tucked beneath the daunting Grand Teton Range. Highlights include the small, outdoor-oriented town of **Driggs** and the nearby **Grand Targhee** ski resort in Wyoming, a powder-snow haven reached only via Idaho. Not far north, down a secluded dead-end road, you'll also find Idaho's only entrance to Yellowstone National Park. To the south of Driggs, a pair of scenic highways meander down towards the active **Bear Lake** area and the Utah border.

East of this mountainous region there's an attractive mix of farms and ranches set in fertile river valleys between arid mountains, along with **Idaho Falls** and the **Fort Hall Indian Reservation**, an easy detour from I-15. The Snake continues west onto a dry and dusty plain as it flows past the city of **Pocatello**, thunders over **Shoshone Falls** (higher than those at Niagara), and then through the city of **Twin Falls**. The river then turns northwest to be funneled between the massive walls of Hell's Canyon some two hundred miles later on. En route, it passes south of Boise, an eclectic place where you can fish for trout downtown, head off to watch a quality theater performance afterward and then finish the day at one of its excellent bars and restaurants. The town's outskirts feature great escapes as well, including quality skiing at the state's second-largest resort, **Bogus Basin**.

Idaho's largest resort, **Sun Valley**, is 150 miles east of Boise. The ski hill and the neighboring town of **Ketchum** are far removed from the stereotypical mountain man image of Idaho, attracting a jet-setting crowd of moguls and movie stars as well as families and ski and boarding junkies. An hour's drive southeast is the bizarre **Craters of the Moon National Monument**, where the surreal volcanic vista of lava cones, tubes, craters, and caves really does look more like a lunar landscape than the Rocky Mountains.

Accommodation price codes

All accommodation prices in this book have been coded using the symbols below. For **hotels**, **motels**, and **B&Bs**, rates are given for the least expensive double room in each establishment during peak season; variations are indicated where appropriate, including winter rates for all ski resorts. For **hostels**, the actual price per bed is given; for **camping**, the overnight cost per site is given. For a full explanation see p.30 in Basics.

❶ up to $30	❹ $60–80	❼ $130–180
❷ $30–45	❺ $80–100	❽ $180–240
❸ $45–60	❻ $100–130	❾ over $240

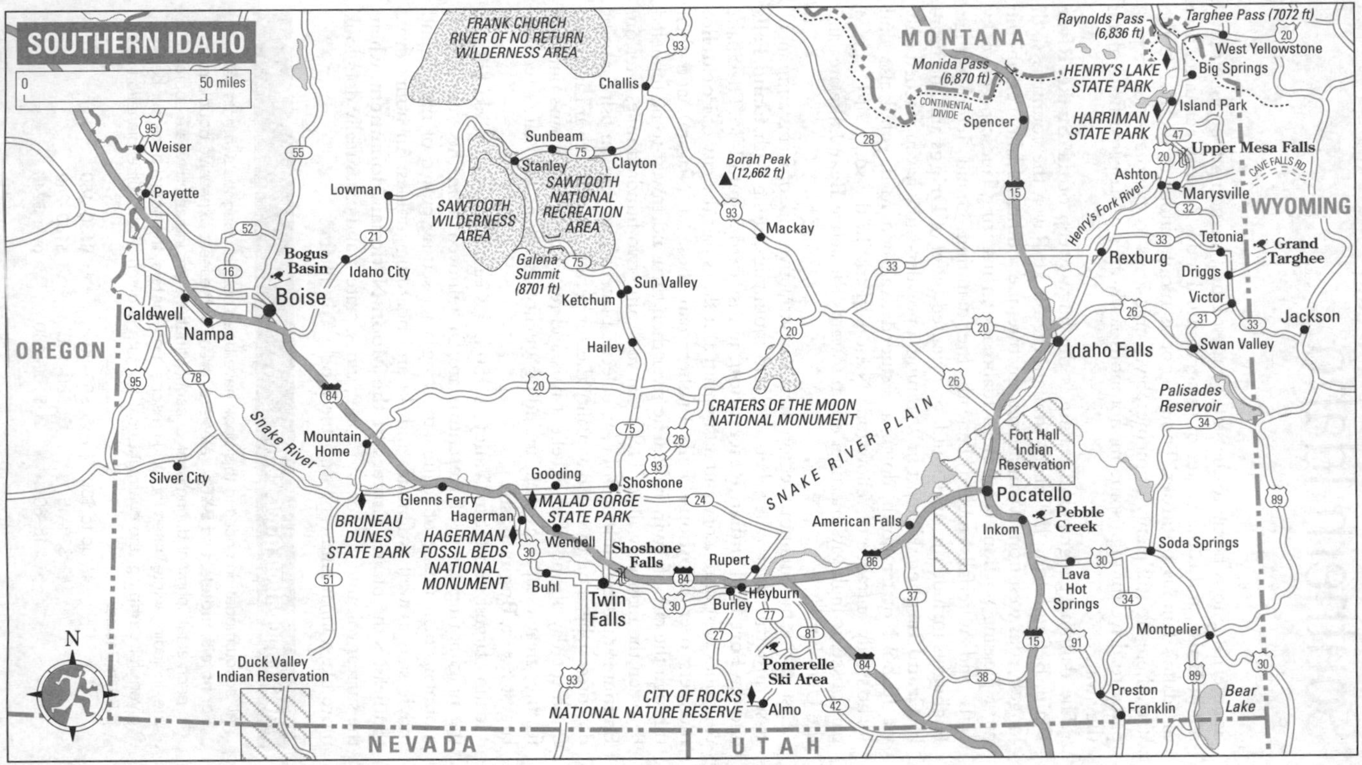

SOUTHERN IDAHO

0 50 miles

FRANK CHURCH RIVER OF NO RETURN WILDERNESS AREA
SAWTOOTH WILDERNESS AREA
SAWTOOTH NATIONAL RECREATION AREA
CRATERS OF THE MOON NATIONAL MONUMENT
SNAKE RIVER PLAIN
Borah Peak (12,662 ft)
Galena Summit (8701 ft)
Monida Pass (6,870 ft)
Raynolds Pass (6,836 ft)
Targhee Pass (7072 ft)
CONTINENTAL DIVIDE
CAVE FALLS RD
Henry's Fork River
Snake River
Palisades Reservoir
Bear Lake
HENRY'S LAKE STATE PARK
HARRIMAN STATE PARK
MALAD GORGE STATE PARK
BRUNEAU DUNES STATE PARK
HAGERMAN FOSSIL BEDS NATIONAL MONUMENT
CITY OF ROCKS NATIONAL NATURE RESERVE
Fort Hall Indian Reservation
Duck Valley Indian Reservation
Bogus Basin
Grand Targhee
Pebble Creek
Pomerelle Ski Area
Upper Mesa Falls
Shoshone Falls
MONTANA
WYOMING
OREGON
NEVADA
UTAH
Weiser
Payette
Caldwell
Nampa
Boise
Lowman
Idaho City
Mountain Home
Silver City
Glenns Ferry
Hagerman
Gooding
Wendell
Buhl
Twin Falls
Shoshone
Hailey
Ketchum
Sun Valley
Stanley
Sunbeam
Clayton
Challis
Mackay
Rupert
Heyburn
Burley
Almo
American Falls
Pocatello
Inkom
Lava Hot Springs
Soda Springs
Preston
Franklin
Montpelier
Idaho Falls
Rexburg
Spencer
Ashton
Marysville
Island Park
Big Springs
West Yellowstone
Tetonia
Driggs
Victor
Swan Valley
Jackson
N

Boise

A friendly city of 170,000 people, Idaho's capital **Boise** ("Boy-see") is proof positive that cities and the environment need not always be at odds. It's a well laid-out place, with an attractive mix of architectural styles and green spaces so unpolluted you can still swim and fish in the river that runs through its center. The downtown area, centered south of the impressive Capitol building, holds a fine collection of bars, restaurants, and galleries, and students from Idaho's biggest university, **Boise State University**, ensure that the nightlife scene remains active. Of course, with a location in the Rocky Mountain's western foothills, it's also home to a wealth of **outdoor activities**, with some of the USA's best skiing, hiking, and rafting all located within a three-hour drive. Some options, like the fine **Bogus Basin Ski Area** (see p.573) and the trails in the sagebrush hills of the 6000ft **Boise Mountains** are much closer.

Boise's beginnings date back to 1834, when a fort was built here as a trading post, used later by local gold miners and emigrants heading west on the Oregon Trail. As legend has it, the name is derived from French-Canadian trappers who, having just crossed the desert to the southwest, exclaimed "Les bois, les bois!" ("The woods, the woods!") upon seeing the lush expanse of greenery. One interesting claim to fame of the city is that it's the most remote urban area in the lower 48 – the closest metropolitan area in any direction is well over 300 miles away. It's actually more cosmopolitan than one might think, though, having over time attracted a mix of nationalities that includes Chinese gold miners, Japanese and Hispanic immigrants, and Basque shepherds – indeed, Boise's 20,000 strong Basque community is the largest such concentration outside the Pyrenees.

Arrival, information, and getting around

On the southeast edge of town is the busy **Boise Airport**, 3201 Airport Way (☎208/383-3110), with traffic to and from several major US cities, including Los Angeles, San Francisco, and Chicago. A **taxi** into town runs around $12 (try ABC Taxi ☎208/344-4444), but several of the major **car rental** companies – Avis, Budget, Hertz, and National – have offices here as well. There's no passenger train service, but Boise is reasonably well served by **bus**. Greyhound (☎208/343-3681) buses stop at 1212 W Bannock St, as do the Boise-Winnemucca/Northwestern Stage Lines (☎208/336-3302), with daily services to Spokane and Reno. If heading east to Sun Valley, Sun Valley Express (☎208/336-4038 or 1-800/821-9064) operates a charter service, including airport transfers, for $59 one-way, $89 return.

The **visitor center** (April–Sept Mon–Fri 10am–6pm; Oct–March Mon–Fri 10am–3.30pm; ☎208/344-5338, Ⓦwww.boise.org) is in the **Boise Center** next to The Grove and has a comprehensive selection of free literature and maps, including self-guided walks around Boise's historic sites. For outdoor information, head to the joint **USFS Boise National Forest** (☎208/373-4100) and **Idaho State BLM** (☎208/373-4000) visitor center (weekdays 7.30am–4.30pm) at 1387 S Vinnel Way.

Getting around the city's fairly compact core on foot or bike is easy enough. One thing to bear in mind, though, is that it can get extremely hot in summer, when temperatures of 100°F are not uncommon. The city's Boise Urban Services (BUS) (☎208/336-1010) run a fairly extensive bus service, including; routes #3 and #13, between downtown and the airport via Capitol Boulevard and Vista Avenue; route #5, between downtown and Towne Square Mall; and route #19 which serves Boise State University. Fares are 75¢ (35¢ Sat).

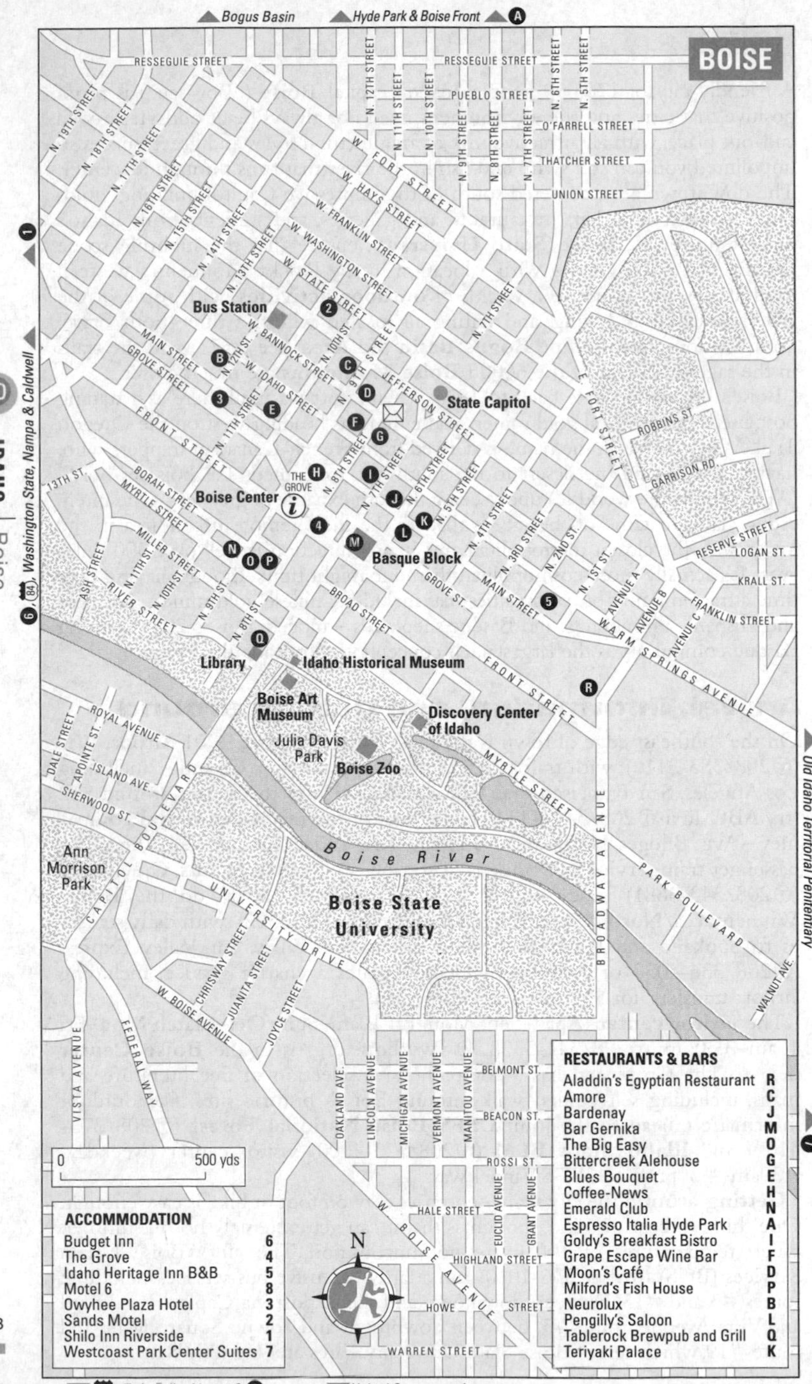
BOISE
Bogus Basin
Hyde Park & Boise Front
A
1
Washington State, Nampa & Caldwell
6 84
Old Idaho Territorial Penitentiary
7
84, Twin Falls, Airport & 8
United Campground
Bus Station
State Capitol
THE GROVE
Boise Center
Basque Block
Library
Idaho Historical Museum
Boise Art Museum
Discovery Center of Idaho
Julia Davis Park
Boise Zoo
Boise River
Ann Morrison Park
Boise State University
RESSEGUIE STREET
PUEBLO STREET
O'FARRELL STREET
THATCHER STREET
UNION STREET
N. 19TH STREET
N. 18TH STREET
N. 17TH STREET
N. 16TH STREET
N. 15TH STREET
N. 14TH STREET
N. 13TH STREET
N. 12TH STREET
N. 11TH STREET
N. 10TH STREET
N. 9TH STREET
N. 8TH STREET
N. 7TH STREET
N. 6TH STREET
N. 5TH STREET
N. 4TH STREET
N. 3RD STREET
N. 2ND ST.
N. 1ST ST.
W. FORT STREET
W. HAYS STREET
W. FRANKLIN STREET
W. WASHINGTON STREET
W. STATE STREET
W. BANNOCK STREET
W. IDAHO STREET
JEFFERSON STREET
MAIN STREET
GROVE STREET
FRONT STREET
BORAH STREET
MYRTLE STREET
MILLER STREET
RIVER STREET
ASH STREET
BROAD STREET
E. FORT STREET
ROBBINS ST.
GARRISON RD.
RESERVE STREET
LOGAN ST.
KRALL ST.
FRANKLIN STREET
AVENUE A
AVENUE B
AVENUE C
WARM SPRINGS AVENUE
ROYAL AVENUE
DALE STREET
APOINTE ST.
ISLAND AVE.
SHERWOOD ST.
CAPITOL BOULEVARD
UNIVERSITY DRIVE
BROADWAY AVENUE
PARK BOULEVARD
WALNUT AVE.
CHRISWAY STREET
JUANITA STREET
JOYCE STREET
W. BOISE AVENUE
FEDERAL WAY
VISTA AVENUE
OAKLAND AVE.
LINCOLN AVENUE
MICHIGAN AVENUE
VERMONT AVENUE
MANITOU AVENUE
EUCLID AVENUE
GRANT AVENUE
BELMONT ST.
BEACON ST.
ROSSI ST.
HALE STREET
HIGHLAND STREET
HOWE STREET
WARREN STREET
0 500 yds
N
ACCOMMODATION
Budget Inn 6
The Grove 4
Idaho Heritage Inn B&B 5
Motel 6 8
Owyhee Plaza Hotel 3
Sands Motel 2
Shilo Inn Riverside 1
Westcoast Park Center Suites 7
RESTAURANTS & BARS
Aladdin's Egyptian Restaurant R
Amore C
Bardenay J
Bar Gernika M
The Big Easy O
Bittercreek Alehouse G
Blues Bouquet E
Coffee-News H
Emerald Club N
Espresso Italia Hyde Park A
Goldy's Breakfast Bistro I
Grape Escape Wine Bar F
Moon's Café D
Milford's Fish House P
Neurolux B
Pengilly's Saloon L
Tablerock Brewpub and Grill Q
Teriyaki Palace K

Accommodation

Boise has a plentiful range of **accommodation** to suit most pockets, although surprisingly there's no hostel. There are, though, good-value motels and hotels within easy reach of downtown, as well as close to the Greenbelt, a pleasant and active route into town. It's a good idea to make reservations at peak periods, and note that if you're planning on **camping**, you'll need your own transportation to reach the closest sites.

Hotels, motels, and B&Bs

Budget Inn 2600 Fairview Ave ⓣ208/344-8617 or 1-800/792-8617. Recently remodeled rooms reasonably close to downtown, with low rates that include continental breakfast and free airport shuttle. ❷

The Grove Hotel 245 S Capitol Blvd ⓣ208/333-8000 or 1-800/426-0670, ⓦwww.westcoasthotels.com. Luxury accommodation in large, well-appointed rooms, many with great views over the city and mountains beyond. Convenient for downtown, facilities here include a fine restaurant, hot tubs, workout room, and a free airport shuttle. ❻

Idaho Heritage Inn B&B 109 W Idaho St ⓣ208/342-8066. This impeccably kept 1904 mansion is listed on the National Register of Historic Places and was once home to State Governor Chase Clark and Senator Frank Church (see p.614). The lovely period rooms, with queen-size beds, all have private baths and air conditioning. The owners can also arrange airport shuttles and rent mountain bikes. ❺

Motel 6 2323 Airport Way ⓣ208/344-3506. Modern, comfortable rooms make this the best bet for budget accommodation close to the airport. It also has an outdoor pool and facilities for the handicapped. ❸

Owyhee Plaza Hotel 1109 Main St ⓣ208/343-4611 or 1-800/233-4611, ⓦwww.owyheeplaza.com. A renovated, older hotel whose one hundred cozy rooms feature large, comfortable beds, cable TV, and dataports. It's right in the heart of downtown and has an outdoor pool and free airport shuttle. ❺

Sands Motel 111 W State St ⓣ208/343-2533. Within easy walking distance of downtown, so worth considering if you're on a budget. The rooms are a bit tatty though, and can be noisy due to thin walls. ❷

Shilo Inn Riverside 3031 W Main St ⓣ208/336-7377 or 1-800/344-3521. Situated in a bright and attractive greenbelt location with comfortable, spacious rooms. There's also a free continental breakfast and free airport shuttle, along with pool, fitness center, and laundromat. ❹

Ustick Inn Residence Hotel 8050 Ustick Rd ⓣ208/322-6277. An old farmhouse dating back to 1900, the *Ustick Inn* provides good-value longer-term (a week or more) accommodation in 26 private rooms and small dorms. It is, however, five miles west of downtown. A week runs $65–105, month $270–450.

Westcoast Park Center Suites 424 E Park Center Blvd ⓣ208/342-1044 or 1-800/325-4000, ⓕ208/342-2763. The large en-suite rooms here are popular with business travelers. Next to the Greenbelt, facilities include swimming pool and hot tubs along with a free continental breakfast. Rates are reduced at weekends. ❻

Camping

Fiesta RV Park 11101 Fairview Ave ⓣ208/375-8207. Two miles from downtown, the tent sites here are a bit pricey ($18), but you do get a pool, laundry room and games room. The sites are pleasantly grassy, though noise from the nearby road can be annoying.

On The River RV Park 6000 N Glenwood ⓣ208/375-7432 or 1-800/375-7432. Shady tent sites for $15, and showers and laundry facilities. The park is a couple of miles northwest of downtown and next to the Greenbelt, and you can swim in the Boise River.

United Campground 7373 Federal Way ⓣ208/343-4379. On the southeast side of town a couple of miles from downtown, complete with showers, laundry, and a small store. Tent sites are $14, but the location between Federal Way and the interstate won't be to everyone's tastes.

Downtown Boise and around

Sprouting up at the north end of Capitol Boulevard in the center of town is the Neoclassical **State Capitol** (Mon–Fri 8am–5pm, Sat–Sun 9am–5pm; free), easily Boise's most majestic building. This elegant native sandstone structure, modeled on the US Capitol, was begun in 1905 and took fifteen years to complete. Though the exterior is dominated by a 208ft-high dome topped with a bronze-plated eagle, it's the interior that's most impressive with its light, open feel, elegant architectural lines, and cool marble – four different types from Vermont, Alaska, Georgia, and Italy. A self-guided tour brochure is available from the visitor information desk on the first floor.

Three blocks south at 8th and Grove streets is **The Grove**, a pleasant traffic-free piazza with an unusual fountain spouting straight out of the street paving – in summer, youngsters drench themselves silly here. The area is a busy shopping and restaurant district, as is the **8th Street Marketplace** (Ⓣ208/344-0641), a trendy renovated early twentieth-century warehouse block a couple of minutes walk south of here.

Due east of The Grove, the unique **Basque Museum and Cultural Center**, 607–611 Grove St (Tues–Fri 10am–4pm, Sat 11am–3pm; $1), celebrates Basque culture through a series of reasonably interesting exhibits (including musical instruments and traditional crafts). Alongside is Boise's oldest brick building, the 1864 **Cyrus Jacobs-Uberuaga House**, built as a lodging house for Basque immigrants who came here in the nineteenth century to work as sheepherders – a job for which their lack of English was no disadvantage. More Basque culture can be found down the block at the **Basque Center**, home of the renowned **Oinkari Dancers**. There's also a pelota court where you can watch a game not unlike squash in which a ball is hurled against a wall using a wicker "sleeve" attached to the player's forearm, to then be returned by his opponent – it's said to be the fastest ball game in the world.

Immediately northeast is **Old Boise**, a quarter of attractive c.1900 residences extending several blocks east along Main Street from Capitol Boulevard; once night falls, the area either side of Capitol Boulevard is the place to be, with a good selection of bars and clubs to choose from.

Julia Davis State Park and around

Just a few hundred yards south of downtown is the inviting **Julia Davis Park**, through which flows the Boise River. Along with the **Ann Morrison Memorial Park** and **Kathryn Albertson Park** – both to the west – Julia Davis Park is linked into the Boise River Greenbelt (see box, opposite), one of Boise's main attractions. It also makes for a well-sited **Boise State University** campus, situated on its south side.

While this parkland is a fine place to laze about, there are also a few cultural attractions worth hitting up. The finest, and also Idaho's largest museum, is the **Idaho State Historical Museum**, 610 N Julia Davis Drive (Mon–Sat 9am–5pm, Sun 1–5pm; admission by donation). Amongst its collections are good displays on Native American and pioneer life – in particular those on the ethnic blend of Idaho's population, including a detailed look at the Chinese miners of the 1870s and 1880s, who were charged an exorbitant $4 monthly fee just to live in the Territory. Opposite is the **Boise Art Museum** (Tues–Fri 10am–5pm, weekends noon–5pm; also open Mon June–Aug; $3), featuring some fine works of photorealism. To the north is the **Discovery Center of Idaho**, 131 Myrtle St (Tues–Sat 10am–5pm, Sun noon–5pm; $4), an amusing interactive science and technology museum featuring such weird stuff as magnetic sand and a bike-riding skeleton. Also in the area is a small **zoo**, 355 N Julia Davis Drive (daily 10am–5pm; $4), and the **Morrison-Knudsen Nature Center**, 600 S Walnut St (Mon–Fri 10am–5pm, Sat–Sun noon–5pm; $2.50). Both feature various forms of captive flora and fauna that are really better viewed out in the wild.

The Boise River Greenbelt

Although Boise is blessed with plenty of wild country right on its doorstep, it also has a patch of it running through the middle of town in the form of the **Boise River Greenbelt**. This excellent nineteen-mile paved-trail crisscrosses the wooded banks of the sparkling Boise River, running from the northeast side of the city to the southeast. Accessible from several points on the river, the Greenbelt offers a great chance to **walk**, **jog**, **cycle**, or **skate** in the heart of an urban environment. Most of the route is **wheelchair** accessible, and it's also possible to **fly-fish** from the banks of the river and various piers.

A great way to escape the heat of the summer is to **float** the Boise River through here. You can hire inner tubes ($5) upstream at Barber Park towards the southeast end of the Greenbelt and enjoy as relaxed or as wild a trip down the river as you like. The journey to Shoreline Park just a few hundred yards southwest of downtown takes about 1.5 hours and there's a shuttle ($2) back to Barber Park.

Old Idaho Territorial Penitentiary

Two miles east of downtown along Warm Springs Avenue is the **Old Idaho Territorial Penitentiary**, 2445 N Penitentiary Rd (daily: June–Aug 10am–5pm, rest of the year noon–5pm; $4), a good and at times chilling demonstration of life in old Boise. Built in 1870, and used until 1973, this imposing sandstone-walled citadel is one of only three territorial prisons still standing in the US. The prison was built by the inmates themselves and was eventually closed by them as well after riots over the conditions occurred. The reasons for the rioting become obvious once you take the self-guided tour through the cramped solitary confinement unit (known as "Siberia") and the gallows room, where the last hanging took place in 1957. A small **museum** contains a unique prison tattoo art exhibition, a display of confiscated weapons, and mugshots of former inmates like Harry Orchard, who blew up the state governor in 1905 and served out his sentence here, dying in 1954 at the age of 88.

Hiking and biking around Boise

To get onto some of the area's fantastic trails, head for the **Boise Front**, the obvious rampart of hills north of the city. It's within hiking distance of the downtown, just past **Hyde Park**, a hip little suburb with good coffee and pizza joints. The views from the sagebrush and forest-speckled hills of the 75,000-acre Front are marvelous, as is the excellent system of more than twenty marked trails set aside for hikers, mountain bikers, and horseback riders, all of whom can get details from Boise Foothills Trail Riders (ⓣ208/387-2658). A couple of the better **hiking** trails here are the two self-guided loops (3.5 and 2.5 miles each) that make up the Hell's Gulch Interpretive Trail, beginning on a dirt road nearly four miles from the end of N 8th Street's pavement.

Besides the trails throughout the Front, **mountain bikers** should also head up for some higher elevation riding on the single-track trails running off the Bogus Basin Road, which climbs some sixteen miles north out of Boise up a switchbacked route to the Bogus Basin Ski Area. A good guide to local bike trails is *Mountain Biking in Southwest Idaho* by Stephen Steubner and Stephen Phipps (High Mountain Adventures). For more information and maps on the trails contact the joint **USFS Boise National Forest/BLM** office (see information, p.567).

Local outfitters

Benchmark 625 Vista Ave ⓣ208/338-1700. A good all-in-one stop as the knowledgeable staff can help out with most backpacking, hiking, rock climbing, fly-fishing, and adventure sports needs.

Bob Greenwood Ski Haus 2400 Bogus Basin Rd ⓣ208/342-6808. Devoted entirely to alpine skiing, the Ski Haus is one of the finest ski stores in Idaho. Located at the base of the road up to Bogus Basin Ski Area (see opposite), and they also do rentals.

The Idaho Angler 1033 Bannock St ⓣ208/389-9957. As well as having a huge range of equipment, the store also arranges fly-fishing trips and has a women's group that happily welcomes newbies to the mysteries of fly-fishing.

Idaho Mountain Touring 1310 Main St ⓣ208/336-3854. A well-stocked bike shop with a good range of road and mountain bikes and a helpful staff.

Idaho River Sport 1521 N 13th St ⓣ208/336-4844. Everything you need for whitewater action can be found here, including canoe and kayak rentals from $35 per day.

Eating, drinking, and nightlife

Boise has quite an eclectic range of **restaurants** and boisterous **bars**, most in the downtown area, meaning meandering about until finding something that strikes your fancy is the way to go. In the evenings, the city has a friendly buzz to it, especially on warm summer nights when outdoor dining is a feature of 8th Street, the main dining and drinking promenade. For entertainment **listings**, look for *The Boise Weekly*. It's also worth getting hold of the Friday edition of *The Idaho Statesman* for details on what's happening over the coming weekend.

Restaurants and cafés

Aladdin's Egyptian Restaurant 111 Broadway ⓣ208/368-0880. A variety of good, reasonably priced Egyptian/Middle Eastern dishes served in a bustling atmosphere. Belly dancing is featured Thurs–Sat, when it's best to reserve a table.

Amore 921 W Jefferson St ⓣ208/343-6435. Good pasta dishes, a fine wine list, and tempting desserts make this friendly Italian restaurant popular with locals, although entrees are slightly expensive at around $15 and up. A pleasant outdoor patio opens in summer.

Coffee-News 801 Main St ⓣ208/344-7661. Good coffee best enjoyed while browsing through the establishment's extensive selection of magazines and newspapers. Internet access is also available.

Espresso Italia Hyde Park 1530 N 13th St ⓣ208/336-5122. A good people-watching spot, this is the place to stop off for coffee and cakes prior to and/or after some exercise up in the nearby hills of Boise Front.

Goldy's Breakfast Bistro 128 S Capital Blvd ⓣ208/345-4100. A great spot for breakfast, with a large menu of equally large dishes, spanning from fresh fruit through to tasty omelettes and steaks. Go early or you'll have to queue, especially at weekends.

Grape Escape Wine Bar 800 W Idaho St ⓣ208/368-0200. Indoor or outdoor dining in the middle of downtown, with a vibrant atmosphere and some good-value Latin dishes, including excellent tapas and pasta dishes. As the name suggests, the wine list is extensive and will suit most tastes.

Moon's Café 815 Bannock St ⓣ208/385-0472. A traditional diner serving very filling breakfasts and lunches for between $5 and $10, along with fifteen different milkshakes, in a 1950s-style atmosphere.

Teriyaki Palace 501 Main St ⓣ208/345-3366. The *Teriyaki Palace* is renowned for its Asian-influenced cuisine – try the teriyaki chicken or beef cooked in the restaurant's own unique sauce. Sushi and a variety of Chinese dishes are also available, and there's a free local delivery service for orders over $15.

Milford's Fish House and Oyster Bar 405 8th St ⓣ208/342-8382. *Milford's* serves top quality seafood often flown directly in from Alaska or Canada, and also features Cajun and Creole dishes, all within a friendly New Orleans-style setting.

Bars and nightclubs

Bar Gernika 202 S Capitol Blvd ⓣ208/344-2175. A Basque bar with a warm and lively old world atmosphere where you'll likely hear Basque spoken, and can try traditional tapas dishes and wines.

Bardenay Restaurant & Distillery 610 Grove St ⓣ208/426-0538, ⓦwww.bardenay.com. The *Bardenay* meticulously distills its own gin, rum, and vodka (you can see the stills in the restaurant) in America's first legal distillery/pub. All drinks are served with fresh-pressed fruit juices or pure fruit liquors that produce superb cocktails. They're also obsessive about their beers and have an extensive and very good lunch and dinner menu, all served up in open, elegant surroundings.

The Big Easy 416 S 9th St ⓣ208/367-1212. Boise's top rock venue opened in 2000 with a performance by none other than James Brown himself. If there's a big-name band playing in Idaho, chances are this is where you'll find them, with cover charges varying depending on who's playing.

Bittercreek Alehouse 246 N 8th St ⓣ208/345-1813. Good beer (including Guinness and an excellent selection of US microbrews and European ales and lagers) are a big attraction in this always busy bar, which also serves fine bar food. In summer, a streetside patio area is opened.

Blues Bouquet 1010 W Main St ⓣ208/345-6605. One of Boise's top music venues, with a huge mahogany bar dating back to 1903 and regular music from local and touring bands. Cover charges vary from $3–15 depending on how big the name is.

Emerald Club 415 S 9th St ⓣ208/342-5442. One of the top dance clubs in town, the *Emerald* has a large dance floor and touts Thursdays as "Straight Night", although you'll usually find a good mix of both orientations every night.

Neurolux 111 N 11th St ⓣ208/343-0886. Pretty much a punk/grunge hangout, although the regular assortment of bands playing here aren't always of that ilk. Cover charge for bands is $3–5, otherwise free.

Pengilly's Saloon 513 W Main St ⓣ208/345-6344. The name may be Welsh but the joint is stylish old-time American, with an imposing dark wood 1880s bar, old-fashioned wooden booths and ancient brass chandeliers. The clientele varies from lawyers and politicians to students and travelers and the staff is wonderfully friendly, plus there's live music several times a week. Recommended.

Tablerock Brewpub and Grill 705 Fulton St ⓣ208/342-0944. Generally busy, this was the first brewpub in Boise and is still one of the best. It has a good selection of homebrewed beers – the Nut Brown is full of flavor – and serves good pub grub too.

Listings

Cinema Flicks Movie Theater, 646 Fulton St (ⓣ208/342-4222). Features both mainstream and art-house movies.

Hospital St Luke's Regional Medical Center, 140 E Bannock St (ⓣ208/381-1200).

Internet *Kinko's*, 691 S Capitol Blvd (ⓣ208/331-5100), is open 24 hours a day and charges 20¢ per min. The Boise Library, corner of Battery St and Capitol Blvd (ⓣ208/384-4114), has free service limited to 30min sittings.

Laundromat Norge Laundry, 515 N 15th St (ⓣ208/336-1917).

Police department 7200 Bannister St (ⓣ208/377-6790).

Post office The downtown post office is located at 750 W Bannock St (ⓣ208/343-5647), but general delivery mail goes to the main post office at 770 S 13th St (ⓣ208/383-4211).

Around Boise

When looking to escape Boise, most locals head either a hundred miles north to McCall and Payette Lake (see p.620) or slightly farther east over to the Sawtooth Recreation Area (see p.604) and Sun Valley (see p.591). There are, however, a couple of closer day-trips – namely the **Bogus Basin Ski Area** and historic **Idaho City** – that are well worth your time if you have some to spare.

Bogus Basin Ski Area

A short drive north of Boise, the **Bogus Basin Ski Area** (ⓣ208/332-5100, ⓦwww.bogusbasin.com) makes for a real feather in the state capital's cap. With an impressive 2600 acres of terrain, it's second in the state in skiable terrain only to Sun Valley. But, unlike its swanky competitor, the prices here allow you to ride or ski all day and still have change left over for a full night out.

The trip up to the resort on Bogus Basin Road is an adventure in itself, with a seemingly endless array of switchbacks on the sixteen-mile drive. The views of Boise are sensational, and once you get up onto the mountain proper the views become even better, especially northeast toward the Sawtooth Mountains. There's been a huge boom in business here since season passes for locals were cut down to $399, and for kids (7–11) to an unbelievable $29. This means it can get pretty busy at weekends, but it's a friendly atmosphere, and lift-lines can be a chatty affair. A day **lift-ticket** costs $37 ($10 kids), not bad considering that it's valid from 9am to 10pm as ninety acres are lit each evening for **night skiing**.

Bogus Basin's **annual snowfall** averages around 250 inches. The top elevation is 7600ft, and the longest groomed run tops out at 1.5 miles. The sixty-odd runs are rated 20 percent beginner, 45 percent intermediate and 35 percent advanced, and are served by seven lifts. Beginners will want to check out Nugget Cat Track and Easy Way Down first, which give a good overall feel for the mountain and the views it offers. Intermediates will find a great selection of wide-open runs such as Ridge and Playboy, and there are plenty of black diamonds, like Lower Nugget or Second Chance, if you want to push yourself a bit. There's also a **terrain park** with a nice selection of quarter pipes, rails, and jumps.

Cross-country skiers should head for the Bogus Basin Nordic Center (ⓣ208/332-5390), located a mile past Bogus Creek Lodge (see below). It has twenty-plus miles of groomed and skate-track skiing. You can also get lessons and rentals here; trail fees are around $8.

Practicalities

If you don't have your own transport, there's a **ski bus** ($8 round-trip; ⓣ208/459-6612) that operates weekends and holidays from various locations in Boise, and the satellite towns of Caldwell, Nampa, Middleton, Eagle, and Meridian. The **Bogus Creek Lodge**, at the base of the mountain, is where you'll find the busy *Deerpoint Café*, ticket sales, and ski and board **rental**. This is also where arrangements for ski lessons can be made. Halfway up the mountain is the **Pioneer Lodge**, home to *Bogus Bob's Grill* and the *Firewater Bar*, where there's good pub grub and a deck with great mountain views. Pioneer Lodge stays open until 11pm, useful not just for night skiers but also for guests at the only **accommodation** on the mountain – the *Pioneer Inn Condominiums* (ⓣ208/332-5200, ⓦwww.pioneercondos.com; ❻). The well-appointed rooms come complete with kitchens and ski lockers, and facilities include two hot tubs, a sauna, and a game room, and marvellous nighttime views over Boise.

Idaho City

It's a delightful forty-mile drive from Boise alongside the Lucky Peak Reservoir then up into the forested hills on the **Ponderosa Pine Scenic Byway** (Hwy-21) to **IDAHO CITY**. Once a booming mining town, Idaho City is not quite a ghost town today – some 300 people still live here full time – but it's certainly a far cry from its heyday in the 1860s when over 20,000 people mined the area. At its peak, it was the largest town between St Louis and San Francisco, with some 33 whiskey shops on its mile-long main street. The mines operated 24 hours a day, with miners working by the light of bon-

Silver City

A couple hours south of Boise into the remote **Owyhee Mountains** lies **Silver City**, an evocative ghost town that a century ago was a rip-roaring silver mining center. Most of the once 2500-strong population were miners who managed to extract a then colossal $60 million worth of silver and gold. Times were so good that, despite a remote mountainous location some 6000ft above desert plains, the city had one of the first telegraphs and the first daily newspaper in the Idaho Territory.

Even so, modern amenities did little to calm the tempers of the lawless town, and miners didn't take lightly to anyone infringing on their claims. A classic showdown occurred in 1868 when workers from two mines, the Ida Elmore and the Golden Chariot, discovered they were both working the same silver vein but from opposite ends of the mountain. Eventually the opposing companies met up underground and a gun battle broke out with at least one man being killed. A truce was negotiated, but when J. Marion More, one of the Ida Elmore's owners, met up with the Golden Chariot's Sam Lockhart on the porch of the town's **Idaho Hotel**, shots rang out again and both men eventually died from the encounter. More's ghost is said to wander the *Idaho Hotel*, PO Box 75, Murphy, ID 83650 (Ⓣ208/583-4104; ❷), *the* place to visit in town. Little has changed here in the past hundred years, and in the evenings, the generator-fed electricity is switched off, giving an even stronger sense of pioneer life.

To reach Silver City from Boise, head south on Hwy-78 from Nampa thirty miles south to the small town of Murphy; from here, it's a rough two-wheel-drive journey up to Silver City. Note that the dirt road up to Silver City is typically closed by early October and opens up again in mid-May.

fires and paying up to $100 per day for the water needed to sluice away the gold. By 1868 the gold was gone and within twenty years the population had fallen to its current state.

Its small grid of streets, fronted by clapboard houses, stores, and hotels mostly dating back to the nineteenth century, is invariably busy with tourists soaking up what remains of the Wild West atmosphere. The best of the historic buildings include the 1864 log-built Territorial Penitentiary, the 1865 Masonic Temple and the Boise Basin Mercantile, the state's first general store. The **Boise Basin Historical Museum**, 402 Montgomery St (June–Aug daily 11am–5pm; May & Sept Sat–Sun 11am–5pm; $2), is worth a look for its extensive collection of yellowed photographs from the boom days. Equally interesting is the **Pioneer Cemetery** on Centerville Road, where the headstones tell the tale of a time when life was cheap. Apparently only 28 of the first 200 residents died of natural causes.

Just 1.5 miles south of Idaho City on Hwy-21 is *Warm Springs Resort* (Ⓣ208/392-4437; ❷), open year-round for bathing in natural **hot springs**. Swimming fees are $4, and you can also rent **cabins** or **camp** ($6 tent/$20 RVs). To the northwest, Hwy-21 climbs through superb scenery to **Mores Creek Summit** (6118ft) before zigzagging down through fire-blackened forests to Lowman (see p.612) and the Sawtooth National Recreation Area beyond.

Southeast to Twin Falls

Besides a few dramatic natural attractions, there's not a lot that draws notice as you head south from Boise along I-84 to **Twin Falls** – brown dusty plains followed by large, heavily irrigated fields are the general order of the day. This is not an area that readily tempted the first pioneers, and until their arrival in the early 1800s it had been inhabited by the **Paiute**, **Bannock**, and **Shoshone** tribes. With the introduction of the horse in the 1700s, these tribes began to travel east over the Continental Divide into present-day Montana to hunt buffalo, and their trails were later used in the 1840s by pioneers heading in the opposite direction on the **Oregon** and **California Trails**. The trails themselves were used so heavily over the next fifty years that in places such as **Bonneville Point** just southeast of Boise the ruts can still be seen. By the early twentieth century, southwest Idaho and the Snake River Plain had become, with the help of massive irrigation projects, major farming areas, growing amongst other things the massive **potato** crops that Idaho is so well known for.

The first settlement of any size that you come to as you drive southeast from Boise on I-84 is **Mountain Home**, 48 miles distant. It's not in the mountains at all but set on a barren stretch of the Snake River Plain at the western end of the Magic Valley. Most notable as the turnoff for the Bruneau Dunes State Park, the town also holds the record for the highest mean temperature in Idaho – in summer, day-after-day of 100°F-plus temperatures are the norm.

Bruneau Dunes State Park

With all the heat and aridity in the area, the presence of the desert-like **Bruneau Dunes State Park**, twenty miles south of Hwy-84 on Hwy-51 ($2, camping $12/hookup $16; ⓣ208/366-7919), should come as no shock. Two interconnected dunes rise to a height of 470ft in a harsh landscape that looks especially dramatic at sunrise and sunset, when gold and russet shades drape themselves over the smooth wind-sculpted outlines. Sand has collected here over the last 15,000 years due in part to constant winds that blow for almost equal amounts of time from opposite directions – which means that unlike other dune systems these barely shift.

From the **visitor center**, located beneath the northern slopes of the dunes, there's a five-mile **hiking trail**, along which blacktail jackrabbits, western whiptail lizards, gopher snakes, and coyote may be spotted. The views from the top of the sand piles across the plains and to the nearby Owyhee Mountains are memorable, as is a leaping run back down them. If you're visiting in summer, it's best to come early in the morning or late afternoon to avoid the extreme heat. The adjacent **Bruneau Dunes Observatory Complex**, is open to the public on some nights – call the above number for details.

Malad Gorge State Park and the Thousand Springs Scenic Byway

About an hour's drive east of Bruneau Dunes along I-84 (exit 147) is the spectacular **Malad Gorge State Park** (daily sunrise–sunset; free). Though right off the freeway, most drive right by, oblivious to the fact that a mile off there's a 250ft rent in the earth's surface with a 60ft **waterfall**, the Devil's Washbowl, pouring into it. Though impressive, the waterfall is overshadowed by the huge, precipitous rocky chasm of the gorge itself, through which the **Malad River** flows to join the Snake River a mile south. A steel footbridge spanning it gives great views of the gorge and the waterfall, though the impact is somewhat marred by the roar of freeway traffic literally yards away. Above the gorge is a grassy **picnic area**, and there's a one-mile hiking **trail** along the north rim and a road along the south rim that can take you down to a spectacular overlook across the Snake River Canyon.

Connecting the towns of Bliss and Twin Falls, the fifty-mile-long **Thousand Springs Scenic Byway** (US-30) is well worth hopping off the interstate for as it cuts through the lush green **Hagerman Valley**. Amazingly, the valley is watered by scores of springs cascading out of the black-lava rock along the northeast wall of the Snake River Canyon. The source of all this water is thought to be the Lost River to the north of Craters of the Moon National Monument – it flows beneath the lava beds there and re-emerges in the canyon walls a hundred years (give or take) later. The springs can be seen from the road easily enough, and although irrigation has seriously reduced the flow of a number of them, they're an impressive site nonetheless.

A couple of miles south of Malad Gorge on the scenic byway is **Hagerman Fossil Beds National Monument**. Head first to the monument's **visitor center**, 221 N State St (June–Sept daily 8.30am–5pm; Oct–May Thurs–Sat 8.30am–5pm, Sun 1–5pm; free; ⓣ208/837-4793), to pick up a good self-guided tour leaflet of the fossil beds, which are viewed from a boardwalk overlook. The region is particularly famous for its horse fossils, including the Hagerman Horse, Idaho's "state fossil," though more than 140 animals – including mastodons and sabre-tooth cats – and 35 plant species have been found in the locality. To reach the fossil beds, head three miles south from Hagerman on US-30 and, after crossing over the Snake River, turn west on the road following its left bank – after about twelve miles, you'll come to signs for the site, which is set amongst 600ft-high bluffs.

If you decide to spend any time in the area, a good option is *The Rock Lodge,* one mile north of Hagerman at 17940 US-30 (ⓣ208/837-4822; ③), which has comfortable rooms and cabins and counts Ernest Hemingway among its past guests. There are also several hot springs nearby, the best being *Banbury Hot Springs* (ⓣ208/543-4098; $15) – turn east off US-30, ten miles north of Buhl, and follow the signs to this tranquil site where facilities include a lovely swimming pool fed by hot and cold springs, showers, and laundry.

Twin Falls and around

The uninspiring farming and ranching city of **TWIN FALLS**, 130 miles southeast of Boise on I-84, doesn't merit a visit of any length. Even the pair of falls it's named after are but a shadow of their former selves, though the nearby **Shoshone Falls** (see below) are worth a look. On your way there, load up on information and take in a grand view at the **Buzz Langdon Visitor Center** (daily 8am–8pm; ⓣ208/733-9458), easily reached from exit 173 off I-84 – it's on US-93 on the south side of the Perrine Bridge. Here, observation decks over the Snake River Canyon give you spectacular views down to the glistening waters nearly five hundred feet below. Two miles upstream of here, **Evel Knievel** made his ludicrous attempt to jump the canyon in 1974, and the ramp he took off from remains rooted to the ground.

Just east of town is the easy-to-find **Shoshone Falls Park** (June–Aug daily 7am–10pm; $3). Known as "The Niagara of the West," the park's horseshoe-shaped falls are 1000ft wide and 212ft high, 52ft higher than their more famous eastern cousins. Take a moment when viewing to think of Harry Wilson, who leapt off them in 1905 – according to the *Twin Falls Daily News*, "he swam to a rock and calmly awaited the arrival of his clothing, which had been removed before making the leap." The best viewing is during the spring snowmelt, when the waters plummet over the falls and are transformed into a mass of fine rainbow-colored spray; at other times, they can slow to a trickle as water is diverted upstream for irrigation.

North of Twin Falls to Sun Valley

From Twin Falls, US-93 heads north past the rather drab little railroad town of **Shoshone** and on across forbidding lava fields to the welcoming sight of the mountains and forests above Sun Valley, eighty miles north (see p.591). Ten miles north of Shashone, you'll pass **Mammoth Cave**, a lava tube about a mile long that can be explored on a self-guided tour ($5). Seven miles further north are **Shoshone Ice Caves** (May–Sept daily 9am–5pm; $5; ⓣ208/886-2058), more lava tubes into which water percolates and remains frozen year-round – a great boon to the area's first settlers. The forty-minute guided tour is moderately interesting, but the tacky tourist shop adds little to the site.

East to Pocatello

The patchwork of flat fields that I-84/86 cuts across from Twin Falls to Pocatello, the center of southeast Idaho about 120 miles away, has only a few attractions of note. First up is the **Pomerelle Ski Area** (ⓣ208/673-5599, snow report ⓣ208/673-5555), twenty miles south of I-84 on Hwy-77. Perched upon the 9265ft Mount Harrison, it's very much a local ski area rather than a visitor resort, with a maximum vertical of 1000ft and 22 runs. The snow is often good-quality powder, though, and lift tickets are only $20. In July and August, you can also use the lifts to access **hiking** and **mountain-biking** trails.

A further twenty miles south of the ski area is the **City of Rocks National Nature Reserve** (ⓣ208/824-5519; free). It's one of the US's premier rock-climbing sites, with over 600 routes on dramatic granite towers rising up for hundreds of feet out of pine and juniper forests. Intermediate to expert climbers will find more than enough to keep them occupied and there's invariably a large international community of climbers **camping** out at the primitive sites here (open April–Nov; $8). If you need **supplies**, Tracy's Merc (ⓣ208/824-5570), a couple miles to the east in **Almo**, is the place to head for.

Southeast Idaho

Squeezed in between a triumvirate of states – Montana to the north, Wyoming to the east and Utah to the south – the hills and mountains of **Southeast Idaho** rise verdantly up from the dry and dusty Snake River Plain. The modest stopover cities of **Pocatello** and **Idaho Falls** are the regional hubs, often used by travelers en route to or from the mountains and ski resorts of neighboring states and Yellowstone National Park. It's a shame that most just drive through, as much of this area is as beautiful – and more secluded – than the more famous landscapes to the east.

Pocatello and around

POCATELLO has an attractive location beneath high, rolling mountains, but the town itself is rather drab both visually and culturally, especially considering the fact that it's Idaho's second-largest city (pop. 53,000). Named after Shoshone chief Po-ca-ta-ro, Pocatello developed as a railroad junction in the late nineteenth century and has grown since as a center for the region's farming industry. The railroad runs right through the center of town (although there's no passenger service), adding a bit of character to an atmosphere that's rather down at heels, even with the presence of almost 13,000 students at **Idaho State University**. Pocatello is thus best seen as an overnight stopover or as a base for forays into the neighboring mountains, including the small **Pebble Creek Ski Area**.

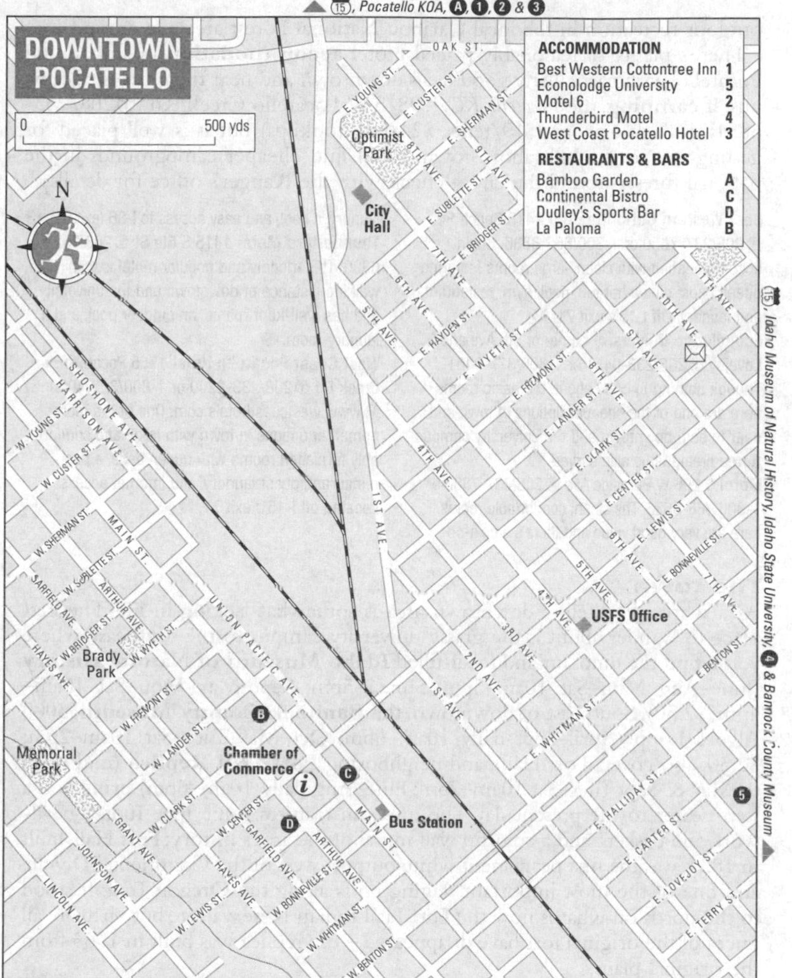

To the west and north of the town is the **Fort Hall Indian Reservation**, home to members of the Shoshone and Bannock tribes. The reservation itself holds little attraction to anyone other than ardent scholars of Native American history, but it's worth considering a visit to the associated **museum**.

Arrival, information, and accommodation

Greyhound **buses** (☎208/232-5365) depart from downtown at 215 W Bonneville to Bozeman and Salt Lake City. Rimrock Trailways Salt Lake Express (☎208/656-8824) also runs a daily service to Salt Lake City ($33 each way) from the Texaco gas station on 1527 Pocatello Creek Rd. For information, call in at the **chamber of commerce**, 343 Center St (Mon–Fri 8am–5pm; ☎208/233-2525). The **Pocatello Ranger District**, in Suite 187 at 250 4th St (Mon–Fri 8am–5pm; ☎208/236-7500), supplies the latest on outdoor recreation in the local Caribou National Forest area and around.

There's plenty of reasonably priced motel **accommodation** in and around Pocatello, with particularly good deals downtown and near the university campus. If **camping**, the *Pocatello KOA*, 9815 W Pocatello Creek Rd (ⓣ208/233-6851), isn't that cheap ($19/tents, $24/full hookups) but it is well placed for getting out to the hills above town. You'll find cheaper campgrounds in the national forests around the city – check with the Ranger's office for details.

Best Western Cottontree Inn 1415 Bench Rd ⓣ208/237-7650 or 1-800/662-6886. Chain accommodation with clean, large rooms featuring queen beds, plus a hot tub, pool, gym, restaurant, and laundry. Off I-15's exit 71. ❹

Econolodge University corner of 5th Ave and E Lovejoy ⓣ208/233-0451 or 1-800/377-0451. Though nothing to crow about, the basic rooms here are one of the cheaper options in town and near to both downtown and the university campus. A free breakfast is also served. ❷

Motel 6 296 W Burnside Ave ⓣ208/237-7880 or 1-800/466-8536. The clean, comfortable rooms here are very good value and there's a coin-op laundry, a pool, and easy access to I-86 (exit 61). ❷

Thunderbird Motel 1415 S 5th St ⓣ208/232-6330. This friendly and popular motel is within walking distance of downtown and the university and has well-kept rooms, an outdoor pool, and a laundry room. ❸

West Coast Pocatello Hotel 1555 Pocatello Creek Rd ⓣ208/233-2200 or 1-800/325-4000, ⓦwww.westcoasthotels.com. One of the more upmarket options in town with large and comfortably furnished rooms with queen beds, a pool, restaurant, guest laundry, and internet access. Located off I-15's exit 71. ❺

The town

As a whole, Pocatello's downtown area is somewhat lacking in life. The best place to wander about is the grassy university campus to the southeast, where you'll find the dinosaur and fossil-filled **Idaho Museum of Natural History** (June–Aug Mon–Sat 10am–5pm, Sun 1–5pm; Sept–May Mon–Sat 10am–4pm; $2.50). Southeast of downtown, the **Bannock County Museum**, 3000 Alvord Loop (April–Sept daily 10am–6pm; Oct–May Tues–Sat 10am–2pm; $2.50, also covers Fort Hall), and neighboring **Fort Hall Replica** (mid April to May & Sept Tues–Sat 10am–2pm; June–Aug daily 10am–6pm) bring you a step nearer to the present day. The museum features some nice Indian beadwork and baskets, and a colorful wall mural of the area's history; Fort Hall, built in 1834, was the first permanent white outpost west of the Continental Divide, and one of the most important staging posts along the Oregon Trail. It stood to the north on what is now the Fort Hall Indian Reservation, but virtually all traces of the original fort have disappeared – the replica was built in 1963 from the original plans.

Outdoor activities and local outfitters

Pocatello's saving grace is that outdoor adventure is on its doorstep. Fifteen miles southeast – just off I-15 at the Inkom exit – **Pebble Creek Ski Area** (ⓣ208/775-4452, snow report ⓣ208/775-4451, ⓦwww.pebblecreekskiarea.com; $25), is one of Idaho's oldest resorts and features 45 runs and nearly 2200ft of vertical drop served by only two triples and one double chair. With an average snowfall of 250 inches, skiers of all abilities have plenty to play on, including some beautiful glade runs. A small lodge at the base serves food and drink and also rents equipment.

The **Mink Creek Recreation Area** (summer 6am–10pm; winter sunrise–sunset; free; ⓣ208/237-9922), fifteen miles south of town on Bannock Highway, also shines in the winter with a fifteen-mile network of cross-country skiing trails. In summer these trails become popular for **hiking** and **mountain biking**. Local **outfitters** who can provide more information, as well as equipment to get you up into the hills, include Gateway Performance Outfitters, 404 S Arthur Ave (☎208/232-3711), and Scott's Ski & Sport, 218 Main St (☎208/232-1449).

Eating and drinking

Bamboo Garden 1200 Yellowstone Ave ☎208/238-2331. Good Szechuan and Hunan dishes served amongst Asian-themed decor. Expect to pay $10–15 for an entree.

Continental Bistro 140 S Main St ☎208/233-4433. A large, friendly restaurant with well-priced dishes – the pasta and seafood dishes are particularly good choices – and a wide selection of beers and wines.

Dudley's Sports Bar 150 S Arthur St ☎208/232-3541. This loud and lively sports bar typically has several big screens blasting out various games. The pub food is dependable, and there's also a decent range of microbrews.

La Paloma 323 N Main St ☎208/232-7712. Though a bit rough looking from the outside, the filling Mexican meals you'll find here are inexpensive and tasty.

Fort Hall Indian Reservation

The **FORT HALL INDIAN RESERVATION**, home to almost 4000 members of the **Shoshone** and **Bannock** tribes, wraps around the north and west sides of Pocatello. The two tribes originally wandered the Great Basin Range of Nevada, Utah, Wyoming, and Idaho and were forced into the reservation in 1868, which at that time was 1.8 million acres in size. The reservation was reduced to 1.2 million acres by a "survey error" in 1872, and then again to its present size of 544,000 acres by the Dawes Act of 1887.

There's little to see here and a tour, which must be arranged in advance from the tribal museum listed below, reveals settlements that would be charitably described as down at heels, although the rolling hills and grassy plains surrounding the reservation's small towns are pleasing on the eye. To learn more about the tribes, head to the small **Shoshone-Bannock Tribal Museum**, off I-15's exit 80 (May–Aug daily 10am–6pm; Sept–April Mon–Fri 10am–5pm; $2), where there are some wonderful c.1900 photographs of tribal members along with superb Indian beadwork and buckskin crafts on sale. Across the road, The Clothes Horse sells more traditional Indian crafts along with an awful lot of tat. There's also a supermarket, restaurant, filling station, and depressing-looking casino, all of which gets heavy traffic during the large **Shoshone Bannock Indian Festival and Rodeo** (☎208/238-3700), held yearly the second week in August.

South of Pocatello

Like many areas in the Rockies, the area to the south of Pocatello is best explored by leaving the main highway for a more picturesque trip down a scenic byway – or two, as is the case here. The first, the **Pioneer Historic Byway**, follows US-34 out of Wyoming from a landscape of high-level lakes and mountains down through forests to **Soda Springs**, then along rolling green agricultural country around **Preston**, just above the Idaho–Utah state line. The second, the **Bear Lake-Caribou National Scenic Byway** (US-30), heads south from Soda Springs through undulating farming country to **Montpelier** where it continues south (now as US-89) to skirt the west shore of **Bear Lake** before crossing into Utah.

Lava Hot Springs and Soda Springs

Ten miles east of I-15 on US-30 is the attractive, small town of **Lava Hot Springs**. Unsurprisingly, the main attraction is the hot springs, best experienced at the **Lava Recreation Complex** (☎208/775-5221 or 1-800/423-8597; $5). You can heat up at the east end of Main Street, where a series of odor-free 110°F pools bubble away above the Portneuf River (daily: April–Sept 8am–11pm; Oct–March 9am–10pm). And then cool off at the west end of town, where three more pools – one an Olympic-size swimming pool – have a constant temperature of 86°F.

If **staying over**, the *Lava Hot Springs Inn*, 94 E Portneuf Ave (☎208/776-5830; ❹), owns its own hot pools and a great deck overlooking the river to go along with pleasant rooms and large breakfasts. If camping, the *River's Edge RV Park & Campground*, 101 Hwy-30 (☎208/775-5209), has tent sites ($18) and hookups ($20) in a fine riverside location. **Dining** options include the *Royal Hotel Pizza*, 11 E Main St (☎208/776-5216), where you can get tasty pizzas in a bright atmosphere, and the lively *Wagon Wheel Lounge*, 225 E Main St (☎208/776-5015), which has a beer garden and live music on summer weekends.

A foil to Lava Hot Springs quaintness, **Soda Springs**, thirty miles east on US-30, is a scraggy little town where you'll find **Geyser Park**, marketed as "the only captive geyser in the world." It was "captured" in 1937 when drillers searching for hot springs hit a pocket of geothermally heated water that blasted 150ft into the air. The constant stream eventually began to discolor the town's buildings and was capped with a timer. It now blasts high into the air every hour on the hour, at the west end of 1st Street S, just off Main Street. On the north side of town is the huge **Monsanto Slag Pour**, produced by the local phosphate plant. There are plans to landscape it, but for now this huge bleached heap of toxic waste is just something to gape at.

South on the Pioneer Historic Byway

The Pioneer Historic Byway rolls south from Soda Springs through attractive farmlands and past the Mormon town of **Preston**. Three miles to the northwest of here is where the **Battle of Bear River**, the worst massacre of Native Americans in US history, took place in the winter of 1863. Between 200 and 400 Shoshone were killed, including at least 90 women, for the loss of 22 soldiers, and reports after the event described how "you could walk on dead Indians for quite a distance without touching the ground." Colonel Patrick Edward Connor, who was in charge of the massacre, was promoted to brigadier-general two months later, while the area's Shoshone were induced to sign peace treaties. There's a small monument to the event on the east side of US-91.

Eight miles south of Preston is the oldest town in Idaho, **Franklin**, located right on the state border – indeed, when the town's Mormon pioneers settled it in 1860, they believed they were still in Utah. The town had the first telegraph, railroad, and telephone connections in Idaho, and today it's a neat, well-kept place. East off US-91 down Franklin's main street is the **Relic Hall**, an attractive log cabin-style building from 1937, and next door is the rustic **FCMI** store, built in the 1860s. Both have rather dull historical collections with irregular opening hours, but the architecture is worth a look. A little further down the street the fine Greek Revival **Bishop Hatch House**, built by English stonemasons in 1872, housed the first mayor of Franklin, Lorenzo Hill Hatch, and his three wives and 24 children; Mormon leader Brigham Young was also an occasional guest.

South on the Bear Lake-Caribou Scenic Byway

From Soda Springs, the Bear Lake-Caribou Scenic Byway passes through thirty miles of the Caribou National Forest south to **Montpelier**, where the drab town center is given over primarily to truck and snowmobile retailers. Sitting abreast of the Oregon Trail, the town first was a wagon train supply point, and the town's **National Oregon Trail Center**, corner of Hwys 89 and 30 (daily 10am–5pm; $6; Ⓦwww.oregontrailcenter.org), is well worth visiting for its re-enactments and interpretations of life on the Oregon Trail. There's also plenty of railroad memorabilia downstairs in the **Rails & Trails Museum** (daily June–Aug 10am–3pm). Beyond that, you may want to pull into *Butch Cassidy's Restaurant & Saloon*, 260 N 4th St (Ⓣ208/847-3501), and have a drink in honor of the bandit (see p.310) who supposedly robbed a bank here back in 1896.

About twenty miles south of Montpelier, the Bear Lake-Caribou Scenic Byway (now US-89) straddles the western shore of the improbably turquoise-blue waters of **Bear Lake**, straddling the Idaho–Utah border and covered in detail on p.347. Immediately to the north is the **Bear Lake National Wildlife Refuge** (Ⓣ208/847-1757), home to one of the largest populations of Canada geese in the western US, along with white-faced ibis, sandhill cranes, egrets, white pelicans, and several species of duck. Spring is the prime time for seeing the best of the birdlife, on one of the walking trails around the refuge.

Idaho Falls

Fifty miles northeast of Pocatello and sitting astride the Snake River is **IDAHO FALLS**, an agricultural hub and the third-largest city in the state with a population of around 48,000. The trim downtown skyline is dominated by a seven-layer "wedding cake" Mormon Temple, the influence of which gives the town a definite air of sobriety. The good news, though, is that Idaho Falls is also the western gateway to a glittering landscape of deep forests, clear mountain lakes, and rocky ranges that grow ever more dramatic as they edge towards the 13,000ft **Teton Range** across the border in Wyoming. As long as you can handle hitting the sheets early, the town makes a fine base.

The finest feature of the town is the **Snake River Greenbelt**, a 29-acre swath of tree-lined banks either side of the river. An attractive two-mile paved loop passes through it from Broadway Bridge to the US-20 bridge, where you'll pass the low, squat waterfalls that give the town its name. Along the way take a break on River Parkway where you'll find a smattering of the town's best bars and restaurants. The nearby **downtown** can be strolled in a matter of minutes and has a number of attractive early twentieth-century buildings. A five-minute walk north along the greenbelt, the white-stone **Idaho Falls Temple of the Church of Jesus Christ of Latter Day Saints**, 1000 Memorial Drive (daily 9am–9pm; free), has a visitor center that welcomes non-Mormons to look around. The **Bonneville County Historical Society Museum**, east of downtown at 200 N Eastern Ave (Mon–Fri 10am–5pm, Sat 1–5pm; $2), is also worth a peek – housed in a redbrick 1916 Carnegie Library, the museum includes a replica Victorian street from the days when the town was known as Eagle Rock.

Arrival, information, and accommodation

Greyhound **buses** (Ⓣ208/522-0912) to and from Bozeman and Salt Lake City stop at 850 Denver St, as do Community and Rural Transport (CART; Ⓣ208/522-2278) buses operating routes to Salmon, the Teton Valley, and Jackson Hole. The **Eastern Idaho Visitor Information Center** is at 505 Lindsay Blvd (Mon–Sat 8am–5pm, also open Sun in summer Ⓣ208/533-1010 or 1-800/634-3246). For information and maps on local trails and campgrounds, contact the **USFS Targhee National Forest office**, located just east of town off US-26 at 3659 E Ririe Hwy (daily Mon–Fri 8am–4.30pm; Ⓣ208/523-1412).

The strip of chain motels along Lindsay Boulevard on the west bank of the Snake River is good place to start looking for **accommodation**. From here, you can walk the attractive Greenbelt into the downtown for a quick meal or to stock up on supplies. For **campers**, the *Idaho Falls KOA*, 1440 Lindsay Blvd (Ⓣ208/523-3362 or 1-800/562-7644), is convenient; facilities include a heated pool and hot tub, and tent sites are $22, full hookups $28.

Best Western Cottontree Inn 900 Lindsay Blvd Ⓣ208/523-6000 or 1-800/662-6886. Large, comfortable rooms with HBO and dataports, plus a pool, hot tub, and fitness center. A free continental breakfast is served as well. ⑤

Days Inn 700 Lindsay Blvd Ⓣ208/522-2910 or 1-800/527-0274. Clean and tidy rooms with large beds, an outdoor pool, hot tubs, and fitness room, plus a restaurant. ⑤

Shilo Inn 780 Lindsay Blvd Ⓣ208/523-0088 or 1-800/222-2244. Friendly chain hotel has spacious and comfortable rooms with plenty of facilities including microwave, fridge- and coffee-maker. There's also a pool, sauna, and steam room plus a hotel bar and restaurant. ⑤

Super 8 Motel 705 Lindsay Blvd Ⓣ208/522-8880. One of the better-value motels, with perfectly adequate rooms, though there are fewer facilities than in some of the surrounding accommodations. ③

Towne Lodge 255 E St Ⓣ208/523-2960. Basic, budget accommodation in a downtown location that can suffer from traffic noise but is close to bars, restaurants, and shops. ②

Eating and drinking

Though Idaho Falls doesn't quite have the range of **bars** and **restaurants** you might expect from a city of this size, several of them are conveniently concentrated on River Parkway off the river's west bank, near the strip of motels on adjacent Lindsay Boulevard.

Brownstone Restaurant & Brewpub 455 River Parkway ☎208/535-0310. More refined than most of the town's bars, *Brownstone*'s offers up a good range of steak, pasta, and seafood dishes along with some decent microbrews.

DD Mudd 439 A St ☎208/535-9088. Good coffee, served amongst free magazines and newspapers in a pleasant interior of brick and galvanized zinc go to make this coffee shop a fine place to start the day or take a midday break.

Frosty Gater 298 D St ☎208/529-3334. A homely and quite busy bar with good pub grub, though the Saturday quiz nights are about as wild as it gets.

Rutabaga's Espresso Bar & Café 415 River Parkway ☎208/529-3990. The attractive riverside location makes for a great place for a relaxing lunch or dinner of omelettes, seafood, and salads for around $10.

Snakebite Restaurant 425 River Parkway ☎208/525-2522. Near the *Brownstone*, and slightly more boisterous, the *Snakebite* has an appetizing range of burgers (including a good veggie) and a wide selection of microbrews.

Thai House 336 Shoup St ☎208/529-2754. One of the few ethnic restaurants in town serves up a tasty range of spicy Thai food including good shrimp dishes.

US-26 east to Wyoming

The quicker of two main routes east into Wyoming from Pocatello, US-26 meanders 75 delightful miles through the verdant **Swan Valley**, between the low peaks of the Caribou Range to the southwest and the higher Snake River Range to the northeast, and past the large **Palisades Reservoir** en route. The original white explorers of this region were the legendary mountain men of the early 1800s, including Jedediah Smith, who by 25 had survived an alleged grizzly attack in which he was able to extricate his head from the bear's jaws. Today, hunters and fishermen, along with hikers and bird watchers, are still drawn to this wild land for its abundant wildlife and superb **trout fishing** on the South Fork of the Snake River. They're certainly not visiting for cosmopolitan comforts, as the towns that dot the area – **Swan Valley**, **Irwin** and **Palisades** – are small one-street settlements strung along the highway. For guided fishing trips, contact the *South Fork Lodge*, by the Snake River in Swan Valley (☎1-877/347-4735, ⓦwww.southforklodge.com; ❼), who will take you out for a day for around $350. They also have very comfortable log motel rooms and tent sites ($15), and the best restaurant in the valley. If you're fishing on your own, self-issuing permits ($6) are available in many of the stores hereabouts. If looking to **camp out**, the cheapest sites are the USFS sites ($8), including *Calamity Campground*, close to the Palisades Dam at the western end of the reservoir, and *Big Elk Creek*, on Forest Road 262 north of US-26.

The Teton Valley and Grand Targhee

From the town of Swan Valley on US-26, the spectacular **Teton Scenic Byway** (Hwy-31 at this point) shoots north over Pine Creek Pass (6764ft) and down into the magnificent **Teton Valley**. The forest and mountain scenery is stunning throughout as the slate-flat valley, fifteen miles wide in places, is hemmed in by Wyoming's 13,000ft Teton Range to the east and the lower, game-rich Big Hole Range to the west, with the Teton River meandering along its length. While the scenic byway snakes it's way north all the way to Ashton (see p.589), it's the portion around **DRIGGS** and **Grand Targhee Resort**, actually across the border in Wyoming, that's most worthwhile. Driggs, a likeable community of around a thousand souls is the valley's urban core, and the compact center has a fair share of good outdoor stores, bars, and restaurants. Of course, it's the mountains on either side that really cry out to be explored, and Driggs makes for a great base for hikes in the area as well as for heading over to Grand Targhee. Reaching the resort is straightforward enough – simply turn east at the crossroads in the center of Driggs and follow the signs to Alta, WY (four miles), then through the village for a further eight miles up to the resort.

Arrival, information, and accommodation

A twice daily **bus** service to Driggs from Idaho Falls (via Rexburg) is run by CART (Ⓣ208/354-2240; $16 round-trip; weekdays only, call for weekend charter service). It also continues up to Grand Targhee from Driggs ($5). They also run a service to Jackson Hole in Wyoming when demand is great enough. For local town **information**, Teton Valley's chamber of commerce is at 10 E Ashley off N Main Street (daily 9am–5pm; Ⓣ208/354-2500, Ⓦwww.tetonvalleychamber.com). The more useful USFS office, 525 Main St (Mon–Fri 8am–5pm; Ⓣ208/354-2312), has loads of information on local summer/winter trails and can help you find campgrounds in the area.

Driggs holds the best **accommodation** options in the valley, with a good range that's within easy reach of the town center. Rates are reasonable year round, but if you're staying in spring or fall it's worth asking about out-of-season discounts. If here to ski and board only, Grand Targhee's ski-and-stay package deals are worth looking into; check Ⓦwww.grandtarghee.com for details. Of the several **campgrounds** in the area, the best is the *Teton Valley Campground* (Ⓣ208/787-2647; $20 tent/$25 hookup), one mile south of Victor on Hwy-31; facilities include a laundry, pool, and showers. Good USFS campgrounds include *Teton Canyon Campground* and *Reunion Flat Campground*, both over 7000ft up in the Teton Canyon ten miles east of Driggs – to get there drive to Alta (on the road to Grand Targhee), take Forest Road 025 east and turn right at Forest Road 009.

Driggs

Best Western Teton West 476 N Main St Ⓣ208/354-2363 or 1-800/528-1234. Though characterless, the standard motel chain rooms here are very clean and comfortable and there's also a guest pool and hot tub. ④

Intermountain Lodge 34 Ski Hill Rd Ⓣ208/354-8153. Conveniently located on the road to Grand Targhee, this lodge has basic two-bed log cabins with kitchens. The hot tub here is greatly appreciated after a day on the nearby slopes. ④

Pines Motel Guest Haus 105 S Main Ⓣ208/354-2774 or 1-800/354-2778, Ⓔthepines@tetonvalley.net. Attractive rooms in a c.1900 log cabin, some with private bath. There's a hot tub and an ice-skating rink in winter, and for $10 extra you get breakfast too. ④

Teton Mountain View Lodge 510 Egbert Ave, Tetonia Ⓣ208/456-2741. Eight miles north of Driggs on the outskirts of the village of Tetonia, this friendly lodge has large rooms (some with fireplaces), chunky pine furniture, and ensuite bathrooms. There are inspiring views to go with a hot tub and free breakfast. In winter, snowmobiles can be rented and driven around the property. ④

Grand Targhee

Alta Lodge B&B State Line Rd at Targhee Town Rd, Alta, WY Ⓣ307/353-2582. One of the few accommodation options in the hamlet of Alta, en route to Grand Targhee. All four guestrooms have queen beds, two are en suite, and the views of the Grand Tetons are sensational. ④

Sioux Lodge Grand Targhee Resort Ⓣ307/353-2300 or 1-800/827-4433. The best slopeside deal if in a group, featuring condo units with full kitchen and living area that can sleep from two to eight people ($260–460). ⑨

Targhee Lodge Grand Targhee Resort Ⓣ307/353-2300 or 1-800/827-4433. The basic rooms, which feature two queen beds, are decent if rather overpriced. The draw is not the rooms, though, but the convenient ski-in/ski-out access. ⑥

Teewinot Lodge Grand Targhee Resort ⓣ307/353-2300 or 1-800/827-4433. Like the *Targhee Lodge*, this accommodation has a handy ski-in/ski-out location. It too is overpriced, though the rooms here are more opulent, each furnished in a Western theme, and facilities include a guest lounge with fireplace and small indoor hot tub. ⑦

Winter Activities

Wyoming's stunning **GRAND TARGHEE** (ⓣ307/353-2300 or 1-800/827-4433, ⓦwww.grandtarghee.com), effectively cut off from its home state by the precipitous Teton Mountains, is hugely undervisited compared with neighboring Jackson Hole – despite Grand Targhee's superior quantities of talc-dry powder snow. Storms strafe the west side of the Tetons all winter long, giving rise to the local expression "a three-inch day" – a day spent skiing in snow three inches above your belly-button. So while accommodation is limited and there's no real nightlife to speak of, this is the perfect resort for those who look forward to a full day of intense skiing or boarding, just to do it all over again the next day.

The ski area, which gets an average **annual snowfall** of 510 inches, is spread across two peaks: Fred's Mountain (10,200ft), which has a **vertical drop** of 2200ft, and Peaked Mountain (10,230ft), whose vertical drop is 2822ft. The 1500 acres of **skiable terrain** on Fred's Mountain (ten percent beginner, seventy percent intermediate, twenty percent advanced) has **63 trails** serviced by two quad **chair-lifts** and one double. Be sure to take a camera on at least one ride up Fred's Dreamcatcher chair and slither across the Teton Vista traverse to snap one of the world's true standout mountain scenes. The majority of Peaked Mountain's mostly advanced 1500 skiable acres are serviced by **snow-cat only** ($265 per day), though a new quad lift has opened up 500 acres of lift-accessed runs. **Lift tickets** cost $47 per day, with a slight discount for multiday passes.

Though the resort attracts the lion's share of winter-sports enthusiasts, experts should take note that some of the Rockies finest **backcountry skiing** can be had at the **Teton Pass**, within easy reach of Hwy-21. Rendezvous Ski Tours, based south in Victor at 219 Highland (ⓣ208/787-2906), leads backcountry ski trips to huts set high in the local mountains – the huts sleep eight and cost around $150 per night. If heading out into the backcountry without guides, check on **snow/avalanche conditions** with the USFS office in Driggs (see opposite).

Summer activities

Once the snow has melted, hundreds of trails in the area open to **hikers** and **bikers**. There's a good, but often busy set of trails in the Teton and Darby canyons, both reached along the obvious right fork in the hamlet of Alta. One of the most popular trails in Teton Canyon is Trail 027 – a forested eight-mile one-way hike that passes several alpine lakes into the lake-strewn **Alaska Basin**. If you want something with fewer folks about, head across the valley to the Big Hole Mountains, where there are good trails in Horseshoe Canyon and Mahogany Canyon, both reached twelve miles down the county road west out of Driggs from the crossroads in the center of town. The USFS office in Driggs has more information on these and other trails. The Grand Targhee resort is also open in summer, offering **horseback riding** ($40 for two hours or $80 half-day), mountain-bike rental ($40 per day), and **lift-served biking** (July–Sept Wed–Sun 10am–3am; June Wed & Sat–Sun only; $16).

Local outfitters

Big Hole Mountain Sports 99 S Main St ⓣ208/354-2209. A snowboard and mountain bike store with a friendly staff who can recommend good local trails. Rental boards for under $30 per day; hardtail bikes cost $28, full suspension $36.

Peaked Sports 70 E Little Ave ⓣ208/354-2354 or 1-800/705-2354. The finest store for downhill skiers, with both overnight servicing and good rentals. They also sell bikes in summer.

Yostmark Mountain Equipment 12 E Little Ave ⓣ208/354-2828. Yostmark specializes in telemark skiing ($18 per day), but also rents alpine skis ($20), snowboards ($25 with boots), snowshoes ($10 with poles), inflatable kayaks ($25), fishing gear ($15), and various pieces of camping gear.

Eating and drinking

As with lodging, Driggs is the place in the Teton Valley to wine and dine. Most places are in the town center, making it easy to flit from one to the other. However, this being Mormon country, the liquor laws can be a little strange and you may find that some bars don't stay open as late as you might expect. If looking for a place to stock up before heading into the wilds, Barrels & Bins, 36 S Main St (ⓣ208/354-2307), has a fine selection of health foods. There's not too much choice when it comes to **eating around Grand Targhee**, though at least you can't get lost trying to find a place in the compact slopeside village. The moderate-to-expensive menu at *Skadi's* includes some excellent seafood, steak, pasta, and vegetarian items (entrees $14–32) and the requisite breakfast buffet is very good too ($10), while the pizzas at the *Wizard of Za* are pretty good value at $9–14. The *Trap Bar* is where everyone – literally everyone – staying at the resort gathers at the end of the day, and regularly features bands during winter.

Aunty M's 189 N Main St ⓣ208/354-2010. Great homemade pies and soups in a Victorian dining room where you can also relax on a couch with an espresso.

Bunk House Bistro 285 N Main St ⓣ208/354-3770. The *Bunk House* serves filling "cowboy cuisine" like prime rib and steaks in a convivial atmosphere. Open for lunch seven days a week, and dinners Fri and Sat only.

Cancun 18 N Main ⓣ208/354-2293. Tasty traditional Mexican and American food with daily specials that won't set you back much over $10. The margaritas are worth checking out as well.

Knotty Pine 58 S Main, Victor ⓣ208/787-2866. Most popular for its full rack of ribs, which will set you back around $15. There's also regular live music.

Main Street Grille 68 N Main St ⓣ208/354-3303. A good place to pull in for a large, traditional American-style breakfast in a friendly atmosphere. Mexican food also makes its way onto the menu.

Royal Wolf Depot St. An excellent smoke-free bar serving up a great array of food, from burgers to seafood, with a few entrees topping out over $15. The nine US and foreign brews on tap help keep this the best bar in town.

Tony's Pizza 364 N Main St ⓣ208/354-8829. Hand-tossed pizzas are the specialty here, which can be delivered throughout the valley. If eating in, you can sit in an antique chair-lift seat while washing down your meal with a beer. Open seven days a week, lunch on weekends only.

US-20 north to Yellowstone National Park

Heading northeast out of Idaho Falls, US-20 is the main route in Idaho to Yellowstone National Park. Though gateway town West Yellowstone is only 112 miles away, you may want to want to spend the night – or at the very least stop for a few hours – along the way. The drive is a scenic delight, passing through mountain meadows, deep forests, and gin-clear lakes and rivers, beneath ever higher mountains, and fantastic **fishing** and **wildlife spotting** is available along much of the way.

Rexburg, Ashton, and the Mesa Falls Scenic Byway

Twenty-five miles north of Idaho Falls is the rather dull town of **REXBURG**, where the only sight of real note is the **Teton Flood Museum**, 51 N Center St (Mon–Sat 10am–5pm; donation; ⓣ208/356-9101), housed in the town's Mormon Temple. The museum describes the tragic local story of the Teton Dam, built twenty miles east on the Teton River. On June 5, 1975, the recently completed dam burst, sending eighty million gallons of water flooding down the valley. Six people and 18,000 head of livestock were drowned, one hundred and fifty homes were lost, and the cost of the damage was estimated at nearly $1 billion. Part of what makes the story so tragic is that most interested parties – the EPA, Idaho Fish and Game Department, and the Army Corps of Engineers – had been opposed to the dam from the start, but were overridden by the US Bureau of Reclamation and the local irrigation district. And with a design that didn't properly take into account the local geology, the dam wall burst open before the reservoir behind it was even completely full.

Some 27 miles on from Rexburg stands the uneventful potato town of **Ashton**. Things are as slow as you might expect from one of the world's largest seed-potato producing regions; better to head down either of two intriguing side-roads. One leads to an isolated entrance to Yellowstone National Park (see box, below), while the other, known as the **Mesa Falls Scenic Byway** (Hwy-47), is a thirty-mile scenic route that ends at Harriman State Park (see below). The road winds north from Marysville, two miles east of Ashton, through forests and past 65ft **Lower Mesa Falls** until you eventually arrive at **Upper Mesa Falls**, where the waters of Henry's Fork hurl themselves over a 114ft precipice. The power of the falls, the rainbow-colored spray and the magnificent wooded surroundings are a mesmerizing sight, easily seen from a flat walkway. There's also an attractive visitor center beside the falls at the Big Falls Inn, an old and recently converted roadhouse from the days when Hwy-47 was a major artery through this part of the state. If you'd like to stay overnight, there's a basic USFS campground at Lower Falls.

Yellowstone's hidden gateway

Though no one could ever claim that **Yellowstone National Park** is Idaho's, one-percent of the park's vast landscape does fall within the state's borders. On top of that, Yellowstone's most isolated entrance, Cave Falls, can only be reached via Idaho. Take Hwy-47 east from Ashton and wind your way up through a glorious landscape of forests, crags, and tumbling rivers four miles past Marysville to Cave Falls Road, which comes to a dead end just inside the park. A world away from the commercialization of other park entrances (and no entrance fee to boot), the road takes you to trailheads that lead into a backcountry paradise that's home to more than half of the park's waterfalls and is prime grizzly country. Trail maps are available from the USFS Bechler Ranger Station (sporadic hours; no phone) en route to the end of Cave Falls Road. The USFS *Cave Falls Campground* ($8), close to the glittering cascade after which it's named, is just outside the entrance and is open July–September but has only sixteen sites and fills up quickly in summer. Like the campground, the Cave Falls Road is not open in winter.

Harriman State Park and north to the border

Around twenty miles north of Ashton on US-20 is **Harriman State Park** (daily: summer 6am–10pm; winter sunrise–sunset; $3, day-use only; ⓣ208/558-7368), once ranch land owned by the family of Averell Harriman, founder of Sun Valley Resort. Sitting at the heart of the 16,000-acre Harriman Wildlife

Refuge, the major attraction here is **trumpeter swans** – up to 5000 winter on the portion of the Henry's Fork (see box, below) that meanders through here. Besides swans, the refuge is also home to moose, black bear, osprey, and eagle. There are twenty miles of hiking, biking, and horseback riding **trails** in the park, which in winter become cross-country ski trails. Two good options at any time are the easy one-mile round-trip Henry's Fork Loop alongside the river, or the more strenuous 5.5-mile round-trip Ridge Loop that takes you up onto a high ridge from where there are great views of the park and nearby mountains. If you're looking for **accommodation** in the area, try *Pond's Lodge* on the west side of US-20 near Island Park (☎208/558-7221; ❸). It's busy year-round and has a good old-fashioned bar and restaurant, and cozy log cabins. Five miles north from here is the riverside *Mack's Inn Resort*, just off US-20 on Forest Road 059 (☎208/558-7272; ❸), which has basic two-person cabins and tent sites ($12). The inn is also a stop for the daily Greyhound **bus** service between Salt Lake City and Bozeman. There are also several USFS **campgrounds** ($8) in the area, including *Buffalo Campground*, on the Buffalo River on the east side of Hwy-20 near Pond's Lodge, and *Big Springs Campground*, to the east of *Mack's Inn*. The latter is close to **Big Springs**, one of the largest springs in the US where twenty million gallons of water a day flow; through the crystal clear water you can see (but not fish for) large trout and salmon. A short trail from the springs takes you to the very rustic **Johnny Sack Cabin**, featuring a homemade water wheel used to supply electricity and water, and built by a German immigrant in the early 1930s.

Just south of the state border and less than fifteen miles from Yellowstone National Park is **Henry's Lake State Park** (June–Oct; ☎208/558-7532; $3), set in a bowl at 6740ft and surrounded on three sides by high mountains. The cutthroat, rainbow, and brook trout fishing is fantastic, and a good spot to pick up tips or rent out gear is the *Wild Rose Ranch* (☎208/558-7201; ❹) on the north shore of the lake and once a haunt of Western writer Zane Grey. The park has a fifty-site **campground** ($10), and facilities include showers, toilets, a boat ramp, and boat docks.

To the east of Henry's Lake, US-20 forks right to head over the Continental Divide at Targhee Pass (7072 ft) into Montana and down the ten miles to West Yellowstone (see p.428). Branching off to the left of the fork is Hwy-87, which crosses the Continental Divide at Raymonds Pass (6836ft) before descending into Montana's Madison Valley towards Ennish (see p.475).

Fishing Henry's Fork

The **Henry's Fork** of the Snake River is widely regarded as one of the finest **fly-fishing** rivers in the US, particularly for its rainbow trout and native Yellowstone cutthroat trout. The headwaters flow from geothermally warmed springs just west of Yellowstone National Park, and the river's flow and temperature are both nearly constant until it joins the Snake near Rexburg.

Throughout its sixty-mile length, the river passes through a beautiful landscape of wide meadows and open forests that's a haven for elk, deer, moose, beaver, otter, eagles, ospreys, and sandhill cranes, meaning you're rarely alone for long when casting a line. To find the best casting spots, either buddy up with a local or hire a **guide**. One of the best is Mike Lawson's Henry's Fork Anglers, HC66 Box 38A, Island Park, ID 83429 (☎208/558-7525), who charge around $300 (one or two anglers) for a day on the river. For more **information** on fishing and other local outdoor activities, contact the USFS Ranger Station in Island Park (☎208/558-7301), located at the south end of town off US-20.

I-15 to Montana

By far the quickest way into Montana from Idaho Falls is on I-15. During the eighty-mile high-speed journey north, the interstate passes through high desert country around the small settlement of Dubois before making a gentle ascent to the Continental Divide at **Monida Pass** (6870ft), huddled beneath the snow-draped 10,000ft Centennial Mountains. En route, you'll pass three **wildlife sanctuaries** – Market Lake Wildlife Management Area, twelve miles north of Idaho Falls, Camas National Wildlife Refuge, another twenty miles north, and Mud Lake Wildlife Management Area, just north again. The sanctuaries, open year-round, are most notable for their spring and fall migratory waterfowl populations, which include Canada and snow geese, trumpeter swans, teal, duck, egrets, and sandhill cranes.

At the small mining town of **Spencer**, some twenty miles south of the border, you can hunt for **opals**. After buying a $20 permit, the Spencer Opal Mine (Ⓣ208/374-5476) will let you spend the day grubbing about in the muck for these semi-precious stones. Even if you don't strike it rich, prospecting in the surrounding high-country scenery is a delight.

Sun Valley

The ski resort of **SUN VALLEY**, taking in the towns of the Wood River Valley – **Ketchum**, **Warm Springs**, and to an extent **Hailey**, twelve miles south – has been attracting moguls and movie stars since its inception in the 1930s. At that time, Union Pacific Railroad chairman Averell Harriman discovered his railroad was obliged to maintain a passenger service. Having nowhere for passengers to travel, he decided an alpine ski center would be an ideal draw and soon after sent Austrian ski champion Count Felix Schaffgotsch on a mission to find snowy, treeless slopes sheltered by higher mountains. Having turned down Aspen for being too high, the Count decided **Dollar Mountain**, here in the relatively gentle foothills of the Sawtooths near the old sheep-ranching village of Ketchum, fit the bill.

The resort was named Sun Valley – the area does indeed get plenty of sunshine, sometimes at the expense of good snow conditions – and was an instant success. The hill itself boasted the world's first chairlift, based on a hoist used for hauling bananas into ship's holds, and Hollywood stars like Marilyn Monroe and Gary Cooper were soon hitching rides up to the top. The area's most famous resident, though, was author **Ernest Hemingway**, who lived in Ketchum and committed suicide here in 1961 (see box on p.599). Today, Sun Valley Resort, its newer neighbor **Elkhorn Resort**, and Ketchum remain the most cosmopolitan and highly priced pieces of real estate in the state, though the downhill action now centers not around Dollar Mountain but the larger and steeper **Bald Mountain** (9150ft), known locally as "Baldy."

Ketchum, slightly more downmarket than the nearby resort villages, is the heart of the Wood River Valley. Still, don't expect the relaxed atmosphere you find in most of Idaho's other mountain towns. The fact that Ketchum is in the business of making money out of tourism is obvious – scores of restaurants, shops, and galleries line the town's streets – and in winter the hard-worked mountain staff are not always as cheerful as at other Idaho ski hills. Just to the north of Ketchum is the village of Warm Springs – a suburb of sorts – which has more accommodation and restaurant facilities and is well placed for skiing Bald Mountain using the Warm Springs lifts and day-lodge. To the south the

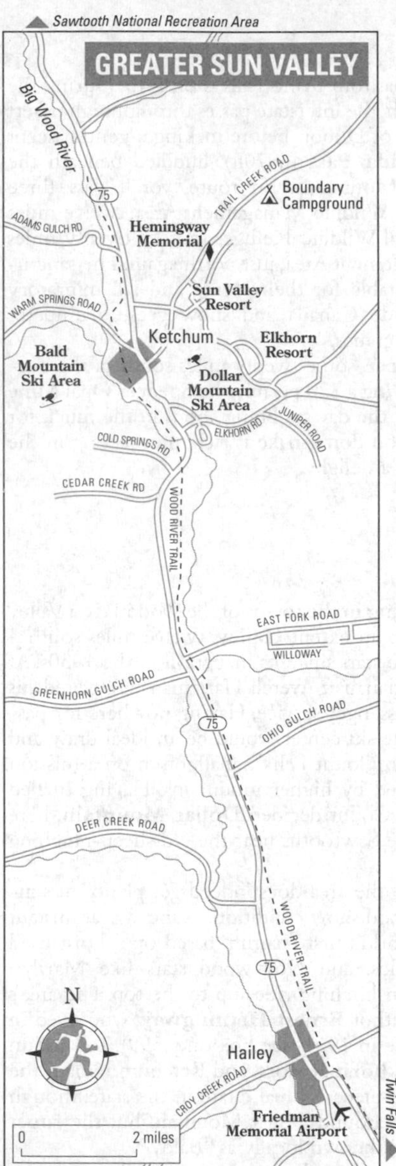

pleasant town of Hailey's claim to fame is that it was the birthplace (1885) of poet **Ezra Pound**, who once lived in the house at the corner of 2nd Avenue and Pine Street. Unfortunately, the house is not open for tours. Though there are no other sights of note, the town does make a better base if you're on a budget – or allergic to the glitz and glamour of the resorts up the valley.

Arrival and getting around

The easiest – and most expensive – way into Sun Valley is by **air** from Boise, Salt Lake City, or Seattle; both Horizon and Skywest fly into Hailey's Friedman Memorial Airport. A bus into town costs $16 one-way, though many hotels offer a complimentary pick-up service. By **car**, Sun Valley is about 150 miles from Boise via I-84, US-20, and Hwy-75, though the longer route following US-21 and Hwy-75 (via Stanley and Galena Pass to the north) is far more picturesque. Sun Valley is also easily reached from the urban centers of southern Idaho via US-93 (off I-84 at Twin Falls, 83 miles south) and Hwy-75. **Parking** can be tight, and in winter especially your best bet may be to park in the large lot on the River Run base area below Bald Mountain, and either walk or take the free shuttle bus into town. Sun Valley Express (☎208/336-4038 or 1-800/821-9064) runs a **bus service** to and from Boise (via Twin Falls), with a fare of $59 one-way, $89 return. There are four daily services each way on weekdays, six at weekends.

Getting around is easy: Ketchum Area Rapid Transit (KART; ☎208/726-7576) runs a free service (every twenty minutes in summer, every fifteen minutes in winter; 7.30am–midnight) between River Run Plaza, Warm Springs Plaza, Ketchum, Sun Valley, and Elkhorn Village. Full schedules and route maps are available from the chamber of commerce. Sun Valley resort also runs a free ski shuttle in winter (see p.597). A **taxi** between Sun Valley Resort and Ketchum will set you back around $7; try Bald Mountain Taxi (T208/726-2650).

Information

For an excellent selection of visitor **information**, stop by the chamber of commerce, 4th and Main streets in Ketchum (daily 8.30am–5pm; T208/726-3423 or 1-800/634-3347, Wwww.visitsunvalley.com). There are a number of useful visitor publications here, including the detailed *Sun Valley Guide* (Wwww.svguide.com). Hailey's chamber of commerce is at W Bullion (Mon–Fri 9am–5pm; T208/788-2700).

The **USFS Ketchum Ranger Station**, 206 Sun Valley Rd (daily 8am–5pm; T208/622-5371), is loaded with information on hiking, biking, camping, and backcountry travel in the area. They also run a useful backcountry weather and **snow conditions hotline** (Dec–April) on T208/622-8027.

Accommodation

Regardless of your budget, the first key to securing suitable **accommodation** in the Sun Valley area is to book as far ahead as possible. During the winter high season, it's not uncommon for hotels and inns to be booked solid months in advance, and summer can be very busy as well. It's a different story in the fall and spring off-seasons, when rates can drop by as much as half at some places. At all times, though, more than half of the available beds in the Sun Valley area are in the two huge resorts, meaning those on a budget will have a hard time finding affordable accommodation. If you're having trouble finding a room, check with the **Sun Valley Central Reservations** (T1-800/634-3347, Wwww.visitsunvalley.com) or call at the chamber of commerce, who can also help with finding **condominiums** and **homes** – often the best deal if you're coming with a group, these vary enormously in the range of facilities and prices, from as little as $60 to several hundred dollars per night.

If you want to pitch a tent, you'll have to use one of the various USFS **campgrounds** out of town; see box, overleaf.

The resorts

Elkhorn Resort 1 Elkhorn Rd T208/622-4511 or 1-800/737-0209, Wwww.elkhornresort.com. The smaller of Sun Valley's two major resorts is located by the base of Dollar Mountain. Set in rolling, grassy grounds, the main building is a 132-room lodge with large, airy, well-appointed and very comfortable rooms, and a snug lobby where you can relax beside the open fire. There are also ninety condominiums, varying from great-value studio apartments (5) to four-bedroom condos (9). Facilities include an excellent eighteen-hole golf course, indoor and outdoor hot tubs, a sauna, a health center, and free shuttles to both ski hills. 5

Sun Valley Resort Sun Valley and Dollar roads T208/622-2151 or 1-800/786-8529, Wwww.sunvalley.com. Purpose built in 1936 as a luxurious mountain resort, Sun Valley proper has expanded considerably over the years to include a wide mix of high-end accommodation that now include the original 600-room lodge (7), the more modern *Sun Valley Inn* (6), *Sun Valley Condominiums* (6), and a small number of luxurious guest cottages starting at $600 per night. Prices can drop considerably in spring and fall, and special ski packages can also be a good deal – four nights accommodation with three days skiing can be as low $245 per person for double occupancy. Even if you don't stay in the lodge, it's worth a visit just to browse the star-filled photographs of past guests, including Clark Gable, Errol Flynn, Gary Cooper, and Clint Eastwood. The entire resort has a vast selection of facilities including two pools, an ice rink, golf course, tennis courts, restaurants, and a movie theater. 6

Ketchum

Best Western Kentwood Lodge 180 S Main St T208/726-9963 or 1-800/805-1001. Comfortably furnished rooms with kitchens, some with balconies and fireplaces, and a good location in downtown Ketchum. There's also an indoor pool, hot tubs, workout room, guest laundry, and restaurant on the premises. 5

Best Western Tyrolean Lodge 260 Cottonwood St ⓣ208/726-5336 or 1-800/333-7912. Designed along the lines of an Austrian ski lodge, the *Tyrolean* is within easy walking distance of both the River Run lifts and downtown. The rooms are big and airy and many have lovely mountain views, and there's a complimentary continental breakfast served daily. An outdoor pool, hot tubs, sauna and exercise room round out the package. 5

Heidelberg Inn 1908 Warm Springs Rd ⓣ208/726-5361 or 1-800/284-4863. Another Swiss-style hotel, trying to bring the Alps to the Rockies, the *Heidelberg* has snug, homey rooms, some with kitchenettes, and an indoor spa and sauna and outdoor pool (summer only). It's convenient for accessing the lifts at Warm Springs, but a couple of miles away from downtown. 5

Knob Hill Inn 960 N Main St ⓣ208/726-8010 or 1-800/526-8010, ⓦwww.knobhillinn.com. Located about a mile from the base of Baldy, this 24-room, Austrian Alps-theme inn is one of Ketchum's finest accommodations. The beautifully appointed rooms include queen beds, marble bathrooms, and balconies with fine mountain views. There's a cozy guest library and bar in which to relax, and an indoor pool and hot tub. 8

Lift Tower Lodge 703 S Main St ⓣ208/726-5163 or 1-800/462-8646. Perhaps the best value in town, with basic but comfortable rooms with two beds, refrigerator, TV, and phone. Amenities include a free continental breakfast and hot tub, and both River Run ski lifts and downtown are within walking distance. 3

River Street Inn 100 Rivers St W ⓣ208/726-3611 or 1-888/746-3611. Ketchum's first B&B has six beautifully furnished, Western-style suites, all with queen-size beds, Japanese-soaking tubs (a deep, one-person tub) and walk-in showers. The lounge is a snug and welcoming spot to relax at the end of the day over free coffee and cookies, or there's a hot tub on the riverside deck outside. Only a minute's walk from downtown and ten minutes from the River Run lifts, this is a wonderfully relaxing place to stay – and the breakfasts are excellent. 7

Ski View Lodge 409 S Main St ⓣ208/726-3441. An affordable option in downtown Ketchum, though there are only eight cabins so you'll need to book in well in advance. The rustic-style design cabins are fairly plain but they're comfortable enough, and they have their own kitchen and phone, plus views of Baldy. Within a couple of minutes walk of downtown. 3

Tamarack Lodge 291 Walnut Ave N ⓣ208/726-3344 or 1-800/521-5379. The *Tamarack* has well-appointed rooms made all the more cozy by their fireplaces, with features including balconies and open-beam ceilings and microwaves, fridges, and coffee-makers. The lodge has an indoor pool and outdoor hot tub, and is right in the middle of town. 6

Hailey

Airport Inn 409 Cedar St ⓣ208/788-2477. Down by the Friedman Memorial Airport, the *Airport Inn* has fairly plain rooms with queen beds, some with kitchenettes, but is better value than most of the accommodation in Ketchum, which means it's well

Camping in Sun Valley

Unfortunately for budget travelers, **camping** options around Sun Valley are limited to six small USFS campgrounds, all open June to mid-October only. If these are full, one option is to drive into the Sawtooth NRA (see p.604) some fifty miles to the north, where you should able to get a space without problem. For information on the USFS campgrounds, contact the USFS Ketchum Ranger Station (see overleaf). Note that the base altitude here is 6000ft, so while it can be hot and sunny in the day, temperatures often fall close to freezing at night even in the height of summer.

Boundary Campground The closest campground to town, with eight shady sites two miles past Sun Valley resort on Trail Creek Rd. $10.

Deer Creek A primitive "dispersed" campground twenty miles west of Ketchum on Deer Creek Rd. Free.

Federal Gulch Set along the East Fork Wood River on Forest Road 118, which branches east off Hwy-75 midway between Ketchum and Hailey. The fifteen units here are nicely set in the mountain's foothills. Free.

Sawmill A short way past the *Federal Gulch* site, though there are only three spaces. Free.

worth making reservations. Facilities include a hot tub and free coffee in the lobby. 4

Hailey Hotel 201 Main St ⓣ208/788-3140. Originally a Basque boarding house, the rooms here are quite plain and the bathroom is down the corridor, but it's popular as a budget option so again reservations are recommended. 4

Povey Pensione 128 W Bullion ⓣ208/788-4682 or 1-800/370-4682. This 110-year-old home is one of the oldest buildings in town and has a welcoming Old West feel to it, as do the homely rooms with antique furnishings, pastel wall coverings, and shared baths. Breakfast is also included in the price. 5

Wood River Inn 601 Main St ⓣ208/578-0600 or 1-877/542-0600. A modern inn with good-sized rooms with queen beds and complimentary continental breakfast, plus an indoor pool and hot tub. 5

Ketchum

Although Ketchum's thirty or so blocks make up the urban heart of the Wood River Valley, there are few sights of note other than the small **Ketchum–Sun Valley Heritage and Ski Museum**, corner of 1st Street and Washington Avenue (daily 11am–4pm; closed April and Nov; free). The museum holds a fairly rote collection of exhibits on local geology, Native Americans, and pioneers along with some interesting notebooks and diaries that belonged to Ernest Hemingway (see box p.599). The skiing section, focusing on local Olympic successes and Sun Valley's Hollywood connection, is sparse considering the area's ski heritage.

The main action in Ketchum is **shopping**. From stores devoted to skiing and climbing gear to high-end galleries and jewelry shops, nearly every block in town is lined with merchants eager to show off their wares. Of the many **galleries**, the most worth stopping by are the *Sun Valley Center for the Arts and Humanities*, 191 5th St E at Washington (ⓣ208/726-9491), a nonprofit organization that displays a wide range of local work, and the superb photographs at *Images of Nature*, 371 Main St (ⓣ1-888/339-1836).

Sun Valley Resort and Elkhorn Village

It's a five-minute drive from Ketchum to the large **Sun Valley and Elkhorn Village resorts**, though in summer it's almost as quick to take the paved cycle paths between the two. Regardless of the season, though, there are few reasons to visit unless you're staying. Unlike Ketchum, neither complex is that suitable for wandering around, though the **Sun Valley Mall** does have a decent range of shops, restaurants, outfitters, and a post office. Besides a couple of fine restaurants and the atmospheric lodge, Sun Valley's main draw is the **ice-skating rink** open to the public year-round ($8; ⓣ208/725-7820).

Winter activities

Sun Valley is synonymous with **winter sports**, and it's hard to imagine anyone getting bored here in the cold season with everything from alpine and cross-country skiing to dog sledding and ice skating on offer. The first snow flurries can start as early as October, but don't expect to get good skiing until well into December through to April. And keep in mind that Sun Valley is called that for a reason – long and sunny dry spells can occur, and its yearly snowfall average is a relatively meager 175 inches.

Bald Mountain

Towering above Ketchum, **Bald Mountain** (ⓣ208/622-2183 or 1-800/786-8259, snow report ⓣ1-800/635-8261, ⓦwww.sunvalley.com), an endearing mix of Alps meets cowboy, has won just about every award going from the

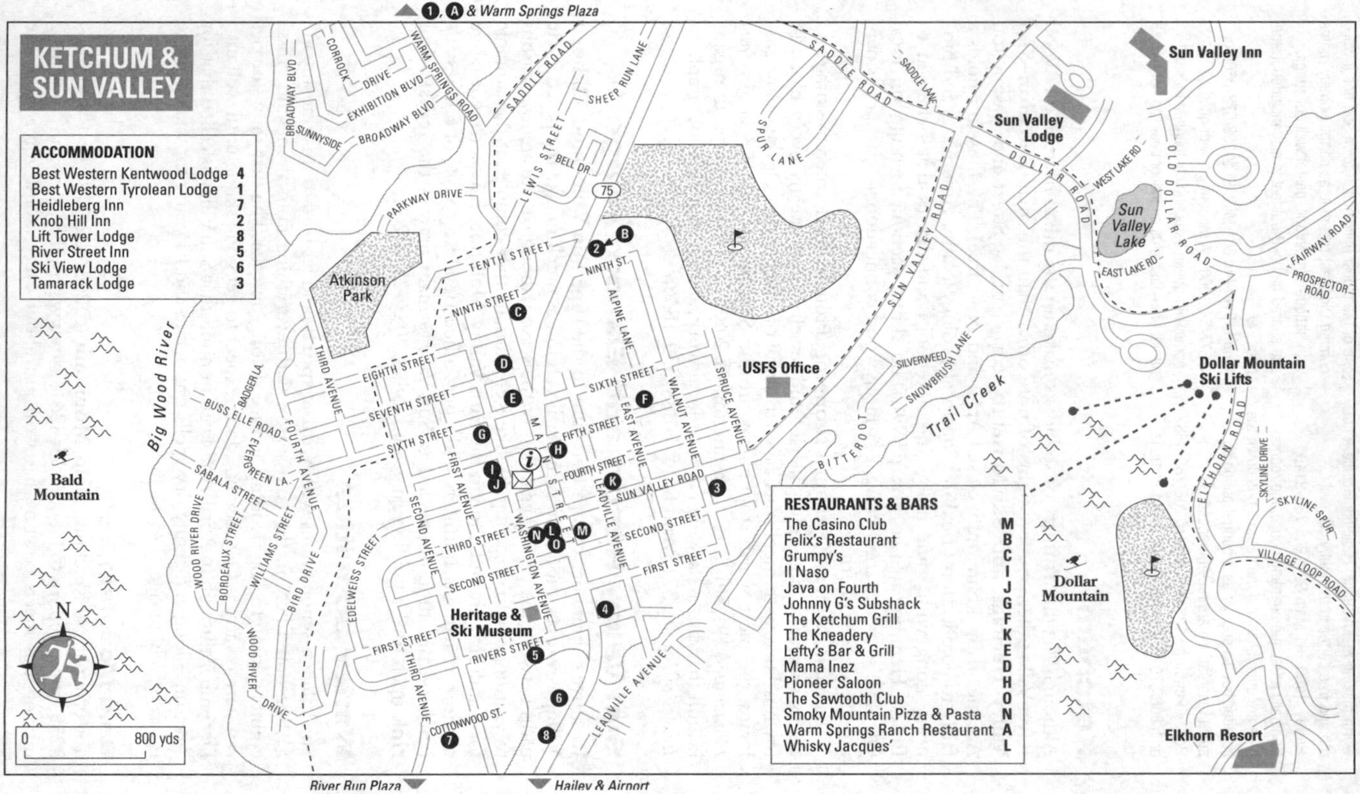

KETCHUM & SUN VALLEY
ACCOMMODATION
Best Western Kentwood Lodge 4
Best Western Tyrolean Lodge 1
Heidleberg Inn 7
Knob Hill Inn 2
Lift Tower Lodge 8
River Street Inn 5
Ski View Lodge 6
Tamarack Lodge 3
RESTAURANTS & BARS
The Casino Club M
Felix's Restaurant B
Grumpy's C
Il Naso I
Java on Fourth J
Johnny G's Subshack G
The Ketchum Grill F
The Kneadery K
Lefty's Bar & Grill E
Mama Inez D
Pioneer Saloon H
The Sawtooth Club O
Smoky Mountain Pizza & Pasta N
Warm Springs Ranch Restaurant A
Whisky Jacques' L
1, A & Warm Springs Plaza
River Run Plaza
Hailey & Airport
Sun Valley Inn
Sun Valley Lodge
Sun Valley Lake
Dollar Mountain Ski Lifts
Dollar Mountain
Elkhorn Resort
USFS Office
Heritage & Ski Museum
Atkinson Park
Bald Mountain
Big Wood River
Trail Creek
SADDLE ROAD
SADDLE LANE
SPUR LANE
DOLLAR ROAD
OLD DOLLAR ROAD
WEST LAKE RD
EAST LAKE RD
FAIRWAY ROAD
PROSPECTOR ROAD
ELKHORN ROAD
SKYLINE DRIVE
SKYLINE SPUR
VILLAGE LOOP ROAD
SUN VALLEY ROAD
SILVERWEED
SNOWBRUSH LANE
BITTEROOT
SPRUCE AVENUE
WALNUT AVENUE
EAST AVENUE
LEADVILLE AVENUE
WASHINGTON AVENUE
MAIN STREET
FIRST AVENUE
SECOND AVENUE
THIRD AVENUE
FOURTH AVENUE
TENTH STREET
NINTH ST.
NINTH STREET
EIGHTH STREET
SEVENTH STREET
SIXTH STREET
FIFTH STREET
FOURTH STREET
THIRD STREET
SECOND STREET
FIRST STREET
RIVERS STREET
COTTONWOOD ST.
ALPINE LANE
EDELWEISS STREET
BIRD DRIVE
WILLIAMS STREET
BORDEAUX STREET
WOOD RIVER DRIVE
SABALA STREET
EVERGREEN LA.
BUSS ELLE ROAD
BADGER LA.
PARKWAY DRIVE
LEWIS STREET
BELL DR.
SHEEP RUN LANE
WARM SPRINGS ROAD
EXHIBITION BLVD
BROADWAY BLVD
CORROCK DRIVE
SUNNYSIDE
75
N
0 800 yds

ski/travel press. Indeed, if you catch Baldy after a good dump of snow, you'll see first-hand why this is so.

Though the **highest point** is only 9150ft, the **vertical drop** is an admirable 3400ft, making for thigh-burning runs of up to three miles in length. There are nearly eighty trails running over the mountain's 2000 skiable acres, all accessed by an impressive **lift system** – eighteen lifts in total – that ensures lines are nearly nonexistent. And the huge **snow-making** system, which covers 630 acres, ensures that even in lean years there's always some fresh snow on the mountain.

Overall, the terrain is broken up into 36 percent beginner, 42 percent intermediate, and 22 percent advanced. Contrary to this breakdown, though, this is not a beginner's hill. Due to the mountain's steep and constant pitch, many of the green runs here would be classified as blue at most other hills – indeed, some even have small mogul fields on them. Intermediates, however, will thrive on runs like the green Southern Comfort or Upper and Lower College, as well as on the Warm Springs face, exhilarating but not too steep to be off-putting. The mountain is dotted with black diamonds, so expert skiers and boarders will have no trouble finding something to keep them occupied; can't-miss areas include the Lookout and Easter Bowls, as well as Limelight, a long and challenging bump run on the Warm Springs face.

A one-day **lift ticket** will set you back around $63 a day ($35 child), $45 half-day ($27), and there's very little saved on extended passes. Outside of the peak times, children under 15 get to ski for free. There's the usual range of **facilities** at the base of the mountain, with ski school desks at Warm Springs Lodge and River Run Plaza and ski and board rental shops in both of these locations too. To get to Bald Mountain, use either Ketchum's free KART buses (see p.592) or Sun Valley Resort's yellow buses, which run a free shuttle service every fifteen minutes from 8.30am to 4.30pm between Sun Valley Resort, Bald Mountain, and Dollar Mountain.

Dollar Mountain

It's hard to believe that **Dollar Mountain** (Ⓣ208/622-2183 or 1-800/786-8259, Ⓦwww.sunvalley.com), sloping up between Sun Valley Resort and Elkhorn Village Resort, was once the resort's star attraction. Nowadays it's very much a **beginners hill**, with seventy percent of the runs reserved for them and the remaining thirty percent designated as intermediate. There's only 718ft of vertical drop, but the wide, easy angled runs provide a great introduction to those not quite ready to tackle the more challenging slopes a couple of miles west. Freestyle snowboarders, though, may want to head here for the solid **half-pipe**.

The mountain is served by four chairs, and **lift tickets** (which can be traded up for tickets for use on Baldy) are around $25 adults, $18 children. Bald Mountain lift tickets are honored here as well.

Cross-country and backcountry skiing

Though nowhere near as impressive as the **cross-country skiing** areas around Galena Lodge (see p.610) in the Sawtooth NRA an hour's drive north, there are a couple of decent spots to work up a sweat in the Sun Valley. The closest option is the **Sun Valley Nordic Center** (Ⓣ208/622-2250; $12; rentals available), just past the *Sun Valley Lodge*, where thirty miles of meticulously groomed trails are open to skiers and snowshoers. It's not much of a backcountry experience, though, as most of the trails are within view of houses. A better choice is the free **Wood River Trails System** that runs twenty miles south from Ketchum to Bellevue along gently inclined slopes. While it doesn't have a real

Winter-sports outfitters

The Sun Valley area is home to scores of outfitters, and you'll have no problem buying or renting anything you need to get you out onto the snow. Below we've listed a few of the best, from which you can expect to pay around $30 a day to rent skis or boards, $15 per day for boots. Of course if you're renting for longer periods, you'll be able to work out a far better deal.

Backwoods Mountain Sports corner of N Main St and Warm Springs Rd ⓣ208/726-8818. One of the valley's best outdoor stores includes a particularly impressive array of cross-country skis and snowshoes.

Board Bin & Girl Street corner of 4th and Washington streets ⓣ208/726-1222, ⓦwww.boardbin.com. Ketchum's best boarding shop, loaded with all the latest gear. If it's one of your first days boarding, stop in to rent a "buttpad," a wise investment that should dull the pain of some of your bigger spills.

Ski Tek 191 Sun Valley Rd W (ⓣ208/726-7503). One of the finest places to hit for high-end demo skis. Also do very good, fast, and affordable tune ups.

Sturtevants 314 N Main St (ⓣ208/726-4501); Warm Springs Village (ⓣ208/726-SKIS). "Sturtos'" stocks a wide range of ski and boarding equipment and the Warm Springs store is handy for dropping off gear after a day on Baldy.

"mountain" feel to it, the trails are well maintained and it's a great place to enjoy a good workout.

Powder-hounds may want to look into a **backcountry** skiing/boarding tour in the nearby Boulder and Sawtooth Mountains. There's a vast amount of skiable terrain here, and with a guide – or without if you're experienced – huge swaths of untracked snow can be found. Backcountry huts and yurts are also available, supplying great overnight stops for multiday tours. Contact Sun Valley Trekking (ⓣ208/788-9585) or Venture Outdoors (ⓣ208/788-5049) for details; prices start from around $100. To experience the ultimate, most expensive ski experience, check in with Sun Valley Heli Ski (ⓣ1-800/872-3108, ⓦwww.svheli-ski.com); prices for a day's worth of **heli-skiing** start at around $500. To check backcountry **avalanche conditions**, call ⓣ208/788-1200 ext 8027.

Summer activities

Sun Valley doesn't sleep in the summer sun – indeed, it's pretty much as busy as in winter with **hikers**, **bikers**, and **anglers** enjoying the surrounding mountains, forests, and rivers. Baldy is open for business whether you want to take the ski lift up or hike or ride to the top, and if you want to get away from the crowds, the stunning **Sawtooth NRA** (see p.604) is less than an hour's drive north on Hwy-75. **Golfers** and **horseback riders** also have several options (see p.602).

Hiking and biking

There's more than forty miles of **hiking** trails within a five-mile radius of Ketchum. One of the finest is the five-mile hike up **Bald Mountain Trail** starting from the River Run Plaza and winding its way up to a superb panorama of the mountains to the north and the Snake River Plain to the south. If tired out, you can take the chairlift back down for free. There are also a number of trails leading down from the summit, often passing through colorful carpets of wildflowers. More mountain views can be had along the loop trails heading

Hemingway in Idaho

Had **Ernest Hemingway** not ended his own life, it's easy to imagine that Sun Valley would have been the setting for a later novel. A one-time resident of Ketchum, he first visited the region in 1939 as a guest of resort founder Averell Harriman. Throughout the next two decades, the Nobel Prize-winning author returned frequently, writing portions or all of *For Whom the Bell Tolls*, *A Moveable Feast*, and *Garden of Eden* during his summer stays. When not writing, he could often be found trekking about the backcountry, taking pleasure in the great hunting and fishing to be had. As often as not, though, Hemingway could be found in the area's bars or at parties around the resort. He enjoyed basking in the celebrity glow of the valley, rubbing elbows with the likes of Gary Cooper and Ingrid Bergman, and the *Casino Club*, *Sawtooth Club* and *Alpine Club* (now *Whisky Jacques'*) on Ketchum's Main Street were all regular haunts.

In the late 1950s, Hemingway left his home in Cuba after Fidel Castro came to power, to become a full-time resident of Ketchum. Unfortunately he was not to enjoy the mountains long. By 1961, a combination of alcoholism and depression proved too much for him, and, after a night out at the *Christiana Restaurant* on July 1, he returned home to end his life with a shotgun. He was buried in Ketchum Cemetery, and a **memorial** to the man who became one of the twentieth century's most influential authors lies in a grove of aspens and willows on Trail Creek Road.

out from the Trail Creek area, two miles east of Sun Valley along Trail Creek Road. Amongst these are the easy two-mile **Aspen Loop Trail**, and the more strenuous six-mile out-and-back **Proctor Mountain Trail**, which rewards the effort with good summit views of Sun Valley. A far less strenuous hike can be had on any portion of the easy twenty-mile long **Wood River Trail** that meanders along the valley from Ketchum to Hailey, dotted with interpretive boards covering the region's history along its route. For more hikes nearby, pick up the *Trails Around Town* leaflet from Ketchum's information center.

Some truly excellent **mountain biking** trails are located around Sun Valley, with enough variety for both beginners and absolute masochists. For serious downhill action, the lifts at River Run Plaza (daily 9am–3.45pm; $20 full day, $15 half-day; ⓣ208/622-2231) take you to the top of **Bald Mountain**. Routes to suit all levels of ability snake their way down from the summit – experienced bikers should hit the superb seven-mile **Warm Springs** and six-mile **Cold Springs** trails, which have a world-class combination of single-track and open riding through alpine meadows and forests. Another great spot is **Adams Gulch**, just under two miles north of Ketchum along Adams Gulch Road west off Hwy-75, where there are both grinding single-track climbs and easier, flatter off-road loops. The flattest option is the **Wood River Trail** (see above), which can also be done on a road bike. To **rent** or get more trail advice, check in at one of Pete Lane's Mountain Sports three locations – River Run Plaza (ⓣ208/622-6123), Sun Valley Village (ⓣ208/622-2279), and Warm Springs Base Lodge (ⓣ208/622-6354) – or the friendly and very knowledgeable Ski Tek, 191 Sun Valley Rd (ⓣ208/726-7503). Rates hover around $35 a day for a full-suspension bike.

Fishing

Silver Creek, a favorite of Ernest Hemingway some 25 miles south of Ketchum, is legendary in trout **fishing** circles. There's good catch-and-release fly-fishing for rainbow trout and other species even closer, though, on the **Big Wood River** that runs right through town. The local creeks flowing into the river, **Warm Springs** to the west and **Trail Creek** to the east, are also worthwhile spots, but look out for public access signs as many sections of the riverbank are privately owned. The trout season runs from June to November, and you can get full details on fishing locally from the brochure *Fishing in the Wood River Valley* available from the Ketchum information center (see p.593). Local guides include Head Waters General Store, 151 S Main St (Ⓣ208/726-5775, Ⓦwww.iflyfishidaho.com), Silver Creek Outfitters, 500 N Main St (Ⓣ208/726-5285), and Sun Valley Outfitters & Sports at Elkhorn Plaza (Ⓣ208/622-3400). Average rates are around $300 for an all-inclusive day-trip.

Eating, drinking, and nightlife

There's an excellent range of **bars** and **restaurants** in Ketchum, the majority either lining Main Street or located off it on either side between 2nd and 6th streets; reservations may be necessary during peak season. There are no major venues for **live music**, but many bars and restaurants still feature bands. As one would expect, the resorts also feature a handful of fine restaurants, though the nightlife is generally low-key. Down the valley, Hailey has a healthy, no-frills approach to evening entertainment and can also be noticeably cheaper than Ketchum or the resorts for dining.

Of course, heading out for an aprés-ski cocktail isn't your only option after a day on the hill. **Cinemas** in town include the Opera House (Ⓣ208/622-2244) in Sun Valley Village, which screens movies nightly (including ski movies in winter), and Ketchum's Magic Lantern, 100 2nd St E (Ⓣ208/726-4274), which has four screens and features mainstream releases. If nothing good is on, you could always go **bowling** at the six-lane Sun Valley Bowling Alley (Ⓣ208/622-2191; $3.75 per game) in the Sun Valley Village.

Restaurants

The resorts

Bald Mountain Pizza & Pasta Sun Valley Mall Ⓣ208/726-3838. Tasty pizzas and pastas at good prices in a family-friendly, relaxed setting. Pizza by the slice and takeout also available.

Gretchen's *Sun Valley Lodge* Ⓣ208/622-2144. Overlooking the ice rink, the lively restaurant features filling breakfasts and a good range of traditional fare (steaks, pastas, and the like) the rest of the day – a full dinner will set you back $15–20.

The Konditorei Sun Valley Village Ⓣ208/622-2235. The best breakfast spot in the village, though also good later in the day for its full range of Austrian cakes and pastries. Beer and wine are also served.

River Rock Steakhouse *Elkkorn Resort* Ⓣ208/622-4411. An elegant restaurant with an excellent variety of steak and seafood dishes that's complemented by an equally fine range of wines and microbrews. An entree here will cost you around $20, though cheaper (and smaller) dishes can be ordered off the bar menu.

Ketchum

Felix's Restaurant 960 N Main St Ⓣ208/726-1166. Located in the *Knob Hill Inn* (see p.594), this restaurant has gained a strong following for its Spanish/Mediterranean-influenced dishes, including a fantastic paella. Entrees can run up to $20; outdoor dining in summer.

Il Naso corner of 5th St and Washington Ave Ⓣ208/726-7776. A popular spot with locals for fine Italian dining in urbane surroundings, with entrees from $15 upwards. If you're looking for something romantic, this is the place to head for.

Java on Fourth 191 4th St Ⓣ208/726-2882. A cool, relaxed atmosphere – perhaps a little too relaxed on the part of the staff – pervades this coffeehouse that also serves pastries and cake. The deck overlooking the sidewalk is a great place to hang out.

Johnny G's Subshack 371 Washington Ave Ⓣ208/725-7827. No-nonsense, filling submarine sandwiches ideal for those on the go.

The Ketchum Grill 5th St and East Ave Ⓣ208/726-4660. Housed in an 1884 postmaster's cabin, this highly recommended restaurant features a wide selection of dishes ranging from burgers and fries to entrees like linguini with quail and sun-dried tomatoes or grilled duck breast with mountain huckleberries, but don't expect much change from $20. Save room for the killer desserts as well. Open for dinner only.

The Kneadery 260 Leadville Ave ☎ 208/726-3856. A Ketchum institution and one of the most popular breakfast spots in town, with good omelettes and a laid-back, woodsy atmosphere. No smoking.

Lefty's Bar & Grill 213 6th St ☎ 208/726-2744. *Lefty's* does basic, good-value bar food that goes perfectly with the typically bustling atmosphere. There's also an assortment of pinball and pool tables to play on after eating.

Mama Inez 7th St and Warm Springs Ave ☎ 208/726-4213. Great Southwestern-style Mexican food served in what feels like someone's home. The salsa is spectacular, and specials include chicken jalapeno, fresh fish, and killer veggie burritos topped with vegan red and green mole. Expect to pay around $10–15 for entrees.

Pioneer Saloon 308 N Main St ☎ 208/726-3139. This atmospheric, old-style pioneer bar is a Ketchum favorite. The prime rib is fantastically done, and the assorted shrimp, scallop, and steak entrees are also quite good ($12–20). It's a popular aprés-ski spot, so it's worth calling in for a beer even if you don't want to eat. Be prepared to queue, though – even Arnold Schwarzenegger has been told to wait his turn.

Smoky Mountain Pizza & Pasta 200 Sun Valley Rd ☎ 208/622-5625. Excellent, affordable pizza and pasta and a friendly atmosphere makes this a hit with families and those on a budget alike. You can dine on the deck in summer, and they'll also deliver.

Warm Springs Ranch Restaurant 1801 Warm Springs Rd ☎ 208/726-2609. A comfortable, relaxing place, with creekside deck dining in summer. There's a wide choice of dishes, including great BBQ chicken and ribs, fresh mountain-trout and filet mignon, none of which should set you back much more than $20. The children's dishes are also very good.

Hailey

Java on Main 310 N Main St ☎ 208/788-2444. Good for a quick coffee and fresh baked goods before heading off for a day in the mountains.

Shorty's Diner 126 S Main St ☎ 208/788-9881. A classic 1950s-style diner where the jukebox plays nonstop early rock'n'roll. Often packed with noisy kids and teenagers, the typical diner menu is well-priced and the staff are consistently cheerful.

Sun Valley Brewing Co. 202 N Main St ☎ 208/788-5777. A highly rated brewpub producing a dozen mouthwatering beers to go along with an eclectic menu than crosses all borders; standouts include Thai curry pasta, homemade bratwurst, and chicken pot pie, all for around $10.

Viva Taqueria 305 N Main St ☎ 208/788-4247. A local favorite for well-priced Mexican meals, including very filling burritos, best enjoyed with one of several beers made south of the border.

Bars and clubs

The resorts

Duchin Bar & Lounge *Sun Valley Lodge* ☎ 208/622-2145. A genteel atmosphere that's reminiscent of Sun Valley's old days, with an orchestra and ballroom dancing for entertainment as you sip your cocktails.

Ketchum

The Casino Club 220 Main St ☎ 208/726-9901. This former casino is a bit quieter than most of Ketchum's other bars, though the earthy atmosphere is still friendly. Pool tables rather than a dance floor provide the main entertainment, though the exuberant bartenders can also be a show.

Grumpy's 860 Warm Springs Rd. The name belies the atmosphere – friendly staff and clientele, great burgers and large quantities of beer make this an excellent place to meet fellow travelers and locals alike. Especially popular for a quick drink after a day on the hill, which can easily turn into an all-night session.

The Sawtooth Club 231 Main St ☎ 208/726-5233. A big hit with the aprés-ski crowd. The attractive pine-paneled bar is a chatty place to have a beer, and upstairs there's a restaurant serving good mesquite-grilled duck, steak, trout, and salmon.

Whisky Jacques' 251 Main St ☎ 208/726-5297. Live bands ($3–5) play some nights in the pleasant log interior, filling the large dance floor with a slightly older crowd. Invariably busy and buzzing with both locals and visitors, you can also get pizza, sandwiches, and burgers, and there are pool tables if dancing isn't your thing.

Hailey

Red Elephant Saloon 107 Main St ☎ 208/788-6047. While not always as lively as those up in Ketchum, this bar still moves and grooves until midnight. The pub grub is decent as well.

Listings

Golf The Sun Valley Golf Course (☎208/622-2251) runs along Trail Creek; green fees are around $90. The longer Elkhorn Golf Course (☎208/622-6400) is ranked among the top hundred in the US and has superb views of the Boulder Mountains; green fees are around $100. The nine-holes Warm Springs Golf Course (☎208/726-3715) and Bigwood Golf Course (☎208/726-4024) are considerably cheaper, with fees of around $25.

Horseback Sun Valley Resort's Horsemen's Center (☎208/622-2387) offers one-hour guided rides in the Trail Creek area for $25, while Elkhorn Stables (☎208/726-1865) in Elkhorn Village offer half-day ($65) and full-day ($100) guided rides in the Sawtooth Mountains.

Internet Email by the hour available at Wood River Technologies, 2nd Floor, Jones Building, corner of Main and 4th streets (☎208/726-5553) and Newslink, cnr Sun Valley Rd and Leadville. Rates vary from $3–5 per half-hour.

Laundry Suds Yer Duds Laundromat, 22 Lewis St (☎208/726-9820).

Post office The main office in Ketchum is at 154 4th St W (☎208/726-5161).

Craters of the Moon National Monument

Though other lava fields exist in southeastern Idaho, **CRATERS OF THE MOON**, named a national monument in 1924, is unusual for the wealth of volcanic features to be found in its 83-square-mile area. Though at first sight the monument looks like little more than a sooty-black wasteland, closer inspection reveals a surreal cornucopia of cinder cones, spatter cones, lava bombs, and lava tubes. Here and there, sagebrush clings to the bleak soil, and any trees have been battered by fierce winds into bonsai-like contortions. All the geological features were formed without the aid of a volcano as such; instead, at roughly two-thousand-year intervals over the last thirteen thousand years, successive waves of lava have oozed from gaping wounds in the earth's crust. The next wave is thought to be due any time now. In summer the heat rises inexorably from the black, dry lava fields in shimmering waves – in winter snow covers it to create a frigid, monochrome landscape. If you've never seen a volcanic landscape before, Craters of the Moon will fascinate you – if you have, you may want to give it a miss.

An hour's drive southeast from Sun Valley will bring you to the park entrance on US-93 between Picabo and Arco, and a seven-mile **loop road**, accessible by car ($5) and bicycle ($2). The loop takes you around the lava fields, where short hiking trails, complete with interpretive boards and well-placed viewpoints, lead past the different volcanic features. Although they appear to be inhospitable, the lava fields are home to 2000 species of insect, nearly 150 birds (including great horned owls) and 47 mammals (including bobcats and mule deer). Large numbers of plants survive here too, and in spring and summer wildflowers can be seen blooming amongst the solidified lava.

The whole area is described in detail in the **visitor center** (daily except winter holidays: June–Aug 8am–6pm; rest of year 8am–4.30pm; ☎208/527-3257), which has informative displays and a dramatic video of volcanoes in action. There's also a basic **campground** ($10 May–Oct, free in winter) bizarrely located amongst the lava flows, and in winter the loop road becomes an unusual **cross-country ski** trail.

Around Craters of the Moon

Twenty miles east, **ARCO** is unremarkable but for the fact that in July 1955 it became the first community in the world to be lit up by atomic energy. That's because some twenty miles southeast is the massive **INEEL** – the Idaho National Engineering & Environmental Laboratory – compound, established in 1949 to build and test nuclear reactors (June–Aug daily 8am–5pm; free;

△ The Sawtooth National Recreation Area's Bench Lakes

☎208/526-0050). The first prototype nuclear submarine was also somehow manufactured and experimented with here amongst the lava fields, as were two nuclear engines designed to power airplanes – thankfully, the latter were never used.

Central and western Idaho

The fact that virtually every major road in central and western Idaho is a designated scenic highway should give you some idea of the truly beautiful mountain landscapes to be found here. And, if you get off the beaten track, things begin to look even better. Here is a landscape where the towering peaks and crags of ranges such as the Bitterroot and Sawtooth Mountains rise up into a brilliant blue sky and where some of the wildest rivers in the US sweep through deep, forested canyons and wildflower meadows. The **Selway-Bitterroot Wilderness**, **Frank Church-River of No Return Wilderness**, **Gospel Hump Wilderness**, and **Sawtooth Wilderness** add up to over 3.9 million acres of wild and untamed landscape – larger than some US states. In addition to this are the 200,000 acres of **Hell's Canyon Wilderness Area** on the western edge of the state.

As one would expect, there are few towns of any size to be found. **Riggins**, **McCall**, **Stanley**, and **Salmon** are the focal points, all best used simply as bases for outdoor types. To see the area at its best, get out of the car and hike, bike, ride, ski, or paddle through it. If you don't have the experience or confidence to do so under your own steam, there are plenty of outfitters in the area that can help out.

Sawtooth National Recreation Area

The mountainous landscape of the 756,000-acre **SAWTOOTH NATIONAL RECREATION AREA** – daunting granite spires shooting up like giant stalagmites, their reflections mirrored in the glassy blue waters of hundreds of lakes – is easily as dramatic as the more famous Grand Tetons in Wyoming. The entire area, which includes 42 peaks over 10,000ft, is breathtaking, though the most spectacular scenery is concentrated within the 217,000-acre **Sawtooth Wilderness** abutting the NRA to the west. Though the Sawtooth Mountains themselves are the most rugged range, several more cut through the NRA. To the east of Hwy-75, the region's main artery, are the denuded slopes of the Boulder Mountains, and in the southeast rise the White Cloud Mountains, a maze of jagged white-limestone ramparts.

Though not very well known out of state, enough locals flock here to make this Idaho's top region for outdoor pursuits. The center for much of the action

is the highway junction town of **STANLEY**, whose year-round population of around seventy rises exponentially in July and August when outdoor enthusiasts flock here in droves. They come to hike and bike on hundreds of miles of trails, and to paddle and fish on the numerous lakes – including busy **Redfish Lake** – and major rivers: the **Salmon**, the **South Fork of the Payette**, the **Big Wood**, and the **Boise**. In winter, things slow down considerably, perhaps not surprising given the heavy snowfalls and sub-zero temperatures, but cross-country skiers, snowshoers, and snowmobilers easily make the most of it.

Arrival and information

One reason that so many locals visit the Sawtooth NRA is that it's readily accessible, the southern boundary a mere nine miles from Ketchum (see p.591) and it's western edge a little over two hours drive northeast of Boise. The main information center is the **Sawtooth NRA Headquarters** (daily 8.30am–5pm; ⓣ208/727-5013 or 1-800/260-5970), located on Hwy-75 on the south side of Galena Summit en route to Ketchum. They have heaps of information including details on camping, hiking, biking, and climbing and sell trailhead parking passes ($5), compulsory within the NRA and the Sawtooth National Forest to the south.

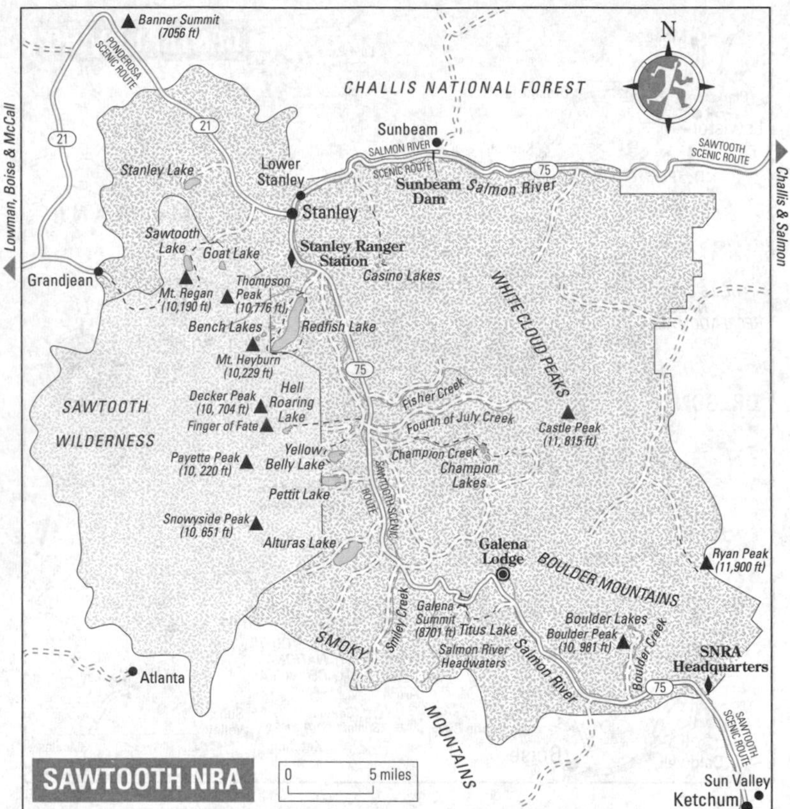

Stanley

It's easy to see why parts of Clint Eastwood's *Pale Rider* were filmed around **STANLEY**. The town has an authentic Western feel to it, with just a handful of unpaved streets shooting off its main drag, evocatively named the **Ace of Diamonds Avenue**. Strung about the crossroads of Hwy-75 and Hwy-21, it's one of the Rockies' most scenic towns, tucked beneath the serrated ridges and peaks of the Sawtooth Mountains at an elevation of 6300ft. The climate here is equally dramatic; it's one of Idaho's coldest towns with an average annual temperature of around 34°F, and in summer a shift from overnight frost to midday highs in the 80's°F is not uncommon.

Originally a supply center for local gold mines and still home to some ranching and logging activities, Stanley now relies most heavily on outdoor recreation. All roads out of town lead into the NRA, and in summer they buzz with campers, hikers, and bikers heading to the numerous nearby trailheads. The town is also an important base for multiday rafting or kayaking trips down the **Middle Fork of the Salmon**. The main drop-in point is at **Boundary Creek**, some two hours drive north, although shorter trips can be undertaken locally. For full details of rafting on the Middle Fork see p.617.

The only real attraction in town is the small **Stanley Museum** (June–Aug 11am–5pm; admission by donation), on Hwy-75 a half-mile north of the junction with Hwy-21. A former ranger station listed on the National Register of Historic Places, it won't take long to view the exhibits in this rustic structure, which focus mostly on the pioneer days.

Information and accommodation

Information is available from the chamber of commerce in the community building just west of the highway junction (June–Aug daily 10am–6pm; ⓣ208/774-3411 or 1-800/878-7950, ⓦwww.stanleycc.org). A good option

Camping in the Sawtooth NRA

With a good selection of scenic sites, **camping** in the Sawtooth region can be a memorable experience. It's worth remembering, though, that nighttime temperatures can fall below freezing even in midsummer, and if you don't come prepared it may be a cold and miserable night. All the sites listed below can get busy, especially during weekends and holiday periods, and where possible you should make reservations. Expect to pay around $12 for a tent site, and up to $28 for an RV site or multiple vehicle pitch. For more details and a full list of campgrounds within the NRA call National Forest Recreation Reservations on ⓣ1-877/444-6777 or the NRA headquarters on ⓣ208/727-5013, or log on to ⓦwww.reserveusa.com.

If **backcountry camping**, you can set up camp just about anywhere, though you should try to camp in a previously used site. Check in with Stanley's Ranger Station or the NRA headquarters near Ketchum for full details.

East of Stanley

Though there are several USFS campgrounds along this stretch of Hwy-75, the two to go for are both close to natural hot springs. *Mormon Bend* (seventeen spaces) is at Mile Marker 193, and *Basin Creek Campground* is seven miles east of Stanley. Come early as both tend to be busy in summer and cannot be reserved.

South of Stanley

Redfish Lake Eight separate campgrounds ring the lake, making a total of 120 spaces. *Mt Heyburn, Outlet, Glacier View* and *Point* are all at the north end, relatively convenient for accessing the laundry and showers by the gas station nearby, and the latter three can be reserved. Further off the north shore, *Sockeye* is a quieter and more remote option.

Alturas Lake Alturas Lake has three quiet and extremely scenic sites just outside the Sawtooth Wilderness Area. *Smokey Bear, North Shore* and *Alturas Inlet* have a total of 55 sites between them and are best if you plan on accessing the wilderness area.

South of Galena Summit South of Galena Summit is a string of campgrounds that can also be used as bases for exploring Ketchum and the Sun Valley area. Listed in order heading south, they include the *Easley Campground* (seventeen spaces; reservable), near natural hot springs, *Wood River Campground* (32 spaces), with a wide range of facilities including showers and a store; and *North Fork Campground* (thirty spaces), close to the NRA headquarters.

West of Stanley

Stanley Lake Located off of Hwy-21 about two miles northwest of Stanley, this lake has three popular sites – *Inlet* (fourteen spaces; open year-round), *Lakeview* (six spaces), and *Stanley Lake* (nineteen spaces; reservable). They can be noisy, but the wonderful views of the Sawtooths and nearby trailheads make up for it.

for outdoor advice is the **Stanley Ranger Station** (June–Aug Mon–Sat 8.30am–5pm; spring and fall Mon–Sat 8.30am–4.30pm; intermittent hours in winter; ⓣ208/774-3000), on Hwy-75 a couple of miles south of town.

If you're not **camping** (see box, overleaf), then Stanley is your main **accommodation** option in the region. Summer reservations are often necessary, and in winter call ahead as many places shut down for the season. Options are split pretty evenly between Upper Stanley, the area of town at the junction of Hwys 21 and 75, and Lower Stanley, the collection of buildings a mile to the northeast strung along Hwy-75. More isolated accommodations can also be found in the lodges off Hwy-75 en route to Ketchum; see "South of Stanley: Redfish Lake to Galena Summit" opposite for more details.

Upper Stanley

Danner's Log Cabin Motel ⓣ208/774-3539, ⓔkrdanner@ruralnetwork.net. Attractive log cabin-themed motel rooms with kitchenettes. A reasonably good value close to downtown. Feb–Oct. ❹

Mountain Village Lodge ⓣ208/774-3661 or 1-800/843-5475, ⓦwww.mountainvillage.com. The largest lodging in town with over sixty rooms, each comfortably furnished along with amenities such as in-room cable TV and coffee-makers. There are some larger suites with kitchenettes, and a guests-only natural hot springs spa. Open year-round. ❹

Triangle C Ranch ⓣ208/774-2266 or 1-800/303-6258. Small, cozy log cabins with fireplaces, located on the west side of town off Hwy-21, open May–Nov. The owners also can arrange rafting trips down the Salmon. ❺

Valley Creek Motel ⓣ208/774-3606. Well-appointed rooms with two queen-beds, private baths, and good views of the Sawtooths – one of the best bets if you're on a budget. No pets and open year-round. ❸

Lower Stanley

Gunter's Salmon River Cabins ⓣ208/774-2290 or 1-888/574-2290. Nicely furnished one- and two-bedroom log cabins, some of which you can fish from directly off the deck. Pets are welcome as well. April–Oct. ❹

Jerry's Country Store and Motel ⓣ208/774-3566 or 1-800/972-4627, ⓦwww.jerrys-country-store.com. Open year round, *Jerry's* has clean and tidy riverfront rooms beside the busy store, which also has an ATM. ❹

McGowan's River Cabins ⓣ208/774-2243, ⓔmcgowan@ruralnetwork.com. A couple of comfortable, reasonably-priced cabins – one sleeps up to eight – with kitchenettes. Located beside the Salmon River. April–Sept. ❹

Redwood Cabins ⓣ208/774-3531, ⓦwww.redwood-stanley.com. No-frills basic motel accommodation in plain cabins by the Salmon. Always clean and one of the best bets for budget travelers. May–Oct. ❸

Salmon River Lodge east of the Salmon River off Hwy-75 ⓣ208/774-3422. Quiet, secluded waterfront cabins with great views of the Sawtooths – one of the best options in Lower Stanley. No-smoking rooms available. ❹

Eating and drinking

The Kasino Club Ace of Diamonds Ave ⓣ208/774-3516. A tastefully furnished bar and restaurant with a good range of microbrews and some of the best food in town – expect to pay around $15 for an excellent steak or pasta dish. They don't take reservations, and advertise tongue in cheek "service with a snarl!" that's anything but.

Mountain Village Restaurant and Lounge junction of Hwy-75 and Hwy-21 ⓣ208/774-3317. Large, centrally located establishment serving reasonably priced home-style meals in a modern setting all day long. The plain menu and atmosphere, though, lack the character of other Stanley dining options.

The Rod and Gun Club Saloon Ace of Diamonds Ave ⓣ208/774-9920. All that's missing in this classic Western bar are swinging doors and spittoons. The jukebox pumps out mostly Country, the folks are friendly, and you can even surf the internet ($5 for 30min) while drinking a brew. One not to miss.

Papa Brunee's ⓣ208/774-2536. Opposite the Post Office on Ace of Diamonds Ave and serving up decent pizzas and filling deli sandwiches (take-out available). A good place to meet outdoor-types over a microbrew or two.

Sawtooth Luce's Hwy-21 and Niece Ave ⓣ208/774-3361. Another popular pizza spot where a good pie and beer on the deck shouldn't set you back more than about $10.

Local Oufitters

McCoy's Tackle & Gift Shop Niece St ☎208/774-3377. Good for information on what's biting where, and for fishing and hunting licenses.

Mystic Saddle Ranch Six miles south of Redfish Lake on Hwy-75 ☎1-888/722-5432, ⓦwww.mysticsaddleranch.com. One of the premier horseback guides in the area, with trips ranging from hour-long jaunts around Red Fish Lake ($32) to extended pack-trips into the Sawtooth Wilderness.

River 1 ☎208/774-2270. Just north of the junction of Hwy-21 and Hwy-75, this outdoor store specializes in rafting and river sports. There's also an espresso bar that makes for a nice place to kick back after emptying your wallet.

Sawtooth Mountain Guides ☎208/774-3324, ⓦwww.sawtoothguides.com. Operating out of Lower Stanley, this full-service guiding company offers everything from fishing trips to backcountry skiing expeditions. Check website for details.

East of Stanley: Sunbeam and around

Snaking alongside the Salmon River and between the peaks of the White Cloud Mountains, Hwy-75 (known as the **Salmon River Scenic Byway** here) passes through the cheerfully named settlement of **SUNBEAM** thirteen miles to the east of Stanley. It's a good spot to **raft** down the Salmon, which flows along the south side of the highway and is relatively calm here. White Otter Outdoor Adventures (☎208/838-2406) have an office in the village where you can rent gear to get on the river; a half-day guided trip runs around $65. While here, take a look at the remains of **Sunbeam Dam** on the opposite side of Hwy-75. Built in 1919, it only operated for one year, and in 1934 it was intentionally breached to give the salmon back their run. Just west of town on the banks of the river are the **Sunbeam Hot Springs** – be careful where you dip, as the waters at the source are nearly 170°F. On the south side of Hwy-75 rise the solitary **White Cloud Mountains**, reaching their highest point at Castle Peak (11,820ft), a serious challenge for mountaineers. There is also some fine hiking in the range (see box p.611).

South of Stanley: Redfish Lake to Galena Summit

South of Stanley, the **Sawtooth Scenic Byway** (Hwy-75) twists by several lakes and mountain passes on its 65-mile journey to the park headquarters and Sun Valley area beyond. You'll only need to drive five miles south of Stanley, though, to reach the turnoff for **Redfish Lake**, one of the region's most popular lakes. Named for the huge numbers of "red" sockeye salmon once found here, it's the largest lake in the recreation area, set in an inspiring spot beneath some of the Sawtooth Mountains' most spectacular peaks. Though busy in summer with all manner of boats, swimmers, and families having picnics, trailheads along the lake's north shore give easy access to the relative seclusion of the surrounding forests and mountains (see box p.611). There are also signposted mountain-bike trails circling the lake, including some very fun semi-technical single-track. If you'd like to get on the lake, one-hour pontoon boat **tours** on the *Lady of the Lake* ($6.50) are on offer, and you can cross the lake on a **shuttle boat** ($5) to trailheads at the far shore – call the *Redfish Lake Lodge* (see below) for times. In **winter** there are good cross-country ski trails around and even across the lake, although many are shared with **snowmobilers**, the noise of which can rather detract from the experience. If you'd rather not camp around its shores (see box p.607), the family-oriented *Redfish Lake Lodge* (Ⓣ208/774-3536, Ⓦwww.redfishlake.com; ④) is the best indoor choice. The various options include basic lodge rooms with shared baths, more comfortable motel rooms sleeping up to four people, and attractive semi-rustic cabins.

Galena Summit and around

Back out on the Sawtooth Scenic Byway, the hour's drive south to Galena Summit is unforgettable. The road meanders below dramatic mountain scenery and alongside the bubbling Salmon River as it flows out of its headwaters in the Smokey Mountains to the south, and there are several idyllic lakes begging for attention only a short detour away. Two particularly good lakes for trout fishing and relaxing, both reached via the same access road, are **Yellow Belly Lake** and **Hell Roaring Lake**, the latter actually in the Wilderness Area and situated beneath the granite spikes of Finger of Fate and Arrowhead Peaks. Further south of these is the turnoff for the larger **Alturas Lake**, a good spot to camp (see box p.607), fish, and cross-country ski in winter. A handful of **lodges** vie for custom along this stretch of the highway and one of the best options before the long haul up to Galena Summit is *Smiley Creek Lodge* (Ⓣ208/774-3547; ③). Along with plain but comfortable cabins and well-appointed lodge rooms, they have tent sites ($10), and large tepees ($35). There's also a general store scooping out excellent ice cream if you're just looking for a sugar fix.

The original wagon road over **Galena Summit** (8701ft) was so steep that early automobiles had to drive up in reverse (so that fuel would drain from the tank through to the engine). Though easier to handle today, the summit is still no less dramatic – as evidenced by the overlook near the summit's north side, where there's also a small tourist information booth.

Once over the pass, the road begins heading down towards the Wood River Valley, past the day-use **Galena Lodge** en route. The beautifully refurbished 1880s mining camp has a cozy restaurant and bar (meals daily from 11am–4pm). It's best known, though, for the nearby network of **cross-country skiers** and **snowshoe** trails, arguably the finest such system in the state (Dec to early April daily 9am–5pm; Ⓣ208/726-4010, Ⓦwww.xcskisv.com; $9, rentals available). With some 35 miles of well-groomed ski trails and eighteen miles of snowshoe trails, everyone from novice to expert can enjoy the quiet, snowmobile-free pine-scented forest and wonderful mountain views. The lodge also rents out a number of **yurts** a short ski or snowshoe away. They're wood heated, sleep six people, and are totally self-contained (or you can have a lodge meal delivered to the door); rates start at $30 per person per night.

There's another excellent system of trails on the south side of Galena Summit in the Upper Wood Valley – the highlight of the **North Valley Nordic Trails** is the eighteen-mile **Boulder Mountain Trail** from Galena Summit south to the Sawtooth NRA headquarters. This is the venue for the annual Boulder Mountain Tour every February, one of the biggest cross-country ski events in the US. Day-passes are $9 adults, $2 kids.

Hiking in the Sawtooth NRA

Wherever you **hike** in the Sawtooth NRA, the scenery is never less than spectacular. However, some of the trails, especially around Redfish Lake, can get quite crowded, and if you're looking for solitude then head into the Sawtooth Wilderness Area or east to the White Cloud Range. Many trails lead up to high elevations, so you may need a day or two to acclimatize (don't forget you're already over 6000ft high in Stanley) and it can **snow** at higher altitudes even in midsummer, so take appropriate clothing and precautions. For more information on hiking trails, call in at the Sawtooth NRA headquarters.

East of Stanley

Big Boulder Chain of Lakes thirteen miles round-trip. A spectacular hike past a chain of lovely alpine lakes on the east side of the White Cloud Peaks to the start of the climb up Castle Peak (11,815 ft). The trailhead is about seventeen miles down the East Fork of the Salmon Rd, accessed off Hwy-75 east of Sunbeam at Clayton.

South of Stanley

Bench Lakes Trail eight-mile round-trip. A moderately strenuous climb that also leaves from the Redfish trailhead parking area and heads up to the Bench Lakes, which sit at 8600ft in an idyllic bowl beneath the splintered towers of Mount Heyburn (10,229ft). The deep-blue alpine lakes at the trail's end are perfect for a picnic stop and warm enough in summer for a quick swim. It will take you about four hours round-trip if you don't push it.

Casino Lakes ten miles round-trip. A strenuous 3000ft climb to the head of Big Casino Creek, past a series of small alpine lakes in the heart of wild and isolated country beneath the White Cloud Peaks. The trailhead is across the highway from Sawtooth Hatchery, just south of Stanley on Hwy-75.

Hell Roaring Lake ten miles round-trip. Accessed from a trailhead off Forest Road 315 on the west side of Hwy-75, this trail passes beneath the imposing Finger of Fate and Arrowhead peaks to Hell Roaring Lake, and although quite a stiff hike you're rewarded for it with some of the best views in the Sawtooths.

Redfish Lake Creek Trail ten miles round-trip. A popular and easy hike, starting from the Redfish trailhead parking area on Redfish Lake Rd at the northeast end of the lake. The trail leads through pine forest along the north shore of the lake and goes into the Wilderness Area at the lake's south end.

Titus Lake five mile round-trip. If you're stuck for time, try this easy trail with good mountain views on the south side of Galena Summit beneath Bromaghin Peak (10,225ft) in the Smoky Mountains. There's only 500ft of climbing involved, but it bear in mind you're already over 8000ft high.

Toxaway-Petit Loop Trail eighteen-mile loop. Best done as a two-day backpacking trip, this popular trail takes you past several alpine lakes and beneath the summits of Payette Peak (10,220ft) and Snowyside Peak (10,651ft). The trailhead is reached by turning west off Hwy-75 at milepost 170.3 onto Pettit Lake Rd and driving to Tin Cup trailhead.

West of Stanley

Sawtooth Lake eight mile round-trip. Turn off Hwy-21 2.6 miles northwest of Stanley onto Iron Creek Rd to the trailhead for the magnificent hike to Sawtooth Lake, a Rocky Mountain classic (chances are you've seen the lake and Mount Regan (10,190ft) reflecting in its waters on at least one scenic calendar). The trail has 1700ft of climbing through lodgepole pine and Douglas fir before emerging at the exposed and dramatic lake and its surrounding mountains.

Mountain biking around the Sawtooth NRA

Mountain biking trails in the NRA vary from easy family rides along the Salmon Valley to demanding single-track beneath the peaks of the Sawtooth and White Cloud ranges. Check at the Sawtooth NRA Headquarters below Galena Lodge (where there are also 25 miles of signposted mountain bike trails) for more details on routes, and where you can and can't ride. The Sawtooth Wilderness Area is completely out of bounds.

Decker Flat Road fourteen miles each way. This route starts at milepost 174.7 south along Hwy-75 and is a popular family ride following the Salmon River north to Redfish Lake Rd, with good views of the Sawtooths to the west and the White Cloud Mountains to the east.

The Fisher Creek-Williams Creek Loop eighteen-mile loop. Starting at Fisher Creek, milepost 176.3 on Hwy-75, this popular loop covers mixed terrain and has plenty of single-track climbing in the foothills of the White Cloud range, with over 1400ft of elevation gain. The exhilarating last half of the trail is almost all downhill.

Fourth of July Creek Trail twenty-mile round-trip. Starting just south of Obsidian on Hwy-75 south, this strenuous route gives access to the White Cloud Mountains where you'll find some of the best riding around, including some good technical and single-track stuff. There's an elevation gain of 2000ft from the start at 6800ft.

Nip and Tuck Road seventeen-mile round-trip. Just outside Lower Stanley on Forest Road 633, this is an easy loop through rolling hills with great views of the northern Sawtooths. It starts and finishes at the junction of Hwy-21 and Valley Creek Rd.

West of Stanley: The Ponderosa Pine and Wildlife Canyon scenic byways

The **Ponderosa Pine Scenic Byway** (Hwy-21) heads west from Stanley some sixty miles to **Lowman**, passing through deep forests of Ponderosa pine and the occasional high-country meadow.The road peaks at **Banner Summit** (7056ft), often blocked by heavy snowfalls and landslides – to check conditions, call ⓣ1-888/432-7623. Past here, the scenic byway swoops out of the Sawtooth NRA and down beside the South Fork of the Payetter River to Lowman, where there are still signs of the huge forest fire that swept through the area in 1989, destroying seventy square miles of woodland. Hwy-21 continues south to Boise from here, while the spectacular **Wildlife Canyon Scenic Byway** branches west to join Hwy-55 at **Banks**, following the twists and turns of the **South Fork of the Payette** as it tumbles and crashes through a gorge hundreds of feet below. At Banks, you have a choice of turning south down Hwy-55 (the Payette River Scenic Byway) to Boise, or north for the pleasant 65-mile drive to McCall (see p.620) alongside the North Fork of the Payette River. On the way you pass through the well-kept lumber town of **Cascade**, and cheerful **Donnelly**, which has regular summer flea markets beside the highway.

The Salmon River region

The **SALMON RIVER** region is renowned for one thing – whitewater rafting. Some of the US's finest rapid-filled stretches of river are found here, and each year thousands come to experience the thrills and chilly spills on offer.

Hiking in the Salmon River Region

You can only hope to scratch the surface of what's available in terms of **hiking** in this region. The best sources of backcountry information in these parts are the USFS and BLM offices in Salmon (see p.615).

Frank Church-River of No Return Wilderness

These hikes run north to south.

Ship Island Lake 22-mile round-trip. A spectacular and accessible hike into the extremely rugged Big Horn Crags region, with good views of Ship Island Lake, surrounded by dense forest. The trail is demanding and rises up high – there can be snow even in summer. To find the trailhead, head for the *Big Horn Crags Campground* ($8; water available) reached from Salmon via Williams Creek Rd south of town. Follow the road for twelve miles to Panther Creek Rd, take this road and then turn right at Porphyry Creek Rd and head another sixteen miles to take a right-hand turn for the final two-mile drive to the campground.

Reflection Lake Trail 26 mile round-trip. Heading off from the same trail-head as Ship Island Lake (see above), this trail switchbacks up to around 9000ft to the eponymous lake, where you can fish and camp out.

Upper Vanity Lakes three-mile round-trip. A short but isolated trek that isn't blazed but is navigable with a map (you'll need the USGS *Langer Peak* 7.5' map). The lakes are reached by turning north off Hwy-21 at the sign for *Lola Creek Campground* to the northwest of Stanley. Forest Road 008 leads eight miles to Vanity Summit (7813ft) from where it's an easy hike east to the lakes.

Blue Bunch Mountain nine-mile round-trip. A good stiff day-hike that takes in 2000ft of climbing, leading to great views over the Middle Fork Salmon Canyon and the mountains surrounding it. This region is also one of the most important habitats in Idaho for gray wolves. To reach the trailhead, take the signposted gravel road to Dagger Falls and Bruce Meadow from Hwy-21 to the east of Banner Summit. After twelve miles take the turnoff sign-posted *Fir Creek Campground* for half a mile.

Around Salmon

Bear Valley Lakes eleven-mile round-trip. A lovely hike in the Lemhi Mountains beside the tumbling waters of Bear Valley Creek to a lake-filled cirque beneath the jagged Lem Peak (10,986ft). To reach the trailhead, head forty miles south from Salmon down Hwy-28, then turn right on Hayden Creek road, then after 3.5 miles left onto Forest Road 009 where the road forks to the trailhead, about eleven miles from Hwy-28.

Freeman Creek ten-mile round-trip. A dozen miles to the northeast of Salmon, this steep hike leads up to the Continental Divide at over 9000ft, from where the views across Idaho and into Montana are awesome. To access the trail, drive to Carmen via US-93, then turn right and follow a road alongside Carmen Creek for seven miles, then right again on Freeman Creek Rd for nearly three miles to a junction with Kirtly Creek Rd. Drive along Kirtly Creek Rd until the road gets too rough for your vehicle and then start hiking.

The majority of the action takes place on the **Main Fork** and **Middle Fork of the Salmon** rivers, both of which flow through the virtually uninhabited **Frank Church-River of No Return Wilderness**, the largest wilderness area in the US outside of Alaska. It's easy to become blasé about the views encountered around every corner – snowtopped peaks rise above heavily forested lower slopes and deep canyons, through which sparkling salmon- and trout-rich rivers flow. Big game is prevalent as well – it's not uncommon to spot

The Gospel Hump Wilderness

To the northwest of the Frank Church-River of No Return Wilderness and the Main Fork of the Salmon is the even more remote **Gospel Hump Wilderness**, named after the region's two highest points, Gospel Peak (8345ft) and Buffalo Hump (8940ft). The landscape in the south tends to be dry and dusty; north of a rugged glaciated divide, it's noticeably wetter and dense forests abound. The Salmon and its tributaries within this 206,000-acre wilderness are spawning and rearing habitats for steelhead and chinook salmon, as well as trout, sturgeon, and whitefish, making for some good fishing.

Access to the region is on unpaved roads and is limited and quite difficult. In the northwest, Forest Road 444 and 444A lead in from around Grangeville (see p.630). In the southwest, Salmon River Road (Forest Road 1614) and Slate Creek Road (Forest Road 354) are the best ways in from around Riggins (see p.626). And in the north, Sourdough Road (Forest Road 492), Orogrande Road (Forest Road 233), and Dixie Road (Forest Road 311) provide entry from around Orogrande (see p.631). **Trails** in the Gospel Hump are likewise remote and difficult, and they're only usually free of snow from mid-July to mid-October. The hike up Gospel Peak is a moderately strenuous trek that is a short and easy walk from Forest Road 444, and you can also access Pyramid Peak (8369ft), another short and not too difficult hike, from the same road about a mile north.

black bears, bighorn sheep, mountain goats, and even the occasional gray wolf and grizzly bear – and, best of all, people are not.

The region's main artery, US-93 (the **Salmon River Scenic Byway**), enters Idaho via Montana at **Lost Trail Pass** (7014ft) and switchbacks down fifty miles through dense forests towards the unassuming town of **Salmon**, which competes with Riggins (see p.626) for the title of whitewater capital of the state. Continuing south, towards the Sawtooth National Recreation area (see p.604), there are few towns of any size and very few roads as well, the vast majority being unpaved loops or dead-ends off of US-93.

The Frank Church-River of No Return Wilderness

The **Frank Church-River of No Return Wilderness** is Idaho as it was when Lewis and Clark first set foot east of the Continental Divide two hundred years ago. It's a vast 2.3-million-square-acre swath of mountain peaks, untrodden forests, and crystalline rivers that contains a wealth of wildlife and very few visitors. Established in 1980 and named in part after Idaho senator Frank Church, the second half of the convoluted name comes from the fact that the Main Fork of the Salmon was known as the "River of No Return" as paddling back up against the current was impossible. You may find it hard to return from a trip as well, seeing as there are some 2600 miles of **trails** and countless **hot springs** in which to soak away your aches at the end of a long day's hike. **Access** to much of the wilderness area is quite good, with several Forest Service roads leading to trailheads on all sides, but as a designated wilderness area no vehicles (including mountain bikes) are allowed inside the boundary. **Backcountry camping** is allowed, though of course "leave no trace" rules are in effect.

Salmon

Sitting beneath bare foothills of the Bitterroots and astride the river that gives the town its name, **SALMON** is a no-nonsense timber and ranching settle-

Local outfitters

Blackadar Boating one mile north of town on US-93 ⓣ208/756-3958. One of the region's best-established outfitters, renting out everything for floating down the river as well as offering a shuttle service to and from put-in and take-out points (see box p.617).

Rendezvous Sports 408 Main St ⓣ208/756-4495. Also serves coffee so you can browse amongst the range of outdoor clothing and equipment and get your caffeine fix at the same time.

Silver Spur Sports 404 Main St ⓣ208/756-2833. The place to go if planning on doing any hunting or fishing; besides gear, they can also supply licenses.

ment that was once a winter campground for fur-trappers like Kit Carson. Refreshingly, it hasn't gone out of its way to spruce itself up for the recent boom in outdoor tourism. That's not to say that the town isn't busy – indeed, it has a fine selection of restaurants, bars, and outdoor stores – but more that art galleries, modern coffeehouses, and the like are not yet part of the scene. Culture comes in the form of **Lemhi County Historical Museum**, 210 Main St (daily 10am–5pm; $1), where there's a comprehensive but rather drably presented array of Native American, fur trapping, and pioneer exhibits that may divert you for half an hour or so.

Thought the majority of visitors are here to **raft**, **fishing** is another major draw. Angling for rainbow, cutthroat, brook and steelhead trout is allowed virtually year-round, with the Salmon River itself being a major draw for steelhead from September to March, when catches of up to twenty pounds are not unknown. There are numerous high elevation lakes in the area where you can hike in and go for various species of trout as well, and ice fishing is possible on **Williams Lake** in winter. The Lemhi River is one of Idaho's blue ribbon trout streams, although permission to fish here must be sought from the owners of ranches bordering the river.

Practicalities

The Community and Rural Transport (CART) service, 102 Van Dreff St (ⓣ208/756-2191), operates a limited **bus service** here from Idaho Falls; the fare is around $22 one-way. The town's **chamber of commerce**, 200 Main St (daily 10am–5pm; ⓣ208/756-2100), has a reasonably good selection of information, including the phenomenally detailed *Salmon River of No Return Adventure Travel Guide*. Other useful sources of information are the **USFS Office** on Hwy-93 just south of town (weekdays 8.30am–5pm; ⓣ208/756-2215), and the **BLM** office next door (same hours; ⓣ208/756-2201).

The main **accommodation** area is a strip of motels on the north side of town along US-93. The *Wagons West Motel*, 503 N US-93 (ⓣ208/756-4281; ❸), has reasonable-sized rooms with comfortable double beds and en-suite bathrooms, plus a laundry. A little closer to town at 201 N US-93 is the *Stagecoach Inn* (ⓣ208/756-4251; ❹), the biggest motel in town with bright, attractive rooms and a laundry. Local B&B accommodation includes the *Country Cottage Inn*, 401 S St Charles St (ⓣ208/756-4319; ❸), which provides big breakfasts and quiet surroundings three blocks away from Main Street. If **camping**, the *Salmon Meadows Campground* at 400 N St Charles St (ⓣ208/756-2640) is only two blocks off Main Street and has tent sites for $12 (RV hookups $15), a laundry, and showers.

With the growing influx of travelers, the selection of **restaurants** and **bars** in Salmon has improved in recent years. One of the best places early in the day

The endangered salmon

The Salmon River, which flows 425 miles from its source in the Sawtooth Mountains to its confluence with the Snake River south of Lewiston, is the longest undammed river in the US within one state. The rivers beyond its convergence with the Snake – the Lower Snake and Columbia – are both dammed though, blocking the progress of the **chinook and sockeye salmon**, and ocean-going **steelhead trout** that all participate in a herculean 900-mile migration between the Upper Salmon and the Pacific Ocean. Due in large part to these dams, these fish are now on the brink of extinction.

It's a sad situation indeed, especially when compared to the wealth of numbers of these migrating fish only a century ago, when the Redfish Lake in the Sawtooth Range was so named because it turned red during the sockeye salmon spawning season. Today there's scarcely a sockeye in the lake, even though $3 billion has been spent since 1981 on (mostly) ineffective salmon recovery measures that have included barging the fish around the dams. Those in the know agree that the only way to save the salmon is to partially remove several dams on the Lower Snake River. Residents of the region who benefit from the electricity produced by the dams have declared their willingness to pay an additional $1–5 per month on their electricity bill if it will help save the fish, but at the time of writing a final decision on the issue had yet to be made. You can find out more about the subject on the Columbia & Snake Rivers Campaign's website, ⓦwww.removedams.org.

is the *Salmon River Coffee Shop,* 606 Main St (ⓣ208/756-3521), which does good-value all-American breakfasts and equally filling lunches. For lunch or dinner, *Food For Thought*, 317B US-93 (ⓣ208/756-3950), is an excellent choice with a wide selection of dishes including tasty vegetarian meals and superb desserts. For a good pizza, head to *Last Chance Pizza*, 605 Lena St (ⓣ208/756-6067), and *The Cabbage Patch*, 206 Van Dreff St, serves good-value fish and vegetarian meals either indoors or out on the patio. Of the town's rowdy but friendly **bars**, the best bet is *Bertram's Salmon Valley Brewery*, corner Main and Andrews, which has a fine selection of eight home-brewed ales (try the Mt. Borah Brown Ale), and good pub grub.

Floating the Salmon River

Whether you choose Salmon or Riggins (see p.626) as the base for a rafting trip down the Salmon River is as much a matter of personal preference as it is geographic location. All trips, from short half-day journeys to an extensive ten-day voyage, are one-way, so you'll have to be **shuttled** to either your put-in or take-out point anyway, and often to both.

Trips down the Main Fork typically begin north of Salmon at North Fork and head west towards Riggins. Trips on the Middle Fork end near Salmon, heading north from put-in points as far as one hundred miles south. We've outlined below the main differences between each river, but along both expect to pass pristine sandy beaches, secluded hot springs, Native American pictographs, and the abandoned mines of early pioneers. Don't forget your binoculars, as your chances of seeing wildlife along the riverbank, particularly bighorn sheep and mountain goats, are excellent. The fishing (on a catch and release basis) is likewise superb. Note that you can **combine** the Middle and Main Fork (the confluence is just upriver of Cache Bar near the small settlement of Shoup) to make an epic eleven–twelve-day trip.

Floating on your own

Permits

River **permits**, of which a limited number are available annually and are distributed on a lottery basis, are required if you're floating the Salmon River on your own. The offices below accept **permit applications** from December 1 to January 31 for the following season, and application forms and information are available from October 1 each year, for which you have to pay a nonrefundable $6 fee. **Permits are issued in February** – if you fail on your first attempt you may pick up a permit from a group that has canceled. Contact the relevant office after Feb 28 to see if any are available, but remember that it's first-come, first-served for cancellations. Permits and information are available from the following addresses:

Middle Fork Salmon Middle Fork Ranger District, N US-93, PO Box 750, Challis, ID 83226-0750 ⓣ208/879-4101 information, ⓣ879-4112 applications, ⓕ879-4198.

Main Fork Salmon North Fork Ranger District, 100 River Rd, PO Box 100, North Fork, ID 83466 ⓣ208/865-2700 information, ⓣ865-2725 applications, ⓕ865-2739.

Shuttle Services

If you book with a river guide, your **shuttles** will be taken care of. Independent rafters and kayakers will, of course, need transport back to their vehicle and/or put-in. Out of Stanley, the well-established River Rat Express (ⓣ208/774-2265 or 1-800/831-8942) will drive your own vehicle from a designated parking lot near your put-in to a designated parking lot at your take-out. Alternatively, they can provide bus transport to shuttle you between put-in and take-out points. Rates vary widely depending on the river and distances – as an example, Middle Fork rafters should expect to pay around $150 for a vehicle shuttle from Boundary Creek to Cache Bar.

The rafting **season** lasts from late May to mid-September, with peak season being June through early August. From July onwards, river levels fall and later in the season there may not be enough water to make the journey, especially in the upper reaches of the rivers. If you're floating the river with a guiding company (see box p.619), they'll take care of river access. However, private parties need to have a **permit**; see box above for more information.

The Main Fork

Of the two rivers, the **Main Fork of the Salmon** is busier, mainly because jet boats are allowed to run the river. Flowing east to west through the northern section of the Frank Church-River of No Return Wilderness, the Main Fork tends to have "bigger" water than the Middle Fork. It drops nearly 2000ft from the put-in at **North Fork**, twenty miles north of Salmon, to the take-out at **Riggins** (a journey of three to six days), which results in a steady stream of Class II and III rapids, with a few more daunting Class IVs sprinkled about. On the way down, trips can call in at the **Buckskin Bill Museum** at **Five Mile Bar**, dedicated to local mountain man Sylvan "Buckskin Bill" Hart and featuring some of his handcrafted guns and clothing, and it's also possible to stay in lodges as well as camp. The Upper Main (in the Stanley/Sunbeam area) is less challenging than the lower river and is ideal for family or novice day-trips.

The easiest way to see the river is by single or multiday **jet boat trips** – these may seem a little incongruous in a relatively pristine aquatic environment like the Main Fork, but they are a heap of fun, despite doing little to bring you closer to nature.

The Salmon River hermit

Idaho has attracted few more solitary individuals than **Earl Parrott**, who built himself a cabin in a remote location above the Middle Fork of the Salmon in the early 1900s and went without a single visit by another person for over twenty years. His only human contact was on yearly trips into **Shoup**, some seventy miles away, where he traded gold dust panned from the river for supplies.

By the 1920s, Forestry Service workers and other backcountry explorers sporadically came across Parrott, but his tiny log cabin remained undiscovered until 1936 when a boating expedition on the Middle Fork stumbled across his gold panning base in **Impassable Canyon**. After pulling over, the boaters followed a trail that climbed 2000ft over two miles up the side of the canyon on a series of log ladders, to find a bigger log cabin and a well-tended garden. A note on the door read "Some of everything in this garden is poison. Nothing in the house is poison. Help yourself."

Parrott emerged with a story that is the stuff of legend: his living costs were 8 cents per day, he made his own shoes with tire tread soles and he carried a Colt .45 pistol with him everywhere so he could shoot himself if he fell and broke his leg. His fondness for human company was limited – as he once said "The more I see of people, the more I like my dog."

You can still see the remains of Earl Parrott's cramped riverside cabin in Impassable Canyon on a float trip down the Middle Fork, but his main cabin was destroyed in a 1989 forest fire.

The Middle Fork

Although relatively few rafters outside the country have heard of it, the **Middle Fork of the Salmon** is regarded in the US as one of the world's top ten whitewater rivers. True or not, floating it is a tremendous adventure, especially in the lower reaches where you careen through spots like **Redside Rapids** (Class III/IV), although it doesn't have the volume of water or quite so many rapid-induced thrills as the Main Fork. What you get instead is a full-on wilderness experience, the more so since jet boats are not allowed on the river. The Middle Fork flows south to north down a narrow-walled canyon through the heart of the Frank Church-River of No Return Wilderness. The main put-in is at **Boundary Creek** (5640ft), a two-hour drive northwest of Stanley (see p.606), and the typical take-out is at **Cache Bar**, five or six days and almost one hundred miles later. As water levels drop in July and August the put-in point moves about twenty miles downstream to the **Indian Creek** airstrip, where access is by single prop planes only, resulting in more expensive tour costs.

South from Salmon on Hwy-28

Heading southeast from Salmon, Hwy-28 cuts between the Beaverhead and Lemhi mountain ranges, and you can get a good feel for the area by turning off onto the **Lewis and Clark National Backcountry Byway** at Tendoy, twenty miles south. Although unpaved, the forty-mile loop road is well graded and in good weather is accessible to vehicles with plenty of clearance. It also makes a fine mountain-bike ride. The byway climbs up to **Lemhi Pass** (7373ft), from where there are magnificent views over both Idaho and Montana. In 1805, Capt Meriwether Lewis first clapped eyes on the west side of the Continental Divide from this point and there's a small free campground just over the pass in Montana if you decide to stay up in the mountains for the night.

Continuing south from Tendoy, Hwy-28 heads over **Gilmore Summit** (7186ft), the road's highest point, then drops down to the flat and dusty Snake River Plain.

River guides and shuttle services

Below are just a few of the many **river guide companies** that can take you down one of the Salmon rivers. The charge for a six-day, fully-inclusive trip on either river will usually be around $1100–1500, while daily rates run from $180–225. The most commonly used raft holds up to eight people, plus your guide. Some companies also use single person "duckies" that are essentially inflatable kayaks with no spray deck, so if you capsize you simply fall out – which is usually fun rather than a threat to life and limb.

Canyon Cats 215 N Main St, Riggins ⓣ208/628-3772 or 1-888/628-3772. Canyon Cats emphasize the "adrenalin" aspect of their trips, which are undertaken in twin-pontoon, state-of-the-art catarafts.

Exodus 606 N Main St, Riggins ⓣ208/628-3484 or 1-800/992-3484, ⓦwww.riverescape.com. A high-end operation with top-quality craft, plus jetboats and fall steelhead fishing trips.

Holiday Expeditions 126 W Main St, Grangeville ⓣ208/983-1518 or 1-800/628-2565. Good for shorter one- and two-day floats down the lower reaches of the Salmon in the Riggins area.

Kookaburra 706 15th St, Salmon ⓣ208/756-4386 or 1-888/654-4386. Good-value one–three-day trips using oar boats, paddle boats, and rubber duckies.

River Odysseys West PO Box 579, Coeur d'Alene 83816 ⓣ208/765-0841 or 1-800/451-6034, ⓦwww.rowinc.com. A high-end, very professional operation with guides who know the rivers intimately.

Wapiti River Guides Main St, Riggins ⓣ1-800/488-9872, ⓦwww.wapitiriverguides.com. Wapiti have traditional wooden dories as used by the first explorers on local rivers for their trips, which ups the price but adds to the character.

Challis and around

South from Salmon, the Salmon River Scenic Byway (US-93) passes through a landscape of sagebrush and brown grasses, smooth-shouldered mountains dotted with pines and desiccated cliffs, and valley sides still harboring the remnants of pioneer ranches that the land could not support. Look out for the curious **ice caves**, signposted one mile north of Elk Bend – these are habitable dugouts built into the hillside by a colorful local character named "Dugout Dick." Ice trapped between gaps in the rock remains frozen year-round, creating a natural storage for food. You can stay there yourself for the princely sum of $2–5 per night – "rooms" have a wood stove and bed but no bedding.

As you approach **CHALLIS**, sixty miles southwest of Salmon, you enter the Round Valley, a fertile, green landscape between the Lost River and Salmon River mountains. Challis' Main Street retains many of its original late nineteenth-century buildings – a good example is the 1894 First Congregational Church, now operating as a friendly coffee shop. The **Land of the Yankee Fork Interpretive Center** (June–Aug daily 8am–6pm; rest of the year Mon–Fri 9am–5pm; free), just off US-93 on the east side of town, has an interesting exhibition on the area's mining history and on the mining sites along the Custer Motorway (see overleaf). If looking to **stay the night**, the best budget option with clean, comfortable rooms is *Northgate Inn*, which has a pleasant location by the Salmon River (ⓣ208/879-2490; ❷). A little more upmarket are rooms at the *Village Inn* on US-93 (ⓣ208/879-2239; ❸), some of which have kitchenettes. **Campers** should make for the *Challis Hot Springs* (ⓣ208/879-4442) campground, five miles north of US-93 at the end of Hot Springs Road, where tent sites go for $11–15 and there's access to nearby hot springs.

Drivers with time to spare and decent ground clearance on their vehicle should consider a detour from US-93 onto the **Custer Motorway Adventure Road**, an unpaved miner's toll road that loops southwest from Challis to Sunbeam through the foothills of the 9000ft Salmon River Mountains. The road passes the ghost towns of **Bonanza** and **Custer** – the latter has a self-guided walking tour and a small museum on the town's heyday in the 1880s (mid-June to Aug daily 10am–5.30pm; admission by donation). To access the road from Challis, take Garden Creek Road off Main Street then turn north onto Forest Road 070. To access the road from Sunbeam, take Forest Road 013 north.

Borah Peak

Not identified as Idaho's highest mountain until 1926, **Borah Peak** (12,662ft) is a bold summit that will provide a strenuous ascent for experienced mountaineers. It's reached by heading southeast from Challis over Willow Creek Summit (7161ft) down the Big Lost River Valley on US-93. Most climbers attempt the southwest ridge, which isn't particularly technical but is long and arduous (5400ft of ascent in under five miles), and has some stretches with serious exposure. Reckon on 8–12 hours for the round-trip, and make sure you have a full complement of mountain gear with you, including an ice axe. You can get more information in **Mackay** at the Lost River Ranger District, 716 W Custer (☎208/588-2224). The little town has a spectacular location, surrounded by nine of the eleven highest peaks in Idaho.

McCall and around

Sitting on the south shores of the sparkling **Payette Lake** and tucked beneath the blue-green peaks of **Brundage Mountain Resort**, **McCALL**, just over a hundred miles north of Boise, is very much devoted to the outdoor life. It's surrounded on three sides by the Payette National Forest, and there are endless opportunities for backpackers, hikers, mountain bikers, and horseback riders to enjoy themselves. In summer, the lake throbs with life as waterskiers, sailboaters, canoeists, and swimmers make the most of the warm waters. **Ponderosa State Park**, a peninsula of huge ponderosa pines, noses up into the lake from its southeast corner. To the south, the **Payette River** flows out of the lake and has great rafting and kayaking. In winter skiers and boarders will find excellent powder and very few lift lines at Brundage Mountain, and there are several cross-country ski trails in the vicinity.

Despite the often heavy traffic running through its center, the small **downtown** area is a vibrant and friendly little hub of activity. Although busiest in summer, it also comes alive in a big way during the week-long **Winter Carnival** in January, when thousands come to ice skate, take sleigh rides, and to view spectacular ice sculptures, firework displays, and sled-dog races. Throughout the rest of the year, the main cultural attraction is the **Central Idaho Cultural Center**, 1001 State St (daily 9am–5pm; free; ☎208/634-7631), based in a complex of eight traditional log buildings. The focal point here is a handsome log-built Fire Warden's House, built in 1936 by the Civilian Conservation Corps and featuring a grand chert fireplace. Also worth a quick look is the **McCall Smokejumper Station** at the airport a mile or so south of downtown (☎208/634-0387), where hour-long tours in summer give you an idea of the drama faced in fighting the wildfires that are so prevalent in the region.

Arrival, information, and accommodation

Daily Northwestern Trailways (☎208/634-2340) **buses** from Boise and Spokane pull in at Bill's Grocery, 147 N 3rd St. McCall's **chamber of commerce**, 1001 State St (daily 9am–5pm; ☎208/634-7631, Ⓦwww.mccall-idchamber.org), has the handy *McCall Activity Guide*, though specific outdoor information is best gotten at the **USFS McCall Ranger Office**, 104 W Lake St (☎208/634-0400, Ⓦwww.mccall.net/pnf).

Easy to reach from Boise, McCall's population swells considerably in summer and on winter weekends, and although the town has a good range of **accommodation**, it's worth making reservations to ensure you get the room you want.

Hotels and motels

Best Western McCall 415 N 3rd St ☎208/634-6300. Comfortable chain-motel accommodation with HBO, fridge, and microwave in each room and a shared hot tub and indoor pool. ❹

Brundage Bungalows 308 W Lake St ☎208/634-8573. Neat self-contained cabins in a shady location on the west side of town. ❹

Manchester at Payette Lake 501 W Lake St ☎208/634-2244, Ⓦwww.manchesterresort.com. Totally refurbished along a theme of "rustic elegance" in 2001, the lakeside *Manchester* (formerly *Shore Lodge*) is one of Idaho's most upmarket hotels, with nearly eighty luxurious en-suite guestrooms, two restaurants, and a fine eighteen-hole golf course beside the lake. Rates begin at $350 a night. ❾

Hotel McCall 1101 N 3rd St ⓣ208/634-8105, ⓕ634-8755, ⓔhotel@micron.net. In the heart of downtown and close to the lake, this attractive 1904 hotel features tastefully decorated queen- or twin-bed rooms (although the walls are a little thin), and all but the cheaper rooms have private baths. There's a good complimentary breakfast buffet, and the cozy library is a great place to enjoy free coffee or wine after a day out. ❹

Scandia Inn Motel 401 N 3rd St ⓣ208/634-7394, ⓦwww.cyberhighway.net/~scandia. A friendly inn with comfortable double rooms, all with TV and air conditioning, located within walking distance of downtown and the lake. ❹

Super 8 Motel 303 S 3rd St ⓣ208/634-4637 or 1-800/800-8000. A better-than-average *Super 8* with large, airy rooms (family rooms feature kitchenettes) and a good range of facilities including a hot tub and guest laundry. The motel also offers Brundage Mountain ski packages. ❹

The Woodsman 402 N 3rd St ⓣ208/634-7671. Basic but clean and comfortable accommodation, popular in winter with budget-minded skiers and boarders. ❸

B&Bs

Bear Creek Lodge PO Box 8, New Meadows, ID 83654 ⓣ208/634-3551 or 1-888/634-2327, ⓕ208/634-7699. Four miles north of town on Hwy-55, this beautiful timber lodge is set in 65 acres of meadows close to the Brundage Mountain turnoff. The eight rooms include queen-size beds and fireplaces, and there are two cabins with huge four-poster beds and hot tubs. The restaurant is excellent, and you can arrange many outdoor activities through the lodge. ❼

Northwest Passage Bed and Breakfast 210 Rio Vista ⓣ208/634-5349 or 1-800/597-6658. A five-room B&B named after the 1940 film *North West Passage*, the cast and crew of which – including Spencer Tracy – stayed at the house during filming. The rooms are well-kept and the home is in a quiet area a few blocks south of Payette Lake. ❹

Campgrounds

McCall Campground 190 Krahn Lane ⓣ208/634-5165. A mile south of town in a rather drab location, but sites are only $12 per night for tents ($16 for hookups). Open all year.

Ponderosa State Park ⓣ208/634-2164. Located beside the lake amongst shady pines, there are three "loops" of tent sites, 137 in all, each of which has a toilet and shower block. $15 per night.

Summer activities

In summer, most visitors turn their backs on McCall and head for **Payette Lake** – the south shore laps up against the town, and the north banks are surrounded by thick forests and high mountains. The frenzy of activity at the city end of the lake can be a little overwhelming, but if you head two miles northeast to **Ponderosa State Park** (ⓣ208/634-2164; $3 per vehicle), things quiet down somewhat. The park occupies a 1000-acre peninsula that juts out into Payette Lake two miles northeast of the city center, with a smaller annex at **North Beach** on the north shore of the lake where there's a lovely sandy beach and a primitive campground. The old-growth forest in the park contains Ponderosa, lodgepole pines and Douglas fir, some of which grow up to 150 feet in height.

If you want to get out onto Payette Lake you'll have no problem **renting** gear in McCall. Cheap Thrills Rentals, 303 N 3rd St (ⓣ1-800/831-1025), have canoes for $50 per day and kayaks for $30 a day. Sports Marina, 1300 E Lake St (ⓣ208/634-8361), rent out jet skis, water-ski boats and fishing boats. Rates vary from around $35 per hour for a fishing boat to $60 an hour for a ski boat with equipment.

Hiking and biking

For a good local half-day hike, head to the **Black Lee Trail** located eleven miles east of McCall along Lick Creek Road from the corner of East Lake Street. Although it's under four miles long, it gains nearly 1900ft from the starting point at 5680ft, with the first two miles being the steepest. In return for the effort, you get up to a ridge above Box Lake from which there are great views. Five miles further down Lick Creek Road is the trailhead for the easy two-mile round-trip to **Duck Lake**, which has little elevation gain, but passes through pleasant meadows and woodland. From Duck Lake, you'll find more trails heading off into the hills, including the **Hum Lake Trail**, which is reached via a steep 1.5-mile climb to almost 7800ft over a saddle and back down 1000ft to Hum Lake. The views of Duck Lake and Hum Lake from the saddle make the climb well worthwhile.

One of the easiest and most popular **bike rides** in the area is the easy nineteen-mile cycle trail around Payette Lake – take your swimming gear and you can also enjoy a swim halfway around at North Beach. For something a bit more hair-raising, there are over fifteen miles of superb single-track at **Brundage Mountain** (see below) that also give access to hundreds of acres of Payette National Forest. The Blue Bird Express (July–Aug Fri 1pm-6pm, Sat–Sun 11am–6pm; $15 full day) accesses trails varying from gentle descents such as the **Elk Trail** to white knuckle, technical downhills like **Zorro** and **Growler**. Suspension bikes and helmets can be rented on the mountain for $23–30 per day. There's also seven miles of trails in Ponderosa State Park (see opposite), the most challenging of which is the technical **Huckleberry Trail**. For more **information** on off-road biking in the area, check out *Mountain Biking in McCall* by Roger Phillips (Boise Front Adventures), available in local book and bike shops, or call in at Gravity Sports, 503 Pine St (Ⓣ208/634-8530), who also rent bikes from $25 a day.

Winter activities

The obvious place to head for in winter is **Brundage Mountain Resort** (Ⓣ208/634-7462 or 1-800/888-7544, snow report Ⓣ208/634-SNOW, Ⓦwww.brundage.com), eight miles northwest of McCall, which has the enviable combination of receiving some of the lightest powder in Idaho and virtually no lift lines. The 1300 acres of terrain here are served by three **chairlifts** and a couple of tows. The top elevation of 7640ft allows for a vertical drop of 1800ft, and from the summit there are great views of the remote Seven Devils Range, the Wallowa Mountains in eastern Oregon, Payette Lake, and the Frank Church-River of No Return Wilderness.

Good beginner runs include Temptation for its fine views and variety of slope angles, and Main Street, an easy, open blue above the day-lodge. Intermediate skiers will enjoy 45th Parallel and Engen which are wide and great for practicing your carves. For advanced skiers there's the bumps of ungroomed Stair Steps or the tree runs of Black Forest, while experts should head towards the steep tree skiing of Hidden Valley.

Facilities at Brundage include a rental and ski shop, a day-lodge, and a ski school. **Lift tickets** are around $32 full day ($26 half), with decent discounts for seniors and those eighteen and younger. There's also a backcountry **snow cat** operation here – the highest peak used is nearby Granite Mountain (8478ft), with runs varying in vertical drop from 800–2800ft. Half-day trips start at around $125 per person, full day $200, and overnight trips staying in a yurt with two full days skiing and all meals are around $495. All prices include rental of powder skis. For more information, call Ⓣ208/634-7462 ext 120.

Closer to town, **cross-country skiers** and **snowshoers** will find fourteen miles of groomed trails, 1.2 miles of which are floodlit, in Ponderosa State Park.

The Payette River

The Payette River flows from the southern end of Payette Lake to eventually join the mighty Snake River in Idaho's southwest corner. The **North Fork of the Payette**, which flows beside Hwy-55 south of Cascade from Smith's Ferry to Banks, has some of the wildest and most challenging whitewater in the USA. This is expert-only territory, though you can still enjoy the experience as a spectator from the turnouts above the river. Below Banks, the North Fork and **South Fork** of the Payette combine to form the **Main Payette**. All three branches of the Payette River offer varying standards of rafting and kayaking and trips from one to three days in length. Local outfitters who can get you onto the river include Bear Valley River Company, Banks (ⓣ1-800/235-2327), and Cascade Raft Company, Horseshoe Bend (ⓣ208/793-2221 or 1-800/292-7238).

Eating and drinking

McCall's compact, lakeside downtown area makes it ideal for wandering between **bars** and **restaurants** on a summer evening, when there's a high-octane buzz on the streets as people return from their outdoor adventures. It can get busy at weekends and holidays, when it may be worth reserving a table.

Bev's Cottage Café and Bakery 1133 E Lake St ⓣ208/634-3737. A popular local haunt close to the lake, with good breakfasts and tasty, filling sandwiches for $5–7.

Blue Moon Outfitters Yurt Ponderosa State Park ⓣ 208/634-3111. A novel alternative in winter, it's great fun to ski or snowshoe out to the lakeside yurt where you can enjoy a menu that features especially good vegetarian dishes, all served in the intimate, cozy surroundings of a traditional yurt. However, at $45 a head it's not cheap, and you have to take your own alcohol.

Bryan's Burger Den 600 N 3rd St ⓣ208/634-7964. Probably the best burgers in town, and the veggie burgers are tasty as well. A full meal should set you back no more than $10.

Lardo's Grill and Saloon 600 Lake St ⓣ208/634-8191. Thanks to a warm, vibrant atmosphere, this bar is one of the most popular in town. The menu includes tasty burgers and pasta ($10–15), and there's a good range of microbrews on tap.

McCall Brewing Company 807 N 3rd St ⓣ208/634-2333. Best enjoyed on the busy large deck overlooking the town, the beers here are finely crafted and there's simple but tasty bar food available as well.

Moxie Java 312 E Lake St ⓣ208/634-3607. Popular with the young boarding/skiing crowd, the coffeehouse serves up all manner of caffeine-rich beverages and is a good place to read and hang out.

Romano's at The Yacht Club 205 E Lake St ⓣ208/634-5649. A good spot for pasta, although you can get traditional American food too in a pleasant lakeside dining room. The *Yacht Club* is also the most reliable spot in town for decent live bands.

Hell's Canyon and around

Although not actually within the Rocky Mountains, a detour and visit to **HELL'S CANYON** is highly recommended. With an average depth of 5500ft this is the deepest river gorge in the USA, though its low-relief formation, hemmed in by a series of gradually ascending false peaks, means that it lacks the impact of the steep-walled Grand Canyon. Nevertheless, it is impressive, with Oregon's Wallowa and Eagle Cap ranges rising behind it and the river glimmering far down below.

The best access point for floating the Snake River that flows through the canyon is **Riggins**, the base for several companies running boating and rafting trips here as well as on the Salmon River. There are unpaved access roads locally that lead to the canyon rim, and Forest Road 493 at **White Bird** leads to the riverbank. You also get superb views of the canyon and the surrounding mountains on the **Kleinschmidt Grade**, reached from **Council**, over the southern flanks of the Seven Devils to Cuprum, from where it plummets down the canyon walls in a series of terrifying white-knuckle switchbacks.

Hell's Canyon National Recreation Area

The **Hell's Canyon National Recreation Area** encompasses over 650,000 acres, and the huge range of elevations within the canyon allows for a very diverse array of flora, varying from alpine flowers to cacti. Black bear, cougar, bobcat, mule deer, elk, mountain goat, and bighorn sheep are all native species, and birdlife is also rich, with numerous species of songbird and raptors such as owls, falcons, and eagles. The **fishing** is excellent too – catches includes the prehistoric-looking white sturgeon, which can be over 10 feet in length.

The canyon is best explored by **raft** or **jet boat**, with the numerous Class II-IV rapids providing a wild, wet adventure. There are also mellower stretches of water where you can kick back and admire the views of the canyon walls, forested upper slopes, and distant mountain peaks, or swim from small sandy beaches. Exploring on foot or horseback is another option as the canyon holds some memorable trails. A classic for backpackers is the multi-day 27-mile **Seven Devils Loop Trail**, accessed from Riggins via Windy Saddle – on a clear day you can see into Oregon and Washington to the west and as far east as the Bitterroot Mountains. You can camp anywhere within the NRA, although the area's heavy snows may keep the roads closed until early July.

Riding the Snake River

There are numerous outfitters running **float trips** through Hell's Canyon. Most operate out of Riggins and start from Hell's Canyon Dam and head north, although some are based in Lewiston (see p.627) and head south up the canyon from the city's Hell's Gate State Park. Prices start at around $30 per person for a two-hour jet boat trip, $95 per person for six hours and $250 per person overnight. **Permits** are required by private parties wishing to float through the canyon; for information contact Hell's Canyon NRA, 2535 Riverside Drive, Clarkston, WA (Ⓣ509/758-0616).

Hell's Canyon Adventures 4200 Hell's Canyon Dam Rd, Oxbow, OR Ⓣ541/785-3352, Ⓕ785-3353, Ⓦwww.hellscanyonadventures.com. One of the best established rafting companies on the Snake, known for the quality of their guides.

Idaho Afloat PO Box 542, Grangeville, ID 83530 Ⓣ208/983-2414 or 1-800/700-2414, Ⓦwww.idafloat.com. Multiday float trips with camping out. This is a good company if you're traveling with kids, for whom they cater especially.

Northwest Voyageurs PO Box 323, Lucile, ID 83542 Ⓣ1-800/727-9977, Ⓕ208/628-3780). A well-established outfitter, based eleven miles north of Riggins, which organizes three- and six-day trips.

River Adventures Riggins Ⓣ208/628-3952 or 1-800/524-9710, Ⓦwww.river-adventures.net. One of the most popular of the jet boat companies and convenient if you want to book while in Riggins.

Snake River Adventures 227 Snake River Ave, Lewiston Ⓣ1-800/262-8874, Ⓦwww.snakeriveradventures.com. Offer an all-day trip to Granite Creek or a jet/float combo that involves floating down the river, overnight lodge accommodation, and jet boating back up the next day. This costs around $400 per person.

There are various **canyon lookouts** at the end of unpaved roads. The classic route (open mid-July to mid-Oct) crosses Windy Saddle and terminates at the rim by the free *Seven Devils Campground*. To get there, turn west on Seven Devils Road south of Riggins and follow the road for seventeen miles over Windy Saddle and to the rim of the canyon. Another two miles along the road leads to the spectacular **Heaven's Gate Lookout** (8430ft). A vehicle with good ground clearance is recommended.

Riggins

The self-proclaimed "narrowest little town in the country," **RIGGINS** is perched above the banks of the Little Salmon River between steep, dry, brown canyon walls. Its streets are lined with outfitters offering rafting and jet boat trips on the Salmon's various forks or through the Hell's Canyon stretch of the Snake River, and the town vies with Salmon (see p.614) for the title of whitewater capital of Idaho. The Salmon River passes just to the north of town where it joins the Little Salmon River, which flows through town from the south. There's a road bridge here over the **Time Zone Rapids** where you pass from Mountain Standard Time to Pacific Time. In summer, Riggins can become unbearably hot, but you can soon solve that problem with a river trip – in fact there's little else to do here.

Practicalities

Northwestern Trailways (Ⓣ208/746-8108) runs a daily **bus** service out of the City Hall on US-95 north to Spokane via Grangeville, Lewiston, and Moscow and south to McCall and Boise. The chamber of commerce (Ⓣ208/628-3441, Ⓦwww.rigginsidaho.com) has an unmanned **information booth** in the center of town on the highway's west side that dispenses information leaflets. For information on rafting and jet boating down Hell's Canyon contact **Hell's Canyon NRA**, PO Box 832, Riggins, ID 83549 (8am–5pm weekdays; Ⓣ208/628-3916), which is located at the south end of town off US-95.

There's a good range of **accommodation** strung along either side of Main Street, the rates of which are usually cheaper outside summer. In the middle of town is the popular and friendly *Riggins Motel* (Ⓣ208/628-3001 or 1-800/669-6739, Ⓦwww.rigginsmotel.com; ④), which has plain but comfortable rooms and a hot tub. To the south is the recently remodeled *Salmon River Motel*, 1203 Main St (Ⓣ208/628-3025 or 1-888/628-3025, Ⓕ208/628-4079; ④), again fairly basic but with clean and airy rooms. In the same part of town is the upmarket *Salmon Rapids Lodge*, 1010 Main St (Ⓣ208/628-2743 or 1-877/957-2743, Ⓦwww.salmonrapids.com; ⑤), which features a splendid river-rock and timber interior and large lodge-style rooms, many overlooking the river. If **camping**, try *River Village RV Park*, 1434 N US-95 (Ⓣ208/628-3441), at the north end of town, which has shady tent sites beside the Salmon River for around $10 (full hookups $15). The most popular place to **eat** is the *Cattleman's Restaurant*, 601 Main St (Ⓣ208/628-3195), where plain but good-value steaks, burgers, and pasta are served up in a congenial environment. The *Salmon River Inn*, 129 Main St (Ⓣ208/628-3813), has a great range of subs and good homemade pizzas and at night the *Seven Devils Saloon*, 312 Main St (Ⓣ208/628-3351), is invariably busy, with good pub grub and the occasional live band.

Lewiston and around

There are few compelling reasons to visit industrial **LEWISTON** other than jet boating down the Snake River (see box p.625). A blue-collar town 110 miles north of Riggins, the town sits at the confluence of the Snake and Clearwater rivers at an elevation of 736ft, making it Idaho's lowest city: in summer it can be stiflingly hot. On the Snake's west bank, in Washington State, is **Clarkston** – the towns are named after Lewis and Clark who passed through the area in 1805/06. The best way to approach the city is to drive down the **Old Spiral Highway** from the top of Lewiston Hill – what seems like an intricate network of roads crisscrossing a series of mounds is, in fact, a single tarmac ribbon twisting through 64 switchbacks as it descends over 2000ft down the steep hillside.

Though there's little to hold you here in Lewiston, a reasonably pleasant way to kill time is to walk or bike the **Clearwater and Snake River National Recreation Trail**, a 25-mile trail running along both sides of the Snake and Clearwater rivers. En route you can also stop off at good interpretive signboards at **Clearwater Landing** (just north of downtown) and the **Lewis and Clark Interpretive Center** (at the rivers' confluence). In front of the center is the unusual Tsceminicum Sculpture (Nez Percé for "meeting of the waters") of a symbolic Earth Mother from whose mane 79 animals from Indian legend extend along both sides of a wall. If you want to bike the parkway, rentals are available from Pedals-n-Spokes, 829 D St (Ⓣ208/743-6567), for $25 per day.

Practicalities

US-95 runs into Lewiston from the north, and connects with Clarkston via the Memorial Bridge across the Clearwater at the northeast corner of town. **Buses** arrive and leave from the *Sportsman Inn Motel*, 3001 North & South Hwy, to the northeast of town across the Clearwater River. Northwestern Trailways (Ⓣ208/746-8108) operate services to Boise via McCall (daily; $59 round-trip) and north to Spokane, WA, via Moscow (daily; $35 round-trip). The **visitor center** is on the north side of the Clearwater at 313 N 2nd St (May–Sept Mon–Fri 9am–5pm; Ⓣ208/746-5172).

Good-value **accommodation** is readily available at the *Sacajawea Motor Inn*, 1824 Main St (Ⓣ1-800/333-1393; ❸), which also has a spa and pool, laundry, and restaurant, though it's a bit far out of town. If you want to be closer, try the *Comfort Inn*, 2128 8th St (Ⓣ208/798-8090; ❹), which has large, well-appointed rooms. One of the best B&Bs in town is the *Carriage House Inn*, 611 5th St (Ⓣ1-800/501-4506; ❺). The elegant rooms include four-poster and antique wrought-iron beds, and cookies and hot drinks are available all day. If you're **camping**, head for Hell's Gate State Park, 3629A Snake River Ave. (Ⓣ208/799-5015; $12 tents, $16 RVs). Although noisy, the sites are well shaded and it has lots of facilities including a beach and nearby hiking and biking. Lewiston is not overburdened with good **eateries**, but *Bojack's Broiler Pit*, 311 Main St (Ⓣ208/746-9532) does good-value steak and seafood dishes, with the house specialty being prime rib. The *Red Lion Hotel* at 621 21st St holds the *M.J. Barleyhoppers Brewery and Sports Pub* (Ⓣ208/746-5300), where good pub grub and a huge range of local and imported microbrews can be had.

Moscow

Located almost on the border with Washington State, and thirty miles north of Lewiston, **MOSCOW** is set amidst the rolling hills of the fertile Palouse Valley

– a patchwork of green lentils, bright yellow rape, soft white wheat, and thick, black topsoil. The roadside red barns and farmhouses of the surrounding countryside complete a lovely rural picture. Moscow's rather incongruous name is pretty ordinary compared to the first settlers' choice of Hog Heaven. A proposal to rename it Paradise was seen as a trifle over-the-top and the present title came from one early resident's hometown in Pennsylvania. Moscow was "given" the **University of Idaho** in 1889 in return for dropping support for a movement for northern Idaho to "secede" from the south. Its student population now helps maintain the array of bookstores, galleries, bars, and cafés that line Moscow's Main Street, a shady and partly-pedestrianized shopping thoroughfare. On the west side of Main Street is the attractive university campus, home to the **Shattuck Arboretum and Botanical Garden** (open year-round; free; ⓣ208/885-6424), where you can enjoy a relaxing stroll amongst an eclectic collection of trees and plants from around the world. If you're in town in late February, check out the renowned **Lionel Hampton Jazz Festival** (ⓣ1-800/345-7402). Named for the late vibrophonist and held at the UI Campus, it draws some of the biggest names in the jazz world.

Three miles west of Moscow on the state border is the **Appaloosa Museum & Heritage Center**, 5070 Hwy-8 (year-round Mon–Fri 8am–5pm; June–Aug also Sat 9am–3pm; free; ⓣ208/882-5578). The spotted Appaloosa is Idaho's "state horse," bred by the Nez Percé and given its distinctive name by early settlers who referred to it as "a palousey" after the Palouse region. The museum includes an "Appaloosa Hall of Fame" cowboy and Nez Percé artifacts, and Appaloosa horses in the center's corral.

Practicalities

Northwestern Trailways (ⓣ208/882-5521) runs a daily **bus** service south to Lewiston (8.40am; $7/12 one-way/round-trip) and Boise (11.20am; $36/66), and also north to Spokane (6.50am, 4pm; $17/31); all three depart from the *Royal Motor Inn*, 120 W 6th St at Jackson. The **chamber of commerce**, 411 Main St (8am–5pm weekdays; ⓣ1-800/380-1801, ⓦwww.moscowchamber.com), is good for current news on local theater, cinema, and festivals, and the **USFS Clearwater National Forest Service Office**, 1221 S Main St (9am–5pm weekdays; ⓣ208/882-3557), has information on outdoor recreation.

A selection of chain **motels** can be found a few blocks west of town around Pullman Road (Hwy-8), convenient for the UI campus, including the *Best Western University Inn*, 1516 W Pullman Rd (ⓣ208/882-0550; ❺). Along Main Street downtown is where you'll find older, independent motels like the *Mark IV Motor Inn*, 414 N Main St (ⓣ1-800/833-4240; ❷), which has clean, basic rooms, pool, and hot tub. Moscow isn't short on vibrant places to **eat and drink**. The *Upper Crust Bakery*, 310 W 3rd St (ⓣ208/883-1024), is a good spot for breakfast, and *Mickey's Gyros*, 527 Main St, serves filling sandwiches in a mellow environment and is popular with the university crowd. *The Treaty Grounds Brew Pub*, 2124 W Pullman Rd (ⓣ208/882-3807) has good-value burgers and steaks for lunch and dinner and a comprehensive selection of home-brewed ales. Alternatively, *West 4th Street Bar and Grill,* 313 S Main St (ⓣ208/882-0743), is a bright, art-filled restaurant serving a wide range of entrees including pasta, scampi, ribs, and chicken for around $15.

The Nez Percé Reservation

About ten miles east of Lewiston is the 137-square-mile Nez Percé **Reservation**, set within the rolling Camas Prairie and encompassing the towns of Spalding, Orofino, Kooskia, and Kamiah. The reservation, home to about 1500 tribe members (see box), contains sections of the abstract **Nez Percé National Historic Park**, established in 1965 with the aim of increasing appreciation of Nez Percé history and culture. The park consists of 38 historic sites spread across Washington, Oregon, Idaho, and Montana, each telling

The Nez Percé

By the time the first white settlers moved into the northwestern states in the early years of the nineteenth century, the **Nez Percé** had been living in what is now north central Idaho and adjacent Washington and Oregon for thousands of years. Known as the *Ni Mii Pu* in their own language, they were based locally in the valleys of the **Clearwater** and **Snake** Rivers and their tributaries, fishing, hunting, and harvesting camas bulbs from the high plateaus.

Their first contact with whites was when **Lewis and Clark** passed through the area in 1805. Relations with the expedition members and whites who followed in their footsteps were friendly, and remained this way for the next half-century. An 1855 treaty moved the peaceable tribe to the **Nez Percé Reservation**, a 5000-square-mile-area that reserved most but by no means all of their traditional lands for their exclusive use. However, after gold was discovered on the reservation at what is now the town of Pierce, a new treaty was drawn up in 1863 which excluded the Nez Percé from the gold fields and left settlers free to work them. It also reduced the reservation to a tenth of its previous size.

The majority of the Nez Percé, under the leadership of **Chief Joseph**, refused to recognize the agreement. In 1877, after much vacillation, the government decided to enact its terms and gave the tribe only thirty days to leave. The Nez Percé asked for more time in order to round up their livestock and avoid crossing the Snake River at a dangerous time; the general in charge refused.

This refusal led to skirmishes that caused the deaths of a handful of settlers – the first whites ever to be attacked by Nez Percé – and a large army was gathered to round them up. Chief Joseph then embarked upon the famous **Retreat of the Nez Percé**. Around 250 warriors (protecting twice as many women, children, and old people) outmaneuvered army columns many times their size, launching frequent guerrilla attacks in a series of hair-breadth escapes. After four months and 1700 miles, the Nez Percé were cornered just thirty miles from the relative safety of the Canadian border. Chief Joseph then (reportedly) made his much-quoted speech of surrender:

"It is cold, and we have no blankets. The little children are freezing to death. Hear me, my chiefs! I am tired. My heart is sick and sad. From where the sun now stands I will fight no more for ever".

The campaign, which had been closely followed out East, created considerable sympathy for the plight of the Nez Percé. Despite this, and although promised that they would be returned to reservations in the northwest, the Nez Percé were soon taken to Fort Leavenworth, Kansas, then moved to Oklahoma. In 1885, the 268 members of the tribe who were still alive were allowed to return to the northwest.

But their problems were not yet over. With the **Dawes Act of 1887**, individual Indians were given title to between 40 and 160 acres of land on their own reservations in the belief that ownership of the land would more swiftly assimilate them into white American culture – which may sound like a positive move were it not for the fact that any land left over after plots had been allotted to the Indians was thrown open for purchase by white settlers. The result of this was that the Nez Percé ended up with a reservation of less than 200,000 acres from the original 5,000 square miles of the 1855 treaty – and, effectively, the end of their traditional lifestyle. In 1948 the tribe became a self-governing body under an approved constitution and bylaws that were revised in 1961.

Wolf tales

Around thirty miles south of Lewiston and just off US-95 at **Winchester** is the engaging **Wolf Education and Research Center** (late May to early Oct daily 9am–5pm; $3, tours $10; ⓣ208/924-9690, ⓦwww.wolfcenter.org). The site is home to the ten-member Sawtooth Pack, wolves born in semi-captivity in the Sawtooth Mountains and the subject of an award-winning documentary (*Wolf: Return of a Legend*) filmed by one of the center's founders. In 1996, the wolves were moved from the Sawtooths to the their present enclosure (the largest of its kind in North America), where they're free to roam over a twenty-acre site and human contact is kept to a minimum. There are viewing platforms off the outer edges of the enclosure; while there's no guarantee you will see the pack at play, it's a fascinating experience if you do. The best chance of seeing the wolves is to join a 1.5-hour interpretive walk around the outside of the enclosure (by reservation Thurs–Mon 7.30am and 7pm).

a part of the tribe's 11,000-year history. Twenty-four of the sites are within Idaho, and include battlefields at White Bird and Camas Meadows; Chief Looking Glass' 1877 campground; and sites of traditional Nez Percé legends. You can get a feel for what it's all about on a three-hour loop drive on the **Clearwater Canyons Scenic Byway** along the northern and eastern edge of the reservation where there are a number of sites with interpretive shelters and/or boards. Information is available from the **Spalding Visitor Center** (daily: June–Aug 8am–5.30pm; rest of year 8am–4.30pm) in the northwest corner of the reservation, where there's also a museum with an excellent display of Nez Percé clothing, beadwork, and other beautifully crafted artifacts.

Grangeville and the Camas Prairie

US-95 rolls south from Lewiston through the wheat and barley fields of the heavily farmed Camas Prairie to the small town of **Cottonwood**. Here, visible from the highway, stands the twin-towered **St Gertrude's Monastery and Museum** (Mon–Sat 9.30am–4.30pm, Sun 1.30–4.30pm; admission by donation; ⓣ208/962-3224). The Romanesque-style priory was built between 1920 and 1925, partly by Benedictine nuns (who still worship and live there); its associated museum has an esoteric range of exhibits, including the handmade tools of Salmon River mountain man Sylvan "Buckskin Bill" Hart.

Another fourteen miles south of Cottonwood lies **GRANGEVILLE**, a reasonably pleasant farming and logging town set amidst the prairie's farms and cattle ranches. You can get general travel information from the friendly **visitor center** (ⓣ208/983-0460) on US-95 just north of town, and hiking and camping information from the Nez Percé National Forest Clearwater Ranger Station, 319 E Main St (ⓣ208/983-1950). Although there's not a great deal to see in town, consider calling in at the friendly Ray Holes Saddle Company, 213 W Main St, to look over their large collection of authentic Western clothing and exquisite hand-tooled saddles on display and being made out back.

Fifteen miles south of here on US-95 is the small town of **White Bird**, site of a famous battle in 1877 between the Nez Percé and the US Cavalry – a turnout here describes the battle in detail. The Salmon River Ranger District in White Bird (ⓣ208/839-2211) is a useful source of **information** if you're planning on heading into the Gospel Hump Wilderness.

Skiing on the Camas Prairie

There are two ski areas standing proud of the Camas Prairie where you can ski all day for under $15. **Cottonwood Butte Ski Area** (Wed 6–10pm, Sat, Sun, and holidays 10am–4pm; ⓣ208/963-3624) seven miles west of Cottonwood on a signposted road has 845ft of vertical served by one T-bar and one rope tow; the similarly low-key **Snowhaven Ski Area** (weekends 10am–4pm except Jan when you can also ski from 10am-9pm on Fri; ⓣ208/983-2299) seven miles south of Grangeville on Forest Road 221 also has a T-bar and one rope tow and 400ft of vertical. Neither spot is exactly Sun Valley, but then neither are the prices with lift tickets at around $12/day for both hills.

East along Highway 14

A dozen miles north of Grangeville on Hwy-13 lies the turnoff for **Hwy-14**, a lonely dead-end highway that follows the South Fork of the Clearwater and lets you explore some truly secluded backwater areas. About forty miles in, an unpaved road heading south to **Orogrande** (Forest Road 233) is one of the few access points to the Gospel Hump Wilderness (see box p.614). You can take a good, short **hike** by driving along the Orogrande-Summit Road (Forest Road 233) to Jumbo Canyon (only accessible by 4WD, or you could walk the worst and final eight miles to the trailhead) where the trail to Oregon Butte Lake (Trail 201) eventually connects with **Oregon Butte Trail** (Trail 202). This climbs moderately up through wildflower meadows to a lookout cabin from where there are superb views of the Salmon River Canyon. Beyond the Orogrande turnoff, Hwy-14 soon ends at small **Elk City**, a former gold mining town founded in 1861. The town now serves as a base for hikers coming to explore the Selway-Bitterroot Wilderness Area to the east. Stock up on supplies at *Carol and Val's Convenience Store*, 110 Main St (ⓣ208/842-2551), where there's also a laundry and shower.

The Clearwater Mountains and the Selway-Bitterroot Wilderness Area

"I could observe high rugged mountains in every direction as far as I could see."

Capt William Clark

Little has changed in this corner of America since William Clark wrote the above line after looking across the massed ranks of hazy blue mountains and boundless forests in 1805. Bounded roughly by the St Joe River in the north, the Frank Church-River of No Return Wilderness Area in the south, the Bitterroot Mountains in the east and in the west by a handful of small towns – Orofino, Kamiah, and Kooskia – the **Clearwater Mountains** and the 1.3-million-acre **Selway-Bitterroot Wilderness Area** is a region where you can lose yourself in a pristine natural landscape. Although the mountains are not especially high by Idaho standards (the highest is the 9001ft Stripe Mountain in the south), they're not readily accessible as there are few roads into them. Most of the region is administered by the US Forest Service through the Clearwater National Forest (ⓣ208/476-4541) in the north, the Nez Percé National Forest (ⓣ208/983-1950) in the southwest, and the Bitterroot National Forest (ⓣ406/363-3131) in the southeast.

One of the best ways to view this wild scenery is by rafting or kayaking down one of the area's major rivers. The hiking and backpacking options could be remarkable, but there are relatively few marked trails, especially in the Selway-Bitterroot, where half of the trails haven't been maintained for twenty years and the USFS allows prescribed-burn wildfires, bears, and wolves to take charge of the landscape. Solitude is easy to find here – to ensure you don't find it for longer than planned always carry a compass and map and let someone know your plans. In winter, visitors are even less common, but a pair of cross-country skis or snowshoes can easily get you out into a magnificent, silent snowbound landscape.

Orofino and Bald Mountain

Located around forty miles east of Lewiston beside the Clearwater River, the tidy but uninspiring lumber town of **OROFINO** is the largest settlement in the Clearwater Valley – it's main claim to fame is that it's home to the world's largest steelhead hatchery. The hatchery is around seven miles northwest of town below the **Dworshak Dam and Reservoir** on the North Fork of the Clearwater, and the associated **Dworshak State Park** (ⓣ208/476-5994; $3) over on the reservoir's north shore. The ethics behind the damming of the North Fork may have been open to question (see below), but today the reservoir is a haven for boaters, water-skiers, anglers, and campers. The deep-blue waters are fringed all around by thick forests, and are crossed at two points by the elegant Dent bridge and the hidden Granddad Bridge, way up the north shores of the reservoir. In the 1970s, the Army Corps of Engineers constructed the 717ft Dworshak Dam and its 53-mile-long reservoir, destroying a prime run of steelhead trout. To compensate, $21 million was spent building the **Dworshak National Fish Hatchery** (daily 7.30am–4pm; free; ⓣ208/476-4591). Self-guided tours show the work of the hatchery and the work of a steelhead migrating from the Pacific.

Loquacious locals, nonexistent lines, and great views of the Clearwater Mountains are the big attractions at **Bald Mountain Ski Area**, 42 miles northeast of town on Grangemont Road (Dec–Jan 9.30am–3.30pm; Feb–March 10am–4pm; lift tickets $15; ⓣ208/464-2311, ⓣ1-800/794-8742 for ski report). It's only open at weekends, but the 5036ft mountain has seventeen runs with a maximum vertical of 975ft, accessed by one T-bar and a free rope tow. The runs are rated 25 percent beginner, 40 percent intermediate, and 35 percent advanced, and facilities at the mountain are limited to a small lodge (with rental gear) and snack bar.

Practicalities

The USFS **Clearwater National Forest Headquarters**, 12730 US-12 (8am–4.30pm weekdays, 8.30am–5pm weekends; ⓣ208/476-4541), has information on Dworshak Reservoir, the Lochsa Valley, and the Selway-Bitterroot Wilderness Area. If you intend to stay in town overnight, two good-value **motels** are the busy *White Pine Motel*, 222 Brown Ave (ⓣ208/476-5711; ❸), and the imposing redbrick *Helgeson Place Motel*, 125 Johnson Ave (ⓣ208/476-5729; ❸), which has clean and spacious rooms. **Campers** will find over 120 primitive free campgrounds scattered around Dworshak Reservoir's shoreline, plus *Dent Acres Campground* on the north shore of the lake, which has fifty sites at $12 per night.

For a hearty, well-priced **breakfast**, head to *Clearwater Bakery and Café* at 214 Johnson Ave (ⓣ208/476-3025; closed Sun), while the bustling *Ponderosa Restaurant*, 220 Michigan Ave (ⓣ208/476-4818), provides large servings of American diner food at reasonable prices.

The North Fork-Superior Adventure Road

The most common route for drivers heading east into Montana is on US-12 (see below). However, if you want to get into the real heart of the Clearwater Mountains, consider taking the **North Fork-Superior Adventure Road**, a 160-mile partially paved road cutting through dense pine forests, under spiky subalpine peaks and beside the clear waters of the North Fork of the Clearwater. This is prime big game country so keep your eyes peeled for moose, deer, elk, and even bears. The route follows Hwy-11 through **Weippe**, where Lewis and Clark met the Nez Percé, and **Pierce**, a boom and bust former gold mining town, to the lumber settlement of Headquarters. From here you hit Forest Road 247 and the pavement ends, then pass onto Forest Road 250 which takes you on its long and winding route across the mountains. You'll need a good map (available from the USFS office in Orofino) and a reliable vehicle (ideally with high clearance), and take spares, and food, gas, and water.

Kamiah and Kooskia

From Orofino, the **Northwest Passage Scenic Byway** (US-12) wends twenty miles south above the Clearwater to the small town of **KAMIAH** ("KAM-ee-eye"). The Kamiah region was a favorite winter camp of the Nez Percé, and the Corps of Discovery spent a month with them here in 1806 waiting for the snows to retreat from Lolo Pass. If here in mid-August you can commune a bit with the Nez Percé yourself at the **Chief Lookingglass Days** powwow, which features traditional Native ceremonies and dancing.

A few miles south of Kamiah on US-12 is **KOOSKIA** ("KOO-skee"), situated beneath the steep slopes of Mount Stuart at the confluence of the Middle and South Forks of the Clearwater River. It's essentially a one-street town, with the renovated Victorian-style **Old Opera House Theatre** (Ⓣ208/926-4411) at the north end of Main Street and the much-touted **Kooskia Mural** – a small, colorful rendition of the valley as it would have looked when Lewis and Clark passed through – a short walk down the road at Pankey's Foods. Nearby on Rt-1 is Kooskia's **Ranger Station** (Ⓣ208/926-4274, Ⓦwww.fs.fed.us/r1/clearwater), useful for trails maps as well as information on the local Lolo Motorway.

Heading east it's immediately obvious how the Clearwater got its name; every rock and boulder on the riverbed appears perfectly visible. On a hot day, it's hard to resist the temptation to stop at one of the small beaches beside the river and take a dip. If you do, bear in mind that the water is chilly and the mid-river current is fast flowing.

US-12 east to Lolo Pass and Montana

US-12 parallels the trail Lewis and Clark forged into Idaho, and to see the best of the region you too should get out and onto the various trails throughout the area, though even from a car the views are still breathtaking. The tumbling, foaming waters of the Lochsa – Nez Percé for "rough water" and pronounced "lock-saw" – bounce down beside the road, bordered either side by steep, seemingly impenetrable forest, as it cuts through the **Lochsa Valley** and the heart of the Clearwater and Bitterroot Mountains. It's a little over one hundred miles from Lowell east to the Continental Divide, and in winter US-12 can see heavy snowfall – call Ⓣ208/746-3005 for road conditions.

Lowell and the Lochsa Historical Ranger Station

Twenty-two miles east of Kooskia, the Middle Fork of the Clearwater is born at the point where the **Lochsa** and the **Selway** rivers merge at **Lowell**, a hamlet that relies almost entirely on tourism for a living. You can stock up on basic foodstuffs and gas here, and also stay at Lowell's focal point, the busy and friendly *Three Rivers Resort* (Ⓣ208/926-4430 or 1-888/926-4430, Ⓦwww.threeriversrafting.com; ❸), which has motel rooms, slightly more expensive log cabins with kitchenettes and river views, and $5 tent sites. The resort also has a pool and hot tubs, and is a good place to get info on the local rafting and hiking/backpacking scene as plenty of like-minded souls stay here.

Around 25 miles northeast of Lowell on US-12 is **Lochsa Historical Ranger Station** (June–Aug daily 9am–5pm; free; Ⓣ208/926-4275). This atmospheric collection of log buildings tucked into a tree-hidden compound dates back to the 1930s, when it was home to 200 forest workers, and it's well worth a visit to get a taste of the spooky solitude inherent in working in such a rustic environment. A self-guided tour takes you around the museum and various outbuildings, including the classic backwoods cabin-style ranger buildings. Note that you can also get recreation and camping information from the rangers here.

From here, the road gradually ascends through high, statuesque pine forests with the waters of the Lochsa on your right, and, on the far bank of the river, a stretch of land known as the Lochsa Face that backs onto the Selway-Bitterroot-Wilderness Area (see opposite). There are footbridges across the river to trailheads at various intervals along the road. If you've been hiking or skiing, you'll welcome the chance to take a dip in one of the region's natural **hot springs**. Weir Hot Springs is near Weir Creek Bridge (just east of milepost 142), and the more popular Jerry Johnson Hot Springs (three pools) is to the east of milepost 152, close to Warm Springs Pack Bridge. There's a hike of around a mile to each spring, and both are signposted from the road. You can also camp close to Jerry Johnson Hot Springs (see box, opposite).

Lolo Pass

Driving onwards and upwards on US-12 you eventually crest the Continental Divide and state border at **Lolo Pass** (5233ft), from where the road descends towards Missoula (see p.513). Lolo Pass is the point where Lewis and Clark were eventually able to descend into Idaho after having failed further south on **Lemhi Pass**; it's also the point where you adjust your watch from Pacific Standard Time to Mountain Standard Time. A **visitor center** (summer 9am–5pm PST; winter Fri–Mon 9am–4pm PST; Ⓣ208/942-3113) has extensive exhibits focusing on the Lewis and Clark Bicentenary, and also sells refreshments and souvenirs. In winter, this is the trailhead for some ten miles of **cross-country ski trails**.

Floating the Lochsa

The Lochsa is a popular **rafting** and **kayaking** river, though after heavy rain or rapid snowmelt it's really for experts only. There are over forty sets of rapids on the river, with nine rated Class IV–V, and the season runs from May to July. A number of guiding companies in the area run one- to three-day trips, including Three Rivers Rafting, out of Lowell (Ⓣ208/926-4430 or 1-888/926-4430, Ⓦwww.threeriversrafting.com), and ROW, out of Coeur d'Alene (Ⓣ208/765-0841 or 1-800/451-6034, Ⓦwww.row-inc.com). Rates range around $100–150 for a day on the river including lunch. **Permits** are not necessary for noncommercial groups.

If you'd like to follow Lewis and Clark's route, take the **Lolo Motorway** from Lolo Pass to Kamiah, above the northern side of US-12. It's a primitive 4WD road that follows the explorers' original trail, and during the Lewis and Clark Bicentennial Period (2003–2007) access will be limited to permit holders only – for more details contact Kooskia Ranger Station (see p.633) or check Ⓦ www.nps.gov/lecl online.

The Selway-Bitterroot Wilderness Area and the Selway River

The **SELWAY-BITTERROOT WILDERNESS AREA** is a landscape of extremes, where irritating or downright dangerous wildlife – from mosquitoes and biting flies to grizzlies and rattlesnakes – are a fact of life. Snow is possible any time of year at higher elevations, and even lower down summer nights can be chilly; in winter, snowfall is heavy and avalanches frequent. Marked trails are scarce and often rough. In short, you'll need good backcountry know-how, the right equipment, and an adventurous mindset if planning on venturing beyond its borders. You will be rewarded for your efforts though, with plenty of glacier-carved mountain peaks, glittering glacial lakes and deep, craggy canyons to marvel at.

The closest **bases** for accessing the wilderness area are Lowell (see opposite) to the north, Elk City and around to the southwest (see p.631), and Hamilton in Montana (see p.509) on the eastern side of the Bitterroots. One of the best access routes is via Selway Road (Forest Road 223) at Lowell, which runs 25 miles alongside the Selway River and past several trailheads before it dead-ends. No vehicles (including mountain bikes) are allowed, so if you intend to spend any time here you'll be carrying all your own supplies on foot or by pack animal. For more **information**, contact the USFS Ranger Station in Kooskia (see p.633) or the Fenn Ranger Station (June–Oct Mon–Sat 7.30am–4.30pm; Sept–May Mon–Fri 7.30am–4pm; Ⓣ 208/926-4258), four miles from Lowell on Selway Road; both sell a vital wilderness map for $3.

Camping in and around the Selway-Bitterroot Wilderness

While you can **backcountry camp** just about anywhere in the Selway-Bitterroot Wilderness, there are a number of USFS **campgrounds** around its borders, all set amongst beautiful forest and mountain scenery. One of the easiest group of camps to reach are strung along the **Selway Road** (Forest Road 223) from Lowell to Selway Falls Guard Station – amongst those you come to as you work your way southeast along the road are:

Johnson Bar: The most accessible campground from US-12 (RV accessible), set four miles from Lowell on Selway Rd, with seven free primitive sites.

O'Hara Bar: Three miles on from Johnson Bar and considerably bigger with 34 sites ($5); RV accessible as well.

Selway Falls: At the end of Selway Rd, a primitive site with seven spaces ($5) that is ideally placed for accessing the wilderness area.

Amongst the campgrounds you'll pass as you travel **east up US-12** are:

Wilderness Gateway: Nearly thirty miles east of Lowell on US-12, with almost one hundred sites ($12). It can be busy here, but as the name implies access to the wilderness area is good.

Jerry Johnson: About fifty miles east of Lowell on US-12 with fifteen sites ($5) close to Jerry Johnson Hot Springs.

Elk Summit: Off US-12 and sixteen miles south of the Powell Ranger Station on Elk Summit Rd (Forest Road 360). The sites are free and near a trailhead into the the Selway-Bitterroot Wilderness Area, but there's no drinking water.

Exploring the Clearwater Mountains and the Selway-Bitterroot Wilderness

In **summer**, hikers, backpackers, and horsepackers will find 2000 miles of rugged trails through pristine mountain country. The best quality trails are along the Selway River – away from this many are steep and poorly defined, meaning good navigational skills and backcountry experience are a must. Consider taking a fishing rod along, as there is excellent **fishing** on the Selway and in over a hundred mountain lakes. In **winter**, many of the trails are used by cross-country skiers and snowshoers. Bear in mind that the drive in to many of the trailheads may require a 4WD vehicle.

Selway River Region

Lower Selway River twelve-mile round-trip. The trailhead for this popular hike is about eighteen miles from Lowell along the Selway Rd at the *Race Creek Campground*. The easy trail is well marked and takes you alongside the Selway River where there are sandy beaches and good summer fishing.

Big Fog Saddle Trailheads. To access the trailheads here, take the Selway Rd (Forest Road 223) southeast from Lowell for about twenty miles to the wide Selway Falls, where you turn onto the rough Fog Mountain Rd for a hard, fourteen-mile drive that gains some 4000ft. There are three trailheads at Big Fog Saddle, all of which take you beneath the rugged Selway Crags that rise above an array of blue alpine lakes. The best route is the **Big Fog Mountain Trail** (seven-mile round-trip) that climbs to a high ridge leading to the Selway Crags. Look out for big game on the way – moose, elk, and deer are quite common, and note the remaining wildfire scars from the massive fires of 1910.

North of US-12

Goat Lake six-mile round-trip. A fine hike for Lewis and Clark enthusiasts. Located to the northwest of Powell Ranger Station on US-12, much of the road to the trailhead follows the Lolo Indian Trail used by Lewis and Clark, and the hike itself takes you beneath the 8000ft peaks of the Continental Divide. To reach the trailhead, take Forest Road 569 north from Powell Ranger Station for 2.2 miles, fork left and after 1.8 miles fork left again. After 1.6 miles follow Forest Road 500 (the Lewis and Clark Trail) and keep straight on for approx. thirteen miles to Cayuse Junction. Here turn right onto Forest Road 581 and head eight miles to the turnoff to Blacklead Mountain (Deer Creek Trail #513), which marks the trailhead. It's best to call in at the ranger station first to check out the state of the road and get a good map of the trail.

The Southwest Corner 18-, 36- or 54-mile multiday round-trip. This hike beneath the Bitterroots in the isolated southwest corner of the Selway-Bitterroot is accessed from Elk City (see p.631). From there, head one mile past the Red River Ranger Station to turn onto the unpaved Magruder Road. Follow signs north off the Magruder Road for twelve miles to Paradise Ranger Station – the trailhead is just past the station. The trail follows the roiling waters of White Cap Creek up into heavily forested backcountry inhabited by black bears, deer, and elk. Give yourself a day in and out for the first nine miles to **Cooper Flat**, two days each way for the next nine miles to a good campground at **Cliff Creek**, and a further two days each way to **White Cap Lakes** (54-mile round-trip). You can make this into an even bigger adventure by following the trail over the Bitterroots to Tin Cup Lake near Darby, Montana (see p.509).

The Panhandle

Jutting up between Montana and Washington, Idaho's **Panhandle** is a wild and narrow strip of remote forests, sparkling lakes, and imposing mountains. From Coeur d'Alene Lake in the south, the fifty-mile-wide Panhandle stretches eighty miles up to the Canadian border, allowing you to conceivably cover much of it in a day. Take your time to explore here, though, as this is a place where you can still see the West as it was when the first fur trappers chanced upon it.

Water is a major feature of the landscape and **Priest Lake**, **Lake Pend Oreille**, and **Coeur d'Alene Lake** are the three main attractions. In summer they're hives of activity with everyone from kayakers to water skiers doing their best to get wet. The whine of two-stroke engines can be irritating at times, but getting away from it all is the least of your problems – people are few and far between on most trails hereabouts, especially in the northern **Selkirk Mountain** and the **Cabinet Mountains**. Animals, though, are most definitely not – **bears**, both black and grizzly, inhabit the dense forests, as do some of the last remaining **woodland caribou** in North America. More common creatures include **moose**, **deer**, and **mountain goat**, often spotted by hikers, and if you see none of these running free you're certain to see the heads of those that didn't move fast enough in bars throughout the area. Also worth looking out for are **osprey** – the area holds the West's highest concentration of this impressive raptor.

In winter, downhill skiing and snowboarding in the quality powder of **Schweitzer Mountain**, **Silver Mountain**, and the small ski area of **Lookout Pass** on the Montana border take over. There are also plenty of cross-country skiing options, including **Fourth of July Pass** near Coeur d'Alene, and snow-mobiling is popular around Priest Lake.

When you want a taste of urban life, **Coeur d'Alene** and the smaller and more appealing **Sandpoint** both have excellent bars and restaurants, making for great lay-overs after leaving the wilds. The well-preserved silver mining town of **Wallace**, the town destroyed by a volcano in the film *Dante's Peak*, is also worth a visit for an authentic taste of the Old West.

Unfortunately, in recent years the Panhandle has also gained a certain notoriety as the base for **white extremists and right-wing survivalists**. Don't believe the hype – they're far fewer in number than the media might have you believe, and their self-imposed isolation means you're highly unlikely to bump into these people unless you go looking. In a nice twist of fate, one of the more notorious groups, Aryan Nations, was recently bankrupted in a court case brought by concerned locals and their compound has now been sold for conversion into a human rights education center.

Accommodation price codes

All accommodation prices in this book have been coded using the symbols below. For **hotels**, **motels**, and **B&Bs**, rates are given for the least expensive double room in each establishment during peak season; variations are indicated where appropriate, including winter rates for all ski resorts. For **hostels**, the actual price per bed is given; for **camping**, the overnight cost per site is given. For a full explanation see p.30 in Basics.

❶ up to $30	❹ $60–80	❼ $130–180
❷ $30–45	❺ $80–100	❽ $180–240
❸ $45–60	❻ $100–130	❾ over $240

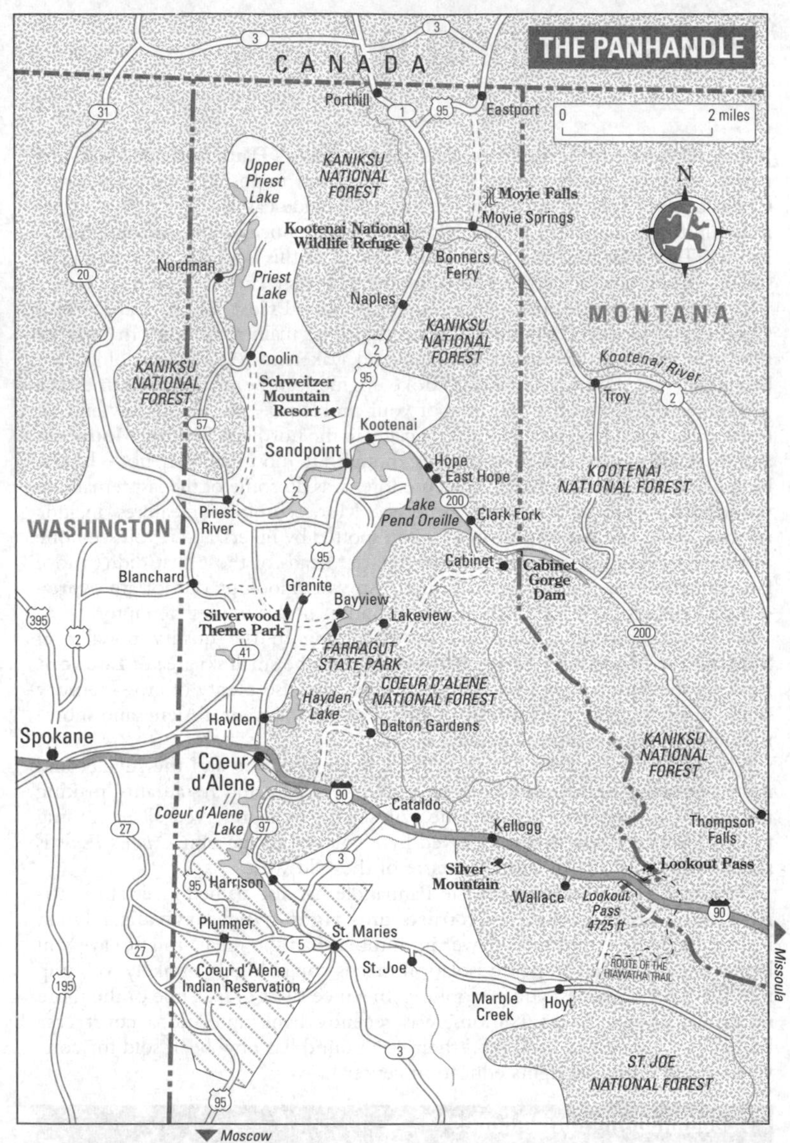

Coeur d'Alene

The Panhandle's largest town, **COEUR D'ALENE** (pronounced "Core da lane") is located in a gem of a setting beneath rolling hills and mountains on the north shore of beautiful Coeur d'Alene Lake. Unsurprisingly, the town has been attracting tourists for almost a century, and thanks to this influx of year-round visitors, its busy lake and a college campus close to downtown, there's always a pleasantly busy atmosphere to the town of 30,000.

The area's original inhabitants were the **Schee-Chu-Umsh Indians**, who acquired the name Coeur d'Alene – meaning "heart like (the point of) an awl" – from French trappers, most likely due to their sharp trading skills. The natives were converted to Catholicism in the 1840s and 1850s by Jesuit missionaries, and together they built Idaho's oldest existing building, The Mission of the Sacred Heart (see p.656) at Cataldo, east of Coeur d'Alene. Around the same time, the US military and white settlers made incursions into the area. **Fort Coeur d'Alene** was built in 1878 by General William Tecumseh Sherman to protect the growing white population from attack by the Native Americans, and as a defense against the possibility of British expansion south from Canada. The name of the fort was later changed to **Fort Sherman** – abandoned in 1901, only remnants remain on the campus of **North Idaho College**.

Today, a much larger structure towers over the north shore of the long, narrow lake; looking not unlike an office block, the five-star **Coeur d'Alene Resort**, which boasts the world's only floating golf green, completely dominates the downtown scene. Not surprisingly, it's a bitter local debating point.

Arrival and information

You'll most likely arrive **by car** – I-90 runs 33 miles west to Spokane and 163 miles east to Missoula; Hwy-95 43 miles north to Sandpoint and south along the lake – though daily Greyhound **buses** from Spokane and Missoula stop at 157 Spruce St (Ⓣ208/664-3343). The local NICE (North Idaho Community Express; Ⓣ208/664-9767) bus service runs from the same terminal, with four daily buses to Sandpoint ($9 round-trip). **Taxi** services include Sunset Taxi (Ⓣ208/664-8000) and Moose Express Ⓣ208/676-1561), who provide a shuttle service between local airports, while **car rental** companies include Auto Rental of Coeur d'Alene (Ⓣ208/664-8000) and Enterprise (Ⓣ208/765-1070).

The **Coeur d'Alene Visitor and Conventions Services**, 1st and Sherman (Mon–Fri 8.30am–5pm; Ⓣ1-877/782-9232, Ⓦwww.coeurdalene.org), has a good range of free helpful publications. For information on hiking and camping, contact the USFS Idaho Panhandle Office at 3815 Schreiber Way (Mon–Sat 8am–5pm; Ⓣ208/765-7223).

Accommodation

Accommodation varies from cheap and cheerful motels to the most ostentatious hotel in the state in the form of *Coeur d'Alene Resort*. A free accommodation reservation service is available by calling Coeur d'Alene Central Reservations (Ⓣ1-800/876-8921), most useful in summer and during public holidays when rooms are often at a premium. The two main accommodation strips are **Sherman Avenue**, close to downtown and the lake, and the rather soulless **Appleway Avenue** a few miles north of downtown, where larger chains are located amidst shopping malls and fast-food joints. Coeur d'Alene also has a great selection of **B&Bs**; for full details, contact the Coeur d'Alene B&B Association (Ⓣ208/667-5081 or 1-800/773-0323).

There's only one **campground** within walking distance of downtown, but plenty of choice if you don't mind driving.

Spokane ▲ Sandpoint & ▲ Priest Lake ▲ Appleway Avenue, 1, 2, 3 & A ▲ 4

COEUR D'ALENE

ACCOMMODATION

Amor's Highwood House	4
Baragar House	8
Bates Motel	12
Coeur d'Alene B&B	7
Coeur d'Alene Resort	13
El Rancho	11
The Flamingo	10
Gregory's McFarland House	6
Hawthorn Inn	9
Motel 6	1
Robin Hood RV Park	5
Shilo Inn	2
Super 8	3

RESTAURANTS & BARS

Beverly's	I
Cricket's Steakhouse and Oyster Bar	H
Dockside Restaurant	J
Hudson's Hamburgers	E
Java on Sherman	G
Jimmy D's	F
Las Palmitas	C
Moon's Saloon	B
Mulligan's Bar and Grille	A
The Wine Cellar	D

Spokane River
Fort Sherman Museum
North Idaho College
Museum of North Idaho
City Park & Beach
Library
Person Field
McEuen Field
Coeur d'Alene Lake
Tubbs Hill
Coeur d'Alene Resort Golf Course
Centennial Trail
Sherman Avenue
Government Way
Lincoln Way
Moscow ▲
Kellogg ▼

0 500 yds

N

Hotels and motels

Bates Motel 2018 Sherman Ave ⓣ208/ 667-1411. Clean, basic rooms in a motel that relies largely on its name for custom. Ask for "Norm's Special" and you may – seriously – get a discount. ❷

Coeur d'Alene Resort Front Ave at 2nd St ⓣ208/765-4000 or 1-800/688-5253, ⓦwww.cdaresort.com. This opulent, though out-of-place creation enjoys a lakefront setting complete with a marina, three lounges, two restaurants, and a fully kitted-out recreation center. Room rates vary enormously, from moderately expensive to over $2500 per night for the penthouse suite. The cheapest rooms are very well furnished and come with cable TV and private baths. The resort also runs "Ski and Stay" packages with Silver Mountain Resort (see p.657). ❼

El Rancho 19th and Sherman Ave ⓣ208/664-8794 or 1-800/359-9791, ⓔelranchomotelcda@juno.com. Excellent value, clean and comfortable rooms with cable TV, coffee-makers, and cooking units, all within walking distance of downtown, the lake, and Tubbs Hill. ❷

The Flamingo 718 Sherman Ave ⓣ1-800/955-2159. *The Flamingo* has spacious rooms with cable TV, private baths, and kitchenettes. There's also a spa, and you're within easy walking distance of the lake and downtown. ❸

Hawthorn Inn & Suites 2209 Sherman Ave ⓣ1-800/522-1173. Near exit 15 on I-90, the *Hawthorn* has well appointed rooms with cable TV and baths, plus a pool and sauna. There's also a free continental breakfast. ❻

Motel 6 416 W Appleway Ave ⓣ208/664-6600. Nothing fancy, but the standard motel rooms here are clean and well-maintained and come with cable TV and private baths. The motel also has a pool. ❷

Shilo Inn 702 W Appleway Ave ⓣ208/664-2300 or 1-800/222-2244. A busy establishment, popular with families and business travelers thanks to the large rooms, small pool, spa, and gym. Free buffet breakfast daily. ❹

Super 8 Motel 505 W Appleway Ave ⓣ208/765-8880 or 1-800/800-8000. Standard chain motel fare with clean rooms, cable TV, and efficient no-frills service. ❸

B&Bs

Amor's Highwood House 1206 Highwood Lane ⓣ208/667-4735, ⓦwww.amors.com. Located in a quiet residential area near the lake and within easy reach of downtown, this pleasant B&B has two homely rooms with king-size beds and private bath. There's a gazebo-covered spa and mountain bikes are available; free evening wine and cookies add a nice touch. ❹

Baragar House 316 Military Drive ⓣ208/664-9125 or 1-800/615-8422, ⓦwww.baragarhouse.com. Situated in the historic Fort Sherman district, *Baragar House* has a hot tub and sauna, and two of the three rooms have ceilings featuring luminous maps of the stars visible only after the lights are turned off. ❺

Coeur d'Alene B&B 906 Foster Ave ⓣ208/667-7527. An attractive colonial-style house dating back to 1906, with a peaceful garden and great mountain views from the porch. There are five luxuriously appointed rooms, four of which are en suite. ❹

Gregory's McFarland House 6th St and Foster ⓣ208/667-1232, ⓦwww.bbhost.com/mcfarlandhouse. This superbly preserved home is listed on the National Historic Register and dates back to 1905. The five rooms are full of tasteful English-style antiques and all have private baths. ❺

Campgrounds

Coeur d'Alene KOA E 10700 Wolf Lodge Bay Rd ⓣ208/664-4471 or 1-800/231-2609. Everything you need for a hassle-free camping experience, with lake access, a pool, and bike, canoe, and boat rental. Rates start at $21 per night.

Mica Bay Campground signposted about seven miles south of town off US-95. A very basic campground with no water, but situated in a pleasant lakeside location with fifteen sites at $10 per site.

Robin Hood RV Park & Campground 703 Lincoln Way ⓣ208/664-2306. Eighty sites plus hookups for RVs. It's not super cheap at $17–19 for a tent, $1 per extra person, but it's close to the Fort Sherman area of town and the lake, and there are clean shower and laundry facilities.

Downtown and around

Coeur d'Alene's **downtown** consists of six rather simple blocks of shops, bars and restaurants leading down to the bustling waterfront. It's become somewhat of a hot spot for **antiques**, and the main drag, **Sherman Avenue**, is home to several shops worth checking out. Also worth a gander is the Idaho Automobile Co., located on the corner of 4th and Indiana, where superb mint condition classic cars are on sale. Worth a peek on a rainy day is the nearby **Museum of**

North Idaho, 115 Northwest Blvd (April–Oct Tues–Sat 11am–5pm; $1.50), on the eastern edge of City Park (see below). It houses fairly rudimentary exhibits on local history, and the black-and-white photos strewn about are particularly interesting, showing the town as an early settlement surrounded completely by raw nature. A half-mile walk north is the pleasant lakefront campus of North Idaho College, home to the **Fort Sherman Museum** (May–Sept Tues–Sat 1–5pm; ⓣ208/664-3448; $1.50). All that remains of the original fort is the 1885 stone powder house in which the museum resides, displaying an absorbing model of the original fort.

Coeur d'Alene Lake

On warm summer evenings, there may be no better place to be in Idaho than the shores of **Coeur d'Alene Lake**. In total, the lake has 135 miles of generally pristine shoreline, and even the stretch bordering Coeur d'Alene is blue and sparkling. This stretch is also where the town really comes alive, bustling with folk paddling and strolling about, or just sitting and gazing across the rippling waters. A paved trail along the shore – part of the 24-mile **North Idaho Centennial Trail** that runs from the northeast shore of Coeur d'Alene Lake to the Washington State line – receives the most action, streaming with friendly locals on foot, bikes, and skates.

Ground zero is **City Park and Beach**, on the north side of Independence Point and within two minutes of downtown. In summer, the water off the lifeguard-patrolled beach is pleasantly warm and usually full of action, with screaming kids leaping about and all manner of vessels buzzing around on the water. Behind the beach, the park's large grassy area, complete with shady trees, basketball courts, and a bandstand, is where you'll find free **live music** on many summer evenings.

Due south of here is the multistory **Coeur d'Alene Resort**, a lovely place to stay but a bit of an eyesore nonetheless. Far prettier is the resort's award-winning **golf course** (ⓣ1-800/688-5253, ⓦwww.floatinggreen.com), where the par-3 14th hole actually floats on the lake – after your tee shot from shore, a small ferry takes you across to the green. A round here costs a whopping $210, though you do get better prices if you're staying at the resort. Due south of the resort is the lakefront's best spot, **Tubbs Hill**. This 120-acre wooded promontory has grand

Getting onto Coeur d'Alene Lake

The most popular way of getting out onto Coeur d'Alene Lake is on a **sightseeing cruise**. Lake Coeur d'Alene Cruises (ⓣ208/765-4000 ext 7143), out of Independence Point next to City Beach, run a variety of tours, including a ninety-minute spin ($13; three times daily), a six-hour jaunt to the secluded southern end of the lake ($25; Sun & Wed), and sunset dinner cruises ($30; Sun–Thurs).

You can also take matters into your own hands by **renting** one of several types of **watercraft**. Next to the *Coeur d'Alene Resort*, Boardwalk Marina (ⓣ208/765-4000 ext 7185) rents eighteen-foot motor boats for around $50 per hour. Island Rentals, 200 Sherman Ave (ⓣ208/666-1626), hire out jet skis from $55 per hour (plus rollerblades and mountain bikes), and canoes and paddleboats can be rented at the dock beside City Beach for $10 per hour.

If none of the above is thrilling enough, there's always the option of a **floatplane** tour or **parasail** above the lake. Brooks Sea Plane (ⓣ208/664-2842; $40 per person) run twenty-minute aerial tours and Coeur d'Alene Parasail (ⓣ208/765-4627; $40) will take you an eye-popping 400ft parasail above the lake; both leave from the city dock.

views across the lake and is braided with pleasant walking trails, many of which lead to small, secluded coves and beaches. The main trailhead at the 3rd Street boat launch leads to an easy mile-and-a-half walk along the shoreline.

Outdoor activities

Some of the area's best **hiking** can be found on and around **Mount Coeur d'Alene** (4439ft), although as with almost all the outdoor activities in the area you'll need a car to get there. There's a pleasant and popular forested five-mile hike on Trail 79 above the lake's east shore to the mountain's summit, starting from *Beauty Creek Campground* just off Hwy-97, which is south of I-90 exit 22. In the same area is the easy three-mile **Mineral Ridge Loop**, which has good views over Lake Coeur d'Alene and is accessed from the Mineral Ridge Scenic Area on Hwy-97.

Mountain bikers are better off heading over to **Canfield Mountain** (4162ft), immediately east of I-90, and within riding distance of town if you're keen enough. There are over thirty miles of forest roads and single-track to suit all abilities across its slopes, and though the climb to the top is a grind, the views over lake and west towards Washington are well worth it. Trailheads are strung along Forest Road 268 off County Road 108 and on Nettleton Gulch Road off 15th Street and a map of the trail system is available from the visitor center.

There's good **fishing** on Coeur d'Alene Lake, mainly for cutthroat trout, chinook salmon, northern pike, and kokanee, and it makes a nice escape from the commotion at City Beach; charters can be organized through Blue Ribbon Charters (☎208/667-3474) and Lake Charters Inc. (☎208/667-3474). Another good spot to drop a line is the 300-acre **Fernan Lake** at the southeast end of town, popular during the winter for ice-fishing. The fishing is even better, though, an hour north in Lake Pend Oreille (see p.649).

In winter there's free **cross-country skiing** at **Fourth of July Pass Park and Ski Area**, twenty-minute's drive east of town on I-90. Trails include two five-mile circuits and a linear two-mile route through thick woods. Downhill skiers and snowboarders are very well catered for at Silver Mountain, forty minutes east on I-90 (see p.657), and Schweitzer Mountain Ski Resort, an hour north on Hwy-95 (see p.651).

Local outfitters

Otter River and Mountain Sports, 423 Sherman ☎208/769-7275. A well-stocked store focusing on kayaking and other river sports in summer and boarding in winter.

Two Wheeler & Ski Dealer, 9551 N Hwy-95, Hayden ☎208/772-8179. Just north of town with a good selection of bikes and rental skis; staff know the local trails inside and out and can help set you up a ride with local cyclists/mountain bikers.

Eating and drinking

Coeur d'Alene has a pleasant bustle to it, especially on summer evenings, yet despite being the largest city in the Panhandle it doesn't exactly have a throbbing **nightlife** – it's more the kind of place to relax over a good meal than burn the midnight oil at a club. The main drag is along Sherman, although there are several chain restaurants along Appleway Avenue for the less discerning.

Beverly's *Coeur d'Alene Resort* ⓣ208/765-4000 or 1-800/688-4142. The place to go if you want to splash out a bit (entrees are $20-plus). The chef creates fantastic dishes using mainly local cuisine like line-caught trout, freshly-picked morel mushrooms, and, of course, potatoes. The views from the seventh floor location are as good as the food; the extensive wine list is also notable.

Cricket's Steakhouse and Oyster Bar 422 Sherman Ave ⓣ208/765-1990. *Cricket's* dishes out good steak and oysters in a lively atmosphere that's part 1950s-style bar, part modern sports bar – a model train runs around the room as you eat and drink. A filling main course won't set you back much more than $10.

Dockside Restaurant *Coeur d'Alene Resort* ⓣ1-800/688-5253 or 208/765-4000. A laid-back, waterside restaurant known for it's great Sunday brunch. It's open daily for breakfast – try the great huckleberry pancakes. Dinner features a massive salad bar and excellent desserts.

Hudson's Hamburgers 207 Sherman Ave ⓣ208/664-5444. Owned and operated by the same family since 1907, *Hudson's* is a local institution and the fine selection of burgers doesn't disappoint.

Java on Sherman 324 Sherman Ave ⓣ208/667-0010. Popular with an active student crowd and a good place to get a decent coffee, breakfast (the granola is good), light lunch, or even evening snacks.

Jimmy D's 320 Sherman Ave ⓣ208/664-9774. One of the most popular_restaurants in town, serving a fine array of steak, seafood and pasta dishes. Typical entrees include lightly breaded pan-fried rainbow trout and roasted baby-back ribs first poached in beer. The sidewalk, open in summer only, is a great people watching spot. Expect to pay $15–20 for a main course.

Las Palmitas 201 N 3rd St ⓣ208/664-0581. A moderately priced Mexican restaurant and bar set in the town's old railroad depot. It's popular with a younger crowd, and the margaritas are well worth checking out.

Moon's Saloon 204 N 2nd St ⓣ208/664-6747. One of the more interesting bars in town that, due to a selection of antiques and stuffed wildlife around the place (including an eight-foot grizzly), also advertises itself as a 'museum.' You'll find a wide selection of microbrews, good burgers for under $10 and occasional live music and/or comedy.

Mulligan's Bar and Grille 414 W Appleway Ave ⓣ208/765-3200. One of the best restaurants in the Appleway Avenue area, serving good skillet breakfasts and renowned stews in the evening. A meal here won't set you back much over $10.

The Wine Cellar 313 Sherman Ave (ⓣ208/664-9463). A popular wine bar that also features an extensive bistro-style menu which includes bouillabaise, steamed mussels and a fine paella. Live jazz and blues nightly.

Listings

Internet Coeur d'Alene Public Library, north of downtown at 201 Harrison Ave (ⓣ208/769-2315), has free access (with a time limit of 15min).

Laundry Cleaning and Laundry Village, 1140 N 4th Ave (ⓣ208/765-8900).

Post office The main post office is at 111 N 7th St (Zip code 83814).

Supermarket Sherman IGA, 1211 Sherman Ave (24 hours).

South of Coeur d'Alene

On the east bank of Lake Coeur d'Alene, the **Lake Coeur d'Alene Scenic Byway** (Hwy-97), heads south toward central Idaho. It's a lovely drive, with postcard-perfect views across the lake to the brilliant-green hills above, and it eventually connects to another picturesque route, the **White Pine Scenic Byway** (Hwy-3). Before doing so, though, the Lake Coeur d'Alene Scenic Byway passes through tiny **Harrison**, located at the mouth of the Coeur d'Alene River. Stop to watch **ospreys**, which nest in great numbers here; you can't fail to see them soaring in the skies, diving for fish or just sunning themselves in their shambolic nests. If you've got the time and the money, one of Idaho's finest guest lodges is located some six miles northeast of here. Tucked away in a sunny basin beneath the St. Joe Mountains, the *Hidden Creek Ranch*, 7600 Blue Lake Rd (ⓣ1-800/446-3833, ⓕ208/689-9115; ⑨), offers lovely log cabin accommodation, fantastic ranch-style cooking, and copious horseback riding, hiking, fishing, and biking options. The ranch owners work in close communion with the environment (one of the owners, John Muir, is an ancestor of *the* John Muir, and is also an avid environmentalist). Six days is the minimum length of stay and will set you back around $1500. The White Pine Scenic Byway turnoff some seven miles south cuts through rolling hills and through the logging town of **St. Maries,** on the banks of the St. Joe River, where the standout feature is a huge statue of John Bunyan on Main Street. Continuing south through the dense green forests of the St. Joe National Forest takes you towards Moscow (see p.627).

North to Sandpoint

Although the drive up Hwy-95 from Coeur d'Alene to Sandpoint can be made in an hour, there are a few worthwhile stops en route. First up, about fifteen miles along, is the **Silverwood Theme Park** (daily mid-June to Aug; weekends from late May to mid-June and Sept; $24 adults; ⓣ208/683-3400, ⓦwww.silverwood4fun.com). The show stoppers here are two of the largest wooden **roller-coasters** in the western USA – the gut-churning *Tremors* (which plummets 103ft into a series of underground tunnels) and the 55mph *Timber Terror*. Those who'd rather stay grounded can explore the re-created mining camp or hitch a ride on an authentic steam train that puffs its way around the park's 500-acre site.

Just north of Silverwood, a signposted turnoff from Hwy-95 leads a few miles east to **Farragut State Park** ($3), a former navel training base located at the southern end of Lake Pend Oreille. There are two campgrounds in the park, *Whitetail Campground* ($12 per tent) and *Snowberry Campground* ($15 tent and RV hookups). **Hikers** should head up the Chilco Mountain Trail (Trail 14), well-marked on Forest Road 290 east off US-95 one-and-a-half miles south of Athol. Though only two miles long, the trail leads up to the summit of Chilco Mountain (5685ft), from where there are magnificent views across the forests and lakes of the Panhandle. There's also some **good mountain biking** – a local favorite being the Bernard Peak Loop, an eighteen-mile circuit that mixes forest road, double-track and single-track and is a solid workout with 2650ft of ascent. The route starts from just south of Bayview on the lake's south shore.

Sandpoint, Lake Pend Oreille, and around

Sixty miles south of the Canadian border, **SANDPOINT**, Idaho's most northerly town of size, sits on the northwest shore of the dazzling blue **Lake Pend Oreille** (pronounced "Pon-du-ray"). There's confusion over the origins of the lake's name – said to have been named by French fur trappers either because it was shaped like an ear ("oreille" in French) or because the local Native Americans wore large earrings, but the origin's of Sandpoint's name are clearer – explorer **David Thompson** (see box p.652) named the area "sandy point" in 1808. Even though named at the beginning of the century, little development took place here until the arrival of the Northern Pacific Railroad in 1882. It only took a short time from then for Sandpoint to grow into a

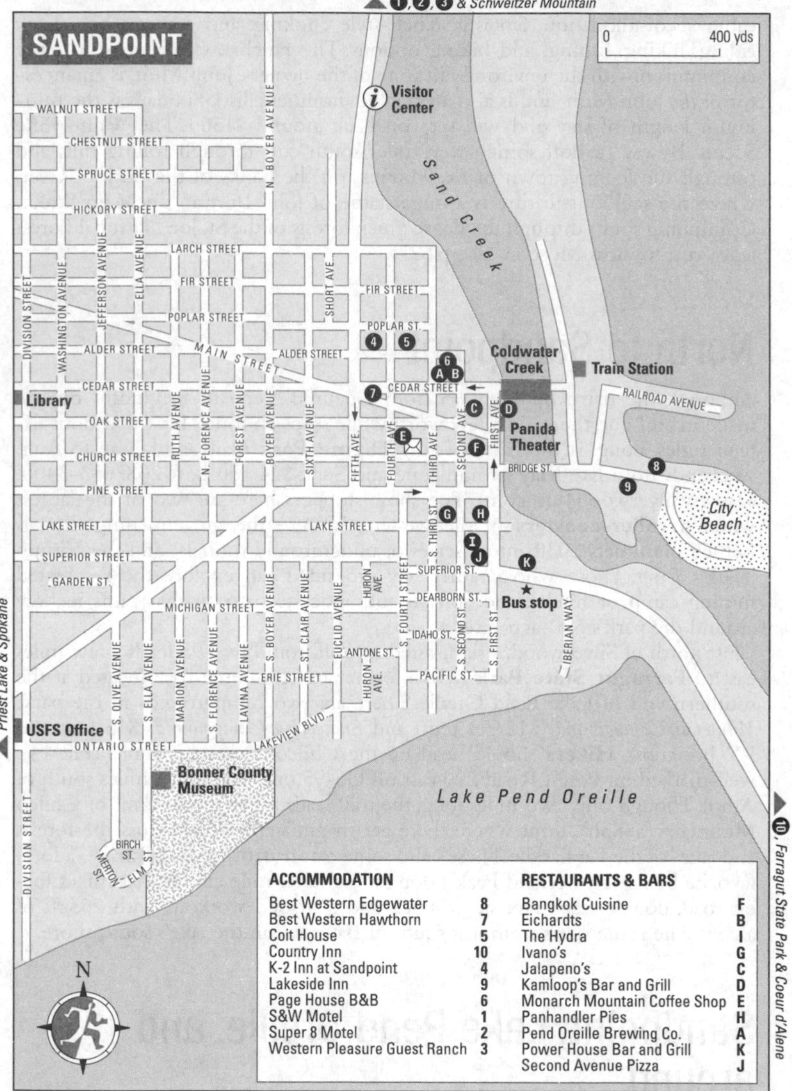

rough community, described by one railroad employee as "a wild town of 100 people with 23 saloons, several houses of ill fame, two hotels, one restaurant and the closest doctor 30 miles away."

Sandpoint further developed around the **logging** industry, and evidence of its operations – from downed swaths of forest to massive lumber trucks – are never very far from sight. But since the 1970s, the area's economic shining light has been **tourism**. Tucked in the shadows of the lofty Selkirk and Cabinet mountains, both ranges attract hikers, bikers, hunters, and fishing fanatics in the warmer months, while the big draw in winter is the nearby and rapidly developing **Schweitzer Mountain Ski Resort**. The town itself has evolved along with this tourist influx, and although it's still a working timber town, a heavy sprinkling of outdoors and artsy types have given this buzzing little town a more bohemian, eclectic feel than anywhere else in the Panhandle.

Arrival and information

Although driving into Sandpoint is impressive from every direction, entering from the south via Hwy-95 – and over the graceful span of **Long Bridge** – is the most memorable approach. The local **bus service**, the North Idaho Community Express (NICE; ⓣ208/263-7287), follows this route four times a day to and from Coeur d'Alene ($9 round-trip), stopping within walking distance of downtown at the Riverside Building on Hwy-95. The town also has the only **train** stop in Idaho. Amtrak's Empire Builder route that runs between Chicago and Seattle pulls in at the station on the north end of Railroad Street (11.30pm westbound, 2.30am eastbound).

Information is available from the helpful chamber of commerce, 900 5th Ave (daily 8.30am–5pm; ⓣ208/263-2161 or 1-800/800-2106, ⓦwww.sandpointchamber.com); the biannual *Sandpoint Magazine* ($2) available here has comprehensive listings of current events. For information on backcountry backpacking and camping, head over to the USFS Idaho Panhandle National Forest Office at 1500 US-2, a mile southwest of downtown (daily 8.30am–5pm; ⓣ208/263-5111).

Accommodation

Sandpoint is very reliant on tourism for its daily bread. Consequently, the range of **accommodation** is very good for a town of this size. Regardless, make reservations if possible as the better places tend to fill up quickly. If visiting Schweitzer Mountain resort, it's usually cheaper to stay in Sandpoint, and in winter many motels and hotels offer money-saving **ski-and-stay packages**. There are no **campgrounds** within Sandpoint proper, but several are within a short drive.

Hotels and motels

Best Western Edgewater Resort Motor Inn 56 Bridge St ⓣ208/263-3194 or 1-800/635-2534, ⓔedgewater@netw.com. Upmarket lodging with large, well-appointed rooms with views of City Beach and cable TV – the more expensive rooms also have hot tubs. The hotel has an indoor pool and offers ski-and-stay packages. ❻

Best Western Hawthorn Inn & Suites 414 Cedar St ⓣ208/282-0660 or 1-800/282-0660. There are seventy large and comfortable rooms here with cable TV, and the location is good for downtown. There's also a pool and spa, and a busy restaurant and cocktail lounge. ❹

Country Inn 470700 Hwy-95 S ⓣ208/263-3333. Basic but good-value rooms with microwaves and fridges two miles south of town. There's also a hot tub. ❷

K-2 Inn at Sandpoint 501 N 4th Ave ⓣ208/263-3441. A popular downtown hotel with small but cozy rooms. The beds are large, and the bathrooms have possibly the world's most powerful showers. Advance reservations recommended. ❺

Lakeside Inn 106 Bridge St ⓣ1-800/543-8126, ⓦwww.sandpointlodging.com. In a pleasant park setting at the mouth of Lake Pend Oreille and Sand Creek, this is one of the best-located hotels in town. Still within walking distance of downtown, the spacious rooms include kitchens, and there's complimentary breakfast, indoor and outdoor hot tubs, and a beach and marina for exclusive use of guests. ❹

S&W Motel 3480 Hwy-200 E ⓣ208/263-5969. A couple of miles out of town on the road to Hope, but very fairly priced and rooms have queen beds, stove, and refrigerator. There's also a hot tub for guests. ❷

Super 8 Motel 476841 Hwy-95 N ⓣ208/263-2210 or 1-800/800-8000. Plain but perfectly adequate rooms with queen beds and complimentary coffee, and a guest hot tub. Close to the Schweitzer Mountain turnoff, so you'll need a car to get downtown. ❷

Western Pleasure Guest Ranch 1413 Upper Gold Creek Rd ⓣ208/263-9066, ⓦwww.westernpleasureranch.com. Located sixteen miles northeast of Sandpoint, this friendly, family-run dude ranch offers quality accommodation in impeccably decorated, handcrafted log rooms for $450 per person for three nights, including horseback riding. They also organize horseback rides through the surrounding Selkirk and Cabinet mountains for nonguests from $35 for two hours, $75 per day. ❼

B&Bs

Coit House 502 N 4th St ⓣ208/265-4035, ⓔwehsetk@juno.com. A Victorian house within walking distance of downtown and the lake. The four guestrooms have been tastefully restored and are decorated with Victorian antiques, and all have their own bath, air-con, and cable TV. ❺

Page House B&B 506 N 2nd Ave ⓣ208/263-6584 or 1-800/500-6584, ⓦwww.keokee.com/pagehouse. The homely, beautifully furnished rooms in this 1918 house each have a separate theme – Victorian, Depression-era, and country-style – and have cable TV and private phones. The house overlooks Sand Creek and is within walking distance of downtown. ❺

Campgrounds

Garfield Bay ⓣ208/265-1438. A lakeside campground twelve miles southeast of town on Garfield Bay Rd. There are 25 spaces with water, toilets, a picnic area, and fire rings and a boat launch. Open June–August. $12.

Round Lake ⓣ208/263-3489. A busy campground ten miles south of town on Dufort Rd with fifty spaces with showers, toilets, and a boat dock. Open year-round. $11.

Samowen Campground ⓣ208/263-5111. In East Hope on the lake's east shore, about twenty minutes' drive from Sandpoint in a lovely shaded lakeside location with spectacular mountain and forest views. There are eighty lakefront sites, open from mid-May to mid-October. Booking in advance is advised. $12.

Springy Point Recreation Area ⓣ208/437-3133. The most convenient site for Sandpoint is located beside the lake one mile south of town. The site has forty spaces and showers, toilets, and a boat ramp. Open May to early Oct. $12.

The town

Thanks to the proximity of the lake a few minutes walk away, Sandpoint's compact downtown has a cheerful holiday feel to it. The town's past is on display at the **Bonner County Historical Museum**, 611 S Ella Ave (Tues–Sat 10am–4pm; $2), although the exhibits on the indigenous Kalispell and Kootenai Indians and the arrival of steamboats, the railways, and the logging industry are really only of passing interest. Another downtown attraction is the **Coldwater Creek** shopping center at the corner of 1st and Cedar. This large, tastefully designed store is visited by shoppers from all over the Northwest for its designer clothing, jewelry, and furniture.

City Beach and Lake Pend Oreille

Most of the summer action takes place due east of downtown along Bridge Street at **City Beach**, which has splendid views across **Lake Pend Oreille** to the surrounding forests and mountains. On warm days, both the lifeguard-patrolled swimming area and grassy park behind it are jammed with locals and tourists. Next to the beach is the dock for lake **cruises**; Lake Pend Oreille Cruises (ⓣ208/263-4598, ⓦwww.lakependoreillecruises.com) offers two-hour trips ($13) at 1.30pm daily from late May to late Sept. You can go out on your own as well as sailboats, paddle boats, canoes, and windsurfers can be rented at the beach from Windbag Sailboat Rentals (ⓣ208/263-7811). Recreational Rentals (ⓣ208/255-2341) at the *Lakeside Inn* (see overleaf) rent ski boats and jet skis. As well as being one of the best fishing lakes in the state (see box), the secluded coves, bays and small islands here are home to a variety of **wildlife**, especially waterfowl, readily seen once you get away from the hubbub around City Beach. An especially good exploring option is a Celtic Kayaks tour (ⓣ208/265-0780) – they offer half-day kayak trips with an experienced wildlife biologist from $50 for a half-day.

Fishing Lake Pend Oreille

Lake Pend Oreille is one of the best fishing holes in the Panhandle, a region that in itself is a superb fishing destination with more than 140 lakes and nearly 2000 miles of rivers. The lake is the biggest in the Panhandle – so large that the US Navy has even used it to test submarines. With a depth of up to 1150ft, it's quite natural to expect there to be some large fish swimming around, and this is probably your best chance in northern Idaho to catch a potentially record-breaking fish.

There are rich stocks of both **bull trout** and **kamloops**, although the latter is listed as a threatened species and therefore catch-and-release only. Other common fish include kokanee, rainbow trout, cutthroat trout, mackinaw, crappie, small- and large-mouth bass, and northern pike. The **world record** kamloops (37 pounds) and the state record for the largest bull trout (32 pounds) were caught here, and although it's not a record, a massive 43-pound lake trout was caught here in 1994.

If stuck on land, the shallow bays at the north and northeast end of the lake make for good shore-based fishing, as does the area around the small east shore settlements of Hope and East Hope (see p.652). However, the fishing is best out on the lake, and there are a number of **outfitters** who can help get you there, including Diamond Charters (ⓣ208/264-2583, ⓦwww.diamondcharters.com) on Hwy-200 in Hope, and Seagull Charters in Kootenai (ⓣ208/263-2770). Prices start at around $250 for four people for half a day. For information on **licences and permits**, see p.58 in Basics.

Outdoor activities

Simply put, Sandpoint is the best base in northern Idaho for outdoor sports enthusiasts. **Hikers** should get hold of the *Sandpoint Ranger District Trails* pamphlet, available from **Sandpoint Ranger District Office**, 1500 Hwy-2 (ⓣ208/263-5111). It features twelve of the best hikes in the area, including the moderately strenuous seven-mile **Gold Hill Trail** (Trail 3), which gives great views over the town and lake – the trailhead is at Bottle Bay Road, to the north of Sagle which is just south of Sandpoint off US-95.

Deep in bear country, the western ranges of the **Cabinet Mountains** above the east shore of Lake Pend Oreille hold some great backcountry hiking as well. A good introduction to the peaks here is the hike along Trail 67 to 6755ft **Mount Pend Oreille**, from where there are magnificent views in all directions. To reach the trailhead, drive along Hwy-200 from Sandpoint and turn left onto Trestle Creek Road (Forest Road 275) about two miles north of Hope. You turn left again off onto Forest Road 1091 to the trailhead at Lunch Peak lookout, from where an easily followed trail climbs gradually north for about two miles through forest before opening out onto a grassy domed peak.

Some of the best **mountain biking** in the area can be had on both Gold Hill, within riding distance of town directly east of Long Bridge, and Mineral Point, overlooking the lake a few miles further south and to the east of Garfield Bay. The trails in these two areas can be linked to make longer rides, forming an exhilarating mix of technical single-track, forest roads, stiff climbs, and high-speed descents. The western Cabinets around the Trestle Creek area also offer some great riding for all abilities, but you'll need to drive out. Schweitzer Mountain (see p.651), the place to head for **winter sports**, has several miles of excellent lift-accessed biking as well.

Anglers will invariably want to head to the shores of Lake Pend Oreille or out onto its waters, details of which are given in the box above.

Local outfitters

Alpine Design Bicycles, 312 N 5th Ave ☎1-800/263-9373. Beyond their own line of custom-built mountain bikes, this store has a wide selection of accessories and is a great source for finding the best local trails – and bars. The friendly staff also organizes a weekly Wednesday evening mountain bike ride open to all.

Alpine Shop, 213 Church St ☎208/263-5157. The best stop for backcountry gear in town has been servicing the local outdoor crowd for over 35 years.

Eating, drinking, and entertainment

There's a surprisingly good selection of **bars** and **restaurants** clustered within a few blocks of each other in Sandpoint's downtown area. If you're in town the first two weeks of August, you'll find the area especially busy during the **Festival at Sandpoint** (☎208/265-4552), which features concerts ranging from classical to rock. Past big names include The Pretenders, Tony Bennett, the Robert Cray Band, and Dwight Yoakam. The focal point of the local entertainment scene during the rest of the year is the **Panida Theater**, 300 N 1st Ave (☎208/263-9191), which hosts stage shows, art-house cinema shows, and concerts.

Restaurants

Bangkok Cuisine 202 N 2nd Ave ☎208/265-4149. Good-value Thai food in an easy-going environment; lunchtime specials start at $5.

Floating Restaurant Hwy-200, East Hope ☎208/264-5311. Based beside the marina at East Hope, the bobbing boats and lakeside views make this one of the most atmospheric restaurants in the area. The food is very good and seafood is unsurprisingly the specialty – try the mouth-watering local salmon. An entree will set you back $15–20, and there's a fine range of microbrews to enjoy while watching the sun set over the lake.

The Hydra 115 Lake St ☎208/263-7123. A friendly, reasonably-priced restaurant with very good prime ribs. Vegetarians will appreciate the huge salad bar, and there's a good selection of wines and microbrews. The subdued lighting and woodland-inspired decor makes for a relaxing atmosphere.

Ivano's 124 S 2nd Ave ☎208/263-0211. A fine Italian restaurant with a good selection of traditional dishes from $10–20. There's a great outside deck in summer. Closed Sundays.

Jalapeno's Mexican Restaurant 314 N 2nd Ave ☎208/263-2995. Housed in an historic brick building, *Jalapeno's* has an eclectic interior self-described as "Northwest by Key West." The meals are large and are especially enjoyable taken on the shady outside deck.

Monarch Mountain Coffee Shop 208 N 4th Ave ☎1-800/599-6702. As a favored haunt of local outdoor types, this is a good place to get information on trails and such, along with a great variety of beverages, from fresh-roasted coffee to tea, chai, and even Argentinian *mate*. The breakfast burritos are a fine way to start the day, and they also serve tasty baked goods. Closed Sundays.

Panhandler Pies 120 S 1st Ave ☎208/263-2912. Famed for its fine home-baked pies, with a selection of over twenty just for dessert. Filling breakfasts cost around $5, and lunch and dinner twice that. Open Mon to Sat from 6am, Sun from 6.30am.

Power House Bar and Grill 120 E Lake St ☎208/265-2449. Located in the town's original powerhouse just north of Long Bridge, with great views across the lake and town and up to Schweitzer Mountain. The atmosphere is casual and prices are reasonable – the burgers in particular are good, as are the weekend breakfast specials.

Second Avenue Pizza 215 S 2nd Ave ☎208/263-9321. Popular with locals for well-priced pizzas – a large will set you back around $12 – and a comprehensive selection of microbrews. If you're really hungry go for the "Juke Box Special," which weighs a massive seven pounds and contains pretty much every ingredient you can think of. The calzones are also recommended.

Bars

Eichardts 212 Cedar St ☎208/263-4005. A lively, friendly bar with a dozen microbrews to choose from. They also serve good bar food which won't set you back more than $10, and there's an upstairs games room with pool table, board games, and darts. Local rock bands perform on weekends.

Kamloop's Bar and Grill 302 N 1st Ave ⓣ208/263-6715. A busy bar popular with Sandpoint's younger residents. The decor is pretty uninspired and the welcome can vary from curious to indifferent, but it can be worth checking out for the regular live music sessions.

Pend Oreille Brewing Co. 220 Cedar St ⓣ208/263-7837. The beer is brewed on the premises and you're encouraged to try something new each round by the friendly bar staff – the Scottish ale is tops. The atmosphere and decor is loosely that of an English pub, and there's a good bar menu. In summer there's a pleasant beer garden where you can bask in the sun with your beer.

Schweitzer Mountain Resort

Looking down on Sandpoint from the rugged Selkirk Mountains to the northeast, **SCHWEITZER MOUNTAIN RESORT** is northern Idaho's best ski and summer resort (ⓣ208/263-9555, snow report ⓣ263-9562, ⓦwww.schweitzer.com). Once a small and quaint hideaway, this ever-expanding resort is now one of Idaho's largest, dominated by two impressive bowls that feature sensational views and fantastic runs.

The small, European-style base village sits 2400ft below the highest point on **Schweitzer Bowl** (6389ft). On the other side of this bowl is **Outback Bowl**, where the skiing tends to be a little quieter, although it's rare to find lift lines on either side. Both bowls have a mix of open slopes and glade skiing, served by six lifts in total. There are nearly sixty trails and a terrain park amongst the mountain's 2500 total acres. Beginners should head for Happy Trails and the Enchanted Forest which drop off below the village, and for intermediates The Great Divide and Loophole offer superb views over the lake. Advanced skiers have heaps to go at, including Schweitzer Bowl's challenging bumps beneath Great Escape, while in the Outback Bowl exciting double-blacks like Misfortune and Whiplash can be accessed from Great Divide.

Lift tickets are $37 per day and $10 for **night skiing** on Fridays and Saturdays. Ski and board rental is available in the village, while ski lessons including lift ticket, ski and boot rental cost $49. Other winter activities include **cross-country skiing** on eighteen miles of groomed trails (passes are $8) and **sleigh rides** with Mountain Horse Adventures (ⓣ1-800/831-8810).

In **summer**, the Great Escape Quad ($8) gives access to some intense **mountain biking** on marked trails. Guided **horseback rides** are another popular way of discovering the trails on and around Schweitzer Mountain, and one of the best established operators is Mountain Horse Adventures (see above) who rent out horses from $45 for two hours.

Practicalities

It's a twenty-minute drive from Sandpoint to Schweitzer – take US-2/95 north out of town and follow the signs. There's a park-and-ride scheme from a large parking lot at the base of the mountain, some four miles from Sandpoint. Though it's cheaper to stay in Sandpoint, there are a couple of very good **accommodation** options at the base. The **Selkirk Lodge** (ⓣ208/265-0257 or 1-800/831-8810; ❼) is a snug alpine-style building with tastefully appointed rooms, three hot tubs, a heated outdoor pool, and a fitness room. Good-value ski-and stay deals are on offer and in summer prices fall significantly. At the time of writing, the **White Pine Lodge** (ⓣ208/255-5483), a large development including new restaurants and retail outlets, was also being built.

There's a reasonable selection of **bars** and **restaurants** in the village, all within seconds of each other. The *Chimney Rock Grill* (ⓣ203/263-9555 ext 2284) in the *Selkirk Lodge* does good bar food in a lively atmosphere and also serves breakfast from 7am. On the mountain, the rustic *Outback Restaurant* serves snacks, lunch, and drinks in a pleasant spot at the base of Outback Bowl.

Southeast to Montana on Hwy-200

East of Sandpoint, Hwy-200 is known as the **Pend Oreille Scenic Byway** as it skirts the east shore of the lake for a 34-mile run to the Montana border. The scenery along the highway is breathtaking, with views west across the glassy lake to near-vertical crags plummeting down into the water, above which the crests of forest-bedecked hills roll blue-tinged to the horizon. Just under half way to the border are the tiny settlements of **Hope** and **East Hope**, sitting almost side by side on the lake's northeast shore. The area is important historically since it was here in 1809 that British explorer **David Thompson** (see box, below) built the first trading post in Idaho. In spots, the landscape has changed little since Thompson first wandered through, and it's worth spending a day wandering about as well. In Hope, the *Pend Oreille Shores Resort* (ⓣ208/264-5828; ❻) has airy and comfortable condo accommodation alongside a marina and the resort's renowned floating restaurant (see p.650). Down the road past East Hope is the more laid-back *Beyond Hope Resort,* 1267 Peninsula Rd (ⓣ208/264-5251 or 1-877/270-4673), where 85 pleasant grassy campsites ($25) sit on a small peninsula within the David Thompson Game Preserve. There's a huge range of facilities, including hot showers, snack bar, cocktail lounge, laundry facilities, and a boat launch.

A further ten miles south on the scenic byway, and last stop before the Montana border, is **Clark Fork**. Essentially a couple of bars and a gas station set in a stunning location in the foothills of the Cabinet Mountains, you'll find remote, top-quality hiking, mountain biking, and horseback riding hereabouts. A popular route for experienced hikers is the steep and rocky Trail 65 to the top of 7009ft **Scotchman Peak**, from where there are fantastic views into Montana. The ten-mile round-trip includes 3500ft of ascent, part of which involves a dizzying exposed ridge scramble, and shouldn't be undertaken lightly. The trailhead is signposted from the road past the University of Idaho Field Campus, just to the east of Clark Fork on Forest Road 276.

From Clark Fork it's a brief but beautiful drive through dense, verdant forest to the Montana border and on to Thompson Falls (see p.558) passing the Cabinet Gorge Dam – not that pretty in itself, but worth a stop to see the waters pounding through the narrow gorge.

The unsung explorer

Although American history is rich with tales of rugged explorers charting new lands and befriending the native populations, few were as successful or went as unrecognized as **David Thompson** (1770–1857). Born in Wales in 1770 and educated in London, Thompson became an apprentice with Britain's Hudson's Bay Company in Canada, where he quickly picked up the twin skills of map making and working with Native Americans. Between 1797 and 1812, the explorer worked for Britain's North West Company, during which time he crossed the Rocky Mountains, mapped out the whole length of the Columbia River and completed more important maps of western Canada. He also explored large tracts of northern Idaho, arriving here in 1808 and constructing the first permanent structure to be built by whites in Idaho. In a shrewd diplomatic move, he named the post **Kullyspell House** after the local Native American tribe with whom he traded and became friendly with. Thompson remained here until 1813, sending huge numbers of beaver pelts back to London. Amazingly, despite being a daring pioneer in a remote and unknown land, Thompson is hardly known to the American public today. Perhaps this is due to the understated success of his explorations, or more so due to the fact that Thompson chose to live in the places he discovered rather than return to "civilization" to enjoy the plaudits he richly deserved.

North towards Canada

From Sandpoint there are two roads north towards the Canadian border – US-95 through **Bonners Ferry**, and the more convoluted route west of Sandpoint on US-2 to Hwy-57, which runs north past **Priest Lake**. The latter doesn't actually make it as far as Canada, petering out into an unpaved road just past the small settlement of **Nordman**, where it forks left to cross the mountains to the town of **Metaline Falls** in Washington State (accessible in summer only).

US-95 to Canada

US-95 north from Sandpoint is often busy with logging trucks, but the peaks of the Selkirk and Cabinet mountains, which hem you in on both sides, will take your mind off things if you get stuck behind one (and you will). Nearly thirty miles north, in the small and woodsy settlement of **Naples**, stands one of the few **hostels** in Idaho. Facilities at the *Naples AYH*, Old Hwy-2 at Hwy-95 (☎208/267-2947 or 267-4118), which charges $10 per person, include a cozy common room with a woodstove and laundry, and there's an old-fashioned general store next door. Despite the great location in the heart of the woods it can be noisy as freight trains pass right beside it. A few miles on is **BONNERS FERRY**, an old logging town set beside the lazy waters of the Kootenai River. The town gained some infamy for a tragic 1992 shootout between the FBI and local resident Randy Weaver in nearby Ruby Ridge, in which Weaver's wife and son were killed (Weaver was a suspected right-wing militia member), but there's nothing particularly compelling about a visit here. Main Street has a reasonably pleasant mix of Western-style buildings, but he real draw is the wealth of nearby rafting, fishing, and hiking options. Both the town's **visitor center**, 7198 US-95 just south of the US-2 junction (daily 9am–5pm summer; reduced hours in winter; ☎208/267-5922), and the local **USFS Kaniksu ranger station**, south of town on US-95 (daily 9am–5pm; ☎208/267-5561), have information on these attractions. Easy hiking trails cut through the nearby **Kootenai National Wildlife Refuge** (☎1-800/267-3888; free; daylight hours only), five miles west of Bonners Ferry. Although primarily a habitat for waterfowl, you may also see moose, elk, and black bear ambling about.

If **staying on**, *Bonners Ferry Log Inn*, two miles north of town on US-95 (☎208/267-3986; ❹), has comfortable rooms, hot tub, and pleasant landscaped grounds. A more adventurous option is a **lookout ranger station**. The US Forestry Service (☎208/267-5561) rents out three very basic stations – bunk beds, gas lighting, wooden stoves, and not always with running water – in the area for $20–25 per night. The best **campgrounds** are in the Twin Rivers Canyon Resort (☎208/267-5932; $13 tent, $21 hookup), located on an impressive setting just east of nearby Moyie Springs at the confluence of the Moyie and Kootenai Rivers.

If heading east from here on Hwy-2 towards Montana, you'll drive over the soaring Moyie Bridge, just outside of **Moyie Springs**. The 450ft-high bridge passes by some impressive waterfalls, and there's a turnoff that allows you to see – albeit not that clearly – the 100ft and 40ft double-drops and the Moyie Dam above. Drivers heading north towards **Canada** will pass through yet more dense forests above which tower the Purcell Mountains, a rugged sub-7000ft range. If heading into Canada, you have a choice of two crossing points; **Eastport** (☎208/267-3966) on US-95 which is open 24 hours, **Porthill** (☎208/267-5309) on Hwy-1 which is only open 7am–11pm.

Priest Lake and around

To reach the majestic mountain landscapes around Priest Lake from Sandpoint, take Hwy-2 ten miles west along the **Pend Oreille River** to the drab logging town of **Priest River**. Look out for the **ospreys** nesting on top of telegraph poles beside the road along the way. From here, Hwy-57 cuts through dense forests 25 miles to the pine-scented Priest Lake area, where the lake's cobalt blue water is rung with over seventy miles of pristine shorelines dotted with small golden-sand beaches. The lake itself harbors seven wooded islands, and it's all shadowed by the spiky granite ridges and peaks of the 7000ft **Selkirk Mountains**, from where the imposing vertical column of **Chimney Rock** (see box, opposite) looks down.

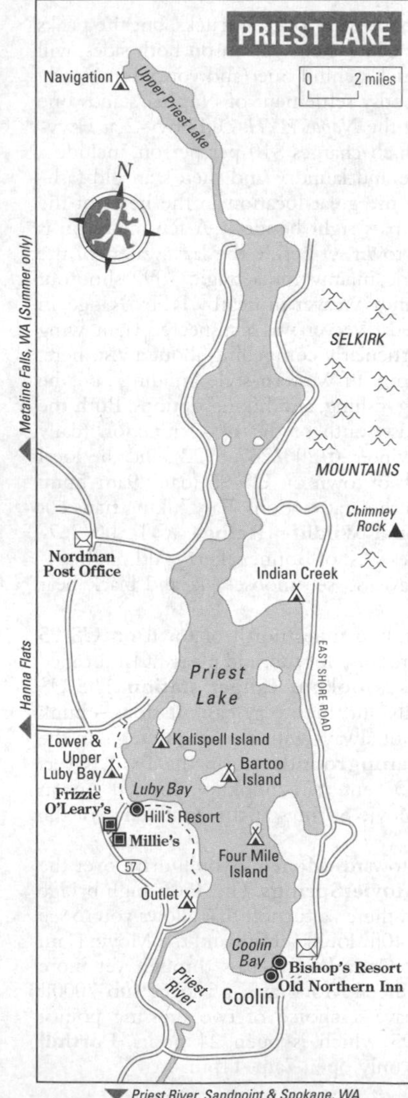

It's not always as quiet as you may like on the lake, though, as a number of popular family-style resorts close to the water's edge have motorized watercraft buzzing about on the lake. Nearly perfect solitude is nearly always available, though, at the much smaller **Upper Priest Lake**, connected to its big brother by a 2.5-mile-long river channel known as the "Thorofare." As a federally designated Scenic Area, motorized vessels are thankfully not allowed on the smaller lake.

One thing that the whole area does have in common, though, is wildlife. A haven for big game, grizzlies, gray wolves, wolverines, moose, and the rare woodland caribou can all live hereabouts. And, if you're looking to spot **black bears**, there's as good a chance here as anywhere else in Idaho – they thrive on the area's tasty huckleberries, so be aware when out picking your evening's dessert.

Outdoor activities

Many of the **hiking** and **biking** trails in the Selkirk Mountains here are poorly marked and mapped, rugged and remote, so don't venture out alone and be prepared for any contingency. A good place to get advice and maps is the Priest Lake Ranger District Office, about four miles south of

Climbing Chimney Rock

Question any experienced climber hanging around northern Idaho and chances are they're day-dreaming about **Chimney Rock** (7124ft), a craggy column rising proudly out of the Selkirk Crest's daunting skyline off the east shore of Priest Lake. First successfully scaled in 1934, the "rock" provides the region's best climbing challenge; the ascent consists of reassuringly solid rock, vertical cracks with good natural protection, and corners of impeccable granite.

The main route up its west face takes in 350ft of clean stemming corners, and is easily protected with a standard rack of cams and nuts. The climb is exposed and exhilarating, and feels harder than its 5.3 rating. Chimney Rock's east face is 100 feet higher and overhangs fifteen feet at the top. Pioneered in 1972, the classic route here is the Cooper Hiser, with a challenging 5.8+ crux on each of the three pitches. If you want to turn up the heat even more, climb Free Friends, a hard four-pitch 5.10 that'll test your full range of crack climbing skills. The 360-degree view from the summit is spectacular – on a clear day you can see Canada, Montana, and Washington.

Give yourself a full day if taking at crack at Chimney Rock. It's a two-hour hike from the **Horton Ridge Trailhead** on the east shore of Priest Lake to the base and then give yourself four–five hours to complete the most popular routes.

Nordman on the east side of Hwy-57. One easy-to-follow trail for both hikers and mountain bikers is the twelve-mile round-trip along Navigation Trail (#291) from Beaver Creek at the north end of Priest Lake. This delightful trail passes alongside the Thorofare, traveling through a forest landscape that varies from almost impenetrable to open, airy glades, and up the west shore of Upper Priest Lake to a backcountry campground. For something more challenging, head to the east shore of the lake and the many trails leading up to the Selkirk Crest – a particularly good access road is **Horton Ridge Road** off East Shore Road, from where there are trails up to Chimney Rock (see box, above) and the triangular summit of Mount Roothaan (7326ft).

As one would expect, the **fishing** – particularly for trout, kokanee, and mackinaw – is excellent. Recommended shoreline fishing spots include the end of Pinto Point on the northeast shore of Priest Lake and the stretch of shoreline off East Shore Road. Priest Lake Outdoor Adventures in Nordman (Ⓣ208/443-5601) rents boats and gear and can also provide a guide. Most of the resorts around the lake rent motorized or non-motorized **water craft** as well; standard rates are around $65 an hour for motor boats, jet skis $45, fishing boats $45, and rowboats $7. Upper Priest Lake is the place for quiet, secluded **canoeing** or **kayaking**.

Things quiet down somewhat in **winter**, when you'll find some excellent groomed **cross-country ski trails** around Indian Creek on Priest Lake's east shore, or Hanna Flats Cedar Grove to the west of Hwy-57 – although the silence is likely to be broken at times by the whine of **snowmobiles**.

Practicalities

Information is available from both the Priest Lake Chamber of Commerce in Coolin on the lake's southern end (daily 9am–5pm; Ⓣ208/443-2200, Ⓦwww.priestlake.org) and at the small Priest Lake Museum and Visitor Center at Luby Bay (daily Memorial Day–Labor Day 10am–4pm; free; Ⓣ208/443-2676).

One of the finest **accommodation** options around the lake is *Hill's Resort* (Ⓣ208/443-2551, Ⓕ443-2363, Ⓦwww.hillsresort.com; ⑥), in Luby Bay on the west shore. They have well-appointed lakeside cabins, condos, chalets, and duplex units featuring fireplaces and rustic decor, helpful staff, a superb restaurant (see below) and access to all lake activities. On the east shore, *Bishop's Resort*, around Coolin (☎208/443-2469; ④), is a good-value base with clean, motel-style rooms, a marina, and a popular restaurant. Of the few **B&Bs** here, the *Old Northern Inn*, PO Box 177, Coolin (☎208/443-2426; ⑤), is one of the best. Housed in a splendid, rustic former hotel, it has elegant, antique-furnished rooms overlooking the lake and a private dock and beach.

The **USFS** has a large number of basic **campgrounds** around the lake (call ☎208/443-2512 for full details). Amongst these are *Outlet* ($8) on the southwest end of Priest Lake, which has a small swimming beach, *Lower Luby Bay* on the west shore and *Upper Luby Bay* across the road in the forest ($10 each), and *Navigation* (free) at the secluded upper end of Upper Priest Lake.

Most of the area's **restaurants** are based within resorts around the lake. Best is the eatery at *Hill's Resort,* featuring fine American and international cuisine though the huckleberry desserts are most memorable. Outside of the resorts, *Frizzie O'Leary's*, corner of Hwy-57 and Luby Bay Road (☎208/443-3043), is a popular and inexpensive spot with good clams and prime rib. When it comes to **supplies**, it's worth noting that while basics can be found in Nordman and Coolin, you'll save money and have greater options if you stock up fully before traveling into this region.

East on I-90 to the Silver Valley, Wallace, and Montana

Travelling east from Coeur d'Alene, I-90 climbs over the Fourth of July Pass (see p.643) and down into the **SILVER VALLEY**, some forty minutes drive away. Once the world's richest mining region and famed for the silver discovered here in the 1880s, the valley still bears some of the scars of decades of digging into the earth. A serious decline in the mining industry in recent years has resulted in both a clean up and a modicum of economic reversal through tourism, particularly at the old mining town of **Wallace** and at **Silver Mountain Resort**. As you continue east towards Montana, up over **Lookout Pass** (4725ft) and the superb **Trail of the Hiawatha** mountain-bike route, the landscape soon reverts back to magnificent high mountains and forests.

Cataldo, Kellogg, and Silver Mountain

Cataldo, twenty miles east of Coeur d'Alene, is worth a stop to look in at Idaho's oldest building, **The Mission of the Sacred Heart** (daily: June–Aug 8am–6pm; 9am–5pm rest of the year; ☎208/862-3814; $3). The striking Greek Revival-style structure, now part of a state park, was built in 1853 by a Jesuit priest named Father Antonio Ravalli, and bearing in mind the remoteness of the region at that time it's an impressive example of one man's faith. The interior is lovely as well, and includes carved wooden statues of the Virgin Mary and St John, skilfully painted to resemble marble.

Some fifteen miles further east along I-90 is **Kellogg**, a former mining town whose main draw is the Silver Mountain resort (see opposite) three miles above town and reached via a gondola from the center. Besides gawking at a 3D silver-mine model in the **Shoshone County Mining and Smelting Museum**, 820 McKinley Ave (June–Aug daily 10am–5pm; ☎208/786-4141;

The lost mine

In 1879, a gold prospector by the name of **Tom Irwin** discovered an impressive gold-bearing vein near Montgomery Gulch, just east of present day Kellogg. Yielding as much as seventy ounces of gold per ton, Irwin worked it for three years before leaving for parts unknown. In a sure sign that he intended to return, Irwin blasted the entrance, sealing off his mining equipment inside. Mysteriously, he never did make it back, and the mine remained unexplored for nearly 120 years. In the 1960s, a road crew drilling for the new I-90 freeway came across the site, but didn't investigate for safety reasons. In 1991, the owner of the land got as far as uncovering the entrance, but he also didn't explore any further. It wasn't until 1996, after the site changed hands, that the current owner, a retired miner, explored the mineshaft and discovered Irwin's mining equipment along with nuggets of gold and native wire silver plainly visible in the walls.

Although it's estimated that the ore in the mine could be worth around $20,000 per ton, the owner of the land decided not to start mining again but instead opened the site as a remarkable tourist attraction. Guided tours of the **Crystal Gold Mine**, 51931 Silver Valley Rd (daily: April–Oct 10am–4pm; until 6pm June–Aug; $10; ⓣ208/783-GOLD, ⓦwww.goldmine-idaho.com), pass the picks, shovels, and trucks that the Victorian miners used, which are still scattered about, while the multicolored mineral Smithsonite and, best of all, real gold and silver still shimmer from the walls. The tour gives a real feel for the sheer hard work and misery that must have been part and parcel of Victorian gold mining. Note that it's a constant 48°F, so take a sweater or fleece to wear during the thirty minute tour. To reach the mine, follow the signs east on I-90 out of Kellogg.

free), there's little else to do here but eat and sleep after spending the day up in the hills.

If **staying on**, the *Super 8 Motel*, 601 Bunker Ave (ⓣ208/783-1234 or 1-800/785-5443; ❸), has spacious rooms, free continental breakfast, a pool, and a great location beside the Silver Mountain gondola. A little more upmarket is the *Silver Ridge Mountain Lodge*, 950 W Cameron Ave (ⓣ208/783-1000 or 1-800/979-1991; ❹), which has pleasant if rather out-of-context Bavarian-style condo units to go along with free continental breakfast and a hot tub. Campers should head for the *Kellogg/Silver Valley KOA Campground*, 801 Division St (ⓣ1-800/562-0799; $20), which has a pool and laundry.

The best **eating** option around these parts is the *Enaville Resort* (ⓣ208/682-3453), a few miles west of town on I-90 (head north off exit 43). A former gold rush bar, railroad way station, whorehouse, and boarding house, much of the restaurant's chequered history is displayed in photographs on the walls, and the locals tend to be loud, fun, and very welcoming. A delicious meal of a buffalo burger with fries, or Rocky Mountain oysters can be had for around $10. In town, *Zany's Restaurant & Bar* (ⓣ208/783-1111) at the gondola's base is good for bar meals, microbrews, and live music at weekends.

Silver Mountain

Of all the mountain resorts in the Rockies, **Silver Mountain** (ⓣ208/783-1111 or 1-800/204-6428, snow report ⓣ1-800/204-6428, ⓦwww.silvermt.com) has probably the most peculiar approach. Instead of driving to the base, resort goers head up on the **world's longest single-stage gondola** from Kellogg, which transports you over three miles and 3400ft up to the Mountain Hause (5700ft), floating directly over the remnants of the area's past mining operations en route. It's not an especially scenic way to start a day, but the ragged landscape is soon left behind as you ascend the steep, forested slopes and it's worth the ride just to enjoy a panorama that features three states (Washington, Idaho, and Montana) and Canada.

From the gondola, a series of five **chairlifts** give riders access to over fifty runs in winter, spread over 1500 acres of rarely crowded terrain. There's a solid 2200ft of **vertical drop**, and the terrain is broken up as fifteen percent beginner, 45 percent intermediate, and the remaining forty percent advanced. Beginners will enjoy Claim Jumper, which has good views of the Silver Valley, while intermediate skiers and boarders will have a field day on runs like the open Silver Belt and Sunrise and the more challenging black-to-blue Steep and Deep. From the easy open glades and powder of South of the Border to the fun steeps of The Meadows, a nice open area that can be traversed for some good tree skiing, the advanced skiing is also great fun. Experts can also climb to the top of **Wardner Peak** (6200ft) for some backcountry action, or in good snow conditions ski down the gondola line to Elizabeth Park at Wardner, from where you'll need a car shuttle to get you the mile or so back to Kellogg. A good terrain park should satisfy all freestyle riders as well. **Lift tickets** are $31 adults ($24 half-day), $22 juniors ($22) and free for under sixes. The ski area is open daily 9am–4pm and for night skiing every Friday during January and February.

In **summer**, the gondola operates Friday to Sunday ($10) and accesses **hiking** and **biking** ($11 day-pass) trails on Kellogg and Wardner peaks – if you like steep downhills you'll enjoy the bike trails as they're more straight down than switchbacked.

Wallace and around

Traveling east from Kellogg on I-90, the Silver Valley constricts, tightening almost into a canyon at the town of **WALLACE** nine miles along. Picturesquely tucked into these narrow confines, the entire place is listed on the US National Register of Historic Places, yet is still a vibrant and lively community that sees its future in tourism but hasn't sold out completely to the tourist dollar.

At the town's core are several blocks of finely preserved buildings, including **Fonk's General Store**, 518 Cedar St, a classic "five and dime" straight from an old black-and-white movie, and the elegant redbrick, chateau-style train depot at 6th and Pine Street built in 1902. The depot now holds the **Northern Pacific Depot Railroad Museum** (daily: June–Aug 9am–7pm; rest of year 10am–3pm; $2), containing a fascinating collection of photographs from the town's early days as a rip-roaring mining town, and an impressive 13ft illuminated glass map of the Northern Pacific route. The most intriguing museum in the area, however, focuses on Wallace's more unsavory history. The **Oasis Rooms Bordello Museum**, 605 Cedar St (ⓣ208/753-0801; May–Oct daily 10am–5pm; Nov–Dec Wed–Sun noon–4.30pm; $5), is a bordello frozen in time. This isn't old Wild West history, though, as the Oasis was shuttered not in 1887, but 1987 following a long stakeout by the law. The rooms have been left as they were when the lingerie-clad residents and their clients made their hasty exits, with 1980s clothes, underwear, books, and magazines strewn about, and even the girl's perfumes and personal mementoes still sitting on the dressing tables. It's a fascinating and by turns amusing and despondent glimpse of the life of the girls who worked here.

A final attraction near town worth checking out is the **Sierra Silver Mine Tour**, which departs from 420 5th St (daily every half-hour May–Oct

9am–4pm, June & July until 6pm; $7.50; ⓣ208/752-5151). An old trolleybus takes you on a narrated tour through the downtown area before heading out on a short ride out to the mine. Once there, you get a rather laconic guided underground tour by a former miner, and are shown how various noisy and potentially lethal pieces of mining equipment operate. It's a revealing exhibition of what life was and largely still is like in the dark, dank, and potentially dangerous world of silver mining.

Lookout Pass

East from Wallace, I-90 climbs up the Bitterroot Range to the Montana border and Lookout Pass (4725ft). Here, straddling the border at exit 0, proudly stands the local favorite and Idaho's second-oldest ski area, **Lookout Pass** (Thurs–Sun 9am–4pm; daily over Christmas–New Year; ⓣ208/744-1301, ⓦwww.skilookout.com). This is low-key skiing at its best, with only one double chair and one tow rope giving access to sixteen runs and two terrain parks over 160 acres of total terrain, with a modest 850ft of vertical drop. However, there's nothing low-key about the average yearly snowfall, which runs close to 400 inches, nor the fabulous views back over Idaho and into Montana. One of the most popular attractions is the free ski school, the cost hinting at the feel-good local atmosphere present here. **Lift tickets** are around $20, and gear can be rented at the mountain, and there are also fifteen miles of groomed **cross-country ski trails** here (ⓣ208/752-1221). In summer the main draw is the **Trail of the Hiawatha** mountain-bike route, passes for which are sold here (see box, overleaf).

Practicalities

Wallace's **Chamber of Commerce**, just off I-90's exit 61 (daily 9am–5pm; ⓣ208/753-7571, ⓦwww.wallace-id.com), is worth popping in for the free guide to the historic center that includes a detailed walking tour. The local **USFS office** (Mon–Fri 8am–5pm; ⓣ208/752-1221) is on Yellowstone Avenue in the small community of Silverton, to the northeast of town.

Accommodation

Beale House 107 Cedar St ⓣ208/752-7151 or 1-888/752-7151). One of the best B&Bs in the area, *Beale House* has five cozy Victorian-style rooms (four with shared bath), a welcoming fire, and a hot tub; the collection of black-and-white photographs recording the house's history is well worth flipping through. ❺

Best Western Wallace Inn 100 Front St ⓣ208/752-1252 or 1-800/6431-386. Located on the outskirts of town, this chain hotel has large rooms with king-size beds, a pool and hot tub, fitness rooms, and a restaurant that serves up particularly good breakfasts. They also offer a shuttle service to both Lookout Pass and the Trail of the Hiawatha, along with Silver Mountain ski packages. ❺

Brooks Hotel 500 Cedar St ⓣ208/556-1471. A popular and well-established old hotel downtown with very fairly priced, quite sumptuous rooms and an attractive garden restaurant and lounge. ❹

The Jameson Hotel 304 6th St (ⓣ208/556-1554. An attractively restored 1900 hotel where the rooms have vintage furnishings and a supposedly friendly female ghost. ❹

Ryan Hotel 608 Cedar St ⓣ208/753-6001. An historic hotel with a flamboyant built from multi-colored bricks, the *Ryan Hotel* was remodeled in the 1980s to its original 1895 style, with cozy rooms reflecting this in the decor. Cheaper rooms have shared baths, more expensive rooms feature kitchenettes, and all come with cable TV and free coffee, juice, and fresh fruit. ❷

Eating, drinking, and entertainment

Wallace's compact downtown has a good range of **restaurants** and an evening stroll alongside the lovely old buildings is a nice way of working up an appetite before you eat. The main entertainment option in town is the **Sixth St Melodrama**, 212 6th St (ⓣ208/752-8871), where you can see deliberately hammed-up productions from the first weekend in July to Labor Day, and more serious musicals in winter.

Albi's Steak House 220 6th St ⓣ208/753-3071. A busy and popular spot serving some of the best steaks in Wallace for around $15. Weekends typically feature a tasty prime rib special.

The Jameson Hotel (see overleaf). A good bet for lunch or dinner surrounded by vintage furnishing and decor in both the dining room and the hotel's Old West-style saloon – a burger or steak dinner costs $10–15.

Metals Bar 514 Cedar St ⓣ208/752-5213. If you want a beer in no-frills surroundings and a chance to meet locals rather than tourists, *Metals Bar* is a good spot to head for.

The Pizza Factory 612 Bank St ⓣ208/753-9003. A variety of excellent and reasonably priced hand-tossed pizzas, served alongside a decent array of microbrews.

Riding the Route of the Hiawatha Trail

As senseless as it sounds, the **Route of the Hiawatha Trail**, a trail with no real ups or downs to speak of, is one of the Rockie's most memorable mountain-biking routes. Beginning a few miles south of Lookout Pass, close to the Idaho–Montana border, this 27.5-mile gravel track follows the old Chicago, Milwaukee and St. Paul Railroad route east–west across the wild and forested Bitterroot Mountains. Suitable for anyone who can ride a mountain bike, the trail, named after a passenger train that ran the line stretching between Chicago and the Pacific coast, follows a gentle downhill two-percent gradient. If you don't want to ride back up, there's even a shuttle service that brings riders back to the start. Once upon the trail, it's hard to imagine the toil that must have gone into constructing the most expensive railroad ever built in the US – the section through the Bitteroots to the Pacific alone cost $260 million by the time it was completed in 1911. Throughout the ride, there are absolutely spectacular views of the mountains, forests, and creeks, most exhilarating from the seven airy wooden **trestle bridges**, crossed en route, some of which are over two hundred feet high. Riders also pass through nine **tunnels**, the longest and darkest of which is the nearly two-mile-long Taft Tunnel. Along much of the route, there's also a good chance of spotting elk, deer, and moose.

There are various **trailheads** where you can access the trail – call in at the Lookout Pass headquarters (see overleaf). The trail is open from late May to early October and **trail fees** are $7 adults, $3 children (3–13), payable at Lookout Pass. A shuttle service ($9 adults, $6 children), running daily 11am–5pm with extended services weekends and holidays, will take you from Lookout Pass Ski Area to the trailheads and collect you from the finish. You can also hire bikes ($22, $26 with front suspension, $16 children's bikes and trailers), compulsory helmets ($6), and lights ($3), which you'll need for the tunnels, at Lookout Pass.

Travel details

Trains

Sandpoint to: Chicago (1 daily; 35hr); East Glacier Park (1 daily; 3hr 30min); Seattle (1 daily; 11hr); Spokane (1 daily; 2hr); West Glacier (1 daily; 3hr); Whitefish (1 daily; 2hr 30min).

Buses

Boise to: Coeur d'Alene (2 daily; 11–14hr); Idaho Falls (2 daily; 12–13hr); Lewiston (1 daily; 17hr); McCall (1 daily; 2hr 30min); Moscow (1 daily; 6hr); Pocatello (2 daily; 10–12hr); Sun Valley (4 daily, 6 weekends; 3hr); Twin Falls (3 daily; 2–3hr; Greyhound).

Coeur d'Alene to: Boise (2 daily; 11–14hr); Missoula (3 daily; 4hr); Sandpoint (4 daily; 1hr);

Spokane (3 daily; 45min).

Idaho Falls to: Boise (2 daily; 15–16hr); Bozeman (2 daily; 6hr); Missoula (2 daily; 6–7hr); Pocatello (2 daily; 1hr); Salmon (1 daily Thu & Fri; 4hr 30min); Salt Lake City (2 daily; 5–6hr).

Pocatello to: Boise (2 daily, 14–15hr); Bozeman (2 daily, 7hr); Idaho Falls (2 daily; 1hr); Missoula (2 daily; 7–9hr).

Salmon to: Idaho Falls (1 daily Tue & Fri; 4hr 30min); Missoula (1 daily Tue, Wed, Fri; 3hr 30min).

contexts

contexts

A brief history

As much as anywhere in the US, the Rocky Mountains are shrouded in the mythology of the American West that is still held dear by the national psyche. Fabled characters from dime novels, tough Mountain Men, hardworking cowboys, savage Indians, grizzled miners, and conniving, fleet-footed outlaws . . . all play into the romanticized image of the Rocky Mountains as a place for the free-spirited – and also pepper the real history of the place.

Native civilizations

The earliest traces of **human presence** in the Rocky Mountains suggest some parts of the region were inhabited as early as 8000 BC, by a primitive society made up of the descendants of those who had migrated from Siberia to Alaska across the Bering Strait around 12,000 BC. Evidence of these nomadic cultures has been pieced together from various archeological finds, including piles of bones from slaughtered mammoths and primitive quartzite quarries in Wyoming. Additionally, records of ancient societies are supplemented by **petroglyphs** (rock etchings) and **pictographs** (rock paintings), scattered in pockets of former settlement throughout the region – though most are estimated to be no older than about 2000 BC.

But the first real civilization to grace the Rockies moved into the southern foothills around 500 AD. Known as the **Basketmaker Culture**, this people were part of a society located in today's southwestern states where their descendants, the Pueblo tribes still live. These **Ancestral Puebloans** occupied the southwest corner of Colorado in a society of increasing sophistication. This culminated in the building of the remarkable stone cities in the **Mesa Verde** area (see p.161), which include some spectacular cliffside dwellings, serviced by advanced water-storage and irrigation systems. After around eight hundred years of habitation in the region, the Ancestral Puebloans seem to have moved away quite suddenly. Quite why this happened is one of the most enduring questions in American archeology; one possibility posits a period of drought in the fourteenth century that made farming in the area impossible.

Much less is known about the early history of the rest of the Rocky Mountain region. By the time of the first European contact, the profusion of native tribes here were broadly divided into two main groups: those of **Shoshonean** and those of **Algonquin** linguistic stock. The former, which included the **Ute** in Colorado, the **Shoshone** of Wyoming and the **Nez Percé** in Idaho, peopled the western slopes of the Rockies and most of the mountainous terrain. Algonquins tended to roam mainly on eastern plains – tribes including the **Apache**, **Comanche**, **Kiowa**, **Cheyenne**, **Arapaho**, **Crow**, **Blackfoot**, and **Sioux**. The number of people living in the mountains themselves was, however, tiny by today's standards.

With so much space to roam, it's not surprising that relations between tribes were punctuated by friction only occasionally. The harmonious balance seems to have been upset by the **first contact with Europeans**, which occurred south of the Rockies, between the Pueblo tribes and the Spanish. In a revolt against the Spanish colonizers in New Mexico in 1680, the Pueblo, along with the Navajo and Apache, who clubbed together to drive the Spanish out, suddenly found themselves in possession of a large number of **horses**. Within fifty years virtually every Rocky Mountain tribe had traded or stolen enough horses to build up a decent herd. Contact with Europeans also led to the spread of **firearms**. These leaked into the many tribes in the northern Rockies during the **Seven Years War** (1756–63), during which both French and British colonial powers courted the support of different tribes. But it was through the trade with trappers that the major influx of guns into Native American cultures came, when animal pelts could be swapped for guns, which were to become a major influence on Native American ways.

Access to horses and guns increased the level of contact between tribes in the Rocky Mountain region, heralding a **golden age** at the end of the eighteenth century for many of them. Those with the greatest herds of horses found hunting easy and generally were able to expand their territory; while tribes in the east were the first to become proficient in the use of firearms, sometimes using their advantage against tribes to the west who still fought with traditional weapons. The Shoshone in Idaho adapted particularly well to a life on horseback, creating a fearsome culture based on warring and living as roving hunters, following the buffalo on the plains. This brought them into contact with plains tribes, attributes of which they readily adopted; using tepees, sporting feather headdresses, and jerking meat. The tribe's influence was extended massively from the mountains into the Great Plains to the east, to include tracts of what's today western Wyoming – where their main concentration, in the **Wind River Reservation** – still is. But the bulk of the Great Plains remained under the control of the Arapaho and Cheyenne, who joined with the Sioux to drive the Crow and Shoshone into the western mountains. The Ute, too, expanded their spheres of operation eastwards throughout the mountains, even occasionally into the eastern plains, frequently fighting with Cheyenne, Arapaho, Comanche, and Kiowa who occupied this territory and were also flourishing thanks to the easy hunting of buffalo enabled by horses.

European exploration

The first whites to lay eyes on the Rockies were probably the Spanish. Though accounts are a little unclear, it seems that in 1541 **Francisco Vasquez de Coronado** approached the mountains from the south before crossing the southeastern corner of Colorado, in search of the of fabled Seven Gold Cities of Cíbola. Discouraged by the absence of these from further exploration, de Coronado turned back to the southwest, where his party raped and pillaged with abandonment.

The early eighteenth-century Old World powers divvied up the Rocky Mountain territory between them, despite their having little or no knowledge of the lands or natives that inhabited them. The **Spanish** had the most significant foothold close to the region; the **French** also made major claims on the territory, though by 1762 had ceded all land west of the Mississippi to the Spanish. In a spate of political wrangling that followed the wilting of British power on the continent after the **War of Independence** (1775–76), the bulk of the Rockies reverted again to French ownership as part of territory attached to Louisiana. Nevertheless, the Spanish maintained a small toehold in the Rockies, in fact sending the first expedition that deliberately set out to explore a portion of the region. The 1775–76 **Domínguez–Escalante** expedition visited portions of both Colorado and Utah, providing the first written accounts of the area, in a search for a useful overland route to connect the Spanish Missions in New Mexico with those in California.

French interest, on the other hand, was minimal. The only French influx came in the form of a small number of mountain men – estimated at around 150 –

who, having ventured in to trap beaver, mostly found homes among the indigenous people, and never left the region. While the French also contributed names to some features in the northern half of the territory – like the **Grand Tetons** (large breasts) – French possession was short-lived. Napoleon, fearing that guarding the territory would spread his armies too thinly, decided to sell the vast and – popularly considered – fairly useless wilderness to President Thomas Jefferson for $15 million as part of the 1803 **Louisiana Purchase**.

American exploration

Keen to prove the worth of the new territory, and no doubt curious as to what he'd just bought through the **Louisiana Purchase**, Jefferson quickly dispatched explorative parties to the west. The most famous and successful such expedition was that of **Lewis and Clark** who set off on what was to be a two-year, 8000-mile trip in 1804, their remit being to detail everything they saw. As a 29-year-old schizophrenic with no expertise in cartography, native languages, or botany, Meriwether Lewis was a bit of a strange choice to head an expedition across the country. Thankfully one of Lewis's best friends, the 33-year-old William Clark, already an army veteran and experienced frontiersman, was duly invited along on the expedition, and within a year they had assembled a party of forty to head west and explore. Having set out from the frontier town of St Louis along the Missouri River, the two expedition leaders took great care to note what they saw en route – Lewis in a romantic and poetic fashion; Clark in an organized scientific fashion. Between them, the explorers named around three hundred plants and animals, including the grizzly bear. One of the most essential members of their entourage was the young Shoshone woman **Sacagawea** (see box on p.390), whose ability to liaise with potentially hostile peoples smoothed the way for the party – although the presence of **York**, Clark's statuesque African-American manservant also helped deter attacks. Incidentally York began the journey as Clark's slave and helpmate and ended as a free man, released from bondage once the men returned from their expedition. During the journey York carried a gun, although it was illegal for a slave to do so, and he cast his vote along with other members of the corps when they voted on a place for their winter quarters on the west coast. Having endured a huge variety of hardships along the way, including treacherous whitewater rapids, dangerous trails, illness, and just plain discomfort – the whole party were, for example, infested with fleas in their winter base on the west coast – Lewis and Clark returned to a hero's welcome in St Louis, receiving high-ranking appointments. Lewis died three years later from what is thought to have been a self-inflicted gunshot wound, most likely due to either schizophrenia or alcholism. Clark went on to be an Indian agent of Indian Affairs in the Louisiana Territory, then governor of the Missouri Territory, and finally US Superintendent of Indian Affairs until his death in 1838.

In 1806 Jefferson dispatched **Zebulon Pike** and sixteen other soldiers to survey the southern end of the range. By all accounts Pike ran a much more bumbling and incompetent expedition, though he did have a crack at bagging what would be later called **Pikes Peak**, failing and declaring it unscaleable. From here he headed southwest into the San Luis Valley, where he was content to hole up for a while – until his arrest by the Spanish, on whose territory he had, apparently unwittingly wandered. He was imprisoned in Santa Fe and the diplomatic horse-trading that followed to secure his release led to an informal agreement that the Arkansas River through Colorado be the boundary between the Spanish and American territories.

Both of these expeditions sparked cautious excitement about what riches the West had in store for courageous explorers. Back East, newspaper ads were placed to recruit trappers to supply local markets with beaver pelts; famous **Mountain Men**, like Jedediah Smith and Jim Bridger and Tom "Broken Hand" Fitzpatrick, being part of this first wave of recruitment. They would go east to join the likes of **John Colter**, who left the Lewis and Clark expedition (with permission) in 1806 to trap in the wilderness. Colter became well-known for determinedly running for his life from the Blackfoot, after they had stripped him naked. His ordeal included hiding out in a freezing river, walking 300 miles to the nearest trading post and eating roots for survival – he later went on to become instrumental in developing the Wyoming fur trade. Another trader, **David Thompson** (see box on p.652), had the distinction of being the first white man in southern Idaho in 1809, and as a trained cartographer he did much to blaze trails for other whites through this part of the country. Mountain Men also helped open up the West by fostering generally good relations with the Native Americans. Each group found the other a useful trading partner – guns being exchanged for pelts; but many Mountain Men also went further, marrying, or at least fathering children by, Native American women. One such Mountain Man was **Kit Carson**, who actually married two natives, and later became crucial, both in his role as guide for Lieutenant John C Fremont in his exploration of the Yellowstone area, and later as a mediator between the US government and native tribes, including the Ute. This era was also infamous for its **Mountain Men Rendezvous**, when trappers and traders all gathered together in a welcome opportunity to leave the quiet mountains and return to the plains, not only to trade but also to raise hell, in an orgy of drinking, fighting, and gambling (see box on p.402). Native Americans would also attend the Rendezvous, evidence of the friendly relations between the two groups.

Territorial divisions and westward migrations

While the first handful of Americans were cautiously settling in the mountains, global political wrangling resulted in the US getting a much firmer grip on the region. The Spanish influence and interest in North and Central America was beginning to wane in the early nineteenth-century, so that in 1821 an independent Mexican State was born. Early Mexican relations with the US were very good and an era of intense trading between them was sparked off; the Santa Fe Trail emerging as an important route across southern Colorado. But the fledgling Mexican state was too weak to hold onto its land claims both in Texas and in Colorado, and after a period of violence and warring, its boundaries were redrawn to more-or-less their present position in the **1848 Treaty of Guadalupe Hidalgo**. Obviously, this left behind significant Hispanic communities in southern Colorado, surrounded by mountain ranges that continued to be known as the San Juan and Sangre de Cristo mountains. At around the same time (1846), political maneuvering between the US and Britain resulted in all land south of the 49th Parallel becoming US territory. The lines were now drawn for the development of the region by the US.

The first great incursion by whites into the West was in the form of **wagon trains** heading for the verdant valleys of Oregon and the gold camps of California. Between 1840 and 1868, around 300,000 pioneers passed through the Rockies on the **Oregon Trail**, a route along the North Platte River in southern Wyoming and then over the gentle South Pass west. Conditions along the dusty trail – in places as much as three miles wide – were harsh, and many travelers were woefully unprepared for the trials of the trip, the bad weather, wild animals, diseases, and stampedes they would encounter. With their oxen tiring, many West-bound émigrés had to discard possessions by the side of the trail. In the words of one traveler: "The road, from morning to night, is crowded like … Broadway … piles of bacon and hard bread thrown by the side of the road…trunks, clothes … boots … spades, picks, guns." And the side of the trail was littered not only with possessions, but with graves, too. An estimated one in seventeen emigrants died along the way, with on average ten graves for every mile of trail. Women had a particularly bad lot, an estimated one in five of them being pregnant, with many dying during childbirth, and nearly all having small children in their care. In turn, the children were particularly susceptible to disease and accidents, like falling out of the wagons or becoming lost and crushed among livestock. Not surprisingly perhaps, emigrants were not overly impressed by the Wyoming they passed through; one wrote "this is a country that may captivate mad poets, but I swear I see nothing but big rocks … high mountains and wild sage. It is a miserable country." But one group to see opportunity where no one else did were the **Mormons** who, persecuted in the Midwest, migrated to the Salt Lake City area to found a Mormon state under Brigham Young (see p.623).

Early settlement and the fate of the natives

The arrival of huge numbers of pioneers, even though they weren't actually settling in the region, marked the start of an important **change in relations** between whites and Native Americans. Whereas relations with the explorers had been reasonably friendly, by the 1850s the sheer number of travelers passing through the region began to cause difficulties. Not only did transient herds of cattle wear out grazing lands, but local buffalo stocks suffered a double setback as settlers killed thousands for meat. Objections were occasionally voiced in the form of raids on passing wagon trains, which met with severe reprisals from the US Army, who moved in to establish trading posts to protect the route. A series of bloody clashes with plains tribes around the Platte River region of the Oregon Trail culminated in the first major agreement with Native Americans in the region, whereby they agreed to retreat to the north of the river, while the US Army agreed to limit its operations to the southern side.

Since few in the wagon trains considered making the Rockies their home, frictions with native peoples for a while subsided, but in the late 1850s and early 1860s the activities of prospectors sparked several **gold rushes** in the region – drawing miners deep into Native American territory. Americans arrived in madding droves digging anywhere that seemed promising – the rather bemused natives looking on with surprise, curiosity, and tacit acceptance. Of the first major strikes, the most famous was the 1858 find in Denver, which sparked the fabled "**Pikes Peak or Bust**" gold rush, which prospectors would proudly scrawl on the side of their westward-bound wagons. The finds in Denver actually proved to be tiny, but by the following year gold had been found around the Clear Creek Valley, a short ways to the west, and the towns of Central City, Idaho Springs, and Georgetown sprung up as a result. At around the same time major finds occurred in both Idaho – 1862 Boise Basin strikes – and Montana, where incredible finds at Grasshopper Creek in the same year created Bannack, a camp that produced $5 million of gold in its first year.

The gold camps in the region provided the first good reason for settlement there, and so heralded the start of the modern-day Rockies. It also marked the beginning of the end for the traditional lives of the Native American people. Not only were the sheer numbers of new arrivals offensive to local populations, but the settlers' complete ignorance of local culture and disrespect for Native American practices caused frictions and triggered a more aggressive role on the part of the natives.

Relations that had traditionally been surprisingly peaceful began to sour, and the US government took the stance that the presence of the Native Americans was an obstacle to industrious development. Two decades of conflict followed, making for one of the most pitiful chapters in American history, during which Native Americans moved from coexistence, to segregation, to marginalization. The milestones in this process were scores of treaties initially guaranteeing exclusive native rights to areas, only to be subsequently broken and reshaped at legendary speed and whenever new economic opportunities, like seams of ore or good grazing lands, presented themselves for exploitation. The Ute, for example, having been granted a huge area of the San Juans in an 1860 treaty, found their rights rescinded a mere five years later after gold strikes in the mountains, leaving them with poor parched lands on the fringes on Colorado and in Utah. In the northern Rockies of Idaho, the Nez Percé got similar treatment, ending in their famous retreat (see p.629).

The loss of rights and territory angered many tribes, who countered with guerilla strikes on various forts and occasionally directed at homesteaders as well; events upon which the American government took a hard stance, particularly once its own instability during the **Civil War** (1861–65) had ended. In the Rockies the major events in the process of subjugating the Native Americans were carnage, such as the 1864 Sand Creek Massacre, when Colonel J.M. Chivington ambushed and massacred a village of 130 Native Americans near the Kansas Border in Colorado, mutilating and torturing many more. One of the major bloodbaths in the north of the region was the 1870 Marias River Massacre in Montana, which saw a friendly tribe of 173 Blackfoot butchered, members of a nation which had already lost around 15,000 people to epidemics of smallpox. Perhaps the only moment of martial glory for the Natives in the so-called Indian Wars, was the 1876 battle at **Little Bighorn** in Montana, in which General George Custer was routed by a combined force of Sioux, Cheyenne, and Arapaho warriors (see p.488). But the wars were only part of the campaign against native tribes and were accompanied by a more insidious core policy to exterminate the buffalo and starve the natives off the land. In total, more than four million buffalo were shot on the plains, their hides taken, but the meat generally left to rot.

Economic and political development

At around the same time as the Native Americans were being pushed out of the mountains, another great obstacle to the area's development – its distance from the east and west coasts – was being overcome with the advent of the **railroad age**. Thanks to huge investment after the end of civil war, the late 1860s saw the transcontinental railroad push its tracks west through the region. The eastern and western ends of the railway were finally joined in Utah's Promontory Mountains on May 10, 1869; an event marked in a momentous ceremony during which four symbolic spikes – two of them gold – were driven into the ground (see p.346).

The coming of the railroad encouraged **ranchers**, who – with the buffalo gone – would not only have access to endless free grazing, but also to the all-important eastern markets. Vast herds came into the region, often owned by absentee businessmen and kept by huge teams of cowboys. **Alexander Swan**, who controlled around half a million acres in Wyoming, ran herds under so many brands that he had to publish a reference book for his cowboys. The dominance of the plains by the large ranchers and their manner of riding roughshod over the interests of homesteaders, precipitated a number of **cattle wars** (see p.378). Soon railroad spurs fed into the mountainous parts of the region, prompting miners to pour in and ore to flow out. The export of logs was also possible and pretty soon the region had built up a formidable economy based on the extractive industries, which helped earn the Rocky Mountain territories **statehood**; Colorado in 1876; Montana in 1889; Idaho and Wyoming in 1890; and Utah the latest in 1896. Wyoming, intriguingly, was the first state to offer **full suffrage to women**, more the result of a desperate shortage of women in the state (outnumbered by men six to one), than a deeply held belief in the equality of the sexes.

Yet dependence on agriculture and the extractive industries provided only a fickle economic base. The brutal **winter of 1887–88** – which included a single blizzard that dumped enough snow to bury cattle completely – saw around 400,000 cattle perish and both smallholders and wealthy ranchers go bankrupt. Similarly, mining in the mountains provided, at best, a precarious basis for livelihoods. The early gold mines were quickly played out, particularly those in Colorado, where silver mining became the main source of income thanks to the discovery of rich lodes around Leadville and Aspen. Both swarmed with miners until the dramatic **silver crash** of 1893, when overnight the US moved off the silver standard, making almost all mines worthless. Thankfully, the lull in the Colorado economy was to be a short one, and in the 1890s major finds at Cripple Creek, near Colorado Springs sparked the **last great gold rush** in the country. Although the area was rich in the mineral, few miners actually made much money from gold, however. Interest in mining the ore was generated by the artificially strong position of stock in mines, owing to the US use of the Gold Standard. Since the economy could only expand as fast as gold was mined, even loss-making mines were good for the national economy, with the result that the 700 working mines around Cripple Creek were represented by some 12,000 mining corporations selling stock. And while all the glamour was focused on the mines of Cripple Creek, the region also developed an extraordinarily strong coal mining industry. In southern Colorado, Pueblo developed as a major steel town; in southern Wyoming, site of the largest coal deposits in the nation, towns like Rock Springs and Cambria boomed.

But the mining industry was **fraught with tensions** in the early twentieth century. Workers in large mines were often severely exploited, forced to live in company housing and paid in coupons to shop at company shops. Morale was poor, and as mines became less profitable, the actions of mine owners often made pay and conditions even worse. Tensions escalated into clashes at many mines. Perhaps the worst conflict of all occurred in Colorado, when the National Guard were called in to keep the peace in Cripple Creek, Telluride, and in Trinidad during the Ludlow Massacre of 1914 (see p.134).

America's playground

The **Great Depression** of the 1930s hit the Rocky Mountain states hard, particularly since the states were yet to develop beyond their dependence on the extractive industries. But the same era yielded a new direction for the region that would grow to become the mainstay of its present-day economy: **tourism**.

The transformation of the region was not unlike that of the celebrated frontiersman Buffalo Bill (see p.384), who nearly a hundred years earlier had gone from Pony Express rider and scout to runner of a Wild West show. Similarly the

Rocky Mountains began to sell its natural features to the leisure industry in the twentieth century. Tourism began tentatively in spa towns like Colorado Springs and Glenwood Springs, which had been attracting the elite since the 1890s; but with the dawn of the motorcar age in the 1920s, the Rocky Mountains began to lure large numbers of ordinary vacationers. Initially, interest was largely centered on the natural wonders of the remarkable **national parks**. Yellowstone National Park, created in 1872, was the best known, but tourists also explored the spate of other national parks that had recently been created in the region, namely Mesa Verde (1906); Glacier (1910); and Rocky Mountain (1915). Numbers of visitors particularly boomed after World War II, when gasoline rationing had ended and tourists withdrew money from bulging savings accounts to mass in the Rockies in record numbers. In the mid-1950s, Yellowstone National Park attracted four times the population of Wyoming in annual visitor numbers. Several towns in the region were quick off the mark to court this new economic opportunity as well: Colorado Springs, for example, built an auto route up Pikes Peak and the Royal Gorge Bridge, both specially designed to give motorists splendid views.

The post-Depression era also saw the first **ski resorts** evolve, mainly first as entertainment for locals. In Idaho, though, the Sun Valley resort, opened in the late 1930s, became the vogue winter destination for Hollywood film stars. Curiously, it was World War II that acted as a catalyst for the development of resorts. Chosen as the location of a large training camp for the **10th Mountain Division** (see box on p.237), the Sawatch and Elk mountains of Colorado would see veterans return from fighting to become a major postwar impetus behind the development of resorts like Vail and Aspen. These resorts especially took off in the late 1960s, and by the 1970s began to overtake summer recreations as the main tourist season. With so much swank new infrastructure in place, ski resorts have subsequently concentrated on developing off-season tourism, based on conferences, golfers, hikers, and, more recently, mountain bikers.

Present-day society

The rise in enthusiasm for outdoor activities was mirrored by an increasingly active **environmental movement**, which steadily gained momentum throughout the second half of the twentieth century. Encouraged by a spate of successful protests – including voting down an initiative to attract the 1976 Olympic games to Colorado on the basis of ecological concerns – the Rockies became known for a brand of hippie-activism centered in university towns like Boulder, even though this has been solid Republican country for the past twenty years or so; indeed, only one of the ten current US senators from Colorado, Utah, Wyoming, Montana, and Idaho is a Democrat, and each state legislature is more or less dominated by Republicans.

Thus it comes as no real surprise that the region has also continued to harbor maverick individualists with beliefs much further to the right than those political activists. Idaho in particular, developed a reputation as a militia hotbed, based partly on an incident near Bonners Ferry (see p.653) in which alleged white separatist **Randy Weaver** spent eleven days under siege from the FBI, his wife and child dying before his surrender. Though compensated for this heavy-handed treatment (a 1995 decision awarded Weaver $3.1 million) by the justice system, the siege later became a rallying cry for militants across the US.

The greatest changes over the last decade or so though have been economical. As a knock-on effect of the closeness of so many splendid recreation opportunities, most major towns in the Rocky Mountains have experienced rapid growth over the last decade, thanks in part to the growth of footloose **high-tech industries**. Not only did towns like Durango become fashionable among teleworkers in the 1990s, but Denver, too, embarked on an orgy of expansion, doubling its population in that decade alone. Such is the rate of economic development that today a major debate in Colorado is how to halt or control its growth – particularly in old mountain towns, where deluxe second homes are pricing locals out of the market. Urban centers like Denver, Bozeman, and Boise are experiencing similar issues as expensive homes encroach on the adjacent mountains, forcing new roads and consequently encouraging more traffic in those areas. And in Utah, both Salt Lake City and Park City experienced extraordinary construction spurts and expansion in the run up to the **2002 Winter Olympics**. Though the contemporary experience of the other Rocky Mountain states is still less crass than Colorado's, developments here may well be pointing to the future for the rest of the region.

Wildlife and landscape

One of the real thrills of traveling the Rocky Mountains region is the chance to see some of North America's most distinctive wildlife in its natural habitat; it should also go without saying that those habitats – alpine meadows, geothermal wonderlands, in addition to the mountain ranges themselves – are among the most dramatic on the continent. The determining factors for the kinds of animals and birds you might encounter while exploring here are altitude, terrain, and vegetation. All three are inextricably linked, with altitude and terrain determining what kinds of vegetation can grow in a given area; the mountains are thus made up of a number of distinct ecosystems, each one supporting particular types of animals and birds. What follows only intends to give an overview to how the Rockies developed, what landscapes you'll see today, and what wildlife inhabits them. For deeper digging, see the recommended books on these topics, p.681.

Geology and terrain

The Rocky Mountains extend some two thousand miles from central New Mexico all the way up to northeastern British Columbia in Canada, effectively dividing North America in a manner not unlike that of the Mississippi River to the east; indeed the mountains basically delineate what is known as the **Continental Divide**, from which the pattern of water flow is dictated in North America. Rivers on the west of the divide drain into the Pacific Ocean, those on the east into the Atlantic or Arctic oceans.

The chain is comprised of a complex series of individual mountain ranges whose hills vary from jagged, incised peaks to flat-topped crags. The Rockies are relatively **young mountains**, formed mainly by the Laramide Revolution, a period of tectonic uplifts that took place in the late Cretaceous Period, around 65 million years ago, which was followed by volcanic activity and folding and faulting that continued into the early Tertiary Period. By contrast, the Blue Ridge Mountains in the eastern United States are thought to have formed some 200 million years ago, with the first great tectonic collision.

The Rockies were later reshaped by heavy **glaciation** during the Pleistocene era, when a sizeable portion of the earth was covered in ice. This process ground down mountains, smoothed out valleys and also left series of mountain lakes when the glaciers receded. Glacial activity continues to affect the landscape of the area's higher mountain ranges – Glacier National Park in northern Montana, for instance, has good examples of these processes in action (see p.538).

Geological activity is still ongoing throughout the Rockies, with earthquakes not uncommon, and, of course, spectacular examples of vulcanism in Yellowstone National Park (see p.409). The geothermal wonders here are most apparent in the form of **geysers**, which violently shoot steam and/or water from a vent in the earth's surface. What's bubbling down below often may just appear in the more docile form of hot springs, not the visual eye-candy of erupting geysers, but far more pleasant to soak in.

The Rockies by region

The Rockies are generally divided into four regions: **Canadian** (outside the scope of this book), Northern, Central, and Southern. The **Northern Rockies** consist of northern Idaho and western Montana, and include the peaks of the Sawtooth, Salmon River, Bitterroot, Clearwater, Selkirk, and Cabinet mountains, as well as Glacier National Park. The highest point in this region is Borah Peak (12,622ft) in Idaho's Lost River Range.

The **Central Rockies** take in southern Montana, eastern Idaho, western Wyoming, and northeastern Utah, encompassing the Absaroka, Beartooth, Big Horn, Teton, Snake River, Wind River, Wasatch, Salt River, and Uinta mountains, the last of these unusual in that they are the only mountains in the Rockies to run east–west – every other range trends north–south. Grand Teton and Yellowstone national parks are within the Central Rockies, so it's no surprise that this is one of the most geologically active regions of the entire range. High points here include rugged Granite Peak (12,799ft), Montana's highest mountain, and Wyoming's magnificent Grand Teton (13,770ft).

The **Southern Rockies** extend from the Wyoming Basin in the south of the state through Colorado to central New Mexico, and have the highest peaks in all the Rocky Mountains, including 14,433ft Mount Elbert, and those of Rocky Mountain National Park. The region is made up of two separate north–south belts of mountains separated by lower lying basins – the main ranges in the west are the Park, Sawatch, and San Juan, and in the east are the Front Range, Laramie, and Sangre de Cristo.

Fauna

The Rockies boasts a line-up of animals that includes the most fascinating and charismatic mammals on the continent: the grizzly bear, the North American bison (or buffalo), the moose, the mountain lion, and the gray wolf, just to mention a few. Inevitably, there's a mix of excitement and frustration that goes with spotting animals, because they don't show up on demand; in fact, the more intelligent and secretive of them make a point of avoiding human contact altogether. You can, however, reliably expect to see certain animals, and even to have quite close encounters with some of them.

Advice on the best spots for wildlife viewing is included in the individual chapters of this guide. If wildlife viewing and photographing is a priority, you should definitely bring along binoculars or a spotting scope, as well as a powerful zoom lens (200–300mm) for your camera.

Large mammals

One of the larger of the animals you're most likely to encounter is the **elk** (also called "wapiti" an appropriately descriptive Native American word meaning "white rump"); the larger bulls weigh up to 900 pounds, and sport huge antlers which alone can weigh as much as fifty pounds. The most dramatic time to observe elk is during the fall rut, which generally begins in September and may go on into early November. The bulls strut and display their necks and antlers to the cows, but the most extraordinary part of their display is an unearthly call to a potential mate called "bugling" – a bizarre ear-piercing squeal. Gatherings of elk are a common sight at many locations in the Rockies, in all sorts of landscapes: low forests, alpine tundra, and so on.

Another beautifully antlered ungulate is the **mule deer**. Roughly one-third the size of an elk – and only a quarter of the weight – the mule deer is further distinguished by the much lighter, almost tan coloring of its coat, an overly generous set of mule-like ears, and a short, black-tipped tail attached to its cream-colored rump. The male's antlers are quite delicate too, flowing with balance and symmetry. You may encounter mule deer almost anywhere below the treeline, including forested areas bisected by hiking trails. A little smaller and heftier than the mule deer is the **pronghorn antelope**, a particularly prominent animal in Wyoming, occupying grassy flatlands and often seen grazing by roadsides and on ranch properties. Pronghorns have a greyish hide and short horns that jut inwards.

The title of Rocky Mountain mascot goes to the extraordinary Rocky Mountain **bighorn sheep** – there is no more indelible image than a lone bighorn perched on a rocky ledge, lord of all he surveys. Both rams and ewes grow horns, although the two are easily distinguished as the ram has the classic "C"-shaped horns, while the ewe's grow as almost vertical spikes, up to eight inches long. Rams put on an extraordinary display during the rutting season, roughly mid-November through December, when they square off and crack horns with a sickening impact to assert their authority and establish mating rights. Bighorns are the archetypal high-country dwellers, great at negotiating rocky ledges and dealing with cool temperatures, and mostly stick to the alpine reaches.

The largest member of the deer family is the **moose**. With the largest bulls reaching seven feet at the shoulder and weighing 1000 pounds, their bulbous heads topped by a broad spread of antlers, and with a pendulous dewlap slung beneath the chin, this marvelous animal, once encountered, is not easily forgotten. Their long gangly legs are built for wading, and moose generally browse the wetland grasses and aquatic plants found along rivers and in riparian meadows. Even bigger than these behemoths are woolly **bison**, weighing up to a ton and found in a few national parks and specially maintained Bison Ranges.

Predators: bears, wolves, and mountain lions

Many visitors to the Rockies are hoping most of all to see potentially dangerous predators such as the grizzly bear, mountain lion, and gray wolf. There are special rules of engagement that go with encountering these animals, particularly the at-times fearsome **grizzly bear**. It's worth noting some of the differences in appearance between the grizzly and its slightly smaller cousin the **black bear** – also a Rockies resident – to be able to distinguish between the two, more for academic reasons than what to do if you spot one. They both come in similar shades of color, so that's of little help: the black bear can range from blond to cinnamon to brown to black, and grizzlies from cinnamon to a deep reddish brown. More useful are distinctions related to the animals' body shape: grizzlies have a fairly pronounced hump behind their necks, a feature the black bear lacks; also, a grizzly's hindquarters slope downwards, while a black bear's tailbone sits level with or just above the height of its shoulders. The best places to see grizzlies are the northernmost national parks (Yellowstone and Glacier), although they are found in smaller numbers in other areas including Wyoming's Wind River Mountains; black bears are occasionally seen in forested areas throughout the Rockies region. For advice on what to do in bear encounters, see the box on p.550.

The **gray wolf** (*canis lupus*) is native to the Glacier region in northern Montana and is making a steady comeback to Greater Yellowstone, with packs now established around the park's borders in forested areas of Montana, Wyoming, and Idaho, as well as within Yellowstone itself (see box on p.428); it's unlikely that there are any wolf packs in either Colorado or Utah. A gray (or "timber") wolf is roughly the size of an Alsatian dog, but with longer, leaner legs. Despite the name, a gray wolf's coat may be any color from snow white to jet black, with most falling somewhere in between as a blend of browns and creams or blueish-grays. Wolves keep very much to themselves so any sighting is well worth bragging about.

Even more secretive – and as well potentially dangerous – is the **mountain lion**; also referred to as a puma or cougar, this sleek, handsome animal has perhaps the most accurate Latin name of all – *felis concolor*, or the one-colored cat. Mountain lion sightings have increased throughout the Rockies in recent years, and while some would suggest that this is evidence of expanding populations, it's more likely that their habitat is shrinking under pressure from suburban development, bringing them into closer proximity with humans (see box on p.286).

Coyotes and various rodents

Affectionately known to some Native American peoples as the "singing trickster," the **coyote** (*canis latrans*) is a highly adaptable and opportunistic predator fairly common in the Rockies. Coyotes hunt small prey such as rodents and rabbits, but also scavenge the carcasses of bigger animals such as elk, deer, and even bison when the opportunity arises. Sometimes confused with wolves from afar, coyotes are much smaller (weighing around thirty pounds, in comparison with 120 pounds for a gray wolf) and unlike wolves, they'll often appear by roadsides and in populated areas where a free meal might present itself.

One of the sorrier tales of human impact on wildlife is that of the **beaver**, nature's most energetic engineer, whose pelt was at one time so desired for making hats that the animal was very nearly wiped from the face of the earth. The largest rodent in North America, the beaver is entrusted with designing and building wetland habitat for countless plants and animals. Its dam-building creates ponds and marshy meadows which in turn support wetland grasses and trees such as willow and cottonwood, as well as waterfowl and grazing animals like moose, elk, and deer. Faced with natural predators such as coyotes, bobcats, and foxes, the beaver is battling to make a comeback – the overall balance of many mountain ecosystems depend upon its success.

Among the other interesting animals that you need a fair bit of luck to see are the bobcat, badger, river otter, raccoon, muskrat, weasel, and pine marten. More common are the **pika**, a small but rotund rodent which announces its presence by squeaking loudly as it pops out from its rocky hideaway, and the **yellow-bellied marmot**, which closely resembles a groundhog. Marmots are inveterate sunbathers, and may be seen on exposed, sunny rock outcrops at lower mountain elevations and almost anywhere on the alpine tundra.

Birds and fish

Nearly every manner of **bird** can be found in the Rockies, often in wildlife refuges, from bald eagles – relatively rare in the lower 48 – to colorful songbirds and trumpeter swans, the world's largest waterfowl. The "Books" section reviews a number of guides incredibly handy for bird-watching and identifying

When animals attack . . . and even when they don't

A small number of animals native to the Rockies have been known occasionally to **attack humans**; bears and mountain lions are the obvious candidates, but others may also react aggressively including elk, moose, and bison. Keep in mind that there isn't an animal alive in the Rockies that can't outrun a human, and if a bear, bison, elk, or moose decided to go after you, it could certainly catch you. The basic **code of conduct** when observing wildlife is to stay at a non-threatening distance – if an animal reacts to your presence, then you're too close. It's actually far more likely that you would pose a threat to an animal than vice versa. Every year thousands of animals are killed on roads in the various national parks and elsewhere, so it's important to **observe speed limits** and be particularly careful while driving early or late in the day when animals are most active.

the species. As for **fish**, there's no shortage of them in the numerous mountain lakes and rivers, and even if you've no interest in casting for them, you can't fail to miss seeing folks throwing a line in any available stream. Various species of trout are most prevalent, notably rainbow, lake, and cutthroat. There are also pockets of **salmon** left, though the future of this once plentiful fish looks grim (see box p.616).

Flora

One feature about traveling through the Rockies is that the region's flora remains fairly uniform, at least as far as simple geography goes; the types of forests, plants, and flowers which you will find depend much more on the altitude you're at, rather than the state you're in. Thus, whether you're in Idaho or Colorado, you will find similar trees and flowers at an altitiude of, say, 10,000 feet.

The mountain environment consists of **three essential ecosystems**: these are the **montane** (6000–9000 feet), **subalpine** (9000–11,500 feet) and **alpine** (above 11,500 feet). The montane is where you'll find forests of lodgepole pine and ponderosa pine as well as stands of aspen and blue spruce. Engelmann spruce, subalpine fir and Douglas fir take over above 9000 feet, where the temperatures get a bit cooler, and wildflowers start to appear in meadows, while alpine tundra supports only slow-growing plants such as mosses, lichens, and a variety of delicate wildflowers, all of which can survive on the thinnest soil and air and with a minimal supply of water. Because they grow so slowly – the tiniest wildflower may take many years to reach maturity – any damage done to these plants impacts dramatically on the alpine ecosytem, so hikers have a special duty of care while exploring these areas.

The various species of **wildflower** that you might come across are too numerous to detail here; among their number are the columbine, alpine sunflower, elephanthead, alpine buttercup, and alpine phlox. There are several excellent books on Rocky Mountain wildflowers that include color photos to help with identification (see "Books" p.681).

Books

It would be hard to argue for the Rocky Mountains as a literary hotbed, though to be sure the rugged lands and postcard images have fired the imagination of many, from the first Native Americans to Lewis and Clark and on. The books below include those most evocative of the Rockies backdrop, as well as ones that proved most entertaining and useful during the research and writing of this guide. The majority should be easy to find on the internet or can be ordered by your favorite bookstore. Some of the specialist trail and climbing guides may only be available in the specific region they cover.

History and biography

★ **Stephen E. Ambrose** *Undaunted Courage*. Perhaps the most accessible account of Lewis and Clark's pioneering journey of discovery from St Louis, over the Montana and Idaho Rockies, to the Pacific coast in 1806.

Richard E. Bennet *We'll Find the Place: The Mormon Exodus*. A well-written and engaging work, recounting the trials and tribulations of early Mormon pioneers. Although researched by a member of the Church of Latter-Day Saints, it resists the urge to preach and is in fact one of the most readable works on the subject.

William Bueler *Roof of the Rockies: A History of Colorado Mountaineering*. A thoroughly readable and engaging history of early mountaineering in Colorado, written by a veteran climber.

John Rolfe Burroughs *Where the Old West Stayed Young*. A homespun history of the deeds and misdeeds of the cattlemen, frontier-folk, and outlaws of northern Colorado, southern Wyoming, and Utah, based largely on first-hand sources and interviews. It's a more compelling read than you might expect, and includes vivid accounts of several cattle wars, as well as episodes from the life and times of Butch Cassidy and the Wild Bunch.

William F. Cody *The Life of Hon William F Cody, Known As Buffalo Bill*. Larger-than-life autobiography of one of the great characters of the Wild West.

Cort Conley *Idaho Loners*. Idaho has long had a reputation for attracting loners, and this book gives the most tragic, heroic, and weird their fifteen minutes of fame.

Aubrey L. Haines *The Yellowstone Story*. Acknowledged as the definitive Yellowstone National Park history. Whether you'll want to wade through both volumes is debatable, but it's a useful reference.

Meriwether Lewis and William Clark *The Journals of the Lewis and Clark Expedition, 1804–1806*. Six volumes of meticulous jottings by the Northwest's first and maybe most intrepid inland explorers, scrupulously following Jefferson's request for details of every aspect of the flora, fauna, and native inhabitants of the West. Interesting to dip into, but you'd be hard pushed to read the lot. Two good alternatives are Frank

Bergon's *The Journals of Lewis & Clark* and Bernard DeVoto's volume of the same name, both of which reconstruct the epic journey using extracts from the original journals. See also Stephen Ambrose, above.

Clyde A. Milner II, Carol A. O'Connor, and Martha A. Sandweiss (eds) *The Oxford History of the American West.* As the title suggests, this doesn't just focus on the Rockies, but it's nonetheless a fascinating collection of essays, covering topics that range from myths and movies to art and religion.

Duane Smith *Mesa Verde National Park.* An informative and wide-ranging history of Mesa Verde, from its earliest inhabitants to the contemporary problems of running – and ruining – a national park.

Elliot West *The Saloon on the Rocky Mountain Mining Frontier.* An academic yet readable volume that emphasizes the centrality of the saloon to Western culture.

Richard White *It's Your Misfortune and None of My Own.* Dense, authoritative and all-embracing history of the American West, that debunks the notion of the rugged pioneer by stressing the role of the federal government.

Culture and society

Alston Chase *Playing God in Yellowstone.* Taking Yellowstone as his example, the iconoclastic Chase explores the truth behind the National Park Service's rhetoric.

★ **Pete Fromm** *The Indian Creek Chronicles.* An engaging and rousing tale of seven winter months spent alone in a tent in the Selway-Bitterroot Wilderness guarding salmon eggs. There are some marvellous descriptions of the author discovering nature in the mountains.

Eleanor Genres, Sandra Dallas, Maxine Benson, Stanley Cuba (eds) *The Colorado Book.* Fascinating and eclectic collection of snippets about Colorado – from literary excerpts to travel writing, poems, and songs.

William Henry Jackson and John Fielder *Colorado: 1870–2000.* An extraordinary photographic essay compiled by renowned Colorado lens-man John Fielder. Armed with a collection of photographs taken by William Henry Jackson (1843–1942), Fielder revisits the sites depicted in Jackson's photos and composes identical shots to illustrate the change – or lack of it – in each subject in the years since. A superb, if somewhat expensive, coffee-table book.

McKay Jenkins *The White Death – Tragedy and Heroism in the Avalanche Zone.* The story of the deaths of five young climbers in an avalanche on Glacier National Park's Mount Cleveland in 1969. The main story is covered with great style, as is the science of avalanches.

Norman Maclean *Young Men and Fire.* An account of Montana's Mann Gulch Fire in 1949 in which twelve young smokejumpers died. It's overlong and a little patronizing at times, but the details of the lifecycle of a wildfire are especially interesting.

Wallace Stegner *Mormon Country*. A collection of 28 essays focusing on Mormon life and the wide range of nonbelievers who lived in Mormon country in the late nineteenth and early twentieth centuries. There are some great tales here, and Stegner tells them superbly.

Lee H. Whitely *Death and Yellowstone – Accidents and Foolhardiness in the First National Park*. Mishaps and near-escapes, drownings and bear stories, from Yellowstone National Park. An offbeat, quirky read.

Travel

Isabella Bird *A Lady's Life in the Rocky Mountains*. An engaging collection of letters written in the 1870s by the intrepid English travel writer. Overall they make for a charming, occasionally humorous portrayal of frontier life.

John Dunning *Denver*. Evocative accounts of the Queen City of the Plains, with a particularly engaging look at the underbelly of life here in the mid-twentieth century.

John Wesley Powell *The Exploration of the Colorado River and its Canyons*. John Wesley Powell and a team of nine men set out to explore the Colorado River in 1869, a scientific expedition that led through the last uncharted territory of the United States. This book details what turned out to be a massive and fearsome adventure, and its best moments compare well with the more harrowing tales of Lewis and Clark.

Flora, fauna, and geology

Peter Alden (ed) *National Audubon Society Field Guide to the Rocky Mountain States*. Lavishly illustrated and extremely informative guide to the flora and fauna of the Rockies, covering everything from lichens and wildflowers, spiders and beetles, to feral horses and mule deer. There's also an appendix detailing parks and preserves, images of the constellations you can see at night, and sections on the topography and geology, ecology, and weather patterns of the region. Invaluable.

Rick Bass *The Book of Yaak*. A passionate book about the Yaak Valley in northwest Montana, one of the last great wild places in the US, and under increasing threat from industry and development.

John Emerick and Cornelia Fliesher Mutel *From Grassland to Glacier: The Natural History of Colorado*. A detailed and readable guide that would be useful to anyone journeying through Colorado and with an interest in its various ecosystems.

John Good and Kenneth Pierce *Interpreting the Landscape: Recent and Ongoing Geology of Grand Teton and Yellowstone National Parks*. A short, sweet exposition on the weird and wonderful geology of the Greater Yellowstone region.

Kim Long *Wolves, A Wildlife Handbook.* A useful guide to wolves that covers everything practical from myths and legends to informative details of wolves in their natural habitat and their relationship with humans.

Scott McMillion *Mark of the Grizzly: True Stories of Recent Bear Attacks and the Hard Lessons Learned.* Grizzly attacks are not uncommon in the mountains, and this book documents eighteen that took place between 1977 and 1997, some of them in the Yellowstone and Glacier national parks. More intriguing than you might think.

T. Scott Bryan *The Geysers of Yellowstone.* A scholarly yet readable work that provides an exhaustive description of the formation, physical characteristics and eruption patterns of the park's most famous features. Good if you're particularly keen on rocks and stuff.

Hiking, biking, and climbing guides

Roger and Carol Shively Anderson *A Ranger's Guide to Yellowstone Day Hikes.* An excellent wrap-up of short hikes in Yellowstone, featuring concise accounts of 29 day-hikes in all.

★ **Caryn Boddie and Peter Boddie** *A Hiker's Guide to Colorado.* This picks out 75 great hikes in the state, with full route descriptions and maps.

John Carrey and Cort Conley *The Middle Fork: A Guide.* An indispensable, mile-by-mile guide for rafters. Great details on the history of early exploration.

★ **Stephen Hlawaty** *Mountain Bike America: Colorado.* If you buy only one book on mountain biking in Colorado, make it this one. The author describes not only fifty of the best rides in the state, but his descriptions, and maps, are consistently reliable.

Brian Litz and Kurt Lankford *Skiing Colorado's Backcountry.* Perhaps the best Colorado backcountry ski guide available, with detailed information on both skiing and boarding – and carrying the seal of approval of the revered Colorado Mountain Club.

Tom Lopez *Idaho, A Climbing Guide: Climbs, Scrambles and Hikes.* An exhaustive guide to virtually all the climbs, scrambles, and hikes in the state, with a good section on the history of climbing in Idaho.

Ralph Maugham and Jackie Johnson Maugham *Hiking Idaho.* The best available introduction to hiking in Idaho, with a large selection of routes throughout the state.

Gerry Roach *Colorado's Fourteeners.* The seminal mountaineering guide to Colorado, packed with detail and useful color maps.

Richard Rossiter *Teton Classics: 50 Selected Climbs in Grand Teton National Park.* This illustrated handbook features succinct descriptions of fifty fine climbing routes in the Tetons.

★ **Bill and Russ Schneider** *Hiking Montana.* The definitive guide to 100 of the state's best hikes.

John Veranth *Hiking the Wasatch.* An easy-to-use hiking and natural history guide to the central Wasatch, which takes you into the mountains and canyons near Salt Lake City.

Rebecca Woods *Walking the Winds; Jackson Hole Hikes.* These guides cover much of the best of northwest Wyoming hikes, and feature simple, clear trail maps to go with their detailed descriptions.

Fiction

James Lee Burke *Bitterroot.* Absorbing crime novel set in and around Montana's Bitterroot Valley.

Zane Gray *Thunder Mountain.* Action-packed pioneer stuff from the celebrated Western writer, set around the Middle Fork of the Salmon in Idaho.

★ **A.B. Guthrie Jr** *The Big Sky.* The novel that gave Montana its nickname, and shattered the romantic Hollywood myth of the West when it was first published in the Thirties. Realistic fiction at its very best, following desperate mountain man and fugitive Boone Caudill, whose idyllic life in Montana was ended by the white settlers.

Dorothy M. Johnson *The Hanging Tree.* A vigorously written psychological Western based on a true episode from Montana's gold mining past by the author who also wrote *A Man Called Horse.*

Jack Kerouac *On the Road.* Cult beatnik meanderings through the US, with an exciting account of time spent in Denver and Central City, Colorado.

William Kittredge (ed) *The Portable Western Reader.* A comprehensive anthology featuring some of the great American writers. Everything from tales of Native Americans to the poems of Walt Whitman, stories of Jack London and travel writing of Steinbeck and Hemingway. Each titbit may only serve to whet your appetite for the complete work, but it does cover a lot of ground and it's scrupulously edited.

★ **Norman Maclean** *A River Runs Through It.* Even non-anglers will revel in this marvellous account of fly-fishing and the landscapes of Montana's Blackfoot River in the early twentieth century. The two associated short stories in the same book also provide memorable descriptions of the Bitterroot Valley and Mountains. You may be familiar with the film of the same name.

Annick Smith and William Kittredge *The Last Best Place.* An exhaustive 1200-page anthology that covers the whole gamut of Montana literature, from poetry to pioneer tales, Native American to contemporary.

index

and small print

Index

Where there's a map of a place listed, this is indicated by the name appearing in colour

G

H

I

J

Q

R

S

T

U

V

W

Y

Z

Twenty Years of Rough Guides

In the summer of 1981, Mark Ellingham, Rough Guides' founder, knocked out the first guide on a typewriter, with a group of friends. Mark had been traveling in Greece after university, and couldn't find a guidebook that really answered his needs.There were heavyweight cultural guides on the one hand – good on museums and classical sites but not on beaches and tavernas – and on the other hand student manuals that were so caught up with how to save money that they lost sight of the country's significance beyond its role as a place for a cool vacation. None of the guides began to address Greece as a country, with its natural and human environment, its politics and its contemporary life.

Having no urgent reason to return home, Mark decided to write his own guide. It was a guide to Greece that tried to combine some erudition and insight with a thoroughly practical approach to travelers' needs. Scrupulously researched listings of places to stay, eat, and drink were matched by careful attention to detail on everything from Homer to Greek music, from classical sites to national parks, and from nude beaches to monasteries. Back in London, Mark and his friends got their Rough Guide accepted by a farsighted commissioning editor at the publisher Routledge and it came out in 1982.

The Rough Guide to Greece was a student scheme that became a publishing phenomenon. The immediate success of the book – shortlisted for the Thomas Cook award – spawned a series that rapidly covered dozens of countries. The Rough Guides found a ready market among backpackers and budget travelers, but soon acquired a much broader readership that included older and less impecunious visitors. Readers relished the guides' wit and inquisitiveness as much as the enthusiastic, critical approach that acknowledges everyone wants value for money – but not at any price.

Rough Guides soon began supplementing the "rougher" information – the hostel and low-budget listings – with the kind of detail that independent-minded travelers on any budget might expect. These days, the guides – distributed worldwide by the Penguin group – include recommendations spanning the range from shoestring to luxury, and cover more than 200 destinations around the globe. Our growing team of authors, many of whom come to Rough Guides initially as outstandingly good letter-writers telling us about their travels, are spread all over the world, particularly in Europe, the USA, and Australia. As well as the travel guides, Rough Guides publishes a series of dictionary phrasebooks covering two dozen major languages, an acclaimed series of music guides running the gamut from Classical to World Music, a series of music CDs in association with World Music Network, and a range of reference books on topics as diverse as the Internet, Pregnancy, and Unexplained Phenomena. Visit **www.roughguides.com** to see what's cooking.

Rough Guide credits

Text editor: Stephen Timblin
Series editor: Mark Ellingham
Editorial: Martin Dunford, Jonathan Buckley, Jo Mead, Kate Berens, Ann-Marie Shaw, Helena Smith, Judith Bamber, Orla Duane, Olivia Eccleshall, Ruth Blackmore, Geoff Howard, Claire Saunders, Gavin Thomas, Alexander Mark Rogers, Polly Thomas, Joe Staines, Richard Lim, Duncan Clark, Peter Buckley, Lucy Ratcliffe, Clifton Wilkinson, Alison Murchie, Matthew Teller, Andrew Dickson (UK); Andrew Rosenberg, Yuki Takagaki, Richard Koss, Hunter Slaton, Julie Feiner (US)
Production: Susanne Hillen, Andy Hilliard, Link Hall, Helen Prior, Julia Bovis, Michelle Draycott, Katie Pringle, Mike Hancock, Zoë Nobes, Rachel Holmes, Andy Turner
Cartography: Melissa Baker, Maxine Repath, Ed Wright, Katie Lloyd-Jones
Picture research: Louise Boulton, Sharon Martins, Mark Thomas
Online: Kelly Cross, Anja Mutic-Blessing, Jennifer Gold, Audra Epstein, Suzanne Welles, Cree Lawson (US)
Finance: John Fisher, Gary Singh, Edward Downey, Mark Hall, Tim Bill
Marketing & Publicity: Richard Trillo, Niki Smith, David Wearn, Chloë Roberts, Demelza Dallow, Claire Southern (UK); Simon Carloss, David Wechsler, Kathleen Rushforth (US)
Administration: Tania Hummel, Julie Sanderson

Publishing information

This first edition published March 2002 by **Rough Guides Ltd**,
62–70 Shorts Gardens, London WC2H 9AH.
Penguin Putnam, Inc., 375 Hudson Street, NY 10014, USA.
Distributed by the Penguin Group
Penguin Books Ltd,
80 Strand, London WC2R ORL
Penguin Putnam, Inc.,
375 Hudson Street, NY 10014, USA
Penguin Books Australia Ltd,
487 Maroondah Highway, PO Box 257, Ringwood, Victoria 3134, Australia
Penguin Books Canada Ltd,
10 Alcorn Avenue, Toronto, Ontario, Canada M4V 1E4
Penguin Books (NZ) Ltd,
182–190 Wairau Road, Auckland 10, New Zealand
Typeset in Bembo and Helvetica to an original design by Henry Iles.

Printed in Italy by LegoPrint S.p.A

728pp includes index
A catalogue record for this book is available from the British Library

ISBN 1-85828-854-1

Help us update

We've gone to a lot of effort to ensure that the first edition of **The Rough Guide to The Rocky Mountains** is accurate and up-to-date. However, things change – places get "discovered," opening hours are notoriously fickle, restaurants and rooms raise prices or lower standards. If you feel we've got it wrong or left something out, we'd like to know, and if you can remember the address, the price, the time, the phone number, so much the better.

We'll credit all contributions, and send a copy of the next edition (or any other Rough Guide if you prefer) for the best letters. Everyone who writes to us and isn't already a subscriber will receive a copy of our full-color thrice-yearly newsletter. Please mark letters: **"Rough Guide Rocky Mountains Update"** and send to: Rough Guides, 62–70 Shorts Gardens, London WC2H 9AH, or Rough Guides, 4th Floor, 345 Hudson St, New York, NY 10014. Or send an email to: **mail@roughguides.co.uk** or **mail@roughguides.com**

Acknowledgments

Alf Alderson Thanks to Karen Ballard at Idaho State Tourism and Pam Gosink at Travel Montana for their invaluable help throughout; to Todd Thesing and Rachel Roach of Big Sky for providing great hospitality and friendship; to Derrek and Lesley Thompson of Whitefish for fun times in North Montana; Rick Shaffer in Wallace; Gray Wolf, somewhere in the mountains; Ruth and Jim May for wild tales in the Lochsa Valley; Pete Grubb of ROW; Anne Baer, and John Wisby and Pat Cox for fine biking in Sun Valley; Laurie McConnel in Helena; Dave Corcoran of The River's Edge, Bozeman; Mary Naylor and Niki LeClair in McCall; Dax Schieffer, Matt and Charley at Big Sky; Ken Wiseman at Grand Targhee; Rusty Houtz at Fort Hall Indian Reservation; Ken Schuman in Kellog; Teri Hills, and Scott Hills for the feature on climbing in the Selkirks; Danny Eddy at Bogus Basin; and Doug Welsh at Bridger Bowl.

Christian Williams Thanks to the people of Colorado for being a laid-back, friendly and accommodating bunch; particularly Barry, Courtney, Bryce, Stoli and Marley in Denver for their unwavering support; Rob and John in Boulder for sofa space and companionship; Nabby for wearing my buff. Thanks also to Raymond for policing punctuation and Heather for preserving my sanity when writing up. At Rough Guides thanks to Martin Dunford and Andrew Rosenberg for deciding I was one of the right men for the job and to Stephen Timblin, for his many hours of patient editorial work, often under huge pressure.

Cameron Wilson In Steamboat, largest thanks to Jim Ruggiero and Heather Sedlack for months of peerless hospitality, for keeping me out of trouble on the slopes and for a real Rocky Mountains Christmas; thanks also to Kris Richards for cheerful chats and for letting me hijack her computer, and to Max (the loopy lab) for frolics in the snow. I'm indebted to Ken Kraus (Utah) and Chuck Coon (Wyoming) for providing me with lots of helpful contacts and generally smoothing the way, and to Kristi Leavitt who made my visit to Yellowstone a breeze. Kudos to our fearless editor Stephen Timblin, whose love of the Rockies saw him abandon the cozy office environs and head off into the wilds of Yellowstone in search of his own adventures among the wolves and grizzlies, and the RG staff at Covent Garden, who continue to patiently endure my noisy forays into their office; among their number, Dave Wearn deserves special mention as provider of lounge-room accommodation and fine baked goods.

Heartfelt thanks go to: Claire Saunders and Martin Dunford for their editing assistance; Melissa Baker, Maxine Repath, and Ed Wright for their mapmaking expertise; Helen Prior, Julia Bovis, and Michelle Draycott for their patience and seamless production work; Andy Turner for his great job in typesetting the color section; Russell Walton for his diligent proofreading; and Andrew Rosenberg for his guidance and support.

Photo credits

Cover credits

Front (small top image) Morning Glory Pool, Yellowstone National Park, Wyoming ©Tony Waltham/Robert Harding
Front (small bottom image) Brown bear © Louise Murray/Robert Harding
Back (top) Slate River Valley, Colorado © Stone
Back (lower) Pioneer Barn, Grand Teton National Park, Wyoming © Stone

Color introduction

Snake River © Pete Saloutos
Glacier National Park, Montana © John Warden/Network Aspen
Cowboys silhouetted at Sunset in the West © John Russell/Network Aspen
Sunrise over Yellowstone Lake, Yellowstone National Park, Wyoming © Geoff Renner/Robert Harding
Sangre De Christo Mountains © Christian Williams
Snowboarder on cliff at Jewel Basin, Montana © Scott Spiker/Robert Harding
Bison © Grand Teton Lodge Company
Leadville © Christian Williams
Brown Bear, Grizzly Discovery Center, West Yellowstone © Louise Murray/Robert Harding
Airborne at The Canyons, Utah © Dan Campbell

Things not to miss

1. Weathered tree and Grand Tetons, Jackson Lake © TRIP/T Mackie
2. A hiker walking the trails in Colorado © Travel Ink/Andrew Watson
3. Festival in Denver, Colorado © TRIP/M Stevenson
4. Lone Mountain, Montana © Big Sky Resort
5. Cliff Palace at Mesa Verde NP, Colorado – Ladders © TRIP/J Dennis
6. View of 'Going-To-The-Sun' Road over Logan Pass, Montana © Nicholas Devore III/Network Aspen
7. Skiing Steamboat © Larry Pierce
8. Silverton, Colorado © Robert Francis/Robert Harding
9. The Silver Dollar Cowboy Bar, Jackson Hole, Wyoming © Bill Bachmann/Network Aspen
10. Buffalo Bill Historical Center in Cody, Wyoming © Robert McLeod/Robert Harding
11. Cheyenne Frontier Days Rodeo © Jeffrey Aaronson/Network Aspen
12. Great Sand Dunes National Monument, Colorado © Conor Caffrey/AXIOM
13. Wind River, Wyoming © Jon Gardey/Robert Harding
14. Vail, Colorado © TRIP/F Torrance
15. Bishops Castle, Colorado © Christian Williams
16. Rocky Mountain National Park, Colorado © Liz Hymans/CORBIS
17. Mountain biking in Sun Valley, Idaho © Alf Alderson
18. Leadville, Colorado © Rebecca Green/Network Aspen
19. Lower Yellowstone Falls from Artists Point, Yellowstone National Park, Wyoming © Geoff Renner/Robert Harding
20. Galena Summit in the Sawtooth National Recreation Area, Idaho © Robert Harding
21. T Rex in front of the Museum of the Rockies in Bozeman, Montana © Celeste Horner
22. Nevada City, Montana © David Hiser/Network Aspen
23. Old Faithful, Yellowstone National Park, Wyoming © TRIP/M Lee
24. Devils Tower, Wyoming © Geoff Renner/Robert Harding
25. Backcountry skiing in the Wasatch Mountains, Utah © James W Kay
26. Raspberry-shaped bakery near Bear Lake, Utah © Scott T Smith/CORBIS
27. Flyfishing in Montana near the Beartooth Mountains © TRIP/B Vikander
28. Maroon Belles, Colorado © TRIP/B Vikander
29. Rendezvous festivals in Wind River Country, Wyoming © Wyoming's Wind River Country
30. Alpine sunflowers in meadow, Medicine Bow Mountains, Wyoming © David Muench/CORBIS
31. The atrium of the Brown Palace Hotel in Denver, Colorado © Robert Reck
32. Moroni Statue, Temple Square, Salt Lake City, Utah © TRIP/B Turner
33. McCall Winter Festival, Idaho © Joel W Rogers/CORBIS
34. W.A. Coughanor Monument outside Capitol, Boise, Idaho © Robert Harding
35. Park City, Utah © Dan Campbell
36. Rafting on the Snake River © TRIP/Viesti Collection

Black and white photos

Boulder, Colorado © Boulder CVB (p.68)
State Capitol Building, Denver, Colorado © TRIP/M Stevenson (p.79)
Garden of the Gods in Colorado Springs, Colorado © TRIP/ F Pirson (p.102)
Cumbres & Toltec Scenic Railroad © Nick Lera (p.128)
Main Street, Telluride, Colorado © Jeffrey Aaronson/Network Aspen (p.179)
Person telemarking at Breckenridge, Colorado © Scott Spike/Robert Harding (p.198)
Grove of aspen trees © David Muench/CORBIS (p.225)
Dream Lake, Rocky Mountain National Park, Colorado © Travel Ink/Andrew Watson (p.262)
Big horn ram and ewes © TRIP/D Ikenberry (p.283)
Temple Square Assembly Hall Tabernacle, Salt Lake City, Utah © TRIP/B Turner (p.314)
Alta, Utah © Lee Cohen (p.329)
Wyoming State Flag © Joseph Sohm; ChromoSohm Inc./CORBIS (p.350)
A statue of Buffalo Bill Cody in Cody, Wyoming © David Hisher/Network Aspen (p.372)
Mail boxes, Hullett, Wyoming © Dave Jacobs/Robert Harding (p.388)
Morning Glory Pool, Yellowstone National Park, Wyoming © T Waltham/Robert Harding (p.408)
Mammoth Hot Springs, Yellowstone National Park, Wyoming © Geoff Renner/Robert Harding (p.426)
Two Medicine Valley in Glacier National Park, Montana © Kirkendall/Spring, Edmonds, WA (p.456)
Big Hole Valley, Montana © Alf Alderson (p.482)
Bull elk with herd © TRIP/T Mackie (p.532)
Sawtooth National Recreation Area, Idaho © Robert Harding (p.562)
Bench Lakes, Sawtooth Wilderness Area, Idaho © Alf Alderson (p.603)

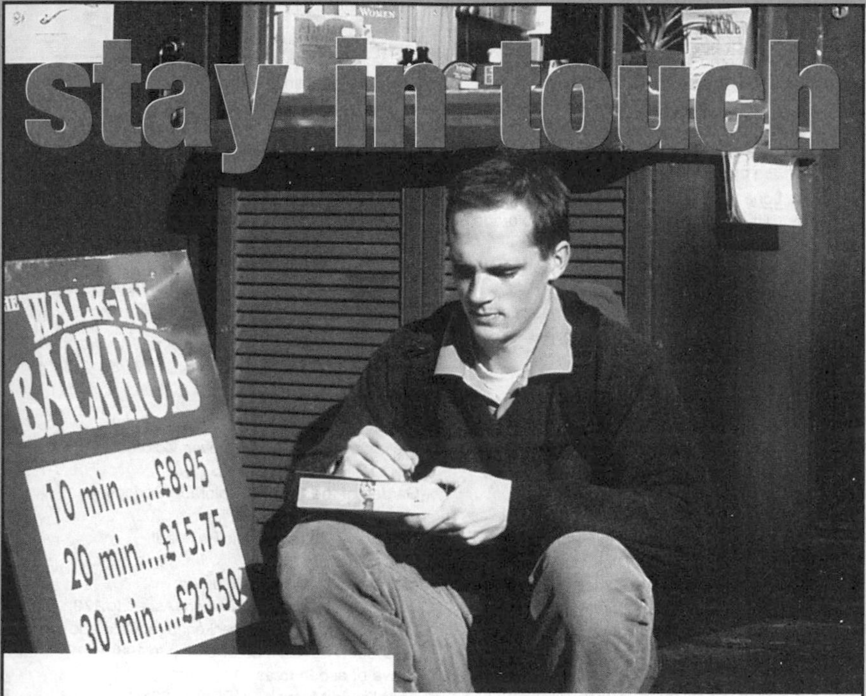

roughnews

Rough Guides' FREE full-colour newsletter

News, travel issues, music reviews, readers' letters and the latest dispatches from authors on the road

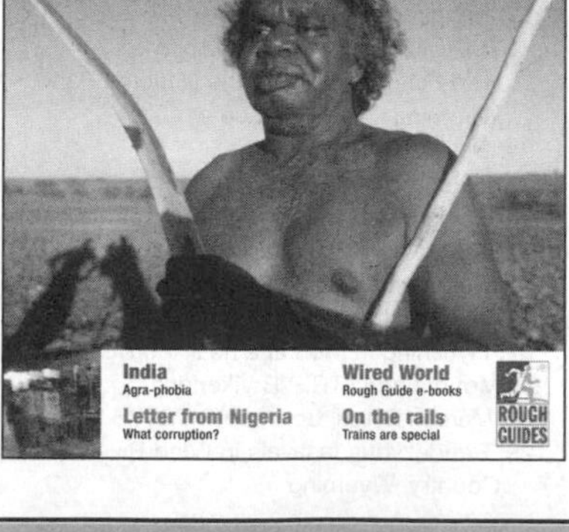

If you would like to receive roughnews, please send us your name and address:

62-70 Shorts Gardens
London, WC2H 9AH, UK

4th Floor, 345 Hudson St,
New York NY10014, USA

newslettersubs@roughguides.co.uk